EYEW

GREAT
BRITAIN

MAIN CONTRIBUTOR: MICHAEL LEAPMAN

LONDON, NEW YORK,
MELBOURNE, MUNICH AND DELHI
www.dk.com

ART EDITOR Stephen Bere
PROJECT EDITOR Marian Broderick
EDITORS Carey Combe, Sara Harper, Elaine Harries,
Kim Inglis, Ella Milroy, Andrew Szudek, Nia Williams
US EDITOR Mary Sutherland
DESIGNERS Susan Blackburn, Elly King,
Colin Loughrey, Andy Wilkinson

CONTRIBUTORS
Josie Barnard, Christopher Catling,
Juliet Clough, Lindsay Hunt, Polly Phillimore,
Martin Symington, Roger Thomas

MAPS
Jane Hanson, Phil Rose, Jennifer Skelley (Lovell Johns Ltd)
Gary Bowes (Era-Maptec Ltd)

PHOTOGRAPHERS
Joe Cornish, Paul Harris, Rob Reichenfeld, Kim Sayer

ILLUSTRATORS
Richard Draper, Jared Gilby (Kevin Jones Assocs), Paul Guest, Roger Hutchins,
Chris Orr & Assocs, Maltings Partnership,
Ann Winterbotham, John Woodcock

Printed and bound by South China Printing Co. Ltd., China

First American edition 1995
13 14 15 16 10 9 8 7 6 5 4 3 2 1
Published in the United States by DK Publishing,
375 Hudson Street, New York, NY 10014

Reprinted with revisions 1996, 1997, 1999, 2000, 2001,
2002, 2003, 2004, 2005, 2006, 2007, 2008, 2009, 2010, 2011, 2013

Copyright © 1995, 2013 Dorling Kindersley Limited, London

Published in Great Britain by Dorling Kindersley Limited.

A catalog record for this book is available
from the Library of Congress.

ISSN 1542-1554
ISBN 978-07566-9480-7

THROUGHOUT THIS BOOK, FLOORS ARE REFERRED TO IN ACCORDANCE
WITH EUROPEAN USAGE, I.E., THE "FIRST FLOOR" IS ONE FLIGHT UP FROM GROUND LEVEL.

Front cover main image: Chatsworth House, Derbyshire

MIX
Paper from
responsible sources
FSC
www.fsc.org   FSC™ C018179

The information in this
DK Eyewitness Travel Guide is checked regularly.
Every effort has been made to ensure that this book is as up-to-date
as possible at the time of going to press. Some details, however,
such as telephone numbers, opening hours, prices, gallery hanging
arrangements and travel information are liable to change. The
publishers cannot accept responsibility for any consequences arising
from the use of this book, nor for any material on third-party
websites, and cannot guarantee that any website address in this
book will be a suitable source of travel information. We value the
views and suggestions of our readers highly. Please write to:
Publisher, DK Eyewitness Travel Guides, Dorling Kindersley, 80 Strand,
London, Great Britain WC2R 0RL, or email travelguides@dk.com

◁ Cricket, England's national game

CONTENTS

HOW TO USE
THIS GUIDE 6

**A 14th-century illustration
of two knights jousting**

INTRODUCING
GREAT BRITAIN

DISCOVERING
GREAT BRITAIN 10

PUTTING GREAT
BRITAIN ON THE MAP 14

A PORTRAIT OF
GREAT BRITAIN 20

THE HISTORY OF
GREAT BRITAIN 38

GREAT BRITAIN
THROUGH THE YEAR 62

Beefeater at the Tower of London

LONDON

INTRODUCING LONDON
72

WEST END AND
WESTMINSTER 76

Eilean Donan Castle on Loch Duich in the Scottish Highlands

SOUTH KENSINGTON AND HYDE PARK **94**

REGENT'S PARK AND BLOOMSBURY **102**

THE CITY AND SOUTHWARK **108**

FURTHER AFIELD **122**

STREET FINDER **127**

SOUTHEAST ENGLAND

INTRODUCING SOUTH-EAST ENGLAND **158**

THE DOWNS AND CHANNEL COAST **164**

EAST ANGLIA **190**

THAMES VALLEY **216**

THE WEST COUNTRY

INTRODUCING THE WEST COUNTRY **240**

WESSEX **246**

DEVON AND CORNWALL **272**

THE MIDLANDS

INTRODUCING THE MIDLANDS **298**

THE HEART OF ENGLAND **306**

EAST MIDLANDS **330**

Jacobean "Old House" in Hereford

THE NORTH COUNTRY

INTRODUCING THE NORTH COUNTRY **346**

LANCASHIRE AND THE LAKES **354**

YORKSHIRE AND THE HUMBER REGION **380**

NORTHUMBRIA **414**

WALES

INTRODUCING WALES **432**

NORTH WALES **440**

SOUTH AND MID-WALES **456**

SCOTLAND

INTRODUCING SCOTLAND **478**

THE LOWLANDS **490**

THE HIGHLANDS AND ISLANDS **524**

TRAVELLERS' NEEDS

WHERE TO STAY **552**

WHERE TO EAT **600**

SHOPPING **658**

ENTERTAINMENT **660**

SPECIALIST HOLIDAYS AND OUTDOOR ACTIVITIES **662**

SURVIVAL GUIDE

PRACTICAL INFORMATION **668**

TRAVEL INFORMATION **680**

GENERAL INDEX **692**

HOW TO USE THIS GUIDE

This guide helps you to get the most from your holidays in Great Britain. It provides both detailed practical information and expert recommendations. *Introducing Great Britain* maps the country and sets it in its historical and cultural context. The six regional chapters, plus *London*, describe important sights, using maps, pictures and illustrations. Features cover topics from houses and famous gardens to sport. Hotel, restaurant, and pub recommendations can be found in *Travellers' Needs*. The *Survival Guide* has practical information on everything from transport to personal safety.

LONDON

The centre of London has been divided into four sightseeing areas. Each has its own chapter, which opens with a list of the sights described. The last section, *Further Afield*, covers the most attractive suburbs. All sights are numbered and plotted on an area map. The information for each sight follows the map's numerical order, making sights easy to locate within the chapter.

All pages relating to London have red thumb tabs.

A locator map shows where you are in relation to other areas of the city centre.

1 Area Map
For easy reference, the sights are numbered and located on a map. Sights in the city centre are also marked on the Street Finder *on pages 127–47.*

Sights at a Glance lists the chapter's sights by category: Historic Streets and Buildings; Museums and Galleries; Churches and Cathedrals; Shops; Parks and Gardens.

2 Street-by-Street Map
This gives a bird's-eye view of the key areas in each chapter.

Stars indicate the sights that no visitor should miss.

A suggested route for a walk is shown in red.

3 Detailed information
The sights in London are described individually. Addresses, telephone numbers, opening hours, admission charges, tours and wheelchair access are also provided, as well as public transport links.

THE LOWLANDS

CLYDE VALLEY · CENTRAL SCOTLAND · FIFE · THE LOTHIANS
AYRSHIRE · DUMFRIES AND GALLOWAY · THE BORDERS

[body text of introduction page, illustrated in reduced form]

1 Introduction

The landscape, history and character of each region is outlined here, showing how the area has developed over the centuries and what it has to offer the visitor today.

GREAT BRITAIN AREA BY AREA

Apart from London, Great Britain has been divided into 14 regions, each of which has a separate chapter. The most interesting towns and places to visit have been numbered on a *Regional Map*.

Each area of Great Britain can be identified quickly by its colour coding, shown on the inside front cover.

Exploring the Lowlands

2 Regional Map

This shows the main road network and gives an illustrated overview of the whole region. All entries are numbered and there are also useful tips on getting around the region by car, train and other forms of transport.

3 Detailed information

All the important sights, towns and other places to visit are described individually. They are listed in order, following the numbering on the Regional Map. *Within each entry, there is detailed information on important buildings and other sights.*

Story boxes explore related topics.

For all the top sights, a Visitors' Checklist provides the practical information you need to plan your visit.

Edinburgh Castle

4 The top sights

These are given one or more full pages. Three-dimensional illustrations reveal the interiors of historic buildings. Interesting town and city centres are given street-by-street maps, featuring individual sights.

EYEWITNESS TRAVEL

GREAT BRITAIN

INTRODUCING
GREAT BRITAIN

DISCOVERING GREAT BRITAIN 10–13

PUTTING GREAT BRITAIN ON THE MAP 14–19

A PORTRAIT OF GREAT BRITAIN 20–37

THE HISTORY OF GREAT BRITAIN 38–61

GREAT BRITAIN THROUGH THE YEAR 62–69

DISCOVERING GREAT BRITAIN

Each one of Great Britain's counties, that have grown out of kingdoms, principalities, shires, fiefs, boroughs, and parishes, has its own special flavour. This derives from Britain's landscape, its resources and its history, all of which have shaped its peoples, too.

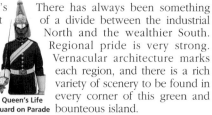

Queen's Life Guard on Parade

There has always been something of a divide between the industrial North and the wealthier South. Regional pride is very strong. Vernacular architecture marks each region, and there is a rich variety of scenery to be found in every corner of this green and bounteous island.

A view of Big Ben and the London Eye

LONDON

- A ride on the London Eye
- Majestic parks
- World-class museums

Britain's capital can be enjoyed in all weathers. So many buildings, from **Big Ben** *(see p77)* to the **Tower of London** *(see pp118–19)*, are emblematic of the city. To get an overview take a bus riverboat or the

London Eye *(see p81)*; visit the West End for the most exciting shops, or stroll through its lovely parks. The **National Gallery** *(see p82–3)* is one of the finest art museums in the world, the **British Museum** *(see pp106–7)* and **Victoria and Albert Museum** *(see pp98–9)* are storehouses of treasures while **Tate Modern** *(see 121)* has set a standard for contemporary art.

THE DOWNS AND CHANNEL COAST

- Great days out from London
- Fairytale castles
- Brighton's brilliant sea front

This is "The Garden of England", green and rural, with rolling Downs. Many places in this corner of the country are accessible on a day trip from London; **Hampton Court** *(see p173)* and **Leeds Castle** *(see p189)* are favourite excursions. Many estates have connections with great

figures from history: Winston Churchill's **Chartwell** *(see p188)*, Queen Victoria's **Osborne** *(see p168)* on the Isle of Wight and J.M.W. Turner's **Petworth** *(see p172)*, an antiques-hunters' paradise. Ancient cathedrals rise from **Chichester** *(see pp171)*, **Winchester** *(see pp170–1)* and **Canterbury** *(see pp186–7)*, which has many tales to tell. Breezy resorts dot the coast. The liveliest is **Brighton** *(see pp174–9)*, known as "London-on-Sea", with its famous Lanes, Palace Pier and seafront promenade.

Punting on the River Cam past King's College Chapel, Cambridge

EAST ANGLIA

- A punt in Cambridge
- Magnificent Ely Cathedral
- A day at the races

This part of the country grew wealthy on the wool trade and its merchants built fabulous half-timbered houses and pretty towns such as **Lavenham** *(see p206)*. In the charming university town of Cambridge *(see p210–15)* try

The promenade and Palace Pier, Brighton, Sussex

◁ *Salisbury Cathedral: from the meadows* by John Constable (1776–1837)

punting on the Backs with the students or, for a less vigourous outing, admire **King's College Chapel** *(see p212–13)*. For another cultural high, visit **Ely Cathedral** *(see pp194–5)*. Spend a day at the races at **Newmarket** *(see p207)*, or visit **Aldeburgh** *(see pp202–203)* during its prestigious annual music festival. The ports on the lovely coast provide seafood for your table.

THAMES VALLEY

- **Attractive riverside pubs**
- **Oxford's dreaming spires**
- **Imposing Blenheim Palace**

The River Thames has long been a pleasure ground. The riverside, from London's outer suburbs to **Windsor** *(see pp235–7)*, **Oxford** *(see pp222–7)* and beyond, has many appealing waterside pubs and restaurants located in attractive towns. Boats can be hired, and the annual rowing regatta at **Henley-on-Thames** *(see p63 and p66)* is the height of the summer season. No wonder that the song of Britain's most exclusive private school, Eton *(see p235)*, which is located by the river, is *The Eton Boating Song*. **Windsor Castle** *(see pp236–7)* is undoubtedly a main draw, easily reached in a day trip from London, as are the beautiful colleges of **Oxford University** *(see pp226–7)*. Not far away are other historic places to visit, including the Churchill family home at **Blenheim Palace** *(see*

Stonehenge, Wiltshire, Great Britain's famous prehistoric monument

pp228–9), the Duke of Bedford's **Woburn Abbey** *(see p230)* and **Stowe** *(see p230)*, which has one of the most magnificent gardens in England.

WESSEX

- **Mysterious Stonehenge**
- **Cheddar cheese and Taunton Cider**
- **Fine architecture in Bath and Salisbury**

The former kingdom of the West Saxons echoes with history and legends. Here are some of the most important Neolithic sites in the country, including the mysterious and magnificent **Stonehenge** *(see pp262–3)*. This is the country of good living, with Cheddar cheese from around the Cheddar Gorge, and Somerset cider. The Georgian spa town of **Bath** *(see pp258–61)* makes an excellent centre to explore the region. There are two coasts – in the north on the Bristol Channel and in the south on the English channel where **Poole** *(see pp270–1)* is a great yachting centre. Bath, **Wells** *(see pp252–3)* and **Salisbury** *(see pp264–5)* all have outstanding cathedrals. There are wild animals at **Longleat** *(see p266)*, wild landscapes on **Exmoor National Park** *(see pp250–1)*, while the **Glastonbury** *(see pp253)* music festival attracts fans in their thousands.

DEVON AND CORNWALL

- **Surfing fit for champions**
- **Seafood and cream teas**
- **Fabulous gardens**

Britain's best beaches are in the West Country, some of which have high cliffs and waves worthy of champion surfers. Its fishing villages have long attracted artists, in particular St Ives, where the **Tate St Ives** gallery *(see p277)* can be visited. Seafood is plentiful, and rich pasturelands brings dairy ice-cream and cream teas. Seafaring is a way of life, as the **National Maritime Museum Cornwall** *(see pp280–1)* in Falmouth attests. **Bodmin Moor** *(see pp284–5)* and **Dartmoor** *(see p81)* present an untamed wilderness but some fine gardens are here, too, including the **Eden Project** *(see pp282–3)*.

A view of Blenheim Palace, Woodstock, Oxfordshire

Eden Project, Cornwall, a garden for the 21st century

THE HEART OF ENGLAND

- Shakespeare's birthplace
- Typically English Cotswold villages
- Half-timbered border towns

There is a great mix of attractions in this region where the Industrial Revolution began *(see pp314–15)*. The most popular sites are **Warwick Castle** *(see pp322–3)* and Shakespeare's birthplace in **Stratford-upon-Avon** *(see pp324–5)*. Cotswold villages built of golden limestone are quintessentially English. Other lovely rural spots include the Malvern Hills and the Wye Vallley. Attractive architecture distinguishes the half-timbered Welsh border towns including the city of **Chester** *(see pp310–11)*.

Anne Hathaway's cottage, Stratford-upon-Avon, Warwickshire

EAST MIDLANDS

- Chatsworth, a fine country house
- Great walking in the Peak District
- Buxton spa and opera house

One of the most impressive country houses, **Chatsworth** *(see pp334–5)*, is a high spot of this region. It sits at the edge of the **Peak District** *(see pp338–9)*, a popular area for walking. There are several attractive towns such as **Buxton** *(see p334)*, a spa town with an opera house while **Lincoln** *(see pp340–1)* has medieval buildings and a fine cathedral.

Mist on Rydal Water, Lake District, Cumbria

LANCASHIRE AND THE LAKES

- England at its most picturesque
- Liverpool, maritime city of Empire
- Manchester, capital of the North

The **Lake District** *(see pp352–68)* is where walking as an activity rather than a chore began, and you will see why when you encounter the stunning scenery of fells and lakes. Serious walkers put on their waterproofs and boots, while Sunday strollers hire row boats, or look in at Dove Cottage, where the poets William and Dorothy Wordsworth lived. To the south is **Liverpool** *(see pp354–5)*, a Unesco World Heritage city, with wonderful architecture and great art galleries. **Blackpool** *(see p371)* is the main resort, known for its illuminations. Inland is **Manchester** *(see pp372–5)* England's second largest city.

YORKSHIRE AND THE HUMBER REGION

- Haunting abbey ruins
- The Brontë sisters' dramatic moors
- The ancient city of York

Yorkshire is known for its striking moors, which the literary Brontë sisters of **Haworth** *(see p412)* knew

so well. It is also known for its great abbeys, such as **Fountains** *(see pp390–1)*, **Rievaulx** *(see p393)* and **Whitby** *(see p396)*, which were reduced to haunting ruins after the English church broke from Rome. **York Minster** *(see pp406–407)* remains the most important church in the north and the ancient town is worth exploring. Sculptures by Henry Moore grace **Yorkshire Sculpture Park** *(see p413)*.

Whitby harbour and St Mary's Church, Yorkshire

NORTHUMBRIA

- The trail of Celtic Christianity
- Life as it was lived, in Beamish Open Air Museum
- Hadrian's Wall from coast to coast

A boat trip to the **Farne Islands** *(see p418)* off Lindisfarne is the starting point to unravelling early Celtic Christianity, a journey that can be followed as far as **Durham Cathedral** *(see pp428–9)*. The **Beamish Open Air Museum** *(see pp424–5)*, which re-creates life in the northeast in the 19th century, makes a great family day out. Castles on Northumberland's coast were built to withstand Viking attack, but it is **Hadrian's Wall** *(see pp422–3)*, erected by the Romans to keep out the Scots, that is particularly impressive.

NORTH WALES

- **Wild Snowdonia National Park**
- **Narrow-gauge railways**
- **Stunning medieval castles**

This is the part of Wales, where Welsh is commonly spoken, and the annual Eisteddfod literary festival is held. Its wildness is captured around Snowdon, the highest mountain in England and Wales. The centre for exploring **Snowdonia National Park** *(see pp450–1)* is Llanberis from where a narrow-gauge railway runs to the top. Another former slate-quarry railway takes passengers up from the coast at Porthmadog near **Portmeirion** *(see p454–5)*. Medieval castles keep watch at **Harlech** *(see p454)*, **Caernarfon** *(see p444)* and **Conwy** *(see p438 and p447)*.

SOUTH AND MID WALES

- **Pony trekking in the hills**
- **Scenic coastal walks**
- **Hay-on-Wye literary festival**

This is a region to tour by car, to go walking or pony trekking, across mountains like the **Brecon Beacons** *(see pp468–9)*. The roads are emptier than England's and the valleys are green and lush. The coast has some delightful ports and long-established resorts. The most attractive are around the **Gower Peninsula** *(see p466)*

Cliffs of the Pembrokeshire Coast National Park, South Wales

and in Pembrokeshire in the south west where there is the diminutive **St Davids Cathedral** *(see pp464–5)*. Wales is known for its male voice choirs – as well as its men of letters – **Hay-on-Wye** *(see p461)* hosts an annual literary festival.

SCOTTISH LOWLANDS

- **Glasgow, dynamic city of art**
- **Medieval Edinburgh and its Georgian New Town**
- **Magnificent abbeys and castles**

The capital **Edinburgh** *(see pp504–11)* and **Glasgow** *(see pp516–21)* are Scotland's dazzling cities, both full of interest and worth several

days' exploration. Charles Rennie Mackintosh left his Art Nouveau mark on Glasgow, while thousands of hopeful performers attempt to find fame in Edinburgh each August at the famous festival. The capital's high points are **Edinburgh Castle** *(see pp506–7)*, keeper of the Scottish Crown jewels and the **Palace of Holyroodhouse** *(see p510)*, the Queen's official Scottish residence. Castles abound in the Lowlands, notably the Renaissance gem **Stirling** *(see pp497–8)*.

SCOTTISH HIGHLANDS AND ISLANDS

- **Mountain climbing and skiing**
- **The castles of Royal Deeside**
- **Remote, idyllic hills**

This is as wild as Britain gets: mountainous, heather-clad and dramatically remote, drifting into offshore islands. You may well see eagles and stags, while on the west coast seals swoop in on the beautiful shores. **Aberdeen** *(see pp538–40)* is the starting point for a tour of the castles of **Royal Deeside** *(see p540–1)*. Climb mountains, go skiing in Aviemore in the **Cairngorms** *(see pp544–5)*, follow the whisky trails and take a ferry to the Western Isles.

A view of Edinburgh Castle, Scotland

Putting Great Britain on the Map

Lying in northwestern Europe, Great Britain is bounded by the Atlantic Ocean, the North Sea and the English Channel. The island's landscape and climate are varied, and it is this variety that even today affects the pattern of settlement. The remote shores of the West Country peninsula and the inhospitable mountains of Scotland and Wales are less populated than the relatively flat and fertile Midlands and Southeast, where the vast majority of the country's 62 million people live. Due to this population density, the south is today the most built-up part of the country.

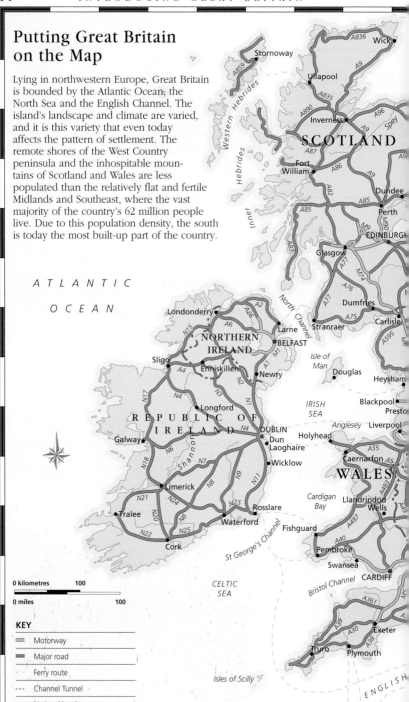

ATLANTIC OCEAN

Stornoway

Western Hebrides

Inner Hebrides

Ullapool

Inverness

SCOTLAND

Fort William

Dundee

Perth

Glasgow

EDINBURGH

Wick

A836

A859

A9

A890

A835

A96

Spey

A87

A86

A9

A82

A85

A85

M9

M90

Londonderry

NORTHERN IRELAND

Larne

BELFAST

Newry

Enniskillen

Sligo

REPUBLIC OF IRELAND

Longford

DUBLIN

Dun Laoghaire

Wicklow

Galway

Limerick

Tralee

Cork

Waterford

Rosslare

A2

A6

N15

A4

N17

N4

N3

N2

N1

N4

N6

N18

Shannon

N7

N8

N9

N11

N21

N24

N8

N20

N22

N25

N25

North Channel

Dumfries

Stranraer

Carlisle

A77

A74

A76

A75

A595

M6

Isle of Man

Douglas

Heysham

Blackpool

Presto

IRISH SEA

Anglesey

Liverpool

Holyhead

Caernarfon

WALES

Cardigan Bay

Llandrindod Wells

Fishguard

Pembroke

Swansea

CARDIFF

A55

A5

A483

A487

A40

St George's Channel

CELTIC SEA

Bristol Channel

A361

A39

A30

A38

Exeter

Truro

Plymouth

ENGLISH

Guernse

Isles of Scilly

Santander

Roscoff

Bilbao

0 kilometres _____ **100**

0 miles _____ **100**

KEY

▭	Motorway
▬	Major road
- - -	Ferry route
•••	Channel Tunnel
▬ ▬	National border

Shetland and Orkney Islands

*These islands form the northern-
most part of Great Britain, with the
Shetlands lying six degrees south of
the Arctic Circle. There are transport links to the mainland.*

Europe

*Great Britain is situated in the northwest
corner of Europe. Its nearest neighbours are
Ireland to the west, and the Netherlands,
Belgium and France across the Channel.
Denmark, Norway and Sweden are also
easily accessible.*

Regional Great Britain: London, the South, the Midlands and Wales

Great Britain has airline connections with most cities in the world. London is the main transport hub with three major international airports, including Heathrow, the world's busiest. The most populous area, Southern Britain, is divided within this book, into four regions – Southeast England, the West Country, Wales and the Midlands – with a separate chapter for London. Road and rail links to the North and Scotland *(see pp18–19)* are plentiful, as are links between all main towns.

KEY TO COLOUR-CODING

■ London

Southeast England

☐ The Downs and Channel Coast

☐ East Anglia

☐ Thames Valley

The West Country

☐ Wessex

■ Devon and Cornwall

Wales

☐ North Wales

■ South and Mid-Wales

The Midlands

■ The Heart of England

■ East Midlands

KEY TO MAP

⛴ Ferry port

✈ Airport

▬ Motorway

▬ Major road

— Railway line

••• Channel Tunnel

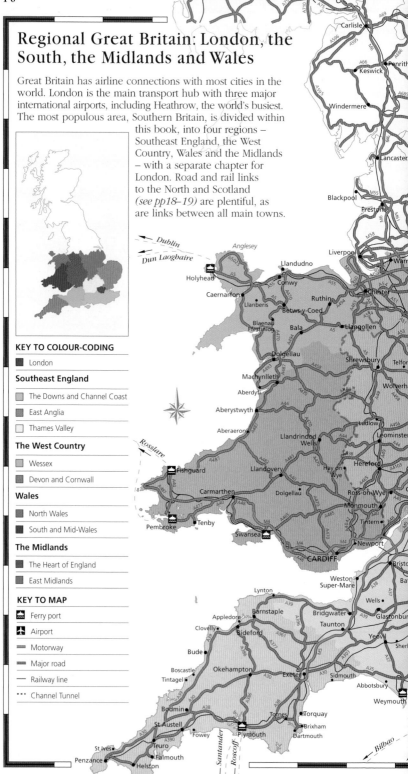

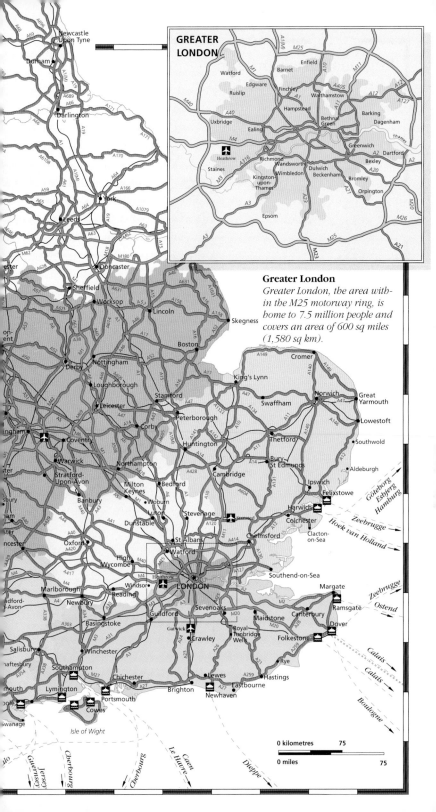

GREATER LONDON

Greater London

*Greater London, the area with-
in the M25 motorway ring, is
home to 7.5 million people and
covers an area of 600 sq miles
(1,580 sq km).*

0 kilometres   75

0 miles   75

Regional Great Britain: The North and Scotland

This part of Great Britain is divided into two sections in this book. Although it is far less populated than the southern sector of the country, there are good road and rail connections, and ferry services link the islands with the mainland.

KEY TO COLOUR-CODING

The North Country

- Lancashire and the Lakes
- Yorkshire and Humber Region
- Northumbria

Scotland

- The Lowlands
- The Highlands and Islands

Isle of Lewis
Stornoway
Tarbert
Ullapool
Lochmaddy
Uig
Western Isles
Lochboisdale
Isle of Skye
Kyle of Lochalsh
Castlebay
Mallaig
Hebrides
Fort William
Arinagour
Tobermory
Scarinish
Craignure
Inner
Oban
Crainlarich
Scalasaig
Jura
Greenock
Kennacraig
Paisley
Ardrossan
Islay
Brodick
Irvine
Port Ellen
Ayr
Campbeltown
Isle of Arran
Larne
Belfast
Cairnryan
Stranraer

Isle of Man
Douglas

0 kilometres   100

0 miles   100

Holyhead

MILEAGE CHART

LONDON

10 = Distance in miles
10 = Distance in kilometres

111 **179**	*BIRMINGHAM*									
150 **241**	102 **164**	*CARDIFF*								
74 **119**	185 **298**	228 **367**	*DOVER*							
372 **599**	290 **466**	373 **600**	442 **711**	*EDINBURGH*						
389 **626**	292 **470**	374 **602**	466 **750**	45 **72**	*GLASGOW*					
529 **851**	448 **721**	530 **853**	600 **966**	158 **254**	167 **269**	*INVERNESS*				
184 **296**	81 **130**	173 **278**	257 **414**	213 **343**	214 **344**	371 **597**	*MANCHESTER*			
274 **441**	204 **328**	301 **484**	343 **552**	107 **172**	145 **233**	265 **426**	131 **211**	*NEWCASTLE*		
112 **180**	161 **259**	235 **378**	167 **269**	360 **579**	383 **616**	517 **832**	185 **298**	260 **418**	*NORWICH*	
212 **341**	206 **332**	152 **261**	287 **462**	427 **784**	426 **785**	545 **1038**	250 **451**	427 **655**	324 **521**	*PLYMOUTH*

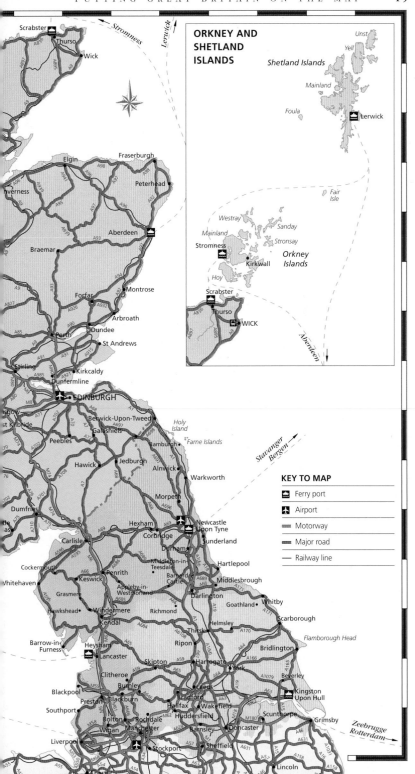

ORKNEY AND SHETLAND ISLANDS

Shetland Islands

Unst

Yell

Mainland

Foula

Lerwick

Fair Isle

Westray

Sanday

Mainland

Stronsay

Stromness

Orkney Islands

Kirkwall

Hoy

Scrabster

Thurso

WICK

Aberdeen

Stromness

Lerwick

Scrabster
Thurso
Wick

Elgin
Fraserburgh
Peterhead
Inverness
Aberdeen
Braemar
Forfar
Montrose
Arbroath
Perth
Dundee
St Andrews
Stirling
Kirkcaldy
Dunfermline
EDINBURGH
Glasgow
East Kilbride
Peebles
Berwick-Upon-Tweed
Galashiels
Holy Island
Hawick
Jedburgh
Bamburgh
Farne Islands
Alnwick
Dumfries
Warkworth
Morpeth
Hexham
Corbridge
Newcastle Upon Tyne
Carlisle
Durham
Sunderland
Cockermouth
Middleton-in-Teesdale
Hartlepool
Keswick
Penrith
Barnard Castle
Middlesbrough
Grasmere
Appleby-in-Westmorland
Darlington
Goathland
Whitby
Hawkshead
Windermere
Richmond
Scarborough
Whitehaven
Kendal
Thirsk
Helmsley
Barrow-in-Furness
Heysham
Ripon
Flamborough Head
Lancaster
Skipton
Harrogate
Bridlington
Clitheroe
York
Beverley
Blackpool
Burnley
Kingston Upon Hull
Southport
Preston
Blackburn
Bradford
Leeds
Wakefield
Bolton
Rochdale
Halifax
Huddersfield
Scunthorpe
Grimsby
Wigan
Manchester
Barnsley
Doncaster
Liverpool
Stockport
Sheffield
Chester
Lincoln

Stavanger
Bergen

Zeebrugge
Rotterdam

KEY TO MAP

- Ferry port
- Airport
- Motorway
- Major road
- Railway line

A PORTRAIT OF GREAT BRITAIN

*B**ritain has been assiduous in preserving its traditions, but offers the visitor much more than stately castles and pretty villages. A diversity of landscape, culture, literature, art and architecture, as well as its unique heritage, results in a nation balancing the needs of the present with those of its past.***

Britain's character has been shaped by its geographical position as an island. Never successfully invaded since 1066, its people have developed their own distinctive traditions. The Roman invasion of AD 43 lasted 350 years but Roman culture and language were quickly overlain with those of the northern European settlers who followed. Ties with Europe were loosened further in the 16th century when the Catholic church was replaced by a less dogmatic established church.

Although today a member of the European Union, Britain continues to delight in its non-conformity, even in superficial ways such as driving on the left-hand side of the

Tudor rose

road instead of the right. The opening of the rail tunnel to France is a topographical adjustment that does not necessarily mark a change in national attitude.

The British heritage is seen in its ancient castles, cathedrals and stately homes with their gardens and Classical parklands. Age-old customs are renewed each year, from royal ceremonies to Morris dancers performing on village greens.

For a small island, Great Britain encompasses a surprising variety in its regions, whose inhabitants maintain distinct identities. Scotland and Wales are separate countries from England with their own legislative assemblies.

Walking along the east bank of the River Avon, Bath

◁ Punting, a popular pastime on the River Cam, Cambridge

Widecombe-in-the-Moor, a Devon village clustered round a church and set in hills

They have different customs, traditions, and, in the case of Scotland, different legal and educational systems. The Welsh and Scots Gaelic languages survive and are sustained by their own radio and television networks. In northern and West Country areas, English itself is spoken in a rich variety of dialects and accents, and these areas maintain their own regional arts, crafts, architecture and food.

The landscape is varied, too, from the craggy mountains of Wales, Scotland and the north, through the flat expanses of the Midlands and eastern England to the soft, rolling hills of the south and west. The long, broad beaches of East Anglia contrast with the picturesque rocky inlets along much of the west coast.

Scottish coat of arms
at Edinburgh Castle

Lake and gardens at Petworth House, Sussex

Despite the spread of towns and cities over the last two centuries, rural Britain still flourishes. Nearly three-quarters of Britain's land is used for agriculture. The main commercial crops are wheat, barley, sugar beet and potatoes, though what catches the eye in early summer are the fields of bright yellow rape or slate-blue flax.

The countryside is dotted with farms and charming villages, with picturesque cottages and lovingly tended gardens – a British passion. A typical village is built around an ancient church and a small, friendly pub. Here the pace of life slows. To drink a pint of ale in a cosy, village inn and relax before a fire is a time-honoured British custom. Strangers will be welcomed cordially, though perhaps with caution; for even if strict formality is a thing of the past, the British have a tendency to be reserved.

In the 19th and early 20th centuries, trade with the extensive British Empire, fuelled by abundant coal supplies, spurred manufacturing and created wealth. Thousands of people moved from the countryside to towns and cities near mines, mills and factories. By 1850 Britain was the world's strongest industrial nation. Now many of these old industrial centres have declined, and today manufacturing employs only 10 per cent of the labour force, while 75 per cent work in the growing service sector. These service industries are located mainly in the southeast, close to London, where modern office buildings bear witness to comparative prosperity.

Crowds at Petticoat Lane market in London's East End

SOCIETY AND POLITICS

British cities are melting-pots for people not just from different parts of the country but also from overseas. Irish immigration has long ensured a flow of labour into the country, and since the 1950s hundreds of thousands have come from former colonies in Africa, Asia and the Caribbean. Today, EU membership has led to another wave of immigration to Britain, mostly from Eastern Europe. Nearly six per cent of Britain's 60 million inhabitants are from non-white ethnic groups – and about

half of these were born in Britain. The result is a multi-cultural society that can boast a wide range of music, art, food and religions. However, prejudice does exist and in some inner-city areas where poorer members of different communities live, racial tensions can occasionally arise. Even though discrimination in housing and employment on the grounds of race is against the law, it does occur. Britain's class structure still intrigues and bewilders many visitors, based as it is on a subtle mixture of heredity and wealth. Even though many of the great inherited fortunes no longer exist,

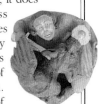

Bosses in Norwich Cathedral cloisters

some old landed families still live on their large estates, and many now open them to the public. Class divisions are further entrenched by the education system. While more than 90 per cent of children are educated free by the state, richer parents often opt for private schooling, and the products of these private schools are disproportionately represented in the higher echelons of government and business.

The monarchy's position highlights the dilemma of a people seeking to preserve its most potent symbol of national unity in an age that is suspicious of inherited privilege. Without real political power, though still head of the Church of England, the Queen and her family are subject to increasing public scrutiny and some citizens advocate the abolition of the monarchy.

Democracy has deep foundations in Britain: there was even a parliament of sorts in London in the 13th century.

Priest in the Close at Winchester Cathedral

Yet with the exception of the 17th-century Civil War, power has passed gradually from the Crown to the people's elected representatives. A series of Reform Acts between 1832 and 1884 gave the vote to all male citizens, though women were not enfranchised on an equal basis until 1928. Margaret Thatcher – Britain's first woman Prime Minister – held office for 12 years from 1979. During the 20th century, the Labour (left wing) and Conservative (right wing) parties have, during their periods in office, favoured a mix of public and private ownership for industry and ample funding for the state health and welfare systems.

Afternoon tea on the back lawn at the Thornbury Castle Hotel, Avon

The position of Ireland has been an intractable political issue since the 17th century. Part of the United Kingdom for 800 years, but divided in 1921, it has seen conflict between Catholics and Protestants for many years. The Good Friday Peace Agreement of 1998 was a huge step forward and the path to lasting peace now seems possible.

CULTURE AND THE ARTS

Britain has a famous theatrical tradition stretching back to the 16th century and William Shakespeare. His plays

The House of Lords, in Parliament

have been performed on stage almost continuously since he wrote them, and the works of 17th- and 18th-century writers are also frequently revived. Contemporary British playwrights such as Tom Stoppard, Alan Ayckbourn and David Hare draw on this long tradition with their vivid language and by using comedy to illustrate serious themes. British actors such as Helen Mirren, Judi Dench, Colin Firth, Ian McKellen, Kate Winslet and Anthony Hopkins have international reputations.

While London is the focal point of British theatre, fine drama is to be seen in many other parts of the country. The Edinburgh Festival and its Fringe are the high point of Great Britain's cultural calendar with theatre and music to suit all tastes. Other music festivals are held across the country, chiefly in summer, while there are annual

Schoolboys at Eton, the famous public school

festivals of literature at Hay-on-Wye and Cheltenham. Poetry has had an enthusiastic following since Chaucer wrote the *Canterbury Tales* in the 14th century: poems from all eras can even be read on the London Underground, where they are interspersed with the advertisements in the carriages and on the station platforms.

In the visual arts, Britain has a strong tradition in portraiture, caricature, landscape and watercolour. In modern times David Hockney and Lucian Freud, and sculptors Henry Moore and Barbara Hepworth, have enjoyed worldwide recognition. Architects including

Christopher Wren, Inigo Jones, John Nash and Robert Adam all created styles that define British cities; and today, Norman Foster and Richard Rogers carry the standard for Post-Modernism. Britain is becoming famous for its inno-

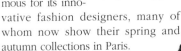
Reading the newspaper in Kensington Gardens

vative fashion designers, many of whom now show their spring and autumn collections in Paris.

The British are avid newspaper readers. There are 10 national newspapers published from London on weekdays: the standard of the serious newspapers is very high; for example, *The Times* is read the world over because of its reputation for strong intentional reporting.

Naomi Campbell, a British supermodel

Most popular, however, are the tabloids packed with gossip, crime and sport, which account for some 80 per cent of the total.

The indigenous film industry has produced international hits such as *The Queen* and *Slumdog Millionaire,* though blockbusters such as the Harry Potter films are often backed by the US. Acclaimed British film directors include Danny Boyle and Mike Leigh. British television is famous for the quality of its news, current affairs and drama programmes. The publicly funded British Broadcasting Corporation (BBC), which controls five national radio networks and two terrestrial television channels, as well as additional radio stations and television channels via digital technology, is widely admired.

The British are great sports fans, and soccer, rugby, cricket and golf are popular. An instantly recognizable English image is that of the cricket match on a village green. Nationwide, fishing is the most popular sporting pastime, and the British make excellent use of their national parks as keen walkers.

British food used to be derided for its lack of imagination, but the creative use of local, seasonal and ethical produce is now the emphasis, along with influences from around the world. Typical English food – plain home cooking and regional dishes – has also enjoyed a revival.

In this, as in other respects, the British are doing what they have done for centuries: accommodating their own traditions to influences from other cultures, while leaving the essential elements of their national life and character intact.

Whitby harbour and St Mary's Church, Yorkshire

Gardens Through the Ages

Styles of gardening in Britain have expanded alongside archi-tecture and other evolving fashions. The Elizabethan knot garden became more elaborate and formal in Jacobean times, when the range of plants greatly increased. The 18th century brought a taste for large-scale "natural" landscapes with lakes, woods and pastures, creating the most distinctively English style to have emerged. In the 19th century, fierce debate raged between supporters of natural and formal gardens, developing into the eclecticism of the 20th century when "garden rooms" in differing styles became popular.

Monumental column

A grotto and cascade brought romance and mystery.

"Capability" Brown (1715–83)
was Britain's most influential garden designer, favouring the move away from formal gardens to man-made pastoral settings.

Blackthorn

Classical temples were a much appreciated feature in 18th-century gardens and were often exact replicas of buildings that the designers had seen in Greece.

Elaborate parterres *were a feature of aristocratic gardens of the 17th century, when the fashion spread from Europe. This is the Privy Garden at Hampton Court Palace, res-tored in 1995 to its design under William III.*

IDEAL LANDSCAPE GARDEN

Classical Greece and Rome inspired the grand gardens of the early 18th century, such as Stourhead and Stowe. In-formal clumps of trees played a critical part in the serene, manicured landscapes.

Maple

Winding paths were carefully planned to allow changing vistas to open out as visitors strolled around the garden.

DESIGN AND FORMALITY

A flower garden is a work of artifice, an attempt to tame nature rather than to copy it. Growing plants in rows or regular patterns, interspersed with statues and ornaments, imposes a sense of order. Designs change to reflect the fashion of the time and the introduction of new plants.

Medieval gardens usually had a herber (a turfed sitting area) and a vine arbour. A good reconstruction is Queen Eleanor's Garden, Winchester.

Tudor gardens featured edged borders and sometimes mazes. The Tudor House Garden, Southampton, also has beehives and heraldic statues.

Herbaceous borders, *full of lush plants, are the glory of the summer garden. Gertrude Jekyll (1843–1932), was high priestess of the mixed border, with her eye for seductive colour combinations.*

Cedar of Lebanon   Yew

Rhododendron

The Palladian bridge was a favourite feature, often decorative rather than practical.

Knot Gardens *were in vogue in the 1500s. Intersecting lines of lavender or box were filled with flowers, herbs or vegetables, as in this restoration at Pitmedden in Scotland.*

DEVELOPMENT OF THE MODERN PANSY

All garden plants derive from wild flowers, bred over the years to produce qualities that appeal to gardeners. The story of the pansy, one of our most popular flowers, is typical.

The wild pansy (Viola tricolor) native to Britain is commonly known as heartsease. It is a small-flowered annual which can vary considerably in colour.

The mountain pansy (Viola lutea) is a perennial. The first cultivated varieties resulted from crossing it with heartsease in the early 19th century.

The Show Pansy was bred by florists after the blotch appeared as a chance seedling in 1840. It was round in form with a small, symmetrical blotch.

The Fancy Pansy, developed in the 1860s, was much larger. The blotch covered all three lower petals save for a thin margin of colour.

Modern hybrids of pansies, violas and violettas, developed by selective breeding, are varied and versatile in a wide range of vibrant new colours.

17th-century gardening was more elaborate. Water gardens like those at Blenheim were often combined with parterres of exotic foreign plants.

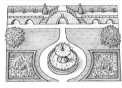

Victorian gardens, their formal beds a mass of colour, were a reaction to the landscapes of "Capability" Brown. Alton Towers has a good example.

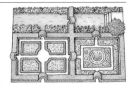

20th-century gardens mix historic and modern styles, as at Hidcote Manor, Gloucestershire. Growing wild flowers is a popular choice.

Stately Homes

Adam sketch (c.1760) for ornate panel

The grand country house reached its zenith in the 18th and 19th centuries, when the old landed families and the new captains of industry enjoyed their wealth, looked after by a retinue of servants. The earliest stately homes date from the 14th century, when defence was paramount. By the 16th century, when the opulent taste of the European Renaissance spread to England, houses became centres of pleasure and showplaces for fine art *(see pp302–03)*. The Georgians favoured chaste Classical architecture with rich interiors, the Victorians flamboyant Gothic. Due to 20th-century social change many stately homes have been opened to the public, some administered by the National Trust.

The saloon, a domed rotunda based on the Pantheon in Rome, was designed to display the Curzon family's Classical sculpture collection to 18th-century society.

The Drawing Room, the main room for entertaining, contains the most important pictures and some exquisite plasterwork.

The Marble Hall *is where balls and other social functions took place among Corinthian columns of pink alabaster.*

The Family Wing is a self-contained "pavilion" of private living quarters; the servants lived in rooms above the kitchen. The Curzon family still live here.

The Music Room is decorated with musical themes. Music was the main entertainment on social occasions.

TIMELINE OF ARCHITECTS

1650				1750
	Colen Campbell (1676–1729) designed Burlington House *(see p81)*	**William Kent** (1685–1748) built Holkham Hall *(see p197)* in the Palladian style	**Robert Adam** (1728–92), who often worked with his brother James (1730–94) was as famous for decorative details as for buildings	**Henry Holland** (1745–1806) designed the Neo-Classical south range of Woburn Abbey *(see p230)*
Sir John Vanbrugh *(see p398)* was helped by **Nicholas Hawksmoor** (1661–1736) on Blenheim Palace *(see pp228–29)*			**John Carr** (1723–1807) designed the Palladian Harewood House *(see p410)*	

Castle Howard (1702) by Sir John Vanbrugh

Adam fireplace, Kedleston Hall, adorned with Classical motifs

NATIONAL TRUST

At the end of the 19th century, there were real fears that burgeoning factories, mines, roads and houses would obliterate much of Britain's historic landscape and finest buildings. In 1895 a group that included the social reformer Octavia Hill formed the National Trust, to preserve the nation's valuable heritage. The first building acquired by the

National Trust oak leaf design

trust was the medieval Clergy House at Alfriston in Sussex, in 1896 *(see p180)*. Today the National Trust is a charity that runs many historic houses and gardens, and vast stretches of countryside and coastline *(see p671)*. It is supported by more than two million members nationwide.

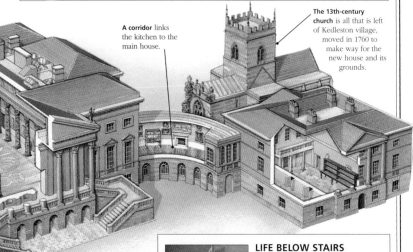

A corridor links the kitchen to the main house.

The 13th-century church is all that is left of Kedleston village, moved in 1760 to make way for the new house and its grounds.

KEDLESTON HALL

This Derbyshire mansion *(see p336)* is an early work of the influential Georgian architect Robert Adam, who was a pioneer of the Neo-Classical style derived from ancient Greece and Rome. It was built for the Curzon family in the 1760s.

Life Below Stairs by Charles Hunt (c.1890)

LIFE BELOW STAIRS

A large community of resident staff was essential to run a country house smoothly. The butler was in overall charge, ensuring that meals were served on time. The housekeeper supervised uniformed maids who made sure the place was clean. The cook ran the kitchen, using fresh produce from the estate. Ladies' maids and valets acted as personal servants.

1800	1850

Philip Webb (1831–1915) was a leading architect of the influential Arts and Crafts movement *(see p328)*, whose buildings favoured the simpler forms of an "Old English" style, instead of flamboyant Victorian Gothic

Sir Edwin Lutyens (1869–1944) designed the elaborate Castle Drogo in Devon *(see p295)*, one of the last grand country houses

Dining Room, Cragside, Northumberland

Norman Shaw (1831–1912) was an exponent of Victorian Gothic, as in Cragside (above), and a pioneer of the Arts and Crafts movement *(see p328)*

Standen, West Sussex (1891–94) by Philip Webb

Heraldry and the Aristocracy

The British aristocracy has evolved over 900 years from the feudal obligations of noblemen to the Norman kings, who conferred privileges of rank and land in return for armed support. Subsequent monarchs bestowed titles and property on their supporters, establishing new aristocratic dynasties. The title of "earl" dates from the 11th century; that of "duke" from the 14th century. Soon the nobility began to choose their own symbols, partly to identify a knight concealed by his armour: these were often painted on the knight's coat (hence the term "coat of arms") and also copied onto his shield.

Order of the Garter medal

The College of Arms, London: housing records of all coats of arms and devising new ones

ROYAL COAT OF ARMS

The most familiar British coat of arms is the sovereign's. It appears on the royal standard, or flag, as well as on official documents and on shops that enjoy royal patronage. Over nearly 900 years, various monarchs have made modifications. The quartered shield in the middle displays the arms of England (twice), Scotland and Ireland. Surrounding it are other traditional images including the lion and unicorn, topped by the crown and the royal helm (helmet).

Edward III *(1327–77) was the founder of the chivalric Order of the Garter. The garter, bearing the motto,* Honi soit qui mal y pense *(evil be to him who thinks of evil), goes round the central shield.*

The lion is the most common beast in heraldry.

The red lion is the symbol of Scotland.

The unicorn is a mythical beast, generally regarded as a Scottish royal beast in heraldry.

Henry II *(1154–89) formalized his coat of arms to include three lions. This was developed by his son Richard I to become the "Gules three lions passant guardant or" seen on today's arms.*

The royal helm with gold protective bars was introduced to the arms by Elizabeth I (1558–1603).

Dieu et mon droit (God and my right) has been the royal motto since the reign of Henry V (1413–22).

Henry VII *(1485–1509) devised the Tudor rose, joining the white and red roses of York and Lancaster.*

ADMIRAL LORD NELSON

When people are ennobled they may choose their own coat of arms if they do not already have one. Britain's naval hero (1758–1805) was made Baron Nelson of the Nile in 1798 and a viscount in 1801. His arms relate to his life and career at sea; but some symbols were added after his death.

A seaman supports the shield.

The motto means "Let him wear the palm (or laurel) who deserves it".

A tropical scene shows the Battle of the Nile (1798).

The San Joseph was a Spanish man o'war that Nelson daringly captured.

TRACING YOUR ANCESTRY

For records of births, deaths and marriages in England and Wales since 1837, contact the **General Register Office** (0845 603 7788; www.gro.gov.uk), and in Scotland **New Register House**, 3 West Register St, Edinburgh EH1 3YT (0131 334 0380; www.gro-scotland. gov.uk). For help in tracing family history, consult the **Society of Genealogists**, 14 Charterhouse Bldgs, London EC1 (020 7251 8799).

Inherited titles *usually pass to the eldest son or the closest male relative, but some titles may go to women if there is no male heir.*

The Duke of Edinburgh (born 1921), husband of the Queen, is one of several dukes who are members of the Royal Family.

The Marquess of Salisbury (1830–1903), Prime Minister three times between 1885 and 1902, was descended from the Elizabethan statesman Robert Cecil.

Earl Mountbatten of Burma (1900–79) was ennobled in 1947 for diplomatic and military services.

Viscount Montgomery (1887–1976) was raised to the peerage for his military leadership in World War II.

Lord Byron (1788–1824), the Romantic poet, was the 6th Baron Byron: the 1st Baron was an MP ennobled by Charles I in 1625.

PEERS OF THE REALM

There are nearly 1,200 peers of the realm. In 1999 the process began to abolish the hereditary system in favour of life peerages that expire on the death of the recipient *(see left and below)*. Ninety-two hereditary peers are entitled to sit in the House of Lords, including the Lords Spiritual – archbishops and senior bishops of the Church of England – and the Law Lords. In 1958 the Queen expanded the list of life peerages to honour people who had performed notable public service. From 1999 the system of "peoples peerages" began to replace inherited honours.

KEY TO THE PEERS

☐	25 dukes
☐	35 marquesses
☐	175 earls and countesses
☐	98 viscounts
☐	800+ barons and baronesses

THE QUEEN'S HONOURS LIST

Twice a year several hundred men and women nominated by the Prime Minister and political leaders for outstanding public service receive honours from the Queen. Some are made dames or knights; a few receive the prestigious OM (Order of Merit); far more receive lesser honours such as OBEs or MBEs (Officers or Members of The Most Excellent Order of the British Empire).

Mother Theresa *received the OM in 1983 for her work in India.*

Terence Conran, *founder of Habitat, was knighted for services to industry.*

The Beatles *were given MBEs in 1965. Paul McCartney was knighted in 1997.*

Rural Architecture

For many, the essence of British life is found in villages. Their scale and serenity nurture a way of life envied by those who live in towns and cities. The pattern of British villages dates back some 1,500 years, when the Saxons cleared forests and established settlements, usually centred around a green or pond. Most of today's English villages existed at the time of the *Domesday Book* in 1086, though few actual buildings survive from then. The settlements evolved organically around a church or manor; the cottages and gardens were created from local materials. Today, a typical village will contain structures of various dates, from the Middle Ages onward. The church is usually the oldest, followed perhaps by a tithe barn, manor house and cottages.

Abbotsbury, in Dorset – a typical village built up around a church

A steep-pitched roof covers the whole house.

Timbers are of Wealden oak.

Eaves are supported by curved braces.

Wealden Hall House *in Sussex is a medieval timber-framed house, of a type found in southeast England. It has a tall central open hall flanked by bays of two floors and the upper floor is "jettied", overhanging the ground floor.*

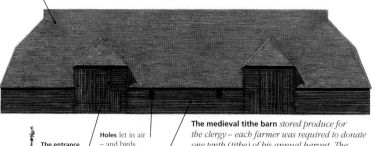

A tiled roof keeps the grain dry.

The entrance is big enough for ox-wagons.

Holes let in air – and birds.

Walls and doors are weatherboarded.

The medieval tithe barn *stored produce for the clergy – each farmer was required to donate one tenth (tithe) of his annual harvest. The enormous roofs may be supported by crucks, large curved timbers extending from the low walls.*

THE PARISH CHURCH

The church is the focal point of the village and, traditionally, of village life. Its tall spire could be seen – and its bells heard – by travellers from a distance. The church is also a chronicle of local history: a large church in a tiny village indicates a once-prosperous settlement. A typical church contains architectural features from many centuries, occasionally as far back as Saxon times. These may include medieval brasses, wall paintings, misericords *(see p341)*, and Tudor and Stuart carvings. Many sell informative guide books inside.

Slender spire from the Georgian era

West elevation

Pinnacled towers dating from the 15th century are situated at the west end.

Bells summon the congregation.

Buttresses support old walls.

Norman arches are rounded.

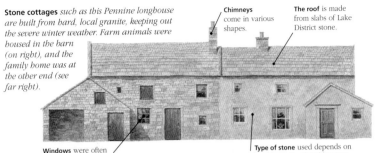

Stone cottages *such as this Pennine longhouse are built from hard, local granite, keeping out the severe winter weather. Farm animals were housed in the barn (on right), and the family home was at the other end (see far right).*

Chimneys come in various shapes.

The roof is made from slabs of Lake District stone.

Windows were often small in cold areas.

The roof is surfaced with tiles.

Type of stone used depends on locality. In Cumbria blue-grey Pennine stone was used.

Weatherboard houses *were built chiefly in southeast England in the 18th and 19th centuries; the timber boarding acted as cladding to keep out the cold and rain.*

Bay windows add light and space.

Thatch is made from reeds or straw.

Thatched cob cottages *of the 17th century have a cob covering a timber frame. The cob is made from a mixture of wet earth, lime, dung, chopped reed, straw, gravel, sand and stones.*

Walls are 1 m (3 ft) thick.

BUILDING MATERIALS

The choice of materials depended on local availability. A stone cottage in east Scotland or Cornwall would be granite, or in the Cotswolds, limestone. Timber for beams was often oak. Flint and pebble were popular in the chalky south and east. Slate is quarried in Wales and brick was widely used from Tudor times.

Welsh slate, making a durable roof

Tiles made from fired clay

Flint and pebble – common in Norfolk

Wood planks used for weatherboarding

Brick, widely used since Tudor times

Local hard granite from South Wales

South elevation

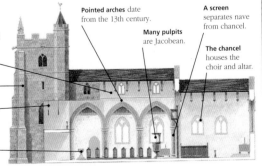

The nave is often the oldest part of the building, with extensions added in later centuries.

Towers are often later additions, due to their tendency to collapse.

Ropes used by bell-ringers.

The font, where babies are baptized, is often a church's oldest feature.

Pointed arches date from the 13th century.

Many pulpits are Jacobean.

A screen separates nave from chancel.

The chancel houses the choir and altar.

The Countryside

For its size, Britain contains an unusual variety of geological and climatic conditions that have shaped diverse landscapes, from treeless windswept moorland to

Common Blue butterfly

boggy marshes and small hedged cattle pastures. Each terrain nurtures its typical wildlife and displays its own charm through the seasons. With the reduction in farming and the creation of footpaths and nature reserves, the countryside is becoming more of a leisure resource.

INDIGENOUS ANIMALS AND BIRDS

There are no large or dangerous wild animals in Britain but a wealth of small mammals, rodents and insects inhabit the countryside, and the rivers and streams are home to many varieties of fish. For bird-watchers there is a great range of songbirds, birds of prey and seabirds.

Livestock graze on low pastures.

Trees provide shelter and protection for wildlife.

Higher land is uncultivated.

Bushes and trees grow between rocks.

Streams flow over a stony bed from mountain springs.

The highest ground is often covered in snow until spring.

WOODED DOWNLAND

Chalk downland, seen here at Ditchling Beacon on the Downs *(see p181)*, has soil of low fertility and is grazed by sheep. However crops are sometimes grown on the lower slopes. Distinctive wild flowers and butterflies thrive here, while beech and yew predominate in the woods.

WILD HILLSIDE

Large tracts of Britain's uplands remain wild terrain, unsuitable for crops or forestry. Purple heather is tough enough to survive in moorland, the haunt of deer and game birds. The highest craggy uplands, such as the Cairngorms *(see p544–45)* in Scotland, pictured here, are the habitat of birds of prey, such as the golden eagle.

Spear thistle *has pink heads in summer that attract several species of butterfly.*

Ling, *a low-growing heather with tiny pink bell-flowers, adds splashes of colour to peaty moors and uplands.*

The dog rose *is one of Britain's best-loved wild flowers; its pink single flower is widely seen in hedgerows.*

Hogweed *has robust stems and leaves with large clusters of white flowers.*

Meadow cranesbill *is a wild geranium with distinctive purple flowers.*

Tormentil *has small yellow flowers. It prefers moist, acid soil and is found near water on heaths and moors in summer.*

Swallows, *swifts and house martins are all summer visitors.*

Kestrels *are small falcons that prey on mammals such as voles.*

Rabbits *are often spotted feeding at the edge of fields or near woods.*

Robins, *common in gardens and hedgerows, have distinctive red breast feathers.*

Foxes, *little bigger than domestic cats, live in hideaways in woods, near farmland.*

Cereal crops ripen in small fields.

Hedgerows provide refuge for wildlife.

Small mixed woods break up the field pattern.

Sheep graze on salty marshes.

Culverts drain water from the field.

Reed beds edge the water.

TRADITIONAL FIELDS

The patchwork fields here in the Cotswolds *(see p304)* reflect generations of small-scale farming. A typical farm would produce silage, hay and cereal crops, and keep a few dairy cows and sheep in enclosed pastures. The tree-dotted hedgerows mark boundaries that may be centuries old.

MARSHLAND

Flat and low-lying wetlands, criss-crossed with dykes and drainage canals, provide the scenery of Romney Marsh *(see also p182)* as well as much of East Anglia. Some areas have rich, peaty soil for crops, or salty marshland for sheep, but there are extensive uncultivated sections, where reed beds shelter wildlife.

Sea lavender *is a saltmarsh plant that is tolerant of saline soils. It flowers in late summer.*

The oxeye daisy *is a larger relative of the common white daisy, found in grassland from spring to late summer.*

Orchids *are among the rarer wild flowers. This species is the Common Spotted Orchid.*

Cowslips *belong to the primrose family. In spring they are often found in the grass on open meadowlands.*

Poppies *glow brilliant red in cornfields.*

Buttercups *are among the most common wild flowers. They brighten meadows in summer.*

Walkers' Britain

Walkers of all levels of ability and enthusiasm are well served in Britain. There is an unrivalled network of long-distance paths through some spectacular scenery, which can be tackled in stages with overnight stays en route, or dipped into for a single day's walking. For shorter walks, Britain is dotted with signposts showing public footpaths across common or private land. You will find books of walk routes in local shops and a large map will keep you on track. Choose river routes for easy walking or take to the hills for a greater challenge.

Walker resting on Scafell Pike, Lake District

The West Highland Way is an arduous 95 mile (153 km) route from Milngavie, near Glasgow, to north of Fort William, across mountainous terrain with fine lochs and moorland scenery *(see p494)*.

Fort William

Glasgow

St Bees Head

The Pennine Way *was Britain's first designated long-distance path. The 268 mile (431 km) route from Edale in Derbyshire to Kirk Yetholm on the Scottish border is a challenging upland hike, with long, lonely stretches of moorland. It is only for experienced hill walkers.*

Offa's Dyke Footpath *follows the boundary between Wales and England. The 168 mile (270 km) path goes through the beautiful Wye Valley (see p461) in the Welsh borders.*

Dales Way runs from Ilkley in West Yorkshire to Bowness-on-Windermere in the Lake District, 81 miles (130 km) of delightful flat riverside walking and valley scenery.

Prestatyn

Pembrokeshire Coastal path *is 186 miles (299 km) of rugged cliff-top walking from Amroth on Carmarthen Bay to the west tip of Wales at Cardigan.*

St Dogmaels

Amroth

Minehead

ORDNANCE SURVEY MAPS

The best maps for walkers are published by the Ordnance Survey, the official mapping agency (08456 050505). Out of a wide range of maps the most useful are the *Explorer* series, which include the more popular regions and cover a large area, on a scale of 1:25,000, and the *Landranger* series, on a scale of 1:50,000.

The Southwest Coastal Path offers varied scenery from Minehead on the north Somerset coast to Poole in Dorset, via Devon and Cornwall – in all a marathon 630 mile (1,014 km) round trip.

SIGNPOSTS

Long-distance paths are well signposted, some of them with an acorn symbol (or with a thistle in Scotland). Many shorter routes are marked with coloured arrows by local authorities or hiking groups. Local councils generally mark public footpaths with yellow arrows. Public bridleways, marked by blue arrows, are paths that can be used by both walkers and horse riders – remember, horses churn up mud. Signs appear on posts, trees and stiles.

TIPS FOR WALKERS

Be prepared: *The weather can change very quickly: dress for the worst. Always take a compass, a proper walking map and get local advice before undertaking any ambitious walking. Pack some food and drink if the map does not show a pub en route.*

On the walk: *Always keep to the footpath and close gates behind you. Never feed or upset farm animals, leave litter, pick flowers or damage plants.*

Where to stay: *The International Youth Hostel Federation (see pp670–71) has a network of hostels which cater particularly for walkers. Bed-and-breakfast accommodation is also available near most routes (see p553).*

Further information: *The Ramblers' Association (020–7339 8500; www.ramblers.org.uk) is a national organization for walkers, with a guide to accommodation.*

The Coast to Coast Walk crosses the Lake District, Yorkshire Dales and North York Moors, on a 190 mile (306 km) route. This demanding walk covers a spectacular range of North Country landscapes. All cross-country routes are best walked from west to east to take advantage of the prevailing wind.

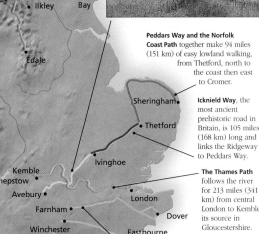

< Yetholm

dermere

Ilkley

Robin Hood's Bay

Edale

The Ridgeway is a fairly easy path that follows an ancient track once used by cattle drovers. Starting near Avebury (see p263) it covers 85 miles (137 km) to Ivinghoe Beacon.

Peddars Way and the Norfolk Coast Path together make 94 miles (151 km) of easy lowland walking, from Thetford, north to the coast then east to Cromer.

Sheringham

Thetford

Icknield Way, the most ancient prehistoric road in Britain, is 105 miles (168 km) long and links the Ridgeway to Peddars Way.

Ivinghoe

Kemble
hepstow

Avebury

Farnham

Winchester

Poole Harbour

London

Dover

Eastbourne

The Thames Path follows the river for 213 miles (341 km) from central London to Kemble, its source in Gloucestershire.

The Isle of Wight Coastal Path circles the entire island on an easy 65 mile (105 km) footpath.

The North Downs Way is an ancient route through 141 miles (227 km) of low-lying hills from Farnham in Surrey to Dover or Folkestone in Kent.

The South Downs Way is a 101 mile (162 km) walk from Eastbourne on the south coast to Winchester (see p170–71). It can be completed in a week.

THE HISTORY OF GREAT BRITAIN

Britain began to assume a cohesive character as early as the 7th century, with the Anglo-Saxon tribes absorbing Celtic and Roman influences and finally achieving supremacy. They suffered repeated Viking incursions and were overcome by the Normans at the Battle of Hastings in 1066. Over centuries, the disparate cultures of the Normans and Anglo-Saxons combined to form the English nation, a process nurtured by Britain's position as an island. The next 400 years saw English kings involved in military expeditions to Europe, but their control over these areas was gradually wrested from them. As a result they extended their domain over Scotland and Wales. The Tudor monarchs consolidated this control and laid the foundations for Britain's future commercial success. Henry VIII recognized the vital importance of sea power and under his daughter, Elizabeth I, English sailors ranged far across the world, often coming into conflict with the Spanish. The total defeat of the Spanish Armada in 1588 confirmed Britain's position as a major maritime power. The Stuart period saw a number of internal struggles, most importantly the Civil War in 1641. But by the time of the Act of the Union in 1707 the whole island was united and the foundations for representative government had been laid. The combination of this internal security with continuing maritime strength allowed Britain to seek wealth overseas. By the end of the Napoleonic Wars in 1815, Britain was the leading trading nation in the world. The opportunities offered by industrialization were seized, and by the late 19th century, a colossal empire had been established across the globe. Challenged by Europe and the rise of the US, and drained by its leading role in two world wars, Britain's influence waned after 1945. By the 1970s almost all the colonies had become independent Commonwealth nations.

Medieval knights, masters of the arts of war

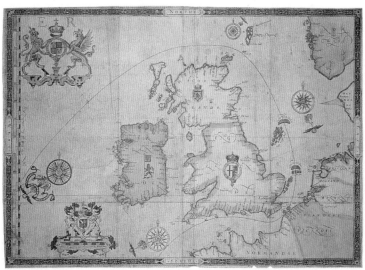

Contemporary map showing the defeat of the Armada (1588), making Britain into a world power

◁ Henry VIII, founder of the British navy, seen here with his son, Edward, and wife Jane Seymour

Kings and Queens

All English monarchs since the Norman Conquest in 1066 have been descendants of William the Conqueror. Scottish rulers, until James VI and the Union of Crowns in 1603 *(see pp482–3),* have been more diverse. When the Crown passes to someone other than the monarch's eldest son, the name of the ruling family usually changes. The rules of succession have been precisely laid down and strongly favour men over women, but Britain has still had six queens since 1553. In Norman times the monarchy enjoyed absolute power, but today the position is largely symbolic.

1413–22 Henry V

1509–47 Henry VIII

1399–1413 Henry IV

1485–1509 Henry VII

1066–87 William the Conqueror

1087–1100 William II

1100–35 Henry I

1135–54 Stephen

1327–77 Edward III

1483–5 Richard III

1050	1100	1150	1200	1250	1300	1350	1400	1450	1500
NORMAN		PLANTAGENET					LANCASTER	YORK	TUDOR
1050	1100	1150	1200	1250	1300	1350	1400	1450	1500

1154–89 Henry II

1189–99 Richard I

1199–1216 John

1216–72 Henry III

1307–27 Edward II

1272–1307 Edward I

1422–61 and 1470–1 Henry VI

1461–70 and 1471–83 Edward IV

1377–99 Richard II

Matthew Paris's 13th-century chronicle showing clockwise from top left, Richard I, Henry II, John and Henry III

1483 Edward V

553–8 Mary I

1660–85 Charles II

1685–8 James II

1689–1702
William III and
Mary II

1702–14
Anne

1714–27
George I

1936 Edward VIII

1603–25
James I

1837–1901 Victoria

1901–10
Edward VII

1727–60
George II

1952– Elizabeth II

50	1600	1650	1700	1750	1800	1850	1900	1950	2000
	STUART			HANOVER		SAXE-COBURG		WINDSOR	
50	1600	1650	1700	1750	1800	1850	1900	1950	2000

1830–37
William IV

1649–60 Commonwealth
under Lord Protector
Oliver Cromwell

1936–52 George VI shown
on the George Medal

1820–30
George IV

1910–36
George V

1625–49 Charles I

1558–1603 Elizabeth I

1760–1820 George III

47–53 Edward VI

Prehistoric Britain

Britain was part of the European landmass until the end of the last Ice Age, around 6000 BC, when the English Channel was formed by melting ice. The earliest inhabitants lived in limestone caves: settlements and farming skills developed gradually through the Stone Age. The magnificent wooden and stone henges and circles are masterworks from around 3000 BC, but their significance is a mystery. Flint mines and ancient pathways are evidence of early trading and many burial mounds (barrows) survive from the Stone and Bronze Ages.

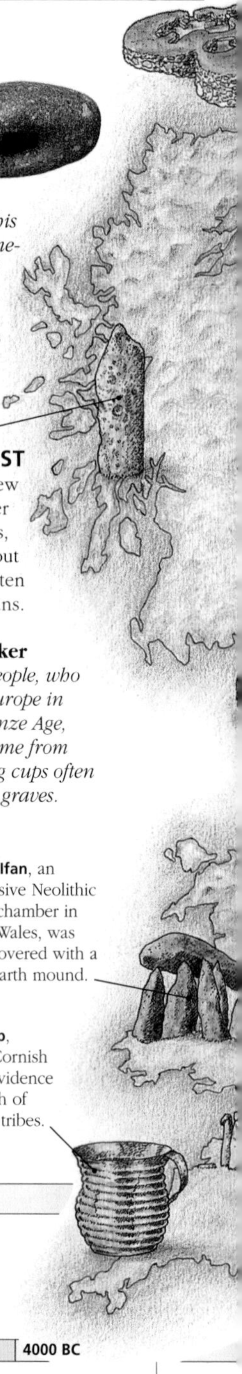

Axe Heads
Stone axes, like this one found at Stonehenge, were used by Neolithic men.

Cup and ring marks were carved on standing stones, such as this one at Ballymeanoch.

MAPPING THE PAST

Monuments from the Neolithic (New Stone), Bronze and Iron Ages, together with artifacts found from these periods, provide a wealth of information about Britain's early settlers, before written history began with the Romans.

Neolithic Tools
Antlers and bones were made into Neolithic leather-working tools. These were found at Avebury (see p263).

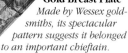

Pottery Beaker
The Beaker People, who came from Europe in the early Bronze Age, take their name from these drinking cups often found in their graves.

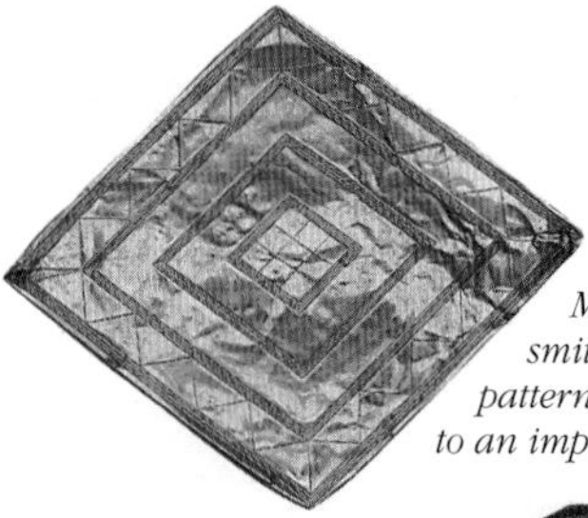

Gold Breast Plate
Made by Wessex goldsmiths, its spectacular pattern suggests it belonged to an important chieftain.

Pentre Ifan, an impressive Neolithic burial chamber in South Wales, was once covered with a huge earth mound.

Mold Cape
Gold was mined in Wales and Cornwall in the Bronze Age. This intricately worked warrior's cape was buried in a grave at Mold, Clwyd.

This gold cup, found in a Cornish barrow, is evidence of the wealth of Bronze Age tribes.

TIMELINE

6000–5000 As the Ice Age comes to an end, sea levels rise, submerging the landlink between Britain and the Continent

Neolithic flint axes

6000 BC	5500 BC	5000 BC	4500 BC	4000 BC

A gold pendant and button (1700 BC), found in Bronze Age graves

3500 Neolithic Age begins. Long barrows and stone circles built around Britain

Skara Brae is a Neolithic village of about 2500 BC (see p529).

Maiden Castle
An impressive Iron Age hill fort in Dorset, its concentric lines of ramparts and ditches follow the contours of the hill top (see p269).

Iron Age Axe
The technique of smelting iron came to Britain around 700 BC, brought from Europe by the Celts.

Iron Age Brochs, round towers with thick stone walls, are found only in Scotland.

Castlerigg Stone Circle is one of Britain's earliest Neolithic monuments (see p361).

WHERE TO SEE PREHISTORIC BRITAIN

Wiltshire, with Stonehenge (p262) and Avebury (p263), has the best group of Neolithic monuments, and the Uffington White Horse is nearby (p221). The Scottish islands have many early sites and the British Museum (pp106–7) houses a huge collection of artefacts.

A circular bank *with over 180 stones encloses the Neolithic site at Avebury (see p263).*

Uffington White Horse
Thought to be 3,000 years old, the shape has to be "scoured" to keep grass at bay (see p221).

A chalk figure, thought to be a fertility goddess, was found at Grimes Graves (see p194).

This bronze Celtic helmet (50 BC) was found in the River Thames, London.

Stonehenge was begun around 3,500 years ago (see pp262–63).

Snettisham Torc
A torc was a neck ring worn by Celtic men. This one, found in Norfolk, dates from 50 BC and is made from silver and gold.

3000 BC	2500 BC	2000 BC	1500 BC	1000 BC	500 BC

2500 Temples, or henges, are built of wood or stone

1650–1200 Wessex is at the hub of trading routes between Europe and the mines of Cornwall, Wales and Ireland

1000 First farmsteads are settled

550–350 Migration of Celtic people from southern Europe

500 Iron Age begins. Hill forts are built

2100–1650 The Bronze Age reaches Britain. Immigration of the Beaker People, who make bronze implements and build ritual temples

Chieftain's bronze sceptre (1700 BC)

1200 Small, self-sufficient villages start to appear

150 Tribes from Gaul begin to migrate to Britain

Roman Britain

Throughout the 350-year Roman occupation, Britain was ruled as a colony. After the defeat of rebellious local tribes, such as Boadicea's Iceni, the Romans remained an unassimilated occupying power. Their legacy is in military and civil construction: forts, walls, towns and public buildings. Their long, straight roads, built for easy movement of troops, are still a feature of the landscape.

Roman jasper seal

Cavalry Sports Helmet
Found in Lancashire, it was used in tournaments by horsemen. Cavalry races and other sports were held in amphitheatres near towns.

Silver Jug
This 3rd-century jug, the earliest known silver item with Christian symbols, was excavated near Peterborough.

Exercise corridor

Main baths

Fishbourne Palace was built at the site of a natural harbour and ships could moor here.

Entrance hall

Hadrian's Wall
Started in 120 as a defence against the Scots; it marked the northern frontier of the Roman Empire and was guarded by 17 forts housing over 18,500 foot-soldiers and cavalry.

Mithras
This head of the god Mithras was found on the London site of a temple devoted to the cult of Mithraism. The sect demanded of its Roman followers loyalty and discipline

TIMELINE

54 BC Julius Caesar lands in Britain but withdraws

Julius Caesar (c.102–44 BC)

AD 61 Boadicea rebels against Romans and burns their towns, including St Albans and Colchester, but is defeated *(see p195)*

AD 70 Romans conquer Wales and the North

Boadicea (1st century), Queen of the Iceni

140–143 Romans occupy southern Scotland and build Antonine Wall to mark the frontier

| 55 BC | AD 1 | AD 50 | | 150 |

AD 43 Claudius invades; Britain becomes part of the Roman Empire

AD 78–84 Agricola advances into Scotland, then retreats

120 Emperor Hadrian builds a wall on the border with Scotland

Flavian Mosaic
Roman floors of the 1st century used patterns in black and white stone. More mosaics survive at Fishbourne than at any other British site.

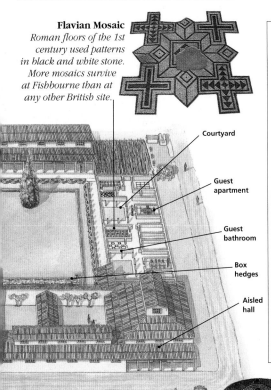

Courtyard

Guest apartment

Guest bathroom

Box hedges

Aisled hall

WHERE TO SEE ROMAN BRITAIN

Many of Britain's main towns and cities were established by the Romans and have Roman remains, including York (*see pp404–09*), Chester (*see pp310–11*), St Albans (*see p232*), Colchester (*see p205*), Bath (*see pp258–61*), Lincoln (*see pp340–41*) and London (*see pp70–155*). Several Roman villas were built in southern England, favoured for its mild climate and proximity to Europe.

The Roman baths in Bath (see pp258–61), *known as Aquae Sulis, were built between the 1st and 4th centuries around a natural hot spring.*

FISHBOURNE PALACE

Built during the 1st century for Togidubnus, a pro-Roman governor, the palace (here reconstructed) had sophisticated functions such as under-floor heating and indoor plumbing for baths (*see p171*).

Battersea Shield
Found in the Thames near Battersea, the shield bears Celtic symbols and was probably made at about the time of the first Roman invasion. Archaeologists suspect it may have been lost by a warrior while crossing the river, or offered as a sacrifice to one of the many river gods. It is now at the British Museum (see pp106–7).

Chi-Rho Symbol
This early Christian symbol is from a 3rd-century fresco at Lullingstone Roman villa in Kent.

206 Tribes from northern Scotland attack Hadrian's Wall

254 St Alban is beheaded, and becomes Britain's first Christian martyr

Aberlemno Pictish stone in Scotland

410 Romans withdraw from Britain

200	250	300	350	400

306 Roman troops in York declare Constantine emperor

350–69 Border raids by Picts and Scots

440–450 Invasions of Angles, Saxons and Jutes

209 Septimius Severus arrives from Rome with reinforcements

Anglo-Saxon Kingdoms

King Canute (1016–35)

By the mid-5th century, Angles and Saxons from Germany had started to raid the eastern shores of Britain. Increasingly they decided to settle, and within 100 years Saxon kingdoms, including Wessex, Mercia and Northumbria, were established over the entire country. Viking raids throughout the 8th and 9th centuries were largely contained, but in 1066, the last invasion of England saw William the Conqueror from Normandy defeat the Anglo-Saxon King Harold at the Battle of Hastings. William then went on to assume control of the whole country.

Viking Axe
The principal weapons of the Viking warriors were spear, axe and sword. They were skilled metal-workers with an eye for decoration, as seen in this axe-head from a Copenhagen museum.

Vikings on a Raiding Expedition
Scandinavian boat-building skills were in advance of anything known in Britain. People were terrified by these large, fast boats with their intimidating figureheads, which sailed up the Thames and along the coasts.

ANGLO-SAXON CALENDAR

These scenes from a chronicle of seasons, made just before the Norman invasion, show life in late Anglo-Saxon Britain. At first people lived in small farming communities, but by the 7th century towns began to spring up and trade increased. Saxon kings were supported by nobles but most of the population were free peasants.

TIMELINE

c.470–495 Saxons and Angles settle in Essex, Sussex and East Anglia

c.556 Saxons move across Britain and set up seven kingdoms

St Augustine (d.604)

635 St Aidan establishes a monastery on Lindisfarne

730–821 Supremacy of Mercia, whose king, Offa (d.796), builds a dyke along the Mercia–Wales border

450	500	550	600	650	700	750

450 Saxons first settle in Kent

563 St Columba lands on Iona

617–85 Supremacy of Northumbrian kingdom

597 St Augustine sent by Rome to convert English to Christianity

Mercian coin which bears the name of King Offa

Ox-drawn plough for tilling

Minstrels entertaining at a feast

Hawks, used to kill game

Alfred Jewel

This 9th-century gold ornament in the Ashmolean Museum (see p224) has the inscription: "Alfred ordered me made". This may refer to the Saxon King Alfred.

Edward the Confessor

In 1042, Edward – known as "the Confessor" because of his piety – became king. He died in 1066 and William of Normandy claimed the throne.

Harold's Death

This 14th-century illustration depicts the victorious William of Normandy after King Harold was killed with an arrow in his eye. The Battle of Hastings (see p181) was the last invasion of Britain.

WHERE TO SEE ANGLO-SAXON BRITAIN

The best collection of Saxon artefacts is from a burial ship unearthed at Sutton Hoo in Suffolk in 1938 and now on display at the British Museum *(see pp106–7)*. There are fine Saxon churches at Bradwell in Essex and Bosham in Sussex *(see p171)*. In York the Viking town of Jorvik has been excavated *(see p408)* and actual relics are shown alongside models of people and dwellings.

The Saxon church *of St Laurence (see p255) was built in the late 8th century.*

Legend of King Arthur

Arthur is thought to have been a chieftain who fought the Saxons in the early 6th century. Legends of his knights' exploits appeared in 1155 (see p285).

An invading Norman ship

800	850	900	950	1000	1050	1100

802–839 After the death of Cenwulf (821), Wessex gains control over most of England

867 Northumbria falls to the Vikings

878 King Alfred defeats Vikings but allows them to settle in eastern England

1016 Danish King Canute *(see p171)* seizes English crown

843 Kenneth McAlpin becomes king of all Scotland

926 Eastern England, the Danelaw, is reconquered by the Saxons

1042 The Anglo-Saxon Edward the Confessor becomes king (d.1066)

1066 William of Normandy claims the throne, and defeats Harold at the Battle of Hastings. He is crowned at Westminster

c.793 Lindisfarne sacked by Viking invaders; first Viking raid on Scotland about a year later

The Middle Ages

Noblemen stag hunting

Remains of Norman castles on English hill tops bear testimony to the military might used by the invaders to sustain their conquest – although Wales and Scotland resisted for centuries. The Normans operated a feudal system, creating an aristo-cracy that treated native Anglo-Saxons as serfs. The ruling class spoke French until the 13th century, when it mixed with the Old English used by the peasants. The medieval church's power is shown in the cathedrals that grace British cities today.

Magna Carta
To protect themselves and the church from arbitrary taxation, the powerful English barons compelled King John to sign a "great charter" in 1215 (see p235). This laid the foundations for an inde-pendent legal system.

Becket is received into heaven.

Craft Skills
An illustration from a 14th-century manuscript depicts a weaver and a copper-beater – two of the trades that created a wealthy class of artisans.

Henry II's knights murder Becket in Canterbury Cathedral.

MURDER OF THOMAS BECKET

The struggle between church and king for ultimate control of the country was brought to a head by the murder of Becket, the Archbishop of Canterbury. After Becket's canonization in 1173, Canterbury became a major centre of pilgrimage.

Ecclesiastical Art
Nearly all medieval art had religious themes, such as this window at Canterbury Cathedral (see pp186–7) depicting Jeroboam.

Black Death
A plague swept Britain and Europe several times in the 14th century, killing mil-lions of people. This illustration, in a religious tract, produced around 100 years later, represents death taking its heavy toll.

TIMELINE

1071 Hereward the Wake, leader of the Anglo-Saxon resistance, defeated at Ely

1154 Henry II, the first Plantagenet king, demolishes castles, and exacts money from barons instead of military service

1170 Archbishop of Canterbury, Thomas à Becket, is murdered by four knights after quar-relling with Henry II

1100	1150	1200	1250

1086 The *Domesday Book*, a survey of every manor in England, is compiled for tax purposes

Domesday Book

1215 Barons compel King John to sign the *Magna Carta*

1256 First Parliament to include ordinary citizens

Battle of Agincourt
In 1415, Henry V took an army to France to claim its throne. This 15th-century chronicle depicts Henry beating the French army at Agincourt.

This casket (1190), in a private collection, is said to have contained Becket's remains.

Becket takes his place in Heaven after his canonization.

Two clergymen look on in horror at Becket's murder.

Richard III
Richard, shown in this 16th-century painting, became king during the Wars of the Roses: a bitter struggle for power between two factions of the royal family – the houses of York and Lancaster.

John Wycliffe (1329–84)
This painting by Ford Madox Brown (1821–93) shows Wycliffe with the Bible he translated into English to make it accessible to everyone.

WHERE TO SEE MEDIEVAL BRITAIN

The university cities of Oxford *(pp222–27)* and Cambridge *(pp210–15)* contain the largest concentrations of Gothic buildings. Magnificent cathedrals rise high above many historic cities, among them Lincoln *(pp340–41)* and York *(pp404–09)*. Both cities still retain at least part of their ancient street pattern. Military architecture is best seen in Wales *(pp438–9)* with the formidable border castles of Edward I.

All Souls College *in Oxford (see p226), which only takes graduates, is a superb blend of medieval and later architecture.*

Castle Life
Every section of a castle was allotted to a baron whose soldiers helped defend it. This 14th-century illustration shows the coats of arms (see p30) of the barons for each area.

1282–3 Edward I conquers Wales

1314 Scots defeat English at the Battle of Bannockburn *(see p482)*

1348 Europe's population halved by Black Death

1387 Chaucer starts writing the *Canterbury Tales* (see p186)

1485 Battle of Bosworth ends Wars of the Roses

Geoffrey Chaucer (c.1345–1400)

1300	1350	1400	1450

1296 Edward I invades Scotland but Scots resist stoutly

Edward I (1239–1307)

1381 Peasants' revolt after the imposition of a poll tax on everyone in the country over 14

1415 English victory at Agincourt

1453 End of Hundred Years' War against France

Tudor Renaissance

Hawking, a popular pastime

After years of debilitating civil war, the Tudor monarchs established peace and national self-confidence, reflected in the split from the church of Rome – due to Henry VIII's divorce from Catherine of Aragon – and the consequent closure of the monasteries. Henry's daughter, Mary I, tried to reestablish Catholicism but under her half-sister, Elizabeth I, the Protestant church secured its position. Overseas exploration began, provoking clashes with other European powers seeking to exploit the New World. The Renaissance in arts and learning spread from Europe to Britain, with playwright William Shakespeare adding his own unique contribution.

Curtains behind the queen are open to reveal scenes of the great English victory over the Spanish Armada in 1588.

Sea Power
Henry VIII laid the foundations of the powerful English navy. In 1545, his flagship, the Mary Rose *(see p169), sank before his eyes in Portsmouth harbour on its way to do battle with the French.*

Theatre
Some of Shakespeare's plays were first seen in purpose-built theatres such as the Globe (see p120) in south London.

The globe signifies that the queen reigns supreme far and wide.

Monasteries
With Henry VIII's split from Rome, England's religious houses, like Fountains Abbey (see pp390–91), were dissolved. Henry stole their riches and used them to finance his foreign policy.

TIMELINE

1497 John Colet denounces the corruption of the clergy, supported by Erasmus and Sir Thomas More

1533–4 Henry VIII divorces Catherine of Aragon and is excommunicated by the Pope. He forms the Church of England

1542–1567 Mary, Queen of Scots rules Scotland

1490 **1510** **1530**

1497 John Cabot *(see p256)* makes his first voyage to North America

1513 English defeat Scots at Flodden *(see p482)*

Henry VIII (1491–1547)

1535 Act of Union with Wales

1536–40 Dissolution of the Monasteries

1549 First Book of Common Prayer introduced

Mary, Queen of Scots
As great-granddaughter of Henry VII, she laid claim to the English throne in 1559. But in 1567, Elizabeth I had her imprisoned for 20 years until her execution for treason in 1587.

Jewels *symbolize triumph.*

WHERE TO SEE TUDOR BRITAIN
Hampton Court Palace *(p173)* has been altered over the centuries but remains a Tudor showpiece. Part of Elizabeth I's former home at Hatfield *(p231)* still survives. In Kent, Leeds Castle, Knole *(pp188–9)* and Hever Castle *(p189)* all have connections with Tudor royalty. Burghley House *(pp342–3)* and Hardwick Hall *(p302)*, both Midlands mansions, retain their 16th-century character.

This astronomical clock at Hampton Court (see p173)*, with its intriguing zodiac symbols, was installed in 1540 by Henry VIII.*

DEFEAT OF THE ARMADA
Spain was England's main rival for supremacy on the seas, and in 1588 Philip II sent 100 powerfully armed galleons towards England, bent on invasion. The English fleet – under Lord Howard, Francis Drake, John Hawkins and Martin Frobisher – sailed from Plymouth and destroyed the Spanish navy in a famous victory. This commemorative portrait of Elizabeth I by George Gower (d.1596) celebrates the triumph.

Protestant Martyrs
Catholic Mary I reigned from 1553 to 1558. Protestants who opposed her rule were burned, such as these six churchmen at Canterbury in 1555.

William Shakespeare (1564-1616)

1570 Sir Francis Drake's first voyage to the West Indies

1584 Sir Walter Raleigh tries to colonize Virginia after Drake's first unsuccessful attempt

1591 First play by Shakespeare performed

1600 East India Company founded, beginning British involvement on the Indian continent

550   **1570**   **1590**

1553 Death of Edward VI; throne passes to the Catholic Mary I

1559 Mary, Queen of Scots lays claim to English throne

1558 Elizabeth I ascends the throne

1587 Execution of Mary, Queen of Scots on the orders of Elizabeth I

1588 Defeat of the Spanish Armada

Sir Walter Raleigh (1552–1618)

1603 Union of Crowns. James VI of Scotland becomes James I of England

Stuart Britain

The end of Elizabeth I's reign signalled the start of internal turmoil. The throne passed to James I, whose belief that kings ruled by divine right provoked clashes with Parliament. Under his son, Charles I, the conflict escalated into Civil War that ended with his execution. In 1660 Charles II regained the throne, but after his death James II was ousted for Catholic leanings. Protestantism was reaffirmed with the reign of William and Mary, who suppressed the Catholic Jacobites (see p483).

A 17th-century barber's bowl

Science

Sir Isaac Newton (1642–1727) invented this reflecting telescope, laying the foundation for a greater understanding of the universe, including the law of gravity.

Charles I stayed silent at his trial.

Oliver Cromwell
A strict Protestant and a passionate champion of the rights of Parliament, he led the victorious Parliamentary forces in the Civil War. He became Lord Protector of the Commonwealth from 1653 to 1658.

On the way to his death, the king wore two shirts for warmth, so onlookers should not think he was shivering with fright.

EXECUTION OF CHARLES I

Cromwell was convinced there would be no peace until the king was dead. At his trial for treason, Charles refused to recognize the authority of the court and offered no defence. He faced his death with dignity on 30 January 1649, the only English king to be executed. His death was followed by a republic known as the Commonwealth.

Theatre
After the Restoration in 1660, when Parliament restored the monarchy, theatre thrived. Plays were performed on temporary outdoor stages.

TIMELINE

1605 "Gunpowder Plot" to blow up Parliament thwarted	**1614** "Addled Parliament" refuses to vote money for James I	**1620** Pilgrim Fathers sail in the *Mayflower* to New England	**1642** Civil War breaks out	**1653–8** Cromwell rules as Lord Protector	
		1625		**1650**	
 *James I (1566–1625)*	**1611** New translation of Bible published, known as King James Version	**1638** Scots sign National Covenant, opposing Charles I's Catholic leanings	**1649** Charles I executed outside Banqueting House and Commonwealth declared by Parliament	**1660** Restoration of the monarchy under Charles II	

Restoration of the Monarchy

This silk embroidery celebrates the fact that Charles II escaped his father's fate by hiding in an oak tree. There was joy at his return from exile in France.

The headless body kneels by the block.

The axeman holds the severed head of Charles I.

Plague

Bills of mortality showed the weekly deaths as bubonic plague swept London in 1665. Up to 100,000 Londoners died.

Onlookers soaked up the king's blood with their handkerchiefs to have a memento.

Anatomy

By dissecting corpses, physicians began to gain an understanding of the working of the human body – a crucial step towards modern surgery and medicine.

WHERE TO SEE STUART BRITAIN

The best work of the two leading architects of the time, Inigo Jones and Christopher Wren, is in London, and includes St Paul's Cathedral (pp114–15). In the southeast two classic Jacobean mansions are Audley End (p208) and Hatfield House (p231). The Palace of Holyrood (p510), in Edinburgh, is another example.

Hatfield House (p231) *is a splendid Jacobean mansion.*

Pilgrim Fathers

In 1620 a group of Puritans sailed to America. They forged good relations with the native Indians; here they are shown being visited by the chief of the Pokanokets.

1665–6 Great Plague

The Great Fire of London

1666 Great Fire of London

1688 The Glorious Revolution: Catholic James II deposed by Parliament

1707 Act of Union with Scotland

1675

1700

1690 Battle of the Boyne: William's English/Dutch army defeats James II's Irish/French army

1692 Glencoe Massacre of Jacobites (Stuart supporters) by William III's forces

William III (1689–1702)

Georgian Britain

The 18th century saw Britain, now recovered from the trauma of its Civil War, develop as a commercial and industrial powerhouse. London became a centre of banking, and a mercantile and professional class grew up. Continuing supremacy at sea laid the foundations of an empire; steam engines, canals and railways heralded the Industrial Revolution. Growing confidence was reflected in stately architecture and elegant fashions but, as cities became more crowded, conditions for the underclass grew worse.

Actress Sarah Siddons (1785), Gainsborough

Slate became the preferred tile for Georgian buildings. Roofs became less steep to achieve an Italian look.

A row of sash windows is one of the most characteristic features of a Georgian house.

Battle of Bunker Hill

In 1775 American colonists rebelled against British rule. The British won this early battle in Massachusetts, but in 1783 Britain recognized the United States of America.

Oak was used in the best dwellings for doors and stairs, but pine was standard in most houses.

The saloon was covered in wallpaper, a cheaper alternative to hanging walls with tapestries or fabrics.

The drawing room was richly ornamented and used for entertaining visitors.

The dining room was used for all family meals.

Watt's Steam Engine

The Scottish engineer James Watt (1736–1819) patented his engine in 1769 and then developed it for locomotion.

Lord Horatio Nelson

Nelson (see p31) became a hero after his death at the Battle of Trafalgar fighting the French.

Steps led to the servants' entrance in the basement.

TIMELINE

1720 "South Sea Bubble" bursts: many speculators ruined in securities fraud

1746 Bonnie Prince Charlie *(see p535)*, Jacobite claimant to throne, defeated at the Battle of Culloden

1715	1730	1745	1760

1714 George, Elector of Hanover, succeeds Queen Anne, ending the Stuart dynasty and giving Britain a German-speaking monarch

1721 Robert Walpole (1646–1745) becomes the first Prime Minister

George I (1660–1727)

1757 Britain's first canal completed

Satirical engraving about the South Sea Bubble, 1720

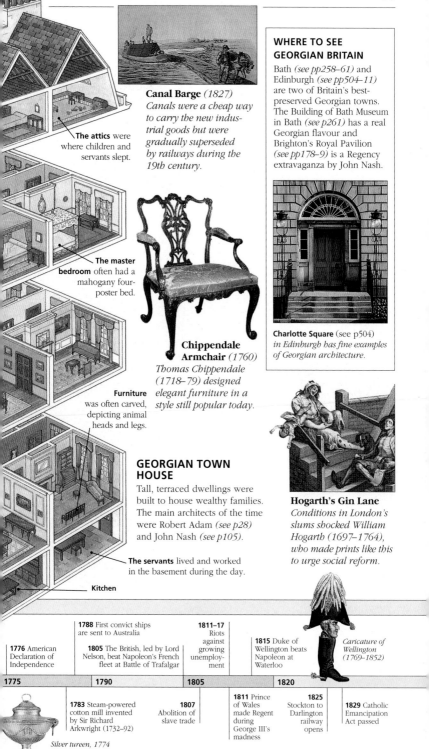

Canal Barge *(1827)*
Canals were a cheap way to carry the new industrial goods but were gradually superseded by railways during the 19th century.

The attics were where children and servants slept.

The master bedroom often had a mahogany four-poster bed.

Furniture was often carved, depicting animal heads and legs.

WHERE TO SEE GEORGIAN BRITAIN

Bath *(see pp258–61)* and Edinburgh *(see pp504–11)* are two of Britain's best-preserved Georgian towns. The Building of Bath Museum in Bath *(see p261)* has a real Georgian flavour and Brighton's Royal Pavilion *(see pp178–9)* is a Regency extravaganza by John Nash.

Charlotte Square (see p504) *in Edinburgh has fine examples of Georgian architecture.*

Chippendale Armchair *(1760)*
Thomas Chippendale (1718–79) designed elegant furniture in a style still popular today.

GEORGIAN TOWN HOUSE

Tall, terraced dwellings were built to house wealthy families. The main architects of the time were Robert Adam *(see p28)* and John Nash *(see p105)*.

The servants lived and worked in the basement during the day.

Kitchen

Hogarth's Gin Lane
Conditions in London's slums shocked William Hogarth (1697–1764), who made prints like this to urge social reform.

1776 American Declaration of Independence

1788 First convict ships are sent to Australia

1805 The British, led by Lord Nelson, beat Napoleon's French fleet at Battle of Trafalgar

1811–17 Riots against growing unemployment

1815 Duke of Wellington beats Napoleon at Waterloo

Caricature of Wellington (1769–1852)

1775

1790

1805

1820

1783 Steam-powered cotton mill invented by Sir Richard Arkwright (1732–92)

1807 Abolition of slave trade

1811 Prince of Wales made Regent during George III's madness

1825 Stockton to Darlington railway opens

1829 Catholic Emancipation Act passed

Silver tureen, 1774

Victorian Britain

When Victoria became Queen in 1837, she was only 18. Britain was in the throes of its transformation from an agricultural country to the world's most powerful industrial nation. The growth of the Empire fuelled the country's confidence and opened up markets for Britain's manufactured goods. The accelerating growth of cities created problems of health and housing and a powerful Labour movement began to emerge. But by the end of Victoria's long and popular reign in 1901, conditions had begun to improve as more people got the vote and universal education was introduced.

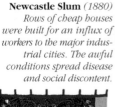

Victoria and Disraeli, 1887

Florence Nightingale *(1820–1910)*
Known as the Lady with the Lamp, she nursed soldiers in the Crimean War and pioneered many improvements in army medical care.

Glass walls and ceiling

Prefabricated girders

Newcastle Slum *(1880)*
Rows of cheap houses were built for an influx of workers to the major industrial cities. The awful conditions spread disease and social discontent.

As well as silk textiles exhibits included carriages, engines, jewels, glass, plants, cutlery and sculptures.

Union Banner
Trade unions were set up to protect industrial workers against unscrupulous employers.

Ophelia by Sir John Everett Millais *(1829–96)*
The Pre-Raphaelite painters chose Romantic themes, reflecting a desire to escape industrial Britain.

TIMELINE

Vase made for the Great Exhibition

1832 Great Reform Bill extends the vote to all male property owners

1841 London to Brighton railway makes resort accessible

1851 Great Exhibition

1867 Second Reform Act gives the vote to all male householders in towns

1830	1840	1850	1860

1834 Tolpuddle Martyrs transported to Australia for forming a union

1833 Factory Act forbids employment of children for more than 48 hours per week

1854–6 Britain victorious against Russia in Crimean War

1863 Opening of the London Underground

Triumph of Steam and Electricity
This picture from the Illustrated London News *(1897) sums up the feeling of optimism engendered by industrial advances.*

Elm trees were incorporated into the building along with sparrows, and sparrow hawks to control them.

WHERE TO SEE VICTORIAN BRITAIN

The industrial cities of the Midlands and the North are built around grandiose civic, commercial and industrial buildings. Notable Victorian monuments include the Manchester Museum of Science and Industry *(see p374)* and, in London, the Victoria and Albert Museum *(see pp98–9)* and St Pancras train station.

The Rotunda, Manchester *is a stately Victorian building.*

GREAT EXHIBITION OF 1851
The brainchild of Prince Albert, Victoria's consort, the exhibition celebrated industry, technology and the expanding British Empire. It was the biggest of its kind held up until then. Between May and October, six million people visited Joseph Paxton's lavish crystal palace, in London's Hyde Park. Nearly 14,000 exhibitors brought 100,000 exhibits from all over the world. In 1852 it was moved to south London where it burned down in 1936.

Cycling Craze
The bicycle, invented in 1865, became immensely popular with young people, as illustrated by this photograph of 1898.

1872 The Ballot Act introduces secret voting

1874 Benjamin Disraeli becomes Prime Minister

1884 Telephones introduced

1893 Gladstone's Irish Home Rule Bill defeated

1901 Queen Victoria dies

Cartoon of Gladstone, Vanity Fair (1869)

1870 — 1880 — 1890 — 1900

1870 Education Act makes school compulsory for children up to the age of 11

1877 Queen Victoria created Empress of India

1892 First Labour MP elected

1899–1902 Britain defeats South African Dutch settlers in Boer War

Early telephone

Britain from 1900 to 1950

When Queen Victoria's reign ended in 1901, British society threw off many of its 19th-century inhibitions, and an era of gaiety and excitement began. This was interrupted by World War I. The economic troubles that ensued, which culminated in the Depression of the 1930s, brought misery to millions. In 1939 the ambitions of Germany provoked World War II. After emerging victorious from this conflict, Britain embarked on an ambitious programme of social, educational and health reform.

Playwright Noel Coward

Welwyn Garden City was based on the Utopian ideals of Sir Ebenezer Howard (1850–1928), founder of the garden city movement.

Suffragettes
Women marched and chained themselves to railings in their effort to get the vote; many went to prison. Women over 30 won the vote in 1919.

The Roaring Twenties
Young flappers discarded the rigid social codes of their parents and instead discovered jazz, cocktails and the Charleston.

NEW TOWNS
A string of new towns was created on the outskirts of London, planned to give residents greenery and fresh air. Welwyn Garden City was originally founded in 1919 as a self-contained community, but fast rail links turned it into a base for London commuters.

World War I
British troops in Europe dug into deep trenches protected by barbed wire and machine guns, only metres from the enemy, in a war of attrition that cost the lives of 17 million.

Wireless
Invented by Guglielmo Marconi, radios brought news and entertainment into homes for the first time.

TIMELINE

1903 Suffragette movement founded	**1911** MPs are given a salary for the first time, allowing working men to be elected	**1914–18** World War I	**1924** First Labour government	

1905	1910	1915	1920

Henry Asquith (1852–1928), Prime Minister

1908 Asquith's Liberal government introduces old age pensions

1918 Vote given to all women over 30

1922 First national radio service begins

Marching for Jobs
These men were among thousands who marched for their jobs after being put out of work in the 1920s. The stock market crash of 1929 and the ensuing Depression caused even more unemployment.

Garden cities all had trees, ponds and open spaces.

World War II
German night-time air raids targeted transport, military and industrial sites and cities, such as Sheffield, in what was known as the "Blitz".

TO LET
PER ANNUM
AL PURCHASE TERMS
EN CITY HERTS
PAVEMENT. E.C.2.

Cheap housing and the promise of a cleaner environment attracted many people to these new cities.

HILLMAN MINX

Family Motoring
By the middle of the century, more families could afford to buy mass-produced automobiles, like the 1950s Hillman Minx pictured in this advertisement.

Modern Homes
Labour-saving devices, such as the vacuum cleaner, invented by William Hoover in 1908, were very popular. This was due to the virtual disappearance of domestic servants, as women took jobs outside the home.

1926 General Strike

Edward VIII (1894–1972) and Wallis Simpson (1896–1986)

1929 Stock market crashes

1928 Votes for all men and women over 21

1936 Abdication of Edward VIII

1936 First scheduled television service begins

1944 Education Act: school leaving age raised to 15; grants provided for university students

1939–45 Winston Churchill leads Britain to victory in World War II

Food ration book

1948 National Health Service introduced

1947 Independence for India and Pakistan

1945 Majority Labour government; national-ization of railways, road haulage, civil aviation, Bank of England, gas, electricity and steel

RATION BOOK

5   1930   1935   1940   1945

Britain Today

1982 British troops set sail to drive the Argentinians from the British-owned Falkland Islands

With the deprivations of war receding, Britain entered the Swinging Sixties, an explosion of youth culture characterized by the mini-skirt and the emergence of pop groups. The Age of Empire came to an end as most colonies gained independence by the 1970s – although Britain went to war again in 1982 when Argentina sought to annexe the tiny Falkland Islands.

1970s The outlandish clothes, hair and make-up of Punk Rockers shock the country

People were on the move; immigration from the former colonies enriched British culture – though it also gave rise to social problems – and increasing prosperity allowed millions of people to travel abroad. Britain joined the European Community in 1973, and forged a more tangible link when the Channel Tunnel opened in 1994.

Designer Vivienne Westwood and Naomi Campbell

1960s The miniskirt takes British fashion to new heights of daring – and Flower Power arrives from California

1981 Charles, Prince of Wales, marries Lady Diana Spencer in "fairytale" wedding at St Paul's Cathedral

1951 Winston Churchill comes back as Prime Minister as Conservatives win general election

1965 Death penalty is abolished

1950	1960	1970	1980

1950	1960	1970	1980

1953 Elizabeth II crowned in first televised Coronation

1975 Drilling begins for North Sea oil

1984 Year-long miners' strike fails to stop pit closures and heralds decline in trade union power

1951 Festival of Britain lifts postwar spirits

1963 The Beatles pop group from Liverpool captures the spirit of the age with numerous chart-topping hits

1959 First motorway, the M1, built from London to the Midlands

VOTE!

...GET BRITAIN OUT

1957 First immigrants arrive from the Caribbean by boat

1973 After years of negotiation, Britain joins the European Community

1979 The "Iron Lady" Margaret Thatcher becomes Britain's first woman Prime Minister; her right-wing Conservative Government privatizes several state-owned industries

2005 The Prince of Wales marries Camilla Parker-Bowles at the Guildhall in Windsor

2005 London's transport system hit by four bombs in a terrorist attack

1991 Then Britain's tallest building, Canada Tower *(see p125),* was erected as part of the huge Docklands development – London's financial centre

2011 Prince William marries Catherine Middleton in Westminster Abbey

2004 One of London's most distinctive buildings, 30 St Mary Axe, also known as "the Gherkin", opens

2010 General Election results in a coalition government with David Cameron as Prime Minister

1992 Conservative Government elected for fourth term – a record for this century

1997 New Labour ends 18 years of Conservative government

2012 Britain hosts the 2012 Olympic Games

1990	2000	2010	2020

1990	2000	2010	2020

2012 Queen Elizabeth II's Diamond Jubilee

1990 Mrs Thatcher forced to resign by Conservative MPs; replaced by John Major

2005 The Labour party is elected for a record third term under Tony Blair

2003 Britain joins the US-led coalition in the Iraq war and thousands take to the streets to protest against the imminent invasion

1999 Formation of Scottish Parliament and Welsh Assembly

1994 Channel Tunnel opens to give direct rail link between Britain and Continental Europe

GREAT BRITAIN
THROUGH THE YEAR

Every British season has its particular charms. Most major sights are open all year round, but many secondary attractions may be closed in winter. The weather is changeable in all seasons and the visitor is as likely to experience a crisp, sunny February day as to be caught in a cold, heavy shower in July. Long periods of

Film festival sign

adverse weather and extremes of temperature are rare. Spring is characterized by daffodils and bluebells, summer by roses and autumn by the vivid colours of changing leaves. In wintertime, country vistas are visible through the bare branches of the trees. Annual events and ceremonies, many stemming from age-old traditions, reflect the attributes of the seasons.

Bluebells in spring in Angrove woodland, Wiltshire

SPRING

As the days get longer and warmer, the countryside starts to come alive. At Easter many stately homes and gardens open their gates to visitors for the first time, and during the week before Whit

Sunday, or Whitsun (the seventh Sunday after Easter), the Chelsea Flower Show takes place. This is the focal point of the gardening year and spurs on the nation's gardeners to prepare their summer displays. Outside the capital, many music and arts festivals mark the middle months of the year.

MARCH

Ideal Home Exhibition (second week), Earl's Court, London. New products and ideas for the home.
Crufts Dog Show, National Exhibition Centre, Birmingham.
St Patrick's Day (17 March). Musical events in major cities celebrate the feast day of Ireland's patron saint.
Oxford and Cambridge Boat Race (late Mar or early Apr), River Thames, London.

APRIL

Maundy Thursday (Thursday before Easter), the Queen gives money to pensioners.
St George's Day (23 April), English patron saint's day.
Antiques for Everyone (last week), National Exhibition Centre, Birmingham.

Water garden exhibited at the Chelsea Flower Show

MAY

Furry Dancing Festival (8 May), Helston, Cornwall. Spring celebration (see p280).
Well Dressings (Ascension Day), Tissington, Derbyshire (see p337).
Chelsea Flower Show (May), Royal Hospital, London.
Brighton Festival (last three weeks). Performing arts.
Glyndebourne Festival Opera Season (mid-May– end Aug), near Lewes, East Sussex. Opera productions.
International Highland Games (last weekend), Blair Atholl, Scotland.

Yeomen of the Guard conducting the Maundy money ceremony

SUMMER

Life moves outdoors in the summer months. Cafés and restaurants place tables on the pavements and pub customers take their drinks outside. The Queen holds garden parties for privileged guests at Buckingham Palace while, more modestly, village fêtes – which include traditional games and local stalls – are organized. Beaches and swimming pools become crowded and office workers picnic in city parks at lunch. The rose, England's national flower, bursts into bloom in millions of gardens. Cultural treats include open-air theatre performances, outdoor concerts, the Proms in London, the National Eisteddfod in Wales, Glyndebourne's opera festival, and Edinburgh's festival of the performing arts.

Glastonbury music festival, a major event attracting thousands of people

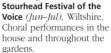
Deck chair at Brighton

JUNE

Hay Festival *(end May–early June)*, Hay-on-Wye, Wales. Family-friendly literature and music festival.
Bath International Music Festival *(late May–early Jun)*, various venues. Arts events.
Royal Academy of Arts Summer Exhibition *(Jun–Aug)*. Large and varied London show of new work by many artists.

Assessment of sheep at the Royal Welsh Show, Builth Wells

Trooping the Colour *(Sat closest to 10 Jun)*, Whitehall, London. The Queen's official birthday parade.
Glastonbury Festival *(late June)*, Somerset.
Aldeburgh Festival *(second and third weeks)*, Suffolk. Arts festival with concerts and opera.
Royal Highland Show *(third week)*, Ingliston, near Edinburgh. Agricultural show.
Stourhead Festival of the Voice *(Jun–Jul)*, Wiltshire. Choral performances in the house and throughout the gardens.
Leeds Castle *(last week Jun–early Jul)*. Open-air concerts.
Glasgow Jazz Festival *(last weekend Jun–early Jul)*. Various venues.

JULY

Henley Royal Regatta *(late Jun–Jul)*, Henley-on-Thames. Rowing regatta on the Thames.
International Eisteddfod *(first week)*, Llangollen, North Wales. International music and dance competition *(see p450)*.
Hampton Court Flower Show *(early July)*, Hampton Court Palace, Surrey.
Cambridge Folk Festival *(last weekend)*. Music festival with top international artists.
Royal Welsh Show *(last weekend)*, Builth Wells, Wales. Agricultural show.
International Festival of Folk Arts *(late Jul–early Aug)*, Sidmouth, Devon *(see p289)*.

AUGUST

Royal National Eisteddfod *(early in month)*. Traditional arts competitions, in Welsh *(see p435)*. Various locations.

Reveller in bright costume at the Notting Hill Carnival

Henry Wood Promenade Concerts *(mid-Jul–mid-Sep)*, Royal Albert Hall, London. Famous concert series popularly known as the Proms.
Edinburgh International Festival *(mid-Aug–mid-Sep)*. The largest festival of theatre, dance and music in the world *(see p481)*.
Edinburgh Festival Fringe. Alongside the festival, there are 400 shows a day.
Brecon Jazz *(mid-Aug)*, jazz festival in Brecon, Wales.
Beatles Festival *(last weekend)*, Liverpool. Music and entertainment related to the Fab Four *(see p377)*.
Notting Hill Carnival *(last weekend)*, London. West Indian street carnival with floats, bands and stalls.

Boxes of apples from the autumn harvest

AUTUMN

After the heady escapism of summer, the start of the new season is marked by the various party political conferences held in October and the royal opening of Parliament. All over the country on 5 November, bonfires are lit and fireworks let off to celebrate the foiling of an attempt to blow up the Houses of Parliament by Guy Fawkes and his co-conspirators in 1605. Cornfields become golden, trees turn fiery yellow through to russet and orchards

Fireworks over Edinburgh on Guy Fawkes Night

are heavy with apples and other autumn fruits. In churches throughout the country, thanksgiving festivals mark the harvest. The shops stock up for the run-up to Christmas, their busiest time of the year.

SEPTEMBER

Blackpool Illuminations *(beg Sep–end Oct)*. A 5 mile (8 km) spectacle of lighting along Blackpool's seafront.
The Braemar Gathering *(first Sat)*, Braemar, Scotland. Kilted clansmen from all over the country toss cabers, shot putt, dance and play the bagpipes. The royal family usually attends.
International Sheepdog Trials *(Jul–Sep)*, all over Britain, with venues changing from year to year.
Great Autumn Flower Show, Harrogate, N Yorks. Displays by nurserymen and national flower organizations.
St Ives Festival *(second and third weeks)*, Cornwall. Open studios, exhibitions, live music, poetry and theatre take place in civic buildings, galleries, pubs and the streets of this picturesque and historic fishing village and artists' community.

Shot putting at Braemar

OCTOBER

Harvest Festivals *(whole month)*, all over Britain especially in farming areas.
Horse of the Year Show *(6–10 Oct)*, NEC, Birmingham.
Nottingham Goose Fair *(first week)*. One of Britain's oldest traditional fairs now has a funfair.
Canterbury Festival *(second and third weeks)*. Music, drama and the arts.
Brighton Early Music Festival *(end Oct)*, Sussex. Choral performances in venues across Brighton and Hove.

Procession leading to the state opening of Parliament

NOVEMBER

State Opening of Parliament *(Oct or Nov)*. The Queen goes from Buckingham Palace to Westminster in a state coach, to open the new parliamentary session.
London Film Festival *(end Oct–beg Nov)*. Forum for new films, various venues.
Lord Mayor's Procession and Show *(second Sat)*. Parade in the City, London.
Remembrance Day *(second Sun)*. Services and parades at the Cenotaph in Whitehall, London, and all over Britain.
RAC London to Brighton Veteran Car Rally *(first Sun)*. A 7am start from Hyde Park, London to Brighton, East Sussex.
Guy Fawkes Night *(5 Nov)*, fireworks and bonfires all over the country.
Regent Street Christmas Lights *(mid-Nov)*, London.

Winter landscape in the Scottish Highlands, near Glencoe

WINTER

Brightly coloured fairy lights and Christmas trees decorate Britain's principal shopping streets as shoppers rush to buy their seasonal gifts. Carol services are held in churches across the country, and pantomime, a traditional entertainment for children deriving from the Victorian music hall, fills theatres in major towns.

Brightly lit Christmas tree at the centre of Trafalgar Square

Many offices close between Christmas and the New Year. Shops reopen for the January sales on 27 December – a paradise for bargain-hunters.

DECEMBER

Christmas Tree *(first Thu)*, Trafalgar Square, London. The tree is donated by the people of Norway and is lit by the Mayor of Oslo; this is followed by carol singing.
Carol concerts *(whole month)*, all over Britain.
Grand Christmas Parade *(beg Dec)*, London. Parade with floats to celebrate myth of Santa Claus.
The Burning of the Clocks *(21 Dec)*, Brighton, Sussex. Parades and fireworks on Brighton beach celebrating the winter solstice.
Midnight Mass *(24 Dec)*, in churches everywhere around Britain.

Sprig of holly

PUBLIC HOLIDAYS

New Year's Day (1 Jan).
2 Jan (Scotland only).
Easter weekend (March or April). In England it begins on **Good Friday** and ends on **Easter Monday**; in Scotland there is no Easter Monday holiday.
May Day (usually first Mon in May).
Late Spring Bank Holiday (last Mon in May).
Bank Holiday (first Mon in August, Scotland only).
August Bank Holiday (last Mon in August, except Scotland).
Christmas and Boxing Day (25–26 December).

JANUARY

Hogmanay and **New Year** *(31 Dec,1 Jan)*, Scottish celebrations. **Burns Night** *(25 Jan)*. Scots everywhere celebrate poet Robert Burns' birth with poetry, feasting and drinking.

FEBRUARY

Chinese New Year *(late Jan or early Feb)*. Lion dances, firecrackers and processions in Chinatown, London.

Morris dancing on May Day in Midhurst, Sussex

The Sporting Year

Many of the world's major competitive sports, including soccer, cricket and tennis, were invented in Britain. Originally devised as recreation for the wealthy, they have since entered the arena of mass entertainment. Some, however, such as the Royal Ascot race meeting and Wimbledon tennis tournament, are still valued as much for their social prestige as for the sport itself. Other delightful sporting events in Britain take place at a local level: village cricket, point-to-point racing and the Highland Games are all popular amateur events.

Kelly Holmes

Royal Ascot *is the four-day social highlight of the horse racing year. The high class of the thoroughbreds is matched by the high style of the fashions, with royalty attending.*

Oxford and Cambridge Boat Race, *first held in 1829 at Henley, has become a national event, with the two university eights now battling it out between Putney and Mortlake on the Thames.*

The FA Cup Final *is the apex of the football season.*

Derby Day horse races, Epsom

January	February	March	April	May	June

Cheltenham Gold Cup steeplechase *(see p328)*

Grand National steeplechase, Aintree *(see p376),* Liverpool

Rugby League Cup Final, Wembley

Embassy World Snooker Championships, Sheffield

Wimbledon Lawn Tennis Tournament *is the world's most prestigious lawn tennis championship.*

Six Nations Rugby Union *is an annual contest between England, France, Italy, Ireland (left), Scotland (right) and Wales. This league-based competition runs through winter ending in March.*

London Marathon *attracts thousands of long-distance runners, from the world's best to fancy-dressed fund raisers.*

Henley Royal Regatta (see p234) *is an international rowing event on the Thames (first held in 1839). It is also a glamorous social occasion.*

British Grand Prix, *held at Silverstone, is Britain's round of the Formula One World Championship.*

TICKETS AND TOUTS

For many big sporting events, the only official source of tickets is the club concerned. Booking agencies may offer hard-to-get tickets – though often at high prices. Unauthorized touts may lurk at popular events but their expensive tickets are not always valid. Check carefully.

Tickets for the Grand Prix

British Open Golf Championship, *a major golf event, is held at one of several British courses. Here, Nick Faldo putts.*

The Cheltenham and Gloucester Trophy *is the final of a season of competition to find the year's county cricket champions. It takes place at Lord's (see p155).*

Cowes week *(see p168),* a yachting festival, covers all classes of racing.

Horse of the Year Show brings together top showjumpers to compete on a tough indoor course *(see p64).*

Oxford versus Cambridge rugby union, Twickenham

August	September	October	November	December

European Show jumping Championships at Hickstead

Braemar Highland Games *(see p64)*

British Figure Skating and Ice Dance Championships *are a feast of elegance on ice (various venues).*

Winmau World Masters Darts Championships

Gold Cup Humber powerboat race, Hull

KEY TO SPORT SEASONS

▦	Cricket
▦	River fishing
▦	Football (soccer)
▦	Hunting and shooting
▦	Rugby (union and league)
▦	Flat racing
▦	Jump racing
▦	Athletics – track and field
▦	Road running and cross-country
▦	Polo

Cartier International Polo, *at the Guards Club, Windsor (see p235), is one of the main events for this peculiarly British game, played mainly by royalty and army officers.*

The Climate of Great Britain

Britain has a temperate climate. No region is far from the sea, which exerts a moderating influence on temperatures. Seldom are winter nights colder than -15°C, even in the far north, or summer days warmer than 30°C in the south and west: a much narrower range than in most European countries. Despite Britain's reputation, the average annual rainfall is quite low – 108 cm (42 inches) – and heavy rain is rare. The Atlantic coast is warmed by the Gulf Stream, making the west slightly warmer, though wetter, than the east.

Wi
Inverness
The Highlands and Islands
EDINBURG
Glasgow
The Lowlands
Lancashire and the Lakes
Liverpo
North Wales
Caernarfon
South and Mid-Wales
CARDIFF
Br
West Coun
Exeter
Devon and Cornwall

LANCASHIRE AND THE LAKES

°C /°F

		19/66		
12/54	13/55	14/57		
5/41			8/46	6/43
				2/36

☀	5.5 hrs	6 hrs	3 hrs	1.5 hrs
☂	53 mm	85 mm	104 mm	90 mm
month	Apr	Jul	Oct	Jan

THE HEART OF ENGLAND

°C /°F

		20/68		
12/54	13/55	13/55		
5/41			8/46	6/43
				2/36

☀	4.5 hrs	5.5 hrs	3 hrs	1.5 hrs
☂	53 mm	69 mm	69 mm	74 mm
month	Apr	Jul	Oct	Jan

Average monthly maximum temperature

Average monthly minimum temperature

Average daily hours of sunshine

Average monthly rainfall

SOUTH AND MID-WALES

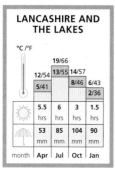

°C /°F

		20/68		
13/55	13/55	14/57		
5/41			8/46	7/45
				2/36

☀	5.5 hrs	6 hrs	3.5 hrs	1.5 hrs
☂	65 mm	89 mm	109 mm	108 mm
month	Apr	Jul	Oct	Jan

NORTH WALES

°C /°F

		17/63		
11/52	11/52	14/57		
5/41			8/46	6/43
				1/34

☀	3 hrs	3.5 hrs	2.5 hrs	1.5 hrs
☂	144 mm	206 mm	261 mm	252 mm
month	Apr	Jul	Oct	Jan

DEVON AND CORNWALL

°C /°F

		19/66		
13/55	13/55	15/59		
6/43			9/48	8/46
				4/39

☀	6 hrs	6.5 hrs	3.5 hrs	2 hrs
☂	53 mm	70 mm	91 mm	99 mm
month	Apr	Jul	Oct	Jan

WEST COUNTRY

°C /°F

		21/70		
14/57	14/57	15/59		
6/43			9/48	7/45
				2/36

☀	5.5 hrs	6.5 hrs	3.5 hrs	2 hrs
☂	49 mm	65 mm	85 mm	74 mm
month	Apr	Jul	Oct	Jan

THAMES VALLEY

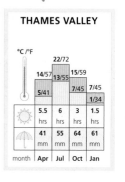

°C /°F

		22/72		
	14/57	13/55	15/59	
5/41			7/45	7/45
				1/34

☀	5.5 hrs	6 hrs	3 hrs	1.5 hrs
☂	41 mm	55 mm	64 mm	61 mm
month	Apr	Jul	Oct	Jan

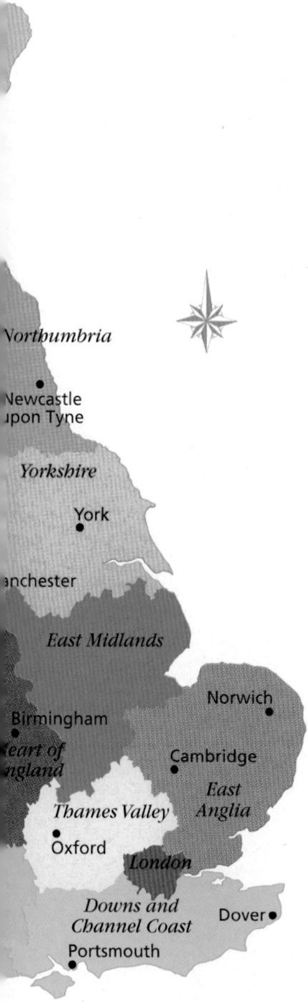

THE HIGHLANDS AND ISLANDS

°C /°F

	Apr	Jul	Oct	Jan
high	11/52	17/63	13/55	7/45
low	3/37	10/50	7/45	1/34
☀	4.5 hrs	3.5 hrs	2 hrs	1 hrs
☂	111 mm	137 mm	215 mm	200 mm
month	Apr	Jul	Oct	Jan

THE LOWLANDS

°C /°F

	Apr	Jul	Oct	Jan
high	11/52	19/66	14/57	6/43
low	4/39	11/52	7/45	1/34
☀	5 hrs	5.5 hrs	3 hrs	1.5 hrs
☂	38 mm	69 mm	56 mm	47 mm
month	Apr	Jul	Oct	Jan

NORTHUMBRIA

°C /°F

	Apr	Jul	Oct	Jan
high	11/52	18/64	13/55	6/43
low	5/41	13/55	8/46	2/36
☀	5 hrs	5.5 hrs	3 hrs	1.5 hrs
☂	38 mm	64 mm	61 mm	62 mm
month	Apr	Jul	Oct	Jan

YORKSHIRE

°C /°F

	Apr	Jul	Oct	Jan
high	13/55	21/70	14/57	6/43
low	5/41	12/54	7/45	1/34
☀	5 hrs	5.5 hrs	3 hrs	1.5 hrs
☂	41 mm	62 mm	56 mm	59 mm
month	Apr	Jul	Oct	Jan

EAST MIDLANDS

°C /°F

	Apr	Jul	Oct	Jan
high	13/55	21/70	14/57	6/43
low	4/39	12/54	6/43	0/32
☀	5 hrs	5.5 hrs	3 hrs	1.5 hrs
☂	38 mm	58 mm	56 mm	56 mm
month	Apr	Jul	Oct	Jan

THE DOWNS AND CHANNEL COAST

°C /°F

	Apr	Jul	Oct	Jan
high	14/57	22/72	14/57	6/43
low	4/39	12/54	6/43	0/32
☀	5.8 hrs	7.3 hrs	4 hrs	2 hrs
☂	38 mm	58 mm	56 mm	56 mm
month	Apr	Jul	Oct	Jan

LONDON

°C /°F

	Apr	Jul	Oct	Jan
high	13/55	22/72	16/61	8/46
low	7/45	15/59	10/50	4/39
☀	5 hrs	6 hrs	3.5 hrs	1.5 hrs
☂	39 mm	45 mm	50 mm	44 mm
month	Apr	Jul	Oct	Jan

EAST ANGLIA

°C /°F

	Apr	Jul	Oct	Jan
high	14/57	22/72	15/59	7/45
low	4/39	12/54	6/43	1/34
☀	5 hrs	6 hrs	3.5 hrs	2 hrs
☂	37 mm	58 mm	51 mm	49 mm
month	Apr	Jul	Oct	Jan

Northumbria

Newcastle upon Tyne

Yorkshire

York

Manchester

East Midlands

Birmingham

Norwich

Heart of England

Cambridge

East Anglia

Thames Valley

Oxford

London

Downs and Channel Coast

Dover

Portsmouth

LONDON

INTRODUCING LONDON 72–75

WEST END AND WESTMINSTER 76–93

SOUTH KENSINGTON AND HYDE PARK 94–101

REGENT'S PARK AND BLOOMSBURY 102–107

THE CITY AND SOUTHWARK 108–121

FURTHER AFIELD 122–126

LONDON STREET FINDER 127–147

SHOPS AND MARKETS 148–151

ENTERTAINMENT IN LONDON 152–155

London at a Glance

The largest city in Europe, London is home to over seven million people and covers 625 sq miles (1,600 sq km). The capital was founded by the Romans in the first century AD as a convenient administrative and communications centre and a port for trade with Continental Europe. For a thousand years it has been the principal residence of British monarchs as well as the centre of business and government, and it is rich in historic buildings and treasures from all periods. In addition to its diverse range of museums, galleries and churches, London is an exciting contemporary city, packed with a vast array of entertainments and shops. The attractions on offer are virtually endless but this map highlights the most important of those described in detail on the following pages.

Buckingham Palace (pp86–7) *is London home and office to the monarchy. The Changing of the Guard takes place on the palace forecourt.*

REGENT'S PARK AND BLOOMSBURY
(see pp102–107)

WEST END AND WESTMINS
(see pp76–

SOUTH KENSINGTON AND HYDE PARK
(see pp94–101)

Hyde Park (p75), *the largest central London park, boasts numerous sports facilities, restaurants, an art gallery and Speakers' Corner. The highlight is the Serpentine Lake.*

```
0 kilometers          1
0 miles        0.5
```

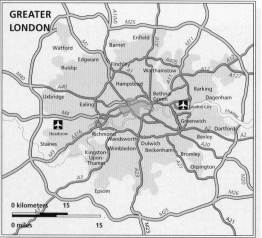

GREATER LONDON

```
0 kilometers     15
0 miles          15
```

The Victoria and Albert Museum (pp98–99) *is the world's largest museum of decorative arts. This German cup is 15th century.*

KEY

▢   Main sightseeing area

◁ **Nelson's Column** (1843) and the National Gallery, Trafalgar Square

The British Museum's
(pp106–7) *vast collection of
antiquities from all over the
world includes this Portland
Vase from the 1st century BC.*

The National Gallery's
*(pp82–3) world-famous
collection of paintings
includes works such as
Christ Mocked (c.1495)
by Hieronymus Bosch.*

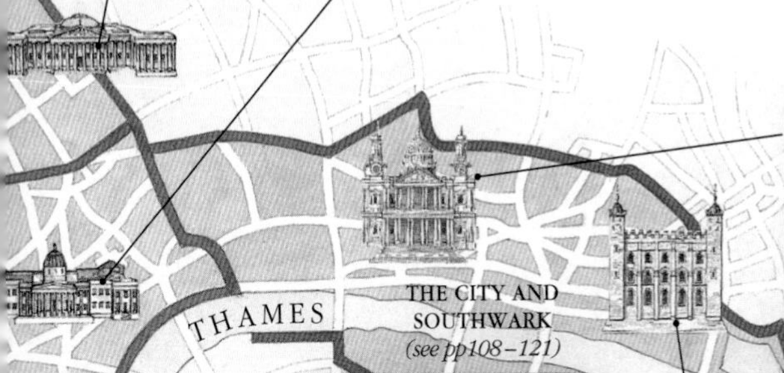

THAMES

THE CITY AND
SOUTHWARK
(see pp108–121)

St Paul's (pp114–15)
*huge dome is the
cathedral's most dis-
tinctive feature.
Three galleries
around the dome
give spectacular
views of London.*

Westminster Abbey (pp92–3)
*has glorious medieval archi-
tecture and is crammed with
impressive tombs and monuments to some of Britain's
greatest public figures.*

Tate Britain (p91) *displays an outstanding collection of British art ranging from stylized Elizabethan
portraiture, such as* The Cholmondeley Ladies, *to
cutting edge installation and film.*

The Tower of London (pp118–19)
*is most famous as the prison where
enemies of the Crown were executed.
The Tower houses the Crown Jewels,
including the Imperial State Crown.*

London's Parks and Gardens

Camellia japonica

London has one of the world's greenest city centres, full of tree-filled squares and large expanses of grass, some of which have been public land since medieval times. From the elegant terraces of Regent's Park to the Royal Botanic Gardens at Kew, every London park and garden has its own charm and character. Some are ancient crown or public land, while others were created from the grounds of private houses or disused land. Londoners make the most of these open spaces: for exercise, listening to music, or simply escaping the bustle of the city.

Holland Park (see pp122–23) *offers acres of peaceful woodland, an open-air theatre (see p153) and a café.*

Kew Gardens (see p126) *are the world's premiere botanic gardens. An amazing variety of plants from all over the world is complemented by an array of temples, monuments and a landscaped lake.*

Richmond Park (see p126), *London's largest Royal Park, remains unspoiled with roaming deer and magnificent river views.*

| 0 kilometres | | 1 |
| 0 miles | 0.5 | |

SEASONAL BEST

As winter draws to a close, spectacular drifts of crocuses, daffodils and tulips are to be found peeping above the ground in Green Park and Kew. Easter weekend marks the start of outdoor events with funfairs on many commons and parks. During the summer months the parks are packed with picnickers and sunbathers and you can often catch a free open-air concert in St James's or Regent's parks. The energetic can play tennis in most

Winter in Kensington Gardens, adjoining Hyde Park

parks, swim in Hyde Park's Serpentine or the ponds on Hampstead Heath, or take rowing boats out on the lakes in Regent's and Battersea parks. Autumn brings a different atmosphere, and on 5 November firework displays and bonfires celebrate Guy Fawkes Night *(see p64)*. Winter is a good time to visit the tropical glasshouses and the colourful outdoor winter garden at Kew. If the weather gets really cold, the Round Pond in Kensington Gardens may be fit for ice-skating.

Hampstead Heath *(see p124)* is a breezy open space embracing a variety of landscapes.

Regent's Park (see p103) *has a large boating lake, an open-air theatre (see p153) and London Zoo. Surrounded by Nash's graceful buildings, it is one of London's most civilized retreats.*

St James's Park, *in the heart of the city, is a popular escape for office workers. It is also a reserve for wildfowl.*

Green Park, *with its shady trees and benches, offers a cool, restful spot in the heart of London.*

Battersea Park is a pleasant riverside site with a man-made boating lake.

Greenwich Park (see p125) *is dominated by the National Maritime Museum. There are fine views from the Old Royal Observatory on the hill top.*

Hyde Park and Kensington Gardens (see p101) *are both popular London retreats. There are sporting facilities, a lake and art gallery in Hyde Park. This plaque is from the ornate Italian Garden in Kensington Gardens.*

HISTORIC CEMETERIES

In the late 1830s, a ring of private cemeteries was established around London to ease the pressure on the monstrously overcrowded and unhealthy burial grounds of the inner city. Today the cemeteries, notably **Highgate** *(see p124)* and **Kensal Green**, are well worth visiting for their flamboyant Victorian monuments.

Kensal Green cemetery on the Harrow Road

WEST END AND WESTMINSTER

The West End is the city's social and cultural centre and the London home of the royal family. Stretching from the edge of Hyde Park to Covent Garden, the district bustles all day and late into the night. Whether you're looking for art, history, street- or café-life, it is the most rewarding area in which to begin an exploration of the city.

Horse Guard on Whitehall

Westminster has been at the centre of political and religious power for a thousand years. In the 11th century, King Canute founded Westminster Palace and Edward the Confessor built Westminster Abbey, where all English monarchs have been crowned since 1066. As modern government developed, the great offices of state were established in the area.

SIGHTS AT A GLANCE

Historic Streets and Buildings

Banqueting House **18**
Buckingham Palace pp86–7 **13**
Cabinet War Rooms and Churchill Museum **16**
Downing Street **17**
Houses of Parliament pp90–91 **19**
Piccadilly Circus **8**
Ritz Hotel **10**
Royal Mews **15**
Royal Opera House **3**
The Mall **12**
The Piazza and Central Market **1**

Museums and Galleries

London Transport Museum **2**
National Gallery pp82–3 **6**
National Portrait Gallery **7**
Royal Academy **9**
Somerset House **4**
Tate Britain **21**
The Queen's Gallery **14**

Churches

Queen's Chapel **11**
Westminster Abbey pp92–3 **20**

Attractions

London Eye **5**

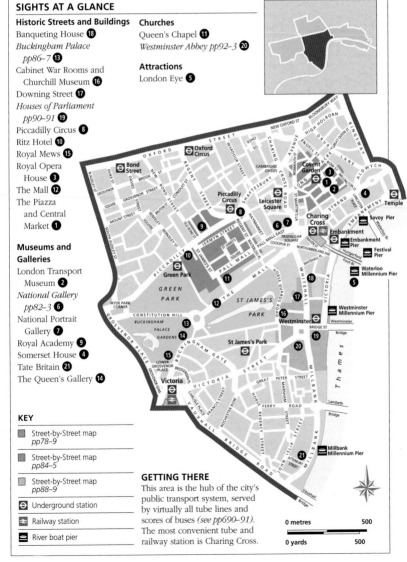

KEY

- ◻ Street-by-Street map *pp78–9*
- ◻ Street-by-Street map *pp84–5*
- ◻ Street-by-Street map *pp88–9*
- ⊖ Underground station
- ⊰ Railway station
- ◻ River boat pier

GETTING THERE

This area is the hub of the city's public transport system, served by virtually all tube lines and scores of buses *(see pp690–91).* The most convenient tube and railway station is Charing Cross.

0 metres   500
0 yards   500

◁ **Big Ben and the Houses of Parliament**

Street-by-Street: Covent Garden

Until 1973, Covent Garden was an area of decaying streets and warehouses, which only came alive after dark when the fruit and vegetable market traders packed up for the day. Since then the Victorian market and elegant buildings nearby have been converted into stylish shops, restaurants, bars and cafés, creating an animated district which attracts a lively young crowd, night and day.

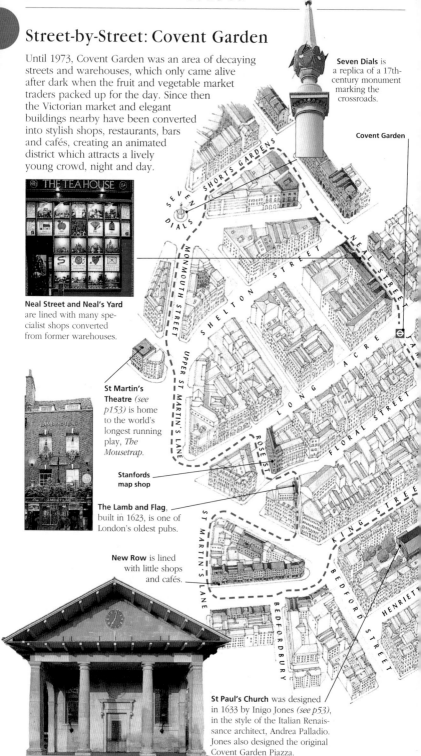

Seven Dials is a replica of a 17th-century monument marking the crossroads.

Covent Garden

Neal Street and Neal's Yard are lined with many specialist shops converted from former warehouses.

St Martin's Theatre *(see p153)* is home to the world's longest running play, *The Mousetrap.*

Stanfords map shop

The Lamb and Flag, built in 1623, is one of London's oldest pubs.

New Row is lined with little shops and cafés.

St Paul's Church was designed in 1633 by Inigo Jones *(see p53)*, in the style of the Italian Renaissance architect, Andrea Palladio. Jones also designed the original Covent Garden Piazza.

Royal Opera House
*Some of the world's
greatest opera singers
and ballet dancers have
performed at the Royal
Opera House* ❸

LOCATOR MAP
See Street Finder map 11

KEY

– – –   Suggested route

0 meters   100

0 yards   100

**London
Transport Museum**
*This museum's
intriguing collec-
tion brings to life
the history of the
city's tubes, buses
and trains. It also
has fine examples
of 20th-century
commercial art* ❷

Jubilee Market

★ **Piazza and
Central Market**
*Shops and cafés fill the
piazza and market* ❶

STAR SIGHTS

★ Piazza and Central
Market

The Piazza and
Central Market ❶

Covent Garden WC2. **Map** 11 C2.
🚇 Covent Garden. ♿ *cobbled
streets.* **Street performers in Piazza:**
10am–dusk daily. **www**.covent
gardenlondonuk.com

The 17th-century architect
Inigo Jones *(see p53)* planned
the Piazza in Covent Garden
as an elegant residential
square, modelled on the
piazza in the Tuscan town of
Livorno, which he had seen
under construction during his
travels in Italy. For a brief period, the Piazza became one of
the most fashionable addresses
in London, but it was superseded by the even grander St
James's Square *(see p85)*
which lies to the southwest.

Decline accelerated when
a fruit and vegetable market
developed. By the mid-18th
century, the Piazza had become a haunt of prostitutes and
most of its houses had turned
into seedy lodgings, gambling
dens, brothels and taverns.

**A mid-18th-century view of
Covent Garden's Piazza**

Meanwhile the wholesale
produce market became the
largest in the country and in
1828 a market hall was erected
to ease congestion. The market, however, soon outgrew
its new home and despite the
construction of new buildings,
such as Floral and Jubilee
halls, the congestion grew
worse. In 1973 the market
moved to a new site in south
London, and over the next
two decades Covent Garden
was redeveloped. Today only
St Paul's Church remains of
Inigo Jones's buildings, and
Covent Garden, with its many
small shops, cafés, restaurants, market stalls and street
entertainers, is one of central
London's liveliest districts.

London Transport Museum ❷

The Piazza, Covent Garden WC2.
Map 11 C2. **Tel** 020 7379 6344.
🚇 *Covent Garden.* 🕐 *10am–6pm Sat–Thu, 11am–6pm Fri.* 🎥 ♿ 🅿
phone in advance. 🍴 📷 📦
www.ltmuseum.co.uk

This collection of buses, trams and underground trains ranges from the earliest horse-drawn omnibuses to a present-day Hoppa bus. Housed in the Victorian Flower Market of Covent Garden built in 1872, the museum is particularly good for children, who can sit in the driver's seat of a bus or an underground train, operate signals and chat to an actor playing a 19th-century tube-tunnel miner.

London's bus and train companies have long been prolific patrons of artists, and the museum holds a fine collection of 19th- and 20th-century commercial art. Copies of some of the best works by distinguished artists, such as Paul Nash and Graham Sutherland, are on sale in the shop. Original works can be seen at the museum's depot in Acton.

METRO-LAND
PRICE TWO-PENCE

Poster by Michael Reilly (1929),
London Transport Museum

Royal Opera House ❸

Covent Garden WC2. **Map** 11 C2.
Tel 020 7304 4000. 🚇 *Covent Garden.* 🕐 *for performances and guided tours (phone to check).* 🍴
www.roh.org.uk

The first theatre on this site was built in 1732, and staged plays as well as concerts. However, the building was destroyed by fire in 1808 and again in 1856. The present structure was designed in 1858 by E M Barry. John Flaxman's portico frieze, depicting tragedy and comedy, survived from the previous building of 1809.

The Opera House is home to the Royal Opera and Royal Ballet companies. After two years of renovation the building reopened in the new millennium, complete with a second auditorium and new rehearsal rooms. Backstage tours are available, and once a month visitors can watch the Royal Ballet rehearse.

Somerset House ❹

Strand WC2. **Map** 11 C2. **Tel** 020 7845 4600. 🚇 *Temple.* 🕐 *8am–11pm daily.* ⛸ *1 Jan, 24–26 Dec.* **Ice rink** 🕐 *two months in winter.* 🎥 📷
Courtauld Institute of Art Gallery.
📦 🏛 ♿ **Tom's Kitchen. Tel** 020 7845 4646. **www**.somersethouse.org.uk

Designed in 1770 by William Chambers, Somerset House presents two great collections of art, the **Courtauld Institute of Art Gallery** and the

Somerset House: Strand façade

Embankment Galleries.

The courtyard forms an attractive piazza (which becomes an ice rink in winter), and the riverside terrace has a café. The Admiralty Restaurant is also highly regarded. Located in Somerset House but famous in its own right is the Courtauld Institute of Art Gallery, which includes important Impressionist and Post-Impressionist works by artists such as Manet, Renoir and Cezanne. In 2008 the riverside Embankment Galleries were launched. Occupying 750 sq m (900 sq yd) of exhibition space on the two lower floors,

---

SOHO AND CHINATOWN

Soho has been renowned for pleasures of the table, the flesh and the intellect ever since it was first developed in the late 17th century. At first a fashionable residential area, it declined when high society shifted west to Mayfair and immigrants from Europe moved into its narrow streets. Furniture-makers and tailors set up shop here and were joined in the late 19th century by pubs, nightclubs, restaurants and brothels. In the 1960s, Hong Kong Chinese moved into the area around Gerrard and Lisle streets and they created an aromatic Chinatown, packed with many restaurants and shops. Soho's raffish reputation has long attracted artists and writers, ranging from the 18th-century essayist Thomas de Quincey to poet Dylan Thomas and painter Francis Bacon. Although strip joints and peep shows remain, Soho has enjoyed something of a renaissance, and today is full of stylish and lively bars and restaurants.

Lion dancer in February's Chinese New Year celebrations

The opulent Palm Court of the Ritz Hotel

the changing programme covers a broad range of contemporary arts, including photography, design, fashion and architecture.

London Eye ❺

Jubilee Gardens, South Bank, SE1. **Map** 12 D2. **Tel** 0870 5000 600 *(information and 24-hr advance booking – recommended as tickets sell out days in advance).* 🚇 *Waterloo, Westminster.* 🚌 *11, 24, 211.* ⏰ *Sep–Mar: 10am–8:30pm daily; Apr–Sep: 10am–9pm daily (Jul & Aug: to 9:30pm).* ⬤ *mid-Jan and 25 Dec (for maintenance).* 🎫 *Pick up tickets at County Hall (adjacent to Eye) at least 30 mins before boarding time.* 🖥 🏪 ♿ www.londoneye.com

The London Eye is a 135-m (443-ft) observation wheel that was installed on the South Bank to mark the Millennium. Its enclosed passenger capsules offer a gentle, 30-minute ride as the wheel makes a full turn, with breathtaking views over London and for up to 42 km (26 miles) around. Towering over one of the world's most familiar riverscapes, it has understandably captured the hearts of Londoners and visitors alike, and is one of the city's most popular attractions. "Flights" on the wheel are on the hour and half-hour.

National Gallery ❻

See pp82–3.

National Portrait Gallery ❼

2 St Martin's Place WC2. **Map** 11 B3. **Tel** 020 7306 0055. 🚇 *Charing Cross, Leicester Sq.* ⏰ *10am–6pm Sat–Wed, 10am–9pm Thu & Fri.* ⬤ *24–26 Dec.* ♿ 🎥 🍴 🏪 🏛 www.npg.org.uk

This museum celebrates Britain's history through portraits, photographs and sculptures; subjects range from Elizabeth I to David Beckham. The 20th-century section contains paintings and photographs of the royal family, politicians, rock stars, designers, artists and writers.

The Statue of Eros

Piccadilly Circus ❽

W1. **Map** 11 A3. 🚇 *Piccadilly Circus.*

Dominated by garish neon advertising hoardings, Piccadilly Circus is a hectic traffic junction surrounded by shopping malls. It began as an early 19th-century crossroads between Piccadilly and John Nash's *(see p105)* Regent Street. It was briefly an elegant space, edged by curving stucco façades, but by 1910 the first electric advertisements had been installed. For years people have congregated at its centre, beneath the delicately poised figure of Eros, erected in 1892.

Royal Academy ❾

Burlington House, Piccadilly W1. **Map** 10 F3. **Tel** 020 7300 8000. 🚇 *Piccadilly Circus, Green Park.* ⏰ *10am–6pm Sat–Thu, 10am–10pm Fri.* ⬤ *24–26 Dec, Good Fri.* 🎥 ♿ 🎫 *by appointment.* 🍴 🏪 🏛 www.royalacademy.org.uk

Founded in 1768, the Royal Academy is best known for its summer exhibition, which has been an annual event for over 200 years and comprises a rewarding mix of around 1,200 new works by established and unknown painters, sculptors and architects. During the rest of the year, the gallery shows prestigious touring exhibitions from around the world, and the courtyard in front of Burlington House, one of the West End's few surviving mansions from the early 18th century, is often filled with people waiting to get in. Quite apart from its aesthetic delights, the Royal Academy provides the weary traveller with a little lacuna of tranquillity. Its interior decoration inspires calm, and seems to be cut off from the stresses and strains of modern city life.

Ritz Hotel ❿

Piccadilly W1. **Map** 10 F3. **Tel** 020 7493 8181. 🚇 *Green Park.* ♿ *See* **Where to Stay** *p557.* www.theritzlondon.com

Cesar Ritz, the Swiss hotelier who inspired the word "ritzy", had virtually settled down to a quiet retirement by 1906 when this hotel was built and named after him. The colonnaded front of the château-style building was erected in 1906 to suggest just the merest whiff of Paris, where the grandest hotels were to be found at the turn of the century. It still maintains its Edwardian air of *fin de siècle* opulence and sophisticated grandeur, and is a popular venue for afternoon tea (reservations are required). A touch of *soigné* danger may be found in the casino.

National Gallery ❻

The National Gallery is London's leading art museum, with over 2,300 paintings, most on permanent display. It has flourished since 1824, when the House of Commons agreed to purchase 38 major paintings. These became the core of a national collection of European art that now ranges from Cimabue in the 13th century to 19th-century Impressionists. The gallery's particular strengths are in Dutch, Italian Renaissance and 17th-century Spanish painting. To the left of the main gallery lies the Sainsbury Wing, financed by the grocery family and completed in 1991. It houses the Early Renaissance collection.

The Adoration of the Kings *(1564)*
This realistic work is by Flemish artist Pieter Bruegel the Elder (c.1525–69).

Sta
and I
to low
galleri

Education Centre entrance ♿

Stairs to lower floor

★ **'The Leonardo Cartoon'** *(c.1499–1500)*
The genius of Leonardo da Vinci glows through this picture of the Virgin and Child, St Anne and St John the Baptist.

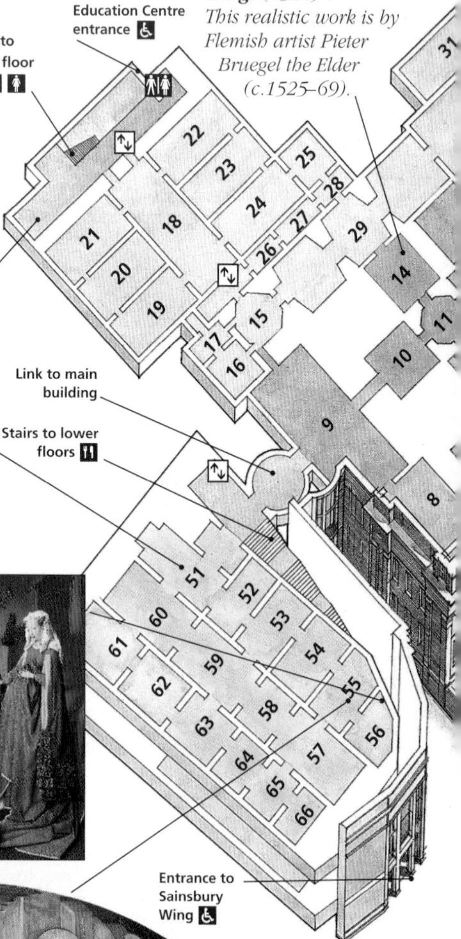

Learning gallery

Link to main building

Stairs to lower floors ᴫᴫ

KEY TO FLOORPLAN

☐	Painting 1250–1500
☐	Painting 1500–1600
☐	Painting 1600–1700
☐	Painting 1700–1900
☐	Special exhibitions
☐	Non-exhibition space

Arnolfini Portrait
Jan van Eyck (c.1385–1441), one of the pioneers of oil painting, shows his mastery of colour, texture, and minute detail in this portrait of 1434.

Entrance to Sainsbury Wing ♿

The Annunciation
This refined work of the early 1450s, by Fra Filippo Lippi, forms part of the gallery's exceptional Italian Renaissance collection.

★ **'The Rokeby Venus'**
*This is Velázquez's only
surviving female nude
(1647–51).*

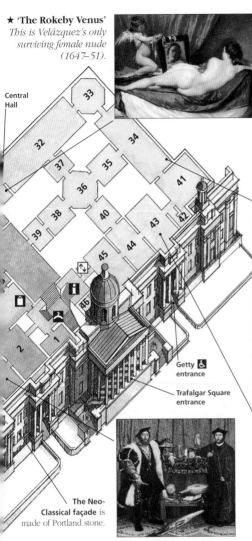

Central
Hall

VISITORS' CHECKLIST

Trafalgar Sq WC2. **Map** 11 B3.
Tel 020 7747 2885.
Charing Cross, Leicester Sq,
Piccadilly Circus. 3, 6, 9, 11,
12, 13, 15, 23, 24, 29, 53, 77A,
88, 91, 139, 159, 176, 453.
Charing Cross.
10am–6pm daily (9pm Fri).
1 Jan, 24–26 Dec. via
Sainsbury Wing and Getty
entrances.
www.nationalgallery.org.uk

★ **The Hay Wain** *(1821)*
*The great age of 19th-century land-
scape painting is represented by
Constable and Turner* (see p91). *
This picture shows how Constable
caught changing light and shadow.*

Getty
entrance

Trafalgar Square
entrance

**The Neo-
Classical façade** is
made of Portland stone.

GALLERY GUIDE

*Most of the collection
is housed on one floor.
The paintings hang
chronologically, with
the earliest works,
1250–1500, in the
Sainsbury Wing.
Lesser paintings of
all periods are dis-
played on the lower
floor of the main
building. There is
a restaurant on the
first floor in the
Sainsbury Wing.*

The Ambassadors
*The strange shape in the fore-
ground of this Hans Holbein
portrait (1533) is a distorted
skull, a symbol of mortality.*

STAR PAINTINGS

★ 'The Leonardo Cartoon'
by Leonardo da Vinci

★ 'The Rokeby Venus'
by Diego Velázquez

★ The Hay Wain by
John Constable

At the Theatre *(1876–7)*
*Renoir was one of the greatest
painters of the Impressionist
movement. The theatre was
a popular subject among
artists of the time.*

Street-by-Street: Piccadilly and St James's

As soon as Henry VIII built St James's Palace in the 1530s, the surrounding area became the centre of fashionable court life. Today Piccadilly forms a contrast between the bustling commercial district full of shopping arcades, eateries and cinemas, with St James's, to the south, which is still the domain of the wealthy and the influential.

St James's Church was designed by Sir Christopher Wren in 1684.

★ Royal Academy
The permanent art collection here includes this Michelangelo relief of the Madonna and Child (1505) **9**

Burlington Arcade, an opulent covered walk, has fine shops and beadles on patrol.

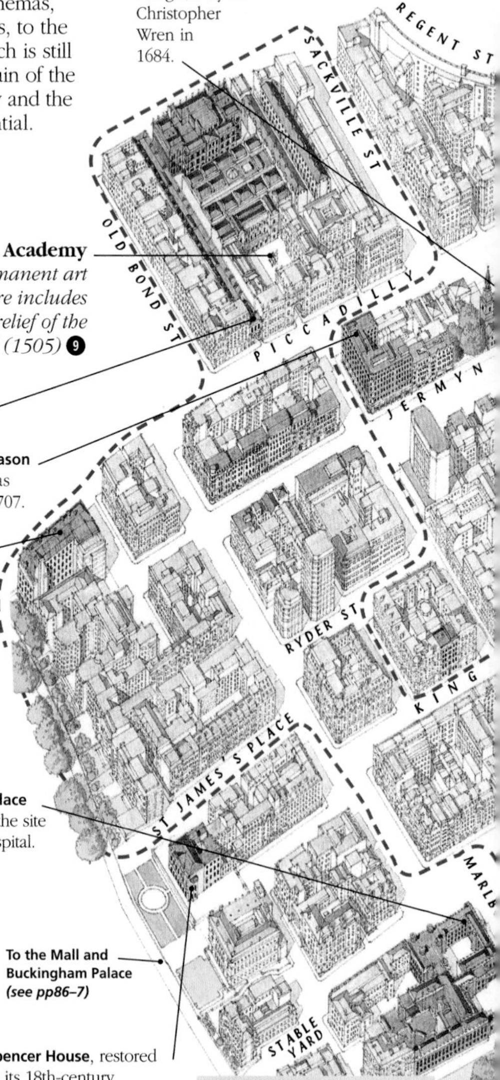

Fortnum & Mason *(see p148)* was founded in 1707.

The Ritz
César Ritz founded one of London's most famous hotels in 1906 **10**

St James's Palace was built on the site of a leper hospital.

To the Mall and Buckingham Palace *(see pp86–7)*

Spencer House, restored to its 18th-century splendour, contains fine period furniture and paintings. This Palladian palace was completed in 1766 for the 1st Earl Spencer, an ancestor of the late Princess of Wales.

STAR SIGHTS

★ Piccadilly Circus

★ Royal Academy

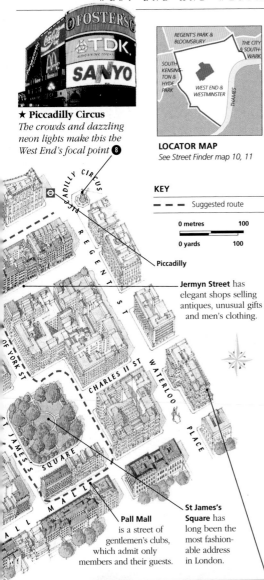

★ **Piccadilly Circus**
The crowds and dazzling neon lights make this the West End's focal point **8**

LOCATOR MAP
See Street Finder map 10, 11

KEY

– – – Suggested route

| 0 metres | 100 |
| 0 yards | 100 |

Piccadilly

Jermyn Street has elegant shops selling antiques, unusual gifts and men's clothing.

St James's Square has long been the most fashionable address in London.

Pall Mall is a street of gentlemen's clubs, which admit only members and their guests.

Queen's Chapel
This was the first Classical church in England **11**

Royal Opera Arcade is lined with quality shops. Designed by John Nash, it was completed in 1818.

Queen's Chapel **11**

Marlborough Rd SW1. **Map** 11 A4. **Tel** 020-7930 4832. ⊖ Green Park. ◯ to the public Sun services: 8:30am, 11:15am ♿

The sumptuous Queen's Chapel was designed by Inigo Jones for the Infanta of Spain, the intended bride of Charles I *(see pp52–3)*. Work started in 1623 but ceased when the marriage negotiations were shelved. The chapel was finally completed in 1627 for Charles's eventual queen, Henrietta Maria. It was the first church in England to be built in a Classical style, with a coffered ceiling based on a reconstruction by Palladio of an ancient Roman temple.

Interior of Queen's Chapel

The Mall **12**

SW1. **Map** 11 A4. ⊖ Charing Cross, Green Park.

This broad triumphal approach from Trafalgar Square to Buckingham Palace was created by Aston Webb when he redesigned the front of the palace and the Victoria Monument in 1911. The spacious tree-lined avenue follows the course of an old path at the edge of St James's Park. The path was laid out in the reign of Charles II, when it became London's most fashionable and cosmopolitan promenade. The Mall is used for royal processions on special occasions. Flagpoles down both sides fly the national flags of foreign heads of state during official visits. The Mall is closed to traffic on Sundays.

Buckingham Palace ⓭

Queen Elizabeth II

Opened to visitors for the first time in 1993 to raise money for repairing fire damage to Windsor Castle (*see pp236–7*), the Queen's official London home and office is an extremely popular attraction in August and September. John Nash (*see p105*) began convert-ing the 18th-century Buckingham House into a palace for George IV in 1826 but was taken off the job in 1831 for overspending his budget. The first monarch to occupy the palace was Queen Victoria, just after she came to the throne in 1837. The tour takes visitors up the grand staircase and through the splendour of the State Rooms, but not into the royal family's private apartments.

Music Room
State guests are presented and royal babies christened in this room.

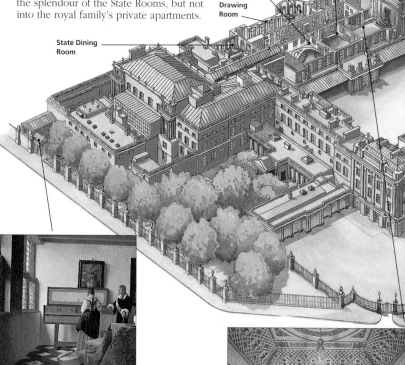

Grand Staircase

White Drawing Room

Green Drawing Room

Blue Drawing Room

State Dining Room

The Queen's Gallery
Masterpieces from the Royal Collection, such as Vermeer's The Music Lesson *(c.1660), are displayed here in a series of changing exhibitions.*

Throne Room
The Queen carries out many formal ceremonial duties here, under the richly gilded ceiling.

View over the Mall
On special occasions the Royal Family wave to crowds from the balcony.

VISITORS' CHECKLIST

SW1. **Map** 10 F5. *Tel 020 7766 7300.* 🚇 *St James's Park, Victoria.* 🚌 *11, 16, 24, 25, 28, 36, 38, 52, 73, 135, C1.* 🚉 *Victoria.* **State Rooms** ◯ *Aug & Sep: 9:30am–5:30pm daily).* 🎟 *Tickets sold in Ambassador's Court. Each ticket has a set entry time; or buy a Royal Day Out ticket to avoid the queues.* ♿ *call first.* **Changing of the Guard:** *11:30am daily; Aug–Apr: alternate days. Subject to change without notice. Tel 020 7321 2233.* www.royalcollection.org.uk

The Royal Standard flies while the Queen is in residence.

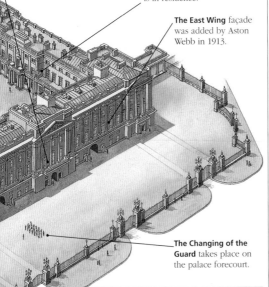

The East Wing façade was added by Aston Webb in 1913.

The Changing of the Guard takes place on the palace forecourt.

THE CHANGING OF THE GUARD

Dressed in brilliant scarlet tunics and tall furry hats called bearskins, the palace guards stand in sentry boxes outside the Palace. Crowds gather to watch the colourful and musical military ceremony as the guards march from Wellington Barracks to Buckingham Palace, parading for half an hour while the palace keys are handed by the old guard to the new.

The Queen's Gallery ⑭

Buckingham Palace Rd SW1. **Map** 10 F5. *Tel 020 7766 7301.* 🚇 *St James's Park, Victoria.* ◯ *10am–5:30pm daily (last admission for exhibitions: 4:30pm).* ⬤ *25, 26 Dec. Call for more details.* www.royalcollection.org.uk

The Queen's art collection is one of the finest and most valuable in the world, rich in the works of old masters such as Rembrandt and Leonardo. The gallery hosts a rotating programme of exhibitions, enabling the year-round display of many masterpieces, drawings and decorative arts from the Queen's collection.

Detail: The Gold State Coach (1762), Royal Mews

Royal Mews ⑮

Buckingham Palace Rd SW1. **Map** 10 E5. *Tel 020 7766 7302.* 🚇 *Victoria.* ◯ *Feb–Mar, Nov–Dec: 10am–4pm Mon–Sat; Apr–Oct: 10am–5pm daily. Subject to closure at short notice.* 📷 *open 9:30am–5pm daily all year (closed 25, 26 Dec).* www.royalcollection.org.uk

Lovers of horses and royal pomp should not miss this working stable and coach house. Designed by John Nash in 1825, it houses horses and state coaches used on official occasions. Among them is the glass coach used for royal weddings and foreign ambassadors. The star exhibit is the ornate gold state coach, built for George III in 1762, which was used by the Queen during the Golden Jubilee celebrations in 2002. The shop sells interesting merchandise.

Street-by-Street: Whitehall and Westminster

The broad avenues of Whitehall and Westminster are lined with imposing buildings that serve the historic seat of both government and the established church. On weekdays the streets are crowded with civil servants whose work is based here, while at weekends the area takes on a different atmosphere with a steady flow of tourists.

Downing Street
Sir Robert Walpole was the first Prime Minister to live here in 1732 ⓱

Cabinet War Rooms and Churchill Museum
Now open to the public, these were Winston Churchill's World War II headquarters ⓰

St Margaret's Church is a favourite venue for political and society weddings.

★ **Westminster Abbey**
The abbey is London's oldest and most important church ⓴

Central Hall (1911) is a florid example of the Beaux Arts style.

Richard I's Statue is an 1860 depiction of the king, killed in battle in 1199.

Dean's Yard is a secluded grassy square surrounded by picturesque buildings from different periods, many used by Westminster School.

The Burghers of Calais is a cast of Auguste Rodin's 1886 original in France.

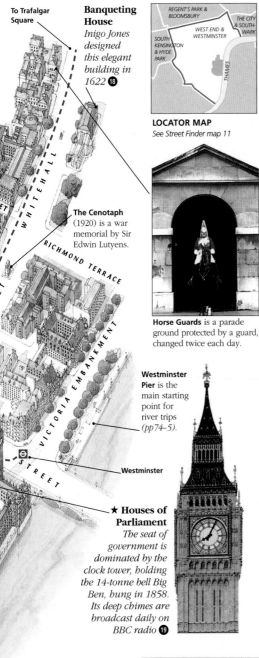

To Trafalgar Square

Banqueting House
Inigo Jones designed this elegant building in 1622 **18**

LOCATOR MAP
See Street Finder map 11

The Cenotaph
(1920) is a war memorial by Sir Edwin Lutyens.

Horse Guards is a parade ground protected by a guard, changed twice each day.

Westminster Pier is the main starting point for river trips *(pp74–5).*

Westminster

★ **Houses of Parliament**
The seat of government is dominated by the clock tower, holding the 14-tonne bell Big Ben, hung in 1858. Its deep chimes are broadcast daily on BBC radio **19**

KEY

– – – Suggested route

0 metres 100

0 yards 100

STAR SIGHTS

★ Westminster Abbey

★ Houses of Parliament

Cabinet War Rooms and Churchill Museum **16**

Clive Steps, King Charles St SW1. **Map** 11 B5. **Tel** 020 7930 6961. ⊜ Westminster. ◯ 9:30am–6pm daily (last adm: 5pm). ⬤ 24–26 Dec. ⬛ & ⬛ ⬛ www.iwm.org.uk

This warren of cellars below a government office building is where the War Cabinet – first under Neville Chamberlain, then Winston Churchill from 1940 – met during World War II when German bombs were falling on London. The rooms include living quarters for ministers and military leaders and a Cabinet Room, where strategic decisions were taken. They are laid out as they were when the war ended, complete with Churchill's desk, communications equipment, and maps for plotting battles and strategies. The Churchill Museum records and illustrates Churchill's life and career.

Telephones in the Map Room, Cabinet War Rooms

Downing Street **17**

SW1. **Map** 11 B4. ⊜ Westminster. ⬤ to the public.

Number 10 Downing Street has been the official residence of the British Prime Minister since 1732. It contains a Cabinet Room in which government policy is decided, an impressive State Dining Room and a private apartment; outside is a well-protected garden.

Next door at No. 11 is the official residence of the Chancellor of the Exchequer, who is in charge of the nation's financial affairs. In 1989, iron gates were erected at the Whitehall end of Downing Street for security purposes.

Banqueting House ®

Whitehall SW1. **Map** 11 B4. *Tel 020 3166 6151.* ⊖ *Charing Cross.* ◻ *10am–5pm Mon–Sat.* ● *pub hols & for functions. Call in advance.* ⬚ ⬚ ⬚ *partial.* **www**.*hrp.org.uk*

Completed by Inigo Jones *(see p53)* in 1622, this was the first building in central London to embody the Palladian style of Renaissance Italy. In 1629 Charles I commissioned Rubens to paint the ceiling with scenes exalting the reign of his father, James I. They symbolize the divine right of kings, disputed by the Parliamentarians, who executed Charles I outside the building in 1649 *(see pp52–3).*

Panels from the Rubens ceiling (1629–34), Banqueting House

Houses of Parliament ®

SW1. **Map** 11 C5. *Tel 020 7219 3000.* ⊖ *Westminster.* **Visitors' Galleries** ◻ *phone ahead for information on debate times. Access to the Visitors' Galleries is by queueing system; or UK residents may apply in advance to local MP.* ● *frequently for parliamentary recesses.* ⬚ ⬚ ⬚ **www**.*parliament.uk/visiting*

There has been a Palace of Westminster here since the 11th century, though only Westminster Hall remains from that time. The present Neo-Gothic structure by Sir Charles Barry was built after the old palace was destroyed by fire in 1834. Since the 16th century it has housed the two Houses of Parliament, the Lords and the Commons. The House of Commons consists of elected Members of Parliament (MPs).

The party with most MPs forms the Government, and its leader becomes Prime Minister. The House of Lords comprises peers, law lords, bishops and archbishops.

Westminster Abbey ®

See pp92–3.

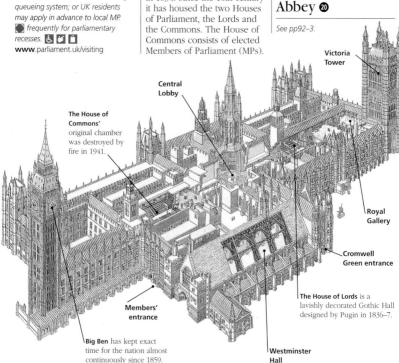

Victoria Tower

Central Lobby

The House of Commons' original chamber was destroyed by fire in 1941.

Royal Gallery

Cromwell Green entrance

Members' entrance

The House of Lords is a lavishly decorated Gothic Hall designed by Pugin in 1836–7.

Big Ben has kept exact time for the nation almost continuously since 1859.

Westminster Hall

Portico of Tate Britain

Tate Britain ㉑

Millbank SW1. **Map** 19 B2. **Tel** 020 7887 8888. 🚇 Pimlico. 🚌 77a, 88, C10. 🚆 Victoria, Vauxhall. 🚤 to Tate Modern every 40 mins. 📷 ⬜ 10am–6pm daily (to 10pm Fri). ⬤ 24–26 Dec. 📷 for major exhibitions. ♿ Atterbury St. 📷 🍴 🛍 📷 www.tate.org.uk

Formerly the Tate Gallery, Tate Britain is the national gallery of British art, and includes works from the 16th to the 21st century. Displays draw on the huge Tate Collection, which also

Recumbent Figure (1938) by Henry Moore

includes the international modern art seen at Tate Modern (p121). A river boat, *Tate to Tate*, takes visitors between the two galleries. Located in the Clore Galleries are works from the Turner Bequest (see box).

The size of the collection necessitates some rotation of displays. Major themes change on a yearly basis, solo artists' rooms and smaller themed rooms more frequently. Loan exhibitions are installed in the ground floor galleries and part of the main floor.

The section on the years 1500–1800 covers a period of dramatic change in British history, from the Tudors and Stuarts through to the age of Thomas Gainsborough. The section ends with a series of changing displays about the poet and artist William Blake.

The years 1800 to 1900 saw dramatic expansion and change in the arts in Britain. This section shows the new themes that began to emerge. Included are the "Victorian Narrative" painters such as William Powell Frith, and the work of the Pre-Raphaelites, such as John Everett Millais and Dante Gabriel Rossetti. The period 1900–1960 includes the work of Jacob Epstein, that of Wyndham Lewis and his Vorticist group, and the celebrated modernist works of Henry Moore, Barbara Hepworth, Ben Nicholson, Francis Bacon and Lucian Freud.

The displays in the outstanding Tate collection of British art from 1960 to the present are changed on a regular basis. From the 1960s, Tate's funding for the purchase of works began to increase substantially, while artistic activity continued to pick up speed, encouraged by public spending. As a result, Tate Britain's collection is particularly rich in this period. Works range from the 1960s Pop

The First Marriage (A Marriage of Styles I) (1962) by David Hockney

artists David Hockney, Richard Hamilton and Peter Blake, through the works of Gilbert and George and the landscape artist Richard Long, to the 1980s paintings of Howard Hodgkin and R B Kitaj. The so-called Young British Artists (YBAs) of the 1990s are well represented by leading figures Damian Hirst, Tracey Emin and Sarah Lucas. A small space called Art Now is dedicated to contemporary artists.

Captain Thomas Lee (1594) by Marcus Gheeraerts II

THE TURNER BEQUEST

The Turner Bequest comprises some 300 oil paintings and 20,000 watercolours and drawings, received by the nation from the great landscape painter J M W Turner some years after his death in 1851. Turner's will had specified that a gallery be built to house his pictures and this was finally done in 1987 with the opening of the Clore Galleries. Most of the oils are on view in the main galleries, and the watercolours are the subject of changing displays.

Shipping at the Mouth of the Thames (c.1806–7)

Westminster Abbey ⓴

Westminster Abbey has been the burial place of
Britain's monarchs since the 11th century and the
setting for many coronations and royal weddings. It
is one of the most beautiful buildings in London, with
an exceptionally diverse array of architectural styles,
ranging from the austere French Gothic of the nave to
the astonishing complexity of Henry VII's chapel. Half
national church, half national museum, the abbey aisles
and transepts are crammed with an extraordinary collection of tombs and monuments honouring some of Britain's
greatest public figures, ranging from politicians to poets.

North Entrance
*The mock-medieval
stonework is
Victorian.*

**Statesmen's
Aisle**

Flying buttresses help
redistribute the great
weight of the roof.

★ **Nave**
*At a height of 31 m
(102 ft), the nave is
the highest in England.
The ratio of height to
width is 3:1.*

CORONATION

The coronation ceremony
is over 1,000 years old
and since 1066, with the
crowning of William the
Conqueror on Christmas
Day, the abbey has been
its sumptuous setting.
The coronation of Queen
Elizabeth II, in 1953, was
the first to be televised.

Coronation Chair
*Constructed in 1301, this is the
chair on which monarchs have
been crowned since 1308.*

STAR FEATURES

★ Nave

★ Henry VII Chapel

★ Chapter House

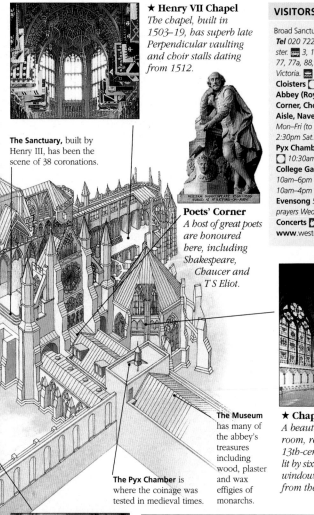

★ Henry VII Chapel
The chapel, built in 1503–19, has superb late Perpendicular vaulting and choir stalls dating from 1512.

The Sanctuary, built by Henry III, has been the scene of 38 coronations.

WILLIAM SHAKESPEARE 1564-1616
BURIED AT STRATFORD-ON-AVON

Poets' Corner
A host of great poets are honoured here, including Shakespeare, Chaucer and T S Eliot.

★ Chapter House
A beautiful octagonal room, remarkable for its 13th-century tile floor. It is lit by six huge stained glass windows showing scenes from the abbey's history.

The Museum has many of the abbey's treasures including wood, plaster and wax effigies of monarchs.

The Pyx Chamber is where the coinage was tested in medieval times.

VISITORS' CHECKLIST

Broad Sanctuary SW1.**Map** 11 B5. **Tel** 020 7222 5152. 🚇 Westminster. 🚌 3, 11, 12, 24, 29, 53, 70, 77, 77a, 88, 109, 159, 170. 🚆 Victoria. 🚢 Westminster Pier. **Cloisters** ⬜ 8am–6pm daily. **Abbey (Royal Chapels, Poets' Corner, Choir, Statesmen's Aisle, Nave)** ⬜ 9:30am–4:30pm Mon–Fri (to 7pm Wed), 9:30am–2:30pm Sat. 🈲 **Chapter House, Pyx Chamber & Museum** ⬜ 10:30am–4pm daily. 🈲 **College Garden** ⬜ Apr–Sep: 10am–6pm Tue–Thu; Oct–Mar: 10am–4pm Tue–Thu. **Evensong** 5pm Mon–Fri (evening prayers Wed), 3pm Sat, Sun. **Concerts** 🎵 🈵 📷 📱 🈲 www.westminster-abbey.org

Cloisters
Built mainly in the 13th and 14th centuries, the cloisters link the Abbey church with the other buildings.

HISTORICAL PLAN OF THE ABBEY

The first abbey church was established as early as the 10th century, but the present French-influenced Gothic structure was begun in 1245 at the behest of Henry III. Because of its unique role as the coronation church, the abbey escaped Henry VIII's onslaught on Britain's monastic buildings *(see pp50–51).*

KEY

⬜	Built between 1055–1350
⬜	Added from 1350–1420
⬜	Built between 1500–1512
⬜	Towers completed 1745
⬜	Restored after 1850

SOUTH KENSINGTON AND HYDE PARK

This exclusive district embraces one of London's largest parks and some of its finest museums, shops, restaurants and hotels. Until the mid-19th century it was a genteel, semi-rural backwater of large houses and private schools lying to the south of Kensington Palace. In 1851, the Great Exhibition, until then the largest arts and science event ever staged *(see pp56–7),* was held in Hyde Park, transforming the area into a celebration of Victorian learning and self-confidence.

Peter Pan statue in Kensington Gardens

The brainchild of Queen Victoria's husband, Prince Albert, the exhibition was a massive success and the profits were used to buy 35 ha (87 acres) of land in South Kensington. Here, Prince Albert encouraged the construction of a concert hall, museums and colleges devoted to the applied arts and sciences; most of them survive. The neighbourhood soon became modish, full of flamboyant red-brick mansion blocks, garden squares and the elite shops still to be found in Knightsbridge.

SIGHTS AT A GLANCE

Historic Buildings
Kensington Palace ❼

Churches
Brompton Oratory ❷

Shops
Harrods ❶

Parks and Gardens
Hyde Park and Kensington Gardens ❻

Museums and Galleries
Natural History Museum ❺
Science Museum ❹
Victoria and Albert Museum pp98–9 ❸

GETTING THERE
South Kensington station (accessible from an entrance on Exhibition Road) is on the Piccadilly, Circle and District lines; only the Piccadilly line passes through Knightsbridge and Hyde Park Corner. The No. 14 bus runs direct from Piccadilly Circus to South Kensington, via Knightsbridge.

KEY
Street-by-Street map pp96–7
Underground station

◁ Ennismore Mews in South Kensington, built 1843–6

Street-by-Street: South Kensington

The numerous museums and colleges created in the wake of the Great Exhibition of 1851 *(see pp56–7)* continue to give this neighbourhood an air of leisured culture. Visited as much by Londoners as tourists, the museum area is liveliest on Sundays and on summer evenings during the Royal Albert Hall's famous season of classical "Prom" concerts *(see p154)*.

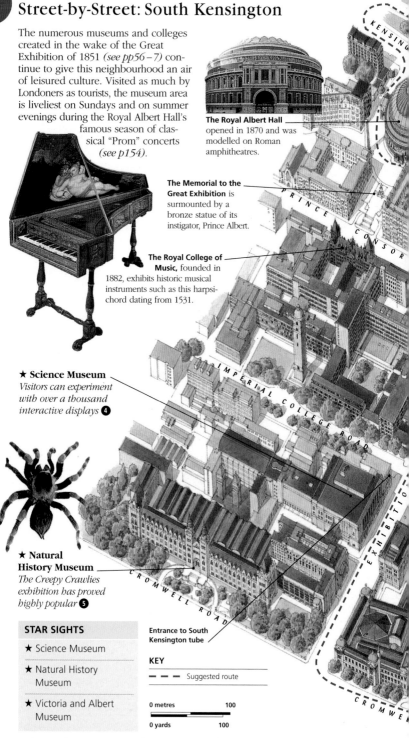

The Royal Albert Hall opened in 1870 and was modelled on Roman amphitheatres.

The Memorial to the Great Exhibition is surmounted by a bronze statue of its instigator, Prince Albert.

The Royal College of Music, founded in 1882, exhibits historic musical instruments such as this harpsichord dating from 1531.

★ **Science Museum**
Visitors can experiment with over a thousand interactive displays ❹

★ **Natural History Museum**
The Creepy Crawlies exhibition has proved highly popular ❺

Entrance to South Kensington tube

STAR SIGHTS

★ Science Museum

★ Natural History Museum

★ Victoria and Albert Museum

KEY

– – – Suggested route

0 metres   100

0 yards   100

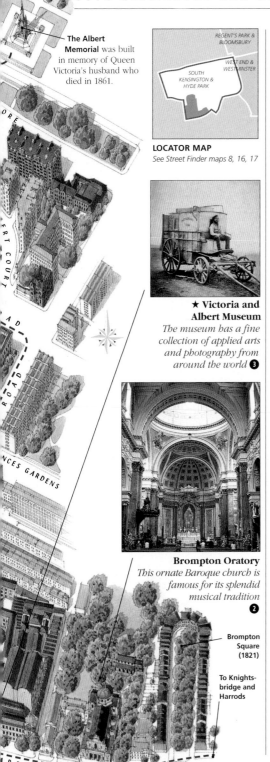

The Albert Memorial was built in memory of Queen Victoria's husband who died in 1861.

LOCATOR MAP
See Street Finder maps 8, 16, 17

REGENT'S PARK & BLOOMSBURY

WEST END & WESTMINSTER

SOUTH KENSINGTON & HYDE PARK

★ Victoria and Albert Museum
The museum has a fine collection of applied arts and photography from around the world ❸

Brompton Oratory
This ornate Baroque church is famous for its splendid musical tradition
❷

Brompton Square (1821)

To Knightsbridge and Harrods

Harrods Food Hall

Harrods ❶

Knightsbridge SW1. **Map** 9 B5. *Tel* 020 7730 1234. ⊖ *Knightsbridge.* ◯ *10am–8pm Mon–Sat, 11:30am–6pm Sun.* See ***Shops and Markets** pp120–21.* **www**.harrods.com

In 1849 Henry Charles Harrod opened a small grocery shop on Brompton Road, which soon became famous for its impeccable service and quality. The store moved into these extravagant premises in Knightsbridge in 1905.

Brompton Oratory ❷

Brompton Rd SW7. **Map** 17 B1. *Tel* 020 7808 0900. ⊖ *South Kensington.* ◯ *6am–8pm daily.* **www**.bromptonoratory.com

The Italianate Oratory is a lavish monument to the 19th-century English Catholic revival. It was established as a base for a community of priests by John Henry Newman (later Cardinal Newman), who introduced the Oratorian movement to England in 1848. The church was opened in 1884, and the dome and façade added in the 1890s.

The sumptuous interior holds many fine monuments. The 12 huge 17th-century statues of the apostles are from Siena Cathedral, the elaborate Baroque Lady Altar (1693) is from the Dominican church at Brescia, and the 18th-century altar in St Wilfred's Chapel is from Rochefort in Belgium.

Victoria and Albert Museum ❸

The Glass gallery, room 131

The Victoria and Albert Museum (the V&A) contains one of the world's widest collections of art and design, ranging from early Christian devotional objects and the mystical art of southeast Asia to cutting-edge furniture design. Originally founded in 1852 as the Museum of Manufactures to inspire students of design, it was renamed by Queen Victoria in 1899 in memory of Prince Albert. The museum has undergone a dramatic redisplay of its collection, including work on the Ceramics galleries, Sackler Education Centre and Medieval and Renaissance galleries, which span three levels. The Gilbert Collection also opened here in 2009.

★ British Galleries
The Great Bed of Ware has been a tourist attraction since 1601, when Shakespeare sparked interest in it by making reference to it in Twelfth Night.

Silver galleries
Radiant pieces such as the Burgess Cup (Britain, 1863) fill these stunning galleries.

★ Fashion gallery
In this gallery, European clothing from the mid-1500s to the present day is displayed, such as these floral Manolo Blahnik shoes.

Exhibition Road entrance

KEY TO FLOORPLAN

- Level 0
- Level 1
- Level 2
- Level 3
- Level 4
- Level 6
- Henry Cole Wing
- Non-exhibition space

STAR EXHIBITS

- ★ British Galleries
- ★ Fashion gallery
- ★ Medieval and Renaissance galleries
- ★ Islamic Middle East gallery

GALLERY GUIDE

The V&A has a 7-mile (11-km) layout spread over six levels. Level 1, houses the China, Japan and South Asia galleries, as well as the Fashion gallery and the Cast Courts. The British Galleries are on levels 2 and 4. Level 3 contains the 20th Century galleries and displays of silver, jewellery, ironwork, paintings and works of 20th-century design. The glass display is also on upper level 4. The Ceramics galleries are on level 6. The Henry Cole Wing houses the Sackler Education Centre, RIBA Architecture Study Rooms and the Prints and Drawings Study Rooms.

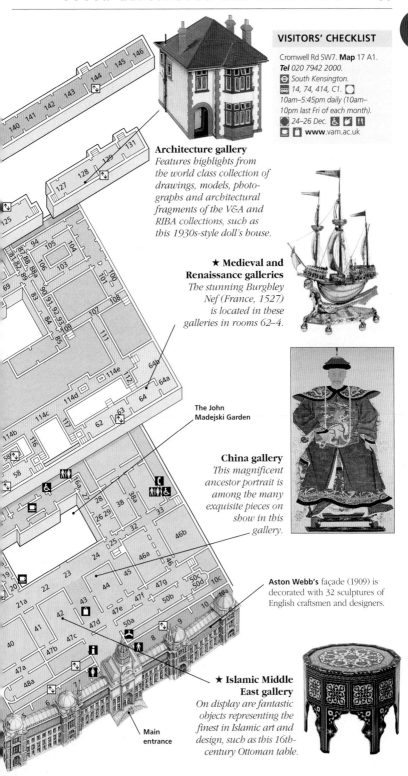

VISITORS' CHECKLIST

Cromwell Rd SW7. **Map** 17 A1.
Tel 020 7942 2000.
⊖ South Kensington.
🚌 14, 74, 414, C1. 🚇
10am–5:45pm daily (10am–
10pm last Fri of each month).
📅 24–26 Dec. 🚻 ♿ 🍴
🏛 📷 www.vam.ac.uk

Architecture gallery
*Features highlights from
the world class collection of
drawings, models, photo-
graphs and architectural
fragments of the V&A and
RIBA collections, such as
this 1930s-style doll's house.*

★ Medieval and
Renaissance galleries
*The stunning Burghley
Nef (France, 1527)
is located in these
galleries in rooms 62–4.*

**The John
Madejski Garden**

China gallery
*This magnificent
ancestor portrait is
among the many
exquisite pieces on
show in this
gallery.*

Aston Webb's façade (1909) is
decorated with 32 sculptures of
English craftsmen and designers.

★ Islamic Middle
East gallery
*On display are fantastic
objects representing the
finest in Islamic art and
design, such as this 16th-
century Ottoman table.*

**Main
entrance**

Science Museum ❹

Exhibition Rd SW7. **Map** 16 F1. *Tel*
0870 870 4868. ⊖ *South Kensing-*
ton. ◯ *10am–6pm daily.* ● *24–26*
Dec. for IMAX, special exhibitions
and simulators only. ♿ 🎥 🛍 🚻
www.sciencemuseum.org.uk

Centuries of continuing
scientific and technological
development lie at the heart
of the Science Museum's
massive collections. The hardware displayed is magnificent:
from steam engines to aero-
engines; spacecraft to the very
first mechanical computers.
Equally important is the social

**Newcomen's Steam Engine (1712),
Science Museum**

context of science – what
discoveries and inventions
mean for day-to-day life – and
the process of discovery itself.
There are many interactive
and hands-on displays which
are very popular with children.
   The museum is spread over
seven floors and includes the
high-tech Wellcome Wing at
the west end of the museum.
The basement features the
excellent hands-on galleries
for children, including The
Garden. The Energy Hall
dominates the ground floor,
and is dedicated to steam
power, with the still-opera-
tional Harle Syke Mill Engine
of 1903. Here too are Space
and Making the Modern
World, a highlight of which
is the display of the scarred
Apollo 10 spacecraft, which
carried three astronauts to the
moon and back in May 1969.
In Challenge of Materials,
located on the
first floor, our

expectations of materials are
confounded with exhibits
such as a bridge made of glass
and a steel wedding dress.
   The Flight gallery on the
third floor is packed with early
flying contraptions, fighter
planes, aeroplanes and the
Launchpad. The fourth and
fifth floors house the medical
science galleries, where Science
and the Art of Medicine has a
17th-century Italian vase for
storing snake bite treatment.
   The high-tech Wellcome
Wing offers four floors of interactive technology, including
"Who Am I?", a fascinating
exhibition exploring the
science of you. With an IMAX
3D Cinema and the SimEx
simulator ride, it is a breathtaking addition to the museum.
The museum cafés and shop
are particularly good.

Natural History Museum ❺

Cromwell Rd SW7. **Map** 16 F1. *Tel*
020 7942 5000. ⊖ *South Kensington.*
◯ *10am–5:50pm daily (to 10:30pm*
last Fri of month). ● *24–26 Dec.*
🍴 ♿ 🎥 🚻 **www**.nhm.ac.uk

This cathedral-like building's
richly sculpted stonework conceals an iron and steel frame;
this construction technique
was revolutionary when the
museum opened in 1881. The
imaginative displays tackle
fundamental issues such as
the ecology and evolution of
the planet, the origin of species and the development of
human beings – all explained
through a dynamic
combination of the
latest technology,
interactive tech-
niques and
traditional
displays.
   The
museum
is divided

**Relief from a decorative panel in
the Natural History Museum**

into four sections: the Blue
Zone, Green Zone, Red Zone
and the Orange Zone. In the
Blue Zone, the Ecology exhibition explores the complex
web of the natural world
through a replica of a moonlit
rainforest buzzing with the
sounds of insects. One of the
most popular exhibits is the
Dinosaur Gallery, which
includes life-like animatronic
models of dinosaurs. The
Vault, located in the Green
Zone, contains a dazzling
collection of the finest gems,
crystals, metals and meteorites
from around the world. The
Darwin Centre, which opened
in 2009, is the largest curved
structure in Europe. The
eight-storey-high cocoon
houses the museum's vast collection of insects and plants.

**The Tuojiangasaurus
skeleton (about 150
million years old),
Natural History Museum**

For hotels and restaurants in this region see pp556–562 and pp608–615

Statue of the young Queen Victoria outside Kensington Palace, sculpted by her daughter, Princess Louise

Hyde Park and Kensington Gardens ❻

W2. **Map** 9 B3. **Tel** 020 7298 2100. **Hyde Park** ⊖ Hyde Park Corner, Knightsbridge, Lancaster Gate, Marble Arch. ◯ dawn–midnight daily. ♿ **Kensington Gardens. Tel** 020 7298 2141. ⊖ Queensway, Lancaster Gate. ◯ dawn–dusk daily. ♿ ▣ See also pp74–5. **Diana, Princess of Wales Memorial Playground** ⊖ Queensway, Bayswater. ◯ 10am–dusk daily. ♿ ▣ www.royalparks.org.uk

The ancient manor of Hyde was part of the lands of Westminster Abbey seized by Henry VIII at the Dissolution of the Monasteries in 1536 (see pp50–51). James I opened the park to the public in the early 17th century, and it was soon one of the city's most fashionable public spaces. Unfortunately it also became popular with duellists and highwaymen, and consequently

William III had 300 lights hung along Rotten Row, the first street in England to be lit up at night. In 1730, the Westbourne River was dammed by Queen Caroline in order to create the Serpentine, an artificial lake that is today used for boating and swimming, and Rotten Row for horse riding. The park is also a rallying point for political demonstrations, while at Speaker's Corner, in the northeast, anyone has had the right to address the public since 1872. Sundays are particularly lively, with many budding orators and a number of eccentrics revealing their plans for the betterment of mankind.

Adjoining Hyde Park is Kensington Gardens, the former grounds of Kensington Palace. Three great attractions for children are the innovative Diana, Princess of Wales Memorial Playground, the bronze statue of J M Barrie's fictional Peter Pan (1912), by George Frampton, and the Round Pond where people sail model boats. Also worth-seeing is the dignified Orangery (1704), once used by Queen Anne as a "summer supper house" and now a summer café.

Detail of the Coalbrookdale Gate, Kensington Gardens

Kensington Palace ❼

Kensington Palace Gdns W8. **Map** 8 D4. **Tel** 0844 482 7777. ⊖ High St Ken, Queensway. ◯ Nov–Feb: 10am–5pm daily; Mar–Oct: 10am–6pm daily (last adm: 1 hr before close). ◯ 1 Jan, 24–26 Dec. ◼️ 🎧 📷 ♿ ground floor. 🖥 www.hrp.org.uk

Kensington Palace was the principal residence of the royal family from the 1690s until 1760, when George III moved to Buckingham Palace. Over the years it has seen a number of important royal events. In 1714 Queen Anne died here from a fit of apoplexy brought on by over-eating and, in June 1837, Princess Victoria of Kent was woken to be told that her uncle William IV had died and she was now queen – the beginning of her 64-year reign. Half of the palace still holds royal apartments, but the other half is open to the public. Among the highlights are the 18th-century state rooms with ceilings and murals by William Kent (see p28). After the death of Princess Diana in 1997, the palace became a focal point for mourners who gathered in their thousands at its gates and turned the area into a field of bouquets.

REGENT'S PARK
AND BLOOMSBURY

Cream stuccoed terraces built by John Nash *(see p105)* fringe the southern edge of Regent's Park in London's highest concentration of quality Georgian housing. The park, named for the Prince Regent, was also designed by Nash, as the culmination of a triumphal route from the Prince's house in St James's *(see pp84–5)*. Today it is the busiest of the royal parks and boasts a zoo, an open air theatre, boating lake, rose garden, cafés and London's largest mosque. To the northeast is Camden Town *(see p124)* with its popular market, shops and cafés, reached by walking, or taking a boat, along the picturesque Regent's Canal.

Ancient Greek vase, British Museum

Bloomsbury, an enclave of attractive garden squares and Georgian brick terraces, was one of the most fashionable areas of the city until the mid-19th century, when the arrival of large hospitals and railway stations persuaded many of the wealthier residents to move west to Mayfair, Knightsbridge and Kensington. Home to the British Museum since 1753 and the University of London since 1828, Bloomsbury has long been the domain of artists, writers and intellectuals, including the Bloomsbury Group *(see p163)*, George Bernard Shaw, Charles Dickens and Karl Marx. Traditionally a centre for the book trade, it remains a good place for literary browsing.

SIGHTS AT A GLANCE

Historic Streets
Bloomsbury **5**

Museums and Galleries
British Museum pp106–7 **4**

Madame Tussaud's **1**
Sherlock Holmes Museum **2**
Wallace Collection **3**

KEY

🚇 Underground station

0 metres   500
0 yards   500

GETTING THERE
For most of Regent's Park, the nearest tube stations are Regent's Park, Great Portland Street and Baker Street. Buses 13, 139 and 159 run from Trafalgar Square to near Baker Street. The closest station to the zoo is Camden Town. Russell Square tube station is in the heart of Bloomsbury.

◁ St Andrew's Place, Regent's Park

Madame Tussauds ❶

Marylebone Rd NW1. **Map** 2 D5.
📶 0870 400 3000. 🚇 Baker St.
🕐 9:30am–5:30pm Mon–Fri,
9am–6pm Sat, Sun & school hols.
● 25 Dec. 🗓 🎫 🚻 phone first.
🖥 www.madametussauds.com

Madame Tussaud began her wax-modelling career making death masks of victims of the French Revolution. She

moved to England and in 1835 set up an exhibition of her work in Baker Street, near the present site. Traditional techniques are still used to create figures of royalty, politicians, actors, pop stars and sporting heroes. The main sections of the exhibition are:

Wax figure of Elizabeth II

Blush, where visitors get to feel what it is like to be at a celebrity A-list party; Première Night, devoted to the giants of the entertainment world; and the World Stage, a collection of various royalty, statesmen, world leaders, writers and artists.

The Chamber of Horrors is the most renowned part of Madame Tussauds for its recreations of murders and executions. In the Spirit of London finale, visitors travel in stylized taxi-cabs through

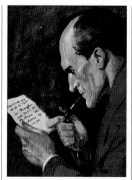

Conan Doyle's fictional detective Sherlock Holmes

the city's history to "witness" events, from the Great Fire of 1666 to the Swinging 1960s. Ticket prices also include entry to temporary exhibitions featuring media icons of the moment. Educational tours are also available for groups.

Sherlock Holmes Museum ❷

221b Baker St NW1. **Map** 1 C4.
Tel 020-7224 3688. 🚇 Baker St. 🕐
9:30am–6pm daily. ● 25 Dec. 🎫 🚻
www.sherlock-holmes.co.uk

Sir Arthur Conan Doyle's fictional detective was supposed to live at 221b Baker Street, which did not exist. The museum, labelled 221b, actually stands between Nos. 237 and 239, and is the only surviving Victorian lodging house in the street. There is a reconstruction of Holmes's front room, and memorabilia from the stories decorate every room. Visitors can buy plaques, Holmes hats, Toby jugs and meerschaum pipes.

Wallace Collection ❸

Hertford House, Manchester Sq W1.
Map 10 D1. 📶 020-7563 9500.
🚇 Bond St, Baker St. 🕐
10am–5pm daily. ● 24–26 Dec, 1
Jan, Good Fri. 🚻 phone first. 🍴 🚻
www.wallacecollection.org

One of the world's finest private collections of European art, it has remained intact since 1897. The product of

passionate collecting by four generations of the Seymour-Conway family who were Marquesses of Hertford, it was bequeathed to the state on the condition that it would go on permanent public display with nothing added or taken away. Hertford House still retains the atmosphere of a grand 19th-century house, and the Centenary Project in 1997 created more gallery space and a stunning high-level glass roof for the central courtyard, which now contains a sculpture garden and an elegant restaurant.

The 3rd Marquess (1777–1842), a flamboyant London figure, used his Italian wife's fortune to buy works by Titian and Canaletto, along with numerous 17th-century Dutch paintings including works by Van Dyck. The collection's particular strength is 18th-century French painting, sculpture and decorative arts, acquired by the 4th Marquess (1800–70) and his natural son, Sir Richard Wallace (1818–90).

A 16th-century Italian majolica dish from the Wallace Collection

The Marquess had a taste for lush romanticism, and notable among his acquisitions are Watteau's *Champs Elysées* (1716–17), Fragonard's *The Swing* (1766) and Boucher's *The Rising and Setting of the Sun* (1753).

Other highlights at the Wallace Collection include Rembrandt's *Titus, the Artist's Son* (1650s), Titian's *Perseus and Andromeda* (1554–6) and Hals's famous *Laughing Cavalier* (1624). There is also an important collection of Renaissance armour, and superb examples of Sèvres porcelain and Italian majolica.

Wax model of Luciano Pavarotti (1990), Madame Tussauds

John Nash's Regency London

John Nash, the son of a Lambeth millwright, was designing houses from the 1780s. However, it was not until the 1820s that he also became known as an inspired town planner, when his "royal route" was completed. This took George IV from his Pall Mall palace, through Piccadilly Circus and up the elegant sweep of Regent Street to Regent's Park, which Nash bordered with rows of beautiful

Statue of John Nash (1752–1835)

Neo-Classical villas, such as Park Crescent and Cumberland Terrace. Though many of his plans were never completed, this map of 1851, which unusually places the south at the top, shows Nash's overall architectural impact on London. His other work included the revamping of Buckingham Palace *(see pp86–7)*, and the building of several theatres and churches.

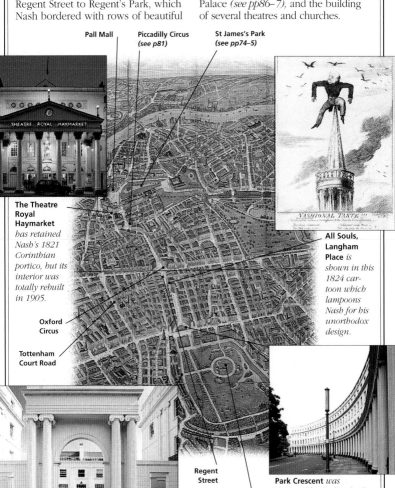

Pall Mall

Piccadilly Circus *(see p81)*

St James's Park *(see pp74–5)*

The Theatre Royal Haymarket *has retained Nash's 1821 Corinthian portico, but its interior was totally rebuilt in 1905.*

All Souls, Langham Place *is shown in this 1824 cartoon which lampoons Nash for his unorthodox design.*

Oxford Circus

Tottenham Court Road

Regent Street

Regent's Park *(see p103)*

Park Crescent *was designed by Nash to be the southern half of a circle, but the northern half was never built. The interiors were refurbished in the 1960s but the dramatic façade was kept intact.*

Cumberland Terrace, *the longest and most ornate of the stuccoed terraces surrounding Regent's Park, was intended to face a royal palace, which was never built.*

British Museum ❹

The oldest public museum in the world, the British Museum was established in 1753 to house the collections of the physician Sir Hans Sloane (1660–1753). Sloane's collection has been added to by gifts and purchases from all over the world, and the museum now contains objects spanning thousands of years. The main part of the building (1823–50) is by architect Robert Smirke, but the architectural highlight is the modern Great Court, with the Reading Room at its centre.

Helmet from Sutton Hoo ship burial

★ **Egyptian Mummies**
Animals such as this cat (30 BC) were preserved alongside humans by the ancient Egyptians.

Upper floors

90
91
67
95
61
59

Bronze Figure Shiva Nataraja
This statue of the Hindu God Shiva Nataraja (c.1100) from South India forms part of the fine collection of Oriental art.

Montague Place entrance

34
33
24

The Egyptian Gallery on the main floor houses the Rosetta Stone, the inscription that enabled 19th-century scholars to decipher Egyptian hieroglyphs.

25
21
20
9
19
22
4
8
17
10
18
16
15

GALLERY GUIDE

The Greek and Roman, and Middle Eastern collections are found on all three levels of the museum, predominantly on the west side. The African collection is located on the lower floor, while Asian exhibits are found on the main and upper floors on the north side of the museum. The Americas collection is located in the northeast corner of the ground floor. Egyptian artifacts are found in the large gallery to the west of the Great Court and on the first floor.

★ **Parthenon Sculptures**
These reliefs from the Parthenon in Athens were brought to London by Lord Elgin around 1802 and are housed in a special gallery.

78
77

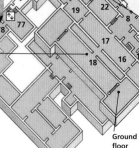

Ground floor

STAR EXHIBITS

★ Egyptian Mummies

★ Parthenon Sculptures

★ Lindow Man

KEY TO FLOORPLAN

☐ Asian collection	☐ Middle Eastern collection
☐ Enlightenment	☐ Europe collection
☐ Coins and medals	☐ Temporary exhibitions
☐ Greek and Roman collection	☐ Non-exhibition space
☐ Egyptian collection	☐ Africa, Oceania and the Americas

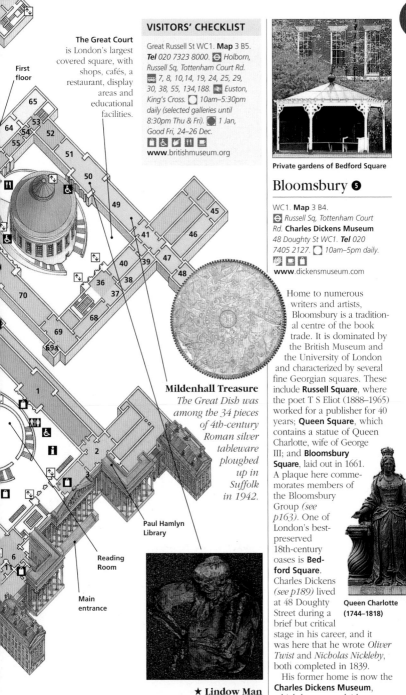

The Great Court is London's largest covered square, with shops, cafés, a restaurant, display areas and educational facilities.

First floor

92

65

64 53
55 54 52
        51
    50
        49
41   45
        46
40 39 47
36 38   48
37

70
68
69
69a

1

2

6
11

Main entrance

Reading Room

Paul Hamlyn Library

Mildenhall Treasure
The Great Dish was among the 34 pieces of 4th-century Roman silver tableware ploughed up in Suffolk in 1942.

★ **Lindow Man**
The skin on this 2,000-year-old human body was preserved by the acids of a peat-bog in Cheshire. He was probably killed in an elaborate ritual.

VISITORS' CHECKLIST

Great Russell St WC1. **Map** 3 B5.
Tel 020 7323 8000. Holborn, Russell Sq, Tottenham Court Rd. 7, 8, 10, 14, 19, 24, 25, 29, 30, 38, 55, 134, 188. Euston, King's Cross. 10am–5:30pm daily (selected galleries until 8:30pm Thu & Fri). 1 Jan, Good Fri, 24–26 Dec.
www.britishmuseum.org

Private gardens of Bedford Square

Bloomsbury ❺

WC1. **Map** 3 B4. Russell Sq, Tottenham Court Rd. **Charles Dickens Museum** 48 Doughty St WC1. **Tel** 020 7405 2127. 10am–5pm daily.
www.dickensmuseum.com

Home to numerous writers and artists, Bloomsbury is a traditional centre of the book trade. It is dominated by the British Museum and the University of London and characterized by several fine Georgian squares. These include **Russell Square**, where the poet T S Eliot (1888–1965) worked for a publisher for 40 years; **Queen Square**, which contains a statue of Queen Charlotte, wife of George III; and **Bloomsbury Square**, laid out in 1661. A plaque here commemorates members of the Bloomsbury Group *(see p163)*. One of London's best-preserved 18th-century oases is **Bedford Square**. Charles Dickens *(see p189)* lived at 48 Doughty Street during a brief but critical stage in his career, and it was here that he wrote *Oliver Twist* and *Nicholas Nickleby*, both completed in 1839.

His former home is now the **Charles Dickens Museum**, which has rooms laid out as they were in Dickens's time, with objects taken from his other London homes and first editions of many of his works.

Queen Charlotte (1744–1818)

THE CITY AND SOUTHWARK

Dominated today by glossy office blocks, the City is the oldest part of the capital. The Great Fire of 1666 obliterated four-fifths of its buildings. Sir Christopher Wren rebuilt much of it and many of his churches survived World War II *(see pp58–9)*. Commerce has always been the City's lifeblood, and the power of its merchants and bankers secured it a degree of autonomy from state control. Humming with activity in business hours, it empties at night.

Old bank sign on Lombard Street

In the Middle Ages Southwark, on the south bank of the Thames, was a refuge for pleasure-seekers, prostitutes, gamblers and criminals. Even after 1550, when the area fell under the jurisdiction of the City, its brothels and taverns thrived. There were also several bear-baiting arenas in which plays were staged until the building of theatres such as the Globe (1598), where many of Shakespeare's works were first performed. Relics of old Southwark are mostly on the waterfront, which has been imaginatively redeveloped and provided with a pleasant walkway.

SIGHTS AT A GLANCE

Historic Sights and Buildings
- HMS Belfast ⓬
- Lloyd's Building ❼
- Monument ❽
- The Old Operating Theatre ⓮
- Temple ❸
- Tower Bridge ❿
- *Tower of London pp118–19* ❾

Pubs
- George Inn ⓯

Museums and Galleries
- Design Museum ⓫
- London Dungeon ⓭
- Museum of London ❻
- Shakespeare's Globe ⓲
- Sir John Soane's Museum ❹
- Tate Modern ⓳

Markets
- Borough Market ⓰

Churches and Cathedrals
- St Bartholomew-the-Great ❺
- *St Paul's Cathedral pp114–15* ❷
- St Stephen Walbrook ❶
- Southwark Cathedral ⓱

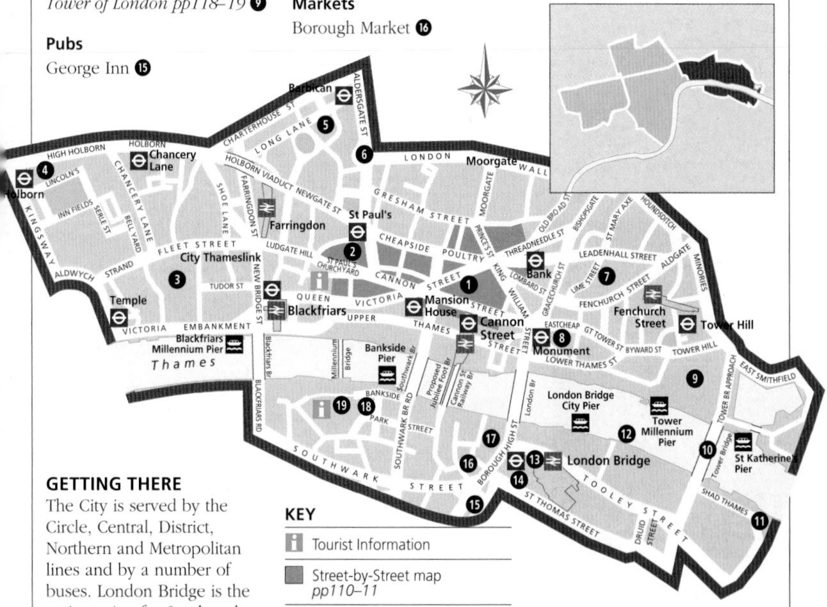

GETTING THERE

The City is served by the Circle, Central, District, Northern and Metropolitan lines and by a number of buses. London Bridge is the main station for Southwark – served by the Northern and Jubilee lines and by trains running from Charing Cross, Cannon Street and Waterloo.

KEY
- Tourist Information
- Street-by-Street map *pp110–11*
- Underground station
- Railway station
- River boat pier

0 metres 500
0 yards 500

◁ **Gothic towers of London's Tower Bridge, built in 1894**

Street-by-Street: The City

This is the financial heart of London and has been ever since the Romans set up a trading post here 2,000 years ago. For years it was London's main residential area but today very few people live here. The City was severely bombed in World War II and the main clues to its past are streets named after vanished inns and markets.

Detail: St Paul's Cathedral

Its numerous churches, many built after the Great Fire of 1666 by the architect Sir Christopher Wren *(see p114)*, are now dwarfed by lavish banks and post-modern developments.

St Mary-le-Bow takes its name from the bow arches in the Norman crypt. Anyone born within earshot of its bells is said to be a true Cockney.

New Change replaces Old Change, a 13th-century street destroyed in World War II.

St Paul's station

Statue of Queen Anne

St Nicholas Cole Abbey was the first church Wren built in the City (in 1677). It had to be restored after World War II bomb damage.

Mansion House station

St James Garlickhythe contains unusual sword rests and hat stands, beneath Wren's elegant spire of 1717.

★ **St Paul's Cathedral**
Built after the Great Fire of 1666, Wren's masterpiece was funded by a tax on coal ❷

The College of Arms is the official repository of the coats of arms and pedigrees of British families *(see p30)*. It was rebuilt here, on its former site, in the 1670s after the Great Fire.

STAR SIGHTS

★ St Paul's Cathedral

★ St Stephen Walbrook

Mansion House (1753), designed by George Dance the Elder, is the official home of the Lord Mayor. The Palladian façade is a familiar City landmark.

LOCATOR MAP
See Street Finder map 13

Bank of England Museum

The Royal Exchange was founded in 1565 by Sir Thomas Gresham as a centre for commerce. The current building dates from 1844.

Bank station

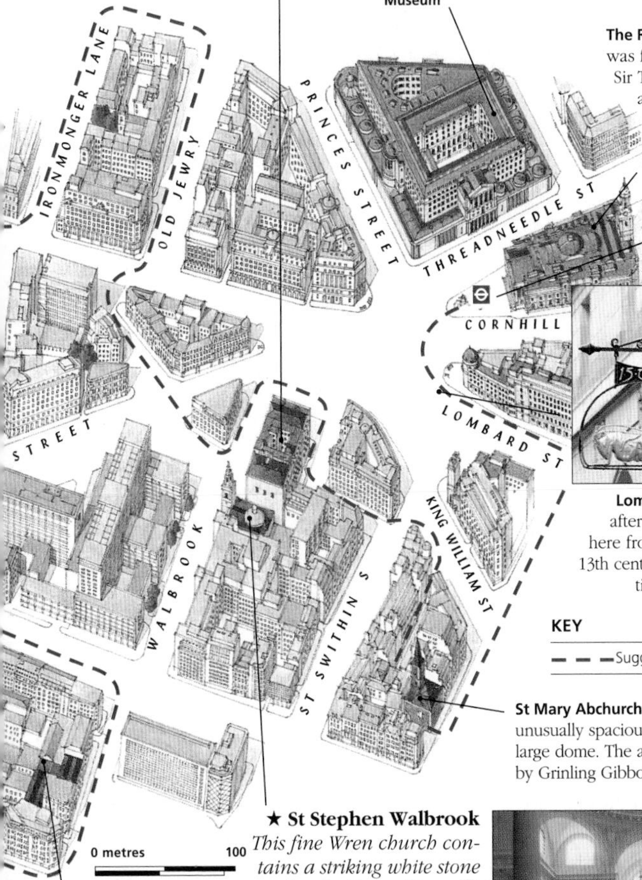

Lombard Street, named after bankers who came here from Lombardy in the 13th century, retains its traditional banking signs.

KEY

━ ━ ━ Suggested route

St Mary Abchurch owes its unusually spacious feel to Wren's large dome. The altar carving is by Grinling Gibbons.

★ St Stephen Walbrook
This fine Wren church contains a striking white stone altar by Henry Moore ❶

0 metres   100
0 yards   100

Skinners' Hall is an 18th-century Italianate building constructed for the ancient guild that controlled trade in fur and leather.

St Stephen Walbrook **①**

39 Walbrook EC4. **Map** 13 B2. *Tel*
020 7626 9000. 🚇 *Bank, Cannon
St.* ⏰ *10am–4pm Mon–Fri.*
⬤ *public hols.* ✝ *12:45am Thu.*
http://ststephenwalbrook.net

The Lord Mayor's parish church
was built by Sir Christopher
Wren in the 1670s and is
among the finest of all his City
churches. The bright, airy interior is flooded with light by a
huge dome that appears to
float above the eight columns
and arches that support it. The
dome, deep and coffered with
ornate plasterwork, was a forerunner of St Paul's. Original
fittings, such as the highly
decorative font cover and
pulpit canopy, contrast with
the stark simplicity of Henry
Moore's massive white stone
altar (1987). The best time to
see the church is during one
of its free organ recitals from
12:30 to 1:30pm on Fridays.

St Paul's **②**

See pp116–17.

Effigies in Temple Church

Temple **③**

Inner Temple, King's Bench Walk
EC4. *Tel 020 7797 8250.* **Map** 12 E2.
🚇 *Temple.* ⏰ *12:30–3pm Mon–Fri
(grounds only).* ♿ **Middle Temple
Hall**, *Middle Temple Ln EC4. Tel 020
7427 4800.* ⏰ *10–11:30am, 3–4pm
Mon–Fri.* ♿ **Temple Church.** *Tel
020 7353 8559.* ⏰ *Wed–Fri; call for
times and services.* 📷 *book ahead.*

A cluster of atmospheric
squares form the Inner and
Middle Temples, two of

London's four Inns of Court,
where law students are trained.
The name Temple derives from
the medieval Knights Templar,
a religious order which protected pilgrims to the Holy Land
and was based here until
1312. Marble effigies of
knights lie on the floor of the
circular Temple Church, part
of which dates from the 12th
century. Middle Temple Hall
has a fine Elizabethan interior.

St Bartholomew-the-Great **⑤**

West Smithfield EC1. **Map** 12 F1.
Tel 020 7606 5171. 🚇 *Barbican,
St Paul's.* ⏰ *8:30am–5pm (4pm in
winter) Mon–Fri, 10:30am–4pm Sat,
8:30am–8pm Sun.* ⬤ *1 Jan, 25, 26
Dec.* 🎁 ♿ 📷 *by appt.* **Concerts.**
www.greatstbarts.com

The historic area of Smithfield
has witnessed a number of
bloody events over the years,
among them the execution
of rebel peasant leader
Wat Tyler in 1381, and, in
the reign of Mary I (1553–58),
the burning of scores of
Protestant martyrs.

Sir John Soane's Museum **④**

13 Lincoln's Inn Fields WC2.
Map 12 D1. *Tel 020 7405 2107.*
🚇 *Holborn.* ⏰ *10am–5pm Tue–Sat,
6–9pm 1st Tue of month.* ⬤ *public
hols, 24 Dec.* ♿ *ground floor only.*
📷 *Sat 11am.* **www.**soane.org

One of the most eccentric
museums in London, this
house was left to the nation
by Sir John Soane in 1837,
with a stipulation that nothing
should be changed. The son
of a bricklayer, Soane became
one of Britain's leading late
Georgian architects developing a restrained Neo-Classical
style of his own. After marrying the niece of a wealthy
builder, whose fortune he
inherited, he bought and reconstructed No. 12 Lincoln's
Inn Fields. In 1813 he and his
wife moved into No. 13 and
in 1824 he rebuilt No. 14,
adding a picture gallery and
the mock medieval Monk's

Parlour. Today, true to Soane's
wishes, the collections are
much as he left them – an
eclectic gathering of beautiful,
instructional and often simply
peculiar artifacts. There are
casts, bronzes, vases, antique
fragments, paintings and a
selection of bizarre trivia which
ranges from a giant fungus
from Sumatra to a scold-bridle,
a device designed to silence
nagging wives. Highlights
include the sarcophagus of
Seti I, Soanes's own designs,
including those for the Bank
of England, models by leading
Neo-Classical sculptors and
the *Rake's Progress* series of
paintings (1734) by William
Hogarth, which Mrs Soane
bought for £520.
    The building itself is full of
architectural surprises and
illusions. In the main ground
floor room, cunningly placed
mirrors play tricks with light
and space, while an atrium
stretching from the basement
to the glass-domed roof
allows light on to every floor.

A glass dome lets light
on to all the floors.

A vast sarcophagus
(1300 BC) stands on
the floor of the crypt.

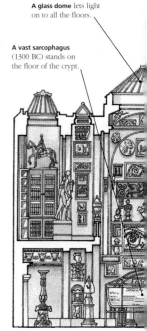

Hidden in a quiet corner behind Smithfield meat market (central London's only surviving wholesale food market), this is one of London's oldest churches. It once formed part of a priory founded in 1123

St Bartholomew's gatehouse

by a monk, Rahere, whose tomb is here. He was Henry I's court jester until he dreamed that St Bartholomew had saved him from a winged monster.

The 13th-century arch, now topped by a Tudor gatehouse, used to be the entrance to the church until the old nave was pulled down during the Dissolution of the Monasteries (*see pp50–51*). The painter William Hogarth was baptized here in 1697. The church featured in the films *Four Weddings and a Funeral* and *Shakespeare in Love*.

Museum of London ❻

London Wall EC2. **Map** 13 A1.
Tel 020 7001 9844. 🚇 *Barbican, St Paul's.* ◯ *10am–6pm daily.*
● *24–26 Dec.* ♿ ▢ ▢ ▢
www.museumoflondon.org.uk

This museum traces life in London from prehistoric times to the outbreak of World War I. Displays of archaeological finds and domestic objects alternate with reconstructed street scenes and interiors.

Delft plate made in London 1600, Museum of London

There is also a working model of the Great Fire of 1666 in the London's Burning section. The Roman London gallery has a brightly coloured 2nd-century fresco from a Southwark bath house.

The museum spent over £20 million redeveloping its lower galleries into the Galleries of Modern London, which opened in 2010. These retell London's history from 1666 to the present day with over 4,000 objects and interactive exhibits. Visitors can also discover the city's many incarnations in the London before London, Roman London and Medieval London galleries.

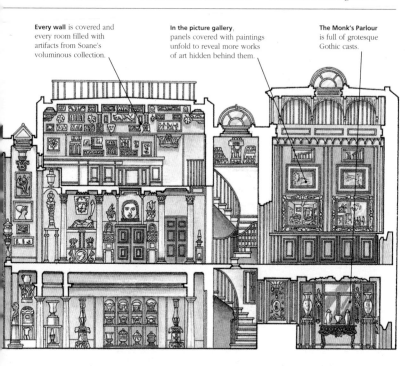

Every wall is covered and every room filled with artifacts from Soane's voluminous collection.

In the picture gallery, panels covered with paintings unfold to reveal more works of art hidden behind them.

The Monk's Parlour is full of grotesque Gothic casts.

St Paul's Cathedral ②

The Great Fire of London in 1666 left the medieval cathedral of St Paul's in ruins. Wren was commissioned to rebuild it, but his design for a church on a Greek Cross plan (where all four arms are equal) met with considerable resistance. The authorities insisted on a conventional Latin cross, with a long nave and short transepts, which was believed to focus the congregation's attention on the altar. Despite the compromises, Wren created a magnificent Baroque cathedral, which was built between 1675 and 1710 and has since formed the lavish setting for many state ceremonies.

★ Dome
At 111 m (360 ft), the elaborate dome is one of the highest in the world.

The balustrade along the top was added in 1718 against Wren's wishes.

★ West Front and Towers
Inspired by the Italian Baroque architect, Borromini, the towers were added by Wren in 1707.

The West Portico consists of two storeys of coupled Corinthian columns, topped by a pediment carved with reliefs showing the Conversion of St Paul.

The Nave
An imposing succession of massive arches and saucer domes open out into the vast space below the cathedral's main dome.

West Porch

Main entrance approached from Ludgate Hill

CHRISTOPHER WREN

Trained as a scientist, Sir Christopher Wren (1632–1723) began his impressive architectural career at the age of 31. He became a leading figure in the rebuilding of London after the Great Fire of 1666, building a total of 52 new churches. Although Wren never visited Italy, his work was influenced by Roman, Baroque and Renaissance architecture, as is apparent in his masterpiece, St Paul's Cathedral.

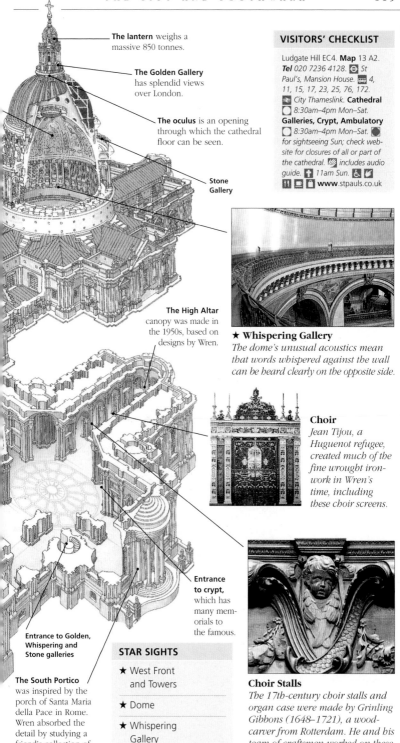

The lantern weighs a massive 850 tonnes.

The Golden Gallery has splendid views over London.

The oculus is an opening through which the cathedral floor can be seen.

Stone Gallery

The High Altar canopy was made in the 1950s, based on designs by Wren.

Entrance to crypt, which has many memorials to the famous.

Entrance to Golden, Whispering and Stone galleries

The South Portico was inspired by the porch of Santa Maria della Pace in Rome. Wren absorbed the detail by studying a friend's collection of architectural engravings.

VISITORS' CHECKLIST

Ludgate Hill EC4. **Map** 13 A2. *Tel* 020 7236 4128. St Paul's, Mansion House. *4, 11, 15, 17, 23, 25, 76, 172.* City Thameslink. **Cathedral** 8:30am–4pm Mon–Sat. **Galleries, Crypt, Ambulatory** 8:30am–4pm Mon–Sat. for sightseeing Sun; check website for closures of all or part of the cathedral. includes audio guide. 11am Sun. www.stpauls.co.uk

★ **Whispering Gallery**
The dome's unusual acoustics mean that words whispered against the wall can be heard clearly on the opposite side.

Choir
Jean Tijou, a Huguenot refugee, created much of the fine wrought ironwork in Wren's time, including these choir screens.

STAR SIGHTS

★ West Front and Towers

★ Dome

★ Whispering Gallery

Choir Stalls
The 17th-century choir stalls and organ case were made by Grinling Gibbons (1648–1721), a woodcarver from Rotterdam. He and his team of craftsmen worked on these intricate carvings for two years.

Richard Rogers's Lloyd's building

Lloyd's Building ❼

1 Lime St EC3. **Map** 13 C2. **Tel** 020 7327 1000. 🚇 *Monument, Bank, Aldgate.* 📧 tours@lloyds.com

Lloyd's was founded in the late 17th century and soon became the world's main

insurers, issuing policies on everything from oil tankers to Betty Grable's legs. The present building, designed by Richard Rogers, dates from 1986 and is one of the most interesting modern buildings in London. Its exaggerated stainless-steel external piping and high-tech ducts echo Rogers' forceful Pompidou Centre in Paris. Lloyd's is well worth seeing floodlit at night.

Monument ❽

Monument St EC3. **Map** 13 C2. **Tel** 020 7626 2717. 🚇 *Monument.* ⏰ 9:30am–5:30pm daily. ⬤ 1 Jan, 24–26 Dec. 🎫 **www**.themonument.info

This doric column, designed by Wren to commemorate the Great Fire of London that devastated the original walled city in September 1666, was, in 1681, the tallest isolated stone column in the world. Topped with a bronze flame, the Monument is 62 m (205 ft) high; the exact distance west to Pudding Lane, where the fire is believed to have started. Reliefs around the column's base show Charles II restoring the city after the tragedy.

The now restored column has 311 tightly spiralled steps that lead to a tiny viewing platform. (In 1842, it was enclosed with an iron cage to prevent suicides.) The steep climb is well worth the effort as the views from the top are spectacular and visitors are rewarded with a certificate.

Tower of London ❾

See pp118–19.

Tower Bridge ❿

SE1. **Map** 14 D3. **Tel** 020 7403 3761. 🚇 *Tower Hill.* **The Tower Bridge Exhibition** ⏰ Apr–Sep: 10am–6:30pm daily; Oct–Mar: 9:30am–6pm daily (last adm: 4pm). ⬤ 24–26 Dec. 🎫 ♿ access lift. 🚻 **www**.towerbridge.org.uk

This flamboyant piece of Victorian engineering, designed by Sir Horace Jones,

was completed in 1894 and soon became a symbol of London. Its two Gothic towers contain the mechanism for raising the roadway to permit large ships to pass through. The towers are made of a supporting steel framework clad in stone, and are linked by two high-level walkways which were closed between 1909 and 1982 due to their popularity

with suicides and prostitutes. The bridge now houses The Tower Bridge Exhibition, with interactive displays bringing the bridge's history to life. There are fine river views from the walkways, and a look at the steam engine room that powered the lifting machinery until 1976, when the system was electrified.

Walkways, open to the public, give panoramic views over the Thames and London.

The roadway, when raised, creates a space 40 m (135 ft) high and 60 m (200 ft) wide, big enough for large cargo ships.

Engine room

Lifts and 300 steps lead to the top of the towers.

The Victorian winding machinery was originally powered by steam.

Entrance

South Bank

North Bank

Design Museum ⓫

Butlers Wharf, Shad Thames SE1.
Map 14 E4. *Tel* 020 7940 8785.
🚇 Tower Hill, London Bridge.
🕐 10am–5:45pm daily (last adm:
5:15pm). ● 25 & 26 Dec. 📷 ♿
🍴 **Blueprint Café** 020 7940 8785
for reservations. ♿ 💻 📱
www.designmuseum.org

This museum was the first
in the world to be devoted
solely to modern and contemporary design when it was
founded in 1989. A frequently
changing programme of
exhibitions explores landmarks in modern design
history and the most exciting
innovations in contemporary
design set against the context
of social, cultural, economic
and technological changes.
The Design Museum embraces
every area of design, from
furniture and fashion, to
household products, cars,
graphics, websites and architecture in exhibitions and
new design commissions.
Each spring the museum
hosts Designer of the Year, a
national design prize, with an
exhibition at which the public
can vote for the winner.

The museum is arranged
over three floors, with major
exhibitions on the first floor.
There is a choice of smaller
displays on the second,
which also houses an
Interaction Space, where
visitors can play vintage video
games and learn about the
designers featured in the
museum in the Design at
the Design Museum online
research archive. The shop
and café are on the ground
floor. On the first floor is the
Blueprint Café restaurant,
which has stunning views of
the Thames (booking ahead
recommended).

Exterior of the Design Museum

**The familiar sight of the naval
gunship HMS Belfast on the Thames**

HMS Belfast ⓬

Morgan's Lane, Tooley St SE1.
Map 13 C3. 📠 020 7940 6300.
🚇 London Bridge, Tower Hill. 🕐
10am–6pm daily (last adm: 5:45pm).
● 24–26 Dec. 📷 ♿ limited. 💻
📱 www.iwm.org.uk/visits/hms-
belfast

Originally launched in 1938
to serve in World War II, the
11,500-ton battle ship HMS
Belfast was instrumental in
the destruction of the German
battle cruiser *Scharnhorst* in
the battle of North Cape, and
also played an important role
in the Normandy Landings.

After the war, the battle
cruiser, designed for offensive
action and for supporting
amphibious operations, was
sent to work for the United
Nations in Korea. The ship
remained in service with the
British navy until 1965.

Since 1971, the cruiser has
been used as a floating naval
museum. Part of it has been
atmospherically recreated
to show what the ship was
like in 1943, when it partici-
pated in sinking the German
battle cruiser. Other displays
portray life on board during
World War II, and there are
also general exhibits which
relate to the history of the
Royal Navy, as well as an
interactive Operations Room.

As well as being a great
family day out, it is also
possible for children to
take part in the educational
activity weekends that take
place on board the ship.

London Dungeon ⓭

Tooley St SE1. **Map** 13 C3. 📠 0207
403 7221. 🚇 London Bridge. 🕐 Jul–
Aug 9:30am–6:30pm; Easter–Jun,
Sep & Oct 10am–5:30pm; Nov–Easter
10:30am–5pm; daily. ● 25 Dec. 📷
book in advance to avoid queues. ♿
💻 📱 www.the-dungeons.co.uk

In effect a much expanded
version of the chamber of
horrors at Madame Tussaud's
(see p104), this museum is
a great hit with children. It
illustrates the most bloodthirsty events in British history.
It is played strictly for terror,
and screams abound as Druids
perform a human sacrifice at
Stonehenge, Henry VIII's wife
Anne Boleyn is beheaded,
and a room full of people die
in agony during the Great
Plague. Other displays include
torture, murder and witchcraft.

19th-century surgical tools

The Old Operating Theatre ⓮

9a St Thomas St SE1. **Map** 13 B4. *Tel*
020 7188 2679. 🚇 London Bridge.
🕐 10:30am–5pm daily. ● 15 Dec–
5 Jan. 📷 📱 www.thegarret.org.uk

St Thomas's Hospital stood
here from its foundation in
the 12th century until it was
moved west in 1862. At this
time most of its buildings
were demolished to make
way for the railway. The
women's operating theatre
(The Old Operating Theatre
Museum and Herb Garret)
survived only because it was
located away from the main
buildings, in a garret over the
hospital church. It lay, bricked
up and forgotten, until the
1950s. Britain's oldest operating theatre, dating back to
1822, it has now been fitted
out as it would have been in
the early 19th century.

Tower of London 🄹

Soon after William the Conqueror became king in 1066, he built a fortress here to guard the entrance to London from the Thames Estuary. In 1097 the White Tower was completed in sturdy stone; other fine buildings have been added over the centuries. The tower has served as a royal residence, armoury, treasury and, most famously, as a prison. Some were tortured here and among those who met their death were the "Princes in the Tower", the sons and heirs of Edward IV. Today the tower is a popular attraction, housing the Crown Jewels and other exhibits, such as the displays about the Peasants' Revolt of 1381, the only time the Tower's walls were breached. The most celebrated residents are the ravens; legend has it that the kingdom will fall if they desert the tower. Some guided tours are led by the colourful Beefeaters.

Beauchamp Tower
Many high-ranking prisoners were held here, often with their own retinues of servants. The tower was built by Edward I around 1281.

"Beefeaters"
Thirty-seven Yeomen Warders guard the Tower and live here. Their uniforms hark back to Tudor times.

Two 13th-century curtain walls protect the tower.

Tower Green was the execution site for favoured prisoners, away from crowds on Tower Hill, where many had to submit to public execution. Seven people died here, including two of Henry VIII's six wives, Anne Boleyn and Catherine Howard.

Queen's House
This Tudor building is the sovereign's official residence at the Tower.

Main entrance from Tower Hill

THE CROWN JEWELS

The world's best-known collection of precious objects, now displayed in a splendid exhibition room, includes the gorgeous regalia of crowns, sceptres, orbs and swords used at coronations and other state occasions. Most date from 1661, when Charles II commissioned replacements for regalia destroyed by Parliament after the execution of Charles I (see pp52–3). Only a few older pieces survived, hidden by royalist clergymen until the Restoration – notably, Edward the Confessor's sapphire ring, now incorporated into the Imperial State Crown (see p73). The crown was made for Queen Victoria in 1837 and has been used at every coronation since.

The Sovereign's Ring (1831)

The Sovereign's Orb (1661), a hollow gold sphere encrusted with jewels

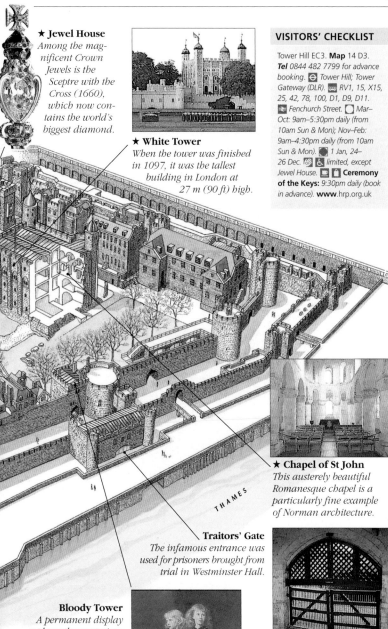

★ **Jewel House**
Among the magnificent Crown Jewels is the Sceptre with the Cross (1660), which now contains the world's biggest diamond.

★ **White Tower**
When the tower was finished in 1097, it was the tallest building in London at 27 m (90 ft) high.

VISITORS' CHECKLIST

Tower Hill EC3. **Map** 14 D3.
Tel 0844 482 7799 for advance booking. ⊖ Tower Hill; Tower Gateway (DLR). 🚌 RV1, 15, X15, 25, 42, 78, 100, D1, D9, D11. 🚆 Fenchurch Street. ◯ Mar–Oct: 9am–5:30pm daily (from 10am Sun & Mon); Nov–Feb: 9am–4:30pm daily (from 10am Sun & Mon). ◯ 1 Jan, 24–26 Dec. 🎫 🚻 limited, except Jewel House. ◯ 📷 **Ceremony of the Keys:** 9:30pm daily (book in advance). **www**.hrp.org.uk

★ **Chapel of St John**
This austerely beautiful Romanesque chapel is a particularly fine example of Norman architecture.

Traitors' Gate
The infamous entrance was used for prisoners brought from trial in Westminster Hall.

Bloody Tower
A permanent display explores the mysterious disappearance of Edward IV's two sons, who were put here by their uncle, Richard of Gloucester (later Richard III), after their father died in 1483. The princes disappeared, and Richard was crowned later that year. In 1674 the skeletons of two children were found nearby.

STAR SIGHTS

★ Jewel House

★ White Tower

★ Chapel of St John

The George Inn, now owned by the National Trust

George Inn ⓯

(NT) 77 Borough High St SE1. **Map** 13 B4. *Tel* 020 7407 2056. ⊖ *London Bridge, Borough.* ⬡ *11am–11pm Mon–Sat, noon–10:30pm Sun* ⬤ *25 & 26 Dec.* 🍴

Dating from the 17th century, this building is the only traditional galleried coaching inn left in London and is mentioned in Dickens's *Little Dorrit*. It was rebuilt after the Southwark fire of 1676 in a style that dates back to the Middle Ages. There were originally three wings around a courtyard, where plays were staged in the 17th century. In 1889 the north and east wings were demolished, so there is only one wing remaining.

The inn is still a popular pub with a well-worn, comfortable atmosphere, perfect on a cold, damp day. In the summer, the yard fills with picnic tables, and patrons are occasionally entertained by actors and morris dancers. The house bitter is highly recommended.

Borough Market ⓰

8 Southwark St SE1. **Map** 13 B4. ⊖ *London Bridge.* **Retail market** ⬡ *11am–5pm Thu, noon–6pm Fri, 9am–5pm Sat.*

Borough Market was until recently a wholesale fruit and vegetable market, which had its origins in medieval times, and moved to its current position beneath the railway tracks in 1756. This hugely popular fine-food market has now become well established, selling gourmet foods from Britain and abroad, as well as quality fruit and vegetables, to locals and tourists alike.

Shakespeare window (1954), Southwark Cathedral

Southwark Cathedral ⓱

Montague Close SE1. **Map** 13 B3. *Tel* 020 7367 6700. ⊖ *London Bridge.* ⬡ *8am–6pm daily (from 8:30am Sat & Sun).* 🖥 🚻 ♿ 🛍 **www.** cathedral.southwark.anglican.org

Although some parts of this building date back to the 12th century, it was not until 1905 that it became a cathedral. Many original medieval features remain, notably the tomb of the poet John Gower (c.1325–1408), a contemporary of Chaucer *(see p172)*. There is a monument to Shakespeare, carved in 1912, and a memorial window *(above)* installed in 1954.

Shakespeare's Globe ⓲

New Globe Walk SE1. **Map** 13 A3. *Tel* 020 7902 1500. Box office: 020 7401 9919. ⊖ *Southwark, London Bridge.* **Exhibition** ⬡ *Late Apr–early Oct: 9am–5:30pm daily; early Oct–late Apr: 10am–5:30pm daily.* ⬤ *24, 25 Dec.* 📷 ♿ 🛍 *every 30 mins. (Rose Theatre tours for groups of 15 or more by appt only).* **Performances** *late Apr–early Oct.* ♿ *limited.* 🍴 🖥 🛍 🛍 **www.** shakespearesglobe.com

Opened in 1997, this circular building is a faithful reproduction of an Elizabethan theatre, close to the site of the original Globe where many of Shakespeare's plays were first performed. It was built using handmade bricks and oak laths, fastened with wooden pegs rather than metal screws, and has the first thatched roof allowed in London since the Great Fire of 1666. The theatre was erected thanks to a heroic campaign by the American actor and director Sam Wanamaker. Open to the elements (although the seats are protected), it operates only in the summer, and seeing a play here can be a thrilling experience, with top-quality acting under the artistic direction of Mark Rylance among others.

Beneath the theatre, Shakespeare's Globe Exhibition is open all year and covers many aspects of Shakespeare's work and times. Groups of 15 or more may book to see the foundations of the nearby Rose Theatre.

Shakespeare's *Henry IV* (performed at the Globe Theatre around 1600)

Tate Modern ⑲

Holland St, SE1. **Map** 13 A3. *Tel 020
7887 8888.* ⊖ *Blackfriar's,
Southwark.* 🚤 *to Tate Britain every
40 mins.* ◯ *10am–6pm Sun–Thu,
10am–10pm Fri & Sat.* ⬤ *24–26
Dec.* 🖼 *major exhibitions.* ♿ 🚻
📷 🛈 **www**.tate.org.uk/modern

Looming over the southern
bank of the Thames, Tate
Modern occupies the converted
Bankside power station, a
dynamic space for one of the
world's premier collections of
contemporary art. Tate Modern
draws its main displays from
the expansive Tate Collection,
also shown at the other Tate
galleries: Tate St Ives *(p277)*,
Tate Liverpool *(p377)* and Tate
Britain *(p91)*. The displays
change frequently and works
are sometimes moved tempo-
rarily, loaned out or removed
for restoration. Works shown
on these pages are examples
of what might be on display.
A river boat, *Tate to Tate,*

Inverno from *Quattro Stagioni*
(1993–4) by Cy Twombly

transports visitors between
Tate Modern and Tate Britain.

The gallery's west entrance
leads straight into the massive
Turbine Hall. Each year an
artist is commissioned to install
in this space. Louise Bourgeois
was the first to do so, creating
three giant towers and a gargantuan spider, *Maman* (2000).
In 2010, Ai Weiwei's *Sunflower Seeds* filled part of the Turbine Hall with 100 million
hand-crafted porcelain seeds.

An escalator whisks visitors
from the Turbine Hall, up to
level 3 where the main
galleries are located. In a break
with convention, Tate Modern
organizes its displays by
theme rather
than chronology
or school – a
practice that
cuts across
movements
and mixes up
media. Four themes based
on traditional genres
reveal how traditions have
been confronted, extended
or rejected by artists
throughout the 20th and
into the 21st centuries.

Tate Modern's displays
are arranged into two
thematic wings on levels 3,
4 and 5. The collection
focuses on key periods of
twentieth-century art history including:
Cubism;
Surrealism;
Abstract Expres-
sionism; Construc-
tivism; and Minimalism.
At the centre of each of
the four exhibitions is a focal
display, from which all the
other displays rotate.

Soft Drainpipe – Blue (Cool)
(1967) by Claes Oldenburg

Spatial Concept "Waiting" (1960)
by Lucio Fontana

The collection includes works
such as the iconic paintings
The Snail by Henri Matisse
and *Quattro
Stagioni* by Cy
Twombly, as
well as the
sculpture, *Fish*
by Constantin
Brancusi and
other important pieces
by the likes of Francis
Picabia and Mark Rothko.
To complement its per-
manent collection, Tate
Modern presents a
dynamic programme of
temporary exhibitions,
including three large-
scale shows per year.
Major live events are
staged each year, taking
their inspiration from
the Collection.

A striking
new extension
is currently
being added to
the south side of the gallery,
which will double exhibition
space. Three oil turbines, from
the original power station,
will form the foundations.

BANKSIDE POWER STATION

This forbidding fortress was designed in 1947 by Sir Giles
Gilbert Scott, the architect of Battersea Power Station, Waterloo
Bridge and London's famous red telephone boxes. The power
station is of a steel-framed brick skin construction, comprising
over 4.2 million bricks. The Turbine Hall was designed to
accommodate huge oil-burning generators and three vast oil
tanks are still in situ, buried under the ground just south of
the building. The tanks are to be employed in a future stage
of Tate Modern development. The power station itself was converted by Swiss architects Herzog and de Meuron who designed
the two-storey glass box, or lightbeam, which runs the length
of the building. This serves to flood the upper galleries with
light and also provides wonderful views of London.

The façade, chimney and light beam of Tate Modern

FURTHER AFIELD

Over the centuries London has steadily expanded to embrace the scores of villages that surrounded it, leaving the City as a reminder of London's original boundaries. Although now linked in an almost unbroken urban sprawl, many of these areas have maintained their old village atmosphere and character. Hampstead and Highgate are still distinct enclaves, as are artistic Chelsea and literary Islington. Greenwich, Chiswick and Richmond have retained features that hark back to the days when the Thames was an important artery for transport and commerce, while just to the east of the City the wide expanses of the former docks have, in the last 20 years, been imaginatively rebuilt as new commercial and residential areas.

SIGHTS AT A GLANCE

Camden and Islington **7**
Chelsea **1**
Chiswick **10**
East End and Docklands **8**

Greenwich **9**
Hampstead **4**
Hampstead Heath **5**
Highgate **6**

Holland Park **2**
Notting Hill and
    Portobello Road **3**
Richmond and Kew **11**

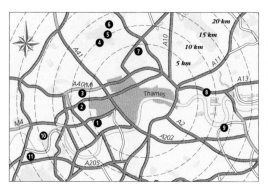

KEY

▦	Main sightseeing areas
☐	Greater London
☐	Parks
═	Motorway
▬	Major road
═	Minor road

10 miles = 15 km

Chelsea **1**

SW3. ⊖ *Sloane Square.* **Map** 17 B2.

Riverside Chelsea has been fashionable since Tudor times when Sir Thomas More, Henry VIII's Lord Chancellor

**Statue of Sir Thomas More
(1478–1535), Cheyne Walk**

(see p50), lived here. The river views attracted artists and the arrival of the historian Thomas Carlyle and essayist Leigh Hunt in the 1830s began a literary connection. Blue plaques on the houses of **Cheyne Walk** celebrate former residents such as J M W Turner *(see p91)* and writers George Eliot, Henry James and T S Eliot.

Chelsea's artistic tradition is maintained by its galleries and antique shops, many of them scattered among the clothes boutiques on **King's Road**. This begins at **Sloane Square**, named after the physician Sir Hans Sloane, who bought the manor of Chelsea in 1712. Sloane expanded the **Chelsea Physic Garden** (1673) along Swan Walk to cultivate plants and herbs.

Wren's **Royal Hospital**, on Royal Hospital Road was built in 1692 as a retirement home for old soldiers and still houses 400 Chelsea Pensioners.

Arab Hall, Leighton House (1866)

Holland Park **2**

W8, W14. ⊖ *Holland Park.* **Map** 7 B5.

This park is more intimate than the large royal parks such as Hyde Park *(see p101).* It was opened in 1952 on the grounds of **Holland House**, a centre of social and political intrigue in its 19th-century heyday.

Around the park are some magnificent late Victorian houses. **Linley Sambourne**

House was built about 1870 and has received a much-needed facelift, though it remains much as Sambourne furnished it, in the Victorian manner, with china ornaments and heavy velvet drapes. He was a political cartoonist for the satirical magazine *Punch* and drawings cram the walls.

Leighton House, built for the Neo-Classical painter Lord Leighton in 1866, has been preserved as an extraordinary monument to the Victorian Aesthetic movement. The highlight is the Arab Hall, which was added in 1879 to house Leighton's stupendous collection of 13th- to 17th-century Islamic tiles. The best paintings include some by Leighton himself and by his contemporaries Edward Burne-Jones and John Millais.

🏛 Linley Sambourne House
18 Stafford Terrace W8. **Tel** 020 7602 3316 (tours: 020 7938 1295).
🚇 High St Ken. ⬤ Mar–Dec: tours only, Wed, Sat & Sun (times vary).
🖼 🎥 🚻

🏛 Leighton House
12 Holland Park Rd W14. **Tel** 020 7602 3316. 🚇 High St Ken. ⬤ 10am–5:30pm Wed–Mon. ⬤ public hols. 🖼 🎥 Wed. 🚻

Notting Hill and Portobello Road ❸

W11. 🚇 Notting Hill Gate. **Map** 7 B2.

In the 1950s and 60s, Notting Hill became a centre for the Caribbean community and today it is a vibrant cosmopolitan part of London. It is also home to Europe's largest street carnival *(see p63)* which began in 1965 and takes over the entire area on the August bank holiday weekend, when costumed parades flood through the crowded streets.

Nearby, Portobello Road market *(see pp148–9)* has a bustling atmosphere with hundreds of stalls and shops selling a variety of collectables.

Hampstead ❹

NW3, N6. 🚇 Hampstead. 🚆 Hampstead Heath.

On a high ridge north of the metropolis, Hampstead is essentially a Georgian village with many perfectly maintained mansions and houses. It is one of London's most desirable residential areas, home to a community of artists and writers since Georgian times.

Situated in a quiet Hampstead street, **Keats House** (1816) is an evocative tribute to the life and work of the poet John Keats (1795–1821). Keats lived here for two years before his tragic death from consumption at the age of 25, and it was under a plum tree in the garden that he wrote his celebrated *Ode to a Nightingale*. Mementoes of Keats and of Fanny Brawne, the neighbour

Georgian house, Hampstead

to whom he was engaged, are on show. Renovated in 2009, Keats House now benefits from more extensive displays.

The **Freud Museum**, which opened in 1986, is dedicated to the dramatic life of Sigmund Freud (1856–1939), the founder of psychoanalysis. At the age of 82, Freud fled from Nazi persecution in Vienna to this Hampstead house where he lived and worked for the last year of his life. His daughter Anna, pioneer of child psychoanalysis, continued to live here until her death in 1982. Inside, Freud's rich Viennese-style consulting rooms remain unaltered, and 1930s home movies show moments of Freud's life, including scenes of the Nazi attack on his home in Vienna.

🏛 Keats House
Keats Grove NW3. 🏢 020 7332 3868. 🚇 Hampstead, Belsize Pk. ⬤ 1–5pm Tue–Sun (Nov–Mar: Fri–Sun). 🖥 www.keatshouse.cityoflondon.gov.uk

🏛 Freud Museum
20 Maresfield Gdns NW3. **Tel** 020 7435 2002. 🚇 Finchley Rd. ⬤ noon–5pm Wed–Sun. 🖼 ♿ limited. 🖥 www.freud.org.uk

Antique shop on Portobello Road

View east across Hampstead Heath to Highgate

Hampstead Heath ❺

N6. 🚇 Hampstead, Highgate.
🚉 Hampstead Heath.

Separating the hill-top villages of Hampstead and Highgate, the open spaces of Hampstead Heath are a precious retreat from the city. There are meadows, lakes and ponds for bathing and fishing, and fine views over the capital from **Parliament Hill**, to the east.

Situated in landscaped grounds high on the edge of the Heath is the magnificent **Kenwood House**, where classical concerts (*see p154*) are held by the lake in summer. The house was remodelled by Robert Adam (*see p28*) in 1764 and most of his interiors have survived, the highlight of which is the library. The

mansion is filled with Old Master paintings, such as works by Van Dyck, Vermeer, Turner (*see p91*) and Romney; the star attraction is Rembrandt's self-portrait of 1663.

🏛 **Kenwood House**
Hampstead Lane NW3. **Tel** *020 8348 1286.* ⏱ *11:30am–4pm daily.* ♿
🅿 📷 *www.*english-heritage.org.uk

Handmade crafts and antiques, Camden Lock indoor market

Highgate ❻

N6. 🚇 *Highgate, Archway.*

A settlement since the Middle Ages, Highgate, like Hampstead, became a fashionable aristocratic retreat in the 16th century. Today, it still has an exclusive rural feel, aloof from the urban sprawl below, with a Georgian high street and many expensive houses.

Highgate Cemetery (*see p75*), with its monuments and hidden overgrown corners, has an extraordinary, magical atmosphere. Tour guides (daily in summer, weekends in winter) tell of the many tales of intrigue, mystery and vandalism connected with the cemetery since it opened in 1839. In the eastern section is the tomb of Victorian novelist George Eliot (1819–80) and of the cemetery's most famous incumbent, Karl Marx (1818–83).

🏛 **Highgate Cemetery**
Swains Lane N6. **Tel** *020 8340 1834.*
🚇 *Archway, Highgate.* ⏱ *daily.*
⏱ *during burials, 25–26 Dec.* 📷
🌐 *www.*highgate-cemetery.org

Camden and Islington ❼

NW1, N1. **Camden** 🚇 *Camden Town, Chalk Farm.* **Islington** 🚇 *Angel, Highbury & Islington.*

Camden is a lively area packed with restaurants, shops and a busy **market** (*see p148–9*). Thousands of people come here each weekend to browse among the wide variety of stalls or simply to soak up the atmosphere of the lively cobbled area around the canal, which is enhanced by the buskers and street performers.

Neighbouring Islington was once a fashionable spa but the rich moved out in the late 18th century and the area deteriorated rapidly. In the 20th century, writers such as Evelyn Waugh, George Orwell and Joe Orton lived here. In recent decades, Islington has been rediscovered and is again fashionable as one of the first areas in London to become "gentrified", with many professionals buying the old houses.

East End and Docklands ❽

E1, E2, E14. **East End** 🔵 *Aldgate East, Liverpool St, Bethnal Green.* **Docklands** 🔵 *Canary Wharf.*

In the Middle Ages the East End was full of craftsmen practising noxious trades such as brewing, bleaching and vinegar-making, which were banned within the City. The area has also been home to numerous immigrant communities since the 17th century, when French Huguenots, escaping religious persecution moved into Spitalfields and made it a silk-weaving centre. Textiles continued to dominate in the 1880s, when Jewish tailors and furriers set up workshops here, and in the 1950s, when Bengali machinists worked in cramped conditions.

A good way to get a taste of the East End is to explore its Sunday street markets *(see p149)* and sample freshly baked bagels and spicy Indian food. By way of contrast, anyone interested in contemporary architecture should visit the **Docklands**, an ambitious redevelopment of disused docks, dominated by the Canada Tower. Other attractions include the **V&A Museum of Childhood**, a delightful toy museum with lots of activities, **Dennis Severs' House**, in which you are taken on a historic journey from the 17th to the 19th centuries, and the **Museum of London, Docklands** that explores the history of London's river and port. See p113 for the Museum of London's website.

Royal Naval College framing the Queen's House, Greenwich

🏛 V&A Museum of Childhood
Cambridge Heath Rd E2. **Tel** 020 8983 5200. ⬜ 10am–5:45pm daily. ⬤ 1 Jan, 25–26 Dec. ♿ 🔲 📷 **www.**vam.ac.uk/moc

🏛 Dennis Severs' House
18 Folgate St E1. **Tel** 020 7247 4013. ⬜ noon–2pm Mon after 1st & 3rd Sun of month, Mon eve (by candlelight), noon–4pm Sun. 📷 ✔ **www.**dennissevershouse.co.uk

Greenwich ❾

SE10. 🚆 *Greenwich, Maze Hill.* 🔵 *Cutty Sark (DLR).*

The world's time has been measured from the **Royal Observatory Greenwich** (now housing a museum) since 1884. The area is full of maritime and royal history, with Neo-Classical mansions, a park, antique shops and markets *(see pp148–9).* The **Queen's House**, designed by Inigo Jones for James I's wife, was completed in 1637 for Henrietta Maria, the queen of Charles I. Its highlights include the perfectly cubic main hall and the spiral "tulip staircase".

Canada Tower, Canary Wharf

The adjoining **National Maritime Museum** has exhibits that range from primitive canoes, through Elizabethan galleons, to modern ships. The **Old Royal Naval College** was designed by Christopher Wren *(see p114)* in two halves so that the Queen's House kept its river view. The Rococo chapel and the 18th-century *trompe l'oeil* Painted Hall are open to the public.

An 18th-century compass, National Maritime Museum

The majestic **Cutty Sark** was built in 1869 as a tea carrier and made its final voyage in 1938. In 2007 the ship was seriously damaged by fire. It was re-opened in 2012 following major renovations.

🏛 Royal Observatory Greenwich
Greenwich Park SE10. **Tel** 020 8858 4422. ⬜ 10am–5pm daily. ⬤ 24–26 Dec. 📷 **www.**rog.nmm.ac.uk

🏛 Queen's House and National Maritime Museum
Romney Rd SE10. **Tel** 020 8858 4422. ⬜ daily. ⬤ 24–26 Dec. 📷 ♿ limited. 🔲 📷 **www.**rmg.co.uk

🏛 Old Royal Naval College
King William Walk, SE10. **Tel** 020 8269 4747. ⬜ 10am–5pm daily. ⬤ public hols.

🏛 Cutty Sark
King William Walk, SE10. **Tel** 020 8858 2698. ⬜ 10am–5pm Tue–Sun. ⬤ 25 & 26 Dec. 📷

Chiswick ❿

W4. 🌐 *Chiswick.*

Chiswick is a pleasant sub-urb of London, with pubs, cottages and a variety of birdlife, such as herons, along the picturesque riverside. One of the main reasons for a visit is **Chiswick House**, a magnificent country villa inspired by the Renaissance architect Andrea Palladio. It was designed in the early 18th century by the 3rd Earl of Burlington as an annexe to his larger house (demol-ished in 1758), so that he could display his art collec-tion and entertain friends. The gardens are now fully restored.

Heron

🏛 **Chiswick House**
Burlington Lane W4. **Tel** 020 8995 0508. ◯ Apr–Oct: Sun–Wed & bank hols. **Garden** ◯ dawn–dusk daily. 🎟 for house. ♿ call ahead. ◻ ◻ ◻

Richmond and Kew ⓫

SW15. 🌐 🚊 *Richmond.*

The attractive village of Richmond took its name from a palace built by Henry VII (the former Earl of Richmond in Yorkshire) in 1500, the remains of which can be seen off the green. Nearby is the expansive **Richmond Park**, which was once Charles I's royal hunting ground. In summer, boats

sail down the Thames from Westminster Millennium Pier, making a pleasant day's excursion from central London.
The nobility continued to favour Richmond after royalty had left, and some of their mansions have survived. The Palladian villa, **Marble Hill House**, was built in 1724–9 for the mistress of George II and has been restored to its original appearance. On the opposite side of the Thames, the brooding **Ham House**, built in 1610, had its heyday later that century when it became the home of the Duke and Duchess of Lauderdale. Elizabeth Countess of Dysart inherited the house from her father, who had been Charles I's "whipping boy" – meaning that he was punished whenever the future king misbehaved. He was rewarded as an adult by being given a peerage and the lease of Ham estate.
A little further north along the Thames, **Syon House** has been inhabited by the Dukes and Earls of Northumberland for over 400 years. Numerous attractions here include a butterfly house, a museum of historic cars and a spectacular conservatory built in 1830. The lavish Neo-Classical interiors of the house, created by Robert Adam in the 1760s *(see p28)*, remain the highlight.

Brewers Lane, Richmond

On the riverbank to the south, **Kew Gardens**, the world's most complete botanic gardens, fea-ture examples of nearly every plant that can be grown in Brit-ain. There are also conserva-tories displaying thousands of exotic tropical blooms.

🏛 **Marble Hill House**
(EH) Richmond Rd, Twickenham. **Tel** 020 8892 5115. ◯ prebooked tours only. ♿ limited. ◻ ◻ ◻

🏛 **Ham House**
(NT) Ham St, Richmond. **Tel** 020 8940 1950. ◯ Apr–Oct: Sat–Thu. Gardens: open daily. 🎟 ♿ ◻ ◻ ◻

🏛 **Syon House**
London Rd, Brentford. **Tel** 020 8560 0882. **House** ◯ mid-Mar–Oct: Wed, Thu, Sun & pub hols. **Gardens** ◯ daily (winter: Sat & Sun only). 🎟 🎟 ♿ gardens only. ◻ ◻ www.syonpark.co.uk

🌷 **Kew Gardens**
Royal Botanic Gdns, Kew Green, Richmond. **Tel** 020 8332 5655. ◯ daily. ⬤ 1 Jan, 24–25 Dec. 🎟 ♿ 🎟 ◻ ◻ ◻ www.kew.org

Chiswick House

LONDON STREET FINDER

The map references given with the sights, hotels, restaurants, shops and entertainment venues based in central London refer to the following four maps. All the main places of interest within the central area are marked on the maps in addition to useful practical information, such as tube, railway and coach stations. The key map below shows the area of London that is covered by the Street Finder. The four main city-centre areas (colour-coded in pink) are shown in more detail on the inside back cover.

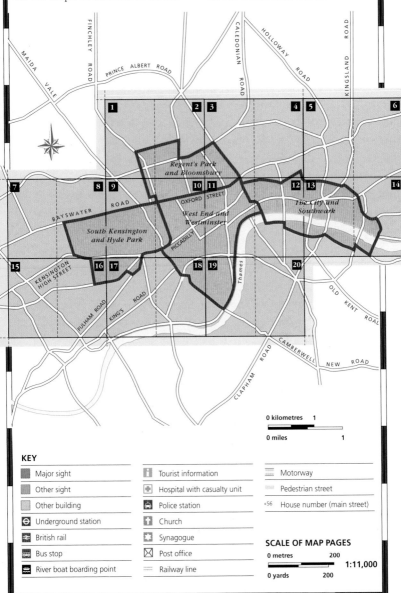

KEY

■ Major sight		🛈 Tourist information		▨ Motorway	
■ Other sight		✚ Hospital with casualty unit		▨ Pedestrian street	
▢ Other building		🚓 Police station		₆56 House number (main street)	
⊖ Underground station		✝ Church			
⇌ British rail		✡ Synagogue		**SCALE OF MAP PAGES**	
🚍 Bus stop		⊠ Post office		0 metres 200	
⇌ River boat boarding point		═ Railway line			**1:11,000**
				0 yards 200	

0 kilometres   1

0 miles   1

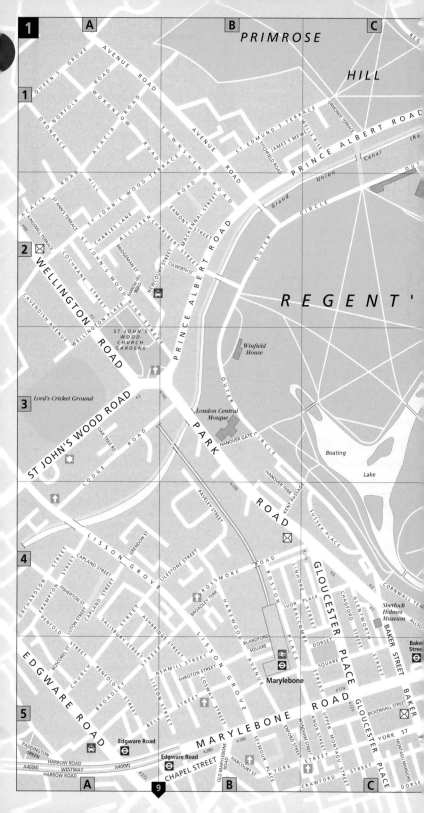

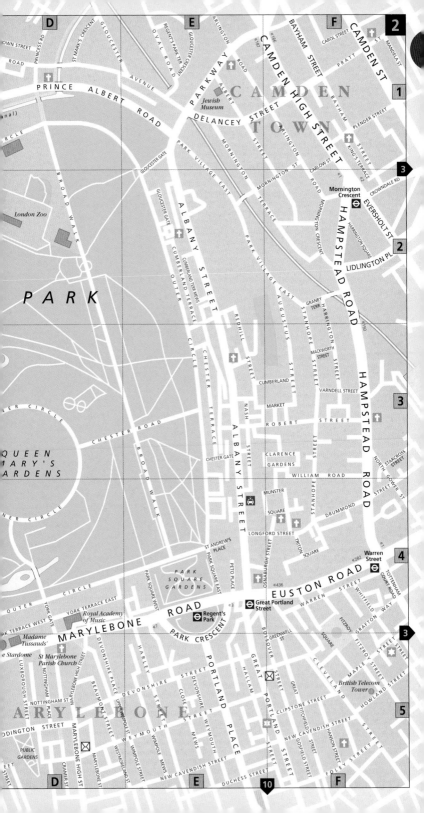

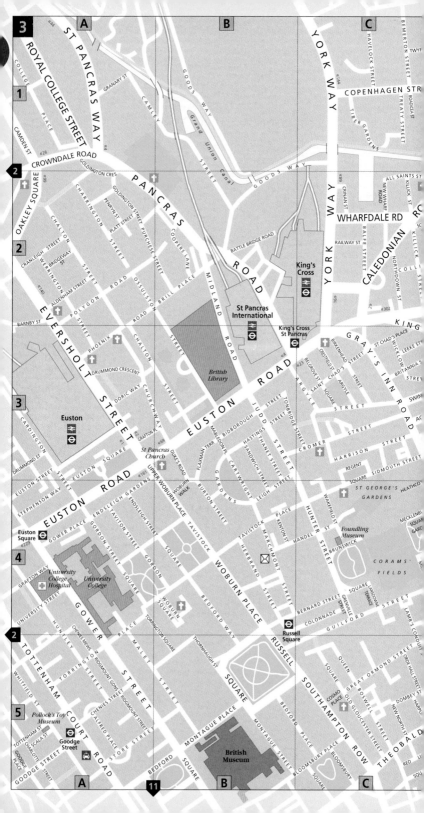

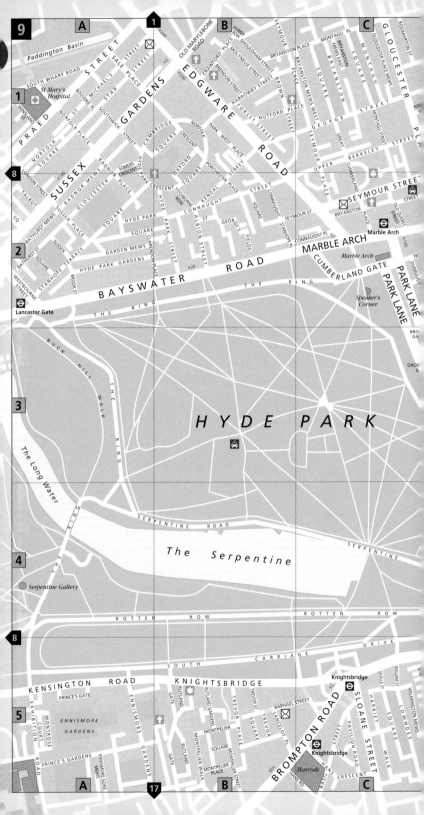

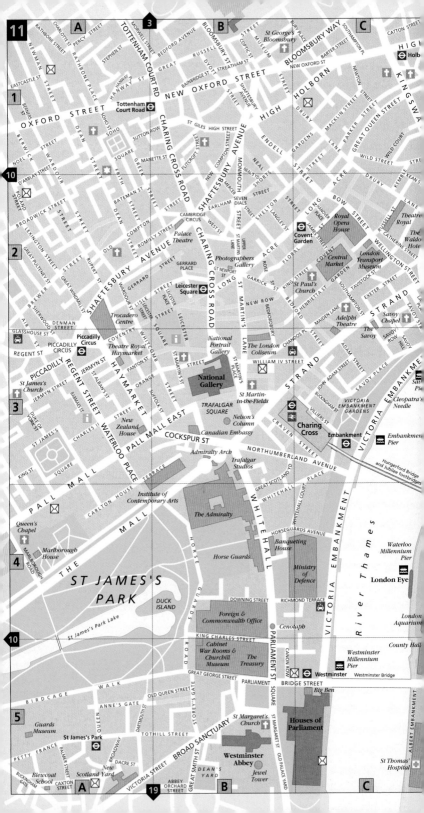

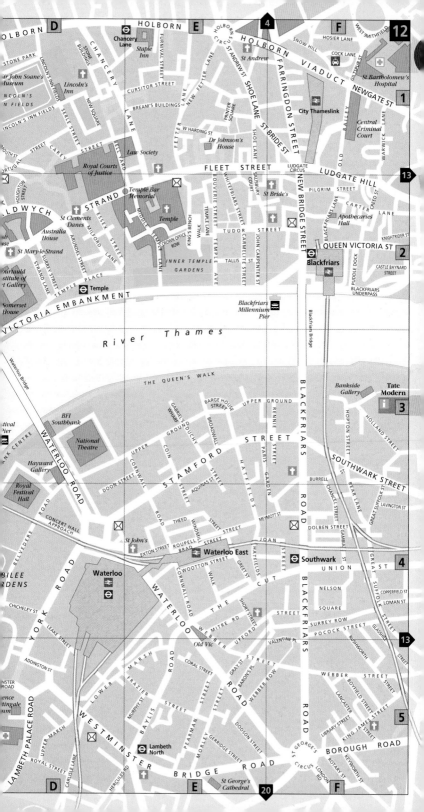

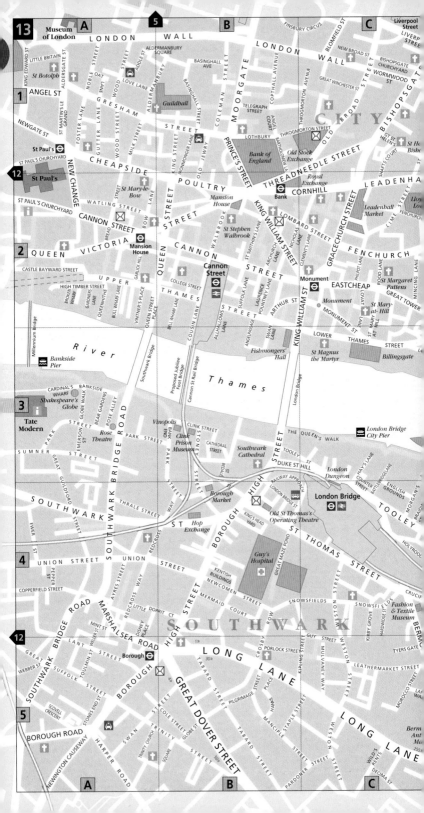

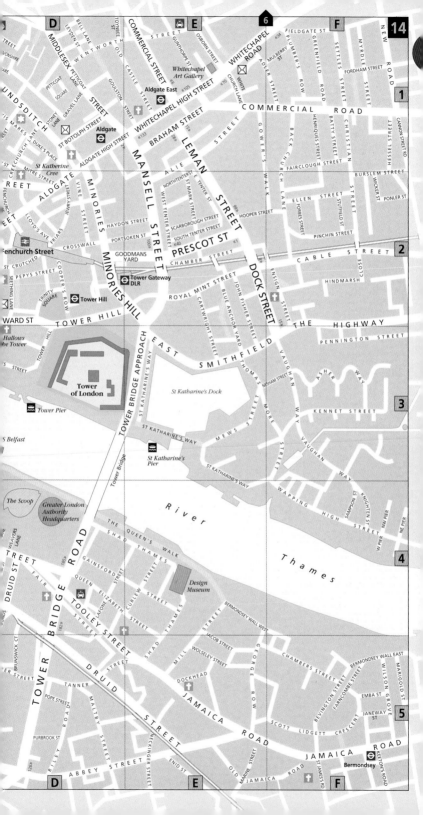

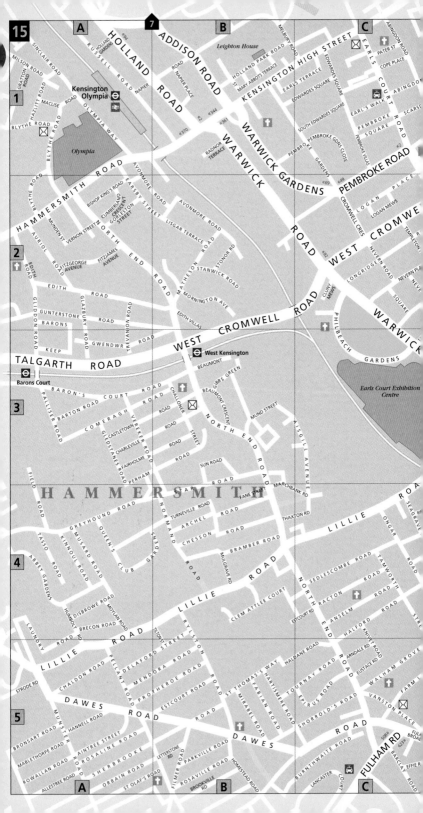

CHENISTON GDNS

STANFORD ROAD

COTTESMORE GDNS

VICTORIA ROAD

VICTORIA GROVE

Queen's Gate Terrace

PETERSHAM PLACE

Petersham Place

IMPERIAL COLLEGE ROAD

KELSO PLACE

ELDON ROAD

LAUNCESTON PLACE

GLOUCESTER ROAD

KYNANCE LANE

ELVASTON PLACE

Science Museum

STRATFORD ROAD

MARLOES ROAD

CORNWALL

GARDENS

CORNWALL

GRENVILLE ROAD

QUEEN'S GATE TE PLACE

QUEEN'S GATE

QUEEN'S GATE

Natural History Museum

1

LEXHAM

GARDENS

K E N S I N G T O N

CORNWALL

GARDENS

EMPEROR'S GATE

MCLEOD'S MEWS

SOUTHWELL GDNS

QUEEN'S GATE GARDENS

ATHERSTONE MEWS

PENNANT MEWS

249»

CROMWELL ROAD

17

CROMWELL ROAD

REDFIELD LANE

KNARESBOROUGH PLACE

COLLINGHAM PLACE

COLLINGHAM GARDENS

ASHBURN GARDENS

COURTFIELD ROAD

Gloucester Road

STANHOPE GARDENS

STANHOPE MEWS WEST

GLOUCESTER ROAD

STANHOPE GARDENS

STANHOPE MEWS EAST

QUEENSBERRY PLACE

HARRINGTON ROAD

KENWAY ROAD

HOGARTH ROAD

COURTFIELD GARDENS

COLLINGHAM ROAD

COLBECK MEWS

HARRINGTON GARDENS

WETHERBY PLACE

CLAREVILLE STREET

CLAREVILLE GROVE

MANSON PLACE

CRANLEY PLACE

2

EARLS COURT

Earls Court

ROAD

PENYWERN ROAD

BARKSTON GARDENS

LAVERTON PL.

COLLINGHAM GARDENS

WETHERBY GARDENS

BINA GARDENS

ROSARY GARDENS

BRECHIN PLACE

OLD BROMPTON

CRANLEY MEWS

CRANLEY GARDENS

ONSLOW GARDENS

ONSLOW GDNS

CRANLEY PLACE

SELWOOD TERRACE

HESPER MEWS

BRAMHAM GARDENS

EARLS COURT SQUARE

BOLTON GARDENS

CRESSWELL GARDENS

ROAD

ROLAND GARDENS

THISTLE GROVE

EVELYN GARDENS

EVELYN

SELWOOD PL.

ELM PLACE

3

EARLS COURT SQUARE

RICK LANE

322»

6243

BROMPTON

ROAD

COLEHERNE COURT

THE LITTLE BOLTONS

CRESSWELL PLACE

THE BOLTONS

DRAYTON

ROLAND WAY

GROVE

GILSTON ROAD

PRIORY WALK

HARLEY GARDENS

MILBORNE GROVE

BEAUFORT STREET

ELM PARK GARDENS

ROAD

278»

West Brompton

COLEHERNE ROAD

REDCLIFFE

SQUARE

HARCOURT TERRACE

REDCLIFFE MEWS

REDCLIFFE ROAD

CALLOW STREET

ELM PARK ROAD

PARK

Chelsea Park Gdns

FINBOROUGH ROAD

WESTGATE TERRACE

TREGUNTER ROAD

SEYMOUR WALK

FULHAM

LIMERSTON STREET

CAMERA PL.

WALK

4

BROMPTON CEMETERY

IFIELD ROAD

REDCLIFFE GARDENS

ROAD

CATHCART ROAD

HOLLYWOOD ROAD

FAWCETT STREET

REDCLIFFE PL.

413»

NETHERTON GROVE

ROAD

GERTRUDE STREET

SHALCOMB STREET

LAMONT ROAD

HOBURY STREET

STREET

BROMPTON PARK CRESCENT

GARDENS

EDITH GROVE

BROMPTON PARK GRES

FERNSHAW ROAD

SLAIDBURN STREET

LANGTON STREET

453»

510»

ANN LANE

WORLD'S END PASSAGE

465»

17

GUNTER GROVE

HORTENSIA ROAD

EDITH TERRACE

EDITH GROVE

BLANTYRE STREET

am ilway

BILLING ROAD

WANDON PL.

CREMORNE ROAD

ASHBURNHAM ROAD

LOTS ROAD

5

FULHAM

WANDON RD.

HILARY CLOSE

HOLMEAD ROAD

ROAD

KING'S

TADEMA ROAD

UPCERNE ROAD

BURNABY STREET

ROAD

BRITANNIA RD.

WATERFORD RD.

CEDARNE RD.

MAXWELL ROAD

RUMBOLD ROAD

MOORE PARK RD.

ROAD

LOTS RD.

TETCOTT ROAD

ROD ROAD

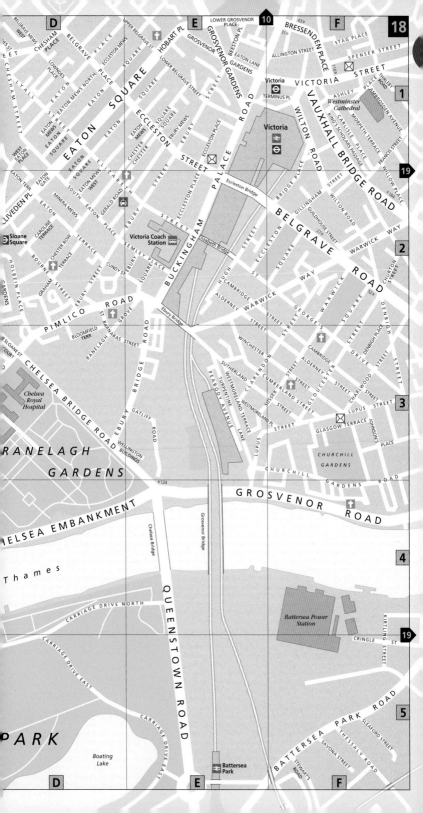

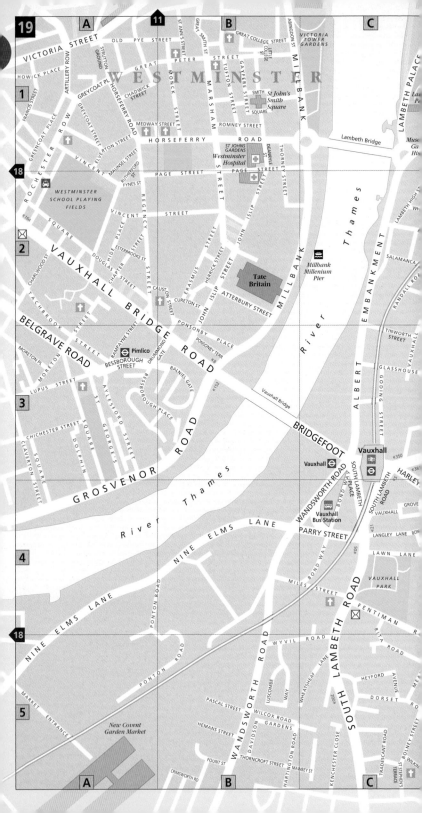

SHOPS AND MARKETS

London is one of the great shopping cities of Europe, with bustling, lively street markets, world-famous department stores and a wide variety of eclectic shops selling clothes, antiques, crafts and much more. The best shopping areas range from up-market districts such as Knightsbridge and Bond Street, which sell expensive designer clothes, to the busy, chaotic stretch of Oxford Street. The vibrant markets of Covent Garden, Berwick Street and Brick Lane are also popular. The city is best known, however, for its huge range of clothes shops selling everything from traditional tweeds to the latest zany designs of the ever-changing high-street fashion trends.

Bags from two famous London department stores

WHEN TO SHOP

In central London, most shops stay open from 10am to about 5.30–6pm Monday to Saturday. Many department stores, however, have longer hours. The "late night" shopping until 7 or 8pm is on Thursday and Friday in Oxford Street and the rest of West End; and on Wednesday in Knightsbridge and Chelsea. Some shops in tourist areas, such as Covent Garden and the Trocadero, are open until 7pm or later every day, including Sunday. Some street markets and a number of other shops are usually open on Sundays as well.

TWICE-YEARLY SALES

The traditional sale season is from January to February and from June to July, when shops slash prices and sell off left-over stock. The department stores have some of the best reductions – queues for the famous Harrods sale start to form long before it opens.

SHOPPING AREAS

London's best shopping areas range from the up-market Knightsbridge, where porcelain, jewellery and couture come at the highest prices, to colourful markets, where getting the cheapest bargains is what it's all about.

The city beckons specialist shoppers with its treasures and collectibles crammed into inviting antiques shops, and streets full of antiquarian booksellers and art galleries.

BEST OF THE DEPARTMENT STORES

Harrods is the king of the city's department stores with over 300 departments and a staff of 5,000. The spectacular food hall with Edwardian tiles displays fish, cheese, fruit and vegetables. Other specialities include fashion, china and glass, kitchenware and electronics. Londoners also often head for the nearby **Harvey Nichols**, which stocks the best of everything. The clothing department is particularly strong, with an emphasis on talented British, European and American names. The food hall, opened in 1992, is one of London's most stylish.

Selfridges, on Oxford Street, has expanded its range in recent years. It has arguably the widest choice of labels, a great lingerie department and a section devoted to emerging designers. It also has a food hall that features delicacies from all over the world.

Originally a drapery, **John Lewis**, to this date, has a good selection of fabrics and haberdashery. Its china, glass and household items make this store and its Sloane Square partner, **Peter Jones**, equally popular with Londoners.

Liberty, near Carnaby Street, has been famous ever since 1875 for its beautiful silks and other Oriental goods. Don't forget to check out the famous scarf department.

Fortnum and Mason's is best known for its ground-floor food department. It has everything from Fortnum's tins of biscuits and tea to cured meats and lovely wicker hampers. In fact, these exquisite delicacies are so engrossing that the upper floors filled with classic fashion and luxury items often remain free of crowds.

Harrods at night, illuminated by 11,500 lights

MARKETS

Whatever you're looking for, it's definitely worth visiting one of London's colourful markets. Many of them mix English traditions with those of more recent immigrants, creating an exotic atmosphere and a truly fascinating array of merchandise. At some, the seasoned hawkers have honed their sales patter to an entertaining art, which reaches fever pitch just before closing, when the plummeting prices at the end of the day are announced. Keep your wits about you, your hand on your purse and join in the fun.

Bustling Petticoat Lane market, officially known as Middlesex Street

Among the best of the West End markets are **Grays Antiques** and **Jubilee and Apple** markets in Covent Garden. Although it is somewhat touristy, **Piccadilly Crafts** is also very popular. In Soho, the spirited costermongers of **Berwick Street** peddle some of the cheapest and freshest fruit and vegetables in the area.

In the East End, **Petticoat Lane** is probably the most famous of London's street markets. Those in search of the latest street fashions make a beeline for **Old Spitalfields**, while **Brick Lane** is massively popular due to its trendy location. Here you can find everything from shellfish to trainers. Nearby, **Columbia Road** is perfect for greenery and blossoms.

South of the river, **East Street** also has a flower market, but the majority of its traders sell clothes. **Bermondsey Market** is a gathering point for London's antiques traders. Collectors set off early to scrutinize the fine paintings and old jewellery. **Borough** (see p120) caters to the restaurant trade with it's fine food and farmer's market. **Brixton Market** stocks a superb assortment of Afro-Caribbean foods, often to the pounding beat of reggae music.

In north London, **Camden Lock Market** offers a vibrant atmosphere and stalls selling everything from vintage clothes to lovely crafts. In nearby Islington, **Camden Passage** is a quiet cobbled street where charming cafés nestle among quaint antiques shops.

In Notting Hill, **Portobello Road** is actually a bunch of markets rolled into one, and an entire afternoon can be spent browsing there.

DIRECTORY

DEPARTMENT STORES

Fortnum & Mason
181 Piccadilly W1. **Map 11 A3. Tel** 020 7734 8040.

Harrods
87–135 Brompton Rd SW1. **Map** 9 C5. **Tel** 020 7730 1234.

Harvey Nichols
109–125 Knightsbridge SW1. **Map** 9 C5. **Tel** 020 7235 5000.

John Lewis
278–306 Oxford St W1. **Map** 10 E1. **Tel** 020 7629 7711.

Liberty
210–20 Regent St W1. **Map** 10 F2. **Tel** 020 7734 1234.

Peter Jones
Sloane Sq, SW1. **Map** 18 D2. **Tel** 020 7730 3434.

Selfridges
400 Oxford St W1. **Map** 10 D2. **Tel** 0870 837 7377.

MARKETS

Bermondsey Market
Long Lane & Bermondsey St SE1. **Map** 13 C5. ⏰ 4am–1pm Fri.

Berwick Street
Berwick St W1. **Map** 11 A2. ⏰ 9am–6pm Mon–Sat.

Borough
8 Southwark St SE1. **Map** 13 B4. ⏰ 11am–5pm Thu, noon–6pm Fri, 8am–5pm Sat.

Brick Lane
Brick Lane E1. **Map** 6 E5. ⏰ dawn–1pm Sun.

Brixton Market
Electric Ave SW9. ⏰ 8am–6pm Tue–Sat (to 3pm Wed).

Camden Lock Market
Chalk Farm Rd NW1. 🚇 Camden Town, Chalk Farm. ⏰ 10am–6pm daily.

Camden Passage
Camden Passage N1. **Map** 4 F1. ⏰ 9am–6pm Wed & Sat.

Columbia Road
Columbia Rd E2. **Map** 6 D3. 🚇 Shoreditch, Old St. ⏰ 8am–3pm Sun.

East Street
East St SE17. 🚇 Elephant & Castle. ⏰ 8am–5pm Tue–Sun (to 6:30pm Sat and 2pm Sun).

Grays Antiques
58 Davies St, Mayfair. **Map** 10 E2. ⏰ 10am–6pm Mon–Fri; 11am–5pm Sat.

Greenwich
College Approach SE10. ⏰ 10am–5:30pm Wed–Sun.

Jubilee and Apple
Covent Gdn Piazza WC2. **Map** 11 C2. ⏰ 9am–5pm daily.

Old Spitalfields
Commercial St E1. 🚇 Liverpool St. **Map** 6 D1. ⏰ 10am–4pm Mon–Sat, 9am–5pm Sun.

Petticoat Lane
Middlesex St E1. **Map** 14 E2. ⏰ 9am–2pm Sun.

Piccadilly Crafts
St James's Church, Piccadilly W1. **Map** 11 A3. ⏰ 10am–6pm Wed–Sat.

Portobello Road
Portobello Rd W10. **Map** 7 C3. ⏰ daily (main market Sat).

Exclusive designer clothes on sale at Harrods, Knightsbridge

CLOTHES

British tailoring and fabrics are world-renowned for their high quality. **Henry Poole & Co, H Huntsman & Sons** and **Gieves & Hawkes** are among the most highly respected tailors on Savile Row.

A new generation of trend-conscious tailors who specialize in modern cuts and fabrics has firmly established itself on the fashion scene. The line-up includes **Richard James** and **Ozwald Boateng**. Several stalwarts of classic British style have also reinvented themselves as fashion labels. **Burberry** is the best example, although it still does a brisk trade in its famous trenchcoats, and distinctive accessories. Designers **Margaret Howell** and **Nicole Farhi** create trend-setting versions of British country garments for men as well as women.

London designers are known for their eclectic, irreverent style. *Grande dames* of fashion, **Zandra Rhodes** and **Vivienne Westwood** have been on the scene since the 1970s. Many other British designers of international stature also have their flagship stores in the capital, including **Stella McCartney**, the late **Alexander McQueen**, **Paul Smith** and **Matthew Williamson**. Designer clothes, however, are not just the preserve of the rich. If you want to flaunt a bit of British design but can't afford the high prices, it's worth visiting **Debenhams**, which has harnessed the talents of numerous leading designers. Cheaper versions of all the latest styles appear in the shops almost as soon as they have been sashayed down the catwalk. **Topshop** and **Oasis** have both won celebrity fans for their up-to-the-minute ensembles of hip and youthful fashions for women; young professionals head to **French Connection**. The up-market chains **Jigsaw** and **Whistles** are more expensive, with their emphasis on beautiful fabrics and shapes. Fashion-conscious young men can turn to **Reiss** and **Ted Baker** for trendy clothing.

SHOES

Some of the most famous names in the footwear industry are based in Britain. If you can spare a few thousand pounds, you can have a pair custom-made by the Royal Family's shoemaker, **John Lobb**. Ready-made, traditional brogues and Oxfords are the mainstay of **Church's Shoes**. **Oliver Sweeney** gives classics a contemporary edge. **The British Boot Company** in Camden has the widest range of funky Dr Martens, appropriated by rock'n'rollers and the grunge set. **Jimmy Choo** and **Manolo Blahnik** are two all-time favourites of most fashionable women all over the world. Less expensive, yet good quality designs can be found in **Hobbs** or **Pied à Terre**, while **Faith** and **Office** turn out young, voguish styles.

GIFTS AND SOUVENIRS

The market in Covent Garden Piazza stocks uniquely British pottery, knitwear and other crafts, and **Neal's Yard Remedies** sells organic health and beauty treats. To buy all your gifts under one roof, visit Liberty *(see p148)*, where all kinds of exquisite items can be found in every department.

Leading museums such as the Victoria and Albert *(see pp98–9)*, Natural History and Science Museums *(see p100)* sell unusual mementos. Try **Hamley's** for gifts and toys.

BOOKS AND MAGAZINES

The bookshops in London rank among its most illustrious specialities. Charing Cross Road is a treasure-trove for those hunting for antiquarian, second-hand and rare volumes. It is the home of **Foyles**, famous for its massive stock. Large branches of chains such as **Waterstone's** co-exist with many specialist stores in this highly learned street.

Hatchards in Piccadilly is the city's oldest bookshop and also one of its finest, offering an extensive and varied choice of titles.

Vintage Magazines in Soho, as its name suggests, stocks publications dating back to the early 1900s – collectors of back issues will be delighted.

Foyles bookshop on the legendary Charing Cross Road

ART AND ANTIQUES

Art and antiques shops abound in London, and you are sure to find something of beauty and value within your means.

Cork Street is the centre of Britain's contemporary art world. **Waddington Galleries** is the best known, while **Redfern Art Gallery** and **Flowers** exhibit unusual modern art.

Visit **Roger's Antiques Galleries** and Grays Antiques *(see p148)* for striking vintage jewellery and objets d'art.

The East End is a growing area for contemporary art. The cutting-edge **White Cube Gallery** is there, as is the internationally renowned **Whitechapel Art Gallery**.

For photography, visit the **Photographers' Gallery**, which has the largest collection of originals for sale in Britain. **Hamiltons Gallery** also hosts interesting exhibitions.

DIRECTORY

CLOTHES

Alexander McQueen
4–5 Old Bond St W1.
Map 10 F3.
Tel 020 7355 0088.

Burberry
21–23 New Bond St W1.
Map 10 F2.
Tel 020 7930 3343.
One of several branches.

Debenhams
334–348 Oxford St W1.
Map 10 E2.
Tel 08445 616 161.

French Connection
249–251 Regent St W1.
Map 10 F2.
Tel 020 7493 3124.
One of several branches.

Gieves & Hawkes
1 Savile Row W1. **Map** 10
F3. *Tel 020 7432 6403.*

H Huntsman & Sons
11 Savile Row W1. **Map**
10 F3. *Tel 020 7734 7441.*

Henry Poole & Co
15 Savile Row W1. **Map**
10 F3. *Tel 020 7734 5985.*

Jigsaw
6 Duke of York Sq, Kings
Rd SW3. **Map** 17 C2.
Tel 020 7730 4404.

Margaret Howell
34 Wigmore St W1. **Map**
10 E1. *Tel 020 7009 9009.*

Matthew Williamson
28 Bruton St W1.
Map 10 E3.
Tel 020 7629 6200.

Nicole Farhi
158 New Bond St W1.
Map 10 E2.
Tel 020 7499 8368.

Oasis
12–14 Argyll St W1.
Map 10 F2.
Tel 020 7434 1799.

Ozwald Boateng
12a Savile Row &
9 Vigo St W1. **Map** 10 F3.
Tel 020 7437 2030.

Paul Smith
Westbourne House
120 & 122 Kensington
Park Rd W11. **Map** 7 B2.
Tel 020 7727 3553.

Reiss
Kent House, 14–17
Market Place W1.
Map 10 F1.
Tel 020 7637 9112.
One of several branches.

Richard James
29 Savile Row W1.
Map 10 F2.
Tel 020 7434 0605.

Stella McCartney
30 Bruton St W1.
Map 10 E3.
Tel 020 7518 3100.

Ted Baker
9–10 Floral St W1.
Map 11 C2.
Tel 020 7836 7808.
One of several branches.

Topshop
Oxford Circus W1.
Map 10 F1.
Tel 08448 487 487.
One of several branches.

Vivienne Westwood
44 Conduit St W1.
Map 10 F2.
Tel 020 7439 1109.

Whistles
12–14 St Christopher's Pl
W1. **Map** 10 E2.
Tel 020 7487 4484.

Zandra Rhodes
79 Bermondsey St, SE1.
Map 11 C5.
Tel 020 7403 5333.

SHOES

The British Boot Company
5 Kentish Town Rd NW1.
Map 2 F1.
Tel 020 7485 8505.

Church's Shoes
201 Regent St W1.
Map 10 F2.
Tel 020 7734 2438.

Faith
192–194 Oxford St W1.
Map 10 F1.
Tel 020 7580 9561.

Hobbs
124 Long Acre WC2.
Map 11 C2.
Tel 020 7836 0625.
One of several branches.

Jimmy Choo
27 New Bond St W1.
Map 10 F2.
Tel 020 7493 5858.

John Lobb
88 Jermyn St SW1.
Map 10 F4.
Tel 020 7930 8089.

Manolo Blahnik
49–51 Old Church St,
Kings Road SW3. **Map** 17
A4. *Tel 020 7352 3863.*

Office
57 Neal St WC2.
Map 11 B1.
Tel 020 7379 1896.
One of several branches.

Oliver Sweeney
5 Conduit St W1.
Map 10 F2.
Tel 020 7491 9126.

Pied à Terre
19 South Molton St W1.
Map 10 E2.
Tel 020 7629 1362.

GIFTS AND SOUVENIRS

Hamley's
188–196 Regent St W1.
Map 10 F2.
Tel 0871 7041977.

Neal's Yard Remedies
15 Neal's Yard WC2.
Map 11 2C.
Tel 020 7379 7222.

BOOKS AND MAGAZINES

Foyles
113–119 Charing
Cross Rd WC2.
Map 11 B1.
Tel 020 7437 5660.

Hatchards
187 Piccadilly W1.
Map 10 F3.
Tel 020 7439 9921.

Vintage Magazines
39–43 Brewer St W1.
Map 11 A2.
Tel 020 7439 8525.

Waterstone's
203–205 Piccadilly W1.
Map 11 A3.
Tel 020 7851 2400.
One of several branches.

ART AND ANTIQUES

Flowers
21 Cork St W1.
Map 10 F3.
Tel 020 7439 7766.

Hamiltons Gallery
13 Carlos Place W1.
Map 10 E3.
Tel 020 7499 9493.

Photographers' Gallery
16–18 Ramillies St W1.
Map 10 F2.
Tel 0845 262 1618.

Redfern Art Gallery
20 Cork St W1.
Map 10 F3.
Tel 020 7734 1732.

Roger's Antiques Galleries
65 Portobello Road W11.
Map 7 A1.
Tel 020 7467 5787.

Waddington Galleries
11, 12, 34 Cork St W1.
Map 10 F3.
Tel 020 7851 2200.

White Cube Gallery
48 Hoxton Square N1.
Map 5 C3.
Tel 020 7930 5373.

Whitechapel Art Gallery
77–82 Whitechapel
High St E1.
Map 14 E1.
Tel 020 7522 7888.

ENTERTAINMENT IN LONDON

London has the enormous variety of entertainment that only the great cities of the world can provide. The historical backdrop and the lively bustling atmosphere add to the excitement. Whether dancing the night away at a famous disco or making the most of London's varied arts scene, the visitor has a bewildering choice. A trip to London is not complete without a visit to the theatre which ranges from glamorous West End musicals to experimental Fringe plays. There is world-class ballet and opera in fabled venues such as Sadler's Wells and the Royal Opera House. The musical menu covers everything from classical, jazz and rock to rhythm and

Many London cafés have free live music

blues performed in atmospheric basement clubs, old converted cinemas and outdoor venues such as Wembley. Movie buffs can choose from hundreds of films each night. Sports fans can watch cricket at Lord's or participate in a host of activities from water sports to ice skating.

Time Out, published every Tuesday, is the most comprehensive guide to what is on in London, with detailed weekly listings and reviews. *The Evening Standard, The Guardian* (Saturday) and *The Independent* also have reviews and information on events. If you buy tickets from booking agencies rather than direct from box offices, do compare prices – and only buy from ticket touts if you are desperate.

WEST END AND NATIONAL THEATRES

Palace Theatre poster (1898)

The glamorous, glittering world of West End theatreland, emblazoned with the names of world-famous performers, offers an extraordinary range of entertainment.

West End theatres (see Directory for individual theatres) survive on their profits and rely on financial backers, known as "angels". Consequently, they tend to stage commercial productions with mass appeal: musicals, classics, comedies

and plays by bankable contemporary playwrights.

The state-subsidized **National Theatre** is based in the Southbank Centre *(see p154)*. It has three auditoriums – the large, open-staged Olivier, the proscenium-arched Lyttelton, and the small studio space of the Cottesloe.

The **Royal Shakespeare Company** (RSC) regularly stages Shakespeare plays, but its repertoire includes Greek tragedies, Restoration comedies and modern works. Based at Stratford-upon-Avon *(see pp325–27)*, its major productions perform at London West End theatres. The RSC ticket hotline has information. **The Old Vic** has been rejuvenated under the artistic directorship of Kevin Spacey, whose exciting programme of drama attracts wide audiences.

Theatre tickets generally cost from £5 to £90 (for a top price West End show) and can be bought direct from box offices, by telephone or post. The "tkts" discount theatre ticket booth in Leicester Square sells tickets for a wide range of shows on the day of performance. It is open Monday to Saturday (10am–7pm) for matinees and evening shows, and Sundays (noon–3pm) for matinees only.

OFF-WEST END AND FRINGE THEATRES

Off-West End theatre is a middle category bridging the gap between West End and Fringe theatre. It includes venues that, regardless of location, have a permanent management team and often provide the opportunity for established directors and actors to turn their hands to more adventurous works in a smaller, more intimate, environment. Fringe theatres, on the other hand, are normally venues hired out to visiting companies. Both offer a vast array of innovative productions, serving as an outlet for new, often experimental writing.

Venues (too numerous to list – see newspaper listings),

The Old Vic, the first home of the National Theatre from 1963

Open-air theatre at Regent's Park

range from tiny theatres or rooms above pubs such as the Gate, which produces neglected European classics, to theatres such as the Donmar Warehouse, which attracts major directors and actors.

OPEN-AIR THEATRE

In summer, a performance of one of Shakespeare's airier creations such as *A Midsummer Night's Dream*, takes on an atmosphere of enchantment among the green vistas of Regent's Park (0870-060 1811). Lavish summer opera productions are staged at Holland Park (020-7602 7856). Shakespeare's Globe (*see p120*) offers open-air theatrical performances in a beautifully recreated Elizabethan theatre.

CINEMAS

The West End abounds with multiplex cinema chains (MGM, Odeon, UCI) which show big budget Hollywood films, usually in advance of the rest of the country, although release dates tend to lag well behind the US and many other European countries.

The Odeon Marble Arch has the largest commercial screen in Europe, while the Odeon Leicester Square boasts London's biggest auditorium with almost 2,000 seats.

Londoners are well-informed cinema-goers and even the larger cinema chains include some low-budget and foreign films in their repertoire. The majority of foreign films are subtitled, rather than dubbed. A number of independent cinemas, such as the Renoir and Prince Charles in central London, and the Curzon in Mayfair, show foreign-language and art films.

The largest concentration of cinemas is in and around Leicester Square although there are local cinemas in most areas. Just off Leicester Square, the Prince Charles is the West End's cheapest cinema. Elsewhere in the area you can expect to pay as much as £10 for an evening screening – almost twice the price of the local cinemas. Monday and afternoon performances in the West End are often cheaper.

BFI IMAX Cinema, at Waterloo

The BFI Southbank, at the Southbank Centre, is London's flagship repertory cinema. Subsidized by the British Film Institute, it screens a wide range of films, old and new, from all around the world. Nearby at Waterloo is the BFI IMAX, with one of the world's largest screens.

DIRECTORY

Adelphi
Strand. **Map** 11 C3.
Tel 0844 412 4651.

Aldwych
Aldwych. **Map** 11 C2.
Tel 0844 847 2330.

Apollo
Shaftesbury Ave.
Map 11 B2.
Tel 0844 579 1971.

Cambridge
Earlham St. **Map** 11 B2.
Tel 0844 412 4652.

Criterion
Piccadilly Circus. **Map**
11 A3. *Tel 0844 847 1778.*

Dominion
Tottenham Court Rd. **Map**
11 A1. *Tel 0844 847 1775.*

Duchess
Catherine St. **Map** 11 C2.
Tel 0844 412 4659.

Duke of York's
St Martin's Lane. **Map** 11
B2. *Tel 0844 871 7623.*

Fortune
Russell St. **Map** 11 C2.
Tel 0844 871 7626.

Garrick
Charing Cross Rd. **Map**
11 B2. *Tel 0844 579 1974.*

Gielgud
Shaftesbury Ave. **Map**
11 B2. *Tel 0844 482 5141.*

Harold Pinter
Panton St. **Map** 11 A3.
Tel 0844 871 7612.

Her Majesty's
Haymarket. **Map** 11 A3.
Tel 0844 482 5158.

Lyceum
Wellington St. **Map** 11
C2. *Tel 0844 844 0085.*

Lyric
Shaftesbury Ave. **Map** 11
B2. *Tel 0844 412 4661.*

National
South Bank. **Map** 12 D3.
Tel 020 7452 3000.

New London
Drury Lane. **Map** 11 C1.
Tel 020 7907 7090.

Noel Coward
St Martin's Lane. **Map** 11
B2. *Tel 0844 482 5120.*

Novello Theatre
Aldwych. **Map** 12 D2.
Tel 0844 482 5120.

The Old Vic
Waterloo Rd SE1.
Map 12 E4.
Tel 0870 060 6628.

Palace
Cambridge Circus W1. **Map**
11 B2. *Tel 0844 755 0016.*

Phoenix
Charing Cross Rd. **Map** 11
B2. *Tel 0870 060 6629.*

Piccadilly
Denman St. **Map** 11 A2.
Tel 0844 412 6666.

Prince Edward
Old Compton St. **Map** 11
D5. *Tel 0844 482 5151.*

Prince of Wales
Coventry St. **Map** 11 A3.
Tel 0844 482 5115.

Queen's
Shaftesbury Ave. **Map**
11 B2. *Tel 0844 482 5160.*
RSC Tel *01789 403 444.*

Shaftesbury
Shaftesbury Ave. **Map**
11 B2. *Tel 020 7379 5399.*

St Martin's
West St. **Map** 11 B2.
Tel 0844 499 1515.

**Theatre Royal:
Drury Lane**
Catherine St. **Map** 11 C2.
Tel 0844 412 2955.

**Theatre Royal:
Haymarket**
Haymarket. **Map** 11 A3.
Tel 0845 481 1870.

Vaudeville
Strand. **Map** 11 C3.
Tel 0844 412 4663.

Wyndham's
Charing Cross Rd. **Map**
11 B2. *Tel 0844 482 5138.*

Royal Festival Hall, South Bank
Centre

CLASSICAL MUSIC, OPERA AND DANCE

London is one of the world's
great centres for classical
music, with five symphony
orchestras, internationally
renowned chamber groups
such as the Academy of St-
Martin-in-the-Fields and the
English Chamber Orchestra,
as well as a number of contemporary groups. There are
performances virtually every
week by major international
orchestras and artists, reaching a peak during the summer
Proms season at the **Royal
Albert Hall** *(see p63)*. The
newly restored **Wigmore
Hall** has excellent acoustics
and is a fine setting for chamber music, as is the converted
Baroque church (1728) of
St John's, Smith Square.

Although televised and outdoor
performances by major stars
have greatly increased the popularity of opera, prices at the
Royal Opera House *(see p80)*
are still aimed at corporate
entertainment but the policy
now is to keep a few cheaper
seats. The refurbished building
is elaborate and productions
are often extremely lavish.
English National Opera, based
at the **London Coliseum**, has
more adventurous produc-
tions, appealing to a younger
audience (nearly all operas
are sung in English). Tickets
range from £5 to £200 and it is
advisable to book in advance.

The Royal Opera House is
also home to the Royal Ballet,
and the London Coliseum to
the English National Ballet, the
two leading classical ballet
companies in Britain. Visiting
ballets also perform in both.
There are numerous young
contemporary dance com-
panies, and **The Place** is a
dedicated contemporary

dance theatre where many
companies perform. Other
major dance venues are
Sadler's Wells, the **ICA**, the
Peacock Theatre and the
Chisenhale Dance Space.

The **Barbican Concert Hall**
and **Southbank Centre**
(comprising the Royal Festival
Hall, Queen Elizabeth Hall
and Purcell Room) host an
impressive variety of events
ranging from touring opera
and classical music performances to free foyer concerts.

Elsewhere in London many
outdoor musical events take
place in summer *(see pp62–3)*
at venues such as **Kenwood
House**. Events to look out for
are: the London Opera Festival
(June) with singers from all
over the world; the City of
London Festival (July) which
hosts a range of varied musical
events; and contemporary
dance festivals Spring Loaded
(February–April) and Dance
Umbrella (October) – see *Time
Out* and newspaper listings.

Kenwood House on Hampstead Heath *(see p124)*

DIRECTORY

CLASSICAL MUSIC, OPERA AND DANCE

Barbican Concert Hall
Silk St EC2. **Map** 5 A5.
Tel 020 7638 8891.
www.barbican.org.uk

Chisenhale Dance Space
64–84 Chisenhale Rd E3.
🚇 *Bethnal Green, Mile End.* **Tel** 020 8981 6617.
www.chisenhaledance space.co.uk

ICA
The Mall SW1. **Map** 11
A4. **Tel** 020 7930 3647.
www.ica.org.uk

Kenwood House
(EH) Hampstead Lane
NW3. **Tel** 020 8348 1286.

London Coliseum
St Martin's Lane WC2.
Map 11 B3. **Tel** 0871 911
0200. www.eno.org

Peacock Theatre
Portugal St WC2. **Map** 12
D1. **Tel** 0844 412 4322.

The Place
17 Duke's Rd WC1. **Map**
3 B3. **Tel** 020 7121 1100.
www.theplace.org.uk

Royal Albert Hall
Kensington Gore SW7.
Map 8 F5. **Tel** 0845 401
5045. www.royal
alberthall.com

Royal Opera House
Floral St WC2. **Map** 11
C2. **Tel** 020 7304 4000.
www.roh.org.uk

Sadler's Wells
Rosebery Ave EC1.
Tel 0844 412 4300.
www.sadlerswells.com

St John's, Smith Sq
Smith Sq SW1. **Map** 19
B1. **Tel** 020 7222 1061.
www.sjss.org.uk

Southbank Centre
SE1. **Map** 12 D3. **Tel**
0844 875 0073. www.
southbankcentre.co.uk

Wigmore Hall
Wigmore St W1. **Map** 10
D1. **Tel** 020 7935 2141.
www.wigmore-hall.org.uk

ROCK, POP, JAZZ AND CLUBS

100 Club
100 Oxford St W1. **Map**
10 F1. **Tel** 020 7636 0933.
www.the100club.co.uk

333
333 Old St EC1.
Tel 020 7739 1800.

Brixton Academy
211 Stockwell Rd SW9.
🚇 *Brixton.* **Tel** 0844 477
2000. www.brixton-
academy.co.uk

Café de Paris
3 Coventry St W1. **Map** 4
D5. **Tel** 020 7734 7700.

Jazz Café, Camden

ROCK, POP, JAZZ AND CLUBS

London features scores of concerts, ranging from rock and pop, to jazz, Latin, world, folk and reggae. Among the city's largest venues are **The O2** and the **Royal Albert Hall**; smaller venues include **Brixton Academy** and the **HMV Forum**.

There are a number of live jazz venues. Best of the old crop is **Ronnie Scott's**, although the **100 Club**, **Jazz Café** and **Vortex Jazz Club** have good reputations. The **Hippodrome** (on Leicester Square) also hosts jazz as well as cabaret nights.

London's club scene is one of the most innovative in Europe. It is dominated by big-name DJs, who host different nights in different clubs (see *Time Out* and newspaper listings). The West End venues **Ruby Blue** and the **Café de Paris** are glitzy, expensive and very much on the tourist

circuit. The New York-style **Ministry of Sound**, the camp cabaret of **Madame Jojo's**, the trendy Shoreditch clubs **333** and **Cargo**, and a host of other venues ensure that you will never be short of choice. Alternatives are the great laser and light shows at **Heaven**, the glamorous super-club **Pacha London**, or the live music venue **Koko** in Camden, which also hosts a variety of club nights. **Heaven** and the **Queen of Hoxton** are among the most popular of London's gay clubs.

Opening times are usually 10pm–3am, but on weekends many clubs open until 6am.

SPORTS

An impressive variety of public sports facilities are to be found in London, and they

are generally inexpensive to use. Swimming pools, squash courts, gyms and sports centres, with an assortment of keep-fit classes, can be found in most districts, and tennis courts hired in most parks. Water sports, ice skating and golf are among the variety of activities on offer. Spectator sports range from football and rugby at various club grounds to cricket at **Lord's** or the **Oval**, and tennis at the **All England Lawn Tennis Club**, Wimbledon. Tickets for the most popular matches can often be hard to come by *(see p67)*. More traditional sports include polo at **Guards**, croquet at **Hurlingham** (private members only) and medieval "real tennis" at **Queen's Club**. See pages 662–665 for more on sporting activities.

Booth selling discounted tickets in Leicester Square

Cargo
83 Rivington St EC2. 🚇
Old St. **Tel** *020 7749 7840.*

Forum
9–17 Highgate Rd NW5.
🚇 *Kentish Town.*
Tel *0844 847 2405*

Heaven
Under the Arches, Villiers St WC2. **Map** 11 C3.
Tel *020 7930 2020.*

Jazz Café
3–5 Parkway NW1.
🚇 *Camden Town.*
Tel *020 7485 6834.*

Koko
1A Camden High St NW1.
🚇 *Mornington Crescent.*
Tel *0870 432 5527.*

Madame Jojo's
8–10 Brewer St W1. **Map**
11 A2. **Tel** *020 7734 3040.*

Ministry of Sound
103 Gaunt St SE1.
🚇 *Elephant & Castle.*
Tel *0870 060 0010.*

Pacha London
Terminus Place, SW1. **Map**
18 F1. **Tel** *0845 371 4489.*
www.pachalondon.com

Queen of Hoxton
1 Curtain Rd EC2.
🚇 *Shoreditch High St.*
Tel *020 7422 0958.*

Ronnie Scott's
47 Frith St W1. **Map** 11 A2.
Tel *020 7439 0747.*
www.ronniescotts.co.uk

Ruby Blue
Leicester Sq WC2. **Map**
4 E5. **Tel** *020 7287 8050.*

The O2
Peninsula Square SE10.
🚇 *North Greenwich.*
Tel *020 8463 6718.*

Vortex Jazz Club
11 Gillett Sq N16.
🚇 *Dalston Kingsland.*
Tel *020 7254 4097.*

SPORTS

All England Lawn Tennis Club
Church Rd, Wimbledon
SW19. 🚇 *Southfields.*
Tel *020 8944 1066.*

Guards Polo Club
Windsor Great Park.
🚂 *Egham.*
Tel *01784 434212.*

Hurlingham Club
Ranelagh Gdns SW6.
Map 18 D3. **Tel** *020 7736 8411.*

Lord's Cricket Ground
St John's Wood NW8.
🚇 *St John's Wood.*
Tel *020 7432 1000.*

Oval Cricket Ground
Kennington SE11. 🚇
Oval. **Tel** *020 7820 5700.*

Queen's Club
Palliser Rd W14.
🚇 *Barons Court.*
Tel *020 7385 3400.*

SOUTHEAST
ENGLAND

INTRODUCING SOUTHEAST
ENGLAND 158–163

THE DOWNS AND CHANNEL COAST 164–189

EAST ANGLIA 190–215

THAMES VALLEY 216–237

Southeast England at a Glance

The old Saxon kingdoms covered the areas surrounding London, and today, while their accessibility to the capital makes them a magnet for commuters, each region retains a character and history of its own. The attractions include England's oldest universities, royal palaces, castles, stately homes and cathedrals, many of which played critical roles in the nation's early history. The landscape is soft, with the green and rounded hills of the south country levelling out to the flat fertile plains and fens of East Anglia, fringed by broad, sandy beaches.

Blenheim Palace (see pp228–9) *is a Baroque masterpiece. The Mermaid Fountain (1892) is part of the spectacular gardens.*

Bedfordshire

Hertford

Buckinghamshire

THAMES VALLEY
(see pp216–37)

Oxfordshire

Oxford University's *buildings (see pp222–7) amount to a textbook of English architecture from the Middle Ages to the present. Christ Church College (1525) is the largest in the university.*

Surrey

Hampshire

West Sussex

Windsor Castle (see pp236–7) *is Britain's oldest royal residence. The Round Tower was built in the 11th century when the palace guarded the western approaches to London.*

Winchester Cathedral (see pp170–1) *was begun in 1097 on the ruins of a Saxon church. The city has been an important centre of Christianity since the 7th century. The cathedral's northwest door is built in a characteristic medieval style.*

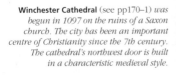

◁ **The white cliffs of Dover, Kent**

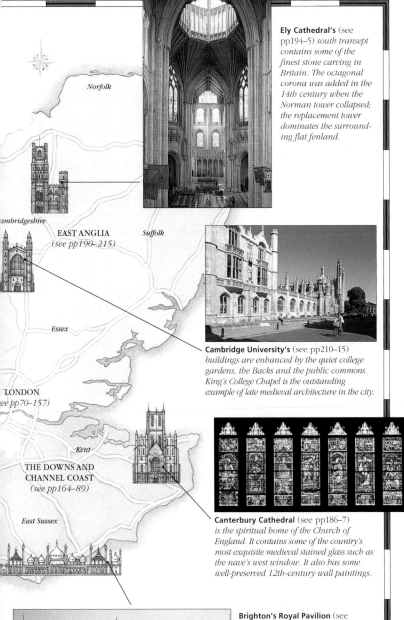

Ely Cathedral's (see pp194–5) *south transept contains some of the finest stone carving in Britain. The octagonal corona was added in the 14th century when the Norman tower collapsed; the replacement tower dominates the surrounding flat fenland.*

Norfolk

Cambridgeshire

EAST ANGLIA
(see pp190–215)

Suffolk

Essex

Cambridge University's (see pp210–15) *buildings are enhanced by the quiet college gardens, the Backs and the public commons. King's College Chapel is the outstanding example of late medieval architecture in the city.*

LONDON
(see pp70–157)

Kent

THE DOWNS AND CHANNEL COAST
(see pp164–89)

East Sussex

Canterbury Cathedral (see pp186–7) *is the spiritual home of the Church of England. It contains some of the country's most exquisite medieval stained glass such as the nave's west window. It also has some well-preserved 12th-century wall paintings.*

Brighton's Royal Pavilion (see pp178–9) *was built for the Prince Regent and is one of the most lavish buildings in the land. Its design by John Nash (see p107) is based on Oriental themes, and it has been restored to its original splendour.*

| 0 kilometres | 25 |
| 0 miles | 25 |

The Garden of England

With its fertile soil, mild climate and regular rainfall, the Kentish countryside has flourished as a fruit-growing region ever since its first orchards were planted by the Romans. Wine-making has also been established here, as the vine-covered hillsides around Lamberhurst show, and several vineyards may be visited. The orchards are dazzling in the blossom season, and in the autumn the branches sag with ripening fruit – a familiar sight which inspired William Cobbett (1762–1835) to describe the area as "the very finest as to fertility and diminutive beauty in the whole world". Near Faversham, the fruit research station of Brogdale is open to the public, offering orchard walks, tastings and informative displays.

White wine from the southeast

HOPS AND HOPPING

Hop-picking, a family affair

Oast houses, topped with distinctive angled cowls, are a common feature of the Kentish landscape, and many have now been turned into houses. They were originally

SEASONAL FRUIT

This timeline shows the major crops in each month of the farming year. The first blossoms may appear when the fields are still dusted with snow. As the petals fall, fruit appears among the leaves. After ripening in the summer sun, the fruit is harvested in the autumn.

Raspberries *are a luscious soft fruit. Many growers allow you to pick your own from the fields, and then pay by weight.*

Peach blossom *is usually to be found on south-facing walls, as its fruit requires warm conditions.*

Orchards *are used to grow plums, pears and apples. The latter (blossoming above) remain Kent's most important orchard crop.*

| MARCH | APRIL | MAY | JUNE | JULY |

Strawberries *are Britain's favourite and earliest soft fruit. New strains allow them to be picked all summer.*

Sour cherry blossom *is the earliest flower. Its fruit is used for cooking.*

Pear blossom *has creamy white flowers which appear two or three weeks before apple blossom.*

Cherry plum blossom *is one of the most beautiful blossoms; the plum is grown more for its flowers than its fruit.*

Gooseberries *are not always sweet enough to eat raw, though all types are superb in pies and other desserts.*

uilt to dry hops, an ingredient
 brewing beer *(see pp604–5).*
 any are still used for that, for
 hough imports have reduced
 omestic hop-growing, more
 an four million tonnes are
 roduced in Britain annually,
 ostly in Kent.
  In summer, the fruiting plants
 n be seen climbing the rect-
 gular wire frames in fields by
 e roadside. Until the middle of
 e 20th century thousands of
 milies from London's East End
 ould move to the Kentish hop
 elds every autumn for working
 olidays harvesting the crop and
 mping in barns. That tradition
 as faded, because now the
 ops are picked by machine.

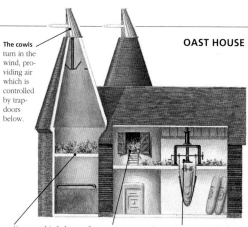

OAST HOUSE

The cowls turn in the wind, providing air which is controlled by trap-doors below.

Hops are dried above a fan which blows hot air from the underlying radiators.

After drying, the hops are cooled and stored.

A press packs the hops into bags, ready for the breweries.

Cherries *are the sweetest of Kent's fruit: two popular varieties are Stella (top) and Duke.*

Plums *are often served stewed, in pies, or dried into prunes. The Victoria plum (left) is the classic English dessert plum and is eaten raw. The Purple plum is also popular.*

Greengages *are green plums. They have a distinctive taste and can be made into jam.*

Bramley Seedling *is one of the best cooking apples, but it is not sweet enough to eat raw.*

Pears, *such as the William (left), should be eaten at the height of ripeness. The Conference keeps better.*

AUGUST	SEPTEMBER	OCTOBER	NOVEMBER

The Kentish cob, *a variety of hazelnut, is undergoing a revival, having been eclipsed by European imports. Unlike many nuts, it is best picked fresh from the tree.*

Dessert apples, *such as Cox's Orange Pippin (right), are some of England's best-loved fruits. The newer Discovery is easier to grow.*

urrants *are
 mong the most assertively
 avoured fruit and are
 sed in desserts and jams.*

Peaches, *grown in China
 4,000 years ago, came to
 England in the 19th century.*

Vineyards *are now a familiar sight in Kent (as well as Sussex and Hampshire). Most of the wine produced, such as Lamberhurst, is white.*

Houses of Historical Figures

Visiting the homes of artists, writers, politicians
and royalty is a rewarding way of gaining an
insight into their private lives. Southeast England,
near London, boasts many historic houses that
have been preserved as they were when their
illustrious occupants were alive. All these houses,
from large mansions such as Lord Mountbatten's
Broadlands to the more modest dwellings, like
Jane Austen's House, contain exhibits relating to
the life of the famous people who lived there.

Florence Nightingale
*(1820–1910), the "Lady with
the Lamp", was a nurse
during the Crimean
War (see p56). She
stayed at Claydon
with her sister,
Lady Verney.*

Nancy Astor *(1879–1964) was the first
woman to sit in Parliament in 1919. She
lived at Cliveden until her death and
made it famous for political hospitality.*

*Claydon House, Winslow,
nr Milton Keynes*

**The Duke of
Wellington**
*(1769–1852)
was given this
house by the
nation in
1817, in
gratitude
for leading
the British
to victory at
Waterloo (see p55).*

THAMES VALLEY
(see pp216–17)

*Cliveden House,
nr Maidenhead*

Stratfield Saye, Basingstoke, nr Windsor

Jane Austen
*(1775–1817) wrote
three of her novels,
including* Emma,
*and revised
the others at
this house
where she
lived for
eight years
until shortly
before her death
(see p172).*

*Broadlands, nr
Southampton*

*Jane Austen's House,
Chawton, nr Winchester*

*Osborne House,
Isle of Wight*

Lord Mountbatten (1900–79), a British
naval commander and statesman, was the
last Viceroy of India in 1947. He lived
here all his married life and remodelled
the original house considerably.

Queen Victoria (1819–1901)
and her husband, Prince Albert,
built Osborne House *(see p168)* in
1855 as a seaside retreat for their family
because they never truly warmed to the
Royal Pavilion in Brighton.

BLOOMSBURY GROUP

A circle of avant-garde artists, designers and writers, many of them friends as students, began to meet at a house in Bloomsbury, London, in 1904 and soon gained a reputation for their Bohemian lifestyle. When Duncan Grant and Vanessa Bell moved to Charleston in 1916 *(see p180)*, it became a Sussex outpost of the celebrated group. Many of the prominent figures associated with the circle, such as Virginia Woolf, EM Forster, Vita Sackville-West and JM Keynes paid visits here. The Bloomsbury Group was also known for the Omega Workshops, which made innovative ceramics, furniture and textiles.

Vanessa Bell at Charleston by Duncan Grant (1885–1978)

Gainsborough's House,
Sudbury, nr Ipswich

EAST ANGLIA
(see pp190–215)

Thomas Gainsborough *(1727–88), one of Britain's greatest painters, was born in this house (see p194). He was best known for his portraits, such as this one of* Mr and Mrs Andrews.

Charles Darwin *(1809–82), who developed the theory that man and apes have a common ancestor, wrote his most famous book,* On the Origin of Species, *at the house where he lived.*

Down House, Downe,
nr Sevenoaks

THE DOWNS AND
CHANNEL COAST
(see pp164–89)

Bleak House,
Broadstairs,
nr Margate

Charles Dickens (1812–70), the prolific and popular Victorian novelist *(see p189)*, had many connections with Kent. He took holidays at Bleak House, later named after his famous novel.

Chartwell,
Westerham,
nr Sevenoaks

Batemans, Burwash,
nr Hastings

Winston Churchill (1874–1965), Britain's inspirational Prime Minister in World War II *(see p189)*, lived here for 40 years until his death. He relaxed by rebuilding parts of the house.

Charleston,
Lewes

Vanessa Bell (1879–1961), artist and member of the Bloomsbury Group, lived here until her death in 1961. The 18th-century farmhouse reflects her decorative ideas and is filled with murals, paintings and painted furniture *(see p180)*.

Rudyard Kipling *(1865–1936), the poet and novelist, was born in India, but lived here for 34 years until his death. His most famous works include* Kim, *the two* Jungle Books *and the* Just So Stories.

THE DOWNS AND CHANNEL COAST

HAMPSHIRE · SURREY · EAST SUSSEX · WEST SUSSEX · KENT

When settlers, invaders and missionaries came from Europe, the southeast coast was their first landfall. The wooded chalk ridges and lower-lying weald beyond them made an ideal base for settlement and proved to be productive farmland.

The Romans were the first to build major fortifications along the Channel Coast to discourage potential attackers from the European mainland. The remains of many of these can be seen today, and some, like Portchester Castle just outside Portsmouth, were incorporated into more substantial defences in later centuries. There also exists substantial evidence of Roman domestic buildings, such as Fishbourne Palace, in coastal areas and further inland.

The magnificence of cathedrals such as Canterbury and Winchester bear witness to their role as important bases of the medieval church, then nearly as powerful as the state. Many Kent and Sussex ports grew prosperous on trade with the Continent – as did the hundreds of smugglers who operated from them. From Tudor times on, monarchs, noblemen and courtiers acquired estates and built manor houses in the countryside between London and the coast, appreciating the area's moderate climate and proximity to the capital. Many of these survive and are popular attractions for visitors.

Today the southeast corner of England is its most prosperous and populous region. Parts of Surrey and Kent, up to 20 miles (32 km) from the capital, are known as the Stockbroker Belt: the area has many large, luxurious villas belonging to wealthy people prominent in business and the professions, attracted by the same virtues that appealed to the Tudor gentry.

The fertile area of Kent has long been known as the Garden of England, and despite the incursion of bricks and mortar, it is still a leading area for growing fruit *(see pp160–1)*, being in a prime position for the metropolitan market nearby.

Aerial view of the medieval and moated Leeds Castle

◁ **A lush covering of bluebells in the deciduous woodlands of Kent**

Exploring the Downs and Channel Coast

The North and South Downs, separated by the lower-lying Weald are ideal walking country as well as being the site of many stately homes. From Tudor times, wealthy, London-based merchants and courtiers built their country residences in Kent, a day's ride from the capital, and many are open to the public. On the coast are the remains of sturdy castles put up to deter invaders from across the Channel. Today, though, the seashore is largely devoted to pleasure. Some of Britain's earliest beach resorts were developed along this coast, and sea bathing is said to have been invented in Brighton.

View of Brighton Pier from the promenade

Oast houses at Chiddingstone near Royal Tunbridge Wells

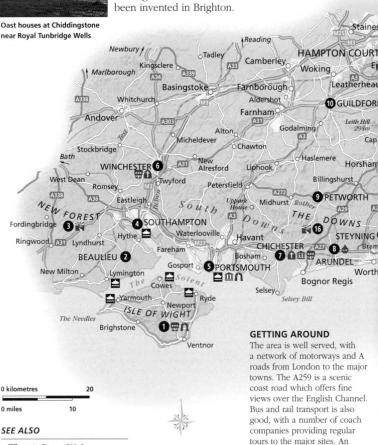

0 kilometres   20

0 miles   10

SEE ALSO

• *Where to Stay* pp563–5

• *Where to Eat* pp615–18

GETTING AROUND

The area is well served, with a network of motorways and A roads from London to the major towns. The A259 is a scenic coast road which offers fine views over the English Channel. Bus and rail transport is also good, with a number of coach companies providing regular tours to the major sites. An InterCity train service runs to all the major towns.

SIGHTS AT A GLANCE

Arundel **8**
Beaulieu **2**
Bodiam Castle **18**
Brighton pp174–9 **13**
Canterbury pp186–7 **23**
Chichester **7**
Dover **21**
The Downs **16**
Eastbourne **15**
Guildford **10**
Hampton Court p173 **11**
Hastings **17**
Hever Castle **27**
Isle of Wight **1**

Knole **26**
Leeds Castle **24**
Lewes **14**
Margate **22**
Rochester **25**
New Forest **3**
Petworth House **9**
Portsmouth **5**
Romney Marsh **20**
Royal Tunbridge Wells **28**
Rye pp184–5 **19**
Southampton **4**
Steyning **12**
Winchester pp170–71 **6**

KEY

━━ Motorway
━━ Major road
━ Secondary road
╌╌ Minor road
━ Scenic route
┅ Main railway
── Minor railway
△ Summit

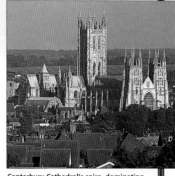

Canterbury Cathedral's spire, dominating the skyline

The Victorian Osborne House, Isle of Wight

Isle of Wight ❶

Isle of Wight. 🏚 138,000.
🛳 from Lymington, Southampton,
Portsmouth. 🛈 Union Street,
Ryde (01983 813813).
www.islandbreaks.co.uk

A visit to **Osborne House**,
the favoured seaside retreat
of Queen Victoria and Prince
Albert (see p160), is alone
worth the ferry ride from the
mainland. Furnished much
as they left it, the house
provides a marvellous insight
into royal life and is dotted
with family mementoes.

The **Swiss Cottage** was
built for the royal children to
play in. It is now a museum
attached to Osborne House.
Adjacent to it you can see the
bathing machine used by the
queen to preserve her modesty
while taking her to the edge
of the sea (see p369).

The other main sight on the
island is **Carisbrooke Castle**,
built in the 11th century. A
walk on its outer wall and the
climb to the top of its keep
provides spectacular views. It
was here that Charles I (see
pp52–3) was held prisoner in
1647; an attempt to escape
was foiled when he got stuck
between the bars of a window.

The island is a base for
ocean sailing, especially during
Cowes Week (see p67). The
scenic highlight is the
Needles – three towers of
rock jutting out of the sea at
the island's western end. This
is only a short walk from

Alum Bay, famous for its
multi-coloured cliffs and sand.

🏛 **Osborne House**
(EH) East Cowes. **Tel** 01983 200022.
🕐 10am–4pm daily (Nov–Mar: Sat &
Sun). 🈺 🅰 limited. 🍴 🖵 (also 🖵
in Swiss Cottage Apr–Oct only). 🗐

🏰 **Carisbrooke Castle**
Newport. **Tel** 01983 522107.
🕐 daily. 🌑 1 Jan, 24–26 Dec. 🈺
🅰 limited. 🖼 🖵 in summer. 🗐

Beaulieu ❷

Brockenhurst, Hampshire. **Tel** 01590
612345. 🚆 Brockenhurst then taxi.
🕐 daily. 🌑 25 Dec. 🈺 🅰 🖼
by appt. 🖵 **www**.beaulieu.co.uk

Palace House, once the gatehouse of Beaulieu Abbey,
has been the home of Lord
Montagu's family since 1538. It
now contains the finest collection of vintage cars in the
country at the **National Motor
Museum**, along with boats
used in the James Bond films.

There is also an exhibition
of monastic life in the ruined
ancient **abbey**, founded in

1204 by King John (see p48)
for Cistercian monks. The
original refectory now serves
as the parish church.

Environs: Just south is the
maritime museum at **Buckler's
Hard**, telling the story of shipbuilding in the 18th century.
The yard employed 4,000
men at its peak but declined
when steel began to be used.
Boat trips are available.

🏛 **Buckler's Hard**
Beaulieu. **Tel** 01590 614645. 🕐
daily. 🌑 25 Dec. 🈺 🅰 ltd. 🖵 🗐

New Forest ❸

Hampshire. 🚆 Brockenhurst. 🚌
Lymington then bus. 🛈 main car
park, Lyndhurst (023 8028 2269).
🕐 10am–4pm Mon–Sat. 🌑 1 Jan,
24–26 Dec. **www**.thenewforest.co.uk

This unique expanse of heath
and woodland is, at 145 sq
miles (375 sq km), the largest
area of unenclosed land in
southern Britain.

Despite its name, this is
one of the few primeval oak
woods in England. It was the
popular hunting ground of
Norman kings, and in 1100
William II was fatally wounded
here in a hunting accident.

Today it is enjoyed by up to
seven million visitors a year,
who share it with the New Forest ponies, unique to the area,
and over 1,500 fallow deer.

Southampton ❹

Hampshire. 🏚 220,000. ✈ 🚆 🚌
🛳 🛈 9 Civic Centre Road (023 8083
3333). **www**.visit-southampton.co.uk

For centuries this has been
a flourishing port. The
Mayflower sailed from here
to America in 1620 with the

A 1909 Rolls-Royce Silver Ghost at Beaulieu's National Motor Museum

Pilgrim Fathers, as did the *Titanic* on its maiden and ultimately tragic voyage in 1912.

Sea City Museum's galleries focus on the lives and times of those who have sailed from the port of Southampton over the past 2,000 years.

There is a walk around the remains of the medieval city wall. At the head of the High Street stands the old city gate, **Bargate**, the most elaborate gate to survive in England. It still has its 13th-century drum towers and is decorated with intricate, 17th-century armorial carvings. **God's House Tower Museum of**

The luxurious liner the *Titanic*, which sank in 1912

Archaeology consists of a 13th-century gatehouse and 15th-century gallery and tower, and includes displays from the Roman to medieval periods.

🏛 Sea City Museum
Havelock Rd. **Tel** 023 8083 4127.
⬜ 10am–4pm daily. 🖼 ♿ 🚻 🛍
www.seacity.co.uk

🏛 God's House Tower Museum
Winkle St. **Tel** 023 8091 5732.
⬜ 10am–4pm Tue–Sat, 1–4pm Sun.
♿ foyer & shop only. 🛍

Portsmouth ➎

Hampshire. 🏘 190,000. 🚢 🚉 ℹ
The Hard (023 9282 6722). 🛍 Thu–Sat. **www**.visitportsmouth.co.uk

Once a vital naval port, Portsmouth is today a quiet town but fascinating for those interested in English naval history. Under the banner of **Portsmouth Historic Dockyard**, the city's historic dockyard is the hub of Portsmouth's most important sights. Among these is the hull of the *Mary Rose*, the favourite of Henry VIII *(see p50)*, which capsized on its maiden voyage as it left to fight the French in 1545. It was recovered from the sea bed in 1982 along with thousands of 16th-century objects now on display nearby, giving an absorbing insight into life at sea in Tudor times.

Alongside it is **HMS Victory**, the English flagship on which Admiral Nelson was killed at Trafalgar *(see p31)* and now restored to its former glory. You can also visit the **Royal Naval Museum** which deals with naval history from the 16th century to the Falklands War, the 19th-century **HMS Warrior,** and galleries telling the story of Nelson.

Portsmouth's other military memorial is the **D-Day Museum**. This is centred on the *Overlord Embroidery*, a masterpiece of needlework commissioned in 1968 from the Royal School of Needlework, depicting the World War II Allied landing in Normandy in 1944.

The figurehead on the bow of HMS *Victory* at Portsmouth

Portchester Castle, on the north edge of the harbour, was fortified in the third century and is the best example of Roman sea defences in northern Europe. The Normans later used the Roman walls to enclose a castle – only the keep survives – and a church. Henry V used the castle as a garrison before the Battle of Agincourt *(see p49)*. In the 18th–19th centuries it was a prisoner-of-war camp.

Among less warlike attractions is the **Charles Dickens Birthplace Museum** *(see p189)*, the house where the author was born in 1812.

The striking **Spinnaker Tower** rises to 170 m (558 ft) above Portsmouth; the views over the harbour and beyond are quite magnificent.

🏛 Portsmouth Historic Dockyard
The Hard. **Tel** 023 9272 8060.
⬜ daily (last adm: 4pm).
⬤ 24–26 Dec. 🖼 ♿ 🚻 🛍

🏛 D-Day Museum
Museum Rd. **Tel** 023 9282 7261.
⬜ daily. ⬤ 24–26 Dec. ♿
🖼 🛍

🏰 Portchester Castle
Church Rd, Porchester. **Tel** 023
9237 8291. ⬜ phone for details.
⬤ 1 Jan, 24–26 Dec. 🖼 ♿ 🛍

🏛 Charles Dickens Birthplace Museum
393 Old Commercial Rd. **Tel** 023
9282 7261. ⬜ daily; 7 Feb
(Dickens's birthday). 🖼 🛍 🚻

🔭 Spinnaker Tower
Gunwharf Quays. **Tel** 023 9285
7520. ⬜ daily. 🖼 🛍 🛍

A wild pony and her foal roaming freely in the New Forest

Winchester ❻

Hampshire. 🏘 36,000. 🚉 🚌
ℹ Guildhall, High St (01962
840500). 🛒 Wed–Sat.
www.visitwinchester.co.uk

Capital of the ancient kingdom of Wessex, the city of
Winchester was also the headquarters of the Anglo-Saxon
kings until the Norman
Conquest (see p47).

William the Conqueror built
one of his first English castles
here. The only surviving part
of the castle is the **Great Hall**,
erected in 1235 to replace the
original. It is now home
to the legendary Round
Table. The story
behind the table is a
mix of history and
myth. King Arthur (see
p285) had it shaped so
no knight could claim
precedence. It was said
to have been built by the
wizard Merlin but was
actually made in the
13th century.

The **Westgate Museum** is
one of the two surviving 12th-
century gatehouses in the city
wall. The room (once a prison)
above the gate has a 16th-
century painted ceiling. It was
moved here from Winchester
College, England's oldest fee-
paying, or "public" school.
Winchester has been an

The 13th-century Round Table,
Great Hall, Winchester

ecclesiastical centre for many
centuries. **Wolvesey Castle**
(built around 1110) was the
home of the **cathedral's**
bishops after the Conquest.
The **Hospital of St Cross** is
an almshouse built in 1446.

Author Izaac Walton (1593–1683) is
depicted in the stained glass Anglers'
Window made in 1914.

These magnificent
choir-stalls (c.1308)
are England's
oldest.

The Perpendicular nave is the
highlight of the building.

Jane Austen's
grave

Main
entrance

Visitors'
centre

The Lady Chapel was
rebuilt by Elizabeth of York
(c.1500) after her son was
baptized in the cathedral.

STUDY TO BE QUIET

The 12
century bla
Tournai marble f

WINCHESTER
CATHEDRAL

The Close. **Tel** 01962 857200.
⬜ daily. 📷 ♿ 🍴 🛍
www.winchester-cathedral.org.uk
The first church was built here in
648, but the present building was begun
in 1079. Originally a Benedictine monastery,
much of the Norman architecture remains despite
continual modifications until the early 16th century.

Weary strangers may claim the "Wayfarer's Dole" a horn (cup) of ale and bread, given out since medieval times.

🏛 **Great Hall & Visitor Centre**
Castle Ave. *Tel* 01962 846476.
◯ *daily.* ⬤ *25, 26 Dec.* ♿

🏛 **Westgate Museum**
High St. *Tel* 01962 869864.
◯ *Sat & Sun.* 🅿

🏛 **Hospital of St Cross**
St Cross Rd. *Tel* 01962 878218.
◯ *Mon–Sat (daily in summer).*
⬤ *Good Fri, 25 Dec.* 🅿 ♿
www.stcrosshospital.co.uk

The Library
has over 4,000 books. This "B" from Psalm 1 is found in the Winchester Bible, an exquisite work of 12th-century illumination.

The Norman chapter house ceased to be used in 1580. Only the Norman arches survive.

Prior's Hall

The Close originally contained the domestic buildings for the monks of the Priory of St Swithun – the name before it became Winchester Cathedral. Most of the buildings, such as the refectory and cloisters, were destroyed during the Dissolution of the Monasteries (see p50).

Chichester ❼

West Sussex. 🏘 *26,000.* 🚉 🚌 ℹ
29A South St (01243 775888). 🏪
Wed, alternate Fri (Farmers' market), Sat. www.visitchichester.org

This wonderfully preserved market town, with an elaborate early 16th-century market cross at its centre, is dominated by its **cathedral**, consecrated in 1108. The cathedral's graceful spire dominates the town and is said to be the only English cathedral spire visible from the sea. Also of interest is the cathedral's unique detached bell tower dating from 1436.

There are two carved stone panels in the choir, dating from 1140. Modern works include paintings by Graham Sutherland (1903–80) and a stained-glass window by Marc Chagall (1887–1985).

Environs: Just west at Bosham is the Saxon **Holy Trinity Church**, thought to have been used by King Canute (see p46). Myth has it that this was where Canute failed to stop the incoming tide and so proved to his courtiers that his powers had limits. The church appears in the *Bayeux Tapestry,* held in France, because Harold heard mass here in 1064 before he was shipwrecked off Normandy and then rescued by William the Conqueror (see p47).

The refurbished **Fishbourne Roman Palace** (see p45), between Bosham and Chichester, is the largest Roman villa in Britain. It covers 3 ha (7 acres) and was discovered in 1960 by a workman. Constructed from AD 75, it was destroyed by fire in 285. The north wing has some of

Chagall's stained-glass window (1978), Chichester Cathedral

the finest mosaics in Britain, including one of Cupid.

To the north is the 18th-century **Goodwood House**. Its magnificent art collection features works by Canaletto (1697–1768) and Stubbs (1724–1806). Home to the Earl of March, it has a motor racing circuit, where the popular Festival of Speed is held in July, and a horseracing course on the Downs.

🏰 **Chichester Cathedral**
West St. *Tel* 01243 782595. ◯
daily. ⬤ *for Mass.* ♿ 📷 🚻 🅿

🏛 **Fishbourne Roman Palace**
Fishbourne. *Tel* 01243 785859. ◯
Feb–mid-Dec: daily; mid-Dec–Jan (café closed): Sat, Sun. 🅿 ♿
🚻 🅿 www.sussexpast.co.uk

🏛 **Goodwood House**
Goodwood. *Tel* 01243 755048. 📠
01243 755000. ◯ *mid-Mar–mid-Oct: Sun–Mon (pm); Aug: Sun–Thu (pm).* ⬤ *special events, last-minute closures. Call ahead.* 🅿 ♿ 🚻 🅿

WILLIAM WALKER

At the beginning of the 20th century, the cathedral's east end seemed certain to collapse unless its foundations were underpinned. But because the water table lies only just below the surface, the work had to be done under water. From 1906 to 1911, Walker, a deep-sea diver, worked six hours a day laying sacks of cement beneath the unsteady walls until the building was safe.

William Walker in his diving suit

The dominating position of Arundel Castle, West Sussex

Arundel Castle ❽

Arundel, West Sussex. *Tel 01903 882173.* 🚉 *Arundel.* ⬤ *Apr–Oct: 10am–5pm Tue–Sun.* ⬤ *public hols.* 🖼️ ♿ 📷 *by arrangement.* 🍽️ ▯ ▯ www.arundelcastle.org

Dominating the small river-side town below, this vast, grey hill-top castle, surrounded by castellated walls, was first built by the Normans.

During the 16th century it was acquired by the powerful Dukes of Norfolk, the country's senior Roman Catholic family, whose descendants still live here. They rebuilt it after the original was virtually destroyed by Parliamentarians in 1643 *(see p52),* and restored it again in the 19th century.

In the castle grounds is the parish church of **St Nicholas**. The small Catholic Fitzalan chapel (c.1380) was built into its east end by the castle's first owners, the Fitzalans, and can only be entered from the grounds.

Petworth House ❾

(NT) Petworth, West Sussex. *Tel 01798 342207.* 🚉 *Pulborough then bus.* **House** ⬤ *Mar–Nov: Sat–Wed.* **Park** ⬤ *daily.* 🖼️ ♿ *limited.* 🍽️ ▯ www.nationaltrust.org.uk/ petworth

This late 17th-century house was immortalized in a series of famous views by the painter J M W Turner *(see p91).* Some of his best paintings are on display here and are part of Petworth's outstanding art

collection, which also includes works by Titian (1488–1576), Van Dyck (1599–1641) and Gainsborough *(see p163).* Also extremely well represented is ancient Roman and Greek sculpture, such as the 4th-century BC *Leconfield Aphrodite,* widely thought to be by Praxiteles.

The Carved Room is decorated with intricately carved wood panels of birds, flowers and musical instruments, by Grinling Gibbons (1648–1721).

The large deer park includes some of the earliest work of "Capability" Brown *(see p26).*

The Restoration clock on the Tudor Guildhall, Guildford

Guildford ❿

Surrey. 🚶 *63,000.* 🚉 ▯ ▯ *14 Tunsgate (01483 444333).* 🚩 *Fri, Sat.* www.visitguildford.com

The county town of Surrey, settled since Saxon times, incorporates the remains of a small refurbished Norman

castle. The high street is lined with Tudor buildings, such as the impressive **Guildhall**, and the huge modern red-brick cathedral, completed in 1954, dominates the town's skyline.

Environs: Guildford stands on the end of the North Downs, a range of chalk hills that are popular for walking *(see p37).* The area also has two famous beauty spots: **Leith Hill** – the highest point in southeast England – and **Box Hill**. The view from the latter is well worth the short, gentle climb from West Humble.

To the north of Guildford is **RHS Wisley** with 97 ha (240 acres) of beautiful gardens. To the south of the town is **Clandon Park**, an 18th-century house with a sumptuous interior. Its Marble Hall boasts an intricate Baroque ceiling.

Southwest is Chawton, where **Jane Austen's House** *(see p162)* is located. This red-brick house is where Austen wrote most of her popular, witty novels, including *Pride and Prejudice,* exploring middle-class manners in Georgian England.

🏛️ **RHS Wisley**
(RHS) Off A3. *Tel 0845 260 9000.* ⬤ *daily.* 🖼️ ♿ ▯ 🍽️ ▯

🏛️ **Clandon Park**
(NT) West Clandon, Surrey. *Tel 01483 222482.* ⬤ *Mar–Oct: Tue–Thu, Sun; public hols.* 🖼️ 📷 ♿ *call 01483 224462.* 🍽️ ▯

🏛️ **Jane Austen's House**
Alton, Hants. *Tel 01420 83262.* ⬤ *Jan–mid-Feb: Sat & Sun; mid-Feb–Dec: daily.* ⬤ *25 & 26 Dec.* 🖼️ ♿ *limited.* ▯

Hampton Court ⓫

East Molesey, Surrey. ☎ 0844 482 7777. 🚆 Hampton Court. ☐ daily. ● 24–26 Dec. 🅿 ♿ 🎁 🍴 🛍
www.hrp.org.uk

The powerful chief minister and Archbishop of York to Henry VIII (see pp50–51), Cardinal Wolsey, leased a small manor house in 1514 and transformed it into a magnificent country residence. In 1528, to retain royal favour,

Wolsey gave it to the king. After the royal takeover, Hampton Court was extended twice, first by Henry himself and in the 1690s by William and Mary, who used Christopher Wren (see p114) as the architect. From the outside the palace is a harmonious blend of Tudor and English Baroque; inside there is a striking contrast between Wren's Classical royal rooms,

Ceiling decoration, Hampton Court

which include the King's Apartments, and Tudor architecture, such as the Great Hall. Many of the state apartments are decorated with paintings and furnishings from the Royal Collection.

The Baroque gardens, with their radiating avenues of majestic limes, collections of rare plants and formal plant beds, have been painstakingly restored.

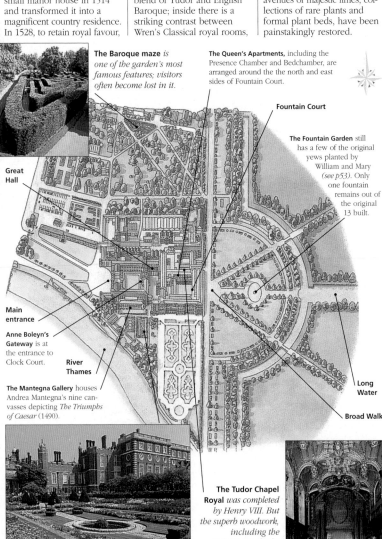

The Baroque maze is one of the garden's most famous features; visitors often become lost in it.

The Queen's Apartments, including the Presence Chamber and Bedchamber, are arranged around the the north and east sides of Fountain Court.

Fountain Court

The Fountain Garden still has a few of the original yews planted by William and Mary (see p53). Only one fountain remains out of the original 13 built.

Great Hall

Main entrance

Anne Boleyn's Gateway is at the entrance to Clock Court.

River Thames

The Mantegna Gallery houses Andrea Mantegna's nine canvasses depicting *The Triumphs of Caesar* (1490).

Long Water

Broad Walk

The Pond Garden, a sunken water garden, was part of Henry VIII's elaborate designs. The small pond in the middle contains a single-jet fountain.

The Tudor Chapel Royal was completed by Henry VIII. But the superb woodwork, including the massive reredos by Grinling Gibbons, all date from a major refurbishment by Queen Anne (c.1711).

Steyning ⑫

West Sussex. 🏘 *5,000* 🚆 🚌 *9 The Causeway, Horsham (01403 211661).*

This lovely little town in the lee of the Downs is packed with timber-framed houses from the Tudor period and earlier, with some built of flint and others in sandstone.

In Saxon times, Steyning was an important port and ship-building centre on the River Adur: King Ethelwulf, father of King Alfred *(see p47)*, was buried here in 858; his body was later moved to Winchester. The *Domesday Book (see p48)* records that Steyning had 123 houses, making it one of the largest towns in the south. The 12th-century church is spacious and splendid, evidence of the area's ancient prosperity; the tower, of chequered stone and flint, was added around 1600.

In the 14th century the river silted up and changed course away from the town, putting an end to its days as a port. Later it became an important coaching stop on the south coast road: the **Chequer Inn** recalls this prosperous period, with its unusual 18th-century flint and stone façade.

Environs: The remains of a **Norman castle** can be visited at Bramber, east of Steyning. This small, pretty village also contains the timber-framed **St Mary's House** (1470). It has fine panelled rooms, including the Elizabethan Painted Room, and one of the oldest trees in the country, a *Ginkgo biloba*. **Chanctonbury Ring** and **Cissbury Ring**, on the hills west of Steyning, were Iron Age forts and the latter has the remains of a Neolithic flint mine. Worthing is the resort where Oscar Wilde (1854–1900) wrote *The Importance of Being Earnest*.

🏛 **St Mary's House**
Bramber. **Tel** 01903 816205.
🕙 May–Sep: Sun (pm), Thu (pm), public hols (pm). 🚻 📷 🛍

Street-by-Street: Brighton ⑬

A stick of Brighton rock

As the nearest south coast resort to London, Brighton is perennially popular, but has always been more refined than its boisterous neighbours further east, such as Margate *(see p183)* and Southend. The spirit of the Prince Regent *(see p179)* lives on, not only in the magnificence of his Royal Pavilion, but in the city's reputation as a venue for adulterous weekends in discreet hotels. Brighton has always attracted actors and artists – Laurence Olivier made his final home here.

Old Ship Hotel
Built in 1559, it was later bought by Nicholas Tettersells, with the money given to him by Charles II as a reward for taking him to France during the Civil War (see p52).

★ Brighton Pier
Built in 1899, this typical late-Victorian pier now caters for today's visitors with amusement arcades.

KEY

– – – Suggested route

STAR SIGHTS

★ Brighton Pier

★ Royal Pavilion

★ Royal Pavilion
The Prince Regent's fantastic Oriental palace helped turn Brighton into a fashionable resort, and is today its principal attraction.

inset

VISITORS' CHECKLIST

East Sussex. 🚃 249,000. 🚉 Brighton. 🚌 Pool Valley. 🛈 Royal Pavilion shop (01273 290 337). 🛍 Mon–Sat. 🎭 International Arts Festival: May.

Many new plays are first staged in the charming Theatre Royal, established in 1807, before they move to the West End of London.

Brighton Dome, an Indian-style building opposite the Royal Pavilion and once George IV's stables, is now a major arts venue.

NEW ROAD

ALBERT STREET

NORTH STREET

CHURCH STREET

Art Deco
This 1920s Art Deco bronze lamp is on display at the Brighton Museum and Art Gallery.

GRAND PARADE

OLD STEINE

OLD STEINE

0 metres 100
0 yards 100

MARINE PARADE

MADEIRA DRIVE

↓ Eastbourne

Sea Life Centre
Built in 1872 as a menagerie, it became an aquarium in 1929. Don't miss the sharks and other British marine life.

THE LANES

PRINCE ALBERT ST
BLACK LION ST
UNION ST
MEETING HOUSE LA
MEETING HOUSE LA
NILE ST
MEETING HOUSE LA
BRIGHTON PL
BARTHOLOMEWS
REGENT ARCADE
MARKET ST
NORTH ST
EAST ST

LANES

The Lanes
Today a maze of antique and independent shops, the Lanes were the original streets of the village of Brighthelmstone.

Brighton: Royal Pavilion

As sea bathing became fashionable in the mid-18th century, Brighton was transformed into England's first seaside resort. Its gaiety soon appealed to the rakish Prince of Wales, who became George IV in 1820. When, in 1785, he secretly married Mrs Fitzherbert, it was here that they conducted their liaison. He moved to a farmhouse near the shore and had it enlarged by Henry Holland *(see p28)*. As his parties grew more lavish, George needed a suitably extravagant setting for them, and in 1815 he employed John Nash *(see p105)* to transform the house into a lavish Oriental palace. Completed in 1823, the exterior has remained largely unaltered. Queen Victoria sold the Pavilion to the town of Brighton in 1850.

Central Dome
Nash adopted what he called the Hindu Style, as in this delicate tracery on one of the imposing turban domes.

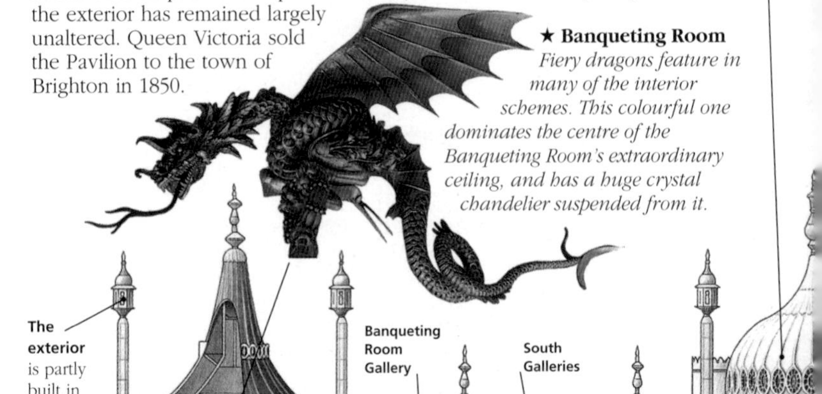

★ Banqueting Room
Fiery dragons feature in many of the interior schemes. This colourful one dominates the centre of the Banqueting Room's extraordinary ceiling, and has a huge crystal chandelier suspended from it.

The exterior is partly built in Bath stone.

Banqueting Room Gallery

South Galleries

The banqueting table, which seats 24 people, is laid as for a splendid feast.

The eastern façade of the Pavilion

Standard Lamps
More dragons, along with dolphins and lotus flowers, figure on the Banqueting Room's eight original standard lamps, made of porcelain, ormolu and gilded wood.

STAR SIGHTS

★ Banqueting Room

★ Great Kitchen

★ Great Kitchen
The Prince's epic banquets required a kitchen of huge proportions. The vast ranges and long shelves of gleaming copper pans were used by famous chefs of the day.

◁ **Front façade of George IV's extravagant Royal Pavilion, Brighton**

Saloon

The original farmhouse that stood on the site was transformed into a villa by architect Henry Holland. The saloon, decorated with Chinese wallpaper, was the central room of the villa.

Long Gallery

Mandarin figures, which can nod their heads, line the pink and blue walls of this 49 m (162 ft) gallery.

Queen Victoria's Bedroom
This reproduction four-poster is on display in the upper floor apartments that were used by Queen Victoria (see pp56–7).

The Music Room, with its crimson and gold murals, was where a 70-piece orchestra played to the Prince's guests.

The domes are made of cast iron.

Music Room Gallery

Yellow Bow Rooms

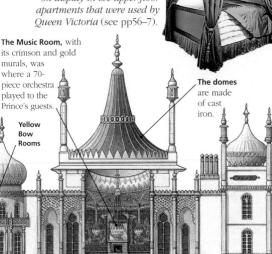

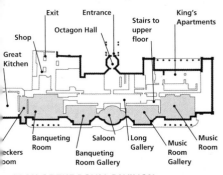

Exit   Entrance   Stairs to upper floor   King's Apartments

Octagon Hall

Shop

Great Kitchen

Banqueting Room   Saloon   Long Gallery   Music Room Gallery   Music Room

Banqueting Room Gallery

eckers oom

PLAN OF THE ROYAL PAVILION

Both Holland and Nash made additions and changes to the original farmhouse. The upper floor contains bedrooms, such as the Yellow Bow Rooms, which George's brothers used. The shaded areas represent the artwork above.

PRINCE OF WALES AND MRS FITZHERBERT

The Prince of Wales was only 23 years old when he fell in love with Maria Fitzherbert, a 29-year-old Catholic widow, and secretly married her. They lived in the farmhouse together and were the toast of Brighton society until George's official marriage took place to Caroline of Brunswick in 1795. Mrs Fitzherbert moved into a small house nearby.

Upstairs interior of Anne of Cleves House, Lewes

Lewes ⑭

East Sussex. 🚶 *16,000.* 🚉
ℹ️ *187 High St (01273 483448).*
🎭 *Glyndebourne Festival: May–Aug.*

The ancient county town of
Sussex was a vital strategic site
for the Saxons, because of its
high vantage point looking
out over the coastline. William
the Conqueror built a wooden
castle here in 1067 but this
was soon replaced by a large
stone structure whose remains
can be visited today.

In 1264 it was the site of a
critical battle in which Simon
de Montfort and his barons
defeated Henry III, enabling
them to establish the first
English Parliament.

The Tudor **Anne of Cleves
House** is a museum of local
history, although Anne of
Cleves, Henry VIII's fourth
wife, never actually lived here.

On Guy Fawkes Night *(see
p64)* lighted tar barrels are
rolled to the river and various
effigies, including of the Pope
and Guy Fawkes, are burned.
This commemorates the town's
17 Protestant martyrs burnt at
the stake by Mary I *(see p51).*

Environs: Nearby are the 16th-
century **Glynde Place**, a fine
courtyard house, and the charming **Charleston**, home to the
Bloomsbury Group *(see p163).*

🏛 **Anne of Cleves House**
Lewes. *Tel 01273 474610.*
🕐 daily (Feb–Oct): phone
for details). 🌐 24–26 Dec. 📷 🏪

🏰 **Glynde Place**
Lewes. *Tel 01273 858224.* 🕐 May–
Aug: Wed, Sun, pub hols. 📷 🖥 🏪

🏰 **Charleston**
Lewes. *Tel 01323 811265.* 🕐 Apr–
Oct: Wed–Sun, Bank Hol Mon. 📷
📷 🖥 🏪 www.charleston.org.uk

Eastbourne ⑮

East Sussex. 🚶 *93,000.* 🚉 🚌 ℹ️
Cornfield Rd (0871 663 0031). 🚌
Tue, Sat. **www**.visiteastbourne.com

This Victorian seaside resort
is a popular place for
retirement, as well as a first-
rate centre for touring the
Downs. The South Downs
Way *(see p37)* begins at
Beachy Head, the spectacular
163 m (536 ft) chalk cliff just
on the outskirts of the town.
From here it is a bracing walk
to the cliff top at Birling Gap,
with views to the **Seven
Sisters**, the chalk hills that end
abruptly as they meet the sea.

Environs: To the west of Eastbourne is **Seven Sisters Country
Park**, a 285 ha (700 acre) area
of chalk cliffs and Downland
marsh that is open all year.
The **Park Visitor's Centre** contains information on the local
area, history and geology.

Just north is the pretty
village of **Alfriston**, with an
ancient market cross and a
15th-century inn, **The Star**, in
its quaint main street. Near
the church is the 14th-century
Clergy House that, in 1896,
became the first National
Trust property *(see p29)*. To
the east is the huge prehistoric
chalk carving, the **Long Man
of Wilmington** *(see p221).*

ℹ️ **Park Visitor's Centre**
Exceat, Seaford. *Tel 0345 6080194.*
🕐 Apr–Oct: daily; Feb, Mar, Nov:
Sat & Sun. 🌐 Jan, Dec. 🏪 ♿ 🍴

🏰 **Clergy House**
(NT) Alfriston. *Tel 01323 870001.*
🕐 Sat–Mon, Wed, Thu.
🌐 Jan. 📷 🏪

The lighthouse (1902) at the foot of Beachy Head, Eastbourne

The meandering River Cuckmere flowing through the South Downs to the beach at Cuckmere Haven

The Downs 🔟

East Sussex. 🚆 🚌 *Eastbourne, Petersfield, Chichester & others.* 🛈 *Cornfield Rd, Eastbourne (0871 663 0031).* **www**.southdowns.gov.uk

The North and South Downs are parallel chalk ridges that run from east to west all the way across Kent, Sussex and Surrey, separated by the lower-lying and fertile Kent and Sussex Weald.

The smooth Downland hills are covered with springy turf, kept short by grazing sheep, making an ideal surface for walkers. The hill above the precipitous **Devil's Dyke**, just north of Brighton, offers spectacular views across the Downs. The legend is that the Devil cut the gorge to let in the sea and flood the countryside, but was foiled by divine intervention. The River Cuckmere runs through one of the most picturesque parts of the South Downs.

Located at the highest point of the Downs is **Uppark House**. This neat square building has been meticulously restored to its mid-18th-century appearance after a fire in 1989.

🏛 Uppark House
(NT) Petersfield, West Sussex. *Tel* 01730 825857. ⬜ Apr–Oct: Sun–Thu (pm). 📷 ♿ 🍴 🎁

Hastings 🔢

East Sussex. 👥 *83,000.* 🚆 🚌 🛈 *Priory Meadow, Queens Square (0845 2741001).* www.visithastings.com

This fascinating seaside town was one of the first Cinque Ports *(see p182)* and is still a thriving fishing port. The town is characterized by the unique tall wooden "net shops" on the beach, where for hundreds of years fishermen have stored their nets.

In the 19th century, the area to the west of the Old Town was built up as a seaside resort, which left the narrow, characterful streets of the old

The wooden net shops, on Hastings' shingle beach

fishermen's quarter intact. There are two cliff railways and smugglers' caves displaying where contraband used to be stored *(see p280)*.

Environs: Seven miles (11 km) from Hastings is Battle. The centre square of this small town is dominated by the gatehouse of **Battle Abbey**. William the Conqueror built this on the site of his great victory, reputedly placing the high altar where Harold fell, But the abbey was destroyed in the Dissolution *(see p50)*. There is an evocative walk around the actual battlefield.

⛪ Battle Abbey
(EH) High St, Battle. **Tel** 01424 775705. ⬜ daily: Easter–Sep: 10am–6pm; Oct–Easter: 10am–4pm. ⬛ 1 Jan, 24–26 Dec. 📷 ♿ 🖥 🎁

BATTLE OF HASTINGS

In 1066, William the Conqueror's *(see p47)* invading army from Normandy landed on the south coast, aiming to take Winchester and London. Hearing that King Harold and his army were camped just inland from Hastings, William confronted them. He won the battle after Harold was mortally wounded by an arrow in his eye. This last successful invasion of England is depicted on the *Bayeux Tapestry* in Normandy, France.

King Harold's death, Bayeux Tapestry

The fairy-tale 14th-century Bodiam Castle surrounded by its moat

Bodiam Castle ⑱

(NT) Nr Robertsbridge, E Sussex. **Tel** 01580 830196. ⊞ Robertsbridge then taxi. ◯ mid-Feb–Oct: daily; Nov–23 Dec: Wed–Sun; 27 Dec–mid-Feb: Sat, Sun. ⬤ 24–26 Dec. 🖼 🖾 ltd. 🔲 🔲

Surrounded by its wide, glistening moat, this late 14th-century castle is one of the most romantic in England.

It was previously thought to have been built as a defence against French invasion, but is now believed to have been intended as a home for a Sussex knight. The castle saw action during the Civil War *(see p52)*, when it was damaged in an assault by Parliamentary soldiers. They removed the roof to reduce its use as a base for Charles I's troops.

It has been uninhabited since, but its grey stone has proved indestructible. With the exception of the roof, it was restored in 1919 by Lord Curzon who gave it to the nation.

Environs: To the east is **Great Dixter**, a 15th-century manor house restored by Sir Edwin Lutyens in 1910. The late Christopher Lloyd created a magnificent garden with a blend of terraces and borders, and a great nursery, too.

🏠 **Great Dixter**
Northiam, Rye. **Tel** 01797 252878. ◯ Apr–Oct: 2–5:30pm Tue–Sun & public hols. 🖼 🔲
www.greatdixter.co.uk

Rye ⑲

See pp184–5.

Romney Marsh ⑳

Kent. ⊞ Ashford. 🚌 Ashford, Hythe. 🛈 Dymchurch Rd, New Romney (01797 369487). ◯ Feb–Dec.

Until Roman times Romney Marsh and its southern neighbour Walland Marsh were entirely covered by the sea at high tide. The Romans drained the Romney section, and Walland Marsh was gradually reclaimed during the Middle Ages. Together they formed a large area of fertile land, particularly suitable for the Romney Marsh sheep bred for the quality of their wool.

Dungeness, a desolate and lonely spot at the southeastern tip of the area, is dominated by a lighthouse and two nuclear power stations. It is also the southern terminus of

---

COASTAL DEFENCE AND THE CINQUE PORTS

Before the Norman Conquest *(see pp46–7)*, national government was weak and, with threats from Europe, it was important for Saxon kings to keep on good terms with the Channel ports. So, in return for keeping the royal fleet supplied with ships and men, five ports – Hastings, Romney, Hythe, Sandwich and Dover – were granted the right to levy taxes; others were added later. "Cinque" came from the old French word for five. The privileges were revoked during the 17th century. In 1803, in response to the growing threat from France, 74 fixed defences were built along the coast. Only 24 of these Martello towers still exist.

The cliff-top position of Dover Castle

A Martello tower, built as part of the Channel's defences

---

the popular **Romney, Hythe and Dymchurch Light Railway** which was opened in 1927. During the summer this takes passengers 14 miles (23 km) up the coast to Hythe on trains a third the conventional size.

The northern edge of the marsh is crossed by the Royal Military Canal, built to serve both as a defence and supply line in 1804, when it was feared Napoleon was planning an invasion (see p55).

The Kent Wildlife Trust Visitor Centre explores the history of the Marsh and its wildlife. For more information visit www.kentwildlifetrust.org.uk

Dover ㉑

Kent. 30,000. 🚃 🖭 ⛴
ℹ️ Old Town Gaol, Biggin St (01304 205108). 🖭 Sat.
www.whitecliffscountry.org.uk

Its proximity to the European mainland makes Dover the leading port for cross-Channel travel. Its famous white cliffs exert a strong pull on returning travellers.

Dover's strategic position and large natural harbour mean the town has always had an important role to play in the nation's defences.

Built on the original site of an ancient Saxon fortification, **Dover Castle**, has helped defend the town from 1198, when Henry II first built the keep, right up to World War II, when it was used as the command post for the Dunkirk evacuation. Exhibits in the castle and in the labyrinth of tunnels beneath made by prisoners in the Napoleonic Wars (see p55) cover all these periods.

Environs: One of the most significant sites in England's early history is the ruin of **Richborough Roman Fort**. Now a large grassy site two miles (3 km) inland, this was where, in AD 43, Claudius's Roman invaders (see p44) made their first landing. For hundreds of years afterwards, Rutupiae, as it was known, was one of the most important ports of entry and military bases in the country.

♜ Dover Castle
(EH) Castle Hill. **Tel** 0870 333 118. ◯ daily (Nov–Jan: Thu–Mon). ◯ 1 Jan, 24–26 Dec. 🎟️ 📷 of the tunnels, by appt. ♿ 🏪 🅿️

⋔ Richborough Roman Fort
(EH) Richborough. **Tel** 01304 612 013. ◯ Apr–Sep: daily. 🎟️ ♿ 🅿️

Margate ㉒

Kent. 40,000. 🚃 🖭
ℹ️ 12–13 The Parade (0870 2646111). **www**.visitthanet.co.uk

A boisterous seaside resort on the Isle of Thanet, Margate has long been a popular destination. Nowadays **Turner Contemporary** is the big draw, both architecturally and for its exhibitions, including a look at Turner's fascination with light.

Environs: Just south is a 19th-century gentleman's residence, **Quex House**, which has two unusual towers in its grounds. The adjoining museum has a fine collection of African and Oriental art, as well as unique dioramas of tropical wildlife. To the west is a Saxon church, built within the remains of the

Visitors relaxing on Margate's popular sandy beach

bleak Roman coastal fort of **Reculver**. Dramatic twin towers, known as the Two Sisters, were added to the church in the 12th century. The church now stands at the centre of a very pleasant, if rather windy, 37 ha (91 acre) camp site.

🏛 Turner Contemporary
Rendezvous. **Tel** 01843 233 000. ◯ Tue–Sun. 🏪 🅿️ www.turnercontemporary.org

🏤 Quex House
Birchington. **Tel** 01843 842168. ◯ Easter–Oct: Tue–Sun. **House** ◯ pm only. 🎟️ ♿ 📷 for groups. 🍴 🅿️

⋔ Reculver Fort
(EH) Reculver. **Tel** 01227 740 676 (Herne Bay Tourist Information). ◯ daily (exterior only).

A drainage dyke running through the fertile plains of Romney Marsh

Street-by-Street: Rye ⑲

This ancient and charming fortified town was added to the original Cinque ports *(see p182)* in the 12th–13th century. A huge storm in 1287 diverted the River Rother so that it met the sea at Rye, and for more than 300 years it was one of the most important Channel ports. However, in the 16th century the harbour began to silt up and the town is now 2 miles (3 km) inland. Rye was frequently attacked by the French, culminating in 1377 when it was burnt to the ground.

The Mermaid Inn sign

★ **Mermaid Street**
This delightful cobbled street, its huddled houses jutting out at unlikely angles, has hardly altered since it was rebuilt in the 14th century.

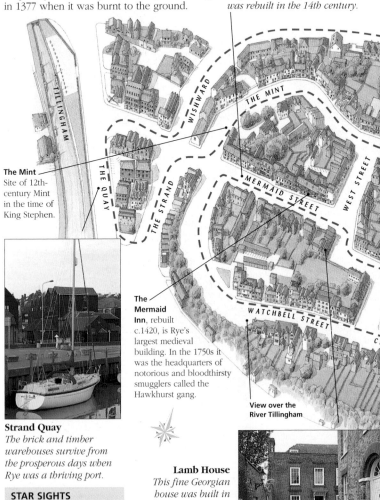

The Mint
Site of 12th-century Mint in the time of King Stephen.

The Mermaid Inn, rebuilt c.1420, is Rye's largest medieval building. In the 1750s it was the headquarters of notorious and bloodthirsty smugglers called the Hawkhurst gang.

View over the River Tillingham

Strand Quay
The brick and timber warehouses survive from the prosperous days when Rye was a thriving port.

Lamb House
This fine Georgian house was built in 1722. George I stayed here when stranded in a storm, and author Henry James (1843– 1916) lived here.

STAR SIGHTS

★ Mermaid Street

★ Ypres Tower

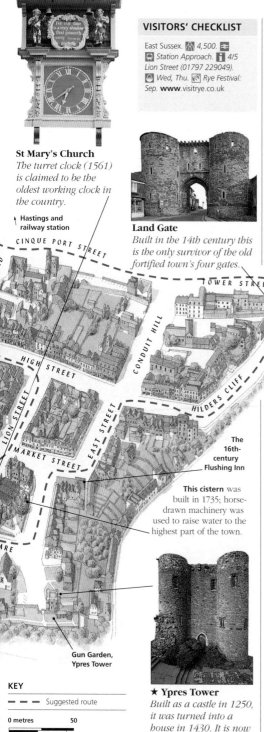

St Mary's Church
The turret clock (1561) is claimed to be the oldest working clock in the country.

↟ Hastings and railway station

Land Gate
Built in the 14th century this is the only survivor of the old fortified town's four gates.

This cistern was built in 1735; horse-drawn machinery was used to raise water to the highest part of the town.

Gun Garden,
Ypres Tower

★ **Ypres Tower**
Built as a castle in 1250, it was turned into a house in 1430. It is now used as the museum.

KEY

- - - Suggested route

| 0 metres | 50 |
| 0 yards | 50 |

VISITORS' CHECKLIST

East Sussex. 🏠 4,500. 🚉
🚏 Station Approach. 🛈 4/5
Lion Street (01797 229049).
🗓 Wed, Thu. 🎭 Rye Festival:
Sep. www.visitrye.co.uk

Environs: Just 2 miles (3 km) to the south of Rye is the small town of **Winchelsea**. At the behest of Edward I, it was moved to its present position in 1288, when most of the old town on lower land to the southeast, was drowned by the same storm that diverted the River Rother in 1287.

Winchelsea is probably Britain's first coherently planned medieval town. Although not all of it was built as originally planned, its rectangular grid survives today, as does the **Church of St Thomas Becket** (begun c.1300) at its centre. Several raids during the 14th century by the French damaged the church and burned down scores of houses. The church has three tombs, and there are also two well-preserved medieval tombs in the chantry. The three windows (1928–33) in the Lady Chapel were designed by Douglas Strachan as a memorial to those who died in World War I.

Just beyond the edges of present-day Winchelsea are the remains of three of the original gates – showing just how big a town was first envisaged. The beach below is one of the finest on the southeast coast.

Camber Sands, to the east of the mouth of the Rother, is another excellent beach. Once used by fishermen, it is now popular with swimmers and edged with seaside bungalows and a bustling holiday camp. Camber Sands is also a favourite spot in the UK for kite- and windsurfing.

The ruins of **Camber Castle** are west of the sands, near Brede Lock, Rye. This was one of the forts built along this coast by Henry VIII when he feared an attack by the French. When the castle was built it was on the edge of the sea but it was abandoned in 1642 when it became stranded inland as the river silted up.

🏰 **Camber Castle**
(EH) Camber, Rye.
Tel 01797 223862. ☐ Jul–Sep:
Sat, Sun pm for 🖾 only.

Jesus on Christ Church Gate,
Canterbury Cathedral

Canterbury ㉓

Kent. 🏠 *50,000.* 🚆 🚌 🛈 *Sun
St, Buttermarket (01227 378100).* 🏪
Wed, Fri. **www**.canterbury.co.uk

Its position on the London to
Dover route meant Canterbury
was an important Roman town
even before the arrival of St
Augustine in 597, sent by the
pope to convert the Anglo-
Saxons to Christianity. The
town rose in importance, soon
becoming the centre of the
Christian church in England.

With the building of the
cathedral and the martyrdom
of Thomas Becket *(see p48),*
Canterbury's future as a
religious centre was assured.
Today, the town is a UNESCO
World Heritage Site.

Adjacent to the ruins of **St
Augustine's Abbey**, destroyed
in the Dissolution *(see p50),* is
St Martin's Church, the oldest
in England. This was where
St Augustine first worshipped
and it has impressive Norman
and Saxon work.

West Gate Museum, with its
round towers, is an imposing
medieval gatehouse. It was
built in 1381 and contains a
display of arms and armoury.

The Poor Priests' Hospital,
founded in the 12th century, is
now the **Museum of Canterbury**.

🏛 **West Gate Museum**
St Peter's St. **Tel** *01227 789576.*
⬜ *Sat.* ⬛ *1 Jan, Good Fri, 24–28
Dec.* 📷 🚻

🏛 **Museum of Canterbury**
Stour St. **Tel** *01227 475202.* ⬜ *Jun–
Sep: daily; Oct–May: Mon–Sat.* 📷 🚻
www.canterbury-museums.co.uk

Canterbury Cathedral

To match Canterbury's growing ecclesiastical rank as
a major centre of Christianity, the first Norman archbishop, Lanfranc, ordered a new cathedral to be built on
the ruins of the Anglo-Saxon cathedral in 1070. It was
enlarged and rebuilt many times and as a result embraces
examples of all styles of medieval architecture. The most
poignant moment in its history came in 1170 when
Thomas Becket was murdered here *(see p48).* Four
years after his death a fire devastated the cathedral and
the Trinity Chapel was built to house Becket's remains.
The shrine quickly became an important
religious site and until the Dissolution
(see p50) the cathedral was
one of Christendom's chief
places of pilgrimage.

The nave at 60 m (188 ft)
makes Canterbury one of the
longest medieval churches.

The South West Porch
(1426) may have been built
to commemorate the victory
at Agincourt *(see p49).*

Main
entrance

★ **Medieval
Stained Glass**
*This depiction of the
1,000-year-old
Methuselah is a detail
from the southwest
transept window.*

GEOFFREY CHAUCER

Considered to be the first
great English poet, Geoffrey
Chaucer (c.1345–1400), a
customs official by profession,
wrote a rumbustious and witty
account of a group of pilgrims
travelling from London to Becket's
shrine in 1387 in the *Canterbury
Tales.* The pilgrims represent a
cross-section of 14th-century English
society and the tales remain one of
the greatest and most entertaining
works of early English literature.

Wife of Bath,
Canterbury Tales

Bell Harry Tower
The central tower, dominating the skyline, was built in 1498 to house a bell donated by Henry of Eastry 100 years before. The fan vaulting is a superb example of the late Perpendicular style.

VISITORS' CHECKLIST

11 The Precincts, Canterbury.
Tel 01227 762862. ◯ 9am–
4:30pm Mon–Sat, 12:30–2pm
Sun. Contact advised. ◯ for
services & concerts; Good Friday,
24 & 25 Dec. 📷 ✝ 8am daily;
5:30pm Mon–Fri; 3:15pm Sat,
Sun; 11am Sun. ♿ 📷
www.canterbury-cathedral.org

★ **Site of the Shrine of St Thomas Becket**
This Victorian illustration (anon) portrays Becket's canonization. The Trinity Chapel was built to house his tomb which stood here until it was destroyed in 1538. The spot is now marked by a lighted candle.

Great Cloister

Chapter House

The Great South Window has four stained glass panels (1958) by Erwin Bossanyi.

★ **Black Prince's Tomb**
This copper effigy is on the tomb of Edward III's son, who died in 1376.

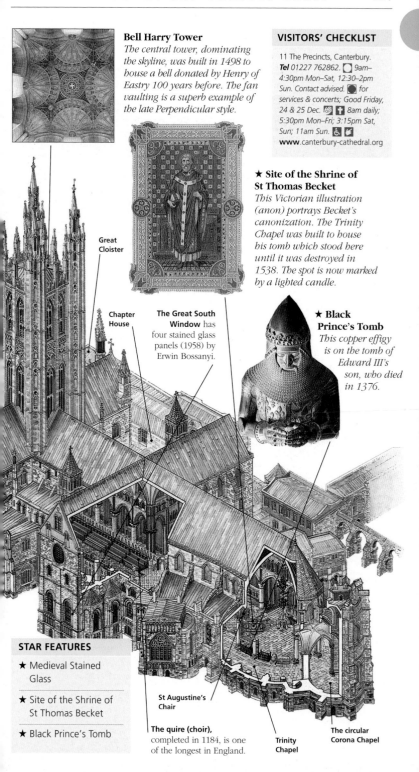

STAR FEATURES

★ Medieval Stained Glass

★ Site of the Shrine of St Thomas Becket

★ Black Prince's Tomb

St Augustine's Chair

The quire (choir), completed in 1184, is one of the longest in England.

Trinity Chapel

The circular Corona Chapel

The keep of Rochester Castle, dominating Rochester and the Medway Valley

Leeds Castle ㉔

Maidstone, Kent. **Tel** 01622 765400.
🚋 Bearsted then bus. ⬚ 10am–5pm
daily. ⬤ for concerts & 25 Dec. 🅿️ ♿
🍴 🛍️ 🏠 **www**.leeds-castle.com

Surrounded by a lake that
reflects the warm buff stone
of its crenellated turrets, Leeds
is often considered to be
the most beautiful castle in
England. Begun in the early
12th century, it has been
continuously inhabited and its
present appearance is a result
of centuries of rebuilding and
extensions, most recently in
the 1930s. Leeds has royal connections going back to 1278,
when it was given to Edward I
by a courtier seeking favour.

Henry VIII loved the castle
and visited it often, escaping
from the plague in London.
It contains a life-sized bust of
Henry from the late 16th century. Leeds passed out of royal
ownership when Edward VI
gave it to Sir Anthony St Leger
in 1552 as a reward for helping to pacify the Irish.

Rochester ㉕

Kent. 🏘️ 145,000. 🚋 🚌
ℹ️ 95 High Street (01634 843666).

Clustered at the mouth of
the River Medway are the
towns of Rochester, Chatham
and Gillingham, all rich in
naval history, but none more
so than Rochester, which

occupied a strategic site on
the London to Dover road.

England's tallest Norman
keep is at **Rochester Castle**,
worth climbing for the views
over the Medway. The town's
medieval history is still visible,
with the original city walls –
which followed the lines of the
Roman fortifications – on view
in the High Street, and some
well-preserved wall paintings
in the **cathedral**, built in 1088.

Environs: In Chatham, the
Historic Dockyard is now a
museum of shipbuilding and
nautical crafts. **Fort Amherst**
nearby was built in 1756 to
protect the dockyard and river
entrance from attack, and has
1,800 m (5,570 ft) of tunnels
to explore that were hewn by
Napoleonic prisoners of war.

♜ Rochester Castle
Castle Hill. **Tel** 0870 333 1181. ⬚
10am–4pm (5pm Apr–Sep) daily (last
adm: 45 mins before close). ⬤ 1 Jan,
24–26 Dec. 🅿️ ♿ grounds only. 🏠

A gladiator,
Knole

🏛️ Historic Dockyard
Dock Rd, Chatham. **Tel** 01634
823800. ⬚ mid-Feb–Oct: daily;
Nov–mid-Feb: call for details. 🅿️ ♿
🍴 🛍️ 🏠

🏹 Fort Amherst
Dock Rd, Chatham. **Tel** 01634
847747. ⬚ call for details. 🅿️ 🛍️

Knole ㉖

(NT) Sevenoaks, Kent. **Tel** 01732
462100. 🚋 Sevenoaks then taxi.
House ⬚ Mar–Jul: Wed–Sun (pm);
Aug: Tue–Sun; Sep–Oct: Wed–Sun
(pm), Good Fri & pub hols. **Park** ⬚
daily. 🅿️ ♿ ltd. 🐾 by appt. 🛍️ 🏠

This huge Tudor mansion
was built in the late 15th
century, and was seized by
Henry VIII from the Arch-
bishop of Canterbury at the
Dissolution (see p50). In 1566
Queen Elizabeth I gave it to
her cousin Thomas Sackville.
His descendants have lived
here ever since, including the
writer Vita Sackville-West,
(1892–1962). The house is
well known for its
17th-century furni-
ture, such as the
elaborate bed
made for James II.
The 405-ha (1,000-acre) park
has deer and lovely walks.

Environs: A small manor
house, **Ightham Mote**, east
of Knole, is one of the finest
examples of English medieval
architecture. Its 14th-century
timber-and-stone building

encloses a central court and is encircled by a moat.

At **Sissinghurst Castle Garden** are gardens created by Vita Sackville-West and her husband Harold Nicolson in the 1930s.

⌂ Ightham Mote
(NT) Ivy Hatch, Sevenoaks.
Tel 01732 810378. ◯ *Mar–Oct: Thu–Mon; Nov & Dec: Thu–Sun.*

♣ Sissinghurst Castle Garden
(NT) Cranbrook. *Tel* 01580 710700.
◯ *mid-Mar–Oct: 11am–6:30pm Fri–Tue.* 💷 ⓑ *limited.*

Hever Castle ㉗

Edenbridge, Kent. *Tel* 01732 865224.
🚉 *Edenbridge Town.* ◯ *Apr–Oct: daily; Nov, Dec, Mar: Wed–Sun (phone for times).* 💷 ⓑ *limited.* 🍴 🎁 *groups by arrangement.* 🖥 **www. hevercastle.co.uk**

This small, moated castle is famous as the 16th-century home of Anne Boleyn, the

CHARLES DICKENS

Charles Dickens (1812–70), a popular writer in his own time, is still widely read today. He was born in Portsmouth but moved to Chatham aged five. As an adult, Dickens lived in London but kept up his Kent connections, taking holidays in Broadstairs, just south of Margate – where he wrote *David Copperfield* – and spending his last years at Gad's Hill, near Rochester. The town celebrates the famous connection with an annual Dickens festival.

The façade of Chartwell, Winston Churchill's home

doomed wife of Henry VIII, executed for adultery. She lived here as a young woman and the king often visited her while staying at Leeds Castle. In 1903 Hever was bought by William Waldorf Astor, who undertook a restoration programme, building a Neo-Tudor village alongside it to accommodate guests and servants. The moat and gatehouse date from around 1270.

Environs: To the northwest of Hever is **Chartwell**, the family home of Sir Winston Churchill (*see p59*). It remains furnished as it was when he lived here. Some 140 of his paintings are on display.

⌂ Chartwell
(NT) Westerham, Kent. 📞 01732 868381. ◯ **House** 11am–5pm Wed–Sun (Jul & Aug: Tue–Sun). Gardens & exhibitions vary; phone for details. 💷 ⓑ limited. 🍴 🎁

Royal Tunbridge Wells ㉘

Kent. 👥 55,000. 🚉 🚌
ℹ Old Fish Market, The Pantiles (01892 515 675). 🛍 Sat.
www.visittunbridgewells.com

Helped by royal patronage, the town became a popular spa in the 17th and 18th centuries after mineral springs were discovered in 1606. The Pantiles – the colonnaded and paved promenade – was laid out in the 1700s.

Environs: Nearby is a superb manor house, **Penshurst Place**. Built in the 1340s, it has an 18-m- (60-ft-) high Great Hall.

⌂ Penshurst Place
Tonbridge, Kent. *Tel* 01892 870307.
◯ Apr–Oct: daily; Mar: Sat & Sun:
House noon–4pm; **Gardens** 10:30am–6pm; **Toy Museum** noon–5pm. 💷 ⓑ limited. 🍴 🎁

An early 18th-century astrolabe to measure the stars, Hever Castle garden

EAST ANGLIA

NORFOLK · SUFFOLK · ESSEX · CAMBRIDGESHIRE

The bulge of land between the Thames Estuary and the Wash, flat but far from featureless, sits aside from the main north – south axis through Britain, and for that reason it has succeeded in maintaining and preserving its distinctive architecture, traditions and rural character in both cities and countryside.

East Anglia's name derives from the Angles, the people from northern Germany who settled here during the 5th and 6th centuries. East Anglians have long been a breed of plain-spoken and independent people. Two prominent East Anglians – Queen Boadicea in the 1st century and Oliver Cromwell in the 17th century – were famous for their stubbornness and their refusal to bow to constituted authority. During the Civil War, East Anglia was Cromwell's most reliable source of support. The hardy people who made a difficult living hunting and fishing in the swampy fens, which were drained in the 17th century, were called the Fen Tigers. After draining, the peaty soil proved ideal for arable farming, and today East Anglia grows about a third of Britain's vegetables. The rotation of crops, heralding Britain's agricultural revolution, was perfected in Norfolk in the 18th century. Many of the region's towns and cities grew prosperous on the agricultural wealth, including Norwich. The sea also plays a prominent role in East Anglian life. Coastal towns and villages support the many fishermen who use the North Sea, rich in herring in former days but now known mainly for flat fish.

In modern times, the area has become a centre of recreational sailing, both off the coast and on the inland waterway system known as the Norfolk Broads. East Anglia is also home to one of Britain's top universities: Cambridge.

Lavender fields in full bloom in July, Heacham, Norfolk

◁ Cley windmill overlooking the sea marshes on the north Norfolk coast

Exploring East Anglia

As you move away from London, you soon reach the countryside immortalized by the painter Constable (see p204), scattered with churches, windmills and medieval agricultural barns. Nature lovers will find it fruitful territory, especially North Norfolk with its bird reserves and seal colonies. Boating enthusiasts, too, are well catered for in this, Britain's driest and sunniest region. The local architecture ranges from a mix of medieval to modern. The distinctive pink-washed cottages in Suffolk, flint cottages in Norfolk and thatched roofs everywhere, are also much in evidence.

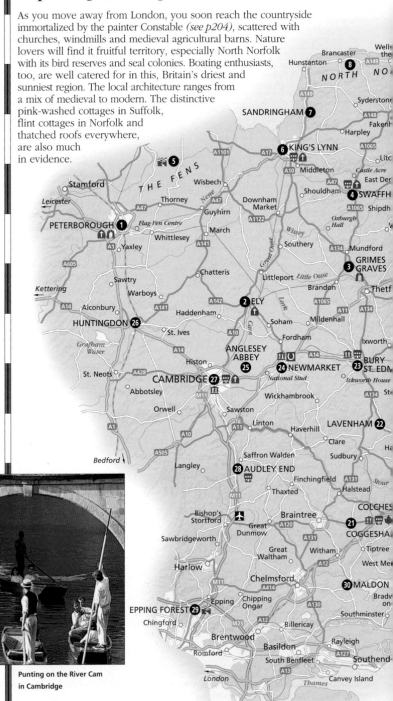

Punting on the River Cam in Cambridge

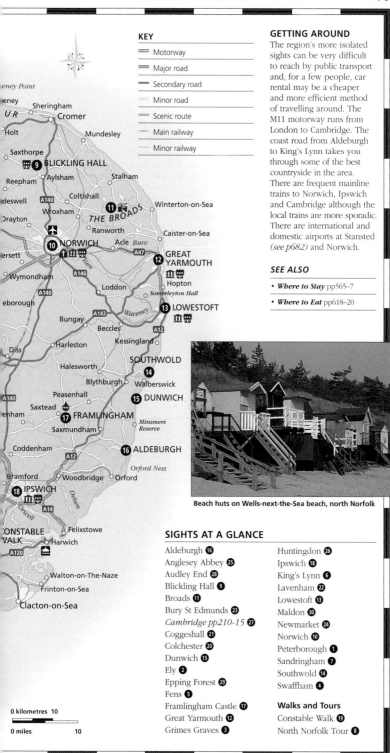

KEY

▬▬ Motorway

▬▬ Major road

▬▬ Secondary road

▭▭ Minor road

▬▬ Scenic route

━━ Main railway

─── Minor railway

GETTING AROUND

The region's more isolated sights can be very difficult to reach by public transport and, for a few people, car rental may be a cheaper and more efficient method of travelling around. The M11 motorway runs from London to Cambridge. The coast road from Aldeburgh to King's Lynn takes you through some of the best countryside in the area. There are frequent mainline trains to Norwich, Ipswich and Cambridge although the local trains are more sporadic. There are international and domestic airports at Stansted (see p682) and Norwich.

SEE ALSO

• **Where to Stay** pp565–7

• **Where to Eat** pp618–20

Beach huts on Wells-next-the-Sea beach, north Norfolk

SIGHTS AT A GLANCE

Aldeburgh **16**
Anglesey Abbey **25**
Audley End **28**
Blickling Hall **9**
Broads **11**
Bury St Edmunds **23**
Cambridge pp210-15 **27**
Coggeshall **21**
Colchester **20**
Dunwich **15**
Ely **2**
Epping Forest **29**
Fens **5**
Framlingham Castle **17**
Great Yarmouth **12**
Grimes Graves **3**

Huntingdon **26**
Ipswich **18**
King's Lynn **6**
Lavenham **22**
Lowestoft **13**
Maldon **30**
Newmarket **24**
Norwich **10**
Peterborough **1**
Sandringham **7**
Southwold **14**
Swaffham **4**

Walks and Tours

Constable Walk **19**
North Norfolk Tour **8**

0 kilometres 10

0 miles 10

Peterborough ❶

Cambridgeshire. 🚶 156,000.
🚌 🚉 ℹ️ 9 Bridge Street
(01733 452336). 🛍️ Tue–Sat.
www.visitpeterborough.com

Although one of the oldest
settlements in Britain, Peterborough was designated a
New Town in 1967, and is
now a mixture of ancient
and modern.

The city centre is dominated
by the 12th-century **St Peter's
Cathedral** which gave the city
its name. The interior of this
classic Norman building, with
its vast yet simple nave, was
badly damaged by Cromwell's
troops (see p52), but its unique
painted wooden ceiling (1220)
has survived intact. Catherine
of Aragon, the first wife of

**Peterborough's coat of arms with
a Latin inscription: Upon this Rock**

Henry VIII, is buried here,
although Cromwell's troops
also destroyed her tomb.

Environs: The oldest wheel in
Britain (1,300 BC) was found
preserved in peat at **Flag Fen
Bronze Age Centre**. The site
provides a fascinating glimpse
into prehistory.

🏛️ **Flag Fen Bronze Age Centre**
The Droveway, Northey Rd. **Tel** 01733
313414. 🛍️ Mar–Sep: Tue–Sun,
public hols (winter: Sat & Sun only).
🎫 ♿ 🚻 💻 www.flagfen.com

Grimes Graves ❸

(EH) Lynford, Norfolk. **Tel** 01842
810656. 🚉 Brandon then taxi. 🛍️
Apr–Sep: daily; Oct, Mar: Thu–Mon.
🎫 🚻 ♿ exhibition area only.

One of the most important
Neolithic sites in England,
this was once an extensive
complex of flint mines – 433
shafts have been located –
dating from before 2000 BC.

Using antlers as pickaxes,
Stone Age miners hacked
through the soft chalk to
extract the hard flint below
to make weapons and tools.
The flint may have been transported long distances around
England on the prehistoric
network of paths. You can
descend 9 m (30 ft) by ladder
into one of the shafts and see

Ely ❷

Cambridgeshire. 🚶 18,000. 🚉
ℹ️ 29 St Mary's St (01353 662062).
🛍️ daily. 🛍️ Thu (general), Sat
(craft & antiques); farmers' market
every 2nd Sat. www.visitely.org.uk

Built on a chalk hill, this
small city is thought to be
named after the eels in the
nearby River Ouse. The hill
was once an inaccessible
island in the then marshy and
treacherous Fens (see p196).
It was also the last stronghold
of Anglo-Saxon resistance,
under Hereward the Wake
(see p48), who hid in the
cathedral until the Normans
crossed the Fens in 1071.

Today this small prosperous
city, totally dominated by the
huge **cathedral**, is the market
centre for the rich agricultural
area surrounding it.

The lantern's glass
windows admit light
into the dome.

**This painted
wooden angel** is
one of hundreds
of bosses that were
carved all over the
south and north
transepts in the 13th
and 14th centuries.

**Stained glass
museum**

The tomb is that of
Alan de Walsingham,
designer of the
unique Octagon.

The Octagon,
made of wood, was built
in 1322 when the Norman
tower collapsed. Its roof,
the lantern, took an extra
24 years to build and
weighs 200 tonnes.

Octagon   **Area of cutaway**

ELY CATHEDRAL
Ely. **Tel** 01353 667735. 🛍️ daily.
🛍️ special events. 🎫 ♿ 🚻 🍴 📷 🛍️
Begun in 1083, the cathedral took 268 years to
complete. It survived the Dissolution (see p50)
but was closed for 17 years by Cromwell (see
p52) who lived in Ely for a time.

the galleries where the flint was mined. During excavations, unusual chalk models of a fertility goddess *(see p43)* and a phallus were discovered.

Environs: Nearby, at the centre of the once fertile plain known as the Breckland, is the small market town of **Thetford**.

Once a prosperous trading town, its fortunes dipped in the 16th century, when its priory was destroyed *(see p50)* and the surrounding land deteriorated due to excessive sheep grazing. The area was later planted with pine trees. A mound in the city marks the site of a pre-Norman castle.

The revolutionary writer and philosopher Tom Paine, author of *The Rights of Man*, was born here in 1737.

The huge cathedral dominates the flat Fens countryside surrounding Ely.

Painted ceiling, 19th century

The Prior's Door (c.1150)

The south aisle has 12 classic Norman arches at its foot, with pointed Early English windows above.

Oxburgh Hall surrounded by its medieval moat

Swaffham ➍

Norfolk. 🚶 6,700. 🚉 ℹ️
4 London St (01760 722255).
📅 Sat.
www.aroundswaffham.co.uk

The best-preserved Georgian town in East Anglia and a fashionable resort during the Regency period, Swaffham is at its liveliest on Saturdays when a market is held in the square around the market cross of 1783. In the centre of the town is the 15th-century **Church of St Peter and St Paul**, with a small spire added in the 19th century. It has a magnificent Tudor north aisle, said to have been paid for by John Chapman, the Pedlar of Swaffham. He is depicted on the two-sided town sign near the market place. Myth has it that he went to London and met a stranger who told him of hidden treasure at Swaffham. He returned, dug it up and used it to embellish the church, where he is shown in a window.

Environs: Castle Acre, north of the town, has the remains of a massive Cluniac **priory**. Founded in 1090, its stunning Norman front still stands.

A short drive south is **Oxburgh Hall and Garden**, built by Sir Edmund Bedingfeld in 1482. The hall, entered through a huge 24 m (80 ft) fortified gatehouse, displays the velvet Oxburgh Hangings, embroidered by Mary, Queen of Scots *(see p511)*.

🏰 **Castle Acre Priory**
(EH) Castle Acre.
Tel 01760 755394.
⭘ daily (Oct–Mar: Thu–Mon. 1 Jan, 24–26 Dec. 🎟️ 👩‍🦽 ltd. 🅿️

🏛️ **Oxburgh Hall & Garden**
(NT) Oxborough. **Tel** 01366 328258. ⭘ Mar–Oct: Sat–Wed (Aug: daily). **Garden** ⭘ Dec: Sat, Sun. 🎟️ 👩‍🦽 ltd. 🍴 🅿️

Swaffham town sign

BOADICEA AND THE ICENI

When the Romans invaded Britain, the Iceni, the main tribe in East Anglia, joined forces with them to defeat the Catuvellauni, a rival tribe. But the Romans then turned on the Iceni, torturing Queen Boadicea (or Boudicca). In AD 61, she led a revolt against Roman rule: her followers burned down London, Colchester and St Albans. The rebellion was put down and the queen took poison rather than submit. At Cockley Cley, near Swaffham, an Iceni camp has been excavated.

Illustration of Queen Boadicea leading her Iceni followers

A windmill on Wicken Fen

The Fens ❺

Cambridgeshire/Norfolk. Ely. 29 St Mary's St, Ely (01353 662062). **www**.visitely.org.uk

This is the open, flat, fertile expanse that lies between Lincoln, Cambridge, Bedford and King's Lynn. Up until the 17th century it was a swamp, and settlement was possible only on "islands", such as Ely *(see p194)*.

Through the 17th century, speculators, recognizing the value of the peaty soil for farmland, brought in Dutch experts to drain the fens. However, as the peat dried, it contracted, and the fens have slowly been getting lower. Powerful electric pumps now keep it drained.

Nine miles (14 km) from Ely is Wicken Fen, 243 ha (600 acres) of undrained fen providing a habitat for a wide range of water life, wildfowl and wild flowers.

King's Lynn ❻

Norfolk. 42,000. Custom House, Purfleet Quay (01553 763044). Tue, Fri, Sat. **www**.visitwestnorfolk.com

Formerly Bishop's Lynn, its name was changed at the Reformation *(see p50)* to reflect the changing political reality. In the Middle Ages it was one of England's most prosperous ports, shipping grain and wool from the surrounding countryside to Europe. There are still a few warehouses and merchants' houses by the River Ouse surviving from this period. At the north end of the town is **True's**

Trinity Guildhall, King's Lynn

North Norfolk Coastal Tour ❽

This tour takes you through some of the most beautiful areas of East Anglia; nearly all of the north Norfolk coast has been designated an Area of Outstanding Natural Beauty. The sea has dictated the character of the area. With continuing deposits of silt, once busy ports are now far inland and the shingle and sand banks that have been built up are home to a huge variety of wildlife. Do bear in mind when planning your journey that this popular route can get congested during summer.

TIPS FOR DRIVERS

Tour length: *28 miles (45 km).*
Stopping-off points: *Holkham Hall makes a pleasant stop for a picnic lunch. There are some good pubs in Wells-next-the-Sea.* (See also pp684–5.)

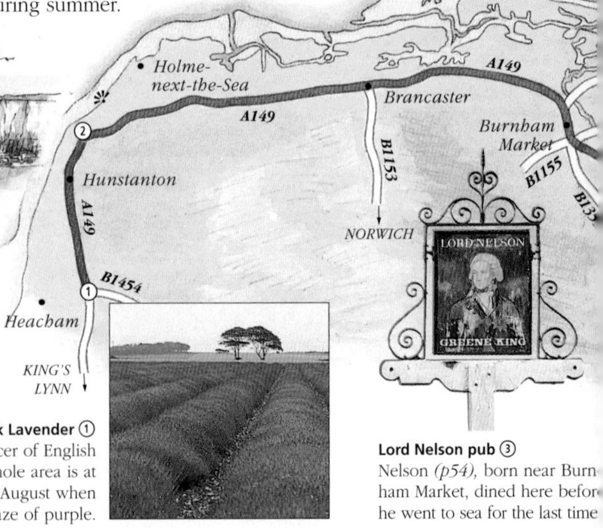

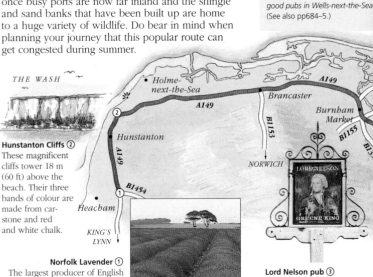

Hunstanton Cliffs ②
These magnificent cliffs tower 18 m (60 ft) above the beach. Their three bands of colour are made from carstone and red and white chalk.

Norfolk Lavender ①
The largest producer of English Lavender, this whole area is at its best in July and August when the fields are a blaze of purple.

Lord Nelson pub ③
Nelson *(p54)*, born near Burnham Market, dined here before he went to sea for the last time

Yard, a relic of the old fishermen's quarter.

The **Trinity Guildhall**, located in the Saturday Market Place, dates back to the 15th century and was formerly a prison. The handsome **Custom House**, overlooking the river, was built in the 17th century as a merchant exchange. It is now a museum dedicated to the town's colourful maritime history. The Tourist Information Centre is also located here. **St Margaret's Church**, on the Market Place, dates back to 1101, and the interior includes a fine Elizabethan screen. In 1741 the tall spire on the southwest tower collapsed in a storm.

Custom House
Purfleet Quay. ***Tel*** *01553 763044.* *daily.* *ground floor.*

Sandringham House, where the Royal Family spend every Christmas

Sandringham ❼

Norfolk. ***Tel*** *01485 545408.* *from King's Lynn.* *Easter–Oct: daily.* *one wk Jul.* *all year.* *all year.* **www**.sandringhamestate.co.uk

This sizeable Norfolk estate has been in royal hands since 1862 when it was bought by the Prince of Wales, who later became Edward VII. The 18th-century house was elaborately embellished and refurbished by the prince and now retains an appropriately Edwardian atmosphere.

The large stables are now a museum and contain several trophies that relate to hunting, shooting and horse racing – all favourite royal activities. A popular feature is a display of royal motor cars spanning nearly a century. In the park there are scenic nature trails.

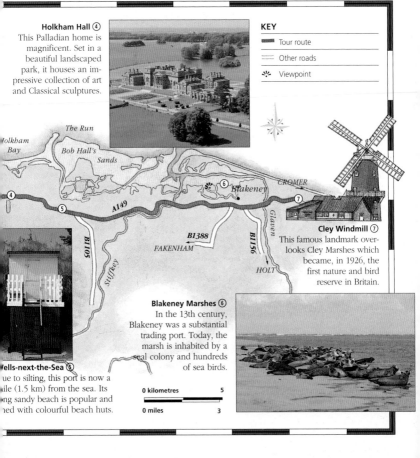

Holkham Hall ④
This Palladian home is magnificent. Set in a beautiful landscaped park, it houses an impressive collection of art and Classical sculptures.

KEY
- Tour route
- Other roads
- Viewpoint

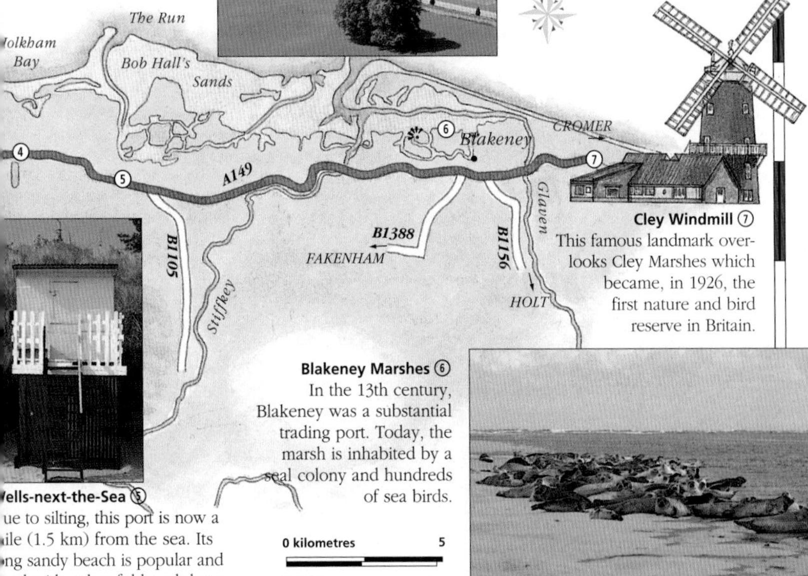

Cley Windmill ⑦
This famous landmark overlooks Cley Marshes which became, in 1926, the first nature and bird reserve in Britain.

Blakeney Marshes ⑥
In the 13th century, Blakeney was a substantial trading port. Today, the marsh is inhabited by a seal colony and hundreds of sea birds.

ells-next-the-Sea ⑤
ue to silting, this port is now a ile (1.5 km) from the sea. Its ng sandy beach is popular and ned with colourful beach huts.

0 kilometres 5
0 miles 3

The symmetrical red-brick façade of the 17th-century Blickling Hall

Blickling Hall ❾

(NT) Aylsham, Norfolk. *Tel 01263 738 030.* ⭑ *Norwich, then bus.* **House** ⬚ *Mar–Oct: Wed–Sun (also open Mon mid-Jul–Aug).* **Garden** ⬚ *dawn–dusk daily.* **Park** ⬚ *daily.* ♿ ⬚ ▯ ▯ **www**.nationaltrust.org.uk

Approached from the east, its symmetrical Jacobean front framed by trees and flanked by two yew hedges, Blickling Hall offers one of the most impressive vistas of any country house in the area.

Anne Boleyn, Henry VIII's tragic second queen, spent her childhood here, but very little of the original house remains. Most of the present structure dates from 1628, when it was home to James I's Chief Justice Sir Henry Hobart. Later in 1767 the 2nd Earl of Buckinghamshire, John Hobart, celebrated the Boleyn connection with reliefs in the Great Hall depicting Anne and her daughter, Elizabeth I. The Long Gallery is the most spectacular room to survive from the 1620s. Its ceiling depicts symbolic representations of learning.

The Peter the Great Room marks the 2nd earl's service as ambassador to Russia and was built to display a huge spectacular tapestry (1764) of the tsar on horseback, a gift from, Catherine the Great. It also has portraits (1760) of the ambassador and his wife by Gainsborough *(see p163)*.

Norwich ❿

See pp200–201.

The Broads ⓫

Norfolk. ⭑ *Hoveton, Wroxham.* ▯ *Norwich, then bus.* ▯ *Station Rd, Hoveton (01603 782281) Apr–Oct, or The Forum, Norwich (01603 213 999).* **www**.broads-authority.gov.uk

These shallow lakes and waterways south and north-east of Norwich, joined by six rivers – the Bure, Thurne, Ant, Yare, Waveney and Chet – were once thought to have been naturally formed, but in actual fact they are medieval peat diggings which flooded when the water level rose in the 13th century.

In summer the 125 miles (200 km) of open waterways, uninterrupted by locks, teem with thousands of boating enthusiasts. You can either hire a boat yourself or take one of the many trips on offer to view the plants and wildlife of the area. Look out for Britain's largest butterfly, the swallowtail. Wroxham, the unofficial capital of the Broads, is the starting point for many of these excursions.

The waterways support substantial beds of strong and durable reeds, much in demand for thatching *(see p33)*. They are cut in winter and carried to shore in the distinctive Broads punts.

For a more detailed look at the origins of the Broads and their varied wildlife, visit the **Norfolk Wildlife Trust** – a large thatched floating information centre on Ranworth Broad, with displays on all aspects of the area, and a bird-watching gallery.

In the centre of Ranworth is **St Helen's Church** which has a painted medieval screen, a well-preserved 14th-century illuminated manuscript and spectacular views over the entire area from its tower.

🗡 **Norfolk Wildlife Trust**
Norwich. *Tel 01603 625540.*
⬚ *Apr–Oct: daily.* ♿ ▯

Sailing boat, Wroxham Broad, Norfolk

Great Yarmouth ⑫

Norfolk. 🔺 90,000. 🚉 🚌
ℹ️ Marine Parade (01493 846346).
🗓️ Wed, Fri (summer), Sat.
www.great-yarmouth.co.uk

Herring fishing was once the major industry of this port, with 1,000 boats engaged in it just before World War I. Over-fishing led to a depletion of stocks and, for the port to survive, it started to earn its living from servicing container ships and North Sea oil rigs.

It is also the most popular seaside resort on the Norfolk coast and has been since the 19th century, when Dickens *(see p189)* gave it useful publicity by setting part of his novel *David Copperfield* here.

The **Elizabethan House Museum** has a large, eclectic display which illustrates the social history of the area.

In the old part of the town, around South Quay, are a number of charming houses including the 17th-century **Old Merchant's House**. It retains its original patterned plaster ceilings as well as examples of old ironwork and architectural fittings from

Fishing trawlers at Lowestoft's quays

nearby houses, which were destroyed during World War II. The guided tour of the house includes a visit to the adjoining cloister of a 13th-century friary.

🏛️ **Elizabethan House Museum**
(NT) 4 South Quay. **Tel** 01493 855746. ⏰ Apr–Oct: daily (pm only weekends). 🏷️ 🚻

🏚️ **Old Merchant's House**
(EH) South Quay. **Tel** 01493 857900. ⏰ Apr–Sep: pm daily. 🏷️ 🎫 🚻

Lowestoft ⑬

Suffolk. 🔺 55,000. 🚉 🚌
ℹ️ East Point Pavilion, Royal Plain (01502 533600). 🗓️ Tue–Sat.
www.visit-lowestoft.co.uk

The most easterly town in Britain was long a rival to Great Yarmouth, both as a holiday resort and a fishing port. Its fishing industry has only just survived. The coming of the railway in the 1840s gave the town an advantage over other resorts, and the solid Victorian and Edwardian boarding houses are evidence of its popularity.

Lowestoft Museum, in a 17th-century house, has a good display of the fine porcelain made here in the 18th century, as well as exhibits on local archaeology and domestic life.

Environs: Somerleyton Hall is built in Jacobean style on the foundations of a smaller mansion. Its gardens are a real delight, and there is a genuinely baffling yew hedge maze.

🏛️ **Lowestoft Museum**
Oulton Broad. **Tel** 01502 511457. ⏰ May–Oct: 1–4pm daily (from 2pm Sun). 🚻 ♿ 🏷️ by appt. **www**.lowestoftmuseum.org

🏚️ **Somerleyton Hall**
On B1074. **Tel** 01502 734901. ⏰ Easter Sun–Oct: Tue, Sun & pub hols (Jul–Aug: also Wed). 🚻 🏷️ ♿ 🎫 by appt. **www**.somerleyton.co.uk

---

WINDMILLS ON THE FENS AND BROADS

The flat, open countryside and the stiff breezes from the North Sea made windmills an obvious power source for East Anglia well into the 20th century, and today they are an evocative and recurring feature of the landscape. On the Broads and Fens, some were used for drainage, while others, such as that at Saxtead Green, ground corn. On the boggy fens they were not built on hard foundations, so few survived, but elsewhere, especially on the Broads, many have been restored to working order. The seven-storey Berney Arms Windmill is the tallest on the Broads. Thurne Dyke Drainage Mill is the site of an exhibition about the occasionally idiosyncratic mills and their more unusual mechanisms.

Corn mill at Saxtead Green, near Framlingham

Herringfleet Smock Mill, near Lowestoft

Norwich ❿

In the heart of the fertile East Anglian countryside, Norwich, one of the best-preserved cities in Britain, is steeped in a relaxed provincial atmosphere. The city was first fortified by the Saxons in the 9th century and still has the irregular street plan of that time. With the arrival of Flemish settlers in the early 12th century and the establishment of a textile industry, the town soon became a prosperous market and was the second city of England until the Industrial Revolution in the 19th century *(see pp56–7).*

The cobbled street, Elm Hill

Exploring Norwich

The oldest parts of the city are Elm Hill, one of the finest medieval streets in England, and Tombland, the old Saxon market place by the cathedral. Both have well-preserved medieval buildings, which are now incorporated into pleasant areas of small shops.

With a trading history spanning hundreds of years, the colourful market in the city centre is well worth a visit. A good walk meanders around the surviving sections of the 14th-century flint city wall.

🛈 Norwich Cathedral

The Close. *Tel 01603 218300.*
⬜ *daily.* **Donations.** 🚻 📷 🍴 🛈
www.cathedral.org.uk
This magnificent building was founded in 1096 by Bishop Losinga and built with stone from Caen in France and Barnack.

The precinct originally included a monastery, and the surviving cloister is the most extensive in England. The thin cathedral spire was added in the 15th century, making it, at 96 m (315 ft), the second tallest in England after Salisbury *(see pp264–5).* In the

majestic nave, soaring Norman pillars and arches support a 15th-century vaulted roof whose stone bosses, many of which illustrate well-known Bible stories, have been beautifully restored.

Easier to appreciate at close hand is the elaborate wood carving in the choir – the canopies over the stalls and the misericords beneath the seats, one showing a small boy being smacked. Not to be missed is the 14th-century Despenser Reredos in St Luke's Chapel. It was hidden for years under a carpenter's table to prevent its destruction by Puritans.

Two gates to the cathedral close survive: **St Ethelbert's,**

One of over a thousand carved bosses in the cathedral cloisters

a 13th-century flint arch, and the **Erpingham Gate** at the west end, built by Sir Thomas Erpingham, who led the triumphant English archers at the Battle of Agincourt in 1415 *(see p49).*

Beneath the east outer wall is the grave of Edith Cavell, the Norwich-born nurse who was arrested and executed in 1915 by the Germans for helping Allied soldiers escape from occupied Belgium.

🏛 Castle Museum

Castle Meadow. *Tel 01603 495897.*
⬜ *daily (Sun pm only).* 🌑 *1 Jan, 25 & 26 Dec.* 💷 🚻 🖼 📷 🛈
www.museums.norfolk.gov.uk
The brooding keep of this 12th-century castle has been a museum since 1894, when it ended 650 years of service as a prison. The most important Norman feature is a carved door that used to be the main entrance.

Exhibits include significant collections of archaeology,

A view of Norwich Cathedral's spire and tower from the southeast

COLMAN'S MUSTARD

It was said of the Colmans that they made their fortune from what diners left on their plate. In 1814 Jeremiah Colman started milling mustard at Norwich because it was at the centre of a fertile plain where mustard was grown. Today at 15 Royal Arcade a shop sells mustard and related items, while a small museum illustrates the history of the company.

It's nicer with
MUSTARD

A 1950s advertisement for Colman's Mustard

natural history, fine art as well as the world's largest collection of ceramic teapots.

The art gallery is dominated by works from the Norwich School of painters. This group of early 19th century landscape artists painted directly from nature, getting away from the stylized studio landscapes that had been fashionable up to then. Chief among the group were John Crome (1768–1821), whom many compare with Constable *(see p204),* and John Sell Cotman (1782–1842), known for his watercolours. There are also regular exhibitions held here.

🔒 Church of St Peter Mancroft

Chantry Rd. *Tel 01603 610443.* ◯ *10am–4pm Mon–Sat; 10am–4pm Sat (summer), 10am–1pm (winter); Sun (services only).* **Donations.** ♿

This imposing Perpendicular church, built around 1455, so dominates the city centre that many visitors assume it is the cathedral. John Wesley *(see p279)* wrote of it, "I scarcely ever remember to have seen a more beautiful parish church".

The large windows make the church very light, and the dramatic east window still has most of its 15th-century glass. The roof is unusual in having wooden fan tracery – it is normally in stone – covering the hammerbeam construction. The famous peal of 13 bells rang out in 1588 to celebrate the defeat of the Spanish Armada *(see p51)* and is still heard every Sunday.

Its name derives from the Latin *magna crofta* (great meadow) which described the area in pre-Norman times.

🏛 Bridewell Museum

Bridewell Alley. *Tel 01603 629127.* ◯ *call for opening times.* 📷 🔒 ♿

One of the oldest houses in Norwich, this 14th-century flint-faced building was used for years as a jail for women and beggars. It now houses an exhibition of local industries, with displays of old machines and reconstructed shops. A section about the people of Norwich is being developed.

🏨 Guildhall

Gaol Hill. *Tel 01264 781611.* 📷

Above the city's ancient market place is the imposing 15th-century flint and stone Guildhall with its gable of checkered flushwork (now a café).

VISITORS' CHECKLIST

Norfolk. 👥 *125,000.* ✈ 🚆 *Thorpe Road.* 🚌 *Surrey St.* ℹ *The Forum, Millennium Plain (01603 213999).* 🏛 *Mon–Sat.* **www.visitnorwich.co.uk**

🏛 Strangers' Hall

Charing Cross. *Tel 01603 493625.* ◯ *10:30am–4pm Wed–Sat (tickets from Castle Museum).* 🔴 *24 Dec–mid-Feb.* 📷 🔒 🔒

This 14th-century merchant's house gives a glimpse into English domestic life through the ages. The house was lived in by immigrant weavers – the "strangers". It has a fine 15th-century Great Hall and a costume display featuring a collection of underwear.

🏛 The Sainsbury Centre for Visual Arts

University of E Anglia (on B1108). *Tel 01603 593199.* ◯ *9am–8pm daily.* 🔴 *23 Dec–20 Jan.* ♿ 🔒 *by arrangement.* 🖥 🔒 **www.scva.ac.uk**

This important art gallery was built in 1978 to house the collection of Robert and Lisa Sainsbury given to the University of East Anglia in 1973.

The collection's strength is in its modern European paintings, including works by Modigliani, Picasso and Bacon, and in its sculptures by Giacometti and Moore. There are also displays of ethnographic art from Africa, the Pacific and the Americas.

The centre, designed by Lord Norman Foster, one of Britain's most innovative architects, was among the first to display its steel structure openly.

Back of the New Mills (1814) by John Crome of the Norwich School

Purple heather in flower on Dunwich Heath

Southwold ⑭

Suffolk. 🏠 3,900. 🚉 ℹ️ *High Street (01502 724729).* 🅿️ *Mon, Thu. Shops closed Wed pm.* **www**.visit-southwold.co.uk

This picture-postcard seaside resort, with its charming white-washed villas clustered around small greens, has, largely by historical accident, remained unspoiled. The railway line which connected it with London was closed in 1929, which effectively isolated this Georgian town from an influx of day-trippers.

This was also once a large port, as testified by the size of the 15th-century **St Edmund King and Martyr Church**, worth a visit for the 16th-century painted screens.

Jack o'the Clock, Southwold

On its tower is a small figure dressed in the uniform of a 15th-century soldier and known as Jack o'the Clock. **Southwold Museum** tells the story of the Battle of Sole Bay, which was fought offshore between the English and Dutch navies in 1672.

Environs: The pretty village of **Walberswick** lies across the creek. By road it is a long detour and the only alternatives are a rowing-boat ferry across the harbour (summer only) or a footbridge across the river half a mile inland. Further inland at Blythburgh, the 15th-century **Holy Trinity Church** dominates the surrounding land. In 1944 a US bomber blew up over the church, killing Joseph Kennedy Jr, brother of the future American president.

🏛 **Southwold Museum**
9–11 Victoria St. **Tel** 01502 726097. ⏲ Easter–Oct: 2–4pm daily (also am in Aug). ♿

Dunwich ⑮

Suffolk. 🏠 1,400.

This tiny village is all that remains of a "lost city" consigned to the sea by erosion. In the 7th century Dunwich was the seat of the powerful East Anglian kings. In the 13th century it was still the biggest port in Suffolk and some 12 churches were built. But the land was being eroded at about a metre (3 ft) a year, and the last original church collapsed into the sea in 1919.

Dunwich Heath, to the south, runs down to a sandy beach and is an important nature reserve. **Minsmere Reserve** has observation hides for watching a huge variety of birds.

🦌 **Dunwich Heath**
(NT) Nr Westleton. **Tel** 01728 648501. ⏲ dawn–dusk. 🚻 ♿

🦌 **Minsmere Reserve**
Minsmere, Westleton. **Tel** 01728 648281. ⏲ daily. 🚫 25, 26 Dec. 🅿️ ♿ 🚻 **www**.rspb.org.uk

Aldeburgh ⑯

Suffolk. 🏠 3,840. 🚉
ℹ️ High St (01728 453637).

Best known today for the music festivals at Snape Maltings, Aldeburgh has been a port since Roman times (the Roman area is under water).

Intricate carving on the exterior of the Tudor Moot Hall, Aldeburgh

For hotels and restaurants in this region see pp565–567 and pp618–620

Erosion has resulted in the fine Tudor **Aldeburgh Museum**, once far inland, today being close to the beach. Its ground floor, originally the market, is now a museum. The large timbered court room above can only be reached by the original outside staircase.

The **church**, also Tudor, contains a large stained-glass window placed in 1979 as a memorial to the composer, Benjamin Britten. **The Red House** was Britten's home from 1957 to 1976.

🏛 **Aldeburgh Museum**
Moot Hall, Market Cross Pl. *Tel* 01728 454666. ⬤ Apr–Oct: daily (pm). 🎫 🚻 www. aldeburghmuseum.org.uk

🏛 **The Red House**
Golf Lane. *Tel* 01728 451700. ⬤ until June 2013. 🎫 🚻

Framlingham Castle ⓱

(EH) Framlingham, Suffolk. *Tel* 01728 724189. ➤ Wickham Market then taxi. ⬤ call to check times. ⬤ 1 Jan, 24–26 Dec. ♿ partial. 🚻 🎫

Perched on a hill, the small village of Framlingham has long been an important strategic site, even before the present castle was built in 1190 by the Earl of Norfolk.

Little of the castle from that period survives except the powerful curtain wall and its towers; walk round the top of it for fine views of the town.

Mary Tudor, daughter of Henry VIII, was staying here in 1553 when she heard she was to become queen.

Environs: To the southeast, on the coast, is the 27 m (90 ft), 16-sided keep of **Orford Castle**, built for Henry II as a coastal defence at around the same time as Framlingham. A short climb to the top of the castle gives fantastic views.

🏰 **Orford Castle**
(EH) Orford. *Tel* 01394 450472. ⬤ daily (Oct–Mar: Thu–Mon). ⬤ 1 Jan, 24–26 Dec. 🎫 🚻

ALDEBURGH MUSIC FESTIVAL

Composer Benjamin Britten (1913–76), born in Lowestoft, Suffolk, moved to Snape in 1937. In 1945 his opera *Peter Grimes* – inspired by the poet George Crabbe (1754–1832), once a curate at Aldeburgh – was performed in Snape. Since then the area has become the centre of musical activity. In 1948, Britten began the Aldeburgh Music Festival, held every June *(see p63)*. He acquired the Maltings at Snape and converted it into a music venue opened by the Queen in 1967. It has since become the focus of an annual series of East Anglian musical events in churches and halls throughout the entire region.

Benjamin Britten in Aldeburgh

Ipswich ⓲

Suffolk. 🏘 120,000. ➤ 🚌 🚇 🚻 St Stephen's Lane (01473 258070). ⬤ Tue, Thu–Sat. 🎭 IPART (music & arts): last 2 wks Jun–1st 2 wks Jul. www.visit-ipswich.com

Suffolk's county town has a largely modern centre but several buildings remain from earlier times. It rose to prominence after the 13th century as a port for the rich Suffolk wool trade *(see p207)*. Later, with the Industrial Revolution, it began to export coal.

The **Ancient House** in Buttermarket has a superb example of pargeting – the ancient craft of ornamental façade plastering. The town's museum and art gallery, **Christchurch Mansion**, is a Tudor house from 1548, where Elizabeth I stayed in 1561. It also boasts the best collection of Constable's paintings out of London *(see p204)*, including four marvellous Suffolk landscapes, as well as paintings by Gainsborough *(see p163)*.

Ipswich Museum contains replicas of the Mildenhall and Sutton Hoo treasures, the originals being in the British Museum *(see pp106–7)*.

In the centre of the town is **St Margaret's**, a 15th-century church built in flint and stone with a double hammerbeam roof and 17th-century painted ceiling panels. **Wolsey's Gate**, a Tudor gateway of 1527, provides a link with Ipswich's most famous son, Cardinal Wolsey *(see p173)*. He started to build an ecclesiastical college in the town, but fell from royal favour before it was finished.

🏛 **Christchurch Mansion**
Soane St. *Tel* 01473 433554. ⬤ 10am–5pm Tue–Sun. ⬤ 1 Jan, Good Fri, 24–27 Dec. ♿ limited. 🎫 by appt. 🚻 🚻

🏛 **Ipswich Museum**
High St. *Tel* 01473 433551. ⬤ Tue–Sat. 🚻 ♿

Pargeting on the Ancient House in Ipswich

Constable Walk ⑲

This walk in Constable country follows one of the most picturesque sections of the River Stour. The route taken would have been familiar to the landscape painter John Constable (1776–1837). Constable's father, a wealthy merchant, owned Flatford Mill, which was depicted in many of the artist's important paintings. Constable claimed to know and love "every stile and stump, and every lane" around East Bergholt.

The River Stour, used as a backdrop for Constable's *Boatbuilding* **(1814)**

TIPS FOR WALKERS

Starting point: Park off Flatford Lane, East Bergholt (charge to park). ℹ 01206 299460; **(NT)** Bridge Cottage (01206 298260). *Getting there:* A12 to East Bergholt, then follow signs to Flatford. ⤢ Manningtree is within walking distance of Flatford. 🚌 from Ipswich or Colchester. *Stopping-off point:* Dedham. *Length:* 3 miles (5 km). *Difficulty:* Flat trail along riverside footpath with kissing gates.

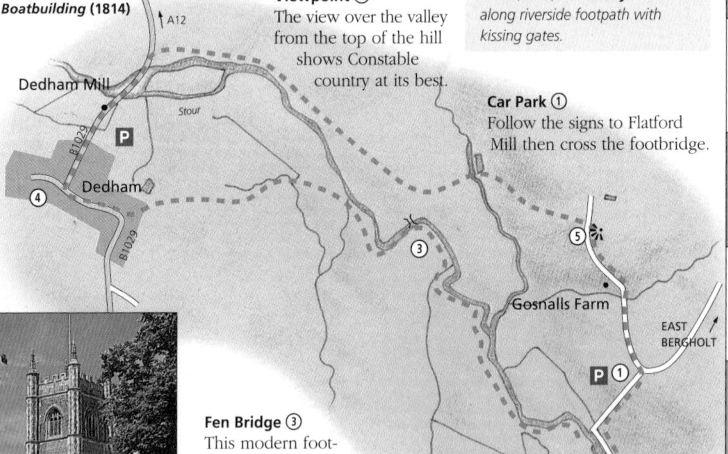

Viewpoint ⑤
The view over the valley from the top of the hill shows Constable country at its best.

Car Park ①
Follow the signs to Flatford Mill then cross the footbridge.

Dedham Mill

Stour

B1029

Dedham

④

③

⑤

Gosnalls Farm

EAST BERGHOLT

P ①

Fen Bridge ③
This modern foot-bridge replaced one that Constable used as a focus for many of his paintings.

Ram Lock •

Flatford Mill •

②

Dedham Church ④
The tall church tower appears in many of Constable's pictures including the *View on the Stour near Dedham* (1822).

KEY

▬ ▬	Route
▭	B road
▭	Minor road
☀	Viewpoint
P	Parking

0 metres   500

0 yards   500

Willy Lott's Cottage ②
This cottage remains much the same as it did when featured in Constable's painting *The Hay-Wain* (see p83).

Colchester ❷⓿

Essex. 160,000. Queen St (01206 282920). Fri, Sat. www.visitcolchester.com

The oldest recorded town in Britain, Colchester was the effective capital of south-east England when the Romans invaded in AD 43, and it was here that the first permanent Roman colony was established.

After Boadicea *(see p195)* burnt the town in AD 60, a 2 mile (3 km) wall was built, 3 m (10 ft) thick and 9 m (30 ft) high, to deter future attackers. You can still see these walls and the surviving Roman town gate, the largest in Britain.

During the Middle Ages Colchester developed into an important weaving centre. In the 16th century, a number of immigrant Flemish weavers settled in an area west of the castle, known as the **Dutch Quarter**, which still retains the original tall houses and steep, narrow streets.

Colchester was besieged for 11 weeks during the Civil War *(see p52)* before being captured by Cromwell's troops.

🏛 Hollytrees Museum

Castle Park. *Tel* 01206 282940. Tue–Sat. 1 Jan, 24–27 Dec. www.cimuseums.org.uk

This elegant Georgian townhouse was built in 1719. Now a charming museum of social history, you can experience the day-to-day lives of Colchester people and changing technology over 300 years. Clock-making was an important craft in Colchester, and it is celebrated in displays here.

Young visitors especially will enjoy exploring the miniature world of the doll's house, and learning about the origin of the famous nursery rhyme "Twinkle, twinkle, little star", which was written in Colchester.

🏛 Castle Museum

Castle Park. *Tel* 01206 282939. 10am–5pm daily (from 11am Sun). 1 Jan, 24–27 Dec. www.cimuseums.org.uk

This is the oldest and largest Norman keep still standing in England. Twice the size of the White Tower at the Tower of

The Norman keep of the Castle Museum, Colchester

London *(see pp118–19)*, it was built in 1076 on the platform of a Roman temple dedicated to Claudius *(see p44)*, using stones and tiles from other Roman buildings. The museum's displays relate the story of the town from prehistoric times to the Civil War. There is also a medieval prison.

🏛 Layer Marney Tower

Off B1022. *Tel* 01206 330784. Apr–Sep: Wed & Sun (Jul & Aug: Sun–Thu). limited. by appt. www.layermarneytower.co.uk

This remarkable Tudor gatehouse is the tallest in Britain: its pair of six-sided, eight-storey turrets reach to 24 m (80 ft). It was intended to be part of a larger complex, but the designer, Sir Henry Marney, died before it was completed. The brickwork and terracotta ornamentation around the roof and windows are models of Tudor craftsmanship.

🌿 Beth Chatto Garden

Elmstead Market. *Tel* 01206 822007. Mar–Oct: 9am–5pm daily (pm only Sun); Nov–Feb: 9am–4pm daily (from 10am Sun). 22 Dec–5 Jan. www.bethchatto.co.uk

One of Britain's most eminent gardening writers, Beth Chatto began this experiment in the 1960s to test her belief that it is possible to create a garden in the most adverse conditions. The dry and windy slopes, boggy patches, gravel beds and wooded areas support an array of plants best suited to that particular environment.

Coggeshall ❷❶

Essex. 4,000. Thu. www.coggeshall-pc.gov.uk

This town has two of the most important medieval and Tudor buildings in the country. Dating from 1140, **Coggeshall Grange Barn** is the oldest surviving timber-framed barn in Europe. Inside is a display of historic farm wagons. The half-timbered merchant's house, **Paycocke's**, was built around 1500 and has a beautifully panelled interior. There is a display of Coggeshall lace.

🏛 Coggeshall Grange Barn

(NT) Grange Hill. 01376 562226. Apr–Oct: Thu–Sun & public hols (pm). Good Fri.

🏛 Paycocke's

(NT) West St. *Tel* 01376 561305. Apr–Oct: Tue, Thu, Sun & public hols (pm). Good Fri.

Beth Chatto Garden, Colchester, in full summer bloom

Lavenham ㉒

Suffolk. 🏘 *1,800.*
ℹ *Lady St (01787 248207).*

Often considered the most perfect of all English small towns, Lavenham is a treasure trove of beautiful timber-framed houses ranged along streets whose pattern is virtually unchanged from medieval times. For 150 years, between the 14th and 16th centuries, Lavenham was the prosperous centre of the Suffolk wool trade. It still has many outstanding and well-preserved buildings; indeed no less than 300 of the town's buildings are listed, including the magnificent **Little Hall**.

Environs: Gainsborough's House, Sudbury, is a museum on this painter *(see p163)*.

🏛 **Little Hall** *Tel 01787 247 019.* ◻ *Apr–Oct: Mon am; Wed, Thu, Sat, Sun pm; public hols.* 🈸

🏛 **Gainsborough's House**
Sudbury. *Tel 01787 372958.* ◻ *Mon–Sat.* ● *24 Dec–2 Jan, Good Fri.* 🈺
🈸 🖼 🈸 www.gainsborough.org

LITTLE HALL

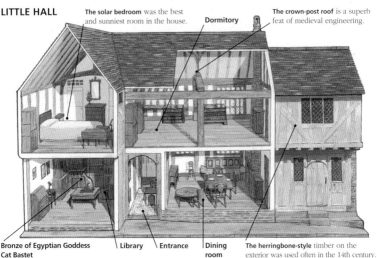

The solar bedroom was the best and sunniest room in the house.

Dormitory

The crown-post roof is a superb feat of medieval engineering.

Bronze of Egyptian Goddess Cat Bastet

Library

Entrance

Dining room

The herringbone-style timber on the exterior was used often in the 14th century.

Bury St Edmunds ㉓

Suffolk. 🏘 *34,000.* 🚆 🚌 ℹ
Angel Hill (01284 764667). 🛒 *Wed, Sat.* www.stedmundsbury.gov.uk

St Edmund was the last Saxon king of East Anglia, decapitated by Danish raiders in 870. Legend has it that a wolf picked up M severed head – an image that appears in a number of medieval carvings. Edmund was canonized in 900 and buried in Bury, where in 1014 King Canute *(see p171)* built an **abbey** in his honour, the wealthiest in England until its destruction in the Dissolution of the Monasteries *(see p351)*. The abbey ruins now lie in the town centre.

Nearby are two large 15th-century churches, built when the wool trade made the town wealthy. **St James's** was designated a cathedral in 1914. The best features of **St Mary's** are the north porch and the hammerbeam roof over the nave. A stone slab in the north-east corner marks the tomb of Mary Tudor *(see pp50–51)*.

Just below the **market cross** in Cornhill – remodelled by Robert Adam *(see p28)* in 1714 – stands the large 12th-century **Moyse's Hall**, a merchant's house that serves as the local history museum, displaying archaeology from the area.

Illustration of St Edmund

Environs: Three miles (5 km) southwest of Bury is the late 18th-century **Ickworth House**. This eccentric Neo-Classical mansion features an unusual rotunda with a

The 18th-century rotunda of Ickworth House, Bury St Edmunds

domed roof flanked by two huge wings. The art collection includes works by Reynolds and Titian. There are also fine displays of silver, porcelain and sculpture, for example, John Flaxman's (1755–1826) moving *The Fury of Athamas*. The house is set in a large park.

The stallion unit at the National Stud, Newmarket

🏛 **Moyse's Hall**
Cornhill. *Tel* 01284 757160.
⬜ *daily (last adm: 4pm).* ⬤
public hols, 24 Dec. 🎦 ♿ 🏠

🎫 **Ickworth House (NT)**
Horringer. *Tel* 01284 735270. ⬜
Mar–Oct: Fri–Tue. 🎦 ♿ 🍴 🏠

Newmarket ㉔

Suffolk. 🏠 *17,000.* 🚆 🏥 🛈 *Palace House, Palace St (01638 667200).* ⬤
Tue, Sat. www.forest-heath.gov.uk

A walk down the short main street tells you all you need to know about this busy and wealthy little town. The shops sell horse feed and all manner of riding accessories; the clothes on sale are tweeds, jodhpurs and the soft brown hats rarely worn by anyone except racehorse trainers.

Newmarket has been the headquarters of British horse racing since James I decided that its open heaths were ideal for testing the mettle of his fastest steeds against those of his friends. The first ever recorded horse race was held here in 1622. Charles II shared his grandfather's enthusiasm and after the Restoration *(see p53)* would move the whole court to Newmarket, every spring and summer, for the sport – he is the only British king to have ridden a winner.

A horse being exercised on Newmarket Heath

The modern racing industry began to take shape here in the late 18th century. There are now over 2,500 horses in training in and around the town, and two racecourses staging regular race meetings from around April to October *(see pp66–7)*. Training stables are occasionally open to the public but you can view the horses being exercised on the heath in the early morning. Tattersall's, the auction house for thoroughbreds, is in the centre of Newmarket.

The **National Stud** can also be visited. You will see the five or six stallions on stud, mares in foal and if you are lucky a newborn foal – most likely in April or May.

The **National Horseracing Museum** tells the history of the sport and contains many offbeat exhibits such as the skeleton of Eclipse, one of the greatest horses ever, unbeaten in 18 races and the ancestor of most of today's fastest performers. It also has a large display of sporting art.

🅿 **National Stud**
Newmarket. *Tel* 01638 663464. ⬜
mid-Feb–Sep: tours only. 🎦 ♿ 🅿
🖥 🏠 www.nationalstud.co.uk

🏛 **National Horseracing Museum**
99 High St, Newmarket. *Tel* 01638 667333. ⬜ *Mar–Oct: daily.* 🎦 ♿
🅿 🖥 🏠 www.nhrm.co.uk

St Mary's Church, Stoke-by-Nayland, southeast of Bury St Edmunds

THE RISE AND FALL OF THE WOOL TRADE

Wool was a major English product from the 13th century and by 1310 some ten million fleeces were exported every year. The Black Death *(see p48)*, which swept Britain in 1348, perversely provided a boost for the industry: with labour in short supply, land could not be cultivated and was grassed over for sheep. Around 1350 Edward III decided it was time to establish a home-based cloth industry and encouraged Flemish weavers to come to Britain. Many settled in East Anglia, particularly Suffolk, and their skills helped establish a flourishing trade. This time of prosperity saw the construction of the sumptuous churches, such as the one at Stoke-by-Nayland, that we see today – East Anglia has more than 2,000 churches. The cloth trade here began to decline in the late 16th century with the development of water-powered looms. These were not suited to the area, which never regained its former wealth. Today's visitors are the beneficiaries of this decline, because the wool towns such as Lavenham and Bury St Edmunds never became rich enough to destroy their magnificent Tudor halls and houses and construct new buildings.

The façade of Anglesey Abbey

Anglesey Abbey 25

(NT) Lode, Cambridgeshire.
Tel 01223 810080. Cambridge
then bus. **House** Mar–Oct: Wed–
Sun; **Garden** Wed–Sun.
limited.

The original Abbey was built
in 1135 for an Augustinian
order. But only the crypt – also
known as the monks' parlour
– with its vaulted ceiling on
marble and stone pillars, survived the Dissolution (see p50).
This was later incorporated
into a manor house whose
treasures include furniture
from many periods and a rare
seascape by Gainsborough
(see p206). The superb garden
was created in the 1930s by
Lord Fairhaven as an ambitious, Classical landscape of
trees, sculptures and borders.

Huntingdon 26

Cambridgeshire. 18,000.
Princes St (01480 388588).
Wed, Sat.

More than 300 years after
his death, Oliver Cromwell
(see p52) still dominates this
small town. Born here in 1599,
a record of his baptism can be
seen in the County Records
Office in Huntingdon. You can
see his name and traces of
ancient graffiti scrawled all
over it which says "England's
plague for five years".
Cromwell Museum, his
former school, traces his life
with pictures and mementos,
including his death mask.
Cromwell remains one of the
most disputed figures in British
history. An MP before he was
30, he became embroiled in
the disputes between Charles
I and Parliament over taxes
and religion. In the Civil War
(see p52) he proved an
inspired general and, after
refusing the title of king, was
made Lord Protector in 1653,
four years after the King was
beheaded. Just two years after
his death the monarchy was
restored by popular demand,
and his body was taken out
of Westminster Abbey (see
pp92–3) to hang on gallows.
There is a 14th-century
bridge across the River Ouse
which links Huntingdon with
Godmanchester, the site of a
Roman settlement.

Cromwell Museum
Grammar School Walk.
Tel 01480 375830. Tue–Sun
(Nov–Mar: pm only except Sat).
1 Jan, 24–27 Dec, some public
hols.

Cambridge 27

See pp210–15.

Audley End 28

(EH) Saffron Walden, Essex. **Tel**
01799 522842. Audley End then
taxi. **House** Apr–Oct: Wed–Sun.
Garden Apr–Oct: Wed–Sun (Jul–
Sep: daily); Nov–Mar: Sat & Sun.
24 Dec–Jan. limited.
www.english-heritage.org.uk

This was the largest house in
England when built in 1603–14
for Thomas Howard, Lord
Treasurer and 1st Earl of Suffolk.
James I joked that Audley End
was too big for a king but not
for a Lord Treasurer. Charles
II, his grandson, disagreed
and bought it in 1667. He
seldom went there, however,
and in 1701 it was given back
to the Howards, who demolished two thirds of it.
What remains is a Jacobean
mansion, retaining its original
hall and many fine plaster
ceilings. Robert Adam (see
p28) remodelled some of the
interior in the 1760s, and these
rooms have been restored
to his original designs. At the
same time, "Capability" Brown
(see p26) landscaped the
magnificent 18th-century park.

The Chapel was completed
in 1772 to a Gothic design.
The furniture was made to
complement the wooden
pillars and vaulting which
are painted to imitate stone.

Main entrance

Stained glass window,
installed in 1771, represents
the Last Supper.

The Great Hall,
hung with family
portraits, is the highlight
of the house, with the
massive oak screen and
elaborate hammerbeam
roof surviving in their
Jacobean form.

Epping Forest 🅸

Essex. 🚆 Chingford. 🚇 Loughton, Theydon Bois. 🚌 High Beach, Loughton (020–8508 0028) & Highbridge St, Waltam Abbey (01992 652295).

As one of the large open spaces near London, the 2,400 ha (6,000 acre) forest is popular with walkers, just as, centuries ago, it was a favourite hunting ground for kings and courtiers – the word forest

Epping Forest contains oaks and beeches up to 400 years old

A depiction of the Battle of Maldon (991) on the *Maldon Embroidery*

denoted an area for hunting. Henry VIII had a lodge built in 1543 on the edge of the forest. His daughter Elizabeth I often used the lodge and it soon became known as **Queen Elizabeth's Hunting Lodge**.

This three-storey timbered building has been fully renovated and now houses an exhibition explaining the lodge's history and other aspects of the forest's life.

The tracts of open land and woods interspersed with a number of lakes, make an ideal habitat for a variety of plant, bird and animal life: deer roam the northern part, many of a special dark strain introduced by James I. The

Corporation of London bought the forest in the mid-19th century to ensure it remained open to the public.

🏛 **Queen Elizabeth's Hunting Lodge**
Rangers Rd, Chingford. **Tel** 020–8529 6681. ☐ Oct–Mar: Fri–Sun; Apr–Sep: Wed–Sun, pm only. ● 1 Jan, 24–26 Dec. ♿ limited. 📷 by appt. 🏠 🅿

Maldon 🅹

Essex. 🏠 21,000. 🚆 Chelmsford then bus. 🚌 Wenlock Way (01621 856503). 🛍 Thu, Sat. **www**.visitmaldon.co.uk

This delightful old town on the River Blackwater, its High Street lined with shops and inns from the 14th century on, was once an important harbour. One of its best-known industries is the production of Maldon sea salt, panned in the traditional way.

A fierce battle here in 991, when Viking invaders defeated the Saxon defenders, is told in *The Battle of Maldon*, one of the earliest known Saxon poems. The battle is also celebrated in the *Maldon Embroidery* on display in the **Maeldune Centre**. This 13-m- (42-ft-) long embroidery, made by locals, depicts the history of Maldon from 991 to 1991.

Environs: East of Maldon at Bradwell-on-Sea is the sturdy Saxon church of **St Peter's-on-the-Wall**, a simple stone building that stands isolated on the shore. It was built in 654, from the stones of a former Roman fort, by St Cedd, who used it as his cathedral. It was restored in the 1920s.

🏛 **Maeldune Centre**
Market Hill. **Tel** 01621 851628 ☐ Feb: Sat; Mar: Thu–Sat; Apr–Nov: Tue–Sat; Dec: call ahead. 📷

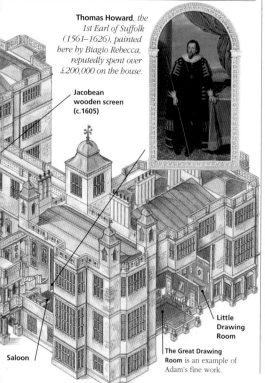

Thomas Howard, *the 1st Earl of Suffolk (1561–1626), painted here by Biagio Rebecca, reputedly spent over £200,000 on the house.*

Jacobean wooden screen (c.1605)

Little Drawing Room

The Great Drawing Room is an example of Adam's fine work.

Saloon

Street-by-Street: Cambridge ㉗

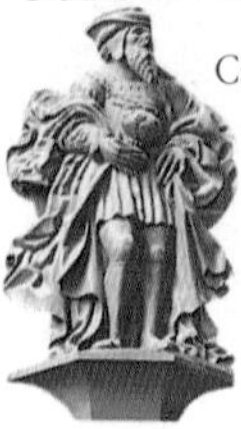

Carving, King's College Chapel

Cambridge has been an important town since Roman times as it was sited at the first navigable point on the River Cam. In the 11th century religious orders began to be established in the town and, in 1209, a group of religious scholars broke away from Oxford University *(see pp222–27)* after academic and religious disputes and came here. Student life dominates the city but it is also a thriving market centre serving a rich agricultural region.

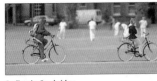

Cyclists in Cambridge

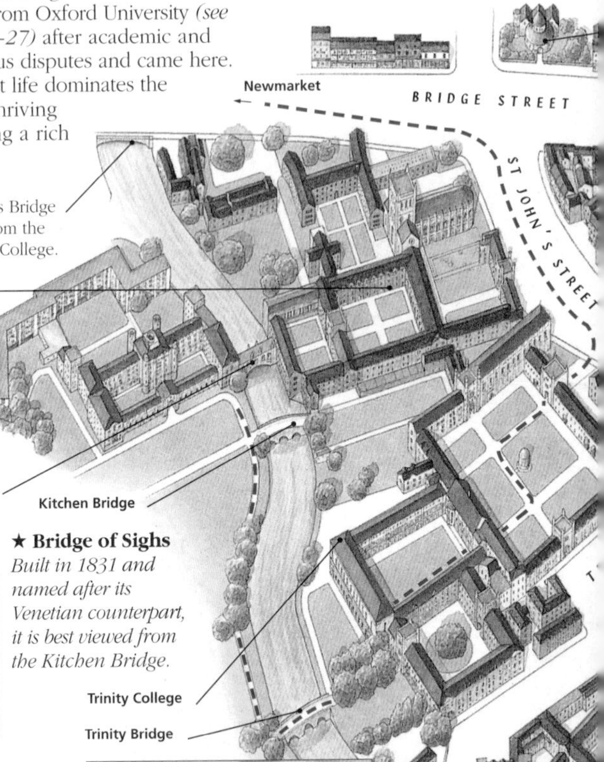

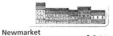

Newmarket
BRIDGE STREET
ST JOHN'S STREET
Grantchester
0 metres 75
0 yards 75

Magdalene Bridge carries Bridge Street across the Cam from the city centre to Magdalene College.

St John's College has superb Tudor and Jacobean architecture.

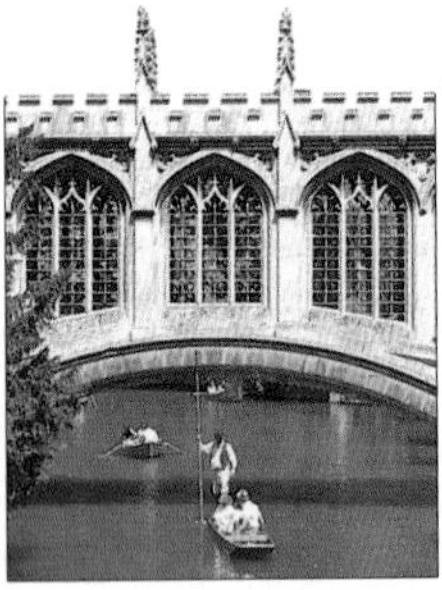

Kitchen Bridge

★ Bridge of Sighs
Built in 1831 and named after its Venetian counterpart, it is best viewed from the Kitchen Bridge.

Trinity College

Trinity Bridge

The Backs
This is the name given to the grassy strip lying between the backs of the big colleges and the banks of the Cam – a good spot to enjoy this classic view of King's College Chapel.

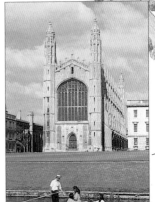

Clare College

Clare Bridge

KEY

– – – Suggested route

STAR SIGHTS

★ Bridge of Sighs

★ King's College Chapel

For hotels and restaurants in this region see pp565–567 and pp618–620

Round Church
The 12th-century
Church of the Holy
Sepulchre has one of
the few round naves in
the country. Its design
is based on the Holy
Sepulchre in Jerusalem.

Gonville and Caius
(pronounced "keys"),
founded in 1348, is one
of the oldest colleges.

Great St Mary's Church
This clock is over the west door
of the university's official church.
Its tower offers fine views.

VISITORS' CHECKLIST

Cambridgeshire. 120,000.
Stansted. Cambridge.
Station Rd. Drummer St.
Wheeler St (0871 2268006).
01223 457574. daily.
Folk Festival: July; Strawberry Fair:
June. **www**.visitcambridge.org

★ **King's College Chapel**
This late medieval masterpiece took
70 years to build (see pp212–13).

Market square

Bus and
Coach
station →

King's College
Henry VIII, king when
the chapel was com-
pleted in 1515, is
commemorated in
this statue near
the main gate.

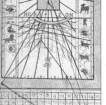

**Queens'
College**
Its Tudor courts
are among the
university's
finest. This 18th-
century sundial
is over the old
chapel – now a
reading room.

Corpus Christi College

To London and
railway station

Mathematical Bridge
It is a myth that this bridge over
the Cam at Queens' College was
first built without nuts or bolts.

Fitzwilliam Museum

Trumpington St. **Tel** *01223 332900.* ☐ *Tue–Sun; public hols.* 🌑 *24–27 Dec, 1 Jan, Good Fri.* **Donation.** ♿ 📷 *by arrangement.* 📖 🏠 www.fitzmuseum.cam.ac.uk

One of Britain's oldest public museums, this massive Classical building has works of exceptional quality and rarity, especially antiquities, ceramics, paintings and manuscripts.

The core of the collection was bequeathed in 1816 by the 7th Viscount Fitzwilliam. Other gifts have since greatly added to the exhibits.

Works by Titian (1488–1576) and the 17th-century Dutch masters, including Hals, Cuyp and Hobbema's *Wooded Landscape* (1686), stand out among the paintings. French Impressionist gems include Monet's *Le Printemps* (1866) and Renoir's *La Place Clichy* (1880), while Picasso's *Still Life* (1923) is notable among the modern works. Most of the important British artists are represented, from Hogarth in the 18th century through Constable in the 19th to Ben Nicholson in the 20th.

The miniatures include the earliest surviving depiction of Henry VIII. In the same gallery are some dazzling illuminated manuscripts, notably the 15th-century *Metz Pontifical,* a French liturgical work.

The impressive Glaisher collection of European earthenware and stoneware includes a unique display of English delftware from the 16th and 17th centuries.

Handel's bookcase contains folios of his work, and nearby is Keats's original manuscript for *Ode to a Nightingale* (1819).

Portrait of Richard James (c.1740s) by William Hogarth

Cambridge: King's College

King's College Coat of Arms

Henry VI founded this college in 1441. Work on the chapel – one of the most important examples of late medieval English architecture – began five years later, and took 70 years to complete. Henry himself decided that it should dominate the city and gave specific instructions about its dimensions: 88 m (289 ft) long, 12 m (40 ft) wide and 29 m (94 ft) high. The detailed design is thought to have been by master stonemason Reginald Ely, although it was altered in later years.

★ **Fan Vaulted Ceiling**
This awe-inspiring ceiling, supported by 22 buttresses, was built by master stonemason John Wastell in 1515.

The Fellows' Building was designed in 1724 by James Gibbs, as part of an uncompleted design for a Great Court.

Henry VI's statue
This bronze statue of the college's founder was erected in 1879.

KING'S COLLEGE CHOIR

When he founded the chapel, Henry VI stipulated that a choir of six lay clerks and 16 boy choristers – educated at the College school – should sing daily at services. This still happens in term time but today the choir also gives concerts all over the world. Its broadcast service of carols has become a much-loved Christmas tradition.

Choristers in King's College Chapel

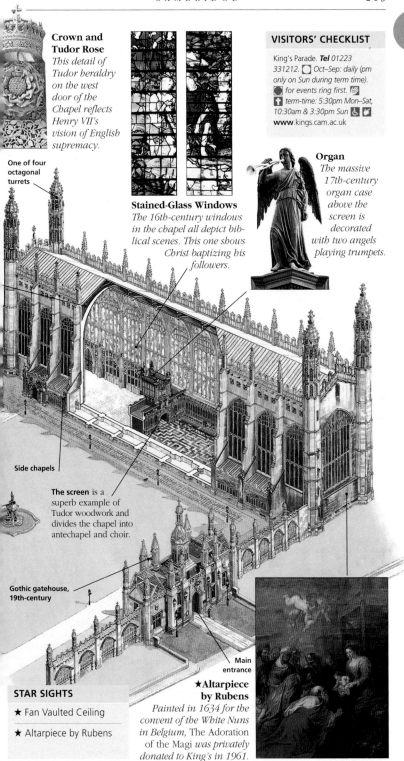

Crown and Tudor Rose
This detail of Tudor heraldry on the west door of the Chapel reflects Henry VII's vision of English supremacy.

VISITORS' CHECKLIST

King's Parade. *Tel 01223 331212.* ☐ Oct–Sep: daily (pm only on Sun during term time). ☐ for events ring first. ☐ term-time: 5:30pm Mon–Sat, 10:30am & 3:30pm Sun ☐ ☐ www.kings.cam.ac.uk

One of four octagonal turrets

Stained-Glass Windows
The 16th-century windows in the chapel all depict biblical scenes. This one shows Christ baptizing his followers.

Organ
The massive 17th-century organ case above the screen is decorated with two angels playing trumpets.

Side chapels

The screen is a superb example of Tudor woodwork and divides the chapel into antechapel and choir.

Gothic gatehouse, 19th-century

Main entrance

★Altarpiece by Rubens
Painted in 1634 for the convent of the White Nuns in Belgium, The Adoration of the Magi *was privately donated to King's in 1961.*

STAR SIGHTS

★ Fan Vaulted Ceiling

★ Altarpiece by Rubens

Exploring Cambridge University

Cambridge University has 31 colleges *(see also pp210–11)*, the oldest being Peterhouse (1284) and the newest being Robinson (1979). Clustered around the city centre, many of the older colleges have peaceful gardens backing onto the River Cam, which are known as the "Backs". The layout of the older colleges, as at Oxford *(see pp226–7)*, derives from their early connections with religious institutions, although few escaped heavy-handed modification in the Victorian era. The college buildings are generally grouped around squares called courts and offer an unrivalled mix of over 600 years of architecture from the late medieval period through Wren's masterpieces and up to the present day.

The nave of the Wren Chapel at Pembroke College

The imposing façade of Emmanuel College

Emmanuel College
Built in 1677 on St Andrew's Street, Sir Christopher Wren's *(see p114)* chapel is the highlight of the college. Some of the intricate interior details, particularly the plaster ceiling and Amigoni's altar rails (1734), are superb. Founded in 1584, the college has a Puritan tradition. One notable graduate was the clergyman John Harvard, who emigrated to America in 1636 and left all his money to the Massachusetts college that now bears his name.

Senate House
King's Parade is the site of this Palladian building, which is used primarily for university ceremonies. It was designed by James Gibbs in 1722 as part of a grand square of university buildings – which was never completed.

Corpus Christi College
Just down from Senate House, this was founded in 1352 by the local trade guilds, anxious to ensure that education was not the sole prerogative of church and nobility. Its Old Court is remarkably well preserved and looks today much as it would have done when built in the 14th century.

The college is connected by a 15th-century gallery of red brick to St Bene't's Church (short for St Benedict's), whose large Saxon tower is the oldest structure in Cambridge.

King's College
See pp212–13.

Pembroke College
The college chapel was the first building completed by Wren *(see pp114–15)*. A formal classical design, it replaced a 14th-century chapel that was turned into a library. The college, just off Trumpington Street, also has fine gardens.

Jesus College
Although founded in 1497, some of its buildings on Jesus Lane are older, as the college took over St Radegond's nunnery, built in the 12th century. There are traces of Norman columns, windows and a well-preserved hammerbeam roof in the college dining hall.

The chapel keeps the core of the original church but the stained glass windows are modern and contain work by William Morris *(see pp220–21)*.

Queens' College
Built in 1446 on Queens' Land, the college was endowed in 1448 by Margaret of Anjou, queen of Henry VI, and again in 1465 by Elizabeth Woodville, queen of Edward IV, which explains the position of the apostrophe. Queens' has a

PUNTING ON THE CAM

Punting captures the essence of carefree college days: a student leaning on a long pole, lazily guiding the flat-bottomed river craft along, while others stretch out and relax. Punting is still popular both with students and visitors, who can hire punts from boat-yards along the river – with a chauffeur if required. Punts do sometimes capsize, and novices should prepare for a dip.

Punting by the King's College "Backs"

marvellous collection of Tudor buildings, notably the half-timbered President's Gallery, built in the mid-16th century on top of the brick arches in the charming Cloister Court. The Principal Court is 15th century, as is Erasmus's Tower, named after the Dutch scholar.

Pepys Library in Magdalene College

The college has buildings on both sides of the Cam, linked by the bizarre Mathematical Bridge, built in 1749 to hold together without the use of nuts and bolts – although they have had to be used in subsequent repairs.

Magdalene College
Pronounced "maudlin" – as is the Oxford college (see p226) – the college, on Bridge Street, was established in 1482. The diarist Samuel Pepys (1633–1703) was a student here and left his large library to the college on his death. The 12 red-oak bookcases have over 3,000 books. Magdalene was the last all-male Cambridge college and it admitted women students only in 1987.

St John's College
Sited on St John's Street, the imposing turreted brick and stone gatehouse of 1514, with its colourful heraldic symbols, provides a fitting entrance to the second largest Cambridge college and its rich store of 16th- and 17th-century buildings. Its hall, most of it Elizabethan, has portraits of the college's famous alumni, such as the poet William Wordsworth (see p366) and the statesman Lord Palmerston. St John's spans the Cam and boasts two bridges, one built in 1712 and the other, the Bridge of Sighs, in 1831, based on its Venetian namesake.

Peterhouse
The first Cambridge college, on Trumpington Street, is also one of the smallest. The hall still has original features from 1286 but its best details are later – a Tudor fireplace which is backed with 19th-century tiles by William Morris (see pp220–21). A gallery connects the college to the 12th-century church of St Mary the Less, which used to be called St Peter's Church – hence the college's name.

William Morris tiles, Peterhouse

VISITORS' CHECKLIST

Cambridge Colleges can usually be visited from 2–5pm daily, but there are no set opening hours. See noticeboards at each college for daily opening times. Some colleges charge admission.

Trinity College
The largest college, situated on Trinity Street, was founded by Henry VIII in 1547 and has a massive court and hall. The entrance gate, with statues of Henry and James I (added later), was built in 1529 for King's Hall, an earlier college incorporated into Trinity. The Great Court features a late Elizabethan fountain – at one time the main water supply. The chapel, built in 1567, has life-size statues of college members, notably Roubiliac's statue of the scientist Isaac Newton (1755).

University Botanic Garden
A delightful place for a leisurely stroll, just off Trumpington Street, as well as an important academic resource, the garden has been on this site since 1846. It has a superb collection of trees and a sensational water garden. The winter garden is one of the finest in the country.

The Bridge of Sighs over the River Cam, linking the buildings of St John's College

THAMES VALLEY

BUCKINGHAMSHIRE · OXFORDSHIRE · BERKSHIRE
BEDFORDSHIRE · HERTFORDSHIRE

The mighty tidal river on which Britain's capital city was founded has modest origins, meandering from its source in the hills of Gloucestershire through the lush countryside towards London. Almost entirely agricultural land in the 19th century, the Thames Valley maintains its pastoral beauty despite the incursion of modern industry.

There are ancient royal connections with the area. Windsor Castle has been a residence of kings and queens for more than 900 years, and played a critical role in history in 1215, when King John set out from here to sign the *Magna Carta* at Runnymede on the River Thames. Further north, Queen Anne had Blenheim Palace built for her military commander, the 1st Duke of Marlborough. Elizabeth I spent part of her childhood at Hatfield House, and part of the Tudor palace still stands.

Several towns in this region, most notably Burford in Oxfordshire, developed as coach staging posts on the important trunk routes between London and the West Country. With the introduction of commuter transportation in the early 20th century, much of the area became an extension of suburbia and saw some imaginative experiments in Utopian town planning such as the garden city of Welwyn and the Quaker settlement at Jordons.

Oxford, the Thames Valley's principal city, owes its importance to the foundation of Britain's first university there in 1167; many of its colleges are gems of medieval architecture. In the 17th century, a number of battles during the Civil War *(see p52)* were fought around Oxford, which for a time was the headquarters of King Charles I, who was supported by the students. When the royalists were forced to flee Oxford, Cromwell made himself chancellor of the university.

Punting on the River Cherwell, Oxford

◁ **Medieval staircase in Christchurch College, Oxford**

Exploring the Thames Valley

The pleasant countryside of the Chiltern Hills and of the Thames Valley itself appealed to aristocrats who built stately homes close to London. Many of these are among the grandest in the country, including Hatfield House and Blenheim. Around these great houses grew picturesque villages, with half-timbered buildings and, as you move towards the Cotswolds, houses built in attractive buff-coloured stone. That the area has been inhabited for thousands of years is shown by the number of prehistoric remains, including the most remarkable chalk hillside figure, the White Horse of Uffington.

SIGHTS AT A GLANCE

Blenheim Palace pp228–9 ❻
Burford ❷
Gardens of the Rose ⓯
Great Tew ❶
Hatfield House ⓭
Kelmscott ❸
Knebworth House ⓬
Oxford pp222–7 ❺
Roald Dahl Museum ❿
St Albans ⓮
Stowe ❼
Vale of the White
   Horse ❹
Waddesdon Manor ❾
Warner Bros. Studio Tour – The
   Making of Harry Potter ⓰
Windsor pp235–7 ⓲
Woburn Abbey ❽
ZSL Whipsnade Zoo ⓫

Walks and Tours
Touring the Thames ⓱

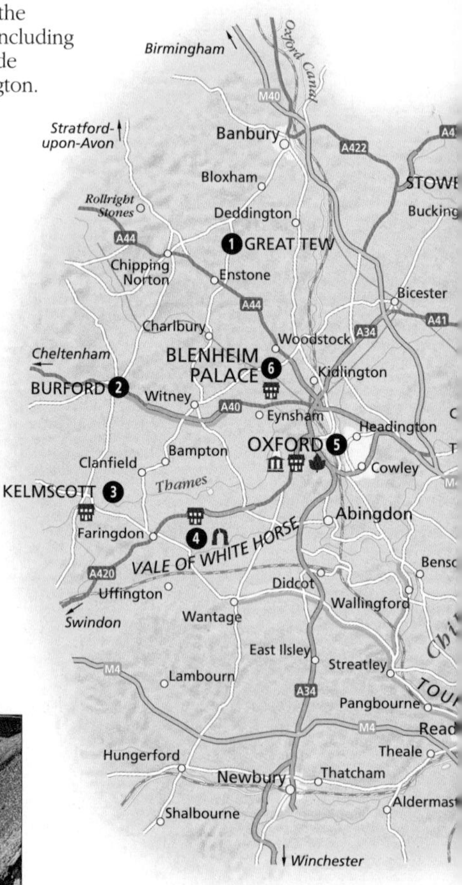

A thatched cottage, Upper Swarford, Banbury

GETTING AROUND

As an important commuter belt, the Thames Valley is well served by public transport, as well as a good network of motorways and major roads into London. Mainline trains travel to all the major towns and there are many coach services that run from London to the major sights and attractions.

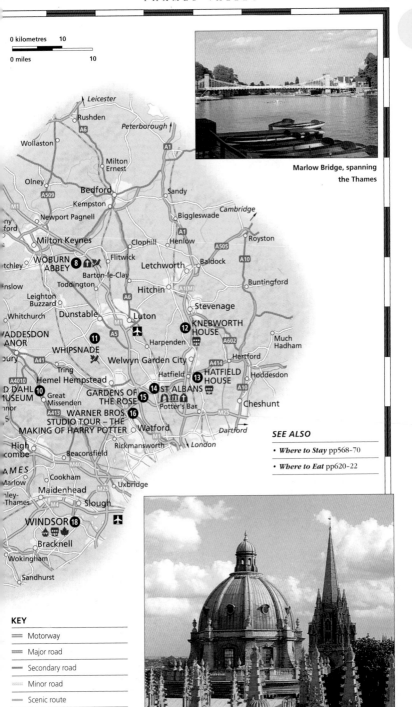

0 kilometres   10

0 miles   10

Marlow Bridge, spanning
the Thames

Leicester

Rushden
A6

Wollaston

Peterborough

Milton
Ernest

A1

Olney

Bedford

Sandy

A509

Kempston

Cambridge

ny
ford

Newport Pagnell

Biggleswade

M1

A1

Milton Keynes

Clophill

Henlow

Royston

A505

tchley

WOBURN
ABBEY 8

Flitwick

Letchworth

Baldock

A10

Barton-le-Clay

nslow

Toddington

Hitchin

A1(M)

Buntingford

Leighton
Buzzard

A6

Whitchurch

Dunstable

Luton

Stevenage

M1

ADDESDON
ANOR

11

KNEBWORTH
HOUSE 12

Much
Hadham

Harpenden

A602

bury

A41

WHIPSNADE

Welwyn Garden City

Hertford

Tring

A414

Hatfield

HATFIELD
HOUSE

Hoddesdon

A4010

Hemel Hempstead

13

A10

D DAHL
USEUM 10

Great
Missenden

GARDENS OF
THE ROSE 15

14 ST ALBANS

Cheshunt

Potter's Bar

A413

WARNER BROS.
STUDIO TOUR – THE
MAKING OF HARRY POTTER

16

Watford

M25

High
combe

Rickmansworth

M1

Dartford

AMES

Beaconsfield

London

SEE ALSO

- *Where to Stay* pp568–70

- *Where to Eat* pp620–22

M40

Marlow

Cookham

Uxbridge

nley-
Thames

Maidenhead

M25

M4

Slough

WINDSOR 18

Bracknell

Wokingham

Sandhurst

KEY

▬	Motorway
▬	Major road
▬	Secondary road
▬	Minor road
▬	Scenic route
▬	Main railway
▬	Minor railway

Radcliffe Camera, surrounded by Oxford's spires

Great Tew ❶

Oxfordshire. 🏠 250. 🚆 Oxford or Banbury then taxi. 🛈 Castle Quay Shopping Centre, Banbury (01295 753752). www.visitnorth oxfordshire.com

This secluded village of ironstone was founded in the 1630s by Lord Falkland for estate workers. It was heavily restored between 1809 and 1811 in the Gothic style. Thatched cottages stand in gardens with clipped box hedges, and in the village centre is the 16th-century pub, the **Falkland Arms**, with its original period atmosphere.

Environs: Five miles (8 km) west are the **Rollright Stones**, three Bronze Age monuments. They comprise a stone circle of 77 stones, about 30 m (100 ft) in diameter, known as the King's Men; the remains of a burial chamber called the Whispering Knights; and the solitary King Stone.

Further north is **Banbury**, well known for its spicy flat cakes and its market cross, immortalized in the nursery rhyme, *Ride a Cock-horse to Banbury Cross*. The original medieval cross was destroyed but it was replaced in 1859.

🍺 **Falkland Arms Pub**
Great Tew. *Tel* 01608 683653.
◯ daily. ● 25 Dec. 🍴 🎵

The 19th-century Banbury Cross

Burford ❷

Oxfordshire. 🏠 1,000.
🛈 High St (01993 823558).

A charming small town, Burford has hardly changed from Georgian times, when it was an important coach stop between Oxford and the West Country. Cotswold stone houses, inns and shops, many built in the 16th century, line its main street. **Tolsey Hall** is a Tudor house with an open ground floor where stalls are still set up. The house is located on the corner of Sheep Street, itself a reminder of the importance of the medieval wool trade *(see p207)*.

Environs: Just east of Burford is **Swinbrook**, whose church contains the Fettiplace Monuments, six carved figures from the Tudor and Stuart periods.

Two miles (3 km) beyond are the ruins of **Minster Lovell Hall**, a 15th-century manor house whose unusual dovecote survives intact.

A few miles south of Burford is **Cotswold Wildlife Park**, home to a diverse collection of mammals, reptiles and birds. **Witney**, to the west, has a town hall dating from 1730.

🏛 **Minster Lovell Hall**
(EH) Minster Lovell. ◯ daily.

🐾 **Cotswold Wildlife Park**
Burford. *Tel* 01993 823006. ◯ daily. ● 25 Dec. 🎨 ♿ 🍴 📷
www.cotswoldwildlifepark.co.uk

Kelmscott ❸

Oxfordshire. 🏠 100. 🛈 The Corn Exchange, Faringdon (01367 242191). www.faringdon.org

The imaginative designer and writer William Morris lived in this pretty Thameside village from 1871 until his death in 1896. He shared his house, the classic Elizabethan **Kelmscott Manor**, with fellow painter Dante Gabriel Rossetti (1828–82), who left after an affair with Morris's wife Jane – the model for many pre-Raphaelite paintings.

Morris and his followers in the Arts and Crafts movement were attracted by the

Cotswold stone houses, Burford, Oxfordshire

For hotels and restaurants in this region see pp568–570 and pp620–622

The formal entrance of the Elizabethan Kelmscott Manor

medieval feel of the village and several cottages were later built in Morris's memory.

Today Kelmscott Manor has works of art by members of the movement – including some William de Morgan tiles. Morris is buried in the village churchyard, with a tomb designed by Philip Webb.

Two miles (3 km) to the east is **Radcot Bridge**, thought to be the oldest bridge still standing over the Thames. Built in the 13th century from the local Taynton stone, it was a strategic river crossing, and in 1387 was damaged in a battle between Richard II and his barons.

Kelmscott Manor
Kelmscott. ***Tel*** *01367 252486.* *Apr–Sep: Wed & some Sat; Gardens & shop: Thu.* *limited.*
www.kelmscottmanor.co.uk

Vale of the White Horse ❹

Oxfordshire. *Didcot.* *25 Bridge St, Abingdon (01235 522711); 19 Church St, Wantage (01235 760176).* **www**.abingdon.gov.uk

This lovely valley gets its name from the huge chalk horse, 100 m (350 ft) from nose to tail, carved into the hillside above Uffington. It is believed to be Britain's oldest hillside carving and has sparked many legends: some say it was cut by the Saxon leader Hengist (whose name means stallion in German), while others believe it is to do with Alfred the Great, thought to have been born nearby.

It is, however, a great deal older than either of these stories suggest, having been dated at around 1000 BC.

Nearby is the Celtic earth ramparts of the Iron Age hill fort, **Uffington Castle**. A mile (1.5 km) west along the Ridgeway, an ancient trade route, *(see p37)*, is an even older monument, a large Stone Age burial mound which is known as **Wayland's Smithy**. This is immersed in legends that Sir Walter Scott *(see p512)* used in his novel *Kenilworth*.

The best view of the horse is to be had from Uffington village, which is also worth visiting for the **Tom Brown's School Museum**. This 17th-century school house contains exhibits devoted to the author Thomas Hughes (1822–96). Hughes set the early chapters of his Victorian novel, *Tom Brown's Schooldays*, here. The museum also contains material about excavations on White Horse Hill.

Tom Brown's School
Broad St, Uffington. *01367 820259.* *Easter–Oct: Sat, Sun & public hols (pm).* *limited.*
www.museum.uffington.net

HILLSIDE CHALK FIGURES

It was the Celts who first saw the potential for creating large-scale artworks on the chalk hills of southern England. Horses – held in high regard by both the Celts and later the Saxons, and the objects of cult worship – were often a favourite subject, but people were also depicted, notably Cerne Abbas, Dorset *(see p269)* and the Long Man of Wilmington *(see p180)*. The figures may have served as religious symbols or as landmarks by which tribes identified their territory. Many chalk figures have been obliterated, because without any attention they are quickly overrun by grass. Uffington is "scoured", to prevent encroachment by grass, a tradition once accompanied by a fair and other festivities. There was a second flush of hillside carving in the 18th century, especially in Wiltshire. In some cases – for instance at Bratton Castle near Westbury – an 18th-century carving has been superimposed on an ancient one.

Britain's oldest hillside carving, the White Horse of Uffington

Street-by-Street: Oxford ❺

Oxford has long been a strategic point on the western routes into London – its name describes its position as a convenient spot for crossing the river (a ford for oxen). The city's first scholars, who founded the university, came from France in 1167. The development of England's first university created the spectacular skyline of tall towers and "dreaming spires".

Old Ashmolean
Now the Museum of the History of Science, this resplendent building was designed in 1683 to show Elias Ashmole's collection of curiosities. The displays were moved in 1845.

The Ashmolean Museum displays one of Britain's foremost collections of fine art and antiquities.

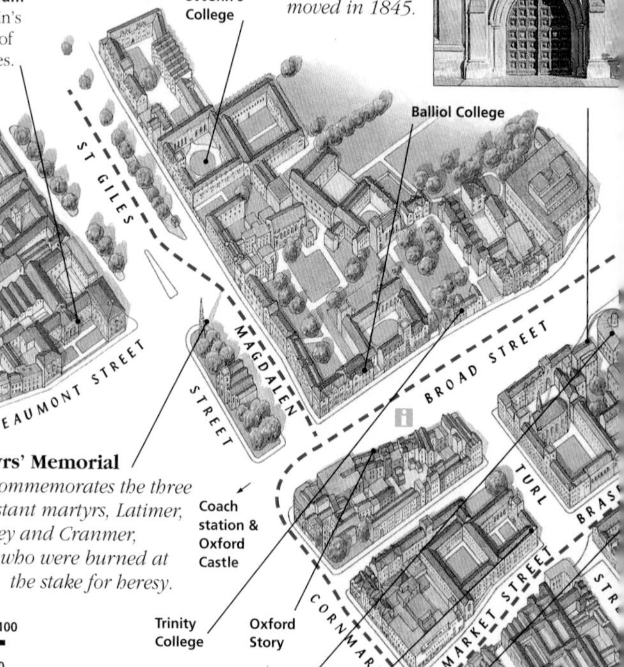

St John's College

Balliol College

ST GILES

BEAUMONT STREET

MAGDALEN STREET

BROAD STREET

TURL STREET

BRAS...

CORNMARKET STREET

MARKET STREET

Martyrs' Memorial
This commemorates the three Protestant martyrs, Latimer, Ridley and Cranmer, who were burned at the stake for heresy.

Coach station & Oxford Castle

Trinity College

Oxford Story

Jesus College

Lincoln College

Covered market

Railway station

Lincoln College Library

ST ALD...

Museum of Oxford

```
0 meters        100
0 yards         100
```

KEY

– – – – Suggested route

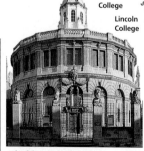

Sheldonian Theatre
The first building designed by Wren (see p114) is the scene of Oxford University's traditional graduation ceremonies.

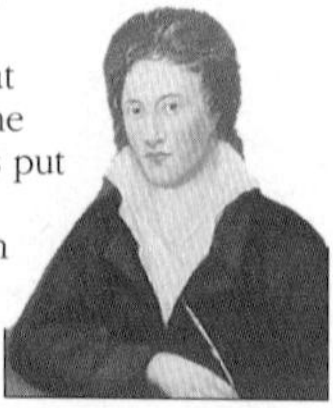

STAR SIGHTS

★ Radcliffe Camera

★ Christ Church

★ Radcliffe Camera
This Classical rotunda is Oxford's most distinctive building and is now a reading room of the Bodleian. It was one of the library's original buildings (see p227).

VISITORS' CHECKLIST

Oxfordshire. 🚶 134,248. 🚉 Botley Rd. 🚌 Gloucester Green. 🛈 15–16 Broad St (01865 25 2200). 🏪 Wed, 1st & 3rd Thu of mth (farmers' market), Thu (flea market). **www**.visitoxford.org

Bridge of Sighs
Resembling the steeply arched bridge in Venice of the same name, this picturesque landmark was built in 1914 and joins the old and new buildings of Hertford College.

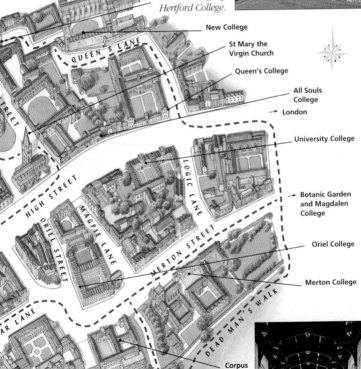

New College

St Mary the Virgin Church

Queen's College

All Souls College

→ London

University College

→ Botanic Garden and Magdalen College

Oriel College

Merton College

QUEEN'S LANE

CATTE STREET

HIGH STREET

ORIEL STREET

MAGPIE LANE

LOGIC LANE

MERTON STREET

BEAR LANE

DEAD MAN'S WALK

Corpus Christi College

★ Christ Church
Students still eat at long tables in all the college halls. Senior academics sit at the high table and grace is almost always said in Latin.

Exploring Oxford

A herm on the Sheldonian Theatre

Oxford is more than just a university city; it has one of Britain's most important car factories in the suburb of Cowley. Despite this, Oxford is dominated by institutions related to its huge academic community: like Blackwell's bookshop which has over 20,000 titles in stock. The two rivers, the Cherwell and the Isis (the name given to the Thames as it flows through the city), provide lovely riverside walks, or you can hire a punt and spend an afternoon on the Cherwell.

🏛 Ashmolean Museum

Beaumont St. **Tel** 01865 278002.
◯ Tue–Sun & public hols.
⬤ 24–26 Dec. ♿ 📷 Tue, Fri, Sat.
📷 📱 www.ashmolean.org

One of the best museums in Britain outside London, the Ashmolean – the first purpose-built museum in England – opened in 1683, based on a display known as "The Ark" collected by the two John Tradescants, father and son.

On their many voyages to the Orient and the Americas they collected stuffed animals and tribal artifacts. On their death, the collection was acquired by the antiquarian Elias Ashmole, who donated it to the university and had a building made for the exhibits on Broad Street – the Old Ashmolean, now the Museum of the History of Science. In the 1800s, part of the Tradescant collection was moved to the University Galleries, a Neo-Classical building of 1845. This greatly expanded museum is now known as the Ashmolean.

What is left of the original curio collection is overshadowed by the other exhibits in the museum, in particular the paintings. These include Bellini's *St Jerome Reading in a Landscape* (late 15th century); Raphael's *Heads of Two Apostles* (1519); Turner's *Venice: The Grand Canal* (1840), Picasso's *Blue Roofs* (1901) and a large group of Pre-Raphaelites, including Rossetti and Millais. There are also fine Greek and Roman carvings and a collection of stringed musical instruments. Items of more local interest include a Rowlandson watercolour of Radcliffe Square in about 1790 and the Oxford Crown. This silver coin was minted here during the Civil War in 1644 *(see p52)* and forms part of the second-largest coin collection in Britain. Perhaps the single most important item is the gold enamelled ornament known as the Alfred Jewel *(see p47)*, which is over 1,000 years old.

A building designed by Rick Mather, which opened in 2009, provides the museum with twice as much space as it previously had, as well as a spectacular rooftop restaurant.

The entrance to the Ashmolean Museum

🌿 The University of Oxford Botanic Garden

Rose Lane. **Tel** 01865 286690.
◯ Mon–Fri. ⬤ Good Fri, 25 Dec.
📷 Mar–Oct. **Donation** Nov–Feb.
♿ www.botanic-garden.ox.ac.uk

Britain's oldest botanic garden was founded in 1621 – one ancient yew tree survives from that period. The entrance gates were designed by Nicholas Stone in 1633 and paid for, like the garden itself, by the Earl of Danby. His statue adorns the gate, along with those of Charles I and II. This delightful garden has an original walled garden, a more recent herbaceous border and rock garden, and an insectivorous house.

The 17th-century Botanic Gardens

🗼 Carfax Tower

Carfax Sq. **Tel** 01865 790522. ◯ daily. ⬤ 1 Jan, 25 & 26 Dec. 📷 📱

The tower is all that remains of the 14th-century Church of St Martin, demolished in 1896 so that the adjoining road could be widened. Watch the clock strike the quarter hours, and climb the 99 steps to the top for panoramic views of the city. Carfax was the crossing point of the original north-to-south and east-to-west routes through Oxford, and the word comes from the Latin *quadrifurcus* (four-forked).

🎵 Holywell Music Room

Holywell St. ◯ concerts only. 📷 ♿

This was the first building in Europe designed, in 1752, specifically for public musical performances. Previously, concerts had been held in private houses for invited guests only. Its two splendid chandeliers originally adorned Westminster Hall at the coronation of George IV in 1820, and were given by the king to Wadham College, of which the music room technically forms a part. The room is regularly used for contemporary and classical concerts.

🏛 Museum of Oxford

St Aldates. **Tel** 01865 252761. ◐ call to check times. ● 1 Jan, 24–26 Dec, 31 Dec. ▣

A well-organized display in the Victorian town hall illustrates the long history of Oxford and its university. Exhibits include a Roman pottery kiln. The main features are a series of well-reconstructed rooms, including one from an Elizabethan inn and an 18th-century student's room.

♜ Martyrs' Memorial

Magdalen St.

This commemorates the three Protestants burned at the stake on Broad Street – Bishops Latimer and Ridley in 1555, and Archbishop Cranmer in 1556. On the accession of Queen Mary in 1553 (see p51), they were committed to the Tower of London, then sent to Oxford to defend their views before the doctors of divinity who, after the hearing, condemned them as heretics.

The memorial was designed in 1843 by George Gilbert Scott and based on the Eleanor crosses erected in 12 English towns by Edward I (1239–1307) to honour his queen.

♜ Oxford Castle

44–46 Oxford Castle. **Tel** 01865 260666. ◐ daily. ♿ ▣ ▣

Following a £40-million development, this 1,000-year-old castle opened in 2005. It forms part of an urban space that includes shops, restaurants and a hotel.

🏛 Oxford Castle Unlocked

44–46 Oxford Castle. **Tel** 01865 260666. ◐ daily. ● 25 Dec. ▣ ▣ ▣ ♿

The secrets of the castle are revealed in this exhibition that looks at the site's turbulent past. Climb St George's Tower for panoramic views over the city.

♜ Sheldonian Theatre

Broad St. **Tel** 01865 277299. ◐ call for details. ● Christmas period, Easter & public hols. ▣ ♿ limited. www.sheldon.ox.ac.uk

Completed in 1669, this was designed by Christopher Wren (see p114), and paid for by Gilbert Sheldon, the Archbishop of Canterbury, as a location for university degree ceremonies. The Classical design of the D-shaped building is based on the Theatre of Marcellus in Rome. The octagonal cupola was built in 1838 and boasts a famous view from its huge Lantern. The theatre's painted ceiling depicts the triumph of religion, art and science over envy, hatred and malice.

⛪ St Mary the Virgin Church

High St. **Tel** 01865 279111. ◐ daily. ● Good Fri, 25, 26 Dec. ▣ ▣ www.university-church.ox.ac.uk

This, the official university church, is said to be the most visited parish church in England. The oldest parts date from the early 13th century and include the tower, from which there are fine views. Its Convocation House served as the university's first

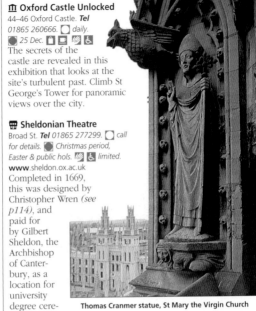

Thomas Cranmer statue, St Mary the Virgin Church

library until the Bodleian was founded in 1488 (see p227). The church is where the three Oxford Martyrs were pronounced heretics in 1555. An architectural highlight is the Baroque south porch.

🏛 University Museum

Parks Rd. **Tel** 01865 272950. ◐ daily. ● Easter, 24–26 Dec. ♿ ▣ www.oum.ox.ac.uk

🏛 Pitt Rivers Museum

Parks Rd. **Tel** 01865 270927. ◐ daily. ● Easter, 24–26 Dec. ♿ ▣ www.prm.ox.ac.uk

Two of Oxford's most interesting museums adjoin each other. The first is a museum of natural history containing relics of dinosaurs as well as a stuffed dodo. This flightless bird has been extinct since the 17th century, but was immortalized by Lewis Carroll (an Oxford mathematics lecturer) in his book Alice in Wonderland. The Pitt Rivers Museum has an extensive ethnographic collection – masks and totems from Africa and the Far East – and archaeological displays, including exhibits collected by the explorer Captain Cook.

The impressive frontage of the University Museum

Exploring Oxford University

Many of the 36 colleges which go to make up the university were founded between the 13th and 16th centuries and cluster around the city centre. As scholarship was then the exclusive preserve of the church, the colleges were designed along the lines of monastic buildings but were often surrounded by beautiful gardens. Although most colleges have been altered over the years, many still incorporate a lot of their original features.

The spectacular view of All Souls College from St Mary's Church

All Souls College
Founded in 1438 on the High Street by Henry VI, the chapel on the college's north side has a classic hammerbeam roof, unusual misericords *(see p341)* on the choir stalls and 15th-century stained glass.

Christ Church College
The best way to view this, the largest of the Oxford colleges, is to approach through the meadows from St Aldate's. Christ Church dates from 1525 when Cardinal Wolsey founded it as an ecclesiastical college to train cardinals. The upper part of the tower in Tom Quad – a rectangular courtyard – was built by Wren *(see p114)* in 1682 and is the largest in the city. When its bell, Great Tom, was hung in 1648, the college had 101 students, which is why the bell is rung 101 times at 9:05pm, to mark the curfew for students (which has not been enforced since 1963). The odd timing is because noon falls here five minutes later than at Greenwich *(see p125)*. Christ Church has produced 13 British prime ministers in the last 200 years. Beside the main quad is the 12th-century Christ Church Cathedral, one of the smallest in England.

Lincoln College
One of the best-preserved of the medieval colleges, it was founded in 1427 on Turl Street, and the front quad and façade are 15th century. The hall still has its original roof, including the gap where smoke used to escape. The Jacobean chapel is notable for its stained glass. John Wesley *(see p279)* was at college here and his rooms, now a chapel, can be visited.

Magdalen College
At the end of the High Street is perhaps the most typical and beautiful Oxford college. Its 15th-century quads in contrasting styles are set in a park by the Cherwell, crossed by Magdalen Bridge. Every May Day at 6am, the college choir sings from the top of Magdalen's bell tower (1508) – a 16th-century custom to mark the start of summer.

New College
One of the grandest colleges, it was founded by William of Wykeham in 1379 to educate clergy to replace those killed by the Black Death of 1348 *(see p49)*.

Magdalen Bridge spanning the River Cherwell

Its magnificent chapel on New College Lane, restored in the 19th century, has vigorous 14th-century misericords and El Greco's (1541–1614) famous painting of *St James*.

Queen's College
Most of the college buildings date from the 18th century and represent some of the finest work from that period in Oxford. Its superb library was built in 1695 by Henry Aldrich (1647–1710) The front screen with its bell-topped gatehouse is a feature of the High Street.

STUDENT LIFE
Students belong to individual colleges and usually live in them for the duration of their course. The university gives lectures, sets exams and awards degrees but much of the students' tuition and social life is based around their college. Many university traditions date back hundreds of years, like the graduation ceremonies at the Sheldonian, which are still held in Latin.

Graduation at the Sheldonian *(see p224)*

Merton College seen from Christ Church Meadows

VISITORS' CHECKLIST

Oxford Colleges can usually be visited from 2pm–dusk daily all year, but there are no set opening hours. See noticeboards outside each college entrance to check opening times.
Bodleian Library (Duke Humphrey's Library & Divinity School), Broad St. *Tel* 01865 277224.
⏰ 9am–5pm Mon–Fri, 9am–4:30pm Sat. ● 24 Dec–2 Jan, Easter, 4–5 Jun. www.bodley.ox.ac.uk

St John's College

The impressive frontage on St Giles dates from 1437, when it was founded for Cistercian scholars. The library has lovely 17th-century bookcases and stained glass, and the college owns a magnificent collection of early embroidered vestments.

Trinity College

The oldest part of the college on Broad Street, Durham Quad, is named after the earlier college of 1296, which was incorporated into Trinity in 1555. The late 17th-century chapel has a magnificent reredos and wooden screen.

Corpus Christi College

The whole of the charming front quad on Merton Street dates from 1517, when the college was founded. The quad's sundial, topped by a pelican – the college symbol – bears an early 17th-century calendar. The chapel has a rare 16th-century eagle lectern.

Merton College

Off Merton Street, this is the oldest college (1264) in Oxford. Much of its hall dates from then, including a sturdy decorated door. The chapel choir contains allegorical reliefs representing music, arithmetic, rhetoric and grammar. Merton's Mob Quad served as a model for the later colleges.

BODLEIAN LIBRARY

Founded in 1320, the library was expanded in 1426 by Humphrey, Duke of Gloucester (1391–1447) and brother of Henry V, when his collection of manuscripts would not fit into the old library. It was refounded in 1602 by Thomas Bodley, a wealthy scholar, who insisted on strict rules: the keeper was forbidden to marry. The library is one of the six copyright deposit libraries in the country – it is entitled to receive a copy of every book published in Britain.

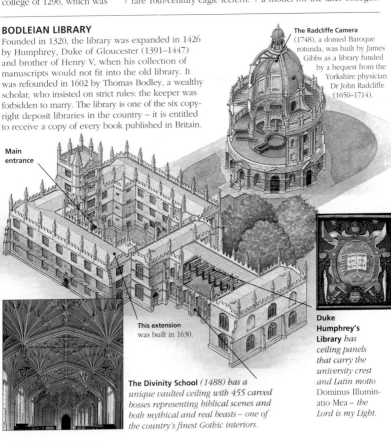

The Radcliffe Camera (1748), a domed Baroque rotunda, was built by James Gibbs as a library funded by a bequest from the Yorkshire physician Dr John Radcliffe (1650–1714).

Main entrance

This extension was built in 1630.

Duke Humphrey's Library *has ceiling panels that carry the university crest and Latin motto Dominus Illumin-atio Mea – the Lord is my Light.*

The Divinity School *(1488) has a unique vaulted ceiling with 455 carved bosses representing biblical scenes and both mythical and real beasts – one of the country's finest Gothic interiors.*

Blenheim Palace ❻

After John Churchill, the 1st Duke of Marlborough, defeated the French at the Battle of Blenheim in 1704, Queen Anne gave him the Manor of Woodstock and had this palatial house built for him in gratitude. Designed by both Nicholas Hawksmoor and Sir John Vanbrugh *(see p398)*, it is a Baroque masterpiece. It was also the birthplace of Britain's World War II leader, Winston Churchill, in 1874.

Winston Churchill and his wife, Clementine

★ **Long Library**
*This 55 m (183 ft) room was design...
by Vanbrugh as...
picture gallery. T...
portraits include...
of Queen Anne b...
Sir Godfrey Knel...
(1646–1723). Th...
stucco on the...
ceiling is by Isaa...
Mansfield (1725)...*

The Grand Bridge was begun in 1708. It has a 31 m (101 ft) main span and contains rooms within its structure.

Chapel
The marble monument to the 1st Duke of Marlborough and his family was sculpted by Michael Rysbrack in 1733.

Water Terraces
These magnificent gardens were laid out in the 1920s by French architect Achille Duchêne in 17th-century style, with detailed patterned beds and fountains.

STAR SIGHTS

★ Long Library

★ Saloon

★ Park and Gardens

Great Hall
This splendid ceiling by Thornhill in 1716, shows the 1st Duke of Marlborough presenting his plan for the Battle of Blenheim to Britannia.

The Italian Garden contains the Mermaid Fountain (early 1900s) by US sculptor Waldo Story.

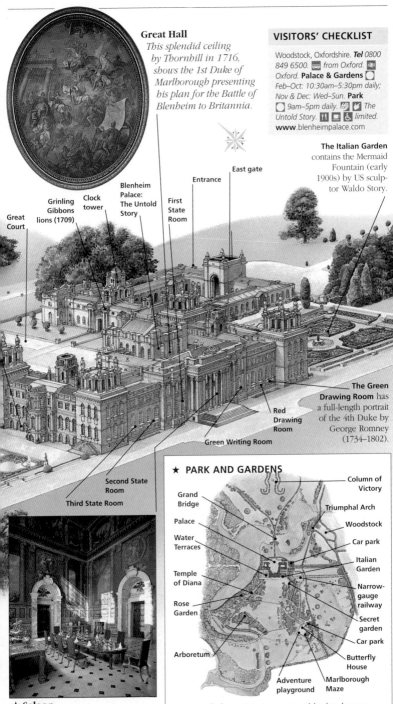

Great Court

Grinling Gibbons lions (1709)

Clock tower

Blenheim Palace: The Untold Story

First State Room

Entrance

East gate

The Green Drawing Room has a full-length portrait of the 4th Duke by George Romney (1734–1802).

Red Drawing Room

Green Writing Room

Second State Room

Third State Room

★ PARK AND GARDENS

Grand Bridge

Palace

Water Terraces

Temple of Diana

Rose Garden

Arboretum

Adventure playground

Marlborough Maze

Column of Victory

Triumphal Arch

Woodstock

Car park

Italian Garden

Narrow-gauge railway

Secret garden

Car park

Butterfly House

A house fit for a victorious general had to be surrounded by a park with suitably heroic monuments. They were kept when "Capability" Brown *(see p26)* re-landscaped the park (1764–74) and created the lake.

★ Saloon
French artist Louis Laguerre (1663–1721) painted the detailed scenes on the walls and ceiling.

Canaletto's Entrance to the Arsenal (1730) hangs at Woburn Abbey

Stowe Gardens ❼

(NT) Buckingham, Buckinghamshire.
Tel 01494 755568. 🚆 Milton
Keynes then bus. ⭕ Mar–Nov: Wed–
Sun; Dec–Feb: Sat & Sun, public hols.
Stowe House ⭕ Access may be
restricted due to a 20-year restoration
project. 🎫 👤 limited. 🖥 🚻 www.
nationaltrust.org.uk/stowegardens

This is the most ambitious
and important landscaped
garden in Britain, as well as
being one of the finest examples of the 18th-century
passion for improving on
nature to make it conform to
fashionable notions of taste.

In the space of nearly 100
years the original garden, first
laid out around 1680, was
enlarged and transformed by
the addition of monuments,
Greek and Gothic temples,
grottoes, statues, ornamental
bridges, artificial lakes and
"natural" tree plantings.

Most of the leading designers
and architects of the period
contributed to the design,
including Sir John Vanbrugh,
James Gibbs and "Capability"
Brown *(see p26)*.

From 1593 to 1921 the property was owned by the Temple
and Grenville families – later
the Dukes of Buckingham –
until the large Palladian house
at its centre was converted
into an elite boys' school.

The family were soldiers
and politicians in the liberal
tradition, and many of the
buildings and sculptures in
the garden symbolize Utopian
ideals of democracy and freedom. Some features deteriorated in the 19th century but a
major restoration programme
has returned much of the
statuary to its former glory.

Woburn Abbey ❽

Woburn, Bedfordshire. **Tel** 01525
290333. 🚆 Flitwick then taxi.
⭕ Apr–Sep: daily. ⚫ Oct–Mar.
Grounds ⭕ daily. 🎫 📷 👤 ring
first. 📷 by arrangement. 🚻
www.woburnabbey.co.uk

The Dukes of Bedford have
lived here for over 350 years
and were among the first
owners of an English stately
home to open their house to
the public some 40 years ago.

The abbey was built in the
mid-18th century on the
foundations of a large 12th-
century Cistercian monastery.
Its mix of styles range from
Henry Flitcroft and Henry
Holland *(see p28)*. The abbey's
grounds are also popular for
their 142-ha (350-acre) safari
park and attractive deer park,
home to nine species including
the Manchurian Sika deer
from China.

The home's magnificent
state apartments house an
important private art collection
which includes works by
Reynolds (1723–92) and
Canaletto (1697–1768).

Waddesdon Manor ❾

Nr Aylesbury, Buckinghamshire. **Tel**
01296 653226. 🚆 Aylesbury then
taxi. **House** ⭕ Mar–Dec: Wed–Sun;
Jan–Feb: Sat & Sun. **Grounds** ⭕
Mar–23 Dec: 10am–5pm Wed–Sun
(11am Sat & Sun), bank hol Mon. 🎫
🚻 🖥 👤 www.waddesdon.org.uk

Waddesdon Manor was built
between 1874–89 by Baron
Ferdinand de Rothschild and
designed by French architect
Gabriel-Hippolyte Destailleur.

Built in the style of a French
16th-century chateau, the
manor houses one of the
world's finest collections of
French 18th-century decorative
art as well as Savonnerie
carpets and Sèvres porcelain.

The garden, originally laid out
by French landscape gardener
Elie Lainé, is renowned for its
seasonal displays.

Roald Dahl Museum ❿

81–83 High St, Great Missenden,
Buckinghamshire. **Tel** 01494 892192.
🚆 Great Missenden. ⭕ 10am–5pm
Tue–Fri, 11am–5pm Sat & Sun. 🎫
🎫 👤 www.roalddahlmuseum.org

The magical world of Roald
Dahl's stories comes to life in
this award-winning museum.
A series of biographical
galleries explore the life and
work of the children's writer,
while the Story Centre's
interactive exhibits allow
children to make their own
animation film, record dreams
in a "dream bottle" or try their
hand at creative writing.

The 17th-century Palladian bridge over the Octagon Lake in Stowe Park

Hatfield House, one of the largest Jacobean mansions in the country

ZSL Whipsnade Zoo ⓫

Nr Dunstable, Bedfordshire. **Tel** 0844 2251826. ⇄ Hemel Hempsted or Luton then bus. ◯ daily. ◯ 25 Dec. 🅿 ♿ 🔲 **www**.zsl.org

The rural branch of London Zoo, this was one of the first zoos to minimize the use of cages, confining animals safely but without constriction.

At 240 ha (600 acres), it is Europe's largest conservation park, with more than 2,500 species. You can drive through some areas or go by steam train. Also popular are the adventure playground, the Cheetah Rock exhibit and the sea lions' underwater display.

Knebworth House ⓬

Knebworth, Hertfordshire. **Tel** 01438 812661. ⇄ Stevenage then taxi. ◯ Sat, Sun; two weeks at Easter: daily; Jul–Aug: daily. 🅿 📷 ♿ limited. 🎫 🔲 **www**.knebworthhouse.com

A notable Tudor mansion, with a beautiful Jacobean banqueting hall, Knebworth was overlain with a 19th-century Victorian Gothic exterior by Lord Lytton, the head of the family. His eldest son, the 1st Earl of Lytton, was Viceroy of India, and exhibits illustrate the Delhi Durbar of 1877, when Queen Victoria became Empress of India.

A visit includes the house, gardens, park, and a dinosaur trail for children.

Hatfield House ⓭

Hatfield, Hertfordshire. **Tel** 01707 287010. ⇄ Hatfield. ◯ Easter–Sep: Wed–Sun & public hols. 🅿 📷 ♿ 🍴 **www**.hatfield-house.co.uk

One of England's finest Jacobean houses, Hatfield House was built between 1607 and 1611 for the powerful statesman Robert Cecil.

Its chief historical interest, though, lies in the surviving wing of the original Tudor Hatfield Palace, where Queen Elizabeth I (see pp50–51) spent much of her childhood. She held her first Council of State here when she was crowned in 1558. The palace was partly demolished in 1607 to make way for the new house, which contains mementoes of her life, including the *Rainbow* portrait painted around 1600 by Isaac Oliver. Visitors can attend medieval banquets in the old palace's Great Hall.

Originally laid out by Robert Cecil with help from John Tradescant, the gardens have been restored to reflect these Jacobean origins.

FAMOUS PURITANS

Three major figures connected with the 17th-century Puritan movement are celebrated in the Thames area. John Bunyan (1628–88), who wrote the allegorical tale *The Pilgrim's Progress*, was born at Elstow, near Bedford. A passionate Puritan orator, he was jailed for his beliefs for 17 years. The Bunyan Museum in Bedford is a former site of Puritan worship. William Penn (1644–1718), founder of Pennsylvania in the USA, lived, worshipped and is buried at Jordans, near Beaconsfield. A bit further north at Chalfont St Giles is the cottage where the poet John Milton (1608–74) stayed to escape London's plague. There he completed his greatest work, *Paradise Lost*. The house is now a museum based on his life and works.

18th-century engraving of John Bunyan

William Penn, founder of Pennsylvania

John Milton painted by Pieter van der Plas

St Albans ⑭

Today a thriving market town and a base for London commuters, St Albans was for centuries at the heart of some of the most stirring events in English history. A regional capital of ancient Britain, it became a major Roman settlement and then a key ecclesiastical centre – so important that during the Wars of the Roses (see p49), two battles were fought for it. In 1455 the Yorkists drove King Henry VI from the town and six years later the Lancastrians retook it.

The martyr
St Alban

Exploring St Albans

Part of the appeal of this ancient and fascinating town, little more than an hour's drive from London, is that its 2,000-year history can be traced vividly by visiting a few sites within easy walking distance of one another. There is a large car park within the walls of the Roman city of Verulamium, between the museum and St Michael's Church and across the road from the excavated theatre. From there it is a pleasant lakeside walk across the park, passing more Roman sites, Ye Olde Fighting Cocks inn, the massive cathedral and the historic High Street. Marking the centre of the town, the High Street is lined with several Tudor buildings and a clock tower dating from 1412, from which the curfew bell used to ring at 4am in the morning and 8:30pm at night.

⋔ Verulamium

Just outside the city centre are the walls of Verulamium, one of the first British cities the Romans established after their invasion of Britain in AD 43. Boadicea (see p195) razed it to the ground during her unsuccessful rebellion against the Romans in AD 62, but its position on Watling Street, an important trading route, meant that it was quickly rebuilt on an even larger scale and the city flourished until 410.

⛁ Verulamium Museum

St Michael's St. *Tel 01727 751814.*
◯ *daily.* ● *25 Dec–2 Jan.* 🖼
& 🖥 www.stalbansmuseum.
org.uk

This excellent museum tells the story of the city, but its main attraction is its splendid collection of well-preserved Roman artefacts, notably some breathtaking mosaic floors, including one depicting the head of a sea god, and another of a scallop shell. Other finds included burial urns and lead coffins.

On the basis of excavated plaster fragments, a Roman room has been painstakingly recreated, its walls painted in startlingly bright colours and geometric patterns.

Between here and St Albans Cathedral are a bath house with a mosaic, remnants of the ancient city wall and one of the original gates.

A scallop shell, one of the mosaic floors at the Verulamium Museum

♨ Ye Olde Fighting Cocks

Abbey Mill Lane. *Tel 01727 869152.*
◯ *daily.*

Believed to be England's oldest surviving pub, Ye Olde Fighting Cocks is certainly, with its

One of the oldest surviving pubs in England

octagonal shape, one of the most unusual. It originated as the medieval dovecote of the old abbey and moved here after the Dissolution (see p50).

♫ Roman Theatre

Bluehouse Hill. *Tel 01727 835035.*
◯ *daily.* ● *1 Jan, 25, 26 Dec.* 🖼
🖥 www.romantheatre.co.uk

Just across the road from the museum are the foundations of the open-air theatre, first built around AD 140 but enlarged several times. It is one of only six known to have been built in Roman Britain. Alongside it are traces of a row of Roman shops and a house, from which many of the museum's treasures – such as a bronze statuette of Venus – were excavated in the 1930s.

⛪ St Michael's Church

St Michael's. *Tel 01727 835037.*
◯ *Apr–Sep: phone for details.* &

This church was first founded during the Saxon reign and is built partly with bricks taken from Verulamium, which by then was in decline. Numerous additions have been made since then, including a truly splendid Jacobean pulpit.

The church contains an early 17th-century monument to the statesman and writer Sir Francis Bacon; his father owned nearby Gorhambury, a large Tudor house, now in ruins.

🔒 **St Albans Cathedral**

Sumpter Yard. *Tel* 01727 860780.
☐ daily. & ✎ 11:30am & 2:30pm.
www.stalbanscathedral.org.uk
This outstanding example
of medieval architecture has
some classic features such as
the 13th- and 14th-century wall
paintings on the Norman piers.

It was begun in 793, when
King Offa of Mercia founded
the abbey in honour of St
Alban, Britain's first Christian
martyr, put to death by the
Romans in the third century
for sheltering a priest. The

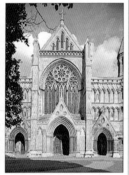

**The imposing west side of
St Albans Cathedral**

oldest parts, which still stand,
were first built in 1077 and
are easily recognizable as
Norman by the round-headed
arches and windows. They
form part of the 84 m (276 ft)
nave – the longest in England.

The pointed arches further
east are Early English (13th
century), while the decorated
work of the 14th century was
added when some of the
Norman arches collapsed.

East of the crossing is
what remains of St Alban's
shrine – a marble pedestal
made up of more than 2,000
tiny fragments. Next to it is the
tomb of Humphrey, Duke of
Gloucester *(see p227)*.

It was here at the cathedral
that the English barons drafted
the *Magna Carta* document
(see p48), which King John
was then forced to sign.

The splendour of the Gardens of the Rose in June

Gardens of the Rose 🅗

Chiswell Green, Hertfordshire. *Tel*
01727 850461. ⊟ St Albans then
bus. ☐ summer: daily, but always
call ahead. 🔵 sometimes Mon, Tue.
🎫 🖼 & 🛒 www.rnrs.org

The 5 ha (12 acre) garden
of the Royal National Rose
Society, with over 30,000
plants and 1,700 varieties, is
at its peak in late June. The
gardens trace the history of
the flower as far back as the
white rose of York, the red
rose of Lancaster *(see p49)*
and the Rosa Mundi – named
by Henry II for his mistress
Fair Rosamond after she was
poisoned by Queen Eleanor
in 1177. In 2005–7 the gardens
were extensively redeveloped
by leading garden designer
Michael Balston.

Warner Bros. Studio Tour – The Making of Harry Potter 🅖

Leavesden, Hertfordshire. *Tel* 08450
840900. ⊟ Watford Junction then
shuttle bus. ☐ daily. 🔵 25 & 26
Dec. 🎫 🖼 & 🍴

Visitors to the Warner Bros.
studio can see original scenery, costumes and props from
all eight Harry Potter movies.
Among the sets are the iconic
Great Hall and Diagon Alley.
The largely self-guided tour
offers glimpses into the
off-camera world of the film-
makers, including how anima-
tronics and green-screen
effects brought to life the monsters and marvels of Harry's
world. Children can even ride
broomsticks here. Tickets
must be booked in advance.

GEORGE BERNARD SHAW

Although a controversial playwright and known
as a mischievous character, the Irish-born
George Bernard Shaw (1856–1950) was a man
of settled habits. He lived near St Albans in a
house at Ayot St Lawrence, now called Shaw's
Corner, for the last 44 years of his life,
working until his last weeks in a
summer-house at the bottom
of his large garden. His plays,
combining wit with a powerful
political and social message, still
seem fresh today. One of the most
enduring is *Pygmalion* (1913),
on which the musical *My Fair
Lady* is based. The house and
garden are now a museum
of his life and works.

Touring the Thames ⑰

The Thames between Pangbourne and Eton is leafy and romantic and best seen by boat. But if time is short, the road keeps close to its bank for much of the way. Swans glide gracefully below ancient bridges, voles dive into the water for cover, and elegant herons stand impassive at the river's edge. Huge beech trees overhang the banks which are lined with fine houses, their gardens sloping to the water. The tranquil scene has inspired painters and writers through the ages as well as operating, until recently, as an important transport link.

Hambledon Mill ⑥
The white weather-boarded mill, which was operational until 1955, is one of the largest on the Thames as well as one of the oldest in origin. There are traces of the original 16th-century mill.

Beale Park ①
The philanthropist Gilbert Beale (1868–1967) created a 10 ha (25 acre) park to preserve this beautiful stretch of river intact and breed endangered birds like owls, ornamental water fowl, pheasants and peacocks.

Henley ⑤
This lovely old river town boasts houses and churches dating from the 15th and 16th centuries and an important regatta, first held in 1829 (*see p66*).

Pangbourne ②
Kenneth Grahame (1859–1932), author of *The Wind in the Willows*, lived here. Pangbourne was used as the setting by artists Ernest Shepard in 1908 and Arthur Rackham in 1951 to illustrate the book.

Sonning Bridge ④
The 18th-century bridge is made up of 11 brick arches of varying width.

TIPS FOR DRIVERS

Tour length: 50 miles (75 km).
Stopping-off points: The picturesque town of Henley has a large number of riverside pubs which will make good stops for lunch. If you are boating you can often moor your boat alongside the river bank. (See also pp684–5.)

Whitchurch Mill ③
This charming village, linked to Pangbourne by a Victorian toll bridge, has a picturesque church and one of the many disused watermills that once harnessed the power of this stretch of river.

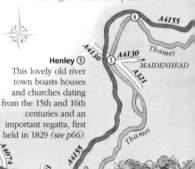

Cookham ⑦

This is famous as the home of Stanley Spencer (1891–1959), one of Britain's leading 20th-century artists. The former Methodist chapel, where Spencer worshipped as a child, has been converted into a gallery that contains some of his paintings and equipment. This work, entitled *Swan Upping* (1914–19), recalls a Thames custom.

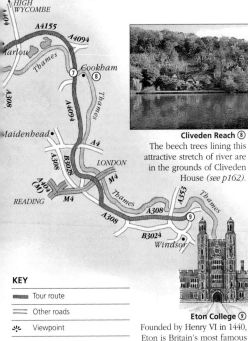

Cliveden Reach ⑧

The beech trees lining this attractive stretch of river are in the grounds of Cliveden House *(see p162)*.

KEY

▬▬▬	Tour route
═══	Other roads
☆	Viewpoint

0 kilometres   10

0 miles   5

Eton College ⑨

Founded by Henry VI in 1440, Eton is Britain's most famous public school. It has a superb Perpendicular chapel (1441) with a series of English wall paintings (1479–88).

BOATING TOURS

In summer, scheduled river services run between Henley, Windsor, Runnymede and Marlow. Several companies operate from towns along the route. You can hire boats by the hour or the day or, for a longer tour, you can rent cabin cruisers and sleep on board *(see also p689)*. Ring Salter Bros on 01753 865 832 for more information.

Salter Bros hire boats, moored at Henley

Windsor ⑱

Berkshire. 🏠 *30,000* 🚆
ℹ️ *Thames St (01753 743900).*
www.windsor.gov.uk

The town of Windsor is dwarfed by the enormous **castle** *(see pp236–7)* on the hill above – in fact its original purpose was to serve the castle's needs. The town is full of quaint Georgian shops, houses and inns. The most prominent building on the High Street is the **Guildhall** completed by Wren *(see p114)* in 1689, where Prince Charles and Camilla Parker-Bowles were married in 2005. **Eton College**, the most prestigious school in Britain, lies just a short walk away.

The huge 1,940-ha (4,800-acre) **Windsor Great Park** stretches from the castle three miles (5 km) to Snow Hill, where there is a statue of George III.

Environs: Four miles (7 km) to the southeast is the level grassy meadow, **Runnymede**. This is one of England's most historic sites, where in 1215 King John was forced by his rebellious barons to sign the *Magna Carta (see p48)*, thereby limiting his royal powers. The dainty memorial pavilion at the top of the meadow was erected in 1957.

🏛 **Eton College**
Tel 01753 671177. 🕐 mid-Mar–Oct: by guided tour only. Always call ahead. **www**.etoncollege.com

King John signing the *Magna Carta*, Runnymede

Windsor Castle

Henry II rebuilt the castle

The oldest continuously inhabited royal residence in Britain, the castle, originally made of wood, was built by William the Conqueror in around 1080 to guard the western approaches to London. He chose the site as it was on high ground and just a day's journey from his base in the Tower of London. Successive monarchs have made alterations that render it a remarkable monument to royalty's changing tastes. King George V's affection for it was shown when he chose Windsor for his family surname in 1917. The castle is an official residence of the Queen and her family who stay here many weekends.

Albert Memorial Chapel
First built in 1240, it was rebuilt in 1485 and finally converted into a memorial for Prince Albert in 1863.

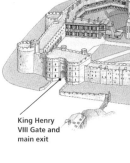

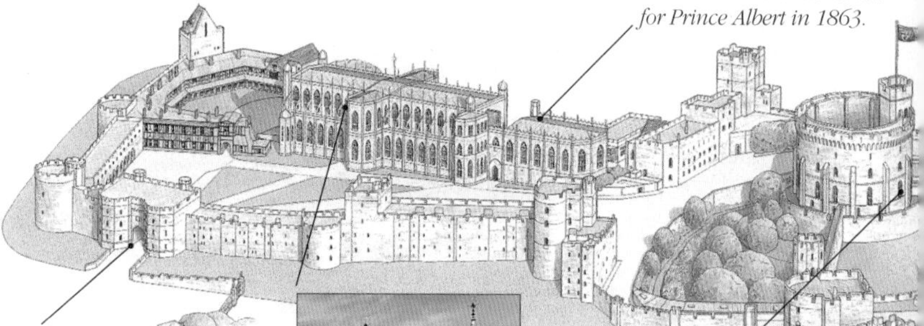

King Henry VIII Gate and main exit

★ St George's Chapel
The architectural highlight of the castle, it was built between 1475 and 1528 and is one of England's outstanding Perpendicular Gothic churches. Ten monarchs are buried here.

The Round Tower was first built in wood by William the Conqueror. In 1170 it was rebuilt in stone by Henry II *(see p48)*. It now houses the Royal Archives and Photographic Collection.

Statue of Charles II

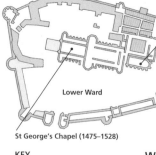

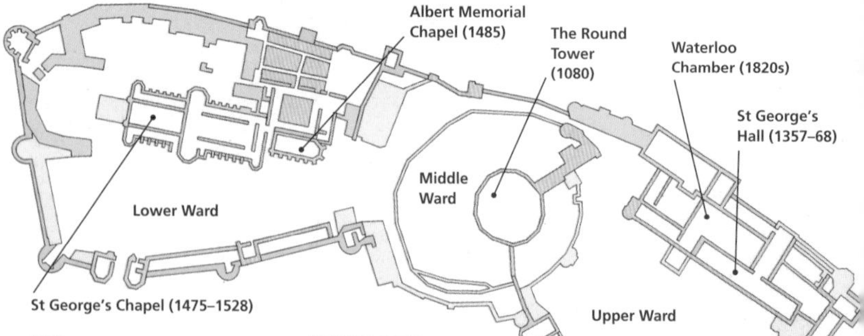

Albert Memorial Chapel (1485)

The Round Tower (1080)

Waterloo Chamber (1820s)

St George's Hall (1357–68)

Middle Ward

Lower Ward

Upper Ward

St George's Chapel (1475–1528)

KEY

- 11th–13th centuries
- 14th century
- 15th–18th centuries
- 19th–20th centuries

WINDSOR CASTLE'S HISTORY
Founded in 1080 as a motte and bailey (see p486), Henry II and Edward III were responsible for the bulk of the work until the castle was remodelled by George IV in 1823.

Drawings Gallery
This chalk etching of Christ by Michelangelo is part of the Royal Collection. Various pieces in the collection are on display here, including works by Holbein and Leonardo da Vinci among others.

VISITORS' CHECKLIST

Castle Hill. ***Tel*** *020 7766 7304.* *9:45am–5:15pm (Nov–Feb: to 4:15pm). (Last adm: 1 hr 15 mins before close.)* *Good Fri, 25 & 26 Dec.* *St Georges Chapel (closed for services).* **www**.royalcollection.org.uk

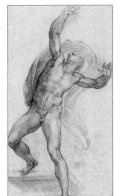

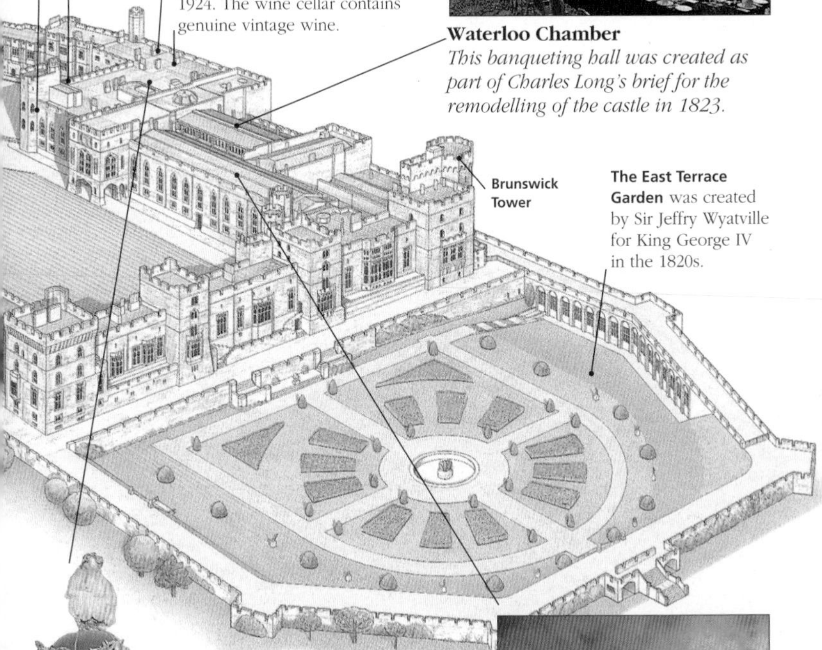

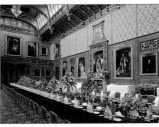

Waterloo Chamber
This banqueting hall was created as part of Charles Long's brief for the remodelling of the castle in 1823.

The Audience Chamber is where the Queen greets her guests.

The Queen's Ballroom

Queen Mary's Dolls' House, designed by Sir Edwin Lutyens, was given to Queen Mary in 1924. The wine cellar contains genuine vintage wine.

Brunswick Tower

The East Terrace Garden was created by Sir Jeffry Wyatville for King George IV in the 1820s.

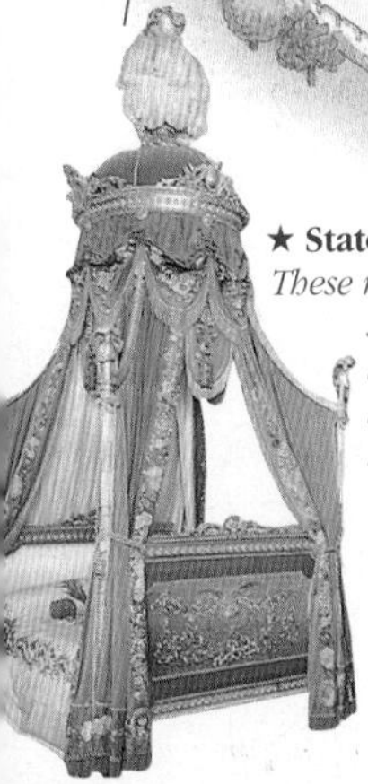

★ State Apartments
These rooms contain many treasures, such as this 18th-century bed in the King's State Bedchamber, hung in its present splendour for the visit in 1855 of Napoleon III.

The Fire of 1992
A devastating blaze began during maintenance work on the State Apartments. St George's Hall was destroyed but has been rebuilt.

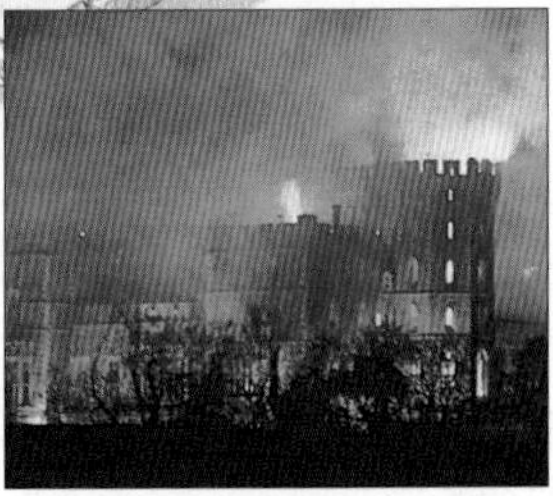

STAR SIGHTS

★ St George's Chapel

★ State Apartments

THE WEST COUNTRY

INTRODUCING THE
WEST COUNTRY 240–245

WESSEX 246–271

DEVON AND CORNWALL 272–295

The West Country at a Glance

The West Country forms a long peninsula bounded by the Atlantic to the north
and the English Channel to the south,
tapering down to Land's End, mainland
Britain's westernmost point. Whether
exploring the great cities and cathedrals,
experiencing the awesome solitude of
the moors and their prehistoric
monuments, or simply enjoying
the miles of coastline and mild
climate, this region has an enduring appeal for holiday-makers.

Wells (see pp252–3) *is a
charming town nestling at the
foot of the Mendip Hills. It is
famous for its exquisite three-
towered cathedral with an
ornate west façade, featuring a
array of statues. Alongside stan
the moated Bishop's Palace and
the 15th-century Vicar's Close.*

Exmoor's (see
pp250–51)
*heather-clad moors
and wooded
valleys, grazed by
wild ponies and
red deer, lead
down to some
of Devon and
Somerset's
most dramatic
cliffs and coves.*

St Ives (see p277) *has a
branch of the Tate Gallery
that shows modern
works by artists
associated with the
area. Patrick Heron's
bold coloured glass
(1993) is on
permanent
display.*

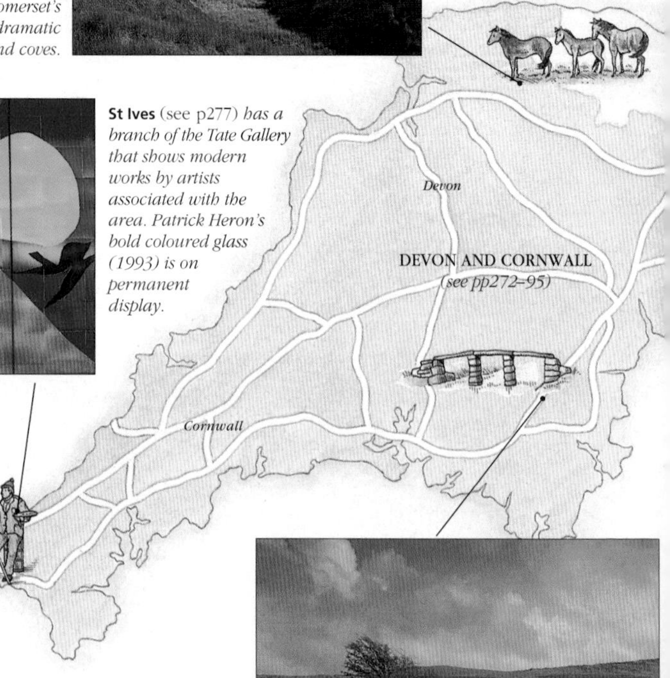

Devon

DEVON AND CORNWALL
(see pp272–95)

Cornwall

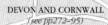

Dartmoor (see pp294–5) *is a wilderness of great natural beauty
covering an area of 365 sq miles
(945 sq km). Stone clapper bridges,
picturesque villages and weathered
granite tors punctuate the landscape.*

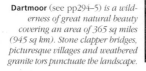

◁ **Stunning views of the Lizard Peninsula**

Bath (see pp258–9) *is named after the Roman baths that stand at the heart of the old city next to the splendid medieval abbey. It is one of Britain's liveliest and most rewarding cities, full of elegant Georgian terraces, built in local honey-coloured limestone by the two John Woods (Elder and Younger).*

Stonehenge (see pp262–3), *the world-famous prehistoric monument, was built in several stages from 3000 BC. Moving and erecting its massive stones was an extraordinary feat for its time. It is likely that this magical stone circle was a place of worship to the sun.*

WESSEX
(see pp246–71)

Wiltshire

Somerset

Dorset

Salisbury's (see pp264–5) *cathedral with its soaring spire was the inspiration for one of John Constable's best-loved paintings. The picturesque Cathedral Close has a number of fine medieval buildings.*

0 kilometres 25

0 miles 25

Stourhead *garden (see pp266–7) was inspired by the paintings of Claude and Poussin. Created in the 18th century, the garden is itself a work of art. Contrived vistas, light and shade and a mixture of landscape and gracious buildings, such as the Neo-Classical Pantheon at its centre, are vital to the overall effect.*

Coastal Wildlife

The long and varied West Country coastline, ranging from the stark, granite cliffs of Land's End to the pebble-strewn stretch of Chesil Bank, is matched with an equally diverse range of wildlife. Beaches are scattered with colourful shells, while rock pools form miniature marine habitats teeming with life. Caves are used by larger creatures, such as grey seals, and cliffs provide nest sites for birds. In the spring and early summer, an astonishing range of plants grow on the foreshore and cliffs which can be seen at their best from the Southwest Coastal Path *(see p36)*. The plants in turn attract numerous moths and butterflies.

Cliff-tops of Land's End with safe ledges for nesting birds

Chesil Bank *is an unusual ridge of pebbles* (see p256) *stretching 18 miles (29 km) along the Dorset coast. The bank was created by storms and the pebbles increase in size from northwest to southeast due to varying strengths of coastal currents. The bank encloses a lagoon called the Fleet, habitat of the Abbotsbury swans, as well as a large number of wildfowl.*

The Painted Lady, *often seen on cliff-top coastal plants, migrates to Brita[in] in the spring.*

High tides wash up driftwood and she[lls]

Cliff-top turf contains many species of wild flowers.

Thrift, *in hummocks of honey-scented flowers, is a familiar sight on cliff ledges in spring.*

Yellowhammers *are to be seen perched on cliff-top bushes.*

Marram grass roots help hold back sand against wind erosion.

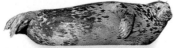

Grey seals *come on land to give birth to their young. They can be spotted on remote beaches.*

A BEACHCOMBER'S GUIDE

The best time to observe the natural life of the s[ea] shore is when the tide begins to roll back, before the scavenging seagulls pick up the stranded cra[b] fish and sandhoppers, and the seaweed dries up. Much plant and marine life can be found in the secure habitat provided by rock pools.

COLLECTING SHELLS

Most of the edible molluscs, such as scallops and cockles, are known as bivalves; others, such as whelks and limpets, are known as gastropods.

Great scallop

Common cockle

Common whelk

Common limpet

Durdle Door *was formed by waves continually eroding the weaker chalk layers of this cliff* (see p270) *in Dorset, leaving the stronger oolite to create a striking arch, known in geology as an eyelet.*

Seaweed, *such as bladder wrack, can resemble coral or lichen when in water.*

Rocks are colonized by clusters of barnacles, mussels and limpets.

Oystercatchers *have a distinctive orange beak. They hunt along the shore, feeding on all kinds of shellfish.*

Starfish *can be aggressive predators on shellfish. The light-sensitive tips of their tentacles help them to "see" the way.*

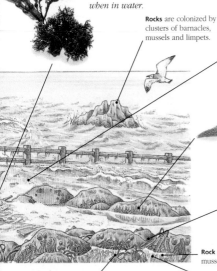

Mussels *are widespread and can be harvested for food.*

Rock pools teem with crabs, mussels, shrimps and plant life.

The Velvet Crab, *often found hiding in seaweed, is covered with fine downy hair all over its shell.*

Grey mullet, *when newly hatched, can often be seen in rock pools.*

West Country Gardens

Gardeners have long been attracted to the West Country. Its mild climate is perfect for growing tender and exotic plants, many of which were brought from Asia in the 19th century. As a result, the region has some of England's finest and most varied gardens, covering the whole sweep of garden styles and history *(see pp26–7)*, from the clipped formality of Elizabethan Montacute, to the colourful and crowded cottage-garden style of East Lambrook Manor.

Lanhydrock's (p284) *clipped yews and low box hedges frame a blaze of colourful annuals.*

Trewithen (p281) *is renowned for its rare camellias, rhododendrons and magnolias, grown from seed collected in Asia. The huge garden is at its most impressive in March and June.*

Cotehele *(p293)* has a lovely lush valley garden.

DEVON AND CORNWALL *(see pp272–*

Trelissick *(p281)* has memorable views over the Fal Estuary through shrub-filled woodland.

Glendurgan *(p281)* is a plant-lover's paradise set in a steep, sheltered valley.

Mount Edgcumbe *(p292)* preserves its 18th-century French, Italian and English gardens.

Trengwainton (p276) *has a fine stream garden, whose banks are crowded with moisture-loving plants, beneath a lush canopy of New Zealand tree ferns.*

Lost Gardens of Heligan

Overbecks *(near Salcombe) enjoys a spectacular site overlooking the Salcombe Estuary. There are secret gardens, terraces and rocky dells.*

CREATIVE GARDENING

Gardens are not simply collections of plants; they rely for much of their appeal on man-made features. Whimsical topiary, ornate architecture, fanciful statuary and mazes help to create an atmosphere of adventure or pure escapism. The many gardens dotted around the West Country offer engaging examples of the vivid imagination of designers.

Mazes *were created in medieval monasteries to teach patience and persistence. This laurel maze at Glendurgan was planted in 1833.*

Fountains *and flamboyant statuary have adorned gardens since Roman times. Such eye-catching embellishments add poetic and Classical touches to the design of formal gardens, such as Mount Edgcumbe.*

Knightshayes Court (p289) *is designed as a series of formal garden "rooms", planted for scent, colour or seasonal effect.*

WESSEX
(see pp246–71)

East Lambrook Manor *(near South Petherton) is a riot of colours, as old-fashioned cottage plants grow without restraint.*

Stourhead *(see pp266–7)* is a magnificent example of 18th-century landscape gardening.

Athelhampton's *(p269)* gardens make use of fountains, statues, pavilions and columnar yews.

Montacute House *(p268)* has pavilions and a centuries-old yew hedge, and is renowned for its collection of old roses.

0 kilometres   25

0 miles   25

Parnham *(near Beaminster), like many West Country gardens, has several parts devoted to different themes. Here conical yews complement the formality of the stone balustrade; elsewhere there are woodland, kitchen, shade and Mediterranean gardens.*

Many garden buildings *are linked by an element of fantasy; while country houses had to conform to everyday practicalities, the design of many smaller buildings gave more scope for imagination. This fanciful Elizabethan pavilion on the forecourt at Montacute House was first and foremost decorative, but sometimes served as a lodging house.*

Topiary *can be traced back to the Greeks. Since that time the sculpting of trees into unusual, often eccentric shapes has been developed over the centuries. The yew topiary of 1920s Knightshayes features a fox being chased by a pack of hounds. The figures form a delightful conceit and come into their own in winter when little else is in leaf.*

WESSEX

WILTSHIRE · SOMERSET · DORSET

The natural and diverse beauty of this predominantly rural region is characterized by rolling hills and charming villages. The area is enriched by a wealth of historical and architectural attractions, ranging from the prehistoric stone circle of Stonehenge to the Roman baths and magnificent Georgian townscape of Bath.

Vast swathes of bare windswept downland give way to lush river valleys, and the contrast between the two may explain the origin in medieval times of the saying, "as different as chalk and cheese". The chalk and limestone hills provided pasture for sheep whose wool was exported to Europe or turned to cloth in mill towns such as Bradford-on-Avon. Meanwhile the rich cow-grazed pastures of the valleys produced the Cheddar cheese for which the region has become famous.

The area's potential for wealth was first exploited by prehistoric chieftains whose large, mysterious monuments, such as Stonehenge and Maiden Castle, are striking features of the landscape. From this same soil sprang King Arthur *(see p285)* and King Alfred the Great, about whom there are numerous fascinating legends. It was King Arthur who is thought to have led British resistance to the Saxon invasion in the 6th century. The Saxons finally emerged the victors and one of them, King Alfred, first united the West Country into one political unit, called the Kingdom of Wessex *(see p47)*.

Wilton House and Lacock Abbey, both former monasteries, were turned into splendid stately homes during the 16th century, due to the Dissolution of the Monasteries *(see pp50–51)*. Today, their previous wealth can be gauged by the size and grandeur of their storage barns.

Matching the many man-made splendours of the region, Wessex is rich in rare wildlife and plants.

Two visitors enjoying the Elizabethan gardens of Montacute House, Somerset

◁ Eighteenth-century cottages lining Gold Hill, Shaftesbury

Exploring Wessex

From the rolling chalk plains around Stonehenge
to the rocky cliffs of Cheddar Gorge and the
heather-covered uplands of Exmoor, Wessex
is a scenically varied microcosm of England.
Reflecting the underlying geology, each part
of Wessex contributes its own distinctive
architecture, with the Neo-Classically inspired
buildings of Bath giving way to the mellow brick
and timber of Salisbury and the thatched flint-
and-chalk cottages of the Dorset landscape.

Bath's abbey and Georgian townscape

KEY

▭▭	Motorway
▭▭	Major road
▬▬	Secondary road
⋯⋯	Minor road
▬	Scenic route
⊶	Main railway
—	Minor railway
▲	Summit

Exmoor National Park

SEE ALSO

- *Where to Stay* pp570–74
- *Where to Eat* pp622–6

SIGHTS AT A GLANCE

Abbotsbury **18**
Avebury **12**
Bath pp258–9 **7**
Bournemouth **25**
Bradford-on-Avon **8**
Bristol pp256–7 **6**
Cheddar Gorge p254 **5**
Corfe Castle **21**
Corsham **9**
Dorchester **20**
Exmoor pp250–51 **1**
Glastonbury **4**
Isle of Purbeck **22**
Lacock **10**
Longleat House **14**
Poole **23**
Salisbury pp264–5 **13**
Shaftesbury **16**
Sherborne **17**
Stonehenge pp262–3 **11**
Stourhead pp266–7 **15**
Taunton **2**
Wells pp252–3 **3**
Weymouth **19**
Wimborne Minster **24**

GETTING AROUND

Bath and Bristol are served by fast mainline trains, other major towns and seaside resorts by regional railways and long-distance bus services. Popular sights such as Stonehenge feature on many tour operators' bus excursions. The rural heart of Wessex, however, has little in the way of public transport and unless you have the time to walk the region's footpaths, you will need a car.

Huge sarsen stones of Stonehenge, dating from around 3000 BC

Exmoor National Park ●

The majestic cliffs plunging into the Bristol Channel along Exmoor's northern coast are interrupted by lush, wooded valleys carrying rivers from the high moorland down to sheltered fishing coves. Inland, wild rolling hills are grazed by sturdy Exmoor ponies, horned sheep and the local wild red deer. Buzzards are also a common sight wheeling over the bracken-clad terrain looking for prey. For walkers, Exmoor offers 1,000 km (620 miles) of wonderful public paths and varied, dramatic scenery, while the tamer perimeters of the National Park offer less energetic attractions – everything from traditional seaside entertainments to picturesque villages and ancient churches.

Curlew

View east along the South West Coast Path

Heddon's Mouth
The River Heddon passes through woodland and meadows down to this attractive point on the coast.

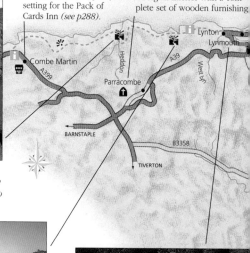

Combe Martin is a pretty setting for the Pack of Cards Inn *(see p288).*

Parracombe Old Church has a Georgian interior with a complete set of wooden furnishing

Combe Martin

Parracombe

Lynton
Lynmouth

BARNSTAPLE

TIVERTON

B3358

The Valley of Rocks
Sandstone outcrops, eroded into fantastical shapes, characterize this natural gorge.

KEY

ℹ	Tourist information
▬▬	A road
▭▭	B road
══	Minor road
- -	Coast path
☀	Viewpoint

Lynmouth
Above the charming fishing village of Lynmouth stands hill-top Lynton. The two villages are connected by a cliff railway (see p288).

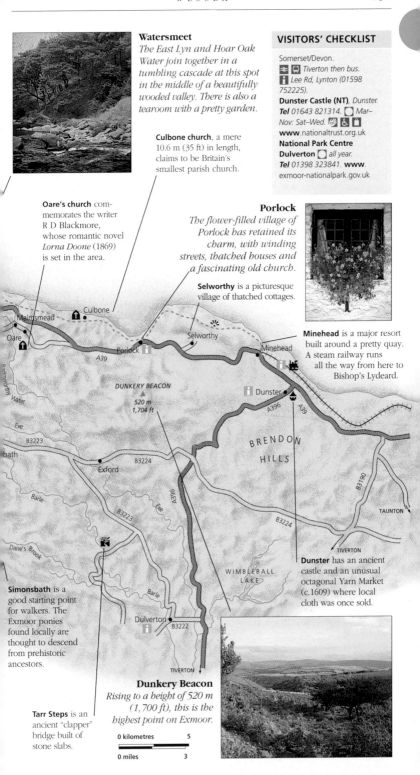

Watersmeet
The East Lyn and Hoar Oak Water join together in a tumbling cascade at this spot in the middle of a beautifully wooded valley. There is also a tearoom with a pretty garden.

Culbone church, a mere 10.6 m (35 ft) in length, claims to be Britain's smallest parish church.

VISITORS' CHECKLIST

Somerset/Devon.
🚆 🚌 *Tiverton then bus.*
ℹ *Lee Rd, Lynton (01598 752225).*
Dunster Castle (NT), *Dunster.*
Tel *01643 821314.* 🕐 *Mar–Nov: Sat–Wed.* 🎫 ♿ 🏛
www.nationaltrust.org.uk
National Park Centre
Dulverton 🕐 *all year.*
Tel *01398 323841.* **www.**
exmoor-nationalpark.gov.uk

Oare's church commemorates the writer R D Blackmore, whose romantic novel *Lorna Doone* (1869) is set in the area.

Porlock
The flower-filled village of Porlock has retained its charm, with winding streets, thatched houses and a fascinating old church.

Selworthy is a picturesque village of thatched cottages.

Minehead is a major resort built around a pretty quay. A steam railway runs all the way from here to Bishop's Lydeard.

Culbone
Malmsmead
Oare
Porlock
A39
Selworthy
Minehead
Dunster
DUNKERY BEACON
▲
520 m
1,704 ft
Exe
B3223
Exford
B3224
BRENDON HILLS
A396
A39
B3190
TAUNTON
Barle
B3223
Eve
A396
B3224
Dane's Brook
TIVERTON
WIMBLEBALL LAKE
Barle
Dulverton
B3222
TIVERTON

Simonsbath is a good starting point for walkers. The Exmoor ponies found locally are thought to descend from prehistoric ancestors.

Dunster has an ancient castle and an unusual octagonal Yarn Market (c.1609) where local cloth was once sold.

Tarr Steps is an ancient "clapper" bridge built of stone slabs.

Dunkery Beacon
Rising to a height of 520 m (1,700 ft), this is the highest point on Exmoor.

0 kilometres   5
0 miles   3

Taunton ❷

Somerset. 🏘 *63,000.* 🚆 🚌 ℹ️
Paul St (01823 336 344). 🛍 *Thu
(farmers').* **www**.*heartofsomerset.
co.uk*

Taunton lies at the heart of a
fertile region famous for its
apples and cider, but it was
the prosperous wool industry
that financed the massive
church of **St Mary Magdalene**
(1488–1514) with its glorious
tower. Taunton's **castle** was
the setting for the notorious
Bloody Assizes of 1685 when
"Hanging" Judge Jeffreys dispensed harsh retribution on
the Duke of Monmouth and
his followers for an uprising
against King James II. The

12th-century building now
houses the **Museum of Somerset**.
A star exhibit is the Roman
mosaic from a villa at Low
Ham, Somerset, showing the
story of Dido and Aeneas.

**Environs: Hestercombe
Garden** is one of Sir Edwin
Lutyens and Gertrude
Jekyll's great masterpieces.

🏛 **Museum of Somerset**
Castle Green.
Tel *01823 255088.* 🕐 *Tue–
Sat.* ♿ *ground floor.* 🚫
www.*somerset.gov.uk/
museums*
🌺 **Hestercombe Garden**
Cheddon Fitzpaine. ***Tel*** *01823
413923.* 🕐 *daily.* 📷 🚫 🚫
♿ **www**.*hestercombe.com*

SOMERSET CIDER

Somerset is one of the few
English counties where
real farmhouse cider,
known as "scrumpy",
is still made using
the traditional
methods. Cider
once formed
part of the farm
labourer's wages
and local folk-
lore has it that
various unsav-
oury additives,
such as iron
nails, were added to give
strength. Cider-making can
be seen at **Sheppy's** farm,
on the A38 near Taunton.

**Scrumpy
cider**

Wells ❸

Somerset. 🏘 *10,000.* 🚌 ℹ️ *Cathedral
Green (01749 671770).* 🛍 *Wed, Sat.*
www.*wellssomerset.com*

Wells is named after St
Andrew's Well, the sacred
spring that bubbles up from
the ground near the 13th-

century **Bishop's
Palace**, residence
of the Bishop of
Bath and Wells. A
tranquil city, Wells
is famous for its
magnificent cathe-
dral which was
begun in the late
1100s. Penniless
Porch, where
beggars once
received alms,
leads from the
bustling market
place to the calm
of the cathedral

**Cathedral
clock
(1386–92)**

close. **Wells & Mendip Museum**
has prehistoric finds from nearby
Wookey Hole and other caves.

Environs: To the northeast of
Wells lies the impressive cave
complex of **Wookey Hole**,
which has an extensive range
of popular amusements.

🏛 **Wells & Mendip Museum**
8 Cathedral Green. ***Tel*** *01749 673477.*
🕐 *daily* 📷 ♿ *limited.* 🚫
www.*wellsmuseum.org.uk*
🔦 **Wookey Hole**
Off A371. ***Tel*** *01749 672243.* 🕐 *daily.*
📷 🎥 🍴 🚫 **www**.*wookey.co.uk*

The West Front
*features 300 fine
medieval statues of
kings, knights and
saints – many of
them life-size.*

**The Vicars'
Close**, built in
the 14th century
for the Vicars'
Choir, is one
of the oldest
complete streets
in Europe.

The Chain Gate (1460)

Cloisters

**Path leading
round the moat**

This graceful flight of steps
*curves up to the octagonal
Chapter House which has delicate vaulting dating from 1306.
The 32 ribs springing from the
central column create a
beautiful palm-tree effect.*

Glastonbury Abbey, left in ruins in 1539 after the Dissolution

Bishops' tombs *circle the chancel. This sumptuous marble tomb, in the south aisle, is that of Bishop Lord Arthur Hervey, who was Bishop of Bath and Wells (1869–94).*

The palace moat *is home to swans which ring a bell by the gatehouse when they want to be fed. Feeding times are at 11am and 4pm.*

The Bishop's Palace (1230–40)

13th-century ruins of the Great Hall

WELLS CATHEDRAL AND THE BISHOP'S PALACE

The Close. **Tel** *01749 988111.*
◻ *daily.* ♿ *limited.*
Bishop's Palace Tel *01749 678691.*
◻ *mid-Feb–mid-Dec: daily.* 📷 ♿

Wells has maintained much of its medieval character with its cathedral, Bishop's Palace and other buildings around the close forming a harmonious group. The most striking features of the cathedral are the west front and the "scissor arches" installed in 1338 to support the tower.

Glastonbury ❹

Somerset. 🏘 *9,000.* 🚆 ℹ️ *Tribunal, High St (01458 832954).* 🛒 *Tue.*
www.glastonburytic.co.uk

Shrouded in Arthurian myth and rich in mystical association, the town of Glastonbury was once one of the most important destinations for pilgrims in England. Now thousands flock here for the annual rock festival *(see p63)* and for the summer solstice on Midsummer's Day (21 June).

Over the years history and legend have become intertwined, and the monks who founded **Glastonbury Abbey**, around 700, found it profitable to encourage the association between Glastonbury and the mythical "Blessed Isle" known as Avalon – alleged to be the last resting place of King Arthur and the Holy Grail *(see p285)*.

The great abbey was left in ruins after the Dissolution of the Monasteries *(see p50)*. Even so, some magnificent relics survive, including parts of the vast Norman abbey church, the unusual Abbot's Kitchen, with its octagonal roof, and the Victorian farmhouse, now the **Somerset Rural Life Museum**.

Growing in the abbey grounds is a cutting from the famous Glastonbury thorn which is said to have miraculously grown from the staff of St Joseph of Arimathea. According to myth, he was sent around AD 60 to convert England to Christianity. The English hawthorn flowers at Christmas as well as in May.

The **Lake Village Museum** has some interesting finds from the Iron Age settlements that once fringed the marshlands around **Glastonbury Tor**. Seen for miles around, the Tor is a hill crowned by the remains of a 14th-century church.

🏛 **Somerset Rural Life Museum**
Chilkwell St. **Tel** *01749 831197.*
◻ *10am–5pm Tue–Sat.* ● *1 Jan, Good Fri, 24–26 Dec.* ♿ *limited.*
📷 *closed winter.* 🅿

🏛 **Lake Village Museum**
Tribunal, High St. **Tel** *01458 832954.*
◻ *Mon–Sat.* ● *25, 26 Dec.*
📷 🅿

Cheddar Gorge ❺

Described as a "deep frightful chasm" by novelist Daniel Defoe in 1724, Cheddar Gorge is a spectacular ravine cut through the Mendip plateau by fast-flowing streams during the interglacial phases of the last Ice Age. Cheddar has given its name to a rich cheese that originates from here and is now produced worldwide. The caves in the gorge provide the perfect environment of constant temperature and high humidity for storing and maturing the cheese.

VISITORS' CHECKLIST

On B3135, Somerset. *from Wells and Weston-super-Mare.* **Cheddar Gorge Cheese Co.** ***Tel*** *01934 742810.* *daily.* **www**.cheddar-gorge cheeseco.co.uk **Cheddar Caves & Gorge** ***Tel*** *01934 742343.* *daily.* *24, 25 Dec.* *entrance to all sites listed below is with a Caves & Gorge Explorer ticket only.* *limited.* **www**.cheddar gorge.co.uk

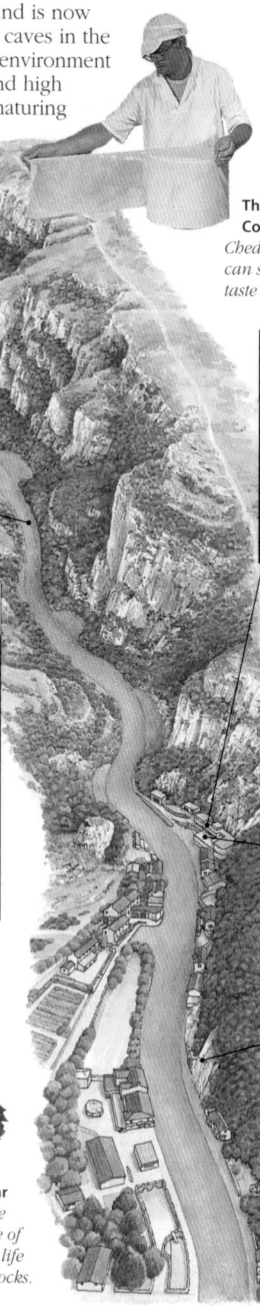

The Cheddar Gorge Cheese Company *is the only working Cheddar dairy in Cheddar. Visitors can see Cheddar being made, and taste and buy cheese in the store.*

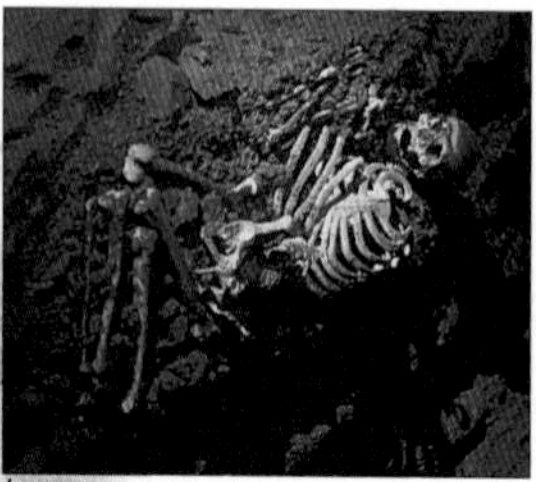

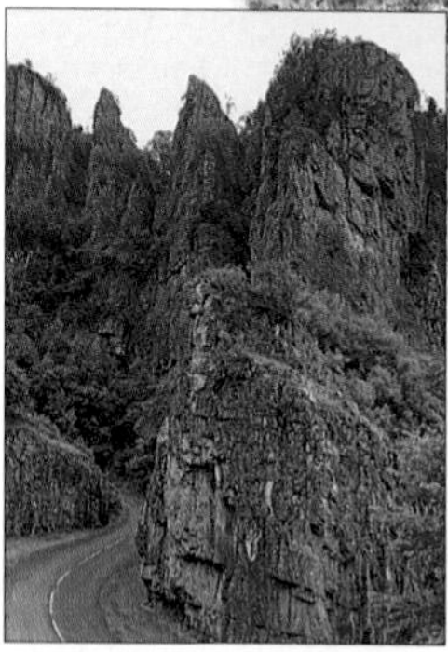

"Cheddar Man", *a 9,000-year-old skeleton, is on display at Cheddar Caves and Gorge. The museum here looks at the pre-historic world of our cannibal ancestors.*

The B3135 road winds round the base of the 3 mile (5 km) gorge.

The gorge *is a narrow, winding ravine with limestone rocks rising almost vertically on either side to a height of 140 m (460 ft).*

A footpath follows the top of the gorge on its southern edge.

Gough's Cave is noted for its cathedral-like proportions.

Cox's Cave contains unusually shaped stalactites and stalagmites.

A flight of 274 steps leads to the top of the gorge.

Lookout Tower has far-reaching views over the area to the south and west.

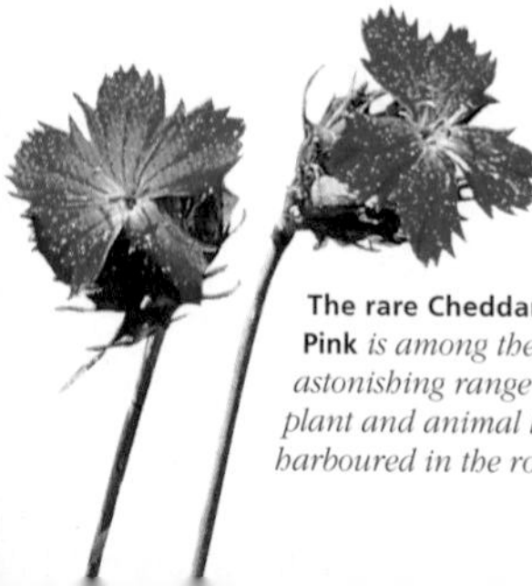

The rare Cheddar Pink *is among the astonishing range of plant and animal life harboured in the rocks.*

Bristol 6

See pp256–7.

Bath 7

See pp258–61.

Bradford-on-Avon 8

Wiltshire. 🚶 11,000. 🚉 ℹ️ *St Margaret St (01225 865797).* 🛒 *Thu.* www.bradfordonavon.co.uk

This lovely Cotswold-stone town is full of flamboyant houses built by wealthy wool and cloth merchants in the 17th and 18th centuries. One fine Georgian example is **Abbey House**, on Church Street. Further along, **St Laurence Church** is a remarkably complete Saxon building founded in 705 *(see p47)*. Converted to a school and cottage in the 12th century,

Typical Cotswold-stone architecture in Bradford-on-Avon

it was rediscovered in the 19th century when a vicar recognized the characteristic cross-shaped roof.

At one end of the medieval **Town Bridge** is a small stone cell, built as a chapel in the 13th century but later used as a lock-up for 17th-century vagrants. A short walk away, near converted mill buildings and a stretch of the Kennet and Avon Canal, is the 14th-century **Tithe Barn** *(see p32)*. There are several teashops in the town and canoe trips down the canal are popular.

🏛 **Tithe Barn**
(EH) Pound Lane. ☐ *daily.* ● *25, 26 Dec.* ♿

Corsham 9

Wiltshire. 🚶 12,000.
ℹ️ *31 High St (01249 714660).*
www.corshamheritage.org.uk

The streets of Corsham are lined with stately Georgian houses in Cotswold stone. **St Bartholomew's Church** has an elegant spire and a lovely carved alabaster tomb (1960) to the late Lady Methuen, whose family founded Methuen publishers. The family acquired **Corsham Court** in 1745 with its picture gallery and a remarkable collection of Flemish, Italian and English paintings, including works by Van Dyck, Lippi and Reynolds. Peacocks wander through the grounds, adding their colour and elegance to the façade of the Elizabethan mansion.

Peacock in grounds, Corsham Court

🏛 **Corsham Court**
off A4. **Tel** 01249 701610. ☐ *mid-Mar–Sep: Tue–Thu, Sat, Sun; Oct–mid-Mar: Sat, Sun (pm).* ● *Dec.* 🎟 ♿

Lacock 10

Wiltshire. 🚶 1,000.

Maintained in its pristine state by the National Trust, the picturesque village of Lacock has provided the backdrop to numerous BBC costume dramas, including *Larkrise to Candleford*. The meandering River Avon forms the boundary to the north side of the churchyard, while humorous stone figures look down from **St Cyriac Church**. Inside the 15th-century church is the splendid Renaissance-style tomb of Sir William Sharington (1495–1553). He acquired **Lacock Abbey** after the Dissolution of the Monasteries *(see p50)*, but it was a later owner, John Ivory Talbot,

who had the buildings remodelled in the Gothic revival style, in vogue in the early 18th century. The abbey is famous for the window (in the south gallery) from which his descendant William Henry Fox Talbot, an early pioneer of photography, took his first picture in 1835. A 16th-century barn at the abbey gates has been converted to the **Fox Talbot Museum**, which has displays on his experiments.

Environs: Designed by Robert Adam *(see pp32–3)* in 1769, **Bowood House** includes the laboratory where Joseph Priestley discovered oxygen in 1774, and a rich collection of sculpture, costumes and paintings. Italianate gardens surround the house while the lake-filled grounds, landscaped by "Capability" Brown *(see p30)*, contain a Doric temple, grotto, cascade and an adventure playground.

🔒 **Lacock Abbey**
(NT) Lacock. **Tel** 01249 730459. ☐ *Feb–Oct: Wed–Mon (pm).* ● *Good Fri.* 🎟 ♿ *limited in house.* www.nationaltrust.org.uk

🏛 **Fox Talbot Museum**
(NT) Lacock. **Tel** 01249 730459. ☐ *daily (Nov–Feb: Sat & Sun only).* ● *Good Fri.* 🎟 ♿

🏛 **Bowood House**
Derry Hill, nr Calne. **Tel** 01249 812102. ☐ *Apr–Oct: daily.* 🎟 ♿ 🍴 ☐ 🔲

William Henry Fox Talbot (1800–77)

Bristol 6

It was in 1497 that John Cabot sailed from Bristol on his historic voyage to North America. The city, at the mouth of the Avon, became the main British port for transatlantic trade, pioneering the era of the ocean-going steam liner with the construction of Brunel's ss *Great Britain*. The city flourished as a major trading centre, growing rich on the distribution of wine, tobacco and, in the 17th century, slaves.

King Brennus, St John's Gate

Because of its docks and aero-engine factories, Bristol was heavily bombed during World War II. In 2008, a multimillion-pound development programme was completed with the opening of Cabot Circus, a vast shopping centre. The old dock area has been brought back to life with bars, cafés, restaurants and art galleries lining the waterside.

Exploring Bristol

The oldest part of the city lies around Broad, King and Corn streets, known as the Old Quarter. The lively St Nicholas covered market, part of which occupies the **Corn Exchange**, was built by John Wood the Elder *(see p258)* in 1743. Outside are the famous Bristol Nails, four bronze 16th–17th-century pedestals which Bristol merchants used as tables when paying for goods – hence the expression "to pay on the nail". **St John's Gate**, at the head of Broad Street, has medieval statues of Bristol's two mythical founders, King Brennus and King Benilus. Between Lewins Mead and Colston Street, **Christmas Steps** is a steep lane lined with specialist shops and cafés. The **Chapel of the Three Kings** at the top was founded in 1504.

A group of buildings around the cobbled King Street include the 17th-century timber-framed **Llandoger Trow** inn. It is here that Daniel Defoe is said to have met Alexander

The Two Sisters (c.1889) by Renoir, City Museum and Art Gallery

Selkirk, whose true-life island exile served as the inspiration for Defoe's novel *Robinson Crusoe* (1719). Just up from here is the **Theatre Royal**, built in 1766, and home to the famous Bristol Old Vic.

Not far away, the renowned gallery the **Arnolfini**, on Narrow Quay, is a showcase for contemporary art, drama, dance and cinema.

On the Harbourside, **At-Bristol** (www.at-bristol. org.uk) combines an exciting, interactive science centre with an aquarium.

Not far from the Harbourside, elegant **Clifton** revels in ornate Regency crescents. The impressive **Clifton Suspension Bridge** by Brunel, completed in 1864, perfectly complements the drama of the steep Avon gorge. **Bristol Zoo Gardens** houses over 400 exotic and endangered species set in stunning gardens.

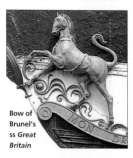

Bow of Brunel's ss Great Britain

Memorial to William Canynge the Younger (1400–74)

🔒 St Mary Redcliffe

Redcliffe Way. **Tel** *0117 9291487.*
⏱ *daily.* ♿ 🎧 *by arrangement.*
💻 **www**.stmaryredcliffe.co.uk

This magnificent 14th-century church was claimed by Queen Elizabeth I to be "the fairest in England". The church owes much to the generosity of William Canynge the Elder and Younger, both famous mayors of Bristol. Inscriptions on the tombs of merchants and sailors tell of lives devoted to trade in Asia and the West Indies. Look out for the Bristol maze in the north aisle.

🏛 Brunel's ss *Great Britain*

Gas Ferry Rd. 📞 *0117 9260680.*
⏱ *daily.* 🚫 *24, 25 Dec.* 🎫 *ticket valid for one year.* ♿ 🎧 *by appt.*
💻 **www**.ssgreatbritain.org

Designed by Isambard Kingdom Brunel, this is the world's first large iron passenger ship. Launched in 1843, she travelled 32 times round the world before being abandoned in the Falkland Islands in 1886. The ship has been fully restored.

🏠 Georgian House

7 Great George St. **Tel** *0117 9211362.*
⏱ *Sat–Wed.* **www**.bristol-city.gov.uk/museums

Life in a wealthy Bristol merchant's house of the 1790s is illustrated by furnishings in the elegant drawing room and the servants' area.

🏛 M-Shed

Princes Wharf, Harbourside. **Tel** *0117 3526600.* ⏱ *Tue–Sun.* **www**. mshed.org

After a massive rebuild, the old Industrial Museum re-opened in 2011 as the M-Shed. The focus is on the individual lives, stories and memories of the city's residents while retaining the best of the original building's industrial heritage. There are also train, boat and crane rides. This project is part of the regeneration of Bristol's Harbourside.

Warehouses overlooking the Floating Harbour

🏛 Bristol Blue Glass Factory and Shop

Brislington. **Tel** *0117 972 0818*.
⬤ *daily.* **www**.bristol-glass.co.uk
The Bristol Blue Glass name is over 350 years old and represents the best tools, techniques and traditions from the past. Every piece of glass is free blown and hand-made, making each one unique and collectable. Glass blowing demonstrations take place at the visitor centre, where there is also a gallery shop.

🏛 Bristol Museum and Art Gallery

Queen's Rd. **Tel** *0117 922 3571*. ⬤
daily. ⬤ *24, 25 Dec.* ♿ *limited.* ▯
🖥 **www**.bristol-city.gov.uk/museums
Varied collections include Egyptology, dinosaur fossils, Roman tableware, Chinese glass and a fine collection of European paintings with works by Renoir and Bellini. Bristol artists include Sir Thomas Lawrence, Francis Danby and the notorious graffiti artist, Banksy.

🛐 Bristol Cathedral

College Green. **Tel** *0117 9264879*.
⬤ *daily.* **Donation.** ♿ *limited.*
www.bristol-cathedral.co.uk
Bristol's cathedral, begun in 1140, took an unusually long time to build. Rapid progress was made between 1298 and 1330, when the inventive choir was rebuilt; the transepts and tower were finished in 1515, and another 350 years passed before the Victorian architect, G E Street, built the nave. Humorous medieval carving abounds – a snail crawling across the stone foliage in the Berkeley Chapel, musical monkeys in the Elder Lady Chapel, and a fine set of wooden misericords in the choir.

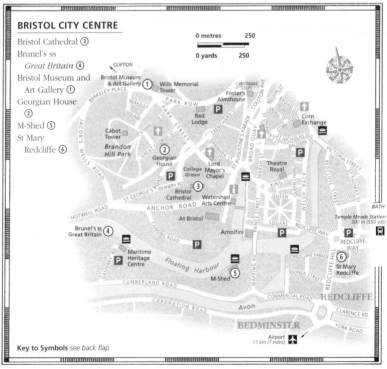

BRISTOL CITY CENTRE

Bristol Cathedral ③
Brunel's ss
   Great Britain ④
Bristol Museum and
   Art Gallery ①
Georgian House
   ②
M-Shed ⑤
St Mary
   Redcliffe ⑥

0 metres 250
0 yards 250

Key to Symbols *see back flap*

Street-by-Street: Bath ❼

Bath owes its magnificent Georgian town-scape to the bubbling pool of water at the heart of the Roman Baths. The Romans transformed Bath into England's first spa resort and it regained fame as a spa town in the 18th century. At this time the two John Woods (Elder and Younger), both architects, designed the city's Palladian-style buildings. Many houses bear plaques recording the numerous famous people who have resided here.

The Circus
This is a daring departure from the typical Georgian square, by John Wood the Elder (1705–54)

No. 1 Royal Crescent

No. 17 is where the 18th-century painter Thomas Gainsborough lived *(see p163).*

Assembly Rooms and Museum of Costume

★ Royal Crescent
Hailed the most majestic street in Britain, this graceful arc of 30 houses (1767–74) is the masterpiece of John Wood the Younger. West of the Royal Crescent, Royal Victoria Park (1830) is the city's largest open space.

Jane Austen *(see p162),* the writer, stayed at No. 13 Queen Square on one of many visits to Bath in her youth.

Milsom Street and New Bond Street contain some of Bath's most elegant shops.

Theatre Royal (1805)

KEY

- – – Suggested route

| 0 metres | 100 |
| 0 yards | 100 |

STAR SIGHTS

★ Royal Crescent

★ Roman Baths

★ Bath Abbey

Pump Rooms
These tearooms once formed the social hub of the 18th-century spa community. They contain this decorative drinking fountain.

THE KING'S SPRING

VISITORS' CHECKLIST

Bath. 85,000. Bristol, 20 miles (32 km) W Bath. Dorchester St. Abbey Chambers, Abbey Church Yard (0906 7112000 – premium rate). daily. International Music Festival: May–Jun. www.visit bath.co.uk

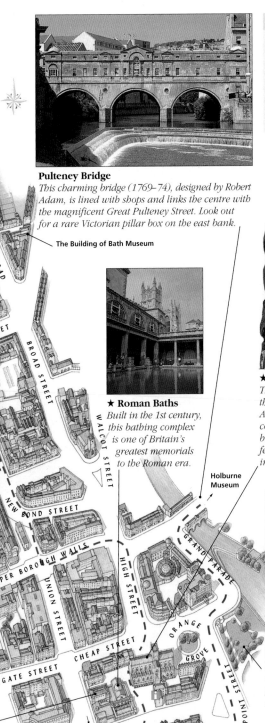

Pulteney Bridge

This charming bridge (1769–74), designed by Robert Adam, is lined with shops and links the centre with the magnificent Great Pulteney Street. Look out for a rare Victorian pillar box on the east bank.

The Building of Bath Museum

★ Bath Abbey

The splendid abbey stands at the heart of the old city in the Abbey Church Yard, a paved courtyard enlivened by buskers. Its unique façade features stone angels climbing Jacob's Ladder to heaven.

★ Roman Baths

Built in the 1st century, this bathing complex is one of Britain's greatest memorials to the Roman era.

Holburne Museum

Parade Gardens

Courting couples came to this pretty riverside park for secret liaisons in the 18th century.

Rail & coach stations

Sally Lunn's House (1482) is one of Bath's oldest houses.

Exploring Bath

The beautiful and compact city of Bath is set among the rolling green hills of the Avon valley, and wherever you walk you will enjoy spendid views of the surrounding countryside. The traffic-free heart of this lively city is full of street musicians, museums, cafés and enticing shops, while the elegant honey-coloured Georgian houses, so characteristic of Bath, form an elegant backdrop to city life.

Piazza cellist

Bath Abbey, at the heart of the old city, begun in 1499

🏠 Bath Abbey

13 Kingston Bldgs, Abbey Churchyard. **Tel** 01225 422462. ◯ daily. ● during services. **Donation.** 🚹 🅿
www.bathabbey.org

This splendid abbey was supposedly designed by divine agency. According to legend, God dictated the form of the church to Bishop Oliver King in a dream; this story has been immortalized in the wonderfully eccentric carvings on the west front. The bishop began work in 1499, rebuilding a church that had been founded in the 8th century. Memorials cover the walls and the varied Georgian inscriptions make fascinating reading. The spacious interior is remarkable for the fan vaulting of the nave, an addition made by Sir George Gilbert Scott in 1874.

🏛 National Trust Assembly Rooms and Fashion Museum

Bennett St. **Tel** 01225 477173. ◯ daily. ● 25, 26 Dec. 🅿 for Fashion Museum. 🚹 🅿 ⚓
www.fashionmuseum.co.uk

The Assembly Rooms were built by Wood the Younger in 1769, as a meeting place for the fashionable elite and as an elegant backdrop for many glittering balls. Jane Austen's novel *Northanger Abbey* (1818) describes the atmosphere of gossip and flirtation here. In the basements is a collection of costumes in period settings. The display illustrates fashions from the 16th century to the present day.

🏛 No. 1 Royal Crescent

Royal Crescent. **Tel** 01225 428 126. ◯ Tue–Sun & public hols. ● Jan, Good Fri, Dec. 🅿 🚹
www.bath-preservation-trust.org.uk

This museum lets you inside the first house of this beautiful Georgian crescent, giving a glimpse of what life was like for 18th-century aristocrats, such as the Duke of York, who probably lived here. It is furnished down to such details as the dog-powered spit used to roast meat in front of the fire.

🏛 Holburne Museum of Art

Great Pulteney St. **Tel** 01225 388588. ◯ daily. 🅿 🚹 limited. 🅿 🚹
www.bath.ac.uk/holburne

This historic building is named after William Holburne of Menstrie (1793–1874), whose collections form the nucleus of the display of fine and decorative arts, including superb silver and porcelain. Paintings can be seen by British artists such as Gainsborough and Stubbs.

ROMAN BATHS

Entrance in Abbey Churchyard. 🎫 01225 477785. ◯ daily. ● 25, 26 Dec. 🅿 🚹 limited.
www.romanbaths.co.uk

According to legend, Bath owes its origin to the Celtic King Bladud who discovered the curative properties of its natural hot springs in 860 BC. Cast out from his kingdom as a leper, Bladud cured himself by imitating his swine and rolling in the hot mud at Bath.

In the first century, the Romans built baths around the spring, and a temple dedicated to the goddess Sulis Minerva, who combined the attributes of the Celt water goddess Sulis and the Roman goddess Minerva. Among the Roman relics is a bronze head of the goddess.

Medieval monks of Bath Abbey also exploited the springs' properties, but it was when Queen Anne visited in 1702–3 that Bath reached its zenith as a fashionable watering place.

Gilded bronze head of Sulis Minerva

🏛 Thermae Bath Spa

Hot Bath St. **Tel** 0844 888 0844.
🕐 9am–10pm daily (last adm:
7:30pm). 🕐 1 Jan, 25 & 26 Dec.
🈲 under 16s not permitted. ♿ ▯
🌐 www.thermaebathspa.com

Tourists have bathed in the
warm, mineral-rich waters of
the spa town of Bath since
Roman times and the opening
of the Thermae Bath Spa, in
2006, has once again made
Bath a popular day-spa
destination. There are three
pools fed by natural thermal
waters: the New
Royal Bath has two
baths including an
open-air rooftop pool
with superb views over
the city; across the road, the
oval Cross Bath is a more
intimate open-air bath, ideal
for shorter sessions. The spa
also offers scented steam
rooms, footbaths and an array
of treatments, bookable in
advance. The signature therapy
is watsu, a water-based version
of the shiatsu massage.

🏛 American Museum

Claverton Manor, Claverton
Down. **Tel** 01225 460503.
🕐 Mar–Oct: Tue–Sun (daily
in Aug). 🈲 ♿ limited. ▯ 🛈
www.americanmuseum.org

Founded in 1961, this was the
first American museum to be
established in this country.
The rooms in the 1820 manor
house are decorated in many
styles, from the rudimentary
dwellings
of the first
settlers to
the opulent
style of
19th-
century
homes. The
museum has
special sections
on Shaker furniture,
quilts and Native
American art, and a
replica of George
Washington's
Mount Ver-
non garden
of 1785.

**A 19th-century
American Indian
weathervane**

RICHARD "BEAU" NASH (1674–1762)

Elected in 1704 as Master
of Ceremonies, "Beau"
Nash played a crucial role
in transforming Bath into
the fashionable centre of
Georgian society. During
his long career, he devised
a never-ending round of
games, balls and entertainment (including gambling)
that kept the idle rich
amused and ensured a
constant flow of visitors.

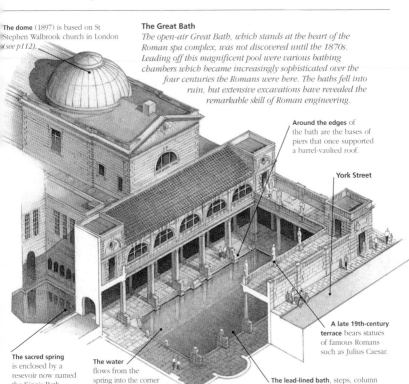

The dome (1897) is based on St
Stephen Walbrook church in London
(see p112).

The Great Bath

*The open-air Great Bath, which stands at the heart of the
Roman spa complex, was not discovered until the 1870s.
Leading off this magnificent pool were various bathing
chambers which became increasingly sophisticated over the
four centuries the Romans were here. The baths fell into
ruin, but extensive excavations have revealed the
remarkable skill of Roman engineering.*

Around the edges of
the bath are the bases of
piers that once supported
a barrel-vaulted roof.

York Street

**A late 19th-century
terrace** bears statues
of famous Romans
such as Julius Caesar.

The sacred spring
is enclosed by a
reservoir now named
the King's Bath.

The water
flows from the
spring into the corner
of the bath at a constant
temperature of 46° C (115° F).

The lead-lined bath, steps, column
bases and paving stones around the
edge all date from Roman times.

Stonehenge ⑪

Built in several stages from about 3000 BC, Stonehenge is Europe's most famous prehistoric monument. We can only guess at the rituals that took place here, but the alignment of the stones leaves little doubt that the circle is connected with the sun and the passing of the seasons, and that its builders possessed a sophisticated understanding of both arithmetic and astronomy.

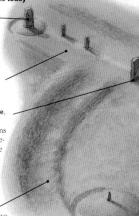

Stonehenge as it is today

Despite popular belief, the circle was not built by the Druids, an Iron Age priestly cult that flourished in Britain from around 250 BC – more than 1,000 years after Stonehenge was abandoned.

Finds from a burial mound near Stonehenge (Devizes Museum)

The Heel Stone casts a long shadow straight to the heart of the circle on Midsummer's day.

The Avenue forms a ceremonial approach to the site.

The Slaughter Stone, named by 17th-century antiquarians who believed Stonehenge to be a place of human sacrifice, was in fact one of a pair marking the entrance to the interiors.

The Outer Bank, dug around 3000 BC, is the oldest known phase of Stonehenge.

BUILDING OF STONEHENGE

Stonehenge's monumental scale is more impressive given that the only tools available were made of stone, wood and bone. The labour involved in quarrying, transporting and erecting the huge stones was such that its builders must have been able to command immense resources and vast numbers of people. One method is explained below.

RECONSTRUCTION OF STONEHENGE

This illustration shows what Stonehenge probably looked like about 4,000 years ago.

A sarsen stone *was moved on rollers and levered into a pit.*

With levers *supported by timber packing, it was gradually raised.*

The stone *was then pulled upright by about 200 men hauling on ropes.*

The pit *round the ba was packed tightly u stones and chalk.*

WILTSHIRE'S OTHER PREHISTORIC SITES

The open countryside of the Salisbury Plain made this area an important centre of prehistoric settlement, and today it is covered in many ancient remains. Ringing the horizon around Stonehenge are scores of circular barrows, or burial mounds, where members of the ruling class were honoured with burial close to the temple site. Ceremonial bronze weapons and other finds excavated around Stonehenge and the other local prehistoric sites can be seen in the museum at Salisbury *(see pp264–5)* and the main museum at Devizes.

Silbury Hill (NT) is Europe's largest prehistoric earthwork,

Silbury Hill

but despite extensive excavations its purpose remains a mystery. Built out of chalk blocks around 2750 BC, the hill covers 2 ha (5 acres) and rises to a height of 40 m (131 ft). Nearby **West Kennet Long Barrow** (NT) is the biggest

The Sarsen Circle was erected around 2500 BC and is capped by lintel stones held in place by mortise and tenon joints.

The Bluestone Circle was built around 2500 BC out of some 80 slabs quarried in the Preseli Hills in south Wales.

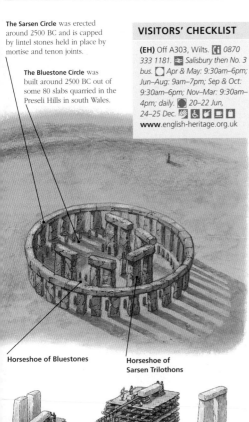

Horseshoe of Bluestones

Horseshoe of Sarsen Trilothons

Alternate ends of the lintel were levered up.

The weight of the lintel was supported by a timber platform.

The lintel *was then levered sideways on to the uprights.*

Sarsen stone forming part of the Avebury Stone Circle

Avebury ⑫

(EH/NT) Wiltshire. 🕿 500. ⛕ Swindon then bus. ℹ Green St (01672 539250). ◻ daily. 🚻 📷
www.nationaltrust.org.uk

Built around 2500 BC, the **Avebury Stone Circle** surrounds the village of Avebury and was probably once some form of religious centre. Although the stones used are smaller than those at Stonehenge, the circle itself is larger. Superstitious villagers smashed many of the stones in the 18th century, believing the circle to have been a place of pagan sacrifice.

The original form of the circle is best appreciated by a visit to the excellent **Alexander Keiller Museum** to the west of the site, which illustrates in detail the construction of the circle. There is also a fascinating exhibition called "6,000 Years of Mystery", which explains the changing landscape of Avebury.

St James's Church has a Norman font carved with sea monsters, and a rare 15th-century choir screen.

Environs: A few minutes' drive east, **Marlborough** is an attractive town with a long and broad High Street lined with colonnaded Georgian shops.

🏛 **Alexander Keiller Museum**
(NT) Off High St. *Tel* 01672 538015. ◻ daily. ● 24, 25 Dec. 🅿♿🍴 📷 www.nationaltrust.org.uk

chambered tomb in England, with numerous stone-lined "rooms" and a monumental entrance. Built as a communal cemetery around 3250 BC, it was in use for several centuries – old bodies were taken away to make room for newcomers.

Old Sarum is set within the massive ramparts of a 1st-century Romano-British hill fort. The Norman founders of Old Sarum built their own motte and bailey castle inside this ready-made fortification, and the remains of this survive along with the foundations of the huge cathedral of 1075. Above ground nothing remains of the town that once sat within the ramparts. The town's occupants moved to the fertile river valley site that became Salisbury during the early 12th century *(see pp264–5).*

🏰 **Old Sarum**
(EH) Castle Rd. *Tel* 01722 335398. ◻ daily. ● 1 Jan, 24–26 Dec. 🅿♿

The chambered tomb of West Kennet Long Barrow (c.3250 BC)

Salisbury ⑬

The "new" city of Salisbury was founded in 1220, when the old hill-top settlement of Old Sarum *(see p263)* was abandoned, being too arid and windswept, in favour of a new site among the lush water meadows where the rivers Avon, Nadder and Bourne meet. Locally sourced Purbeck marble and Chilmark stone were used for the construction of a new cathedral which was built mostly in the early 13th-century, over the remarkably short space of 38 years. Its magnificent landmark spire – the tallest in England – was an inspired afterthought added in 1280–1310.

The early 14th-century house of John A'Port, Queen's Street

Bishop's Walk and a sculpture by Elisabeth Frink (1930–93), Cathedral Close

Exploring Salisbury

The spacious and tranquil **Close**, with its schools, alms-houses and clergy housing, makes a fine setting for Salisbury's cathedral. Among the numerous elegant buildings here are the **Matrons' College**, built in 1682 as a home for widows and unmarried daughters of the clergy, and 13th-century **Malmesbury House** with its splendid early Georgian façade (1719), fronted by lovely wrought-iron gates. Other buildings of interest include the 13th-century **Medieval Hall**, the 13th-century **Wardrobe**, now a regimental museum, and the **Cathedral School**, housed in the 13th-century Bishop's Palace and famous for the quality of its choristers.

Beyond the walls of the Cathedral Close, Salisbury

developed its chessboard layout, with areas devoted to different trades, perpetuated in street names such as Fish Row and Butcher Row. Leaving the Close through **High Street Gate**, you reach the busy High Street leading to the 13th-century **Church of St Thomas**, which has a lovely carved timber roof (1450), and a late 15th-century Doom painting, showing Christ seated in judgement and demons seizing the damned. Nearby in Silver Street, **Poultry Cross** was built in the 14th century as a covered poultry market. An intricate network of alleys

fans out from this point with a number of fine timber-framed houses. In the large bustling **Market Place** the **Guildhall** is an unusual cream stone building from 1787–95, used for civic functions. More attractive are the brick and tile-hung houses on the north side of the square, many with Georgian façades concealing medieval houses.

The Cloisters are the largest in England. They were added between 1263 and 1284 in the Decorated style.

The Chapter House has an original of the *Magna Carta*. Its walls have stone friezes of the Old Testament.

The Trinity Chapel contains the grave of St Osmund who was bishop of Old Sarum from 1078–1099.

Choir stalls

Bishop Audley's Chantry, a magnificent 16th-century monument to the bishop, is one of several small chapels clustered round the altar.

Street signs reflecting trades of 13th-century Salisbury

Mompesson House

(NT) The Close. **Tel** 01722 420980. Mar–Oct: Sat–Wed. limited. www.nationaltrust.org.uk

Built by a wealthy Wiltshire family in 1701, the handsomely furnished rooms of this house give an indication of life for the Close's inhabitants in the 18th century. The delightful garden, bounded by the north wall of the Close, has fine herbaceous borders.

Salisbury and South Wiltshire Museum

The Close. **Tel** 01722 332151. Mon–Sat (Jun–Sep: Sun pm). www.salisburymuseum.org.uk

In the medieval King's House, this museum has displays on early man, Stonehenge and nearby Old Sarum (see p263).

Environs: The town of Wilton is renowned for its carpet industry, founded by the 8th Earl of Pembroke using French Huguenot refugee weavers. The town's ornate **church** (1844) is a brilliant example of Neo-Romanesque architecture, incorporating genuine Roman columns, Flemish Renaissance woodwork, German and Dutch stained glass and Italian mosaics.

Wilton House has been home to the Earls of Pembroke since it was converted from a nunnery after the Dissolution (see p50). The house, largely rebuilt by Inigo Jones in the 17th century, includes one of the original Tudor towers, a fine collection of art and a landscaped park with a Palladian bridge (1737). The Single and Double Cube State Rooms have magnificently frescoed ceilings and gilded stucco work, and were designed to hang a series of family portraits by Van Dyck.

The graceful spire soars to a height of 123 m (404 ft).

The West Front is decorated by rows of lavish symbolic figures and saints in niches.

A roof tour takes you up to an external gallery at the base of the spire with views of the town and Old Sarum.

Wilton House

Wilton. **Tel** 01722 746729. Easter weekend, May–Aug: Sun–Thu, bank hol Sat.

The clock dating from 1386 is the oldest working clock in Europe.

The nave is divided into ten bays by columns of polished Purbeck marble.

North transept

Numerous windows add to the airy and spacious atmosphere of the interior.

SALISBURY CATHEDRAL

The Close. **Tel** 01722 555120. daily. **Donation.** www.salisburycathedral.org.uk

The cathedral was mostly built between 1220 and 1258. It is a fine example of Early English Gothic architecture, typified by tall, sharply pointed lancet windows.

Double Cube room, designed by Inigo Jones in 1653

The Longleat Tree tapestry (1980) depicting a 400-year history

Longleat House ⑭

Warminster, Wiltshire. *Tel* 01985 844400. ≋ *Warminster then taxi.*
House ☐ *Mar–Oct: daily.* ● *25 Dec.*
Safari Park ☐ *Feb–Nov: daily.* ☐
🕭 ▮▮ ▯ ▯ **www**.longleat.co.uk

The architectural historian John Summerson coined the term "prodigy house" to describe the exuberance and grandeur of Elizabethan architecture that is so well represented at Longleat. The house was started in 1540, when John Thynne bought the ruins of a priory on the site for £53. Over the centuries subsequent owners have added their own touches. These include the Breakfast Room and Lower Dining Room (dating from the 1870s), modelled on the Venetian Ducal Palace, and erotic murals painted by the present owner, the 7th Marquess of Bath. Today, the Great Hall is the only remaining room which belongs to Thynne's time.

In 1949, the 6th Marquess was the first landowner in Britain to open his stately home to the public, in order to fund the maintenance and preservation of the house and its estate. Parts of the grounds, landscaped by "Capability" Brown *(see p26)*, were turned into an expansive safari park in 1966, where lions, tigers and other wild animals roam freely. This, along with other additions such as England's longest hedge maze, the Adventure Castle and Blue Peter Maze, and special events, now draw even more visitors than the house.

Stourhead ⑮

Stourhead is among the finest examples of 18th-century landscape gardening in Britain *(see pp26–7)*. The garden was begun in the 1740s by Henry Hoare (1705–85), who inherited the estate and transformed it into a breathtaking work of art. Hoare created the lake, surrounding it with rare trees and plants, and Neo-Classical Italianate temples, grottoes and bridges. The Palladian-style house, built by Colen Campbell *(see p28)*, dates from 1724.

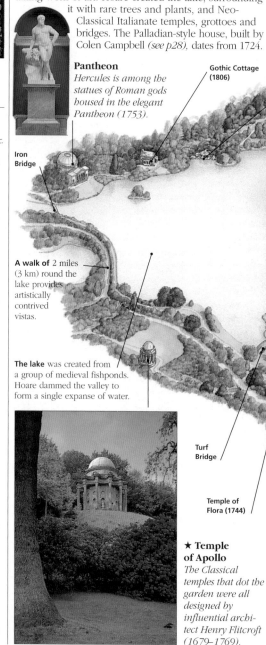

Pantheon
Hercules is among the statues of Roman gods housed in the elegant Pantheon (1753).

Iron Bridge

Gothic Cottage (1806)

A walk of 2 miles (3 km) round the lake provides artistically contrived vistas.

The lake was created from a group of medieval fishponds. Hoare dammed the valley to form a single expanse of water.

Turf Bridge

Temple of Flora (1744)

★ Temple of Apollo
The Classical temples that dot the garden were all designed by influential architect Henry Flitcroft (1679–1769).

Grotto
Tunnels lead to an artificial cave with a pool and a life-size statue of the guardian of the River Stour, sculpted by John Cheere in 1748.

VISITORS' CHECKLIST

(NT) Stourton, Wiltshire. *Tel* 01747 841152. ☰ Gillingham (Dorset) then taxi. **House** ◯ Mar–Oct: 11am–5pm Fri–Tue (Aug: daily). **Gardens** ◯ 9am–7pm (or dusk if earlier) daily. 🅿 🛦 limited. 🔲 ⬛ 🔲 🔲
www.nationaltrust.org.uk/stourhead

★ Stourhead House
Reconstructed after a fire in 1902, the house contains fine Chippendale furniture. The art collection reflects Henry Hoare's Classical tastes and includes The Choice of Hercules *(1637) by Nicolas Poussin.*

Colourful shrubs around the house include fragrant rhododendrons in spring.

Stourton village was incorporated into Hoare's overall design. 🔲 🔲

Pelargonium House is a historical collection of over 100 species and cultivars.

The reception offers information to help you enjoy your visit.

Entrance and car park

St Peter's Church
The parish church contains monuments to the Hoare family. The medieval Bristol Cross, nearby, was brought from Bristol in 1765.

STAR SIGHTS

★ Temple of Apollo

★ Stourhead House

Shaftesbury ⓰

Dorset. 🏛 *8,000.* 🛈 *8 Bell St (01747 853514).* 🗓 *Thu.*
www.shaftesburydorset.com

Hilltop Shaftesbury, with its cobbled streets and 18th-century cottages is often used as a setting for films to give a flavour of Old England. Picturesque **Gold Hill** is lined on one side by a wall of the demolished **abbey**, founded by King Alfred in 888. Only the excavated remains of the abbey church survive, and many masonry fragments are found in the local museum.

The Almshouse (1437) adjoining the Abbey Church, Sherborne

Sherborne ⓱

Dorset. 🏛 *9,500.* 🚂 🚌 🛈 *Digby Rd (01935 815341).* 🗓 *Thu, Sat.*
www.visit-dorset.com

Few other towns in Britain have such a wealth of unspoilt medieval buildings. Edward VI *(see p41)* founded the famous Sherborne School in 1550, saving intact the splendid **Abbey Church** and other monastic buildings that might otherwise have been demolished in the Dissolution *(see p50)*. Remains of the Saxon church can be seen in the abbey's façade, but the most striking feature is the 15th-century fan-vaulted ceiling.

Sherborne Castle, built by Sir Walter Raleigh *(see p51)* in 1594, is a wonderfully varied building that anticipates the flamboyant Jacobean style. Raleigh also lived briefly in the early 12th-century **Old Castle**, which now stands in ruins, demolished during the Civil War *(see p52)*.

Environs: West of Sherborne, past Yeovil, is the magnificent Elizabethan **Montacute House** *(see p245)*, set in 120 ha (300 acres) of grounds. It is noted for tapestries, and for the Tudor and Jacobean portraits in the vast Long Gallery.

⚜ **Sherborne Castle**
Off A30. *Tel* 01935 813182.
Castle and grounds ⬭ *Apr–Oct: Tue–Thu, Sat, Sun & bank hols (pm).*
🎫 🅿 🅰 **www**.sherbornecastle.com

⚜ **Old Castle**
(EH) Off A30. *Tel* 01935 812730.
⬭ *Easter–Oct: daily.* 🎫 🅰 🅿

🏰 **Montacute House**
(NT) Montacute. *Tel* 01935 823289.
House ⬭ *Mar–Oct: Wed–Mon.*
Grounds ⬭ *Apr–Nov: Wed–Mon; Dec–Mar: Wed–Sun.* 🎫 🍴 🅿

Abbotsbury ⓲

Dorset. 🏛 *500.* 🛈 *Bakehouse Market St (01305 871990).*
www.abbotsbury-tourism.co.uk

The name Abbotsbury recalls the town's 11th-century Benedictine abbey of which little but the huge tithe barn, built around 1400, remains.
Nobody knows when the **Swannery** here was founded, but the earliest record dates to 1393. Mute swans come to nest in the breeding season, attracted by the reed beds along the Fleet, a brackish lagoon protected from

The Swannery at Abbotsbury

the sea by a high ridge of pebbles called **Chesil Bank** *(see p242)*. Its wild atmosphere makes an appealing contrast to the south coast resorts, although strong currents make swimming too dangerous.
Abbotsbury Sub-Tropical Gardens are the frost-free home to many new plants, discovered by botanists travelling in South America and Asia.

🦢 **Swannery**
New Barn Rd. *Tel* 01305 871858. ⬭
mid-Mar–Oct: daily. 🎫 🅰 🅿

🌿 **Abbotsbury Sub-Tropical Gardens**
Off B3157. *Tel* 01305 871387. ⬭
daily. ● *24 Dec–1 Jan.* 🎫 🅰 🅿 🅿

Weymouth ⓳

Dorset. 🏛 *53,000.* 🚂 🚌 🚢
🛈 *Pavilion Theatre, The Esplanade (01305 785747).* 🗓 *Thu.*

Weymouth's popularity as a seaside resort began in 1789, when George III paid the first of many summer visits here. His statue is a prominent feature on the seafront. Here gracious Georgian terraces

Weymouth Quay, Dorset's south coast

For hotels and restaurants in this region see pp570–574 and pp622–626

look across to the beautiful expanse of Weymouth Bay. Different in character is the old town around Custom House Quay with its fishing boats and old seamen's inns. In 1944 the town played host to over 500,000 troops in advance of the D-Day Landings, and **Nothe Fort** has displays of World War II memorabilia.

🏛 **Nothe Fort**
Barrack Rd. *Tel 01305 766626.*
◯ *daily (Sun only in winter).*

Dorchester ㉒

Dorset. 🏘 *16,000.* 🚉 🛈 *Antelope Walk (01305 267992).* 🛒 *Wed.*
www.westdorset.com

Dorchester, the county town of Dorset, is still recognizably the town in which Thomas Hardy based his novel *The Mayor of Casterbridge* (1886). Here, among the many 17th- and 18th-century houses lining the High Street, is the **Dorset County Museum**, where the original manuscript of the novel is displayed. Dorchester also has the only example of a **Roman town house** in Britain. The remains reveal architectural details including a fine mosaic. There are also finds from Iron Age and Roman sites on the outskirts of the

A 55 m (180 ft) giant carved on the chalk hillside, Cerne Abbas (NT)

town. **Maumbury Rings** (Weymouth Avenue), is a Roman amphitheatre, originally a Neolithic henge. To the west, many Roman graves have been found below the Iron Age hill fort, **Poundbury Camp**.

Environs: Just southwest of Dorchester, **Maiden Castle** *(see p43)* is a massive monument dating from around 100 BC. In AD 43 it was the scene of a battle when the Romans fought the Iron Age people of southern England.

To the north lies the charming village of **Cerne Abbas** with its magnificent medieval tithe barn and monastic buildings. The huge chalk figure of a giant on the hillside here is a fertility figure thought to represent either

the Roman god Hercules or an Iron Age warrior.

East of Dorchester are the churches, thatched villages and rolling hills immortalized in Hardy's novels. Picturesque **Bere Regis** is the Kingsbere of *Tess of the D'Urbervilles,* where the tombs of the family whose name inspired the novel may be seen in the Saxon **church**. **Hardy's Cottage** is where the writer was born and **Max Gate** is the house he designed and lived in from 1885 until his death. His heart is buried with his family at

Hardy's statue, Dorchester

Stinsford church – his body was given a public funeral at Westminster Abbey *(pp92–3).*

There are beautiful gardens *(see p245)* and a magnificent medieval hall at 15th-century **Athelhampton House**.

🏛 **Dorset County Museum**
High West St. *Tel 01305 262735.*
◯ *Mon–Sat (Jul–Sep: daily).* ◗ *25, 26 Dec.* 🎟 *valid for one year.* 🚻 *ltd.*
🖥 **www**.dorsetcountymuseum.org

🏚 **Hardy's Cottage**
(NT) *Higher Bockhampton. Tel 01305 262366.* ◯ *Apr–Oct: Sun–Thu.* 🎟
🚻 🚻 *garden only.*

🏛 **Max Gate**
(NT) *Alington Ave, Dorchester. Tel 01305 262538.* ◯ *Apr–Sep: Sun, Mon & Wed (pm).* 🎟 🚻 🚻

🏚 **Athelhampton House**
Athelhampton. Tel 01305 848363. ◯ *Sun–Thu (Nov–Feb: Sun).* 🎟 🚻 *gardens only.* 🛍 🍴 🚻 ⬚
🖥 **www**.athelhamptonhouse.co.uk

THOMAS HARDY (1840–1928)

The vibrant, descriptive novels and poems of Thomas Hardy, one of England's best-loved writers, are set against the background of his native Dorset. The Wessex countryside provides a constant and familiar stage against which his characters enact their fate. Vivid accounts of rural life record a key moment in history, when mechanization was about to destroy ancient farming methods, just as the Industrial Revolution had done in the towns a century before *(see pp54–5).* Hardy's powerfully visual style has made novels such as *Tess of the D'Urbervilles* (1891) popular with modern film-makers, and drawn literary pilgrims to the villages and landscapes that inspired his fiction.

Nastassja Kinski in Roman Polanski's film *Tess* (1979)

Corfe Castle ㉑

(NT) Dorset. *Tel* 01929 481294. 🚆 *Wareham then bus.* ⬜ *daily.* ⬤ *25 & 26 Dec.* 🖼️ 🚻 *limited.* 📷 *Mar–Oct; Nov–Feb by arrangement.* 💻 🏠 www.nationaltrust.org.uk

The spectacular ruins of Corfe Castle romantically crown a jagged pinnacle of rock above the charming un-spoilt village that shares its name. The castle has domi-nated the landscape since the 11th century, first as a royal fortification, then as the dra-matic ruins seen today. In 1635 the castle was purchased by Sir John Bankes, whose wife and her retainers – mostly women – courageously held out against 600 Parliamentary troops, in a six-week siege during the Civil War *(see pp52–3)*. The castle was eventually taken through trea-chery and in 1646 Parliament voted to have it "slighted" – deliberately blown up to prevent it being used again. From the ruins there are far-reaching views over the Isle of Purbeck and its coastline.

The ruins of Corfe Castle, dating mainly from Norman times

Isle of Purbeck ㉒

Dorset. 🚆 *Wareham.* ⛴️ *Shell Bay, Studland.* 🛈 *Swanage (01929 422885).* www.swanage.gov.uk

The Isle of Purbeck, which is in fact a peninsula, is the source of the grey shelly limestone, known as Purbeck marble, from which the castle and surrounding houses were built. The geology changes to the southwest at **Kimmeridge**, where the muddy shale is rich in fossils and oil reserves.

The Isle, a World Heritage site, is fringed with unspoilt beaches. **Studland Bay** (NT) – with its white sand and its sand-dune nature reserve, rich in birdlife – has been rated one of Britain's best beaches. Sheltered **Lulworth Cove** is almost encircled by white cliffs, and there is a fine cliff-top walk to Durdle Door *(see p243)*, a natural chalk arch.

The main resort in the area is **Swanage**, the port where Purbeck stone was trans-ported by ship to London, to be used for everything from street paving to church building. Unwanted masonry from demolished buildings was shipped back and this is how Swanage got its wonderfully ornate **Town Hall** façade, designed by Wren around 1668.

Poole ㉓

Dorset. 🏘️ *142,000.* 🚆 🚌 ⛴️ 🛈 *Poole Quay (0845 2345560).* www.pooletourism.com

Situated on one of the largest natural harbours in the world, Poole is an ancient, still thriving, seaport. The quay is lined with old warehouses, modern apartments and a marina, overlooking a safe sheltered bay. The **Poole Museum**, partly housed in 15th-century cellars alongside the quay, has four floors of galleries.

Nearby **Brownsea Island** (reached by boat from the quay) is given over to a woodland nature reserve with a waterfowl and heron

Beach adjoining Lulworth Cove, Isle of Purbeck

For hotels and restaurants in this region see pp570–574 and pp622–626

sanctuary. The fine views of the Dorset coast add to the appeal of the island.

🏛 **Poole Museum**
High St. **Tel** 01202 262600.
⬤ Apr–Sep: daily; Oct–Mar: Tue–Sun. ⬤ 1 Jan, 25, 26 Dec. ♿
www.poole.gov.uk

🦌 **Brownsea Island**
(NT) Poole. **Tel** 01202 707744.
⬤ Apr–Nov: daily (boat trips leave the quayside every 30 mins during the season). 🎦 ♿ ✉ ⬛ ⬛

Boats in Poole harbour

Wimborne Minster ㉔

Dorset. 🏠 6,500. 🚌 ℹ 29 High St (01202 886116). ⬤ Fri–Sun.
www.visit-dorset.co.uk

The fine collegiate church of Wimborne's **Minster** was founded in 705 by Cuthburga, sister of King Ina of Wessex. It fell prey to marauding Danish raiders in the 10th century, and the imposing grey church we see today dates from the refounding by Edward the Confessor *(see p47)* in 1043. Stonemasons made use of the local Purbeck marble, carving beasts, biblical scenes, and a mass of zig-zag decoration.

The 16th-century **Priest's House Museum** has rooms furnished in the style of different periods and an enchanting hidden garden.

Environs: Designed for the Bankes family after the destruction of Corfe Castle, **Kingston Lacy** was acquired by the National Trust in 1981. The estate has always been farmed by traditional methods

and is astonishingly rich in wildlife, rare flowers and butterflies. This quiet, forgotten corner of Dorset is grazed by rare Red Devon cattle and can be explored using paths and "green lanes" that date back to Roman and Saxon times. The fine 17th-century house on the estate contains an outstanding collection of paintings, including works by Rubens, Velázquez and Titian.

🏛 **Priest's House Museum**
High St. **Tel** 01202 882533. ⬤ Apr–Oct: Mon–Sat. 🎦 ♿ limited. ⬛ ⬛

🏯 **Kingston Lacy**
(NT) on B3082. **Tel** 01202 883402.
House ⬤ Apr–Oct: Wed–Sun; 2 wks at Christmas. **Gardens** ⬤ Apr–Oct: daily; Nov–Mar: Sat & Sun. 🎦 ♿ gardens only. 🍽 ⬛

Bournemouth ㉕

Dorset. 🏠 165,000. ✈ 🚆 🚌.
ℹ Westover Road (0845 0511700).
www.bournemouth.co.uk

Bournemouth's popularity as a seaside resort is due to an almost unbroken sweep of sandy beach, extending from the mouth of Poole Harbour to Hengistbury Head. Most of the seafront is built up, with large seaside villas and exclusive hotels. To the west there are numerous clifftop parks and gardens, interrupted by beautiful wooded river ravines, known as "chines". The varied and colourful garden of **Compton Acres** was conceived as a museum of many different garden styles.

In central Bournemouth the amusement arcades, casinos, nightclubs and shops cater for the city's many visitors. In the summer, pop groups, TV comedians and the highly

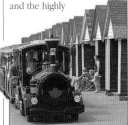

A road train on the popular seafront at Bournemouth

Marchesa Maria Grimaldi by Sir Peter Paul Rubens (1577–1640), **Kingston Lacy**

regarded Bournemouth Symphony Orchestra perform at various venues in the city. The **Russell-Cotes Art Gallery and Museum**, housed in a late Victorian villa, has an extensive collection, with many fine Oriental and Victorian artefacts.

Environs: The magnificent **Christchurch Priory**, east of Bournemouth, is 95 m (310 ft) in length – the longest church in England. It was rebuilt between the 13th and 16th centuries and presents a sequence of different styles. The original nave, built around 1093, is an impressive example of Norman architecture, but the highlight is the intricate stone reredos, which features a Tree of Jesse, tracing the lineage of Christ. Next to the Priory are the ruins of a Norman **castle**.

Between Bournemouth and Christchurch, **Hengistbury Head** is well worth climbing for grassland flowers, butterflies and sea views, while **Stanpit Marsh**, to the west of Bournemouth, is an excellent spot for viewing herons and other wading birds.

🌸 **Compton Acres**
Canford Cliffs Rd. **Tel** 01202 700778. ⬤ daily. ⬛ 🎦 ♿ 🍽
www.comptonacres.co.uk

🏛 **Russell-Cotes Art Gallery and Museum**
Eastcliff. **Tel** 01202 451858.
⬤ Tue–Sun. ♿ 🍽 ⬛ www. russell-cotes.bournemouth.gov.uk

DEVON AND CORNWALL

DEVON · CORNWALL

Miles of magnificently varied coastline dominate this magical corner of Britain. Popular seaside resorts alternate with secluded coves and unspoilt fishing villages rich in maritime history. In contrast there are lush, exotic gardens and the wild terrain of the moorland interior, dotted with tors and historic remains.

Geographical neighbours, the counties of Devon and Cornwall are very different in character. Celtic Cornwall, with its numerous villages named after early Christian missionaries, is mostly stark and treeless at its centre. In many places it is still scarred by the remains of tin and copper mining that has played an important part in the economy for some 4,000 years. Yet this does not detract from the beauty and variety of the coastline dotted with lighthouses and tiny coves, and penetrated by deep tidal rivers.

Devon, by contrast, is a land of lush pasture divided into a patchwork of tiny fields and threaded with narrow lanes, whose banks support a mass of flowers from the first spring primroses to summer's colourful mixture of campion, foxglove, oxeye daisies and blue cornflowers. The leisurely pace of rural life here, and in Cornwall, contrasts with life in the bustling cities. Exeter with its magnificent cathedral, historic Plymouth, elegant Truro and Elizabethan Totnes are urban centres brimming with life and character.

The spectacular coastline and the mild climate of the region attract families, boating enthusiasts and surfers. For those in search of solitude, the Southwest Coastal Path provides access to the more tranquil areas. There are fishing villages and harbours whose heyday was in the buccaneering age of Drake and Raleigh *(see p51)*, and inland the wild moorland of Bodmin and Dartmoor, which provided inspiration for many romantic tales. Many of these are associated with King Arthur *(see p285)* who, according to legend, was born at Tintagel on Cornwall's dramatically contorted north coast.

Beach huts on the seafront at Paignton, near Torquay

◁ Fishing boats in Port Isaac, on Cornwall's north coast

Exploring Devon and Cornwall

Romantic Moorland dominates the inland parts of
Devon and Cornwall, ideal walking country with
few roads and magnificent views stretching for miles.
By contrast the extensive coastline is indented by
hundreds of sheltered river valleys, each one seem-
ingly isolated from the rest of the world – one reason
why Devon and Cornwall can absorb so many visitors
and yet still seem uncrowded. Wise tourists get to
know one small part of Devon or Cornwall intimately,
soaking up the atmosphere of the region, rather than
rushing to see everything in the space of a week.

KEY

- ═══ Motorway
- ═══ Major road
- ─── Secondary road
- ┈┈┈ Minor road
- ─── Scenic route
- ╍╍╍ Main railway
- ─── Minor railway
- △ Summit

SIGHTS AT A GLANCE

Appledore ⑯
Barnstaple ⑰
Bideford ⑮
Bodmin ⑪
Buckfastleigh ㉓
Buckland Abbey ㉖
Bude ⑬
Burgh Island ㉔
Clovelly ⑭
Cotehele ㉗
Dartmoor pp294–5 ㉙
Dartmouth ㉑
Eden Project pp282–3 ⑨
Exeter ⑲
Falmouth ⑥
Fowey ⑩
Helston and the
  Lizard Peninsula ⑤
Lynton and Lynmouth ⑱
Morwellham Quay ㉘
Penzance ③
Plymouth ㉕
St Austell ⑧
St Ives ②
*St Michael's Mount
  pp278–9* ④
Tintagel ⑫
Torbay ⑳
Totnes ㉒
Truro ⑦

Walks and Tours

Penwith Tour ❶

The dramatic cliffs of Land's End,
England's most westerly point

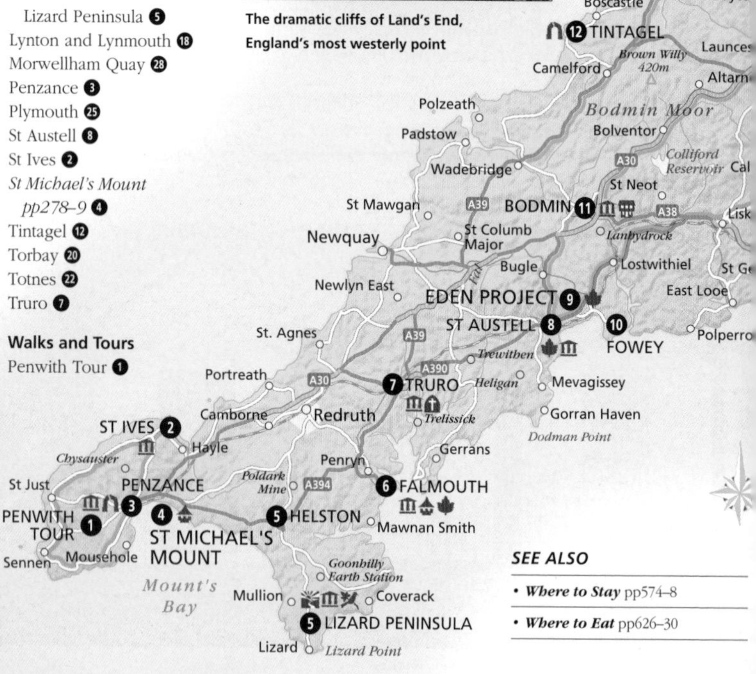

SEE ALSO

- *Where to Stay* pp574–8
- *Where to Eat* pp626–30

Sub-tropical gardens at Torquay, the popular seaside resort

GETTING AROUND

Large numbers of drivers, many towing caravans (trailers), travel along the M5 motorway and A30 trunk road from mid-July to early September and travel can be slow, especially on Saturdays. Once in Devon and Cornwall, allow ample time if you are travelling by car along the region's narrow and high-banked lanes.

The regular train services, running from Paddington to Penzance, along Brunel's historic Great Western Railway, stop at most major towns. Aside from this, you are dependent on taxis or infrequent local buses.

Combe Martin
mbe
18 LYNTON & LYNMOUTH
Parracombe
Minehead
Woolacombe
Arlington Court
Braunton
Brayford
Exmoor
NSTAPLE **17** 🏛 🏫
APPLEDORE
South Molton
Molland
BIDEFORD
A361
Oakford
Bampton
Taunton
Great Torrington
A377
Witheridge
Tiverton
Yeovil
Merton
Chulmleigh
Lapford
Bickleigh
Upottery
M5
therleigh
A386
Winkleigh
Crediton
Killerton House
Talaton
Honiton
North Tawton
Tedburn St Mary
A30
A35
Okehampton
Whiddon Down
Broad Clyst
Ottery St. Mary
High Willhays 621m
EXETER **19** 🏛 🏫
Otter
Beer
Dunsford
ydford
Chagford
Topsham
Sidmouth
A386
DARTMOOR
Bovey Tracy
A38
Budleigh Salterton
Postbridge
🏕 **29**
Chudleigh
Exmouth
Lyme Bay
Two Bridges
A380
Dawlish
MORWELLHAM QUAY
Ashburton
Newton Abbot
Babbacombe Bay
26 BUCKLAND ABBEY
23
Kingskerswell
Torquay
TEHELE
BUCKFASTLEIGH
🏛 🍁 **22**
🏛 🗡 **20** TORBAY
Itash
South Brent
TOTNES
Paignton
Plympton
A38
Dart
Brixham
25 PLYMOUTH
Modbury
Kingswear
Newton Ferrers
DARTMOUTH **21**
🏛 Stoke Fleming
24 BURGH ISLAND
Torcross
Salcombe
Start Point
Prawle Point

0 kilometres 15

0 miles 10

Typical thatched, stone cottages, Buckland-in-the-Moor, Dartmoor

Penwith Tour ●

This tour passes through a spectacular, remote Cornish landscape, dotted with relics of the tin mining industry, picturesque fishing villages and many prehistoric remains. The magnificent coast-line varies between the gentle rolling moorland in the north and the rugged, windswept cliffs that characterize the dramatic south coast. The beauty of the area, combined with the clarity of light, has attracted artists since the late 19th century. Their work can be seen in Newlyn, St Ives and Penzance.

TIPS FOR DRIVERS

Tour length: 31 miles (50 km)
Stopping-off points: There are pubs and cafés in most villages. Sennen Cove makes a pleasant mid-way stop. (See also pp684–5.)

Zennor ①
The carved mermaid in the church recalls the legend of the mermaid who lured the local squire's son to her ocean lair.

Lanyon Quoit ②
One of many prehistoric monuments, this chambered tomb is visible on the left from the road to Madron.

Botallack Mine ⑧
Derelict engine-houses clinging to the cliffside are a vivid reminder of the region's former industry of tin-mining.

Trengwainton ③
These gardens are noted for their luxuriance (*p244*).

Land's End ⑦
England's most westerly point is noted for its dramatic and wild landscape. A local exhibition reveals its history, geology and wildlife.

Newlyn ④
Cornwall's largest fishing port gave its name to a school of artists founded in the 1880s (*p278*). Examples of their work can be seen in the art gallery here.

Merry Maidens ⑤
This Bronze Age stone circle is said to be 19 girls turned to stone for dancing on Sunday.

Minack Theatre ⑥
This Ancient Greek-style theatre (1923) overlooks a magical bay of Porthcurno. It forms a magnificent backdrop for productions in summer.

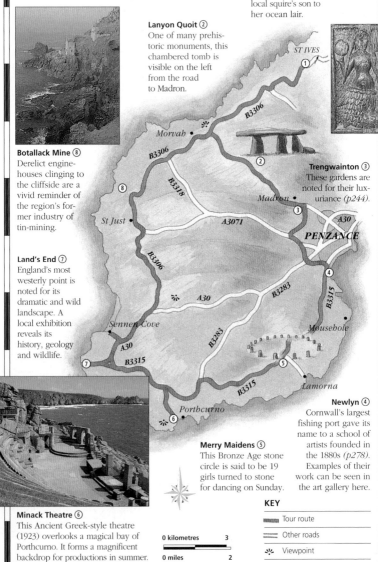

KEY

▨▨▨ Tour route

═══ Other roads

☼ Viewpoint

0 kilometres 3
0 miles 2

St Ives ❷

Cornwall. 🏘 11,000. ✈ 🚌
ℹ️ Street-an-Pol (01736 797600).
www.stives.co.uk

St Ives's **Barbara Hepworth Museum and Sculpture Garden** and **Tate St Ives** celebrate the work of a group of artists who set up a seaside art colony here from the 1920s. The former presents the sculptor's work in the house and garden where she lived and worked for many years. Tate St Ives, designed to frame a panoramic view of Porthmeor Beach, reminds visitors of the natural surroundings that inspired the art on display within. A museum at the Leach Pottery (www.leachpottery.com) celebrates the life and work of potter Bernard Leach, another luminary of the St Ives Society of Artists.

The Lower Terrace, Tate St Ives

The town of St Ives remains a typical English seaside resort, surrounded by a crescent of golden sands. Popular taste rules in the many other art galleries tucked down winding alleys with names such as Teetotal Street, a legacy of the town's Methodist heritage. Many galleries are converted cellars and lofts where fish were once salted and packed. In between are whitewashed cottages with tiny gardens brimming with flowers, their vibrant colours made intense by the unusually clear light that first attracted artists to St Ives.

🏛 **Barbara Hepworth Museum and Sculpture Garden**
Barnoon Hill. **Tel** 01736 796226. ⭕ daily (Nov–Feb: Tue–Sun). ⬤ 24–26 Dec. ♿ ♿ by appt. 📷

🏛 **Tate St Ives**
Porthmeor Beach. **Tel** 01736 796226. ⭕ daily (Nov–Feb: Tue–Sun). ⬤ 24–26 Dec; occasionally for rehanging – phone to check. ♿ ♿ 🍴 📷 **www**.tate.org.uk/stives

---

TWENTIETH-CENTURY ARTISTS OF ST IVES

Ben Nicholson and Barbara Hepworth formed the nucleus of a group of artists that made a major contribution to the development of abstract art in Europe. In the 1920s, St Ives together with Newlyn *(see p276)* became a place for aspiring artists. Among the prolific artists associated with the town are the potter Bernard Leach (1887–1979) and the painter Patrick Heron (1920–99), whose *Coloured Glass Window (see p240)* dominates the Tate St Ives entrance. Much of the art on display at Tate St Ives is abstract and illustrates new responses to the rugged Cornish landscape, the human figure and the ever-changing patterns of sunlight on sea.

Barbara Hepworth *(1903–75) was one of the foremost abstract sculptors of her time.* Madonna and Child *(1953) can be seen in the church of St Ia.*

John Wells' *(1907–2000) key interests are in light, curved forms and birds in flight, as revealed in* Aspiring Forms *(1950).*

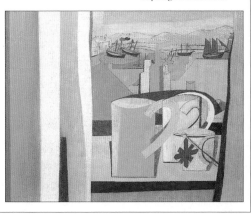

Ben Nicholson's *(1894–1982) work shows a change in style from simple scenes, such as the view from his window, to a preoccupation with shapes – as seen in this painting* St Ives, Cornwall *(1943–5). Later, his interest moved towards pure geometric blocks of colour.*

Penzance ❸

Cornwall. 🏘 22,000. 🚆 🚌 ✈ ℹ *Station Approach (01736 362207).* **www**.penzance.co.uk

Penzance is a bustling resort with a climate so mild that palm trees and sub-tropical plants grow happily in the lush **Morrab Gardens**. The town commands fine views of St Michael's Mount and a great sweep of clean sandy beach.

The main road through the town is Market Jew Street, at the top of which stands the magnificent domed Market House (1837), fronted by a statue of Sir Humphrey Davy (1778–1829). Davy, who came from Penzance, invented the miner's safety lamp which detected lethal gases.

Chapel Street is lined with curious buildings, none more striking than the flamboyant **Egyptian House** (1835), with its richly painted façade and lotus bud decoration. Just as curious is **Admiral Benbow Inn** (1696) on the same street, which has a pirate perched on the roof looking out to sea. The **Penlee House Gallery and Museum** has pictures by the Newlyn School of artists.

Environs: A short distance south of Penzance, **Newlyn** *(see p276)* is Cornwall's largest fishing port, which has given its name to the local school of artists founded by Stanhope Forbes (1857–1947). They painted outdoors, aiming to capture the fleeting impressions of wind, sun and sea. Continuing south, the coastal road ends at **Mousehole** (pronounced Mowzall), a pretty, popular village with a

The Egyptian House (1835)

tiny harbour, tiers of cottages and a maze of narrow alleys.

North of Penzance, overlooking the magical Cornish coast, **Chysauster** is a fine example of a Romano-British village. The site has remained almost undisturbed since it

St Michael's Mount ❹

(NT) Marazion, Cornwall. *Tel* 01736 710507; tide and ferry information 01736 710265. 🚢 from Marazion (Mar–Oct) or on foot at low tide. ◯ Apr–Oct: Sun–Fri; Nov–Mar: Tue & Fri (tours only – call ahead). 🏷 🍴 📷 🏪 **www**.stmichaelsmount.co.uk

St Michael's Mount emerges dramatically from the waters of Mounts Bay. According to ancient Roman historians, the mount was the island of Ictis, an important centre for the Cornish tin trade during the Iron Age. It is dedicated to the archangel St Michael who, according to legend, appeared here in 495.

When the Normans conquered England in 1066 *(see pp46–7)*, they were struck by the island's resemblance to their own Mont-St-Michel, whose Benedictine monks were invited to build a small abbey here. The abbey was absorbed into a fortress at the Dissolution *(see p351)*, when Henry VIII set up a chain of coastal defences to counter an expected attack from France. In 1659 St Michael's Mount was purchased by Colonel John St Aubyn, whose descendants subsequently turned the fortress into a magnificent house.

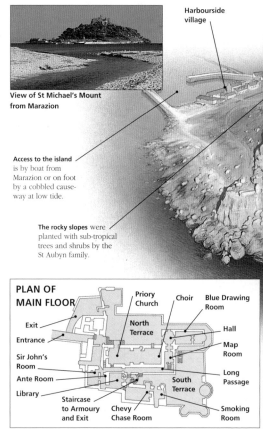

View of St Michael's Mount from Marazion

Harbourside village

Access to the island is by boat from Marazion or on foot by a cobbled causeway at low tide.

The rocky slopes were planted with sub-tropical trees and shrubs by the St Aubyn family.

PLAN OF MAIN FLOOR

Exit
Entrance
Sir John's Room
Ante Room
Library
Staircase to Armoury and Exit
Chevy Chase Room
Priory Church
North Terrace
South Terrace
Choir
Blue Drawing Room
Hall
Map Room
Long Passage
Smoking Room

was abandoned during the 3rd century.

From Penzance, regular boat and helicopter services depart for the **Isles of Scilly**, a beautiful archipelago forming part of the same granite mass as Land's End, Bodmin Moor and Dartmoor. Along with tourism, flower-growing forms the main source of income here.

🏛 Penlee House Gallery and Museum

Morrab Rd.
Tel 01736 363625.
☐ May–Sep: 10am–5pm Mon–Sat; Oct–Apr: 10:30am–4:30pm Mon–Sat. ◐ 1 Jan, 25–26 Dec. 🏷 🚫 but free admission on Sat. ♿ 🏷
www.penleehouse.org.uk

⛏ Chysauster

(EH) Off B3311.
Tel 07831 757934.
☐ Apr–Oct: daily. 🚫 🏷

THE GROWTH OF METHODISM

The hard-working and independent mining and fishing communities of the West Country had little time for the established church, but they were won over by the new Methodist religion, with its emphasis on hymn singing, open-air preaching and regular or "methodical" Bible reading. When John Wesley, the founder of Methodism, made the first of many visits to the area in 1743, sceptical Cornish-

John Wesley (1703–91)

men pelted him with stones. His persistence, however, led to many conversions and by 1762 he was preaching to congregations of up to 30,000 people. Simple places of worship were built throughout the county; one favoured spot was the amphitheatre **Gwennap Pit**, at Busveal, south of Redruth. Methodist memorabilia can be seen in the Royal Cornwall Museum in Truro (*see p281*).

Castle entrance

The South Terrace forms the roof of the large Victorian wing. Beneath it there are five floors of private quarters.

The Blue Drawing Room *was formed from the Lady Chapel in the mid-18th century and is decorated in charming Rococo Gothic style. It contains fine plaster work, furniture and paintings by Gainsborough and Thomas Hudson.*

The Armoury displays sporting weapons and military trophies brought back by the St Aubyn family from various wars.

The Priory Church, *rebuilt in the late 14th century, forms the summit of the island. Beautiful rose windows are found at both ends.*

The Chevy Chase Room *takes its name from a plaster frieze (1641) representing hunting scenes.*

Pinnacles of serpentine rock at Kynance Cove (NT), Lizard Peninsula

Helston and the Lizard Peninsula ❺

Cornwall. 🚌 from Penzance.
ℹ Menage St, Helston (01326 565431). www.visitcornwall.com

The attractive town of Helston makes a good base for exploring the windswept coastline of the Lizard Peninsula. The town is famous for its Furry Dance, which welcomes spring with dancing through the streets (see p62); the **Folk Museum** explains the history of this ancient custom. The Georgian houses and inns of Coinagehall Street are a reminder that Helston was once a thriving stannary town where tin ingots were brought for weighing and stamping before being sold.

Locally mined tin was brought down river to a harbour at the bottom of this street until access to the sea was blocked in the 13th century by a shingle bar that formed across the estuary. The bar created the freshwater lake, Loe Pool, and an attractive walk skirts its wooded shores. In 1880, Helston's trade was taken over by a new harbour created to the east on the River Helford, at Gweek. Today, Gweek is the home of the **National Seal Sanctuary**, where sick seals are nursed before being returned to the sea.

Cornwall's tin mining industry, from Roman to recent times, is covered at **Poldark Mine** where underground tours show the working conditions of 18th-century miners.

Another attraction is **Flambards Experience**, with its recreations of a Victorian village and of Britain during the Blitz.

Further south is Britain's most southerly tourist attraction, the **Lizard Lighthouse Heritage Centre**. Built in 1619, the tower was automated in 1998. Interactive displays describe the workings of a lighthouse.

Local shops sell souvenirs carved from serpentine, a soft greenish stone which forms the unusual-shaped rocks that rise from the sandy beach at picturesque **Kynance Cove**.

🏛 **Folk Museum**
Market Place, Helston. Tel 01326 564027. ⏰ Mon–Sat (am only). ⬤ Christmas week. 🎫 👍 🅿
www.cornwall.gov.uk

🐾 **National Seal Sanctuary**
Gweek. Tel 01326 221361. ⏰ daily. ⬤ 25 Dec. 🎫 👍 🅿
www.sealsanctuary.com

🏛 **Poldark Mine**
Wendron. Tel 01326 573173. ⏰ 2 wks at Easter, Jul & Aug: daily; Apr–Jun, Sep & Oct: Sun–Fri; Nov–Mar: tours only, by appt. 🎫 👍 🅿
www.poldark-mine.co.uk

🏛 **Flambards Experience**
Culdrose Manor, Helston. Tel 01326 573404. ⏰ Easter–Oct: daily; Nov–Mar: call to check. 🎫 👍 🍴 🅿 www.flambards.co.uk

🏛 **Lizard Lighthouse Heritage Centre**
Helston. Tel 01326 290202. ⏰ call ahead for opening hours.

Falmouth ❻

Cornwall. 🏘 22,000. 🚉 🚌 🚏 🛥 ℹ 11 Market Strand (01326 313394). www.falmouth.co.uk

Falmouth stands at the point where seven rivers flow into a long stretch of water called the **Carrick Roads**. The drowned river valley is so deep that huge ocean-going ships can sail up almost as far as Truro. Numerous creeks are ideal for boating excursions to view the varied scenery and birdlife.

Falmouth has the third largest naturally deep harbour after Sydney and Rio de Janeiro, and it forms the most interesting part of this seaside resort. On the

CORNISH SMUGGLERS

In the days before income tax was invented, the main form of government income came from tax on imported luxury goods, such as brandy and perfume. Huge profits were to be made by evading these taxes, which were at their height during the Napoleonic Wars (1780–1815). Remote Cornwall, with its coves and rivers penetrating deep into the mainland, was prime smuggling territory; estimates put the number of people involved, including women and children, at 100,000. Some notorious families resorted to deliberate wrecking, setting up deceptive lights to lure vessels onto the sharp rocks, in the hope of plundering the wreckage.

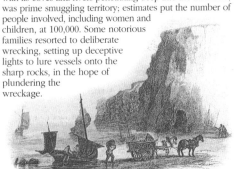

harbour waterfront stands the **National Maritime Museum Cornwall**, part of a large waterside complex, which includes cafés, shops and restaurants. The museum is dedicated to the great maritime tradition of Cornwall and contains Britain's finest public collection of historic and contemporary small craft. Exhibits look at maritime themes and the story of those whose lives depended on the sea.

Ship's figure-head, Falmouth

The many old houses on the harbour include the **Customs House** and the chimney alongside, known as the "King's Pipe" because it was used for burning contraband tobacco seized from smugglers in the 19th century. **Pendennis Castle** and St Mawes Castle opposite, were built by King Henry VIII.

Towards the town centre is the **Falmouth Art Gallery**, with one of Cornwall's most important art collections.

Environs: To the south, **Glendurgan** (see p244) and **Trebah** gardens are both set in sheltered valleys leading down to delightful sandy coves on the Helford River.

⚓ **National Maritime Museum Cornwall**
Discovery Quay, Falmouth.
Tel 01326 313388. ☐ daily.
● 25 & 26 Dec. 🗺 🔊 🖵 🖬

⚓ **Pendennis Castle**
(EH) The Headland. **Tel** 01326 316594. ☐ Apr–Oct: daily; Nov–Mar: Sat & Sun. ● 1 Jan, 24–26 Dec. 🖬 🔊 limited. 🗺 🖵 🖬

🏛 **Falmouth Art Gallery**
The Moor. **Tel** 01326 313863. ☐ Mon–Sat.

🌿 **Glendurgan**
(NT) Mawnan Smith. **Tel** 01326 252020. ☐ mid-Feb–Oct: Tue–Sat & pub hols (Aug: Mon–Sat). ● Good Fri. 🗺 🖵 🖬

🌿 **Trebah**
Mawnan Smith. **Tel** 01326 252200. ☐ daily. 🖬 🗺 🔊 🖵
www.trebah-garden.co.uk

Truro ❼

Cornwall. 🚶 19,000. 🚉 🚌
🛈 Boscawen St (01872 274555).
🛒 Wed (cattle), Wed & Sat (farmers' market). www.discovertruro.gov.uk

Once a market town and port, Truro is now the administrative capital of Cornwall. Truro's many gracious Georgian buildings reflect its prosperity during the tin mining boom of the 1800s. In 1876 the 16th-century parish church was rebuilt to create the first new **cathedral** to be built in England since Wren built St Paul's (see pp114–15) in the 17th century. With its central tower, lancet windows and spires, the cathedral is an exuberant building that looks more French than English.

Truro's cobbled streets and alleys lined with craft shops are also a delight to explore. The **Royal Cornwall Museum** provides an excellent introduction to the history of the county with displays on tin mining, Methodism (see p279) and smuggling.

Environs: On the outskirts of the city lie **Trewithen** and **Trelissick** gardens (see p244). The former has a rich collection of Asiatic plants.

🏛 **Royal Cornwall Museum**
River St. **Tel** 01872 272205. ☐ Tue–Sat. ● public hols. 🔊 🖵 🖬
www.royalcornwallmuseum.org.uk

🌿 **Trewithen**
Grampound Rd. **Tel** 01726 883647.
☐ Mar–May: daily; Jun–Sep: Mon–Sat. 🗺 🔊 🗺 by arrangement. 🖵
🖬 www.trewithengardens.co.uk

🌿 **Trelissick**
(NT) Feock. **Tel** 01872 862090.
☐ Mar–May: daily; Jun–Sep: Mon–Sat. 🗺 🔊 🍴 🖬

The "Cornish Alps": china-clay spoil tips north of St Austell

St Austell ❽

Cornwall. 🚶 20,000. 🚉 🚌 🛈
Texaco Service Station, Southbourne Rd (01726 879500). 🛒 Sat–Sun.
www.visitthecornishriviera.co.uk

The busy industrial town of St Austell is the capital of the local china-clay industry which rose to importance in the 18th century. Clay is still a vital factor here; until recently, China was the only other place where such quality and quantity of clay could be found. Spoil tips are a prominent feature; on a sunny day they look like snow-covered peaks, meriting the local name the "Cornish Alps".

Environs: The famous **Lost Gardens of Heligan** are an amazing restoration project to recreate the extraordinary gardens created by the Tremayne family from the 16th century to World War I. At the **Wheal Martyn China Clay Museum**, nature trails weave through clay works that operated from 1878 until the 1920s.

🌿 **Lost Gardens of Heligan**
Pentewan. **Tel** 01726 845100.
☐ daily. ● 24 & 25 Dec. 🗺 🔊
🍴 🖵 🖬 www.heligan.com

🏛 **Wheal Martyn China Clay Museum**
Carthew. **Tel** 01726 850362.
☐ Feb–Sep: daily. 🗺 🔊 limited.
🖵 🖬 www.wheal-martyn.com

Truro Cathedral, designed by J L Pearson and completed in 1910

Eden Project ❾

Built in a china clay pit that had reached the end of its useful life, the Eden Project is a global garden for the 21st century, and a dramatic setting in which to tell the fascinating story of mankind's dependence on plants. Two futuristic conservatories called Biomes have been designed to mimic the environments of warmer climes: one hot and humid, the other warm and dry. The outer Biome is planted with species that thrive in the Cornish climate. The Eden Project seeks to educate by telling the story of plants, people and places. The relationship between humans and nature is interpreted by artists throughout the site. An impressive education centre, the Core, was opened in 2006 and is used for exhibitions, films and workshops.

④ **Tropical South America**
Some plants in this area reach enormous proportions. The leaves of the giant waterlily can be up to 2 m (6 ft) across.

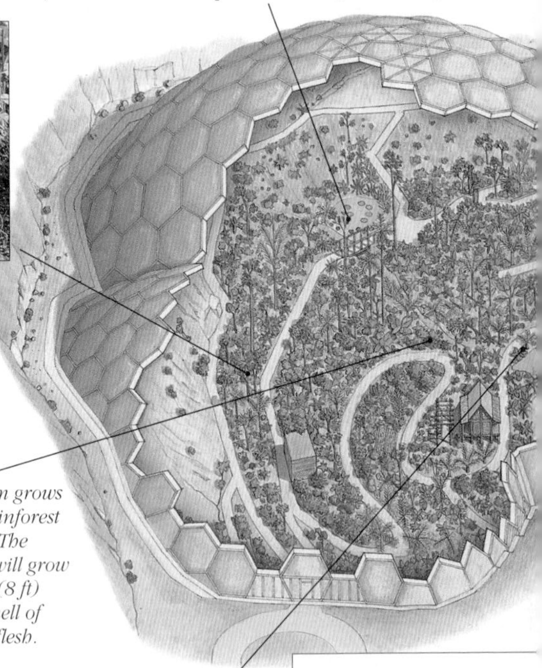

③ **West Africa**
Iboga is central to the African religion Bwiti. Highly hallucinogenic, it is an integral part of initiation ceremonies.

② **Malaysia**
The Titan arum grows within this rainforest display. The flower will grow to 3 m (8 ft) and smell of rotting flesh.

① **Tropical Islands**
Set apart from the rest of the world, these islands have many fascinating plants. The rare Madagascar Periwinkle (Catharanthus roseus) is thought to help cure leukemia.

THE SITE

Access to the outdoor and the covered Biomes is via the Visitor Centre.

Rainforest Biome
① Tropical Islands
② Malaysia
③ West Africa
④ Tropical South America
⑤ Crops & cultivation

Mediterranean Biome
⑥ The Mediterranean
⑦ South Africa
⑧ California
⑨ Crops & cultivation

VISITORS' CHECKLIST

Bodelva, St Austell, Cornwall.
Tel 01726 811911. St Austell.
dedicated bus service from St
Austell. *Apr–Oct: 10am–
6pm daily (last adm 5pm); Nov–
Mar: 10am–4:30pm daily (last
adm 3pm).* 24, 25 Dec.
For events details
see **www**.edenproject.com

Building Eden

*Cornwall's declining china clay industry has left behind
many disused pits. The Eden Project makes ingenious use
of this industrial landscape. After partly infilling a pit,
the massive Biomes were nestled into its base and walls.*

**Transparent hexagons
made of ultra-light hi-
tech plastic**

⑤ Crops and cultivation

*The coffee plant (Coffea
arabica) is one of the many
plants on display that are
used in our everyday lives.*

The entrance to both
the Rainforest and
Mediterranean Biomes is
via the Link, where the
Eden Bakery is located.

⌐NFOREST BIOME

vast conservatory houses a lush jungle of trees
plants. The dome is high enough to allow some
forest trees to grow to their full height.

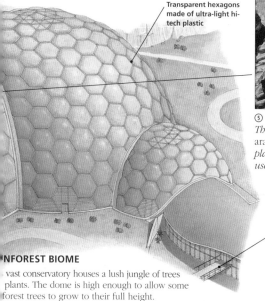

⌐door Biome	㉕ Play
⌐ollination	㉖ Flowers in the making
⌐ornish crops	㉗ Health
⌐lants for taste	㉘ Flowerless garden
⌐lobal gardeners	
⌐eer & brewing	
⌐ope & fibre	
⌐emp	
⌐teppe & Prairie	
⌐co-engineering	
⌐ea	
⌐avender	
⌐echanical theatre	
⌐uel	
⌐yth & folkore	
⌐iodiversity & Cornwall	

KEY

Land Train

The Stage

The Core

Eden Arena

Visitor Centre

0 metres   150

0 yards   150

View of Polruan across the estuary from Fowey

Fowey ❿

Cornwall. 🏠 *2,000.* 🚉
ℹ️ *5 South St (01726 833616).*
www.fowey.co.uk

Fowey (pronounced Foy), has been immortalized under the name of Troy Town in the humorous novels of Sir Arthur Quiller-Couch (1863–1944), who lived here in a house called **The Haven**. A resort favoured by many wealthy Londoners with a taste

DAPHNE DU MAURIER

The period romances of Daphne du Maurier (1907–89) are inextricably linked with the wild Cornish landscape where she grew up. *Jamaica Inn* established her reputation in 1936, and with the publication of *Rebecca* two years later she found herself one of the most popular authors of her day. *Rebecca* was made into a film directed by Alfred Hitchcock, starring Joan Fontaine and Lord Laurence Olivier.

for yachting and expensive seafood restaurants, Fowey is the most gentrified of the Cornish seaside towns. The picturesque charm of the flower-filled village is undeniable, with its tangle of tiny steep streets and its views across the estuary to Polruan. The church of **St Fimbarrus** marks the end of the ancient Saint's Way footpath from Padstow – a reminder of the Celtic missionaries who arrived on the shores of Cornwall to convert people to Christianity. Its flower-lined path leads to a majestic porch and carved tower. Inside there are some fine 17th-century memorials to the Rashleigh family whose seat, Menabilly, became Daphne du Maurier's home and featured as Manderley in *Rebecca* (1938).

Jamaica Inn, Bodmin Moor

Environs: For a closer look at the town of **Polruan** and the ceaseless activity of the harbour there is a number of river trips up the little creeks. At the estuary mouth are the twin towers from which chains were once hung to demast invading ships – an effective form of defence.

A fine stretch of coast leads further east to the picturesque fishing villages of **Polperro**, nestling in a narrow green ravine, and neighbouring **Looe**.

Upriver from Fowey is the tranquil town of **Lostwithiel**. Perched on a hill just to the north are the remains of the Norman **Restormel Castle**.

⚜️ **Restormel Castle**
(EH) Lostwithiel. **Tel** *01208 872687.*
☐ *Apr–Oct: daily.* 📷 🅿️

Bodmin ⓫

Cornwall. 🚉 *Bodmin Parkway.* 🚌
Bodmin. ℹ️ *Mount Folly Sq, Bodmin
(01208 76616).* **www**.bodminlive.com

Bodmin, Cornwall's ancient county town, lies on the sheltered western edge of the great expanse of moorland that shares its name. The history and archaeology of the town and moor is covered by **Bodmin Town Museum**, while **Bodmin Jail**, where public executions took place until 1909, is a gruesome tourist attraction. The churchyard is watered by the ever-gushing waters of a holy spring, and it was here that St Guron established a Christian cell in the 6th century. The **church** is dedicated to St Petroc, a Welsh missionary who founded a monastery here. The monastery has disappeared, but the bones of St Petroc remain, housed in a splendid 12th-century ivory casket in the church.

For a pleasant day out, ride the **Bodmin & Wenford Railway**, a steam train which departs from Bodmin Station, or take part in a Victorian murder trial at **The Courtroom Experience**, run by the tourist office.

South of Bodmin is the **Lanhydrock** estate. Amid its extensive wooded acres and formal gardens *(see p244)* lies the massive Victorian manor house, rebuilt after a fire in 1881, but retaining some Jacobean features. The fine 17th-century plaster ceiling in the Long Gallery depicts scenes from the Bible.

The desolate wilderness of Bodmin Moor is noted for its network of prehistoric field boundaries. The main attraction, however, is the 18th-century **Jamaica Inn**, made famous by Daphne du Maurier's tale of smuggling and romance. Today there is a restaurant and bar based on du Maurier's novel, and a small museum. A 30-minute walk from the Inn is **Dozmary Pool**, reputed to be bottomless until it dried up in 1976.

The ruins of Tintagel Castle on the north coast of Cornwall

According to legend, the dying King Arthur's sword Excalibur was thrown into the pool.

To the east is **Altarnun**. Its spacious 15th-century church of **St Nonna** is known as the "Cathedral of the Moor".

🏛 **Bodmin Town Museum**
Mt Folly Sq, Bodmin. *Tel* 01208 77067. ☐ Easter–Oct: Mon–Sat, Good Fri. ⬤ pub hols. ♿ ltd. 📷

🏰 **Bodmin Jail**
Berrycombe Rd, Bodmin. *Tel* 01208 76292. ☐ daily. ⬤ 25 Dec. 📷 🎦
🍴 🖥 www.bodminjail.org

🏰 **Lanhydrock**
(NT) Bodmin. *Tel* 01208 265950.
House ☐ Apr–Oct: Tue–Sun & public hols. **Gardens** ☐ daily.
📷 🎦 ♿ 🍴

Tintagel ⑫

Cornwall. 🏠 1,700. 🚌 Bossiney Rd (01840 779084). 🛒 Thu (summer). www.visitboscastleandtintagel.com

The romantic and mysterious ruins of **Tintagel Castle**, built around 1240 by Earl Richard of Cornwall, sit high on a hill-top surrounded by slate cliffs. Access to the castle is via two steep staircases clinging to the cliffside where pink thrift and purple sea lavender abound.

The earl was persuaded to build in this isolated, wind-swept spot by the popular belief, derived from Geoffrey of Monmouth's fictitious

KING ARTHUR

Historians think the legendary figure of King Arthur has some basis in historical fact. He was probably a Romano-British chieftain or warrior who led British resistance to the Saxon invasion of the 6th century *(see pp46–7)*. Geoffrey of Monmouth's *History of the Kings of Britain* (1139) introduced Arthur to literature with an account of the many legends connected with him – how he became king by removing the sword Excalibur from a stone, his final battle with the treacherous Mordred, and the story of the Knights of the Round Table *(see p170)*. Other writers, such as Alfred, Lord Tennyson, took up these stories and elaborated on them.

King Arthur, from a 14th-century chronicle by Peter of Langtoft

History of the Kings of Britain, that this was the birthplace of the legendary King Arthur.

Large quantities of fine eastern Mediterranean pottery dating from around the 5th century have been discovered, indicating that the site was an important trading centre, long before the medieval castle was built. Whoever lived here, perhaps the ancient Kings of Cornwall, could evidently afford a luxurious lifestyle.

A clifftop path leads from the castle to Tintagel's **church**, which has Norman and Saxon masonry. In Tintagel village the **Old Post Office** is a rare example of a 14th-century restored and furnished Cornish manor house.

Environs: A short distance to the east, **Boscastle** is a pretty National Trust village. The River Valency runs down the middle of the main street to the fishing harbour, which is sheltered from the sea by high slate cliffs. Access from the harbour to the sea is via a channel cut through the rocks.

⚓ **Tintagel Castle**
(EH) Off High St. *Tel* 01840 770328. ☐ Apr–Oct: daily; Nov–Mar: Sat & Sun. ⬤ 1 Jan, 24–26 Dec. 🎦
www.english-heritage.org.uk/tintagel

🏰 **Old Post Office**
(NT) Fore St. *Tel* 01840 770024. ☐ Mar–Oct: daily. 📷 🎦

Bude ⑬

Cornwall. 🏠 9,000. 🚌 Crescent car park (01288 354240). 🛒 alternate Fri (summer). www.visitbude.info

Wonderful beaches around this area make Bude a popular resort for families. The expanse of clean golden sand that attracts visitors today once made Bude a bustling port. Shelly, lime-rich sand was transported along a canal to inland farms where it was used to neutralize the acidic soil. The canal was abandoned in 1880 but a short stretch survives, providing a haven for birds such as kingfishers and herons.

Kingfisher

Clovelly ⑭

Devon. 🏘 350. **Tel** 01237 431781.
Town & Visitors' Centre ☐ daily.
🔴 25 & 26 Dec. 🈴 🕭 Visitors'
Centre. **www**.clovelly.co.uk

Clovelly has been a noted
beauty spot since the novelist
Charles Kingsley (1819–75)
wrote about it in his stirring
story of the Spanish Armada,
Westward Ho! (1855). The
whole village is privately
owned and has been turned
into a tourist attraction, with
little sign of the flourishing
fishing industry to which it
owed its birth. It is a charming
village with steep, traffic-free
cobbled streets rising up the
cliff from the harbourside,
white-washed houses and
gardens brimming with brightly
coloured flowers. There are
superb views from the lookout
points and fine coastal paths
to explore from the tiny quay.
   Hobby Drive is a scenic
3-mile (5-km) approach on
foot to the village which runs
through woodland along the
coast. The road was con-
structed in 1811–29 to give
employment to local men

Bideford's medieval bridge, 203 m (666 ft) long with 24 arches

who had been made redundant
at the end of the Napoleonic
Wars *(see pp54–5)*.

Bideford ⑮

Devon. 🏘 14,000. 🚉 🛈 Burton
Art Gallery, Kingsley Rd (01237
471455). 🛒 Tue, Sat.

Strung out along the estuary of
the River Torridge, Bideford
grew and thrived on importing
tobacco from the New World.
Some 17th-century merchants'
houses survive in Bridgeland
Street, including the splendid
bay-windowed house at No. 28
(1693). Beyond is Mill Street,
leading to the parish church

and the fine medieval bridge.
The quay stretches from here
to a pleasant park and a statue
that commemorates Charles
Kingsley, whose novels
helped bring visitors to the
area in the 19th century.

Environs: To the west of
Bideford, the village **Westward
Ho!** was built in the late 19th
century and named after
Kingsley's popular novel. The
development failed, and the
Victorian villas and hotels are
now part of a holiday resort.
Rudyard Kipling *(see p163)*
was at school here and the
hill to the south, known as
Kipling Tors, was the background for *Stalky & Co* (1899).
   Also to the west is **Hartland
Abbey**, built as a monastery
c.1157, now a family home.
The BBC filmed parts of *Sense
and Sensibility* here. Visitors
can enjoy a museum, art and
antiques, as well as gardens.
   Henry Williamson's *Tarka
the Otter* (1927) describes the
otters of the **Torridge Valley**
and naturalists are hoping to
reintroduce otters here. Part
of a Tarka Trail has been laid
out along the Torridge and
bicycles can be hired from the
old railway station. The trail
passes close to the magnificent **Rosemoor Garden**.
   Day trips run from either
Bideford or Ilfracombe
(depending on the tide) to
Lundy island, which is abundant in birds and wildlife.

🌺 **RHS Rosemoor Garden**
Great Torrington. **Tel** 01805
624067. ☐ daily. 🔴 25 Dec. 🈴
🕭 🔢 🏠 **www**.rhs.org.uk

🏛 **Hartland Abbey**
nr. Bideford. **Tel** 01237 441264.
☐ Apr–May: Wed, Thu, Sun;
Jun–Sep: Sun–Thu. 🈴 🖥 🏠 🕭
limited. **www**.hartlandabbey.com

Fishing boats in Clovelly's harbour

Fishermen's cottages, Appledore

Appledore ⑯

Devon. 🏘 2,500. ℹ Bideford
(01237 477676).

Appledore's remote position at the tip of the Torridge Estuary has helped to preserve its charms intact. Busy boatyards line the long riverside quay, which is also the departure point for fishing trips and ferries to the sandy beaches of Braunton Burrows on the opposite shore. Timeworn Regency houses line the main street which runs parallel to the quay, and behind is a network of narrow cobbled lanes with 18th-century fishermen's cottages. Several shops retain their original bow-windows and sell an assortment of crafts, antiques and souvenirs.

Uphill from the quay is the **North Devon Maritime Museum**, with an exhibition on the experiences of Devon emigrants in Australia and displays explaining the work of local shipyards. The tiny **Victorian Schoolroom** which is affiliated to the museum, shows various documentary videos on local trades such as fishing and shipbuilding.

🏛 **North Devon Maritime Museum**
Odun Rd. *Tel* 01237 422064. ⬜ *May–Sep: daily; Apr, Oct: Mon–Fri.* 🖼 ♿ ltd. 🅿 **www. northdevonmaritimemuseum.co.uk**

Barnstaple ⑰

Devon. 🏘 33,000. 🚆 🚌 ℹ The Square (01271 375000). 🛒 Mon–Sat (Apr–Nov only).

Although Barnstaple is an important distribution centre for the whole region, its town centre remains calm due to the exclusion of traffic. The massive glass-roofed **Pannier Market** (1855) has stalls of organic food, much of it produced by farmers' wives to supplement their income. Nearby is **St Peter's Church** with its twisted broach spire, said to have been caused by a lightning strike which warped the timbers in 1810.

On the Strand is a wonderful arcade topped with a statue of Queen Anne, now the **Heritage Centre**. This was built as an exchange where merchants traded the contents of their cargo boats moored on the River Taw alongside. Nearby is the 15th-century bridge and the **Museum of Barnstaple and North Devon**, where displays cover local history and the 700-year-old pottery industry, as well as local wildlife, such as the otters. The 180-mile (290 km) Tarka Trail circuits around Barnstaple; 35 miles (56 km) of it can be cycled.

Environs: Just west of Barnstaple, **Braunton "Great Field"** covers over 120 ha (300 acres) and is a well-preserved relic of medieval open-field

Barnstaple's Pannier Market

Statue of Queen Anne (1708)

cultivation. Beyond lies **Braunton Burrows**, one of the most extensive wild-dune reserves in Britain. It is a must for plant enthusiasts who would like to spot sea kale, sea holly, sea lavender and horned poppies growing in their natural habitat. The sandy beaches and pounding waves at nearby Croyde and Woolacombe, are favourites among surfing enthusiasts, but there are also calmer areas of warm shallow water and rock pools.

Arlington Court, north of Barnstaple, has a collection of model ships, magnificent perennial borders and a lake. The stables house a collection of horse-drawn vehicles, and rides are available in summer.

🏛 **Museum of Barnstaple and North Devon**
The Square. *Tel* 01271 346747. ⬜ *Mon–Sat.* ⬤ 24 Dec–1 Jan. ♿ ltd. 🅿 **www.devonmuseums.net**

🏰 **Arlington Court**
(NT) Arlington. *Tel* 01271 850296. ⬜ *Easter–Oct: daily.* 🖼 ♿ limited. 🅿 ⬜

DEVONSHIRE CREAM TEAS

Devon people claim all other versions of a cream tea are inferior to their own. The essential ingredient is Devonshire clotted cream which comes from Jersey cattle fed on rich Devon pasture – anything else is second best, or so it is claimed. Spread thickly on freshly baked scones, with lashings of homemade strawberry jam, this makes a seductive, delicious, but fattening, tea-time treat.

A typical cream tea with scones, jam and clotted cream

The village of Lynmouth

Lynton and Lynmouth ⑱

Devon. 🚹 2,000. 🚌 🚉 ℹ️ Town Hall,
Lee Rd, Lynton (01598 752225).
www.lynton-lynmouth-tourism.co.uk

Situated at the point where
the East and West Lyn rivers
meet the sea, Lynmouth is a
picturesque, though rather
commercialized, fishing village.
The pedestrianized main street,
lined with shops selling seaside
souvenirs, runs parallel to the
Lyn, now a canal with high
embankments to protect
against flash floods. One flood
devastated the town at the
height of the holiday season
in 1952. The scars caused by
the flood, which was fuelled
by heavy rain on Exmoor, are
now overgrown by trees in
the pretty **Glen Lyn Gorge**,
which leads north out of the
village. Lynmouth's sister town,
Lynton, is a mainly Victorian
village perched on the clifftop
130 m (427 ft) above, giving
lovely views across the Bristol
Channel to the Welsh coast.
It can be reached from the
harbour front by a cliff railway
(open March to October), by
road or by a steep path.

Environs: Lynmouth makes an
excellent starting point for
walks on Exmoor. There is a
2 mile (3 km) trail that leads
southeast to tranquil **Watersmeet** (see p251). On the
western edge of Exmoor,
Combe Martin (see p250) lies
in a sheltered valley. On the
main street, lined with Victorian villas, is the 18th-century
Pack of Cards Inn, built by
a gambler with 52 windows,
for each card in the pack.

Exeter ⑲

Exeter is Devon's capital, a bustling and lively city with
a great deal of character, despite the World War II
bombing that destroyed much of its city centre. Built
high on a plateau above the River Exe, the city is encircled by substantial sections of Roman and medieval wall,
and the street plan has not changed much since the
Romans first laid out what is now the High Street.
Elsewhere the Cathedral Close forms a pleasant green,
and there are cobbled streets and narrow alleys which
invite leisurely exploration. For shoppers there is a wide
selection of big stores and smaller speciality shops.

Exploring Exeter
The intimate green and the
close surrounding Exeter's
distinctive cathedral were the
setting for Anthony Trollope's
novel He Knew He Was Right
(1869). Full of festive crowds
listening to buskers in the
summer, the close presents an
array of architectural styles.
One of the finest buildings
here is the Elizabethan **Mol's
Coffee House**. Among the
other historic buildings that
survived World War II are the
magnificent **Guildhall** (1330)
on the High Street (one of
Britain's oldest civic buildings), the opulent **Custom
House** (1681) by the quay,
and the elegant 18th-century
Rougemont House which
stands near the remains of a
Norman **castle** built by William
the Conqueror (see pp46–7).

The port area has been transformed into a tourist attraction
with its early 19th-century
warehouses converted into
craft shops, antique galleries
and cafés. Boats can be hired
for cruising down the short
stretch of canal. The **Quay
House Interpretation Centre**

The timber-framed Mol's Coffee
House (1596), Cathedral Close

West front and south tower,
Cathedral Church of St Peter

(open daily April–October;
weekends November–March)
has audio-visual and other displays on the history of Exeter.

⛪ Cathedral Church
of St Peter
Cathedral Close. **Tel** 01392 255573.
⬜ daily. 🏠 ♿ 🍴
Exeter's cathedral is one of
the most gloriously ornamented
in Britain. Except for the two
Norman towers, the cathedral
is mainly 14th century and
built in the style aptly known
as Decorated because of the
swirling geometric patterns
of the stone work. The West
Front, the largest single
collection (66) of medieval
figure sculptures in England,
includes kings, apostles and
prophets. Started in the 14th
century, it was completed by
1450. Inside, the splendid
Gothic vaulting sweeps from
one end of the church to the
other, impressive in its unifor-
mity and punctuated by gaily
painted ceiling bosses.

Among the tombs around
the choir is that of Edward II's
treasurer, Walter de Stapledon
(1261–1326), who was mur-
dered by a mob in London.
Stapledon raised much of the
money needed to fund the
building of this cathedral.

Collection of shells and other objects in the library of A La Ronde

VISITORS' CHECKLIST

Devon. 120,000. 5 miles (8 km) east. Exeter St David's, Bonhay Rd; Exeter Central, Queen St. Paris St. Dix's Field (01392 665700). www. heartofdevon.com

Underground Passages

Paris St. **Tel** 01392 665 887. Jun–Sep: daily; Oct–May: Tue–Sun.
Under the city centre lie the remains of Exeter's medieval water-supply system. An excellent video and guided tour explain how the stone-lined tunnels were built in the 14th and 15th centuries on a slight gradient in order to bring in fresh water for townspeople from springs outside the town. The site was refurbished in 2007 and includes the Heritage Centre.

St Nicholas Priory

The Mint. **Tel** 01392 665858. phone for details.
Built in the 12th century, this building has retained many of its original features and rooms. These help visitors to trace its fascinating history from austere monastic beginnings, through its secular use as a Tudor residence for wealthy merchants, to its 20th-century incarnation as five separate business premises occupied by various tradesmen including a bootmaker and an upholsterer.

Royal Albert Memorial Museum and Art Gallery

Queen St. **Tel** 01392 265858. Tue–Sun.
This museum has a wonderfully varied collection, including Roman remains, a zoo of stuffed animals, West Country art and a particularly good ethnographic display. Highlights include displays on silverware, watches and clocks.

19th-century head of an Oba, Royal Albert Museum

Environs: South of Exeter on the A376, the eccentric **A La Ronde** is a 16-sided house built in 1796 by two spinster cousins, who decorated the interior with shells, feathers and souvenirs gathered while on tours of Europe.

Further east, the unspoilt Regency town of **Sidmouth** lies in a sheltered bay. There is an eclectic array of architecture, the earliest buildings dating from the 1820s when Sidmouth became a popular summer resort. Thatched cottages stand opposite huge Edwardian villas, and elegant terraces line the seafront. In summer the town hosts the famous International Festival of Folk Arts (see p63).

North of Sidmouth lies the magnificent church at **Ottery St Mary**. Built in 1338–42 by Bishop Grandisson, the church is clearly a scaled-down version of Exeter Cathedral, which he also helped build. In the churchyard wall is a memorial to the poet Coleridge who was born in the town in 1772.

Nearby **Honiton** is famous for its extraordinarily intricate and delicate lace, made here since Elizabethan times.

To the north of Exeter, **Killerton** is home to the National Trust's costume collection. Here, displays of bustles and corsets and vivid tableaux illustrate aristocratic fashions from the 18th century to the present day.

Further north near Tiverton, is **Knightshayes Court**, a Victorian Gothic mansion with fine gardens (see p245).

A La Ronde

(NT) Summer Lane, Exmouth. **Tel** 01395 265514. Mar–Oct: Sat–Wed (Jul–Aug: daily).

Killerton

(NT) Broadclyst. **Tel** 01392 881345. **House** mid-Feb–Dec: daily. **Garden** daily.

Knightshayes Court

(NT) Bolham. **Tel** 01884 254665. mid-Mar–Oct: Sat–Thu. **Gardens** Apr–Nov: daily. limited.

Mexican dancer at Sidmouth's International Festival of Folk Arts

Torbay ⑳

Torbay. 🚃 ✈ Torquay, Paignton. ℹ
Vaughan Parade, Torquay (01803
211211). www.englishriviera.co.uk

The seaside towns of Torquay,
Paignton and Brixham form
an almost continuous resort
around the great sweep of
sandy beach and blue waters
of Torbay. Because of its mild
climate, semi-tropical gardens
and exuberant Victorian hotel
architecture, this popular
coastline has been dubbed the
English Riviera. In the Victorian
era Torbay was patronized by
the wealthy. Today, the theme
is mass entertainment, and
there are plenty of attractions,
mostly in and around Torquay.

Torre Abbey includes the
remains of a monastery founded in 1196. It is currently
undergoing a massive restoration programme, the first phase
of which focused on the
abbey's oldest part. Future
phases will redevelop the
abbey's galleries and restore
the historic gardens. **Torquay
Museum** nearby covers natural
history and archaeology,
including finds from **Kents
Cavern**, on the outskirts of
the town. This is one of England's most important prehistoric sites, and the spectacular
caves include displays on
people and animals who lived
here up to 350,000 years ago.

The charming miniature
town of **Babbacombe Model
Village** is north of Torquay,
while a mile (1.5 km) inland
is the lovely village of
Cockington. Visitors travel by
horse-drawn carriage to the
preserved Tudor manor house,
church and thatched cottages.

In Paignton, the celebrated
Paignton Zoo teaches children about the planet's wildlife,
and from here you can take
the steam railway – an ideal
way to visit Dartmouth.

Continuing south from
Paignton, the pretty town of
Brixham was once England's
most prosperous fishing port.

🏰 **Torre Abbey**
King's Drive, Torquay. **Tel** 01803
293593. ● for renovation. 🎫 📷
🔌 📷 📷

Bayards Cove, Dartmouth

🏛 **Torquay Museum**
Babbacombe Rd, Torquay. **Tel** 01803
293975. ● daily (Nov–Easter: Mon–
Sat). ● Christmas wk. 🎫 🔌 📷
📷 www.torquaymuseum.org

🦇 **Kents Cavern**
Ilsham Rd, Torquay. 📠 01803 215
136. ● daily. ● 25 & 26 Dec. 🎫
🎫 🍴 📷 www.kents-cavern.co.uk

🏛 **Babbacombe Model
Village**
Hampton Ave, Torquay. **Tel** 01803
315315. ● daily. 🎫 🔌 📷

🐾 **Paignton Zoo**
Totnes Rd, Paignton. 📠 0844 474
2222. ● daily. ● 25 Dec. 🎫 🔌
🍴 📷 www.paingtonzoo.org.uk

Dartmouth ㉑

Devon. 🏘 5,500. 🚃 ℹ Mayors Ave
(01803 834224). ● Tue–Fri am.
www.discoverdartmouth.com

Sitting high on the hill
above the River Dart is the
Royal Naval College, where
British naval officers have
trained since 1905. Dartmouth
has always been an important
port and it was from here that
English fleets set sail to join
the Second and Third Cru-
sades. Some 18th-century
houses adorn the cobbled
quay of Bayards Cove, while
carved timber buildings line
the 17th-century Butterwalk,
home to **Dartmouth Museum**.
To the south is **Dartmouth
Castle** (1388).

🏛 **Dartmouth Museum**
Butterwalk. **Tel** 01803 832923. ●
Mon–Sat. ● 1 Jan, 25 & 26 Dec.
🎫 📷 www.devonmuseums.net

🏰 **Dartmouth Castle**
(EH) Castle Rd. **Tel** 01803 833588.
● daily (Nov–Easter: Sat & Sun).
● 1 Jan, 24–26 Dec. 🎫 📷

Torquay, on the "English Riviera"

Stained-glass window in Blessed Sacrament Chapel, Buckfast Abbey

Totnes ②

Devon. 🏠 7,500. 🚉 🚌 ⛴
ℹ️ Town Mill (01803 863168).
🚌 Tue am (May–Sep), Fri, Sat.
www.totnesinformation.co.uk

Totnes sits at the highest navigable point on the River Dart with a Norman **castle** perched high on the hill above. Linking the two is the steep High Street, lined with bow-windowed Elizabethan houses. Bridging the street is the **Eastgate**, part of the medieval town wall. Life in the town's heyday is explored in the **Totnes Elizabethan Museum**, which also has a room devoted to the mathematician Charles Babbage (1791–1871), who is regarded as the pioneer of modern computers. There is a **Guildhall**, and a **church** with a delicately carved and gilded rood screen. On Tuesdays in the summer, market stallholders dress in Elizabethan costume.

Environs: A few miles north of Totnes, **Dartington Hall** has 10 ha (25 acres) of lovely gardens and a famous music school where concerts are held in the timbered 14th-century Great Hall.

Stallholders in Totnes market

♠ **Totnes Castle**
(EH) Castle St. **Tel** 01803 864406.
⬜ Apr–Oct: daily; Nov–Mar: Sat & Sun. 🅿️

🏛 **Totnes Elizabethan Museum**
Fore St. **Tel** 01803 863821. ⬜ Easter–Oct: Mon–Fri. 🅿️ 🚻 limited.

🎪 **Guildhall**
Rampart Walk. **Tel** 01803 862147.
⬜ Apr–Oct: Mon–Fri. 🅿️

🌿 **Dartington Hall Gardens**
Tel 01803 862367. ⬜ daily.
www.dartington.org

Buckfastleigh ②

Devon. 🏠 3,300. 🚉 ℹ️ Fore St (01364 644522).

This market town, situated on the edge of Dartmoor (see pp294–5), is dominated by **Buckfast Abbey**. The original abbey, founded in Norman times, fell into ruin after the Dissolution of the Monasteries and it was not until 1882 that a small group of French Benedictine monks set up a new abbey here. Work on the present building was financed by donations and carried out by the monks. The abbey was completed in 1938 and lies at the heart of a thriving community. The fine mosaics and modern stained-glass window are also the work of the monks.

Nearby is the **Buckfast Butterfly Farm and Otter Sanctuary**, and the **South Devon Steam Railway** terminus where steam trains leave for Totnes.

🔵 **Buckfast Abbey**
Buckfastleigh. **Tel** 01364 645500.
⬜ daily. 🔴 Good Fri, 25–27 Dec.
🅿️ 🚻 🏪 www.buckfast.org.uk

🦋 **Buckfast Butterfly Farm and Otter Sanctuary**
Buckfastleigh. **Tel** 01364 642916.
⬜ Easter–Nov: daily. 🅿️ 🅿️
www.ottersandbutterflies.co.uk

Burgh Island ②

Devon. 🚉 Plymouth, then taxi. ℹ️ The Quay, Kingsbridge (01548 853 195). www.kingsbridgeinfo.co.uk

The short walk across the sands at low tide from Bigbury-on-Sea to Burgh Island takes you back to the era of the 1920s and 1930s. It was here that the millionaire Archibald Nettlefold built the luxury **Burgh Island Hotel** (see p567) in 1929. Created in Art Deco style with a natural rock sea-bathing pool, this was the exclusive retreat of figures such as the Duke of Windsor and Noel Coward. The restored hotel is worth a visit for the photographs of its heyday and the Art Deco fittings. You can also explore the island and **Pilchard Inn** (1336), reputed to be haunted by the ghost of a smuggler.

The Art Deco style bar in Burgh Island Hotel

Plymouth ㉕

Plymouth. 🏙 250,000. ✈ 🚢 🚉
🚌 ℹ The Mayflower, The Barbican
(01752 306330). 🏪 daily.
www.visitplymouth.co.uk

The tiny port from which Drake, Raleigh, the Pilgrim Fathers, Cook and Darwin all set sail on pioneering voyages has now grown to a substantial city, much of it boldly rebuilt after wartime bombing. Old Plymouth clusters around the **Hoe**, the famous patch of turf on which Sir Francis Drake is said to have calmly finished his game of bowls as the Spanish Armada approached the port in 1588 (*see pp50–51*). Today the Hoe is a pleasant park and parade ground surrounded by memorials to naval men, including Drake himself. Alongside is Charles II's **Royal Citadel**, built to guard the harbour in

Drake's coat of arms

the 1660s. On the harbour is the **National Marine Aquarium**. Nearby is the **Mayflower Stone and Steps**, the spot where the Pilgrim Fathers set sail for the New World in England's third and successful attempt at colonization in 1620. The popular **Plymouth Mayflower Exhibition** explores the story of the Mayflower and the creation of the harbour. Interactive graphics are used to tell the tales of merchant families and emigration to the New World.

Environs: A boat tour of the harbour is the best way to see the dockyards where warships have been built since the Napoleonic Wars. There are also splendid views of various fine gardens, such as **Mount Edgcumbe Park** (*see p244*), scattered around the coastline. East of the city, the 18th-century **Saltram House** has two rooms

Mid-18th-century carved wood chimneypiece, Saltram House

by Adam (*see pp28–9*) and portraits by Reynolds, who was born in nearby Plympton.

🏰 **Royal Citadel**
(EH) The Hoe. ⬜ May–Sep: Tue & Thu. 🎫 only. 🖼 www.english heritage.org.uk

🐟 **National Marine Aquarium**
Rope Walk, Coxside. **Tel** 01752 600 301. ⬜ daily. ⬛ 25 Dec. 🖼 ♿ 🛍
www.national-aquarium.co.uk

🏛 **Plymouth Mayflower Exhibition**
3–5 The Barbican. **Tel** 01752 306 331. ⬜ daily (Nov–Apr: Mon–Sat).

🌿 **Mount Edgcumbe Park**
Cremyll, Torpoint. 🚌 from Torpoint car park. **Tel** 01752 822236. **House** ⬜ Apr–Sep: Sun–Thu. **Grounds** ⬜ all year. 🖼 🎫 ♿ 🛍 🛍 🍴

🏰 **Saltram House**
(NT) Plympton. **Tel** 01752 333500. **Gallery** ⬜ mid-Mar–Dec: daily; Feb–mid-Mar: Sat & Sun. **Gardens** ⬜ all year. 🖼 ♿ 🍴 🛍 🛍

Buckland Abbey ㉖

(NT) Yelverton, Devon. **Tel** 01822 853607. 🚌 from Yelverton. ⬜ Fri–Wed (Jul–Aug: daily; Nov–Mar: Fri–Sun). ⬛ Christmas–mid-Feb. 🖼 ♿ 🍴 🛍 www.nationaltrust.org.uk

Founded by the Cistercian monks in 1278, Buckland Abbey was converted to a house after the Dissolution of the Monasteries and became the home of Drake from 1581–96. Many of the monastic buildings survive in a garden setting, notably the 14th-century tithe barn (*see p28*). Drake's life is explained through paintings and memorabilia in the house.

View of Plymouth Harbour from the Hoe

Cotehele ㉗

(NT) St Dominick, Cornwall.
Tel 01579 351346. ⊞ *Calstock.*
House ⬚ *Apr–Oct: Sat–Thu &
Good Fri.* Grounds ⬚ *daily.* ⬚ ⬚
⬚ *limited.* ⬚ ⬚

Magnificent woodland and lush river scenery make Cotehele (pronounced Coteal) one of the most delightful spots on the River Tamar and a rewarding day can be spent exploring the estate. Far from civilization, tucked into its wooded fold in the Cornish countryside, Cotehele has slumbered for 500 years. The main attraction is the house and valley garden at its centre. Built mainly between 1489 and 1520, it is a rare example of a medieval house, set around three courtyards with a magnificent open hall, kitchen, chapel and a warren of private parlours and chambers. The romance of the house is enhanced by colourful terraced gardens to the east, leading via a tunnel into a richly planted valley garden. The path through this garden passes a large domed medieval dovecote and descends to a quay, to which lime and coal were once shipped. There are fine views up and down the winding reed-fringed Tamar from Prospect Tower, and a gallery on the quayside specializes in local arts and crafts. The estate includes a village, a quay with a small maritime museum, working mill buildings, ancient lime kilns and workshops with 19th-century equipment.

Spanish Armada and British fleets in the English Channel, 1588

SIR FRANCIS DRAKE

Sir Francis Drake (c.1540–1596) was the first Englishman to circumnavigate the globe and he was knighted by Elizabeth I in 1580. Four years later he introduced tobacco and potatoes to England, after bringing home 190 colonists who had tried to establish a settlement in Virginia. To many, however, Drake was no more than an opportunistic rogue, renowned for his exploits as a "privateer", the polite name for a pirate. Catholic Spain was the bitter enemy and Drake further endeared himself to queen and people by his part in the victory over Philip II's Armada *(see pp50–51)*, defeated by bad weather and the buccaneering spirit of the English.

Morwellham Quay ㉘

Near Tavistock, Devon.
Tel 01822 832766. ⊞ *Gunnislake.*
⬚ *daily.* ⬚ *1 Jan, 24–26 Dec.*
⬚ ⬚ ⬚ *limited.* ⬚ ⬚
www.morwellham-quay.co.uk

Morwellham Quay was a neglected and overgrown industrial site until 1970, when members of a local trust began restoring the abandoned cottages, schoolhouse, farmyards, quay and copper mines to their original condition.

Today, Morwellham Quay is a thriving and rewarding industrial museum, where you can easily spend a whole day partaking in the typical activities of a Victorian village, from preparing the shire horses for a day's work, to riding a tramway deep into a copper mine in the hillside behind the village. The museum is brought to life by characters in costumes, some of whom give demonstrations throughout the day. You can watch, or lend a hand to the

Medieval dovecote in the gardens of Cotehele estate

Industrial relics at Morwellham Quay in the Tamar Valley

cooper while he builds a barrel, attend a lesson in the schoolroom, take part in Victorian playground games or dress up in 19th-century hooped skirts, bonnets, top hats or jackets. The staff, who convincingly play the part of villagers, lead you through their lives and impart a huge amount of information about the history of this small copper-mining community.

Dartmoor National Park ㉘

Buzzard

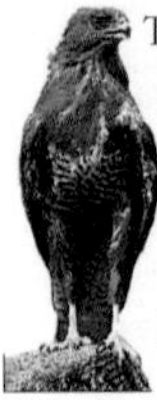

The high, open moorland of central Dartmoor provides the eerie background for Conan Doyle's thriller, *The Hound of the Baskervilles* (1902). Here at Princetown, surrounded by weathered outcrops of granite tors is one of Britain's most famous prisons. Also dotting the landscape are scores of prehistoric remains which have survived because of the durability of granite. Elsewhere the mood is very different. Streams tumble through wooded and boulder-strewn ravines forming cascades and waterfalls, and thatched cottages nestle in the sheltered valleys around the margins of the moor. Many establishments offer cream teas and warming fires to weary walkers.

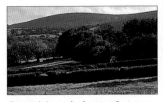

Characteristic moorland, eastern Dartmoor

Okehampton has the Museum of Dartmoor Life and a ruined 14th-century castle.

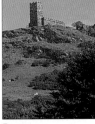

Brentor

This volcanic hill crowned by a tiny church (first built in 1130) is visible for miles.

Lydford Gorge (NT) (open Apr–Oct) is a dramatic ravine, leading to a waterfall.

The Ministry of Defence uses much of this area for training but access is available on non-firing days (0800 458 4868 to check).

High Moorland Visitor Centre

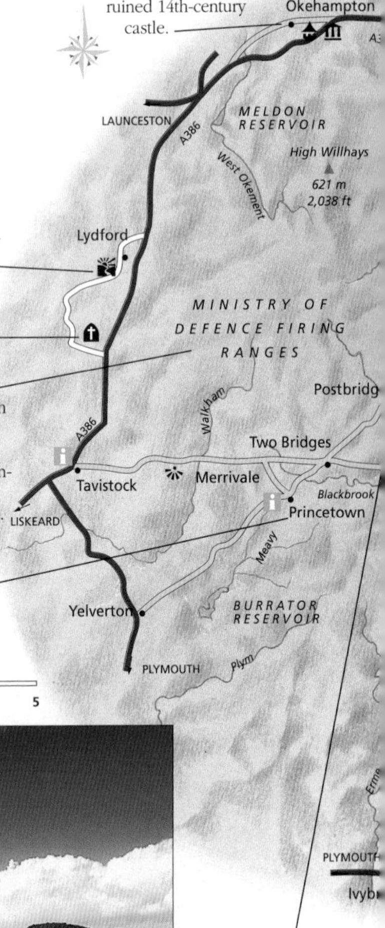

Okehampton
LAUNCESTON
A386
MELDON RESERVOIR
West Okement
High Willhays
621 m
2,038 ft
Lydford
MINISTRY OF DEFENCE FIRING RANGES
Postbridg
Walkham
Two Bridges
Tavistock
Merrivale
Blackbrook
Princetown
LISKEARD
Meavy
BURRATOR RESERVOIR
Yelverton
PLYMOUTH
Plym
Erme
PLYMOUTH
Ivybr

KEY

- Information centre
- A road
- B road
- Minor road
- Viewpoint

0 kilometres 5

0 miles 5

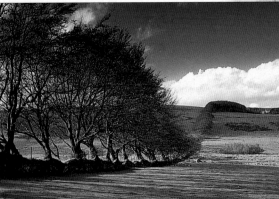

Postbridge

Dartmoor's northern moor can be explored from the village of Postbridge. The gently rolling moorland is crossed by many dry-stone walls.

Dartmoor Ponies
These small, tough ponies have lived on the moor since at least the 10th century.

Grimspound is the impressive remains of a Bronze Age settlement.

Castle Drogo (NT) is a magnificent mock-castle built by the architect Sir Edwin Lutyens *(see p29)* in 1910–30.

VISITORS' CHECKLIST

Devon. ⊟ ⊞ *Exeter, Plymouth, Totnes then bus.* ⓘ *Dartmoor National Park Authority's Centre (01822890414),* www.*dartmoor-npa.gov.uk.* **Okehampton Castle**, Castle Lane, Okehampton. *Tel 01837 52844.* ◯ *Apr–Sept daily.* ◪ **Museum of Dartmoor Life**, West St, Okehampton. *Tel 01837 52295.* ◯ *Apr–mid-Dec: Mon–Sat.* ● *24 Dec–1 Jan.* ◪ ⏃ *limited.* **Castle Drogo (NT)**, Drewsteignton. *Tel 01647 433 306.* ◯ *mid-Feb–Oct: daily.* **Gardens** ◯ *daily.* ◪ ⏃ *gardens only.* �️ ☐ ☐

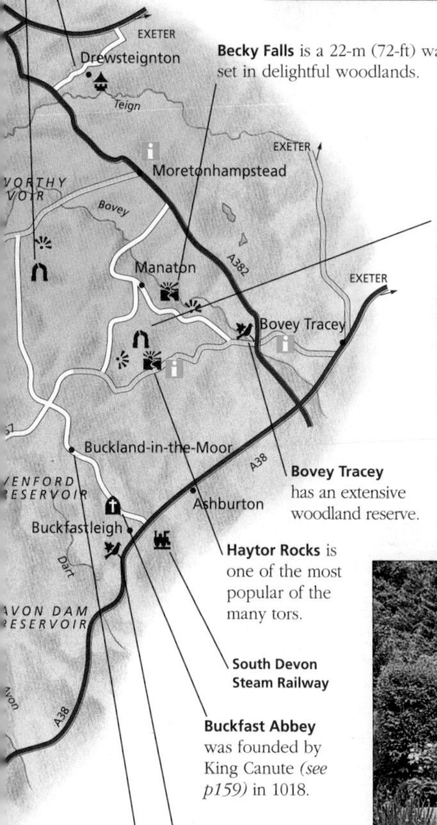

Becky Falls is a 22-m (72-ft) waterfall set in delightful woodlands.

EXETER
Drewsteignton
Teign

VORTHY
VOIR

Bovey

EXETER
Moretonhampstead

Manaton

Bovey Tracey

EXETER

Buckland-in-the-Moor

A38

Ashburton

VENFORD
RESERVOIR

Buckfastleigh

Dart

AVON DAM
RESERVOIR

A38

Hound Tor
Nearby lie the remains of a Medieval settlement abandoned in the 14th century.

Bovey Tracey has an extensive woodland reserve.

Haytor Rocks is one of the most popular of the many tors.

South Devon Steam Railway

Buckfast Abbey was founded by King Canute *(see p159)* in 1018.

Dartmoor Butterfly and Otter Sanctuary

Dartmeet marks the lovely confluence point of the East and West Dart rivers.

Buckland-in-the-Moor
One of the many picturesque villages on Dartmoor.

THE
MIDLANDS

INTRODUCING THE MIDLANDS 298–305

THE HEART OF ENGLAND 306–329

EAST MIDLANDS 330–343

The Midlands at a Glance

The Midlands is an area that embraces wonderful landscapes and massive industrial cities. Visitors come to discover the wild beauty of the rugged Peaks, cruise slowly along the Midlands canals on gaily painted narrowboats and explore varied and enchanting gardens. The area encompasses the full range of English architecture from mighty cathedrals and humble churches to charming spa towns, stately homes and country cottages. There are fascinating industrial museums, many in picturesque settings.

Tissington Trail (see p337) *combines a walk through scenic Peak District countryside with an entertaining insight into the ancient custom of well-dressing.*

Cheshire

Staffordshire

Shropshire

THE HEART OF ENGLAND
(see pp304–329)

Ironbridge Gorge (see pp314–15) *was the birthplace of the Industrial Revolution (see pp348–9). Now a World Heritage Site, it is a reminder of the lovely countryside in which the original factories were located.*

Worcestershire

Herefordshire

Gloucestershire

The Cotswolds (see pp304–5) *are full of delightful houses built from local limestone, on the profits of the medieval wool trade. Snowshill Manor (left) is situated near the unspoilt village of Broadway.*

| 0 kilometres | 25 |
| 0 miles | 25 |

Chatsworth House (see pp334–5), *a magnificent Baroque edifice, is famous for its gorgeous gardens. The "Conservative" Wall, a greenhouse for exotic plants, is pictured above.*

Lincoln Cathedral (see p341), *a vast, imposing building, dominates the ancient town. Inside are splendid misericords and the superb 13th-century Angel Choir, which has 30 carved angels.*

Nottinghamshire

Lincolnshire

Derbyshire

EAST MIDLANDS
(see pp330–343)

Burghley House (see pp342–3) *is a dazzling landmark for miles around in the flat East Midlands landscape, with architectural motifs from the European Renaissance.*

Leicestershire

Warwickshire

Warwick Castle (see pp322–3) *is an intriguing mixture of medieval power base and country house, complete with massive towers, battlements, a dungeon and state apartments, such as the Queen Anne Bedroom.*

Northamptonshire

Stratford-upon-Avon (see pp324–7) *has many picturesque houses connected with William Shakespeare's life, some of which are open to visitors. These black and white timber-framed buildings, which abound in the Midlands, are a typical example of Tudor architecture (see pp302–3).*

Canals of the Midlands

One of England's first canals was built by the 3rd Duke of Bridgewater in 1761 to link the coal mine on his Worsley estate with Manchester's textile factories. This heralded the start of a canal-building boom and by 1805, a 3,000 mile (4,800 km) network of waterways had been dug across the country, linking into the natural river system. Canals provided the cheapest, fastest way of transporting goods, until competition began to arrive from the railways in the 1840s. Cargo transport ended in 1963 but today nearly 2,000 miles (3,200 km) of canals are still navigable, for travellers who wish to take a leisurely cruise on a narrowboat.

The Grand Union Canal *(pictured in 1931) is 300 miles (485 km) long and was dug in the 1790s to link London with the Midlands.*

The Farmer's Bridge *is a flight of 13 locks in Birmingham. Locks are used to raise or lower boats from one level of the canal to another. The steeper the gradient, the more locks are needed.*

Lock-keepers were provided with canalside houses.

Lockside inns cater for narrowboats.

Heavy V-shaped timber gates close off the lock.

Water pressing against the gate keeps it shut.

The towpath is where horses pulled the canal boats before engines were invented. They were changed periodically for fresh animals.

Narrowboats *have straight sides and flat bottoms and are pointed at both ends. Cargo space took up most of the boat, with a small cabin for the crew. Exteriors were brightly painted.*

NO 7   BILL O TOMS   NEW MARTON LOCK

MIDLANDS CANAL NETWORK

The industrial Midlands was the birthplace of the English canal system and still has the biggest concentration of navigable waterways.

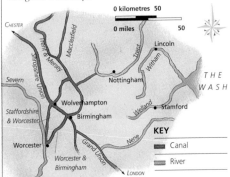

0 kilometres 50

0 miles 50

CHESTER

Trent & Mersey

Macclesfield

Shropshire Union

Severn

Trent

Lincoln

Witham

Nottingham

THE WASH

Wolverhampton

Staffordshire & Worcester

Birmingham

Welland

Stamford

Worcester

Grand Union

Nene

Worcester & Birmingham

LONDON

KEY

■ Canal

■ River

VISITORS' CHECKLIST

Canal boat holidays:
Blake's Holidays *Tel 0844 856 7060*; Hoseasons *Tel 01502 501010*; Canal Cruising Co *Tel 01785 813982*; Black Prince Holidays *Tel 01527 575115*; ABC Leisure Group Ltd *Tel 0330 333 0590*;

Canal museums: Phone to check opening times: Gloucester Waterways Museum *(see p329)*; The Canal Museum, Stoke Bruerne *Tel 01604 862229*; National Waterways Museum, Ellesmere Port. *Tel 0151 3555017.* **www.** canalrivertrust.org.uk

Canal

Footbridge

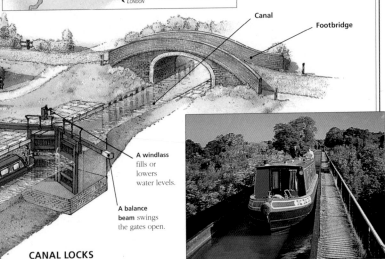

A **windlass** fills or lowers water levels.

A **balance beam** swings the gates open.

CANAL LOCKS

Canals used tunnels, embankments and locks for the speedy transportation of goods across country. Locks were used to convey boats up or down hills.

The Edstone Aqueduct, *just north of Stratford-upon-Avon, carries the canal in a cast iron trough. This is supported on brick piers for 180 m (495 ft), over roads and a busy railway line.*

CANAL ART

Canal boat cabins are very small and every inch of space is utilized to make a comfortable home for the occupants. Interiors were enlivened with colourful paintings and attractive decorations.

Furniture was designed to be functional and to brighten up the cramped cabin.

Narrowboats are often decorated with ornamental brass.

Water cans were also painted. The most common designs were roses and castles, with local variations in style.

Tudor Manor Houses

Many striking manor houses were built in central England during the Tudor Age *(see pp50–51)*, a time of relative peace and prosperity. The abolition of the monasteries meant that vast estates were broken up and sold to secular landowners, who built houses to reflect their new status *(see p28)*. In the Midlands, wood was the main building material, and the gentry flaunted their wealth by using timber panelling for flamboyant decorative effect.

The Lucy family arms

The decorative moulding *on the south wing dates from the late 16th century. Ancient motifs, such as vines and trefoils, are combined with the latest imported Italian Renaissance styles.*

The rectangular moat *was for decoration rather than defence. It surrounds a recreated knot garden (see p26) that was laid out in 1972 using plants known to have been available in Tudor times.*

The Long Gallery *was the last part of the Hall to be built (c.1560–1562). It has original plasterwork portraying* Destiny *(left) and* Fortune.

Brickwork chimney

Jetties (overhanging upper stories)

TUDOR MANSIONS AND TUDOR REVIVAL

There are many sumptuously decorated Tudor mansions in the Midlands. In the 19th century Tudor Revival architecture became a very popular "Old English" style, intended to invoke family pride and values rooted in the past.

Hardwick Hall *in Derbyshire, whose huge kitchen is pictured, is one of the finest Tudor mansions in the country. These buildings are known as "prodigy" houses (see p342) due to their gigantic size.*

Charlecote Park, *Warwickshire, is a brick mansion built by Sir Thomas Lucy in 1551–59. It was heavily restored in Tudor style in the 19th century, but has a fine original gatehouse. According to legend, the young William Shakespeare (see pp324–7) was caught poaching deer in the park.*

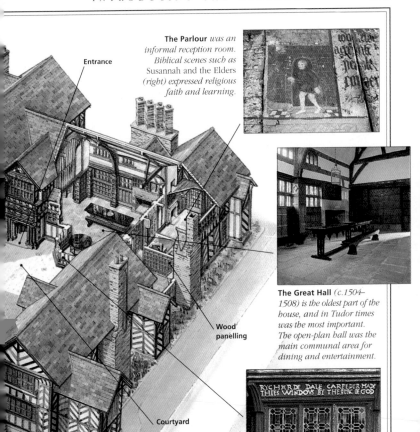

Entrance

The Parlour *was an informal reception room. Biblical scenes such as Susannah and the Elders (right) expressed religious faith and learning.*

Wood panelling

The Great Hall *(c.1504–1508) is the oldest part of the house, and in Tudor times was the most important. The open-plan hall was the main communal area for dining and entertainment.*

Courtyard

LITTLE MORETON HALL

The Moreton family home *(see p311)* was built between 1504 and 1610, from a number of box-shapes, fitted together. Wood panelling and jetties displayed the family's wealth.

The patterned glazing *in the great bay window is typically 16th century: small pieces of locally made glass were cut into diamond shapes and held in place by lead glazing bars.*

Packwood House *in Warwickshire is a timber-framed mid-Tudor house with extensive 17th–century additions. The unusual garden of clipped yew trees dates from the 17th century and is supposed to represent the Sermon on the Mount.*

Moseley Old Hall, *Staffordshire, has a red brick exterior concealing its early 17th-century timber frame. The King's Room is where Charles II hid after the Battle of Worcester (see pp52–3).*

Wightwick Manor, *West Midlands, was built in 1887–93. It is a fine example of Tudor Revival architecture and has superb late 19th-century furniture and decorations.*

Building with Cotswold Stone

The Cotswolds are a range of limestone hills running over 50 miles (80 km) in a north-easterly direction from Bath *(see pp258–61)*. The thin soils are difficult to plough but ideal for grazing sheep, and the wealth engendered by the medieval wool trade was poured into building majestic churches and opulent town houses. Stone quarried from these hills was used to build London's St Paul's Cathedral *(see pp114–15)*, as well as the villages, barns and manor houses that make the landscape so picturesque.

Dragon, Deerhurst Church

Arlington Row Cottages *in Bibury, a typical Cotswold village, were built in the 17th century for weavers whose looms were set up in the attics.*

Windows were taxed and glass expensive. Workers' cottages had only a few, not very large windows made of small panes of glass.

A drip mould keeps rain off the chimney.

The roof is steeply pitched to carry the weight of the tiles. These were made by master craftsmen who could split blocks of stone into sheets by using natural fault lines.

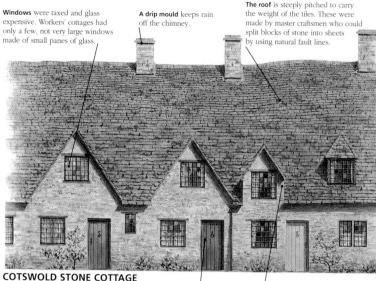

COTSWOLD STONE COTTAGE

The two-storey Arlington Row Cottages are asymmetrical and built of odd-shaped stones. Small windows and doorways make them quite dark inside.

Timber lintels and doors

Timber framing was cheaper than stone, and was used for the upper rooms in the roof.

VARIATIONS IN STONE

Cotswold stone is warmer-toned in the north, pearly in central areas and light grey in the south. The stone seems to glow with absorbed sun-light. It is a soft stone that is easily carved and can be used for many purposes, from buildings to bridges, headstones and gargoyles.

"Tiddles" is a cat's gravestone in Fairford churchyard.

Lower Slaughter *gets its name from the Anglo-Saxon word* slough, *or muddy place. It has a low stone bridge, over the River Eye.*

COTSWOLD STONE TOWNS AND VILLAGES

The villages and towns on this map are prime examples of places built almost entirely from stone. By the 12th century almost all of the villages in the area were established. Huge deposits of limestone resulted in a wealth of stone buildings. Masons worked from distinctive local designs that were handed down from generation to generation.

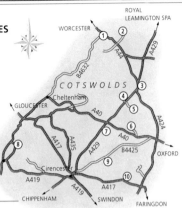

① Winchcombe
② Broadway
③ Stow-on-the-Wold
④ Upper and Lower Slaughter
⑤ Bourton-on-the-Water
⑥ Sherborne
⑦ Northleach
⑧ Painswick
⑨ Bibury
⑩ Fairford

Wool merchants' houses were built of fine ashlar (dressed stone) with ornamental cornerstones, doorframes and windows.

The eaves here have a dentil frieze, so-called because it resembles a row of teeth.

STONE GARGOYLES

In Winchcombe's church, 15th-century gargoyles reflect a combination of pagan and Christian beliefs.

Pagan gods warded off pre-Christian evil spirits.

Fertility figures, always important in rural areas, were incorporated into Christian festivals.

Human faces often caricatured local church dignitaries.

Animal gods represented qualities such as strength in pagan times.

COTSWOLD STONE HOUSE

This early Georgian merchant's house in Painswick shows the fully developed Cotswold style, which borrows decorative elements from Classical architecture.

The door frame has a rounded pediment on simple pilasters.

Dry-stone walling *is an ancient technique used in the Cotswolds. The stones are held in place without mortar.*

A stone cross *(16th century) in Stanton village, near Broadway, is one of many found in the Cotswolds.*

Table-top and "tea caddy", *fine 18th-century tombs, can be found in Painswick churchyard.*

THE HEART OF ENGLAND

CHESHIRE · GLOUCESTERSHIRE · HEREFORDSHIRE
SHROPSHIRE · STAFFORDSHIRE · WARWICKSHIRE · WORCESTERSHIRE

*B*ritain's great attraction is its variety, and nowhere is this more true than at the heart of the country, where the Cotswold hills, enfolding stone cottages and churches, give way to the flat, fertile plains of Warwickshire. Shakespeare country borders on the industrial heart of England, once known as the workshop of the world.

Coventry, Birmingham, the Potteries and their hinterlands have been manufacturing iron, textiles and ceramics since the 18th century. In the 20th century these industries have declined, and a new type of museum has developed to commemorate the towns' industrial heyday and explain the manufacturing processes which were once taken for granted. Ironbridge Gorge and Quarry Bank Mill, Styal, where the factories are now living museums, are fascinating industrial sites and enjoy beautiful surroundings.

These landscapes may be appreciated from the deck of a narrowboat, making gentle progress along the Midlands canals, to the region on the border with Wales known as the Marches. Here the massive walls of Chester and the castles at Shrewsbury and Ludlow recall the Welsh locked in fierce battle with Norman barons and the Marcher Lords. The Marches are now full of rural communities served by the peaceful market towns of Leominster, Malvern, Ross-on-Wye and Hereford. The cities of Worcester and Gloucester both have modern shopping centres, yet their majestic cathedrals retain the tranquillity of an earlier age.

Cheltenham has Regency terraces, Cirencester a rich legacy of Roman art and Tewkesbury a solid Norman abbey. Finally, there is Stratford-upon-Avon, where William Shakespeare, the Elizabethan dramatist, lived and died.

Leisurely village pastimes, reminiscent of a more tranquil age

◁ Cotswold stone: an extremely popular building material in the Heart of England

Exploring the Heart of England

The heart of England, more than any other region, takes its character from the landscape. Picturesque houses, pubs and churches, made from timber and Cotswold stone, create a harmonic appearance that delights visitors and adds greatly to the pleasures of exploration. The area around Birmingham and Stoke-on-Trent, however – once the industrial hub of England – contrasts sharply. The bleak concrete skyline may not appeal, but the area has a fascinating history that is reflected in the self-confident Victorian art and architecture, and a series of award-winning industrial heritage museums.

Arlington Row: stone cottages in the Cotswold village of Bibury

SIGHTS AT A GLANCE

Birmingham **13**
Cheltenham **20**
Chester **2**
Chipping Campden **18**
Cirencester **22**
Coventry **14**
Gloucester **21**
Great Malvern **11**
Hereford **8**
Ironbridge pp314–15 **5**
Ledbury **10**
Leominster **7**
Ludlow **6**
Quarry Bank Mill, Styal **1**
Ross-on-Wye **9**
Shrewsbury **4**
Stoke-on-Trent **3**
Stratford-upon-Avon pp324–7 **17**
Tewkesbury **19**
Warwick pp321–3 **16**
Worcester **12**

Walks and Tours
Midlands Garden Tour **15**

GETTING AROUND

The Heart of England is easily reached by train, with mainline rail services to Cheltenham, Worcester, Birmingham, and Coventry. The M5 and M6 motorways are the major road routes but are frequently congested. Long-distance buses provide regular shuttle services to Cheltenham and Birmingham. Travelling within the region is best done by car. Rural roads are delightfully empty, although major attractions, such as Stratford-upon-Avon, may be very crowded during the summer.

SEE ALSO

• *Where to Stay* pp578–80
• *Where to Eat* pp630–32

0 kilometres   10

0 miles   10

Warring
Runcorn   *Mersey*   M56
Ellesmere Port
CHESTER **2**   Tarvin
A55 🏛 ⛪
Aldford   Bunb
A41
Wrexbam
Chirk   Whitchurch
A5   A495   Prees
Oswestry
West Felton   W
A483   A49
Nesscliffe
Severn
Middletown
SHREWSBURY **4**
A458   ⚓ 🏛 ⛪
Minsterley
A483
Chirbury   Church Stretton
A489   *Long Mynd*
Lydham
Newcastle   *Wenlock E*
Teme   Craven Ar
Stokesay Castle   A489
Knighton   LUDLOW **6**
Wigmore   Wooffe
Presteigne   Be Ha
LEOMINSTER **7**
Pembridge   A49
Eardisley   Hope under Dinmore
Clifford
🏛 🏛 🎪
HEREFORD **8**
Kingston   A465
Kilpeck   A49
Abbey Dore
Abergavenny   ROSS-W
Goodrich Castle
A40
Monmouth
Chepstow

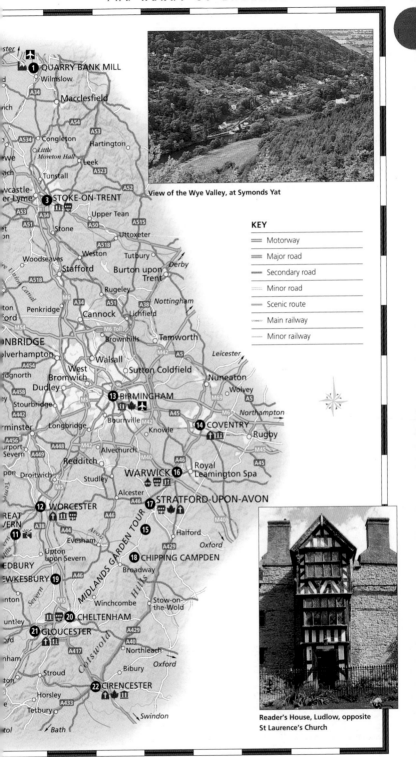

View of the Wye Valley, at Symonds Yat

1 QUARRY BANK MILL
Wilmslow
Macclesfield
A34
A54
A534 Congleton
A53 Hartington
Little
Moreton Hall
Leek
Tunstall A523
A52
3 STOKE-ON-TRENT
Upper Tean
A53
A51 Stone A50 A515
Uttoxeter
A518
Woodseaves Weston Tutbury
Stafford Burton upon Derby
A518 Trent
Rugeley
M6 A51 Nottingham
Penkridge A34 A38 Lichfield
Cannock
M54 M6 Toll
NBRIDGE Brownhills Tamworth
lverhampton M42 A5 Leicester
A454 Walsall
West Sutton Coldfield Nuneaton
idgnorth Bromwich M69 Wolvey
A458 Dudley M6 A5
Stourbridge M5 Northampton
A442 **13** BIRMINGHAM
rminster Longbridge M42 A45
A456 Bournville Knowle **14** COVENTRY
urport Rugby
Severn A449 A448 Alvechurch M45
Redditch M40 A46 A45
pon Droitwich Studley Royal
A46 WARWICK **16** Leamington Spa
Alcester
12 WORCESTER A46 **17** STRATFORD-UPON-AVON
REAT
ERN A38 A46
11 A44 Avon **15** Halford
Evesham A429 Oxford
Upton MIDLANDS GARDEN TOUR **18** CHIPPING CAMPDEN
upon Severn Broadway
EDBURY A46
WKESBURY **19** Winchcombe Stow-on-
the-Wold
nton M5 Cotswold
untley **20** CHELTENHAM
A429
21 GLOUCESTER A40
rd Northleach
nham A417 Oxford
Stroud Bibury
ton Cotswold
22 CIRENCESTER
Horsley A433
Tetbury Swindon
tol Bath

KEY

═══	Motorway
▬▬▬	Major road
───	Secondary road
┄┄┄	Minor road
───	Scenic route
╌╌╌	Main railway
───	Minor railway

Reader's House, Ludlow, opposite
St Laurence's Church

Quarry Bank Mill, a working reminder of the Industrial Revolution

Quarry Bank Mill, Styal ❶

(NT) Cheshire. **Tel** 01625 445896.
🚊 Manchester Airport, then bus.
⬜ Mar–Oct: daily; Nov–Feb: Wed–Sun
(& Mon in school hols). ⬤ 24 & 25
Dec. 🅿️ ♿ limited. 🍴 🛍
www.nationaltrust.org.uk

The history of the Industrial Revolution (see pp54–5) is brought vividly to life at Quarry Bank Mill, an early factory now transformed into a museum and private garden. Here, mill master Samuel Greg first used the waters of the Bollin Valley in 1784 to power the water frame, a machine for spinning raw cotton fibres into thread. By the 1840s, the Greg cotton empire was one of the biggest in Britain, and the mill produced bolts of material to be exported all over the world.

Today the massive old mill buildings have been restored to house a living museum of the cotton industry. This dominated the Manchester area for nearly 200 years, but was finally destroyed by foreign competition. The entire process, from the spinning and weaving to the bleaching, printing and dyeing, is shown through a series of reconstructions, demonstrations and hands-on displays. The weaving shed is full of clattering looms producing textiles. There are fascinating contraptions that demonstrate how water can be used to drive machinery, including an enormous wheel, 50 tons in weight and 7 m (24 ft) high, that is still used to power the looms.

The Greg family realized the importance of having a healthy, loyal and stable workforce. A social history exhibition explains how the mill workers were housed in the purpose-built village of Styal, in spacious cottages which had vegetable gardens and toilets. Details of their wages, working conditions and medical facilities are displayed on information boards.

There are guided tours of the nearby **Apprentice House**. Local orphans lived here, and were sent to work up to 12 hours a day at the mill when they were just six or seven years old. Visitors can try the beds in the house and even sample the medicine they were given. Quarry Bank Mill is surrounded by over 115 ha (284 acres) of woodland.

Chester ❷

Cheshire. 🏘 120,000. 🚆 🚌
ℹ️ Town Hall, Northgate St
(0845 6477868). 🅰️ Mon–Sat.
www.visitchester.com

First settled by the Romans (see pp44–5), who established a camp in AD 79 to defend fertile land near the River Dee, the main streets of Chester are now lined with timber buildings. These are the **Chester Rows**, which, with their two tiers of shops and continuous upper gallery, anticipate today's multi-storey shops by several centuries.

Although their oriel windows and decorative timber-work are mostly 19th century, the Rows were first built in the 13th and 14th centuries, and the original structures can be seen in many places. The façade of the 16th-century **Bishop Lloyd's House** in Watergate Street is the most richly carved in Chester. The Rows are at their most varied and attractive where Eastgate Street meets Bridge Street. Here, views of the cathedral and the town walls give the impression of a perfectly preserved medieval city. This illusion is helped by the Town Crier, who calls the hour and announces news in summer from the Cross, a reconstruction of the 15th-century stone crucifix that was destroyed in the Civil War (see pp52–3).

The **Grosvenor Museum**, south of the Cross, explains the town's history. To the north is the **cathedral**. The choir stalls have splendid misericords (see p341), with

Chester's 1897 clocktower

Examples of the intricate carving on Bishop Lloyd's House, a Tudor building in Watergate Street, Chester

For hotels and restaurants in this region see pp578–580 and pp630–632

The **Gladstone Pottery Museum** is a Victorian complex of workshops, kilns, galleries and an engine house. There are demonstrations of traditional pottery techniques. The **Potteries Museum and Art Gallery** in Hanley has historic and modern ceramics, and items from the Anglo-Saxon "Staffordshire Horde".

Josiah Wedgwood founded his pottery in 1769 and built a workers' village, Etruria. The last surviving steam-powered pottery mill is on display at the **Etruria Industrial Museum**.

Environs: About 10 miles (16 km) north of Stoke-on-Trent is **Little Moreton Hall** (see p303), a Tudor manor house.

🏛 **Gladstone Pottery Museum**
Uttoxeter Rd, Longton. *Tel* 01782 237777. ◻ daily. ● 24 Dec–2 Jan. 🦽 🖈 🔊 🗂
www.stokemuseums.org.uk/gpm

🏛 **Potteries Museum and Art Gallery**
Bethesda St, Hanley. *Tel* 01782 232323. ◻ daily. ● 25 Dec–1 Jan. 🦽 🔊 🗂 www.stokemuseums. org.uk/pmag

🏛 **Etruria Industrial Museum**
Lower Bedford St, Etruria. *Tel* 01782 233144. ◻ Apr–Nov: Wed–Sun; Dec–Mar: tour only, book ahead. 🦽 📷 🔊 🗂 www.stokemuseums. org.uk/eim

🏚 **Little Moreton Hall**
(NT) Congleton, off A34. *Tel* 01260 272018. ◻ Apr–Oct: Wed–Sun & public hols; Nov–mid-Dec: Sat & Sun. 🦽

The Chester Rows, where shops line the first-floor galleries

scenes including a quarrelling couple. In sharp contrast are the delicate spire-lets on the stall canopies. The cathedral is surrounded on two sides by the **city walls**, originally Roman but rebuilt at intervals. The best stretch is from the cathedral to Eastgate, where a wrought-iron **clock** was erected in 1897. The route to Newgate leads to a **Roman amphitheatre** built in AD 100.

🏛 **Grosvenor Museum**
Grosvenor St. *Tel* 01244 402033. ◻ Mon–Sat, Sun pm. ● 1 Jan, Good Fri, 25 & 26 Dec. 🖈 🦽 limited. www.visitchester.com

⛩ **Roman Amphitheatre**
Little St John St. *Tel* 01244 402009. ◻ daily.

Stoke-on-Trent ❸

Stoke-on-Trent. 🚶 240,000. ✈ 🚆 🔊 🛈 Victoria Hall, Cultural Quarter, Hanley (01782 236000). 🛒 Mon–Sat. www.visitstoke.co.uk

From the mid-18th century, Staffordshire became a leading centre for mass-produced ceramics. Its fame arose from the fine bone china and porcelain products of Wedgwood, Minton, Doulton and Spode, but the Staffordshire potteries also make a wide range of utilitarian products such as baths, toilets and wall tiles.

In 1910 a group of six towns – Longton, Fenton, Hanley, Burslem, Tunstall and Stoke – merged to form the conurbation of Stoke-on-Trent, also known as the Potteries. Writer Arnold Bennett (1867–1931) depicted this area as the "Five Towns" in his novels.

STAFFORDSHIRE POTTERY

An abundance of water, marl, clay and easily mined coal to fire the kilns enabled Staffordshire to develop as a ceramics centre; and local supplies of iron, copper and lead were used for glazing. In the 18th century, pottery became widely accessible and affordable. English bone china, which used powdered animals' bones for strength and translucence, was shipped all over the world, and Josiah Wedgwood (1730–95) introduced simple, durable crockery – though his best known design is the blue jasperware decorated with white Classical themes. Coal-powered bottle kilns fired the clay until the 1950s Clean Air Acts put them out of business. They have been replaced by electric or gas-fired kilns.

Wedgwood candlesticks, 1785

Timber-framed, gabled mansions in Fish Street, Shrewsbury

Shrewsbury ❹

Shropshire. 🚶 70,000. 🚉 🚌
ℹ️ *Rowley's House Museum (01743 281200).* 🏪 *Tue, Wed, Fri, Sat.* 🎪 *Shrewsbury Flower Show (mid-Aug).*

Shrewsbury is almost an island, enclosed by a great loop of the River Severn. A gaunt **castle** of red sandstone, first built in 1083, guards the entrance to the town, standing on the only section of land not surrounded by the river. Such defences were necessary on the frontier between England and the wilder Marches of Wales, whose inhabitants fiercely defied Saxon and Norman invaders *(see pp46–7)*. The castle, rebuilt over the centuries, now houses the Shropshire Regimental Museum.

In AD 60 the Romans *(see pp44–5)* built the garrison town of Viroconium, modern Wroxeter, 5 miles (8 km) east of Shrewsbury. Finds from the excavations are displayed at **Shrewsbury Museum and Art Gallery**, including a decorated silver mirror from the 2nd century and other luxury goods imported by the Roman army.

The town's medieval wealth as a centre of the wool trade is evident in the many timber-framed buildings found along the High Street, Butcher Row,

Roman silver mirror in Rowley's House Museum

and Wyle Cop. Two of the grandest High Street houses, **Ireland's Mansions** and **Owen's Mansions**, are named after Robert Ireland and Richard Owen, the wealthy wool merchants who built them in 1575 and 1570 respectively. Similarly attractive buildings in Fish Street frame a view of the **Prince Rupert Hotel**, which was briefly the headquarters of Charles I's nephew, Rupert, in the English Civil War *(see pp52–3)*.

Outside the loop of the river, the **Abbey Church** survives from the medieval monastery. It has a number of interesting memorials, including one to Lieutenant WES Owen MC, better known as the war poet Wilfred Owen (1893–1918), who taught at the local Wyle Cop school and was killed in the last days of World War I.

Environs: To the south of Shrewsbury, the road to Ludlow passes through the landscapes celebrated in the 1896 poem by AE Housman (1859–1936), *A Shropshire Lad*. Highlights include the bleak moors of **Long Mynd**, with 15 prehistoric barrows, and **Wenlock Edge**, wonderful walking country with glorious, far-reaching views.

Shrewsbury Castle
⚓ **Shrewsbury Castle**
Castle St. **Tel** *01743 358516.*
🕐 *Tue–Sat.* 🌙 *late Dec–mid-Feb.*
📷 ♿ 🛍️

🏛 **Shrewsbury Museum and Art Gallery**
The Music Hall, Market Sq. **Tel** *01743 281205.* 🕐 *May–Sep: daily; Apr, Oct: Mon–Sat.* ♿ *limited.* 🛍️
www.shrewsburymuseums.com

Ironbridge Gorge ❺

See pp314–15.

Ludlow ❻

Shropshire. 🚶 10,000. 🚉 ℹ️ *Castle St (01584 875053).* 🏪 *Mon, Wed, Fri, Sat.* 🎪 *music & drama (end Jun).*
www.visitshropshire.co.uk

Ludlow attracts large numbers of visitors to its splendid castle, but there is much else to see in this town, with its small shops and its lovely Georgian and half-timbered Tudor buildings. Ludlow is an important area of geological research and the **museum**, just off the town centre, has fossils of the oldest known animals and plants.

The ruined **castle** is sited on cliffs high above the River Teme. Built in 1086, it was damaged in the Civil War *(see pp52–3)* and abandoned in 1689. *Comus*, a court masque using music and drama, by John Milton (1608–74) was first performed here in 1634 in the Great Hall.

The 13th-century south tower and hall of Stokesay Castle, near Ludlow

Prince Arthur (1486–1502), elder brother of Henry VIII *(see pp50–51),* died at Ludlow Castle. His heart is buried in **St Laurence Church** at the other end of Castle Square, as are the ashes of the poet A E Housman. The east end of the church backs onto the **Bull Ring**, with its timber buildings. Two inns vie for attention across the street: **The Bull**, with its Tudor back yard, and **The Feathers**, with its flamboyant façade, whose name recalls the feathers used in arrow-making, once a local industry.

Environs: About 5 miles (8 km) north of Ludlow, in a lovely setting, is **Stokesay Castle**, a fortified manor house with a colourful moated garden.

♣ **Ludlow Castle**
The Square. *Tel* 01584 873355.
☐ daily (Dec & Jan: Sat & Sun only).
🚫 🚻

🏛 **Ludlow Museum**
Castle St. *Tel* 01584 813665. ☐ Apr–
Oct: Mon–Sat (Jun–Aug: daily). 🚻

♣ **Stokesay Castle**
(EH) Craven Arms, A49. *Tel* 01588
672544. ☐ Apr–Sep: daily; Oct:
Wed–Sun; Nov–Mar: Sat & Sun. 🚫
🚻

Leominster ➐

Herefordshire. 🏠 *11,000.* 🚂
🛈 *Corn Sq (01568 616460).*
🗓 *Fri.* www.herefordshire.gov.uk

Farmers come to Leominster (pronounced "Lemster") from all over this rural region to buy supplies. There are two buildings of note in the town, which has been a wool-manufacturing centre for 700 years. In the town centre stands the magnificent **Grange Court**, carved with bold and bizarre figures in 1633. Nearby is the **priory**, whose imposing Norman portal is carved with an equally strange mixture of mythical birds and beasts. The lions, at least, can be explained: medieval monks believed the name of Leominster was derived from *monasterium leonis,* "the monastery of the lions". In fact, *leonis* probably comes from medieval, rather than Classical Latin, and it means

A view of Leominster, set on the River Lugg in rolling border country

"of the marshes". The aptness of this description can readily be seen in the green lanes around the town, following the lush river valleys.

Environs: South of the town, the magnificent gardens and parkland at **Hampton Court** have been restored and include island pavilions and a maze. To the west of the town, along the River Arrow, are the villages of **Eardisland** and **Pembridge**, with their well-kept gardens and timber-framed houses. **Berrington Hall**, 3 miles (5 km) north of Leominster, is a Neo-Classical

Gatehouse of Stokesay Castle, near Ludlow

house set in grounds by "Capability" Brown. Inside are beautifully preserved ceiling decorations and period furniture.

To the northeast of Leominster is **Tenbury Wells**, which enjoyed brief popularity as a spa in the 19th century. The River Teme flows through it, full of minnows, trout and other fish and beloved of the composer Sir Edward Elgar *(see p317),* who came to seek inspiration on its banks. The river also feeds **Burford House Gardens**, on the western outskirts of Tenbury Wells, where the water is used to create streams, fountains and pools that are rich in unusual moisture-loving plants.

🌸 **Hampton Court Gardens**
nr Hope Under Dinmore. *Tel* 01568
797 777. ☐ Apr–Oct: 10:30am–5pm
(call for winter opening times). 🚫 🚻
🍴 🎁 www.hamptoncourt.org.uk

🏛 **Berrington Hall**
(NT) Berrington. *Tel* 01568 615721.
☐ Mar–Oct, mid-late Dec: daily;
Nov–mid-Dec: Sat & Sun. 🚫 🍴 🎁

🌸 **Burford House Gardens**
Tenbury Wells. *Tel* 01584 810777.
☐ daily. ● 1 Jan, 25 & 26 Dec.
🚫 🍴 🎁 www.burford.co.uk

Ironbridge Gorge ❺

Ironbridge Gorge was one of the most important centres of the Industrial Revolution (see pp54–5). It was here, in 1709, Abraham Darby I (1678–1717) pioneered the use of inexpensive coke, rather than charcoal, to smelt iron ore. The use of iron in bridges, ships and buildings transformed Ironbridge Gorge into one of the world's great iron-making centres. Industrial decline in the 20th century led to the Gorge's decay, although today it has been restored as an exciting complex of industrial archaeology, with several museums strung along the wooded banks of the River Severn.

VISITORS' CHECKLIST

Shropshire. 🏠 2,900. ✈ Telford then bus (0871 2002233). 🚉 Museum of the Gorge (01952 884391). ◯ daily. ● 1 Jan, 24, 25 Dec. Some sites closed Nov–Apr, call for details. ♿ most sites. 📷 📹 by arrangement. 🅿 🍴 🛏 www.ironbridge. org.uk

The Museum of Iron, topped by a cast- and wrought-iron clock

COALBROOKDALE MUSEUM OF IRON

The history of iron and the men who made it is traced in this remarkable museum. Abraham Darby I's discovery of how to smelt iron ore with coke allowed the mass production of iron, paving the way for the rise of large-scale industry. His original blast furnace forms the museum's centrepiece.

One of the museum's themes is the history of the Darby dynasty, a Quaker family who had a great impact on the Coalbrookdale community.

Ironbridge led the world in industrial innovation, producing the first iron wheels and cylinders for the first steam engine. Cast-iron statues, many of them commissioned for the 1851 Great Exhibition (see pp56–7), are among the many Coalbrookdale Company

products on display. They include a bronze figure of Andromeda and many sculptures of stags and hounds.

One of the Darby family's homes in the nearby village of Coalbrookdale, **Rosehill House** (open during the summer), has been furnished in mid-Victorian style.

MUSEUM OF THE GORGE

This partly castellated, Victorian building was a warehouse for storing products from the ironworks before they were shipped down the River Severn. The warehouse is now home to the Museum of the Gorge, and has displays illustrating the history of the Severn and the development of the water industry.

Until the arrival of the railways in the mid-19th century, the Severn was the main form of transport and communication to and from the Gorge. Sometimes too shallow, at other times in flood, the river was not a particularly reliable means of transportation; by the 1890s river trading had stopped completely.

The highlight of the museum is a wonderful 12 m (40 ft) model of the Gorge as it would have appeared in 1796, complete with foundries, cargo boats and growing villages.

Europe (1860), statue in the Museum of Iron

JACKFIELD TILE MUSEUM

There have been potteries in this area since the 17th century, but it was not until the Victorian passion for decorative tiles that Jackfield became famous. There were two tile-making factories here – Maw and Craven Dunnill – that produced a tremendous variety of tiles from clay mined nearby.

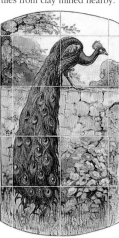

Peacock Panel (1928), one of the tile museum's star attractions

Talented designers created an astonishing range of images. The Jackfield Tile Museum, in the old Craven Dunnill works, has a collection of the decorative floor and wall tiles that were produced here from the 1850s to the 1960s. On certain days, visitors can watch small-scale demonstrations of traditional methods of tile-making in the old factory buildings, including the kilns and the decoration workshops.

IRONBRIDGE GORGE SIGHTS

Blists Hill Victorian Town ⑥
Coalbrookdale
   Museum of Iron ①
Coalport China
   Museum ⑤
Iron Bridge ③
Jackfield Tile
   Museum ④
Museum of the Gorge ②

0 kilometres   2

0 miles   1

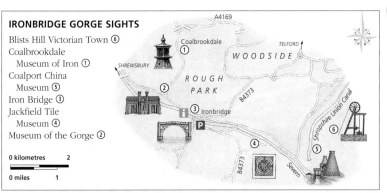

COALPORT CHINA MUSEUM

In the mid-19th century the Coalport Works was one of the largest porcelain manufacturers in Britain, and its name was synonymous with fine china. The Coalport Company still makes porcelain but has long since moved its operations to Stoke-on-Trent *(see p311).* Today the china workshops have been converted into a museum, where visitors can watch demonstrations of the various stages of making porcelain, including the skills of pot-throwing, painting and gilding. There is a superb collection of 19th-century china housed in one of the museum's distinctive bottle-shaped kilns.

Coalport China Museum with its bottle-shaped kiln

Nearby is the **Tar Tunnel**, an important source of natural bitumen discovered 110 m (360 ft) underground in the 1700s. It once yielded 20,500 litres (4,500 gal) of tar every week. Visitors can still explore part of the tunnel (Apr–Oct).

THE IRON BRIDGE

Abraham Darby III (grandson of the first man to smelt iron with coke) cast the world's first iron bridge in 1779, revolutionizing building methods in the process. Spanning the Severn, the bridge is a monument to the ironmasters' skills. The toll-house on the south bank charts its construction.

BLISTS HILL VICTORIAN TOWN

This enormous open-air museum recreates Victorian life in an Ironbridge Gorge town. A group of 19th-century buildings has been reconstructed on the 20 ha (50 acre) site of Blists Hill, an old coal mine that used to supply the ironworks in the Gorge. Here, people in period costume enact roles and perform tasks such as iron forging.

The site has period housing, a church and even a Victorian school. Visitors can change money into old coinage to buy items from the baker or even pay for a drink in the local pub.

The centrepiece of Blists Hill is a complete foundry that still produces wrought iron. One of the most spectacular sights is the Hay Inclined Plane, which was used to transport canal boats up and down a steep slope. Other attractions include steam engines, a saddlers, a doctors, a chemist, a candlemakers and a sweetshop.

Hereford ❽

Herefordshire. 🚶 55,700. 🚲 ⬛
ℹ️ King St (01432 268430).
📅 Wed (cattle, general), Sat (general).
www.visitherefordshire.co.uk

Once the capital of the
Saxon kingdom of West
Mercia, Hereford is today an
attractive town which serves
the needs of a primarily rural
community. A cattle market is
held here every Wednesday,
and local produce is sold at
the covered market in the
town centre. Almost opposite,
the Jacobean timber-framed
Old House of 1621 is now a
museum of local history.

In the **cathedral**, only a
short stroll away, interesting
features include the Lady
Chapel, in richly ornamented
Early English style, the
Mappa Mundi (see below)
and the Chained Library,
whose 1,500 books are
tethered by iron chains to
bookcases as a precaution
against theft. The
story of these
national treasures is
told through models,
original artifacts and
interactive computer
technology. The best
place for an overall
view of the cathedral
is at the Bishop's
Meadow, south of
the centre, leading
down to the banks
of the Wye.

**Detail of figures on
Kilpeck Church**

Hereford's many
rewarding museums include
the **City Museum and Art
Gallery**, noted for its Roman
mosaic and for watercolours
by local artists, and the **Cider**

Hereford's 17th-century Old House, furnished in period style

Museum. In the museum,
visitors can discover the history
of traditional cider making.
This includes exploring the
champagne cellars and learning how the barrels are made.

There are still over
30 traditional cider-
makers operating
in Herefordshire.

Environs: During the
12th century, Oliver
de Merlemond made
a pilgrimage from
Hereford to Spain.
Impressed by
several churches he
saw on the way, he
brought French
masons over to
England and introduced their
techniques to this area. One
result was **Kilpeck Church**,
6 miles (10 km) southwest,
full of splendid carvings

including lustful figures
showing their genitals, tail-
biting dragons and snakes. At
Abbey Dore, 4 miles (6 km)
west, the Cistercian abbey
church is complemented by
the serene riverside gardens
and tranquil arboretum of
Abbey Dore Court.

🏛️ **Old House**
High Town. **Tel** 01432 260694.
⬚ Apr–Sep: Tue–Sun; Oct–Mar:
Tue–Sat; public hols. ● 25 & 26
Dec, 1 Jan, Good Fri. ♿ limited.
🖥️ www.herefordshire.gov.uk

🏛️ **City Museum
and Art Gallery**
Broad St. **Tel** 01432 260692.
⬚ Tue–Sat. ● 1 Jan, Good Fri,
25 & 26 Dec. ♿ 🖥️ www.
herefordshire.gov.uk

🏛️ **Cider Museum**
Ryelands St. **Tel** 01432 354207.
⬚ Tue–Sat. ● 1 Jan , 25 & 26
Dec, Good Fri. ♿ limited.
📷 by arrangement.
www.cidermuseum.co.uk

MEDIEVAL VIEW

Hereford Cathedral's most
celebrated treasure is the
Mappa Mundi, the Map of
the World, drawn in 1290
by a clergyman, Richard of
Haldingham. The world is
depicted here on Biblical
principles: Jerusalem is at
the centre, the Garden of
Eden figures prominently
and monsters inhabit the
margins of the world.

Central detail, *Mappa Mundi*

Ross-on-Wye ❾

Herefordshire. 🚶 10,000. 🚲 ℹ️
Market House (01989 562768). 📅 Thu,
Sat; farmers' market 1st Fri of month.
www.visitherefordshire.co.uk

The fine town of Ross sits
on a cliff of red sandstone
above the water meadows of
the River Wye. There are wonderful views over the river
from the cliff-top gardens,

The Wye Valley at Symond's Yat

given to the town by a local benefactor, John Kyrle (1637–1724). Kyrle was lauded by the poet Alexander Pope (1688–1744) in his *Moral Essays on the Uses of Riches* (1732) for using his wealth in a practical way, and he came to be known as "The Man of Ross". There is a memorial to Kyrle in **St Mary's Church**.

Environs: Downstream from Ross, the river Wye negotiates a huge, incised meander at **Symond's Yat**. Viewing points and forest walks offer dramatic views across wooded gorges.

Goodrich Castle, 5 miles (8 km) south of Ross, is a 12th-century red sandstone fort on a rock above the river.

🏰 **Goodrich Castle**
(EH) Goodrich. *Tel* 01600 890538.
◯ mid-Feb, Apr–Oct: daily; Nov–Mar: Sat & Sun). 🎦 ▯ (Apr–Sep).

Ledbury ❿

Herefordshire. 🏘 9,900. 🚄 ◲ ℹ
Ice Bytes, 38 The Homend (01531 634700). **www**.visitledbury.info

Ledbury's main street is lined with timbered houses, including the **Market Hall** which dates from 1655. Church Lane, a cobbled lane running up from the High Street, has lovely 16th-century buildings: the **Heritage Centre** and **Butcher Row House** are both now museums. **St Michael and All Angels Church** has a massive detached bell tower, ornate Early English decoration and interesting monuments.

Medieval tile from the Priory at Great Malvern

🏛 **Heritage Centre**
Church Lane. ◯ *Easter–Oct: daily.* ♿

🏛 **Butcher Row House**
Church Lane. ◯ *Easter–Oct: daily.*

Great Malvern and the Malverns ⓫

Worcestershire. 🏘 35,000. 🚄 ◲
ℹ 21 Church St (01684 892289).
◲ Fri; farmers' market 3rd Sat of month. **www**.visitthemalverns.org

The ancient granite rock of the Malvern Hills rises from the plain of the River Severn, its 9 miles (15 km) of glorious scenery visible from afar. Composer Sir Edward Elgar (1857–1934) wrote many of his greatest works here, including the oratorio *The Dream of Gerontius* (1900), inspired by what the diarist John Evelyn (1620–1706) described as "one of the goodliest views in England". Elgar's home was in **Little Malvern**, whose truncated Church of St Giles, set on a steep, wooded hill, lost its nave when the stone was stolen during the Dissolution *(see p339)*. **Great Malvern**, capital of the hills, is graced with 19th-century buildings which look like Swiss sanitoria: patients would stay at institutions such as Doctor Gulley's Water Cure Establishment. The water gushing from the hillside at St Ann's Well, above the town, is bottled and sold throughout Britain. The town is home to the famous Morgan cars (contact 01684 584580 to arrange a factory visit).

Malvern's highlight is the **Priory**, with its 15th-century stained-glass windows and medieval misericords. The old monastic fishponds below the church form the lake of the **Priory Park**. Here the theatre hosts performances of Elgar's music and plays by George Bernard Shaw.

A view of the Malverns range, formed of hard Pre-Cambrian rock

Worcester ⑫

Worcestershire. 🚶 95,000.
🚆 🏠 ℹ️ High St (01905 726311).
🅿️ Mon–Sat.
www.visitworcester.com

Worcester is one of many
English cities whose character
has been transformed by
modern development. The
architectural highlight remains
the **cathedral**, off College
Yard, which suffered a collapsed tower in 1175 and a
disastrous fire in 1203, before
the present structure was
started in the 13th century.

The nave and central tower
were completed in the 1370s,
after building was severely
interrupted by the Black Death,
which decimated the labour
force (see p48). The most
recent and ornate addition
was made in 1874, when Sir
George Gilbert Scott (see p465)
designed the High Gothic
choir, incorporating 14th-
century carved misericords.

There are many interesting
tombs, including King John's,

Charles I holding a symbol of the
Church on Worcester's Guildhall

a masterpiece of medieval
carving, in front of the altar.
Prince Arthur, Henry VIII's
brother (see p313), who died
at the age of 15, is buried in
the chantry chapel south of
the altar. Underneath, the
huge Norman crypt survives
from the first cathedral (1084).

From the cathedral cloister,
a gate leads to College Green
and out into Edgar Street and

its Georgian houses. Here the
Worcester Porcelain Museum
displays Royal Worcester porcelain dating back to 1751.
On the High Street, north of
the cathedral, the **Guildhall**
of 1723 is adorned with
statues of Stuart monarchs,
reflecting the city's Royalist
allegiances. In Cornmarket
is **Ye Olde King Charles
House,** in which Prince
Charles, later Charles II, hid
after the Battle of Worcester
in 1651 (see pp52–3).

Some of Worcester's finest
timber buildings are found
in Friar Street: **The Greyfriars,**
built around 1480, has been
restored in period style. The
Commandery was originally
an 11th-century hospital. It
was rebuilt in the 15th century
and used by Prince Charles
as a base during the Civil
War. Now a museum, it has
a fine hammerbeam roof.

Elgar's Birthplace was the
home of composer Sir Edward
Elgar (see p318) and contains
memorabilia of his life.

🏛 **Worcester Porcelain
Museum**
Severn St. **Tel** 01905 21247.
🕐 Easter–Oct: Mon–Sat; Nov–
Easter: Tue–Sat. 🔴 public hols. 🈲
🈳 🈴 🈵 🈶 www.worcester
porcelainmuseum.org

🏛 **The Greyfriars**
(NT) Friar St. **Tel** 01905 23571.
🕐 mid-Feb–mid-Dec: Tue–Sat. 🈲

🏛 **Commandery**
Sidbury. **Tel** 01905 361821. 🕐
daily. 🔴 1 Jan, 25–26 Dec. 🈵 🈲

🏛 **Elgar's Birthplace**
Lower Broadheath. **Tel** 01905
333224. 🕐 daily. 🔴 24 Dec–
mid-Jan. 🈲 🈳 limited. 🈵
www.elgarmuseum.org

Birmingham ⑬

Birmingham. 🚶 1,037,000.
✈️ 🚆 🚌 ℹ️ New St (0844 888
3883). 🅿️ Mon–Sat. www.
visitbirmingham.com

Brum, as it is affectionately
known to its inhabitants, grew
up as a major centre of the
Industrial Revolution in the
19th century. A vast range
of manufacturing trades was
based in Birmingham and
was responsible for the rapid
development of grim factories
and cramped housing. Since

Worcester Cathedral, overlooking the River Severn

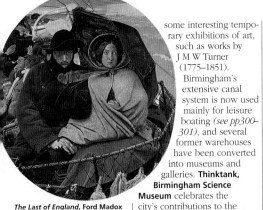

The Last of England, Ford Madox Brown, Birmingham Art Gallery

the clearance of several of these areas after World War II, Birmingham has raised its cultural profile. The city succeeded in enticing Sir Simon Rattle to conduct the City of Birmingham Symphony Orchestra (1980–98), and persuaded the former Royal Sadler's Wells Ballet (now the Birmingham Royal Ballet) to leave London for the more up-to-date facilities of Birmingham. The **National Exhibition Centre**, 8 miles (13 km) east of the centre, draws thousands of people to its conference, lecture and exhibition halls.

Set away from the massive Bullring shopping centre, Birmingham's 19th-century civic buildings are excellent examples of Neo-Classical architecture. Among them are the **Birmingham Museum and Art Gallery**, where the collection includes outstanding works by pre-Raphaelite artists such as Sir Edward Burne-Jones (1833–98), who was born in Birmingham, and Ford Madox Brown (1821–93). The museum also organizes

some interesting temporary exhibitions of art, such as works by J M W Turner (1775–1851).

Birmingham's extensive canal system is now used mainly for leisure boating *(see pp300–301)*, and several former warehouses have been converted into museums and galleries. **Thinktank, Birmingham Science Museum** celebrates the city's contributions to the world of railway engines, aircraft, and the motor trade. The old jewellery quarter has practised its traditional crafts here since the 16th century.

Suburban Birmingham has many attractions, including the **Botanical Gardens** at Edgbaston, and **Cadbury World** at Bournville, where there is a visitor centre dedicated to chocolate (booking ahead is advisable). Bournville village was built in 1890 by the Cadbury brothers for their workers and is a pioneering example of a garden suburb.

🏛 **Birmingham Museum and Art Gallery**
Chamberlain Sq. **Tel** *0121 303 2834*. ⬜ *daily*. ● *25 & 26 Dec.* ♿ 📷 📖

🏛 **Thinktank**
Millennium Point. **Tel** *0121 202 2222*. ⬜ *daily*. ● *24–26 Dec.*

🌿 **Botanical Gardens**
Westbourne Rd, Edgbaston. **Tel** *0121 454 1860*. ⬜ *daily*. ● *25 Dec.* 📷 ♿ 📖 *by appt.* 🍴

🏛 **Cadbury World**
Linden Rd, Bournville. **Tel** *0845 450 3599*. ⬜ *daily (Nov–Jan: call for details)*. ● *first two weeks Jan.* ♿

Coventry ⓵⓸

Coventry. 🏛 *316,000*. ✈ 🚉 ℹ *Cathedral Tower (024 7622 5616)*. 🏠 *Mon–Sat*. **www**.visitcoventryand warwickshire.co.uk

As an armaments centre, Coventry was a prime target for German bombing raids in World War II, and in 1940 the **cathedral** in the city centre was hit. After the war the first totally modern cathedral by Sir Basil Spence (1907–76) was built alongside the ruins. It

Epstein's *St Michael Subduing the Devil*, on Coventry Cathedral

includes sculptures by Sir Jacob Epstein and a tapestry by Graham Sutherland.

The **Herbert Gallery and Museum** has displays on the 11th-century legend of Lady Godiva, who rode naked through the streets. The **Coventry Transport Museum** has the largest collection of Britain's road transport in the world, including cars, cycles and models, and features the fastest car in the world as well as interactive displays.

🏛 **Herbert Gallery and Museum**
Jordan Well. **Tel** *024 7683 2386*. ⬜ *daily (Sun: pm) 1 Jan.* 📷 🍴

🏛 **Coventry Transport Museum**
Hales St. **Tel** *024 7623 4270*. ⬜ *daily*. ● *24–26 Dec.* ♿ 📷 🌐 *www*.transport-museum.com

Stately civic office buildings in Victoria Square, Birmingham

Midlands Garden Tour ⑮

The charming Cotswold stone buildings perfectly complement the lush gardens for which the region is famous. This picturesque route from Warwick to Cheltenham is designed to show every type of garden, from tiny cottage plots, brimming with bell-shaped flowers and hollyhocks, to the deer-filled, landscaped parks of stately homes. The route follows the escarpment of the Cotswold Hills, taking in spectacular scenery and some of the prettiest Midlands villages on the way.

Plum tree in blossom

TIPS FOR DRIVERS

Tour length: 35 miles (50 km). *Stopping-off points:* Hidcote Manor has excellent lunches and teas; there are refreshments at Kiftsgate Court and Sudeley Castle. Travellers will find a good choice in Broadway, from traditional pubs and tea shops to the de luxe Lygon Arms. (See also pp684–5.)

Cheltenham Imperial Gardens ⑨
These colourful public gardens on the Promenade were laid out in 1817–18 to encourage people to walk from the town to the spa *(see p328).*

Sudeley Castle ⑧
The restored castle is complemented by box hedges, topiary and an Elizabethan knot garden *(see p26).* Catherine Parr, Henry VIII's widow, died here in 1548.

Broadway ⑤
Wisteria and cordoned fruit trees cover 17th-century cottages, fronted by immaculate gardens.

Stanway House ⑦
This Jacobean manor has many lovely trees in its grounds and a pyramid above a cascade of water.

Snowshill Manor ⑥
This Cotswold stone manor contains an extraordinary collection, from bicycles to Japanese armour. There are walled gardens and terraces full of *objets d'art* such as the clock (left). The colour blue is a recurrent theme.

Warwick Castle ①
The castle's gardens *see pp322–3)* include [th]e Mound, planted in medieval style, with [gr]ass, oaks, yew trees and box hedges.

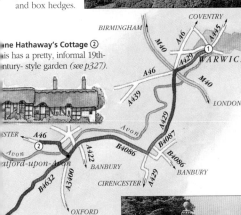

[A]ne Hathaway's Cottage ②
[Th]is has a pretty, informal 19th-[ce]ntury- style garden *(see p327).*

Hidcote Manor Gardens ③
Started in the early years of the last century, these beautiful gardens pioneered the idea of a garden as a series of outdoor "rooms", enclosed by high yew hedges and planted according to themes.

Kiftsgate Court Garden ④
This charmingly naturalistic garden lies opposite Hidcote Manor. It has many rare and unusual plants on a series of hillside terraces, including the enormous "Kiftsgate" Rose, nearly 30 m (100 ft) high.

KEY

▬▬▬	Motorway
▬▬▬	Tour route
═══	Other roads
☀	Viewpoint

0 kilometres 5

0 miles 5

Warwick ⑯

Warwickshire. 🏠 *23,350.*
🚉 🅿 ℹ *The Courthouse, Jury St (01926 492212).* 🛒 *Sat.*
www.visitwarwick.co.uk

Warwick suffered a major fire in 1694, but some medieval buildings survived. **St John's House Museum** in St John's is a charming Jacobean mansion housing reconstructions of a Victorian parlour, kitchen and classroom. At the west end of the High Street, a row of medieval guild buildings were transformed in 1571 by the Earl of Leicester, who founded the **Lord Leycester Hospital** as a refuge for his old soldiers.

The arcaded **Market Hall** (1670) is part of the Warwick-shire Museum, renowned for its unusual tapestry map of the county, woven in 1558.

In Church Street, to the south of St Mary's Church, is the **Beauchamp Chapel** (1443–64). It is a superb example of Perpendicular architecture and has tombs of the Earls of Warwick. There is a view of **Warwick Castle** *(see pp322–3)* from St Mary's tower.

🏛 **St John's House Museum**
St John's. *Tel 01926 412132.*
🕙 *Tue–Sat.* 🔘 *limited.*

🏰 **Lord Leycester Hospital**
High St. *Tel 01926 491422.* 🕙 *Tue–Sun & public hols.* ⬤ *Good Fri, 25 Dec.* **Gardens** 🕙 *same as house but Easter–Sep only.* 📷 ⬜ 🔘 *ltd.* 📱

🏛 **Market Hall**
Market Place. *Tel 01926 412500.*
🕙 *Tue–Sat (Apr–Sep: Tue–Sun).*
🔘 *limited.* 📱

The Lord Leycester Hospital, now a home for ex-servicemen

Warwick Castle

Neville family at prayer (c.1460)

Warwick's magnificent castle is the finest medieval fortress in the country. The original Norman castle was rebuilt in the 13th and 14th centuries, when huge outer walls and towers were added, mainly to display the power of the great feudal magnates, the Beauchamps and, in the 1400s, the Nevilles, the Earls of Warwick. The castle passed in 1604 to the Greville family who, in the 17th and 18th centuries, transformed it into a great country house. In 1978 the owners of Madame Tussaud's (*see p104*) bought the castle and set up tableaux of wax portraits to illustrate its history.

Merlin: The Dragon Tower houses characters from the BBC TV series *Merlin*, including the great dragon itself.

The Mound has remains of the motte and bailey cas (*see p486*) and the 13 century keep.

Princess Tower

Royal Weekend Party
The portrait of the valet is part of the award-winning exhibition of the Prince of Wales's visit in 1898.

RIVER AVON

The Mill and Engine House

Kingmaker
Dramatic displays recreate medieval life as "Warwick the Kingmaker", Richard Neville, prepared for battle in the Wars of the Roses.

★ **Great Hall and State Rooms**
Medieval apartments were transformed into the Great Hall and State Rooms. A mark of conspicuous wealth, they display a collection of family treasures from around the world.

View of Warwick Castle, south front, by Antonio Canaletto (1697–1768)

Ramparts and towers, of local grey sandstone, were added in the 14th and 15th centuries.

★ **Guy's Tower**
Completed around 1393, the tower had lodgings for guests and members of the Earl of Warwick's retinue.

The Castle Dungeon is a chilling, live dramatisation of plague-ridden medieval Warwick.

Entrance

STAR SIGHTS

★ Great Hall and State Rooms

★ Guy's Tower

The Gatehouse is defended by portcullises and "murder holes" through which boiling pitch was dropped onto attackers beneath.

Caesar's Tower

TIMELINE

Richard Neville

Shield (1745)

1068 Norman motte and bailey castle built	**1264** Simon de Montfort, champion of Parliament against Henry III, attacks Warwick Castle		**1478** Castle reverts to Crown after murder of Richard Neville's son-in-law	**1890s–1910** Visits from future Edward VII

1000	1200	1400	1600	1800

1268–1445 Much of the present castle built by the Beauchamp family, Earls of Warwick

1449–1471 Richard Neville, Earl of Warwick, plays leading role in Wars of the Roses

1604 James I gives castle to Sir Fulke Greville

1600–1800 Interiors remodelled and gardens landscaped

1642 Siege of the Castle of Royalist Troops

1871 Fire damages the Great Hall

Street-by-Street: Stratford-upon-Avon ⑰

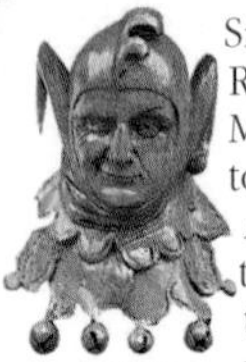

A 1930s jester

Situated on the west bank of the River Avon, in the heart of the Midlands, is one of the most famous towns in England. Stratford-upon-Avon dates back to at least Roman times but its appearance today is that of a small Tudor market town, with mellow, half-timbered architecture and tranquil walks beside the tree-fringed Avon. This image belies its popularity as the most visited tourist attraction outside London, with eager hordes flocking to see buildings connected to William Shakespeare or his descendants.

Bancroft Gardens
There is an attractive boat-filled canal basin here and a 15th-century causeway.

Tourist information

WATER

★ Shakespeare's Birthplace
This building was almost entirely reconstructed in the 19th century, but in the style of the Tudor original.

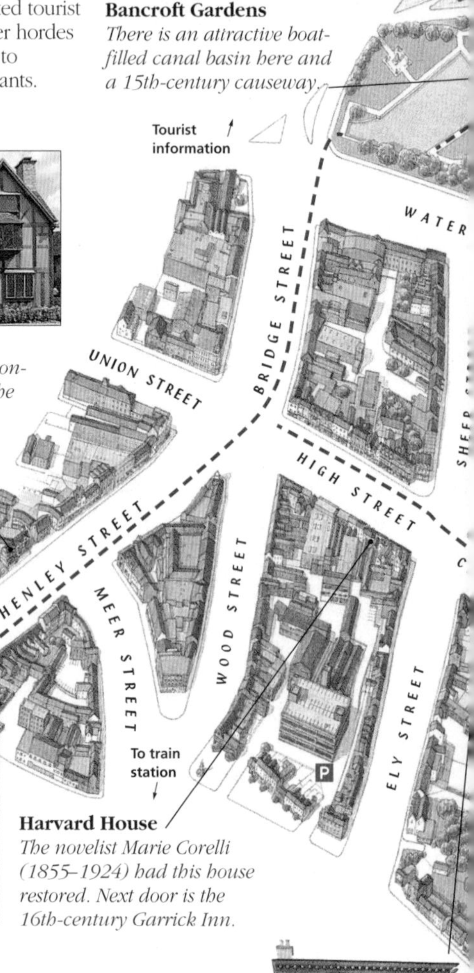

0 metres   100
0 yards   100

Shakespeare Centre

UNION STREET

BRIDGE STREET

HIGH STREET

SHEEP S

HENLEY STREET

MEER STREET

WOOD STREET

ELY STREET

C

To train station

P

Harvard House
The novelist Marie Corelli (1855–1924) had this house restored. Next door is the 16th-century Garrick Inn.

STAR SIGHTS

★ Shakespeare's Birthplace

★ Hall's Croft

★ Holy Trinity Church

Town Hall
Built in 1767, there are traces of 18th-century graffiti on the front of the building saying God Save the King.

Royal Shakespeare Theatre and Swan Theatre
*Home of the Royal Shakespeare Company (RSC), the Swan
Theatre is located on the western bank of the River Avon.*

VISITORS' CHECKLIST

Warwickshire. 🚗 25,000.
✈ 20 miles (32 km) NW of
Stratford-upon-Avon. 🚉
Alcester Rd. 🚌 Bridge St.
ℹ Bridgefoot **Tel** 0870 160
7930. 🛒 Fri. 🎭 Shakespeare's
Birthday: Apr; Stratford Festival:
Jul. **www**.shakespeare-country.
co.uk

Nash's House
*The foundations of New
Place, where Shakespeare
died, form the garden
beside this house.*

★ Holy Trinity Church
*Shakespeare's grave
and copies of the parish
register entries record-
ing his birth and
death are here.*

CHAPEL LANE

AVON

SOUTHERN LANE

OLD TOWN

CHURCH STREET

OLD TOWN

Edward VI
Grammar
School

Guild
Chapel

KEY

- - - Suggested route

e
...away's
...age

★ Hall's Croft
*John Hall, Shakespeare's son-in-law, was
a doctor. This delightful house includes
an exhibition of medicine in
Shakespeare's time.*

Exploring Stratford-upon-Avon

Mosaic of Shakespeare on the beautiful Old Bank (1810)

William Shakespeare was born in Stratford-upon-Avon on St George's Day, 23 April 1564. Admirers of his work have been coming to the town since his death in 1616. In 1847 a public appeal successfully raised the money to buy the house in which he was born. As a result Stratford has become a literary shrine to Britain's greatest dramatist. It also has a thriving cultural reputation as the provincial home of the prestigious Royal Shakespeare Company, whose dramas are usually performed in Stratford before playing a second season in London (see pp152–3).

Anne Hathaway's Cottage, home of Shakespeare's wife

Around Stratford

The centre of Stratford-upon-Avon has many buildings that are connected with William Shakespeare and his descendants. On the High Street corner is the **Cage**, a 15th-century prison. It was converted into a house where Shakespeare's daughter Judith lived, and is now a shop. At the end of the High Street, the **Town Hall** has a statue of Shakespeare on the façade given by David Garrick (1717–79), the actor who in 1769 organized the first Shakespeare festival.

The High Street leads into Chapel Street where the half-timbered **Nash's House** is a museum of local history. It is also the site of **New Place**, where Shakespeare died in 1616, and which is now a herb and knot garden (see p26). In Church Street opposite, the **Guild Chapel** (1496) has a *Last Judgement* painting (c.1500) on the chancel wall. Shakespeare is thought to have attended the **Edward VI Grammar School** (above the former Guildhall) next door.

A left turn into Old Town leads to **Hall's Croft**, home of Shakespeare's daughter Susanna, which displays 16th- and 17th-century medical artefacts. An avenue of lime trees leads to **Holy Trinity Church**, where Shakespeare is buried. A walk along the river follows the Avon to **Bancroft Gardens**, which lies at the junction of the River Avon and the Stratford Canal.

Holy Trinity Church, seen across the River Avon

🎭 Shakespeare's Birthplace

Henley St. **Tel** 01789 204016. 🔘 daily. 🔘 23–26 Dec. 📷 👤 limited. 🔲 www.shakespeare.org.uk
Bought for the nation in 1847, when it was a public house, Shakespeare's Birthplace was converted back to Elizabethan style. Objects associated with Shakespeare's father, John, a glovemaker and wool merchant, are on display. There is a birth room, in which Shakespeare was supposedly born, and another room has a window etched with visitors' autographs, including that of Sir Walter Scott (see p512).

🏛 Harvard House

High St. ⬤ *not open to the public.*
Built in 1596, this ornate house was the home of Katherine Rogers, whose son, John Harvard, emigrated to America in 1637. He died the following year, leaving money and a small library to the New College in Cambridge, Massachusetts. They expressed their gratitude by renaming the college in his honour. Harvard never actually lived in this house, however.

Environs: At Shottery, 1 mile (1.5 km) west of Stratford, is **Anne Hathaway's Cottage**, home of Shakespeare's wife before their marriage *(see p321).* Also worth a visit is **Mary Arden's Farm** in Wilmcote, home of Shakespeare's grand-parents and childhood home of his mother, Mary Arden.

🏛 Anne Hathaway's Cottage

Cottage Lane. *Tel 01789 292100.*
⬤ *daily.* ⬤ *23–26 Dec.* 🅿 🔲

🏛 Mary Arden's Farm

Station Rd. *Tel 01789 293455.*
⬤ *Apr–Oct: daily.* 🅿 🔲 🔲 **www.**
shakespeare.org.uk

Kenneth Branagh in *Hamlet*

THE ROYAL SHAKESPEARE COMPANY

The Royal Shakespeare Company is renowned for its new interpretations of Shakespeare's work. It was established in the 1960s as a resident company for the 1932 Shakespeare Memorial Theatre, now the Royal Shakespeare Theatre. It has seen the brightest and best theatrical talent tread its boards, from Laurence Olivier and Vivien Leigh to Helen Mirren and Kenneth Branagh. The RSC also tours, with regular seasons in London, Newcastle and even New York.

Grevel House, the oldest house in Chipping Campden

Chipping Campden ⑱

Gloucestershire. 🚶 *2,500.*
🛈 *High St (01386 841206).*
www.visitchippingcampden.com

This perfect Cotswold town is kept in pristine condition by the Campden Society. Set up in the 1920s, the Society has kept alive the traditional skills of stonecarving and repair that make Chipping Campden such a unified picture of golden-coloured and lichen-patched stone. Visitors travelling from the northwest along the B4035 first see a group of ruins: the remains of **Campden Manor**, begun around 1613 by Sir Baptist Hicks, 1st Viscount Campden. The manor was burned by Royalist troops to stop it being sequestered by Parliament at the end of the Civil War *(see pp52–3),* but the almshouses opposite the gateway were spared. They were designed in the form of the letter "I" (which is Latin for "J"), a symbol of the owner's loyalty to King James I.

The town's **Church of St James**, one of the finest in the Cotswolds, was built in the 15th century, financed by merchants who bought wool from Cotswold farmers and exported it at a high profit. Inside the church there are many elaborate tombs, and

a magnificent brass dedicated to William Grevel, describing him as "the flower of the wool merchants of England". He built **Grevel House** (c.1380) in the High Street, the oldest in a fine row of buildings, which is distinguished by a double-storey bay window.

Viscount Campden donated the **Market Hall** in 1627. His contemporary, Robert Dover, founded in 1612 the "Cotswold Olimpicks", long before the modern Olympic Games had been established. The 1612 version included such painful events as the shin-kicking con-test. It still takes place on the first Friday after each Spring Bank Holiday, followed by a torchlight procession into town ready for the Scuttlebrook Wake Fair on the next day. The setting for the games is a spectacular natural hollow on **Dover's Hill** above the town, worth climbing on a clear day for the marvellous views over the Vale of Evesham.

The 17th-century Market Hall in Chipping Campden

Tewkesbury's abbey church overlooks the town, crowded onto the bank of the River Severn

Tewkesbury ⑲

Gloucestershire. 🏠 11,000.
ℹ Church St (01684 855040).
🏪 Wed, Sat. www.visitcotswolds
andsevernvale.gov.uk

This lovely town sits on the confluence of the rivers Severn and Avon. It has one of England's finest Norman abbey churches, **St Mary the Virgin**, which locals saved during the Dissolution of the Monasteries *(see p50)* by paying Henry VIII £453. Around the church, with its bulky tower and Norman façade, timbered buildings are crammed within the bend of the river. Warehouses are a reminder of past wealth, and Borough Mill on Quay Street, the only mill left harnessed to the river's energy, still grinds corn.

Pump Room detail, Cheltenham

Environs: Boat trips run from the river to **Twyning**'s riverside pub, 6 miles (10 km) north.

Cheltenham ⑳

Gloucestershire. 🏠 110,000. 🚉 🚌
ℹ 77 Promenade (01242 522878).
🏪 Sun; farmers' market 2nd & last Fri of month. www.visitcheltenham.com

Cheltenham's reputation for elegance was first gained in the late 18th century, when high society flocked to the spa

town to "take the waters", following the example set by George III *(see pp54–5)*. Many gracious terraced houses were built, in a Neo-Classical style, along broad avenues. These survive around the Queen's Hotel, near **Montpellier**, a lovely Regency arcade lined with craft and antique shops, and in the **Promenade**, with its smart department stores and couturiers. A more modern atmosphere prevails in the Regency Arcade, where the star attraction is the 1987 **clock** by Kit Williams: visit on the hour to see fish blowing bubbles over the onlookers' heads. The **Museum and Art Gallery** is worth a visit to see its unusual collection of furniture and other crafts made by members of the influential Arts and Crafts Movement *(see p29)*, whose strict principles of utilitarian design were laid down by William Morris *(see p220)*.

The **Pittville Pump Room** (1825–30), modelled on the Greek Temple of Ilissos in Athens, is frequently used for performances during the town's renowned annual festivals of music (July) and literature (October).

The event that really attracts the crowds is the Cheltenham Gold Cup – the premier event of the National Hunt season – held in March *(see p66)*.

🏛 **Museum and Art Gallery**
Clarence St. **Tel** 01242 237431.
◻ Mon–Sat. ◻ 1 Jan, 25 Dec & public hols. ♿ 📷 by arrangement.
🖥 📷 www.cheltenham museum.org.uk

🏛 **Pittville Pump Room**
Pittville Park. **Tel** 0844 5762210.
◻ Wed–Mon. ◻ 1 Jan, 25 & 26 Dec, public hols & frequently for functions: call to check. ♿
www.pittvillepumproom.org.uk

Fantasy clock, by Kit Williams, in Cheltenham's Regency Arcade

Gloucester Cathedral's nave

Gloucester ㉑

Gloucestershire. 👥 110,000.
🚉 🚌 🛈 28 Southgate St
(01452 396572). 🏪 Wed, Sat.
www.thecityofgloucester.co.uk

Gloucester has played a
prominent role in the history
of England. It was here that
William the Conqueror
ordered a vast survey of all the
land in his kingdom, that was
to be recorded in the *Domesday Book* of 1086 *(see p48)*.

The city was popular with
the Norman monarchs and in
1216 Henry III was crowned
in its magnificent **cathedral**.
The solid, dignified nave was
begun in 1089. Edward II *(see
p439)*, who was murdered in
1327 at Berkeley Castle, 14
miles (22 km) to the southwest, is buried in a tomb near
the high altar. Many pilgrims
came to honour Edward's
tomb, leaving behind generous donations, and Abbot
Thoky was able to begin
rebuilding in 1331. The result
was the wonderful east
window and the cloisters,
where the fan vault was
developed and then copied
in other churches all over
the country.

The impressive buildings
around the cathedral include
College Court, with its **House
of the Tailor of Gloucester**
museum, in the house that
the children's author Beatrix
Potter used as the setting *(see
p367)* for her illustrations of
that story. A museum complex
has been created in the
Gloucester Docks, part of
which is still a port, linked
to the Bristol Channel by the

Gloucester and Sharpness
Canal (opened in 1827). In
the old port, and housed in
a Victorian warehouse, the
Gloucester Waterways Museum
relates the history of canals.
A gallery called Move It looks
at how canals were built.

🏛 **House of the Tailor of
Gloucester**
College Court. *Tel 01452 422856.*
⭕ Mon–Sat (Sun: pm only).
⬤ public hols. 📷

🏛 **Gloucester Waterways
Museum**
Llanthony Warehouse, Gloucester
Docks. *Tel 01452 318200.*
⭕ daily. ⬤ 25 Dec. 📷 🎥 ♿
🖥 www.gloucesterwaterways
museum.org.uk

Cirencester ㉒

Gloucestershire. 👥 20,000. 🚌
🛈 Market Place (01285 654180).
🏪 Mon, Tue (cattle) & Fri.
www.cotswold.gov.uk

Known as the capital of the
Cotswolds, Cirencester has as
its focus a market place, where
there is a market every Monday and Friday. Overlooking
the market is the **Church of St
John Baptist**, whose "wine-
glass" pulpit (1515) is one
of the few pre-Reformation
pulpits to survive in England.
To the west, **Cirencester Park**
was laid out by the 1st Earl
of Bathurst from 1714, with
help from the poet Alexander
Pope *(see p317)*. The mansion
is surrounded by a massive
yew hedge. Clustering round

the park entrance are the
17th- and 18th-century wool
merchants' houses of Cecily
Hill, built in grand Italianate
style. Much humbler Cots-
wold houses are to be found
in Coxwell Street, and
underlying this is a Roman
town, evidence of which
emerges whenever the
ground is dug.

The **Corinium Museum** is an
impressive modern museum.
It features excavated objects
in a series of tableaux illustrating life in a Roman
household.

🌿 **Cirencester Park**
Cirencester Park. *Tel 01285
640410.* ⭕ daily. ♿
www.cirencesterpark.co.uk

🏛 **Corinium Museum**
Park St. *Tel 01285 655611.*
⭕ daily (Sun pm only). ⬤ 1 Jan,
25 & 26 Dec. 🎥 ♿ 🖥 📷
www.cotswold.gov.uk

**Cirencester's fine parish church,
one of the largest in England**

ART AND NATURE IN THE ROMAN WORLD

Cirencester was an important centre of mosaic production
in Roman days. Fine examples of the local style are shown
in the Corinium Museum and mosaics range from Classical
subjects, such as Orpheus taming lions and tigers with the
music of his lyre, to the naturalistic depiction of a hare. At

Chedworth Roman Villa, 8
miles (13 km) north, mosaics
are inspired by real life. In
the *Four Seasons* mosaic,
Winter shows a peasant,
dressed in a woollen hood
and a wind-blown cloak,
clutching a recently caught
hare in one hand and a
branch for fuel in the other.

Hare mosaic, Corinium Museum

EAST MIDLANDS

DERBYSHIRE · LEICESTERSHIRE · LINCOLNSHIRE
NORTHAMPTONSHIRE · NOTTINGHAMSHIRE

Three very different kinds of landscape greet visitors to the East Midlands. In the west, wild moors rise to the craggy heights of the Peak District. These give way to the low-lying plain and the massive industrial towns at the region's heart. In the east, hills and limestone villages stretch to a long, flat seaboard.

The East Midlands owes much of its character to a conjunction of the pastoral with the urban. The spa resorts, historical villages and stately homes coexist within a landscape shaped by industrialization. Throughout the region there are swathes of scenic countryside – and grimy industrial cities.

The area has been settled since prehistoric times. The Romans mined lead and salt, and they built a large network of roads and fortresses. Anglo-Saxon and Viking influence is found in many of the place names. During the Middle Ages profits from the wool industry enabled the development of towns such as Lincoln, which still has many fine old buildings. The East Midlands was the scene of ferocious battles during the Wars of the Roses and the Civil War, and insurgents in the Jacobite Rebellion reached as far as Derby.

In the west of the region is the Peak District, Britain's first national park. Created in 1951, it draws crowds in search of the wild beauty of the heather-covered moors, or the wooded dales of the River Dove. The peaks are very popular with rock climbers and hikers.

The eastern edge of the Peaks descends through stone-walled meadows to sheltered valleys. The Roman spa of Buxton adds a final note of elegance before the flatlands of south Derbyshire, Leicestershire and Nottinghamshire are reached. An area of coal mines and factories since the late 18th century, the landscape was improved greatly by a 10-year planting scheme of the National Forest.

Well-dressing dance, an ancient custom at Stoney Middleton in the Peak District

◁ **West front of Chatsworth House, a superb Baroque stately home in the Peak District**

Exploring the East Midlands

The East Midlands is a popular tourist destination, easily accessible by road, but best explored on foot. Numerous well-marked trails pass through the Peak District National Park. There are superb country houses at Chatsworth and Burghley and the impressive historic towns of Lincoln and Stamford to discover.

SIGHTS AT A GLANCE

Burghley pp342–3 ❽
Buxton ❶
Chatsworth pp334–5 ❷
Lincoln pp340–41 ❼
Matlock Bath ❸
Northampton ❿
Nottingham ❻
Stamford ❾

Walks and Tours
Peak District Tour ❺
Tissington Trail ❹

GETTING AROUND

The M6, M1 and A1 are the principal road routes to the East Midlands, but they are subject to frequent delays because of the volume of traffic they carry. It can be faster and more interesting to find cross-country routes to the region, for example through the attractive countryside and villages around Stamford and Northampton. Roads in the Peak District become very congested during the summer and an early start to the day is advisable. Lincoln and Stamford are well served by fast mainline trains from London. Rail services in the Peak District are far more limited, but local lines run as far as Matlock and Buxton.

KEY

━━ Motorway

━━ Major road

━━ Secondary road

┄┄ Minor road

━━ Scenic route

┄┄ Main railway

── Minor railway

△ Summit

View of Burghley House from the north courtyard

SEE ALSO

• **Where to Stay** pp581–2

• **Where to Eat** pp632–4

Peak District countryside seen from the Tissington Trail

Map labels:
Barnsley
Manchester A628
Peak District National Park
Kinder Scout 636m
Edale
Hathersage
BUXTON ❶
Eyam ❺
CHATSWORTH ❷
Chester
A515
Bakewell
Stoke-on-Trent
A6
MATLOCK ❸
TISSINGTON TRAIL ❹
Dovedale
Wirksworth
Ashbourne
Kedleston Hall
A515
Derby
Sudbury
A50
Burton upon Trent
A38
A511
A42
Twycross
Birm

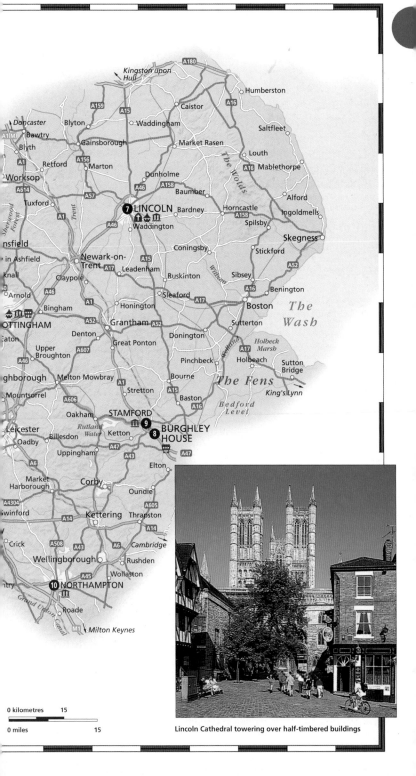

Kingston upon Hull

A180

Humberston

A159   A15   Caistor   A16

Doncaster   Blyton   Waddingham   Saltfleet

Bawtry   Gainsborough   Market Rasen   Louth

Blyth   A1   Marton   A16   Mablethorpe

Worksop   Retford   A156   Dunholme   The Wolds

A614   A57   A46   A158   Alford

Tuxford   A1   Baumber   Ingoldmells

Sherwood Forest   **7** LINCOLN   Horncastle

nsfield   A46   Bardney   A158   Spilsby   Skegness

in Ashfield   Waddington   Coningsby   Stickford

Knall   Newark-on-Trent   A17   A15   Leadenham   Ruskinton   A52

Arnold   Claypole   Sleaford   A17   Sibsey   Benington

A46   Honington   A16

Bingham   A1   Donington   Boston   *The Wash*

OTTINGHAM   Denton   Grantham   A52   Sutterton

aton   Great Ponton   Pinchbeck   A17   Holbeck Marsh   Holbeach   Sutton Bridge

Upper Broughton   A607

A46   Melton Mowbray   Bourne   *The Fens*

ghborough   A1   Stretton   A15   Baston   King's Lynn

Mountsorrel   A606   A16   *Bedford Level*

Oakham   STAMFORD   **9**

Leicester   *Rutland Water*   Ketton   **8** BURGHLEY HOUSE

Oadby   Billesdon   A47   A47

Uppingham   A43

Market Harborough   Elton

A4304   Corby   Oundle

winford   A605

Crick   Kettering   Thrapston

A508   A43   A6   Cambridge

Wellingborough   Rushden

ntry   A45   Wollaston

10 NORTHAMPTON

Grand Union Canal   Roade

M1   Milton Keynes

0 kilometres   15

0 miles   15

Lincoln Cathedral towering over half-timbered buildings

Buxton Opera House, a late 19th-century building restored in 1979

Buxton ❶

Derbyshire. 21,300. Pavilion Gardens (01298 25106). Tue, Sat. **www**.highpeak.gov.uk

Buxton was developed as a spa town by the 5th Duke of Devonshire during the late 18th century. It has many fine Neo-Classical buildings, including the **Devonshire Royal Hospital** (1790), originally stables, at the entrance to the town. The **Crescent** was built (1780–90) to rival Bath's Royal Crescent *(see p258)* and is being restored.

The town baths were at the southwest end. Here, a spring where water surges from the ground at a rate of 7,000 litres (1,540 gallons) an hour can be seen. Buxton water is bottled and sold but there is a public fountain at **St Ann's Well**, opposite.

Steep gardens known as the Slopes lead from the Crescent to the small, but worthwhile, **Museum and Art Gallery**, with geological and archaeological displays. Behind the Crescent, overlooking the Pavilion Gardens, is the striking 19th-century iron and glass **Pavilion**, and the splendidly restored **Opera House**, where a music and arts festival is held in summer.

Buxton Museum and Art Gallery
Terrace Rd. ***Tel*** *01629 533540.* *Easter–Sep: Tue–Sun; Oct–Easter: Tue–Sat.* *1 Jan, 25 & 26 Dec.* **www**.derbyshire.gov.uk

Pavilion Gardens
St John's Rd. ***Tel*** *01298 23114.* *daily.* *25 Dec.*

Chatsworth House and Gardens ❷

Chatsworth is one of Britain's most impressive stately homes. Between 1687 and 1707, the 4th Earl of Devonshire replaced the old Tudor mansion with this Baroque palace. The house has beautiful gardens, landscaped in the 1760s by "Capability" Brown *(see p26)* and developed by the head gardener, Joseph Paxton *(see pp56–7)*, in the mid-19th century.

First house built in 1552 by Bess of Hardwick

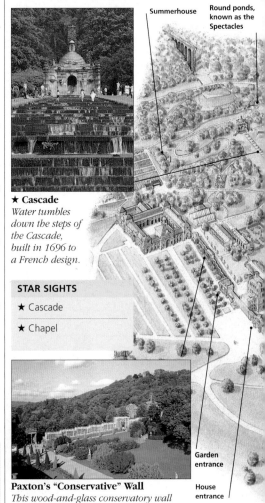

★ Cascade
Water tumbles down the steps of the Cascade, built in 1696 to a French design.

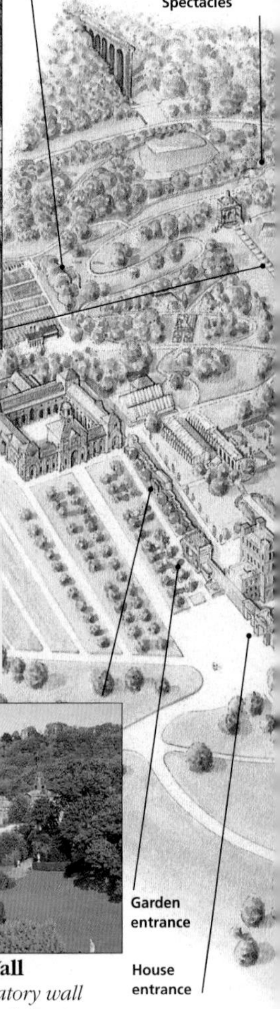

STAR SIGHTS

★ Cascade

★ Chapel

Paxton's "Conservative" Wall
This wood-and-glass conservatory wall was designed in 1848 by Joseph Paxton, the creator of Chatsworth's Great Conservatory (now demolished).

South front and canal pond with Emperor fountain

VISITORS' CHECKLIST

Derbyshire. ⬛ Chesterfield,
then bus. **Tel** 01246 565300.
⬜ mid-Mar–Dec: 11am–4:30pm
(gardens: 11am–5pm) daily. 🎫
♿ gardens & some of house. 🍴
⬛ 🅿 www.chatsworth.org

Maze: site of Paxton's Great Conservatory

Rhododendron Walk

Grotto

★ **Chapel**
*The chapel (1693) is
resplendent with
art and marble.*

War Horse
*This sculpture
(1991) is by
Elisabeth Frink.*

Canal pond

Sea-horse fountain

State Rooms
*The rooms have
fine interiors and
superb art, such as
this* trompe l'oeil *by Jan
van der Vaart (1651–1727).*

Matlock ❸

Derbyshire. 🏘 9,500. 🚆
ℹ️ *Matlock Station (01629 583388).*
www.visitpeakdistrict.com

Matlock was developed as a
spa from the 1780s. Interesting
buildings include a former
hydrotherapy centre (1853)
on the hill above the town,
which is now used for council
offices. On the hill opposite is
the mock-Gothic **Riber Castle**.

From Matlock, the A6 winds
through the beautiful **Derwent
Gorge** to **Matlock Bath**. Here,
cable cars ascend to the **Heights
of Abraham** pleasure park,
with caves, nature trail and
extensive views. Lead-mining is
the subject of the **Peak District
Mining Museum**, and visitors
can inspect the old **Temple
Mine** nearby. **Sir Richard Arkwright's Cromford Mill** (1771),
a World Heritage Site and the
first ever water-powered cotton
spinning mill, lies at the southern end of the gorge *(see p339)*.

🎿 **Heights of Abraham**
On A6. *Tel 01629 582365.* ⬜ Feb–
Oct: daily. 🎫 & limited. 🅿️ 🏪
www.heightsofabraham.com

🏛 **Peak District Mining
Museum**
The Pavilion, off A6. *Tel 01629
583834.* ⬜ Apr–Oct: daily; Nov–
Mar: Wed–Sun. 🎫 & 🅿️ 🏪
www.peakmines.co.uk

⛏ **Temple Mine**
Temple Rd, off A6. *Tel 01629
583834.* ⬜ call for details. 🎫

⛏ **Cromford Mill**
Mill Lane, Cromford. *Tel 01629
824297.* ⬜ daily. ⬤ 25 Dec.
& 🍴 🏪 **www**.arkwrightsociety.
org.uk

Cable cars taking visitors to the Heights of Abraham

Tissington Trail ❹

See p337.

Peak District Tour ❺

See pp338–9.

Nottingham ❻

Nottinghamshire. 🏘 269,000. 🚆
✈️ ℹ️ *Smithy Row (0844 477 5678).*
🛒 daily. **www**.nottinghamcity.gov.uk

The name of Nottingham
often conjures up the image
of the evil Sheriff, adversary
of Robin Hood. **Nottingham
Castle** stands on a rock riddled
with underground passages.
The castle houses a museum,
with displays on the city's
history, and what was Britain's
first municipal art gallery, featuring works by Sir Stanley
Spencer (1891–1959) and Dante
Gabriel Rossetti (1828–82). At
the foot of the castle, Britain's

oldest tavern, **Ye Olde Trip to
Jerusalem** (1189), is still in
business. Its name may refer
to the 12th- and 13th-century
crusades, but much of it is
17th-century.

There are several museums
nearby, including the **Museum
of Nottingham Life**, which
looks at life in Nottingham
over the last 300 years, and
Wollaton Hall and Deer Park,
an Elizabethan mansion housing a natural history museum.
Nottingham's redeveloped
city centre includes an award-
winning Old Market Square.

Environs: Stately homes
within a few miles of Nottingham include the Neo-
Classical **Kedleston Hall** *(see
pp28–9)*. "Bess of Hardwick",
Countess of Shrewsbury *(see
p334)*, built the spectacular
Hardwick Hall *(see p302)*.

♠ **Nottingham Castle
and Museum**
Friar Lane. *Tel 0115 9153700.*
⬜ Tue–Sun. ⬤ 1 Jan, 24–27 Dec.
🎫 & 🏪 of the caves. 🖥 🏪

🏛 **Wollaton Hall and Deer
Park**
Wollaton. *Tel 0115 9153900.* ⬜
daily. ⬤ 25 & 26 Dec. & 🖥 🏪
🅿️ fee.

🏛 **Museum of
Nottingham Life**
Castle Boulevard. *Tel 0115 915
3700.* ⬜ daily. ⬤ 1 Jan, 24–26 Dec.
& 🏪 **www**.nottinghamcity.gov.uk

🏛 **Kedleston Hall**
(NT) off A38. *Tel 01332 842191.*
⬜ mid-Feb–Oct: Sat–Wed (pm). 🎫
& 🏪

🏛 **Hardwick Hall**
(NT) off A617. *Tel 01246 850430.*
⬜ mid-Feb–Oct: Wed–Sun. 🎫 &
limited. 🍴 🏪

ROBIN HOOD OF SHERWOOD FOREST

England's most colourful folk hero was a
legendary bowman, whose adventures are
depicted in numerous films and
stories. He lived in Sherwood Forest,
near Nottingham, with a band of
"merry men", robbing the rich to
give to the poor. As part of an
ancient oral tradition, Robin Hood
figured mainly in ballads; the first
written records of his exploits date
from the 15th century. Today historians think that he was not one
person, but a composite of many
outlaws who refused to conform
to medieval feudal constraints.

**Victorian depiction of Friar
Tuck and Robin Hood**

Tissington Trail ❹

The full-length Tissington Trail runs for 13 miles (22 km), from the town of Ashbourne to Parsley Hay, where it meets the High Peak Trail. This is a short version, taking an easy route along a dismantled railway line around Tissington village and providing good views of the beautiful White Peak countryside. The Derbyshire custom of well-dressing is thought to have originated in pre-Christian times. It was revived in the early 17th century, when the Tissington village wells were decorated in thanksgiving for deliverance from the plague, in the belief that the fresh water had had a medicinal effect. Well-dressing is still an important event in the Peakland calendar, and can be seen in other villages where the water supplies were prone to dry up.

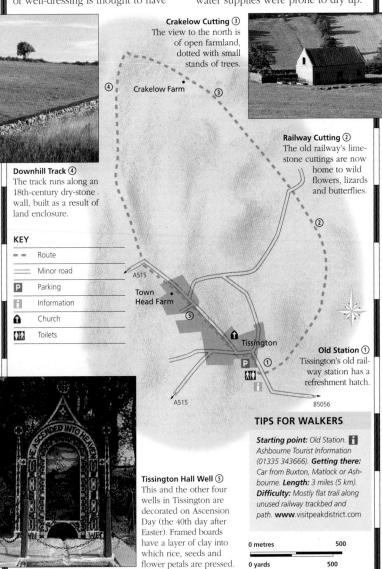

Crakelow Cutting ③
The view to the north is of open farmland, dotted with small stands of trees.

Railway Cutting ②
The old railway's limestone cuttings are now home to wild flowers, lizards and butterflies.

Downhill Track ④
The track runs along an 18th-century dry-stone wall, built as a result of land enclosure.

KEY

– –	Route
═══	Minor road
P	Parking
ℹ	Information
🕀	Church
🚻	Toilets

Crakelow Farm

A515

Town Head Farm

Tissington

Old Station ①
Tissington's old railway station has a refreshment hatch.

A515

B5056

Tissington Hall Well ⑤
This and the other four wells in Tissington are decorated on Ascension Day (the 40th day after Easter). Framed boards have a layer of clay into which rice, seeds and flower petals are pressed.

TIPS FOR WALKERS

Starting point: *Old Station.* ℹ *Ashbourne Tourist Information (01335 343666).* **Getting there:** *Car from Buxton, Matlock or Ashbourne.* **Length:** *3 miles (5 km).* **Difficulty:** *Mostly flat trail along unused railway trackbed and path.* **www**.visitpeakdistrict.com

0 metres	500
0 yards	500

Peak District Tour ❺

The Peak District's natural beauty and sheep-grazed crags contrast with the factories of nearby valley towns. Designated Britain's first National Park in 1951, the area has two distinct types of landscape. In the south are the gently rolling hills of the limestone White Peak. To the north, west and east are the wild, heather-clad moorlands of the Dark Peak peat bogs, superimposed on millstone grit.

Detail, Buxton Opera House

Edale ⑤

The high plateau above scenic Edale marks the starting point of the 256 mile (412 km) Pennine Way footpath *(see p36)*.

Buxton ⑥

This lovely spa town's opera house *(see p334)* is known as the "theatre in the hills" because of its magnificent setting.

Arbor Low ⑦

This stone circle, known as the "Stonehenge of the North", dates from around 2000 BC and consists of 46 recumbent stones enclosed by a ditch.

TIPS FOR DRIVERS

Tour length: 40 miles (60 km).
Stopping-off points: There are refreshments at Crich Tramway Village and Arkwright's Mill in Cromford. Eyam has good old-fashioned tea shops. The Nag's Head in Edale is a charming Tudor inn. Buxton has many pubs and cafés. (See also pp684–5.)

KEY

▰▰▰	Tour route
═══	Other roads
☀	Viewpoint

Dovedale ⑧

Popular Dovedale is one of the prettiest of the Peak District's river valleys, with its stepping stones, thickly wooded slopes and wind-sculpted rocks. Izaac Walton (1593–1683), author of *The Compleat Angler,* used to fish here.

STOCKPORT, MANCHESTER

HOLLINS
410
1,345
A625
A6
A623
A5004
A53
A515
A5270
Wye
A6
⑤
⑥

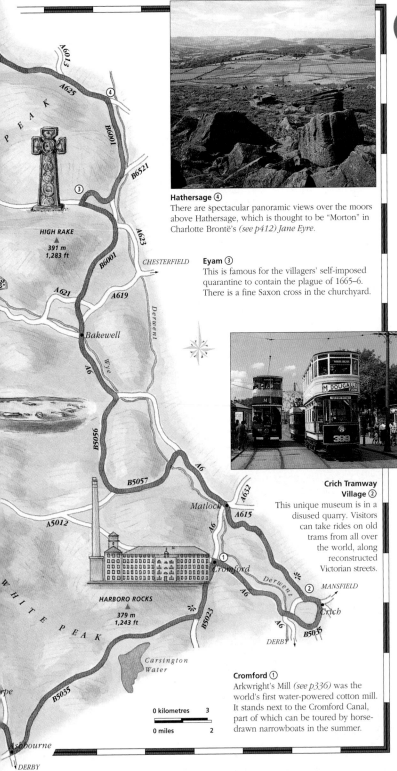

Hathersage ④
There are spectacular panoramic views over the moors above Hathersage, which is thought to be "Morton" in Charlotte Brontë's *(see p412) Jane Eyre.*

Eyam ③
This is famous for the villagers' self-imposed quarantine to contain the plague of 1665–6. There is a fine Saxon cross in the churchyard.

Crich Tramway Village ②
This unique museum is in a disused quarry. Visitors can take rides on old trams from all over the world, along reconstructed Victorian streets.

Cromford ①
Arkwright's Mill *(see p336)* was the world's first water-powered cotton mill. It stands next to the Cromford Canal, part of which can be toured by horse-drawn narrowboats in the summer.

HIGH RAKE
391 m
1,283 ft

HARBORO ROCKS
379 m
1,243 ft

Carsington Water

0 kilometres 3
0 miles 2

Street-by-Street: Lincoln 🐾

Carving in Angel Choir

Surrounded by the flat landscape of the Fens, Lincoln rises dramatically on a cliff above the River Witham, the three towers of its massive cathedral visible from afar. The Romans *(see pp44–5)* founded the first fortress here in AD 50. By the time of the Norman Conquest *(see p47)*, Lincoln was one of the most important cities in England (after London, Winchester and York). The city's wealth was due to its strategic importance for the export of wool from the Lincolnshire Wolds to Europe. Lincoln has managed to retain much of its historic character. Many remarkable medieval buildings have survived, most of which are along the aptly named Steep Hill, leading to the cathedral.

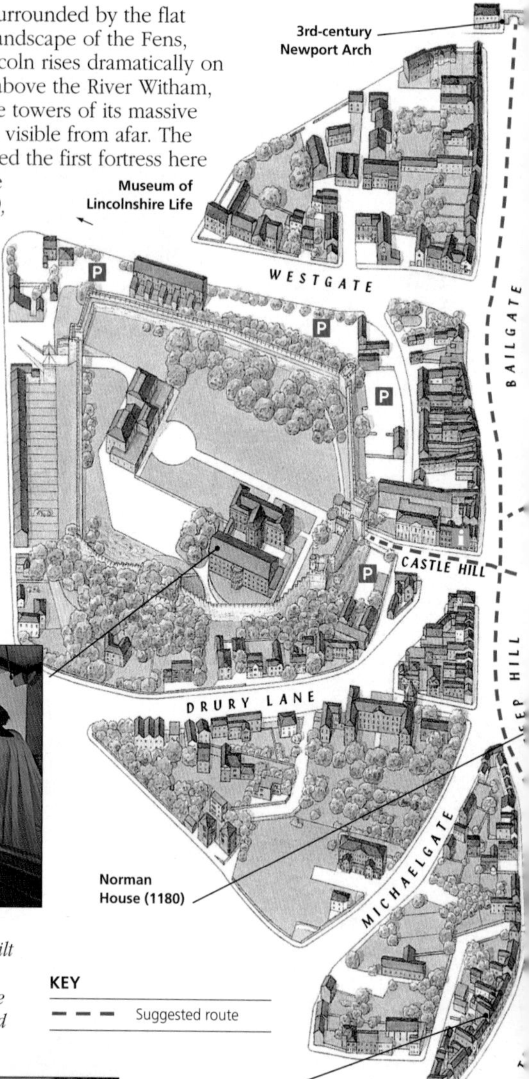

3rd-century Newport Arch

Museum of Lincolnshire Life

WESTGATE

BAILGATE

CASTLE HILL

STEEP HILL

DRURY LANE

MICHAELGATE

Norman House (1180)

★ Lincoln Castle
The early Norman castle, rebuilt at intervals, acted as the city prison from 1787 to 1878. The chapel's coffin-like pews served to remind felons of their fate.

KEY

– – – Suggested route

Jew's House
Lincoln had a large medieval Jewish community. This mid-12th-century stone house, one of the oldest of its kind, was owned by a Jewish merchant.

15th-century Stonebow Gate and bus and railway stations

```
0 meters          100
0 yards           100
```

STAR SIGHTS

★ Lincoln Castle

★ Lincoln Cathedral

VISITORS' CHECKLIST

Lincoln. 👥 90,000. ✈ Humberside, 30 miles (48 km); E Midlands, 51 miles (82 km). 🚉 St Mary St. 🚌 Melville St. ℹ Castle Hill (01522 545458). www.visitlincolnshire.com

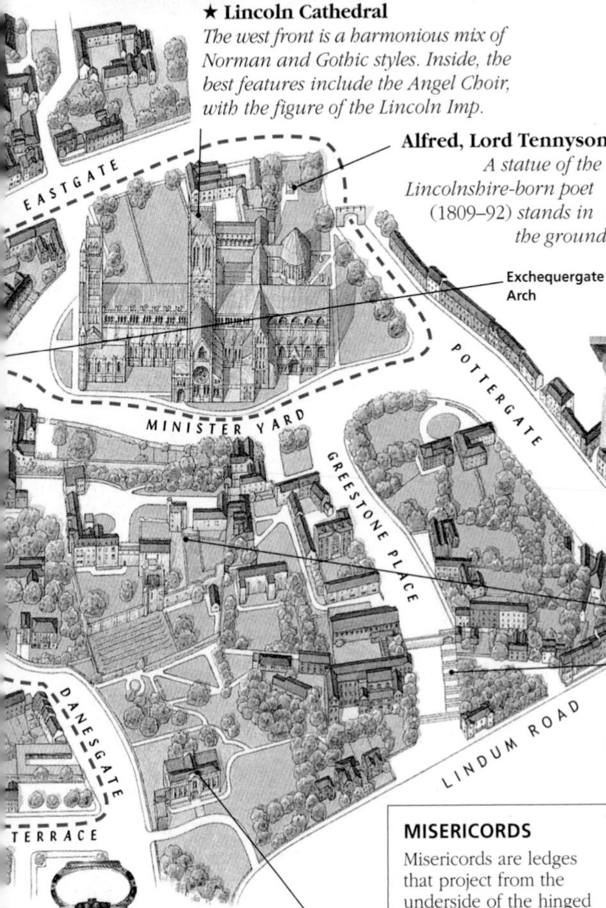

★ Lincoln Cathedral
The west front is a harmonious mix of Norman and Gothic styles. Inside, the best features include the Angel Choir, with the figure of the Lincoln Imp.

Alfred, Lord Tennyson
A statue of the Lincolnshire-born poet (1809–92) stands in the grounds.

EASTGATE

Exchequergate Arch

POTTERGATE

MINSTER YARD

GREESTONE PLACE

The 14th-century Pottergate Arch

Victorian Arboretum

Ruins of Medieval Bishop's Palace

Greestone Stairs

DANESGATE

LINDUM ROAD

TERRACE

MISERICORDS
Misericords are ledges that project from the underside of the hinged seat of a choir stall, which provide support while standing.

St Francis of Assisi

Lincoln Cathedral's misericords in the early Perpendicular-style canopied choir stalls are some of the best in England. The wide variety of subjects includes parables, fables, myths, biblical scenes and irreverent images from daily life.

One of a pair of lions

The Collection – Usher Gallery
This is packed with clocks, ceramics, and silver. There are paintings by Peter de Wint (1784–1849) and JMW Turner (see p91).

Burghley House ⑧

Portrait of Sir Isaac Newton, Billiard Room

William Cecil, 1st Lord Burghley (1520–98) was Queen Elizabeth I's adviser and confidant for 40 years and built the wonderfully dramatic Burghley House in 1555–87. The roof line bristles with stone pyramids, chimneys disguised as Classical columns and towers shaped like pepper pots. The busy skyline resolves itself into a symmetrical pattern when viewed from the west, where a lime tree stands, one of many planted by "Capability" Brown *(see p26)* when the surrounding deer park was landscaped in 1760. The interior walls are lavishly decorated with Italian paintings of Greek gods enacting their dramas. An Elizabethan "Garden of Surprises" and an education and visitor centre opened in 2007.

★ Old Kitchen
Gleaming copper pans hang from the walls of the fan-vaulted kitchen, little altered since the Tudor period.

North Gate
Intricate examples of 19th-century wrought-iron work adorn the principal entrances.

The Billiard Room
has many fine portraits inset in oak panelling.

Cupolas were very fashionable details, inspired by European Renaissance architecture.

A chimney has been disguised as a Classical column.

Mullioned windows were added in 1683 when glass became less expensive.

The Gatehouse, with its side turrets, is a typical feature of the "prodigy" houses of the Tudor era *(see p302).*

West Front
Featuring the Burghley crest, the West Front was finished in 1577 and formed the original main entrance.

STAR SIGHTS

- ★ Old Kitchen
- ★ Heaven Room
- ★ Hell Staircase

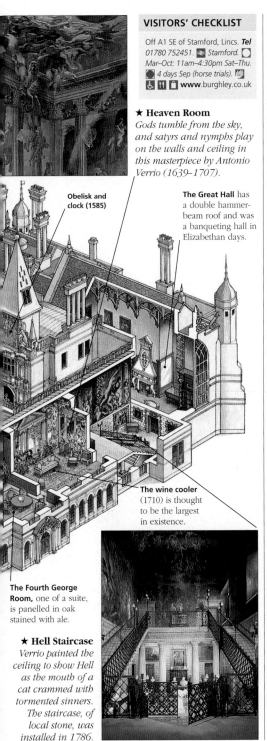

★ **Heaven Room**
*Gods tumble from the sky,
and satyrs and nymphs play
on the walls and ceiling in
this masterpiece by Antonio
Verrio (1639–1707).*

**Obelisk and
clock (1585)**

The Great Hall has
a double hammer-
beam roof and was
a banqueting hall in
Elizabethan days.

The wine cooler
(1710) is thought
to be the largest
in existence.

**The Fourth George
Room,** one of a suite,
is panelled in oak
stained with ale.

★ **Hell Staircase**
*Verrio painted the
ceiling to show Hell
as the mouth of a
cat crammed with
tormented sinners.
The staircase, of
local stone, was
installed in 1786.*

Stamford ❾

Lincolnshire. 🚶 20,000. ≡ 🚌 ℹ️
27 St Mary's St (01780 755611). 🛒
Fri. **www**.southwestlincs.com

Stamford is a showpiece town,
famous for its churches and
Georgian townhouses. The
town retains a medieval street
plan, with a warren of winding
streets and cobbled alleys.

The spires of the medieval
churches (five survive of the
original eleven) give Stamford
the air of a miniature Oxford.

Barn Hill, leading up from
All Saints Church, is the best
place for a view of Stamford's
Georgian architecture in all
its variety. Below it is Broad
Street and High Street, where
the Public Library is fronted
by Tuscan columns. Inside is
the **Discovering Stamford**
exhibition, which tells the
town's development through
the ages, as well as the 6-m
(20-ft) Stamford Tapestry,
a depiction of the town's
history in wool.

🏛 **Discovering Stamford**
Stamford Library, High St. **Tel**
01522 782010. ◯ Mon–Sat.
♿ **www**.lincolnshire.gov.uk

Northampton ❿

Northamptonshire. 🚶 212,000. ≡
🚌 ℹ️ Sessions House, George Row
(01604 838800). 🛒 Mon–Sat (Thu:
antiques). **www**.northamptonshire.
gov.uk

This market town was once a
centre for shoe-making, and
the **Museum and Art Gallery**
holds the world's largest
collection of footwear. One
of many fine old buildings is
the Victorian Gothic **Guildhall**.
Six miles west of the town is
Althorp, family home of Diana
Princess of Wales. Visitors can
tour the house, grounds, see
an exhibition on Diana and
her island resting place.

🏛 **Northampton Museum
and Art Gallery**
Guildhall Rd. **Tel** 01604 838111. ◯
daily (Sun: pm). ⬤ 25, 26 Dec. ♿
🏛 **Althorp**
Great Brington (off A428). **Tel** 01604
770107. ◯ Jul & Aug. ⬤ 31 Aug.
♿ **www**.althorp.com

THE NORTH COUNTRY

INTRODUCING THE NORTH
COUNTRY 346–353

LANCASHIRE AND THE LAKES 354–379

YORKSHIRE AND THE HUMBER
REGION 380–413

NORTHUMBRIA 414–429

The North Country at a Glance

Rugged coastlines, spectacular walks and climbs, magnificent stately homes and breathtaking cathedrals all have their place in the north of England, with its dramatic history of Roman rule, Saxon invasion, Viking attacks and border skirmishes. Reminders of the industrial revolution are found in towns such as Halifax, Liverpool and Manchester, and peace and inspiration in the dramatic scenery of the Lake District, with its awe-inspiring mountains and waters.

Hadrian's Wall (see pp422–3), *built around 120 to protect Roman Britain from the tribes to the north, cuts through rugged Northumberland National Park scenery.*

NORTHUMBR
(see pp414–42

Northumberl

The Lake District (see pp354–69) *is a combination of superb peaks, tumbling rivers and falls and shimmering lakes such as Wast Water.*

Durha

Cumbria

Yorkshire Dales National Park (see pp384–86) *creates a delightful environment for walking and touring the farming landscape, scattered with attractive villages such as Thwaite, in Swaledale.*

Lancashire

LANCASHIRE AND THE LAKES *(see pp354–379)*

Manchester

The Walker Art Gallery (see pp378–9) *in Liverpool is one of the jewels in the artistic crown of the north, with an internationally renowned collection ranging from Old Masters to modern art. Sculpture includes John Gibson's* Tinted Venus *(c.1851–6).*

Liverpool

◁ **The 11th-century Alnwick Castle, Alnwick, Northumberland, from across the River Aln**

Durham Cathedral (see pp428–9), *a striking Norman structure with an innovative southern choir aisle and fine stained glass, has towered over the city of Durham since 995.*

Fountains Abbey (see pp390–91), *one of the finest religious buildings in the north, was founded in the 12th century by monks who desired simplicity and austerity. Later the abbey became extremely wealthy.*

Castle Howard (see pp398–9), *a triumph of Baroque architecture, offers many magnificent settings, including this Museum Room (1805–10), designed by CH Tatham.*

York (see pp404–409) *is a city of historical treasures, ranging from the medieval to Georgian. Its magnificent minster has a large collection of stained glass and the medieval city walls are well preserved. Other sights include churches, narrow alleyways and notable museums.*

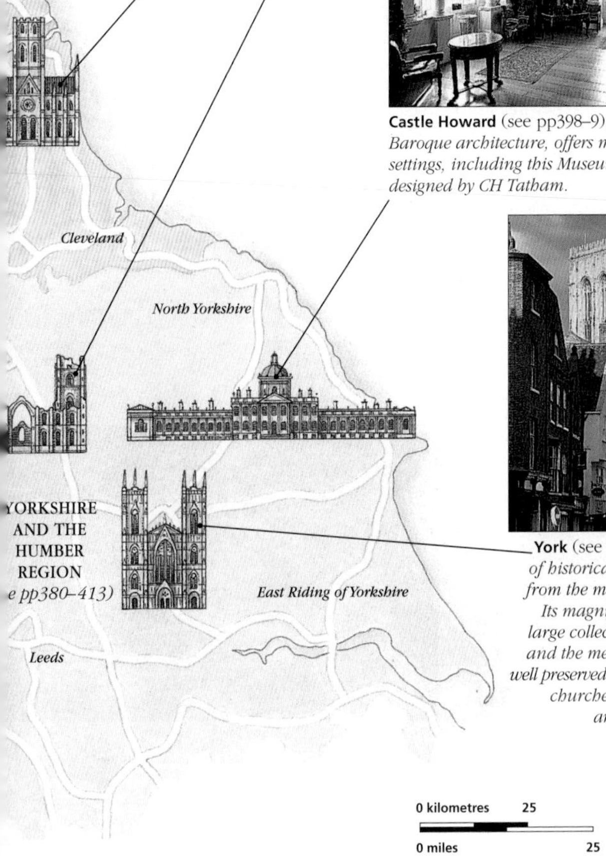

Cleveland

North Yorkshire

YORKSHIRE AND THE HUMBER REGION
e pp380–413)

East Riding of Yorkshire

Leeds

0 kilometres   25

0 miles   25

The Industrial Revolution in the North

The face of Northern England in the 19th century was dramatically altered by the development of the coal mining, textile and shipbuilding industries. Lancashire, Northumberland and the West Riding *(see p381)* of Yorkshire all experienced population growth and migration to cities. The hardships of urban life were partly relieved by the actions of several wealthy industrial philanthropists, but many people lived in extremely deprived conditions. Although most traditional industries have now declined sharply or disappeared as demand has moved elsewhere, a growing tourist industry has developed in many of the former industrial centres.

Back-to-backs *or colliers' rows, such as these houses at Easington, were provided by colliery owners from the 1800s onwards. They comprised two small rooms for cooking and sleeping, and an outside toilet.*

1815 Sir Humphrey Davy invented a safety oil lamp for miners. Light shone through a cylindrical gauze sheet which prevented the heat of the flame igniting methane gas in the mine. Thousands of miners benefited from this device.

Coal mining *was a family industry in the North of England with women and children working alongside the men.*

1750		1800	
PRE-STEAM		STEAM AGE	
1750		1800	

1781 Leeds-Liverpool Canal opened. The building of canals facilitated the movement of raw materials and finished products, and aided the process of mechanization immeasurably.

1830 Liverp and Manchester railv opened, connecting twe the biggest cities outs London. Within a month railway carried 1, passeng

Halifax's Piece Hall (see p413), *restored in 1976, is the most impressive surviving example of industrial architecture in northern England. It is the only complete 18th-century cloth market building in Yorkshire. Merchants sold measures of cloth known as "pieces" from rooms lining the cloisters inside.*

Hebden Bridge (see p412), *a typical West Riding textile mill town jammed into the narrow Calder Valley, typifies a pattern of workers' houses surrounding a central mill. The town benefited from its position when the Rochdale Canal (1804) and then the railway (1841) took advantage of this relatively low-level route over the Pennines.*

Saltaire (see p411) *was a model village built by the wealthy cloth merchant and mill-owner Sir Titus Salt (1803–76), for the benefit of his workers. Seen here in the 1870s, it included houses and facilities such as shops, gardens and sportsfields, with almshouses, a hospital, school and chapel. A disciplinarian, Salt banned alcohol and pubs from Saltaire.*

George Hudson *(1800–71) built the first railway station in York (see p408) in 1840–42. In the 1840s he owned more than a quarter of the railways in Britain and was known as the "railway king".*

1842 Coal Mines Act prevented women and children from working in harsh conditions in the mines.

Port Sunlight (see p379) *was founded by William Hesketh Lever (1851–1925) to provide housing for workers at his Sunlight soap factory. Between 1889 and 1914 he built 800 cottages. Amenities included a pool.*

Strikes to improve working conditions were common. Violence flared in July 1893 when colliery owners locked miners out of their pits and stopped their pay after the Miners' Federation resisted a 25 per cent wage cut. Over 300,000 men struggled without pay until November, when work resumed at the old rate.

1850	1900
FULL MECHANIZATION	
1850	1900

Power loom weaving *transformed the textile industry while creating unemployment among skilled hand loom weavers. By the 1850s, the West Riding had 30,000 power looms, used in cotton and woollen mills. Of 79,000 workers, over half were to be found in Bradford alone.*

Furness dry dock *was built in the 1890s when the shipbuilding industry moved north, in search of cheap labour and materials. Barrow-in-Furness, Glasgow (see pp516–19) and Tyne and Wear (see p424) were the new centres.*

Joseph Rowntree *(1836–1925) founded his chocolate factory in York in 1892, having formerly worked with George Cadbury. As Quakers, the Rowntrees believed in the social welfare of their workers (establishing a model village in 1904), and, with Terry's confectionary (1767), they made a vast contribution to York's prosperity. Today, Nestlé Rowntree makes one of the most popular chocolate bars, the Kit Kat, and York is Britain's chocolate capital.*

North Country Abbeys

Northern England has some of the finest and best preserved religious houses in Europe. Centres of prayer, learning and power in the Middle Ages, the larger of these were designated abbeys and were governed by an abbot. Most were located in rural areas, considered appropriate for a spiritual and contemplative life. Viking raiders had destroyed many Anglo-Saxon religious houses in the 8th and 9th centuries *(see pp46–7)* and it was not until William the Conqueror founded the Benedictine Selby Abbey in 1069 that monastic life revived in the north. New orders, Augustinians in particular, arrived from the Continent and by 1500 Yorkshire had 83 monasteries.

Cistercian monk

Ruins of St Mary's Abbey today

ST MARY'S ABBEY

Founded in York in 1086, this Benedictine abbey was one of the wealthiest in Britain. Its involvement in the wool trade in York and the granting of royal and papal privileges and land led to a relaxing of standards by the early 12th century. The abbot was even allowed to dress in the same style as a bishop, and was raised by the pope to the status of a "mitred abbot". As a result, 13 monks left in 1132, to found Fountains Abbey *(see pp390–91).*

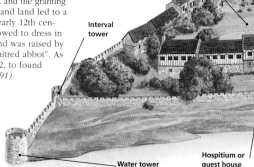

The Liberty of St Mary was the name given to the land around the abbey, almost a city within a city. Here, the abbot had his own market, fair, prison and gallows – all exempt from the city authorities.

Gatehouse and St Olave's church

Interval tower

Water tower

Hospitium or guest house

MONASTERIES AND LOCAL LIFE

As one of the wealthiest landowning sections of society, the monasteries played a vital role in the local economy. They provided employment, particularly in agriculture, and dominated the wool trade, England's largest export during the Middle Ages. By 1387 two thirds of all wool exported from England passed through St Mary's Abbey, the largest wool trader in York.

Cistercian monks tilling their land

WHERE TO SEE ABBEYS TODAY

Fountains Abbey *(see pp390–91),* founded by Benedictine monks and later taken over by Cistercians, is the most famous of the numerous abbeys in the region. Rievaulx *(see p393),* Byland *(see p392)* and Furness *(see p368)* were all founded by the Cistercians, and Furness became the second wealthiest Cistercian house in England after Fountains. Whitby Abbey *(see p396),* sacked by the Vikings, was later rebuilt by the Benedictine order. The northeast is famous for its early Anglo-Saxon monasteries, such as Hexham, Lindisfarne and Jarrow *(see pp418–19).*

Mount Grace Priory (see p394) *founded in 1398, is the best-preserved Carthusian house in England. The former individual gardens and cells of each monk are still clearly visible.*

THE DISSOLUTION OF THE MONASTERIES (1536–40)

By the early 16th century, the monasteries owned one-sixth of all English land and their annual income was four times that of the Crown. Henry VIII ordered the closure of all religious houses in 1536, acquiring their wealth in the process. His attempt at dissolution provoked a large uprising of Catholic northerners led by Robert Aske later that year. The rebellion failed and Aske and others were executed for conspiracy. The dissolution continued under Thomas Cromwell, who became known as "the hammer of the monks".

Thomas Cromwell (c.1485–1549)

The large Abbot's House testified to the grand lifestyle that late medieval abbots adopted.

The Chapter House, an assembly room, was the most important building after the church.

Lavatory

Kitchen

The Warming House was the only room in the monastery, apart from the kitchen, which had a fire.

Refectory

The Abbey Wall had battlements added in 1318 to protect it against raids by Scottish armies.

Common parlour

Cloister

Kirkham Priory, *an Augustinian foundation of the 1120s, enjoys a tranquil setting on the banks of the River Derwent, near Malton. The finest feature of the ruined site is the 13th-century gatehouse which leads into the priory complex.*

Kirkstall Abbey *was founded in 1152 by monks from Fountains Abbey. The well-preserved ruins of this Cistercian house near Leeds include the church, the late Norman chapter house and the abbot's lodging. This evening view was painted by Thomas Girtin (1775–1802).*

Easby Abbey *lies beside the River Swale, outside the pretty market town of Richmond. Among the remains of this Premonstratensian house, founded in 1155, are the 13th-century refectory and sleeping quarters and 14th-century gatehouse.*

The Geology of the Lake District

Honister Pass, *with its distinctive U-shape, is an example of a glaciated valley, once completely filled with ice.*

The Lake District contains some of England's most spectacular scenery. Concentrated in just 900 sq miles (231 sq km) are the highest peaks, deepest valleys and longest lakes in the country. Today's landscape has changed little since the end of the Ice Age 10,000 years ago, the last major event in Britain's geological history.

Piece of Lake District slate

But the glaciated hills which were revealed by the retreating ice were once part of a vast mountain-chain whose remains can also be found in North America. The mountains were first raised by the gradual fusion of two ancient landmasses which, for millions of years, formed a single continent. Eventually the continent broke into two, forming Europe and America, separated by the widening Atlantic Ocean.

GEOLOGICAL HISTORY

The oldest rock formed as sediment under an ocean called Iapetus. Some 450 million years ago, Earth's internal movements made two continents collide, and the ocean disappear.

1 **The collision** *buckled the former sea bed into a mountain range. Magma rose from Earth's mantle, altered the sediments and cooled into volcanic rock.*

2 **In the Ice Age,** *glaciers slowly excavated huge rock basins in the mountainsides, dragging debris to the valley floor. Frost sculpted the summits.*

3 **The glaciers retreated** *10,000 years ago, their meltwaters forming lakes in valleys dammed by debris. As the climate improved, plants colonized the fells.*

RADIATING LAKES

The diversity of lakeland scenery owes much to its geology: hard volcanic rocks in the central lakes give rise to rugged hills, while soft slates to the north produce a more rounded topography. The lakes form a radial pattern, spreading out from a central volcanic rock zone.

Scafell Pike is the highest peak in England. One of the three Scafell Pikes, its two neighbours are Broad Crag and Ill Crag.

Great Gable

Old Man of Coniston

Coniston Water

Wast Water *is the deepest of the lakes. Its southeastern cliffs are streaked with granite scree – the debris formed each year as rock shattered by the winter frost tumbles down during the spring thaw.*

MAN ON THE MOUNTAIN

The sheltered valley floors with their benign climate and fertile soils are ideal for settlement. Farmhouses, dry-stone walls, pasture and sheep pens are an integral part of the landscape. Higher up, the absence of trees and bracken are the result of wind and a cooler climate. Old mine workings and tracks are the relics of once-flourishing industries.

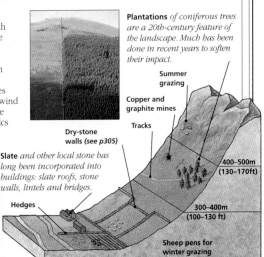

Plantations *of coniferous trees are a 20th-century feature of the landscape. Much has been done in recent years to soften their impact.*

Summer grazing

Copper and graphite mines

Tracks

400–500m (130–170ft)

Dry-stone walls *(see p305)*

Slate *and other local stone has long been incorporated into buildings: slate roofs, stone walls, lintels and bridges.*

Hedges

300–400m (100–130 ft)

Sheep pens for winter grazing

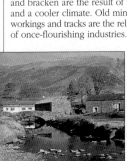

waite

▲ *Blencathra*

nt Water

Helvellyn

Ullswater

▲ *Place Fell*

High Street

Windermere

Skiddaw *is composed of slate, formed when the muddy sediment of the ancient ocean floor was altered by extreme pressure.*

Striding Edge *is a long, twisting ridge which leads to the summit of Helvellyn. It was sharpened by the widening of the valleys on either side caused by the build up of glaciers.*

The Langdale Pikes *are remnants of the volcanic activity which once erupted in the area. They are made of hard igneous rocks, known as Borrowdale Volcanics. Unlike the Skiddaw Slates, they have not eroded smoothly, so they leave a craggy skyline.*

LANCASHIRE AND THE LAKES

CUMBRIA · LANCASHIRE

The landscape painter John Constable (1776–1837) declared that the Lake District, now visited by 18 million people annually, had "the finest scenery that ever was". The Normans built many religious houses here, and William II created estates for English barons. Today, the National Trust is its most important landowner.

Within the 30 mile (45 km) radius of the Lake District lies an astonishing number of fells and lakes. Today, all looks peaceful, but from the Roman occupation to the Middle Ages, the northwest was a turbulent area, as successive kings and rulers fought over the territory. Historians can revel in the various Celtic monuments, Roman remains, stately homes and monastic ruins. Although the scenery is paramount, there are many outdoor activities as well as spectator sports, such as Cumbrian wrestling, and wildlife to observe.

Lancashire's portfolio of tourist attractions includes the fine county town of Lancaster, bright Blackpool with its autumn illuminations and fairground attractions, and the peaceful seaside beaches to the south. Inland, the most appealing regions are the Forest of Bowland, a sparse expanse of heathery grouse moor, and the picturesque Ribble Valley.

Further south still are the industrial conurbations of Manchester and Merseyside, where the attractions are more urban.

There are many fine Victorian buildings in Manchester, where the industrial quarter of Castlefield has been revitalized. Liverpool, with its restored Albert Dock, is best known as the seaport city of the Beatles. It has a lively club scene and is increasingly used as a film location. Both cities have good art galleries and museums.

Jetty at Grasmere, one of the most popular lakes in the Lake District

◁ Restored Albert Dock, lining the River Mersey in Liverpool

Exploring Lancashire and the Lakes

The Lake District's natural scenery outweighs any of its man-made attractions. Its natural features are the result of geological upheavals over millennia (*see pp352–3*), and at 978 m (3,210 ft), Scafell Pike is its highest peak. Human influences have left their mark too: the main activities are quarrying, mining, farming and tourism.

The Lakes are most crowded in summer when activities include lake trips and hill-walking. The best bases are Keswick and Ambleside, while there are also good hotels on the shores of Windermere and Ullswater and in the Cartmel area.

Lancashire's Bowland Forest is an attractive place to explore on foot, with picturesque villages. Further south, Manchester and Liverpool have excellent museums and galleries.

Watersports on Derwentwater in the Northern Fells and Lakes area

GETTING AROUND

For many, the first glimpse of the Lake District is from the M6 near Shap, but the A6 is a more dramatic route. You can reach Windermere by train, but you need to change at Oxenholme, on the mainline route from Euston to Carlisle. Penrith also has rail services and bus links into the Lakes. La'al Ratty, the miniature railway up Eskdale, and the Lakeside & Haverthwaite railway, which connects with the steamers on Windermere,

make for enjoyable outings. Regular buses link all the main centres where excursions are organized. Seasonal minibus services connect some of the more remote passes and valleys.

Lancaster, Liverpool and Manchester are on the main rail and bus routes and also have airports. For Blackpool, you may need to change trains in Preston. Wherever you go in the area, one of the best means of getting around is on foot.

For additional map symbols *see back flap*

View over Crummock Water, north of Buttermere,
one of the quieter Western Lakes

SIGHTS AT A GLANCE

Ambleside **16**
Blackpool **27**
Borrowdale **10**
Buttermere **9**
Carlisle **1**
Cartmel **21**
Cockermouth **7**
Coniston Water **18**
Dalemain **3**
Duddon Valley **13**
Eskdale **12**
Furness Peninsula **20**
Grasmere and Rydal **15**
Kendal **19**
Keswick **5**
Lancaster **25**
Langdale **14**
Leighton Hall **24**
Levens Hall **22**
Liverpool pp376–9 **30**
Manchester pp372–5 **29**
Morecambe Bay **23**
Newlands Valley **8**
*Northern Fells and Lakes
    pp360–61* **6**
Penrith **2**
Ribble Valley **26**
Salford Quays **28**
Ullswater **4**
Wastwater **11**
Windermere **17**

KEY

▬▬	Motorway
▬▬	Major road
▬▬	Secondary road
▭▭	Minor road
▬▬	Scenic route
▬▬	Main railway
—	Minor railway
△	Summit

0 kilometres   20

0 miles   10

SEE ALSO

• *Where to Stay* pp582–5

• *Where to Eat* pp635–8

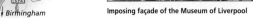

Imposing façade of the Museum of Liverpool

Carlisle ●

Cumbria. 🏛 *72,000.* ✈ 🚃 🚌 🛈
*The Old Town Hall, Green Market
(01228 625600).* **www**.discover
carlisle.co.uk

Due to its proximity to the
Scottish border, this city has
long been a defensive site.
Known as Luguvalium
by the Romans, it was
an outpost of Hadrian's
Wall *(see pp422–3).* Carlisle
was sacked and pillaged
repeatedly by the
Danes, the Normans
and border raiders, and
suffered damage as a
Royalist stronghold under
Cromwell *(see p52).*

Today, Carlisle is the
capital of Cumbria. In its
centre its timber-
framed Guildhall and
market cross, and forti-
fications still exist around
its West Walls, drum-
towered gates and its
Norman **castle**. The
castle tower has a small
museum devoted to the
King's Own Border Regi-
ment. The cathedral dates
from 1122 and features a
decorative east window.
Carlisle's **Tullie House
Museum** recreates the
city's past with sections
on Roman history and
Cumbrian wildlife. Nearby
lie the evocative ruins of

Façade of Hutton-in-the-Forest with medieval tower on the right

**Saxon iron sword in the
Tullie House Museum**

Lanercost Priory (c.1166)
and **Birdoswald Roman Fort**.

⚜ Carlisle Castle
(EH) Castle Way. *Tel 01228 591922.*
⬜ *Apr–Oct: daily; Nov–Mar: Sat &
Sun.* ● *1 Jan, 24–26 Dec.* 🔲 ♿ *ltd.*
🔲 🛈

🏛 Tullie House Museum
Castle St. *Tel 01228 618718.* ⬜ *daily
(Sun: pm).* ● *1 Jan, 25 & 26 Dec* 🔲
♿ 🛈 🔲

♫ Lanercost Priory
(EH) Nr Brampton. *Tel 016977 3030.*
⬜ *Apr–Sep: daily, Oct: Thu–Mon;
Nov–Mar: Sat & Sun.* 🛈 🔲 ♿ *ltd.*

⚜ Birdoswald Roman Fort
(EH) Gilsland, Brampton. *Tel*
016977 47602. ⬜ *Apr–Oct: daily;
Nov–Mar: Sat & Sun.* ● *1 Jan,
24–26, 31 Dec.* 🔲 🔲 🛈

Penrith ●

Cumbria. 🏛 *15,000.* 🛈 *Robinson's
School, Middlegate (017688 67466).* ●
Tue, Sat, Sun. **www**.visiteden.gov.uk

Timewarp shopfronts on the
market square and a 14th-
century **castle** of sandstone

are Penrith's main attractions.
There are some strange hogback stones in St Andrew's
churchyard, allegedly a giant's
grave, but more likely Anglo-
Viking headstones.

Environs: Just northeast of
Penrith at Little Salkeld is a
famous Bronze Age circle
(with 66 tall stones) known
as **Long Meg and her
Daughters**. Six miles (9 km)
northwest of Penrith lies
Hutton-in-the-Forest. The
oldest part of this house is the
13th-century tower. Inside is a
magnificent Italianate staircase,
a sumptuously panelled
17th-century Long Gallery, a
delicately stuccoed Cupid
Room dating from the 1740s,
and several Victorian rooms.
Outside, you can walk around
the walled garden and topiary
terraces, or explore the woods.

⚜ Penrith Castle
(EH) Ullswater Rd. *Tel 0870 333
1181.* **House** ⬜ *daily.* ♿ *grounds.*

♰ Hutton-in-the-Forest
Off B5305. *Tel 017684 84449.*
House ⬜ *Easter–Sep: Wed, Thu,
Sun & pub hols (pm).* **Grounds** ⬜
Apr–Oct: Sun–Fri. 🔲 ♿ *ltd.* 🔲 🛈

Dalemain ●

Penrith, Cumbria. *Tel 017684
86450.* 🚃 🚌 *Penrith then taxi.* ⬜
Apr–Oct: Sun–Thu. 🔲 ♿ *limited.*
🔲 🔲 🛈 **www**.dalemain.com

A seemly Georgian façade
gives this fine house near
Ullswater the impression of
architectural unity, but hides
a much-altered medieval and
Elizabethan structure with a
maze of rambling passages.
Public rooms include a superb
Chinese drawing room with

TRADITIONAL CUMBRIAN SPORTS

Cumberland wrestling is one of the most interesting sports
to watch in the summer months. The combatants, often clad
in longjohns and embroidered velvet pants, clasp one
another in an armlock and attempt to topple each other
over. Technique and good balance outweigh physical force.
Other traditional Lakeland sports include fell-racing, a
gruelling test of speed and stamina up and down local
peaks at ankle-breaking speed. Hound-trailing is also a
popular sport in which
specially bred hounds
follow an aniseed trail
over the hills. Sheep-
dog trials, steam fairs
and flower shows take
place in summer. The
Egremont Crab Fair in
September is famous
for its face-pulling, or
"gurning", competition.

Cumberland wrestlers

Sheep resting at Glenridding, on the southwest shore of Ullswater

hand-painted wallpaper, and a panelled 18th-century drawing room. Several small museums occupy various outbuildings, and the gardens contain a fine collection of fragrant shrub roses and a huge silver fir.

Sumptuous Chinese drawing room at Dalemain

Ullswater ❹

Cumbria. 🚋 Penrith. 🛈 Main car park, Glenridding, Penrith (017684 82414). www.golakes.co.uk

Often considered the most beautiful of all Cumbria's lakes, Ullswater stretches from gentle farmland near Penrith to dramatic hills and crags at its southern end. The main western shore road can be very busy. In summer, two restored Victorian steamers ply

regularly from Pooley Bridge to Glenridding. One of the best walks crosses the eastern shore from Glenridding to Hallin Fell and the moorland of Martindale. The western side passes Gowbarrow, where Wordsworth's immortalized "host of golden daffodils" bloom in spring (see p366).

Keswick ❺

Cumbria. 👥 5,000. 🛈 Moot Hall, Market Sq (017687 72645). www.golakes.co.uk

Popular as a tourist venue since the end of the 18th century, Keswick has guest houses, a summer repertory theatre, outdoor equipment shops and a popular street market. Its most striking central building is the **Moot Hall**, dating from 1813, now used as the tourist office. The town prospered on wool and leather until, in Tudor times, deposits of graphite and copper were discovered. Mining then took over as the main industry and Keswick became an important centre for pencil manufacture. In World War II, hollow pencils were made to hide espionage maps on thin paper. The factory includes the **Pencil Museum** with interesting audiovisual shows. Among the

many fine exhibits at the **Keswick Museum and Art Gallery** are the original manuscripts of Lakeland writers, musical stones and many other curiosities.

To the east of the town lies the ancient stone circle of Castlerigg, thought to be older than Stonehenge.

🏛 **Pencil Museum**
Carding Mill Lane. **Tel** 017687 73626. 🕘 9:30am–5pm daily. ● 1 Jan, 25, 26 Dec. 📷 ♿ 🖥 🛈 www. pencilmuseum.co.uk

🏛 **Keswick Museum and Art Gallery**
Fitz Park, Station Rd. **Tel** 017687 73263. 🕘 10am–4pm Tue–Sat & public hols. ♿ 🛈

Outdoor equipment shop in Keswick

Northern Fells and Lakes ❻

The rare red squirrel, native to the area

Many visitors praise this northern area of the Lake District National Park for its scenery and geological interest *(see pp352–3)*. It is ideal walking country, and nearby Derwentwater, Thirlmere and Bassenthwaite provide endless scenic views, rambles and opportunities for watersports. Large areas surrounding the regional centre of Keswick *(see p359)* are accessible only on foot, particularly the huge mass of hills known as Back of Skiddaw – located between Skiddaw and Caldbeck – or the Helvellyn range, east of Thirlmere.

The Whinlatter Pass is an easy route from Keswick to the farmland of Lorton Vale. It gives a good view of Bassenthwaite Lake and a glimpse of Grisedale Pike.

Bassenthwaite is best viewed from the east shore; however accessibility is limited. Parking is easier from the west side.

CARLISLE

B5291

WORKINGTON

A66

BASSENTHWAITE LAKE

A591

River Derwent

High Lorton

WHINLATTER PASS

B5292

LORTON VALE

Braithwaite

B5289

LOWESWATER

Newlands Beck

DERWE

Grange

BUTTERMERE

Lorton Vale

The lush, green farmland south of Cockermouth creates a marked contrast with the more rugged mountain landscapes of the central Lake District. In the village of Low Lorton is the private manor house of Lorton Hall, dating from the 15th century.

Derwentwater

Surrounded by woodland slopes and fells, this attractive oval lake is dotted with tiny islands. One of these was inhabited by St Herbert, a disciple of St Cuthbert (see p419), who lived there as a hermit until 687. Boats from Keswick provide lake excursions.

THE MAJOR PEAKS

The Lake District hills are the highest in England. Although they seem small by Alpine or world standards, the scale of the surrounding terrain makes them look extremely grand. Some of the most important peaks are shown on the following pages. Each peak is regarded as having its own personality. This section shows the Skiddaw fells, which are north of Keswick.

① Blencathra
②
③
Skiddaw
Grisedale Pike
Grasmoor
Knott Rigg
Helvellyn
Great Gable
High Street
Wastwater Screes
Scafell
Hard Knott
The Old Man of Coniston
④
⑤
⑥

KEY

▬ From ① Blencathra to ② Cockermouth *(see opposite)*

▬ From ③ Grisedale Pike to ④ the Old Man of Coniston *(see pp362–3)*

▬ From ⑤ the Old Man of Coniston to ⑥ Windermere and Tarn Crag *(see pp364–5)*

— National Park boundary

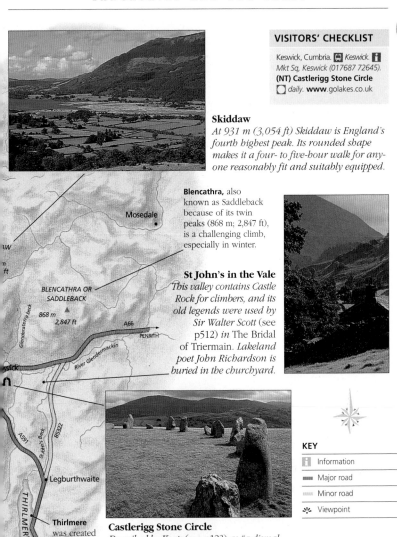

VISITORS' CHECKLIST

Keswick, Cumbria. 🚉 *Keswick.* ℹ️
Mkt Sq, Keswick (017687 72645).
(NT) Castlerigg Stone Circle
⭕ *daily.* **www**.golakes.co.uk

Skiddaw

At 931 m (3,054 ft) Skiddaw is England's fourth highest peak. Its rounded shape makes it a four- to five-hour walk for anyone reasonably fit and suitably equipped.

Blencathra, also known as Saddleback because of its twin peaks (868 m; 2,847 ft), is a challenging climb, especially in winter.

St John's in the Vale

This valley contains Castle Rock for climbers, and its old legends were used by Sir Walter Scott (see p512) in The Bridal of Triermain. Lakeland poet John Richardson is buried in the churchyard.

KEY

ℹ️	Information
▬▬	Major road
▪▪▪	Minor road
☼	Viewpoint

Thirlmere was created as a reservoir to serve Manchester in 1879.

Castlerigg Stone Circle

Described by Keats (see p123) as "a dismal cirque of Druid stones upon a forlorn moor", these ancient stones overlook Skiddaw, Helvellyn and Crag Hill.

0 kilometres — 5
0 miles — 3

Map labels:
Mosedale
BLENCATHRA OR SADDLEBACK — 868 m — 2,847 ft
A66 — PENRITH
River Glendermackin
Glenderaterra beck
Keswick
St John's Beck
B5322
A591
Legburthwaite
THIRLMERE
WINDERMERE
Thirlmere

Panorama labels:
Blencathra 868 m (2,847 ft) — Hart Side — Great Dodd — Ullock Pike — Helvellyn 950 m (3,116 ft) — Dodd Wood — Keswick — Derwentwater — Sale Fell — Lord's Seat — Ullscarf — Lorton Fell — Grisedale Pike 790 m (2,591 ft)
Great Cockup — Great Calva — Skiddaw 931 m (3,054 ft) — A591 — B5291 — Bassenthwaite Lake — A66 to Cockermouth
Bassenthwaite Village

① ②

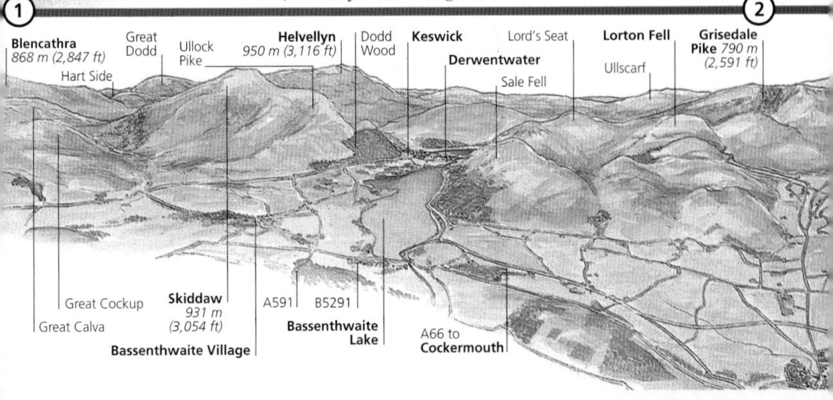

Crummock Water, one of the quieter "western lakes"

Cockermouth 7

Cumbria. 🏘 8,000. 🚆 Workington. 🚌 ℹ Town Hall, Market St (01900 822634). www.western-lakedistrict.co.uk

Colourwashed terraces and restored workers' cottages beside the river are especially attractive in the busy market town of Cockermouth, which dates from the 12th century. The place not to miss is the handsome **Wordsworth House**, in the Main Street, where the poet was born *(see p366)*. This fine Georgian building still contains a few of the family's possessions, and is furnished in the style of the late 18th century. Wordsworth mentions the attractive terraced garden, which overlooks the River Derwent, in his *Prelude*. The local parish church contains a Wordsworth memorial window.

Cockermouth **castle** is partly ruined but still inhabited and closed to the public. The town was badly damaged by serious flooding in 2009 but has recovered well since. The **Jennings Brewery** invites visitors for tours and tastings.

Kitchen, with an old range and tiled floor, at Wordsworth House

🏛 **Wordsworth House** (NT) Main St. *Tel* 01900 824805. ☐ Mar–Oct: Sat–Wed. 🖼 non-members. 🌐 www.wordsworthhouse.org.uk

🍺 **Jennings Brewery** Castle Brewery. *Tel* 0845 1297190. ☐ Mon–Sat (Jan: Sat only; Jul, Aug: daily). 🛒 🌐 www.jennings brewery.co.uk

Newlands Valley 8

Cumbria. 🚆 Penrith then bus. 🚌 Cockermouth. ℹ Market Sq, Keswick (017687 72645). www.lake-district.gov.uk

From the gently wooded shores of Derwentwater, the Newlands Valley runs through a scattering of farms towards rugged heights of 335 m (1,100 ft) at the top of a pass, where steps lead to a waterfall, Moss Force. Grisedale Pike, Cat Bells and Robinson all provide excellent fell walks. Local mineral deposits of copper, graphite, lead and even small amounts of gold and silver were extensively mined here from Elizabethan times onwards. **Little Town** was used as a setting by Beatrix Potter *(see p367)* in *The Tale of Mrs Tiggywinkle*.

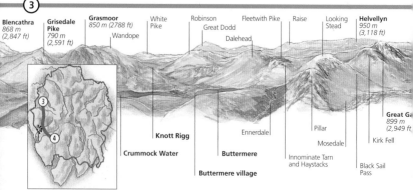

③

Blencathra 868 m (2,847 ft)

Grisedale Pike 790 m (2,591 ft)

Grasmoor 850 m (2788 ft)
Wandope

White Pike

Robinson
Great Dodd
Dalehead

Fleetwith Pike

Raise

Looking Stead

Helvellyn 950 m (3,118 ft)

Great Ga 899 m (2,949 ft

Knott Rigg

Ennerdale

Pillar

Mosedale

Kirk Fell

Crummock Water

Buttermere

Innominate Tarn and Haystacks

Black Sail Pass

Buttermere village

Buttermere ❾

Cumbria. 🚉 *Penrith.* 🚌 *Keswick.* 🚌 *Penrith to Keswick; Keswick to Buttermere.* 🛈 *Town Hall, Market St, Cockermouth (01900 822634).*

Interlinking with Crummock Water and Loweswater, Buttermere and its surroundings contain some of the most appealing countryside in the region. Often known as the "western lakes", the three are remote enough not to become too crowded. Buttermere is a jewel amid grand fells: High Stile, Red Pike and Haystacks. Here the ashes of the celebrated hill-walker and author of fell-walking books, A W Wainwright, were scattered.

The village of Buttermere, with its handful of houses and inns, is a popular starting point for walks round all three lakes. Loweswater is the furthest and therefore the quietest, surrounded by woods and hills. Nearby Scale Force is the highest waterfall in the Lake District, plunging 52 m (170 ft).

Verdant valley of Borrowdale, a favourite with artists

Borrowdale ❿

Cumbria. 🚉 *Penrith.* 🚌 *Keswick.* 🛈 *Moot Hall, Keswick (01768 772645).*

This romantic valley, subject of a myriad sketches and watercolours before photography stole the scene, lies beside the densely wooded shores of Derwentwater under towering crags. It is a popular trip from Keswick and a great variety of walks are possible along the valley.

The tiny hamlet of **Grange** is one of the prettiest spots, where the valley narrows dramatically to form the "Jaws of Borrowdale". Nearby Castle Crag has superb views.

From Grange you can complete the circuit of Derwentwater along the western shore, or move southwards to the more open farmland around Seatoller. As you head south by road, look out for a National Trust sign *(see p29)* to the **Bowder Stone**, a delicately poised block weighing nearly 2,000 tonnes, which may have fallen from the crags above or been deposited by a glacier millions of years ago.

Two attractive hamlets in Borrowdale are **Rosthwaite** and **Stonethwaite**. Also worth a detour, preferably on foot, is Watendlath village, off a side road near the famous beauty spot of **Ashness Bridge**.

WALKING IN THE LAKE DISTRICT

Typical Lake District stile over dry-stone wall

Two long-distance footpaths pass through the Lake District's most spectacular scenery. The 70 mile (112 km) Cumbria Way runs from Carlisle to Ulverston via Keswick and Coniston. The western section of the Coast-to-Coast Walk *(see pp36–7)* passes through this area. There are hundreds of shorter walks along lake shores, nature trails or following more challenging uphill routes. Walkers should stick to paths to avoid erosion, and check weather conditions at: www.lakedistrictweatherline.co.uk.

Scafell Pike
78 m
3,210 ft)

Langdale Pikes

Hard Knott
550 m (1,803 ft)

Hardknott Pass

Carrs

Grey Friar

Swirl How

Dow Crag

Old Man of Coniston
803 m (2,633 ft)

Caw

ast-
ter

Wastwater
crees

Crinkle Crags
815 m
(2,674 ft)

Blea Tarn

Harter Fell

Eskdale

Seathwaite Tarn

Seathwaite

Ravenglass and Eskdale Railway

River Duddon

④

Convivial Wasdale Head Inn at
Wasdale Head

Wastwater ⓫

Wasdale, Cumbria. 🚆 *Whitehaven.*
ℹ️ *Lowes Court Gallery, Egremont
(01946 820693).*

A silent reflection of truly
awesome surroundings,
black, brooding **Wastwater** is
a mysterious, evocative lake.
The road from Nether Wasdale
continues along its northwest
side. Along its eastern flank
loom walls of sheer scree over
600 m (2,000 ft) high. Beneath
them the water looks inky
black, whatever the weather,
plunging an icy 80 m (260 ft)
from the waterline to the
bottom to form England's
deepest lake. You can walk
along the screes, but it is an
uncomfortable and dangerous
scramble. Sailing and power
boats are banned, but fishing
permits are available from the
nearby National Trust camp site.

At **Wasdale Head** lies one
of Britain's grandest views:
the austere pyramid of **Great
Gable,** centrepiece of a fine
mountain composition, with

the huge forms of Scafell and
Scafell Pike. The scenery is
utterly unspoilt, and the only
buildings lie at the far end of
the lake: an inn and a tiny
church commemorating fallen
climbers. Here the road ends,
and you must turn back or
take to your feet, following
signs for Black Sail Pass and
Ennerdale, or walk up the
grand fells ahead. Wasdale's
irresistible backdrop was the
inspiration of the first serious
British mountaineers, who
flocked here during the 19th
century, insouciantly clad in
tweed jackets, carrying little
more than a length of rope
slung over their shoulders.

Eskdale ⓬

Cumbria. 🚆 *Ravenglass then narrow-
gauge railway to Eskdale (Easter–Oct:
daily; Dec–Feb: phone to check).*
www.ravenglass-railway.co.uk
ℹ️ *Lowes Court Gallery, Egremont
(01946 820693).* www.eskdale.info

The pastoral delights of
Eskdale are best encountered
over the gruelling **Hardknott**

Pass, which is the most taxing
drive in the Lake District, with
steep gradients. You can pause
below the 393-m (1,291-ft)
summit to explore the Roman
Hardknott Fort or enjoy the
lovely view. As you descend
into Eskdale, rhododendrons
and pines flourish in a landscape of small hamlets, narrow
lanes and gentle farmland.
The main settlements are the
villages of Boot and Eskdale
Green, and Ravenglass, the
only coastal village in the
Lake District National Park.

Just south of Ravenglass is
the impressive **Muncaster
Castle**, the richly furnished
home of the Pennington
family. Another way to enjoy
the scenery is to take the
miniature railway (known as
La'al Ratty) from Ravenglass
to Dalegarth.

🏰 **Muncaster Castle**
Ravenglass. *Tel* 01229 717614.
Castle ⬜ mid-Mar–Oct:
Sun–Fri (pm) & public hols.
Garden ⬜ Feb–Dec: daily. 🚻 🅿️
♿ ground floor and garden.
www.muncaster.co.uk

Remains of the Roman Hardknott Fort, Eskdale

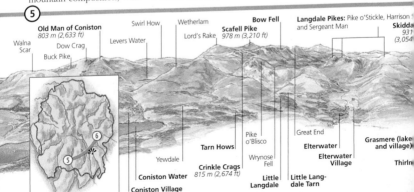

(5)

Old Man of Coniston
803 m (2,633 ft)

Swirl How

Wetherlam

Lord's Rake

Bow Fell

Scafell Pike
978 m (3,210 ft)

Langdale Pikes: Pike o'Stickle, Harrison
and Sergeant Man

Skidda
*931
(3,054*

Walna
Scar

Dow Crag

Levers Water

Buck Pike

Great End

Yewdale

Tarn Hows

Pike
o'Blisco

Crinkle Crags
815 m (2,674 ft)

Wrynose
Fell

Elterwater

**Little Lang-
dale Tarn**

Elterwater
Village

**Grasmere (lake
and village)**

Thirln

Coniston Water

Coniston Village

**Little
Langdale**

Autumnal view of Seathwaite, in the Duddon Valley, a popular centre for walkers and climbers

Duddon Valley ⑬

Cumbria. ⊞ Foxfield, Ulverston.
ℹ The Square, Broughton-in-Furness
(01229 716115; Easter–Oct only).
www.duddonvalley.co.uk

Also known as Dunnerdale,
this picturesque tract of
countryside inspired 35 of
Wordsworth's sonnets (see
p366). The prettiest stretch lies
between Ulpha and Cockley
Beck. In autumn the colours
of heather moors and a light
sprinkling of birch trees are
particularly beautiful. Stepping
stones and bridges span the
river at intervals, the most
charming being Birk's Bridge,
near Seathwaite. At the southern end of the valley, where

the River Duddon meets the
sea at Duddon Sands, is the
pretty village of Broughton-
in-Furness. Note the stone
slabs once used for fish on
market day in the square.

Langdale ⑭

Cumbria. ⊞ Windermere. ℹ Market
Cross, Ambleside (0844 2250544).
www.golakes.co.uk

Stretching from Skelwith
Bridge, where the Brathay
surges powerfully over waterfalls, to the summits of Great
Langdale is the two-pronged
Langdale Valley. Walkers and
climbers throng here to take
on **Pavey Ark, Pike o'Stickle,**

Crinkle Crags and **Bow Fell**.
The local mountain rescue
teams are the busiest in Britain.

Great Langdale is the more
spectacular valley and it is
often crowded, but quieter
Little Langdale has many
attractions too. It is worth
completing the circuit back to
Ambleside via the southern
route, stopping at Blea Tarn.
Reedy **Elterwater** is a picturesque spot, once a site of the
gunpowder industry. Wrynose
Pass, west of Little Langdale,
climbs to 390 m (1,281 ft), a
warm-up for Hardknott Pass
further on. At its top is Three
Shires Stone, marking the
former boundary of the old
counties of Cumberland,
Westmorland and Lancashire.

⑥

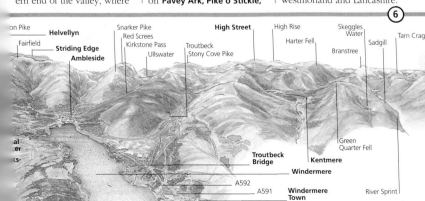

Rydal Water, one of the major attractions of the Lake District

Grasmere and Rydal ⑮

Cumbria. **Grasmere** 🧍 700.
Rydal 🧍 100. 🚃 Grasmere.
🛈 Central Buildings, Market Cross,
Ambleside (0844 2250544).
www.golakes.co.uk

The poet William Wordsworth lived in both these villages on the shores of two lakes. Fairfield, Nab Scar and Loughrigg Fell rise steeply above their reedy shores and offer good opportunities for walking. Grasmere is now a sizable settlement, and the famous Grasmere sports (*see p358*) attract large crowds every August.

The Wordsworth family is buried in St Oswald's Church, and crowds flock to the annual ceremony of strewing the church's earth floor with fresh rushes. Most visitors head for **Dove Cottage**, where the poet spent his most creative years. The museum in the barn behind includes such artefacts as the great man's socks. The Wordsworths moved to **Rydal Mount**, in Rydal in 1813 and

lived here until 1850. The grounds have waterfalls and a summerhouse. Dora's Field nearby is a blaze of daffodils in spring and the Fairfield Horseshoe offers an energetic walk.

🏛 Dove Cottage and the Wordsworth Museum
Off A591 nr Grasmere. **Tel** 015394 35544. ◯ daily (Nov–Feb: Wed–Mon). ● 24–26 Dec, mid-Jan–mid-Feb. 🏷 🚻 🚹 ◻ 🐕 **www**.
wordsworth.org.uk

🏛 Rydal Mount
Rydal. **Tel** 015394 33002. ◯ Mar–Oct: daily; Nov–Feb: Wed–Sun. ●
Jan, 25 & 26 Dec. 🏷 🚹 limited. 🏺

Ambleside ⑯

Cumbria. 🧍 3,400. 🚌
🛈 Central Buildings, Market Cross
(0844 2250544). 🚃 Wed.
www.golakes.co.uk

Ambleside has good road connections to all parts of the Lakes and is an attractive base, especially for walkers and climbers. Mainly Victorian in character, it has a range of outdoor clothing, crafts and specialist food shops. An enterprising little cinema and a summer classical music festival add life in the evenings. Sights in town are small-scale: the remnants of the Roman fort of Galava, AD 79, Stock Ghyll Force waterfall and **Bridge House**, now a National Trust information centre.

Environs: Within easy reach of Ambleside is the scenic Loughrigg Fell. At nearby Troutbeck is the restored farmhouse of **Townend**, dating from 1626, whose interior gives an insight into Lakeland domestic life.

The tiny Bridge House over Stock Beck in Ambleside

WILLIAM WORDSWORTH (1770–1850)

Best known of the Romantic poets, Wordsworth was born in the Lake District and spent most of his life there. After school in Hawkshead and a period at Cambridge, a legacy enabled him to pursue his literary career. He settled at Dove Cottage with his sister Dorothy and in 1802 married an old school friend, Mary Hutchinson. They lived simply, walking, bringing up their children and receiving visits from poets such as Coleridge and de Quincey. Wordsworth's prose works include one of the earliest guidebooks to the Lake District.

BEATRIX POTTER AND THE LAKE DISTRICT

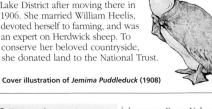

Although best known for her children's stories with characters such as Peter Rabbit and Jemima Puddle-duck, which she also illustrated, Beatrix Potter (1866–1943) became a champion of conservation in the Lake District after moving there in 1906. She married William Heelis, devoted herself to farming, and was an expert on Herdwick sheep. To conserve her beloved countryside, she donated land to the National Trust.

Cover illustration of *Jemima Puddleduck* (1908)

🏛 Townend
(NT) Troutbeck, Windermere. *Tel 015394 32628.* ◯ *Apr–Oct: Wed–Sun; Sun & bank hol Mon: pm.*

Windermere ⑰

Cumbria. 🚆 *Windermere.* 🚌 *Victoria St.* 🛈 *Victoria St (015394 46499) or Glebe Rd, Bowness-on-Windermere (015394 42895).*

At over 10 miles (16 km) long, this dramatic watery expanse is England's largest lake. Industrial magnates built mansions around its shores long before the railway arrived. Stately **Brockhole**, now a national park visitor centre, was one such grand estate. When the railway reached Windermere in 1847, it enabled crowds of workers to visit the area on day trips.

Today, a year-round car ferry service connects the lake's east and west shores (it runs between Ferry Nab and Ferry House), and summer steamers link Lakeside, Bowness and Ambleside on the north-south axis. Belle Isle, a wooded island on which a unique round house stands, is one of the lake's most attractive features, but landing is not permitted. **Fell Foot Park** is at the south end of the lake, and there are good walks on the northwest shore. A quite stunning viewpoint is Orrest Head 238 m (784 ft), northeast of Windermere town.

Environs: Bowness-on-Windermere, on the east shore, is a popular centre. Many of its buildings display Victorian details, and St Martin's Church dates back to the 15th century. The **Blackwell Arts and Crafts House** is one of Britain's most beautiful houses from the early 20th century. It still boasts all of its original features. The **Stott Park Bobbin Mill** is the last working example of over 70 such mills in Cumbria that once served the textiles industry. The **World of Beatrix Potter** recreates her characters in an exhibition, and a film tells her life story.

Beatrix Potter wrote many of her books at **Hill Top**, the 17th-century farmhouse at Near Sawrey, northwest of Windermere. The house is furnished with many of Potter's possessions and left as it was in her lifetime. The **Beatrix Potter Gallery** in Hawkshead holds annual exhibitions of her manuscripts and illustrations.

🛈 Brockhole Visitor Centre
On A591. *Tel 015394 46601.* ◯ *daily.*

🍂 Fell Foot Park
(NT) Newby Bridge. *Tel 015395 31273.* ◯ *daily.*

🏛 Blackwell Arts and Crafts House
Bowness-on-Windermere. *Tel 015394 46139.* ◯ *daily.*

🏛 Stott Park Bobbin Mill
(EH) Finsthwaite. *Tel 01539 531087.* ◯ *Apr–Oct: Mon–Fri & public hols.*

🏛 World of Beatrix Potter
The Old Laundry, Crag Brow. *Tel 015394 88444.* ◯ *daily.* ● *25 Dec, mid-Jan–mid-Feb.*

🏛 Hill Top
(NT) Near Sawrey, Ambleside. *Tel 015394 36269.* ◯ *Feb–Oct: Sat–Thu (house); Feb–Dec: daily (garden).*

🏛 Beatrix Potter Gallery
(NT) The Square, Hawkshead. *Tel 015394 36355.* ◯ *Feb–Oct: Sat–Thu.*

Boats moored along the shore at Waterhead, near Ambleside, the north end of Windermere

For hotels and restaurants in this region see pp582–585 and pp635–638

Peaceful Coniston Water, the setting of Arthur Ransome's novel, *Swallows and Amazons* (1930)

Coniston Water ⑱

Cumbria. 🚆 *Windermere then bus.* 🚌 *Ambleside then bus.* ℹ️ *Coniston car park, Ruskin Ave (015394 41533);* **Coniston Boating Centre** *Tel* 015394 41366. **www.**conistontic.org

For the finest view of this lovely lake, you need to climb a little. The 19th-century art critic, writer and philosopher John Ruskin had a fine view from his house, **Brantwood**, where his paintings can be seen today. Contemporary art exhibitions and events take place throughout the year.

An enjoyable excursion is the summer lake trip from Coniston Pier on the National Trust steam yacht, *Gondola*, calling at Brantwood. Alternatively, boats can be hired at the Coniston Boating Centre. The lake was also the scene of Donald Campbell's fatal attempt on the world water speed record in 1967. The green slate village of Coniston, once a centre for copper-mining, now caters for walkers.

To the northwest is **Hawkshead**, a quaint, traffic-free village with timber-framed houses. To the south is the vast Grizedale Forest, dotted with woodland sculptures and popular with mountain bikers.

Just north of Coniston Water is the man-made **Tarn Hows**, a landscaped tarn surrounded by woods. There is a pleasant climb up the 803 m (2,635 ft) Old Man of Coniston.

🏛 **Brantwood**
Off B5285, nr Coniston. *Tel* 015394 41396. 🕐 *mid-Mar–mid-Nov: 11am–5pm daily; mid-Nov–mid-Mar: 11am–4:30pm Wed–Sun.* 🎫 ♨ 🅿 📷 ♿ *limited.*

Kendal ⑲

Cumbria. 🏘 *28,000.* 🚆 ℹ️ *25 Stramongate (01539 735891).* 🛥 *Wed, Sat.* **www.**southlakeland.gov.uk

A busy market town, Kendal is the administrative centre of the region and the southern gateway to the Lake District. Built in grey limestone, it has an arts centre, the **Brewery**, and a central area which is best enjoyed on foot. **Abbot Hall,**

Kendal mint cake, the famous lakeland energy-booster for walkers

built in 1759, has paintings by Turner and Romney, as well as Gillows furniture. In addition, the hall's stable block contains the **Museum of Lakeland Life**, with occasional workshops demonstrating local crafts and trades. There are dioramas of geology and wildlife in the **Kendal Museum**.

About 3 miles (5 km) south of the town is 14th-century **Sizergh Castle**, with a fortified tower, carved fireplaces and a lovely garden.

🏛 **Abbot Hall Art Gallery & Museum of Lakeland Life**
Kendal. *Tel* 01539 722464. 🕐 *Gallery: mid-Jan–mid-Dec: Mon–Sat; Museum: Mon–Sat all year (mid-Jul–mid-Sep: both daily).* 🎫 ♿ *gallery.* 📷 *by arrangement.* 🅿 📷
www.abbothall.org.uk

🏛 **Kendal Museum**
Station Rd. *Tel* 01539 815597. 🕐 *Wed–Sat.* ● *Christmas week.* 📷 **www.**kendalmuseum.org.uk

⛰ **Sizergh Castle**
(NT) off A591 & A590. *Tel* 01539 60951. 🕐 *Mar–Oct: Sun–Thu.* 🎫 ♿ *ground floor & grounds.* 🅿 📷

Furness Peninsula ⑳

Cumbria. 🚆 🚌 *Barrow-in-Furness.* ℹ️ *Forum 28, Duke St, Barrow-in-Furness (01229 876505).* **www.**barrowbc.gov.uk

Barrow-in-Furness *(see p349)* is the peninsula's main town. Its **Dock Museum**, built over a Victorian dock where ships were repaired, traces the history of Barrow using interactive computer displays.

Ruins of the red sandstone walls of **Furness Abbey** remain in the wooded Vale of Deadly Nightshade, with a small exhibition of monastic life. The historic town of Ulverston received its charter in 1280. Stan Laurel, of Laurel and Hardy fame, was born here in 1890. His memorabilia **museum** has a cinema. In the nearby village of Gleaston is the **Gleaston Water Mill**, a 400-year-old, working corn mill.

🏛 Dock Museum
North Rd, Barrow-in-Furness. *Tel 01229 876400.* ⏰ *Easter–Oct: Wed–Sun; Nov–Easter: Wed–Sun; public hols.* ♿ 🖥 🅿 **www**. dockmuseum.org.uk

🛈 Furness Abbey
(EH) Vale of Deadly Nightshade. *Tel 01229 823420.* ⏰ *Apr–Sep: Thu–Mon; Oct–Mar: Sat & Sun.* ⚫ *1 Jan, 24–26 Dec.* 🅿 📷 ♿ *limited.*

🏚 Gleaston Water Mill
Gleaston. *Tel 01229 869244.* ⏰ *Tue–Sun.* **www**.watermill.co.uk

🏛 Laurel and Hardy Museum
Upper Brook St, Ulverston. *Tel 01229 582292.* ⏰ *Feb–Dec: daily; Jan: Thu, Sat & Sun.* ⚫ *25–26 Dec.* 📷 ♿ **www**.laurel-and-hardy.co.uk

Staircase at Holker Hall

Cartmel ㉑

Cumbria. 🏘 *700.* 🛈 *Main St, Grange-over-Sands (015395 34026).* **www**.grangeoversands.net

The highlight of this pretty village is its 12th-century **priory**, one of the finest Cumbrian churches. Little remains of the original priory except the gatehouse in the village centre. The restored church has an attractive east window, a stone-carved 14th-century tomb, and beautiful misericords.

Cartmel also boasts a small racecourse. The village has given its name to its surroundings, a hilly district of green farmland with mixed woodland and limestone scars.

A major local attraction is **Holker Hall**, former residence of the Dukes of Devonshire. Inside are lavishly furnished rooms, with fine marble fireplaces, and a superb oak staircase. Outside are stunning gardens and a deer park.

🏚 Holker Hall
Cark-in-Cartmel. *Tel 015395 58328.* ⏰ *Apr–Nov: daily.* 🖼 ♿ *limited.* 📷 *by arrangement.* 🅿 🖥 **www**.holker-hall.co.uk

Levens Hall ㉒

Nr Kendal, Cumbria. *Tel 015395 60321.* 🚌 *from Kendal or Lancaster.* ⏰ *Easter–mid-Oct: Sun–Thu.* 🅿 🖼 ♿ *gardens only.* 🖥 **www**.levenshall.co.uk

The outstanding attraction of this Elizabethan mansion is its topiary, but the house itself has much to offer. Built around a 13th-century tower, it contains a fine collection of Jacobean furniture and watercolours by Peter de Wint (1784–1849). Also of note are the ornate ceilings, Charles II dining chairs, the earliest example of English patchwork and the gilded hearts on the drainpipes.

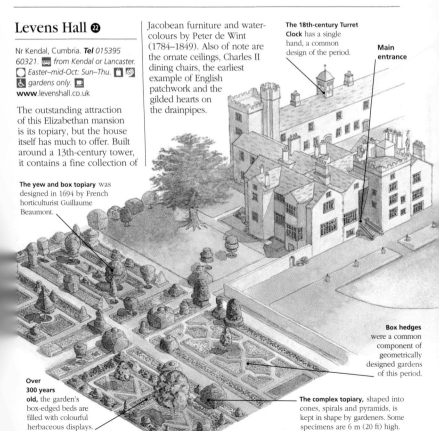

The 18th-century Turret Clock has a single hand, a common design of the period.

Main entrance

The yew and box topiary was designed in 1694 by French horticulturist Guillaume Beaumont.

Box hedges were a common component of geometrically designed gardens of this period.

Over 300 years old, the garden's box-edged beds are filled with colourful herbaceous displays.

The complex topiary, shaped into cones, spirals and pyramids, is kept in shape by gardeners. Some specimens are 6 m (20 ft) high.

Morecambe Bay, looking northwest towards Barrow-in-Furness

Morecambe Bay ㉓

Lancs. 🚆 Morecambe. ⛴ Heysham (to Isle of Man). 🛈 Marine Rd. (01524 582808). **www**.citycoastcountryside.co.uk

The best way to explore Morecambe Bay is by train from Ulverston to Arnside. The track follows a series of low viaducts across a huge expanse of glistening tidal flats where thousands of wading birds feed and breed. The bay is one of the most important bird reservations in the country. On the Cumbrian side of the bay, retirement homes have expanded the sedate Victorian resort of Grange-over-Sands. Nearby, **Hampsfell** and **Humphrey Head Point** give fine views.

Leighton Hall ㉔

Carnforth, Lancashire. **Tel** 01524 734 474. 🚌 to Yealand Conyers (from Lancaster). ⬜ May–Sep: 2–5pm Tue–Fri & bank hols (also Sun in Aug). 📷 ♿ ground floor only. 🛈 💻 📷 www.leightonhall.co.uk

Leighton Hall's estate dates back to the 13th century, but most of the building is 19th-century, including its Neo-Gothic façade. It is owned by the Gillow family, of the Lancastrian furniture business, whose products are prized antiques. Excellent pieces can be seen here, including a ladies' work-box inlaid with biblical scenes. In the afternoons the hall's large collection of birds of prey display their aerial prowess.

Lancaster ㉕

Lancashire. 🏚 46,000. 🚆 📷 🛈 Meeting House Lane (01524 582394). 🛒 Mon–Sat. **www**.citycoastcountryside.co.uk

Despite its size, the small county town of Lancaster has a long history. The Romans named it after their camp over the River Lune. Originally a defensive site, it developed into a prosperous port. Today, its university and cultural life thrive. The Norman **Lancaster Castle** was expanded in the 14th and 16th centuries. From the 13th century right up to 2011, it was a crown court

Tawny eagle at Leighton Hall

and a prison. The Shire Hall is decorated with 600 heraldic shields. Some fragments from Hadrian's Tower are 2,000 years old.

The nearby priory church of **St Mary** is on Castle Hill. Its main features include a Saxon doorway and carved 14th-century choir stalls. There is an outstanding museum of furniture in the 17th-century **Judge's Lodgings**, while the **Maritime Museum** contains displays on the port's history. The **City Museum**, based in the old town hall, concentrates on the history of Lancaster.

The splendid **Lune Aqueduct** carries the canal over the River Lune on five wide arches. Other attractions are found in **Williamson Park**, site of the 1907 Ashton Memorial. This folly was built by the linoleum magnate and politician, Lord Ashton. There are fine views from the top of this 67 m (220 ft) domed structure. Opposite is a tropical butterfly house.

Environs: North of Lancaster, the small town of **Carnforth** has some interesting sights. **Leighton Moss Nature Reserve** is the largest reedbed in the northwest and home to birds such as Breeding Bitterns and

CROSSING THE SANDS

Morecambe Bay sands are very dangerous. Travellers used to cut across the bay at low tide to shorten the long trail around the Kent estuary. Many perished as they were caught by rising tides or quicksand, and sea fogs hid the paths. Locals who knew the bay became guides, and today you can travel with a guide from Kents Bank to Hest Bank near Arnside.

The High Sheriff of Lancaster Crossing Morecambe Sands (anon)

For hotels and restaurants in this region see pp582–585 and pp635–638

Bearded Tits. The restored **Carnforth Station** is the setting for David Lean's classic film *Brief Encounter*, shot here in 1945. Information on Carnforth sights is available at www.citycoastcountryside.co.uk

♦ Lancaster Castle
Castle Parade. **Tel** 01524 64998. ⬤ *daily.* ⬤ *1 Jan, 25 & 26 Dec.* ⬤ *only (limited when court is in session).* ⬤ www.lancastercastle.com

🏛 Judge's Lodgings
Church St. **Tel** 01524 32808. ⬤ *Apr–Jun, Oct: daily (Sat & Sun: pm only); Jul–Sep: daily.* ⬤ *Nov–Good Fri.* ⬤ ⬤ *limited.*

🏛 Maritime Museum
Custom House, St George's Quay. **Tel** 01524 64637. ⬤ *daily (Nov–Easter: pm).* ⬤ *24–26, 31 Dec, 1 Jan.* ⬤ ⬤ www.lancashire.gov.uk

🏛 City Museum
Market Sq. **Tel** 01524 64637. ⬤ *Mon–Sat.* ⬤ *24 Dec–2 Jan.* ⬤ ⬤

♣ Williamson Park
Wyresdale Rd. **Tel** 01524 33318. ⬤ *daily.* ⬤ *1 Jan, 25 & 26 Dec.* ⬤ ⬤ *limited.* ⬤ ⬤

Ribble Valley 🟤

Lancashire. 🚆 *Clitheroe.* 🛈 *Market Place, Clitheroe (01200 425566).* ⬤ *Tue, Thu, Sat.* www.ribblevalley.gov.uk

Clitheroe, a small market town with a hilltop castle, is a good centre for exploring the Ribble Valley's rivers and old villages, such as Slaidburn. Ribchester has a **Roman Museum**, and there is a ruined **Cistercian abbey** at Whalley. To the east is 560 m (1,830 ft) Pendle Hill, with a Bronze Age burial mound at its peak.

🏛 Roman Museum
Ribchester. **Tel** 01254 878261. ⬤ *daily.* ⬤ ⬤ *by arrangement.* ⬤

♠ Whalley Abbey
Whalley. **Tel** 01254 828400. ⬤ *daily.* ⬤ *24 Dec–2 Jan.* ⬤ ⬤ ⬤ www.whalleyabbey.co.uk

Blackpool 🟤

Lancashire. 🏠 *150,000.* ✈ 🚆 ⬤ 🛈 *Festival House, Promenade (01253 478222).* www.visitblackpool.com

Blackpool is no longer the apogee of seaside entertainment that it once was, but it

Coming from the Mill (1930) by L S Lowry (See p375)

remains a unique experience. A wall of amusement arcades, piers, bingo halls and fast-food stalls stretch behind the sands. At night, entertainers strut their stuff under the bright lights. The town attracts thousands of visitors in September and October when the Illuminations trace the skeleton of the 158 m (518 ft) Blackpool Tower. Blackpool's resort life dates back to the 18th century, but it burst into prominence when the railway first arrived in 1840, bringing Lancastrian workers to their holiday resort.

Blackpool Tower, painted gold for its centenary in 1994

Salford Quays 🟤

Salford. 🚋 *Harbour City (from Manchester).* 🛈 *The Lowry, Pier 8 (0161 848 8601).* www.thequays.org.uk

The Quays, to the west of Manchester city centre (15 minutes by tram), were once the terminal docks for the **Manchester Ship Canal**. After the docks closed in 1982, the area became sadly run down but since the 1990s a massive redevelopment plan has changed the area dramatically. A world-class business, cultural and residential area of great architectural and regional significance has been created and more people are now employed at the Quays than in its heyday as a major seaport.

There is a wealth of entertainment, leisure and cultural facilities on offer, including **The Lowry** *(see p375)*, the **Manchester United Museum** *(see p375)*, the **Imperial War Museum North** *(see p375)*, the **Salford Museum and Art Gallery** and The Lowry Outlet Mall, as well as numerous bars, restaurants and shops.

There are various water-based activities and ship-canal cruises. Media City, opposite the Lowry, is an important centre for radio and television production.

🏛 Salford Museum and Art Gallery
Peel Park, The Crescent. **Tel** 0161 778 0800. ⬤ *Mon–Fri, Sat & Sun pm.* ⬤ *25 & 26 Dec.*

Manchester ㉙

Sign for the John Rylands Library

Manchester dates back to Roman times, when in AD 79, Agricola set up a base called Mamucium. It rose to prominence in the late 18th century, when Richard Arkwright introduced cotton processing. By 1830, the first railway linked Manchester and Liverpool, and in 1894 the Manchester Ship Canal (see p371) opened, allowing cargovessels inland. Civic buildings sprang up from the proceeds of cotton wealth, but these were in stark contrast to the slums of the millworkers. Social discontent led writers, politicians and reformers to espouse liberal or radical causes.

The achievements of football team Manchester United and the international success of bands such as The Smiths and The Stone Roses, gave Manchester a cachet of cool during the 1980s and 1990s. Devastation caused by an IRA carbombing of the city centre in 1996 was seized as an opportunity to redevelop the main shopping areas. This regeneration has since spread to other areas of the city, notably the old dockside area of Salford Quays.

The National Football Museum (formerly Urbis)

Exploring Manchester

Manchester is a fine, compact city with much to see in its central areas. The Victorian era of cotton wealth has gifted the city an imposing heritage of industrial architecture, much of which is providing sites for development. The former central railway station, for example, is now **Manchester Central**, a huge exhibition and conference complex. Among other fine 19th-century buildings are the dramatic **John Rylands Library** on Deansgate, founded over 100 years ago by the widow of a local cotton millionaire, and the 1856 Renaissance-style **Free Trade Hall**, now the Radisson Edwardian hotel, which stands on the site of the Peterloo Massacre.

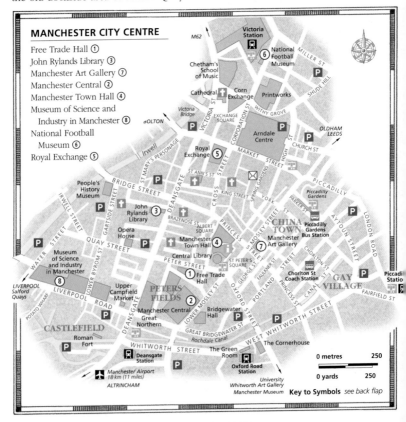

MANCHESTER CITY CENTRE

Free Trade Hall ①
John Rylands Library ③
Manchester Art Gallery ⑦
Manchester Central ②
Manchester Town Hall ④
Museum of Science and Industry in Manchester ⑧
National Football Museum ⑥
Royal Exchange ⑤

0 metres 250
0 yards 250

Key to Symbols *see back flap*

The Neo-Gothic Town Hall by Alfred Waterhouse

🏛 Manchester Town Hall

Albert Square. **Tel** 0161 234 5000.
☐ Mon–Fri. ♿ 🚹 once a month
on Wed & Sat – call 0161 440 0277.

Manchester's majestic town hall was designed by Liverpool-born Alfred Waterhouse (1830–1905), an architect who would later find fame with his Natural History Museum in London. Waterhouse won the commission for the building in an architectural competition, his design finding favour for making best use of the awkward triangular site.

The building was completed in 1877 in an English Gothic style with its roots in the 13th century. Tours are available, but visitors can also explore the building on their own. Sign in inside the main entrance, where a statue of General Agricola, the Roman who founded Manchester in AD 79, looks down on passersby. The highlight is the Great Hall adorned by 12 murals painted by Ford Maddox Brown, the celebrated Pre-Raphaelite painter.

Throughout the building the decoration includes numerous examples of cotton flowers and bees, the latter a symbol of Manchester's industriousness. In the square in front of the town hall is Manchester's **Albert Memorial**, dedicated to the consort of Queen Victoria, which is similar in style but predates the one in London's Hyde Park.

🏛 Royal Exchange Theatre

St Ann's Square.
Tel 0161 833 9833.
☐ Mon–Sat. ♿
📧 🖥 www.royal exchange.co.uk

Built in 1729, the Manchester Royal Exchange, as it was then known, was once claimed to be the "biggest room in the world". It was built as the main trading hall of the cotton industry and at the end of the 19th century it was reckoned that over 80 per cent of world trade in cloth was controlled from these premises. During the Second World War the building was severely damaged by bombs. This coincided with the decline of the cotton trade in the United Kingdom and when the Exchange was rebuilt it was reduced to half its original size. The doors were finally closed to trading in 1968. A daring scheme saw the main hall converted into a theatre in the mid-1970s with the auditorium enclosed in a high-tech structure supported by the old building's pillars; it nestles like a lunar module beneath the great dome. The rest of the Exchange building contains an arcade, shops and cafés.

🏛 National Football Museum

Cathedral Gdns. **Tel** 0161 605 8200.
☐ 10am–5pm Mon–Sat, 11am–5pm Sun. ♿ 🍴 🖥 🎁

The National Football Museum has relocated from its original location in Preston to Manchester. It is housed in a striking, ski slope-shaped glass building, originally the Urbis museum which opened in 2002. The visit begins with a glass-elevator-ride up the incline, then proceeds down through three staggered floors of exhibits.

The museum has a huge collection of football memorabilia. Especially worth admiring is the ball from the 1966 World Cup Final.

Across the plaza from the museum is **Manchester Cathedral**, which largely dates from the 19th century but stands on a site that has been occupied by a church for over a millennium.

THE PETERLOO MASSACRE

In 1819, the working conditions of Manchester's factory workers were so bad that social tensions reached breaking point. On 16 August, 50,000 people assembled in St Peter's Field to protest at the oppressive Corn Laws. Initially peaceful, the mood darkened and the poorly trained mounted

troops panicked, charging the crowd with their sabres. Eleven were killed and many wounded. The incident was called Peterloo (the Battle of Waterloo had taken place in 1815). Reforms such as the Factory Act came in that year.

G Cruikshank's Peterloo Massacre cartoon

Museum of Science and Industry, set in old passenger railway buildings

🏛 Manchester Art Gallery

Mosley St & Princess St. *Tel 0161 235 8888.* ◯ *Tue–Sun.* ◉ *Mon (except Bank Holidays), 24–26, 31 Dec, 1 Jan, Good Fri.* 🎨 ♿ 🍴 📷 📷 www.manchestergalleries.org

The gallery reopened in 2002, doubling its display space after a £35 million makeover and a brand new extension by architect Sir Michael Hopkins. The original building was designed by Sir Charles Barry (1795–1860) in 1824 and contains an excellent collection of British art, notably Pre-Raphaelites such as Holman Hunt and Dante Gabriel Rossetti. Early Italian, Flemish and French Schools are also represented.

The gallery has a fine collection of decorative arts, from the Greeks to Picasso to contemporary craftworkers, in the Gallery of Craft & Design. There is also a changing programme of special exhibitions in two fantastic galleries on the top floor. Most exhibitions are free, and there is a programme of accompanying events for adults and families.

A lively space called the Clore Interactive Gallery offers a combination of real artworks and hands-on activities for children.

🏛 Museum of Science and Industry

Liverpool Rd. *Tel 0161 832 2244.* ◯ *daily.* ◉ *1 Jan, 24–26 Dec.* ♿ 📷 🍴 📷 www.mosi.org.uk

One of the largest science museums in the world, the spirit of scientific enterprise and industrial might of Manchester's heyday is conveyed here. Among the best sections are the Power Hall, a collection of working steam engines, the Electricity Gallery, tracing the history of domestic power, and an exhibition on the Liverpool and Manchester Railway. A collection of planes that made flying history are displayed in the Air and Space Gallery.

🏛 Manchester Museum

Oxford Road. *Tel 0161 275 2648.* ◯ *daily.* ◉ *1 Jan, 24–26 Dec.* ♿ 🍴 📷 📷 www.museum.manchester.ac.uk

Part of Manchester University, this venerable museum (opened 1885) houses around six million items from all ages and all over the world, but it specializes in Egyptology and zoology. The collection of ancient Egyptian artefacts is one of the largest in the United Kingdom and numbers about 20,000 objects including monumental stone sculpture and mummies, displayed with their coffins and funerary

goods. There are also various sections that deal with funerary masks, tomb models and mummified animals. The zoological collections number over 600,000 objects, ranging from stuffed animals to a cast of one of the most complete skeletons of a T Rex dinosaur, which was added to the museum in November 2004.

The original museum building was designed by Alfred Waterhouse, the same architect responsible for the city's magnificent Town Hall (*see p373*).

🏛 Whitworth Art Gallery

University of Manchester, Oxford Rd. *Tel 0161 275 7450.* ◯ *daily (Sun: pm).* ◉ *24 Dec–2 Jan, Good Fri.* ♿ 📷 📷 www.whitworth.manchester.ac.uk

Jacob Epstein's *Genesis*, Whitworth Art Gallery

The Stockport-born machine tool manufacturer and engineer Sir Joseph Whitworth bequeathed money for this gallery, originally intended to be a museum of industrial art and design that would inspire the city's textile trade. Founded in 1889, it has been a part of the University of Manchester since 1958. The fine red-brick building is from the Edwardian period, while the modern interior dates from the 1960s.

The gallery houses a superb collection of drawings, sculpture, contemporary art, textiles and prints. Jacob Epstein's *Genesis* nude occupies the entrance, and there is an important collection of British watercolours by Turner (*see p91*), Girtin and others. Look out for the Japanese woodcuts and the Collection of historic and modern wallpapers, built up from donations from wallpaper manufacturers, as well as through the gallery's active Collecting Policy.

There is a well-developed Education Department that organizes a full programme of activities for groups and individuals of all ages and abilities, for both formal and informal learning.

Lawrence Alma-Tadema, *Etruscan Vase Painters*, Manchester Art Gallery

Exterior of the Imperial War Museum North, designed by Daniel Libeskind to represent a globe shattered by conflict

🏛 Lowry Centre

Pier 8, Salford Quays. *Tel 0843 208 6000.* ◯ *daily. Admission free, but donations requested.* ♿ 🍴 🛍 🛗 www.thelowry.com.

On a prominent site beside the Manchester Ship Canal, the Lowry is a shimmering, silvery arts and entertainment complex that combines two theatres, a restaurant, terrace bars and cafes, art galleries and a shop.

The centre is named after celebrated reclusive artist Laurence Stephen Lowry (1887–1976), who was born locally and lived all his life in the Manchester area. A rent collector by day, in his leisure hours he painted cityscapes dominated by the smoking chimneys of industry beneath heavy soot filled skies.

However, he is most famous as a painter of "matchstick men", the term frequently applied to the crowds of slight and ghostly figures peopling his canvases. Some of Lowry's work is displayed in one of the galleries here; another hosts regularly changing temporary exhibitions. There is also a room where a 20-minute documentary "Meet Mr Lowry" is screened throughout the day.

The centre provides many facilities and activities for children, and is perfect for a family day out.

🏛 Imperial War Museum North

Trafford Wharf Road, Salford Quays. *Tel 0161 836 4000.* ◯ *daily.* ● *24–26 Dec.* 🎫 ♿ 🍴 🛍 🛗 www.iwm.org.uk.

This most striking piece of modern architecture comes courtesy of Daniel Libeskind, the architect nominated to design a replacement for New York's World Trade Center. His Manchester building is a waterfront collision of three great aluminium shards, representing a globe shattered by conflict. Inside, a vast, irregular space is used to display a small but well presented collection of military hardware and ephemera, with nine "silos" devoted to exhibits on people's experiences of war.

On the hour the lights are extinguished for an audio-visual display using the angled walls of the main hall.

As visitors leave they are invited to take the elevator up the 55-metre (180-ft) "Air Shard" for views over the city.

🏛 Manchester United Museum

Salford Quays. *Tel 0161 868 8000.* ◯ *daily (except match days). Tours must be booked in advance.* 🎫 🛗 🛍 📷 www.manutd.com

Premier League football (soccer) team Manchester United's ground Old Trafford also includes a purpose-built museum. In addition to the historic displays there is much interactive fun such as a chance to test your own penalty-taking skills.

The museum tour takes in the dressing rooms, the trophy room and the players' lounge and culminates in a walk down the tunnel tracing the route taken by players at every home game.

Manchester United Museum on the grounds of Old Trafford football stadium

Liverpool ⑳

Traces of settlement on Merseyside date back to the 1st century. In 1207 "Livpul", a fishing village, was granted a charter by King John. The population was only 1,000 in Stuart times, but during the 17th and 18th centuries Liverpool's westerly seaboard gave it a leading edge in the lucrative Caribbean slave trade. The first docks opened in 1715 and eventually stretched 7 miles (11 km) along the Mersey. Liverpool's first ocean steamer set out from here in 1840, and would-be emigrants to the New World poured into the city from Europe, including a flood of Irish refugees from the potato famine. Many settled permanently in Liverpool, and a large, mixed community developed. Today, the port handles even greater volumes of cargoes than in the 1950s and 1960s, but container ships use Bootle docks. Despite economic and social problems, the irrepressible "Scouse" or Liverpudlian spirit re-emerged in the Swinging Sixties, when four local lads stormed the pop scene. Many people still visit Liverpool to pay homage to the Beatles, but the city is also known for its orchestra, the Liverpool Philharmonic, its sport and its universities. Liverpool was the Capital of Culture in 2008.

Liver Bird on the Royal Liver Building

Victorian ironwork, restored and polished, at Albert Dock

Exploring Liverpool

Liverpool's waterfront by the Pier Head, guarded by the mythical Liver Birds (a pair of cormorants with seaweed in their beaks) on the **Royal Liver Building**, is one of the most easily recognized in Britain. Nearby are the famous ferry terminal across the River Mersey and the revitalized

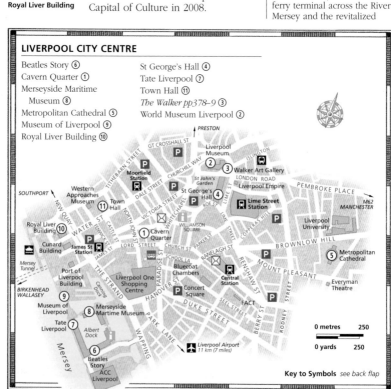

LIVERPOOL CITY CENTRE

Beatles Story ⑥
Cavern Quarter ①
Merseyside Maritime Museum ⑧
Metropolitan Cathedral ⑤
Museum of Liverpool ⑨
Royal Liver Building ⑩
St George's Hall ④
Tate Liverpool ⑦
Town Hall ⑪
The Walker pp378–9 ③
World Museum Liverpool ②

docklands. Other attractions include top-class museums and fine galleries, such as the **Walker** (*see pp378–9*). Its wealth of interesting architecture includes some fine Neo-Classical buildings in the city centre, such as the gargantuan **St George's Hall**, and two cathedrals.

Albert Dock

i 0151 708 7334. ☐ daily. ● 1 Jan, 25 Dec. 🗓 some attractions. 🚻 www.albertdock.com

There are five warehouses surrounding Albert Dock, all designed by Jesse Hartley in 1846. The docks were closed by 1972. After a decade of dereliction, these Grade I listed buildings were restored in a development that includes museums, galleries, shops, restaurants, bars and businesses.

Albert Dock quay beside the River Mersey

🏛 Merseyside Maritime Museum

Albert Dock. **Tel** 0151 478 4499. ☐ 10am–5pm daily. ● 1 Jan, 24–26 Dec. 🗓 limited. 🖵 📷 www.liverpoolmuseums.org.uk

Devoted to the history of the Port of Liverpool, this large complex has good sections on ship-building and the Cunard and White Star liners. The area on the Battle of the Atlantic in World War II includes models and charts. Another gallery deals with emigration to the New World. The **UK Border Agency National Museum** is also located here, and examines the history of the subject, including smuggling, as well as customs and excise today. Next door is the **International Slavery Museum**. Across the quayside is the rebuilt Piermaster's House and the Cooperage.

Ship's bell in the Maritime Museum

🏛 Museum of Liverpool

Pier Head, Albert Dock. **Tel** 0151 478 4545. ☐ 10am–5pm daily. ● 1 Jan, 24–26 Dec. 🗓 🖵 📷 www. liverpoolmuseums.org.uk/mol

Opened in 2011, the Museum of Liverpool is housed in a stunning building on the waterfront. Inside, visitors learn the story of this famous city, including its contributions to the fields of music, popular culture, sport and industry, as well as its role in the wider world.

🏛 Beatles Story

Britannia Vaults. **Tel** 0151 709 1963. ☐ 10am–6pm daily. ● 25, 26 Dec. 🗓 🚻 📷 www.beatlesstory.com

In a walk-through exhibition, this museum records the history of The Beatles' meteoric rise to fame, from their first record, *Love Me Do*, through Beatlemania to their last live appearance together in 1969, and their eventual break-up. The hits that mesmerized a generation can be heard.

🏛 Tate Liverpool

Albert Dock. **Tel** 0151 702 7400. ☐ 10am–5pm Tue–Sun (Jun–Aug: daily). ● Good Fri, 24–26 Dec. 🗓 some exhibitions. 🚻 🖵 📷 www. tate.org.uk/liverpool

Tate Liverpool has one of the best contemporary art collections outside London. Marked by bright blue and orange panels and arranged over three floors, the gallery was converted from an old warehouse by architect James Stirling. It opened in 1988 as Tate Britain's (*see p91*) first outstation.

THE BEATLES

Liverpool has produced many good bands and a host of singers, comedians and entertainers before and since the 1960s. But the Beatles – John Lennon, Paul McCartney, George Harrison and Ringo Starr – were the most sensational, and locations associated with the band, however tenuous, are revered as shrines in Liverpool. Bus and walking tours trace the hallowed ground of the Salvation Army home at *Strawberry Fields* and *Penny Lane* (both outside the city centre), as well as the boys' old homes. The most visited site is Mathew Street, near Moorfields Station, where the Cavern Club first throbbed to the Mersey Beat. The original site is now a shopping arcade, but the bricks have been used to create a replica. Nearby are statues of the Beatles and *Eleanor Rigby*.

Liverpool: The Walker Art Gallery

Italian dish (c. 1500)

Founded in 1877 by Sir Andrew Barclay Walker, a local brewer and Mayor of Liverpool, this gallery houses one of the finest art collections in Britain. Paintings range from early Italian and Flemish works to Rubens, Rembrandt, and French Impressionists such as Degas's *Woman Iron-ing* (c.1892–5). Among the strong collection of British artists from the 18th century onward are works by Millais and Turner and Gainsbor-ough's *Countess of Sefton* (1769). There is 20th-century art by Hockney and Sickert, and the sculpture collection includes works by Henry Moore and the contemporary artist Banksy.

Seashells *(1874)* *Albert Moore painted female figures based on antique statues. Influenced by Whistler (see p519), he adopted subtle shading.*

Interior at Paddington
(1951) Lucian Freud's friend Harry Diamond posed for six months for this picture, intended by the artist to "make the human being uncomfortable".

Big Art for Little Artists Gallery

Ground floor

First floor

Façade was designed by H H Vale and Cornelius Sherlock.

Main entrance

GALLERY GUIDE

All the picture galleries are on the first floor.
Rooms 1–2 house medieval and Renaissance paintings; Rooms 3 and 4 have 17th-century Dutch, French, Italian and Spanish art. British 18th- and 19th-century works are in Rooms 5–9. Rooms 11–15 have 20th-century and contemporary British art, and Room 10 has Impressionists and Post-Impressionists.

The Sleeping Shepherd Boy
(c.1835) The great Neo-Classical sculptor of the mid-19th century, John Gibson (1790–1866), used traditional colours to give his statuary a smooth appearance.

VISITORS' CHECKLIST

William Brown St. **Tel** 0151 478 4199. 🚆 Lime St. 🚌 Empire Theatre, Lime St, Queen Sq, Paradise St. ◯ 10am–5pm daily. ◑ 1 Jan, 25–26 Dec. 🚻 🔲 🔲 **www.** liverpoolmuseums.org.uk/walker

The 7th-century Kingston Brooch in World Museum Liverpool

🏛 World Museum Liverpool

William Brown St. **Tel** 0151 478 4393. ◯ 10am–5pm daily. ◑ 25 & 26 Dec. 🚻 🔲 🔲 **www.** liverpoolmuseums.org.uk/wml

Six floors of exhibits in this excellent museum include collections of Egyptian, Greek and Roman pieces, natural history, archaeology, space and time. Highlights include the hands-on Weston Discovery Centre, a planetarium, the Clore Natural History Centre, an aquarium and a Bug House.

🔒 Anglican Cathedral

St James' Mount. **Tel** 0151 709 6271. ◯ 7:30am–6pm daily. 📷 🚻 🔲 🔲 www.liverpoolcathedral.org.uk

Although Gothic in style, this building was only completed in 1978. The largest Anglican cathedral in the world is a fine red sandstone edifice designed by Sir Giles Gilbert Scott. The foundation stone was laid in 1904 by Edward VII but, dogged by two world wars, building work dragged on to modified designs.

🔒 Metropolitan Cathedral of Christ the King

Mount Pleasant. **Tel** 0151 709 9222. ◯ 7:30am–6pm daily. **Donation.** 🔲 🚻 🔲 www.liverpoolmetro cathedral.org.uk

Liverpool's Roman Catholic cathedral rejected traditional forms in favour of a striking modern design. Early plans, drawn up by Pugin and later by Lutyens (see p29) in the 1930s, proved too expensive. The final version, brainchild of Sir Frederick Gibberd and built from 1962–7, is a circular building surmounted by a stylized crown of thorns 88 m (290 ft) high. It is irreverently known as "Paddy's Wigwam" by non-Catholics (a reference to Liverpool's large Irish

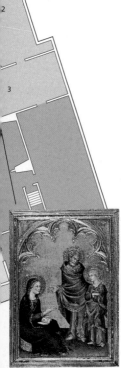

Christ Discovered in the Temple (1342)
Simone Martini's Holy Family conveys emotional tension through highly expressive body language.

KEY TO FLOOR PLAN

- 13th–17th-century European
- 18th–19th-century British, Pre-Raphaelites and Victorian
- Impressionist/Post-Impressionist
- 20th-century and contemporary British
- Sculpture gallery
- Craft and design gallery
- Merseyside people and places
- Special exhibitions
- Non-exhibition space

population). Inside, the stained-glass lantern, designed by John Piper and Patrick Reyntiens, floods the circular nave with diffused blueish light. There is a fine bronze of Christ by Elisabeth Frink (1930–94).

Environs: A spectacular, richly-timbered building dating from 1490, **Speke Hall** lies 6 miles (10 km) east of Liverpool's centre, on the banks of the River Mersey. The oldest parts of the hall enclose a cobbled courtyard dominated by two yew trees, Adam and Eve.

Birkenhead on the Wirral peninsula has been linked to Liverpool by ferry for over 800 years. Now, road and rail tunnels supplement access. The Norman Priory is still in use on Sundays, and stately Hamilton Square was designed from 1825–44 by J Gillespie Graham, one of the architects of Edinburgh's New Town.

On the Wirral side is **Port Sunlight Village** (see p349), a Victorian garden village built by enlightened soap manufacturer William Hesketh Lever for his factory workers. He also founded the **Lady Lever Art Gallery** here for his collection of works of art, including Pre-Raphaelite paintings.

🏰 Speke Hall

(NT) The Walk, Speke. **Tel** 0151 427 7231. ◯ mid-Feb–mid-Mar, Nov–early Dec: Sat & Sun; mid-Mar–mid-Jul, Sep–Oct: Wed–Sun; mid-Jul–Aug: Tue–Sun. 📷 🚻 limited. 🔲 🔲

🏰 Port Sunlight Museum and Garden Village

23 King George's Drive, Port Sunlight, Wirral. **Tel** 0151 644 6466. ◯ 10am–5pm daily. ◑ 1 Jan, 25 & 26 Dec. 📷 📷 🚻 🔲 **www.portsunlightvillage.com**

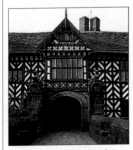

Entrance to the half-timbered manor house of Speke Hall

YORKSHIRE AND THE HUMBER REGION

NORTH YORKSHIRE · EAST RIDING OF YORKSHIRE

With the historic city of York at its heart, this is an area of picturesque moorland and valleys. To the north lie the Yorkshire Dales and the North York Moors; eastwards, a coastline of beaches; and southwards, a landscape of lush meadows.

Yorkshire was originally made up of three separate counties, formerly known as "Ridings". Today it covers over 5,000 sq miles (12,950 sq km). The northeast section has dramatic limestone scenery that was carved by glaciers in the Ice Age. Farming was the original livelihood, and the dry-stone walls weaving up precipitous scars and fells were used to divide the land. Imposed on this were the industries of the 19th century; blackened mill chimneys and crumbling viaducts are as much a part of the scenery as the grand houses of those who profited from them.

Close to the Humber, the landscape is very different, dominated historically by the now flagging fishing industry, and geographically by lush, sprawling meadows. Its coastline is exceptional, and further north are the attractions of wide, sandy beaches and bustling harbour towns. Yet it is the contrasting landscapes that make the area so appealing, ranging from the bleak moorland of the Brontë novels to the ragged cliff coast around Whitby, and the flat expanse of Sunk Island.

The city of York, where Roman and Viking relics exist side by side, is second only to London in the number of visitors that tread its streets. Indeed the historical centre of York is the region's foremost attraction. Those in search of a real taste of Yorkshire, however, should head for the countryside. In addition to excellent touring routes, a network of rewarding walking paths range from mellow ambles along the Cleveland Way to rocky scrambles over the Pennine Way at Pen-y-Ghent.

Lobster pots on the quayside at the picturesque fishing port of Whitby

◁ The peaceful valley of Rosedale, North York Moors

Exploring Yorkshire and the Humber Region

Yorkshire covers a wide area, once made up of three counties or "Ridings". Until the arrival of railways, mining and the wool industry in the 19th century, the county was a farming area. Dry-stone walls dividing fields still pepper the northern part of the county, alongside 19th-century mill chimneys and country houses. Among the many abbeys are Rievaulx and the magnificent Fountains. The medieval city of York is a major attraction, as are Yorkshire's beaches. The Humber region is characterized by the softer, rolling countryside of the Wolds, and its nature reserves attract enormous quantities of birds.

Rosedale village in the North York Moors

SIGHTS AT A GLANCE

Bempton and Flamborough Head **26**
Beverley **27**
Bradford **35**
Burton Agnes **25**
Burton Constable **28**
Byland Abbey **10**
Castle Howard pp398–9 **22**
Coxwold **11**
Eden Camp **23**
Fountains Abbey pp390–91 **7**
Grimsby **31**
Halifax **38**
Harewood House **33**
Harrogate **3**
Haworth **36**
Hebden Bridge **37**
Helmsley **13**
Holderness and Spurn Head **30**
Hutton-le-Hole **16**
Kingston upon Hull **29**
Knaresborough **4**

Leeds **34**
Magna **41**
Mount Grace Priory **15**
National Coal Mining Museum for England **39**
Newby Hall **6**
North York Moors **17**
North York Moors Railway **18**
Nunnington Hall **12**
Rievaulx Abbey **14**
Ripley **5**
Ripon **8**
Robin Hood's Bay **20**
Scarborough **21**
Sutton Bank **9**
Whitby **19**
Wharram Percy **24**
York pp404–9 **32**
Yorkshire Dales **1**
Yorkshire Sculpture Park **40**

Walks
Malham Walk **2**

(Map area)

Penrith
Durham
A66
A66
Scotch Corner
Richmond
Thwaite
Swaledale
Reeth
Catterick
Hardraw
Castle Bolton
Leyburn
Hawes
Wensleydale
Aysgarth
Middleham
YORKSHIRE
DALES
1
NATIONAL
Kendal
PARK
Kettlewell
Horton in Ribblesdale
A65
FOUNTAINS ABBEY
MALHAM
WALK **2**
Grassington
Pateley B
Settle
Burnsall
RIPLE
Malham
Long Preston
Bolton Abbey
A59
HARROGA
Skipton
Wharfe
A629
Ilkley
HAREWO
HO
Keighley
Bingley
HAWORTH **36**
Burnley
BRADFORD **35**
LEE
HEBDEN
BRIDGE **37**
Sowerby Bridge
A646
38 **HALIFAX**
De
NATIONAL COAL MINING
MUSEUM FOR ENGLAND **39**
Huddersfield
YORKSHIRE
Manchester
SCULPTURE PARK **4**
Holmfirth
Penistone
A628
Stocksbridge
Peak
Distric

SEE ALSO

• *Where to Stay* pp586–8

• *Where to Eat* pp638–40

For additional map symbols *see back flap*

Section of Lendal Bridge (1863) crossing the Ouse in York

KEY

═══	Motorway
═══	Major road
───	Secondary road
┄┄┄	Minor road
───	Scenic route
───	Main railway
───	Minor railway

0 kilometres   15

0 miles   10

GETTING AROUND

The area is served by the A1, the M1, the M62 and the A59. Trains run to major cities such as York and Leeds, and there are train or coach (bus) links between many towns and hamlets. The Yorkshire Dales and North York Moors national parks are good for walkers, and cyclists can enjoy rides around York and the River Humber.

Yorkshire Dales ●

The Yorkshire Dales is a farming landscape, formed from three principal dales, Swaledale, Wharfedale and Wensleydale, and a number of smaller ones, such as Deepdale. Glaciation in the Ice Age helped carve out these steep-sided valleys, and this scenery contrasts with the high moorlands. However, 12 centuries of settlement have altered the landscape in the form of cottages, castles and villages which create a delightful environment for walking. A national park since 1954, the area provides recreation while serving local community needs.

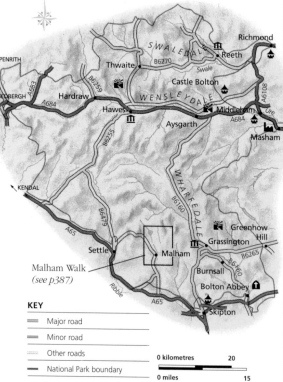

Monk's Wynd – one of Richmond's narrow, winding streets

Exploring Swaledale

Swaledale's prosperity was founded largely on wool, and it is famous for its herds of sheep that graze on the wild higher slopes in the harshest weather. The fast-moving river Swale that gives the northern-most dale its name travels from bleak moorland down magnificent waterfalls into the richly wooded lower slopes, passing through the village of Reeth and the town of Richmond.

♜ Richmond Castle

(EH) Tower Street. *Tel* 01748 822493. ◻ Apr–Sep: daily; Oct: Thu–Mon; Nov–Mar: Sat & Sun. ● 1 Jan, 24–26 Dec. ▨ &. limited. ▯
Swaledale's main point of entry is the medieval market town of Richmond. Alan Rufus, the Norman 1st Earl of Richmond, began building the castle in 1071, and some of the masonry on the curtain walls probably dates from that time. It has a fine Norman keep, 30 m (100 ft) high with walls 3.3 m (11 ft) thick. An 11th-century arch leads into a courtyard containing Scolland's Hall (1080), one of England's oldest buildings.

Richmond's marketplace was once the castle's outer bailey. Its quaint, narrow streets gave rise to the song, *The Lass of Richmond Hill* (1787), written by Leonard McNally for his wife, Frances I'Anson, who was brought up in Hill House, on Richmond Hill. Turner

KEY

═══	Major road
═══	Minor road
═══	Other roads
───	National Park boundary

0 kilometres   20
0 miles   15

Malham Walk
(see p387)

The green, rolling landscape of Deepdale, near Dent

For hotels and restaurants in this region see pp586–588 and pp638–640 *(see p91)* depicted the town many times. The Georgian Theatre (1788) is the only one of its age still surviving.

🏛 Swaledale Folk Museum

Reeth Green. *Tel 01748 884118.* ☐ *Easter–Oct: daily; Nov–Mar: call to check.* 📷 📖 🎁

Reeth, a town that became known as the centre of the lead-mining industry, houses this museum in a former Methodist Sunday school (1830). Included in it are mining and wool-making artifacts (wool from the hardy Swaledale sheep was another mainstay of the economy) and brass band memorabilia.

🎋 Buttertubs

Near Thwaite, on the B6270 Hawes road, are a series of fluted limestone potholes that streams fall into. These became known as the Buttertubs when farmers going to market lowered their butter into the holes to keep it cool.

Buttertubs, near Thwaite

Exploring Wensleydale

The largest of the Yorkshire dales, Wensleydale is famous for its cheese and more recently for James Herriot's books and the television series, *All Creatures Great and Small.* It is easy walking country for anyone seeking an alternative to major moorland hikes.

🏛 Dales Countryside Museum

Station Yard, Hawes. *Tel 01969 666210.* ☐ *10am–5pm daily.* ● *24–26 Dec, 1 Jan.* 📷 👣 🎁

In a former railway goods warehouse in Hawes, capital of Upper Wensleydale, is a

Barrels at the Theakston Brewery

fascinating museum, filled with items from life and industry in the 18th- and 19th-century Upper Dales. This includes cheese- and butter-making equipment. Wensleydale cheese was created by monks at nearby Jervaulx Abbey. There is also a rope-making works a short walk away.

Hawes is one of the highest market towns in England, at 259 m (850 ft) above sea level. It is a thriving centre where thousands of sheep and cattle are auctioned each summer.

🎋 Hardraw Force

📷 *at Green Dragon Inn, Hardraw.*

At the tiny village of Hardraw, nearby, is England's tallest single-drop waterfall, with no outcrops to interrupt its 29 m (96 ft) fall. It became famous in Victorian times when the daredevil Blondin walked across it on a tightrope. Today, you can walk right under it and look through the stream without getting wet.

🎋 Aysgarth Falls

ℹ️ *National Pk Centre (01969 662910).* ☐ *Apr–Oct: daily; Nov–Dec & Feb–Mar: Fri–Mon.* 📷

An old packhorse bridge gives a clear view of the point at which the previously placid River Ure suddenly begins to plunge in foaming torrents over wide limestone shelves. Turner painted the impressive lower falls in 1817.

🏛 Theakston Brewery

Masham. *Tel 01765 680000.* ☐ *daily.* ● *23 Dec–early Jan.* 📷 📷 🎁 *www.theakstons.co.uk*

The pretty town of Masham is the home of Theakston's brewery, creator of the potent ale Old Peculier. The history

VISITORS' CHECKLIST

N Yorkshire. 🚉 *Skipton.*
🚌 ℹ️ *0300 4560030.*
www.yorkshiredales.org.uk

of this local family brewery from its origin in 1827 is on display in the visitors' centre. Masham village itself has an attractive square once used for sheep fairs, surrounded by 17th- and 18th-century houses.

♣ Bolton Castle

Castle Bolton, nr Leyburn. *Tel 01969 623981.* ☐ *daily.* ● *Nov–weekend before Easter.* 📷 👣 🎁 *www.boltoncastle.co.uk*

Situated in the village of Castle Bolton, this spectacular medieval fortress was built in 1379 by the 1st Lord Scrope, Chancellor of England. Its most notorious period was from 1568 to 1569 when Mary, Queen of Scots *(see p511)* was held prisoner here by Elizabeth I *(see pp50–51).*

♣ Middleham Castle

(EH) Middleham, nr Leyburn. *Tel 01969 623899.* ☐ *Apr–Sep: daily; Oct: Sat–Wed; Nov–Mar: Sat & Sun.* ● *1 Jan, 24–26 Dec.* 🎁 📷 👣 *ltd.*

Owned by Richard Neville, Earl of Warwick, it was built in 1170. The castle is better known as home to Richard III *(see p49)* when he was made Lord of the North. It was once one of the strongest fortresses in the north but became uninhabited during the 15th century, when many of its stones were used for nearby buildings. The keep provides a fine view of the landscape.

Remains of Middleham Castle, once residence of Richard III

Extensive ruins of Bolton Priory, dating from 1154

Exploring Wharfedale

This dale is characterized by gritstone moorland, contrasting with quiet market towns along meandering sections of river. Many consider Grassington a central point for exploring Wharfedale, but the showpiece villages of Burnsall, overlooked by a 506 m (1,661 ft) fell, and Buckden, near Buckden Pike (701 m/2,302 ft), also make excellent bases.

Nearby are the Three Peaks of Whernside, 736 m (2,416 ft), Ingleborough, 724 m (2,376 ft) and Pen-y-Ghent 694 m (2,278 ft). They are known for their potholes and tough terrain, but this does not deter keen walkers from attempting to climb them all in one day. If you sign in at the Pen-y-Ghent café at Horton-in-Ribblesdale, at the centre of the Three Peaks, and complete the 20 mile (32 km) course, reaching the summit of all three peaks in less than 12 hours, you can qualify for membership of the Three Peaks of Yorkshire Club.

Burnsall

St Wilfrid's, Burnsall. *Tel* 01756 720331. ⬜ *Apr–Oct: daily to dusk.* &

Preserved in St Wilfrid's church graveyard are the original village stocks, gravestones from Viking times and a headstone carved in memory of the Dawson family by sculptor Eric Gill (1882–1940). The village has a five-arched bridge and hosts Britain's oldest fell race every August.

🏛 Grassington Folk Museum

The Square, Grassington. *Tel* 01756 752801. ⬜ *Apr–Oct: daily (pm).* 📷 & *limited.*

This museum is set in two 18th-century lead miners' cottages. Its exhibits illustrate the domestic and working history of the area, including farming and lead mining.

🏠 Bolton Priory

Bolton Abbey, Skipton. *Tel* 01756 718000. ⬜ *daily.* &

One of the most beautiful areas of Wharfedale is around the village of Bolton Abbey, set in an estate owned by the Dukes of Devonshire. While preserving its astounding beauty, its managers have incorporated over 30 miles (46 km) of footpaths, many suitable for the disabled and young families.

The ruins of Bolton Priory, established by Augustinian canons in 1154 on the site of a Saxon manor, are extensive. They include a church, chapter house, cloister and prior's lodging. These all demonstrate the wealth accumulated by the canons from the sale of wool from their flocks of sheep. The priory nave is still used as a parish church. Another attraction of the estate is the "Strid", a point where the River Wharfe surges spectacularly through a gorge, foaming yellow and gouging holes out of the rocks.

🏔 Stump Cross Caverns

Greenhow Hill, Pateley Bridge. *Tel* 01756 752780. ⬜ *Mar–Nov: daily; Dec–Feb: Sat, Sun & pub hols.* 📷 ▢ 🏠 www.stumpcrosscaverns.co.uk

These caves were formed over a period of half a million years: trickles of underground water formed intertwining passages and carved them into fantastic shapes and sizes. Sealed off in the last Ice Age, the caves were only discovered in the 1850s, when lead miners sank a mine shaft into the caverns.

♣ Skipton Castle

High St. *Tel* 01756 792442. ⬜ *daily (Sun: pm).* ● *25 Dec.* 📷 ▢ 🏠 www.skiptoncastle.co.uk

The market town of Skipton is still one of the largest auctioning and stockraising centres in the north. Its 11th-century castle was almost entirely rebuilt by Robert de Clifford in the 14th century. Beautiful Conduit Court was added by Henry, Lord Clifford, in Henry VIII's reign. The central yew tree was planted by Lady Anne Clifford in 1659 to mark restoration work to the castle after Civil War damage.

Conduit Court (1495) and yew tree at Skipton Castle

For hotels and restaurants in this region see pp586–588 and pp638–640

Malham Walk ❷

The Malham area, shaped by glacial erosion 10,000 years ago, has one of Great Britain's most dramatic limestone landscapes. The walk from Malham village can take over four hours if you pause to enjoy the viewpoints and take a detour to Gordale Scar. Those who are short of time tend to go only as far as Malham Cove. This vast natural amphitheatre, formed

Sandpiper at Malham Tarn

by a huge geological tear, is like a giant boot-heel mark in the landscape. Above lie the deep crevices of Malham Lings, where rare flora such as hart's-tongue flourishes. Unusual plants grow in the lime-rich Malham Tarn, said to have provided inspiration for Charles Kingsley's *The Water Babies* (1863). Coot and mallard visit the tarn in summer and tufted duck in winter.

Where the path meets the road ⑤
From here, you can catch a bus back to Malham village.

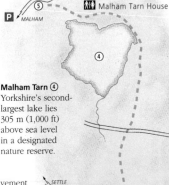

Malham Tarn House

Malham Tarn ④
Yorkshire's second-largest lake lies 305 m (1,000 ft) above sea level in a designated nature reserve.

Gordale Scar ⑥
Guarded by steep limestone cliffs, this deep gorge was created by meltwater from Ice Age glaciers.

Malham Lings ③
This fine limestone pavement was formed when Ice Age meltwater seeped into cracks in the rock, then froze and expanded.

Malham Cove ②
The black streak in the centre of this 76 m (250 ft) cove is the site of a former waterfall.

Malham ①
An attractive riverside village, it has an information centre with details of drives and walks.

KEY

▪▪	Walk route
═══	Minor road
✲	Viewpoint
P	Parking
ℹ	Tourist information
🚻	Toilets

0 kilometres 1
0 miles ½

TIPS FOR WALKERS

Starting point: *Malham.* **Getting there:** *Leave M65 at Junction 14 and take A56 to Skipton, then follow signs to Malham which is off A65.* **Length:** *7 miles (11 km).* **Difficulty:** *Malham Cove is steep but the Tarn area is flatter.*
ℹ *01729 833200.*

A 1920s poster advertising the spa town of Harrogate

Harrogate ❸

North Yorkshire. 🚶 72,000.
🚆 🚌 🛈 The Royal Baths,
Crescent Rd (0845 389 3223).
www.harrogate.gov.uk

Between 1880 and World War I, Harrogate was the north's leading spa town, with nearly 90 medicinal springs. It was ideal for aristocrats who, after a tiring London season, were able to stop for a health cure before journeying on to grouse-shooting in Scotland.

Today, Harrogate's main attractions are its spa town atmosphere, fine architecture, public gardens and its convenience as a centre for visiting North Yorkshire and the Dales.

The naturally welling spa waters may not currently be in use, but you can still go for a Turkish bath in one of the country's most attractive steam rooms. The entrance at the side of the Royal Bath Assembly Rooms (1897) is unassuming, but once inside, the century-old **Harrogate Turkish Baths** are a visual feast of tiled Victoriana.

The town's spa history is recorded in the **Royal Pump Room Museum**. At the turn of the century, the waters were thought to be rich in iron early in the day. So, between 7am and 9am the 1842 octagonal building would have been filled with rich and fashionable people drinking glasses of water. Poorer people could take water from the pump outside. Today you can sample the waters and enjoy the museum's exhibits, including a Penny Farthing bicycle.

Harrogate is also known for the rainbow-coloured flower-beds in **The Stray**, a common space to the south of the town centre, and for the ornamental **RHS Harlow Carr Gardens**, owned by the Royal Horticultural Society. Visitors can enjoy the delicious cakes at **Bettys Café Tea Rooms** (see p628).

🔲 **Harrogate Turkish Baths**
The Royal Baths, Crescent Rd. *Tel*
01423 556746. ◯ *Women: Mon,
Tue & Thu (pm); Fri (am); Sun.*
Mixed (in bathing suits): Mon (eve),
Wed, Thu (eve), Sat & Sun. ♿

🏛 **Royal Pump Room Museum**
Crown Pl. *Tel* 01423 556188.
◯ daily (Sun: pm only).
● 1 Jan, 24–26 Dec. ♿ ♿ 🅿

🔲 **Bettys Café Tea Rooms**
1 Parliament St. *Tel* 01423
814070. ◯ daily. ● 1 Jan, 25 &
26 Dec. www.bettys.co.uk

♣ **RHS Harlow Carr Gardens**
Crag Lane. *Tel* 01423 565418.
◯ daily. ● 25 Dec. ♿ ♿ 🍴 ♿
www.rhs.org.uk

Knaresborough ❹

North Yorkshire. 🚶 15,000. 🚆 🚌
from Harrogate. 🛈 9 Castle
Courtyard, Market Place (08453
890177). ◳ Wed.

Perched precipitously above the River Nidd is one of England's oldest towns, mentioned in the Domesday Book of 1086 (see p48). Its historic streets – which link the church, John of Gaunt's ruined castle, and the market place with the river – are now lined with fine 18th-century houses.

Nearby is **Mother Shipton's Cave**, reputedly England's oldest tourist attraction. It first went on show in 1630 as the birthplace of Ursula Sontheil,

Mother Shipton's cave, with objects encased in limestone

For hotels and restaurants in this region see pp586–588 and pp638–640

The south front of Newby Hall

a famous local prophetess. Today, people can view the effect the well near her cave has on objects hung below the dripping surface. Almost any item, from umbrellas to soft toys, will become encased in limestone within a few weeks.

🏚 Mother Shipton's Cave
Prophesy House, High Bridge. **Tel** 01423 864600. ⭕ *Easter–Oct: daily; Feb–Easter: Sat, Sun.* ⬤ *Nov–Jan.* 📷 🖊 🛒 🏠

Ripley ❺

North Yorkshire. 🏘 *250.*
🚌 *from Harrogate or Ripon.*
ℹ *Harrogate (0845 893223).*
www.harrogate.gov.uk

Since the 1320s, when the first generation of the Ingilby family lived in an early incarnation of **Ripley Castle**, the village has been made up almost exclusively of castle employees. The influence of one 19th-century Ingilby had the most visual impact. In the 1820s, Sir William Amcotts Ingilby was so entranced by a village in Alsace Lorraine that he created a similar one in French Gothic style, complete with an *Hôtel de Ville*. Present-day Ripley has a cobbled market square, and quaint cottages line the streets.

Ripley Castle, with its 15th-century gatehouse, was where Oliver Cromwell *(see p52)* stayed following the Battle of Marston Moor. The 28th generation of Ingilbys live here, and it is open for tours. The attractive grounds contain two lakes and a deer park, as well as more formal gardens.

⚓ Ripley Castle
Ripley. **Tel** 01423 770152. ⭕ *Apr–Oct: daily; Mar, Nov: Tue, Thu, Sat & Sun; Dec–Feb: Sat & Sun.*
Gardens ⭕ *daily all year.* ⬤ *1 Jan, 25 & 26 Dec.* 📷 ♿ 🖊 🛒 🏠

Newby Hall ❻

Nr Ripon, North Yorkshire. **Tel** 0845 4504068. ⭕ *Apr–Jun & Sep: Tue–Sun; Jul & Aug: daily.* 📷 ♿ 🍴 🛒
www.newbyhall.com

Newby Hall stands on land once occupied by the de Nubie family in the 13th century and has been in the hands of the current family since 1748. The central part of the present house was built in the late 17th century, in the style of Sir Christopher Wren.

Visitors will find 25 acres of gardens to explore. Laid out in a series of compartmented areas off a main axis, each garden is planted to come into flower during a different season. There is also a Woodland Discovery Walk, with contemporary sculpture.

For children, there is an adventure garden with activities and a miniature railway that runs through the gardens alongside the river Ure. River boat rides are also available. Each year a number of special events are staged, including Plant Fairs, a Historic Vehicle Rally and two Craft fairs.

Fountains Abbey ❼

See pp390–91.

Ripon ❽

North Yorkshire. 🏘 *16,000.*
🚌 *from Harrogate.* ℹ *Minster Rd (0845 389 0178).* ⬤ *Thu.*
www.visitripon.org

Ripon, a charming small city, is best known for the cathedral and "the watch", which has been announced since the Middle Ages by the Wakeman. In return for protecting Ripon citizens, he would charge an annual toll of two pence per household. Today, a man still blows a horn in the Market Square each evening at 9pm, and every Thursday a handbell is rung to open the market.

The **Cathedral of St Peter and St Wilfrid** is built above a 7th-century Saxon crypt. At less than 3 m (10 ft) high and just over 2 m (7 ft) wide, it is held to be the oldest complete crypt in England. The cathedral is known for its collection of misericords *(see p341)*, which include both pagan and Old Testament examples. The architectural historian Sir Nikolaus Pevsner (1902–83) considered the cathedral's West Front the finest in England.

Ripon's **Prison and Police Museum**, housed in the 1686 "House of Correction", looks at police history and the conditions in Victorian prisons.

🏛 Prison and Police Museum
St Marygate. **Tel** 01765 690799. ⭕ *Apr–Oct: daily (pm only).* ⬤ *Nov–Mar.* 📷 ♿ 🏠
www.riponmuseums.co.uk

Ripon's Wakeman, blowing his horn in the Market Square

Fountains Abbey ⑦

Nestling in the wooded valley of the River Skell are the extensive sandstone ruins of Fountains Abbey and the outstanding water garden of Studley Royal. Fountains Abbey was founded by Benedictine monks in 1132 and taken over by Cistercians three years later. By the mid-12th century it had become the wealthiest abbey in Britain, though it fell into ruin during the Dissolution (see p50). In 1720, John Aislabie, the MP for Ripon and Chancellor of the Exchequer, developed the land and forest of the abbey ruins. He began work, continued by his son William, on the famous water garden, statuary and Classical temples in the grounds. Studley Royal and the Abbey became a World Heritage Site in 1986.

Fountains Hall
Built by Sir Stephen Proctor around 1611, with stones from the abbey ruins, its design is attributed to architect Robert Smythson. It included a great hall with a minstrels' gallery and an entrance flanked by Classical columns.

THE ABBEY

The abbey buildings were designed to reflect the Cistercians' desire for simplicity and austerity. The abbey frequently dispensed charity to the poor and the sick, as well as travellers.

The Chapel of Nine Altars *at the east end of the church was built from 1203 to 1247. It is ornate, compared to the rest of the abbey, with an 18-m (60-ft) high window complemented by another at the western end of the nave.*

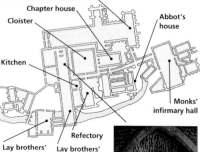

Chapter house
Cloister
Kitchen
Abbot's house
Monks' infirmary hall
Refectory
Lay brothers' infirmary
Lay brothers' refectory

Cellarium and dormitory undercroft, *with vaulting 90 m (300 ft) long, was used for storing fleeces which the abbey monks sold to Venetian and Florentine merchants.*

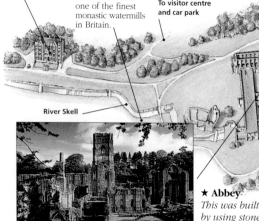

Fountains Mill is one of the finest monastic watermills in Britain.

To visitor centre and car park

River Skell

Paths leading to the estate park

★ **Abbey**
This was built by using stones taken from the Skell valley.

STAR SIGHTS

★ Abbey

★ Temple of Piety

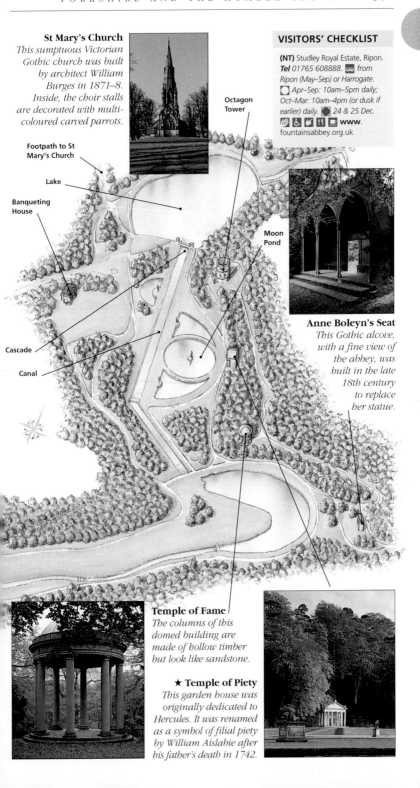

St Mary's Church
This sumptuous Victorian Gothic church was built by architect William Burges in 1871–8. Inside, the choir stalls are decorated with multi-coloured carved parrots.

Octagon Tower

Footpath to St Mary's Church

Lake

Banqueting House

Moon Pond

Cascade

Canal

Anne Boleyn's Seat
This Gothic alcove, with a fine view of the abbey, was built in the late 18th century to replace her statue.

Temple of Fame
The columns of this domed building are made of hollow timber but look like sandstone.

★ Temple of Piety
This garden house was originally dedicated to Hercules. It was renamed as a symbol of filial piety by William Aislabie after his father's death in 1742.

The 19th-century white horse above Kilburn, seen on one of the walks around Sutton Bank

Sutton Bank 9

North Yorkshire. ☎ *Thirsk.* ⓘ *Sutton Bank (01845 597426).*

Notorious among motorists for its 1 in 4 gradient, which climbs for about 107 m (350 ft), Sutton Bank itself is known for its panoramic views. On a clear day you can see across the Vale of York to the Dales *(see pp384–5)*. William and his sister Dorothy Wordsworth stopped here to admire the vista in 1802, on their way to visit his future wife, Mary Hutchinson, at Brompton.

There is a visitor centre at the top of the Bank, from which it is a pleasant walk to the white horse above Kilburn.

Byland Abbey 10

(EH) Coxwold, York. **Tel** *01347 868 614.* 🚌 *from York or Helmsley.* ☎ *Thirsk.* ◯ *Apr–Jun, Sep: Thu–Mon; Jul–Aug: daily; Oct–Mar: Sat & Sun.* ⓦ ♿ *limited.* **www**.english-heritage.org.uk

This Cistercian monastery was founded in 1177 by monks from Furness Abbey in

Cumbria. It featured what was then the largest Cistercian church in Britain, 100 m (328 ft) long and 41 m (135 ft) wide across the transepts. The layout of the monastery, including cloisters and the west front of the church, is still visible, as is the green and yellow glazed tile floor. Fine workmanship is shown in carved stone details and in the capitals, kept in the small museum.

In 1322 the Battle of Byland was fought nearby, and King Edward II *(see p40)* narrowly escaped capture when the invading Scottish army learned that he was dining with the Abbot. In his hurry to escape, the king had to leave many treasures behind, which were looted by the invading soldiers.

Coxwold 11

North Yorkshire. 🚗 *185.* ⓘ *49 Market Place, Thirsk (01845 522755).* **www**.hambleton.gov.uk

Situated just inside the bounds of the North York Moors National Park *(see p395)*, this charming village nestles at the foot of the Howardian Hills. Its pretty houses are built from local stone, and the 15th-century church has some fine Georgian

Shandy Hall, home of author Laurence Sterne, now a museum

box pews and an impressive octagonal tower. But Coxwold is best known as the home of the author Laurence Sterne (1713–68), whose writings include *Tristram Shandy* and *A Sentimental Journey*.

Sterne moved here in 1760 as the church curate. He rented a rambling house that he named **Shandy Hall** after a Yorkshire expression meaning eccentric. Originally built as a timber-framed, open-halled house in the 15th century, it was modernized in the 17th century and Sterne later added a façade. His grave lies beside the porch at Coxwold's church.

 Shandy Hall
Coxwold. *Tel* 01347 868465.
May–Sep: Wed & Sun (pm).
limited. **Gardens** May–Sep:
Sun–Fri.

Nunnington Hall ⑫

(NT) Nunnington, York. *Tel* 01439 748283. Malton, then bus or taxi. Feb–Oct: Tue–Sun; Nov–mid-Dec: Sat & Sun. mid-Dec–Jan. ground floor.

Set in alluring surroundings, this 17th-century manor house is a combination of architectural styles, including features from the Elizabethan and Stuart periods. Both inside and outside, a notable architectural feature is the use of the broken pediment (the upper arch is left unjoined).

Nunnington Hall was a family home until 1952, when Mrs Ronald Fife donated it to the National Trust. A striking

The miniature Queen Anne drawing room at Nunnington Hall

feature is the panelling in the Oak Hall. Formerly painted, it extends over the three-arched screen to the Great Staircase. Nunnington's collection of 22 miniature furnished period rooms is popular with visitors.

A mid-16th-century tenant Dr Robert Huickes, physician to Henry VIII (*see pp50–51*), is best known for advising Elizabeth I that she should not, at the age of 32, consider having any children.

Helmsley ⑬

North Yorkshire. 1,600. from Malton or Scarborough. Helmsley Castle (01439 770173). Fri.
www.discovernorthyorkshire.co.uk

This pretty market town is noted for its castle, now an imposing ruin. Built from 1186 to 1227, its main function and strength as a fortress is illustrated by the remaining keep, tower and curtain walls. The original D-shaped keep had one part blasted away in the Civil War (*see p52*), but remains the

dominant feature. The castle was so impregnable that there were few attempts to force entry. However, in 1644, after holding out for a three-month seige against Sir Thomas Fairfax, the Parliamentary general, the castle was finally taken.

Helmsley church tower

Rievaulx Abbey ⑭

(EH) Nr Helmsley, North Yorkshire. *Tel* 01439 798228. Thirsk or Scarborough, then bus or taxi. Apr–Sep: daily; Oct: Thu–Mon; Nov–Mar: Sat & Sun. 1 Jan, 2 weeks late Feb, 24–26 Dec. limited.

Rievaulx is perhaps the finest abbey in the area, due to both its dramatic setting in the steep wooded valley of the River Rye and its extensive remains. It is surrounded by steep banks that form natural barriers from the outside world. Monks of the French Cistercian order from Clairvaux founded this, their first major monastery in Britain, in 1132. The main buildings were finished before 1200. The layout of the chapel, kitchens and infirmary give an idea of monastic life.

Rievaulx Abbey, painted by Thomas Girtin (1775–1802)

Mount Grace Priory ruins, with farm and mansion in foreground

Mount Grace Priory **⑮**

(EH/NT) On A19, NE of Northallerton, North Yorks. *Tel* 01609 883494. ⬛ Northallerton then bus 89. ◯ Apr–Sep: Thu–Mon; Oct: Thu–Sun; Nov: Sat & Sun. 🈳 ♿ ground floor, shop & grounds. 🗂

Founded by Thomas Holland, Duke of Surrey, and in use from 1398 until 1539, this is the best-preserved Carthusian or charterhouse monastery *(see pp350–51)* in England. The monks took a vow of silence and lived in solitary cells, each with his own garden and an angled hatch so that he would not even see the person serving his food. They only met at matins, vespers and feast-day services. Attempts at escape by those who could not endure the rigour of the rules were punished by imprisonment.

The ruins of the priory include the former prison, gatehouse and outer court, barns, guesthouses, cells and the church. The 14th-century church, the best-preserved section of the site, is particularly small, as it was only rarely used by the community. A cell has been reconstructed to give an impression of monastic life.

Hutton-le-Hole **⑯**

North Yorkshire. 🈂 400. ⬛ Pickering then bus (seasonal service). 🛈 The Ropery, Pickering (01751 473791). **www**.ryedale.co.uk

This picturesque village is characterized by a spacious green, grazed by roaming sheep, and surrounded by houses, an inn and shops. Lengths of white wood, replacing stone bridges, span the moorland stream. Its cottages, some with date panels over the doors, are made from limestone, with red pantiled roofs. In the village centre is the excellent

Wheelwright's workshop at Ryedale Folk Museum

Ryedale Folk Museum, which records the lifestyle of an agricultural community using ancient artifacts and reconstructed buildings.

🏛 **Ryedale Folk Museum**
Hutton-le-Hole. *Tel* 01751 417367. ◯ late Jan–mid-Dec: daily. 🈳 ♿ 🗂

North York Moors **⑰**

See p395.

North Yorkshire Moors Railway **⑱**

Pickering & Grosmont, North Yorkshire. *Tel* 01751 472508. ◯ Apr–Oct: daily; Nov–Mar: some weekends (call for details). 🈳 ♿ 🗂 🗂 **www**.nymr.co.uk

Designed in 1831 by George Stephenson as a route through the North York Moors and linking with the Esk Valley, Pickering and Whitby *(see p382)*, this railway was considered an engineering miracle. Due to budget constraints, Stephenson was not able to build a tunnel, so had to lay the route down the mile-long (1.5 km) incline between Beck Hole and Goathland. The area around Fen Bog had to be stabilized using timber, heather, brushwood and fleeces so that a causeway could be built over it. A horse was used to pull a coach along the track at 10 miles (16 km) per hour. After horsepower came steam, and for almost 130 years the railway linked Whitby to the rest of the country. In the early 1960s the line to Pickering was closed, but in 1967 a group of locals began a campaign to relaunch it, and in 1973 it reopened. Today, steam engines run the 18-mile (29-km) line from Pickering via Levisham, Newtondale Halt and Goathland before stopping at Grosmont, through the scenic heart of the North York Moors.

North York Moors ⑰

The area between Cleveland, the Vale of York and the Vale of Pickering is known as the North York Moors National Park. The landscape consists of bleak yet beautiful moors interspersed with lush green valleys. Agriculture is still the main source of income here as it has been for centuries, and until the advent of coal, the communities' local source of fuel was turf. In the 19th century, the geology of the area created extractive industries which included ironstone, lime, coal and building stone.

Mallyan Spout
A footpath leads to this waterfall from Goathland.

Farndale
During springtime, this area is famous for the beauty and profusion of its daffodils.

"Fat Betty" White Cross Crosses and standing stones are a feature of the Moors.

Goathland
A centre for forest and moorland walks, it is a terminus for the North Yorkshire Moors railway.

THE MOORS CENTRE, DANBY

EGTON BRIDGE

West Beck

WHITBY

LEAHOLM

Wheeldale Gill

THORGILL

Seven

Hartoft Beck

Rutmoor Beck

Blawarth Beck

Dove

Rosedale Abbey
Named after the priory that has long since gone, this beautiful village still has some remains of the kilns from its 19th-century ironstone mining industry.

Hutton-le-Hole
This lovely village has the excellent Ryedale Folk Museum.

Spaunton

Wade's Causeway
Often called the Roman Road, its origins and destination are unknown. Long considered Roman in date, this is now less certain, although it may date from towards the end of the Roman occupation.

VISITORS' CHECKLIST

North Yorkshire. 🚇 *Danby.* 🚌 *Pickering (Easter–Oct).* **Moorsbus Tel** 01845 597000. 🛈 *Sutton Bank (01845 597426); Moors Centre (01439 772737).* **www.** northyorkmoors.org.uk

Lastingham
Lastingham's church, dating from 1078, has a Norman crypt with stone carving.

0 kilometres   2

0 miles   2

Whitby ⑲

Whitby's known history dates back to the 7th century, when a Saxon monastery was founded on the site of today's famous 13th-century abbey ruins. In the 18th and early 19th centuries it became an industrial port and shipbuilding town, as well as a whaling centre.

Jet comb (c.1870)

In the Victorian era, the red-roofed cottages at the foot of the east cliff were filled with workshops crafting jet into jewellery and ornaments. Today, the tourist shops that have replaced them sell antique-crafted examples of the distinctive black gem.

VISITORS' CHECKLIST

North Yorkshire. 👥 13,500. ✈ Teeside, 44 miles (70 km) NW Whitby. 🚆 Station Sq. ℹ Langborne Rd (01723 383617). 🚌 Tue, Sat. 🎣 Angling Festival: Apr, Jun, Sep; Lifeboat Day: Jun; Folk Week: Aug; Whitby Regatta: Aug. **www**.discover yorkshirecoast.com

Exploring Whitby

Whitby is divided into two by the estuary of the River Esk. The Old Town, with its pretty cobbled streets and pastel-hued houses, huddles round the harbour. High above it is St Mary's Church with a wood interior reputedly fitted by ships' carpenters. The ruins of the 13th-century Whitby Abbey, nearby, are still used as a landmark by mariners. From them you get a fine view over the still-busy harbour, strewn with colourful nets. A pleasant place for a stroll, the harbour is overlooked by an imposing bronze clifftop statue of the explorer Captain James Cook (1728–79), who was apprenticed as a teenager to a Whitby shipping firm.

Lobster pots lining the quayside of Whitby's quaint harbour

Medieval arches above the nave of Whitby Abbey

♟ Whitby Abbey

(EH) Abbey Lane. **Tel** 01947 603568. ⬜ Apr–Sep: daily; Oct: Thu–Mon; Nov–Mar: Sat & Sun. ⬤ 1 Jan, 24–26 Dec. 📷 ♿ 🛍

The monastery founded in 657 was sacked by Vikings in 870. In the 11th century it was rebuilt as a Benedictine Abbey. The ruins date mainly from the 13th century.

♟ St Mary's Parish Church

East Cliff. **Tel** 01947 606578. ⬜ daily. Stuart and Georgian alterations to this Norman church have left a mixture of twisted wood columns and maze-like 18th-century box pews. The 1778 triple-decker pulpit has rather avant-garde decor – ear-trumpets used by a Victorian rector's deaf wife.

🏛 Captain Cook Memorial Museum

Grape Lane. **Tel** 01947 601900. ⬜ Mar–Oct & Feb half-term: daily. 📷 🛍 ♿ limited. **www**.cookmuseum whitby.co.uk

The young James Cook slept in the attic of this 17th-century harbourside house when he was apprenticed nearby. The museum has displays of period furniture and watercolours by artists who travelled on his voyages.

🏛 Whitby Museum and Pannett Art Gallery

Pannett Park. **Tel** 01947 602908 (museum), 01947 602051 (gallery). ⬜ Tue–Sun & public hols. ⬤ 24 Dec–2 Jan. 📷 museum only. ♿ limited. 🛍 **www**.whitbymuseum.org.uk

The Pannett Park grounds, museum and gallery were a gift of Whitby solicitor, Robert Pannett (1834–1920), to house his art collection. Among the museum's treasures are objects illustrating local history, such as jet jewellery, and Captain Cook artifacts.

The three-storey extension at the museum, completed in 2005, houses a costume gallery and photography and map collections.

♟ Caedmon's Cross

East Cliff.
On the path side of the abbey's clifftop graveyard is the cross of Caedmon, an illiterate labourer who worked at the abbey in the 7th century. He experienced a vision that inspired him to compose cantos of Anglo-Saxon religious verse, which are still sung today.

Cross of Caedmon (1898)

Robin Hood's Bay ⑳

North Yorkshire. 🚶 1,400.
🚉 🚌 Whitby. 🛈 Langbourne Rd, Whitby (01723 383637).
www.robin-hoods-bay.co.uk

Legend has it that Robin Hood (see p336) kept his boats here in case he needed to make a quick getaway. The village has a history as a smugglers' haven, and many houses have ingenious hiding places for contraband. The cobbled main street is so steep that visitors need to leave their vehicles in the car park at the top. In the village centre, narrow streets full of colour-washed stone cottages huddle around a quaint quay. There is a rocky beach with rock pools for children to play in. At low tide, the pleasant walk south to Boggle Hole is 15 minutes, but you need to keep an eye on the tides.

Cobbled alley in the Bay Town area of Robin Hood's Bay

The fishing port and town of Scarborough nestling round the harbour

Scarborough ㉑

North Yorkshire. 🚶 51,000. 🚉
🚌 🛈 Brunswick Shopping Centre (01723 383636). 🛒 Mon–Sat.
www.discoveryorkshirecoast.com

The history of Scarborough as a resort can be traced back to 1626, when it became known as a spa. In the Industrial Revolution (see pp348–9) it was nicknamed "the Queen of the Watering Places", but the post-World War II trend for holidays abroad has meant fewer visitors. The town has two beaches; the South Bay amusement arcades contrast with the quieter North Bay. Playwright Alan Ayckbourn premieres his work at the Stephen Joseph theatre, and Anne Brontë (see p412) is buried in St Mary's Church.

Bronze and Iron Age relics have been found on the site of **Scarborough Castle**. The **Rotunda** (1828–9), which underwent a major refurbishment during 2007, was one of Britain's first purpose-built museums. Works by the local artist Atkinson Grimshaw (1836–93) hang in **Scarborough Art Gallery**. The **Sea Life and Marine Sanctuary**'s baby seals are its main attraction.

🏰 **Scarborough Castle**
(EH) Castle Rd. **Tel** 01723 372451.
🕐 Apr–Sep: daily; Oct: Thu–Mon; Nov–Mar: Sat & Sun. ⬤ 1 Jan, 24–26 Dec. 🎫 ♿ 🖥 🏠

🏛 **Rotunda Museum**
Vernon Rd. **Tel** 01723 353665.
🕐 Tue–Sun. ⬤ 1 Jan, 25 & 26 Dec. 🏠 🎫

🏛 **Scarborough Art Gallery**
The Crescent. **Tel** 01723 374753.
🕐 Tue–Sun. ⬤ 1 Jan, 25 & 26 Dec. 🏠 🎫 🖥 www.scarborough museumstrust.co.uk

🐟 **Sea Life and Marine Sanctuary**
Scalby Mills Rd. **Tel** 01723 373414.
🕐 daily. ⬤ 25 Dec. 🎫 ♿ 🖥 🏠
www.visitsealife.com

THE GROWING POPULARITY OF SWIMMING

During the 18th century, sea-bathing came to be regarded as a healthy pastime, and from 1735 onwards men and women, on separate stretches of the coast, could be taken out into the sea in bathing huts, or "machines". In the 18th century, bathing was segregated although nudity was permitted. The Victorians brought in fully clothed bathing, and 19th-century workers from Britain's industrial heartlands used the new steam trains to visit the coast for their holidays. At this time, British seaside resorts such as Blackpool (see p371) and Scarborough expanded to meet the new demand.

A Victorian bathing hut on wheels

Castle Howard 🔢

Pillar detail in the Great Hall, carved by Samuel Carpenter

Still owned and lived in by the Howard family, Castle Howard was created by Charles, 3rd Earl of Carlisle. In 1699, he commissioned Sir John Vanbrugh, a man of dramatic ideas but with no previous architectural experience, to design a palace for him. Vanbrugh's grand designs of 1699 were put into practice by architect Nicholas Hawksmoor *(see p28)*, and the main body of the house was completed by 1712. The West Wing was built in 1753–9, using a design by Thomas Robinson, son-in-law of the 3rd Earl. In the 1980s, Castle Howard was used as the location for the television version of Evelyn Waugh's novel *Brideshead Revisited* (1945) and again for the film version in 2008.

Temple of the Four Winds
Vanbrugh's last work, designed in 1724, has a dome and four Ionic porticoes. Situated in the grounds at the end of the terrace, it is typical of an 18th-century "landscape building".

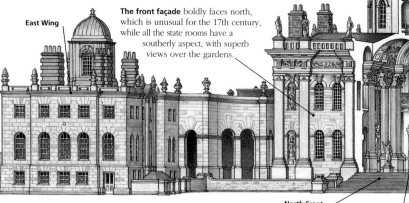

East Wing

The front façade boldly faces north, which is unusual for the 17th century, while all the state rooms have a southerly aspect, with superb views over the gardens.

North Front

★ Great Hall
Rising 20 m (66 ft), from its 515 sq m (5,500 sq ft) floor to the dome, the Great Hall has columns by Samuel Carpenter (1660–1713), wall paintings by Pellegrini and a circular gallery.

SIR JOHN VANBRUGH

Vanbrugh (1664–1726) trained as a soldier, but became better known as a playwright, architect and member of the Whig nobility. He collaborated with Hawksmoor over the design of Blenheim Palace, but his bold architectural vision, later greatly admired, was mocked by the establishment. He died while working on the garden buildings and grounds of Castle Howard.

Chapel Stained Glass
Admiral Edward Howard altered the chapel in 1870–75. The windows were designed by Edward Burne-Jones and made by William Morris & Co.

Bust of the 7th Earl
J H Foley sculpted this portrait bust, which stands at the top of the Grand Staircase in the West Wing, in 1870.

★ Long Gallery
Displayed here are paintings and sculptures commissioned by the Howard family, including works by Reynolds and Pannini.

West Wing

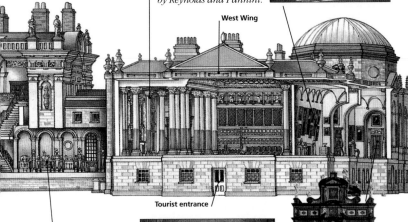

Tourist entrance

Antique Passage
Antiquities collected in the 18th and 19th centuries by the various Earls of Carlisle are on display here. The plethora of mythical figures and gods reflects contemporary interest in Classical civilizations.

STAR SIGHTS
* ★ Great Hall
* ★ Long Gallery

Museum Room
Furniture here includes Regency chairs, a bronze collection and this 17th-century cabinet.

Eden Camp ㉓

Malton, North Yorkshire. *Tel 01653 697777.* 🚆 *Malton then taxi.* ⭘ *daily.* 📷 🖼 ♿ 🖥 *www.* edencamp.co.uk

This is an unusual, award-winning theme museum which pays tribute to the British people during World War II. Italian and German prisoners of war were kept at Eden Camp between 1939 and 1948. Today, some original huts built by Italian prisoners in 1942 are used as a museum, with period tableaux and a soundtrack. Each hut adopts a theme to take the visitor through civilian life in war-time, from Chamberlain's radio announcement of the outbreak of hostilities to the coming of peace. Visitors, including schoolchildren and nostalgic veterans, can see the Doodle-bug V-1 bomb which crashed outside the Officers' Mess, take tea in the canteen or experience a night in the Blitz. A tour can last for several hours.

British and American flags by the sign for Eden Camp

Wharram Percy ㉔

(EH) North Yorkshire. Tel 0870 333 1181. 🛈 *01653 600 048.* 🚆 *Malton, then taxi.* ⭘ *daily.* *www.* english-heritage.org.uk

This is one of England's most important deserted medieval village sites. Excavations have unearthed evidence of a 30-household community, with two manors, and the remains of a medieval church. There is also a millpond which has beautiful wild flowers in late spring. Wharram Percy is set in a pretty valley, sign-posted off the B1248 from Burdale, in the heart of the Wolds. It is about 20 minutes' walk from the car park and makes an ideal picnic stop.

Alabaster carving on the chimney-piece at Burton Agnes

Burton Agnes ㉕

On A614, nr Driffield, East Riding. *Tel 01262 490324.* 🚆 *Driffield, then bus.* ⭘ *Apr–Oct: daily.* 🖼 ♿ *limited.* 🖥 📷 *www.* burtonagnes.com

Of all the grand houses in this area, Burton Agnes Hall is a firm favourite. This is partly because the attractive, red-brick Elizabethan mansion has such a homely atmosphere. One of the first portraits you see in the Small Hall is of Anne Griffith, whose father, Sir Henry, built the house. There is a monument to him in the local church.

Burton Agnes has remained in the hands of the original family and has changed little since it was built, between 1598 and 1610. You enter it by the turreted gatehouse, and the entrance hall has a fine Elizabethan alabaster chimney piece. The massive oak staircase is an impressive example of Elizabethan woodcarving.

In the library is a collection of Impressionist and Post-Impressionist art, pleasantly out of character with the rest of the

house, including works by André Derain, Renoir and Augustus John. The extensive grounds include a purpose-built play area for children.

Bempton Cliffs and Flamborough Head ㉖

East Riding. 🚆 *Bempton.* 📷 *Bridlington.* 🛈 *Bempton Cliffs Visitor Centre (01262 851179).* *www.* rspb.org.uk

Bempton, which consists of 5 miles (8 km) of steep chalk cliffs between Speeton and Flamborough Head, is the largest seabird-breeding colony in England, and is famous for its puffins. The ledges and fissures provide ideal nest-sites for more

Nesting gannet on the chalk cliffs at Bempton

than 100,000 pairs of birds. Today, eight different species, including skinny black shags and kittiwakes, thrive on the Grade 1 listed *(see p671)* Bempton cliffs. Bempton is the only mainland site for goose-sized gannets, well known for their dramatic fishing techniques. May, June and July are the best bird-watching months.

The spectacular cliffs are best seen from the north side of the Flamborough Head peninsula.

Beverley 27

East Riding of Yorkshire. 🚶 30,000. 🚉 34 Butcher Row (01482 391672). 🅿 Sat. **www**.realyorkshire.co.uk

The history of Beverley dates back to the 8th century, when Old Beverley served as a retreat for John, later Bishop of York, who was canonized for his healing powers. Over the centuries Beverley grew as a medieval sanctuary town. Like York, it is an attractive combination of both medieval and Georgian buildings.

The inspiration for Lewis Carroll's White Rabbit, St Mary's Church

The best way to enter Beverley is through the last of five medieval town gates, the castellated North Bar (rebuilt 1409–10). The bars were constructed so that market goods had to pass through them and a toll (levy) paid.

The skyline is dominated by the twin towers of the magnificent **Beverley Minster**. This was co-founded in 937 by Athelstan, King of Wessex, in place of the church that John of Beverley had chosen as his final resting place in 721. The decorated nave is the earliest surviving building work which dates back to the early 1300s. It is particularly famous for its 16th-century choir stalls and 68 misericords *(see p341)*.

The minster contains many early detailed stone carvings, including a set of four from about 1308 that illustrate figures with ailments such as toothache and lumbago. On the north side of the altar is the richly carved 14th-century Gothic Percy tomb, thought to be that of Lady Idoine Percy. Also on the north side is the Fridstol, or Peace Chair, said to date from 924-39, the time of Athelstan. Anyone who sat on it would be granted 30 days' sanctuary. Within the North Bar, **St Mary's Church** has a 13th-century chancel and houses Britain's largest number of medieval stone

Minstrel Pillar in St Mary's Church

carvings of musical instruments. The brightly painted 16th-century Minstrel Pillar is particularly notable. Painted on the panelled chancel ceiling are portraits of monarchs after 1445. On the richly sculpted doorway of St Michael's Chapel is the grinning pilgrim rabbit said to have inspired Lewis Carroll's White Rabbit in *Alice in Wonderland*.

There is a great day out to be had at **Beverley Races**, with various theme days throughout the season and excellent food and drink.

🛈 **Beverley Minster**
Minster Yard. **Tel** 01482 868 540.
☐ daily. 🅰 🅱 🅾 🅿 🏛 www.
beverleyminster.org.uk

Beverley Minster, one of Europe's finest examples of Gothic architecture

Burton Constable ㉘

Nr Hull, East Yorkshire. *Tel 01964 562400.* 🚆 *Hull then taxi.* ⬜ *Easter–Oct: Sat–Thu.* 📷 ♿ 📹 🖥 🏠 www.burtonconstable.com

The Constable family have been leading landowners since the 13th century, and have lived at Burton Constable Hall since work began on it in 1570. It is an Elizabethan house, altered in the 18th century by Thomas Lightholer, Thomas Atkinson and James Wyatt. Today, its 30 rooms include Georgian and Victorian interiors. It has a fine collection of Chippendale furniture and family portraits dating from the 16th century. Most of the collections of prints, textiles and drawings belong to Leeds City Art Galleries. The family still lives in the south wing.

Painting of Burton Constable (c.1690) by an anonymous artist

The Princes' Dock in Kingston upon Hull's restored docks area

Kingston upon Hull ㉙

Kingston upon Hull. 🏛 263,000. 🚆 🚌 ⛴ 🚶 *Paragon St. (01482 223559).* 🛒 *Mon–Sat.* www.visithullandeastyorkshire.com

There is a lot more to Hull than the heritage of a thriving fishing industry. The restored town centre docks are attractive, and Hull's Old Town, laid out in medieval times, is all cobbled, winding streets and quaintly askew red-brick houses. You can follow the "Seven Seas" Fish Trail, a path of inlaid metal fishes on the city's pavements that illustrates the many different varieties that have been landed in Hull, from anchovy to shark.

In Victoria Square is the **Maritime Museum**. Built in 1871 as the offices of the Hull Dock Company, it traces the city's maritime history. Among its exhibits are an ornate whale-bone and vertebrae bench and a display of complicated rope knots such as the Eye Splice and the Midshipman's Hitch.

An imposing Elizabethan building, **Hands on History**, explores Hull's story through a collection of some of its families' artifacts.

In the heart of the Old Town, the **William Wilberforce House** is one of the surviving examples of the High Street's brick merchants' dwellings. Its first-floor oak-panelled rooms date from the 17th century. As well as examining the transatlantic slave trade, and contemporary forms of slavery, there are exhibitions on West African culture and the Wilberforce family.

Nearby is the **Streetlife Museum of Transport**, Hull's most popular and noisiest museum, loved by children. It features Britain's oldest tramcar. At the mouth of the River Hull, **The Deep** is the world's only "submarium", in a stunning building and dramatic setting. With lots of exciting sea life and state-of-the-art technology, it is ideal for families.

🏛 **Maritime Museum**
Queen Victoria Sq *Tel 01482 300300.* ⬜ *daily (Sun: pm).* ♿🖥 www.hullcc.gov.uk/museums

🏛 **Hands on History**
South Churchside. *Tel 01482 300300.* ⬜ *daily (Sun: pm).*⬤ *1 Jan, Good Fri, 24–28 Dec.* 🏠 ♿

WILLIAM WILBERFORCE (1758–1833)

William Wilberforce, born in Hull to a merchant family, was a natural orator. After studying Classics at Cambridge, he entered politics and in 1784 gave one of his first public addresses in York. The audience was captivated, and Wilberforce realized the potential of his powers of persuasion. From 1785 onwards, adopted by the Pitt government as spokesman for the abolition of slavery, he conducted a determined and conscientious campaign. But his speeches won him enemies, and in 1792, threats from a slave-importer meant that he needed a constant armed guard. In 1807 his bill to abolish the lucrative slave trade became law.

A 19th-century engraving of Wilberforce by J Jenkins

🏛 **William Wilberforce House**
High St, Hull. Tel 01482 300300.
⬜ daily (Sun: pm). 🔲 🚻 limited.

🏛 **Streetlife Museum
of Transport**
High St, Hull. Tel 01482 300300.
⬜ Mon–Sat, Sun pm. 🚻 🔲

🚾 **The Deep**
Hull (via Citadel Way). Tel 01482 381
000. ⬜ daily. ⬤ 24, 25 Dec. 🚻 🖼
🔲 📷 🅿 www.thedeep.co.uk

Holderness and Spurn Head ㉚

East Riding of Yorkshire. 🚉 Hull
(Paragon St) then bus. 🛈 120
Newbegin, Hornsea (01964 536404).

This curious flat area east of
Hull, with straight roads and
delicately waving fields of oats
and barley, in many ways
resembles Holland, except that
its windmills are mostly disused. Beaches stretch for 30
miles (46 km) along the coastline. The main resort towns
are **Withernsea** and **Hornsea**.

The Holderness landscape
only exists because of erosion
higher up the coast. The sea
continues to wash down tiny
bits of rock which accumulate.
Around 1560, this began to
form a sandbank, and by 1669
it had became large enough
to be colonized as Sonke
Sand. The last bits of silting
mud and debris joined the
island to the mainland as
recently as the 1830s. Today,
you can drive through the
eerie, lush wilderness of Sunk
Island on the way east to
Spurn Head. This is located at
the tip of the Spurn Peninsula,
a 3.5 mile (6 km) spit of land
that has also built up as the
result of coastal erosion
elsewhere. Flora, fauna and
birdlife have been protected
here by the Yorkshire
Wildlife Trust since 1960.
Walking here gives the eerie
feeling that the land could be
eroded from under your feet
at any time. A surprise
discovery at the end of Spurn
Head is a tiny community of
pilots and lifeboat crew,
constantly on call to guide
ships into the Humber estuary,
or help cope with disasters.

**Fishing boat at Grimsby's
National Fishing Heritage Centre**

Grimsby ㉛

NE Lincs. 🏘 92,000. 🚉 🔲 🛈
Cleethorpes Library, Alexandra Road,
Cleethorpes (01472 323111). **www.**
nelincs.gov.uk

Perched at the mouth of the
River Humber, legend claims
Grimsby was founded in the
9th century by a Danish
fisherman by the name of
Grim. It rose to prominence in
the 19th century as one of the
world's largest fishing ports.
Its first dock was opened in
1800 and, with the arrival of
the railways, the town secured
the means of transporting its
catch all over the country.
Even though the traditional
fishing industry had declined
by the 1970s, dock area
redevelopment has ensured
that Grimsby's unique heritage
is retained.

This is best demonstrated by
the award-winning **National
Fishing Heritage Centre**, a
museum that recreates the
industry in its 1950s heyday,
capturing the atmosphere of
the period. Visitors sign on as
crew members on a trawler
and, by means of vivid interactive displays, travel from
the back streets of Grimsby to
the Arctic fishing grounds. On
the way, they can experience
the roll of the ship, the smell
of the fish and the heat of the
engine. The tour ends with a
look at the restored 1950s
trawler, the *Ross Tiger*.

Other attractions in Grimsby
include a restored Victorian
shopping street called Abbey-
gate, a market and a wide
selection of restaurants. Nearby
seaside resorts of Cleethorpes,
Mablethorpe and Skegness
offer miles of golden sands.

🏛 **National Fishing
Heritage Centre**
Heritage Sq, Alexandra Dock. Tel
01472 323345. ⬜ Tue–Sun. ⬤ 1
Jan, 25–26 Dec. 🖼 🚻 🔲 📷 🔲

Isolated lighthouse at Spurn Head, at the tip of Spurn Peninsula

Street-by-Street: York ❷

The city of York has retained so much of its medieval structure that walking into its centre is like entering a living museum. Many of the ancient timbered houses, perched on narrow, winding streets, such as the Shambles, are protected by a conservation order. Much of the centre is pedestrianised and there are always student bikes bouncing over cobbled streets. Its strategic position led to its development as a railway centre in the 19th century.

Monk Bar coat of arms

Stonegate
The medieval red devil is a feature of this street, built over a Roman road.

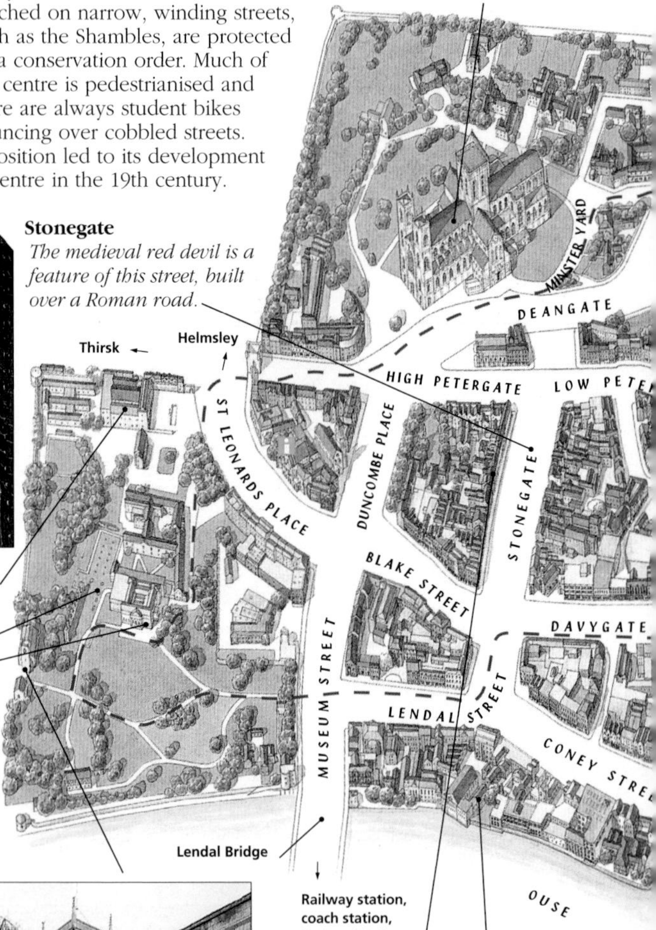

★ **York Minster**
England's largest me[di]eval church was beg[un] in 1220 (see pp406–[7])

← Thirsk   Helmsley

DEANGATE

HIGH PETERGATE   LOW PETE[R]

ST LEONARDS PLACE

DUNCOMBE PLACE

STONEGATE

BLAKE STREET

DAVYGATE

MUSEUM STREET

LENDAL STREET

CONEY STREE[T]

York Art Gallery

St Mary's Abbey

Yorkshire Museum is home to some of the most fascinating archeology in the country.

Lendal Bridge

↓
Railway station, coach station, National Railway Museum, and Leeds

OUSE

Ye Old Starre Inne is one of the oldest pubs in York.

St Olave's Church
The 11th-century church, next to the gate-house of St Mary's Abbey (see p350), was founded by the Earl of Northumbria in memory of St Olaf, King of Norway. To the left is the Chapel of St Mary on the Walls.

Guildhall
This two-headed medieval roof boss is on the 15th-century Guildhall, situated beside the River Ouse and restored after bomb damage during World War II.

WHIP·MA·WHOP·MA·GATE

Whip-ma-whop-ma-gate
York's tiniest street has the city's longest name, which dates from Saxon times and means "neither one thing nor the other".

VISITORS' CHECKLIST

York. 202,500. Leeds Bradford, 32 miles (50 km) NW. Station Rd. Station Rd. 1 Museum St (01904 550099). daily. Jorvik Festival: Feb; Early Music Festival: Jul. (Association of Voluntary Guides, from Exhibition Sq): Apr–Oct: 10:15am & 2:15pm daily (Jun–Aug: also 6:45pm); Nov–Mar: 10:15am daily, 1:15pm Fri–Sun. www.visityork.org

★ Jorvik
The many artifacts on show here illustrate the time when York was a strategic Viking town. The street names ending in "gate" come from the Danish word gata, *meaning "street" or "way".*

Merchant Adventurer's Hall, built for a guild of merchant adventurers in the 14th century, is now a visitor attraction.

★ York Castle Museum
Converted from two prisons, this museum (see p408) features print and blacksmith work-shops, and the cell formerly used by highwayman Dick Turpin (1706–39).

Clifford's Tower

Holy Trinity Church

King's Square

COLLIERGATE
ST SAVIOURGATE
THE STONEBOW
THE SHAMBLES
FOSSGATE
PAVEMENT
IAMENT STREET
PICCADILLY
IERGATE
CASTLEGATE
OUSEGATE
CLIFFORD STREET
TOWER STREET
FOSS

Hull →

Fairfax House

St Mary's Church

0 meters 100
0 yards 100

KEY
- - - Suggested route

STAR SIGHTS
★ York Minster
★ Jorvik
★ York Castle Museum

York Minster

The largest Gothic cathedral north of the Alps, and seat of the Archbishop of York, York Minster is 158 m (519 ft) long and 76 m (249 ft) wide across the transepts. It is also home to the largest collection of medieval stained glass in Britain (see p409). The word "minster" refers to a missionary teaching church in Anglo-Saxon times. The first minster began as a wooden chapel used to baptize King Edwin of Northumbria in 627. There have been several cathedrals on or near the site, including an 11th-century Norman structure. The present minster was begun in 1220 and completed 250 years later. In 1984, fire damage led to a £2.25 million restoration programme.

Central sunflower in rose window

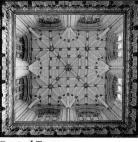

Central Tower
This lantern tower was reconstructed in 1420–65 (after partial collapse in 1407) from a design by the master stonemason William Colchester.

Great East Window (p409)

The Choir has a vaulted entrance with a 15th-century boss of the Assumption of the Virgin.

South transept entrance

The 16th-century rose window

★ **Choir Screen**
Sited between the choir and the nave, this 15th-century stone screen depicts kings of England from William I to Henry VI, and has a canopy of angels.

★ **Chapter House**
A Latin inscription near the entrance of the wooden-vaulted Chapter House (1260–85) reads: "As the rose is the flower of flowers, so this is the house of houses".

The Nave, begun i 1291, was severel damaged by fire 1840. Rebuildin costs were heav but it was re-opene with a new peal bells in 184

Timbered interior of the Merchant Adventurers' Hall

VISITORS' CHECKLIST

Deangate, York. **Tel** 01904 557216. ☐ Mon–Sat: 9am–5pm (from 9:30am Nov–Mar); Sun: noon–3:45pm. Opening times may change subject to major services. ● Good Fri, Easter Sun, 24 & 25 Dec. 🎫 to Minster, Undercroft & the Tower. ✝ Mon–Sat: 7:30am, 7:45am, 12:30pm (also at noon Sat), 5:15pm (evensong); Sun: 8am, 10am, 11:30am, 4pm. ♿ main floors. 📷 🍴 🚻
www.yorkminster.org

The western towers, with their 15th-century decorative panelling and elaborate pinnacles, contrast with the simpler design of the north transept. The southwest tower is the minster belfry.

Great West Door

West Window

STAR SIGHTS

★ Chapter House

★ Choir Screen

🚪 Monk Bar

This is one of York's finest original medieval gates, situated at the end of Goodramgate. It is vaulted on three floors, and the portcullis still works. In the Middle Ages, the rooms above it were rented out, and it was a prison in the 16th century. Its decorative details include men holding stones ready to drop on intruders.

🏛 York Art Gallery

Exhibition Sq. **Tel** 01904 687687. ☐ 10am–5pm daily. ● 1 Jan, 25 & 26 Dec. 🎫 ♿ 🛍 🚻
www.yorkartgallery.org.uk
This Italianate building of 1879 holds a wide-ranging collection of paintings from western Europe dating from the early 14th century. The Gallery of Pots, on the first floor, has rotating exhibitions showcasing the gallery's large collection of British and foreign studio pottery. Work by Bernard Leach, William Staite Murray and Shoji Hamada is on display alongside details of the potters themselves and those who collected their work.

Preparing for a Fancy Dress Ball (1833) by William Etty, York Art Gallery

🚪 Clifford's Tower

(EH) Clifford's St. **Tel** 01904 646940. ☐ Apr–Oct: daily; Nov–Mar: Sat & Sun. ● 1 Jan, 24–26 & 31 Dec. 🚻 🎫 **www.english-heritage.org.uk**
Sited on top of a mound that William the Conqueror built for his original wooden castle, destroyed by fire during anti-Jewish riots in 1190, Clifford's Tower dates from the 13th century. Built by Henry III, it was named after the de Clifford family, who were constables of the castle.

🏛 DIG – An Archaeological Adventure

St Saviourgate. **Tel** 01904 615505. ☐ daily (best to book in advance). ● 24 & 25 Dec. 🎫 ♿ 🛍 🚻

Housed in a restored medieval church, this centre invites visitors to become archaeological detectives and discover how archaeologists have pieced together clues from the past to unravel the history of the Viking age in York.

🚪 Merchant Adventurers' Hall

Fossgate. **Tel** 01904 654818. ☐ Mar–Oct: daily; Nov–Feb: Mon–Sat. ● 24 Dec–3 Jan. 🎫 ♿ 🛍
www.theyorkcompany.co.uk

Built by a guild of Yorkshire merchants in 1357, this is one of the largest timber-framed medieval buildings in Britain. The Great Hall is probably the best example of its kind in Europe. Among its paintings is an unattributed 17th-century copy of Van Dyck's portrait of Charles I's queen, Henrietta Maria. Below the Great Hall is the hospital, which was used by the guild until 1900, and a private chapel.

Exploring York

The appeal of York is its many layers of history. A medieval city constructed on top of a Roman one, it was first built in AD 71, when it became capital of the northern province and was known as Eboracum. It was here that Constantine the Great was made emperor in 306, and reorganized Britain into four provinces. A hundred years later, the Roman army had withdrawn. Eboracum was renamed Eoforwic, under the Saxons, and then became a Christian stronghold. The Danish street names are the reminder that it was a Viking centre from 867, and one of Europe's chief trading bases. Between 1100 and 1500 it was England's second city. The glory of York is the minster *(see pp406–7)*. The city also boasts 18 medieval churches, 3 mile long (4.8 km) medieval city walls, elegant Jacobean and Georgian architecture and fine museums.

The Middleham Jewel, Yorkshire Museum

Grand staircase and fine plaster ceiling at Fairfax House

🏛 York Castle Museum

The Eye of York. **Tel** 01904 687687.
⬜ daily. ⬤ 1 Jan, 25 & 26 Dec. 📷
♿ ground floor only. 🔲 🛈
www.yorkcastlemuseum.org.uk
Housed in two 18th-century prisons, the museum has a fine folk collection, started by Dr John Kirk of the market town of Pickering. Opened in 1938, its period displays include a Jacobean dining room, a moorland cottage, and a 1950s front room. It also contains an exhibition on the traditions of birth, marriages and death in Britain from 1700 to 2000.

The most famous exhibits include the reconstructed Victorian street of Kirkgate, complete with shopfronts, and the Anglo Saxon York Helmet, discovered in 1982.

🛈 York Minster

See pp406–7.

🏛 Jorvik

Coppergate. **Tel** 01904 615505.
⬜ daily (pre-booking advised).
⬤ 24–26 Dec. 📷 ♿ ring first. 🛈
www.jorvik-viking-centre.co.uk
This centre is built on the site of the original Viking settlement which archaeologists uncovered at Coppergate. Using new technology, a dynamic vision of 10th-century York is recreated, with smells bringing the Viking world to life. At the centre's sister attraction, DIG, visitors can take part in an archaeological excavation.

🏛 Yorkshire Museum and St Mary's Abbey

Museum Gardens. **Tel** 01904 687687. ⬜ daily. 📷 ♿ 🛈
Yorkshire Museum made the news when it purchased the 15th-century Middleham Jewel for £2.5 million, one of the finest pieces of English Gothic jewellery found this century. Other exhibits include 2nd-century Roman mosaics and an Anglo-Saxon silver gilt bowl.

St Mary's Abbey *(see p350)* hosts the medieval York Mystery Plays occasionally.

🏠 Fairfax House

Castlegate. **Tel** 01904 655543.
⬜ mid-Feb–Dec: daily (Sun: pm only; Mon: tours only). ⬤ 24–26 Dec, Jan, early Feb. 📷 📷 ♿ limited. 🛈
www.fairfaxhouse.co.uk
From 1755 to 1762 Viscount Fairfax built this fine Georgian town house for his daughter, Anne. The house was designed by John Carr *(see p28),* and restored in the 1980s. Between 1920 and 1965 it was a cinema and dancehall. Today, visitors can see the bedroom of Anne Fairfax (1725–93), and a fine collection of 18th-century furniture, porcelain and clocks.

🏛 National Railway Museum

Leeman Rd. **Tel** 0844 815 3139.
⬜ daily. ⬤ 24–26 Dec. ♿ 🔲 🛈
www.nrm.org.uk
In what is the world's largest railway museum, nearly 200 years of history are explored using a variety of visual aids. Visitors can try wheel-tapping and shunting in the interactive gallery, or find out what made Stephenson's *Rocket* so successful. Exhibits include uniforms, rolling stock from 1797 onward and Queen Victoria's Royal Train carriage, as well as the very latest rail innovations.

Reproduction of Stephenson's Rocket (right) and 1830s first-class carriage in York's National Railway Museum

The Stained Glass of York Minster

York Minster houses the largest collection of medieval stained glass in Britain, some of it dating from the late 12th century. The glass was generally coloured during production, using metal oxides to produce the desired colour, then worked on by craftsmen on site. When a design had been produced, the glass was first cut, then trimmed to shape. Details

Window detail

were painted on, using iron oxide-based paint which was fused to the glass by firing in a kiln. Individual pieces were then leaded together to form the finished window.

Part of the fascination of the minster glass is its variety of subject matter. Some windows were paid for by lay donors who specified a particular subject, others reflect ecclesiastical patronage.

Miracle of St Nicholas (late 12th century) was put in the nave over 100 years after it was made. It shows a Jew's conversion.

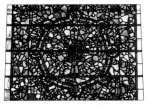

The Five Sisters in the north transept are the largest examples of grisaille glass in Britain. This popular 13th-century technique involved creating fine patterning on clear glass and decorating it with black enamel.

St John the Evangelist, in part of the Great West Window (c.1338), is holding an eagle, itself an example of stickwork, where paint is scraped off to reveal clear glass.

Noah's Ark with its distinct boat-like shape is easily identified in the Great East Window.

The Great East Window (1405–8), the size of a tennis court, is the largest area of medieval painted glass in the world. The Dean and Chapter paid master glazier John Thornton four shillings a week for this celebration of the Creation.

Edward III is a fine example of the 14th-century "soft" style of painting, achieved by stippling the paint.

Walter Skirlaw, whose bishopric was revoked in favour of Richard Scrope, donated this window on its completion in 1408.

Harewood House ⑬

Leeds. *Tel* 0113 2181010. ☷ *Leeds then bus.* ◯ *Apr–31 Oct: daily.* 🅿 ♿ 🎥 *by arrangement.* ▣ 📷
www.harewood.org

Designed by John Carr in 1759, Harewood House is the Yorkshire home of the Earl and Countess of Harewood.

The grand Palladian exterior is impressive, with interiors created by Robert Adam and an unrivalled collection of 18th-century furniture made specifically for Harewood by Yorkshire-born Thomas Chippendale (1711–79). There are paintings by Italian and English artists, including Reynolds and Gainsborough, and two watercolour rooms. The grounds by "Capability" Brown *(see p26)* include the **Harewood Bird Garden**, which has exotic species and a breeding programme of certain endangered varieties.

Bali starling, one of Harewood's rare birds

Leeds ⑭

Leeds. 👥 750,000. ✈ ☷ 🚌
🈯 *Leeds City Station (0113 2425242).* 🛍 *Mon–Sat.*
www.leedsliveitloveit.com

The third-largest of Britain's provincial cities, Leeds was at its most prosperous during the Victorian period. The most impressive legacy from this era is a series of ornate, covered shopping arcades. Also of note is the **Town Hall**, designed by Cuthbert Brodrick and opened by Queen Victoria in 1858.

Today, although Leeds is primarily an industrial city, it also offers a thriving cultural scene. Productions at **The Grand** by Opera North, one of Britain's top operatic companies, are of a high quality.

The **Leeds Art Gallery** has impressive collections of British 20th-century art and of Victorian paintings, including works by local artist Atkinson Grimshaw (1836–93). Among the late 19th-century French art are works by Signac, Courbet and Sisley. The Henry Moore Institute, added in 1993, is devoted to the research and display of sculpture of all periods. It comprises a study centre, library, galleries and an archive of material on Moore and other sculptural pioneers.

The **Armley Mills Museum**, in a 19th-century woollen mill, explores the industrial heritage of Leeds. Filled with original equipment, recorded sounds and models in 19th-century workers' clothes, it traces the history of the ready-to-wear industry. The **Leeds City Museum** charts the history of Leeds with ethnographical and archaeological exhibits.

A striking waterfront development by the River Aire has attracted two museums. The **Royal Armouries Museum** is the UK's national museum of arms and armour, home to a vast array of weaponry from around the world. The **Thackray Medical Museum** is an interactive display of medical advances, from a re-created Victorian slum to modern-day medical challenges.

For children, **Tropical World** features crystal pools, a rainforest house, butterflies and tropical fish. There is also a farm and a Rare Breeds

The County Arcade, one of Leeds' restored shopping arcades

centre in the grounds of the Tudor-Jacobean **Temple Newsam House**, which has major art and furniture collections.

🏛 **Leeds Art Gallery**
The Headrow. *Tel* 0113 2478256.
◯ *daily (Sun: pm).* ● *pub hols.*
♿ 📷 ▣

🏛 **Armley Mills Museum**
Canal Rd, Armley. *Tel* 0113 2637 861. ◯ *Tue–Sun (Sun: pm), pub hols.*
● *1 Jan, 25, 26 Dec.* 🎥 ♿ 📷

🏛 **Leeds City Museum**
Millennium Sq. *Tel* 0113 2243732.
◯ *Tue–Sun.* ● *pub hols.* ♿ ▣ 📷

🏛 **Royal Armouries**
Armouries Drive. *Tel* 0113 2201999.
◯ *daily.* ● *24–26 Dec.* ♿ 🍴 📷

🏛 **Thackray Medical Museum**
Beckett St. 🛗 *0113 2444343.* ◯
daily. ● *1 Jan, 24–26, 31 Dec.*
♿ 📷 www.thackraymuseum.org

🍂 **Tropical World**
Canal Gdns, Princes Ave. *Tel* 0113 3957400. ◯ *daily.* ● *25, 26 Dec.*
🎥 ♿ ▣ 📷

🏯 **Temple Newsam House**
Off A63. *Tel* 0113 2645535. ◯ *Tue–Sun.* ● *Jan, 25 & 26 Dec.* 🎥 ▣ 📷

Working loom at the Armley Mills Museum in Leeds

The Other Side (1990–93) by David Hockney at Bradford's 1853 Gallery in Saltaire

Bradford ③⑤

Bradford. 🏘 294,000. ✈ 🚆 ☐
🛈 City Hall, Centenary Square
(01274 433678). 🛍 Mon–Sat.
www.visitbradford.com

In the 16th century, Bradford was a thriving market town, and the opening of its canal in 1774 boosted trade. By 1850, it was the world's capital for worsted (fabric made from closely twisted wool). Many of the city's well-preserved civic and industrial buildings date from this period, such as the Wool Exchange on Market Street. In the 1800s a number of German textile manufacturers settled in what is now called Little Germany. Their houses are characterized by decorative stone carvings that illustrated the wealth and standing of the occupants.

Daguerreotype camera by Giroux (1839)

The **National Media Museum**, founded in 1983, explores the technology and art of these media. There is a television section called TV Heaven, where visitors can ask to watch their favourite programme. They are also encouraged to see themselves read the news on TV. The giant IMAX screen uses the world's largest film format. Film subjects include journeys into space, the ocean and the natural world.

The **Cartwright Hall Art Gallery** displays 19th- and 20th-century British art and collections of contemporary art from South Asia. **Bradford Industrial Museum** is housed in an original spinning mill. As well as seeing and hearing all the mill machinery, you can ride on a horse-drawn tram. Saltaire, a Victorian industrial village (*see p349*), is on the outskirts of the city. Built by Sir Titus Salt for his Salts Mill workers, it was completed in 1873. The **1853 Gallery** has the world's largest collection of works by David Hockney, born in Bradford.

🏛 **National Media Museum**
Pictureville. *Tel* 0870 7010200.
☐ daily (school hols); Tue–Sun (school terms); public holidays. ● 24–26 Dec. 🅿 ♿ 🍴 www.nationalmediamuseum.org.uk

🏛 **Cartwright Hall Art Gallery**
Lister Park. *Tel* 01274 431212.
☐ Tue–Sat. ● Good Fri, 25–26 Dec. 🅿 🍴 ♿

🏛 **Bradford Industrial Museum**
Moorside Mills, Moorside Rd. *Tel* 01274 435900. ☐ Tue–Sat, Sun (pm), public hols. ● Good Fri, 25–26 Dec. ♿ 🅿 www.bradfordmuseums.org

🏛 **1853 Gallery**
Salts Mill, Victoria Rd. *Tel* 01274 531 163. ☐ daily. ● 1 Jan, 25–26 Dec. ♿ 🍴 🖵 🅿 www.saltsmill.org.uk

---

BRADFORD'S ASIAN COMMUNITY

Immigrants from the Indian subcontinent originally came to Bradford in the 1950s to work in the mills, but with the decline of the textile industry many began small businesses. By the mid-1970s there were 1,400 such enterprises in the area. Almost one fifth were in the food sector, born out of simple cafés catering for millworkers whose families were far away. As Indian food became more popular, these restaurants thrived, and today there are over 200 serving the highly spiced dishes of the Indian subcontinent.

Curry in a Bradford restaurant

Haworth Parsonage, home to the Brontë family, now a museum

Haworth 36

Bradford. 5,000. Keighley.
i 2–4 West Lane (01535 642329).
www.visithaworth.com

The setting of Haworth, in bleak Pennine moorland dotted with farmsteads, has changed little since it was home to the Brontë family. The village boomed in the 1840s, when there were more than 1,200 hand-looms in operation, but it is more famous today for the Brontë connection.

You can visit the **Brontë Parsonage Museum**, home from 1820–61 to novelists Charlotte, Emily and Anne, their brother Branwell and their father, the Revd Patrick Brontë. Built in 1778–9, the house remains decorated as it was during the 1850s. Eleven rooms, including the children's study and Charlotte's room, display letters, manuscripts, furniture and personal objects.

The nostalgic Victorian **Keighley and Worth Valley Railway** runs through Haworth. It stops at Oakworth station, where parts of *The Railway Children* were filmed. At the end of the line is the Railway Museum at Oxenhope.

🏛 Brontë Parsonage Museum

Church St. **Tel** *01535 642323*.
◯ daily. ◯ 24–27 Dec; Jan. 🏛 🏛
♿ limited. www.bronte.org.uk

Charlotte Brontë's childhood story book, for her sister, Anne

THE BRONTË SISTERS

Charlotte Brontë (1816–55)

During a harsh, motherless childhood, Charlotte, Emily and Anne retreated into fictional worlds of their own, writing poems and stories. As adults, they had to work as governesses, but still published a poetry collection in 1846. Only two copies were sold, but in the following year Charlotte's *Jane Eyre*, became a bestseller, arousing interest in Emily's *Wuthering Heights* and Anne's *Agnes Grey*. After her siblings' deaths in 1848–9, Charlotte published her last novel, *Villette*, in 1852. She married the Revd Nicholls, her father's curate, in 1854, but died shortly afterwards.

Hebden Bridge 37

Calderdale. 12,500. 🚲 i
Butlers Wharf (01422 843831). 🏠
Thu. www.visitcalderdale.com

Hebden Bridge is a delightful South Pennines former mill town, surrounded by steep hills and former 19th-century mills. The houses seem to defy gravity as they cling to the valley sides. Due to the gradient, one house is made from two bottom floors, and the top two floors form another unit. To separate ownership of these "flying freeholds", an Act of Parliament was devised.

There is a superb view of Hebden Bridge from nearby **Heptonstall**, where the poet Sylvia Plath (1932–63) is buried. The village contains a Wesleyan chapel (1764).

Halifax 38

Calderdale. 88,000. 🚲 🏠
i Piece Hall (01422 368725). 🏠
Thu–Sat. www.visitcalderdale.com

Halifax's history has been influenced by textiles since the Middle Ages, but today's visual reminders date mainly from the 19th century, with stone-built terraced housing and several fine buildings. The wool trade helped to make the Pennines into Britain's industrial backbone.

Until the mid-15th century cloth production was modest, but vital enough to contribute towards the creation of the 13th-century Gibbet Law, which stated that anyone caught stealing cloth could be executed. There is a replica of the gibbet, a forerunner of the guillotine, used for decapitation at the bottom of Gibbet Street. Many of Halifax's 18th- and 19th-century buildings owe their existence to wealthy cloth traders. Sir Charles Barry (1795–1860), architect of the Houses of Parliament, was commissioned by the Crossley family to design the Town Hall. They also paid for the landscaping of the People's Park by the creator of the Crystal Palace, Sir Joseph Paxton (1801–65). Thomas Bradley's

Large Two Forms (1966–9) by Henry Moore at Yorkshire Sculpture Park

18th-century **Piece Hall** was where wool merchants once sold their cloth, trading in one of the 315 "Merchants' Rooms". It has a beautifully restored Italianate courtyard where Halifax's market takes place.

Eureka! is the hands-on National Children's Museum with exhibits such as the Giant Mouth Machine. **Shibden Hall Museum** is a fine period house, parts of which date to the 15th century.

Environs: The nearby village of **Sowerby Bridge** was an important textile centre from the Middle Ages to the 1960s. Today visitors come to enjoy the scenic canals.

🏛 **Eureka!**
Discovery Rd. 📱 *01422 330069.*
🕐 *Tue–Sun (daily in school hols).*
⬤ *24–26 Dec.* 🈲 🛗 🖥 www.
eureka.org.uk

🏛 **Shibden Hall Museum**
Listers Rd. *Tel 01422 352246.*
🕐 *daily (Sun: pm).* ⬤ *24 Dec–2 Jan.* 📷 🈲 🖥

National Coal Mining Museum ❸❾

Wakefield. *Tel 01924 848806.* 🚆 *Wakefield then bus.* 🕐 *daily (last tour 3:15pm – booking advised). Children under 5 not allowed underground.*
⬤ *24–26 Dec, 1 Jan.* 🦽 📷 🖥 🈲
www.ncm.org.uk

Housed in the old Caphouse Colliery, this museum offers the chance to go into a real mine shaft: warm clothing is advised. An underground tour takes you 137 m (450 ft) down,

equipped with a hat and a miner's lamp. Enter narrow seams and see exhibits such as life-size working models. Other displays depict mining from 1820 to the present day.

Yorkshire Sculpture Park ❹⓿

Wakefield. *Tel 01924 832631.*
🚆 *Wakefield then bus.* 🕐 *daily.*
⬤ *24, 25, 29–31 Dec.* 🦽 🖥 🈲
www.ysp.co.uk

This is one of Europe's leading open-air galleries, situated in 200 ha (500 acres) of 18th-century parkland dotted with changing exhibitions of the work of Henry Moore, Anthony Caro, Eduardo Chillida, Barbara Hepworth, Antony Gormley and others. The indoor display spaces include the ambitious visitor centre, which leads on to the stunning Underground Gallery exhibition space.

Magna ❹❶

Rotherham. *Tel 01709 720002.*
🚆 *Rotherham Central or Sheffield then bus (No. 69).* 🕐 *daily.*
⬤ *1 Jan, 24–26 & 31 Dec.*
🈲 🦽 🛗 🖥 🈲
www.visitmagna.co.uk

A former steel works has been imaginatively converted into a huge science adventure centre, with an emphasis on interactive exhibits, noise and spectacle designed to appeal to 4–15-year-olds. In the Air, Fire, Water and Earth Pavilions visitors can get close to a tornado, operate real diggers or discover what it's like to detonate a rock face. There are also multimedia displays on the lives of steelworkers and on how a giant furnace operated, as well as a show that features robots with artificial intelligence that evolve and learn as they hunt each other down.

The Face of Steel display at Magna

NORTHUMBRIA

NORTHUMBERLAND · COUNTY DURHAM

England's northeast extremity is a tapestry of moorland, ruins, castles, cathedrals and huddled villages. With Northumberland National Park and Kielder Water reservoir to the north, a rugged eastern coastline, and the cities of Newcastle and Durham to the south, the area combines a dramatic history with abundant natural beauty.

The empty peaceful hills, elusive wildlife and panoramic vistas of Northumberland National Park belie the area's turbulent past. Warring Scots and English, skirmishing tribes, cattle drovers and whisky smugglers have all left traces on ancient routes through the Cheviot Hills. Slicing through the southern edge of the park is the famous reminder of the Romans' 400-year occupation of Britain, Hadrian's Wall, the northern boundary of their empire.

Conflict between Scots and English continued for 1,000 years after the Romans departed, and even after the 1603 union between the two crowns. A chain of massive crenellated medieval castles punctuates the coastline, while other forts that once defended the northern flank of England along the River Tweed lie mostly in ruins. Seventh-century Northumbria was the cradle of Christianity under St Aidan, but this was sharply countered by Viking violence from 793 onward, as the Scandinavian invaders raided the monasteries. But a reverence for Northumbrian saints is in the local psyche, and St Cuthbert and the Venerable Bede are both buried in Durham Cathedral. The influence of the Industrial Revolution, concentrated around the mouths of the rivers Tyne, Wear and Tees, made Newcastle upon Tyne the north's main centre for coal mining and shipbuilding. Today, the city is famous for its "industrial heritage" attractions and urban regeneration schemes.

Section of Hadrian's Wall, built by the Romans in about 120, looking east from Cawfields

◁ The towers of Durham Cathedral, rising above the River Wear

Exploring Northumbria

Historic sites are plentiful along Northumbria's coast.
South of Berwick-upon-Tweed, a causeway leads to the
ruined priory and castle on Lindisfarne, and there are
major castles at Bamburgh, Alnwick and Warkworth. The
hinterland is a region of wide open spaces, with wilderness
in the Northumberland National Park, and fascinating Roman
remains of Hadrian's Wall at Housesteads and elsewhere.
The glorious city of Durham is dominated by its castle and
cathedral, and Newcastle upon Tyne has a lively nightlife.

SIGHTS AT A GLANCE

Alnwick Castle **5**
Bamburgh **4**
Barnard Castle **17**
Beamish Open Air Museum **13**
Berwick-upon-Tweed **1**
Cheviot Hills **8**
Corbridge **10**
Durham pp428–9 **14**
Farne Islands **3**
Hadrian's Wall pp422–3 **11**
Hexham **9**
Kielder Water **7**
Lindisfarne **2**
Middleton-in-Teesdale **16**
Newcastle upon Tyne **12**
Warkworth Castle **6**

Walks and Tours
North Pennines Tour **15**

SEE ALSO

- *Where to Stay* pp588–90
- *Where to Eat* pp640–42

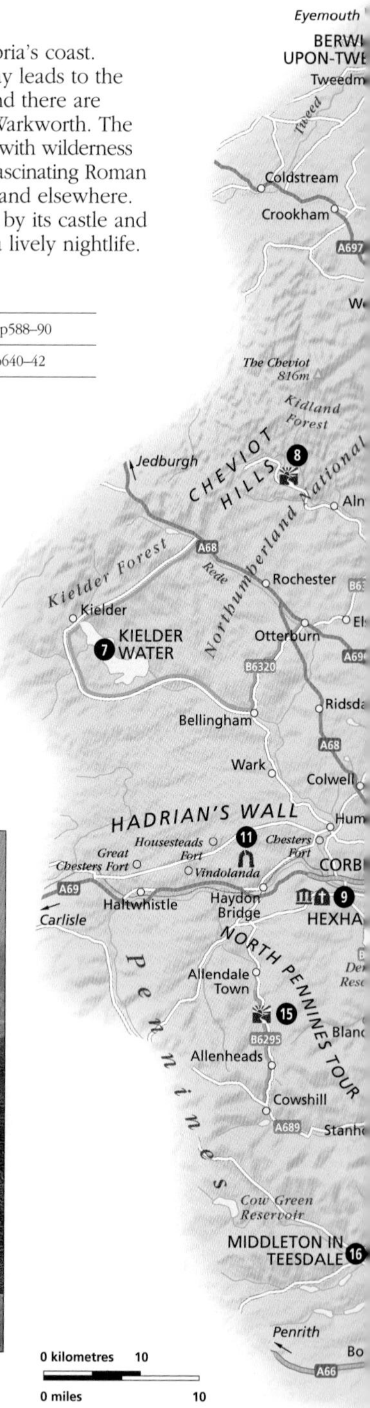

The wilderness of Upper Coquetdale in the sparsely
populated Cheviot Hills

Eyemouth
BERWI
UPON-TWE
Tweedm

Tweed

Coldstream

Crookham

A697

W

The Cheviot
816m

Kidland
Forest

Jedburgh

CHEVIOT HILLS **8**

Aln

Kielder Forest

A68   *Rede*

Rochester   B6

El

Kielder

Northumberland National

Otterburn

KIELDER
7 WATER

B6320

A69

Ridsda

Bellingham

A68

Wark

Colwell

HADRIAN'S WALL

Hum

Housesteads   **11**   Chesters
Great   Fort   Fort
Chesters Fort   *Vindolanda*   CORB

A69

Haltwhistle   Haydon   **9**
    Bridge   HEXHA

Carlisle

NORTH PENNINES TOUR

Allendale   *Der*
Town   *Rese*

15

B6295   Blanc

Allenheads

Cowshill

A689   Stanhe

Cow Green
Reservoir

MIDDLETON IN
TEESDALE **16**

Penrith

Bo

A66

0 kilometres   10

0 miles   10

ARNE ⌂⚓ 2

E ISLANDS 3

4 BAMBURGH ⚓🏛 Seahouses

B1340

Embleton

K CASTLE 5 ⚓🏛 Alnmouth

Shilbottle

WARKWORTH 6 CASTLE ⚓ Amble

Broomhill

Felton

Widdrington

A697 A1068

Ashington

Morpeth

Bedlington Blyth

A189

Cramlington

A19 Whitley Bay

Gosforth Tynemouth

South Shields

12 NEWCASTLE UPON TYNE

Gateshead Boldon

A692

Washington

BEAMISH OPEN AIR MUSEUM 13 🏛 Sunderland

A1(M)

Chester-le-Street

Consett Stanley

Houghton-le-Spring

A691 A690 Hetton-le-Hole

14 DURHAM ⌂⚓🏛 Peterlee

Brandon

Wheatley Hill

Willington Coxhoe A19

Spennymoor Hartlepool

Ferryhill

op Auckland Sedgefield

Shildon Seaton Carew

A688 A68 Newton Aycliffe Redcar

Staindrop Billingham Saltburn-by-the-Sea

RNARD Stockton-on-Tees Middlesbrough Loftus
STLE A1(M) A66

Darlington Whitby

York A171

Northallerton

The rugged coastline of Northumberland, with Bamburgh Castle in the distance

GETTING AROUND

North of Newcastle, the A1068 meets the A1 linking the sights of the Northumbrian coast, and continuing on to Scotland. Two spectacular inland routes, the A696 and the A68, merge near Otterburn to skirt the Northumberland National Park. A mainline railway links Durham, Newcastle and Berwick, but a car is necessary to explore Northumbria comprehensively.

KEY

▬	Motorway
▬	Major road
▬	Secondary road
⋯	Minor road
▬	Scenic route
▬	Main railway
—	Minor railway
△	Summit

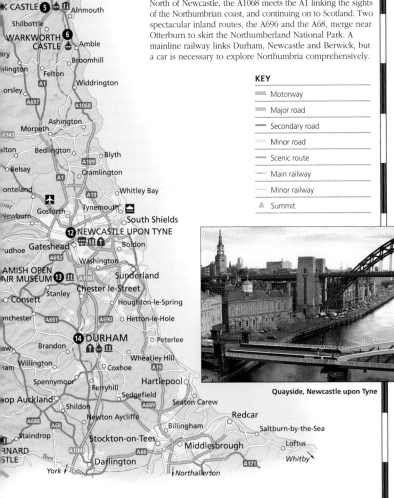

Quayside, Newcastle upon Tyne

View over Berwick-upon-Tweed's three bridges

Berwick-upon-Tweed ❶

Northumberland. 🏛 *13,000.* 🚉
ℹ *106 Mary Gate (01289 301780).*
🛒 *Wed, Sat.*
www.visitnorthumberland.com

Between the 12th and 15th centuries Berwick-upon-Tweed changed hands 14 times in the wars between the Scots and English. Its position, at the mouth of the river which divides the two nations, made the town strategically vital.

The English finally gained permanent control in 1482 and maintained Berwick as a fortified garrison. Ramparts dating from 1555, 1.5 miles (2.5 km) long and 23 ft (7 m) thick, offer superb views over the Tweed. Within the 18th-century barracks are the **King's Own Scottish Borderers Regimental Museum**, an **art gallery**, and **By Beat of Drum**, charting the history of British infantrymen.

🏛 King's Own Scottish Borderers Regimental Museum
The Barracks. *Tel 01289 307426.*
🔲 *Easter–Sep: Mon–Fri.*
⚫ *public hols.* 🖼 📷
www.kosb.co.uk/museum

Lindisfarne ❷

Northumberland. 🚉 *Berwick-upon-Tweed then bus.* ℹ *106 Mary Gate, Berwick-upon-Tweed (01289 301780).* **www**.lindisfarne.org.uk

Twice daily a long, narrow neck of land sinks under the North Sea tide for five hours, separating Lindisfarne, or Holy Island, from the coast. At low tide, visitors stream over the causeway to the island made famous by St Aidan, St Cuthbert and the Lindisfarne gospels. Nothing remains of the Celtic monks' monastery, finally abandoned in 875 after successive Viking attacks, but the magnificent arches of the 11th-century **Lindisfarne Priory** are still visible.

After 1540, stones from the priory were used to build **Lindisfarne Castle**, which was restored and made into a private home by Sir Edwin Lutyens *(see p29)* in 1903. It includes a walled garden by Gertrude Jekyll *(see p27)*.

⛪ Lindisfarne Castle
(NT) Holy Island. *Tel 01289 389244.* **Castle** 🔲 *Mar–Oct & Feb half-term: Tue–Sun.* **Gardens** 🔲 *Tue–Sun all year. Opening times depend on tide – phone to check.* 🖼

Farne Islands ❸

(NT) Northumberland. 🛥 *from Sea-houses (Apr–Oct).* ℹ *106 Mary Gate, Berwick-upon-Tweed (01289 301780); Seahouses (01655 301777).*

There are between 15 and 28 Farne Islands off the coast from Bamburgh, some of them periodically covered by sea. Nature wardens and light-house keepers share them with seals, puffins and other seabirds. Boat tours depart from **Seahouses** harbour and can land on Staple and Inner Farne, site of St Cuthbert's 14th-century chapel, or Long-stone, where Grace Darling's lighthouse is located.

Lindisfarne Castle (1540), the main landmark on the island of Lindisfarne

Celtic Christianity

St Cuthbert on a sea voyage

The Irish monk St Aidan arrived in Northumbria in 635 from the island of Iona, off western Scotland, to evangelize the north of England. He founded the monastery on the island of Lindisfarne, and it became one of the most important centres for Christianity in England. This and other monastic communities thrived in Northumbria, becoming rich in scholarship, although the monks lived simply. It also emerged as a place of pilgrimage after miracles were reported at the shrine of St Cuthbert, Lindisfarne's most famous bishop. But the monks' pacifism made them defenceless against 9th-century Viking raids.

St Aidan's Monastery *was added to over the centuries to become Lindisfarne Priory. This 8th-century relic with interlaced animal decorations is from a cross at the site.*

The Venerable Bede *(673–735), the most brilliant early medieval scholar, was a monk at the monastery of St Paul in Jarrow. He wrote* The Ecclesiastical History of the English People *in 731.*

St Aidan *(600–651), an Irish missionary, founded a monastery at Lindisfarne and became Bishop of Northumbria in 635. This 1960 sculpture of him, by Kathleen Parbury, is in Lindisfarne Priory grounds.*

St Cuthbert *(635–87) was the monk and miracle worker most revered of all. He lived as a hermit on Inner Farne (a chapel was built there in his memory) and later became Bishop of Lindisfarne.*

Lindisfarne Priory *was built by Benedictines in the 11th century, on the site of St Aidan's earlier monastery.*

THE LINDISFARNE GOSPELS

Held in the British Library, this book of richly illustrated portrayals of Gospel stories is one of the masterpieces of the "Northumbrian Renaissance" which left a permanent mark on Christian art and history-writing. The work was carried out by monks at Lindisfarne under the direction of Bishop Eadfrith, around 700. Monks managed to save the book and took it with them when they fled from Lindisfarne in 875 after suffering Viking raids. Other treasures were plundered.

Elaborately decorated initial to the *Gospel of St Matthew* (c.725)

Illustration of Grace Darling from the 1881 edition of *Sunday at Home*

Bamburgh ➍

Northumberland. 🏘 *1,100*. 🚆 *Berwick*. 🛈 *Seahouses (01665 301777; Apr–Oct); 106 Mary Gate, Berwick-upon-Tweed (01289 301780)*.

Due to Northumbria's history of hostility against the Scots, there are more strongholds and castles here than in any other part of England. Most were built from the 11th to the 15th centuries by local warlords, as was Bamburgh's red sandstone **castle**. Its coastal position had been fortified since prehistoric times, but the first major stronghold was built in 550 by a Saxon chieftain, Ida the Flamebearer.

In its heyday between 1095 and 1464, Bamburgh was the royal castle that was used by the Northumbrian kings for coronations. By the end of the Middle Ages it had fallen into obscurity, then in 1894 it was bought by Newcastle arms tycoon Lord Armstrong, who restored it. Works of art are exhibited in the cavernous Great Hall, and there are suits of armour and medieval artifacts in the basement.

Bamburgh's other main attraction is the tiny **Grace Darling Museum** which celebrates the bravery of the 23-year-old, who, in 1838, rowed through tempestuous seas with her father, the keeper of the Longstone lighthouse, to rescue nine people from the wrecked *Forfarshire* steamboat.

Carrara marble fireplace (1840) at Alnwick Castle

🏰 **Bamburgh Castle**
Bamburgh. *Tel 01668 214515*.
🔲 *mid-Feb–Oct: daily; Nov–mid-Feb: Sat & Sun.* 🈯 🔊 🖥 🔲
www.bamburghcastle.com

🏛 **Grace Darling Museum**
Radcliffe Rd. *Tel 01688 214910*.
🔲 *daily (closed Mon in winter)*. 🔊

Alnwick Castle ➎

Alnwick, Northumberland. *Tel 01665 510777*. 🚆 *Alnmouth*. 🔲 *April–Oct: daily.* 🈯 🔊 *limited.* 🖥 🔲 *www*.alnwickcastle.com

Dominating the pretty market town of Alnwick on the River Aln, this castle doubled as Hogwarts in the first two Harry Potter movies. It is the main seat of the Duke of Northumberland, whose family, the Percys, have lived here since 1309. This border stronghold has survived many battles, but now sits peacefully amongst landscape designed by "Capability" Brown. The stern medieval exterior belies the treasure house within, furnished in palatial Renaissance style with a collection of Meissen china and paintings by Titian, Van Dyck and Canaletto. The Postern Tower contains early British and Roman relics. The **Regimental Museum of Royal Northumberland Fusiliers** is in the Abbot's Tower. Other attractions are the Percy State coach and the dungeon.

Warkworth Castle ➏

(EH) Warkworth, nr Amble. *Tel 01665 711423*. 🚆 🚌 *518 from Newcastle*. 🔲 *Apr–Oct: daily; Nov–mid-Feb: Sat & Sun.* 🔲 *1 Jan, 24–26 Dec.* 🔲 🈯 🔊 *limited*.

Warkworth Castle sits on a green hill overlooking the River Coquet. It was one of the Percy family homes. Shakespeare's *Henry IV* features the castle in the scenes between the Earl of Northumberland and his son, Harry Hotspur. Much of the present-day castle remains date from the 14th century. The unusual turreted, cross-shaped keep is a central feature of the castle tour.

Warkworth Castle reflected in the River Coquet

Kielder Water ➐

Northumberland. 🛈 *Tower Knowe Visitor Centre, Falstone (0845 1550236)*. 🔲 *daily*. 🔊 *www*.visitkielder.com

One of the top attractions of Northumberland, Kielder Water lies close to the Scottish border, surrounded by spectacular scenery. With a perimeter of 27 miles (44 km), it is Britain's largest man-made lake, and offers facilities for sailing, windsurfing, canoeing, water-skiing and fishing. In summer, the cruiser *Osprey* departs from Leaplish on trips around the lake. The Kielder Water Exhibition, at the Visitor Centre, depicts the history of the valley from the Ice Age to the present day.

Cheviot Hills 8

These bare, lonely moors, smoothed into rounded humps by Ice Age glaciers, form a natural border with Scotland. Walkers and outdoor enthusiasts find a near-wilderness unmatched anywhere else in England. This remotest extremity of the Northumberland National Park nevertheless has a long and vivid history. Roman legions, warring Scots and English border raiders, cattle drovers and whisky smugglers have all left traces along the ancient routes and tracks they carved out here.

VISITORS' CHECKLIST

Northumberland. *Hexham.* *Wooler.* ***Tel*** *01668 282123.* **www**.northumberlandnational park.org.uk

The Cheviots' *isolated burns and streams are a stronghold in England for the shy, elusive otter.*

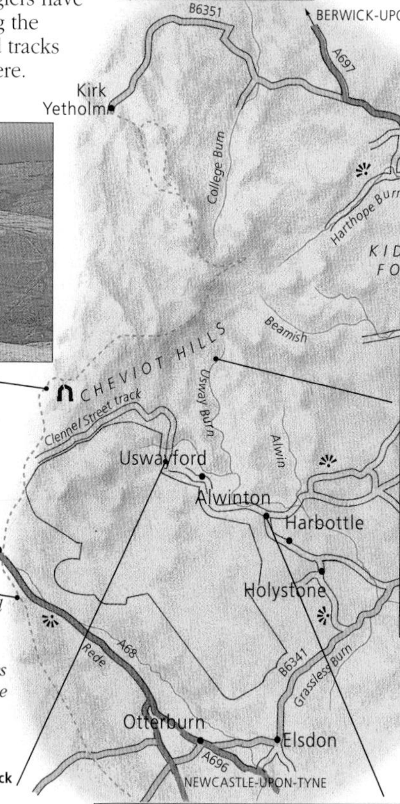
B6351
BERWICK-UPON-TWEED
A697
Kirk Yetholm
Wooler
College Burn
Harthope Burn
KIDLAND FOREST
Beamish
CHEVIOT HILLS
Clennel Street track
Usway Burn
Alwin
Uswayford
Alwinton
Harbottle
Byrness
Holystone
Rede
A68
B6341
Grassless Burn
Otterburn
Elsdon
A696
NEWCASTLE-UPON-TYNE

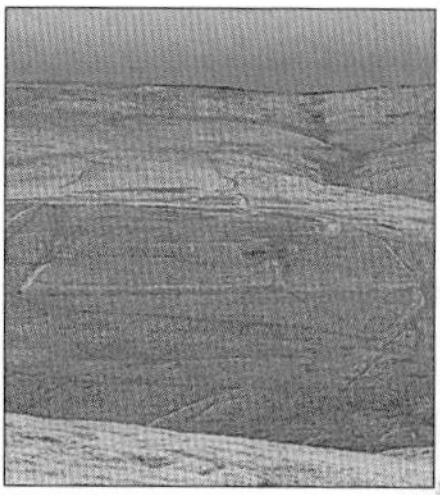

Chew Green Camp, *which to the Romans was* ad fines, *or, "towards the last place", has fine views from the remaining fortified earthworks.*

The Pennine Way *starts in Derbyshire and ends at Kirk Yetholm in Scotland. The final stage (shown here) goes past Byrness, crosses the Cheviots and traces the Scottish border.*

Uswayford Farm track

Uswayford Farm, *is perhaps the most remote farm in England, and one of the hardest to reach. It is set in deserted moorland.*

KEY

- A roads
- B roads
- Minor roads
- Pennine Way
- Viewpoint

0 kilometres 5

0 miles 5

Alwinton, *a tiny village built mainly from grey stone, is situated beside the River Coquet. It is an access point for many fine walks in the area, and the wild landscape is deserted except for sheep.*

Hexham ❾

Northumberland. 🏘 11,500. 🚉
🚌 ℹ Wentworth Car Park
(01434 652220). 🗓 Tue.
www.visitnorthumberland.com

The busy market town of Hexham was established in the 7th century, growing up around the church and monastery built by St Wilfrid, but the Vikings sacked and looted it in 876. In 1114, Augustinians began work on a priory and abbey on the original church ruins to create **Hexham Abbey**, which still towers over the market square. The Saxon crypt, built partly with stones from the former Roman fort at Corbridge, is all

Ancient stone carvings at Hexham Abbey

that remains of St Wilfrid's Church. The south transept has a 12th-century night stair: stone steps leading from the dormitory. In the chancel is the Frith Stool, a Saxon throne in the centre of a circle which protected fugitives.

Medieval streets, many with Georgian and Victorian shopfronts, spread out from the market square, The 15th-century Moot Hall was once a council chamber and the old gaol (jail) contains a **museum** of border history.

Hadrian's Wall ⓫

On the orders of Emperor Hadrian, work began in AD 120 on a 73-mile (117-km) wall to be erected across northern England, to mark and defend the northern limits of the British province and the northwest border of the Roman Empire. Troops were stationed at milecastles along the wall, and large turrets, later forts, were built at 5-mile (8-km) intervals. The wall was abandoned in 383 as the Empire crumbled, but much of it remains. In 1987 it was declared a World Heritage Site.

Location of Hadrian's Wall

Vindolanda *is the site of several forts. The first timber fort dated from AD 90 and a stone fort was not built until the 2nd century. The museum has a collection of Roman writing tablets providing details of food, clothes and work.*

Carvoran Fort is probably pre-Hadrianic. Little of the fort survives, but the Roman Army museum nearby covers the wall's history.

Great Chesters Fort was built facing east to guard Caw Gap, but there are few remains today. To the south and east of the fort are traces of a civil settlement and a bathhouse.

Housesteads Settlement includes the remains of terraced shops or taverns.

Emperor Hadrian *(76–138) came to Britain in 120 to order a stronger defence system. Coins were often cast to record emperors' visits, such as this bronze* sestertius. *Until 1971, the penny was abbreviated to* d, *short for* denarius, *a Roman coin.*

Cawfields, *2 miles (3 km) north of Haltwhistle, is the access point to one of the highest and most rugged section of the wall. To the east, the wall and a series of milecastle sit on volcanic cra*

🔒 Hexham Abbey
Market Place. *Tel* 01434 602031.
⭘ 9:30am–5pm daily. 🔖 ▣ ▢

🏛 Border History Museum
Old Gaol, nr Hallgate. *Tel* 01434
652349. ⭘ Feb–Oct: daily; Nov:
Mon, Tue, Sat. 🔖 🔖 ▢

Corbridge ❿

Northumberland. 🏚 *3,500.* 🚉
🛈 *Hill St (01434 632815).*

This quiet town conceals
a few historic buildings
constructed with stones from
the Roman garrison town of

**The parson's 14th-century fortified
tower house at Corbridge**

nearby Corstopitum. Among
these are the thickset Saxon
tower of St Andrew's Church
and the 14th-century fortified
tower house built to protect
the local clergyman. Excavations of Corstopitum, now
known as **Corbridge Roman
Town–Hadrian's Wall**, have
exposed earlier forts, a well-
preserved granary, temples,
fountains and an aqueduct.

**🏛 Corbridge Roman Town–
Hadrian's Wall**
(EH) *Tel* 01434 632349. ⭘ Apr–Oct:
daily; Nov–Mar: Sat & Sun. ⬤ 1 Jan,
24–26 Dec. 🔖 🔖 limited. 🔖 ▢

THE WALL COAST-TO-COAST

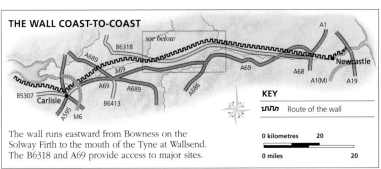

see below

A1

B6318

A689

Newcastle

A69

A69   A689

A68

A1(M)   A19

A69

B5307   Carlisle   B6413

A595   M6

A686

KEY

〰〰〰 Route of the wall

0 kilometres   20

0 miles   20

The wall runs eastward from Bowness on the
Solway Firth to the mouth of the Tyne at Wallsend.
The B6318 and A69 provide access to major sites.

Carrawburgh Fort, a 500-man
garrison, guarded the Newbrough
Burn and North Tynedale approaches.

Limestone Corner Milecastle is
sited at the northernmost part of
the wall and has magnificent views
of the Cheviot Hills (*see p421*).

Sewingshields Milecastle, *with
magnificent views west to Housesteads,
is one of the best places for walking.
This reconstruction shows the layout
of a Roman milecastle on the wall.*

Chesters Fort was a
bridgehead over the
North Tyne. In the
museum are altars, sculp-
tures and inscriptions.

Chesters Bridge crossed the
Tyne. The original Hadrianic
bridge was rebuilt in 207. The
remains of this second bridge
abutment can still be seen.

Housesteads Fort *is the best-
preserved site on the wall, with
fine views over the countryside.
The excavated remains include
the commanding officer's house
and a Roman hospital.*

0 metres   500

0 yards   500

Newcastle upon Tyne ⑫

273,000. ✈ ≈ 🚉 ⛴ ✚ ⓘ
Quayside (0191 277 8000). 🏠 *Sun.*
www.newcastlegateshead.com

Newcastle owes its name to its Norman **castle** which was founded in 1080 by Robert Curthose, the eldest son of William the Conqueror *(see p47).* The Romans had bridged the Tyne and built a fort on the site 1,000 years earlier. During the Middle Ages it was used as a base for English campaigns against the Scots. From the Middle Ages, the city flourished as a coal mining and exporting centre. It was known in the 19th century for engineering, steel production and later as the world's foremost shipyard. The city's industrial base has recently declined, but "Geordies", as inhabitants of the city are known, have refocused their civic pride on the Metro Centre shopping mall at Gateshead, southwest of the city, and Newcastle United soccer team.

The city's lively night scene includes clubs, pubs and ethnic restaurants. The visible trappings of its past are reflected in the magnificent **Tyne Bridge** and in **Earl Grey's Monument**, as well as the grand façades in the city centre thoroughfares, such as Grey Street. On the quayside there are some dramatic new features, notably **Baltic**, the contemporary art centre, **The Sage Gateshead**, the international centre for music, and the tilting **Gateshead Millennium Bridge**.

♣ **The Castle**
St Nicholas St. **Tel** *0191 232 7938.* 🕐 *daily.* 🔴 *1 Jan, Good Fri, 24–26 Dec.* 📷 🔊
Curthose's original wooden "new castle" was rebuilt in stone in the 12th century. Only

Bridges crossing the Tyne at Newcastle

Beamish, The North of England Open Air Museum ⑬

This giant open air museum, spread over 120 ha (300 acres) of County Durham, recreates an authentic picture of family, working and community life in the northeast in the 19th and early 20th centuries.

It has a 1913 Town Street, colliery village with drift mine, working farm and railway station. A tramway serves the different parts of the museum, which carefully avoids romanticizing the past.

Tram symbol

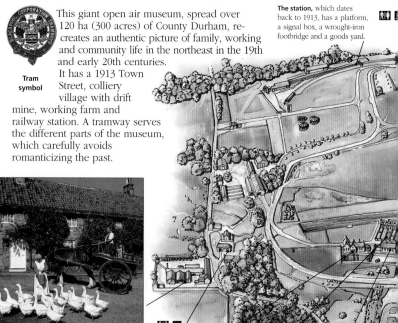

The station, which dates back to 1913, has a platform, a signal box, a wrought-iron footbridge and a goods yard.

Home Farm *recreates the atmosphere of an old-fashioned farm. Rare breeds of cattle and sheep, more common before the advent of mass breeding, can be seen.*

School

Miners' houses were tiny, oil-lit dwellings, backing onto vegetable gardens and owned by the colliery.

Chapel

the thickset, crenellated keep remains intact with two suites of royal apartments. A series of staircases spiral up to the renovated battlements, from which there are fine views over the city and the Tyne.

🔒 St Nicholas Cathedral

St Nicholas Sq. *Tel* 0191 232 1939.
⬜ daily. ♿
This is one of Britain's tiniest cathedrals. There are remnants inside of the original 11th-century Norman church on which the present 14th- and 15th-century structure was founded. Its most striking feature is its ornate "lantern tower" – half tower, half spire – of which there are only three others in Britain.

🏛 Bessie Surtees' House

(EH) 41–44 Sandhill. *Tel* 0191 2691200. ⬜ Mon–Fri. 🚫 24 Dec–7 Jan, public hols. ♿ limited. 📷
The story of beautiful, wealthy Bessie, who lived here before

Reredos of the Northumbrian saints in St Nicholas Cathedral

eloping with penniless John Scott, later Lord Chancellor of England, is the romantic tale behind these half-timbered 16th- and 17th-century houses. The window through which Bessie escaped now has a blue glass pane.

🏛 Tyne Bridge

Newcastle–Gateshead.
⬜ daily. ♿
Opened in 1928, this steel arch was the longest of its type in Britain with a span of 162 m (531 ft). Designed by Mott, Hay and Anderson, it soon became the city's most potent symbol.

🏛 Earl Grey's Monument

Grey St.
Benjamin Green created this memorial to the 2nd Earl Grey, Liberal Prime Minister from 1830 to 1834.

🏛 BALTIC

The Centre for Contemporary Art Gateshead. *Tel* 0191 478 1810. ⬜ daily. 📷 🍴 📷 www.balticmill.com
This former grain warehouse has been converted by architect Dominic Williams into a major international centre for contemporary art, one of the biggest in Europe, with amazing views of Tyneside from its rooftop restaurant.

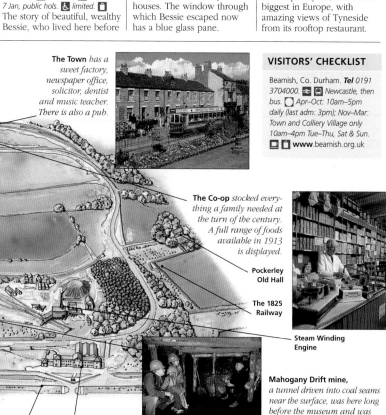

The Town *has a sweet factory, newspaper office, solicitor, dentist and music teacher. There is also a pub.*

VISITORS' CHECKLIST

Beamish, Co. Durham. *Tel* 0191 3704000. 🚃 🚌 Newcastle, then bus. ⬜ Apr–Oct: 10am–5pm daily (last adm: 3pm); Nov–Mar: Town and Colliery Village only 10am–4pm Tue–Thu, Sat & Sun. 📷 📷 www.beamish.org.uk

The Co-op *stocked everything a family needed at the turn of the century. A full range of foods available in 1913 is displayed.*

Pockerley Old Hall

The 1825 Railway

Steam Winding Engine

Entrance ♿ 📷 📷
P

Mahogany Drift mine, *a tunnel driven into coal seams near the surface, was here long before the museum and was worked from the 1850s to 1958. Visitors are given guided tours underground.*

Houses built by the London Lead Company in Middleton-in-Teesdale

Durham 14

See pp428–9.

North Pennines Tour 15

See p427.

Cotherstone cheese, a speciality of the Middleton-in-Teesdale area

Middleton-in-Teesdale 16

Co. Durham. 🏘 1,100.
🚆 Darlington. 🛈 10 Market Place (03000 262626).

Clinging to a hillside amid wild Pennine scenery on the River Tees is this old lead mining town. Many of its rows of grey stone cottages were built by the London Lead Company, a paternalistic, Quaker-run organization who influenced every corner of its employees' daily lives.

The company began mining in 1753, and soon it virtually owned the town. Workers were expected to observe strict temperance, send their children to Sunday school and conform to the many company maxims. Today, mining has all but ceased in Teesdale, with Middleton standing as a monument to the 18th-century idea of the "company town". The offices of the London Lead Company can still be seen, as well as Nonconformist chapels from the era and a memorial fountain made of iron.

The crumbly Cotherstone cow's milk cheese, a speciality of the surrounding dales, is available in the shops.

Barnard Castle 17

County Durham. 🏘 5,000.
🚆 Darlington. 🛈 Woodleigh, Flatts Rd (03000 262626). 🛒 Wed. www.thisisdurham.com

Barnard Castle, known in the area as "Barney", is a little town full of character, with old shopfronts and a cobbled market overlooked by the ruins of the Norman castle from which it takes its name. The original Barnard Castle was built around 1125–40 by Bernard Balliol, ancestor of the founder of Balliol College, Oxford (see p222). Later, the market town grew up around the fortification.

Today, Barnard Castle is known for the extraordinary French-style château to the east of the town, surrounded by acres of formal gardens. Started in 1860 by the local aristocrat John Bowes and his French wife Josephine, an artist and actress, it was never a private residence, but always intended as a museum and public monument. The château finally opened in 1892, by which time the couple were both dead. Nevertheless, the **Bowes Museum** stands as a monument to his wealth and her extravagance.

The museum houses a strong collection of Spanish art which includes El Greco's *The Tears of St Peter,* dating from the 1580s, and Goya's *Don Juan Meléndez Váldez,* painted in 1797. Clocks, porcelain, furniture, musical instruments, toys and tapestries are among its treasures.

🏛 **Bowes Museum**
Barnard Castle. *Tel 01833 690606.*
◯ 10am–5pm daily. ● 1 Jan, 25 & 26 Dec. 📷 ♿ 🎫 (summer). 🖥 🖱 www.bowesmuseum.org.uk

The Bowes Museum, a French-style château near Barnard Castle

North Pennines Tour ⓖ

Starting just to the south of Hadri-an's Wall, this tour ex-plores the South Tyne Valley, and Upper Weardale. It crosses one of England's wildest and most remote tracts of moorland, then heads north again. The high ground is mainly blanketed with heather, dotted with sheep or criss-crossed with dry-stone walls, a

Sheep grazing on the moors

feature of this region. Harriers and other birds hover above, and streams tumble into valleys of tightly huddled villages.

Celts, Romans and other settlers have left imprints on the North Pennines. The wealth of the area was based on lead mining and stone quarrying which has long co-existed with farming.

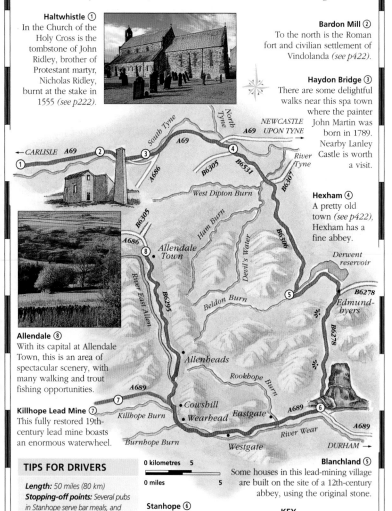

Haltwhistle ①
In the Church of the Holy Cross is the tombstone of John Ridley, brother of Protestant martyr, Nicholas Ridley, burnt at the stake in 1555 (see p222).

Bardon Mill ②
To the north is the Roman fort and civilian settlement of Vindolanda (see p422).

Haydon Bridge ③
There are some delightful walks near this spa town where the painter John Martin was born in 1789. Nearby Lanley Castle is worth a visit.

Hexham ④
A pretty old town (see p422), Hexham has a fine abbey.

Allendale ⑧
With its capital at Allendale Town, this is an area of spectacular scenery, with many walking and trout fishing opportunities.

Killhope Lead Mine ⑦
This fully restored 19th-century lead mine boasts an enormous waterwheel.

Blanchland ⑤
Some houses in this lead-mining village are built on the site of a 12th-century abbey, using the original stone.

Stanhope ⑥
An 18th-century castle over-looks the market square. The giant stump of a fossilized tree, said to be 250 million years old, guards the graveyard.

TIPS FOR DRIVERS

Length: 50 miles (80 km)
Stopping-off points: Several pubs in Stanhope serve bar meals, and the Durham Dales Centre provides teas all year round. Horsley Hall Hotel at Eastgate serves meals all day. (See also pp684–5.)

0 kilometres   5
0 miles   5

KEY

▬▬▬ Tour route
═══ Other roads
☆ Viewpoint

Durham ⑭

The city of Durham was built on Island Hill or "Dunholm" in 995. This rocky peninsula, which defies the course of the River Wear's route to the sea, was chosen as the last resting place for the remains of St Cuthbert. The relics of the Venerable Bede were brought to the site 27 years later, adding to its attraction for pilgrims. Durham

Cathedral Sanctuary knocker

Cathedral was treated by architects as an experiment for geometric patterning, while the Castle served as the Episcopal Palace until 1832, when Bishop William van Mildert gave it up and surrendered part of his income to found Britain's third university. The 23 ha (57 acre) peninsula has many footpaths, views and fine buildings.

Old Fulling Mill, a largely 18th-century building, houses a museum of archaeology.

★ **Cathedral**
Built from 1093 to 1274, it is a striking Norman structure.

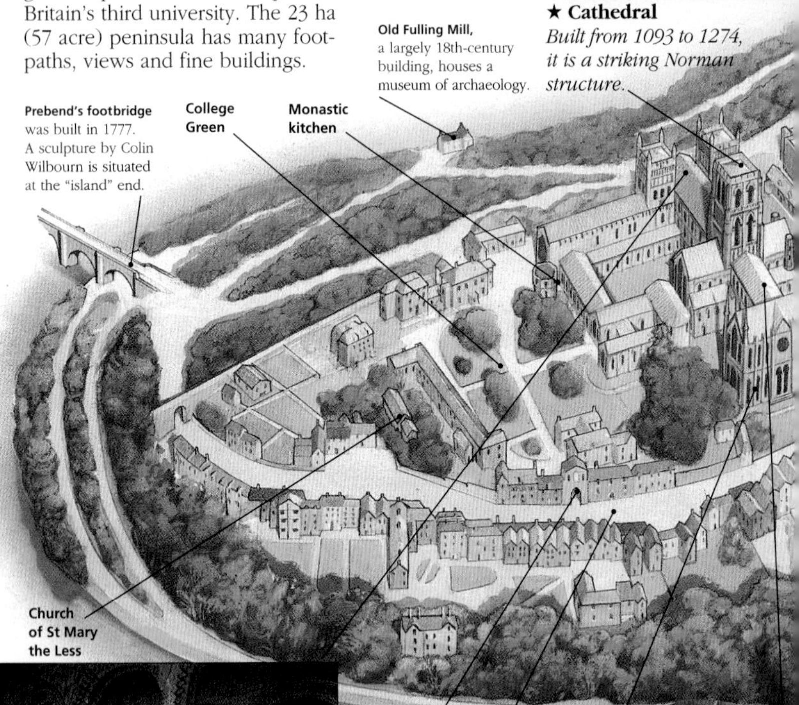

Prebend's footbridge was built in 1777. A sculpture by Colin Wilbourn is situated at the "island" end.

College Green

Monastic kitchen

Church of St Mary the Less

College gatehouse **South Bailey** **St Cuthbert's Tomb**

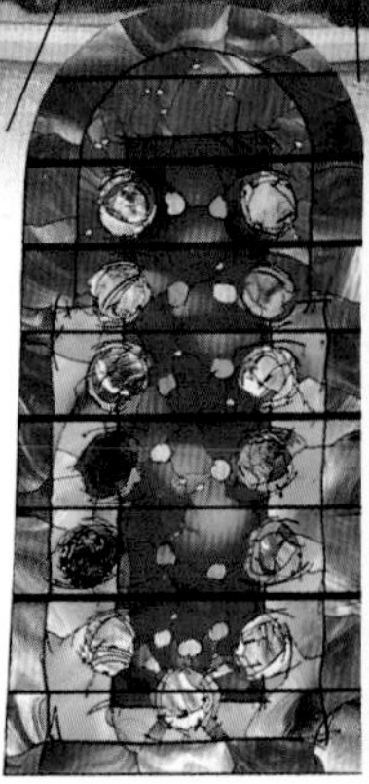

"Our Daily Bread" Window
This modern stained-glass window in the north nave aisle was donated in 1984 by a local department store.

Galilee Chapel
Architects began work on the exotic Galilee Chapel in 1170, drawing inspiration from the Great Mosque of Cordoba in Andalusia. It was altered by Bishop Langley (d.1437) whose tomb is by the west door.

STAR SIGHTS

★ Cathedral
★ Castle

★ Castle

Begun in 1072, the castle is a fine Norman fortress. The keep, sited on a mound, is now part of the university.

Town Hall (1851)

St Nicholas' Church (1857)

...lace ...reen

VISITORS' CHECKLIST

Co.Durham. Durham. Owengate (03000 262626). **Cathedral. Tel** 0191 386 4266. 9:30am–6:15pm daily (12:45–5:30pm Sun, 9:30am–8pm Jul & Aug). limited. **Castle. Tel** 0191 334 3800. daily (pm only in termtime). mandatory. **www**.thisisdurham.com

Tunstal's Chapel

Situated at the end of the Tunstal's Gallery, the castle chapel was built c.1542. Its fine woodwork includes this unicorn misericord (see p341).

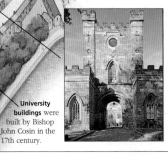

Castle Gatehouse

Traces of Norman stonework can be seen in the outer arch, while the sturdy walls and upper floors are 18th century, rebuilt in a style dubbed "gothick" by detractors.

University buildings were built by Bishop John Cosin in the 17th century.

CATHEDRAL ARCHITECTURE

The vast dimensions of the 900-year-old columns, piers and vaults, and the inventive giant lozenge and chevron, trellis and dogtooth patterns carved into the stone columns, are the main innovative features of Durham Cathedral. It is believed that 11th- and 12th-century architects such as Bishop Ranulph Flambard tried to unify all parts of the structure. This can be seen in the south aisle of the nave below.

Ribbed vaults, *criss-crossing above the nave, are now common in church ceilings. One of the major achievements of Gothic architecture, they were first built at Durham.*

...rch of St ...y le Bow

Kingsgate ...ootbridge, built from ...2–3, leads to North Bailey.

The lozenge *shape is a pattern from prehistoric carving, but never before seen in a cathedral.*

Chevron patterns *on some of the piers in the nave are evidence of Moorish influence.*

WALES

INTRODUCING WALES 432–439
NORTH WALES 440–455
SOUTH AND MID-WALES 456–475

Wales at a Glance

Wales is a country of outstanding natural beauty with varied landscapes. Visitors come to climb dramatic mountain peaks, go walking in the forests, fish in the broad rivers and enjoy the miles of unspoilt coastline. The country's many seaside resorts have long been popular with English holidaymakers. As well as outdoor pursuits there is the vibrancy of Welsh culture, with its strong Celtic roots, to be experienced. Finally there are many fine castles, ruined abbeys, mansions and cities full of magnificent architecture.

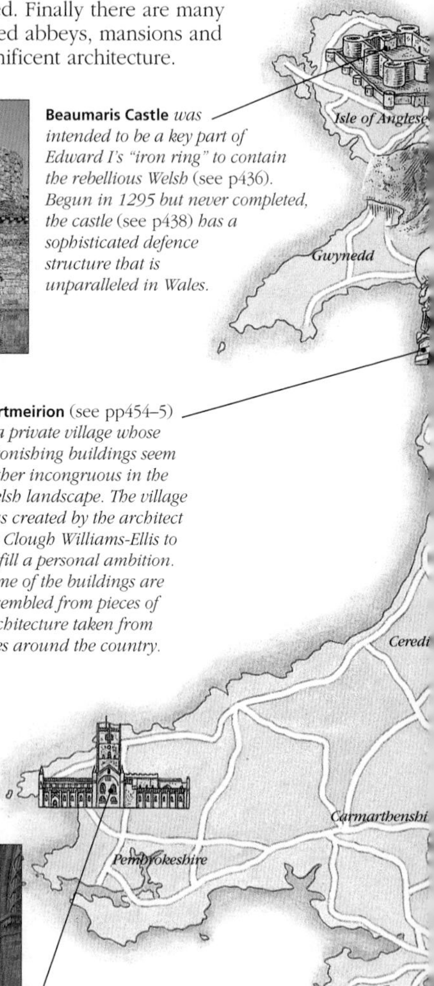

Beaumaris Castle *was intended to be a key part of Edward I's "iron ring" to contain the rebellious Welsh (see p436). Begun in 1295 but never completed, the castle (see p438) has a sophisticated defence structure that is unparalleled in Wales.*

Isle of Anglesey

Gwynedd

Portmeirion *(see pp454–5) is a private village whose astonishing buildings seem rather incongruous in the Welsh landscape. The village was created by the architect Sir Clough Williams-Ellis to fulfill a personal ambition. Some of the buildings are assembled from pieces of architecture taken from sites around the country.*

Ceredi

Carmarthenshi

Pembrokeshire

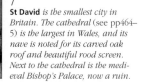

St David *is the smallest city in Britain. The cathedral (see pp464–5) is the largest in Wales, and its nave is noted for its carved oak roof and beautiful rood screen. Next to the cathedral is the medieval Bishop's Palace, now a ruin.*

◁ Caernarfon's colourful quayside marina

Llanberis and Snowdon
(see p451) *is an area
famous for dramatic, high
peaks, long popular with
climbers. Snowdon's summit
is most easily reached from
Llanberis. Its Welsh name,
Yr Wyddfa Fawr, means
"great tomb" and it is
the legendary burial place
of a giant slain by King
Arthur* (see p285).

Flintshire

*rconwy
olwyn*   *Denbighshire*

NORTH WALES
(see pp440–55)

Wrexham

Conwy Castle *guards one of the
best-preserved medieval fortified
towns in Britain* (see pp446–7).
*Built by Edward I, the castle
was besieged and came close
to surrender in 1294. It was
taken by Owain Glyndŵr's
supporters in 1401.*

Powys

SOUTH AND MID-WALES
(see pp456–75)

The Brecon Beacons (see pp468–9) *is a national park,
a lovely area of mountains, forest and moorland in South
Wales, which is a favourite with walkers and naturalists.
Pen-y-Fan is one of the principal summits.*

Cardiff Castle's
(see pp472–3) *Clock
Tower is just one of
many 19th-century
additions by the
eccentric but gifted
architect William
Burges. His flamboy-
ant style still delights
and amazes visitors.*

Monmouthshire

rdiff, Swansea, Newport & the Valleys

0 kilometres   25

0 miles   25

A PORTRAIT OF WALES

*L*ong popular with British holidaymakers, the many charms of Wales are now becoming better known internationally. They include spectacular scenery and a vibrant culture specializing in male-voice choirs, poetry and a passionate love of team sports. Governed from Westminster since 1536, Wales has its own distinct Celtic identity and in 1999 finally gained partial devolution.

Much of the Welsh landmass is covered by the Cambrian Mountain range, which effectively acts as a barrier from England. Wales is warmed by the Gulf Stream and has a mild climate, with more rain than most of Britain. The land is unsuitable for arable farming, but sheep and cattle thrive; the drove roads, along which sheep used to be driven across the hills to England, are now popular walking trails. It is partly because of the rugged terrain that the Welsh have managed to maintain their separate identity and their ancient language.

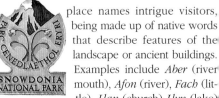

One of Wales's splendid National Parks

Welsh is an expansive, musical language, spoken by only one-fifth of the 3 million inhabitants, but in parts of North Wales it is still the main language of conversation. There is an official bilingual policy: road signs are in Welsh and English, even in areas where Welsh is little spoken. Welsh place names intrigue visitors, being made up of native words that describe features of the landscape or ancient buildings. Examples include *Aber* (river mouth), *Afon* (river), *Fach* (little), *Llan* (church) *Llyn* (lake) and *Nant* (valley).

Wales was conquered by the Romans, but not by the Saxons. The land and the people therefore retained Celtic patterns of settlement and husbandry for six centuries before the Norman Conquest in 1066. This allowed time for the development of a distinctive Welsh nation whose homogeneity continues to this day.

The early Norman kings subjugated the Welsh by appointing "Marcher Lords" to control areas bordering England. A string

Rugby: the popular Welsh sport

of massive castles provides evidence of the turbulent years when Welsh insurrection was a constant threat. It was not until 1535 that Wales formally became part of Britain, and it would take nearly 500 years before the people of Wales regained partial autonomy.

Religious non-conformism and radical politics are deeply rooted in Welsh consciousness. Saint David converted the country to Christianity in the 6th century. Methodism, chapel and teetotalism became firmly entrenched in

Mountain sheep: a familiar sight in rural Wales

A *gorsedd* (assembly) of bards at the eisteddfod

ancient bards: minstrels and poets, who may have been associated with the Druids. Bardic tales of quasi-historical figures and magic were part of the oral tradition of the Dark Ages. They were first written down in the 14th century as the *Mabinogion,* which has inspired Welsh poets up to the 20th century's Dylan Thomas. The male-voice choirs found in many towns, villages and factories, particularly in the industrial south, express the Welsh musical heritage. Choirs compete in eisteddfods: festivals that celebrate Welsh culture.

the Welsh psyche during the 19th century. Even today some pubs stay closed on Sundays. A long-standing oral tradition in Wales has produced many outstanding public speakers, politicians and actors. Welsh labour leaders have played important roles in the British trade union movement and the development of socialism.

Welsh heritage is steeped in song, music, poetry and legend rather than handicrafts, although one notable exception is the carved Welsh lovespoon – a craft recently revived. The well-known Welsh love of music derives from the

Welsh lovespoon

In the 19th century, the opening of the South Wales coalfield in Mid-Glamorgan – for a time the biggest in the world – led to an industrial boom, with mass migration from the countryside to the iron and steelworks. This prosperity was not to last: apart from a brief respite in World War II, the coal industry has been in terminal decline for decades, causing severe economic hardship. Today tourism is being promoted in the hope that the wealth generated, by outdoor activities in particular, will be able to take "King Coal's" place.

Conwy's picturesque, medieval walled town, fronted by a colourful harbour

The History of Wales

Wales has been settled since prehistoric times, its history shaped by many factors, from invasion to industrialization. The Romans set up bases in the mountainous terrain, but it was effectively a separate Celtic entity when Offa's Dyke was built as the border with England in 770. Centuries of cross-border raids and military campaigns followed before England and Wales were formally united by the Act of Union in 1535. The rugged northwest, the former stronghold of the Welsh princes, remains the heartland of Welsh language and culture.

St David, patron saint of Wales

Owain Glyndwr, heroic leader of Welsh opposition to English rule

THE CELTIC NATION

Ornamental Iron Age bronze plaque from Anglesey

Wales was settled by waves of migrants in prehistoric times. By the Iron Age *(see pp42–3)*, Celtic farmers had established hillforts and their religion, Druidism. From the 1st century AD until the legions withdrew around 400, the Romans built fortresses and roads, and mined lead, silver and gold. During the next 200 years, Wales was converted to Christianity by missionaries from Europe. St David *(see pp464–5)*, the Welsh patron saint, is said to have turned the leek into a national symbol. He persuaded soldiers to wear leeks in their hats to distinguish themselves from Saxons during a 6th-century skirmish.

The Saxons *(see pp46–7)* failed to conquer Wales, and in 770 the Saxon King Offa built a defensive earthwork along the unconquered territory *(see p461)*. Beyond Offa's Dyke the people called

themselves *Y Cymry* (fellow countrymen) and the land *Cymru*. The Saxons called the land "Wales" from the Old English *wealas*, meaning foreigners. It was divided into kingdoms of which the main ones were Gwynedd in the north, Powys in the centre and Dyfed in the south. There were strong trade, cultural and linguistic links between each.

MARCHER LORDS

The Norman invasion of 1066 *(see p47)* did not reach Wales, but the border territory ("the Marches") was given by William the Conqueror to three powerful barons based at Shrewsbury, Hereford and Chester. These Marcher Lords made many incursions into Wales and controlled most of the lowlands. But the Welsh

Edward I designating his son Prince of Wales in 1301

princes held the mountainous northwest and exploited English weaknesses. Under Llywelyn the Great (d.1240), North Wales was almost completely independent; in 1267 his grandson, Llywelyn the Last, was acknowledged as Prince of Wales by Henry III.

In 1272 Edward I came to the English throne. He built fortresses and embarked on a military campaign to conquer Wales. In 1283 Llywelyn was killed in a skirmish, a shattering blow for the Welsh. Edward introduced English law and proclaimed his son Prince of Wales *(see p444)*.

OWAIN GLYNDWR'S REBELLION

Welsh resentment against the Marcher Lords led to rebellion. In 1400 Owain Glyndŵr (c.1350–1416), a descendant of the Welsh princes, laid waste to English-dominated towns and castles. Declaring himself Prince of Wales, he found Celtic allies in Scotland, Ireland, France and Northumbria. In 1404 Glyndŵr captured Harlech and Cardiff, and formed a parliament in Machynlleth *(see p462)*. In 1408 the French made a truce with the English king, Henry IV. The rebellion then failed and Glyndŵr went into hiding until his death.

UNION WITH ENGLAND

Wales suffered greatly during the Wars of the Roses *(see p49)* as Yorkists and Lancastrians tried to gain control of the strategically important Welsh castles. The wars ended in 1485, and the Welshman Henry Tudor, born in Pembroke, became Henry VII. The Act of Union in 1535 and other laws abolished the Marcher Lordships, giving Wales parliamentary representation in London instead. English practices replaced inheritance customs and English became the language of the courts and administration. The Welsh language survived, partly helped by the church and by Dr William Morgan's translation of the Bible in 1588.

Vernacular Bible, which helped to keep the Welsh language alive

INDUSTRY AND RADICAL POLITICS

The industrialization of south and east Wales began with the development of open-cast coal mining near Wrexham and Merthyr Tydfil in the 1760s. Convenient ports and the arrival of the railways helped the process. By the second half of the 19th century open-cast mines had been superseded by deep pits in the Rhondda Valley.

Living and working conditions were poor for industrial and agricultural workers. A series of "Rebecca Riots" in

Miners from South Wales pictured in 1910

South Wales between 1839 and 1843, involving tenant farmers (dressed as women) protesting about tithes and rents, was forcibly suppressed. The Chartists, trade unions and the Liberal Party had much Welsh support.

The rise of Methodism *(see p279)* roughly paralleled the growth of industry: 80 per cent of the population was Methodist by 1851. The Welsh language persisted, despite attempts by the British government to discourage its use, which included punishing children caught speaking it.

WALES TODAY

In the 20th century the Welsh became a power in British politics. David Lloyd George, although not born in Wales, grew up there and was the first British Prime Minister to come from a Welsh family. Aneurin Bevan, a miner's son who became a Labour Cabinet Minister, helped create the National Health Service *(see p59)*.

Welsh nationalism continued to grow: in 1926 Plaid Cymru, the Welsh Nationalist Party, was formed. In 1955 Cardiff was recognized as the capital of Wales

(see p470) and four years later the red dragon became the emblem on Wales' new flag. Plaid Cymru won two parliamentary seats at Westminster in 1974, and in a 1998 referendum the Welsh espoused limited home rule. The National Assembly for Wales is housed in the stunning Y Senedd, on the waterfront in Cardiff Bay.

The 1967 Welsh Language Act made Welsh compulsory in schools, and the television channel S4C (Sianel 4 Cymru), formed in 1982, broadcasts many programmes in Welsh.

From the 1960s the steel and coal industries declined, creating mass unemployment. This has been partly alleviated by the emergence of high-tech industries, and by growth in tourism: Cardiff is home to many major tourist attractions including the Millennium Stadium and Cardiff Bay, Europe's largest waterfront development *(see pp470–71)*.

Girl in traditional Welsh costume

Castles of Wales

A French 15th-century painting of Conwy Castle

Wales is rich in romantic medieval castles. Soon after the Battle of Hastings, in 1066 *(see p47)*, the Normans turned their attentions to Wales. They built earth and timber fortifications, later replaced by stone castles, initiating a building programme that was pursued by the Welsh princes and invading forces. Construction reached its peak during the reign of Edward I *(see p436)*. As the need for security lessened in the later Middle Ages, some castles became stately homes.

The north gatehouse was planned to be 18 m (60 ft) high, providing lavish royal accommodation, but its top storey was never built.

The inner ward was lined with a hall, granary, kitchens and stables.

Rounded towers, with fewer blind spots than square ones, gave better protection.

Arrow slit

Moat

Curtain wall

BEAUMARIS CASTLE

The last of Edward I's Welsh castles *(see p444)*, this perfectly symmetrical, concentric design was intended to combine impregnable defence with comfort. Invaders would face many obstacles before reaching the inner ward.

WHERE TO SEE WELSH CASTLES

In addition to Beaumaris, in North Wales there are medieval forts at Caernarfon *(see p444)*, Conwy *(see p446)* and Harlech *(see p454)*. Edward I also built Denbigh, Flint (near Chester) and Rhuddlan (near Rhyll). In South and mid-Wales, Caerphilly (near Cardiff), Kidwelly (near Carmarthen) and Pembroke were built between the 11th and 13th centuries. Spectacular sites are occupied by Cilgerran (near Cardigan), Criccieth (near Porthmadog) and Carreg Cennen *(see p468)*. Chirk Castle, near Llangollen, is a good example of a fortress that has since become a stately home.

Caerphilly, *6 miles (10 km) north of Cardiff, is a huge castle with concentric stone and water defences that cover 12 ha (30 acres).*

Harlech Castle *(see p454) is noted for its massive gatehouse, twin towers and the fortified stairway to the sea. It was the headquarters of the Welsh resistance leader Owain Glyndŵr (see p436) from 1404–8.*

CASTELL-Y-BERE

This native Welsh castle at the foot of Cader Idris *(see p440)* was founded by Llywelyn the Great in 1221 *(see p422)*, to secure internal borders rather than to resist the English.

Entrance

The D-shaped, elongated tower is a typical feature of Welsh castles.

The castle's construction follows the shape of the rock. The curtain walls are too low and insubstantial to be of much practical use.

Drawbridge

e Chapel Tower has a
autiful medieval chapel.

The protected dock, on a channel that originally led to the sea, received supplies during sieges.

inner wall, with an
r passage, was higher
the curtain wall to
nit simultaneous firing.

Twin-towered gatehouse

EDWARD I AND MASTER JAMES OF ST GEORGE

In 1278 Edward I brought over from Savoy a master stonemason who became a great military architect, James of St George. Responsible for planning and building at least 12 of Edward's fine Welsh castles, James was paid well and liberally pensioned off, indicating the esteem in which he was held by the king.

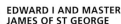

Edward I (see p436) *was the warrior king whose castles played a key role in the subjugation of the Welsh people.*

A plan of Caernarfon Castle *illustrates how its position, on a promontory surrounded by water, has determined the building's shape and defence.*

Caernarfon Castle (see p444), *birthplace of the ill-fated Edward II (see p327), was intended to be the official royal residence in North Wales, and has palatial private apartments.*

Castell Coch *was restored in Neo-Gothic style by Lord Bute and William Burges (see p472). Mock-castles were built by many Victorian industrialists.*

Conwy Castle (see p447), *like many other castles, required forced labour on a massive scale for its construction.*

NORTH WALES

CONWY · ISLE OF ANGLESEY · GYWNEDD · DENBIGHSHIRE · FLINTSHIRE · WREXHAM

The North Wales landscape has a dramatic quality reflected in its history. In prehistoric times, Anglesey was a stronghold of the religious elite known as the Druids. Roman and Norman invasions concentrated on the coast, leaving the mountains to the Welsh. These wild areas are the centre of Welsh language and culture.

Defence and conquest have been constant themes in Welsh history. North Wales was the scene of ferocious battles between the Welsh princes and Anglo-Norman monarchs determined to establish English rule. The string of formidable castles which still stand in North Wales are as much a testament to Welsh resistance as to the wealth and strength of the invaders. Several massive fortresses, including Beaumaris, Caernarfon and Harlech, almost surround the rugged high country of Snowdonia, an area that even today maintains an untamed quality.

Sheep and cattle farming are the basis of the rural economy here, though there are also large areas of forestry. Along the coast, tourism is a major activity. Llandudno, a purpose-built Victorian resort, popularized the sandy northern coastline in the 19th century. The area continues to attract large numbers of visitors, though major development is confined to the narrow coastal strip that lies between Prestatyn and Llandudno, leaving the island of Anglesey and the remote Lleyn Peninsula largely untouched.

The Lleyn Peninsula remains one of the strongholds of the Welsh language, along with rather isolated inland communities, such as Dolgellau and Bala.

No part of North Wales can truly be called industrial, though there are still remnants of the once-prosperous slate industry in Snowdonia, where the stark, grey quarries provide a striking contrast to the natural beauty of the surrounding mountains. At the foot of Snowdon (the highest mountain in Wales), the villages of Beddgelert, Betws-y-Coed and Llanberis are popular bases for walkers who come to enjoy the spectacular views and striking beauty of this remote region.

Caernarfon Castle, one of the forbidding fortresses built by Edward I

◁ The River Dee at Llangollen, still an area of unspoilt natural beauty

Exploring North Wales

The dominant feature of North Wales is Snowdon, the highest mountain in Wales. Snowdonia National Park extends dramatically from the Snowdon massif south beyond Dolgellau, with thickly wooded valleys, mountain lakes, moors and estuaries. To the east are the softer Clwydian Hills, and unspoilt coastlines can be enjoyed on Anglesey and the beautiful Lleyn Peninsula.

A lighthouse perched on the sea cliffs of Anglesey

KEY

═══ Major road

─── Minor road

┈┈┈ Secondary road

─── Scenic route

━━━ Main railway

─── Minor railway

△ Summit

Carmel Head

Cemaes — A5025 — Amlwch

Holyhead Bay

Llyn Alaw

A5111

Moelfre

Holyhead

Holy Island

Benllech

A n g l e s e y

Great Ormes Head

LLANDUDN

Pentraeth

BEAUMARIS
2

CONW

Gwalchmai

A5

Llangefni

A5025

Llanfairfechan

Penm

Rhosneigr

A55

Bangor

Aberffraw

A4080

Port Dinorwic

Bethesda

Dolgarro

Newborough

Carnedd La
1064m

CAERNARFON 1

A4086

Llanberis

Capel Curig

Caernarfon Bay

LLANBERIS AND
SNOWDON 10

BETW

Penygroes

Snowdon
1085m

Dolwyc

Llanllyfni

A498

A470

BEDDGELERT 11

BLA
9 FFES

Llanaelhaearn

A487

A498

Ffesti

Nefyn

Tan-y-Bwlch

Maentwrog

LLEYN PENINSULA

Porthmadog

13 PORTMEIRION

Trav

Tudweiliog

A4417

Criccieth

Pwllheli

Tremadog Bay

A470

12

A499

Llanbedrog

HARLECH 14

Rhinog Fawr
720m

Plas-yn-Rhiw

Abersoch

Llanbedr

Y Llethr
754m

Aberdaron

Porth Neigwl

Braich y Pwll

*C a r d i g a n
B a y*

Snowdo

National

Bardsey Island

Llanaber

DOLGELLAU 15

Barmouth

Cader Id
892m

Barmouth Bay

Fairbourne

A493

Llwyngwril

Abergynolwyn

A

Tywyn

A493

Aberystwyth ↓

16 ABERDYFI

The peaks and moorland of Snowdonia

GETTING AROUND
The main route into North Wales from the northwest of England is the A55, a good dual carriageway which bypasses several places that used to be traffic bottlenecks, including Conwy. The other main route through the region is the A5 Shrewsbury to Holyhead road, which follows a trail through the mountains pioneered by the 19th-century engineer Thomas Telford *(see p447)*. Rail services run along the coast to Holyhead, connecting with ferries across the Irish Sea to Dublin and Dun Laoghaire. Scenic branch lines travel from Llandudno Junction to Blaenau Ffestiniog (via Betws-y-Coed) and along the southern Lleyn Peninsula.

SIGHTS AT A GLANCE
Aberdyfi ⑯
Bala ⑦
Beaumaris ②
Beddgelert ⑪
Betws-y-Coed ⑧
Blaenau Ffestiniog ⑨
Caernarfon ①
Conwy pp446–7 ③
Dolgellau ⑮
Harlech ⑭
Llanberis and Snowdon ⑩
LLandudno ④
LLangollen ⑥
Lleyn Peninsula ⑫
Portmeirion pp454–5 ⑬
Ruthin ⑤

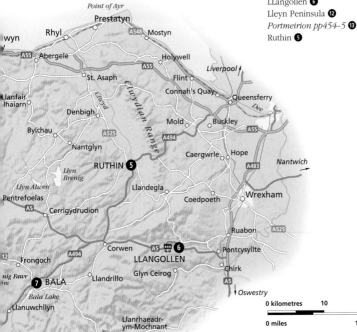

SEE ALSO
• *Where to Stay* pp590–91
• *Where to Eat* pp642–4

The imposing castle built at Conwy by Edward I in the 13th century

Caernarfon Castle, built by Edward I as a symbol of his power over the conquered Welsh

Caernarfon ❶

Gwynedd. 🏛 10,000. 🚆
ℹ️ Castle St (01286 672232).
📅 Sat. www.gwynedd.gov.uk

One of the most famous castles in Wales, Caernarfon Castle, looms over this busy town set at the mouth of the Seiont River. Both town and castle were created after Edward I's defeat of the last native Welsh prince, Llywelyn ap Gruffydd (Llywelyn the Last) in 1283 *(see p436)*. The town walls merge with modern streets that spread beyond the medieval centre to a market square.

THE INVESTITURE

In 1301 the future Edward II became the first English Prince of Wales *(see p436)*, a title since held by the British monarch's eldest son. In 1969 the investiture in Caernarfon Castle of Prince Charles *(above)* as Prince of Wales drew 500 million TV viewers.

Overlooking the town and its harbour, **Caernarfon Castle** *(see p439)*, with its polygonal towers, was built as a seat of government for North Wales. Caernarfon was a thriving port in the 19th century, and during this period the castle ruins were restored by the architect Anthony Salvin. Displays in the castle include the Royal Welch Fusiliers Museum, and exhibitions tracing the history of the Princes of Wales and exploring the importance of the castle in Welsh history.

Situated on the hill above the town are the ruins of **Segontium**, a Roman fort built in about AD 78. Local legend claims that the first Christian Emperor of Rome, Constantine the Great, was born here in 280.

♣ **Caernarfon Castle**
Y Maes. **Tel** 01286 677617.
🔲 daily. 🅿️ 🔲 call for details. 🔲
www.cadw.wales.gov.uk

🏛 **Segontium**
(NT) Beddgelert Rd. 🔲 Tue–Sun.
🔲 1 Jan, 24, 26 Dec. 🔲 limited.
www.segontium.org.uk

Beaumaris ❷

Isle of Anglesey. 🏛 2,000. 🚆 ℹ️
Llanfair PG, Station Site, Holyhead Rd, Anglesey (01248 713177).
www.visitanglesey.co.uk

Handsome Georgian and Victorian architecture gives Beaumaris the air of a resort on England's southern coast. The buildings reflect this

sailing centre's past role as Anglesey's chief port, before the island was linked to the mainland by the road and railway bridges built across the Menai Strait in the 19th century. This was the site of Edward I's last, and possibly greatest, **castle** *(see p438)*, which was built to command this important ferrying point to the mainland of Wales.

Ye Olde Bull's Head inn, on Castle Street, was built in 1617. Its celebrated literary patrons have included Dr Samuel Johnson (1709–84) and Victorian novelist Charles Dickens *(see p189)*.

The town's **Courthouse**, was built in 1614, and the restored 1829 **Gaol** preserves its soundproofed punishment room and a huge treadmill for prisoners. Two public hangings took place here. Richard Rowlands, the last victim, protested his innocence and cursed the church clock as he was led to the gallows, declaring that its four faces would never show the same times again. It failed to show consistent times until it had an overhaul in 1980.

♣ **Beaumaris Castle**
Castle St. **Tel** 01248 810361.
🔲 daily. 🅿️ 🔲 **www**.cadw.
wales.gov.uk

🏛 **Courthouse**
Castle St. **Tel** 01248 811691.
🔲 Apr–Sep: Sat–Thu. 🅿️ 🔲 🔲

🏛 **Gaol**
Bunkers Hill. **Tel** 01248 810921.
🔲 Apr–Sep: Sat–Thu. 🅿️ 🔲 ltd.
🔲 **www**.visitanglesey.co.uk

ALICE IN WONDERLAND

Penmorfa, Llandudno, was the summer home of the Liddells. Their friend, Charles Dodgson (1832–98), would entertain young Alice Liddell with stories of characters such as the White Rabbit and the Mad Hatter. As Lewis Carroll, Dodgson wrote his magical tales in *Alice's Adventures in Wonderland* (1865) and *Through the Looking-Glass* (1871).

Arthur Rackham's illustration (1907) of *Alice in Wonderland*

🏛 **Llandudno Museum**
Gloddaeth St. *Tel* 01492 876517.
◯ *Easter–Oct: 10:30am–1pm, 2–5pm Tue–Sat, (from 2:15pm Sun); Nov–Easter: 1:30–4:30pm Tue–Sat.*
♿ *limited.*

⛏ **Great Orme Copper Mines**
Off A55. *Tel* 01492 870447. ◯ *mid-Mar–Oct: daily.* 📷 ♿ *limited.*
🖥 📷 www.greatormemines.info

Conwy ❸

See pp446–7.

Llandudno ❹

Conwy. 🏘 *20,000.* 🚆 🚌 **i**
Library Building, Mostyn St (01492 577577). www.visitllandudno.org.uk

Llandudno's crescent-shaped bay

Llandudno retains much of the holiday spirit of the 19th century, when the new railways brought crowds to the coast. Its **pier**, more than 700 m (2,295 ft) long, and its canopied walkways recall the heyday of seaside holidays. The town is also proud of its association with the author Lewis Carroll *(see above)*. The exhibits at the **Llandudno Museum** explore Llandudno's history from Roman times onwards.

Llandudno's cheerful seaside atmosphere owes much to a strong sense of its Victorian roots – unlike many British seaside towns, which embraced the flashing lights and funfairs of the 20th century. To take full advantage of its sweeping beach, Llandudno was laid out between its two headlands, Great Orme's Head and Little Orme's Head.

Great Orme's Head, now a Country Park and Nature Reserve, rises to 207 m (670 ft) and has a long history. In the Bronze Age copper was mined here; the **copper mines** and their excavations are open to the public. The **church** on the headland was built from timber in the 6th century by St Tudno, rebuilt in stone in the 13th century, restored in 1855 and is still in use. Local history and wildlife can be traced in an information centre on the summit.

There are two effortless ways to reach the summit: on the **Great Orme Tramway**, one of only three cable-hauled street tramways in the world (the others are in San Francisco and Lisbon), or by the **Llandudno Cable Car**. Both run from April to October.

Ruthin ❺

Denbighshire. 🏘 *5,200.*
🚌 **i** *Craft Centre, Park Rd (01824 703992).* 🛒 *1st Tue of every month; Thu (indoor).*
www.visitruthin.com

Ruthin's long-standing prosperity as a market town is reflected in its fine half-timbered medieval buildings. These include the NatWest and Barclays banks in St Peter's Square. The former was a 15th-century courthouse and prison, the latter the home of Thomas Exmewe, Lord Mayor of London in 1517–18. **Maen Huail** ("Huail's stone"), a boulder outside Barclays, is said to be where King Arthur *(see p285)* beheaded Huail, his rival in a love affair.

St Peter's Church, on the edge of St Peter's Square, was founded in 1310 and has a Tudor oak roof in the north aisle. Next to the Castle Hotel is the 17th-century pub **The Myddleton Arms**, whose seven unusual, Dutch-style, dormer windows are known locally as the "eyes of Ruthin".

The "eyes of Ruthin", an unusual feature in Welsh architecture

Street-by-Street: Conwy ➌

Conwy is one of Britain's most underrated historic towns. Until the early 1990s it was famous as a traffic bottleneck, but thanks to a town bypass, its concentration of architectural riches – unparalleled in Wales – can now be appreciated. The castle dominates: a brooding, intimidating monument built by Edward I *(see p438)*. But Conwy is set apart from other medieval towns by its amazingly well-preserved town walls. Fortified with 21 towers and three gateways, the walls form an almost unbroken shield around the old town.

Smallest House
This fisherman's cottage on the quayside, just over 3 m (10 ft) high, is said to be the smallest house in Britain.

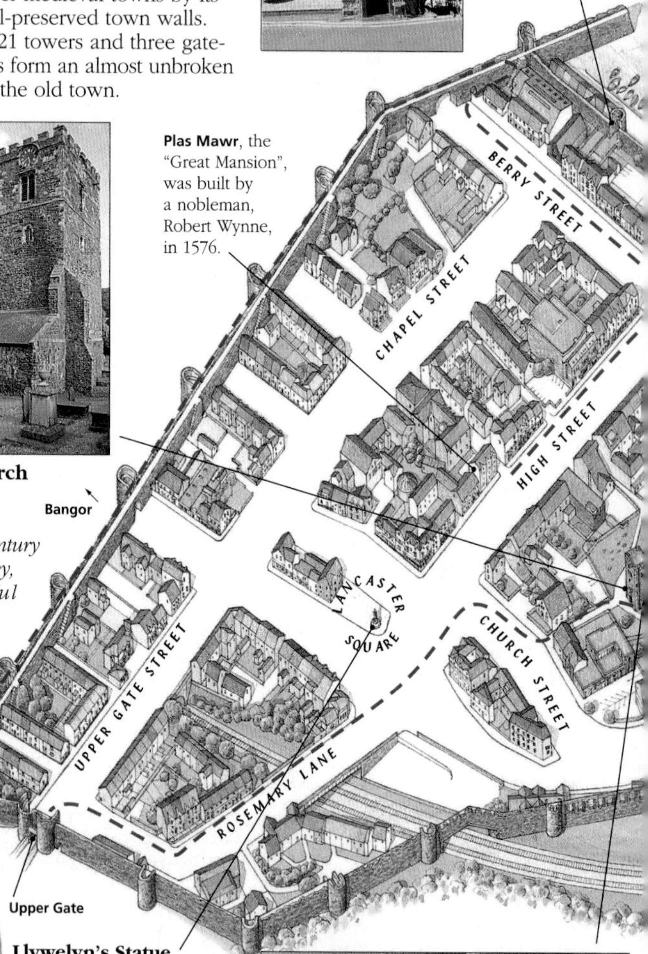

Plas Mawr, the "Great Mansion", was built by a nobleman, Robert Wynne, in 1576.

St Mary's Church
This medieval church, on the site of a 12th-century Cistercian abbey, is set in peaceful grounds.

Bangor

BERRY STREET

CHAPEL STREET

HIGH STREET

LANCASTER SQUARE

CHURCH STREET

UPPER GATE STREET

ROSEMARY LANE

Upper Gate

Llywelyn's Statue
Llywelyn the Great (see p436) was arguably Wales's most successful medieval leader.

Aberconwy House
This restored 14th-century house was once the home of a wealthy merchant.

THOMAS TELFORD

Thomas Telford (1757–1834) was the gifted Scottish engineer responsible for
many of Britain's roads, bridges and
canals. The Menai Bridge *(see
p444)*, the Pontcysyllte Aqueduct
(see p450) and Conwy Bridge
are his outstanding works in Wales.
Telford's graceful bridge at Conwy
has aesthetic as well as practical qualities.
Completed in 1826
across the mouth of the Conwy estuary, it was designed in
a castellated style to blend with the castle. Before the bridge's
construction the estuary could only be crossed by ferry.

VISITORS' CHECKLIST

Conwy. 🏠 8,000. 🚂 Conwy.
🛈 01492 577566. **Aberconwy
House (NT). Tel** 01492 592246.
⬜ Wed–Mon (Jul–Aug: daily).
⬤ Nov–Mar. 🎫 🏠 **Conwy
Castle Tel** 01492 592358. ⬜
daily. 🎫 🏠 **Smallest House
Tel** 01492 593484. ⬜ Apr–Oct:
daily. 🎫 🖥 **www**.conwy.com

★ Town Walls
*These remarkably
well-preserved
medieval walls are
1,280 m (4,200 ft)
long and over 9 m
(30 ft) high.*

Chester

NEW BRIDGE

CASTLE STREET

CASTLE STREET

HILL STREET

Telford's bridge

Railway
bridge

| 0 metres | 50 |
| 0 yards | 50 |

Entrance
to castle

KEY

– – – Suggested route

STAR SIGHTS

★ Town Walls

★ Conwy Castle

★ Conwy Castle
This atmospheric watercolour, Conway Castle
(c.1770), is by the Nottingham artist Paul Sandby.

Pontcysyllte Aqueduct, built in 1795–1805, carrying the Llangollen Canal

Llangollen 6

Denbighshire. 5,000. *y Capel, Castle St (01978 860828).* *Tue.* **www**.llangollen.org.uk

Best known for its annual Eisteddfod (festival), this pretty town sits on the River Dee, which is spanned by a 14th-century bridge. The town became notorious in the 1700s, when two Irishwomen, Sarah Ponsonby and Lady Eleanor Butler, the "Ladies of Llangollen", set up house together in the half-timbered **Plas Newydd**. Their unconventional dress and literary enthusiasms attracted such celebrities as the Duke of Wellington *(see p162)* and William Wordsworth *(see p366)*. The ruins of a 13th-century castle, **Castell Dinas Brân**, occupy the summit of a hill overlooking the house.

Environs: Boats on the **Llangollen Canal** sail from Wharf Hill in summer and cross the spectacular 300 m (1,000 ft) long Pontcysyllte Aqueduct, built by Thomas Telford *(see p447)*.

Plas Newydd
(NT) Hill St. ***Tel*** *01978 862834.* *Apr–Oct: Wed–Sun.* *limited.*

Bala 7

Gwynedd. 2,000. from Llangollen. Penllyn, Pensarn Rd (01678 521021). **www**.visitsnowdonia.info

Bala Lake, Wales's largest natural lake, lies between the Aran and Arenig mountains at the fringes of Snowdonia National Park. It is popular for water-sports and boasts a unique fish called a *gwyniad,* which is related to the salmon.

The little grey-stone town of Bala is a Welsh-speaking community, its houses strung out along a single street at the eastern end of the lake. Thomas Charles (1755–1814), a Methodist church leader, once lived here. A plaque on his former home recalls Mary Jones who walked 28 miles (42 km) barefoot from Abergynolwyn to buy a Bible. This led to Charles establishing the Bible Society, providing cheap bibles to the working classes.

The narrow-gauge **Bala Lake Railway** follows the lake shore from Llanuwchllyn, 4 miles (6 km) southwest.

Betws-y-Coed 8

Conwy. *600. Royal Oak Stables (01690 710426).* **www**.betws-y-coed.co.uk

This village near the peaks of Snowdonia has been a hill-walking centre since the 19th century. To the west are the **Swallow Falls**, where the River Llugwy flows through a wooded glen. The bizarre **Ty Hyll** ("Ugly House"), is a *tŷ unnos* ("one-night house"); traditionally, houses erected between dusk and dawn on common land were entitled to freehold rights, and the owner could enclose land as far as he could throw an axe from the door. To the east is **Waterloo Bridge**, built by Thomas Telford to celebrate the victory against Napoleon.

Ty Hyll
Capel Curig. ***Tel*** *01286 685498.* **House** *Easter–Sep: daily.* **Grounds** *daily.* *limited.*

WORLD CULTURES IN LLANGOLLEN

Llangollen's International Eisteddfod *(see p63)* in the first half of July draws musicians, singers and dancers from around the world. First held in 1947 as a gesture of post-war international unity, it now attracts over 12,000 performers from nearly 50 countries to the six-day-long competition-cum-fair.

Choristers at the Eisteddfod, a popular Welsh festival

The ornate Waterloo Bridge, built in 1815 after the famous battle

◁ The picturesque village of Beddgelert in Snowdonia National Park

A view of the Snowdonia countryside from Llanberis Pass, the most popular route to Snowdon's peak

Blaenau Ffestiniog ❾

Gwynedd. 🏔 4,800. 🚆
ℹ Betws-y-Coed (01690 710426).
🛒 Tue (Jun–Sep).

Blaenau Ffestiniog, once the slate capital of North Wales, sits among mountains riddled with quarries. The **Llechwedd Slate Caverns**, overlooking Blaenau, opened to visitors in the early 1970s, marking a new role for the declining industrial town. The electric Miners' Tramway takes passengers on a tour into the original caverns.

On the Deep Mine tour, visitors descend on Britain's steepest passenger incline railway to the underground chambers, while sound effects recreate the atmosphere of a working quarry. The dangers included landfalls and floods, as well as the more gradual threat of slate dust breathed into the lungs.

There are slate-splitting demonstrations on the surface, a quarryman's cottage and a re-creation of a Victorian village to illustrate the cramped and basic living conditions endured by workers between the 1880s and 1945.

The popular narrow-gauge **Ffestiniog Railway** (see pp452–3) runs from Blaenau to Porthmadog.

🏛 **Llechwedd Slate Caverns**
Off A470. **Tel** 01766 830306. ◯
Mar–Oct: daily; Nov–Feb: Sat–Thu.
🎫 ♿ except Deep Mine. ▢ 🗌 🗍
www.llechwedd-slate-caverns.co.uk

Llanberis and Snowdon ❿

Gwynedd. 🏔 2,100. ℹ High St, Llanberis (01286 870765).
www.gwynedd.gov.uk

Snowdon, which at 1,085 m (3,560 ft) is the highest peak in Wales, is the main focus of the vast Snowdonia National Park, whose scenery ranges from this rugged mountain country to moors and sandy beaches.

The easiest route to Snowdon's summit begins in Llanberis: the 5 mile (8 km) **Llanberis Track**. From Llanberis Pass, the Miners' Track (once used by copper miners) and the Pyg Track are alternative paths. Walkers should beware of sudden weather changes and dress accordingly. The narrow-gauge **Snowdon Mountain Railway**, which opened in 1896, is an easier option.

Llanberis was a major 19th-century slate town, with grey terraces hewn into the hills. Other attractions are the 13th-century shell of **Dolbadarn Castle**, and, above Llyn (Lake) Peris, the **Electric Mountain**, which has tours of Europe's biggest hydro-electric pumped storage station.

♦ **Dolbadarn Castle**
Off A4086 nr Llanberis.
Tel 01286 870765. ◯ daily.

ℹ **Electric Mountain**
Llanberis. **Tel** 01286 870636.
◯ daily. 🎫 ♿ 🗌 🗍
www.fhc.co.uk

BRITAIN'S CENTRE OF SLATE

Welsh slates provided roofing material for Britain's new towns in the 19th century. In 1898, the slate industry employed nearly 17,000 men, a quarter of whom worked at Blaenau Ffestiniog. Foreign competition and new materials later took their toll. Quarries such as Dinorwig in Llanberis and Llechwedd in Blaenau Ffestiniog now survive on the tourist trade.

The dying art of slate-splitting

The village of Beddgelert, set among the mountains of Snowdonia

Beddgelert ⑪

Gwynedd. 🚉 500.
ℹ Canolfan-Hebog (01766 890615).
www.beddgelerttourism.com

Beddgelert enjoys a spectacular location in Snowdonia. The village sits on the confluence of the Glaslyn and Colwyn rivers at the approach to two mountain passes: the beautiful Nant Gwynant Pass, which leads to Snowdonia's highest reaches, and the Aberglaslyn Pass, a narrow wooded gorge which acts as a gateway to the sea.

Business was given a boost by Dafydd Pritchard, the landlord of the Royal Goat Hotel, who in the early 19th century adapted an old Welsh legend to associate it with Beddgelert. Llywelyn the Great (see p436) is said to have left his faithful hound Gelert to guard his infant son while he went hunting. He returned to find the cradle overturned and Gelert covered in blood. Thinking the dog had savaged his son, Llywellyn slaughtered Gelert, but then discovered the boy, unharmed, under the cradle. Nearby was the corpse of a wolf, which Gelert had killed to protect the child. To support the tale, Pritchard created **Gelert's Grave** (bedd Gelert in Welsh) by the River Glaslyn, a mound of stones a short walk south of the village.

Environs: There are many fine walks in the area: one leads south to the Aberglaslyn Pass and along a disused part of the Welsh Highland Railway. The **Sygun Copper Mine**, 1 mile (1.5 km) northeast of Beddgelert, offers self-guided tours of caverns recreating the life of Victorian miners.

🔩 Sygun Copper Mine
On A498. **Tel** 01766 890595.
⬜ Mar–Oct: daily; Feb half term.
🎟 ♿ limited. 🅿 🚻 🏪
www.syguncoppermine.co.uk

Ffestiniog Railway

The Ffestiniog narrow-gauge railway takes a scenic 14 mile (22 km) route from Porthmadog Harbour to the mountains and the slate town of Blaenau Ffestiniog (see p451). Designed to carry slate from the quarries to the quay, the railway replaced a horse-drawn tramway constructed in 1836, operating on a 60 cm (2 ft) gauge. After closure in 1946, it was reconstructed by volunteers and re-opened in sections from 1955–82.

Railway crest

Steam traction trains were first used on the Ffestiniog Railway in 1863. There are some diesel engines but most trains on the route are still steam-hauled.

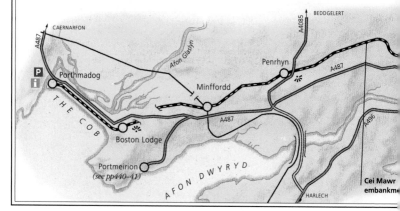

Lleyn Peninsula ⑫

Gwynedd. 🚆 🚌 *Pwllheli.* 🚤
Aberdaron to Bardsey Island. 🛈
Min-y-don, Station Sq, Pwllheli (01758 613000). **www**.nwt.co.uk

This 24-mile (38-km) finger of land points southwest from Snowdonia into the Irish Sea. Although it has popular beaches, notably at Pwllheli, Criccieth, Abersoch and Nefyn, the coast's overriding feature is its untamed beauty. Views are at their most dramatic in the far west and along the mountain-backed northern shores.

The windy headland of **Braich-y-Pwll**, to the west of Aberdaron, looks out towards Bardsey Island, the "Isle of 20,000 Saints". This became a place of pilgrimage in the 6th century, when a monastery was founded here. Some of the saints are said to be buried in the churchyard of the ruined 13th-century **St Mary's Abbey**. Close by is **Porth Oer**, a small bay also known as "Whistling Sands" (the sand is meant to squeak, or whistle, underfoot).

East of Aberdaron is the 4 mile (6.5 km) bay of **Porth Neigwl**, known in English as Hell's Mouth, the scene of many shipwrecks due to the bay's treacherous currents. Hidden in sheltered grounds above Porth Neigwl bay, 1 mile (1.5 km) northeast of Aberdaron, is **Plas-yn-Rhiw**, a small, medieval manor house with Tudor and Georgian additions and lovely gardens.

The former quarrying village and "ghost town" of **Lithfaen**, tucked away below the sheer cliffs of the mountainous north coast, is now a centre for Welsh language studies.

🏠 Plas-yn-Rhiw
(NT) off B4413. **Tel** *01758 780219.*
⭕ *Apr & Oct: Thu–Sun; May–Aug: Wed–Mon; Sep: Thu–Mon.* 🅿 ♿ *limited.*

Lithfaen village, now a language centre, on the Lleyn Peninsula

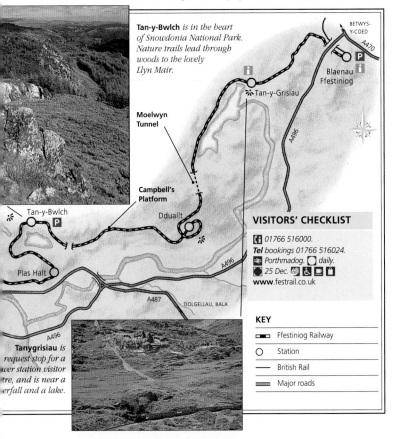

Tan-y-Bwlch is in the heart of Snowdonia National Park. Nature trails lead through woods to the lovely Llyn Mair.

BETWYS-Y-COED

🅿 🛈 Blaenau Ffestiniog

🏔 Tan-y-Grisiau

Moelwyn Tunnel

Campbell's Platform

Dduallt

Tan-y-Bwlch 🅿

Plas Halt

A487

A496

A470

DOLGELLAU, BALA

Tanygrisiau is ... *request stop for a* ... *wer station visitor* ... *re, and is near a* ... *erfall and a lake.*

VISITORS' CHECKLIST

🛈 *01766 516000.*
Tel *bookings 01766 516024.*
🚆 *Porthmadog.* ⭕ *daily.*
⭕ *25 Dec.* 🅿 ♿ 🍴 🛍
www.festrail.co.uk

KEY

▭▬	Ffestiniog Railway
○	Station
—	British Rail
▬	Major roads

Portmeirion ⑬

Gwynedd. **Tel** 01766 770000.
Minffordd. daily 25 Dec.
limited.
www.portmeirion-village.com

This bizarre Italianate village on a private peninsula at the top of Cardigan Bay was created by Welsh architect Sir Clough Williams-Ellis (1883–1978). He fulfilled a childhood dream by building a village "to my own fancy on my own chosen site". About 50 build-ings surround a central piazza, in styles from Oriental to Gothic. Visitors can stay at the luxurious hotel or in one of the charming village cottages. Portmeirion has been an atmo-spheric location for many films and television programmes, including the popular 1960s television series *The Prisoner*.

Sir Clough Williams-Ellis at Portmeirion

Hercules *is a life-size 19th-century copper statue near the Town Hall, where a 17th-century ceiling, rescued from a demolished mansion, depicts his legend.*

Fountain Cottage is where Noel Coward (1899–1973) wrote *Blithe Spirit*.

The *Amis Reunis* is a stone replica of a boat that sank in the bay.

Swimming pool

The Portmeirion Hotel *overlooks the bay. In 2005 its dining room was redesigned by Sir Terence Conran.*

Harlech ⑭

Gwynedd. 2,000. High St (01766 780658). Sun (summer).
www.gwynedd.gov.uk

This small town with fine beaches is dominated by **Harlech Castle**, a medieval fortress *(see p438)* built by Edward I between 1283 and 1289. The castle sits on a pre-cipitous crag, with superb views of Tremadog Bay and the Lleyn Peninsula to the west, and Snowdonia to the north. When the castle was built, the sea reached a fortified stairway cut into the cliff, so that sup-plies could arrive by ship, but now the sea has receded. A towering gatehouse protects the inner ward, enclosed by walls and four round towers.

Despite its defences, Harlech Castle fell to Owain Glyndŵr *(see p436)* in 1404, and served as his court until its recapture four years later. The song *Men of Harlech* is thought to have been inspired by the castle's heroic resistance during an eight-year siege in the Wars of the Roses *(see p49)*.

♣ **Harlech Castle**
Castle Sq. **Tel** 01766 780552.
daily. 1 Jan, 24–26 Dec.
www.cadw.wales.gov.uk

Dolgellau ⑮

Gwynedd. 2,700. Eldon Sq (01341 422888). Fri (livestock).

The dark local stone gives a stern, solid look to this market town, where the Welsh language and customs are still very strong. It lies in the long shadow of the 892 m (2,927 ft) mountain of Cader Idris where, according to legend, anyone who spends a night on its summit will awake a poet or a madman – or not at all.

Dolgellau was gripped by gold fever in the 19th century, when high-quality gold was

Harlech Castle's strategic site overlooking mountains and sea

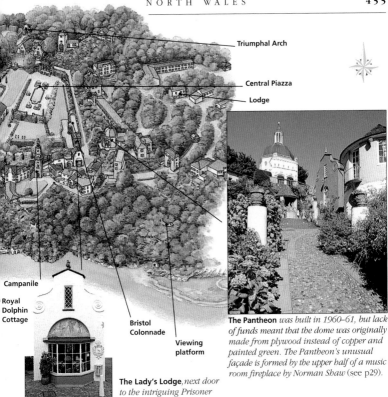

Triumphal Arch

Central Piazza

Lodge

Campanile

Royal Dolphin Cottage

Bristol Colonnade

Viewing platform

The Lady's Lodge, *next door to the intriguing Prisoner Shop.*

The Pantheon *was built in 1960–61, but lack of funds meant that the dome was originally made from plywood instead of copper and painted green. The Pantheon's unusual façade is formed by the upper half of a music room fireplace by Norman Shaw (see p29).*

Dolgellau's grey-stone buildings, dwarfed by the mountain scenery

discovered in the Mawddach Valley nearby. The deposits were not large enough to sustain an intensive mining industry for long. Nevertheless, up until 1999, small amounts were mined and crafted locally into fine jewellery.

Dolgellau is a good centre for walking, whether you wish to take gentle strolls through beautiful leafy countryside or strenuous hikes across extreme terrain with dramatic mountain views. The lovely **Cregennen lakes** are set high in the hills above the thickly wooded **Mawddach Estuary** to the northwest; north are the harsh, bleak **Rhinog moors**, one of Wales's last true wilderness.

Aberdyfi ⑯

Gwynedd. ⚑ 780. ⊟ ⓘ *Wharf Gardens (01654 767321).* www.gwynedd.gov.uk

Perched on the mouth of the Dyfi Estuary, this little harbour resort and sailing centre makes the most of its splendid but rather confined location, its houses occupying every yard of a narrow strip of land between mountain and sea. In the 19th century, local slate was exported from here, and between the 1830s and the 1860s about 100 ships were built in the port. *The Bells of Aberdovey*, a song by Charles Dibdin for his opera *Liberty Hall* (1785), tells the legend of Cantref-y-Gwaelod, thought to have been located here, which was protected from the sea by dykes. One stormy night, the sluice gates were left open by Prince Seithenyn, when he was drunk, and the land was lost beneath the waves. The submerged church bells are said to peal under the water to this day.

Neat Georgian houses by the sea, Aberdyfi

SOUTH AND MID-WALES

CARDIFF, SWANSEA & ENVIRONS · CEREDIGION
CARMARTHENSHIRE · MONMOUTHSHIRE · POWYS · PEMBROKESHIRE

*S*outh and mid-Wales are less homogeneous regions than North
Wales. Most of the population lives in the southeast corner. To
the west is Pembrokeshire, the loveliest stretch of Welsh coastline. To the north the industrial valleys give way to the wide hills of
the Brecon Beacons and the rural heartlands of central Wales.

South Wales's coastal strip has been settled for many centuries. There are prehistoric sites in the Vale of Glamorgan and Pembrokeshire. The Romans established a major base at Caerleon, and the Normans built castles all the way from Chepstow to Pembroke. In the 18th and 19th centuries, coal mines and ironworks opened in the valleys of South Wales, attracting immigrants from all over Europe. Close communities developed here, focused on the coal trade, which turned Cardiff from a sleepy coastal town into the world's busiest coal-exporting port.

The declining coal industry has again changed the face of this area: spoil heaps have become green hills, and the valley towns struggle to find alternative forms of employment. Coal mines such as Blaenafon's Big Pit are now tourist attractions; today, many of the tour guides taking visitors underground are ex-miners, who can offer a first-hand glimpse of the hard life found in mining communities before the pits closed.

The southern boundary of the Brecon Beacons National Park marks the beginning of rural Wales. With a population sparser than anywhere in England, this is an area of small country towns, hill-sheep farms, forestry plantations and spectacular man-made lakes.

The number of Welsh-speakers increases and the sense of Welsh culture becomes stronger as you travel further from the border with England, with the exception of an English enclave in south Pembrokeshire.

The changing face of the coal industry: former miners take visitors down the Big Pit in Blaenafon

◁ Magnificent coastal scenery near St David's, Pembrokeshire

Exploring South and Mid-Wales

Magnificent coastal scenery marks the Pembrokeshire
Coast National Park and cliff-backed Gower Peninsula,
while Cardigan Bay and Carmarthen Bay offer quieter
beaches. Walkers can enjoy grassy uplands in the Brecon
Beacons and gentler country in the leafy Wye Valley. Urban
life is concentrated in the southeast of Wales, where old
mining towns line the valleys north of Cardiff, the capital.

GETTING AROUND
The M4 motorway is the major route
into Wales from the south of England,
and there are good road links west of
Swansea running to the coast. The
A483 and A488 give access to mid-
Wales from the Midlands. Frequent
rail services connect London with
Swansea, Cardiff and the ferry
port of Fishguard.

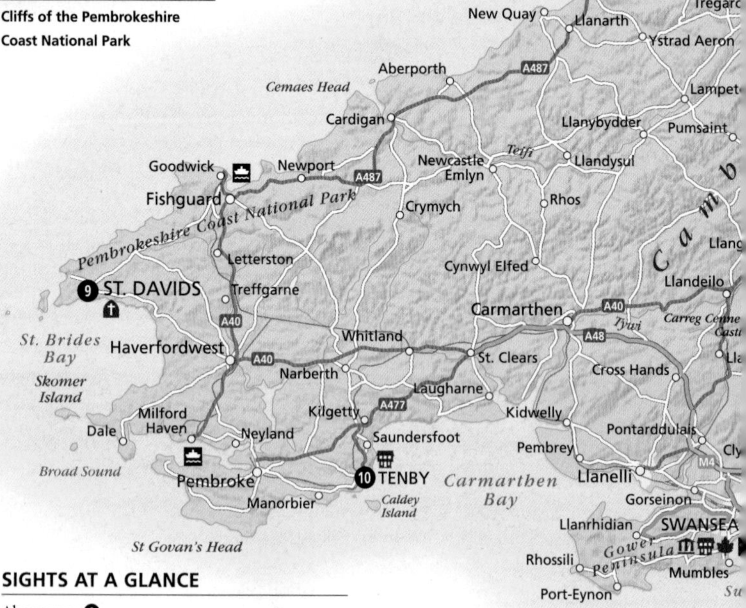

**Cliffs of the Pembrokeshire
Coast National Park**

MACHYNLLE

Aberdyfi

Borth

A487

ABERYSTWYTH 7

*Cardigan
Bay*

Devil's

Llanon   Pontrhydfenc
        Strata Florid

ABERAERON 8

New Quay   Llanarth   Tregarc

Aberporth   Ystrad Aeron

Cemaes Head   A487   Lampet

Cardigan   Llanybydder   Pumsaint

Newcastle   *Teifi*   Llandysul
Emlyn

Goodwick   Newport   Crymych   Rhos   *Ca m b*

Fishguard   A487   Cynwyl Elfed   Llang

Pembrokeshire Coast National Park   Llandeilo

Letterston   Carmarthen   A40   *Tywi*   Carreg Cenne
                      Castl

9 **ST DAVIDS**   Treffgarne   A48

A40   Whitland   St Clears   Lla

*St. Brides
Bay*   Haverfordwest   A40   Narberth   Cross Hands   Lla

*Skomer
Island*   Laugharne   Kidwelly   Pontarddulais

Dale   Milford   Kilgetty   A477   M4
     Haven   Neyland   Saundersfoot   Pembrey   Cly

Broad Sound   Pembroke   10 **TENBY**   *Carmarthen*   Llanelli   Gorseinon

Manorbier   *Caldey
Island*   *Bay*   Llanrhidian   **SWANSEA**

St Govan's Head   *Gower*

Rhossili   *Peninsula*   Mumbles

Port-Eynon   *Su*

SIGHTS AT A GLANCE

Aberaeron 8
Aberystwyth 7
Blaenafon 16
*Brecon Beacons
   pp468–9* 13
Caerleon 15
Cardiff pp470–71 14
Elan Valley 5
Hay-on-Wye 3
Knighton 2
Llandrindod Wells 4

Machynlleth 6
Monmouth 17
Powis Castle 1
St Davids pp464–5 9
Swansea and the
   Gower Peninsula 11
Tenby 10
Tintern Abbey 18

Walks and Tours

Wild Wales Tour 12

SEE ALSO

• *Where to Stay* pp591–4

• *Where to Eat* pp644–6

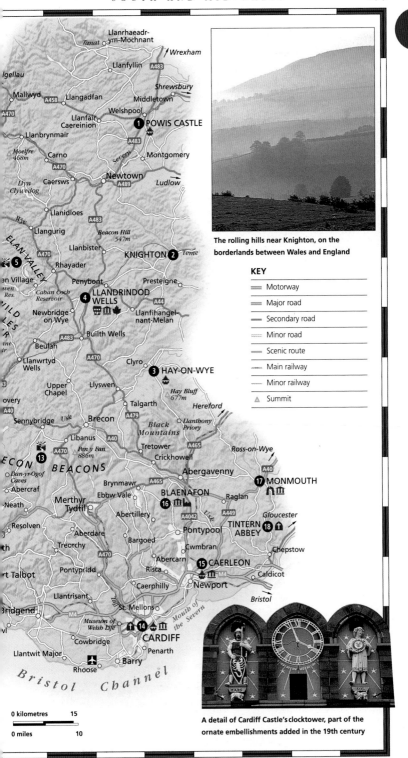

The rolling hills near Knighton, on the borderlands between Wales and England

KEY

═══ Motorway

═══ Major road

─── Secondary road

···· Minor road

─── Scenic route

▬▬▬ Main railway

─── Minor railway

△ Summit

A detail of Cardiff Castle's clocktower, part of the ornate embellishments added in the 19th century

0 kilometres 15

0 miles 10

Italianate terraces and formal gardens at Powis Castle, adding a Mediterranean air to the Welsh borderlands

Powis Castle ❶

(NT) Welshpool, Powys. 📷 01938 551944. 🚌 Welshpool then bus. ⭕ Mar–Dec: daily. 🅿️ 🔌 limited. 📷 🍴 www.nationaltrust.org.uk

Powis Castle – the spelling is an archaic version of "Powys" – has outgrown its military roots. Despite its sham battlements and dominant site, 1 mile (1.6 km) to the southwest of the town of Welshpool, this red-stone building has served as a country mansion for centuries. It began life in the 13th century as a fortress, built by the princes of Powys to control the border with England.

The castle is entered through one of few surviving medieval features: a gateway, built in 1283 by Owain de la Pole. The gate is flanked by two towers.

The castle's lavish interiors soon banish all thoughts of war. A **Dining Room**, decorated with fine 17th-century panelling and family portraits, was originally designed as the castle's Great Hall. The **Great Staircase**, added in the late 17th century and elaborately decorated with carved fruit and flowers, leads to the main apartments: an early 19th-century library, the panelled **Oak Drawing Room** and the Elizabethan **Long Gallery**, where ornate plasterwork on the fireplace and ceiling date from the 1590s. In the **Blue Drawing Room** there are three 18th-century Brussels tapestries.

The Herbert family bought the property in 1587 and were proud of their Royalist connections; the panelling in the **State Bedroom** bears the royal monogram. Powis Castle

The richly carved 17th-century Great Staircase

was defended for Charles I in the Civil War (see pp52–3), but fell to Parliament in 1644. The 3rd Baron Powis, a supporter of James II, had to flee the country when William and Mary took the throne in 1688 (see pp52–3).

The castle's **Clive Museum** has an exhibition concerning "Clive of India" (1725–74), the general and statesman who helped strengthen British control in India in the mid-18th century. The family's link with Powis Castle was established by the 2nd Lord Clive, who married into the Herbert family and became the Earl of Powis in 1804.

The **gardens** at Powis are among the best-known in Britain, with their series of elegant Italianate terraces, adorned with statues, niches, balustrades, hanging gardens and sinuous mounded yew trees, all stepped into the steep hillside beneath the castle walls. Created between 1688 and 1722, these are the only formal gardens of this period in Britain that are still kept in their original form (see pp26–7).

Knighton ❷

Powys. 👥 3,500. 🚆 ℹ️ Offa's Dyke Centre, West St (01547 528753). 🛒 Thu. www.visitknighton.co.uk

Knighton's Welsh name, Tref y Clawdd ("The Town on the Dyke"), reflects its status as the only original settlement on **Offa's Dyke**. In the 8th century, King Offa of Mercia (central and southern England) constructed a ditch and bank to mark out his territory, and to enable the enforcement of a Saxon law: "Neither shall a Welshman cross into English land without the appointed man from the other side, who should meet him at the bank and bring him back again without any offence being committed." Some of the best-preserved sections of the 6-m-(20-ft-) high earthwork lie in the hills around Knighton. The Offa's Dyke Footpath runs for 177 miles (285 km) along the border between England and Wales.

Knighton is set on a steep hill, sloping upwards from **St Edward's Church** (1877) with its medieval tower, to the summit, where a castle once stood. The main street leads via the market square, marked by a 19th-century clock tower, along **The Narrows**, a Tudor street with little shops. **The Old House** on Broad Street is a medieval "cruck" house (curved timbers form a frame to support the roof), with a hole in the ceiling instead of a chimney.

Knighton's clock

Hay-on-Wye ❸

Powys. 👥 1,500. ℹ️ Oxford Rd (01497 820144). 🛒 Thu. www.hay-on-wye.co.uk

Book-lovers from all over the world come to this quiet border town in the Black Mountains. Hay-on-Wye has over 30 second-hand bookshops stocking millions of titles, and in early summer hosts a prestigious Festival of Literature and the Arts. The town's love affair with books began when a bookshop was opened in the 1960s by Richard Booth, who claims the (fictitious) title of King of Independent Hay and lived in **Hay Castle**, a 17th-century mansion in the grounds of the original 13th-century castle (now owned by a charitable trust).

Hay's oldest inn, the 16th-century **Three Tuns** on Bridge Street, is still functioning and has an attractive half-timbered façade.

Environs: Hay sits on the approach to the Black Mountains and is surrounded by rolling hills. To the south are the heights of Hay Bluff and the Vale of Ewyas, where the 12th-century ruins of **Llanthony Priory** (see p469) retain fine pointed arches.

⛪ **Hay Castle**
🔘 until further notice.
www.haycastletrust.com

Llandrindod Wells ❹

Powys. 👥 5,000. 🚆 ℹ️ Memorial Gardens (01597 822600). 🛒 farmers' market last Thu of month; Fri.

Llandrindod is a perfect example of a Victorian town, with canopied streets, delicate wrought ironwork,

One of Hay-on-Wye's bookshops

gabled villas and ornamental parklands. This purpose-built spa town became Wales's premier inland resort of the 19th century. Its sulphur and magnesium spring waters were taken to treat skin complaints and a range of other ailments.

The town now makes every effort to preserve its Victorian character, with a lake and the well-tended **Rock Park Gardens**. The restored 19th-century **Pump Room** in Temple Gardens is where, during the last full week of August, residents don period costume and cars are banned from the town centre.

The **Radnorshire Museum** traces the town's past as one of a string of 19th-century Welsh spas which included Builth, Llangammarch and **Llanwrtyd** (now a pony trekking centre).

🏛 **Radnorshire Museum**
Temple Street. *Tel* 01597 824513.
🔘 Tue–Sat. 🔘 1 Jan, 25 & 26 Dec. 📷 ♿

Victorian architecture on Spa Road, Llandrindod Wells

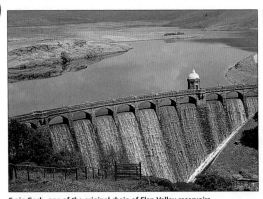
Craig Goch, one of the original chain of Elan Valley reservoirs

Elan Valley ❺

Powys. 🚌 *Llandrindod.*
🚆 *Rhayader (01597 810898).*
www.elanvalley.org.uk

A string of spectacular reservoirs, the first of the country's man-made lakes, has made this one of Wales's most famous valleys. **Caban Coch, Garreg Ddu, Pen-y-Garreg** and **Craig Goch**, were created between 1892 and 1903 to supply water to Birmingham, 73 miles (117 km) away. They form a chain of lakes about 9 miles (14 km) long, holding 50 billion litres (13 billion gallons) of water. Victorian engineers selected these high moorlands on the Cambrian Mountains, for their high annual rainfall of 1,780 mm (70 inches). The choice created bitter controversy and resentment: more than 100 people had to move from the valley that was flooded in order to create Caban Coch.

Unlike their more utilitarian modern counterparts, these dams were built during an era when decoration was seen as an integral part of any design. Finished in dressed stone, they have an air of grandeur which is lacking in the huge **Claerwen** reservoir, a stark addition built during the early 1950s to double the lakes' capacity. Contained by a 355 m (1,165 ft) dam, it lies 4 miles (6 km) along the B4518 that runs through Elan Valley and offers magnificent views.

The remote moorlands and woodlands surrounding the lakes are an important habitat for wildlife; the red kite can often be seen here. The **Elan Valley Visitors' Centre**, beside the Caban Coch dam, describes the construction of the lakes, as well as the valley's own natural history. **Elan Village**, set beside the centre, is an unusual example of a model workers' village, built during the 1900s to house the water-works staff. Outside the centre is a statue of the poet Percy Bysshe Shelley *(see p222),* who stayed in the valley at the mansion of Nantgwyllt in 1810 with his wife, Harriet. The house now lies underneath the waters of Caban Coch, along with the rest of the old village. Among the buildings submerged were the village school and a church.

The trail from Machynlleth to Devil's Bridge, near Aberystwyth

Machynlleth ❻

Powys. 🏚 *2,200.* 🚆 🚌
Aberystwyth (01970 612125). 🛥
Wed. **www**.exploremidwales.com

Half-timbered buildings and Georgian façades appear among the grey-stone houses in Machynlleth. It was here that Owain Glyndŵr, Wales's last native leader *(see p436),* held a parliament in 1404. The restored Parliament House now houses the **Owain Glyndŵr Centre**.

The ornate **Clock Tower**, in the middle of Maengwyn Street, was erected in 1874 by the Marquess of Londonderry to mark the coming of age of his heir, Lord Castlereagh. The Marquess lived in **Plas Machynlleth**, a 17th-century house in parkland off the main street, which now houses a restaurant and offices.

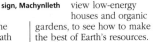
Parliament House sign, Machynlleth

Environs: In an old slate quarry 2.5 miles (4 km) to the north, a "village of the future" is run by the **Centre for Alternative Technology**. A water-balanced cliff railway takes summer visitors to view low-energy houses and organic gardens, to see how to make the best of Earth's resources.

🏛 **Owain Glyndŵr Centre**
Maengwyn St. **Tel** 01654 702932.
⬤ *Mar–Dec: Tue–Sat.* ♿ 🚻
🏛 **Centre for Alternative Technology** On A487. **Tel** 01654 705950. ⬤ *daily.* ⬤ *early Jan.* 📷
📷 ♿ 🚻 🔲 **www**.cat.org.uk

Aberystwyth ❼

Ceredigion. 🏚 *16,000.* 🚆 🚌
🚆 *Terrace Rd (01970 612125).*
www.ceredigion.gov.uk

This seaside and university town claims to be the cultural capital of mid-Wales. By the standards of this rural area, "Aber" is a big place, its population increased for much of the year by students.

To Victorian travellers, Aberystwyth was the "Biarritz

of Wales". There have been no great changes along the promenade, with its gabled hotels, since the 19th century. **Constitution Hill**, a steep outcrop at the northern end, can be scaled in summer on the electric **Cliff Railway**, built in 1896. At the top, in a *camera obscura*, a lens

Buskers on Aberystwyth's seafront

projects views of the town. The ruined **Aberystwyth Castle** (1277) is located south of the promenade. In the town centre, the **Ceredigion Museum**, set in a former music hall, traces the history of the town.

To the northeast of the town centre, **The National Library of Wales**, next to Aberystwyth University, has a valuable collection of ancient Welsh manuscripts.

SAVIN'S HOTEL

When the Cambrian Railway opened in 1864, businessman Thomas Savin put £80,000 into building a new hotel in Aberystwyth for package tourists. The scheme made him bankrupt, but the seafront building, complete with mock-Gothic tower, was bought by campaigners attempting to establish a Welsh university. The "college by the sea" opened in 1872, and is now the University of Aberystwyth.

Mosaics on the college tower

Environs: During the summer the narrow-gauge Vale of Rheidol Railway runs 12 miles (19 km) to **Devil's Bridge**, where a dramatic series of waterfalls plunges through a wooded ravine and a steep trail leads to the valley floor.

🏛 **Ceredigion Museum**
Terrace Rd. *Tel* 01970 633088. ⬜
Mon–Sat. ⬤ Good Fri, 25 Dec–2
Jan. 🅿 ♿ www.ceredigion.gov.uk

Aberaeron ❽

Ceredigion. 🚶 *1,500.*
🚌 *Aberystwyth, then bus.*
ℹ Quay Parade (01545 570602).
www.tourism.ceredigion.gov.uk

Aberaeron's harbour, lined with Georgian houses, became a trading port and shipbuilding centre in the early 19th century. Its orderly streets were laid out in pre-railway days, when the ports along Cardigan Bay enjoyed considerable wealth. The last boat was built here in 1994 and its harbour is now full of holiday sailors. The harbour can be crossed via a wooden footbridge.

On the quayside, the popular Hive honey ice cream parlour serves world-renowned ice creams to a loyal clientele. There is also a centre of local crafts in the town, Clos Pengarreg.

Rows of brightly painted Georgian houses lining the purpose-built harbour at Aberaeron

St Davids ❾

St David, the patron saint of Wales, founded a monastic settlement in this remote corner of southwest Wales in about 550, which became one of the most important Christian shrines. The present cathedral, built in the 12th century, and the Bishop's Palace, added a century later, are set in a grassy hollow below St Davids town, officially Britain's smallest city. The date of St David's death, 1 March, is commemorated throughout Wales.

Icon of Elijah, south transept

St Davids' Cathedral, the largest in Wales

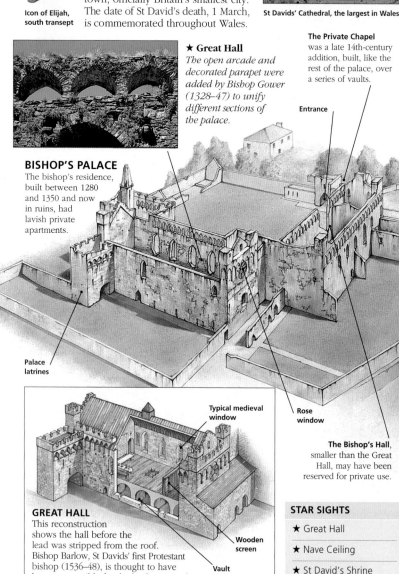

★ Great Hall
The open arcade and decorated parapet were added by Bishop Gower (1328–47) to unify different sections of the palace.

The Private Chapel
was a late 14th-century addition, built, like the rest of the palace, over a series of vaults.

Entrance

BISHOP'S PALACE
The bishop's residence, built between 1280 and 1350 and now in ruins, had lavish private apartments.

Palace latrines

Typical medieval window

Rose window

The Bishop's Hall, smaller than the Great Hall, may have been reserved for private use.

GREAT HALL
This reconstruction shows the hall before the lead was stripped from the roof. Bishop Barlow, St Davids' first Protestant bishop (1536–48), is thought to have been responsible for the lead's removal.

Wooden screen

Vault

STAR SIGHTS

★ Great Hall

★ Nave Ceiling

★ St David's Shrine

★ **Nave Ceiling**
The roof of the nave is lowered and hidden by an early 16th-century oak ceiling. A beautiful 14th-century rood screen divides the nave from the choir.

VISITORS' CHECKLIST

Cathedral Close, St Davids.
Tel 01437 720202.
Haverfordwest then bus.
9am–5:30pm daily (Sun: pm).
www.stdavidscathedral.org.uk

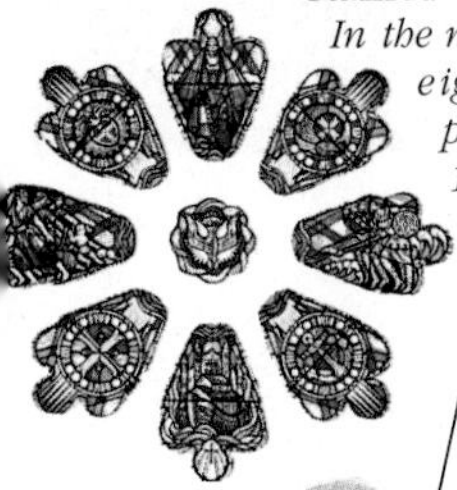

Stained-Glass Window
In the nave's west end, eight panels, produced in the 1950s, radiate from a central window showing the dove of peace.

CATHEDRAL
St David was one of the founders of the 6th-century monastic movement, so this was an important site of pilgrimage. Three visits here equalled one to Jerusalem.

St Mary's College Chapel

Bishop Vaughan's Chapel has a fine fan-vaulted early Tudor roof.

Entrance

Tower Lantern Ceiling
The medieval roof was decorated with episcopal insignia when restored in the 1870s by Sir George Gilbert Scott.

Sixteenth-Century Choir Stalls
The royal coat of arms on one of the carved choir stalls shows that the sovereign is a member of St Davids' Chapter. There are some interesting misericords (see p341) in these stalls.

★ **St David's Shrine**
A statue of the saint is placed near the shrine. Thought to symbolize the Holy Spirit, a dove is said to have landed on David's shoulder as he spoke to a gathering of bishops.

Tenby ⑩

Pembrokeshire. 🏠 5,000. 🚂 🚌 📍
🛈 Upper Park Road (01834 842
402). www.visitsouthwales.com

Tenby has successfully trodden the fine line between over-commercialization and popularity, refusing to submit its historic character to the garish excesses of some seaside towns. Georgian houses overlook its handsome harbour, which is backed by a well-preserved medieval clifftop town of narrow streets and passages. The old town was defended by a headland fortress, now ruined, flanked by two wide beaches and a ring of 13th-century walls. These survive to their full height in places, along with a fortified gateway, the **Five Arches**.

The three-storeyed **Tudor Merchant's House** is a 15th-century relic of Tenby's highly prosperous seafaring days, with original fireplaces and chimneys. There are regular boat trips from the harbour to **Caldey Island**, 3 miles (5 km) offshore, home of a perfume-making monastic community.

🏛 **Tudor Merchant's House**
(NT) Quay Hill. **Tel** 01834 842279.
◷ Apr–Oct: Wed–Mon (Aug:
daily); Nov–Dec, Feb: Sat & Sun. 📷
🎫 for pre-booked parties.

**A partly medieval restaurant next
to the Tudor Merchant's House**

Swansea and the Gower Peninsula ⑪

Swansea. 🏠 232,500. 🚂 🚌 📍
🛈 Plymouth St (01792 468321). 🛒
Mon–Sat. www.visitswanseabay.com

Swansea, Wales's second city, is set along a wide, curving bay. The city centre was rebuilt after heavy bombing in World War II but, despite the modern buildings, a traditional Welsh atmosphere prevails. This is particularly noticeable in the excellent food market, full of Welsh delicacies such as laverbread (see p606) and locally caught cockles.

The award-winning **Maritime Quarter** redevelopment has transformed the old docklands, and is worth a visit.

A statue of copper magnate John Henry Vivian (1779–1855) overlooks the marina. The Vivians, a leading Swansea family, founded the **Glynn Vivian Art Gallery**, which has exquisite Swansea pottery and porcelain. Archaeology and Welsh history feature at the **Swansea Museum**, the oldest museum in Wales.

**Swansea's most celebrated son,
the poet Dylan Thomas**

The life and work of local poet Dylan Thomas (1914–53) is celebrated in the **Dylan Thomas Centre**. A permanent exhibition, Man and Myth, includes the original drafts of his poems, letters and memorabilia. His statue overlooks the Maritime Quarter. Thomas spent his childhood in the city's suburbs. **Cwmdonkin Park** was the scene of an early poem, The Hunchback in the Park, and its water garden has a memorial stone quoting from his Fern Hill.

The **National Waterfront Museum** tells the story of industry and innovation in Wales over the past 300 years. The ultra-modern slate and glass building incorporates historic warehouses.

**Picturesque fishermen's cottages
at the Mumbles seaside resort**

Swansea Bay leads to the **Mumbles**, a popular water-sports centre at the gateway to the 19-mile-long (30 km) Gower Peninsula, which in 1956 was the first part of Britain to be declared an Area of Outstanding Natural Beauty. A string of sheltered, south-facing bays leads to Oxwich and Port-Eynon beaches.

Rhossili's enormous beach leads to north Gower and a coastline of low-lying burrows, salt marshlands and cockle beds. The peninsula is littered with ancient sites such as **Parc Le Breose**, a prehistoric burial chamber.

Near Carmarthen is the **National Botanic Garden of Wales**, with formal gardens centred on The Great Glasshouse which contains a Mediterranean ecosystem.

🏛 **Glynn Vivian Art Gallery**
Alexandra Rd. ◷ until 2014 for
refurbishment.
🌐 www.swansea.gov.uk

🏛 **Swansea Museum**
Victoria Rd. **Tel** 01792 653763. ◷
Tue–Sun & public hols. ♿ limited.
🌐 www.swansea.gov.uk

🏛 **Dylan Thomas Centre**
Somerset Pl. **Tel** 01792 463980.
◷ daily. ♿ 📷 by arrangement.
🍴 🎁 🛒 www.swansea.gov.uk

🏛 **National Waterfront
Museum**
Oystermouth Rd. **Tel** 01792
638950. ◷ daily. ♿ 🛒 www.
museumwales.ac.uk

🌷 **National Botanic Garden
of Wales**
Middleton Hall, Llanarthne.
Tel 01558 668768. ◷ daily.
● 25 Dec. 📷 ♿ 🍴 🛒 🎁
www.gardenofwales.org.uk

Wild Wales Tour ⑫

This tour weaves across the Cambrian Mountains' windswept moors, green hills and high, deserted plateaux. New roads have been laid to the massive Llyn Brianne Reservoir, north of Llandovery, and the old drover's road across to Tregaron has a tarmac surface. But the area is still essentially a "wild Wales" of hidden hamlets, isolated farmsteads, brooding highlands and traditional, quiet market towns.

Llanidloes ⑥
The town was a centre of religious and social unrest in the 17th and 18th centuries *(see p437)*. There is a rare example of a free-standing Tudor market hall. The medieval church was restored in the late 19th century.

Devil's Bridge ④
This is a popular, romantic beauty spot with waterfalls, rocks, wooded glades and an ancient stone bridge – built by the Devil, according to legend.

Strata Florida ③
This famous ruined abbey was an important political, religious and educational centre during the Middle Ages.

Elan Valley ⑤
This is an area of lakes and important wildlife habitats *(see p462)*.

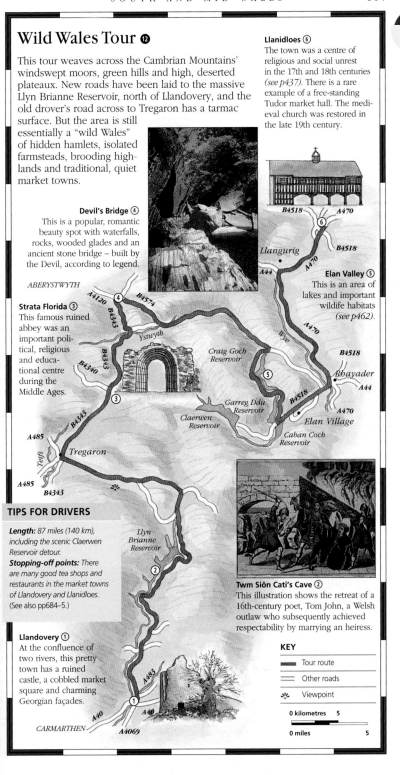

ABERYSTWYTH

Llangurig

Ystwyth

Craig Goch Reservoir

Wye

Rhayader

Garreg Ddu Reservoir

Claerwen Reservoir

Caban Coch Reservoir

Elan Village

Tregaron

Teifi

Llyn Brianne Reservoir

Twm Siôn Cati's Cave ②
This illustration shows the retreat of a 16th-century poet, Tom John, a Welsh outlaw who subsequently achieved respectability by marrying an heiress.

TIPS FOR DRIVERS

Length: *87 miles (140 km), including the scenic Claerwen Reservoir detour.*
Stopping-off points: *There are many good tea shops and restaurants in the market towns of Llandovery and Llanidloes. (See also pp684–5.)*

Llandovery ①
At the confluence of two rivers, this pretty town has a ruined castle, a cobbled market square and charming Georgian façades.

CARMARTHEN

KEY

▰▰▰	Tour route
═══	Other roads
☀	Viewpoint

0 kilometres 5

0 miles 5

Brecon Beacons ⑬

Trekking in the Beacons

The Brecon Beacons National Park covers 520 sq miles (1,345 sq km) from the Wales–England border almost all the way to Swansea. There are four mountain ranges within the park: the Black Mountain (to the west), Fforest Fawr, the Brecon Beacons and the Black Mountains (to the east). Much of the area consists of high, open country with smooth, grassy slopes on a bedrock of red sandstone. The park's southern rim has limestone crags, wooded gorges, waterfalls and caves. Visitors can enjoy many outdoor pursuits, from fishing in the numerous reservoirs to pony trekking, caving and walking.

Llyn y Fan Fach
This remote, myth-laden glacial lake is a 4 mile (6.5 km) walk from Llanddeusant.

The Black Mountain, a largely overlooked wilderness of knife-edged ridges and high, empty moorland, fills the western corner of the National Park.

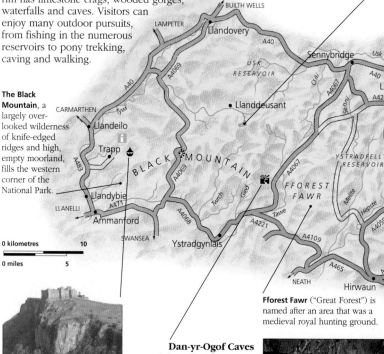

BUILTH WELLS
LAMPETER
Llandovery
A40
Sennybridge
Usk
USK RESERVOIR
A4069
A40
A421
Lli
CARMARTHEN
Tywi
Llanddeusant
Glai
A4067
Isge nni
Llandeilo
Trapp
B L A C K   M O U N T A I N
YSTRADFELLT RESERVOIR
A4067
A483
A4069
Twrch
Gled
FFOREST FAWR
Mellte
Hepste
A4059
Llandybie
A471
Tawe
A4221
A4109
LLANELLI
Ammanford
A4068
A465
SWANSEA
Ystradgynlais
NEATH
Hirwaun
A4

0 kilometres   10
0 miles   5

Fforest Fawr ("Great Forest") is named after an area that was a medieval royal hunting ground.

Dan-yr-Ogof Caves
A labyrinth of caves runs through the Brecon Beacons. Guided tours of two large caves are offered here.

Carreg Cennen Castle
Spectacularly sited, the ruined medieval fortress of Carreg Cennen (see p438) stands on a sheer limestone cliff near the village of Trapp.

KEY

▬▬▬	A road
▭▭▭	B road
═══	Minor road
– –	Footpath
☀	Viewpoint

Hay Bluff

At 677 m (2,221 ft), Hay Bluff looks out across border country. A narrow mountain road climbs from Hay-on-Wye to the Gospel Pass before dropping to Llanthony.

Brecon is an old market town with handsome Georgian buildings.

The Black Mountains form part of the border with England.

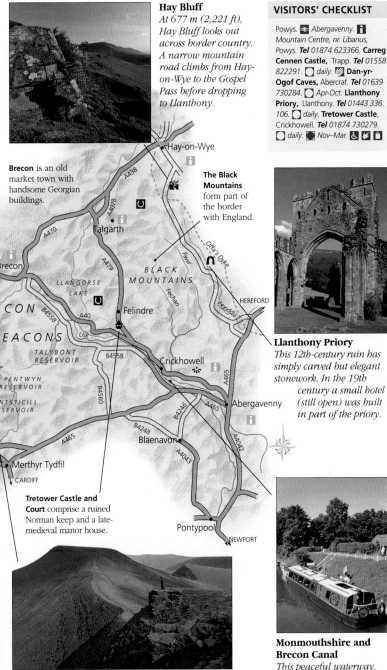

Llanthony Priory

This 12th-century ruin has simply carved but elegant stonework. In the 19th century a small hotel (still open) was built in part of the priory.

Tretower Castle and Court comprise a ruined Norman keep and a late-medieval manor house.

Monmouthshire and Brecon Canal

This peaceful waterway, completed in 1812, was once used to transport raw materials between Brecon and Newport. It is now popular with leisure boats.

Pen y Fan

At 886 m (2,907 ft), Pen y Fan is the highest point in South Wales. Its distinctive, flat-topped summit, once a Bronze Age burial ground (see pp42–3), can be reached by footpaths from Storey Arms on the A470.

Cardiff ⑭

Cardiff was first occupied by the Romans, who built a fort here in AD 55 *(see pp44–5)*. Little is known of its subsequent history until Robert FitzHamon *(see p472)*, a knight in the service of William the Conqueror, was given land here in 1093. By the 13th century, the settlement was substantial enough to be granted a royal charter, but it remained a quiet country town until the 1830s when the Bute family, who inherited land in the area, began to develop it as a port. By 1913 this was the world's busiest coal-exporting port, profiting from rail links with the South Wales mines. Its wealth paid for grandiose architecture, while the docklands became a raucous boom-town. Cardiff was confirmed as the first Welsh capital in 1955, by which time demand for coal was falling and the docks were in decline. The city is now being transformed by urban renewal programmes.

Fireplace detail in the Banqueting Hall, Cardiff Castle

City Hall's dome, adorned with a dragon, the emblem of Wales

Exploring Cardiff

Cardiff is a city with two focal points. The centre, laid out with Victorian and Edwardian streets and gardens, is the first of these. There is a Neo-Gothic castle and Neo-Classical civic buildings, as well as indoor shopping malls and a 19th-century **covered market**. Canopied arcades, lined with shops, lead off the main streets, the oldest being the **Royal Arcade** of 1858. The **Millennium Stadium** (on the site of Cardiff Arms Park, the first home of Welsh rugby) opened in 1999 with the Rugby World Cup, and is open for tours most days.

To the south of the centre, the docklands are now being transformed into the second focal point by the creation of a freshwater lake and waterfront. **Y Senedd**, which opened in 2006, houses the National Assembly for Wales. Free guided tours are available but

booking is essential. Other attractions in the area are **Techniquest**, a hands-on science museum, and the impressive **Wales Millennium Centre**. A leading cultural venue, it stages a range of arts performances including musicals, ballet and stand-up comedy. It is also home to the Welsh National Opera.

The wooden **Norwegian Church** was first erected in 1868 for Norwegian sailors bringing wooden props for use in the coal pits of the South Wales valleys. Once surrounded by warehouses, it was taken apart and rebuilt during the dockland development.

Also in Cardiff Bay, the Red Dragon Centre houses a range of entertainment and food outlets, while the **Doctor Who Experience**, featuring memorabilia and props from the show, is also based on the waterfront. The classic BBC television series has been made in Cardiff since 2004, and many of the city's landmarks appear on screen.

♣ Cardiff Castle
See pp472–3.

🏛 City Hall and Civic Centre
Cathays Park. **Tel** 029 2087 1727.
🕐 Mon–Fri. ◑ public hols.   ♿ ✓
www.cardiffcityhall.com

Cardiff's civic centre of Neo-Classical buildings in white Portland stone is set among parks and avenues around Alexandra Gardens. The City Hall (1905), one of its first buildings, is dominated by its 60 m (200 ft) dome and clock tower. Members of the public

The entrance to the Wales Millennium Centre

can visit the first-floor Marble Hall, which is furnished with Siena marble columns and statues of Welsh heroes, among them St David, Wales's patron saint *(see pp464–5).* Cardiff University is based in the Civic Centre, Cathays Park.

🏛 National Museum Cardiff
Cathays Park. *Tel 029 2039 7951.*
⬜ Tue–Sun, public hols. ⬤ 1, 2 Jan & 24, 25 Dec. ♿ ▢ 🎁 www.museum wales.ac.uk

Opened in 1927, the museum occupies an impressive civic building with a colonnaded portico, guarded by a statue of David Lloyd George *(see p437).* The art collection is among the finest in Europe, with works on display by Renoir, Monet and Van Gogh.

Statue of Welsh politician David Lloyd George

🏛 Craft in the Bay
The Flourish, Lloyd George Ave, Cardiff Bay. *Tel 029 2048 4611.*
⬜ 10:30am–5:30pm daily. ♿ ▢

An extensive craft gallery, organized by the Makers' Guild in Wales, opened here in 2002. The building now houses a wide variety of craft displays and demonstrations, including textile weaving and ceramic making.

Environs: Established during the 1940s at St Fagans, on the western edge of the city, the open-air **St Fagans National History Museum** was one of the first of its kind. Buildings from all over Wales, including workers' terraced cottages, farmhouses, a tollhouse, row of shops, chapel and old schoolhouse have been carefully reconstructed within the 40-ha (100-acre) parklands, along with a recreated Celtic village. There is also a Tudor mansion which can be visited, boasting

its own beautiful gardens in the grounds.

Llandaff Cathedral lies in a deep, grassy hollow beside the River Taf at Llandaff, 2 miles (3 km) northwest of the city centre. The cathedral was first a medieval building, occupying the site of a 6th-century monastic community.

Restored after suffering severe bomb damage during World War II, it was eventually reopened in 1957 with the addition of Sir Jacob Epstein's huge, stark statue, *Christus,* which is mounted on a concrete arch.

🏛 St Fagans National History Museum
St Fagans. *Tel 029 2057 3500.*
⬜ daily. ♿ 🍴
www.museumwales.ac.uk

CARDIFF CITY CENTRE

Cardiff Castle pp472–3 ③
Cardiff Market ⑤
City Hall & Civic Centre ②
Craft in the Bay ⑥
Millennium Stadium ④
National Museum Cardiff ①
Norwegian Church ⑨
Techniquest ⑦
Y Senedd ⑧

0 metres 500
0 yards 500

Key to Symbols *see back flap*

Cardiff Castle

Cardiff Castle began life as a Roman fort, whose remains are separated from later work by a band of red stone. A keep was built within the Roman ruins in the 12th century. Over the following 700 years, the castle passed to several powerful families and eventually to John Stuart, son of the Earl of Bute, in 1776. His great-grandson, the 3rd Marquess of Bute, employed the "eccentric genius", architect William Burges, who created an ornate mansion between 1869 and 1881, rich in medieval images and romantic detail.

Arab Room
The gilded ceiling, with Islamic marble and lapis lazuli decorations, was built in 1881.

Herbert Tower

Animal Wall
A lion and other creatures guard the wall to the west of the castle. They were added between 1885 and 1930.

★ Summer Smoking Room
This was part of a complete bachelor suite in the Clock Tower, that also included a Winter Smoking Room.

Clock Tower

Main entrance to apartments

TIMELINE					
	1107 Castle inherited by Mabel FitzHamon, whose husband is made Lord of Glamorgan		**1423–49** Beauchamp family adds the Octagon Tower and Great Hall ceiling		**1869** 3rd Marquess of Bute begins reconstruction
AD 75 Roman fort constructed	**1183** Castle damaged during Welsh uprising		**1445–1776** Castle passes in turn to Nevilles, Tudors and Herberts		
1000	**1200**	**1400**	**1600**	**1800**	
1093 First Norman fort built by Robert FitzHamon of Gloucester		**1308–1414** Despenser family holds castle		**1776** Bute family acquires the castle	
			Chaucer Room wall detail	**1947** The castle is given in trust to the city of Cardiff	

VISITORS' CHECKLIST

Castle St, Cardiff. **Tel** 029-2087
8100. ◯ Mar–Oct: 9am–6pm
daily; Nov–Feb: 9:30am–5pm
daily. 🅟 🖼 🎫 🖼
www.cardiffcastle.com

★ Banqueting Hall
*The design and decoration of
this room depicts the castle's
history, making impressively
ingenious use of the murals
and castellated fireplace.*

The Octagon Tower, also
called the Beauchamp
Tower, is the setting for
Burges's Chaucer Room,
decorated with themes
from the *Canterbury
Tales (see p186).*

★ Roof Garden
*Using tiles, shrubs and
a central fountain,
Burges aimed to create
a Mediterranean feel
in this indoor garden,
turning it into the
crowning glory of the
castle's apartments.*

**The Bute
Tower** had
a suite of
private rooms
added in 1873,
including a
dining room,
bedroom and
sitting room.

★ Library
*Carved figures representing ancient characters
of Greek, Assyrian, Hebrew and Egyptian
alphabets decorate the library's chimneypiece.*

STAR SIGHTS

★ Banqueting Hall

★ Library

★ Summer Smoking
   Room

★ Roof Garden

Remains of Caerleon's amphitheatre, built in the 2nd century

Caerleon **⑮**

Newport. 🏠 *11,000.*
🛈 *5 High St (01633 422656).*
www.*newport.gov.uk*

Together with York *(see pp404–5)* and Chester *(see pp310–11)*, Caerleon was one of only three fortress settlements in Britain built for the Romans' elite legionary troops. From AD 74 Caerleon (*Isca* to the Romans, after the River Usk, which flows beside the town) was home to the 2nd Augustan Legion, which had been sent to Wales to crush the native Silures tribe. The remains of their base now lie between the modern town and the river.

An altar at Caerleon's Legion Museum

The excavations at Caerleon are of great social and military significance. The Romans built not just a fortress for their crack 5,500-strong infantry division but a complete town to service their needs, including a stone amphitheatre. Judging by the results of the excavation work carried out since the archaeologist Sir Mortimer Wheeler unearthed the amphitheatre in 1926, Caerleon is one of the largest and most important Roman military sites in Europe. The defences enclosed an area of 20 ha (50 acres), with 64 rows of barracks, arranged in pairs, a hospital, and a bath-house complex.

Outside the settlement, the amphitheatre's large stone foundations have survived in an excellent state of preservation.

Six thousand spectators could enjoy the blood sports and gladiators' combat.

More impressive still is the fortress baths complex, which opened to the public in the mid-1980s. The baths were designed to bring all the home comforts to an army posted to barbaric Britain. The Roman troops could take a dip in the open-air swimming pool, play sports in the exercise yard or covered hall, or enjoy a series of hot and cold baths.

Nearby are the foundations of the only Roman legionary barracks on view in Europe. The many excavated artifacts, including a collection of engraved gemstones, are displayed at the **National Roman Legion Museum**.

🏛 National Roman Legion Museum
High St. **Tel** *01633 423134.* ⬜ *Mon–Sat, Sun (pm).* ● *1 Jan, 24–26 Dec.*
♿ 🅿 www.*museumwales.ac.uk*

Big Pit Mining Museum, reminder of a vanished industrial society

Blaenafon **⑯**

Torfaen. 🏠 *6,350.* 🛈 *Monmouth Rd, Abergavenny (01873 853254).* www.*world-heritage-blaenafon.org.uk*

Commercial coal-mining has now all but ceased in the South Wales valleys – an area which only 100 years ago was gripped by the search for its "black gold". Though coal is no longer produced at **Big Pit** in Blaenafon, the **National Coal Museum** provides a vivid reminder of this tough industry. The Big Pit closed as a working mine in 1980, and opened three years later as a museum. Visitors follow a marked-out route around the mine's surface workings to the miners' baths, the blacksmith's forge, the workshops and the engine house. There is also a replica of an underground gallery, where mining methods are explained. But the climax of any visit to Big Pit is beneath the ground. Kitted out with helmets, lamps and safety batteries, visitors descend by cage 90 m (300 ft) down the mineshaft and then are guided by ex-miners on a tour of the underground workings and pit ponies' stables.

Across the valley from Big Pit stand the 18th-century smelting furnaces and workers' cottages that were once part of the **Blaenavon Ironworks**, and which are now a museum.

🏛 Big Pit National Coal Museum
Blaenafon. **Tel** *01495 790311.* ⬜ *mid-Feb–Nov: daily; Dec & Jan: phone for details.* ♿ *phone first.* 🎦 🅿 🛈

🏛 Blaenavon Ironworks
North St. **Tel** *01495 792615.*
⬜ *Apr–Oct: daily; Nov–Mar: Fri–Sun.*
🎦 🅿 🛈

Monmouth **⑰**

Monmouthshire. 🏠 *9,000.* 🚌 🛈
Shire Hall (01600 775257). 🅿 *Fri, Sat.* www.*visitwyevalley.com*

This market town, which sits at the confluence of the Wye and Monnow rivers, has many historical associations. The 11th-century castle, behind Agincourt Square, is in ruins but the **Regimental Museum**,

Monnow Bridge in Monmouth, once a watchtower and jail

beside it, remains open to the public. The castle was the birthplace of Henry V *(see p49)* in 1387. Statues of Henry V (on the façade of Shire Hall) and Charles Stewart Rolls stand in the Square. Rolls, born at nearby Hendre, co-founded Rolls-Royce cars, and died in a flying accident in 1910.

Lord Horatio Nelson *(see p54)*, the famous admiral, visited Monmouth in 1802. An excellent collection of Nelson memorabilia, gathered by Lady Llangattock, mother of Charles Rolls, is displayed at the **Nelson Museum**.

Monmouth was the county town of the old Monmouthshire. The wealth of elegant Georgian buildings, including the elaborate **Shire Hall**,

which dominates Agincourt Square, reflect its former status. The most famous architectural feature in Monmouth is **Monnow Bridge**, a narrow 13th-century gateway on its western approach, thought to be the only surviving fortified bridge gate in Britain.

For a lovely view over the town, climb the Kymin, a 256 m (840 ft) hill crowned by a **Naval Temple** built in 1801.

Monmouth Castle and Regimental Museum
The Castle. *Tel 01600 772175.* ⬜ *Apr–Oct: daily; Nov–Mar: on request.* ● *25 Dec.* & www.monmouth castlemuseum.org.uk

Nelson Museum
Priory St. *Tel 01600 710630.* ⬜ *daily (Sun: pm).* & ⬜

Tintern Abbey ⑱

Monmouthshire. *Tel 01291 689251.* ⬛ *Chepstow then bus.* ⬜ *daily* ● *1 Jan, 24–26 Dec.* 🏠 & www.cadw.wales.gov.uk

Ever since the 18th century, travellers have been enchanted by Tintern's setting in the steep and wooded Wye Valley and by the majestic ruins of its abbey. Poets were often inspired by the scene. Wordsworth's sonnet, *Lines composed a few miles above Tintern Abbey*, embodied his romantic view of landscape:

> *once again*
> *Do I behold these steep and*
>   *lofty cliffs,*
> *That on a wild, secluded*
>   *scene impress*
> *Thoughts of more deep*
>   *seclusion*

The abbey was founded in 1131 by Cistercian monks, who cultivated the surrounding lands (now forest), and developed it as an influential religious centre. By the 14th century this was the richest abbey in Wales, but along with other monasteries it was dissolved in 1536. Its skeletal ruins are now roofless and exposed, the soaring arches and windows giving them a poignant grace and beauty.

Tintern Abbey in the Wye Valley, in the past a thriving centre of religion and learning, now a romantic ruin

SCOTLAND

INTRODUCING SCOTLAND 478–489

THE LOWLANDS 490–523

THE HIGHLANDS AND ISLANDS 524–549

Scotland at a Glance

Stretching from the rich farmlands of the Borders to a chain of isles only a few degrees south of the Arctic Circle, the Scottish landscape has a diversity without parallel in Britain. As you travel northwest from Edinburgh, the land becomes more mountainous and its archaeological treasures more numerous. In the far northwest, Scotland's earliest relics stand upon the oldest rock on Earth.

Western Isles

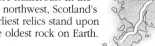

THE HIGHLANDS AND ISLANDS *(see pp524–4...*

Skye (see pp534–5) *renowned for its dramatic scenery, has one of Scotland's most striking coastlines. On the east coast, a stream plunges over Kilt Rock, a cliff of hexagonal basalt columns named after its likeness to an item of Scottish national dress.*

Argyll and Bute

Clyde Valley

Ayrs...

The Trossachs (see pp494–5) *are a beautiful range of hills straddling the border between the Highlands and the Lowlands. At their heart, the forested slopes of Ben Venue rise above the still waters of Loch Achray.*

Culzean Castle (see pp522–3) *stands on a cliff's edge on the Firth of Clyde, amid an extensive country park. One of the jewels of the Lowlands, Culzean is a magnificent showcase of work by the Scottish-born architect, Robert Adam (see p28).*

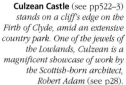

◁ **Loch Lomond, the Lowlands**

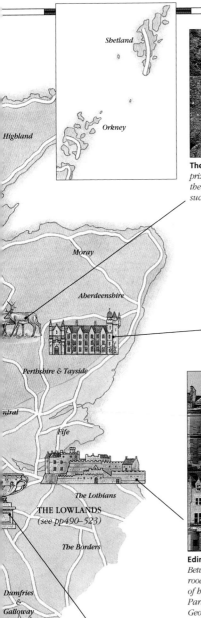

Shetland

Orkney

Highland

Moray

Aberdeenshire

Perthshire & Tayside

ntral

Fife

The Lothians

THE LOWLANDS
(see pp490–523)

The Borders

Dumfries
&
Galloway

The Cairngorms (see pp544–45) cover an area prized for its beauty and diversity of wildlife, though there are also many historical relics to be found, such as this early 18th-century arch at Carrbridge.

Royal Deeside (see pp540–41) in the Grampians has been associated with British royalty since Queen Victoria bought Balmoral Castle in 1852.

Edinburgh (see pp504–11) is the capital of Scotland. Between its medieval castle and the Palace of Holyroodhouse stretches the Royal Mile – a concentration of historic sights, ranging from the old Scottish Parliament buildings to the house of John Knox. Georgian terraces predominate in the New Town.

The Burrell Collection (see pp520–21), on the southern outskirts of Glasgow, is a museum of some of the city's greatest art treasures. It is housed in a spacious, glass building opened in 1983.

0 kilometres   50

0 miles   50

A PORTRAIT OF SCOTLAND

From the grassy hills of the Borders to the desolate Cuillin Ridge of Skye, the landscape of Scotland is breathtaking in its variety. Lonely glens, sparkling lochs and ever-changing skies give the land a challenging character, which is reflected in the qualities of the Scottish people. Tough and self-reliant, they have made some of Britain's finest soldiers, its boldest explorers and most astute industrialists.

The Scots are proud of their separate identity and their own systems of law and education and, in 1998, voted overwhelmingly for their own parliament. Many Scots welcomed this as a long-awaited reversal of the Act of Union that united the English and Scottish parliaments in 1707. But despite their national pride, they are not a homogeneous people, the main division is between traditionally Gaelic-speaking Highlanders, and the Lowlanders who spoke Scots, a form of Middle English which is now extinct. Today, though Gaelic survives (chiefly in the Western Isles), most people speak regional dialects or richly accented English. Many Scottish surnames derive from Gaelic: the prefix "mac" means "son of". A Norse heritage can be found in the far north, where Shetlanders welcome the annual return of the sun during the Viking fire festival, Up Helly Aa.

A hammer-thrower at the Braemar Games

In the 16th century, a suspicion of authority and dislike of excessive flamboyance attracted many Scots to the Presbyterian church with its absence of bishops and its stress on simple worship. The Presbyterian Church of Scotland was established in 1689, though a substantial Catholic minority remained which today predominates in the crofting (small-scale farming) communities of the Western Isles. Now sparsely populated, the Isles preserve a rural culture that once dominated the Highlands, a region that is the source of much that is distinctively Scottish. The clan system originated there, along with the tartans, the bagpipes and such unique sports as tossing the caber – a large tree trunk. Highland sports, along with traditional dances, are still performed at annual games *(see p64).*

Edinburgh bagpiper

Resourcefulness has always been a prominent Scottish virtue, and Scotland has produced a disproportionately high number of Britain's geniuses. James Watt designed the first effective steam engine to power the Industrial Revolution, while Adam Smith became the 18th century's most influential economist. In the 19th century, James Simpson discovered the anaesthetic qualities of

The Viking festival, Up Helly Aa, in Lerwick, Shetland

A traditional stone croft on the Isle of Lewis

With some of the harshest weather conditions in Europe it is perhaps less surprising that Scotland has bred numerous explorers, including polar explorer William Speirs Bruce and African missionary David Livingstone. There is also a strong intellectual and literary tradition, from the 18th-century philosopher David Hume, through novelists Sir Walter Scott and Robert Louis Stevenson, to the poetry of Robert Burns. Today Scotland hosts a variety of arts festivals, such as Edinburgh's.

chloroform, James Young developed the world's first oil refinery and Alexander Bell revolutionized communications by inventing the telephone. The 20th century saw one of the greatest advances in medicine with the discovery of penicillin by Alexander Fleming.

The Scots are also known for being shrewd businessmen, and have always been prominent in finance: both the Bank of England and the Royal Bank of France were founded by Scots, while Andrew Carnegie created one of 19th century-America's biggest business empires.

Detail of Edinburgh's Festival Fringe office

With a population density only one-fifth of England and Wales, Scotland has vast tracts of untenanted land which offer numerous outdoor pleasures. It is richly stocked with game, and the opening of the grouse season on 12 August is a highlight on the social calendar. Fishing and hill-walking are popular and in winter thousands flock to the Cairngorms and Glencoe for skiing. Though the weather may be harsher than elsewhere, the Scots will claim that the air is purer – and that enjoying rugged conditions is what distinguishes them from their soft southern neighbours.

The blue waters of Loch Achray in the heart of the Trossachs, north of Glasgow

The History of Scotland

Bonnie Prince Charlie, by G Dupré

Since the Roman invasion of Britain, Scotland's history has been characterized by its resistance to foreign domination. The Romans never conquered the area, and when the Scots extended their kingdom to its present boundary in 1018, a long era of conflict began with England. After many wars, the Scots finally accepted union with the "auld enemy": first with the union of crowns, and then with the Union of Parliament in 1707. In 1999 the inauguration of the Scottish Parliament was a dramatic change.

An elaborately carved Pictish stone at Aberlemno, Angus

EARLY HISTORY

There is much evidence in Scotland of important prehistoric population centres, particularly in the Western Isles, which were peopled mostly by Picts who originally came from the Continent. By the time Roman Governor Julius Agricola invaded in AD 81, there were at least 17 independent tribes, including the Britons in the southwest, for him to contend with.

The Romans reached north to the Forth and Clyde valleys, but the Highlands deterred them from going further. By 120, they had retreated to the line where the Emperor Hadrian had built his wall to keep the Picts at bay (not far from today's border). By 163 the Romans had retreated south for the last time. The Celtic influence began when

"Scots" arrived from Ireland in the 6th century, bringing the Gaelic language with them.

The Picts and Scots united under Kenneth McAlpin in 843, but the Britons remained separate until 1018, when they became part of the Scottish kingdom.

THE ENGLISH CLAIM

The Norman Kings regarded Scotland as part of their territory but seldom pursued the claim. William the Lion of Scotland recognized English sovereignty by the Treaty of Falaise (1174), though English control never spread to the northwest. In 1296 William Wallace, supported by the French (the start of the Auld Alliance, which lasted two centuries), began the long war of independence. During this bitter conflict, Edward I seized the sacred Stone of Destiny from Scone *(see p498)*, and took it to Westminster Abbey. The war lasted for more than 100 years. Its great hero was Robert the Bruce, who defeated the English in 1314 at Bannockburn. The English held the upper hand after that, even though the Scots would not accept their rule.

John Knox statue in Edinburgh

THE ROAD TO UNION

The seeds of union between the crowns were sown in 1503 when James IV of Scotland married Margaret Tudor, daughter of Henry VII. When her brother, Henry VIII, came to the throne, James sought to assert independence but was defeated and killed at Flodden Field in 1513. His granddaughter, Mary, Queen of Scots *(see p511)*, married the French Dauphin in order to cement the Auld Alliance and gain assistance in her claim to

Bruce in Single Combat at Bannockburn (1906) by John Hassall

the throne of her English
cousin, Elizabeth I. She had
support from the Catholics
wanting to see an end to
Protestantism in England
and Scotland. However, fiery
preacher John Knox won
support for the Protestants
and established the Presbyterian Church in 1560. Mary's
Catholicism led to the loss of
her Scottish throne in 1568,
and her subsequent flight to
England, following defeat at
Langside. Finally, after nearly
20 years of imprisonment
she was executed for treason
by Elizabeth in 1587.

The factories on Clydeside, once creators of the world's greatest ships

UNION AND REBELLION

On Elizabeth I's death in
1603, Mary's son, James VI
of Scotland, succeeded
to the English throne and
became James I, king of both
countries. Thus the crowns
were united, though it was
100 years before the formal
Union of Parliaments in 1707.
During that time, religious
differences within the country

**Articles of Union between
England and Scotland, 1707**

reached boiling point. There
were riots when the Catholic-
influenced Charles I restored
bishops to the Church of
Scotland and authorized the
printing of a new prayer
book. This culminated in the
signing, in Edinburgh in 1638,
of the National Covenant, a
document that condemned
all Catholic doctrines. Though
the Covenanters were sup-
pressed, the Protestant
William of Orange took over
the English throne in 1688
and the crown passed out
of Scottish hands.

In 1745, Bonnie Prince
Charlie *(see p535)*, descended
from the Stuart kings, tried to
seize the throne from the
Hanoverian George II. He

marched far into England,
but was driven back and
defeated at Culloden field
(see p537) in 1746.

INDUSTRIALIZATION AND SOCIAL CHANGE

In the late 18th and 19th
centuries, technological progress transformed Scotland
from a nation of crofters to
an industrial powerhouse.
In the notorious Highland
Clearances *(see p531)*, from
the 1780s on, landowners
ejected tenants from their
smallholdings and gave the
land over to sheep and other
livestock. The first ironworks
was established in 1760 and
was soon followed by coal
mining, steel production and
shipbuilding on the Clyde.
Canals were cut, railways
and bridges built.

A strong socialist movement
developed as workers sought
to improve their conditions.
Keir Hardie, an Ayrshire coal
miner, in 1892 became the
first socialist elected to parliament, and in 1893 founded
the Independent Labour Party.
The most enduring symbol
of this time is the spectacular
Forth rail bridge *(see p502)*.

SCOTLAND TODAY

Although the status of the
country appeared to have
been settled in 1707, a strong
nationalist sentiment remained
and was heightened by the
Depression, which had severe
effects on the heavily industrialized Clydeside. This was
when the Scottish National
Party formed, advocating self-
rule. The Nationalists asserted
themselves in 1950 by stealing the Stone of Scone from
Westminster Abbey.

The discovery of North Sea
oil in 1970 sparked a nationalist revival and, in 1979, the
Government promised to
establish a separate assembly
if 40 per cent of the Scottish
electorate endorsed the plan
in a referendum. This figure
was finally surpassed in 1998,
and the Scottish Parliament
was inaugurated in 1999. A
referendum on full independence is earmarked for 2014.

**A North Sea oil rig, helping to
provide prosperity in the 1970s**

Clans and Tartans

The clan system, by which Highland society was divided into tribal groups led by autocratic chiefs, can be traced to the 12th century, when clans were already known to wear the chequered wool cloth later called tartan. All members of the clan bore the name of their chief, but not all were related by blood. Though they had noble codes of hospitality, the clansmen had to be warriors to protect their herds, as can be seen from their mottoes. After the Battle of Culloden *(see p537)*, all the clan lands were forfeited to the Crown, and the wearing of tartan was banned for nearly 100 years.

The Mackays, *also known as the Clan Morgan, won lasting renown during the Thirty Years War.*

The MacLeods *are of Norse heritage. The clan chief still lives in Dunvegan Castle, Skye (see p534).*

The Mackenzies *received much of the lands of Kintail (see p530) from David II in 1362.*

The MacDonalds *were the most power-ful of all the clans, holding the title of Lords of the Isles.*

CLAN CHIEF

The chief was the clan's patriarch, judge and leader in war, commanding absolute loyalty from his clansmen who gave military service in return for his protection. The chief summoned his clan to do battle by sending a runner across his land bearing a burning cross.

Bonnet with eagle feathers, clan crest and plant badge.

Dirk

Sporran, or pouch, made of badger's skin.

Feileadh-mor, or "great plaid" (the early kilt), wrapped around waist and shoulder.

Basket-hilted sword

The Campbells *were a widely feared clan who fought the Jacobites in 1746 (see p537).*

The Black Watch, *raised in 1729 to keep peace in the Highlands, was one of the Highland regiments in which the wearing of tartan survived. After 1746, civilians were punished by exile for up to seven years for wearing tartan.*

The Sinclairs *came from France in the 11th century and became Earls of Caithness in 1455.*

The Frasers *came to Britain from France with William the Conqueror (see p47) in 1066.*

George IV, *dressed as a Highlander, visited Edinburgh in 1822, the year of the tartan revival. Many tartan "sets" (patterns) date from this time, as the original ones were lost.*

The Gordons *were famously good soldiers; the clan motto is "by courage, not by craft".*

The Stuarts *were Scotland's royal dynasty. Their motto was "no one harms me with impunity".*

CLAN TERRITORIES

The territories of 10 prominent clans are marked here with their clan crests. Dress tartans tend to be colourful, while hunting tartans are darker.

The Douglas *clan were prominent in Scottish history, though their origin is unknown.*

PLANT BADGES

Each clan had a plant associated with its territory. It was worn on the bonnet, especially on the day of battle.

Scots pine was worn by the MacGregors of Argyll.

Rowan berries were worn by the Clan Malcolm.

Ivy was worn by the Clan Gordon of Aberdeenshire.

Spear thistle, now a national symbol, was a Stuart badge.

Cotton grass was worn by the Clan Henderson.

HIGHLAND CLANS TODAY

Once the daily dress of the clansmen, the kilt is now largely reserved for formal occasions. The one-piece *feileadh-mor* has been replaced by the *feileadh-beag*, or "small plaid", made from approximately 7 m (23 ft) of material with a double apron fastened at the front with a silver pin. Though they exist now only in name, the clans are still a strong source of pride for Scots, and many still live in areas traditionally belonging to their clans. Many visitors to Britain can trace their Scots ancestry *(see p31)* to the Highlands.

Modern Highland formal dress

Evolution of the Scottish Castle

There are few more romantic sights in the British Isles than a Scottish castle on an island or at a lochside. These formidable retreats, often in remote settings, were essential all over the Highlands, where incursions and strife between the clans were common. From the earliest Pictish *brochs (see p43)* and Norman-influenced motte and bailey castles, the distinctively Scottish stone tower-house evolved, first appearing in the 14th century. By the mid-17th century fashion had become more important than defence, and there followed a period in which numerous huge Scottish palaces were built.

Detail of the Baroque façade, Drumlanrig

MOTTE AND BAILEY

These castles first appeared in the 12th century. They stood atop two adjacent mounds enclosed by a wall, or palisade, and defensive ditches. The higher mound, or motte, was the most strongly defended as it held the keep and chief's house. The lower bailey was where the people lived. Of these castles little more than earthworks remain today.

Keep, with chief's house, lookout and main defence

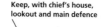

All that remains today of Duffus Castle, Morayshire

Duffus Castle, *(c.1150), was atypically made of stone rather than wood. Its fine defensive position dominates the surrounding flatlands north of Elgin.*

Bailey enclosing dwellings and storehouses

Motte of earth or rock, sometimes partially man-made

EARLY TOWER-HOUSE

Designed to deter local attacks rather than a major assault, the first tower-houses appeared in the 13th century, though their design lived on for 400 years. They were built initially on a rectangular plan, with a single tower divided into three or four floors. The walls were unadorned, with few windows. Defensive structures were on top, and extra space was made by building adjoining towers. Extensions were made as vertically as possible, to minimize the area open to attack.

Crenellated parapet for sentries

Featureless, straight walls with arrow slits for windows

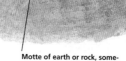

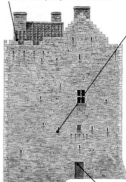

Claypotts Castle (c.1570) with uniquely projecting garrets above its towers

Braemar Castle (c.1630), a conglomeration of extended towers

Neidpath Castle, *standing upon a steep rocky crag above the River Tweed, is an L-shaped tower-house dating from the late 14th century. Once a stronghold for Charles II, its walls still bear damage from a siege conducted by Oliver Cromwell (see p52).*

Small, inconspicuous doorway

LATER TOWER-HOUSE

Though the requirements of defence were being replaced by those of comfort, the style of the early tower-house remained popular. By the 17th century, wings for accommodation were being added around the original tower (often creating a courtyard). The battlements and turrets were kept more for decorative than defensive reasons.

Drum Castle (*see p541*), a 13th-century keep with a mansion house extension from 1619

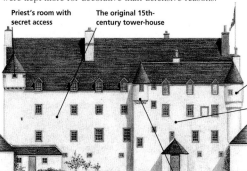

Priest's room with secret access

The original 15th-century tower-house

Round angle tower, containing stairway

A 16th-century horizontal extension

Traquair House (see p513), *by the Tweed, is reputedly the oldest continuously inhabited house in Scotland. The largely unadorned, roughcast exterior dates to the 16th century, when a series of extensions were built around the original 15th-century tower-house.*

Decorative, corbelled turret

Blair Castle (*see p543*), incorporating a medieval tower

CLASSICAL PALACE

By the 18th century, the defensive imperative had passed and castles were built in the manner of country houses, rejecting the vertical tower-house in favour of a horizontal plan (though the building of imitation fortified buildings continued into the 19th century with the mock-Baronial trend). Outside influences came from all over Europe, including Renaissance and Gothic revivals, and echoes of French châteaux.

Dunrobin Castle (c.1840), Sutherland

Larger windows due to a lesser need for defence

Balustrades instead of battlements

Decorative cupola

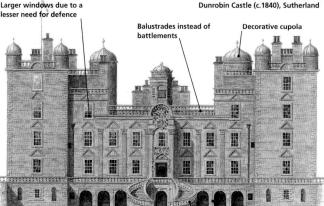

Drumlanrig Castle (see p514) *was built in the 17th century. There are many traditional Scots aspects as well as such Renaissance features as the decorated stairway and façade.*

Renaissance-style colonnade

Baroque horseshoe stairway

The Flavours of Scotland

At its best, Scottish food is full of the natural flavour of the countryside. Served with few sauces or spices, its meat is lean and tasty. Beef doesn't get better than Aberdeen Angus, the lamb is full flavoured, and the venison superb. Scottish salmon and trout are renowned, but there are also excellent mussels, lobster and crabs. Wheat does not grow here, so oatcakes and bannocks (flat, round loaves) replace bread. The Scots have a sweet tooth, not just for cakes and shortbread but also for toffee and butterscotch.

Smoked Salmon

Pedigree Aberdeen Angus cattle grazing the Scottish moors

THE LOWLANDS

The pasturelands of southern Scotland nourish dairy cattle and sheep, producing cheeses such as Bonnet, Bonchester and Galloway Cheddar. To accompany them are summer fruits such as loganberries, tayberries and strawberries that ripen in the Carse of Gowrie beside the River Tay. Oats, the principal cereal,

appears in much Scottish cookery, from porridge to oatcakes. Pearl barley is also a staple, used in Scotch Broth (made with mutton and vegetables) or in a milk pudding. Oats are also used in the making of haggis, a round sausage of sheep or venison offal – the "chieftain o' the puddin' race", as the poet Robert Burns described it. It is often served with "neeps and tatties" (mashed swede and potato).

THE HIGHLANDS

From the Highlands comes wonderful game, including grouse, partridge, caper-caillie (a large type of grouse) and deer. Fish are smoked around the coast, the west coast producing kippers, the east coast Finnan haddock, notably Arbroath Smokies. Smoked white fish is the main ingredient of Cullen Skink, a soup served on Burns' Night.

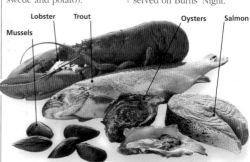

Lobster   Trout

Mussels

Oysters   Salmon

Selection of fresh Scottish fish and seafood

TRADITIONAL SCOTTISH FOOD

Kippers (oak-smoked herrings) are one way to start the day in Scotland, and porridge – traditionally served with salt rather than sugar – is another, although oatcakes or some other kind of griddled scone are usually present. A bowl of porridge would once last all week, just as one-pot Scotch broths bubbled in iron cauldrons over peat fires for days. Sometimes broths were made with kale or lentils, or they might contain an old boiling fowl and leeks, in which case they were known as cock-a-leekie. Any leftover meat went into making stovies, a potato and onion hash. The evening meal in Scotland is traditionally "high tea" taken in the early evening which might start with smoked fish, cold meats and pies, followed by shortbread, fruit cake or drop scones, all washed down with cups of tea.

Oats

Haggis with neeps and tatties
This is the definitive Scottish dish, traditionally served on Burns' Night (25 January).

HOW WHISKY IS MADE

Traditionally made from just barley, yeast and stream water, Scottish whisky (from the Gaelic *usquebaugh*, or the "water of life") takes a little over three weeks to produce, though it must be given at least three years to mature. Maturation usually takes place in oak casks, often in barrels previously used for sherry. The art of blending was pioneered in Edinburgh in the 1860s.

Barley grass

1 Malting is the first stage. Barley grain is soaked in water and spread on the malting floor. With regular turning the grain germinates, producing a "green malt". Germination stimulates the production of enzymes which turn the starches into fermentable sugars.

2 Drying of the barley halts germination after 12 days of malting. This is done over a peat fire in a pagoda-shaped malt-kiln. The peat-smoke gives flavour to the malt and eventually to the mature whisky. The malt is gleaned of germinated roots and then milled.

3 Mashing of the ground malt, or "grist", occurs in a large vat, or "mash tun", which holds a vast quantity of hot water. The malt is soaked and begins to dissolve, producing a sugary solution called "wort", which is then extracted for fermentation.

4 Fermentation occurs when yeast is added to the cooled wort in wooden vats, or "washbacks". The mixture is stirred for hours as the yeast turns the sugar into alcohol, producing a clear liquid called "wash".

5 Distillation involves boiling the wash twice so that the alcohol vaporizes and condenses. In copper "pot stills", the wash is distilled – first in the "wash still", then in the "spirit still". Now purified, with an alcohol content of 57 per cent, the result is young whisky.

6 Maturation is the final process. The whisky mellows in oak casks for a legal minimum of three years. Premium brands give the whisky a 10- to 15-year maturation, though some are given up to 50 years.

Traditional drinking vessels, or *quaichs,* **made of silver**

Blended whiskies *are made from a mixture of up to 50 different single malts.*

Single malts *vary according to regional differences in the peat and stream water used.*

THE LOWLANDS

CLYDE VALLEY · CENTRAL SCOTLAND · FIFE · THE LOTHIANS
AYRSHIRE · DUMFRIES AND GALLOWAY · THE BORDERS

*S*outheast of the Highland boundary fault line lies a part of
Scotland very different in character from its northern neighbour.
If the Highlands embody the romance of Scotland, the Lowlands
have traditionally been her powerhouse. Lowlanders have always prospered in agriculture and, more recently, in industry and commerce.

Being the region of Scotland closest to the English border, the
Lowlands inevitably became
the crucible of Scottish history. For centuries after the
Romans built the Antonine
Wall *(see p44)* across the Forth–
Clyde isthmus, the area was
engulfed in conflict. The Borders
are scattered with the castles of
a territory in uneasy proximity
to rapacious neighbours, and
the ramparts of Stirling Castle
overlook no fewer than seven different battlefields fought over in the
cause of independence.

The ruins of medieval abbeys, such
as Melrose, also bear witness to the
dangers of living on the invasion route
from England, though the woollen
trade founded by their monks still
flourishes in Peebles and Hawick.

North of the Borders lies Edinburgh,
the cultural and administrative capital of Scotland. With its Georgian
squares dominated by a medieval castle, it is one of Europe's most elegant
cities. While the 18th and 19th centuries saw a great flowering of the
arts in Edinburgh, the city of
Glasgow became a merchant
city second only to London.
Fuelled by James Watt's development of the steam engine in
the 1840s, Glasgow became the cradle
of Scotland's Industrial Revolution,
which created a prosperous cotton
industry and launched the world's
greatest ships.

Both cities retain this dynamism
today: Edinburgh annually hosts the
world's largest open-access arts
festival, and Glasgow is acclaimed as
a model of post-industrial renaissance.

A juggler performing at the annual arts extravaganza, the Edinburgh Festival

◁ Glamis Castle, 12 miles (19 km) north of Dundee, with its typically Scottish turreted exterior

Exploring the Lowlands

The Lowlands are traditionally all the land south of the fault line stretching northeast from Loch Lomond to Stonehaven. Confusingly, they include plenty of wild upland country. The region illustrates the diversity of Scotland's scenery. The wooded valleys and winding rivers of the borders give way to the stern hills of the Cheviots and Lammermuirs. Fishing villages cling to the rocky east coast, while the Clyde coast and its islands are dotted with holiday towns. Inland lies the Trossachs, a romantic area of mountain, loch and woodland east of Loch Lomond that is a magnet for walkers *(see pp36–7)* and well within reach of Glasgow.

Loch Katrine seen from the Trossachs

SEE ALSO

- *Where to Stay* pp594–6
- *Where to Eat* pp646–9

SIGHTS AT A GLANCE

Abbotsford House 20
Biggar 22
Burns Cottage 31
Culross 11
Culzean Castle pp522–3 30
Doune Castle 3
Drumlanrig Castle 27
Dundee 6
Dunfermline 10
East Neuk 8
Edinburgh pp504–11 16
Falkirk Wheel 13
Falkland Palace 9
Forth Bridges 15
Glamis Castle 5
Glasgow pp516–21 25
Hopetoun House 14
Linlithgow Palace 12
Melrose Abbey 19
New Lanark 24
Pentland Hills 23
Perth 4
St Abb's Head 17
St Andrews 7
Sanquhar 26
Stirling pp496–7 2
Threave Castle 28
Traquair House 21
Trossachs pp494–5 1
Whithorn 29

Walks and Tours
Tour of the Borders 18

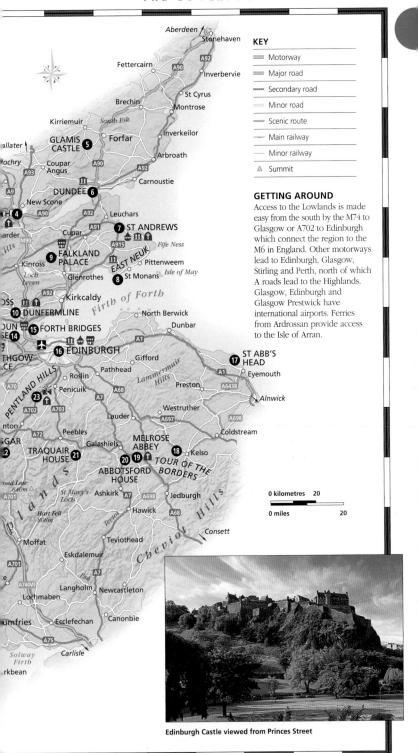

KEY

═══ Motorway

━━━ Major road

━━ Secondary road

╌╌╌ Minor road

━━ Scenic route

⊶⊶ Main railway

━━ Minor railway

△ Summit

GETTING AROUND

Access to the Lowlands is made easy from the south by the M74 to Glasgow or A702 to Edinburgh which connect the region to the M6 in England. Other motorways lead to Edinburgh, Glasgow, Stirling and Perth, north of which A roads lead to the Highlands. Glasgow, Edinburgh and Glasgow Prestwick have international airports. Ferries from Ardrossan provide access to the Isle of Arran.

0 kilometres   20

0 miles   20

Edinburgh Castle viewed from Princes Street

The Trossachs ❶

Golden eagle

Combining the ruggedness of the Grampians with the pastoral tranquillity of the Borders, this beautiful region of craggy hills and sparkling lochs is the colourful meeting place of the Lowlands and Highlands. Home to a wide variety of wildlife, including the golden eagle, peregrine falcon, red deer and the wildcat, the Trossachs have inspired numerous writers, including Sir Walter Scott *(see p512)* who made the area the setting for several of his novels. It was the home of Scotland's folk hero, Rob Roy, who was so well known that, in his own lifetime, he was fictionalized in *The Highland Rogue* (1723), a novel attributed to Daniel Defoe.

Loch Katrine
The setting of S... Walter Scott's L... of the Lake (18... this freshwater loch can be ex- plored on the Victorian steam... SS Sir Walter Sc... which cruises fr... the Trossachs P...

Loch Lomond
Britain's largest freshwater lake was immortalized in a ballad composed by a local Jacobite soldier, dying far from home. He laments that though he will return home before his companions who travel on the high road, he will be doing so on the low road (of death).

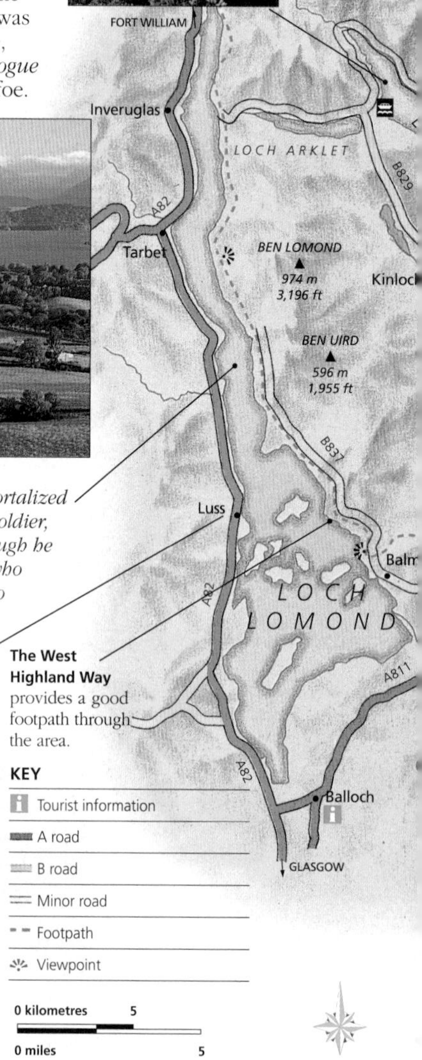

Luss
With its exceptionally picturesque cottages, Luss is one of the prettiest villages in the Lowlands. Surrounded by grassy hills, it occupies one of the most scenic parts of Loch Lomond's western shore.

The West Highland Way provides a good footpath through the area.

FORT WILLIAM

Inveruglas

LOCH ARKLET

Tarbet

BEN LOMOND
▲
974 m
3,196 ft

BEN UIRD
▲
596 m
1,955 ft

Kinloc...

Luss

Balm...

LOCH LOMOND

Balloch

GLASGOW

KEY

🛈	Tourist information
▬▬	A road
▭▭	B road
═══	Minor road
- -	Footpath
🔅	Viewpoint

0 kilometres   5

0 miles   5

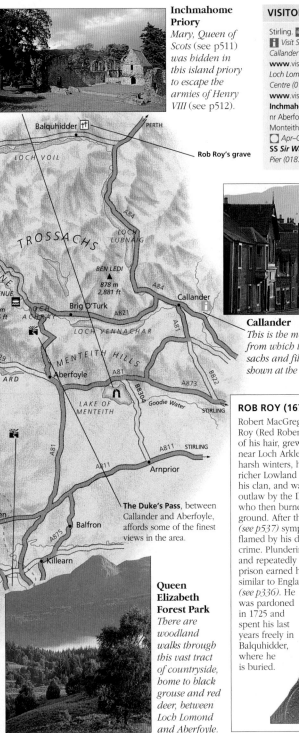

Inchmahome Priory

Mary, Queen of Scots (see p511) was hidden in this island priory to escape the armies of Henry VIII (see p512).

Balquhidder

PERTH

LOCH VOIL

Rob Roy's grave

A84

TROSSACHS

LOCH LUBNAIG

BEN LEDI
▲
878 m
2,881 ft

A84

ENUE

LOCH ACHRAY

Brig O'Turk

A821

Callander

Callander

This is the most popular town from which to explore the Trossachs and films of the area are shown at the information centre.

LOCH VENNACHAR

A81

MENTEITH HILLS

A29

Aberfoyle

A81

A873

B822

ARD

LAKE OF MENTEITH

B8034

Goodie Water

STIRLING

ROB ROY (1671–1734)

Robert MacGregor, known as Rob Roy (Red Robert) from the colour of his hair, grew up as a herdsman near Loch Arklet. After a series of harsh winters, he took to raiding richer Lowland properties to feed his clan, and was declared an outlaw by the Duke of Montrose who then burned his house to the ground. After this, Rob's Jacobite *(see p537)* sympathies became inflamed by his desire to avenge the crime. Plundering the duke's lands and repeatedly escaping from prison earned him a reputation similar to England's Robin Hood *(see p336).* He was pardoned in 1725 and spent his last years freely in Balquhidder, where he is buried.

A81

A811

STIRLING

A811

Arnprior

The Duke's Pass, between Callander and Aberfoyle, affords some of the finest views in the area.

en

A875

Balfron

Killearn

Queen Elizabeth Forest Park

There are woodland walks through this vast tract of countryside, home to black grouse and red deer, between Loch Lomond and Aberfoyle.

The 17th-century town house of the Dukes of Argyll, Stirling

Stirling ❷

Stirling. 🏘 *41,000.* 🚉 🚌 🗂 *St John St (01786 475019).* **www.** visitscottishheartlands.com

Situated between the Ochil Hills and the Campsie Fells, Stirling grew up around its castle, historically one of Scotland's most important fortresses. Below the castle the Old Town is still protected by the original 16th-century walls, built to keep Mary Queen of Scots safe from Henry VIII. The medieval **Church of the Holy Rude**, on Castle Wynd, where the infant James VI was crowned in 1567, has one of Scotland's few surviving hammerbeam oak roofs. The ornate façade of **Mar's Wark** is all that remains of a grand palace which, though never completed, was commissioned in 1570 by the 1st Earl of Mar. It was destroyed by the Jacobites *(see p537)* in 1746. Opposite stands the beautiful 17th-century town house of the Dukes of Argyll.

Environs: Two miles (3 km) south, the **Bannockburn Heritage Centre** stands by the field where Robert the Bruce defeated the English *(see p482)*. After the battle, he dismantled the castle so it would not fall back into English hands. A bronze equestrian statue commemorates the man who is an icon of Scottish independence.

🗂 **Bannockburn Heritage Centre**
(NTS) Glasgow Rd. **Tel** *0844 493 2139.* ☐ *Mar–Oct: 10am–5:30pm daily; other times by appointment.* ● *24 Dec–Feb.* ♿ ♿

Stirling Castle

Rising high on a rocky crag, this magnificent castle, which dominated Scottish history for centuries, now remains one of the finest examples of Renaissance architecture in Scotland. Legend says that King Arthur *(see p285)* wrested the original castle from the Saxons, but there is no evidence of a castle before 1124. The present building dates from the 15th and 16th centuries and was last defended, against the Jacobites *(see p537)*, in 1746. From 1881 to 1964 the castle was a depot for recruits into the Argyll and Sutherland Highlanders, though now it serves no military function.

Gargoyle on castle wall

Robert the Bruce
In the esplanade, this modern statue shows Robert the Bruce sheathing his sword after the Battle of Bannockburn in 1314.

Prince's Tower

Forework

Entrance

***Stirling Castle in the Time of the Stuarts**, painted by Johannes Vorsterman (1643–99)*

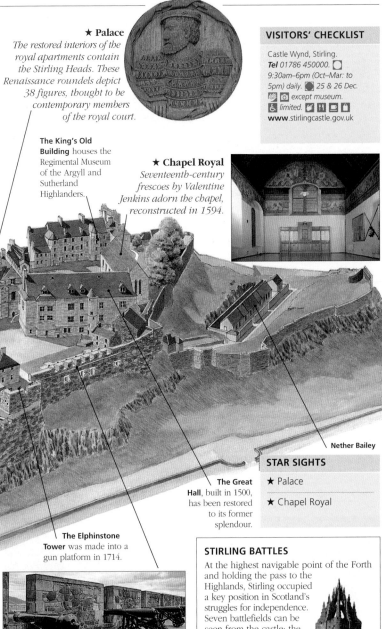

★ **Palace**
The restored interiors of the royal apartments contain the Stirling Heads. These Renaissance roundels depict 38 figures, thought to be contemporary members of the royal court.

The **King's Old Building** houses the Regimental Museum of the Argyll and Sutherland Highlanders.

★ **Chapel Royal**
Seventeenth-century frescoes by Valentine Jenkins adorn the chapel, reconstructed in 1594.

Nether Bailey

The **Great Hall**, built in 1500, has been restored to its former splendour.

The **Elphinstone Tower** was made into a gun platform in 1714.

STAR SIGHTS

★ Palace

★ Chapel Royal

STIRLING BATTLES

At the highest navigable point of the Forth and holding the pass to the Highlands, Stirling occupied a key position in Scotland's struggles for independence. Seven battlefields can be seen from the castle; the 67-m (220-ft) Wallace Monument at Abbey Craig recalls William Wallace's defeat of the English at Stirling Bridge in 1297, foreshadowing Bruce's victory in 1314 *(see p482)*.

The Victorian Wallace Monument

Grand Battery
Seven guns stand on this parapet, built in 1708 during a strengthening of defences following the revolution of 1688 (see p53).

Perth seen from the east across the Tay

Doune Castle ❸

Doune, Stirling. **Tel** *01786 841742.*
🚉 🚌 *Stirling then bus.* ⬜ *Apr–Sep: 9:30am–5:30pm daily; Oct: 9:30am–4:30pm daily; Nov–Mar: 9:30am–4:30pm Mon–Wed, Sat & Sun; last entry 30 mins before close.*
⬤ *21 Dec–8 Jan.* 🅿️ ♿ *limited.*
www.historic-scotland.gov.uk

Built as the residence of Robert, Duke of Albany, in the 14th century, **Doune Castle** was a Stuart stronghold until it fell into ruin in the 18th century. Now fully restored, it is one of the most complete castles of its time and offers a unique insight into the royal household.

The Gatehouse, once a self-sufficient residence, leads to the central courtyard off which is the Great Hall. Complete with its reconstructed open-timber roof, minstrels' gallery and central fireplace, the Hall adjoins the Lord's Hall and Private Room. A number of private stairs and narrow passages reveal the ingenious ways the royal family tried to hide during times of danger. The castle was the setting for the 1975 film, *Monty Python and the Holy Grail*.

Perth ❹

Perthshire. 🏘 *45,000.* 🚉 🚌
ℹ️ *West Mill St (01738 450600).*
www.perthshire.co.uk

Once the capital of medieval Scotland, Perth's rich heritage is reflected in many of its buildings. It was in the **Church of Saint John**, founded in 1126, that John Knox *(see p483)* delivered many of his fiery sermons. The Victorianized **Fair Maid's House**, on North Port, is one of the oldest houses in town (c.1600) and was the fictional home of the heroine of Sir Walter Scott's *(see p512) The Fair Maid of Perth* (1828).

In **Balhousie Castle**, the Museum of the Black Watch commemorates the first Highland regiment, while the **Perth Museum & Art Gallery** has displays on local industry and exhibitions of Scottish art.

Environs: Two miles (3 km) north of Perth, the Gothic mansion of **Scone Palace** stands on the site of an abbey destroyed in 1559. Between the 9th and 13th centuries, Scone guarded the sacred Stone of Destiny *(see pp482–3)*, now kept in Edinburgh Castle *(see pp506–7)*. Some of Mary, Queen of Scots' *(see p511)* embroideries are on display.

♜ **Balhousie Castle**
RHQ Black Watch, Hay St. **Tel** *0173 863 8152.* ⬜ *9:30am–5pm Mon–Sat, 10am–4pm Sun (Nov–Apr: to 5pm Mon–Sat).*

🏛 **Perth Museum & Art Gallery**
78 George St. **Tel** *01738 632488.*
⬜ *10am–5pm Mon–Sat (also May–Sep: 1–4:30pm Sun).* ♿

♜ **Scone Palace**
A93 to Braemar. **Tel** *01738 552300.*
⬜ *Apr–Oct: 9:30am–5pm daily (to 4pm Sat); Nov–Mar: 10am–4pm Fri.*
🅿️ ♿ **www**.scone-palace.net

Glamis Castle ❺

Forfar, Angus. **Tel** *01307 840393.*
🚉 🚌 *Dundee then bus.* ⬜ *Mar–Oct: 10am–6pm (last adm: 4:30pm) daily; Nov & Dec: 10:30am–4:30pm (last adm: 3pm) daily.* 🅿️ 🎟
www.glamis-castle.co.uk

With the pinnacled fairytale outline of a Loire chateau,

Glamis Castle with statues of James VI (left) and Charles I (right)

the imposing medieval towerhouse of **Glamis Castle** began as a royal hunting lodge in the 11th century but underwent extensive reconstruction in the 17th century. It was the childhood home of Queen Elizabeth the Queen Mother, and her former bedroom can be seen with a youthful portrait by Henri de Laszlo (1878–956).

Many rooms are open to the public, including Duncan's Hall, the oldest in the castle and Shakespeare's setting for the king's murder in *Macbeth*.

Dundee ❻

Dundee City. 🏛 144,000. ✈ 🚃 🚌 🛈 Discovery Point, Discovery Quay (01382 527527). 🏧 daily; farmers' market 3rd Sat of month. **www. angusanddundee.co.uk**

Famed for its three Js of jam, jute mills and journalism – see the statues of publisher DC Thomson's *Beano* and *Dandy* comic characters near the grand venue of Caird Hall – **Dundee** is a hub of creative industries and science.

Due in 2015 is Kengo Kuma's stunning V&A design museum, set on the waterfront with dramatic views across the Tay, Britain's most powerful river.

Nearby is the royal research ship *Discovery*, built here in 1901 for Captain Scott's first voyage to the Antarctic. At Victoria Dock is **HMS** *Unicorn* (1824), Britain's oldest warship still afloat. The North Carr lightship (1932) sets sail from May to September for dolphin-watching trips from beachside Broughton Ferry.

View of St Andrews over the ruins of the cathedral

The **McManus Galleries'** collection of Dundee-related art and artefacts is housed in a splendid Victorian Gothic building. Walk along Riverside to the Tay Rail Bridge (1887) to learn about the famous disaster and spot seals on the sandbanks.

🏛 **HMS** *Unicorn*
Victoria Docks, City Quay. **Tel** 01382 200 900. 🕐 Apr–Oct: daily; Nov–Mar: Wed–Sun. 🅿 ♿ limited. **www.frigateunicorn. org**

🏛 *Discovery*
Discovery Point. **Tel** 01382 309060. 🕐 daily (Sun pm). 🅿 ♿ **www.rrsdiscovery.com**

🏛 **McManus Galleries**
Albert Sq. **Tel** 01382 307200. 🕐 10am–5pm Mon–Sat, 12:30–4:30pm Sun. ♿ **www.mcmanus.co.uk**

St Mary's College insignia, St Andrews University

St Andrews ❼

Fife. 🏛 16,000. 🚃 Leuchars. 🚌 Dundee. 🛈 70 Market St (01334 472021). **www.visitscotland.com**

Scotland's oldest university town and one-time ecclesiastical capital, **St Andrews** is now a shrine to golfers from all over the world *(see below)*. Its three main streets and numerous cobbled alleys, full of crooked housefronts, dignified university buildings and medieval churches, converge on the venerable ruins of the 12th-century **cathedral**. Once the largest in Scotland, the cathedral was later pillaged for stones to build the town. **St Andrew's Castle** was built for the bishops of the town in 1200. The dungeon can still be seen. The city's golf courses to the west are each open for a modest fee. The **British Golf Museum** tells how the city's Royal and Ancient Golf Club became the ruling arbiter of the game.

♣ **St Andrew's Castle**
The Scores. **Tel** 01334 477196. 🕐 Apr–Sep: 9:30–5:30pm daily; Oct–Mar: 9:30–4:30pm daily. ● 1 & 2 Jan, 25 & 26 Dec. 🅿 ♿

🏛 **British Golf Museum**
Bruce Embankment. **Tel** 01334 460 046. 🕐 Jan–Mar: 10am–4pm daily; Apr–Oct: 9:30am–5pm daily; Nov–Dec: 10am–4pm daily. 🅿 ♿

THE ANCIENT GAME OF GOLF

Scotland's national game was pioneered on the sandy links around St Andrews. The earliest record dates from 1457, when golf was banned by James II on the grounds that it was interfering with his subjects' archery practice.

Mary, Queen of Scots *(see p511)* enjoyed the game and was berated in 1568 for playing straight after the murder of her husband Darnley.

Mary, Queen of Scots at St Andrews in 1563

The central courtyard of Falkland Palace, bordered by rose bushes

East Neuk ❽

Fife. 🚉 *Leuchars*. 🚌 *Glenrothes & Leuchars*. 🛈 *70 Market Street, St Andrews (01334 472021).*

A string of pretty fishing villages scatters the shoreline of the **East Neuk** (the eastern "corner") of Fife, stretching from Earlsferry to Fife Ness. Much of Scotland's medieval trade with Europe passed through these ports, a connection reflected in the Flemish-inspired crow-stepped gables of many of the cottages. Although the herring industry has declined and the area is now a peaceful holiday centre, the sea still dominates village life. Until the 1980s, fishing boats were built at St Monans, a charming town of narrow twisting streets, while Pittenweem is the base for the East Neuk fishing fleet.

The town is also known for **St Fillan's Cave**, the retreat of a 9th-century hermit whose relic was used to bless the army of Robert the Bruce *(see p482)* before the Battle of Bannockburn. A church stands among the cobbled lanes and colourful cottages of Crail; the stone by the church gate is said to have been hurled to the mainland from the Isle of May by the Devil.

Several 16th- to 19th-century buildings in the village of Anstruther contain the **Scottish Fisheries Museum** which tells the area's history with the aid of interiors, boats and displays on whaling. From the village you can embark for the nature reserve on the **Isle of May** which teems with seabirds and grey seals. The statue of Alexander Selkirk in Lower Largo recalls the local boy whose adventures inspired Daniel Defoe's *Robinson Crusoe* (1719). Disagreeing with his captain, he was dumped on a desert island for four years.

🏛 **Scottish Fisheries Museum**
St Ayles, Harbourhead, Anstruther. **Tel** 01333 310628. ⬜ *Apr–Sep: 10am–5:30pm Mon–Sat (to 4:30pm Oct–Mar), 11am–5pm Sun (from noon Oct–Mar).* ⬤ *25 & 26 Dec, 1 & 2 Jan.* 📷 ♿ www.scotfishmuseum.org

THE PALACE KEEPER

Due to the size of the royal household and the necessity for the king to be itinerant, the office of Keeper was created by the medieval kings who required custodians to maintain and replenish the resources of their many palaces while they were away. Now redundant, it was a hereditary title and gave the custodian permanent and often luxurious lodgings.

James VI's bed in the Keeper's Bedroom, Falkland Palace

Falkland Palace ❾

(NTS) Falkland, Fife. **Tel** 0844 4932186. 🚉 🚌 *Ladybank, Kirkcaldy, then bus.* ⬜ *Mar–Oct: 11am–5pm Mon–Sat, 1–5pm Sun.* 🏠 📷 ♿ 🚫 www.nts.org.uk

This stunning Renaissance palace was designed as a hunting lodge of the Stuart kings. Although its construction was begun by James IV in 1500, most of the work was carried out by his son, James V *(see p510)*, in the 1530s. Under the influence of his two French wives he employed French workmen to redecorate the façade of the East Range with dormers, buttresses and medallions, and to build the beautifully proportioned South Range. The palace fell into ruin during the years of the Commonwealth *(see p52)* and was occupied briefly by Rob Roy *(see p495)* in 1715.

After buying the estates in 1887, the 3rd Marquess of Bute became the Palace Keeper and restored it. The richly panelled interiors are filled with superb furniture and portraits of the Stuart monarchs. The royal tennis court is the oldest in Britain.

Dunfermline ❿

Fife. 🏘 *55,000.* 🚉 🚌 🛈 *1 High St (01383 720999).* www.visitdunfermline.com

Scotland's capital until 1603, Dunfermline is dominated by the ruins of the 12th-century abbey and palace which recall its royal past. In the 11th century, the town was the seat of King Malcolm III, who founded a priory on the present site of the **Abbey Church**. With its Norman nave and 19th-century choir, the church contains the tombs of 22 Scottish kings and queens, including Robert the Bruce *(see p482)*.

The ruins of King Malcolm's **palace** soar over the beautiful gardens of Pittencrieff Park. Dunfermline's most famous son, philanthropist Andrew Carnegie (1835–1919), had been forbidden entrance to the park as a boy. After making his fortune, he bought the entire Pittencrieff estate and gave it to the people of Dunfermline. He was born in the town, though moved to Pennsylvania in his teens. There he made a vast fortune in the iron and steel industry. The **Carnegie Birthplace Museum** is still furnished as it was when he lived there, and tells the story of his meteoric career.

🏛 **Carnegie Birthplace Museum**
Moodie St. *Tel* 01383 724302.
⭕ Mar–Nov: 10am–5pm Mon–Sat; 2–5pm Sun. 🔲 ♿

The 12th-century Norman nave of Dunfermline Abbey Church

Culross ⑪

(NTS) Fife. 🏠 450. 🚆 Dunfermline. 🚌 Dunfermline. 🛈 NTS, The Palace (0844 4932189). ⭕ Apr–Aug: noon–5pm Mon–Thu (daily Jun–Aug); Sep–Oct: noon–4pm Thu–Mon. **Garden** ⭕ 10am–6pm (or dusk if earlier). 🏠 ♿ ltd. 🔲 🔲 🎵 Music & Arts: Jun.

An important religious centre in the 6th century, the town of Culross is said to have

been the birthplace of St Mungo in 514. Now a beautifully pre- served 16th- and 17th-century village, Culross prospered in the 16th century with the growth of its coal and salt industries, most notably under Sir George Bruce. He took charge of the Culross colliery in 1575 and created a drainage system called the "Egyptian Wheel" which cleared a mile-long (1.5 km) mine beneath the River Forth.

During its subsequent decline Culross stood unchanged for over 150 years. The National Trust for Scotland began restoring the town in 1932 and now provides a guided tour, which starts at the **Visitors' Centre**.

Built in 1577, Bruce's **palace** has the crow-stepped gables, decorated windows and red pantiles typical of the period. The interior retains its original early 17th-century painted ceilings. Crossing the Square, past the **Oldest House**, dating from 1577, head for the **Town House** to the west. Behind it, a cobbled street known as the Back Causeway (with its raised section for nobility) leads to the turreted **Study**, built in 1610 as a house for the Bishop of Dunblane. The main room is open to visitors and should be seen for its original Norwegian ceiling. Continuing northwards to the ruined abbey, fine church and Abbey House, don't miss the Dutch-gabled **House with the Evil Eyes**.

The 16th-century palace of industrialist George Bruce, Culross

Linlithgow Palace ⑫

Linlithgow, West Lothian. *Tel* 01506 842896. 🚆 🚌 ⭕ Apr–Sep: 9:30am–5:30pm daily; Oct–Mar: 9:30am–4:30pm daily. ⭕ 25, 26 Dec, 1, 2 Jan. 🏠 ♿ limited.
www.historic-scotland.gov.uk

On the edge of Linlithgow Loch stands the former royal palace of **Linlithgow**. Today's remains are mostly of the palace of James I in 1425. The scale of the building is demonstrated by the 28 m (94 ft) long Great Hall, with its huge fireplace and windows. Mary, Queen of Scots (see p511), was born here in 1542.

Falkirk Wheel ⑬

Lime Rd, Falkirk. *Tel* 08700 500208 (booking line). 🚆 Falkirk. ⭕ Feb–Nov: **Boat trips** from 5 trips Wed–Sat in winter to 3 trips per hour daily in summer. **Visitor Centre** daily. Nov–Feb: phone for times. 🏠 boat trip. 🔲 🔲 www.thefalkirkwheel.co.uk

This impressive boat lift is the first ever to revolve, and the centrepiece of Scotland's canal regeneration scheme. Once important for commercial transport, the Union and the Forth and Clyde canals were blocked by several roads in the 1960s. Now the Falkirk Wheel gently swings boats between the two waterways creating an uninterrupted link between Glasgow and Edinburgh. Visitors can ride the wheel on boats that leave from the Visitor Centre.

The rotating Falkirk Wheel boat lift

Hopetoun House ⑭

West Lothian. **Tel** 0131 331 2451.
🚉 Dalmeny then taxi. ⬜ mid-Mar–late Sep: 10:30am–5pm (last entry 4pm). 📷 ♿ ⬜ limited.
🎫 for groups – book ahead. ⬜
www.hopetounhouse.com

An extensive parkland by the Firth of Forth, designed in the style of Versailles, is the setting for one of Scotland's finest stately homes. The original house was built by 1707; it was later absorbed into William Adam's grand extension. The dignified, horseshoe-shaped plan and lavish interior plasterwork represent Neo-Classical 18th-century architecture at its finest. The drawing rooms, with their Rococo plasterwork and highly ornate mantelpieces, are particularly impressive. The Marquess of Linlithgow, whose family still occupies part of the house, is a descendant of the 1st Earl of Hopetoun, for whom the house was built.

A wooden panel above the main stair, depicting Hopetoun House

Forth Bridges ⑮

Edinburgh. 🚉 Dalmeny, North Queensferry. 🚌 South Queensferry.

The small town of South Queensferry is dominated by the two great bridges that span the mile (1.6 km) across the River Forth to North Queensferry. The spectacular rail bridge, the first major steel-built bridge in the world, was opened in 1890 and remains one of the greatest

The shattered crags and cliffs of St Abb's Head

engineering achievements of the late Victorian era. Its massive cantilevered sections are held together by more than 6.5 million rivets, and the painted area adds up to some 55 ha (135 acres). The saying "like painting the Forth Bridge" has become a byword for non-stop, repetitive endeavour. The bridge also inspired *The Bridge* (1986) by writer Iain Banks.

The neighbouring road bridge was the largest suspension bridge outside the USA when it opened in 1964. There are plans to perch a viewing platform atop the 101-m (330-ft) rail bridge, and a new road bridge is due to be completed in 2016.

South Queensferry got its name from the 11th-century Queen Margaret *(see p507)*, who used the ferry here on her journeys between Edinburgh and the royal palace at Dunfermline *(see p501)*.

Edinburgh ⑯

See pp504–11.

St Abb's Head ⑰

(NTS) Scottish Borders. 🚉 Berwick-upon-Tweed. 🚌 from Edinburgh.

The jagged cliffs of St Abb's Head, rising 91 m (300 ft) from the North Sea near the southeastern tip of Scotland, offer a spectacular view of thousands of seabirds wheeling and diving below. This 80 ha (200 acre) nature reserve is an important site for cliff-nesting sea birds and becomes, during the May to June breeding season, the home of more than 50,000 birds, including fulmars, guillemots, kittiwakes and puffins that throng the headland near the fishing village of St Abbs. The village has one of the few unspoiled working harbours on Britain's east coast. A clifftop trail begins at the **Visitors' Centre**, where displays include identification boards and a touch table where young visitors can get to grips with wings and feathers.

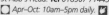

ℹ Visitors' Centre
St Abb's Head. **Tel** 018907 71443.
⬜ Apr–Oct: 10am–5pm daily. 🎫

The huge, cantilevered Forth Rail Bridge, seen from South Queensferry

A Tour of the Borders ⓲

Because of their proximity to England, the Scottish Borders are scattered with the ruins of many ancient buildings destroyed in the conflicts between the two nations. Most poignant of all are the Border abbeys, whose magnificent architecture bears witness to their former spiritual and political power. Founded during the 12th-century reign of David I, the abbeys were destroyed by Henry VIII *(see p512)*.

Kelso Abbey ②
The largest of the Border Abbeys, Kelso was once the most powerful ecclesiastical establishment in Scotland.

Melrose Abbey ⑥
Once one of the richest abbeys in Scotland, it is here that Robert the Bruce's heart is buried *(see p512)*.

Floors Castle ①
The largest inhabited castle in Scotland, it is the Duke of Roxburghe's ancestral home and was built in the 18th century by William Adam.

Scott's View ⑤
This was Sir Walter Scott's favourite view of the Borders. Out of habit his horse stopped here during Scott's funeral procession.

BERWICK-UPON-TWEED

GALASHIELS

Melrose

Kelso

Bonjedward

Jedburgh

A6089
B6361
A6091
A68
B6356
B6352
A699
B6404
Kale Water
B6401
Ale Water
B6400
Teviot
A698
Teviot
A698
Jed Water

KEY

▬▬▬	Tour route
═══	Other roads
᠅	Viewpoint

Dryburgh Abbey ④
Set on the banks of the Tweed, Dryburgh is considered the most evocative monastic ruin in Scotland. Sir Walter Scott is buried here.

TIPS FOR DRIVERS

Length: 32 miles (50 km).
Stopping-off points: There is a delightful walk northwards from Dryburgh Abbey to the footbridge over the River Tweed.

0 kilometres	5
0 miles	3

Jedburgh Abbey ③
Though established in 1138, fragments of 9th-century Celtic stonework survive from an earlier structure. A Visitors' Centre illustrates the lives of the Augustinian monks who once lived here.

Edinburgh ⑯

Royal Scots soldiers from the castle

With its striking medieval and Georgian districts, overlooked by the extinct volcano of Arthur's Seat and, to the northeast, Calton Hill, Edinburgh is widely regarded as one of Europe's most handsome capitals. The city is famous for the arts (it was once known as "the Athens of the North"), a pre-eminence reflected in its hosting every year of Britain's largest arts extravaganza, the Edinburgh Festival *(see p509)*. Its museums and galleries display the riches of many cultures.

The doorway of the Georgian House, 7 Charlotte Square

Exploring Edinburgh

Edinburgh falls into two main sightseeing areas, divided by Princes Street, the city's most famous thoroughfare and commercial centre. The Old Town straddles the ridge between the castle and the Palace of Holyroodhouse, with most of the city's medieval history clustered in the alleys of the Grassmarket and Royal Mile areas. The New Town, to the north, evolved after 1767 when wealthy merchants expanded the city beyond its medieval walls. This district contains Britain's finest concentration of Georgian architecture.

🏛 National Gallery of Scotland

The Mound. **Tel** *0131 624 6200.*
⬜ *10am–5pm Fri–Wed, 10am–7pm Thu (extended during the festival).* 🈲 *for special exhibitions.* ♿ 🖥 📷 *by appt.* **www**.*nationalgalleries.org*
One of Britain's finest art galleries, the National Gallery of Scotland is worth visiting for its 15th- to 19th-century British and European

paintings alone, though plenty more can be found to delight the art-lover. Highlights among the Scottish works include portraits by Allan Ramsay and Henry Raeburn, such as his *Reverend Robert Walker Skating on Duddingston Loch* (c.1800). The Early German collection includes Gerard David's almost comic-strip treatment of the *Three Legends of Saint Nicholas* (c.1500). Works by Raphael, Titian and Tintoretto accompany southern European paintings such as Velázquez's *An Old Woman Cooking Eggs* (1620) and the entire room devoted to *The Seven Sacraments* (c.1640) by Nicholas Poussin.

The Weston Link is an underground complex that connects the gallery with the Royal Scottish Academy. It contains a lecture theatre/cinema, shop, restaurant, café, and an IT and education room.

Raeburn's *Rev. Robert Walker Skating on Duddingston Loch*

🏛 Georgian House

(NTS) 7 Charlotte Sq. **Tel** *0844 493 2118.* ⬜ *Mar: 11am–4pm daily; Nov: 11am–3pm daily; Apr–Jun & Sep–Oct: 10am–5pm daily; Jul–Aug: 10am–6pm daily. (Last adm: half an hour before closing.)* 🈲 ♿ *limited.* **www**.*nts.org.uk*
In the heart of the New Town, Charlotte Square is a superb example of Georgian architecture, its north side, built in the 1790s, being a masterwork by the architect Robert Adam *(see pp28–9)*. The Georgian House at No. 7 has been furnished and repainted in its original 18th-century colours which provide a memorable introduction to the elegance of wealthy New Town life. In stark contrast, "below stairs" is the household staff's living quarters, demonstrating how Edinburgh's working class lived and worked.

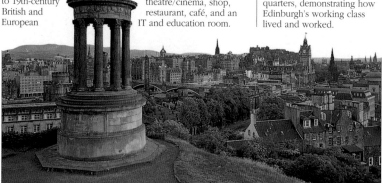

The view from Dugald Stewart Monument on Calton Hill, looking west towards the castle

🏛 Scottish National Gallery of Modern Art One and Two

Belford Rd. *Tel* 0131 624 6200. ⬜ 10am–5pm daily (Aug: to 6pm). ♿ www. nationalgalleries.org

Housed in a 19th-century school to the northwest of the city centre, the Modern

Medieval chessmen, National Museum of Scotland

One gallery features most European and American 20th-century greats, from Vuillard and Picasso, to Magritte and Lichtenstein. Work by John Bellany can be found among the Scottish painters. Sculpture by Henry Moore is on display in the grounds. The adjacent Modern Two gallery show-cases Dada and Surrealist art.

Lichtenstein's *In the Car*, National Gallery of Modern Art

🏛 National Museum of Scotland

Chambers St. *Tel* 0131 225 7534. ⬜ 10am–5pm daily. ⬤ 25 Dec. 📷 ♿ ✉ free. 🍴 www.nms.ac.uk

This purpose-built museum houses the Scottish Collections of the National Museums of Scotland. Exhibitions tell the story of Scotland, the land and its people, dating from its geological beginnings right up to the constitutionally exciting events of today.

The museum's key exhibits include the famous medieval *Lewis Chessmen; Pictish Chains,* known as Scotland's earliest crown jewels, and the *Ellesmere* railway locomotive. There is also a special exhibition gallery which houses fascinating temporary displays.

VISITORS' CHECKLIST

Edinburgh. 🏠 450,000. ✈ 8 miles (13 km) W Edinburgh. 🚆 North Bridge (Waverley Station). 🚌 St Andrew Sq. ℹ 3 Princes St (0845 22 55 121). 🎭 Edinburgh International: Aug; Military Tattoo: Aug; Fringe: Aug. www.edinburgh.org

🏛 Scottish National Portrait Gallery

1 Queen St. *Tel* 0131 624 6200. ⬜ 10am–5pm daily (to 7pm Thu). ♿ 📷 by appointment. www.nationalgalleries.org

The Scottish National Portrait Gallery provides a unique visual history of Scotland told through the portraits of those who shared it, from Robert the Bruce (*see p482*) to Queen Anne. Portraits of other famous Scots include Robert Burns (*see p515*) by Alexander Nasmyth. Since a major refurbishment, there is a greater emphasis on photog-raphy at the gallery, such as Alexander Hutchinson's moving record of the lost com-munity of St Kilda, and Scottish art, alongside a dynamic exhibition programme.

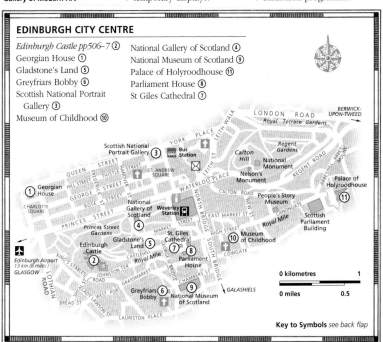

EDINBURGH CITY CENTRE

Edinburgh Castle pp506–7 ②
Georgian House ①
Gladstone's Land ⑤
Greyfriars Bobby ⑥
Scottish National Portrait Gallery ③
Museum of Childhood ⑩

National Gallery of Scotland ④
National Museum of Scotland ⑨
Palace of Holyroodhouse ⑪
Parliament House ⑧
St Giles Cathedral ⑦

Key to Symbols *see back flap*

Edinburgh Castle

Standing upon the basalt core of an extinct volcano, Edinburgh Castle is an assemblage of buildings dating from the 12th to the 20th centuries, reflecting its changing role as fortress, royal palace, military garrison and state prison. Though there is evidence of Bronze Age occupation of the site, the original fortress was built by the 6th-century Northumbrian King Edwin, from whom the city takes its name. The castle was a favourite royal residence until the Union of Crowns (see p483) in 1603, after which the king resided in England. After the Union of Parliaments in 1707, the Scottish regalia were walled up in the Palace for over a hundred years. The castle is now the zealous possessor of the so-called Stone of Destiny, a relic of ancient Scottish kings which was seized by the English in 1296 from Scone Palace, Perthshire and not returned until 1996.

Beam support in the Great Hall

Scottish Crown
On display in the palace, the Crown was restyled by James V of Scotland in 1540.

Military Prison

Governor's House
Complete with Flemish-style crow-stepped gables, this building was constructed for the governor in 1742. It can only be viewed from the outside only as it is still reserved for ceremonial use.

Old Back Parade

Vaults
This French graffiti, dating from 1780, recalls the many prisoners who were held in the vaults during the wars with France in the 18th and 19th centuries.

MONS MEG

Positioned outside St Margaret's Chapel, the siege gun (or *bombard*) Mons Meg was made in Belgium in 1449 for the Duke of Burgundy, who gave it to his nephew, James II of Scotland. It was used by James against the Douglas family in their stronghold of Threave Castle (see p515) in 1455, and later by James IV against Norham Castle in England. After exploding during a salute to the Duke of York in 1682, it was kept in the Tower of London until it was returned to Edinburgh in 1829, at Sir Walter Scott's request.

STAR SIGHTS

★ Great Hall

★ Royal Palace

VISITORS' CHECKLIST

Castle Hill. *Tel* 0131 225 9846.
⬚ 9:30am–6pm daily (Oct–Mar:
to 5pm). (Last adm: 45 mins
before closing.) ⬚ 25, 26 Dec.
⬚ book tickets online to avoid
queuing. ⬚⬚⬚⬚⬚
www.edinburghcastle.gov.uk

Argyle Battery
*This fortified wall commands a spec-
tacular view to the north beyond the
city's Georgian district of New Town.*

★ **Royal Palace**
*Mary, Queen of
Scots (see p511)
gave birth to James
VI in this 15th-
century palace,
where the Scottish
regalia are on
display.*

Entrance

**Royal
Mile** →

The Esplanade is the
location of the Military
Tattoo *(see p509)*.

**The Half Moon
Battery** was built in the
1570s as a platform for
the artillery defending
the northeastern wing
of the castle.

St Margaret's Chapel
*This stained-glass
window depicts Malcolm
III's saintly queen, to
whom the chapel is
dedicated. Probably built
by her son, David I, in
the early 12th century,
the chapel is the castle's
oldest existing building.*

★ **Great Hall**
*With its restored open-timber
roof, the Hall dates from the
15th century and was the
meeting place of the Scottish
parliament until 1639.*

Exploring the Royal Mile: Castlehill to High Street

The Royal Mile is a stretch of four ancient streets (from Castlehill to Canongate) which formed the main thoroughfare of medieval Edinburgh, linking the castle to the Palace of Holyroodhouse. Confined by the city wall, the "Old Town" grew upwards, with some tenements climbing to 20 storeys. It is still possible, among the 66 alleys and closes off the main street, to sense the city's medieval past.

Eagle sign outside Gladstone's Land

Locator map

Gladstone's Land is a preserved 17th-century merchant's house.

Scotch Whisky Heritage Centre introduces visitors to Scotland's national drink.

The Camera Obscura contains an observatory from which to view the city, plus optical illusions and giant kaleidoscopes.

LAWNMARKET

Edinburgh Castle ←   CASTLE HILL

Lady Stair's House
This 17th-century house is now a museum of the lives and works of Burns, Scott (see p512) and Stevenson.

The "Hub" (c.1840) has the city's highest spire.

🏛 Gladstone's Land

(NTS) 477B Lawnmarket. **Tel** 0844 493 2120. ◯ Easter–Oct: 10am–5pm daily (Jul & Aug: to 6:30pm). (Last adm: 30 mins before closing.) 🚫 ♿ 🚫
This 17th-century merchant's house provides a window on life in a typical Old Town house before overcrowding drove the rich to the Georgian New Town. "Lands", as they were known, were tall, narrow buildings erected on small plots of land. The six-storey Gladstone's Land was named after Thomas Gledstanes, the merchant who built it in 1617. The house still has the original arcade booths on the street front and a painted ceiling with fine Scandinavian floral designs. Though extravagantly furnished, it also contains items which are a reminder of the less salubrious side of the old city, such as wooden overshoes which had to be worn in the dirty streets. A chest in the beautiful Painted Chamber is said to have been given by a Dutch sea captain to a Scottish merchant who saved him from a shipwreck. A similar house, Morocco Land, can be found on Canongate *(see p511)*.

🏛 Parliament House

Parliament Sq, High St. **Tel** 0131 225 2595. ◯ 9am–5pm Mon–Fri. ● public hols. ♿ limited.
This majestic, Italianate building was constructed in the 1630s for the Scottish parliament. Parliament House has been home to the Court of Session and the Supreme Court since the Union of Parliaments *(see p483)* in 1707. It is worth seeing, as much for the spectacle of its gowned and wigged advocates as for the stained-glass window in its Great Hall, commemorating the inauguration of the Court of Session by James V, in 1532.

The bedroom of Gladstone's Land

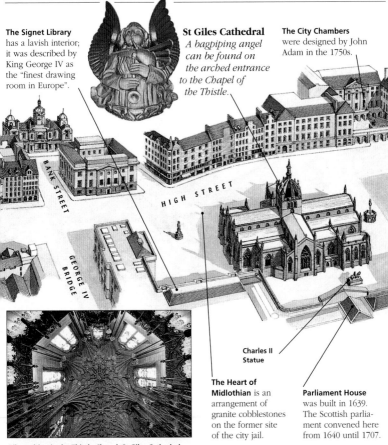

The Signet Library has a lavish interior; it was described by King George IV as the "finest drawing room in Europe".

St Giles Cathedral
A bagpiping angel can be found on the arched entrance to the Chapel of the Thistle.

The City Chambers were designed by John Adam in the 1750s.

BANK STREET

HIGH STREET

GEORGE IV BRIDGE

Charles II Statue

The Heart of Midlothian is an arrangement of granite cobblestones on the former site of the city jail.

Parliament House was built in 1639. The Scottish parliament convened here from 1640 until 1707.

Rib-vaulting in the Thistle Chapel, St Giles Cathedral

🔒 St Giles Cathedral

Royal Mile. *Tel 0131 225 9442.* ⬭ *May–Sep: 9am–7pm Mon–Fri, 9am–5pm Sat, 1–5pm Sun; Oct–Apr: 9am–5pm Mon–Sat, 1–5pm Sun.* ⬤ *1 & 2 Jan, 25 & 26 Dec.* 📷 *donation.* 🏛️ **www.stgilescathedral.org.uk**

Properly known as the High Kirk (church) of Edinburgh, it is ironic that St Giles is popularly known as a cathedral. Though it was twice the seat of a bishop in the 17th century, it was from here that John Knox *(see p483)* directed the Scottish Reformation with its emphasis on individual worship freed from the authority of bishops. A tablet marks the place where Jenny Geddes, a stallholder from a local market, scored a victory for the Covenanters *(see p483)* by hurling her stool at a preacher reading from an English prayer book in 1637.

The Gothic exterior is dominated by a 15th-century tower.

Inside, the impressive Thistle Chapel can be seen, with its elaborate rib-vaulted roof and carved heraldic canopies. The chapel honours the knights, past and present, of the Order of the Thistle. The carved royal pew in the Preston Aisle is used by the Queen when she stays in Edinburgh.

EDINBURGH FESTIVAL

Every year, for three weeks in late summer *(see p63)*, Edinburgh hosts one of the world's most important arts festivals, with every available space (from theatres to street corners) overflowing with performers. It has been held in Edinburgh since 1947 and brings together the best in international contemporary theatre, music, dance and opera. The alternative Festival Fringe balances the classic productions with a host of innovative performances. The most popular event is the Edinburgh Military Tattoo, held on the Castle Esplanade – a spectacle of Scottish infantry battalions marching to pipe bands. Also popular are the Edinburgh Book Festival and Edinburgh Film Festival (held in June).

Street performer from the Edinburgh Festival Fringe

Exploring the Royal Mile: High Street to Canongate

The second section of the Royal Mile passes two monuments to the Reformation: John Knox House and the Tron Kirk. The latter is named after a medieval *tron* (weighing beam) that stood nearby. The Canongate was once an independent district, owned by the canons of the Abbey of Holyrood, and sections of its south side have been restored. Beyond Morocco's Land, the road stretches for the final half-mile (800 m) to the Palace of Holyroodhouse.

THE PALACE OF HOLYROODHOUSE

EDINBURGH CASTLE

LOCATOR MAP

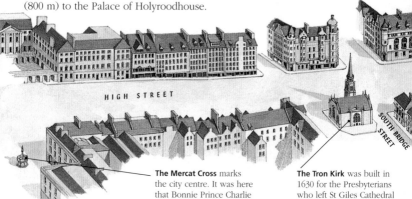

HIGH STREET

SOUTH BRIDGE STREET

The Mercat Cross marks the city centre. It was here that Bonnie Prince Charlie (*see p535*) was proclaimed king in 1745.

The Tron Kirk was built in 1630 for the Presbyterians who left St Giles Cathedral when it came under the Bishop of Edinburgh's control.

🏛 Museum of Childhood

42 High St. *Tel* 0131 529 4142.
◯ 10am–5pm Mon–Sat (& Sun pm).
⬤ 25–27 Dec. ♿ limited. **www.cac.org.uk**

This lovely museum is not merely a toy collection but a magical insight into childhood. Founded in 1955 by a city councillor, Patrick Murray (who claimed to enjoy eating children for breakfast), it was the first museum in the world to be devoted to the history and theme of childhood. The collection includes medicines, school books and prams as well as galleries full of old-fashioned toys. With its nickel-odeon, antique slot machines

An 1880 automaton of the Man on the Moon, Museum of Childhood

The entrance to the Palace of Holyroodhouse, seen from the west

and the general enthusiasm of visitors, this has been called the world's noisiest museum.

🏰 Palace of Holyroodhouse

East end of Royal Mile. *Tel* 0131 556 5100. ◯ Apr–Oct: 9:30am–6pm; Nov–Mar: 9:30am–4:30pm daily. ⬤ 25 & 26 Dec and during royal visits. 📷 ♿ limited. **www.royalcollection.org.uk**

Now the Queen's official Scottish residence, the Palace of Holyroodhouse is named after the "rood", or cross, which King David I is said to have seen between the antlers of a stag he was hunting here in 1128. The present palace was built in 1529 to accommodate James V (*see p501*) and his French wife, Mary of Guise,

though it was remodelled in the 1670s for Charles II. The Royal Apartments (including the Throne Room and Royal Dining Room) are used for investitures and banquets whenever the Queen visits the palace. A chamber in the James V tower is associated with the unhappy reign of Mary, Queen of Scots. It was here, in 1566, that she saw the murder of her trusted Italian secretary, David Rizzio, by her jealous husband, Lord Darnley. She had married Darnley a year earlier in Holyroodhouse chapel.

Bonnie Prince Charlie held court here in 1745 in the Jacobite (*see p537*) rising.

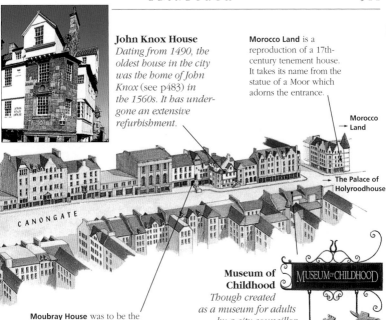

John Knox House

Dating from 1490, the oldest house in the city was the home of John Knox (see p483) in the 1560s. It has undergone an extensive refurbishment.

Morocco Land is a reproduction of a 17th-century tenement house. It takes its name from the statue of a Moor which adorns the entrance.

→ Morocco Land

→ The Palace of Holyroodhouse

CANONGATE

Museum of Childhood

Though created as a museum for adults by a city councillor who was known to dislike children, this lively museum now attracts flocks of young visitors.

MUSEUM OF CHILDHOOD

Moubray House was to be the signing place of the Treaty of Union in 1707 *(see p469)*, until a mob forced the authorities to retreat to another venue.

🏛 National Museum of Scotland

Chambers St. **Tel** *0300 123 6789.*
⬭ *10am–5pm daily.* ⬤ *25 Dec.*
📷 ♿ 🅿 🍴 www.nms.ac.uk

Two adjoining buildings, the Victorian former Royal Gallery and a modern sculptural edifice of Moray sandstone, house collections that tell the story of Scotland – its geology, natural history, scientific advancements, art and design. The exhibits include the Columbia Printing Press and a Stevenson lighthouse lens as well as Baird's first television and a model of the famous "Rocket" steam locomotive. The Scottish Galleries span the millennia with artifacts from pre-history to the present day.

Parvati, at the National Museum of Scotland

The soaring Grand Gallery houses Window on the World, the single largest museum installation in the UK. It features a spectacular array of exhibits from around the world, covering everything from culture and creativity to the diversity of our planet.

🐕 Greyfriars Bobby

Near the gateway to Greyfriars Church stands the statue of a Skye terrier. It commemorates the dog who, for 14 years, is said to have guarded the grave of his master, John Gray. The people of Edinburgh cared for Bobby until his death in 1872.

MARY, QUEEN OF SCOTS (1542–87)

Born only days before the death of her father, James V, the young Queen Mary spent her childhood in France, after escaping Henry VIII's invasion of Scotland *(see p512)*. A devout Catholic, she married the French Dauphin, and made claims on the English throne. This alarmed Protestants throughout England and Scotland, and when she returned as a widow to Holyroodhouse, aged 18, she was harangued for her faith by John Knox *(see p483)*. In 1567 she was accused of murdering her second husband, Lord Darnley. Two months later, when she married the Earl of Bothwell (also implicated in the murder), rebellion ensued. She lost her crown and fled to England where she was held prisoner for 20 years, before being charged with treason and beheaded at Fotheringhay.

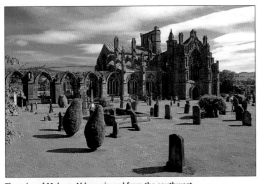

The ruins of Melrose Abbey, viewed from the southwest

Melrose Abbey ⑲

Abbey Street, Melrose, Scottish
Borders. *Tel* 01896 822562. ◯
9:30am–4:30pm daily (Apr–Sep: to
5:30pm). (Last adm: 30 mins before
closing.) ● 1, 2 Jan, 25, 26 Dec. ▨
◻ ltd. www.historic-scotland.gov.uk

The rose-pink ruins of this
beautiful Border abbey *(see
p503)* bear testimony to the
hazards of standing in the path
of successive English invasions.
Built by David I in 1136 for
Cistercian monks from Yorkshire, and also to replace a
7th-century monastery, Melrose
was repeatedly ransacked by
English armies, notably in
1322 and 1385. The final blow,
from which none of the
abbeys recovered, came in
1545 during Henry VIII's
destructive Scottish policy
known as the "Rough Woo-
ing". This resulted from the
failure of the Scots to ratify
a marriage treaty between
Henry VIII's son and the
infant Mary, Queen of Scots
(see p511). What remains of
the abbey are the outlines
of cloisters, the kitchen and
other monastic buildings and
the shell of the abbey church
with its soaring east window
and profusion of medieval
carvings. The rich decorations
of the south exterior wall
include a gargoyle shaped like
a pig playing the bagpipes.

An embalmed heart, found
here in 1920, is probably that
of Robert the Bruce *(see
p482)*, who had decreed that
his heart be taken on a crusade to the Holy Land. It was
returned to Melrose after its
bearer, Sir James Douglas *(see
p515)*, was killed in Spain.

Abbotsford House ⑳

Galashiels, Scottish Borders. *Tel*
01896 752043. ▥ from Galashiels.
◯ mid-Mar–late Oct: 9:30am–5pm
Mon–Sat, 11am–4pm Sun (Jun–Sep:
9:30am–5pm). ▨ ◻ limited. ▨
www.scottsabbotsford.co.uk

Few houses bear the stamp
of their creator so intimately as
Abbotsford House, the home
of Sir Walter Scott for the last
20 years of his life. He bought
a farm here in 1811, known
as Clartyhole ("dirty hole"
in Scots), though he soon
renamed it Abbotsford, after
the monks of Melrose Abbey
who used to cross the River
Tweed nearby. He later
demolished the house to
make way for the turreted
building we see today, funded
by the sales of his novels.

Scott's library contains more
than 9,000 rare books and his
collections of historic relics
reflect his passion for the
heroic past. An extensive
collection of arms and armour
includes Rob Roy's broad-
sword *(see p495)*. Stuart
mementos include a crucifix
that belonged to Mary, Queen
of Scots and a lock of Bonnie
Prince Charlie's *(see p535)*
hair. The small study in which
he wrote his *Waverley* novels
can be visited as can the
room, overlooking the river,
in which he died in 1832.

SIR WALTER SCOTT

Sir Walter Scott (1771–1832)
was born in Edinburgh and
trained as a lawyer. He is best
remembered as a major champion and literary figure of
Scotland, whose poems and
novels (most famously his
Waverley series) created
enduring images of a heroic
wilderness filled with the
romance of the clans. His
orchestration, in 1822, of the
state visit of George IV to
Edinburgh *(see p485)* was an
extravaganza of Highland culture that helped re-establish
tartan as the national dress of Scotland. He served as Clerk of
the Court in Edinburgh's Parliament House *(see p508)* and for
30 years was Sheriff of Selkirk in the Scottish Borders, which
he loved. He put the Trossachs *(see pp494–5)* firmly on the
map with the publication of the *Lady of the Lake* (1810). His
final years were spent writing to pay off a £114,000 debt following the failure of his publisher in 1827. He died with his
debts paid, and was buried at Dryburgh Abbey *(see p503)*.

The Great Hall at Abbotsford,
adorned with arms and armour

Traquair House ㉑

Peebles, Scottish Borders. *Tel 01896 830 323.* from Peebles. Apr, May & Sep: 11am–5pm daily; Jun–Aug: 10:30am–5pm daily; Oct: 11am–4pm daily; Nov: 11am–3pm Sat & Sun. limited. **www.**traquair.co.uk

As Scotland's oldest continuously inhabited house, Traquair has deep roots in Scottish religious and political history, stretching back over 900 years. Evolving from a fortified tower to a stout-walled 17th-century mansion *(see p487)*, the house was a Catholic Stuart stronghold for 500 years. Mary, Queen of Scots *(see p511)* was among the many monarchs to have stayed here and her bed is covered by a counterpane which she made. Family letters and engraved Jacobite *(see p537)* drinking glasses are among relics recalling the period of the Highland rebellions.

Mary, Queen of Scots' crucifix, Traquair House

After a vow made by the 5th Earl, Traquair's Bear Gates (the "Steekit Yetts"), which closed after Bonnie Prince Charlie's *(see p535)* visit in 1745, will not reopen until a Stuart reascends the throne.

A secret stairway leads to the Priest's Room which attests to the problems faced by Catholic families until Catholicism was legalized in 1829. Traquair House Ale is still produced in the 18th-century brewhouse.

Biggar ㉒

Clyde Valley. 2,000. High St (01899 221066).

This typical Lowland market town has a number of museums worth visiting. The **Gladstone Court Museum** boasts a reconstructed Victorian street complete with a milliner's, printer's and a village library, while the town's industrial past are recalled at the **Gasworks Museum**, with its collection of engines, gaslights and appliances. Established in 1839 and preserved in the 1970s, the Biggar Gasworks is the only remaining rural gasworks in Scotland.

🏛 **Gladstone Court Museum**
Northback Rd. *Tel 01899 221050.* Easter–Sep: 11am–4:30pm Mon, Tue, Thu–Sat, 2–4:30pm Sun.
🏛 **Gasworks Museum**
Gasworks Rd. *Tel 01899 221070.* Jun–Sep: 2–5pm daily.

Pentland Hills ㉓

The Lothians. Edinburgh, then bus. Regional Park Headquarters, Biggar Rd, Edinburgh (0131 4453383).

The Pentland Hills, stretching for 16 miles (26 km) southwest of Edinburgh, offer some of the best hill-walking country in the Lowlands. Leisurely walkers can saunter along the many signposted footpaths, while the more adventurous can take the chairlift at the Hillend dry ski slope to reach the higher ground leading to the 493 m (1,617 ft) hill of Allermuir. Even more ambitious is the classic scenic route along the ridge from Caerketton to West Kip.

To the east of the A703, in the lee of the Pentlands, stands the exquisite and ornate 15th-century **Rosslyn Chapel**. It was originally intended as a church, but after the death of its founder, William Sinclair, it was also used as a burial ground for his descendants. The delicately wreathed Apprentice Pillar recalls the legend of the apprentice carver who was killed by the master stonemason in a fit of jealousy at his pupil's superior skill.

🔒 **Rosslyn Chapel**
Roslin. *Tel 0131 4402159.* daily (Sun: pm only).

Details of the decorated vaulting in Rosslyn Chapel

The Classical 18th-century tenements of New Lanark on the banks of the Clyde

New Lanark ㉔

Clyde Valley. ▲ 185. ▓ ▢ Lanark.
🛈 Horsemarket, Ladyacre Rd
(01555 661345). ♿ 🏠 daily.
www.newlanark.org

Situated by the falls of the
River Clyde, the village of
New Lanark was founded in
1785 by the industrial entrepreneur David Dale. Ideally

DAVID LIVINGSTONE

Scotland's great missionary
doctor and explorer was
born in Blantyre where he
began working life as a
mill boy at the age of ten.
Livingstone (1813–73)
made three epic journeys
across Africa, from 1840,
promoting "commerce and
Christianity". He became
the first European to see
Victoria Falls and died in
1873 while searching for
the source of the Nile. He
is buried in Westminster
Abbey (see pp92–3).

located for the working of its
water-driven mills, the village
had become Britain's largest
cotton producer by 1800.
Dale and his successor, Robert
Owen, were philanthropists
whose reforms proved that
commercial success need not
undermine the wellbeing of
the workforce. Now a museum,
New Lanark is a window on to
working life in the early 19th
century. Audio-visual shows
tell the story of New Lanark
and Robert Owen's progressive
ideals, and how they apply as
much today and in the future
as they did in the 1820s.

Environs: 15 miles (24 km)
north, Blantyre has a memorial to the famous Scottish
explorer David Livingstone.

🏛 **New Lanark**
New Lanark Visitor Centre. **Tel** 01555
661345. ◷ 11am–5pm daily. 📷 ♿
📷 groups only, by appt – book ahead.

Glasgow ㉕

See pp516–21.

Sanquhar ㉖

Dumfries & Galloway. ▲ 2,500. ▓
▢ 🛈 High St (01659 50186).

Now of chiefly historic
interest, the town of
Sanquhar was famous in the
history of the Covenanters
(see p483). In the 1680s,

two declarations opposing
the rule of bishops were
pinned to the Mercat Cross,
the site of which is now
marked by a granite obelisk.
The first protest was led by a
local teacher, Richard Cameron,
whose followers became the
Cameronian regiment. The
Georgian **Tolbooth** was
designed by William Adam
(see p548) in 1735 and houses
a local interest museum and
tourist centre. The Post Office,
opened in 1763, is the oldest
in Britain, predating the mail
coach service.

Drumlanrig
Castle ㉗

Thornhill, Dumfries & Galloway.
Tel 01848 331555. ▓ ▢ Dumfries,
then bus. ◯ Grounds Apr–Oct:
10am–5pm daily; Nov–Mar: 11am–
4pm Sat & Sun. **Castle** Easter–Aug:
11am–4pm daily. 📷 ♿ 📷 www.
drumlanrig.com

Rising squarely from a grassy
platform, the massive fortress-
palace of **Drumlanrig** (see p487)
was built from pink sandstone

The Baroque front steps and
doorway of Drumlanrig Castle

between 1679 and 1691 on the site of a 15th-century Douglas stronghold. A formidable multi-turreted exterior contains a priceless collection of art treasures such as paintings by Holbein and Rembrandt, as well as such Jacobite relics as Bonnie Prince Charlie's camp kettle and sash. The emblem of a crowned and winged heart, shown throughout the castle, recalls Sir James, the "Black Douglas", who bore Robert the Bruce's *(see p482)* heart while on crusade. After being mortally wounded he threw the heart at his enemies with the words "forward brave heart!"

The sturdy island fortress of Threave Castle on the Dee

Threave Castle ㉘

Castle Douglas, Dumfries & Galloway. **Tel** 07711 223101. Dumfries. Apr–Oct: 9:30am–4:30pm last outward boat (Oct: 3:30pm) daily. www.historic-scotland.gov.uk

This menacing giant of a tower, a 14th-century Black Douglas *(see above)* stronghold standing on an island in the Dee, commands the most complete medieval riverside harbour in Scotland. Douglas's struggles against the early Stewart kings culminated in his surrender here after a two-month siege in 1455 – but only after James II had brought the cannon Mons Meg *(see p506)* to batter the castle. Threave was dismantled after Protestant Covenanters *(see p483)* defeated its Catholic defenders in

1640. Inside the tower, only the shell of the kitchen, great hall and domestic levels remains. Over the 15th-century doorway is the "gallows knob", a reminder of when the owners are said to have boasted that it never lacked its noose. Access to the castle is by small boat.

Whithorn ㉙

Dumfries & Galloway. 1,000. Stranraer. Dashwood Sq, Newton Stewart (01671 402431). **www**.visitdumfriesandgalloway.co.uk

The earliest site of continuous Christian worship in Scotland, Whithorn (meaning white house) takes its name from the white chapel built here by St Ninian in 397. Though nothing remains of his chapel, a guided tour of the archaeological dig reveals evidence of Northumbrian, Viking and Scottish settlements ranging from the 5th to the 19th centuries. A visitors' centre, **The Whithorn Story**, provides information on the excavations and contains a collection of carved stones. One, dedicated to Latinus, dates to 450, making it Scotland's earliest Christian monument.

🏛 **The Whithorn Story**
The Whithorn Trust, 45–47 George St. **Tel** 01988 500508. Easter–Oct: 10:30am–5pm daily. **www**.whithorn.com

Culzean Castle ㉚

See pp522–3.

Robert Burns surrounded by his creations, by an unknown artist

Burns Cottage ㉛

Robert Burns Birthplace Museum, Alloway, South Ayrshire. **Tel** 0844 4932601. Ayr, then bus. Oct–Mar: 10am–5pm; Apr–Sep: 10am–5:30pm; daily. 25 & 26 Dec, 1 & 2 Jan. **www**.burnsmuseum.org.uk

Robert Burns (1759–96), Scotland's favourite poet, was born and spent his first seven years in this small thatched cottage in Alloway. Built by his father, the restored cottage still contains much of its original furniture. A modern museum displays many of Burns's manuscripts along with early editions of his works. Much of his poem *Tam o' Shanter* (1790) is set in Alloway, which commemorates him with elegant monuments on the outskirts of the village.
Burns became a celebrity following the publication in 1786 of the Kilmarnock Edition of his poems. Scots everywhere gather to celebrate Burns Night *(see p65)* on his birthday, 25 January.

SCOTTISH TEXTILES

Weaving in the Scottish Borders goes back to the Middle Ages, when monks from Flanders established a thriving woollen trade with the Continent. Cotton became an important source of wealth in the Clyde Valley during the 19th century, when handloom weaving was overtaken by power-driven mills. The popular Paisley patterns were based on Indian designs.

A colourful pattern from Paisley

Glasgow ❷

St Mungo with the Glasgow symbols

Though its Celtic name, *Glas cu*, means "dear green place", Glasgow is more often associated with its industrial past, and once enjoyed the title of Second City of the Empire (after London). Glasgow's architectural standing, as Scotland's finest Victorian city, reflects its era of prosperity, when ironworks, cotton mills and ship-building were fuelled by Lanarkshire coal. The Science Centre sits on the Clyde's revitalized south bank, and Glasgow rivals Edinburgh *(see pp504–11)* in the arts, with galleries such as the Kelvingrove and the Burrell Collection *(see pp520–21)*.

Glasgow's medieval cathedral viewed from the southwest

Exploring Glasgow

With some relics of its grimy industrial past and glossy new image, modern Glasgow is a city of contrasts. The deprived East End, with its busy week-end market, "the Barras", stands by the restored 18th-century Merchant City and Victorian George Square. The more affluent West End prospered in the 19th century as a retreat for wealthy merchants escaping the industrialized Clydeside, and it is here that restaurants, bars, parks and Glasgow University can be found. South Side, next to affluent Pollokshields, is Pollok Country Park, site of the Burrell Collection. An underground network and good bus and rail links provide easy travel around the city.

🛈 Glasgow Cathedral

2 Castle St. **Tel** 0141 5528198. 🔲 Apr–Sep: 9:30am–5:30pm Mon–Sat, 1–5pm Sun; Oct–Mar: 9:30am–4:30pm Mon–Sat, 1–4:30pm Sun. 🔖 As one of the only cathedrals to escape destruction during the Scottish Reformation *(see pp482–3)* – by adapting itself

to Protestant worship – this is a rare example of an almost complete 13th-century church. It was built on the site of a chapel founded by the city's patron saint, St Mungo, a 6th-century bishop of Strathclyde. According to legend, Mungo placed the body of a holy man named Fergus on a cart yoked to two wild bulls, telling them to take it to the place ordained by God. In the "dear green place" at which the bulls stopped he built his church. The cathedral is on two levels.

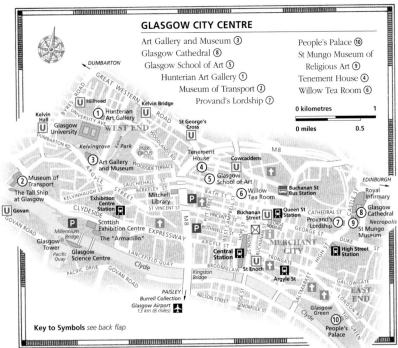

GLASGOW CITY CENTRE

Art Gallery and Museum ③
Glasgow Cathedral ⑧
Glasgow School of Art ⑤
Hunterian Art Gallery ①
Museum of Transport ②
Provand's Lordship ⑦

People's Palace ⑩
St Mungo Museum of Religious Art ⑨
Tenement House ④
Willow Tea Room ⑥

0 kilometres   1

0 miles   0.5

Key to Symbols see back flap

Dali's *Christ of St John of the Cross* at the Kelvingrove Art Gallery *(see p519)*

Situated in the cathedral precinct, this museum is a world first. The main exhibition illustrates religious themes with superb artifacts, including a 19th-century dancing Shiva and an Islamic painting entitled the *Attributes of Divine Perfection* (1986) by Ahmed Moustafa. Other religious paintings on display include *Crucifixion VII* (1988) by Scottish artist Craigie Aitchison. An exhibition on religion in Glasgow throws light on the life of the missionary David Livingstone *(see p514)*. Outside you can visit Britain's only permanent Zen Buddhist garden.

The crypt contains the tomb of St Mungo, surrounded by an intricate forest of columns springing up to end in delicately carved rib-vaulting. The Blackadder Aisle, reputed to have been built over a cemetery blessed by St Ninian *(see p515)*, has a ceiling thick with decorative bosses.

🏛 St Mungo Museum of Religious Life and Art

2 Castle St. **Tel** 0141 2761625. ☐ 10am–5pm Tue–Thu & Sat, 11am–5pm Fri & Sun. 🔊 🖪 by appt. 🖵 🖪

🚇 Tenement House

(NTS) 145 Buccleuch St. **Tel** 0844 4932197. ☐ Mar–Oct: 1–5pm daily. 🖪 🖪 by appt. **www.**nts.org.uk
Less a museum than a time capsule, the Tenement House is an almost undisturbed record of life in a modest Glasgow flat in a tenement estate during the early 20th century. Glasgow owed much of its vitality and neighbourliness to tenement life, though many of these Victorian and Edwardian apartments were to earn a bad name for poverty and overcrowding,

The preserved Edwardian kitchen of the Tenement House

and many have now been pulled down. The Tenement House was first owned by Miss Agnes Toward who lived here from 1911 until 1965. It remained largely unaltered and, since Agnes threw very little away, it is now a treasure trove of social history. The parlour, previously used only on formal occasions, has afternoon tea laid out on a white lace cloth. The kitchen, with its coal-fired range and box bed, is filled with the tools of a vanished era such as a goffering iron for crisping waffles, a washboard and a stone hot-water bottle.

Agnes's lavender water and medicines are still in the bathroom, as though she had stepped out for a minute 70 years ago, and forgotten to return home.

The Kelvingrove Art Gallery and the Glasgow University buildings, viewed from the south

Glasgow's medieval house, Provand's Lordship

Provand's Lordship

3 Castle St. **Tel** 0141 2761625.
◻ 10am–5pm Tue–Thu & Sat,
11am–5pm Fri & Sun. **www.**
glasgowmuseums.com

Now a museum, Provand's Lordship was built as a canon's house in 1471, and is the city's oldest surviving house. Its low ceilings and austere wooden furnishings create a vivid impression of life in a wealthy 15th-century household. It is

Mackintosh's interior of the Willow Tea Room

thought that Mary, Queen of Scots (*see p511*) may have stayed here in 1566 when she made a visit to see her cousin and husband, Lord Darnley.

Willow Tea Room

217 Sauchiehall St (also 97 Buchanan St). **Tel** 0141 332 0521. ◻ 9am–5pm Mon–Sat, 11am–4:15pm Sun.
🖳 **www.**willowtearooms.co.uk

This is the sole survivor of a series of delightful tea rooms created by Charles Rennie Mackintosh in 1904 for the celebrated restaurateur Miss Kate Cranston. Everything from the high-backed chairs to the tables and cutlery was his design. In particular, the 1904 Room de Luxe sparkles with silver furniture and flamboyant leaded glass work. The No. 97 Buchanan Street branch opened in 1997, and recreates Cranston's original Ingram Street Tea Rooms. It features painstaking replicas of Mackintosh's light and airy White Dining Room and atmospheric Chinese, or "Blue", Room.

Riverside Museum

Pointhouse Quay. **Tel** 0141 2872720.
◻ 10am–5pm Mon–Thu & Sat,
11am–5pm Fri & Sun. 🖳 🖳 🖳 🖳
www.glasgowmuseums.com

Model ships and ranks of gleaming Scottish-built steam engines, cars and motorcycles recall the 19th and early 20th centuries, when Glasgow's supremacy in shipbuilding, trade and manufacturing made her the "second city" of the British Empire. Old Glasgow's transition into a modern city can be seen through fascinating footage of the town in the cinema and through a series of three street reconstructions covering 1890–1930, 1930–60 and 1960–80. Don't miss the *Tall Ship Glenlee*, berthed just outside the museum on the River Clyde.

Striking Riverside Museum, housing Glasgow's transport collection

Glasgow Necropolis

Cathedral Sq. **Tel** 0141 2873961.
◻ daily. 🖳 🖳 limited.

Behind the cathedral, the reformer John Knox (*see p483*) surveys the city from his Doric pillar overlooking a Victorian cemetery. It is filled with crumbling monuments to the dead of Glasgow's wealthy merchant families.

CHARLES RENNIE MACKINTOSH

A Mackintosh floral design

Glasgow's most celebrated designer, Charles Rennie Mackintosh (1868–1928), entered Glasgow School of Art at 16. After his first big break with the Willow Tea Room, he became a leading figure in the Art Nouveau movement, developing a unique style that borrowed from Gothic and Scottish Baronial designs. He believed a building should be a fully integrated work of art, creating furniture and fittings that complemented the overall construction. Nowhere is this total design better seen than in the Glasgow School of Art, which he designed in 1896.

Unrecognized in his lifetime, Mackintosh's work is now widely imitated. Its characteristic straight lines and flowing detail are the hallmark of early 20th-century Glasgow style, in all fields of design from textiles to architecture.

🏛 People's Palace

Glasgow Green. *Tel* 0141 2760795.
⬜ 10am–5pm Tue–Thu & Sat,
11am–5pm Fri & Sun. ⬤ 1 & 2 Jan,
25 & 26 Dec. ♿ ⬜ ⬜
www.glasgowmuseums.com
This Victorian sandstone structure was built in 1898 as a
cultural museum for the people
of Glasgow's East End. It
houses everything from temperance tracts to trade-union
banners, suffragette posters
to comedian Billy Connolly's
banana-shaped boots, providing a social history of the
city from the 12th century. A
conservatory at the back contains an exotic winter garden.

🏛 Glasgow School of Art

167 Renfrew St. *Tel (tours)* 0141 566
1472. ⬜ tour only, reserve ahead.
📷 ♿ ♿ limited. **www**.gsa.ac.uk
Widely considered to be
Charles Rennie Mackintosh's
greatest architectural work,
the Glasgow School of Art
was built between 1897 and
1909 to a design he submitted
in a competition. It was built
in two periods due to financial
constraints. The later, western
wing displays a softer design
than the more severe eastern
half, built only a few years
earlier and compared by a
contemporary critic to a prison.

A student guide takes you
through the building to the
Furniture Gallery, Board
Room and the Library, the
latter a masterpiece of spatial
composition. Each room is an
exercise in contrasts between
height, light and shade with
innovative details echoing the
architectural themes of the
structure. How much of the
school can be viewed depends
on curricular requirements at
the time of visiting.

🏛 Hunterian Art Gallery

82 Hillhead St. *Tel* 0141 3304221.
⬜ 10am–5pm Tue–Sat, 11am–4pm
Sun. ⬤ 24 Dec–5 Jan & public hols.
⬜ ♿ ltd. **www**.hunterian.gla.ac.uk
Built to house a number of
paintings bequeathed to
Glasgow University by ex-
student and physician Dr
William Hunter (1718–83), the
Hunterian Art Gallery contains
Scotland's largest print collec-
tion and works by major
European artists stretching
back to the 16th century. A

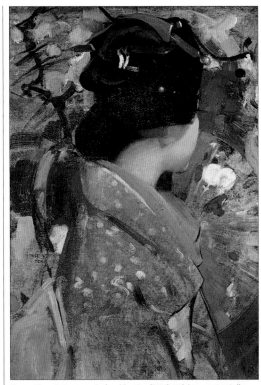

George Henry's *Japanese Lady with a Fan* (1894), Kelvingrove Art Gallery

collection of work by Charles
Mackintosh is supplemented
by a complete reconstruction
of No. 6 Florentine Terrace,
where he lived from 1906 to
1914. A major collection of
19th- and 20th-century Scottish
art includes work by William
McTaggart (1835–1910), but the
gallery's most famous collection
is of work by the painter James
McNeill Whistler (1834–1903).

Whistler's *Sketch for Annabel Lee*
(c.1869), Hunterian Art Gallery

🏛 Kelvingrove Art Gallery and Museum

Argyle St, Kelvingrove. *Tel* 0141 276
9599. ⬜ 10am–5pm Mon–Thu & Sat,
11am–5pm Fri & Sun. ⬤ 1 & 2 Jan,
25 & 26 Dec. **www**.glasgow
museums.com
The imposing red sandstone
building that is Kelvingrove is
a striking Glasgow landmark –
even though it was supposedly
built the wrong way round –
and the gallery and museum
is the most visited in Scotland.
Having undergone a major
(£27.9 million) refurbishment,
the gallery and museum house
an impressive array of art and
artifacts. The outstanding
collection has paintings of
inestimable value, including
works by Botticelli, Giorgione
(*The Adulteress Brought Before
Christ*), Rembrandt and Dalí
(*Christ of St John of the Cross,
see p517*). Its impressive representation of 17th-century Dutch
and 19th-century French art is
augmented by the home-grown
talent of the Glasgow Boys and
the Scottish Colourists.

The Georgian Pollok House, viewed from the south

🏛 Pollok House

(NTS) 2060 Pollokshaws Rd. **Tel** 0844 493 2202. ☐ 10am–5pm daily. ● 1 & 2 Jan, 25 & 26 Dec. ✂ Apr–Oct only. **www**.nts.org.uk

Pollok House is Glasgow's finest 18th-century domestic building and contains one of Britain's best collections of Spanish paintings. The Neo-Classical central block was finished in 1750, the sobriety of its exterior contrasting with the exuberant plasterwork within. The Maxwells have lived at Pollok since the mid-13th century, but the male line ended with Sir John Maxwell, who added the grand entrance hall in the 1890s and designed most of the terraced gardens and parkland beyond.

Hanging above the family silver, porcelain, hand-painted Chinese wallpaper and Jacobean glass, the Stirling Maxwell collection is strong on British and Dutch schools, including William Blake's *Sir Geoffrey Chaucer and the Nine and Twenty Pilgrims* (1745) and William Hogarth's portrait of James Thomson, who wrote the words to *Rule Britannia*.

Spanish 16th- to 19th-century art predominates: El Greco's *Lady in a Fur Wrap* (1541) hangs in the library, while the drawing room contains works by Francisco de Goya and Esteban Murillo. In 1966 Anne Maxwell Macdonald gave the house and 146 ha (361 acres) of parkland to the City of Glasgow. The park provides the site for the city's fascinating Burrell Collection.

Glasgow: The Burrell Collection

Given to the city in 1944 by Sir William Burrell (1861–1958), a wealthy shipping owner, this internationally acclaimed collection is the jewel in Glasgow's crown, with objects of major importance in numerous fields of interest. The building was purpose-built in 1983. In the sun, the stained glass blazes with colour, while the shaded tapestries seem a part of the surrounding woodland.

Figure of a Lohan
This sculpture of Buddha's disciple dates from the Ming Dynasty (1484).

Hutton Castle Drawing Room
This is a reconstruction of the Drawing Room at Burrell's own home – the 16th-century Hutton Castle, near Berwick-upon-Tweed. The Hall and Dining Room can also be seen nearby.

Bull's Head
Dating from the 7th century BC, this bronze head from Turkey was once part of a cauldron handle.

Hornby Portal
This detail shows the arch's heraldic display. The 14th-century portal comes from Hornby Castle in Yorkshire.

Main entrance

STAR EXHIBITS

★ Stained Glass

★ Tapestries

Rembrandt van Rijn
This self-portrait, signed and dated 1632, has pride of place among the paintings hanging in the 16th- and 17th-century room.

Mezzanine floor

VISITORS' CHECKLIST

2060 Pollokshaws Rd, Glasgow.
Tel (0141) 287 2550. Pollok-shaws West. 45, 47, 48, 57 from Glasgow. 10am–5pm Mon–Thu, Sat; 11am–5pm Fri, Sun.
www.glasgowmuseums.com

GALLERY GUIDE
Except for a mezzanine-floor display of paintings, the exhibitions are on the ground floor. Right of the entrance hall, rooms are devoted to tapestries, stained glass and sculpture, while ancient civilizations, Oriental art and the period galleries are ahead.

Matthijs Maris
This popular Dutch painter's ethereal style appealed to late 19th-century tastes. The Sisters (1875) is one of over 50 Maris works acquired by Burrell.

KEY TO FLOORPLAN

☐	Ancient civilizations
☐	Oriental art
☐	Medieval and post-medieval European art, stained glass and tapestries
☐	Period galleries
☐	Hutton Castle Rooms
☐	Paintings and drawings
☐	Temporary exhibition area

Ground floor

Lecture theatre

★ Stained Glass
This 15th-century Norwich School panel, depicting a youth snaring birds, is one of many secular themes illustrated in the stained-glass display.

★ Tapestries
Scenes from the Life of the Virgin (c.1450), a Swiss work in wool and linen, is one of many tapestries on show.

Culzean Castle ㉚

Robert Adam by George Willison

Standing on a cliff's edge in an extensive parkland estate, the 16th-century keep of Culzean (pronounced Cullayn), home of the Earls of Cassillis, was remodelled between 1777 and 1792 by the Neo-Classical architect Robert Adam *(see p28)*. Restored in the 1970s, it is now a major showcase of his later work. The grounds became Scotland's first public country park in 1969 and, with farming flourishing alongside ornamental gardens, they reflect both the leisure and everyday activities of a great country estate.

View of Culzean Castle (c.1815), by Nasmyth

Lord Cassillis' Rooms contain typical mid-18th-century furnishings, including a gentleman's wardrobe of the 1740s.

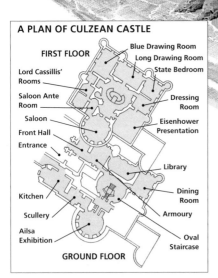

A PLAN OF CULZEAN CASTLE

FIRST FLOOR

- Blue Drawing Room
- Long Drawing Room
- State Bedroom
- Lord Cassillis' Rooms
- Saloon Ante Room
- Saloon
- Front Hall
- Entrance
- Dressing Room
- Eisenhower Presentation

- Kitchen
- Scullery
- Ailsa Exhibition
- Library
- Dining Room
- Armoury
- Oval Staircase

GROUND FLOOR

The clock tower, fronted by the circular carriageway, was originally the coach house and stables. The clock was added in the 19th century, and today the buildings are used for residential and educational purposes and a shop.

STAR SIGHTS

★ Saloon

★ Oval Staircase

Armoury
Displayed on the walls is the world's most important collection of flintlock pistols, used by the British Army and Militia between the 1730s and 1830s.

Fountain Court
This sunken garden is a good place to begin a tour of the grounds to the east.

The Eisenhower Presentation
honours the general who was given the top floor of Culzean in gratitude for his role in World War II.

Carriageway

★ **Saloon**
With its restored 18th-century colour scheme and Louis XVI chairs, this elegant saloon perches on the cliff's edge 46 m (150 ft) above the Firth of Clyde. The carpet is a copy of the one designed by Adam.

★ **Oval Staircase**
Illuminated by an overarching skylight, the staircase, with its Ionic and Corinthian pillars, is considered one of Adam's finest achievements.

THE HIGHLANDS AND ISLANDS

ABERDEENSHIRE · MORAY · ARGYLL & BUTE · PERTH & KINROSS
SHETLAND · ORKNEY · WESTERN ISLES · HIGHLANDS · ANGUS

Most of the stock images of Scottishness – clans and tartans, whisky and porridge, bagpipes and heather – originate in the Highlands and enrich the popular picture of Scotland as a whole. But for many centuries the Gaelic-speaking, cattle-raising Highlanders had little in common with their southern neighbours.

Clues to the non-Celtic ancestors of the Highlanders lie scattered across the Highlands and Islands in the form of stone circles, brochs and cairns some over 5,000 years old. By the end of the 6th century, the Gaelic-speaking Celts had arrived from Ireland, along with St Columba who taught Christianity. Its fusion with Viking culture in the 8th and 9th centuries produced St Magnus Cathedral in the Orkney Isles.

For over 1,000 years, Celtic Highland society was founded on a clan system, built on family ties to create loyal groups dependent on a feudal chief.

However, the clans were systematically broken up by England after 1746, following the defeat of the Jacobite attempt on the British crown, led by Bonnie Prince Charlie *(see p521)*. A more romantic vision of the Highlands started in the early 19th century. Its creation was largely due to Sir Walter Scott, whose novels and poetry depicted the majesty and grandeur of a country previously considered merely poverty-stricken and barbaric. Another great popularizer was Queen Victoria, whose passion for Balmoral helped to establish the trend for acquiring Highland sporting estates. But behind the sentimentality lay harsh economic realities that drove generations of Highlanders to seek a new life overseas.

Today, over half the inhabitants of the Highlands and Islands still live in communities of less than 1,000. Oil and tourism have supplemented fishing and whisky as the main businesses and population figures are rising.

A wintry dawn over the Cairngorms, the home of Britain's only herd of reindeer

◁ The stunningly sited castle of Eilean Donan, Loch Duich in Glen Shiel

Exploring the Highlands and Islands

To the north and west of Stirling (the historic gateway to the Highlands) lie the magnificent mountains and glens, fretted coastlines and lonely isles that are the epitome of Scottish scenery. Inverness, the Highland capital, makes a good starting point for exploring Loch Ness and the Cairngorms, while Fort William holds the key to Ben Nevis. Inland from Aberdeen lie Royal Deeside and the Spey Valley whisky heartland. The romantic Hebrides can be reached by ferry from Oban or Ullapool.

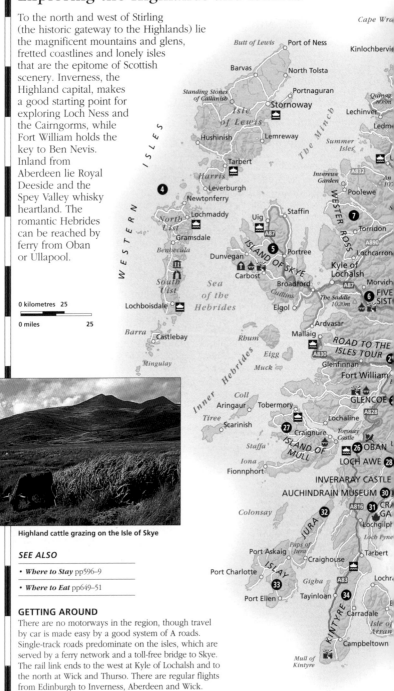

0 kilometres   25

0 miles   25

Highland cattle grazing on the Isle of Skye

SEE ALSO

• **Where to Stay** pp596–9

• **Where to Eat** pp649–51

GETTING AROUND

There are no motorways in the region, though travel by car is made easy by a good system of A roads. Single-track roads predominate on the isles, which are served by a ferry network and a toll-free bridge to Skye. The rail link ends to the west at Kyle of Lochalsh and to the north at Wick and Thurso. There are regular flights from Edinburgh to Inverness, Aberdeen and Wick.

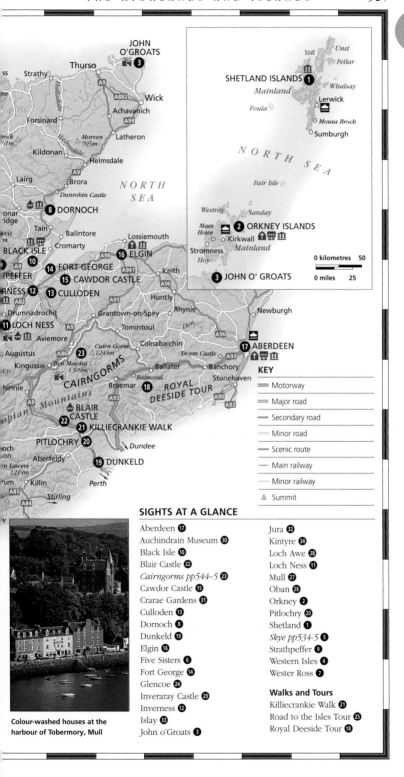

Colour-washed houses at the harbour of Tobermory, Mull

KEY

━━━ Motorway

━━━ Major road

━━━ Secondary road

═══ Minor road

━━━ Scenic route

━━━ Main railway

─── Minor railway

△ Summit

SIGHTS AT A GLANCE

Aberdeen **17**
Auchindrain Museum **30**
Black Isle **10**
Blair Castle **22**
Cairngorms pp544–5 **23**
Cawdor Castle **15**
Culloden **13**
Dornoch **8**
Dunkeld **19**
Elgin **16**
Five Sisters **6**
Fort George **14**
Glencoe **24**
Inveraray Castle **29**
Inverness **12**
Islay **33**
John o'Groats **3**

Jura **32**
Kintyre **34**
Loch Awe **28**
Loch Ness **11**
Mull **27**
Oban **26**
Orkney **2**
Pitlochry **20**
Shetland **1**
Skye pp534–5 **5**
Strathpeffer **9**
Western Isles **4**
Wester Ross **7**

Walks and Tours
Killiecrankie Walk **21**
Road to the Isles Tour **25**
Royal Deeside Tour **18**

Shetland ❶

Shetland. 🚶 22,000. ✈ 🚢 *from Aberdeen and Stromness on mainland Orkney.* ℹ *Lerwick (01595 989898).* **www**.visit.shetland.org

Lying six degrees south of the Arctic Circle, the rugged Shetland islands are Britain's most northerly region and were, with Orkney, part of the kingdom of Norway until 1469. In the main town of Lerwick, this Norse heritage is remembered during the ancient midwinter festival Up Helly Aa *(see p480),* in which costumed revellers set fire to a replica Viking longship. Also in the town, the **Shetland Museum** tells the story of a people dependent on the sea, right up to modern times with the discovery of North Sea oil and gas in the 1970s.

The Iron Age tower, **Mousa Broch**, can be visited on its isle by boat from Sandwick. There is more ancient history at Jarlshof where a museum explains the sprawling sea-front ruins which span 3,000 years.

A boat from Lerwick sails to the isle of Noss where grey seals bask beneath sandstone cliffs crowded with Shetland's seabirds – a spectacle best seen between May and June. Other wildlife includes otters and killer whales.

🏛 **Shetland Museum**
Hay's Dock, Lerwick. **Tel** 01595 695057. ◐ *daily (pm only Sun).* **www**.shetland-museum.org.uk

Orkney ❷

Orkney. 🚶 19,800. ✈ 🚢 *from Gills Bay, Caithness; John o'Groats (May–Sep); Scrabster, Aberdeen.* ℹ *West Castle St, Kirkwall (01856 872856).* **www**.visitorkney.com

The fertile isles of Orkney are remarkable for the wealth of prehistoric monuments which place them among Europe's most treasured archaeological sites. In the town of Kirkwall, the sandstone **St Magnus Cathedral** stands amid a charming core of narrow streets. Its many interesting tombs include that of its 12th-century patron saint.

THE SHETLAND SEABIRD ISLES

As seabirds spend most of their time away from land, nesting is a vulnerable period in their lives. The security provided by the inaccessible cliffs at such sites as Noss and Hermaness on Unst finds favour with thousands of migrant and local birds.

Puffin

Great Skua

Fulmar

Black Guillemot

Razorbills

Herring Gull

Nearby, the early 17th-century **Earl's Palace** is widely held to be one of Scotland's finest Renaissance buildings. To the west of Kirkwall lies Britain's most impressive chambered tomb, the cairn of **Maes Howe**. Dating from 2000 BC, the tomb has runic graffiti on its walls believed to have been left by Norsemen returning from the crusades in 1150.

Nearby, the great **Standing Stones of Stenness** may have been associated with Maes Howe rituals, though these still remain a mystery. Further west, on a bleak heath, stands the Bronze Age **Ring of Brodgar**.

Another archaeological treasure can be found in the Bay of Skail – the complete Stone Age village of **Skara Brae**. It was unearthed by a storm in 1850, after lying buried for 4,500 years. Further south, the

The Norman façade of the St Magnus Cathedral, Orkney

town of Stromness was a vital centre of Scotland's herring industry in the 18th century. Its story is told in the local museum, while the **Pier Arts Centre** displays British and international art.

🏛 **Earl's Palace**
Palace Rd, Kirkwall. **Tel** 01856 871918. ◐ Apr–Oct: 9:30am–5:30pm daily. 🅿 ♿ ltd. **www**.historic-scotland.gov.uk

🏛 **Pier Arts Centre**
Victoria St, Stromness. **Tel** 01856 850209. ◐ 10:30am–5pm Tue–Sat. **www**.pierartscentre.com

John o'Groats ❸

Highland. 🚶 500. ✈ 🚢 🚌 *Wick* 🚢 John o'Groats to Burwick, Orkney (May–Sep). ℹ John o'Groats (01955 611373).

Some 876 miles (1,409 km) north from Land's End, Britain's most northeasterly mainland village faces Orkney, 8 miles (13 km) across the turbulent Pentland Firth. The village takes its name from a 15th-century Dutchman John de Groot, who, to avoid accusations of favouritism, is said to have built an octagonal house here with one door for each of his eight heirs. The spectacular cliffs and rock stacks of Duncansby Head lie a few miles further east.

Western Isles ❹

Western Scotland ends with this remote chain of islands, made of some of the oldest rock on Earth. Almost treeless landscapes are divided by countless waterways, the western, windward coasts edged by miles of white sandy beaches. For centuries, the eastern shores, composed largely of peat bogs, have provided the islanders with fuel. Man has been here for 6,000 years, living off the sea and the thin turf, though such monuments as an abandoned Norwegian whaling station on Harris attest to the difficulties in commercializing the islanders' traditional skills. Gaelic, part of an enduring culture, is widely spoken.

The Black House Museum, a traditional croft on Lewis

The monumental Standing Stones of Callanish in northern Lewis

Lewis and Harris

Western Isles. 🏠 22,000. ✈ Stornoway. ⛴ Uig (Skye), Ullapool, Kyle of Lochalsh. 🛈 Stornoway, Lewis (01851 703088).
www.visitthebrides.com
Black House Museum. *Tel 01851 710395.* ⬜ *9:30am–4:30pm daily (to 5:30pm in summer).* 🚫 ♿ 🚻 🎁

Forming the largest landmass of the Western Isles, Lewis and Harris are a single island, though Gaelic dialects differ between the two areas. From **Stornoway**, with its bustling harbour and colourful house fronts, the ancient **Standing Stones of Callanish** are only 16 miles (26 km) to the west. Just off the road on the way to Callanish are the ruins of **Carloway Broch**, a Pictish *(see p482)* tower over 2,000 years old. The more recent past can be explored at Arnol's **Black House Museum** – a showcase of crofting life as it was until only 50 years ago.

South of the rolling peat moors of Lewis, a range of mountains marks the border with Harris, which one enters as one passes Aline Lodge at the head of Loch Seaforth. Only a little less spectacular than the "Munros" (peaks over 914 m; 3,000 ft) of the

mainland and the Isle of Skye *(see pp534–5)*, the mountains of Harris are a paradise for the hillwalker, and from their summits on a clear day, the distant Isle of St Kilda can be seen 50 miles (80 km) to the west.

The ferry port of Tarbert stands on a slim isthmus separating North and South Harris. Some local weavers of the famous Harris Tweed still follow the old tradition of using plants to make their dyes.

From the port of Leverburgh, close to the southern tip of Harris, a ferry can be taken to the isle of North Uist, where a causeway has been built to Berneray.

The Uists, Benbecula and Barra

Western Isles. 🏠 7,200. ✈ Barra, Benbecula. ⛴ Uig (Skye), Ullapool, Oban. 🚗 🚆 Oban, Mallaig, Kyle of Lochalsh. 🛈 Lochmaddy, North Uist (01876 500321); Lochboisdale, South Uist (01878 700286); Castlebay, Barra (01871 810336).
www.visitthebrides.com

After the dramatic scenery of Harris, the lower-lying, largely waterlogged southern isles may seem an anticlimax, though they nurture secrets well worth discovering. Long, white, sandy beaches fringe the Atlantic coast, edged with one of Scotland's natural treasures: the lime-rich soil known as *machair*. During the summer months, the soil is covered with wild flowers.

From **Lochmaddy**, North Uist's main village, the A867 crosses 3 miles (5 km) of causeway to Benbecula, the isle from which Flora MacDonald smuggled Bonnie Prince Charlie *(see p535)* to Skye. Another causeway leads to South Uist, with its golden beaches renowned as a National Scenic Area. From Lochboisdale, a ferry sails to the tiny isle of Barra. The ferry docks in Castlebay, affording an unforgettable view of **Kisimul Castle**, the ancestral stronghold of the MacNeils of Barra.

The remote and sandy shores of South Uist

The western side of the Five Sisters of Kintail, seen from above Loch Duich

Skye ❺

See pp534–5.

The Five Sisters ❻

Skye & Lochalsh. 🚆 *Kyle of Lochalsh.* 🚌 *Glenshiel.* ℹ️ *Bayfield Road, Portree, Isle of Skye (0845 2255121).* www.visithighlands.com

Dominating one of Scotland's most haunting regions, the awesome summits of the Five Sisters of Kintail rear into view at the northern end of Loch Cluanie as the A87 enters Glen Shiel. The **Visitor Centre** at Morvich offers ranger-led excursions in the summer. Further west, the road passes **Eilean Donan Castle**, connected by a bridge. A Jacobite *(see p537)* stronghold, it was destroyed in 1719 by English warships. In the 19th century it was restored and now contains Jacobite relics.

♟️ Eilean Donan Castle
Off A87, nr Dornie. *Tel 01599 555 202.* ⬜ *Mar–Oct: 10am–6pm (from 9am Jul–Aug) daily.* 📷
www.eileandonancastle.com

Wester Ross ❼

Ross & Cromarty. 🚆 *Achnasheen, Strathcarron.* ℹ️ *Gairloch (01445 712130).* www.visithighlands.com

Leaving Loch Carron to the south, the A890 enters the northern Highlands and the great wilderness of Wester Ross.

The Torridon Estate includes some of the oldest mountains on Earth (Torridonian rock is over 600 million years old), and is home to red deer, wild cats and wild goats. Peregrine falcons and golden eagles nest in the towering sandstone mass of Liathach, above the village of Torridon with its breathtaking views over Applecross to Skye. The **Torridon Countryside Centre** provides guided walks in season and information on the region's natural history. The estate is open all year.

To the north, the A832 cuts through the Beinn Eighe National Nature Reserve in which remnants of the ancient Caledonian pine forest still stand on the banks and isles of Loch Maree.

Along the coast, exotic gardens thrive in the warming currents of the Gulf Stream, most impressive being **Inverewe Garden** created in 1862 by Osgood Mackenzie (1842–1922). May and June are the months to see the display of

Typical Torridonian mountian scenery in the Wester Ross

rhododendrons and azaleas; July and August for the herbaceous borders.

🏛️ Torridon Countryside Centre
(NTS) Torridon. *Tel 0844 493 2229.* ⬜ *Apr–Sep: 10am–5pm daily.* **Estate** ⬜ *daily all year.* 📷 ♿
www.nts.org.uk

🌺 Inverewe Garden
(NTS) off A832, nr Poolewe. *Tel 0844 493 2225.* ⬜ *daily.* 📷 ♿

Dornoch ❽

Sutherland. 🏘️ *2,200.* 🚆 *Golspie, Tain.* ℹ️ *The Square, Dornoch (08452 255121).* www.visithighlands.com

With its first-class golf course and extensive sandy beaches, **Dornoch** is a popular holiday resort, though it has retained a peaceful atmosphere. Now the parish church, the medieval cathedral was all but destroyed in a clan dispute in 1570; it was finally restored in the 1920s for its 700th anniversary. A stone at the beach end of River Street marks the place where Janet Horne, the last woman to be tried in Scotland for witchcraft, was executed in 1722.

Environs: Twelve miles (19 km) northeast of Dornoch is the stately Victorianized pile of **Dunrobin Castle**, magnificently situated in a great park with formal gardens overlooking the sea. Since the 13th century, this has been the seat of the Earls of Sutherland. Many of its rooms are open to visitors. A steam-powered fire engine is among the miscellany of objects on display.

South of Dornoch stands the town of **Tain**. Though patronized by medieval kings as a place of pilgrimage, it became an administrative centre of the Highland Clearances. All is explained in the heritage centre, **Tain Through Time**.

♠ **Dunrobin Castle**
Nr Golspie. *Tel 01408 633177.*
☐ *Apr, May, Sep & Oct: 10:30am–4:30pm daily (from noon Sun); Jun–Aug: 10:30am–5:30pm daily. Falconry displays: 11:30am & 2pm.* 🏷

🏛 **Tain Through Time**
Tower St. *Tel 01862 894089.* ☐
Apr–Oct: 10am–5pm Mon–Sat. 🏷
♿ 🏷 **www.tainmuseum.org.uk**

The serene cathedral precinct in the town of Dornoch

Strathpeffer ❾

Ross & Cromarty. 🏔 *1,400.* 🚉
Dingwall, Inverness. 🚌 *Inverness.*
ℹ *Visit Scotland (01463 252401).*
www.undiscoveredscotland.co.uk

Standing 5 miles (8 km) from the Falls of Rogie and to the east of the Northwest Highlands, the popular town of Strathpeffer still has the refined charm for which it was well known in Victorian times, when it flourished as a spa and health resort. The grand hotels, individually designed buildings and gracious layout of Strathpeffer recall the days when royalty from all over Europe used to flock to the chalybeate- and sulphur-laden springs, which were believed to help in the cure of tuberculosis, and in the treatment of rheumatism.

The shores of the Black Isle in the Moray Firth

The Black Isle ❿

Ross & Cromarty. 🚉 🚌 *Inverness.*
ℹ *Visit Scotland (01463 252401).*

Though the drilling platforms in the Cromarty Firth are reminders of how oil has changed the local economy, the peninsula of the Black Isle is still largely composed of farmland and fishing villages. The town of **Cromarty** was an important port in the 18th century, with thriving rope and lace industries. Many of its merchant houses still stand; the museum in the **Cromarty Courthouse** provides heritage tours of the town. The **Hugh Miller Museum** is a museum to the theologian and geologist Hugh Miller (1802–56), who was born here. **Fortrose** has a ruined 14th-century cathedral, while a stone on Chanonry Point commemorates the Brahan Seer, a 17th-century prophet burnt alive in a tar barrel by the Countess of Seaforth after he foresaw her husband's infidelity. Chanonry Point is also renowned as a great spot for bottlenose dolphin-watching. For local archaeology, visit **Groam House Museum** in Rosemarkie.

🏛 **Cromarty Courthouse**
Church St, Cromarty. *Tel 01381 600 418.* ☐ *Apr–Sep: 11am–4pm Sun–Thu.* 🏷

🏛 **Hugh Miller Museum**
(NTS) Church St, Cromarty. *Tel 0844 493 2158.* ☐ *Apr–Sep: daily; Oct: Tue, Thu & Fri (pm).* 🏷 ♿ *limited.*

🏛 **Groam House Museum**
High St, Rosemarkie. *Tel 01381 620961.* ☐ *Apr–Oct: 11am–4:30pm Mon–Fri, 2–4pm Sat; Nov: 2–4pm Sat.*

THE HIGHLAND CLEARANCES

During the heyday of the clan system *(see p484)*, tenants paid their clan chiefs rent for their land in the form of military service. However, with the decline of the clan system after the Battle of Culloden *(see p537)* and the coming of sheep from the borders, landowners were able to command a financial rent their tenants were unable to afford and the land was bought up by Lowland and English farmers. In what became known as "the year of the sheep" (1792), thousands of tenants were evicted to make way for sheep. Many emigrated to Australia, America and Canada. Ruins of their crofts can still be seen in Sutherland and Wester Ross.

The Last of the Clan **(1865) by Thomas Faed**

Isle of Skye ❺

Otter by the coast at Kylerhea

The largest of the Inner Hebrides, Skye can be reached by the bridge linking Kyle of Lochalsh and Kyleakin. A turbulent geological history has given the island some of Britain's most varied and dramatic scenery. From the rugged volcanic plateau of northern Skye to the ice-sculpted peaks of the Cuillins, the island is divided by numerous sea lochs, leaving the traveller never more than 8 km (5 miles) from the sea. North of the Dunvegan are small caves and white beaches, while Limestone grasslands predominate in the south, where the hillsides, home of sheep and cattle, are scattered with the ruins of crofts abandoned during the Clearances (*see p531*). Historically, Skye is best known for its association with Bonnie Prince Charlie.

Skeabost has the ruins of a chapel which is associated with St Columba. Medieval tombstones can be found in the graveyard.

Grave of Flora MacDonald

Kilm

WESTERN ISLES

Ui

LOCH SNIZORT

● Lusta

B886

Milovaig

A850

Dunvegan

Ske

B884

B

A863

● Portnalong

B8009

● Talisker   Carbost

0 kilometres   10

0 miles   5

C

Se

ALA

9

(3,

Dunvegan Castle

For over seven centuries, Dunvegan Castle has been the seat of the chiefs of the Clan MacLeod. It contains the Fairy Flag, a fabled piece of magic silk treasured for its protection in battle.

The Talisker Distillery produces one of the best Highland malts, often described as "the lava of the Cuillins".

Cuillins

Britain's finest mountain range is within walking distance of Sligachan, and in summer a boat sails from Elgol to the desolate inner sanctuary of Loch Coruisk. As he fled across the surrounding moorland, Bonnie Prince Charlie is said to have claimed: "Even the Devil shall not follow me here!"

KEY

🛈	Tourist information
▬	Major road
▭	Minor road
═	Narrow lane
❃	Viewpoint

◁ Dawn over the desolate tablelands of northern Skye, viewed from the Quiraing

Quiraing
A series of landslides has exposed the roots of this volcanic plateau, revealing a fantastic terrain of spikes and towers. They are easily explored off the Uig to Staffin road.

Staffin

Kilt Rock

SOUND OF RAASAY

RAASAY

ree

B883

Sconser

achan

S C A L P A Y

Luib

A87

B8083

Elgol

L O C H   E I S H O R T

A851

Armadale

MALLAIG

VISITORS' CHECKLIST

The Highlands. 🏠 26,000. ✈ Kyle of Lochalsh. 🚌 Portree. ⛴ from Mallaig or Glenelg (summer only). 🛈 Bayfield House, Portree (01478 614 906). www.visithighlands. com **Dunvegan Castle** Dunvegan. **Tel** 01470 521206. ◯ daily. 🎟 ♿ limited. www.dunvegancastle. com **Armadale Castle**, Armadale. **Tel** 01471 844305. ◯ Apr–Oct: daily (gardens open all year). 🎟 ♿ **Talisker Distillery**, Carbost. **Tel** 01478 614308. ◯ daily: call for details. 🎟 ♿ limited. 🎟

The Storr
The erosion of this basalt plateau has created the Old Man of Storr, a monolith rising to 49 m (160 ft) by the Portree road.

Loch Coruisk

Luib has a beautiful thatched cottage, preserved as it was 100 years ago.

Portree
With its colourful harbour, Portree (meaning "port of the king") is Skye's metropolis. It received its name after a visit by James V in 1540.

Bridge to mainland

Kyleakin

KYLE OF LOCHALSH

Broadford

A87

Otters can be seen from the haven in Kylerhea.

Kilchrist

Kylerhea

Armadale Castle Gardens and Museum of the Isles houses the Clan Donald visitor centre.

Kilchrist Church
This ruined pre-Reformation church's last service was held in 1843. It once served Skye's most populated areas, though the surrounding moors are now deserted.

BONNIE PRINCE CHARLIE

The last of the Stuart claimants to the Crown, Charles Edward Stuart (1720–88), came to Scotland from France in 1745 to win the throne. After marching as far as Derby, his army was driven back to Culloden where it was defeated. Hounded for five months through the Highlands, he escaped to Skye, disguised as the maidservant of a woman called Flora MacDonald, from Uist. From the mainland, he sailed to France in September 1746, and died in Rome. Flora was buried in 1790 at Kilmuir, on Skye, wrapped in a sheet taken from the bed of the "bonnie" (handsome) prince.

The prince, disguised as a maidservant

The ruins of Urquhart Castle on the western shore of Loch Ness

Loch Ness ⓫

Inverness. ⇄ 🚉 *Inverness.* ⓘ *Castle Wynd, Inverness (01463 234353).* **www**.visitlochness.com

At 24 miles (39 km) long, one mile (1.5 km) at its widest and up to 305 m (1,000 ft) deep, **Loch Ness** fills the northern half of the Great Glen fault from Fort William to Inverness. It is joined to lochs Oich and Lochy by the 22-mile (35-km) Caledonian Canal,

THE LOCH NESS MONSTER

First sighted by St Columba in the 6th century, "Nessie" has attracted increasing attention since ambiguous photographs were taken in the 1930s. Though serious investigation is often undermined by hoaxers, sonar techniques continue to yield enigmatic results: plesiosaurs, giant eels and too much whisky are the most popular explanations. Nessie appears to have a close relative in the waters of Loch Morar (*see p546*).

designed by Thomas Telford (*see p447*). On the western shore, the A82 passes the ruins of the 16th-century **Urquhart Castle**, which was blown up by government supporters in 1692 to prevent it falling into Jacobite hands. A short distance west, **Loch Ness Centre and Exhibition** offers a wealth of audio-visual information.

⚓ Urquhart Castle
Nr Drumnadrochit. **Tel** 01456 450551. ◯ 9:30am–6pm daily (Oct–Feb: to 4:30pm). (Last adm: 45 mins before closing.) 🎦 ⓫ 🛈

🏛 Loch Ness Centre and Exhibition
Drumnadrochit. **Tel** 01456 450573. ◯ Nov–Easter: 10am–3:30pm daily; Easter–Oct: 9:30am–5pm daily. 🎦 ♿ 🛈 **www**.lochness.com

Inverness ⓬

Highland. 🏚 60,000. ⇄ 🚉 ⓘ *Castle Wynd (01463 234353).* **www**.visithighlands.com

As the Highland capital, Inverness makes an ideal base from which to explore the surrounding countryside. The Victorian castle dominates the town centre, the oldest buildings of which are found in nearby Church Street. Today

the castle is used as law courts. The **Inverness Museum and Art Gallery** provides a good introduction to the history of the Highlands with exhibits including a lock of Bonnie Prince Charlie's (*see p535*) hair and a fine collection of Inverness silver. The **Scottish Kiltmaker Visitor Centre** explores the history and tradition of Scottish kilts as well as workshops, while those in search of tartans and knitwear should visit the **James Pringle Weavers of Inverness**.

Jacobite Cruises run a variety of year-round cruises along the Caledonian Canal and on to Loch Ness. The unfolding scenery makes this a most pleasant and tranquil way to spend a sunny afternoon.

Kilt maker with royal Stuart tartan

🏛 Museum and Art Gallery
Castle Wynd. **Tel** 01463 237114. ◯ Apr–Oct: Mon–Sat; Nov–Mar: Thu–Sat. ♿ **www**.inverness. highland.museum

🛍 James Pringle Weavers of Inverness
Holm Woollen Mill, Dores Rd. **Tel** 01463 223311. ◯ daily. ♿

🏛 Scottish Kiltmaker Visitor Centre
Huntly St. **Tel** 01463 222781. ◯ call to check. ● 1 Jan, 25 Dec. 🎦

Jacobite Cruises
Glenurquhart Road. **Tel** 01463 233 999. ◯ daily. 🎦 ♿ **www**. jacobite.co.uk

Culloden ⑬

(NTS) Inverness. 🚆 🚌 *Inverness.*
www.nts.org.uk/culloden

A desolate stretch of moorland, Culloden looks much as it did on 16 April 1746, the date of the last battle to be fought on British soil *(see p483)*. Here the Jacobite cause, with Bonnie Prince Charlie's *(see p535)* leadership, finally perished under the onslaught of Hanoverian troops led by the Duke of Cumberland. All is explained in the **NTS Visitor Centre**.

Environs: Signposted for a mile (1.5 km) or so east are the outstanding Neolithic burial sites, the **Clava Cairns**.

> ℹ️ **NTS Visitor Centre**
> On the B9006 east of Inverness.
> *Tel* 0844 4932159. ⬤ Apr–Oct:
> 9am–6pm daily; Nov–Dec & Feb–
> Mar: 10am–4pm daily. ⬤ 24
> Dec–23 Jan. 🖼️ ♿

Fort George ⑭

Inverness. *Tel* 01667 460232.
🚆 🚌 *Inverness, Nairn.* ⬤ Apr–Sep:
9:30am–5:30pm daily (to 4:30pm
Oct–Mar). ⬤ 25 & 26 Dec. 🖼️ ♿
📷 www.historic-scotland.gov.uk

One of the finest works of European military architecture, Fort George stands on a windswept promontory jutting into the Moray Firth, ideally located to suppress the Highlanders. Completed in 1769, the fort was built after the Jacobite risings to discourage further rebellion in the Highlands and has remained a military garrison

THE JACOBITE MOVEMENT

James II, by Samuel Cooper (1609–72)

The first Jacobites (mainly Catholic Highlanders) were the supporters of James II of England (James VII of Scotland) who was deposed by the "Glorious Revolution" of 1688 *(see p53)*. With the Protestant William of Orange on the throne, the Jacobites' desire to restore the Stuart monarchy led to the uprisings of 1715 and 1745. The first, in support of James VIII, the "Old Pretender", ended at the Battle of Sheriffmuir (1715). The failure of the second uprising, with the defeat at Culloden, saw the end of Jacobite hopes and led to the end of the clan system and the suppression of Highland culture for over a century *(see p485)*.

The drawbridge on the eastern side of Cawdor Castle

ever since. The Fort houses the **Regimental Museum** of the Highlanders Regiment, and some of its barrack rooms reconstruct the conditions of the common soldiers stationed here more than 200 years ago. The **Grand Magazine** contains an outstanding collection of arms and military equipment. The battlements also make an excellent place from which to watch dolphins in the Moray Firth.

Cawdor Castle ⑮

On B9090 (off A96). *Tel* 01667
404401. 🚆 Nairn, then bus.
🚌 from Inverness. ⬤ May–Sep:
10am–5:30pm daily. 🖼️ ♿ gardens
& ground floor only. 🚻
www.cawdorcastle.com

With its turreted central tower, moat and drawbridge, Cawdor Castle is one of the most romantic stately homes in the Highlands. Though the castle is famed for being the 11th-century home of Shakespeare's *(see p322)* Macbeth and the scene of his murder of King Duncan, it is not historically proven that either came here.

An ancient holly tree preserved in the vaults is said to be the one under which, in 1372, Thane William's donkey, laden with gold, stopped for a rest during its master's search for a place to build a fortress. According to legend, this was how the site for the castle was chosen. Now, after 600 years of continuous occupation (it is still the home of the Thanes of Cawdor) the house is a treasury of family history, containing a number of rare tapestries and portraits by the 18th-century painters Joshua Reynolds (1723–92) and George Romney (1734–1802). Furniture in the Pink Bedroom and Woodcock Room includes work by Chippendale and Sheraton. In the Old Kitchen, the huge Victorian cooking range stands as a shrine to below-stairs drudgery. The grounds provide nature trails and a nine-hole golf course.

A contemporary picture, *The Battle of Culloden* (1746), by D Campbell

Elgin ⑯

Moray. 🏰 21,000. ✈ 🚉
ℹ 17 High St, Moray (01343 542666).

With its cobbled marketplace and crooked lanes, the popular holiday centre of Elgin still retains much of its medieval layout. The 13th-century **cathedral** ruins next to King Street are all that remain of one of Scotland's architectural triumphs, the design of its tiered windows reminiscent of the cathedral at St Andrews *(see p499)*. Once known as the Lantern of the North, the cathedral was severely damaged in 1390 by the Wolf of Badenoch (the son of Robert II) in revenge for his excommunication by the Bishop of Moray. Worse damage came in 1576 when the Regent Moray ordered the stripping of its lead roofing. Among its remains is a Pictish cross-slab in the nave, and a basin in a corner where one of Elgin's benefactors,

Details of the central tower of Elgin Cathedral

Andrew Anderson, was kept as a baby by his homeless mother. Next to the cathedral are the **Biblical Gardens** with all 110 plants mentioned in the Bible, while the **Elgin Museum** has anthropological displays and the **Moray Motor Museum** has over 40 vehicles.

🏛 Elgin Museum
1 High St. **Tel** 01343 543675.
⬤ Apr–Oct: 10am–5pm Mon–Fri; 11am–4pm Sat. 🎟 ⬤ limited. 📷

🏛 Moray Motor Museum
Bridge St, Bishopmill. **Tel** 01343 544933. ⬤ Easter–Oct: 11am–5pm daily. 🎟 ⬤

Aberdeen ⑰

Scotland's third largest city and Europe's offshore oil capital, Aberdeen has prospered since the discovery of petroleum in the North Sea in 1970. The sea bed has now yielded over 100 oilfields. Widely known as the Granite City, its rugged outlines are softened by sumptuous year-round floral displays in its public parks and gardens, the Duthie Park Winter Gardens being one of the largest indoor gardens in Europe. The picturesque village of Footdee, which sits at the end of the city's 2-mile (3-km) beach, has good views back to the busy harbour.

The spires of Aberdeen, rising behind the city harbour

Exploring Aberdeen
The city centre flanks the mile-long (1.5 km) Union Street ending to the east at the Mercat Cross. The cross stands in Castlegate, the one-time site of the city castle. From here the cobbled Shiprow winds southwest and passes Provost Ross's House *(see p540)* on its way to the harbour with its fish market. A bus can be taken a mile (1.5 km) north of the centre to Old Aberdeen which, with its medieval streets and wynds, has the peaceful character of a separate village. Driving is restricted in some streets.

🚋 King's College
College Bounds, Old Aberdeen. **Tel** 01224 272137. **Chapel** ⬤ 9:30am–3:30pm Mon–Fri. ⬤
King's College was founded in 1495 as the city's first university. The inter-denominational chapel (the only part of the college open to the public), in the past consecutively Catholic and Protestant, has a lantern tower rebuilt after a storm in 1633. Stained-glass windows by Douglas Strachan add a contemporary touch to the interior which contains a 1540 pulpit, later carved with heads of Stuart monarchs.

🔒 St Andrew's Cathedral
King St. **Tel** 01224 640119.
⬤ May–Sep: 11am–4pm Tue–Fri.
⬤ 📷 by appointment.
The Mother Church of the Episcopal Communion in America, St Andrew's has a memorial to Samuel Seabury, the first Episcopalian bishop in the United States, who was consecrated in Aberdeen in 1784. Coats of arms adorn the ceiling above the north and south aisles, contrasting colourfully with the white walls and pillars. They represent the American States and local Jacobite *(see p537)* families.

The elegant lantern tower of the chapel at King's College

PROVOST SKENE'S HOUSE

Guestrow. **Tel** *01224 641086.* ⬜ *10am–5pm Mon–Sat (limited access to upper floors).* ⬤ *25 & 26, 31 Dec–2 Jan.* **www**.aagm.co.uk

Once the home of Sir George Skene, a 17th-century provost (mayor) of Aberdeen, the house was built in 1545. Inside, period rooms span 200 years of design. The Duke of Cumberland stayed here before the Battle of Culloden *(see p537)*.

VISITORS' CHECKLIST

City of Aberdeen. 🏠 *203,500.*
✈ ⇄ 🚌 *Guild St.*
ℹ *23 Union St (01224 288828).*
www.aberdeen-grampian.com

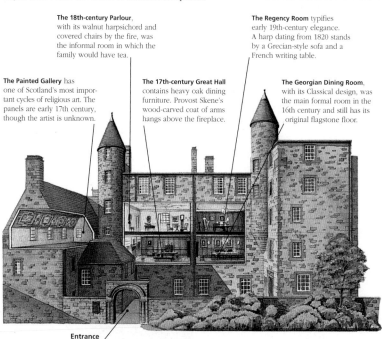

The 18th-century Parlour, with its walnut harpsichord and covered chairs by the fire, was the informal room in which the family would have tea.

The Regency Room typifies early 19th-century elegance. A harp dating from 1820 stands by a Grecian-style sofa and a French writing table.

The Painted Gallery has one of Scotland's most important cycles of religious art. The panels are early 17th century, though the artist is unknown.

The 17th-century Great Hall contains heavy oak dining furniture. Provost Skene's wood-carved coat of arms hangs above the fireplace.

The Georgian Dining Room, with its Classical design, was the main formal room in the 16th century and still has its original flagstone floor.

Entrance

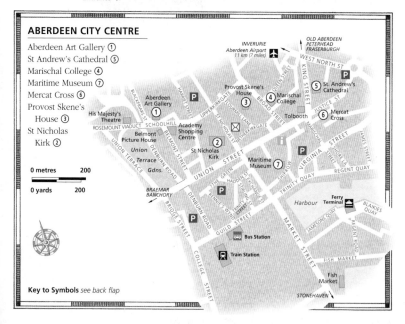

ABERDEEN CITY CENTRE

Aberdeen Art Gallery ①
St Andrew's Cathedral ⑤
Marischal College ④
Maritime Museum ⑦
Mercat Cross ⑥
Provost Skene's House ③
St Nicholas Kirk ②

0 metres   200
0 yards   200

Key to Symbols *see back flap*

🏛 Art Gallery

Schoolhill. **Tel** 01224 523700. ◯ 10am–5pm Tue–Sat, 2–5pm Sun. ● 25 Dec–2 Jan. ♿ www.aagm.co.uk
Housed in a Neo-Classical building, purpose-built in 1884, the Art Gallery has a wide range of exhibitions, with an emphasis on contemporary work. A fine collection of Aberdonian silver can be found among the decorative arts on the ground floor, and is the subject of a video presentation.
A permanent collection of 18th–20th-century fine art features such names as Toulouse-Lautrec, Reynolds and Zoffany. Several of the works were bequeathed in 1900 by a local granite merchant, Alex Macdonald. He commissioned many of the paintings in the Macdonald Room, which displays 92 self-portraits by British artists. Occasional poetry-readings, music recitals and films are on offer.

Aberdonian silver in the Art Gallery

⛪ St Nicholas Kirk

Union St. **Tel** 01224 643494. ◯ 10am–1pm Mon–Fri. ♿ www.kirk-of-st-nicholas.org.uk
Founded in the 12th century, St Nicholas is Scotland's largest parish church. Though the present structure dates from 1752, many relics of earlier times can be seen inside.
After being damaged during the Reformation, the interior was divided into two. A chapel in the East Church contains iron rings used to secure witches in the 17th century, while in the West Church there are some embroidered panels attributed to one Mary Jameson (1597–1644).

🏛 Maritime Museum

Shiprow. **Tel** 01224 337700. ◯ 10am–5pm Tue–Sat, noon–3pm Sun. ♿ ▯ ▯ www.aagm.co.uk
Overlooking the harbour is Provost Ross's House, which dates back to 1593 and is one of the oldest residential buildings in the town. This museum traces the history of Aberdeen's seafaring tradition. Exhibitions include ship-wrecks, rescues, shipbuilding and the oil installations off Scotland's east coast.

⛪ St Machar's Cathedral

The Chanonry. **Tel** 01224 485988. ◯ 9am–5pm daily (10am–4pm winter). ♿
Dominating Old Aberdeen, the 15th-century edifice of St Machar's is the oldest granite building in the city. The stonework of one arch even dates as far back as the 14th century. The impressive nave now serves as a parish church and its magnificent oak ceiling is adorned with the coats of arms of 48 popes, emperors and princes of Christendom.

Royal Deeside Tour ⑱

Since Queen Victoria's purchase of the Balmoral estate in 1852, Deeside has been best known as the summer home of the British Royal Family, though it has been associated with royalty since the time of Robert the Bruce *(see p482)*. The route follows the Dee, formerly a prolific salmon river, through some magnificent Grampian scenery.

Muir of Dinnet Nature Reserve ④
An information centre on the A97 provides an excellent place from which to explore this beautiful mixed woodland area, formed by the retreating glaciers of the last Ice Age.

BRAEMAR, PERTH

Ballater ⑤
The old railway town of Ballater has royal warrants on many of its shop fronts. It grew as a 19th-century spa town, its waters reputedly providing a cure for tuberculosis.

Balmoral ⑥
Bought by Queen Victoria for 30,000 guineas in 1852, after its owner choked to death on a fishbone, the castle was rebuilt in the Scottish Baronial style at Prince Albert's request.

Dunkeld ⑲

Perth & Kinross. 🏠 2,500. 🚆 Birnam.
🚌 🛈 The Cross (01350 727688).
www.perthshire.co.uk

Situated by the River Tay, this ancient and charming village was all but destroyed in the Battle of Dunkeld, a Jacobite (see p537) defeat, in 1689. The **Little Houses** lining Cathedral Street were the first to be rebuilt, and are fine examples of imaginative restoration. The ruins of the 14th-century **cathedral** enjoy an idyllic setting on shady lawns beside the Tay, against a backdrop of steep and wooded hills. The choir is used as the parish church and its north wall contains a Leper's Squint: a hole through which lepers could see the altar during mass. It was while on holiday in the Dunkeld country-side that Beatrix Potter (see p367) found the location for her Peter Rabbit stories.

The ruins of Dunkeld Cathedral

Pitlochry ⑳

Perth & Kinross. 🏠 2,900. 🚆 🚌
🛈 22 Atholl Rd (01796 472215).
www.perthshire.co.uk

Surrounded by pine-forested hills, Pitlochry became famous after Queen Victoria (see p56) described it as one of the finest resorts in Europe. In early summer, salmon swim up the ladder built into the Power Station Dam, on their way to spawning grounds upriver. There is a viewing chamber here to see them. The **Power Station Visitor Centre** outlines the hydro-electric scheme that harnesses the waters of the River Tummel. The tasting tours at **Edradour Distillery** give an insight into traditional whisky-making (see p489). Scotland's famous **Festival Theatre** puts on a summer season when the programme changes daily.

🛈 **Power Station Visitor Centre**
Pitlochry. **Tel** 01796 473152. ⬜
Apr–Oct: 10am–5:30pm Mon–Fri (Jul & Aug: daily). 🎟️ 📷

🎭 **Festival Theatre**
Port-na-Craig. **Tel** 01796 484626.
⬜ daily. 🎟️ ♿ 🅿️

🏭 **Edradour Distillery**
Pitlochry, off A924. **Tel** 01796 472095. ⬜ phone for opening hours and times of tours. 🎟️ ♿ ltd.
📷 🛈 www.edradour.co.uk

TIPS FOR DRIVERS

Length: 69 miles (111 km).
Stopping-off points: Crathes Castle café (May–Sep: daily); Station Restaurant, Ballater (food served all day). (See also pp684–5.)

Drum Castle ①
This impressive 13th-century keep was granted by Robert the Bruce to his standard bearer in 1323, in gratitude for his services.

Banchory ③
Local lavender is a popular attraction here. From the 18th-century Brig o' Feugh, salmon can be seen.

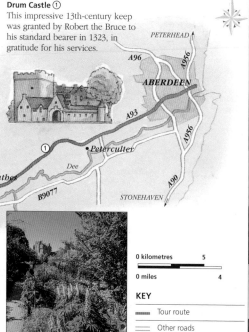

PETERHEAD

A96

ABERDEEN

A93

① • Peterculter

Dee

A980

A93

② • Crathes

③

B9077

STONEHAVEN

A90

A956

A956

B974

Crathes Castle and Gardens ②
This is the family home of the Burnetts, who were made Royal Foresters of Drum by Robert the Bruce. Along with the title, he gave Alexander Burnett the ivory Horn of Leys which is still on display.

0 kilometres		5
0 miles		4

KEY

▬▬▬ Tour route

═══ Other roads

🌼 Viewpoint

Killiecrankie Walk ㉑

In an area famous for its scenery and historical connections, this circular walk offers typical Highland views. The route is fairly flat, though ringed by mountains, and follows the River Garry south to Loch Faskally, meandering through a wooded gorge, passing the Soldier's Leap and a Victorian viaduct. There are several ideal picnic spots along the way. Returning along the River Tummel, the walk crosses one of Queen Victoria's favourite Highland areas, before doubling back along the rivers to complete the circuit.

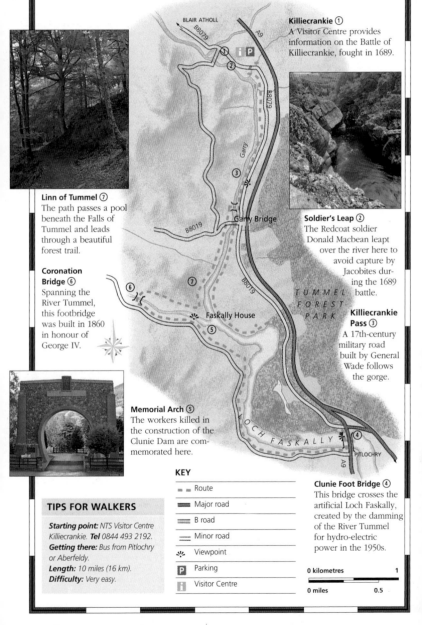

Killiecrankie ①
A Visitor Centre provides information on the Battle of Killiecrankie, fought in 1689.

Linn of Tummel ⑦
The path passes a pool beneath the Falls of Tummel and leads through a beautiful forest trail.

Coronation Bridge ⑥
Spanning the River Tummel, this footbridge was built in 1860 in honour of George IV.

Soldier's Leap ②
The Redcoat soldier Donald Macbean leapt over the river here to avoid capture by Jacobites during the 1689 battle.

Killiecrankie Pass ③
A 17th-century military road built by General Wade follows the gorge.

Memorial Arch ⑤
The workers killed in the construction of the Clunie Dam are commemorated here.

Clunie Foot Bridge ④
This bridge crosses the artificial Loch Faskally, created by the damming of the River Tummel for hydro-electric power in the 1950s.

KEY

▬ ▬	Route
▬▬	Major road
▭▭	B road
═══	Minor road
☆	Viewpoint
P	Parking
i	Visitor Centre

0 kilometres   1

0 miles   0.5

TIPS FOR WALKERS

Starting point: NTS Visitor Centre Killiecrankie. **Tel** 0844 493 2192.
Getting there: Bus from Pitlochry or Aberfeldy.
Length: 10 miles (16 km).
Difficulty: Very easy.

The Three Sisters, Glencoe, in late autumn

Blair Castle ㉒

Blair Atholl, Perthshire. **Tel** 01796 481207. 🚆 Blair Atholl. ◯ Apr–Oct: 9:30am–5:30pm daily; Nov–Mar: 10am–4pm Sat & Sun. ● 1 & 2 Jan, 25–27 Dec. 🏷 ⬧ limited. **www.** blair-castle.co.uk

This rambling, turreted castle has been altered so often in its 700-year history that it provides a unique insight into the history of Highland aristo-cratic life. The 18th-century wing has a display containing the gloves and pipe of Bonnie Prince Charlie (see p535), who spent two days here gathering Jacobite (see p537) support. Family portraits cover 300 years and include paint-ings by such masters as Johann Zoffany and Sir Peter Lely. Sir Edwin Landseer's *Death of a Stag in Glen Tilt* (1850) was painted nearby.

In 1844 Queen Victoria visited the castle and conferred on its owners, the Dukes of Atholl, the distinction of being allowed to maintain a private army. The Atholl Highlanders still flourish.

THE MASSACRE OF GLENCOE

In 1692, the chief of the Glencoe MacDonalds was five days late in registering an oath of submission to William III, giving the government an excuse to root out a nest of Jacobite (p537) supporters. For ten days 130 soldiers, cap-tained by Robert Campbell, were hospitably entertained by the unsuspecting MacDonalds. At dawn on 13 February, in a terrible breach of trust, the soldiers fell on their hosts, killing some 38 MacDonalds. Many more died in their wintry mountain hideouts. The mas-sacre, unsurprisingly, became a political scandal, though there were to be no official reprimands for three years.

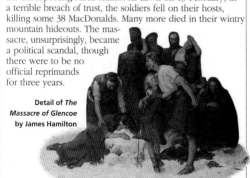

Detail of *The Massacre of Glencoe* by James Hamilton

The Cairngorms ㉓

See pp544–5.

Glencoe ㉔

Highland. 🚆 Fort William. 🚌 Glencoe. ℹ Visit Scotland (0844 493 2222). **www.**glencoescotland.com

Renowned for its awesome scenery and savage history, Glencoe was compared by Dickens to "a burial ground of a race of giants". The precip-itous cliffs of Buachaille Etive Mor and the knife-edged ridge of Aonach Eagach (both over 900 m; 3,000 ft) present a formidable challenge even to experienced mountaineers.

Against a dark backdrop of craggy peaks and the tum-bling River Coe, the Glen offers superb hill-walking in the summer. Stout footwear, waterproofs and attention to safety warnings are essential. Details of routes, ranging from the easy half-hour between the **NTS Visitor Centre** and Signal Rock (from which the signal was given to commence the massacre) to a stiff 6 mile (10 km) haul up the Devil's Staircase can be had from the Visitor Centre. Guided walks are offered in summer by the NTS Ranger service.

🏠 NTS Visitor Centre
Glencoe. **Tel** 01855 811307. ◯ daily. 🏷 ⬧ ltd. **www.**nts.org.uk

The Cairngorms ㉒

Wild Goat

Rising to a height of 1,309 m (4,296 ft), the Cairngorm mountains form the highest landmass in Britain. Cairn Gorm itself is the site of one of Britain's first ski centres. A weather station at the mountain's summit provides regular reports, essential in an area known for sudden changes of weather. Walkers should be sure to follow the mountain code without fail. The funicular railway that climbs Cairn Gorm affords superb views over the Spey Valley. Many estates in the valley have centres which introduce the visitor to Highland land use.

Strathspey Steam Railway
This track between Aviemore and Broomhill dates from 1863.

Aviemore, the commercial centre of the Cairngorms, provides buses to the ski area 13 km (9 miles) away.

INVERNESS   NAI
A 938   Carrbridge
B9153
Boat of Garte
Aviemore
Coylum
Bearaidh
A9   B9152   Spey
LOCH AN EILEIN
Kincraig
LOCH INSH
Feshie
BRAERIACH
1,295 m (4,248 ft)
LOCH EINICH
Kingussie
NEWTONMORE
B970
Tolvah
PERTH

0 kilometres   5
0 miles   5

Kincraig Highland Wildlife Park
Driving through this park, the visitor can see bison alongside wolves and wild boar. All of these animals were once common in the Highlands.

The Cairngorms by Aviemore

Rothiemurchus Estate
Highland cattle can be seen among many other creatures at Rothiemurchus. A visitor centre provides guided walks and illustrates life on a Highland estate.

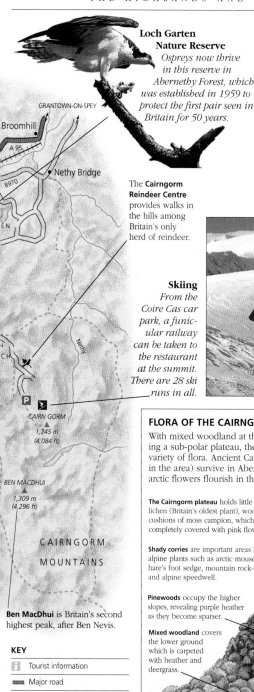

Loch Garten Nature Reserve

Ospreys now thrive in this reserve in Abernethy Forest, which was established in 1959 to protect the first pair seen in Britain for 50 years.

GRANTOWN-ON-SPEY

Broomhill

A 95

Nethy Bridge

B970

The **Cairngorm Reindeer Centre** provides walks in the hills among Britain's only herd of reindeer.

Skiing

From the Coire Cas car park, a funicular railway can be taken to the restaurant at the summit. There are 28 ski runs in all.

CAIRN GORM
1,245 m
(4,084 ft)

BEN MACDHUI
1,309 m
(4,296 ft)

CAIRNGORM MOUNTAINS

Ben MacDhui is Britain's second highest peak, after Ben Nevis.

KEY

Tourist information	
Major road	
Minor road	
Narrow lane	
Footpath	
Viewpoint	

VISITORS' CHECKLIST

The Highlands. ✈ 🚌 Aviemore. 🛈 King St, Kingussie (01540 661000). **Cairngorm Reindeer Centre**, Loch Morlich. **Tel** 01479 861228. ⭘ daily. 🏞 🎟 **Kincraig Highland Wildlife Park. Tel** 01540 651270. ⭘ daily (weather permitting). **www**.highland wildlifepark.org **Rothiemurchus Visitor Centre**, near Aviemore. **Tel** 01479 812345. ⭘ daily. **Loch Garten Nature Reserve. Tel** 01479 831476. ⭘ daily. **Skiing Tel** 01479 861261.

FLORA OF THE CAIRNGORMS

With mixed woodland at their base and the summits forming a sub-polar plateau, the Cairngorms present a huge variety of flora. Ancient Caledonian pines (once common in the area) survive in Abernethy Forest, while arctic flowers flourish in the heights.

The Cairngorm plateau holds little life except lichen (Britain's oldest plant), wood rush and cushions of moss campion, which is often completely covered with pink flowers.

Shady corries are important areas for alpine plants such as arctic mouse-ear, hare's foot sedge, mountain rock-cress and alpine speedwell.

Pinewoods occupy the higher slopes, revealing purple heather as they become sparser.

Mixed woodland covers the lower ground which is carpeted with heather and deergrass.

1,200 m (4000 ft)

1,000 m (3,300 ft)

800 m (2,600 ft)

600 m (2,000 ft)

400 m (1,300 ft)

200 m (650 ft)

0 m (0 ft)

An idealized section of the Cairngorm plateau

Road to the Isles Tour 25

This scenic route goes past vast mountain-corridors, breathtaking beaches of white sand and tiny villages, to the town of Mallaig, one of the ferry ports for the isles of Skye, Rum and Eigg. As well as the stunning scenery, the area is steeped in Jacobite history *(see p537).*

(see p537).

TIPS FOR DRIVERS

Tour length: 45 miles (72 km).
Stopping-off points: Glenfinnan NTS Visitors' Centre (01397 722 250) explains the Jacobite risings and serves refreshments; the Old Library Lodge, Arisaig, has good Scottish food. (See also pp684–5.)

Mallaig ⑦
The Road to the Isles ends at Mallaig, an active little fishing port with a very good harbour and one of the ferry links to Skye *(see pp534–5).*

Morar ⑥
The road continues through Morar, an area renowned for its white sands, and Loch Morar, rumoured to be the home of a 12-m (40-ft) monster known as Morag.

Prince's Cairn ⑤
Crossing the Ardnish Peninsula to Loch Nan Uamh, a cairn marks the spot from which Bonnie Prince Charlie finally left Scotland for France in 1746.

Oban 26

Argyll & Bute. 🏠 8,500. ✈ 🚌 ⛴
🛈 Argyll Sq (01631 563122).
www.oban.org.uk

Located on the Firth of Lorne and commanding a magnificent view of the Argyll coast, the bustling port of Oban is a popular destination for travellers on their way to Mull and the Western Isles *(see p529).*

Dominating the skyline is McCaig's Tower, an unfinished Victorian imitation of the Colosseum in Rome. It is worth making the 10-minute climb from the town centre for the sea views alone. Attractions in the town include working centres for glass, pottery and whisky; the Oban distillery produces one of the country's finest malt whiskies *(see p489).* The **Scottish Sealife Sanctuary** rescues injured and orphaned seals and has displays of underwater life. Car ferries depart for Barra and South Uist, Mull, Tiree and Colonsay islands.

Dunstaffnage Castle, 3 miles (5 km) north of Oban, offers fine views over the Firth of Lorn. This 13th-century stronghold of the MacDougalls has atmospheric ruins, a chapel and the "new house" where Flora MacDonald *(see p535)* is believed to have been imprisoned in 1746.

🏛 Scottish Sealife Sanctuary
Barcaldine. **Tel** 01631 720386.
◯ daily. ● 25 Dec. 🦽 ♿ 🍴 🛍
www.sealsanctuary.co.uk

♜ Dunstaffnage Castle
Dunbeg, off A85. **Tel** 01631 562 465. ◯ daily. 🦽 🛍

Mull 27

Argyll & Bute. 🏠 2,800. ⛴ from Oban, Kilchoan, Lochaline. 🛈 Main Street, Tobermory (01688 302182).

Most roads on this easily accessible Hebridean island follow the sharply indented rocky coastline, affording wonderful sea views. On a promontory to the east lies **Duart Castle**, home of the chief of Clan Maclean. Visitors can see the Banqueting Hall and State Rooms in the 13th-century keep. Its dungeons once held prisoners from a

Looking out to sea across Tobermory Bay, Mull

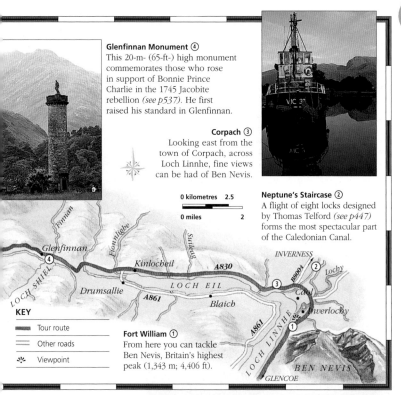

Glenfinnan Monument ④
This 20-m- (65-ft-) high monument
commemorates those who rose
in support of Bonnie Prince
Charlie in the 1745 Jacobite
rebellion *(see p537)*. He first
raised his standard in Glenfinnan.

Corpach ③
Looking east from the
town of Corpach, across
Loch Linnhe, fine views
can be had of Ben Nevis.

Neptune's Staircase ②
A flight of eight locks designed
by Thomas Telford *(see p447)*
forms the most spectacular part
of the Caledonian Canal.

0 kilometres 2.5

0 miles 2

KEY

🟫🟫 Tour route

══ Other roads

🔆 Viewpoint

Fort William ①
From here you can tackle
Ben Nevis, Britain's highest
peak (1,343 m; 4,406 ft).

Spanish Armada galleon sunk
by a Donald Maclean in 1588.
The attractive riverside village
of Dervaig houses a fascinating
heritage centre.

Environs: From Fionnphort,
a ferry goes to **Iona**, where St
Columba *(see p525)* began his
mission in Scotland in 563.
North of Iona, the Isle of
Staffa should be visited for
its magnificent **Fingal's Cave**.

⚓ **Duart Castle**
Off A849, nr Craignure.
Tel 01680 812309. ◯ *Apr–Oct:
10:30am–5:30pm daily.* 🖼

Loch Awe ㉘

Argyll & Bute. 🚆 🚌 *Dalmally.*
ℹ *Inveraray (01499 302063).*
www.loch-awe.com

One of the longest of
Scotland's freshwater lochs,
Loch Awe fills a 25-mile (40-
km) glen in the southwestern
Highlands. A short drive east
of the village of Lochawe

The ruins of Kilchurn Castle on the shore of Loch Awe

leads to the lochside remains
of **Kilchurn Castle**, abandoned
after being struck by lightning
in the 18th century. Dwarfing
the castle is the huge bulk of
Ben Cruachan, whose summit
can be reached by the narrow
Pass of Brander, in which
Robert the Bruce *(see p482)*
fought the Clan MacDougal in
1308. From the A85, a tunnel
leads to the cavernous
Cruachan Power Station.

Near the village of Taynuilt
the preserved Lorn Furnace at
Bonawe is a reminder of the
iron-smelting industry that
caused the destruction of
much of the area's woodland
in the 18th and 19th centuries.
Marked prehistoric cairns are
found off the A816 between
Kilmartin and Dunadd. The
latter boasts a 6th-century hill
fort from which the Stone of
Destiny *(see p482)* originated.

Inveraray Castle

Inveraray, Argyll & Bute.
Arrochar, then bus. **Tel** *01499 302203.* Apr–Oct: 10am–5:45pm daily. limited.
www.inveraray-castle.com

This multi-turreted mock Gothic palace is the family home of the powerful Clan Campbell who have been the Dukes of Argyll since 1701. The castle was built in 1745 by architects Roger Morris and William Adam on the ruins of a 15th-century castle, and the conical towers added later, after a fire in 1877. Magnificent interiors, designed by Robert Mylne in the 1770s, form a backdrop to a huge collection of Oriental and European porcelain and Regency furniture and portraits by Ramsay, Gainsborough and Raeburn. The Armoury Hall features a display of weaponry collected by the Campbells to fight the Jacobites *(see p537).*

The pinnacled, Gothic exterior of Inveraray Castle

Auchindrain Museum ⓪

Inveraray, Argyll & Bute. **Tel** *01499 500235.* Inveraray, then bus.
May–Oct: 10am–5pm daily (last adm: 4pm); Nov–Apr: daily, weather permitting. limited.
www.auchindrain-museum.org.uk

The first open-air museum in Scotland, Auchindrain illuminates the working lives of the kind of farming community that was typical of the Highlands until the late 19th century. Originally a township of some 20 thatched buildings, the site was communally farmed by its tenants until the last one retired in 1962. Visitors can wander through the buildings,

many of which combine living space, kitchen and cattle shed under one roof. Some are furnished with box beds and old rush lamps. The homes of Auchindrain are a fascinating memorial to the time before the transition from of subsistence to commercial farming.

An old hay turner at the Auchindrain Museum

Crarae Gardens ⓪

Crarae, Argyll & Bute. **Tel** *01546 886614 or NTS (0844 4932210).* Inveraray, then bus. 9:30am–sunset daily. **Visitor Centre** Apr–Oct: 10am–5pm Thu–Mon. limited.

Considered the most beguiling of the gardens of the West Highlands, the **Crarae Gardens** were created in the 1920s by Lady Grace Campbell. She was the aunt of explorer Reginald Farrer, whose specimens from Tibet were the beginnings of a collection of exotic plants. The gardens are nourished by the warmth of the Gulf

Stream and the high rainfall. Although there are many unusual Himalayan rhododendrons flourishing here, the gardens are also home to exotic plants from various countries including Tasmania, New Zealand and the USA. Plant collectors still contribute to the gardens, which are best seen in spring and early summer against the blue waters of Loch Fyne.

Jura ⓪

Argyll & Bute. 200. from Kennacraig to Islay, then Islay to Jura. Bowmore (01496 810254).

Barren, mountainous and overrun by red deer, the isle of Jura has only one road which connects the single village of Craighouse to the Islay ferry. Though walking is restricted during the stalking (deer hunting) season between August and October, the island offers superb hill-walking, especially on the slopes of the three main peaks, known as the Paps of Jura. The tallest of these is Beinn An Oir at 784 m (2571 ft). Beyond the northern tip of the isle are the notorious whirlpools of Corryvreckan. The novelist George Orwell (who came to the island to write his final novel, *1984*) nearly lost his life here in 1946 when he fell into the water. A legend tells

Lagavulin distillery, producer of one Scotland's finest malts, on Islay

Mist crowning the Paps of Jura, seen at sunset across the Sound of Islay

of Prince Breackan who, to win the hand of a princess, tried to keep his boat anchored in the whirlpool for three days, held by ropes made of hemp, wool and maidens' hair. The Prince drowned when a single rope, containing the hair of a girl who had been untrue, finally broke.

Islay ③③

Argyll & Bute. 🚶 3,500. 🚢 from Kennacraig. 🛈 The Square, Bowmore (01496 810254). www.visitscotland.com

The most southerly of the Western Isles, Islay (pronounced 'Eyeluh') is the home of respected Highland single malt whiskies Lagavulin and Laphroaig. Most of the island's distilleries produce heavily peated malts with a distinctive tang of the sea. The Georgian village of Bowmore has the island's oldest distillery and a circular church designed to minimize the Devil's possible lurking-places. The **Museum of Islay Life** in Port Charlotte contains fascinating information on social and natural history. Seven miles (11 km) east of Port Ellen stands the Kildalton Cross. A block of local green stone adorned with Old Testament scenes, it is one of the most impressive 8th-

century Celtic crosses in Britain. Worth a visit for its archaeological and historical interest is the medieval stronghold of the Lords of the Isles, **Finlaggan**. Islay's beaches support a variety of bird life, some of which can be observed at the RSPB reserve at Gruinart.

🏛 **Museum of Islay Life**
Port Charlotte. **Tel** 01496 850358. ◻ Apr–Oct: Mon–Sat (times vary – call to check). 🚫 ♿

Kintyre ③④

Argyll & Bute. 🚶 6,000. ✈ Oban. 🚌 Campbeltown. 🛈 MacKinnon House, The Pier, Campbeltown (01586 552056). www.kintyre.org

A long, narrow peninsula stretching far south of Glasgow, Kintyre has superb views across to the islands of Gigha, Islay and Jura. The 9 mile (14 km) Crinan Canal,

opened in 1801, is a delightful inland waterway, its 15 locks bustling with pleasure craft in the summer. The town of Tarbert (meaning "isthmus" in Gaelic) takes its name from the neck on which it stands, which is narrow enough to drag a boat across between Loch Fyne and West Loch Tarbert. This feat was first achieved by the Viking King Magnus Barfud who, in 1198, was granted by treaty as much land as he could sail around. Travelling south past Campbeltown, the B842 ends at the headland known as the Mull of Kintyre, which was made famous when former Beatle Paul McCartney commercialized a traditional pipe tune of the same name. Westward lies the isle of Rathlin, where Robert the Bruce *(see p482)* learned patience in his struggles against the English by watching a spider weaving a web in a cave.

Fishing boats and yachts moored at Tarbert harbour, Kintyre

TRAVELLERS' NEEDS

WHERE TO STAY 552–599

WHERE TO EAT 600–657

SHOPPING IN BRITAIN 658–659

ENTERTAINMENT IN BRITAIN 660–661

SPECIALIST HOLIDAYS AND
OUTDOOR ACTIVITIES 662–665

WHERE TO STAY

Whatever your budget or accommodation preferences, you should be able to find somewhere to suit you from the large choice given in the hotel listings section that follows *(see pp556–99)*. The listings include over 500 suggestions, ranging from palatial five-star establishments to humble guesthouses. The common factor in this selection is that they are all good of their kind, offering distinctive character or exceptional qualities of hospitality, facilities or value for money. Location is another prime consideration for inclusion. All the hotels and guesthouses listed make convenient touring bases for one or more of the destinations featured in this book, or have attractive or interesting settings enjoyable in their own right. On the next few pages we outline some of the types of accommodation available in Britain, along with various aspects of choosing, booking and paying for somewhere to stay.

Hotel doorman, London

COUNTRY-HOUSE HOTELS

The quintessentially British country-house hotel has proliferated in the last few decades. Many indifferent hotels try to claim the title with a cursory decorative makeover, but the genuine article stands head and shoulders above them. Individual examples vary widely, but the best are usually set in buildings of architectural or historic interest filled with antiques or high-quality traditional furnishings. They generally have extensive grounds but are not always in deeply rural locations. Comfort, even luxury, is assured, along with good food and service – frequently with a very high price tag. Many also have extensive spa or health facilities. Some of these hotels are still owned and personally managed by resident proprietors; others belong to groups or chains.

BOUTIQUE AND DESIGNER HOTELS

There is a new breed of sophisticated, contemporary hotel that has been making waves in Britain for some years now. These ultra-cool temples of style revel in innovative architecture, funky decor and hip high-tech gadgetry. Many exude an air of uncluttered minimalism, and some have outstanding restaurants. The best-known examples are perhaps in London (the Metropolitan, *p557*, for instance, or the Sanderson, *p559*), but they can be found elsewhere too, usually in city centres. Trend-setting, upmarket micro-chains like **Malmaison** or **Hotel du Vin** could perhaps be included in this category. Most of these hotels are expensive, but facilities, furnishings, service and privacy justify the cost.

Atholl Palace Hotel *(see p599)*

HOTEL GROUPS

New hotel groups have taken the place of many of the long-established names, providing reliably standardized accommodation at all price levels in most parts of Britain. The majority of chain hotels (operated by the same company under identical corporate branding) lie in accessible, convenient locations. Though lacking in any individuality, they are practical and efficiently run, and usually represent good value for money. They also frequently offer bargain deals and reduced rates depending on the time of year.

Budget chains offering no-frills, motel-lodge-style accommodation include **Ibis**, **Travelodge** and **Premier Inn**; further up the scale are mid-market chains like **Holiday Inn** or **Novotel**.

Buckland Manor *(see p578)*, Gloucestershire

◁ The 11th-century ruins of Corfe Castle, Dorset

The Swan at Lavenham, Suffolk *(see p567)*, a converted coaching inn

Chain-hotel rates generally don't include breakfast, but look out for inclusive leisure-break rates at pricier chains like **Moat House**.

Also found throughout the country are well-known, independently owned franchise hotels, including **Best Western** and **Pride of Britain**. There's also **Wolsey Lodges**, a group of private houses, many beautifully furnished and often sited in buildings of notable architectural or historic interest.

INNS AND PUBS WITH ROOMS

The coaching inn is a familiar concept in Britain. Many of these fine old hostelries date from the 18th century, though some are even older, such as The George of Stamford *(see p582)*, and often provide reliable restaurants, traditional decor and a warm and friendly atmosphere.

Other types of pub or inn now offer accommodation and reputable food, and many have become much more welcoming to families. Britain's best inns are very comfortable and stylish and bear comparison with any good hotel. Gastropubs, informal eateries often with exceptional food, sometimes offer stylish accommodation at reasonable prices.

BED-AND-BREAKFASTS AND GUEST HOUSES

The B&B is probably the best-known and certainly the most widely used type of budget accommodation in Britain. These establishments are generally family-owned private homes or farmhouses. Accommodation and facilities can be simple (bedrooms may not have TV, telephones, or en-suite bathrooms, for instance), but the best can be quite sophisticated. Prices include breakfast (generally a traditional British fry-up, but other options are usually available).

A few B&Bs are reluctant to accept credit cards or travellers' cheques, or may charge a premium for doing so. It's advisable to have some alternative method of payment, preferably cash. Any regional tourist office should be able to supply a list of local registered B&Bs on request, though they cannot make specific recommendations, and may charge a fee or a commission for making bookings on your behalf. Travel websites such as www.enjoy england.com are also a good resource, as is the **London Bed and Breakfast Agency**, who offer rooms in private homes.

HOTEL GRADINGS

Recent but only partially successful attempts have been made to harmonize the confusing and often conflicting systems of accommodation classification used by the various tourist boards and motoring organizations, such as the AA and RAC. In England, hotel gradings are now based on a system of one to five stars awarded for facilities and service (the more stars, the more luxurious you can expect your hotel to be). Guesthouses and B&Bs are also graded with one to five stars, a quality score which is based on various aspects of the accommodation, including cleanliness and hospitality. Special awards (gold and silver, ribbons, rosettes, etc) are given for excellence in certain categories, such as an exceptional breakfast or a warm welcome. Scotland and Wales have their own quality-based gradings.

Number Sixteen, a boutique hotel in London *(see p558)*

PRICES AND BOOKINGS

Make sure you understand clearly what terms you are being offered when you book. Some hotels just quote room rates, but many quote a B&B or half board (dinner, bed and breakfast) rate per person. Rates are generally inclusive of VAT and service but some top-range hotels make additional charges; most charge hefty single-person supplements.

Prices in London start at around £80 per night for a standard en suite double room, including breakfast, but could be well over £200 (without breakfast) at the top end of the scale. Outside London, prices tend to be cheaper, starting from around £70 for an en suite double with

The folly of Doyden Castle, Cornwall, now a National Trust holiday cottage

The elegant hallway of the Gore Hotel in London (see p562)

breakfast. Bed-and-breakfast accommodation outside London starts from around £35 per person per night (though prices vary seasonally and regionally). Farm guesthouses (which occasionally include dinner) can be very good value, at around £45 for half board per person.

Most hotels request confirmation by email and a deposit in advance (a credit card number will generally do). Email bookings are now commonplace, and most hotels have an on-line booking facility on their website. Business or chain hotels often give big discounts; contact central reservations as well as the hotel itself to see which one will give you the best deal. Websites such as

Expedia and Travelocity are often the easiest and most economical means of booking, especially when looking for a room and a flight together.

Any hotel booking is a legally binding contract. If you don't show up, the full cost of your stay may be charged. Most hotels will refund your deposit if they are able to relet the room, but some will charge a penalty, depending how close to your stay you cancel. Most travel insurance policies cover cancellation charges for prebooked UK hotel stays of more than two days, if you have a satisfactory reason.

Watch out for hidden extras. Telephone charges from hotel rooms have a high mark-up, and rates quoted per unit do not always indicate clearly how much time you get for your money. Consider using a lobby payphone instead, if you do not have a mobile phone.

Certain chains have a regrettable policy of charging meals or other extras to your credit card weeks after you have left the hotel; check your card statement carefully.

There is no need to tip staff unless they go out of their way to perform some very exceptional duty, such as booking theatre tickets or restaurants for you.

Roadside signboard for bed-and-breakfast

SELF CATERING

Self catering has many attractions, especially for families on a budget and with young children. Tourist boards give accommodation a one to five star rating for quality and facilities, much the same as for hotels. The range of places to let for holiday rentals is huge, from luxury apartments to log cabins or converted farm buildings. Character properties are available from conservation organizations such as the **Landmark Trust**, which restores buildings of historic or architectural interest and makes them available for short-term lets, or the **National Trust** (see p29), which has a number of holiday cottages on its estates. They tend to be very popular, so book well ahead.

Annually updated self-catering guides are a useful source of listings. Also try specialist agencies, tour operators and the small ads in newspapers. Tourist offices can supply up-to-date regional lists and can also offer a booking service.

Confirm what is included in the price (cleaning, electricity, etc.) and check whether any extra fees, deposits or insurance charges will be added to the bill.

CARAVANNING, CAMPING AND MOTOR HOMES

Most of Britain's campsites and caravan (trailer) parks open only for about six months of the year (typically from Easter to October), but you will need to make reservations in advance. Helpful organizations in Britain include the **Camping and Caravanning Club** and the Caravan Club, which publish lists of their member parks and operate their own grading systems.

Camping or caravanning pitches typically cost between £15 and £20 per night. The **Forestry Commission** operates a number of sites in scenic woodland locations throughout the UK.

Motor homes give greater freedom to explore at your own pace, a wider choice of places to stay – including most campsites and caravan parks. Some operators will let you pick up your vehicle directly from an airport or ferry terminal. The **Motor Caravanners' Club** produces a useful monthly magazine.

Campsite, Ogwen Valley, Snowdonia

DISABLED TRAVELLERS

All the UK's tourist boards provide detailed information about disabled access in their accommodation and sightseeing guides. National Accessible Scheme gradings are awarded to properties approved under the Tourism for All initiative for various categories of disability.

For more information on these gradings, or other advice on accommodation and travel for disabled visitors, contact **Tourism for All**. Another useful organization is **RADAR** (the Royal Association for Disability and Rehabilitation), which publishes a yearly *Holidays in the British Isles: A Guide for Disabled People*. Also good is the Enjoy England website (www.enjoyengland. com), which has dedicated pages on accessible travel. The listings on pp556–99 indicate which hotels have wheelchair access, but you are strongly advised to check when booking that it matches your needs. The same is true of camping and caravan sites.

DIRECTORY

For more tips on different types of accommodation, see **www**.visitbritain.com

HOTELS

Accor Hotels
(Ibis, Novotel)
Tel 0871 702 9469.
www.accorhotels.com

Best Western
Tel 08457 767676.
www.bestwestern.co.uk

Book Direct Rooms
www.bookdirectrooms. com

Hilton International
Tel 0870 590 9090.
www.hilton.co.uk

Intercontinental Hotels Group
Tel 0871 423 4942.
www.ichotelsgroup.com

Hotel du Vin
Tel 0845 365 4438.
www.hotelduvin.com

Malmaison
Tel 08453 654247.
www.malmaison.com

Premier Inn
Tel 0871 527 8000 (UK);
+44 1582 567890
(international).
www.premierinn.com

Pride of Britain
Tel 0800 089 3929.
www.prideofbritain hotels.com

QMH Hotels
Tel 01708 730522.
www.qmh-hotels.com

Travelodge
www.travelodge.co.uk

Wolsey Lodges
Tel 01473 822058. **www**. wolseylodges.com

BED-AND-BREAKFASTS

London Bed and Breakfast Agency
Tel 020 7586 2768.

CARAVANNING, CAMPING AND MOTOR HOMES

Camping and Caravanning Club
Tel 0845 130 7633.
www.campingand caravanningclub.co.uk

Forestry Commission
Tel 0845 130 8223.
www.forestholidays.co.uk

Motor Caravanners' Club
Tel 01684 311677.
www.motorcaravanners.eu

SELF-CATERING

Landmark Trust
Tel 01628 825925.
www.landmarktrust. org.uk

National Trust
Tel 0844 800 2070.
www.nationaltrust cottages.co.uk

National Trust for Scotland
Wemyss Hse, 28 Charlotte Square, Edinburgh EH2 4ET. *Tel* 0844 493 2100.
www.nts.org.uk

Snowdonia Tourist Services
High Street, Porthmadog, Gwynedd LL49 9PG. *Tel* 01766 513829. **www**. snowdoniatourist.com

DISABLED TRAVELLERS

RADAR
Unit 12, City Forum, 250 City Road, London, EC1V 8AF. *Tel* 020 7250 3222.
www.radar.org.uk

Tourism for All
c/o Vitalise, Shap Road Industrial Estate, Kendal, Cumbria LA9 6NZ. *Tel* 0303 303 0146. **www**. tourismforall.org.uk

Choosing a Hotel

The hotels in this guide have been selected across a wide price range for their excellent, facilities, good value and location. Many also have a recommended restaurant. The chart lists the hotels by region, starting with London. For more details on restaurants see pages 608–651.

PRICE CATEGORIES
For a standard double room per night, inclusive of service charge and any additional taxes such as VAT:

£ under £80
££ £80–£120
£££ £120–£180
££££ £180–£220
£££££ over £220

LONDON

WEST END AND WESTMINSTER Vandon House   £
1 Vandon St, SW1 **Tel** *020 7799 6780* **Rooms** *32*   **Map** *11 A5*

The short walk to Westminster and Buckingham Palace is one reason for the popularity of this bright budget hotel. The rooms – singles, twins with or without en suite facilities, and family rooms – are simple but good value. A Continental buffet breakfast is included and there is free Wi-Fi in every room. **www.vandonhouse.com**

WEST END AND WESTMINSTER B&B Belgravia   ££
64–66 Ebury St, SW1 **Tel** *020 7259 8570* **Rooms** *17*   **Map** *18 E2*

Renovated to provide a contemporary interior, this Victorian building caters for the discerning traveller's every need. Facilities include flat screen TVs in all rooms and free Wi-Fi access, and with cooked breakfasts made to order you will really feel at home. **www.bb-belgravia.com**

WEST END AND WESTMINSTER Dover Hotel   ££
42–44 Belgrave Rd, SW1 **Tel** *020 7821 9085* **Rooms** *34*   **Map** *18 F2*

This well-maintained hotel is terrific value for money. It may not be luxurious once past the grand stucco façade, but the decor is refreshingly modern and every room has satellite TV and pristine en suite shower and WC. It's handy for Victoria Station and Pimlico's many pubs and cafés. Free Wi-Fi. **www.dover-hotel.co.uk**

WEST END AND WESTMINSTER Morgan Guest House   ££
120 Ebury St, SW1 **Tel** *020 7730 2384* **Rooms** *11*   **Map** *18 E2*

This comfortable guest house in a listed Georgian building offers excellent value for money, especially if you opt for a room without facilities, or one of the spacious family rooms that sleep four. The decor is light and airy and many rooms contain original features. There is a pretty garden. Wi-Fi available. **www.morganhouse.co.uk**

WEST END AND WESTMINSTER Citadines Covent Garden/Holborn   £££
94–99 High Holborn, WC1 **Tel** *020 7395 8800* **Rooms** *192*   **Map** *11 C1*

This central branch of the apart'hotel chain underwent a refurbishment in 2010. It offers pleasant, good-value accommodation for up to four people. Studios or one-bedroom apartments have kitchenettes, dining tables, satellite TVs and iPod docking. There are also handy business facilities and an on-site breakfast room. **www.citadines.com**

WEST END AND WESTMINSTER Double Tree by Hilton - Westminster   £££
30 John Islip St, SW1 **Tel** *020 7630 1000* **Rooms** *460*   **Map** *19 B2*

Around the corner from Tate Britain, City Inn is unpretentiously modern. Rooms have floor-to-ceiling windows, some of which command Thames views, and luxuries such as robes, flatscreen TVs and DVD players. There's a red cocktail lounge and café with outside tables. Enquire about cheap weekend deals. **www.hilton.com**

WEST END AND WESTMINSTER Hazlitt's   ££££
6 Frith St, W1 **Tel** *020 7434 1771* **Rooms** *30*   **Map** *11 A1*

One of central London's most characterful hotels, Hazlitt's occupies a group of beautiful Georgian buildings in the heart of Soho. Behind the grand doorway are sumptuous rooms full of period decor and antiques, as well as modern electronics cleverly concealed, and Wi-Fi. The lounges are hugely atmospheric, and service is exceptional. **www.hazlittshotel.com**

WEST END AND WESTMINSTER The Trafalgar   ££££
2 Spring Gardens, SW1 **Tel** *020 7870 2900* **Rooms** *129*   **Map** *11 B3*

A "boutique-style" departure for the Hilton group, with one of London's best locations – right on Trafalgar Square. The luxurious and spacious rooms are minimalist in style, with fine electronics (free Wi-Fi throughout) and other fittings. There is a roof garden with fabulous views and the chic Rockwell bar-restaurant offers a global menu. **www.hilton.com**

WEST END AND WESTMINSTER Brown's Hotel   £££££
Albemarle Street, W1 **Tel** *020 7493 6020* **Rooms** *117*   **Map** *10 F3*

A byword for elegant Mayfair luxury since 1837, Brown's occupies several Georgian townhouses. The interior has been beautifully renovated to combine modern facilities and styling with a timeless sense of opulent comfort. The restaurant is excellent; afternoon tea is more intimate than at some grand hotels. Wi-Fi. **www.brownshotel.com**

Key to Symbols *see back cover flap*

WEST END AND WESTMINSTER Claridges   ££££££

Brook St, W1 **Tel** *020 7629 8860* **Rooms** *203*   **Map** *10 E2*

Favoured by the European aristocracy in the 19th century, Empress Eugènie wintered here. Nowadays it attracts show business *glitterati* and business clients alike. Rooms range from Victorian to contemporary by way of fabulous Art Deco suites. Gordon Ramsay's fêted restaurant and a smart bar are further draws. Wi-Fi. **www.claridges.co.uk**

WEST END AND WESTMINSTER Covent Garden Hotel   £££££

10 Monmouth St, WC2 **Tel** *020 7806 1000* **Rooms** *58*   **Map** *11 B2*

This exquisite hotel's Covent Garden location is one reason why it's popular with thespians. Part of the Firmdale chain, it is decorated in contemporary-English style with antiques and fresh fabrics. Brasserie Max is a popular meeting spot and films are shown in the luxurious screening room at weekends. Wi-Fi. **www.firmdalehotels.com**

WEST END AND WESTMINSTER Metropolitan   £££££

19 Old Park Lane, W1 **Tel** *020 7447 1000* **Rooms** *150*   **Map** *10 D3*

The Metropolitan redefined the London luxury hotel when it opened in 1997 and its blond wood, pale fabrics and large plate-glass windows still epitomise modern chic. With holistic spa treatments, a top Japanese–Peruvian restaurant upstairs and entry to the exclusive Met Bar, you won't have to stray far. Wi-Fi. **www.metropolitan.co.uk**

WEST END AND WESTMINSTER One Aldwych   £££££

1 Aldwych, WC2 **Tel** *020 7300 1000* **Rooms** *105*   **Map** *11 C2*

A grand contemporary hotel in former Edwardian newspaper offices. Impressive details include original art and tarazzo-stone bathrooms with heated floors and mini TVs. There's a spacious health club with a swimming pool, two fabulous restaurants and the buzzing, high-ceilinged Lobby Bar. Wi-Fi. **www.onealdwych.com**

WEST END AND WESTMINSTER Radisson Edwardian Hampshire   £££££

31–36 Leicester Square, WC2 **Tel** *020 7839 9399* **Rooms** *127*   **Map** *11 B2*

Leicester Square is a good base if you want to make the most of London's nightlife, as it's well placed for the theatre district, bars, clubs and restaurants. This luxurious Radisson has designer bedrooms with Philippe Starck bathrooms and Bose sound systems in the suites. Conference rooms also available. Wi-Fi. **www.radissonedwardian.com**

WEST END AND WESTMINSTER Ritz   £££££

150 Piccadilly, W1 **Tel** *020 7493 8181* **Rooms** *137*   **Map** *10 F3*

There are two staff for every room in this famous grand hotel on the edge of Green Park. You can even have your luggage unpacked for you. Rooms are in lavish Louis XVI style with antique furnishings and gold leaf, plus all mod cons. The Rivoli Bar has been restored to its Art Deco splendour. Wi-Fi. **www.theritzlondon.com**

WEST END AND WESTMINSTER Savoy   £££££

Strand, WC2 **Tel** *020 7836 4343* **Rooms** *263*   **Map** *11 C2*

This legendary hotel was an afterthought, Richard D'Oyly Carte capitalized on the success of his Savoy Theatre by providing a place to stay. The rest is history. Monet painted the Thames view from his window, Elton John flooded a bathroom and the dry martini was popularized in the bar. There's a rooftop pool as well. Wi-Fi. **www.fairmont.com/savoy**

WEST END AND WESTMINSTER The Connaught   £££££

Carlos Place, W1 **Tel** *020 7499 7070* **Rooms** *121*   **Map** *10 E3*

The Connaught maintains its traditional charm while moving with the times. Facilities include butler service and a state-of-the-art gym. The interior feels less stuffy since many of the public rooms, including The Connaught and the Coburgh Bar, were restyled by renowned designer Nina Campbell. **www.the-connaught.co.uk**

WEST END AND WESTMINSTER The Cumberland   £££££

Great Cumberland Pl, W1 **Tel** *0871 376 9014* **Rooms** *1000*   **Map** *9 C2*

This giant hotel near Marble Arch has been transformed into something of a design showcase, with elegantly stylish lounges and rooms fitted with the latest technology. The exceptional choice of bars and dining areas include hip Carbon Bar and chef Gary Rhodes' flagship restaurant, Rhodes W1. Wi-Fi. **www.guoman.com**

WEST END AND WESTMINSTER The Dorchester   £££££

Park Lane, W1 **Tel** *020 7629 8888* **Rooms** *250*   **Map** *10 D3*

The epitome of the glamorous luxury hotel, with an outrageously lavish lobby and a star-studded history, the Dorchester has been revamped but maintains its tasteful floral bedrooms. The Art Deco-style marble baths are probably the deepest in London. For even more pampering, pop down to the fabulous Art Deco spa. **www.thedorchester.com**

WEST END AND WESTMINSTER The Soho Hotel   £££££

4 Richmond Mews, W1 **Tel** *020 7559 3000* **Rooms** *89*   **Map** *11 A1*

One of the most striking of the Firmdale Group's six luxury boutique hotels in London, The Soho occupies an impressive warehouse-like building. Its guestrooms and stunning apartments mix modern chic and traditional English styles. A fine gym and holistic beauty treatments complete the sophisticated experience. **www.firmdale.com**

SOUTH KENSINGTON AND HYDE PARK Knightsbridge Green Hotel   ££

159 Knightsbridge, SW1 **Tel** *020 7584 6274* **Rooms** *31*   **Map** *9 C5*

A shopaholic's dream, this well-kept hotel is right on Knightsbridge, and rates are reasonable. The tidy, modern rooms are regularly upgraded and feature air conditioning, satellite TVs and wireless internet access. Some have views over Hyde Park. There's also a small business centre on-site. **www.thekghotel.com**

SOUTH KENSINGTON AND HYDE PARK The Rembrandt   ££££

11 Thurloe Place , SW7 **Tel** *020 7589 8100* **Rooms** *193*   **Map** *17 A1*

Well located opposite the Victoria & Albert Museum, this traditional mid-range hotel has been attractively modernized. Guestrooms are comfortable, and all have free Wi-Fi. There is a relaxing lounge bar and a carvery restaurant. Extras include an excellent fitness centre with a pool. **www.sarova.com/rembrandt**

SOUTH KENSINGTON AND HYDE PARK The Rockwell   £££

181–183 Cromwell Rd, SW5 **Tel** *020 7244 2000* **Rooms** *40*   **Map** *16 D2*

Sumptuous and classy, the rooms at The Rockwell are a haven from the bustle of the capital. Egyptian cotton sheets and plush feather pillows, combined with bathroom fittings by Philippe Starck and Hans Grohe, provide guests with a thoroughly rejuvenating experience. **www.therockwell.com**

SOUTH KENSINGTON AND HYDE PARK Number Sixteen   ££££

16 Sumner Place, SW7 **Tel** *020 7589 5232* **Rooms** *42*   **Map** *17 A2*

This smaller, more discreet part of the Firmdale boutique hotel group occupies a Kensington townhouse with a charming garden. Rooms are bright, imaginatively stylish and very well equipped. There's no restaurant, but afternoon tea is served in the lounge or garden, and there is 24-hour room service. **www.firmdale.com**

SOUTH KENSINGTON AND HYDE PARK 41   £££££

41 Buckingham Palace Rd, SW1 **Tel** *020 7300 0041* **Rooms** *30*   **Map** *18 F1*

Plush luxury with a distinctive individuality is the hallmark of this unique, hugely praised hotel. Service is both exceptional and personal, as staff respond to any imaginable need. Lounges and public areas evoke a traditional London club, while the chic bedrooms are decorated in black and white. **www.41hotel.com**

SOUTH KENSINGTON AND HYDE PARK The Capital   £££££

22–24 Basil St, SW3 **Tel** *020 7589 5171* **Rooms** *49*   **Map** *9 C5*

Situated between Harrods and Harvey Nichols, this service-oriented hotel even offers personal shoppers and jogging partners. Its Michelin two-starred restaurant has been refurbished in 1940s-influenced style. Bedrooms feature king-size beds, designer fabrics and the latest technology. **www.capitalhotel.co.uk**

SOUTH KENSINGTON AND HYDE PARK The Halkin   £££££

5 Halkin St, SW1 **Tel** *020 7333 1000* **Rooms** *41*   **Map** *10 D5*

Modern comforts meet Eastern serenity at this gracious luxury hotel. Warm wood, curving lines and creamy bed linen are accented by Southeast Asian art handpicked by the Singaporean owner. Be sure to have a meal at Nahm, it's the only Michelin-starred Thai restaurant outside Thailand. Wi-Fi. **www.halkin.como.bz**

REGENT'S PARK AND BLOOMSBURY Clink261   £

261–265 Grays Inn Rd, WC1 **Tel** *020 7833 9400* **Rooms** *34*   **Map** *3 C3*

This backpackers' hostel offers dorm-style accommodation as well as a few low-cost single and double rooms. Common spaces are bright and comfortable, and the Internet room has Wi-Fi access (charged). The same owners operate the similar Clink Hostel nearby. **www.ashleehouse.co.uk**

REGENT'S PARK AND BLOOMSBURY Arosfa Hotel   ££

83 Gower St, WC1 **Tel** *020 7636 2115* **Rooms** *17*   **Map** *3 A5*

A city B&B, the Arosfa is one of central London's real bargains. Its cosy, well-kept rooms are set in a classic Bloomsbury townhouse that was once home to the painter Millais. The owners are welcoming, and the lounges and breakfast room suitably comfortable. Free Wi-Fi access is provided in all rooms. **www.arosfalondon.com**

REGENT'S PARK AND BLOOMSBURY Crescent Hotel   ££

49–50 Cartwright Gardens, WC1 **Tel** *020 7387 1515* **Rooms** *27*   **Map** *3 B4*

One of several hotels in this striking Regency Street, the Crescent has been run by the same family since the 1950s. Most of the well-kept bedrooms have en suite facilities. Soft drinks and snacks are served in the lounge, and guests can use the tennis courts in the private gardens. **www.crescenthoteloflondon.com**

REGENT'S PARK AND BLOOMSBURY Euston Square Hotel   ££

152–156 North Gower St, NW1 **Tel** *020 7388 0099* **Rooms** *75*   **Map** *3 A4*

A chic stopover close to Euston Station. Rooms may be on the small side, but they are stylishly kitted out in dark wood and cream leather, with flatscreen TVs, a music library and tasteful bathrooms. Complimentary papers and squashy sofas are on offer in the airy lounge and there's also a restaurant. Wi-Fi. **www.euston-square-hotel.com**

REGENT'S PARK AND BLOOMSBURY Harlingford Hotel   ££

61-63 Cartwright Gardens, WC1 **Tel** *020 7387 1551* **Rooms** *43*   **Map** *3 B4*

The Harlingford stands out among Bloomsbury's many mid-range hotels for its fresh approach. The hotel's lounge areas, breakfast room and bedrooms have been renovated in attractive contemporary colours, and guests have access to the private garden square in front. A Continental or full English breakfast is included. **www.harlingfordhotel.com**

REGENT'S PARK AND BLOOMSBURY Hotel Cavendish   ££

75 Gower St, WC1 **Tel** *020 7636 9079* **Rooms** *33*   **Map** *3 A5*

This characterful B&B near London University has a fascinating history, DH Lawrence and the Beatles stayed here once. Rooms are simple yet comfortably furnished, and some have original fireplaces. Original artworks brighten up the breakfast room and there's a pretty garden as well. Shared facilities available. **www.hotelcavendish.com**

Key to Price Guide *see p556* **Key to Symbols** *see back cover flap*

REGENT'S PARK AND BLOOMSBURY 22 York Street
£££

22 York St, W1 **Tel** *020 7224 2990* **Rooms** *10*   **Map** *1 C5*

This beautiful property is a cut above most B&Bs. Liz and Michael Callis ensure that rooms in these two immaculately preserved Georgian houses are spotless and stylishly furnished with antiques and French quilts. A gourmet continental breakfast is served in the rustic kitchen. **www.22yorkstreet.co.uk**

REGENT'S PARK AND BLOOMSBURY Hart House Hotel
£££

51 Gloucester Place, W1 **Tel** *020 7935 2288* **Rooms** *15*   **Map** *9 C1*

This small, family-run hotel in a Georgian house north of Oxford Street has many return visitors. Rooms, all with Wi-Fi and other modern fittings, combine period charm with a contemporary style. The breakfasts are generous and included in the price. Gloucester Place is a busy street, so ask for a room at the back. **www.harthouse.co.uk**

REGENT'S PARK AND BLOOMSBURY myhotel Bloomsbury
£££

11-13 Bayley Street, WC1 **Tel** *020 7667 6000* **Rooms** *78*   **Map** *3 A5*

With just three branches – two in London, one in Brighton – the chic myhotels stand out for deliberately hip design, influenced by feng shui. The comfortable guestrooms boast luxurious linens and free Wi-Fi. There's a choice of three bar-restaurants, including a fashionable tapas bar. **www.myhotels.com**

REGENT'S PARK AND BLOOMSBURY Park Plaza Sherlock Holmes
£££

108 Baker St, W1 **Tel** *020 7486 6161* **Rooms** *119*   **Map** *1 C5*

The name may suggest a tacky theme hotel, yet this is anything but that. You enter this Baker Street boutique hotel via its stylish bar. Contemporary rooms, many with wooden floors, are softened with tactile throws and cushions; there are thoughtful details such as European and US sockets. The gym has spa facilities. Wi-Fi. **www.parkplaza.com**

REGENT'S PARK AND BLOOMSBURY Dorset Square Hotel
££££

39 Dorset Square, NW1 **Tel** *020 7723 7874* **Rooms** *37*   **Map** *1 C5*

Regulars prize this award-winning hotel near Regent's Park for its old-fashioned character and attention to detail. Rooms are opulently decorated to match the Regency building and are equipped with free Wi-Fi and other modern amenities. The Osteria dell'Orologio restaurant offers refined Italian cuisine. **www.dorsetsquarehotel-london.co.uk**

REGENT'S PARK AND BLOOMSBURY Montagu Place
££££

2 Montagu Place, W1 **Tel** *020 7467 2777* **Rooms** *16*   **Map** *9 C1*

Well-located in fashionable Marylebone, this small hotel rings a few changes on the established boutique-hotel style. Rooms are comfortable and well equipped and are divided into "Comfy", "Fancy" or "Swanky" (the largest). Service is individual and helpful, and frequent special offers can make it a bargain. **www.montagu-place.co.uk**

REGENT'S PARK AND BLOOMSBURY The Sumner
££££

54 Upper Berkeley St, W1 **Tel** *020 7723 2244* **Rooms** *20*   **Map** *9 C1*

The Sumner is an intimate boutique hotel located in a quiet street near Marble Arch. The interior has been carefully designed to combine contemporary styling, natural fabrics and state-of-the-art electronics with the original features of the 1820s building. Chic breakfast room and lounges. Free Wi-Fi throughout. **www.thesumner.com**

REGENT'S PARK AND BLOOMSBURY Charlotte Street Hotel
£££££

15 Charlotte St, W1 **Tel** *020 7806 2000* **Rooms** *52*   **Map** *11 A1*

The ground floor bar is always buzzing with local workers as well as guests in this exquisitely designed hotel in a street full of restaurants. Reflecting the area's history, its decor nods to the Bloomsbury Set period with original artworks by Vanessa Bell and others. Weekend films in the screening room. **www.firmdale.com**

REGENT'S PARK AND BLOOMSBURY Durrants Hotel
£££££

26–32 George St, W1 **Tel** *020 7935 8131* **Rooms** *92*   **Map** *10 D1*

Established in 1790, Durrants occupies a row of terraced houses and its warren of creaky rooms is delightfully old fashioned. Decor is traditional, old prints and antiques, but TVs are hidden in cabinets and bathrooms are modern. The restaurant and bar are period pieces. Only a few rooms are air conditioned. **www.durrantshotel.co.uk**

REGENT'S PARK AND BLOOMSBURY Sanderson
£££££

50 Berners St, W1 **Tel** *020 7300 1400* **Rooms** *150*   **Map** *10 F1*

The Sanderson's witty decor, red lips sofa and a framed portrait that seems to hang in mid-air, is like a surreal stage set. Rooms have every comfort, and the Malaysian restaurant, Suki, and two sophisticated cocktail bars are destinations in their own right. The Agua spa offers holistic pampering. **www.sandersonlondon.com**

REGENT'S PARK AND BLOOMSBURY The Langham, London
£££££

1C Portland Place, W1 **Tel** *020 7636 1000* **Rooms** *382*   **Map** *10 E1*

The Langham was Europe's first grand hotel when it opened in 1865 and still offers an ultra-luxurious experience behind its sprawling Victorian façade. Rooms achieve a tasteful middle ground between modern and traditional and there are extensive spa facilities including a swimming pool. Near Regent's Park. **www.langhamhotels.com**

THE CITY AND SOUTHWARK Southwark Rose Hotel
££

47 Southwark Bridge Rd, SE1 **Tel** *020 7015 1480* **Rooms** *106*   **Map** *13 A4*

All Seasons hotels are a boutique-style brand in the French Accor hotel group, and its London outpost has bright, modern rooms with good facilities for leisure and business travellers. The hotel provides excellent value and is well located for the Tate Modern and South Bank attractions. **www.all-seasons-hotel.com**

THE CITY AND SOUTHWARK London County Hall 　　　　　£££

Belvedere Rd, SE1 **Tel** *0870 238 3300* **Rooms** *314* 　　　**Map** *12 D5*

This branch of the budget Premier Inn chain is housed in the massive former County Hall on the Thames. The more expensive Marriott, which shares the building, has all the river views, but it's a good-value option next to the London Eye, near Waterloo and the Southbank Centre. Wireless Internet on-site. **www.premierinn.com**

THE CITY AND SOUTHWARK Novotel London City South 　　　　　£££

53–61 Southwark Bridge Rd, SE1 **Tel** *020 7089 0400* **Rooms** *182* 　　　**Map** *13 A3*

Billed as a "New Generation" Novotel, the interior has an airy, minimalist feel. Rooms are equipped with extras such as wireless Internet, minibar and even a radio in the bathroom. The fitness centre has a sauna and steam room, and the location is convenient for the venues and galleries of the South Bank. **www.novotel.com**

THE CITY AND SOUTHWARK Andaz Liverpool Street 　　　　　£££££

40 Liverpool St, EC2 **Tel** *020 7961 1234* **Rooms** *267* 　　　**Map** *13 C1*

This magnificent 19th-century railway hotel has been given a 21st century makeover. The bedrooms have all been designed to create the ultimate modern hotel experience, and there are four fabulous eateries and three bars. Special weekend deals are available. **www.london.liverpoolstreet.andaz.com**

THE CITY AND SOUTHWARK Rookery 　　　　　£££££

12 Peter's Lane, Cowcross St, EC1 **Tel** *020 7336 0931* **Rooms** *33* 　　　**Map** *4 F5*

Occupying six Georgian houses and shops (with faded butcher's and baker's signs still visible on some), this Dickensian hideaway retains many original features, such as flagstone floors in the hall and ceiling beams in some of the rooms. Decorated with antiques throughout, it also offers all the latest technology. **www.rookeryhotel.com**

THE CITY AND SOUTHWARK The Zetter 　　　　　£££££

86–88 Clerkenwell Rd, EC1 **Tel** *020 7324 4456* **Rooms** *59* 　　　**Map** *4 F4*

In an area known for its loft apartments, this is a loft hotel in a 19th-century warehouse. Rooms have exposed brick, quirky 1970s furniture, old Penguin books, hot-water bottles and high-tech extras, while vending machines on each floor dispense necessities. Hip Italian restaurant at street level. **www.thezetter.com**

THE CITY AND SOUTHWARK Shangri-La Hotel, at The Shard 　　　　　£££££

32 London Bridge Rd, SE1 **Tel** *020 8747 8484* **Rooms** *195* 　　　**Map** *13 C4*

Spread over floors 34–52 of The Shard, London's tallest building, is this luxury hotel, which opened in 2013. Rooms and suites are spacious, luxurious and well-equipped, and many areas of the hotel feature spectacular city views. Facilities include Wi-Fi, an indoor infinity pool and fitness centre, and a range of bars and dining options. **www.shangri-la.com**

FURTHER AFIELD Chelsea Guest House 　　　　　£

372 Wandsworth Rd, SW8 **Tel** *020 7627 6262* **Rooms** *47*

Calling it "Chelsea" is a misnomer (it is actually in Wandsworth, south of the Thames), but this hotel offers an imaginative alternative to the high prices in other parts of town. Rooms are all en suite and are bright, modern and comfortable, with TV and Wi-Fi. **www.chelseaguesthouse.co.uk**

FURTHER AFIELD easyHotel 　　　　　£

14 Lexham Gardens, W8 **Rooms** *34* 　　　**Map** *16 D1*

The easy group's bright and basic budget hotels offer some of the cheapest en suite double rooms in London. The no-frills rooms are clean and well maintained with extra charges for the use of towels. All rooms have a TV and Wi-Fi. All bookings must be made online. **www.easyhotel.com**

FURTHER AFIELD Rushmore 　　　　　£

11 Trebovir Rd, SW5 **Tel** *020 7370 3839* **Rooms** *22* 　　　**Map** *15 C2*

Like the nearby Mayflower, the Rushmore is proof that accommodation doesn't have to be expensive to be stylish. Each room in this Victorian townhouse has been designed in a different style; even the bathrooms have been customized to fit in with the mood. Breakfast is served in a chic conservatory. **www.rushmore-hotel.co.uk**

FURTHER AFIELD The Mitre 　　　　　£

291 Greenwich High Rd, SE10 **Tel** *020 8293 0037* **Rooms** *24*

An inn since 1837, the Mitre is one of historic Greenwich's best-known and most popular pubs. Above its three bars are 15 simple, traditionally furnished rooms available on a bed and breakfast basis. All rooms have bathrooms and TV sets. A hearty menu is served in the bar, and there's a pleasant garden alongside. **www.mitregreenwich.com**

FURTHER AFIELD base2stay 　　　　　££

25 Courtfield Gardens , SW5 **Tel** *020 7244 2255* **Rooms** *67* 　　　**Map** *16 D2*

A unique hotel with an attractive combination of sleek boutique-style design, luxury extras and accessible prices. Rooms range from singles to family-sized suites and even small apartments. All options have mini-kitchens and an exceptional range of high-quality electronics (including free Wi-Fi). **www.base2stay.com**

FURTHER AFIELD Church Street Hotel 　　　　　££

29–33 Camberwell Church St, SE5 **Tel** *020 7703 5984* **Rooms** *30*

A hotel unlike any other in London – the friendly, well-travelled Spanish owners have decorated it with rich colours and quirky Mexican artifacts. There is a lovely, atmospheric bar-restaurant and free Wi-Fi connection. The generous organic breakfasts are included in the price. **www.churchstreethotel.com**

Key to Price Guide *see p556* **Key to Symbols** *see back cover flap*

FURTHER AFIELD Garden Court Hotel
£££

30–31 Kensington Gardens Square, W2 **Tel** *020 7229 2553* **Rooms** *32*   **Map** *8 D2*

An antique Beefeater guards the airy lobby of this well-maintained family hotel on a lovely garden square. The rooms of this Victorian townhouse are tastefully furnished and to keep the cost down, you can opt for shared facilities. Breakfast is included. Good value and close to Portobello Market. **www.gardencourthotel.co.uk**

FURTHER AFIELD Hampstead Village Guesthouse
£££

2 Kemplay Rd, NW3 **Tel** *020 7435 8679* **Rooms** *9*

This Victorian home, in the picturesque village of Hampstead, is intriguingly cluttered with antiques and curios. Breakfast is served in the garden in summer, English weather permitting. Rooms are equipped with hot-water bottles and fridge. The rates are cheaper if you forego en suite facilities. **www.hampsteadguesthouse.com**

FURTHER AFIELD Mayflower Hotel
£££

26–28 Trebovir Rd, SW5 **Tel** *020 7370 0991* **Rooms** *48*   **Map** *16 D2*

This beautifully furnished, budget-boutique hotel is a cut above the rest. The spacious, contemporary rooms have wooden floors and Eastern elements such as elaborately carved beds and rich silks. Marble bathrooms, ceiling fans and CD players are luxurious perks. There are also 35 tasteful apartments nearby. **www.mayflowerhotel.co.uk**

FURTHER AFIELD Mornington
£££

12 Lancaster Gate, W2 **Tel** *020 7262 7361* **Rooms** *69*   **Map** *8 F2*

This formerly Swedish-owned hotel is now part of the quality Best Western chain. Bedrooms in the grand Victorian building near Hyde Park maintain a light, airy Scandinavian feel. There is no restaurant, but light snacks are served in the wood-panelled Library Bar in the evening. Inquire about special rates. **www.bw-morningtonhotel.co.uk**

FURTHER AFIELD Pavilion Hotel
£££

34–36 Sussex Gardens, W2 **Tel** *020 7262 0905* **Rooms** *30*   **Map** *9 A1*

The Pavilion's understated brick exterior may not stand out in this hotel-lined strip, but inside it's a world away from boring B&Bs. The fabulously themed rooms, from the rich panelling and tartan of "Highland Fling" to the antique Chinese chests and silks of "Enter the Dragon" are favoured by rock stars. **www.pavilionhoteluk.com**

FURTHER AFIELD Riverside Hotel
£££

23 Petersham Rd, Richmond, Surrey, TW10 6UH **Tel** *020 8940 1339* **Rooms** *12*

This peaceful B&B is a good-value alternative to staying in central London. The charming rooms have TVs and en suite bathrooms; all enjoy river views, as do the lounge area and breakfast room. Self-contained apartments are also available for short-term rental. **www.riversiderichmond.co.uk**

FURTHER AFIELD Stylotel
£££

160–162 Sussex Gardens, W2 **Tel** *020 7723 1026* **Rooms** *40*   **Map** *9 A2*

Offering some of the cheapest rates in central London, Stylotel is true to its name, although the high-tech style may not suit all tastes. Rooms have wooden floors, aluminium walls, light-box bedside tables and futuristic bathrooms. There's a groovy lounge with curved stainless steel bar and blue leather seats. **www.stylotel.com**

FURTHER AFIELD Twenty Nevern Square
££

20 Nevern Square , SW5 **Tel** *020 7565 9555* **Rooms** *20*   **Map** *15 C2*

Set on a quiet garden square, this intimate boutique hotel features gorgeous fabrics and fine beds including magnificent divans and four-posters. Wi-Fi and other modern electronics are available too, and breakfast is included. This is a very reasonably priced option. **www.20nevernsquare.co.uk**

FURTHER AFIELD Cannizaro House
£££

West Side, Wimbledon Common, SW19 **Tel** *020 8879 1464* **Rooms** *46*

This Georgian mansion on the edge of Wimbledon Common is an ideal base for keen tennis fans. Rooms are decorated in country-house style; some have four-poster beds and air conditioning. There is a restaurant and cocktail bar, and extensive grounds where you can play croquet. There is also free Wi-Fi. **www.cannizarohouse.com**

FURTHER AFIELD Colonnade
£££

2 Warrington Crescent, W9 **Tel** *020 7286 1052* **Rooms** *43*

Near the picturesque canals of Little Venice, this hotel in two Victorian mansions has been operating since the 1930s. Freud stayed here while his house was being redecorated, and JFK paid a visit in the 1960s. The interior is grand yet unintimidating and every luxurious room has a different feel. **www.theetoncollection.com**

FURTHER AFIELD K West
£££

Richmond Way, W14 **Tel** *020 8008 6600* **Rooms** *220*

Housed in a former BBC studio building, this attention-grabbing hotel offers chic accommodation and an equally hip restaurant, Kanteen. This is home to the K Spa, one of the most opulent in London. Wheelchair-accessible rooms are available. **www.k-west.co.uk**

FURTHER AFIELD New Linden Hotel
£££

59 Leinster Square, W2 **Tel** *020 7221 4321* **Rooms** *51*   **Map** *8 D2*

Warm, subtle colour schemes and chic modern design are features of this stylish hotel on the borders of Notting Hill. Rooms combine a fresh, bright feel with sumptuous comforts and state-of-the-art electronics, including free Wi-Fi. Continental breakfasts are included and feature plenty of fresh fruit. **www.newlinden.co.uk**

FURTHER AFIELD Sydney House
9–11 Sydney St, SW3 **Tel** *020 7376 7711* **Rooms** *21*   £££   **Map** *17 A2*

This small hotel is located just steps away from the chic shops of Brompton Cross. Airy rooms are furnished with blond wood furniture, Frette linen, contemporary art and thoughtful features such as American sockets in the ultra-modern bathrooms. Check the website for special rates. **www.sydneyhousechelsea.com**

FURTHER AFIELD The Royal Park
3 Westbourne Terrace, W2 **Tel** *020 7479 6600* **Rooms** *48*   £££   **Map** *8 F2*

This town house hotel near Hyde Park has a discreet luxury, which has attracted celebrity guests. Classic, unfussy rooms are furnished with exquisite fabrics, original prints and stone-tiled bathrooms. All the usual gadgetry, plus complimentary welcome drink and evening champagne in the gracious drawing room. **www.theroyalpark.com**

FURTHER AFIELD The Windmill on the Common
Clapham Common Southside , SW4 **Tel** *020 8673 4578* **Rooms** *29*   £££

The broad terrace of this old pub, facing Clapham Common, has long been a popular place to eat and drink on summer evenings; when it's colder, there are big, cosy rooms inside. Guestrooms are available on a bed and breakfast basis and have been renovated with stylish design and excellent facilities. **www.windmillclapham.co.uk**

FURTHER AFIELD Aster House
3 Sumner Place, SW7 **Tel** *020 7581 5888* **Rooms** *13*   ££££   **Map** *17 A2*

Three-time winner of the Tourist Board's best B&B award, this friendly hotel in a white stucco house has immaculate bedrooms in a typical English-country style. A superior breakfast served in the palm-filled conservatory and a pretty garden complete with pond and resident ducks attract guests. Check the website for special deals. **www.asterhouse.com**

FURTHER AFIELD myhotel Chelsea
35 Ixworth Place, SW3 **Tel** *020 7225 7500* **Rooms** *46*   ££££   **Map** *17 B2*

Sister hotel to myhotel in Bloomsbury, the Chelsea branch is similarly chic but slightly more traditional in style and a little more opulent. There's a very mellow spa, and the hip mybar restaurant-cocktail lounge, in vivid colours, has a lively global menu. **www.myhotels.com**

FURTHER AFIELD The Gore
190 Queen's Gate, SW7 **Tel** *020 7584 6601* **Rooms** *50*   ££££   **Map** *8 F5*

The Gore has been in operation for more than 110 years and, although all the modern amenities are available, it still preserves the atmosphere of a bygone age. Rooms feature four-poster beds, framed pictures, luxurious draperies and opulent fabrics. There's a panelled bar and casual bistro as well. **www.gorehotel.com**

FURTHER AFIELD The Hempel
31–35 Craven Hill Gardens, W2 **Tel** *020 7298 9000* **Rooms** *50*   ££££   **Map** *8 E2*

Designer Anouska Hempel's luxury retreat was one of London's first boutique hotels, and has kept its caché. The style is Japanese-influenced minimalism, emphasizing serenity, with several rooms looking out onto a Zen garden. Suites and apartments are especially stunning. The No. 35 restaurant has a refined global menu. **www.the-hempel.co.uk**

FURTHER AFIELD The Hoxton
81 Great Eastern St, EC2 **Tel** *020 7550 1000* **Rooms** *208*   ££££   **Map** *5 C4*

On the edge of the City, Hoxton is one of London's trendiest areas and has one of its hippest hotels. The Hoxton offers small but inventively styled rooms with plenty of technology including free Wi-Fi. Cutting-edge work by local artists is on show, and the Hoxton Grill bistro is great for people-watching. **www.hoxtonhotels.com**

FURTHER AFIELD The Petersham
Nightingale Lane, Richmond, Surrey, TW10 **Tel** *020 8939 1010* **Rooms** *60*   ££££

This sprawling Victorian hotel perches on Richmond Hill overlooking the Thames. The elegant rooms are in keeping with the building's period grandeur, while integrating modern elements; some have spectacular views of the Thames. Unsurprisingly given its romantic location, it is popular for weddings. **www.petershamhotel.co.uk**

FURTHER AFIELD The Portobello Hotel
22 Stanley Gardens, W11 **Tel** *020 7727 2777* **Rooms** *21*   ££££   **Map** *7 B2*

This divinely decadent Notting Hill mansion has lured rock royalty for over 30 years with its hip location and extravagantly decorated rooms. Choose from such exotic retreats as the serene Japanese room with private grotto garden and the notorious "Round Bed Room", with its freestanding Victorian bath. **www.portobellohotel.com**

FURTHER AFIELD Blakes Hotel
33 Roland Gardens, SW7 **Tel** *020 7370 6701* **Rooms** *42*   £££££   **Map** *16 F2*

Blakes is the original boutique hotel, created by designer Anouska Hempel over two decades ago. Rooms range in style from baronial manor to opulent Oriental and contain pieces collected on her travels. The discreet residential location has made it a favourite celebrity hideaway. Only some suites are air conditioned. **www.blakeshotels.com**

FURTHER AFIELD The Milestone Hotel
1 Kensington Court, W8 **Tel** *020 7917 1000* **Rooms** *57 & 6 apartments*   £££££   **Map** *8 E5*

This plush hotel opposite Kensington Palace features originally designed rooms, from the smart "Savile Row" to the Colonial-style "Safari Suite". Extras include gym and resistance pool, broadband Internet and Penhaligon's toiletries, 24-hour butler and use of the hotel Bentley. **www.milestonehotel.com**

Key to Price Guide *see p556* **Key to Symbols** *see back cover flap*

THE DOWNS AND CHANNEL COAST

BATTLE The Powdermills
Powdermill Lane, Battle, East Sussex , TN33 0SP **Tel** *01424 775511* **Rooms** *42*

A charmingly individual country hotel that was once a Napoleonic-era gunpowder works. The Powdermills is set in a stunning location amid 150 acres of grounds, with a pool and its own fishing lake. The rooms are sumptuously decorated in traditional style, staff are welcoming, and prices are very reasonable. **www.powdermillshotel.com**

BEAULIEU Master Builders House Hotel
Buckler's Hard, Beaulieu, Hampshire, SO42 7XB **Tel** *0844 815 3399* **Rooms** *25*

Marketed by Distinguished Hotels, the Master Builders House stands on the creek where the famed "Hearts of Oak" ships of the Royal Navy were once built. It is on Lord Montagu's estate, which puts the National Motor Museum within minutes while the glorious New Forest is also at the doorstep. Breakfast included. **www.themasterbuilders.co.uk**

BRIGHTON Hotel Seattle
Brighton Marina, Brighton, East Sussex, BN2 5WA **Tel** *01273 679799* **Rooms** *71*

A fresh alternative to old-style seaside hotels, the imaginative Seattle has bright contemporary rooms with excellent facilities, and great sea views. Unlike some boutique hotels, it has fine provision for children, and the light, airy restaurant is delightful. A bargain, and very popular, so book well ahead. **www.hotelseattlebrighton.com**

BRIGHTON De Vere Grand Brighton
97–99 Kings Rd, Brighton, East Sussex, BN1 2FW **Tel** *01273 224300* **Rooms** *201*

Brighton's only five-star hotel, this is arguably the nation's finest big seaside hotel, located right on the seafront. There is a gymnasium and a magnificent Victorian dining room and bar that serves a classic British menu, as well as delicious cream teas. Includes breakfast. **www.devere.co.uk**

BRIGHTON Hotel Du Vin Brighton
2–6 Ship St, Brighton, East Sussex, BN1 1AD **Tel** *01273 718588* **Rooms** *49*

Set in the Lanes conservation area, a stone's throw away from the seafront, this cutting-edge hotel and bistro is housed in a collection of eccentric, Gothic Revival and mock-Tudor buildings. All the bedrooms are decorated with Egyptian linen and handsprung mattresses. A Pub du Vin can be found next door. **www.hotelduvin.com**

BROCKENHURST Cottage Lodge
Sway Rd, Brockenhurst, Hampshire, SO42 7SH **Tel** *01590 622296* **Rooms** *12*

This charming New Forest B&B has won green tourism awards. The setting is delightful, and the rooms, some with balconies, are pretty and comfortable. Extras include free Wi-Fi, and the delicious breakfasts feature fresh local produce. Facilities for disabled travellers are exceptional. **www.cottagehotel.org**

BROCKENHURST Balmer Lawn
Lyndhurst Rd, Brockenhurst, Hampshire, SO42 7ZB **Tel** *01590 623116* **Rooms** *54*

Built in the 1880s as a hunting lodge in the New Forest, Balmer Lawn is now an oasis of comfort and good service. The in-house Beresford's Restaurant has two AA Rosettes for fine dining. Indoor and outdoor heated pools, a health spa and tennis courts are among the leisure amenities. Breakfast is included. **www.balmerlawnhotel.com**

BROCKENHURST Rhinefield House
Rhinefield Rd, Brockenhurst, Hampshire, SO42 7QB **Tel** *0845 072 7516* **Rooms** *50*

Set in a New Forest clearing and surrounded by rhododendrons, Rhinefield is a magnificent 19th-century Jacobean Revival mansion, with Grindling Gibbons wood carvings and other priceless features. Star of the show is the Moorish-style Alhambra Room, now a gracious bar. Breakfast included. **www.handpickedhotels.co.uk/rhinefieldhouse**

CANTERBURY The Abode
30–33 High St, Canterbury, Kent, CT1 2RX **Tel** *01227 766266* **Rooms** *72*

Located on the pedestrianized High Street, The Abode dates from the 16th century and has many original features. All the bedrooms, some furnished in Tudor or Georgian style, have satellite TV. There is a champagne bar, a fine dining restaurant and The Old Brewery for pub food. Breakfast included. **www.abodehotels.co.uk**

CANTERBURY The Falstaff
8–10 St Dunstans St, Canterbury, Kent, CT2 8AF **Tel** *01227 462138* **Rooms** *46*

The Falstaff, at the heart of one of England's most historic cities, celebrated its 600th year in 2005. The one-time coaching inn has been extended into a restored wood mill. All rooms are en suite, and have TV and hot drink facilities. It stands next to the imposing Westgate Tower. **www.thefalstaffincanterbury.com**

DEAL Number One B&B
1 Ranelagh Rd, Deal, Kent, CT14 7BG **Tel** *01304 364459* **Rooms** *4*

Only 10 miles (16 km) from Dover, Georgian Deal has far more charm. The owners of this innovative B&B have renovated their house, just off the beach, in elegant contemporary style, and their attention to detail is seen in fine fabrics, exceptional facilities and delicious breakfasts. **www.numberonebandb.co.uk**

DOVER Wallett's Court Country Hotel & Spa   P ⅰⅰ ≋ ⅿ   ££££

Westcliffe, Dover, Kent, CT15 6EW **Tel** *01304 852424* **Rooms** *17*

Relax in a Tudor-style room in the manor house, with fine sea views and an oak-beamed ceiling, or enjoy a room in one of the converted ancient barns. The Spa, set in the grounds of Wallett's Court, has a Romanesque exercise pool, sauna and a mineral steam room. Breakfast included. Check the website for special deals. **www.wallettscourt.com**

EAST GRINSTEAD Gravetye Manor   P ⅰⅰ   ££££

Vowels Lane, East Grinstead, West Sussex, RH19 4LJ **Tel** *01342 810567* **Rooms** *18*

Regarded by many as the establishment that started the country-house hotel movement. A Relais et Châteaux affiliate, it has an oak-panelled restaurant. In 1884, William Robinson, one of England's great gardeners, laid out the wonderful shrubs and flowerbeds. Activities include croquet and shooting. **www.gravetyemanor.co.uk**

EASTBOURNE The Grand Hotel   ⅶ ⅰⅰ ≋ ⅿ   £££££

King Edwards Parade, Eastbourne, East Sussex, BN21 4EQ **Tel** *01323 412345* **Rooms** *152*

Appropriately named, the imposing Grand is one of Britain's classic seaside hotels. Owners Elite Hotels have lavishly refurbished the property to meet 21st-century five-star requirements. Ideal for touring Sussex or just taking the sea air with strolls down the prom. Prices include breakfast. **www.grandeastbourne.com**

FOLKESTONE Quality Hotel Burlington   ⅶ P ⅰⅰ   ££

3–5 Earls Avenue, Folkestone, Kent, CT20 2HR **Tel** *01303 255301* **Rooms** *70*

This Victorian boutique hotel, situated close to the beach, has extensive public rooms, including a choice of lounges, the Bay Tree restaurant and a large cocktail bar. Bedrooms are pleasantly decorated and equipped with modern facilities. Some rooms have sea views. **www.theburlingtonhotel.com**

GUILDFORD Angel Posting House & Livery   ⅶ ⅰⅰ   ££

91 High St, Guildford, Surrey, GU1 3DP **Tel** *01483 564555* **Rooms** *21*

Jane Austen and Admiral Nelson have been guests at this town centre coaching inn that welcomed its first guests in 1500. Old-world charm and high standards of hospitality ensure popularity. The atmospheric salon has a minstrel gallery, a fireplace and a 1685 coaching clock. **www.angelpostinghouse.com**

LEWES Millers   ▤   ££

134 High St, Lewes, East Sussex, BN7 1XS **Tel** *01273 475631* **Rooms** *2*

Behind a neat Georgian frontage in Lewes's charming conservation area stands a 16th-century timber-framed building, which once belonged to the first Duke of Newcastle. The two double letting rooms have magnificent four-poster beds. Book in advance. The town is renowned for its antiques shops. **www.millersbedandbreakfast.com**

MID LAVANT Rooks Hill Guest House   P ⅾ   £££

Lavant Road, Mid Lavant, Chichester, West Sussex, PO18 0BQ **Tel** *01243 528400* **Rooms** *5*

This charming guesthouse is located within sight of the Goodwood Estate, famed for its horse racing and motor festivals. All the rooms are en suite and have been beautifully furnished to provide a real country feel. Breakfast is included in the price, and there is a great gastropub opposite. **www.rookshill.co.uk**

MIDHURST The Spread Eagle Hotel & Spa   ⅰⅰ ≋ ⅿ P ⅾ   £££

South St, Midhurst, W Sussex GU29 9NH **Tel** *01730 815668* **Rooms** *39*

In the centre of a country market town, but in its own grounds, this hotel dates back to 1430 and was a coaching inn favoured by the rich. Public areas feature oak beams and leaded-light windows; rooms are individually decorated and furnished with antiques. The Aquila spa has an indoor pool, sauna and steam room. **www.hshotels.co.uk**

NEW MILTON Chewton Glen   ⅰⅰ ≋ ⅿ   £££££

Christchurch Rd, New Milton, Hampshire, BH25 6QS **Tel** *01425 275341* **Rooms** *58*

The epitome of Edwardian elegance, Chewton Glen is located close to the sea. It is renowned for its food and the hotel also boasts a magnificent indoor pool and spa in addition to a range of outdoor sports and leisure activities. The rooms are constantly being updated to offer a high standard of comfort. **www.chewtonglen.com**

RINGWOOD Moortown Lodge   ⅾ   ££

244 Christchurch Rd, Ringwood, Hampshire, BH24 3AS **Tel** *01425 471404* **Rooms** *7*

This unpretentious country inn at the gateway to the New Forest, offers all modern in-room amenities, including high-speed Internet via broadband. Guests have access to the adjacent David Lloyd club, with its gym and pool. A full English breakfast is included. **www.moortownlodge.co.uk**

ROYAL TUNBRIDGE WELLS Hotel Du Vin & Bistro   ⅶ ⅰⅰ   £££

Crescent Rd, Tunbridge Wells, Kent, TN1 2LY **Tel** *01892 526455* **Rooms** *34*

Superb quality without unnecessary frills. Sensible prices and trendy service are the key to success for the small but steadily growing Vin & Bistro chain. This branch opened in 1997 and immediately became a favourite for its modern styles of accommodation and cuisine catered in a spacious historic building. **www.hotelduvin.com**

RYE The Apothecary   ££

1 East St, Rye, East Sussex, TN31 7JY **Tel** *01797 229157* **Rooms** *3*

On a cobbled street in the middle of historic Rye, this charming B&B has rooms above a coffee shop. The sloping ceilings, snug corners and views over the old town's rooftops provide plenty of character. All rooms have en suite bathrooms, TVs and mini-fridges. **www.bedandbreakfastrye.com**

Key to Price Guide *see p556* **Key to Symbols** *see back cover flap*

RYE Jeake's House   P   ££

Mermaid St, Rye, East Sussex, TN31 7ET **Tel** *01797 222828* **Rooms** *11*

Creeper-clad Jeake's House is tucked away in Rye's atmospheric jumble of little cobbled streets. Guests are welcomed by the two resident cats and proprietors Jenny Hadfield and Richard Martin. There's an oak-beamed parlour and a book-lined bar, plus roaring fires on colder days. Breakfast included. **www.jeakeshouse.com**

SEAVIEW Seaview   ₦ &   £££

High St, Seaview, Isle of Wight, PO34 5EX **Tel** *01983 612711* **Rooms** *28*

Once described as "the perfect seaside hotel", this is just the spot for an idyllic weekend. It's good for family holidays too. Crisp linen, maritime bric-à-brac and a warren of corridors and stairways all add to the romance. Seaview's restaurant offers deliciously inventive cuisine. **www.seaviewhotel.co.uk**

SOUTHAMPTON Hunters Lodge   P   £

25 Landguard Rd, Southampton, Hampshire, SO15 5DL **Tel** *02380 227919* **Rooms** *14*

Attentive, personal service is a hallmark of this pleasant B&B, set in a Victorian house in a quiet part of Southampton. The guestrooms are traditionally styled, with good modern fittings, quality fabrics and free Wi-Fi. Breakfasts are excellent, and the hotel is well attuned to the needs of cruise-ship passengers. **www.hunterslodgehotel.net**

VENTNOR The Royal Hotel   ▦ ₦ ≈ &   £££

Belgrave Rd, Ventnor, Isle of Wight, PO38 1JJ **Tel** *01983 852186* **Rooms** *53*

The Isle of Wight's largest premier hotel can be found in the elegant Victorian town of Ventnor. Gourmets can indulge in inspired cuisine in a palatial dining room replete with rich drapes, high ceilings and massive chandeliers. Explore the island or the staff can arrange a yacht charter. Breakfast included. **www.royalhoteliow.co.uk**

WICKHAM Old House Hotel & Restaurant   P ₦   ££

The Square, Wickham, Hampshire, PO17 5JG **Tel** *01329 833049* **Rooms** *12*

Located just off the M27 motorway, this is a good option for those wishing to explore the Portsmouth, Southampton, Winchester triangle. Built in 1715 as a gentleman's town house, the building was converted into a hotel in 1970. You can also stay in a three-bedroom cottage a short walk away. Breakfast included. **www.oldhousehotel.co.uk**

WINCHESTER The Wykeham Arms   P ₦   ££

75 Kingsgate St, Winchester, Hampshire, SO23 9PE **Tel** *01962 853834* **Rooms** *14*

On a tiny lane in the middle of old Winchester, the Wykeham Arms, an inn since 1755, is full of historic character. The bedrooms of different sizes, some at the top of creaking staircases, are equally atmospheric, and have modern fittings too. Food is served in the lovely old bar. **www.fullershotels.com**

WINCHESTER Hotel du Vin   ₦   £££

Southgate St, Winchester, SO23 9EF **Tel** *01962 841414* **Rooms** *24*

This chain of luxury boutique hotels began life in historic Winchester. The original Hotel du Vin occupies a fine Georgian building in the centre of town. Each room is sponsored by a different wine house and is individually styled; stay in the main house or in one of the cosy cottage rooms off the walled garden. The French bistro is superb. **www.hotelduvin.com**

WINCHESTER Lainston House   P ₦ ▧ &   ££££

Sparsholt, Winchester, Hampshire, SO21 2LT **Tel** *01962 776088* **Rooms** *50*

One of England's most handsome hotels, Lainston House has country style yet is just minutes from the centre of Winchester. Behind that imposing Queen Anne red-brick frontage is a friendly welcome. There are 63 acres to wander in, a gourmet restaurant and you can always order a DVD from room service. **www.exclusivehotels.co.uk**

EAST ANGLIA

ALDEBURGH Wentworth   P ₦ &   £££

Wentworth Rd, Aldeburgh, Suffolk, IP15 5BD **Tel** *01728 452312* **Rooms** *35*

Replete with antiques and log fires, the Wentworth Hotel has been run by succeeding generations of the Pritt family since 1920. All the bedrooms are well equipped with latest facilities, including satellite TV, and offer fine sea views. There are also three local golf courses. Includes breakfast. **www.wentworth-aldeburgh.com**

BUCKDEN Lion   P ₦ &   £

High St, Buckden, Cambridgeshire, PE19 5XA **Tel** *01480 810313* **Rooms** *14*

Rescued from corporate ownership in 1982, this 15th-century, Grade II listed hotel is a classic country inn. It also has a resident ghost. Well-furnished bedrooms. The oak-panelled restaurant offers excellent wholesome food using the best of local produce. There is also a bar and lounge. Breakfast is included. **www.thelionbuckden.com**

BURNHAM MARKET The Hoste Arms   P ₦ &   £££

The Green, Burnham Market, King's Lynn, Norfolk, PE31 8HD **Tel** *01328 738777* **Rooms** *35*

You can choose to stay in the pretty main part of the inn; in the Zulu wing with its modern African-flavoured styling and leather couches; in an old railway station, a five minutes' walk away; or in the luxury Georgian boutique hotel known as the Vine House. There is a great wine list. Rate includes breakfast. **www.hostearms.co.uk**

BURY ST EDMUNDS Angel Hotel
3 Angel Hill, Bury St Edmunds, Suffolk, IP33 1LT **Tel** *01284 714000* **Rooms** *75*

The virginia creeper-clad Angel dominates Bury St Edmunds' largest square. Rooms are individually decorated with modern flair or classical grace. Its public areas have always been the place for the local elite to meet. These days they are joined by a global clientele drawn by the hotel's reputation for contemporary British fine dining. **www.theangel.co.uk**

BURY ST EDMUNDS Ounce House
Northgate St, Bury St Edmunds, Suffolk, IP33 1HP **Tel** *01284 761779* **Rooms** *5*

A merchant's house dating from 1870, this spacious family home stands at the top of one of the finest residential streets in Bury St Edmunds. Bedrooms have a chintzy, Victorian style and are equipped with all the modern facilities. A bar operates in the drawing room. Includes breakfast. **www.ouncehouse.co.uk**

CAMBRIDGE Regency House
7 Regent Terrace, Cambridge, Cambridgeshire, CB2 1AA **Tel** *01223 329626* **Rooms** *9*

The rooms at this budget guesthouse, many overlooking Parker's Piece park in central Cambridge, have a bright, fresh look, down pillows, TVs and free Wi-Fi. Several rooms share bathrooms. An ample Continental breakfast is included. **www.regencyguesthouse.co.uk**

CAMBRIDGE Arundel House Hotel
Chesterton Rd, Cambridge, Cambridgeshire, CB4 3AN **Tel** *01223 367701* **Rooms** *103*

This hotel, created from a terrace of late 19th-century Victorian houses, overlooks the River Cam and is a short walk across the park from the city centre. The historic façade and gracefully decorated rooms have been retained while providing all the latest amenities, such as free Wi-Fi. Includes continental breakfast. **www.arundelhousehotels.co.uk**

CAMPSEA ASHE The Old Rectory
Campsea Ashe, Woodbridge, Suffolk, IP13 0PU **Tel** *01728 746524* **Rooms** *7*

All the delights of the Suffolk coastline are in easy reach – the music and culture of Snape Maltings, the Sutton Hoo Saxon burial ground and the towns of Woodbridge and Aldeburgh. An elegant Georgian house encircled by gardens, furnished in chic contemporary style. Includes breakfast. Free Wi-Fi. **www.theoldrectorysuffolk.com**

COGGESHALL The White Hart
Market End, Coggeshall, Essex, CO6 1NH **Tel** *01376 561654* **Rooms** *18*

Sleepy Coggeshall once boasted of having more inns and pubs per capita than any other town in the country. The atmospheric White Hart is one of the survivors, offering outstanding value for money in one of East Anglia's secret gems. All the rooms have en suite facilities. Full breakfast is included. Free Wi-Fi. **www.whitehart-coggeshall.com**

DEDHAM Dedham Hall
Brook St, Dedham, Essex, CO7 6AD **Tel** *01206 323027* **Rooms** *22*

A 15th-century farmhouse and cottages on the edge of Dedham village, right beside footpaths to the most beautiful parts of "Constable Country". Rooms are both comfortable and atmospheric, and the pretty Fountain House restaurant has some of the area's most enjoyable cuisine. Residential art courses are offered. **www.dedhamhall.co.uk**

DEDHAM Maison Talbooth
Stratford Rd, Dedham, Colchester, Essex, CO7 6HN **Tel** *01206 322367* **Rooms** *12*

The Milsom family are a legend in Constable country, taking hospitality to new levels of excellence. The essence of Victorian country-house grace and style, the hotel is just a few minutes from the riverside half-timbered Le Talbooth restaurant and the sister Milsom's hotel. There is a pool in the summer and a tennis court. **www.milsomhotels.com**

DUNWICH The Ship
St James St, Dunwich, Suffolk, IP17 3DT **Tel** *01728 648219* **Rooms** *15*

Before it sank into the sea, medieval Dunwich was East Anglia's busiest port and had a population of 3,000. The 500-year old ship survived and offers simple rooms in an out-of-the-way location. The restaurant is renowned for simply prepared home food, including fish and chips. Some rooms are dog-friendly. **www.shipatdunwich.co.uk**

ELY Lamb Hotel
2 Lynn Rd, Ely, Cambridgeshire, CB7 4EJ **Tel** *01353 663574* **Rooms** *15*

The Lamb makes no secret of its 15th-century coaching inn origins at the heart of the Fens *(see p196)*, close to the glorious cathedral. Oak panelling, arched picture-end windows, antique furnishings and candle-lit suppers – it's a haven of traditional values. Includes breakfast. Check the website for special rates. Free Wi-Fi. **www.thelamb-ely.com**

GREAT DUNMOW The Starr
Market Place, Gt Dunmow, Essex, CM6 1AX **Tel** *01371 874321* **Rooms** *8*

The Starr's elegant conservatory is just the place to enjoy the owners', Terry and Louise George, good food and fine wines before retiring to one of the eight comfortable bedrooms located in a cleverly converted stable block. One room has a four-poster and an impressive Victorian bathtub. Breakfast included. **www.the-starr.co.uk**

HARWICH The Pier Hotel & Restaurant
The Quay, Harwich, Essex, CO12 3HH **Tel** *01255 241212* **Rooms** *14*

Set close to where the Pilgrim Fathers set off on their epic voyage, The Pier overlooks neighbouring Felixstowe, the UK's busiest commercial port. Not surprisingly, there's an emphasis on fresh fish in the restaurant. The lovingly and individually furnished rooms are the latest in modern chic style. Includes continental breakfast. **www.milsonhotels.com**

HUNTINGDON Old Bridge   P ⏃   £££
1 High St, Huntingdon, Cambridgeshire, PE29 3TQ   Tel 01480 424300   Rooms 24

While the rooms are comfortable in this ivy-clad hostelry, the focus is very much on food and wine. A light pasta lunch or a full dinner – they cater for it all with aplomb and gusto and will send a menu on request. There is also a wine shop, and they do wine tastings, too. Breakfast is included. Business centre is a plus. **www.huntsbridge.com**

IPSWICH Salthouse Harbour   £££
1 Neptune Quay, Ipswich, Suffolk, IP4 1AX   Tel 01473 226789   Rooms 43

Set right on the River Orwell, from which the writer George Orwell took his name. A substantial old seven-storey warehouse by Neptune Marina has been converted into a trendy loft-style hotel. Bedrooms are en suite with TVs, DVDs and Internet access. The food is equally good and they have an interesting wine list. **www.salthouseharbour.co.uk**

KINGS LYNN Knights Hill Hotel   P ⏃ 🖼 📺 ⚕   ££
South Wootton, Norfolk, PE30 3HQ   Tel 01553 675566   Rooms 79

Close to King's Lynn, the royal estate at Sandringham and the North Norfolk coast, Knights Hill is a restored farm complex in 11 acres of gardens. Style ranges from the relaxed elegance of Rising Lodge to the rustic charms of the Farmers Arms. The health and leisure centre provides a pool and exercise areas. **www.bw-knightshillhotel.co.uk**

LAVENHAM Lavenham Priory   £££
Water St, Lavenham, Sudbury, Suffolk, CO10 9RW   Tel 01787 247404   Rooms 6

At this 13th-century hotel you can have an-out-of-the-world experience at affordable prices, with exposed beams, polished floors and beds carved by a local craftsman. All the rooms are comfortably furnished with all the latest facilities. Breakfast included in the price. Free Wi-Fi is available. **www.lavenhampriory.co.uk**

LAVENHAM Swan   P ⏃   ££££
High St, Lavenham, Sudbury, Suffolk, CO10 9QA   Tel 01787 247477   Rooms 46

Luxuriate below a wealth of exposed beams in a wonderful bedroom named after a local village. Other comforts include rich fabrics, cotton sheets and feather pillows. Some rooms have four-poster beds. The heavily-beamed restaurant has fine food and an extensive wine list. The Garden Bar is much simpler. **www.theswanatlavenham.co.uk**

LOWESTOFT Ivy House Country Hotel   P ⏃ ⚕   £££
Ivy Lane, Beccles Rd, Lowestoft, Suffolk, NR33 8HY   Tel 01502 501353   Rooms 20

Surrounded by countryside, Ivy House has huge gardens, with herbaceous borders and lily ponds. Rooms come with colour TV, tea and coffee making machines and en suite bathrooms. Also has conference rooms and the Crooked Barn restaurant is famous for its cuisine. Includes breakfast. **www.ivyhousecountryhotel.co.uk**

NEWMARKET The Rutland Arms   P ⏃   £££
33 High St, Newmarket, Suffolk, CB8 8NB   Tel 08444 146578   Rooms 46

Newmarket is England's horse-racing capital, and owners, trainers and jockeys are among the regulars at a hotel that is jam-packed with period features. It's one of Newmarket High Street's prime buildings and has a pleasant courtyard for alfresco summer meals. The restaurant serves modern European food. **www.oxfordhotelsandinns.com**

NORTH WALSHAM Beechwood   P ⏃ ⚕   ££
20 Cromer Rd, North Walsham, Norfolk, NR28 0HD   Tel 01692 403231   Rooms 17

In 2003 this establishment became the first two-star hotel ever to win the VisitBritain "Hotel of the Year". Rooms are styled with antique furniture, some with four-poster beds. The highlight of the hotel is chef Steven Norgate's speciality, the "Ten-Mile Dinner", with all ingredients sourced from within 10 miles. **www.beechwood-hotel.co.uk**

NORWICH The Old Rectory   P ⏃ 🏊   £££
103 Yarmouth Rd, Norwich, Norfolk, NR7 0HF   Tel 01603 700772   Rooms 8

The Old Rectory overlooks the River Yare in a pleasant suburb that is now a conservation area. Rooms are beautifully furnished, and chef James Perry has earned a good reputation for his daily changing menus. The outdoor heated pool is a real treat. A self-catering cottage for two is also available. Includes breakfast. **www.oldrectorynorwich.com**

SLOLEY Sloley Hall   P   £££
Sloley, near Norwich, Norfolk, NR12 8HA   Tel 01692 538582   Rooms 4

Within acres of formal gardens, woods and parkland, this elegant late-Georgian manor has been subtly converted into a gracious B&B. The four rooms, each different, are all spacious and very comfortable, and breakfasts are generous. Well located for Norwich and the Norfolk Broads and coast. **www.sloleyhall.com**

SOUTHWOLD The Crown Hotel   P   £££
90 High St, Southwold, Suffolk, IP18 6DP   Tel 01502 722275   Rooms 14

Next to its sister Adnams hotel, the Swan, this traditional hotel with modern facilities stands at the heart of East Anglia's most gracious little seaside resort. The beach is just five minutes walk away. A venue for all four seasons, it's a wonderful retreat from big city pressures and has a delightful bistro-bar. Includes breakfast. **www.adnams.co.uk**

WOODBRIDGE Seckford Hall   P ⏃ 🏊 📺   £££
Woodbridge, Suffolk, IP13 6NU   Tel 01394 385678   Rooms 32

One of East Anglia's most successful country-house hotels, the Tudor façade features mullion windows and giant chimneys above a huge carved oak entrance door. The bedrooms have en suite facilities, and leisure activities include a pool, gym, beauty salon; and a golf club for a small fee. Includes breakfast. **www.seckford.co.uk**

THAMES VALLEY

AYLESBURY Hartwell House
Oxford Rd, Aylesbury, Oxfordshire, HP17 8NR **Tel** *01296 747444* **Rooms** *50*

A member of the Pride of Britain consortium, this hotel was once the home of the exiled King of France. Relax in palatial reception rooms with decorative ceilings, antique furniture and fine paintings. Enjoy the gourmet restaurant, the luxurious spa or walk in the Lancelot "Capability" Brown designed grounds. **www.hartwell-house.com**

BICESTER Bignell Park Hotel
Chesterton, Bicester, Oxfordshire, OX26 1UE **Tel** *01869 326550* **Rooms** *22*

Built in 1740 and set in two and a half well-tended acres, the picturesque Bignell Park Hotel offers outstanding views from its luxurious individually styled rooms. Modern cuisine tempts the taste buds and romantic suppers may be taken on the minstrel's gallery. Includes breakfast. **www.bignellparkhotel.co.uk**

BRACKNELL Coppid Beech Hotel
John Nike Way, Bracknell, Berkshire, RG12 8TF **Tel** *01344 303333* **Rooms** *205*

This popular family and business venue has its own dry ski slope and ice rink. There's a conference room, an evening entertainment programme and a health and fitness suite, which includes a children's pool. The restaurant has a good reputation, and there are also three bistro-pubs and a nightclub. Includes breakfast and Wi-Fi. **www.coppidbeech.com**

BRAY-ON-THAMES Monkey Island Hotel
Bray-on-Thames, Berkshire, SL6 2EE **Tel** *01628 623400* **Rooms** *26*

This unique hotel is set on its own mid-Thames island and is accessible only by boat or footbridge. The large bedrooms are housed in "The Temple", a Palladian fishing lodge built in the 1740s for the Duke of Marlborough. The Pavilion restaurant is housed in a separate building from the same era. **www.monkeyisland.co.uk**

BURFORD The Lamb Inn
Sheep St, Burford, Oxfordshire, OX18 4LR **Tel** *01993 823155* **Rooms** *17*

Among the best in Burford, The Lamb Inn is a classic golden stone building with beamed ceilings. All the bedrooms are comfortably designed with en suite facilities. You can enjoy lunch or a traditional tea here, and dinner is served at the bar or in the main dining room (6:30–9:30pm). Close to many local attractions. **www.cotswold-inns-hotels.co.uk**

CHARLBURY The Bell at Charlbury
Church St, Charlbury, Oxfordshire, OX7 3PP **Tel** *01608 810278* **Rooms** *12*

Mellow golden Cotswold stone gives a handsome air to this convenient town-centre inn. Comfortable accommodation, fine food and drink and proximity to all the Cotswold attractions keep it eternally popular. Charlbury was once a centre for glove makers and Quakers. **www.bellhotel-charlbury.co.uk**

CHIPPERFIELD Two Brewers
The Common, Chipperfield, Hertfordshire, WD4 9BS **Tel** *01923 265266* **Rooms** *20*

Set on the edge of a common in the peaceful village of Chipperfield, the Two Brewers was once the training quarters for great boxers such as Jem Mace and Bob Fitzsimmons. There's a stone-floored taproom and the food is of gastro-pub quality. Bedrooms are furnished in keeping with the country-inn feel. Includes breakfast. Free Wi-Fi is available.

GREAT TEW Falkland Arms
Great Tew, Chipping Norton, Oxfordshire, OX7 4DB **Tel** *01608 683653* **Rooms** *5*

Oak beams, a flagstone floor and an inglenook fireplace set the mood in a Cotswold premises that is part thatch-roofed. This local pub is famous for its drinks and also provides comfortable B&B accommodation. All the rooms have en suite facilities and a colour TV. **www.falklandarms.org.uk**

HARPENDEN Harpenden House
18 Southdown Rd, Harpenden, Hertfordshire, AL5 1PE **Tel** *01582 449955* **Rooms** *76*

Conveniently located close to the M1, Luton Airport and for travelling to London, Harpenden House is a well-integrated mix of modern and traditional, with a loyal following among the business community. The main four-storey building is a handsome Georgian edifice. Also has a cocktail bar. **www.harpendenhouse.co.uk**

HENLEY-ON-THAMES Red Lion
Hart St, Henley-on-Thames, Oxfordshire, RG9 2AR **Tel** *01491 572161* **Rooms** *39*

Overlooking the Royal Regatta course on the Thames and next to the church where the singer Dusty Springfield is buried, the Red Lion is a charming redbrick riverside inn. The pleasant, individually decorated rooms, many of them with river views, offer en suite facilities, and also has a restaurant and a bar. **www.redlionhenley.co.uk**

LONG CRENDON Angel
47 Bicester Rd, Long Crendon, Buckinghamshire, HP18 9EE **Tel** *01844 208268* **Rooms** *4*

In a village 32 km (20 miles) from Oxford, the age-old Angel is renowned for its good food. A Pacific Rim influence pervades the kitchen's mouthwatering output. There are just four elegantly decorated rooms, so personal attention is assured. The Cotswolds are in easy reach, as is Milton Keynes. Includes breakfast. **www.angelrestaurant.co.uk**

Key to Price Guide *see p556* **Key to Symbols** *see back cover flap*

MAIDENHEAD Elva Lodge Hotel   P 🍴   ⓔ

Castle Hill, Maidenhead, Berkshire, SL6 4AD **Tel** *01628 622948* **Rooms** *26*

A standard-style modern hotel close to the centre of Maidenhead, the Elva Lodge is convenient for touring Windsor Castle, Henley and the other attractions of the Thames Valley. Service is efficient and while the hotel is orientated to business travellers, families will also feel welcome. Includes breakfast. Wi-Fi is available. **www.elvalodgehotel.co.uk**

MARLOW Granny Anne's   P   ⓔ

54 Seymour Park Rd, Marlow, Buckinghamshire, SL7 3EP **Tel** *01628 473086* **Rooms** *4*

With a pretty garden, this homely B&B stands out in an expensive area for good value and cosy, traditional comfort. Owners Anne and Roger are especially welcoming, offering afternoon tea to arriving guests. The copious breakfasts feature home-made bread. Two rooms share a bathroom. **www.marlowbedbreakfast.co.uk**

MARLOW MacDonald Compleat Angler   P 🍴 ♿   ⓔⓔⓔ

Marlow Bridge, Marlow, Buckinghamshire, SL7 1RG **Tel** *0844 879 9128* **Rooms** *64*

This is one of England's most renowned historic hostelries. All the rooms are comfortably furnished with en suite facilities and have satellite TV, CD players, playstations and a minibar. Service standards are legendary. Its location overlooking Marlow Weir attracts guests. **www.macdonaldhotels.co.uk/compleatangler**

MARLOW Cliveden   🍴 ≈ 🍴 ♿   ⓔⓔⓔⓔ

Taplow, Berkshire, SL6 0JF **Tel** *01628 668561* **Rooms** *38*

Built by the second Duke of Buckingham in 1666 and once the home of Lord and Lady Astor, this palace above the Thames has welcomed royalty, film stars and writers. All the rooms are handsomely decorated, and they have indoor and outdoor pools and extensive leisure facilities, including tennis, squash and boating. **www.clivedenhouse.co.uk**

MILTON Le Manoir Aux Quat' Saisons   P 🍴 ♿   ⓔⓔⓔⓔⓔ

Church Rd, Great Milton, Oxfordshire, OX44 7PD **Tel** *01844 278881* **Rooms** *32*

This is where French expat Raymond Blanc literally carved his reputation as one of Britain's most acclaimed gourmet chefs. As if the food was not enough, the building is a handsome manor, surrounded by herb gardens, while the bedrooms are a mix of contemporary and traditional styles. **www.manoir.com**

MOULSFORD Beetle & Wedge   P 🍴 ♿   ⓔⓔ

Ferry Lane, Moulsford on Thames, Oxfordshire, OX10 9JF **Tel** *01491 651381* **Rooms** *3*

A gorgeous Thames-side setting is the highlight of this ever-popular upscale hotel and its renowned restaurant, where it always pays to pre-book a table. The style is Anglo-French. The room decor is classic and there are river views and an opulent bathroom. **www.beetleandwedge.co.uk**

NEWBURY The Vineyard At Stockcross   🍴 P 🍴 ≈ 🍴 ♿   ⓔⓔⓔⓔ

Stockcross, Newbury, Berkshire, RG20 8JU **Tel** *01635 528770* **Rooms** *49*

The Vineyard raises the bar when it comes to country-house style. Best rooms are in the original house, but those in the modern wing are also outstanding for their contemporary look. Also available are a spa and treatment rooms. The restaurant serves highly inventive British cuisine. Includes breakfast. **www.the-vineyard.co.uk**

OXFORD Remont   🍴 P ☰ ♿   ⓔⓔ

367 Banbury Road, Summertown, Oxford, OX2 7PL **Tel** *01865 311020* **Rooms** *25*

This boutique B&B in Oxford is a chic, fresh and friendly place to stay. The comfortable rooms range from singles to family size and boast contemporary styling and first-rate electronics including free Wi-Fi. The breakfast buffet is in an airy room overlooking a creatively designed garden. A great bargain. **www.remont-oxford.co.uk**

OXFORD Macdonald Randolph Hotel   🍴 P 🍴 🍴 ♿   ⓔⓔⓔ

Beaumont St, Oxford, Oxfordshire, OX1 2LN **Tel** *0844 879 9132* **Rooms** *151*

The refined Randolph has starred in the TV series *Inspector Morse* and numerous movies, including *Shadowlands*. It's the veritable heart of Oxford, and a favourite for students' parents, American tourists and the business community. Rooms are tastefully decorated. Dining is in classical silver-service mode. **www.macdonaldhotels.co.uk**

OXFORD Old Bank   🍴 P 🍴 ♿   ⓔⓔⓔ

92–94 High St, Oxford, Oxfordshire, OX1 4BJ **Tel** *01865 799599* **Rooms** *42*

This handsome stone building in the heart of this university city used to serve as a bank. Money still flows here as it is often fully booked – tribute to the sharp Armani styling of the rooms and the tempting new British cuisine. Conference room and beauty treatments are a plus; an off-site gym can also be used. **www.oldbank-hotel.co.uk**

OXFORD The Old Parsonage Hotel   P 🍴   ⓔⓔⓔⓔ

1 Banbury Rd, Oxford, Oxfordshire, OX2 6NN **Tel** *01865 310210* **Rooms** *30*

Walls of Cotswold stone screen the Old Parsonage from Oxford's passing hubbub, creating the pleasing illusion of a country retreat. The luxurious bedrooms are air conditioned and now have broadband Internet. Fresh Jersey lobsters are served in the restaurant from May through September. **www.oldparsonage-hotel.co.uk**

READING Millennium Madejski Hotel Reading   🍴 🍴 ≈ 🍴 ♿   ⓔⓔ

Madejski Stadium (Jct 11 on M4), Reading, Berkshire, RG2 0FL **Tel** *0118 925 3500* **Rooms** *201*

John Madejski made his fortune from *Auto Trader* magazines, then saved Reading Football Club from extinction and built them a new stadium of which this hotel is a part. His love of fine food explains the high quality of the fare on offer; the rooms are of an equally high standard. Check the website for special rates. **www.millenniumhotels.com**

ST ALBANS Comfort   £

Ryder House, 27 Holywell Hill, St Albans, Hertfordshire, AL1 1HG **Tel** *01727 442400* **Rooms** *60*

One of America's biggest groups, Choice and their Comfort brand are now making their mark in the UK thanks to consistent quality and value prices. All the rooms are spacious, with big and firm beds. This hotel occupies a historic building in the centre of this hilltop town that was once a Roman stronghold. **www.choicehotels.com**

WINDSOR Sir Christopher Wren's House Hotel & Spa   £££££

Thames St, Windsor, Berkshire, SL4 1PX **Tel** *01753 861354* **Rooms** *96*

Stroll through the pedestrianized Thames Bridge from Eton College and on the right side is this handsome Georgian mansion. The riverside setting makes for a romantic dining experience while the spacious, individualized rooms brim with antiques. They also have a gym and a spa offering beauty treatments. **www.sirchristopherwren.co.uk**

WITNEY Rectory Farm   £

Northmoor, Witney, Oxfordshire **Tel** *01865 300207* **Rooms** *2*

Located 10 miles (16 km) from Oxford, this grand 16th-century farmhouse has soft yellow-stone walls, lofty gables and arching windows. There are just two lovely B&B rooms, as well as self-contained cottages for rent. The Rectory is still a working family farm, and the eggs cooked for breakfast come fresh from the hens. **www.oxtowns.co.uk/rectoryfarm**

YATTENDON Royal Oak   ££

The Square, Yattendon, Thatcham, Berkshire, RG18 OUG **Tel** *01635 201325* **Rooms** *7*

A classic country pub in Berkshire, serving a pretty little village and tourists alike. The mood is smart and informal, and the contemporary take on traditional food is deservedly award-winning. All rooms are individually decorated and en suite. Includes breakfast. **www.royaloakyattendon.com**

WESSEX

ABBOTSBURY The Abbey House   £

Church St, Abbotsbury, Dorset, DT3 4JJ **Tel** *01305 871330* **Rooms** *5*

Set in a large, stone country house, this charming guesthouse is well situated for exploring the beautiful Jurassic coast. The rooms offer a high level of comfort, with flat-screen TVs and king-size beds; most are en suite and one has a private sitting room. The restaurant and tea room is open Mar–Oct. **www.theabbeyhouse.co.uk**

BATH Bath Youth Hostel   £

Bathwick Hill, Bath, Somerset, BS2 6JZ **Tel** *0845 371 9303* **Rooms** *27*

This hostel occupies a beautiful Italianate mansion set in its own gardens, a short walk from the centre of Bath and all its amenities. The rooms are simple and clean, and the hostel is open all year round with 24-hour access. Parking is free on nearby Bathwick Hill. **www.yha.org.uk**

BATH Villa Magdala   ££

Henrietta Rd, Bath, Somerset, BA2 6LX **Tel** *01225 466329* **Rooms** *20*

A boutique B&B hotel, Villa Magdala is set in a peaceful location overlooking lovely Henrietta Park. It's a five-minute flat walk to the Roman baths and city centre shops. This is one of the few local hotels to have on-site guest parking. Includes breakfast and free Wi-Fi. **www.villamagdala.co.uk**

BATH The Queensberry Hotel   £££

Russell St, Bath, Somerset, BA1 2QF **Tel** *01225 447928* **Rooms** *29*

A boutique hotel in the centre of Bath that offers great service including a concierge with plenty of ideas about exploring the city. All rooms are individually designed, and the hotel's Olive Tree restaurant is one of the finest in Bath. The Old Q Bar here is popular for pre-dinner drinks. **www.thequeensberry.co.uk**

BATH The Windsor Guest Hotel   £££

69 Gt Pulteney St, Bath, Somerset, BA2 4DL **Tel** *01225 422100* **Rooms** *15*

Set in an elegant Grade I protected Georgian terrace, just a short walk from Pulteney Bridge and the heart of Bath, the rooms in this hotel are individually decorated. Rooms are elegantly furnished and facilities include Wi-Fi. The price also includes breakfast. **www.bathwindsorguesthouse.co.uk**

BATH Royal Crescent   ££££

16 Royal Crescent, Bath, Somerset, BA1 2LS **Tel** *01225 823333* **Rooms** *45*

Located at the centre of Bath's glorious semi-circle of Georgian grandiosity. The simple but imposing Bath stone façade is the first glimpse of one of Britain's great hotels. Rooms brim with antiques, beds are luxuriant, there's a spa and the restaurant is elegance personified. Stay on B&B or half-board basis. **www.royalcrescent.co.uk**

BATH The Bath Priory Hotel   £££££

Weston Rd, Bath, Somerset, BA1 2XT **Tel** *01225 331922* **Rooms** *32*

Located just outside the centre of Bath, this hotel offers upmarket luxury accommodation. There are lovely gardens for the summer months, and roaring fires and comfortable sofas make for a cosy stay in winter. The restaurant boasts local and regional awards, and there is a superb boutique spa. **www.thebathpriory.co.uk**

BLANDFORD FORUM The Crown Hotel

*West St, Blandford Forum, Dorset, DT11 7AJ Tel 01258 456626 **Rooms** 32*

A former coaching inn at the heart of a pretty market town, on the edge of Salisbury Plain, with strong military connections, including a fascinating tank museum nearby. Rooms are spacious and well equipped. The Georgian hotel boasts en suite rooms throughout and high-speed Wi-Fi. Breakfast is included. **www.innforanight.co.uk**

BOURNEMOUTH Arlington Hotel

*Exeter Park Rd, Bournemouth, Dorset, BH2 5BD Tel 01202 552879 **Rooms** 28*

Situated in the town centre, the Arlington stands in its own grounds among scented pine trees. The well-equipped rooms are comfortable, and the hotel prides itself on friendly hospitality. The hotel's private gateways lead directly into the Bournemouth flower gardens, which are just a short walk from the beach. **www.arlingtonbournemouth.co.uk**

BOURNEMOUTH Avalon Beach Hotel

*43 Grand Av, Southbourne, Bournemouth, Dorset, BH6 3SY Tel 01202 425370 **Rooms** 9*

Just a few minutes from Southbourne's Blue Flag beach is this small, family-run hotel. The fantastic personal service here includes great family options – children's entertainment, babysitting, self-catering and quality home cooking. There are large coastal gardens and a beach hut for hire. Internet access is also available. **www.avalon-beach-hotel.co.uk**

BOURNEMOUTH Bay View Breeze Court

*35 East Overcliff Drive, Bournemouth, Dorset, BH1 3AH Tel 01202 294449 **Rooms** 70*

An East Cliff location gives lovely panoramic views across Bournemouth Bay. This comfortable family-run hotel serves international cuisine. Snooker, pool, darts and games machines are located in the popular Purbeck suite. There are relaxing lounges and sun terraces. **www.bayviewbreeze.co.uk**

BOURNEMOUTH Miramar

*East Overcliff Dr, Bournemouth, Dorset, BH1 3AL Tel 01202 556581 **Rooms** 43*

The Miramar occupies a stunning vantage point, with views to the Isle of Wight and the Purbeck Hills. This attractive Edwardian mansion offers a wide range of rooms and suites. It has a restaurant as well as terraces with lawns sweeping down towards the sea. Guests can use a local gym. **www.miramar-bournemouth.com**

BOURNEMOUTH Urban Beach Hotel

*23 Argyll Rd, Bournemouth, Dorset, BH5 1EB Tel 01202 301509 **Rooms** 12*

This Victorian seaside hotel has had a makeover to create a youthful, funky boutique hotel in the up-and-coming Boscombe area of Bournemouth. It boasts an award-winning bar and bistro and offers access to a nearby health club and swimming pool. Walking distance from the beach and town. Children welcome. **www.urbanbeach.co.uk**

BRADFORD-ON-AVON Bradford Old Windmill

*4 Masons Lane, Bradford-on-Avon, Wiltshire, BA15 1QN Tel 01225 866842 **Rooms** 3*

And now for something completely different. Yes, it really is an old and extremely atmospheric stone windmill – and the round room has a circular bed. Evening meals are vegetarian but breakfast offers hearty fare for meat-eaters, vegetarians and vegans alike. Price includes breakfast. **www.bradfordoldwindmill.co.uk**

BRIDPORT The Bull Hotel

*34 East St, Bridport, Dorset, DT6 3LF Tel 01308 422878 **Rooms** 15*

A step away from Bridport's busy market streets is this glamorous hotel. Housed in a former 17th-century coaching inn, the hotel offers vintage-styled rooms, four-poster beds, rolltop baths and swanky cosmetics. The relaxed restaurant serves anything from brunch to canapés. Children welcome. **www.thebullhotel.co.uk**

BRISTOL Future Inn Cabot Circus

*Bond St South, Bristol, BS1 3EN Tel 0845 094 5588 **Rooms** 149*

A functional, cheap central hotel across the busy road from Cabot Circus shopping centre in the heart of the city. The Chophouse restaurant has live entertainment including jazz. Parking is free and there is a Wi-Fi available. A good choice for business travellers on a budget. **www.futureinns.co.uk/bristol**

BRISTOL Radisson Blu

*Broad Quay, Bristol, BS1 4BY Tel 01179 349500 **Rooms** 176*

This central, modern glass-fronted hotel offers bright and functional rooms, a gym and free high speed Internet access. The hotel's proximity to the waterfront makes it a good choice for dining out. There is also an art-house cinema nearby. **www.radissonblu.co.uk/hotel-bristol**

BRISTOL Hotel du Vin

*The Sugar House, Narrow Lewins Mead, Bristol, BS1 2NU Tel 0117 925 5577 **Rooms** 40*

Bristol's finest hotel is a former sugar house occupying a collection of Grade II listed warehouses dating to the 1700s. The loft suites are sensational, while the classy restaurant is one of the best in town. The hotel is an easy walk to the centre and the waterfront and is good for both business and leisure travellers. **www.hotelduvin.com**

BRISTOL Mercure Brigstow

*5–7 Welsh Back, Bristol, Somerset, BS1 4SP Tel 0117 929 1030 **Rooms** 116*

Occupying a prime city centre position on the banks of the River Avon, the Mercure Brigstow is at the heart of an historic but vigorously modern city. Facilities are first rate, including air conditioning and even a plasma screen in the bathroom. The business centre is well equipped, and guests can use a local health club. **www.mercure.com**

BRISTOL The Avon Gorge Hotel
£££

Sion Hill, Clifton, Bristol, BS8 4LD **Tel** *0117 9738 955* **Rooms** *75*

In Georgian Clifton, this well-placed hotel has the city's best view over the gorge and across to Brunel's famous suspension bridge. Rooms are simple but comfortable, and there is a fantastic outdoor patio for dining in summer. Perfect for university visitors or a romantic break. **www.theavongorge.com**

CALNE Lansdowne Strand Hotel
£

The Strand, Calne, Wiltshire, SN11 0EH **Tel** *01249 812488* **Rooms** *25*

In the centre of the market town, this 16th-century former coaching inn still retains many period features. Individually decorated rooms vary in size. There are two bars; one offers a wide selection of ales and a cosy fire to sit by. An interesting menu and choice of wines is available in the brasserie-style restaurant. **www.lansdownestrand.co.uk**

CASTLE COMBE The Manor House Hotel & Golf Club
££££

Castle Combe, Chippenham, Wiltshire, SN14 7HR **Tel** *01249 782206* **Rooms** *48*

A secluded valley position on its own golf course makes this a truly idyllic retreat within easy reach of both Bath and the Cotswolds. Accommodation is partly in a row of individual cottages and partly in the main Jacobean-styled house. The hotel's Bybrook restaurant has excellent cuisine and a Michelin star. **www.exclusivehotels.co.uk**

DORCHESTER Casterbridge
££

49 High East St, Dorchester, Dorset, DT1 1HU **Tel** *01305 264043* **Rooms** *14*

Here's a peaceful haven in a busy county town. Dorchester was the Casterbridge in Thomas Hardy's novel, *The Mayor of Casterbridge,* hence the name of this hotel. Ground floor rooms enjoy a patio and have wheelchair access. Four-poster room available. Enjoy breakfast in the dining room or the conservatory. **www.thecasterbridge.co.uk**

DULVERTON Three Acres Country House
££

Brushford, Dulverton, Somerset, TA22 9AR **Tel** *01398 323730* **Rooms** *6*

Just south of Dulverton, this award-winning B&B occupies a tranquil setting on a hill at the edge of Exmoor National Park. It is perfect for a real country-house experience, with hearty breakfasts, log fires and lovely views. Light suppers are available at the bar, make sure you try the home-made sloe gin. **www.threeacrescountryhouse.co.uk**

EVERSHOT Summer Lodge
£££££

Evershot, Dorset, DT2 0JR **Tel** *01935 482000* **Rooms** *24*

Set in the picturesque village of Evershot, at the heart of Thomas Hardy's Wessex, this Relais et Châteaux property has a spa as well as a large heated indoor swimming pool. Enjoy croquet, tennis or an alfresco afternoon tea. Rooms are cozy yet highly luxurious. **www.summerlodgehotel.co.uk**

EYPE'S Eype's Mouth Country Hotel
££

Eype, Bridport, Dorset, DT6 6AL **Tel** *01308 423300* **Rooms** *17*

With dramatic sea views and located just a few minutes walk to the beach, this hotel occupies a coveted position on the heritage coast, with immediate access to the much-lauded coastal path. Family-run, it exudes a welcoming and relaxed atmosphere, ensuring a pleasant and comfortable stay. Includes breakfast. **www.eypesmouthhotel.co.uk**

GILLINGHAM Stock Hill Country House Hotel & Restaurant
£££££

Stockhill, Gillingham, Dorset, SP8 5NR **Tel** *01747 823626* **Rooms** *9*

A beech-lined drive leads to the very definition of peace and seclusion. Stock Hill is one of the country's finest country-house hotels. Chef and patron Peter Hauser and his wife Nita have spent two decades refurbishing to exacting standards. Provides business facilities, and price includes dinner. **www.stockhillhouse.co.uk**

LACOCK At the Sign of the Angel
£££

6 Church St, Lacock, Wiltshire, SN15 2LB **Tel** *01249 730230* **Rooms** *6*

If you are looking for character, you've found it. Run by the Levis family since 1953, the hotel has low beams, log fires and squeaky floorboards. Luxuriously furnished bedrooms have oak-panelled walls and antique furniture. Includes breakfast. Lacock is now owned by the National Trust. **www.lacock.co.uk**

LONGLEAT The Bath Arms
£££

Longleat Estate, Horningsham, Warminster, Wiltshire, BA12 7LY **Tel** *01985 844308* **Rooms** *15*

This unusual, ivy-clad pub offers quirky, boutique-styled rooms, some with free-standing Victorian baths. Popular with the hunting set, it is also dog- and child-friendly and offers half price rooms during the week. The Lodge, over-looking Longleat House, provides self-contained family accommodation. **www.batharms.co.uk**

LYME REGIS 1 Lyme Town House
££

1 Pound St, Lyme Regis, Dorset, DT7 3HZ **Tel** *01297 442499* **Rooms** *7*

An upmarket B&B housed in a Grade II listed townhouse. The focus here is on luxury with Osborne & Little wallpaper, Designers Guild fabrics and Molton Brown toiletries. The breakfasts are excellent; picnics are provided on request. A good base from which to explore the Jurassic Coast and nearby seafood restaurants. Free Wi-Fi. **www.1lymetownhouse.com**

LYME REGIS Hotel Alexandra
£££

Pound St, Lyme Regis, Dorset, DT7 3HZ **Tel** *01297 442010* **Rooms** *24*

Lauded for its hospitality, comfort and good food, the Alexandra has sloping lawns and magnificent views of the Cobb. All the bedrooms are finely decorated and have private bathrooms. Elegant dining room with first-class menu and wine list. Management can arrange guided fossil hunting. **www.hotelalexandra.co.uk**

Key to Price Guide *see p556* **Key to Symbols** *see back cover flap*

MALMESBURY The Old Bell

*Abbey Row, Wiltshire, SN16 0BW Tel 01666 822344 **Rooms** 33*

Established in 1220 adjacent to historic Malmesbury Abbey, it is reputed to be Britain's oldest purpose-built hotel. Welcoming rooms and outstanding levels of service amid the ambience of a bygone age. Pretty terrace for outdoor dining in summer. Outstanding wine list. Includes breakfast. **www.oldbellhotel.co.uk**

MALMESBURY The Rectory Hotel

*Crudwell, Malmesbury, Wiltshire, SN16 9EP Tel 01666 577194 **Rooms** 12*

This elegant period retreat in the Cotswolds has had style magazines all in a lather about its modern country cool design. Its three acres of Victorian walled gardens include an outdoor heated sunken swimming pool while the food here is fantastic. A good base from which to explore the area. **www.therectoryhotel.com**

PORLOCK WEIR The Café

*Porlock Weir, Minehead, Somerset, TA24 8PB Tel 01643 863300 **Rooms** 5*

The Café stands on one of Europe's most beautiful stretches of coast, where thick woods sweep down to the sea. Bedrooms are comfortably furnished and the inventively presented food is quite exquisite. It also has a beautiful garden and is close to nearby Exmoor. Breakfast included. Dog friendly. **www.thecafeatporlockweir.co.uk**

ROOKSBRIDGE Bristol Camper Company

Acacia Farm, Bristol Rd, Rooksbridge, Bristol, BS26 2TA Tel 0845 4674147

Half an hour south of Bristol, this unusual operation offers retro and brand new VW campervans to help you explore the West Country in style. Vans sleep up to four and can be delivered to Bristol Airport or central Bristol on request. Rates from £325 for a 3-day weekend. **www.thebristolcampercompany.co.uk**

SALISBURY St Ann's House

*32–34 St Ann St, Salisbury, Wiltshire, SP1 2DP Tel 01722 335657 **Rooms** 8*

In the heart of Salisbury, this much-recommended Georgian B&B has simple, stylish rooms with chandeliers and sash windows. There are pet-friendly rooms and fantastic private dining available from Andrew Lloyd Webber's former personal chef. Limited parking, but bike storage available. **www.stannshouse.co.uk**

SHEPTON MALLET Charlton House

*Charlton Rd, Somerset, BA4 4PR Tel 01749 342008 **Rooms** 27*

Decorated with imagination, flair and a sense of theatre, this country-house hotel is set amid rolling hills just 18 miles (30 km) south of Bath. Relaxation comes easy in an ambience of informal splendour. The outstanding restaurant uses local produce and the spa is special. Includes breakfast. **www.charltonhousehotel.com**

SOMERSET Lord Poulett Arms

*Hinton St George, Somerset, TA17 8SE Tel 01460 73149 **Rooms** 4*

A multi-award-winning pub in the heart of Somerset. The traditional rooms boast antique beds, rolltop baths and Roberts radios. A roaring fire greets visitors in the pub downstairs where punters can enjoy cider and real ales. Minimum stay of two nights at weekends. **www.lordpoulettarms.com**

STON EASTON Ston Easton Park

*Ston Easton, nr Bath, Somerset, BA3 4DF Tel 01761 241631 **Rooms** 22*

An elegant Palladian mansion sited on a romantic estate offering upscale country life at its best. Wonderfully ornate ceilings, masses of antique furniture and priceless paintings make for a comfortable stay while the cuisine is truly sublime. Facilities include conference and business meeting rooms. Inclusive of breakfast. **www.stoneaston.co.uk**

TAUNTON Meryan House

*Bishops Hill Road, Taunton, Somerset, TA1 5EG Tel 01823 337445 **Rooms** 6*

Antique furniture and an eye-catching selection of paintings, ornaments and chandeliers adorn this handsome 600-year-old country-house hotel, in a village just a mile (2 km) from Taunton town centre. The gardens are a year-round delight, and menus in the restaurant feature produce. Free Wi-Fi. **www.meryanhouse.co.uk**

TAUNTON The Mount Somerset

*Lower Henlade, Somerset, TA3 5NB Tel 01823 442500 **Rooms** 19*

Cradled by the Quantock and Blackdown Hills, the Regency-styled Mount is noted for the elegance and warmth of its greeting. Log fires, abundant scatter cushions and a superb sweeping staircase reek of the good life. Just the place for a calm, unhurried stay. Includes breakfast. **www.themountsomersethotelandspa.com**

WAREHAM The Priory

*Church Green, Wareham, Dorset, BH20 4ND Tel 01929 551666 **Rooms** 18*

Landscaped gardens fronting the River Frome, it offers fine views of the Purbeck Hills. Sumptuous yet relaxed in style, this 16th-century masterpiece has moorings for those arriving by boat. Furnished with antiques, all rooms are en suite, and you may stay in the main house or the hotel's houseboats. Includes breakfast. **www.theprioryhotel.co.uk**

WELLS The Crown At Wells

*Market Place, Wells, Somerset, BA5 2RP Tel 01749 673457 **Rooms** 15*

Set in the bustling market place at the centre of one of England's smallest cities, this attractive Grade II listed building is overlooked by the cathedral and the Bishops Palace, with its moat. All the bedrooms are comfortably furnished with en suite facilities, and Anton's Bistrot is well known for its excellent food. **www.crownatwells.co.uk**

WEYMOUTH Seaham   ⓔ
3 Waterloo Place, Dorset, DT4 7NU **Tel** *01305 782010* **Rooms** *5*

A Grade II listed guesthouse, the Seaham dates back to the 19th century and is located close to the town centre and picturesque harbour. The bedrooms are simply decorated and have en suite facilities. Breakfast is included. Children are not welcome. **www.theseahamweymouth.co.uk**

WOOKEY HOLE Wookey Hole Inn   🍴 ♿   ⓔⓔ
Wookey Hole, Somerset, BA5 1BP **Tel** *01749 676677* **Rooms** *5*

Outwardly a traditional pub on the village's main street, inside the decor is Bohemian; so too is its motto: "peace, love and good food". The rooms are funky and stylish, the restaurant is very popular and there is a walled sculpture garden. Just two minutes' walk from Wookey Hole Caves. **www.wookeyholeinn.com**

WOOTTON BASSETT School House Hotel and Restaurant   🍴 ♿   ⓔ
Hook St, Hook, Swindon, Wiltshire, SN4 8EF **Tel** *01793 851198* **Rooms** *11*

Close to Swindon and at the gateway to the Cotswolds, this transformed Victorian school building is just minutes from Junction 16 on the M4. Car hire, station and airport transfers can be arranged. The restaurant has a Victorian beamed ceiling. Suitable for business travellers as well. Includes breakfast. **www.schoolhotel.com**

DEVON AND CORNWALL

BABBACOMBE BEACH The Cary Arms   🅿 🍴 ♿   ⓔⓔⓔ
Babbacombe Beach, South Devon, TQ1 3LX **Tel** *01803 327110* **Rooms** *8*

This highly rated inn on the beach between Exeter and Torquay offers chic rooms that open onto terraces. One-, two- and four-bedroomed cottages are also available. The bar serves gastropub food under beamed ceilings, while the spa offers an array of treatments. Dogs welcome. **www.caryarms.co.uk**

BARNSTAPLE Broomhill Art Hotel   🅿 🍴 ♿   ⓔ
Muddiford, Barnstaple, North Devon, EX31 4EX **Tel** *01271 850262* **Rooms** *6*

Surrounded by a modern sculpture park, this quirky hotel is a short drive from the north Devon beaches and is ideally located for woodland walks. The comfortable rooms have art on the walls, and the restaurant serves "slow food" designed to respect local produce. Jazz nights and dining packages also available. **www.broomhillart.co.uk**

BIGBURY-ON-SEA Burgh Island   🛏 🍴 🏊 🍴   ⓔⓔⓔⓔⓔ
Burgh Island, Bigbury-On-Sea, South Devon, TQ7 4BG **Tel** *01548 810514* **Rooms** *25*

This Art Deco treasure set 200 m (656 ft) off the South Devon coast is where Agatha Christie wrote two of her novels. Rooms are individually decorated with all the modern facilities. Call for the elevated four-wheel drive or stroll by the sea. Guests can swim in a natural rock pool. Inclusive of breakfast and dinner. **www.burghisland.com**

BOSCASTLE The Old Rectory   ⓔⓔ
St Juliot, Boscastle, Cornwall, PL35 0BT **Tel** *01840 250225* **Rooms** *4*

Beautiful gardens surround the house where Thomas Hardy fell in love with Emma Lavinia Gifford, leading to some of his best poetry. A family home that has been renovated and decorated beautifully in period style. The breakfast is all-inclusive in this B&B close to the coast and about 30 miles (50 km) from the Eden Project. **www.stjuliot.com**

BUDE Elements   🅿 🍴 🍴   ⓔ
Marine Drive, Widemouth Bay, Bude, North Cornwall, EX23 0LZ **Tel** *01288 352386* **Rooms** *11*

Between Bude and Widemouth Bay, this clifftop hotel boasts great views. The simple, comfortable rooms are styled in white and navy blue with wooden floors, while facilities include a bistro, bar, gym and sauna. There are panoramic views of the sea from the bistro. Surf coaching, golf, sailing, cycling and more on offer. **www.elements-life.co.uk**

CHAGFORD Three Crowns Hotel   🍴   ⓔⓔ
High St, Chagford, Devon, TQ13 8AJ **Tel** *01647 433444* **Rooms** *18*

This 13th-century stone-built inn evokes a long history with its mullion windows, massive oak beams, great open fireplace and four-poster rooms. It is at the heart of Dartmoor National Park and conveniently located close to the Eden Project and the Lost Gardens of Heligan. Breakfast is included. **www.chagford-accom.co.uk**

CHAGFORD Gidleigh Park   🍴 ♿   ⓔⓔⓔⓔⓔ
Gidleigh, Chagford, Devon, TQ13 8HH **Tel** *01647 432367* **Rooms** *24*

Gidleigh Park has long been established as one of the UK's finest country-house hotels. Family-owned and in the heart of Dartmoor, it has fabulous gardens, tennis and croquet courts, a bowling green and a golf course. The main event is dinner: chef Michael Caines MBE has won two Michelin stars for his work here. **www.gidleigh.com**

CREDITON The Lamb Inn   🅿 🍴   ⓔ
The Square, Sandford, Crediton, Devon, EX17 4LW **Tel** *01363 773676* **Rooms** *6*

The luxury spacious rooms, unexpected above a village pub, have solar-powered underfloor heating, orthopaedic beds and power showers. There is also a cinema and conference rooms. The pub is a 16th-century coaching inn and serves food to order seven days a week. **www.lambinnsandford.co.uk**

DARTMOOR The Cherrybrook
P ⑪ ⓔⓔⓔ

Two Bridges, Dartmoor, Devon, PL20 6SP **Tel** *01822 880260* **Rooms** *7*

A remote, 200-year-old farmhouse, in the heart of Dartmoor National Park, houses this B&B. Rooms are comfortable and have views of the moor. Facilities include free Wi-Fi, flat screen TVs and DVD players, plus a bar and restaurant. Drying facilities are available for walkers and cyclists. Dogs are welcome. **www.thecherrybrook.co.uk**

EXETER Innkeeper's Lodge Exeter East
⑪ & ⓔ

Clyst St George, Exeter, Devon, EX3 OQJ **Tel** *01392 876121* **Rooms** *21*

A fast-growing nationwide chain of modern budget hotels, Innkeeper's Lodge choose their sites well. This one is located just off the M5, making it a suitable jumping off point for forays into the deepest West Country. Continental breakfast is complimentary. **www.innkeeperslodge.com/exetereast**

EXETER Magdalen Chapter
⊠ ⑪ ⟨⟩ ⓔⓔⓔ

Magdalen St, Exeter, Devon, EX2 4HY **Tel** *01392 281000* **Rooms** *46*

This landmark hotel, originally an eye hospital, has a high-tech, contemporary feel inside. Rooms have satellite TV, DVD players, iPads and free mini-bars. The restaurant serves classic British seasonal fare, and there is a modern spa. **www.themagdalenchapter.com**

FALMOUTH Budock Vean Hotel On The River
⊠ ⑪ ⌫ & ⓔⓔ

Helford Passage, Mawnan Smith, Falmouth, Cornwall, TR11 5LG **Tel** *01326 250288* **Rooms** *57*

This formal country hotel is set in 65 acres of grounds that lead down to the Helford River. The bedrooms have all the latest facilities, and some have fine views of the gardens and the golf course. They also have a swimming pool, health spa, two tennis courts and a fine restaurant, and they offer boat trips. Includes breakfast and dinner. **www.budockvean.co.uk**

FOWEY The Old Quay House
P ⑪ ⓔⓔⓔ

28 Fore St, Fowey, Cornwall, PL23 1AQ **Tel** *01726 833302* **Rooms** *11*

The individually styled rooms at this waterside hotel offer an experience of luxurious indulgence, with natural fabrics, warm colours and splendid views of the surrounding area. The Old Quay House blends 150 years of history with boutique hotel style and boasts an award-winning restaurant. **www.theoldquayhouse.com**

ILFRACOMBE Hamptons Hotel
P ⓔⓔ

Excelsior Villas, Torrs Park, Ilfracombe, Devon, EX34 8AZ **Tel** *01271 864246* **Rooms** *6*

This family-run B&B on the north Devon coast overlooks Ilfracombe and has great sea views. The chic rooms have luxury bedding, designer toiletries and mod cons such as free Wi-Fi and DVD players. Well placed for beaches, surfing, golf and the Southwest Coastal Path. **www.thehamptonshotel.com**

ISLES OF SCILLY Star Castle Hotel
⑪ ⌫ & ⓔⓔⓔ

St Mary's, Isles of Scilly, TR21 0JA **Tel** *01720 422317* **Rooms** *38*

A historic, star-shaped castle, dating back to the reign of Elizabeth I, is the setting for this half-board hotel. The refurbished interior has white walls; bright, comfortable rooms; two restaurants and a bar in what was originally the dungeon. Transport from the mainland can be arranged. **www.star-castle.co.uk**

ISLES OF SCILLY Hell Bay
⑪ ⌫ ⟨⟩ & ⓔⓔⓔⓔ

Bryher, Isles of Scilly, TR23 OPR **Tel** *01720 422947* **Rooms** *25*

New England and the Caribbean meet Cornwall's offshore islands. Lloyd Loom furnishing and Malabar fabrics are set against cool ocean blues and greens. Robert and Lucy Dorrien-Smith have filled this secluded haven of tranquility with the works of renowned artists, including Barbara Hepworth. Breakfast and dinner inclusive. **www.hellbay.co.uk**

LANDEWEDNACK Landewednack House
⑪ ⌫ ⓔⓔ

Church Cove, Landewednack, The Lizard, Cornwall, TR12 7PQ **Tel** *01326 290909* **Rooms** *5*

This former rectory is today a quintessential country-house B&B. There is a secluded two-acre walled garden with sea views and a heated swimming pool to keep you on-site, though the surrounding countryside is delightful. There is also a self-contained two-bedroom annexe. Full breakfast is included in the price. **www.landewednackhouse.com**

LUNDY ISLAND Landmark Trust
ⓔⓔⓔⓔ

Lundy Shore Office, The Quay, Bideford, Devon, EX39 2LY **Tel** *01271 863636* **Rooms** *23*

The 17 historic cottages on Lundy ("Puffin") Island, off the coast of Devon, are reached by boat from Ilfracombe and Bideford and can be booked through the Landmark Trust. Lundy Island offers outstanding natural beauty and is small enough to walk round in an afternoon. All accommodation is self catering. **www.lundyisland.co.uk**

LYNMOUTH The Rising Sun
⑪ ⓔⓔⓔ

Harbourside, Lynmouth, Devon, EX35 6EG **Tel** *01598 753223* **Rooms** *14*

Percy Bysshe Shelley honeymooned in this 14th-century thatched smugglers inn. It overlooks Lynmouth's picturesque harbour and the highest hogback cliffs in England. Oak panelling, wonky ceilings, beachstone walls and uneven floorboards – it's atmosphere all the way, with well-appointed rooms. **www.risingsunlynmouth.co.uk**

MAWGAN PORTH Bedruthan Steps
⊠ P ⑪ ⌫ ⟨⟩ & ⓔⓔⓔⓔ

Mawgan Porth, Cornwall, TR8 4BU **Tel** *01637 860555* **Rooms** *101*

A family-friendly hotel with indoor and outdoor playground areas, children's clubs and a surf shack. The Ocean Spa is an ideal place to wind down while the safe, sandy beach just outside is great for children. Other facilities include a restaurant, bar, Internet access and childminding services. Price includes dinner. **www.bedruthan.com**

MAWGAN PORTH The Scarlet

Tredragon Rd, Mawgan Porth, Cornwall, TR8 4DQ **Tel** *01637 861800* **Rooms** *37*

Seriously stylish, this eco-friendly hotel has excellent facilities including a superb restaurant with floor-to-ceiling windows, an Ayurvedic spa, indoor and outdoor pools and sun decks and terraces. All rooms have beach views, and there are plenty of activities from knitting classes to guided wild swimming. Adults only. **www.scarlethotel.co.uk**

MEMBURY Lea Hill

Membury, Axminster, Devon, EX13 7AQ **Tel** *01404 881881* **Rooms** *2*

This group of cottages and apartments lies in peaceful Devon countryside, 9 miles (15 km) from the coast. Converted from an old farmhouse and its barns, Lea Hill offers fully furnished self-catering accommodation set in lovely gardens. Dogs welcome. **www.leahill.co.uk**

MORTEHOE Lundy House Hotel

Chapel Hill, Mortehoe, North Devon, EX34 7DZ **Tel** *01271 870372* **Rooms** *8*

Wet suits and surfboards can be rented at nearby Woolacombe Beach or you can ramble over Exmoor. You might, though, prefer to simply relax while admiring the view over to the romantic offshore Lundy Island and watch the sunset. Five rooms have sea views. Closed Nov–Mar. **www.lundyhousehotel.co.uk**

MOUSEHOLE Old Coastguard Hotel

The Parade, Mousehole, Penzance, Cornwall, TR19 6PR **Tel** *01736 731222* **Rooms** *14*

Razed in 1595 by raiders from the Spanish Armada, tiny Mousehole has survived as a classic Cornish fishing village. As the name implies, this stylish hotel with fluffy towels and crisp white linen, overlooks the local maritime scene. Most rooms have sea views. Breakfast included. **www.oldcoastguardhotel.co.uk**

MULLION The Polurrian Bay Hotel

Mullion, South Cornwall, TR12 7EN **Tel** *01326 240421* **Rooms** *39*

Excellent service is still a hallmark here, but what guests always talk about most is the stunning cliff-top location, set in beautiful landscaped gardens and with glorious views across to St Michael's Mount. All rooms are en suite and most have sea views. Includes breakfast and access to the spa. **www.polurrianhotel.com**

NEWQUAY Sands Resort

Watergate Rd, Porth, Newquay, Cornwall, TR7 3LX **Tel** *01637 872864* **Rooms** *88*

Spacious rooms with separate sleeping space for children await at this North Cornwall family favourite. Close to the golden sand beaches and surf, this full-on holiday resort features the Ocean Breeze Spa's relaxing therapies plus four age-banded children's clubs. Good-value rates include full breakfast. **www.sandsresort.co.uk**

NEWQUAY The Headland Hotel

Fistral Beach, Newquay, Cornwall, TR7 1EW **Tel** *01637 872211* **Rooms** *94*

High Victorian Gothic architecture dominating the cliff above one of Newquay's finest beaches gives this four-star hotel an imposing setting. Inside it is a friendly, family-orientated place and they also run 40 luxurious cottages. The rooms are comfortably furnished, and many have sea views. **www.headlandhotel.co.uk**

NEWQUAY Watergate Bay Hotel

On the beach, Watergate Bay, TR8 4AA **Tel** *01637 860543* **Rooms** *69*

A trendy hotel with a chic, contemporary interior, the Watergate caters for both a young crowd and families. Rooms are well-equipped with iPod docks and Wi-Fi; the family suites sleep up to six. Watersports enthusiasts will welcome the Extreme Academy, while foodies can visit Jamie Oliver's Fifteen, both nearby (*see p628*). **www.watergatebay.co.uk**

OKEHAMPTON Lewtrenchard Manor

Lewdown, nr Okehampton, Devon, EX20 4PN **Tel** *01566 783222* **Rooms** *14*

Barely touched by time, this Jacobean delight is built on the site of an even earlier manor and is now a country-house retreat. It is famed for its heavenly 17th-century gardens and gourmet delights. The rooms are oak-panelled and decorated with rich fabrics and antiques. Full breakfast is inclusive. **www.lewtrenchard.co.uk**

OTTERY ST MARY Tumbling Weir

Canaan Way, Ottery St Mary, nr Exeter, Devon, EX11 1AQ **Tel** *01404 812752* **Rooms** *10*

A thatched hotel set in half-an-acre of beautiful gardens beside a millstream. Conveniently located close to the M5, this gem is a short drive from historic Exeter and the coast. Comfortable beds and en-suite bathrooms, while the restaurant creates wonderful dishes from local produce. **www.tumblingweirhotel.co.uk**

PADSTOW The Seafood Restaurant

Riverside, Padstow, Cornwall, PL28 8BY **Tel** *01841 532700* **Rooms** *16*

Described as "a restaurant-with-rooms" rather than a hotel, this central gem is the perfect showcase for Rick Stein's renowned fish cookery. Rooms are simple and stylish while romantics will enjoy watching the coming and going of the fishing fleet. Breakfast is included. **www.rickstein.com**

PADSTOW St Petroc's Hotel

New St, Padstow, Cornwall, PL28 8EA **Tel** *01841 532700* **Rooms** *10*

Part of seafood chef Rick Stein's empire, this classy, modern hotel sits on a hill overlooking the seaside town of Padstow. The hotel has a fantastic fish restaurant and a courtyard garden for outdoor dining during summer. There is a minimum stay of two nights at weekends, and the price includes breakfast. Dogs welcome. **www.rickstein.com**

Key to Price Guide *see p556* **Key to Symbols** *see back cover flap*

PENZANCE Summer House ⓘ £££

Cornwall Terrace, Penzance, Cornwall, TR18 4HL **Tel** *01736 363744* **Rooms** *5*

This charming Garde II listed Regency house has been converted into a delightfully intimate hotel and lies very close to the sea. Tropical walled garden, fresh-cut flowers, polished wooden floors and inventive Mediterranean inspired cuisine await. Breakfast is inclusive; restaurant open weekends only. Closed Nov–Mar. **www.summerhouse-cornwall.com**

PLYMOUTH Legacy International £

Plymouth Road, Marsh Mills, Plymouth, Devon, PL6 8NH **Tel** *01752 221422* **Rooms** *100*

Marsh Mills is the gateway into Plymouth, with all the delights of Devon and Cornwall within easy reach. Each of the modern rooms features a large double and a single bed and up to two under 16s stay free on a B&B basis when sharing their parents' room. Also has a swimming pool and private parking space. **www.legacy-hotels.co.uk**

ROCK St Enodoc £££

Rock, nr Wadebridge, Cornwall, PL27 6LA **Tel** *01208 863394* **Rooms** *20*

A short drive from the foodie mecca of Padstow, the St Enodoc hotel has a bright, comfortable feel, with original paintings adding wit and colour. Sixteen double rooms and four family suites overlook the Camel Estuary. The hotel is well located for miles of National Trust cliff walking paths. Breakfast included. **www.enodoc-hotel.co.uk**

ST BLAZEY Nanscawen Manor £

Prideaux Rd, Luxulyan Valley, St Blazey, Cornwall, PL24 2SR **Tel** *01726 814488* **Rooms** *4*

Don't be misled by the valley address – this is a hilltop-sited gem with lawns sweeping down to breathtaking views – and you can enjoy these from the sizeable outdoor pool or the hot tubs. The owner adds flair and a gracious welcome to a charming building with 14th-century roots. Breakfast is inclusive. **www.nanscawen.com**

ST HILARY Ennys ££

Trewhella Lane, St Hilary, Penzance, Cornwall, TR20 9BZ **Tel** *01736 740262* **Rooms** *6*

An idyllic country B&B whose private fields stretch down to the delightful River Hayle. Sheltered formal gardens frame a large heated swimming pool and tennis courts. The rooms are comfortably furnished. Ideal for Lands End, St Michael's Mount, the Eden Project and the Lizard peninsula. Rates include an outstanding breakfast. **www.ennys.co.uk**

ST IVES The Gunard's Head ££

Near Zennor, Treen, St Ives, Cornwall, TR26 3DE **Tel** *01736 796928* **Rooms** *7*

A much-lauded, handsome inn set between the coast road and stonewall-crossed countryside. This restaurant with rooms provides the perfect base from which to explore St Ives. The excellent restaurant uses fresh ingredients and serves local beer and the accommodation is comfortable. **www.gunardshead.co.uk**

ST IVES The Garrack Hotel £££

Burthallam Lane, St Ives, Cornwall, TR26 3AA **Tel** *01736 796199* **Rooms** *18*

Unusually for the busy little artists' haunt of St Ives, the Garrack has its own on-site car parking, as well as delightfully themed subtropical gardens. All rooms have private bathrooms and TV while some have Jacuzzi or spa baths. Dine on seafood, meat and vegetarian specialities. Includes breakfast. Dogs welcome by arrangement. **www.garrack.com**

ST MAWES Rising Sun ££

The Square, St Mawes, Truro, Cornwall, TR2 5DJ **Tel** *01326 270233* **Rooms** *8*

Rooms are bright and cheery in this hotel with all the modern comforts. The property fronts directly on to St Mawes' picturesque little harbour, with views of the Roseland Peninsula. Visitors can dine in the Rising Sun's restaurant or bar. Well placed for yachting, sailing and walking. **www.risingsunstmawes.com**

ST MAWES Hotel Tresanton ££££

St Mawes, Truro, Cornwall, TR2 5DR **Tel** *01326 270055* **Rooms** *33*

St Anthony's Lighthouse is a beacon for one of Cornwall's best-loved hotels, formerly a club for yachtsmen. Olga Polizzi has created a casually elegant venue ideal for weddings and holidays alike. Decorated with local Cornish art and antiques, it has a cinema, bar, fish restaurant and therapy room. Includes breakfast and dinner. **www.tresanton.com**

TAVISTOCK The Bedford £

1 Plymouth Road, Tavistock, Devon, PL19 8BB **Tel** *01822 892347* **Rooms** *30*

Formerly a Benedictine Abbey, this elegant hotel was once the residence of the Dukes of Bedford. The rooms are charming and tastefully furnished to a high standard. Situated in the historic market town of Tavistock, the Bedford makes an excellent base for exploring Dartmoor. **www.bedford-hotel.co.uk**

TAVISTOCK The Horn of Plenty ££

Gulworthy, Tavistock, Devon, PL19 8JD **Tel** *01822 832528* **Rooms** *10*

Set in two hectares (five acres) of spectacular gardens and with breathtaking views, this elegant country house hotel has a unique character and charm. Rooms offer a combination of elegance and classic sophistication and the hotel boasts an award-winning restaurant under executive chef Peter Gorton. **www.thehornofplenty.co.uk**

TEIGNMOUTH Thomas Luny House ££

Teign St, Teignmouth, Devon, TQ14 8EG **Tel** *01626 772976* **Rooms** *4*

Once frequented by the captains of Nelson's navy, this Georgian house is furnished with antiques and collectibles. Tea and home-made cake are offered to afternoon arrivals, which may be enjoyed in the secluded garden. All rooms are individually designed, and expect faultless hospitality. Includes breakfast. **www.thomas-luny-house.co.uk**

TORQUAY Palace Hotel

Babbacombe Rd, Torquay, Devon, TQ1 3TG **Tel** *01803 200200* **Rooms** *141*

Overlooking St Anstey's Cove and featuring a nine-hole golf course, tennis courts and indoor and outdoor swimming pools, this uncrowned queen of the English Riviera stands in 26 acres of glorious gardens. Well placed for visiting Dartmoor. Additionals include conference facilities and tennis tutorials. **www.palacetorquay.co.uk**

WIDEGATE Coombe Farm

Widegates, Looe, Cornwall, PL13 1QN **Tel** *01503 240223* **Rooms** *3*

Spacious rooms offer fine views of the wooded valley. Horse riding and sea and lake fishing are among other attractions. The rooms are warmly decorated and in comfortable cottages. Dartmoor, Bodmin Moor and the Cornish Coastal Path are all at hand. Breakfast included. **www.coombefarmhotel.co.uk**

WOOLACOMBE Rocks Hotel

Beach Rd, Woolacombe, Devon, EX34 7BT **Tel** *01271 870361* **Rooms** *10*

Located 300 yards from the beach, this B&B offers small, modern rooms with en suite bathrooms. There are also two family rooms that sleep one and two children, respectively. Wi-Fi is available, and there are handy surfer facilities including outdoor showers and surfboard storage. Full English breakfast is included. **www.therockshotel.co.uk**

THE HEART OF ENGLAND

BIBURY The Swan

Bibury, Gloucestershire, GL7 5NW **Tel** *01285 740695* **Rooms** *22*

A picturesque hotel set in a converted 17th-century coaching inn in the Cotswolds. The rooms are luxurious with views over the peaceful River Coln and expansive hotel gardens. Some rooms have en suite Jacuzzis. The Swan also boasts a fine restaurant. **www.swanhotel.co.uk**

BIRMINGHAM Hotel du Vin & Bistro

Church St, Birmingham, B3 2NR **Tel** *0121 200 0600* **Rooms** *66*

Large, elegant hotel in a converted Victorian building in the city's trendy Jewellery Quarter. Many of the building's original features, including the sweeping staircase and granite pillars, have been retained. Features a well-reputed bistro restaurant and the popular Pub du Vin. Also has a beauty spa. **www.hotelduvin.com**

BIRMINGHAM Malmaison

1 Wharfside St, Birmingham, B1 1RD **Tel** *0121 246 5000* **Rooms** *189*

A stylish, award-winning hotel in a former 1960s Royal Mail sorting office, Malmaison sits amid designer stores and within walking distance of the city centre. The rooms are furnished in chic chocolate and cream, with moody lighting and CD libraries. Also has a spa with sauna, Jacuzzi and choice of treatments. **www.malmaison-birmingham.com**

BLACKWELL Blackwell Grange

Blackwell, Shipston-on-Stour, Warwickshire, CV36 4PF **Tel** *01608 682357* **Rooms** *3*

Small B&B in a 17th-century farmhouse, complete with low-beamed ceilings and stone-flagged floors, to the north of the Cotswolds. Offers two self-catering cottages; one for up to six persons and the other for two. A great spot for walking. Picnics are provided on request. Also functions as a working farm. **www.blackwellgrange.co.uk**

BLOCKLEY The Crown Inn and Hotel

High St, Blockley, Moreton-In-Marsh, Gloucestershire, GL56 9EX **Tel** *01386 700245* **Rooms** *24*

A converted 14th-century coaching inn with wood-beamed ceilings, whitewashed walls and log fires. Has individually furnished rooms with fireplaces and four-poster beds. The restaurant boasts an impressive cellar and an extensive choice of Real Ales. The nearby countryside is great for walking and horse riding. **www.crownhotelblockley.co.uk**

BROAD CAMPDEN Malt House

Broad Campden, Chipping Campden, Gloucestershire, GL55 6UU **Tel** *01386 840295* **Rooms** *7*

Elegant and well-located B&B, which prides itself on its personal touch. Each of the six bedrooms (and one garden suite) is individually decorated with antique furnishings, four-poster beds, fine china and freshly cut flowers from its carefully-tended gardens. Offers a large breakfast with home-made bread and jams. **www.malt-house.co.uk**

BUCKLAND Buckland Manor

Buckland, Gloucestershire, WR12 7LY **Tel** *01386 852626* **Rooms** *13*

This 13th-century country-house hotel, near Broadway, features antiques-filled rooms and fine views over the grounds. Hosts croquet lawns, tennis courts and a private putting green. The award-winning restaurant serves seasonal fruit, vegetables and herbs from the nearby Vale of Evesham. **www.bucklandmanor.co.uk**

CHELTENHAM Montpelier Chapter

Bayshill Rd, Montpellier, Cheltenham, Gloucestershire, GL50 3AS **Tel** *01242 527788* **Rooms** *60*

An eclectic hotel with contrasting Regency exterior, located in the heart of Cheltenham. The rooms are large and luxurious. Features a sunlit conservatory and a large lounge for guests, and has a contract with a local gym, just ten minutes away. Also has a restaurant. **www.themontpelierchapterhotel.com**

Key to Price Guide *see p556* **Key to Symbols** *see back cover flap*

CHELTENHAM Hotel du Vin

Parabola Rd, Cheltenham, Gloucestershire, GL50 3AQ **Tel** *01242 588450* **Rooms** *49*

This luxury Regency hotel is located in leafy Montpellier in the spa town of Cheltenham. It offers superb dining and bar facilities, sumptuous rooms and a superlative honeymoon suite. There is also a spa in the basement. The hotel is a favourite of visiting luminaries to the city's many upmarket festivals. **www.hotelduvin.com**

CHELTENHAM Hotel on the Park

38 Evesham Rd, Cheltenham, Gloucestershire, GL52 2AH **Tel** *01242 511526* **Rooms** *12*

In the heart of the Cotswolds and close to Cheltenham's town centre, the luxurious Hotel on the Park combines exceptional standards of hotel keeping with friendly hospitality. Peace, elegance and refinement with full business facilities and an award-winning restaurant. **www.thehotel.co.uk**

CHIPPING CAMPDEN Badgers Hall

High St, Chipping Campden, Gloucestershire, GL55 6HB **Tel** *01386 840839* **Rooms** *3*

This B&B and traditional English tearoom offers a friendly and comfortable stay in the beautiful old Cotswolds market town of Chipping Campden. The bedrooms are large, with antique pine furnishings and wood-beamed ceilings. Serves plentiful breakfasts and authentic cream teas – everything is home-made on the premises. **www.badgershall.com**

CHIPPING CAMPDEN Nineveh Farm

Campden Rd, Mickleton, Chipping Campden, Gloucestershire, GL55 6PS **Tel** *01386 438923* **Rooms** *5*

Cosy and welcoming B&B in a 200-year-old Cotswold farmhouse, within easy reach of Chipping Campden and Stratford-upon-Avon. Rooms are furnished with oak beams, flagstone floors and log fires, with views over the vast grounds. Provides ample parking space, and offers discounts for longer stays. **www.stayinthecotswolds.co.uk**

CHIPPING CAMPDEN Cotswold House

The Square, Chipping Campden, Gloucestershire, GL55 6AN **Tel** *01386 840330* **Rooms** *28*

Located in a Regency town house, this elegant property offers a luxurious, relaxing break in some of England's most beautiful countryside. The deluxe rooms have fireplaces, hot tubs, king-sized beds and state-of-the-art facilities. **www.cotswoldhouse.com**

COLWALL Colwall Park Hotel

Colwall, Malvern, Worcestershire, WR13 6QG **Tel** *01684 540000* **Rooms** *22*

The Colwall Park Hotel offers comfortable, individually decorated rooms, some with views over the beautiful Malvern Hills. Guests can relax in the cosy lounge with a roaring fire in winter and deep armchairs, or head to the library or the games room. Modern British dishes are served in the restaurant. Wi-Fi access. **www.colwall.co.uk**

EVESHAM Evesham Hotel

Coopers Lane, off Waterside, Evesham, Worcestershire, WR11 1DA **Tel** *01386 765566* **Rooms** *40*

Family-friendly and well-priced hotel, often ranked among the top ten places to stay in Britain. The rooms provide all modern amenities, but are decorated to befit the building's Georgian heritage; some rooms offer great views of the grounds. Has an indoor swimming pool. **www.eveshamhotel.com**

GLEWSTONE Glewstone Court

Near Ross-on-Wye, Herefordshire, HR9 6AW **Tel** *01989 770367* **Rooms** *8*

Ideally located in the Wye Valley Area of Outstanding Natural Beauty. This family-run hotel is well placed for walking, touring and exploring, canoeing and other outdoor activities. Rooms are comfortably furnished to a high standard. The restaurant has open log fires and serves fresh seasonal fare. **www.glewstonecourt.com**

HEREFORD Pilgrim Hotel

Much Birch, Hereford, Herefordshire, HR2 8HJ **Tel** *01981 540742* **Rooms** *20*

Delightful three-star, country-house hotel, set amid a vast parkland in the Wye Valley just outside Hereford. The rooms are cosy, with views over the rolling mountains into Wales. Guests can enjoy scenic walks through the Dore Valley. The Pilgrim also boasts a restaurant that uses local produce. **www.pilgrimhotel.co.uk**

HEREFORD The Priory

Stretton Sugwas, Hereford, Herefordshire, HR4 7AR **Tel** *01432 760264* **Rooms** *8*

Small, but grand, family-run hotel in an 18th-century building, on the outskirts of Hereford. Rooms are large with antique furnishings, including luxurious four-poster beds. The surrounding countryside is stunning and well worth a visit. The restaurant serves local produce (reservations should be made in advance). **www.hotelpriory.co.uk**

HEREFORD Castle House Hotel

Castle St, Hereford **Tel** *01432 356321* **Rooms** *24*

Set in the heart of historic Hereford, Castle House occupies a gracious Georgian town house. Its award-winning restaurant and quiet gardens with views over the old castle moat really make this a special place to stay. The rooms are elegantly furnished with fine antiques and all have modern amenities. **www.castlehse.co.uk**

ILMINGTON Howard Arms

Lower Green, Ilmington, nr Shipston-on-Stour, Warwickshire, CV36 4LT **Tel** *01608 682226* **Rooms** *8*

Traditional Cotswolds pub offering B&B accommodation on the village green. The rooms at this hotel have a beamed ceiling and antique, country-style furnishings. It has a good reputation for serving fresh seasonal produce and for its extensive selection of wine and cask ale. **www.howardarms.com**

IRONBRIDGE Library House   ££

11 Severn Bank, Ironbridge, Telford, Shropshire, TF8 7AN **Tel** *01952 432299* **Rooms** *3*

A distinguished guesthouse, housed in a restored Grade II listed building in the World Heritage Site of Ironbridge Gorge. This hotel sits in a peaceful location among immaculately-tended gardens, and is a short distance from the Telford town centre. Each of the rooms has en suite facilities. **www.libraryhouse.com**

MALVERN Copper Beech House   P   £

32 Avenue Rd, Malvern, Worcestershire, WR14 3BJ **Tel** *01684 565013* **Rooms** *7*

Simply gorgeous, this Victorian establishment in the Malvern Hills has picturesque period features and oozes both charm and character. The delightful rooms are comfortable, and there is a beautiful walled garden. Ideally located for walks in the surrounding hills, with stunning views. A host of sights is also well within reach. **www.copperbeechhouse.co.uk**

MORETON IN MARSH Redesdale Arms   P   ££

High St, Moreton in Marsh, Gloucestershire, GL56 0AW **Tel** *01608 650308* **Rooms** *24*

Originally an old stable inn, this hotel offers all traditional comforts in impressive surroundings. The executive rooms have four-poster beds and two of the guestrooms are fitted with whirlpool baths. The hotel is set in the heart of the north Cotswolds and is an ideal base for walkers. **www.redesdalearms.com**

NORTON Hundred House   ££

Bridgnorth Rd (A442), Norton, nr Shifnal, Shropshire, TF11 9EE **Tel** *01952 580240* **Rooms** *10*

Each room in this friendly, acclaimed hotel offers something a little bit different: one has a four-poster bed and period furniture; another has a velvet covered swing; and another has patchwork drapes and fragrant bed sheets. The pub serves a weekly changing menu using locally sourced ingredients. **www.hundredhouse.co.uk**

PRESTBURY White House Manor   £££

Prestbury, Cheshire, SK10 4HP **Tel** *01625 829376* **Rooms** *12*

Popular manor house, located within easy reach of Manchester. The rooms are luxurious and individually furnished with antiques, collectibles and rich fabrics. All the rooms offer basic amenities such as central heating and TV, as well as a range of tea, coffee and alcoholic beverages. **www.thewhitehousemanor.co.uk**

SHREWSBURY Albright Hussey Manor Hotel & Restaurant   £££

Shrewsbury, Shropshire, SY4 3AF **Tel** *01939 290523/290571* **Rooms** *26*

Converted moated manor house with splendid views over the Shropshire countryside. All the rooms offer en suite facilties, and boast an atmospheric blend of historic oak panelling, open fireplaces, Tudor beams and modern amenities. Six of the rooms feature original four-poster beds, spa baths and antique furnishings. **www.albrighthussey.co.uk**

STAFFORD The Swan   ££

46 Greengate St, Stafford, ST16 2JA **Tel** *01785 258142* **Rooms** *31*

The Swan, a former 16th-century coaching inn, benefits from a central town location. Lovingly restored, many of the rooms have original features including stone fireplaces and exposed beams. There are amenities for business and leisure travellers as well as a brasserie and coffee shop. **www.theswanstafford.co.uk**

STRATFORD-UPON-AVON Victoria Spa Lodge   £

Bishopton Lane, Bishopton, Stratford-upon-Avon, Warwickshire, CV37 9QY **Tel** *01789 267985* **Rooms** *7*

Built in 1837, this Victorian spa hotel was visited by Queen Victoria, hence its name and the appearance of her coat of arms in the hotel gables. The bedrooms face forward onto the hotel grounds; some overlook Stratford-upon-Avon's canal. Family rooms are also available. Serves a generous breakfast. **www.victoriaspalodge.co.uk**

STRATFORD-UPON-AVON Willow Corner   £

Armscote, Stratford-upon-Avon, Warwickshire, CV37 8DE **Tel** *01608 682391* **Rooms** *3*

Small, luxury B&B in a beautiful, 300-year-old thatched cottage, a short drive from Stratford-upon-Avon. The rates include a full English breakfast with home-made bread and jams, served beside the magnificent inglenook fireplace in the main lounge. **www.willowcorner.co.uk**

TEWKESBURY Corse Lawn House Hotel   £££

Corse Lawn, Gloucestershire, GL19 4LZ **Tel** *01452 780771* **Rooms** *18*

On the edge of a quiet village green, this elegant, Grade II listed Queen Anne building has been extended to create a stunning country house hotel. The Corse Lawn is set in 12 acres of beautiful grounds and the atmosphere here is relaxed and the service attentive and unobtrusive. **www.corselawn.com**

TRUMPET Verzon House   £££

Hereford Rd, Trumpet, Nr Ledbury, HR8 2PZ **Tel** *01531 670381* **Rooms** *8*

The Verzon is a stylish boutique hotel situated 2 miles (3 km) from the historic market town of Ledbury. The Mulberry bar and brasserie offer informal dining. Stunning views of the Malvern Hills can be appreciated from the deck terrace. **www.verzonhouse.com**

WINCHCOMBE Wesley House   ££

High St, Winchcombe, Gloucestershire, GL54 5LJ **Tel** *01242 602366* **Rooms** *5*

Historic, half-timbered restaurant-with-rooms. One room overlooks the North Cotswolds; all are small, but cosy. The Almsbury room has a private terrace and the best view, and the Preacher's room once gave shelter to the founder of the Methodist Church, John Wesley. **www.wesleyhouse.co.uk**

Key to Price Guide *see p556* **Key to Symbols** *see back cover flap*

EAST MIDLANDS

BABWORTH The Barns Country Guesthouse   £

*Morton Farm, Babworth, Retford, Nottinghamshire, DN22 8HA **Tel** 01777 706336 **Rooms** 6*

B&B in the heart of Robin Hood Country. Offers peaceful rooms in a converted, 18th-century farmhouse, near the busy market town of Retford. Vine-covered exterior walls, original oak beams and country furniture all add to the rural charm. **www.thebarns.co.uk**

BARNBY MOOR Ye Olde Bell Hotel and Restaurant   £££

*Barnby Moor, Retford, Nottinghamshire, DN22 8QS **Tel** 01777 705121 **Rooms** 49*

Set in expansive, tranquil grounds on the edge of Sherwood Forest, this privately owned converted coaching inn is one of Nottinghamshire's most characterful hotels. The rooms are decorated with oak panelling, log fires and leaded windows, and the restaurant serves award-winning cuisine. **www.yeoldebell-hotel.co.uk**

BASLOW Hotel Cavendish   ££££

*Baslow, Derbyshire, DE45 1SP **Tel** 01246 582311 **Rooms** 24*

This beautiful property is located on the Chatsworth Estate, at the heart of the Peak District National Park. Most of the furnishings – an elegant blend of antiques and modern art – come from Chatsworth House itself. The hotel is within reach of the spa town of Buxton. **www.cavendish-hotel.net**

BIGGIN-BY-HARTINGTON Biggin Hall   ££

*Biggin-by-Hartington, Buxton, Derbyshire, SK17 0DH **Tel** 01298 84451 **Rooms** 20*

A peaceful, 17th-century country-house hotel, in the Peak District National Park. This Grade II listed building is set amid typical Derbyshire landscape, with heather-clad moorlands and deep wooded valleys. Offers spacious rooms, furnished with four-poster beds and open fires, as well as self-contained apartments. **www.bigginhall.co.uk**

BUXTON Old Hall Hotel   £££

*The Square, Buxton, Derbyshire, SK17 6BD **Tel** 01298 22841 **Rooms** 38*

In the centre of Buxton, opposite the Pavilion Garden and the Opera House, the Old Hall can trace its origins back to the 16th century. For a time Mary, Queen of Scots was held captive here. Today it is a stylish, well-appointed hotel at the heart of the Peak District. **www.oldhallhotelbuxton.co.uk**

GLOSSOP Wind in the Willows   £££

*Glossop, Derbyshire, SK13 7PT **Tel** 01457 868001 **Rooms** 12*

Early Victorian country house with great views of the Peak District National Park. Boasts delightful oak-panelled rooms with antique furnishings and modern facilities. The popular restaurant serves traditional English fare in its period dining room. A nine-hole golf course adjoins the hotel. **www.windinthewillows.co.uk**

HOPE Underleigh House   ££

*Off Edale Rd, Hope, Derbyshire, S33 6RF **Tel** 01433 621372 **Rooms** 5*

This small B&B is located in prime walking area, and offers panoramic views over the surrounding Peak District. Set in a converted cottage and barn, it provides comfortable, spacious rooms, and a generous breakfast in its stone-flagged dining room. The staff are friendly and helpful. **www.underleighhouse.co.uk**

HOUGH ON THE HILL The Brownlow Arms   ££

*Grantham Rd, Hough on the Hill, Lincolnshire, NG32 2AZ **Tel** 01400 250234 **Rooms** 4*

Truly exceptional accommodation; the four bedrooms are individually and tastefully furnished to a high standard to provide every comfort for guests. Enjoy exploring diverse local attractions and unspoilt countryside before returning to dine at the hotel's excellent restaurant. **www.thebrownlowarms.com**

LANGAR Langar Hall   £££

*Langar, Nottinghamshire, NG13 9HG **Tel** 01949 860559 **Rooms** 12*

This stately country-house hotel is popular for weddings and other celebrations. The elegant rooms are split between the main house and the chalet next to the croquet lawn. The restaurant serves simple English cuisine, including Stilton from Colston Bassett and fruits from the Belvoir fruit farm. **www.langarhall.com**

LOUTH The Priory   £

*149 Eastgate, Louth, Lincolnshire, LN11 9AJ **Tel** 01507 602930 **Rooms** 9*

This Grade II listed building boasts beautiful gardens, a stunning wood-panelled bar, a Gothic function room (generally used for weddings) and a communal lounge for playing cards. The rooms are modern, but in line with the building's original architecture. **www.theprioryhotel.com**

MATLOCK BATH Hodgkinson's Hotel & Restaurant   ££

*150 S Parade, Matlock Bath, Derbyshire, DE4 3NR **Tel** 01629 582170 **Rooms** 8*

This stylish hotel dates back to the Georgian spa era, and is housed in a Grade II listed building. Offers carefully-renovated, luxurious rooms, furnished with original antiques and four-poster beds. The elegant restaurant serves delicious Mediterranean cuisine. **www.hodgkinsons-hotel.co.uk**

NOTTINGHAM Lace Market Hotel   ££

29–31 High Pavement, The Lace Market, Nottingham, NG1 1HE **Tel** *0115 852 3232* **Rooms** *42*

This trendy hotel is home to a brasserie, gastropub and a cocktail bar. The luxurious rooms are equipped with modern facilities, and offer great views over St Mary's Church and the Galleries of Justice. Serves a variety of good food and drink, and provides free access to the nearby Virgin Active health club. **www.thefinesseconnection.com**

NOTTINGHAM Restaurant Sat Bains   £££

Restaurant Sat Bains, Old Lenton Lane, Nottingham, NG7 2SA **Tel** *0115 986 6566* **Rooms** *8*

Highly regarded and popular restaurant-with-rooms. The rooms feature Molton Brown toiletries, freshly brewed coffee and Egyptian cotton linen. Also boasts a kitchen workshop, and offers a selection of tasting menus and accommodation deals. This is Nottingham's only Michelin-starred restaurant. **www.restaurantsatbains.net**

OAKHAM Hambleton Hall   £££££

Oakham, Rutland, Leicestershire, LE15 8TH **Tel** *01572 756991* **Rooms** *17*

Part of the Relais & Chateaux network of hotels, this sophisticated country-house hotel has a stunning lakeside setting. The spacious rooms are decorated with comfortable furnishings and rich fabrics, and the gourmet restaurant offers a fine wine list. Also has a heated outdoor pool and tennis courts. **www.hambletonhall.com**

STAMFORD George of Stamford   £££

71 St Martins, Stamford, Lincolnshire, PE9 2LB, **Tel** *01780 750750* **Rooms** *47*

Historic coaching inn with magnificent oak-panelled walls. The rooms are comfortable and spacious, equipped with en suite facilities and modern amenities. The well-reputed restaurant serves mouthwatering cuisine, which includes traditional English fare. Also has a business centre. **www.georgehotelofstamford.com**

WASHINGBOROUGH Washingborough Hall Hotel   £££

Church Hill, Washingborough, Lincoln, LN4 1BE **Tel** *01522 790340* **Rooms** *12*

This grand Georgian manor house, not far from Lincoln, is set in large, well-tended grounds and boasts attractive original features. The tranquil setting is ideal for quiet retreats, and the rooms – most with garden views – are comfortable; two have four-poster beds. The restaurant offers a good British menu. **www.washingboroughhall.com**

LANCASHIRE AND THE LAKES

AMBLESIDE Wateredge Inn   £

Waterhead Bay, Ambleside, Cumbria, LA22 OEP **Tel** *01539 432332* **Rooms** *22*

Delightful inn set in two adjoining 17th-century fishermen's cottages, near Lake Windermere. The colourfully decorated rooms have en suite facilities; many offer great views of the lake. Well-placed for exploring the scenic countryside and other local attractions. Includes breakfast. **www.wateredgeinn.co.uk**

AMBLESIDE Drunken Duck   £££

Barngates, Ambleside, Cumbria, LA22 ONG **Tel** *01539 436347* **Rooms** *17*

This lively dining-pub-with-rooms has been welcoming travellers for more than 400 years. Wood fires, oak floors and ales brewed on site add to the appeal. Offers fine views towards Ambleside. The rooms are stylish; ask for the Garden Room with its open-beamed ceiling. Room rate includes breakfast. Use of nearby spa. **www.drunkenduckinn.co.uk**

ARNSIDE No 43   ££££

The Promenade, Arnside, Cumbria, LA5 0AA **Tel** *01524 762 761* **Rooms** *5*

No 43 is inundated with accolades. Looking out onto the serene Kent Estuary, this boutique-style guesthouse is a top-drawer experience throughout, from the hospitable welcome to the tranquil surrounds and great walks. Beautiful rooms and fantastic sunsets. The home-made biscuits are a treat. **www.no43.org.uk**

BASSENTHWAITE Pheasant   £££

Bassenthwaite Lake, Cockermouth, Cumbria, CA13 9YE **Tel** *01768 776234* **Rooms** *15*

This well-loved hostelry retains its traditional and tranquil ambience. Built 500 years ago as a farmhouse, it became an alehouse in 1778. Has bright and cheery bedrooms; all have en suite facilities. The snug bar is highly popular. Also has a spacious lounge. Includes breakfast. **www.the-pheasant.co.uk**

BLACKBURN Millstone   ££

3 Church Lane, Mellor, Blackburn, Lancashire, BB2 7JR **Tel** *01254 813333* **Rooms** *22*

A former coaching inn that retains its original charm, while adding modern amenities. One of the highest-rated, two-star hotels in the country, it offers neat, practical bedrooms. A good base for those interested in exploring the countryside. Room rates include breakfast. **www.millstonehotel.co.uk**

BLACKBURN Northcote   £££££

Northcote Rd, Blackburn, Lancashire, BB6 8BE **Tel** *01254 240555* **Rooms** *14*

A luxurious restaurant-with-rooms, housed in an elegant manor amid lovely gardens. This comfortable house is renowned for its warmth and friendly welcome, as well as superb cuisine. Offers individually decorated rooms, with modern amenities, a traditional English breakfast and complimentary newspaper. **www.northcote.com**

BLACKPOOL Hotel Sheraton

54–62 Queens Promenade, Blackpool, Lancashire, FY2 9RP **Tel** *01253 352723* **Rooms** *104*

Features an entertainment programme every night of the week, as well as several attractions for kids. The public areas and well-appointed bedrooms are exceptionally spacious, and the service standards high. Also has a large indoor pool and sauna. Includes breakfast. **www.hotelsheraton.co.uk**

BLACKPOOL Raffles

73–77 Hornby Rd, Blackpool, Lancashire, FY1 4QJ **Tel** *01253 294713* **Rooms** *20*

Flower-decked, white-and-blue painted B&B close to the famous Blackpool Tower. A decided notch above the usual seaside offering, it offers a warm welcome along with bright and stylish rooms. A great place for afternoon tea; evening meals on request. Includes breakfast. **www.raffleshotelblackpool.co.uk**

BLACKPOOL The Imperial

N Promenade, Blackpool, Lancashire, FY1 2HB **Tel** *01253 623971* **Rooms** *180*

Part of the Barcelo Hotel Group, this opulent hotel is ideally located – it presents spectacular views over the beach and the sea, and is only minutes from the local attractions. Rooms and suites are elegantly furnished. Also has a sauna, steam room and spa. Includes breakfast. **www.barcelo-hotels.co.uk**

BOLTON The Last Drop Village Hotel and Spa

Bromley Cross, Bolton, Lancashire, BL7 9PZ **Tel** *01204 591131* **Rooms** *128*

One of a kind, this charming retreat is a re-creation of a typical North Country moorland village. Features arts and crafts shops and a range of eating options. Rooms are modern and well equipped. The glorious Pennine Hills are close by, and it's a short drive into bustling Manchester. Includes breakfast. **www.mercure.com**

BOWNESS-ON-WINDERMERE Lindeth Fell Country House Hotel

Lyth Valley Rd, Bowness-On-Windermere, Cumbria, LA23 3JP **Tel** *01539 443286* **Rooms** *14*

Relaxing country-house hotel, located in the beautiful hills above Lake Windermere. The decor is fresh and stylish, with original works of art adorning the walls. Has spacious, attractively furnished rooms, equipped with modern amenities. Includes breakfast. **www.lindethfell.co.uk**

BOWNESS-ON-WINDERMERE Linthwaite House

Crook Rd, Bowness-On-Windermere, Cumbria, LA23 3JA **Tel** *01539 488600* **Rooms** *30*

A fine country house, located on a sublime hilltop setting, overlooking the beautiful waters of Lake Windermere. The rooms are elegantly decorated, with modern conveniences and great views. This romantic retreat is an ideal venue for a wedding or honeymoon. Complimentary use of nearby fitness centre. Includes breakfast. **www.linthwaite.com**

BUTTERMERE Wood House

Buttermere, Cockermouth, Cumbria, CA13 9XA **Tel** *01768 770208* **Rooms** *3*

Magnificent views across the Lake District fells. The rooms personify simple elegance, furnished with lovely antiques. However, the greatest appeal of this tiny hideaway is the owner's home-baked bread. Also has a delightful stone cottage that can be rented on a weekly basis. Includes breakfast. **www.wdhse.co.uk**

CARLISLE Number Thirty-One

31 Howard Place, Carlisle, Cumbria, CA1 1HR **Tel** *01228 597080* **Rooms** *4*

A stylish Victorian town house in a quiet residential area, yet just a short distance from the city centre. The decor is bold and full of panache. Offers evening meals, provided they are pre-ordered as only fresh ingredients are used. Charming rooms, equipped with modern conveniences. Includes breakfast. **www.number31.co.uk**

CARLISLE Dalston Hall

Dalston, Carlisle, Cumbria, CA5 7JX **Tel** *01228 710271* **Rooms** *13*

Enveloped in delightful countryside to the north of the Lake District, this Grade II listed castle boasts well-appointed, individually designed rooms. The dining is excellent and the staff attentive. For extra luxury, book into the Knight of the Shires suite. Quiet location with an adjacent golf course. **www.dalston-hall-hotel.co.uk**

CHIPPING The Gibbon Bridge Hotel

Chipping, Forest of Bowland, Preston, Lancashire, PR3 2TQ **Tel** *01995 61456* **Rooms** *30*

Stone-built, luxury hotel located in the Forest of Bowland – designated as an Area of Outstanding Natural Beauty. Offers fine dining, expansive gardens and tastefully decorated rooms. A profusion of country pursuits such as walks, cycling, bird-watching and fishing are available. Includes breakfast. **www.gibbon-bridge.co.uk**

COCKERMOUTH The Trout Hotel

Crown St, Cockermouth, Cumbria, CA13 OEJ **Tel** *01900 823591* **Rooms** *49*

An appropriate name for a comfortable, if a little impersonal hotel that stands by the fast-moving River Derwent in the northern reaches of Lake District. Just a short walk into delightful Cockermouth – if you can tear yourself away from the hotel's lovely gardens. Room rates include breakfast. **www.trouthotel.co.uk**

GRANGE-IN-BORROWDALE Borrowdale Gates

Grange-In-Borrowdale, Keswick, Cumbria, CA12 5UQ **Tel** *01768 777204* **Rooms** *33*

In a wooded valley close to the shores of Derwentwater, "The Queen of the English Lakes". This relaxing hotel is a sensible base for walking, climbing and touring this scenic region. The ever-changing colours of the seasons add to the charm of this smart and well-managed hotel. Includes breakfast and evening meal. **www.borrowdale-gates.com**

GRASMERE How Foot Lodge
Town End, Grasmere, Cumbria, LA22 9SQ **Tel** *01539 435366* **Rooms** *7*

This Victorian guesthouse is owned by the Wordsworth Trust. It stands in landscaped gardens and is furnished with period antiques in keeping with the house. Has pleasant and cheerful rooms, two of which are deluxe standard. An excellent place for outdoor activities such as walks and bicycling. Includes breakfast. **www.howfoot.co.uk**

HAWKSHEAD Queens Head Hotel
Main St, Hawkshead, Cumbria, LA22 ONS **Tel** *01539 436271* **Rooms** *13*

At the heart of one of the prettiest Lakeland villages. Low, exposed oak-beamed ceilings, flagstone floors and a profusion of memorabilia create a relaxed and informal ambience. Some rooms have four-poster beds. Also has family rooms. Food is prepared using fresh local produce. Includes breakfast. **www.queensheadhawkshead.co.uk**

KENDAL Best Western Castle Green Kendal
Castle Green Lane, Kendal, LA9 6BH **Tel** *01539 734000* **Rooms** *99*

Helpful, attentive staff is a plus at this attractively located Kendal hotel. The setting is picturesque, the accommodation is comfortable and the hotel's restaurant combines excellent food with lovely views. The in-house pub here serves good real ales. **www.castlegreen.co.uk**

KESWICK The Grange
Manor Brow, Keswick, Cumbria, CA12 4BA **Tel** *01768 772500* **Rooms** *11*

One of the few five-star establishments in the Keswick area, this small guesthouse was once a hotel and it has retained the hotel-style facilities, which have brought guests back time and again. The scenic views of England's highest mountains are breathtaking, the hospitality faultless. Includes breakfast. **www.grangekeswick.com**

LANCASTER Lancaster House
Green Lane, Ellel, Lancaster, LA1 4GJ **Tel** *01524 844822* **Rooms** *99*

Savour the good things in life in this modern and elegant hotel, with its gourmet restaurant, intimate bars and lounges. The hotel has 19 luxury suites, and all rooms have modern conveniences, as well as a spa and hot tubs in its leisure club. Includes breakfast. **www.elh.co.uk**

LANCASTER The Ashton
Wyresdale Rd, Lancaster, LA1 3JJ **Tel** *01524 68460* **Rooms** *5*

Staying at this exquisite B&B with a personal touch is a memorable experience. The handmade chocolates are tantalising, the superb breakfasts comprise all locally sourced ingredients and the gratis drink on arrival makes for a warm welcome. Rooms are chic and comfortable; bathrooms have underfloor heating. **www.theashtonlancaster.com**

LIVERPOOL Hard Days Night Hotel
Central Buildings, North John St, Liverpool, L2 6RR **Tel** *0151 236 1964* **Rooms** *110*

This stylish boutique hotel in the heart of the city attracts Beatles fans from around the world. Specially commissioned art work and memorabilia adorns the walls of this converted Grade II listed building that pays homage to the Fab Four. Business facilities are available. Check the website for special deals. **www.harddaysnighthotel.com**

LIVERPOOL Hope Street Hotel
40 Hope St, Liverpool, L1 9DA **Tel** *0151 709 3000* **Rooms** *89*

Built in 1860 in the style of a Venetian palazzo, Liverpool's first boutique hotel is set in the city's beautiful Georgian quarter. The contemporary rooms are individually designed and feature solid wood floors, large beds and Egyptian cotton sheets. A good base from which to explore the city. Includes breakfast. **www.hopestreethotel.co.uk**

LIVERPOOL Hotel Indigo
10 Chapel St, Liverpool, L3 9AG **Tel** *0151 559 0111* **Rooms** *151*

The Indigo is a stylish but relaxed modern hotel brand. The decor is contemporary – blocks of colour picking out various themes – and the rooms are well-appointed, with free Wi-Fi. The restaurant was developed by leading chef Marco Pierre White. **www.hotelindigoliverpool.co.uk**

LIVERPOOL Malmaison
William Jessop Way, Princes Dock, Liverpool, L3 1QZ **Tel** *0151 229 5000* **Rooms** *130*

This stylishly dark Malmaison offers sleek design with distinctive charcoal hues and modern, roomy accommodation. The location on Princes Dock is central, and the gym can help shift calories put on at the impressive Malmaison brasserie. Rooms with views of the docks are pricier. **www.malmaison-liverpool.com**

LYTHAM ST ANNES Lindum Hotel
63–67 S Promenade, Lytham St Annes, Lancashire, FY8 1LZ **Tel** *01253 721534* **Rooms** *80*

A delightful, family-run hotel, located within easy walking distance of the city centre. This seaside retreat has attractively decorated rooms, equipped with modern facilities; most rooms have great views and a sauna and Jacuzzi. Serves fresh local produce. Sunday lunch is a much-anticipated affair. Room rates include breakfast. **www.lindumhotel.co.uk**

MANCHESTER Malmaison
Piccadilly, Manchester, Lancashire, M1 3AQ **Tel** *0161 278 1000* **Rooms** *167*

Stylish hotel housed in a converted, 19th-century building, located in the centre of town. Close to the Piccadilly train station, several shops and other downtown attractions. Offers contemporary rooms, decorated in bright, bold colours. Also has a bistro-style restaurant and a spa. **www.malmaison-manchester.com**

Key to Price Guide *see p556* **Key to Symbols** *see back cover flap*

MANCHESTER Velvet

2 Canal St, Manchester, M1 3HE **Tel** *0161 236 9003* **Rooms** *19*

In the heart of Manchester, Velvet is a sumptuous choice with ample wow factor and flair. The plush, highly distinctive rooms are fully equipped and a cut above the rest, while the decor and service throughout is excellent. Many guests experience the signature restaurant to fully round off their stay. **www.velvetmanchester.com**

MANCHESTER The Midland Hotel

Peter St, Manchester, Lancashire, M60 2DS **Tel** *0161 236 3333* **Rooms** *312*

This imposing, red sandstone hotel has been one of Manchester's most familiar landmarks since it opened in 1903. Elegance, luxury and high standards of service, accommodation and cuisine are on offer. Also has an indoor pool and a spa. **www.qhotels.co.uk**

MANCHESTER The Lowry

50 Dearmans Place, Chapel Wharf, Salford, Greater Manchester, M3 5LH **Tel** *0161 827 4000* **Rooms** *165*

This ultra-modern, ultra-chic riverside hotel is frequented by celebrities, fashion icons, pop stars and sports personalities. Rooms are modern and elegant, while the restaurant purveys modernistic British cuisine. **www.thelowryhotel.com**

OLD TRAFFORD Old Trafford Lodge

Lancashire County Cricket Club, Old Trafford, Manchester, Lancashire, M16 OPX **Tel** *0161 874 3333* **Rooms** *68*

Built next to the cricket ground and just minutes from Manchester United's ground and the huge Centre Trafford shopping mall. This modern hotel offers comfortable rooms, with en suite facilities and modern conveniences. A short drive from the city centre. Includes breakfast. **www.oldtraffordlodgehotel.co.uk**

PRESTON Barton Grange Hotel

Garstang Road, Barton, Preston, Lancashire PR3 5AA **Tel** *01772 862551* **Rooms** *51*

This hotel was originally designed as a fine gentlemen's residence. Its most recent refurbishment, inspired by the hotel's history, successfully recreated the Edwardian ambiance of the oak panelled lounge, and restored many of the original features. Staff are friendly and non-intrusive. Includes breakfast. **www.bartongrangehotel.co.uk**

SAWREY Cuckoo Brow Inn

Far Sawrey, Ambleside, Cumbria, LA22 OLQ **Tel** *01539 443425* **Rooms** *14*

Close to Beatrix Potter's Hilltop Farm, this charming property has a homely atmosphere. The bedrooms are spacious and tastefully furnished; most of them offer stunning views of the surroundings. Attractions such as Estwaite Water and Grizedale Forest are located nearby. Includes breakfast. **www.cuckoobrow.co.uk**

ULLSWATER Macdonald Leeming House

Ullswater, Penrith, CA11 0JJ **Tel** *0844 879 9142* **Rooms** *41*

Embedded within vast grounds bordering Ullswater, this traditional Cumbrian hotel offers excellent service, a fine location and a high degree of comfort. Superb breakfasts and fine dining in the Regency Restaurant and activities such as croquet and private fishing are available. **www.macdonaldhotels.co.uk**

ULLSWATER Sharrow Bay

Ullswater, Penrith, Cumbria, CA10 2LZ **Tel** *01768 486301* **Rooms** *24*

An exquisite country-house hotel, located in a magnificent lakeside setting. Renowned for its excellent cuisine, stylish decor and perfect service. The rooms are appropriately luxurious, and the view from the dining room is claimed as one of England's most beautiful. Breakfast is included in the room rate. **www.sharrowbay.co.uk**

WHITEWELL Inn At Whitewell

Whitewell, Forest of Bowland, Lancashire, BB7 3AT **Tel** *01200 448222* **Rooms** *23*

Old-fashioned, yet sophisticated riverside inn. This welcoming and friendly retreat is a favourite with visitors and locals alike. Parts of the building date to the early 1300s. The rooms are stylishly spectacular. Serves delicious food and wines. A memorable experience. Includes breakfast. **www.innatwhitewell.com**

WINDERMERE The Archway

13 College Rd, Windermere, LA23 1BU **Tel** *015394 45613* **Rooms** *4*

Perfectly located for Lake District sojourns, this lovely guesthouse is a picture and is presided over by a helpful owner who makes all guests feel welcome. The views are good, and the cooking – extending to home-made biscuits in every room and soup for cold winter walks – is a triumph. **www.the-archway.com**

WINDERMERE Gilpin Lodge

Crook Rd, Windermere, Cumbria, LA23 3NE **Tel** *01539 488818* **Rooms** *20*

Several acres of gardens, woods and moorland provide a glorious setting for this long-established country-house hotel. The roaring log fires, fine wines and superb food in the AA Rosette-awarded restaurant add to the feeling of utter contentment. Rooms are spacious and beautifully furnished. Includes breakfast and dinner. **www.gilpinlodge.co.uk**

WINDERMERE Holbeck Ghyll

Holbeck Lane, Windermere, Cumbria, LA23 1LU **Tel** *015394 323 75* **Rooms** *23*

An oasis of calm, perfect for relaxing on the terrace and soaking up fantastic views across Windermere to the rugged fells beyond. Food is mouthwateringly good, and the plush armchairs and open fire of the lounge encourage an indulgent way of life. Also has a spa and sauna. Includes breakfast. **www.holbeckghyll.com**

YORKSHIRE AND THE HUMBER REGION

AMPLEFORTH Shallowdale House
£££

Ampleforth, nr York, North Yorkshire, YO62 4DY **Tel** *01439 788325* **Rooms** *3*

Refined guesthouse, just 32 km (20 miles) from York and on the southern edge of the North York Moors National Park. This small retreat was built in the 1960s, and overlooks an exquisite landscape of unspoilt Yorkshire countryside. The rooms are simple, yet stylish. **www.shallowdalehouse.co.uk**

BARNSLEY Holiday Inn
£

Barnsley Rd, Dodsworth, Barnsley, South Yorkshire, S75 3JT **Tel** *01226 299571* **Rooms** *77*

This four-star hotel features well-appointed rooms, blending traditional elegance with modern conveniences. Includes executive suites and some rooms with four-poster beds. Holds a license for conducting civil wedding ceremonies. Also has nine conference rooms. **www.hibarnsley.com**

BEVERLEY Tickton Grange Hotel
£££

Main St, Tickton, Beverley, East Yorkshire, HU17 9SH **Tel** *01964 543666* **Rooms** *20*

A charming Georgian country-house hotel, set amid lovely, landscaped grounds. Offers contemporary, en suite bedrooms, with thoughtful touches adding to the charm. The tranquil setting is ideal for both weddings and conferences. Serves mouthwatering desserts. Includes breakfast. **www.ticktongrange.co.uk**

BRADFORD Dubrovnik Hotel
£

3 Oak Avenue, Bradford, West Yorkshire, BD8 7AQ **Tel** *01274 543511* **Rooms** *45*

Bradford's largest privately owned hotel has spacious, comfortable rooms, and a relaxed atmosphere. Situated in the leafy suburbs, this former mill owner's residence also has a well-renowned restaurant that is popular with locals and guests alike. Special deals are available at weekends, and there is live jazz on Mondays. **www.dubrovnik.co.uk**

EAST WITTON Blue Lion
££

E Witton, Leyburn, North Yorkshire, DL8 4SN **Tel** *01969 624273* **Rooms** *15*

A classy, 18th-century coaching inn, set amid beautiful surroundings. Offers simple, but comfortable rooms, with modern conveniences. Also caters for weddings, conferences and other events. The hotel is located just a short distance from many attractions, including Jervaulx Abbey. Includes breakfast. **www.thebluelion.co.uk**

FLAMBOROUGH Manor House
££

Flamborough, Bridlington, East Yorkshire, YO15 1PD **Tel** *01262 850943* **Rooms** *2*

An elegant Georgian country house in a Grade II listed building. Offers just two rooms, both traditionally decorated, yet with modern amenities. Ideal for those looking for an intimate and quiet retreat. The surrounding countryside is a favourite among walkers and bird-watchers. Includes breakfast. **www.flamboroughmanor.co.uk**

GRASSINGTON Ashfield House
££

Summer Fold, Grassington, North Yorkshire, BD23 5AE **Tel** *01756 752584* **Rooms** *7*

This peaceful 17th-century hotel near Summersfold's cobbled square has elegantly furnished rooms with modern conveniences; the restaurant serves set meals only. Well placed to explore the beauty of the surrounding Yorkshire Dales. Activities such as fishing, sailing and horse riding are available. Includes breakfast. **www.ashfieldhouse.co.uk**

GUISBOROUGH Gisborough Hall
££

Whitby Lane, Guisborough, TS14 6PT **Tel** *0844 879 9149* **Rooms** *71*

This traditional-style hotel is surrounded by woodland and offers scenic views of the Cleveland Hills. Set in an ivy-clad, grand Victorian building, the accommodation includes feature rooms. Fine walking opportunities in the surrounding Yorkshire countryside are at hand. **www.macdonaldhotels.co.uk/gisborough**

HALIFAX Holdsworth House
££

Holdsworth Rd, Holmfield, Halifax, West Yorkshire, HX2 9TG **Tel** *01422 240024* **Rooms** *39*

Grand, 17th-century Jacobean manor, just a short distance from Halifax. Has individually decorated rooms and suites, with modern amenities; some with four-poster beds. The expansive gardens are ideal for hosting weddings. Also offers conference facilities. Includes breakfast. **www.holdsworthhouse.co.uk**

HARROGATE Balmoral
£££

Franklin Mount, Harrogate, North Yorkshire, HG1 5EJ **Tel** *01423 508208* **Rooms** *23*

A mock-Tudor frontage makes this luxurious hotel easy to spot. Offers tastefully furnished rooms, as well as well-equipped business facilities. The decor here is a perfect mix of traditional and contemporary. Boasts an award-winning restaurant. Room rate includes breakfast. **www.balmoralhotel.co.uk**

HAWORTH Old White Lion Hotel
££

Main St, Haworth, Keighley, West Yorkshire, BD22 8DU **Tel** *01535 642313* **Rooms** *14*

A 300-year-old family-run coaching inn, set at the top of the cobbled main street in Haworth, a Yorkshire town redolent with memories of the Brontë sisters. The parsonage and the museum are a few steps away, and the Keighley & Worth Valley steam railway stops nearby. Comfortable rooms. Includes breakfast. **www.oldwhitelionhotel.com**

Key to Price Guide *see p556* **Key to Symbols** *see back cover flap*

HELMSLEY Feversham Arms

1–8 High St, Helmsley, North Yorkshire, YO62 5AG **Tel** *01439 770766* **Rooms** *33*

This comfortable, refurbished coaching inn has been around for more than 150 years. Located next to the parish church, the hotel offers pleasant rooms. The cuisine here is impeccable, yet unpretentious. Also has a heated swimming pool. Includes breakfast. **www.fevershamarmshotel.com**

HOVINGHAM Worsley Arms

Main St, Hovingham, Yorkshire, YO62 4LA **Tel** *01653 628234* **Rooms** *20*

Built in the 1840s as a spa hotel, this exquisite and timeless country house features open log fires and stylish furnishings. The informal and relaxing environment, in the depths of the Yorkshire countryside, is perfect for a stress-relieving break. Room rate includes breakfast. **www.worsleyarms.co.uk**

HUDDERSFIELD Huddersfield Central Lodge

11/15 Beast Market, Huddersfield, West Yorkshire, HD1 1QF **Tel** *01484 515551* **Rooms** *21*

A well-run, centrally located hotel with spacious, comfortable rooms and friendly service. The reception is manned 24 hours, and there is a porter service available. A bar gets going in the evenings, while the breakfasts are excellent. On-site secure parking; for non-drivers it is a short walk from the train station. **www.centrallodge.com**

LEEDS Bewley's Hotel Leeds

City Walk, Sweet St, Leeds, West Yorkshire, LS11 9AT **Tel** *0113 234 2340* **Rooms** *334*

Opened in 2003, this is Leeds' largest hotel. Conveniently situated close to the city's commercial and shopping district, it offers great value for money. The rooms are large and stylishly furnished, with Internet access, TVs, en suite facilities and more. The city station is just a ten-minute walk away. Includes breakfast. **www.bewleyshotels.com**

LEEDS Haley's Hotel & Restaurant

Shire Oak Rd, Headingley, Leeds, West Yorkshire, LS6 2DE **Tel** *0113 278 4446* **Rooms** *26*

Located in a leafy suburb, just a short distance from the city centre. The bedrooms are individually furnished with style and flair, and equipped with many modern conveniences. The cuisine is inventive and well presented by people who really care. Room rate includes breakfast. **www.haleys.co.uk**

LEEDS 42 The Calls

42 The Calls, Leeds, West Yorkshire, LS2 7EW **Tel** *0113 244 0099* **Rooms** *41*

A refreshingly different town-house hotel that manages to be trendy without becoming a cliché. This converted cornmill, set beside River Aire, features beamed ceilings, original mill mechanisms, modern handmade beds and a collection of original works of art. Offers luxurious rooms. Includes breakfast. **www.42thecalls.co.uk**

LEEDS Malmaison Leeds

1 Swine Gate, Leeds, West Yorkshire, LS1 4AG **Tel** *0113 398 1000* **Rooms** *100*

Conceived as a chic brasserie and bar with themed rooms, this stylish hotel has grown into a chain with its finger on the pulse of contemporary-style hospitality. Situated in the centre of town, it is an easy walk from all local attractions. Offers striking views of the town's skyline. Includes breakfast. **www.malmaison-leeds.com**

PICKERING White Swan

Market Place, Pickering, North Yorkshire, YO18 7AA **Tel** *01751 472288* **Rooms** *21*

Set in the picturesque Vale of Pickering, at the foot of the North York Moors, this delightful country-house inn is priced affordably. Offers pleasant, comfortable rooms. Also has conference facilities. The restaurant serves highly appreciated food. Includes breakfast. **www.white-swan.co.uk**

RICHMOND King's Head

Market Place, Richmond, North Yorkshire, DL10 4HS **Tel** *01748 850220* **Rooms** *26*

Close to King Henry VIII's favourite castle and overlooking the fast-flowing River Swale. The rooms at this hotel are individually styled and tastefully furnished. Local attractions such as the Georgian Theatre Royal are also nearby. Boasts an acclaimed bar, and serves afternoon tea in the lounge. Includes breakfast. **www.kingsheadrichmond.com**

RIPON The Old Deanery

Minster Rd, Ripon, HG4 1QS **Tel** *01765 600 003* **Rooms** *11*

Located opposite Ripon Cathedral and priding itself on good service, the historic Old Deanery is housed in a building dating to 1625. Period features include a 17th-century oak staircase, and there are lovely terraced gardens. Rooms are bright; some have four-poster beds and views over the cathedral. Dining is excellent. **www.theolddeanery.co.uk**

ROYDHOUSE Three Acres Inn

Roydhouse, Shelley, West Yorkshire, HD8 8LR **Tel** *01484 602606* **Rooms** *17*

A rambling old millstone building with lots of character. The rooms are simple, yet comfortably furnished; many offer views of the open moorland. Has independent cottages as well, each with its own garden. Also hosts a traditional shop with pickles, spices and preserves. Ample car parking space. Room rate includes breakfast. **www.3acres.com**

SCARBOROUGH Raven Hall Hotel

Ravenscar, Scarborough, North Yorkshire, YO13 0ET **Tel** *01723 870353* **Rooms** *60*

This dramatically sited clifftop hotel is conveniently placed between Scarborough and Whitby on Yorkshire's Heritage Coast. Originally a country house, it became the focus for an ambitious resort in the 19th century. The resort failed, leaving the hotel in splendid isolation amid extensive grounds which include a golf course. **www.ravenhall.co.uk**

THORNTON WATLASS The Buck Inn

Thornton Watlass, Ripon, North Yorkshire, HG4 4AH **Tel** *01677 422461* **Rooms** *7*

An archetypal village hostelry with real ale, quality home-cooked food and comfortable bedrooms. The pub wall marks the boundary of the village cricket green. At the rear is a large and secluded garden with a children's play area. Located a short distance from the bustling A1 trunk road. Includes breakfast. **www.thebuckinn.net**

WHITBY Broom House

Broom House Lane, Egton Bridge, Whitby, YO21 1XD **Tel** *01947 895 279* **Rooms** *9*

Within the picturesque village of Egton Bridge, Broom House provides traditional accommodation in a lovely garden setting. All rooms are of a high standard and have en suite facilities, while the Yorkshire breakfasts are first rate. This is a good base from which to explore the North York Moors and the seaside town of Whitby. **www.egton-bridge.co.uk**

YARM Judges Country House Hotel

Kirklevington Hall, Yarm, Cleveland, North Yorkshire, TS15 9LW **Tel** *01642 789000* **Rooms** *21*

A luxury hotel housed in Kirklevington Hall, a glorious country mansion. The bedrooms and suites are stylishly decorated, with modern amenities such as Jacuzzis, CD players, hairdryers, complimentary newspapers and more. Showcases several antiques and works of art as well. Includes breakfast. **www.judgeshotel.co.uk**

YORK Mount Royale Hotel

119 The Mount, York, YO24 1GU **Tel** *01904 628856* **Rooms** *24*

Housed in a William IV listed building, the Mount Royale exudes a charming old-world charm, while a thorough attention to cleanliness is matched by helpful staff. Rooms are comfortable and spacious; some have lovely views over the garden. Outdoor hot tub and heated pool (open May to September). **www.mountroyale.co.uk**

YORK The Churchill Hotel

65 Bootham, York, YO30 7DQ **Tel** *01904 644456* **Rooms** *32*

Occupying a grand Georgian house, the Churchill is a cosy hotel with a pleasant old-fashioned atmosphere. The well-equipped rooms combine traditional features with contemporary fittings; all are en suite. Staff are attentive, and the hotel offers fine dining. Close to the centre of town and York Minster. **www.churchillhotel.com**

YORK The Royal York

Station Parade, York, Yorkshire, YO24 1AA **Tel** *01904 653681* **Rooms** *167*

Part of the Principal Hotels chain, this magnificent Victorian retreat is set in vast, landscaped gardens. Offers en suite, luxury rooms, with all modern amenities; has two, specially designed rooms for the disabled as well. Also has a conference centre. Just a few steps from the centre of town. Includes breakfast. **www.royalhotelyork.co.uk**

YORK Middlethorpe Hall

Bishopthorpe Rd, York, Yorkshire, YO23 2GB **Tel** *01904 641241* **Rooms** *36*

One of the National Trust's Historic House hotels and, arguably, its finest. Set on 20 acres of outstanding gardens and parkland, this country-house hotel is filled with antiques and works of art. Built in 1699, it offers elegant accommodation in the main house and the adjacent mews cottages. Includes breakfast. **www.middlethorpe.com**

NORTHUMBRIA

BEAL Lindisfarne Inn

Beal, Berwick-upon-Tweed, Northumberland, TD15 2PD **Tel** *01289 381223* **Rooms** *21*

This roadside inn with rooms is perfectly placed for touring north Northumberland, or just stopping off on your way to other destinations. The en-suite rooms are motel-style at the back of the inn, which is on a quieter section of the A1, and have free Wi-Fi. Meals are taken in the inn itself. **www.lindisfarneinn.co.uk**

BELFORD Waren House Hotel

Waren Mill, Belford, Northumberland, NE70 7EE **Tel** *01668 214581* **Rooms** *15*

This small hotel enjoys outstanding views of the Cheviot Hills from its six acres of mature woodlands and formal gardens. Features individually decorated rooms and suites. Its location next to Budle Bay, a bird life sanctuary, makes it a favourite with bird-watchers. Includes breakfast. **www.warenhousehotel.co.uk**

BERWICK-UPON-TWEED The Walls Bed and Breakfast

8 Quay Walls, Berwick-upon-Tweed, Northumberland, TD15 1HB **Tel** *01289 330 233* **Rooms** *3*

This charming, award-winning B&B has delightful rooms and views over the River Tweed. The Walls occupies a period townhouse that sits on the medieval Walls in the historic centre of Berwick-upon-Tweed. The delectable, home-made fishcakes and other delights served for breakfast make for a memorable stay. **www.thewallsberwick.com**

CHESTER-LE-STREET Lumley Castle

Chester-le-Street, Durham, DH3 4NX **Tel** *0191 389 1111* **Rooms** *73*

A genuine medieval castle, complete with battlements and arrow slits, that has been converted into a luxurious hotel. The en suite rooms are elegantly decorated; some with antiques and four-poster beds. A perfect choice for a romantic break. Located a short distance from Durham and Newcastle. Includes breakfast. **www.lumleycastle.com**

Key to Price Guide *see p556* **Key to Symbols** *see back cover flap*

CROOKHAM Coach House 🍴 ⭐ ££

Crookham, Cornhill-on-Tweed, Northumberland, TD12 4TD **Tel** *01890 820293* **Rooms** *10*

Welcoming guesthouse set in a complex of renovated farm buildings that include a 1680s cottage and an old-smithy, all surrounding a sun-trap courtyard. The Coach House offers excellent home cooking and comfortable rooms, and has a reputation for maintaining high, award-winning standards. Includes breakfast. **www.coachhousecrookham.com**

DARLINGTON Headlam Hall 🅿 🍴 ≋ 📺 ⭐ ££

Headlam, nr Gainford, Darlington, DL2 3HA **Tel** *01325 730238* **Rooms** *39*

With simply exquisite views and a wonderful sense of solitude and grandeur, this stunning 17th-century Durham Dales mansion is a great getaway. The comfortable rooms are well equipped and come in a range of sizes; the spa rooms have private rooftop balconies. Luxury spa, golf course and good walks nearby. **www.headlamhall.co.uk**

DURHAM Whitworth Hall Country Park Hotel 🗔 🍴 ££

Near Spennymoor, Durham, County Durham, DL16 7QX **Tel** *01388 811772* **Rooms** *29*

A Grade II listed building set amid several acres of lovely gardens. Offers stately en suite rooms; some with views. The deer grazing in the surrounding grounds enhance the hotel's tranquil and relaxing ambience. An idyllic location for weddings. Also provides conference facilities. Includes breakfast. **www.whitworthhall.co.uk**

DURHAM Durham Marriott Hotel Royal County 🗔 🅿 🍴 ≋ 📺 £££

Old Elvet, Durham, County Durham, DH1 3JN **Tel** *0191 386 6821* **Rooms** *147*

Well placed in a historic city, dominated by a massive Norman cathedral and castle. This large hotel offers spacious, tastefully furnished rooms, equipped with modern conveniences. Local attractions such as Beamish North Country Museum are nearby. Includes breakfast. **www.marriott.com**

HALTWHISTLE Centre Of Britain 🍴 ££

Main St, Haltwhistle, Northumberland, NE49 0BH **Tel** *01434 322422* **Rooms** *12*

Part of the 15th-century Pele Tower, this building served as a manor house, post office, coaching inn and more before it was converted into a hotel. The original architectural features have been retained and tastefully combined with modern touches. Has simple rooms. Includes breakfast. **www.centre-of-britain.org.uk**

HEXHAM Battlesteads Hotel 🅿 🍴 ⭐ ££

Wark on Tyne, Hexham, Northumberland, NE48 3LS **Tel** *01434 230 209* **Rooms** *17*

From the attentive service and high degree of comfort to the actively green, carbon-neutral ethos, it's hard to fault the Battlesteads. The lovely rural setting is complemented by great food and a good selection of real ale in the hotel bar. The curtained bunk bed in the family room is popular with children. **www.battlesteads.com**

HEXHAM Langley Castle Hotel 🗔 🅿 🍴 🗏 ⭐ £££

Langley-on-Tyne, Hexham, NE47 5LU **Tel** *01434 688 888* **Rooms** *27*

The Langley enjoys a 14th-century castle setting not far from Hadrian's Wall. The medieval magnificence extends to the guestrooms, while the enveloping woodland is perfect for walks. Expect fine cuisine and much pageantry: battlements, sumptuous furnishings and log fires, plus a host of surrounding sights. **www.langleycastle.com**

MORPETH Linden Hall 🗔 🅿 🍴 ≋ 📺 ££

Longhorsley, Morpeth, Northumberland, NE65 8XF **Tel** *0844 879 9084* **Rooms** *50*

Several hundred acres of woods and parkland, including an award-winning 18-hole golf course, frame this magnificent Georgian mansion. Boasts a health, leisure and fitness spa, a traditional pub and a much-acclaimed restaurant. Has well-appointed and stylish rooms. Includes breakfast. **www.macdonaldhotels.co.uk**

NEWCASTLE UPON TYNE Malmasion Newcastle 🗔 🍴 📺 ⭐ ££

104 Quayside, Newcastle Upon Tyne, NE1 3DX **Tel** *0191 245 5000* **Rooms** *122*

Sophisticated warehouse conversion on the quayside, adjacent to the Millennium Bridge and opposite the outstanding Baltic arts centre. Part of the Malmaison chain of boutique hotels, which is renowned for its finger-on-the-pulse modern style, with much use of primary colours. Includes breakfast. **www.malmaison.com**

NEWCASTLE UPON TYNE Sandman Signature Hotel 🗔 🗏 📺 ⭐ ££

Gallowgate, Newcastle upon Tyne, NE1 4SD **Tel** *0191 229 2601* **Rooms** *174*

One of a slew of modern hotel developments in Newcastle, the stylish Sandman Signature is a hit with weekend tourists and business visitors alike. Newcastle United FC's St James's Park is across the road from this imposing tower block, and the vibrant city centre is a stroll away. Free Wi-Fi. **www.sandmansignature.co.uk**

NEWCASTLE UPON TYNE Hotel du Vin 🗔 🍴 🗏 ⭐ £££

City Rd, Newcastle upon Tyne, NE1 2BE **Tel** *0191 229 2200* **Rooms** *42*

One of a chain of boutique hotels, the Newcastle Hotel du Vin is housed in a former Tyne Teas Steam Shipping Company building. There are excellent quayside views and modern, elegant rooms, equipped with handsprung mattresses, plasma TVs, DVD players and stunning bathrooms. Superb bistro and wine cellar. **www.hotelduvin.com**

ROMALDKIRK Rose & Crown 🍴 ⭐ £££

Romaldkirk, Barnard Castle, County Durham, DL12 9EB **Tel** *01833 650213* **Rooms** *12*

Picture postcard England at its best. The village green makes a charming backdrop for this delightful little inn. Inside, it is smart, yet reassuringly traditional. Serves home-made soup and delicious food. The rooms are small, but cosy. Ideal for an intimate getaway. Includes breakfast. **www.rose-and-crown.co.uk**

STANNERSBURN Pheasant
Stannersburn, Kielder Water, Northumberland, NE48 1DD **Tel** *01434 240382* **Rooms** *8*

An ivy-covered inn near Kielder Water, the largest man-made lake in Britain. A friendly and warm place, full of character, offering spacious en suite rooms, many with countryside views. Food is freshly prepared, using local produce. Located close to Newcastle and Edinburgh. Includes breakfast. **www.thepheasantinn.com**

TILLMOUTH PARK Tillmouth Park Country House Hotel
Cornhill-On-Tweed, Northumberland, TD12 4UU **Tel** *01890 882255* **Rooms** *14*

Hunting, shooting, fishing and golf are all on the menu at this elegant venue. Serves contemporary British cuisine in an award-winning dining room. Rooms are traditionally furnished, but the stylish decor is well-maintained and appropriate. Includes breakfast. **www.tillmouthpark.co.uk**

NORTH WALES

ABERDYFI Penhelig Arms
Aberdyfi, Gwynedd, LL35 0LT **Tel** *01654 767215* **Rooms** *15*

This whitewashed, seafront hotel is spread over three buildings – Penhelig House, Bodhelig and The Cottage. Offers lavish, contemporary rooms and suites, well-equipped with modern amenities. Most rooms boast splendid views of the sea. Serves tasty cuisine, and features an extensive wine list. **www.penheligarms.com**

ABERSOCH Porth Tocyn Country Hotel
Abersoch, Gwynedd, LL53 7BU **Tel** *01758 713303* **Rooms** *17*

Country-house hotel renowned for its fine cuisine. Boasts fine views across Cardigan Bay. The rooms are furnished with antiques; those on the ground floor are suitable for disabled travellers (call in advance). Also hosts a children's play area, equipped with a TV, Nintendo, video and board games. Open Apr–Oct. **www.porthtocynhotel.co.uk**

BEAUMARIS Ye Olde Bull's Head Inn and Townhouse
Castle St, Beaumaris, Isle of Anglesey, LL58 8AP **Tel** *01248 810329* **Rooms** *26*

This charming inn on the Isle of Anglesey occupies a Grade II listed building dating back to the 15th century. The rooms combine modern facilities with ancient oak-beamed ceilings and antique furniture and fittings. Hosts an award-winning restaurant and a traditional freehouse bar that serves real ale. **www.bullsheadinn.co.uk**

BEDDGELERT Sygun Fawr Country House
Beddgelert, Gwynedd, LL55 4NE **Tel** *01766 890258* **Rooms** *12*

Set in a truly rural setting, this four-star, country-house hotel sits amid a vast expanse of mountains and gardens. The rooms at this former, 17th-century manor feature exposed stone work, oak beams and inglenook fireplaces. The dining room, located in the oldest part of the building, has antique furniture. **www.sygunfawr.co.uk**

BETWS-Y-COED Craig-y-Dderwen Riverside Hotel
Betws-y-Coed, Snowdonia National Park, North Wales, LL24 0AS **Tel** *01690 710293* **Rooms** *16*

Country-house hotel, set amid 16 acres of gardens in the heart of Snowdonia National Park. Boasts tastefully furnished rooms, with four-poster beds, log fires and modern amenities; a specially equipped room is available for disabled guests. This tranquil retreat also has a play area for children and free parking. **www.snowdoniahotel.com**

CAPEL GARMON Tan-y-Foel Country House
Near Betws-y-Coed, Capel Garmon, Conwy, LL26 0RE **Tel** *01690 710507* **Rooms** *6*

This quiet and luxurious, family-run hotel is located within striking distance of the Conwy Valley and Snowdonia. The rooms in this 17th-century, Welsh stone building are beautifully crafted to fuse traditional and modern styles. Activities such as hiking, horse riding and bird-watching are available nearby. **www.tyfhotel.co.uk**

CONWY Tir Y Coed Country House
Rowen, LL32 8TP **Tel** *01492 650219* **Rooms** *7*

Nestled in one of North Wales' prettiest villages, this small, award-winning country-house hotel is the place to go for affordable luxury. The renowned restaurant is a "must-visit": Welsh beef and lamb take pride of place. Walled Conwy, with its imposing medieval castle, is 4 miles (6 km) away. **www.tirycoed.com**

CRICCIETH Mynydd Ednyfed Country House Hotel
Caernarfon Rd, Criccieth, Gwynedd, LL52 0PH **Tel** *01766 523269* **Rooms** *9*

Secluded, 400-year-old, country-house hotel. Small, intimate rooms overlook expansive gardens, woods, an orchard and a paddock. Offers striking views of Tremadog Bay and Criccieth Castle as well. This family-run, Welsh retreat is licensed to conduct civil marriage ceremonies too. Tennis courts and a holistic therapy room are available. **www.criccieth.net**

HARLECH Gwrach Ynys
Harlech, Talsamau, Gwynedd, LL47 6TS **Tel** *01766 780742* **Rooms** *6*

A secluded B&B overlooking Snowdonia National Park. The rooms are cosy and modern, and the ground floor has two lounges. This Edwardian country house is located within reach of Harlech Castle, Royal St David's Golf Club, the Morfa Harlech Nature Reserve and the beach. **www.gwrachynys.co.uk**

LLANABER Llwyndu Farmhouse

Llanaber, Barmouth, Gwynedd, LL42 1RR **Tel** *01341 280144* **Rooms** *6*

Historic farmhouse set in a Grade II listed building, overlooking Cardigan Bay. This early 17th-century hotel has been renovated to provide en suite accommodation, and features oak-beamed ceilings, inglenook fireplaces and modern amenities, as well as many antiques and curios. **www.llwyndu-farmhouse.co.uk**

LLANBERIS Plas Coch

High St, Llanberis, Gwynedd, LL55 4HB **Tel** *01286 872122* **Rooms** *7*

Welcoming guesthouse at the foot of Snowdon. Offers modern B&B accommodation in a spacious Victorian house, built around 1865. All rooms are en suite. This family-friendly hotel is located a short distance from Snowdon Mountain Railway, Llanberis Lake Railway and Padarn Country Park. **www.plascochsnowdonia.co.uk**

LLANDRILLO Tyddyn Llan

Near Corwen, Denbighshire, LL21 0ST **Tel** *01490 440264* **Rooms** *13*

Award-winning restaurant-with-rooms occupying an elegant Georgian house, and located in the Vale of Edeyrnion. Rooms are spacious and tastefully furnished, with en suite facilties; most rooms have great views. Sports activities such as fishing, golf, sailing, horse riding and walking are all within easy reach. **www.tyddynllan.co.uk**

LLANDUDNO St Tudno Hotel & Restaurant

The Promenade, Llandudno, Conwy, LL30 2LP **Tel** *01492 874411* **Rooms** *18*

Luxurious hotel with a highly acclaimed restaurant. Occupies a Victorian seafront terrace with great views over the town's promenade, gardens and beach, and the nearby Great Orme headland. The lavish rooms and suites are individually decorated, with modern facilities. Also has spacious lounges. **www.st-tudno.co.uk**

LLANDUDNO Bodysgallen Hall

Llandudno, Conwy, LL30 1RS **Tel** *01492 584466* **Rooms** *32*

Impressive, historic country-house hotel, owned by the National Trust and set amid an expansive wooded parkland. Features a fabulous 17th-century rockery and walled garden. The luxurious rooms offer stunning views over Conwy Castle and the mountains of Snowdonia. Hosts an award-winning restaurant. **www.bodysgallen.com**

LLANGOLLEN Cornerstones Guesthouse

15 Bridge St, Llangollen, Denbighshire, LL20 8PF **Tel** *01978 861569* **Rooms** *5*

A colourful town centre B&B, Cornerstones has five rooms and suites spread over three historic 16th-century town houses in the bustling heart of Llangollen. All the rooms are well-appointed, with modern facilities. Rooms at the back have dramatic views of the fast-flowing River Dee. **www.cornerstones-guesthouse.co.uk**

PENMAENPOOL Penmaenuchaf Hall

Dolgellau, Gwynedd, LL40 1YB **Tel** *01341 422129* **Rooms** *14*

Relaxing country-house retreat situated in Snowdonia National Park. The tastefully decorated rooms have wonderful views over the surrounding mountains. Outdoor pursuits such as mountain biking, fishing, walking, golf and horse riding are available nearby. The up-market restaurant serves modern British food. **www.penhall.co.uk**

PORTMEIRION Portmeirion

Portmeirion, Gwynedd, LL48 6ET **Tel** *01766 770000* **Rooms** *53*

This village-like complex, built initially by Clough Williams-Ellis as a private peninsula, is now a holiday retreat with a popular hotel, self-catering cottage, shops and restaurants. The lavish rooms and suites are furnished in a contemporary style, and are well-equipped with modern facilities. **www.portmeirion-village.com**

RUTHIN Ruthin Castle Hotel

Ruthin, Denbighshire, LL15 2NU **Tel** *01824 702664* **Rooms** *58*

This luxurious, converted, 13th-century castle once belonged to the Crown. The castle sits amid an ancient walled dry moat, with acres of landscaped gardens and parkland alongside the pretty River Clwyd. Offers fine dining, a beauty spa and private fishing. Medieval banquets are a speciality. **www.ruthincastle.co.uk**

TALSARNAU Maes-y-Neuadd

Talsarnau, Harlech, Gwynedd, LL47 6YA **Tel** *01766 780200* **Rooms** *15*

Charming, 14th-century manor house, beautifully placed at the base of Snowdonia National Park. Houses lavish, well-equipped rooms. The award-winning restaurant is noted for Wales's lamb, fish and farmhouse cheese, while the intimate bar features an ancient inglenook fireplace and period curios. **www.neuadd**

SOUTH AND MID-WALES

ABERGAVENNY Clytha Arms

Clytha, nr Abergavenny, Monmouthshire, NP7 9BW **Tel** *01873 840206* **Rooms** *4*

Small, welcoming hotel-restaurant just outside the market town of Abergavenny with an award-winning pub for its real ale. Well placed for exploring the Brecon Beacons and the Sugar Loaf Mountain. The rooms are homely and cheerful, with views over the large grounds. Fishing trips can be arranged on request. **www.clytha-arms.com**

ABERYSTWYTH Gwesty Cymru

19 Marine Terrace, SY23 2AZ **Tel** *01970 612252* **Rooms** *8*

On Aberystwyth's promenade, this restaurant with rooms offers a boutique, contemporary twist to the traditional seaside boarding house. The stylish rooms boast bespoke oak furniture, designer bathrooms and stunning sea and sunset views. There is a cosy cellar bar and dining area overlooking the sea. **www.gwestycymru.com**

BRECON Cantre Selyf

5 Lion St, Brecon, Powys, LD3 7AU **Tel** *01874 622904* **Rooms** *3*

Small, historic B&B in a 17th-century town house. This hotel is situated in Brecon's town centre. The rooms are cosy with beamed ceilings, Georgian fireplaces and cast-iron beds. Ask for a room overlooking the large walled garden and the Norman Town Wall that encloses it. **www.cantreselyf.co.uk**

BROAD HAVEN Druidstone

Broad Haven, Haverfordwest, Pembrokeshire, SA62 3NE **Tel** *01437 781221* **Rooms** *11*

Perched high above the sandy beach of Druidstone Haven, this seaside hotel offers splendid views. Accommodation here is split between en suite rooms in the main house and five, individually decorated cottages. Dining room, sitting room and cellar bar overlook the sea. Children and pets are welcome. **www.druidstone.co.uk**

CARDIFF The Big Sleep Hotel

Bute Terrace, Cardiff, CF10 2FE **Tel** *02920 636363* **Rooms** *81*

A stylish hotel at affordable prices, housed in a converted 1960s office block. The interior is self-consciously retro, but the rooms are contemporary and comfortable, with en suite amenities. Offers stunning views as far as the Severn Bridge. Highly popular with both business and leisure travellers. **www.thebigsleephotel.com**

CARDIFF St David's Hotel & Spa

Havannah St, Cardiff, CF10 5SD **Tel** *02920 454045* **Rooms** *142*

Overlooking Cardiff's trendy waterfront bay, this five-star hotel and spa is one of Wales's most luxurious hotels. Offers plush rooms and state-of-the-art leisure amenities. Each room has a private, deck-style balcony with views across the bay. Tailormade spa packages are available, as are conference facilities. **www.thestdavidshotel.com**

CRICKHOWELL Gliffaes Country House

Crickhowell, Powys, NP8 1RH **Tel** *01874 730371* **Rooms** *23*

Welcoming, Victorian country-house, set on expansive gardens and grouse-filled woodland. This scenic retreat is located just outside Crickhowell, on the road to Brecon Beacons National Park. It's proximity to River Usk makes it a popular destination for fly fishing enthusiasts. **www.gliffaeshotel.com**

EGLWYSFACH Ynyshir Hall

Eglwysfach, Machynlleth, Powys, SY20 8TA **Tel** *01654 781209* **Rooms** *9*

Nestled in secluded, picturesque countryside above the Dovey estuary, this 16th-century house was once owned by Queen Victoria. Its nearness to one of Britain's finest wildfowl reserves makes it a favourite with bird-watchers. The rooms are tastefully decorated with antique furnishings. **www.ynyshirshall.co.uk**

LAKE VYRNWY Lake Vyrnwy

Llanwyddyn, nr Welshpool, Powys, SY10 0LY **Tel** *01691 870692* **Rooms** *52*

Converted Victorian fishing lodge on the massive Vyrnwy Estate. Boasts fabulous views over mountains, untamed moorland, forests and, of course, Lake Vyrnwy itself. Has elegant rooms; some with luxuries such as Jacuzzis, four-poster beds and balconies. Leisure facilities include a sauna and lakeside gym. **www.lakevyrnwy.co.uk**

LAMPETER Falcondale Mansion Hotel

Falcondale Drive, Lampeter, Ceredigion, SA48 7RX **Tel** *01570 422910* **Rooms** *19*

This Victorian mansion is set within a vast parkland, a short drive from the market town of Lampeter. The en suite rooms have four-poster beds and small balconies overlooking the well-tended gardens. The award-winning restaurant serves Welsh cuisine. **www.thefalcondale.co.uk**

LANGLAND Little Langland Hotel

2 Rotherslade Road, SA3 4QN **Tel** *01792 369696* **Rooms** *5*

A 15-minute walk from the heart of bustling Mumbles, this end-of-terrace Victorian villa is the perfect base to explore the Gower Peninsula. The bedrooms are beautifully uncluttered with white-washed walls. Guests can enjoy the likes of pan-fried wild boar with apple and cider sauce in the restaurant. **www.littlelangland.co.uk**

LAUGHARNE Seaview

Market Lane, SA33 4SB **Tel** *01994 427030* **Rooms** *4*

Follow in the footsteps of T S Eliot and Arthur Miller for a sophisticated stay in the one-time home of Dylan Thomas. As well as the sweeping views over the Taf Estuary, guests will love the bright, contemporary rooms and the French-Welsh menu in this quaint Victorian house. **www.seaview-laugharne.co.uk**

LLANIGON Old Post Office

Llanigon, Hay-on-Wye, Powys, HR3 5QA **Tel** *01497 820008* **Rooms** *3*

Small, but charming, 17th-century B&B on the edge of Brecon Beacons, just outside Hay-on-Wye. The rooms are located beneath wood-beamed ceilings at the top of a winding oak staircase. Serves a vegetarian breakfast. **www.oldpost-office.co.uk**

Key to Price Guide *see p556* **Key to Symbols** *see back cover flap*

LLANTHONY Llanthony Priory
Llanthony, Abergavenny, Monmouthshire, NP7 7NN **Tel** *01873 890487* **Rooms** *4*

Stunning, retreat-style B&B in a 12th-century Augustinian priory on the edge of the Black Mountains. The rooms, housed in former abbey cells, are simple, with minimal furnishings. The low ceilings add to their character and charm. Perfectly located for exploring the scenic countryside. **www.llanthonyprioryhotel.co.uk**

MILEBROOK Milebrook House
Knighton, Powys, LD7 1LT **Tel** *01547 528632* **Rooms** *10*

A converted, stone-built Georgian house, located on the border of England and Wales. This small hotel is perfectly placed for exploring Offa's Dyke, the man-made earthwork that marks the border. The comfortable rooms and restaurant overlook some fabulous countryside. Also has a croquet lawn. **www.milebrookhouse.co.uk**

MONMOUTH The Crown at Whitebrook
Near Monmouth, Monmouthshire, NP25 4TX **Tel** *01600 860254* **Rooms** *8*

This acclaimed restaurant-with-rooms sits in large gardens, in a tiny village on the edge of the Wye Valley Area of Outstanding Natural Beauty. The rooms at this 17th-century eatery are luxurious and beautifully decorated, but it is the gourmet cuisine that draws most visitors. **www.crownatwhitebrook.co.uk**

NEWPORT Cnapan Country House Hotel
East St, Newport, SA42 0SY **Tel** *01239 820575* **Rooms** *5*

A charming and intimate country house with a cheerful and welcoming ambience. Offers spacious rooms, carefully decorated with traditional oak Welsh furnishings. Serves excellent Welsh cuisine. The service is efficient and the hotel is ideally located to explore the countryside. **www.cnapan.co.uk**

PEN-Y-CAE Craig-y-Nos Castle
Brecon Rd, Pen-y-cae, Powys, SA9 1GL **Tel** *01639 731167* **Rooms** *26*

Located in the Brecon Beacons, this impressive castle offers a not-to-be-missed glimpse into Wales's feudal history. Houses en suite rooms; some with great views of the gardens. This popular wedding venue once belonged to the renowned opera singer, Adelina Patti. Ideal for walkers and bird-watchers. **www.craigynoscastle.co.uk**

REYNOLDSTON Fairyhill
Reynoldston, Gower, Swansea, SA3 1BS **Tel** *01792 390139* **Rooms** *8*

Secluded country house set amid vast, mature woodlands on the Gower Peninsula Area of Outstanding Natural Beauty. Hosts luxurious rooms and an award-winning restaurant that serves a fusion of Welsh and European cuisine. Therapy treatments such as massages, reflexology and reiki are available on request. **www.fairyhill.net**

ST DAVID'S Lochmeyler Farm Guest House
Pen-y-Cwm, near Solva, St David's, Pembrokeshire, SA62 6LL **Tel** *01348 837724* **Rooms** *7*

This quiet guesthouse, on a huge working dairy farm, is a popular stopping off point on the Pembrokeshire Long Distance Coast Path. The accommodation is split between the main 16th-century farmhouse, the cottages and the barn. The rooms are tastefully furnished and equipped with modern amenities. **www.lochmeyler.co.uk**

ST DAVID'S The Old Cross Hotel
Cross Sq, St David's, Pembrokeshire, SA62 6SP **Tel** *01437 720387* **Rooms** *16*

This friendly and comfortable hotel is situated in the centre of the town, just a short walk from the famous cathedral. Bedrooms are spacious and have a good range of facilities. Public areas include comfortable lounges, a popular bar and an airy restaurant where good wholesome food is offered. **www.oldcrosshotel.co.uk**

SWANSEA Windsor Lodge
Mount Pleasant, Swansea, SA1 6EG **Tel** *01792 642158* **Rooms** *16*

Small hotel in a 200-year-old, Grade II listed building. This two-star lodge, near the city centre, provides a reasonably priced break. The rooms are modern and comfortable, with free Wi-Fi for guest use.
www.windsor-lodge.co.uk

TENBY Fourcroft Hotel
North Beach, Tenby, Pembrokeshire, SA70 8AP **Tel** *01834 842886* **Rooms** *40*

This charming hotel offers striking views of Tenby's sheltered North Beach and the fishing harbour. Boasts secluded trails leading down to the beach. The rooms are simple, yet comfortably furnished, with most modern amenities. The restaurant serves local produce with an emphasis on fresh seafood. **www.fourcroft-hotel.co.uk**

THE MUMBLES The Shoreline Hotel
648 Mumbles Rd, Mumbles, Swansea, SA3 4EA **Tel** *01792 366322* **Rooms** *11*

Located on the seafront and close to local amenities, The Shoreline Hotel offers high levels of comfort. All rooms have TVs and there is a communal bar area and beautiful views across Swansea Bay. Ideally located to explore the area or play a round of golf at the course nearby. **www.shorelinehotel.co.uk**

TINTERN Parva Farmhouse Guesthouse
Tintern, Chepstow, Monmouthshire, NP16 6SQ **Tel** *01291 689411/689511* **Rooms** *8*

Farmhouse and restaurant on the banks of River Wye. This welcoming stone house is well placed for exploring Tintern Abbey and its surrounding countryside. The rooms offer great views over the river; some have four-poster beds. There is a guest lounge area and a restaurant with a 4 m (14 ft) high beamed fireplace. **www.parvafarmhouse.co.uk**

USK Clearvewe Bed and Breakfast 🅿 ££

Ty Wilson Barn, near Usk, Monmouthshire, NP15 1LT **Tel** *01291 671515* **Rooms** *3*

Three stylishly modernized rooms, fashioned from a range of old barns, make up this charming B&B. One delightful room, particularly popular with children, is tucked into the eves and accessed by a steep staircase. Full Welsh breakfasts are made from the finest locally sourced produce and include home-baked bread. **www.clearvewe.com**

THE LOWLANDS

AUCHTERARDER The Gleneagles Hotel ££££££

A9, Auchterarder, Perthshire, PH3 1NF **Tel** *0800 3893737* **Rooms** *266*

World-renowned château-style resort hotel with high standards of service, cuisine, and amenities. Boasts championship golf courses and state-of-the-art spa and leisure facilities. Well equipped to accommodate the most demanding of guests. Popular with both business travellers and families. **www.gleneagles.com**

BALQUHIDDER Monachyle Mhor ££££

Balquhidder, Lochearnhead, Perthshire, FK19 8PQ **Tel** *01877 384622* **Rooms** *14*

A beautiful, family-run hotel situated in the heart of Highland Perthshire, near the picturesque shores of Loch Voil. Offers luxury rooms and suites, some with log fires, as well as self-catering cottages. Service is outstanding. Also has an award-winning restaurant, farm shop and cookery school. **www.mhor.net**

BLAIRGOWRIE Kinloch House ££££

By Blairgowrie, Perthshire, PH10 6SG **Tel** *01250 884237* **Rooms** *18*

This family-run, country-house hotel is set in a particularly scenic locale at the end of a remote lochside glen road. Has an especially warm and welcoming atmosphere. The rooms and suites are comfortable and well equipped with modern facilities. Hosts a sauna and spa, and serves good food. **www.kinlochhouse.com**

CUPAR Peat Inn ££££

Peat Inn, by St Andrews, Fife, KY15 5LH **Tel** *01334 840206* **Rooms** *8*

Relaxed and informal award-winning restaurant-with-rooms. Boasts luxury suites, elegantly decorated with plush furnishings. The renowned restaurant serves mouthwatering dishes by Michelin-starred chef Geoffrey Smeddle. Located just a short distance from St Andrews and other sightseeing attractions. **www.thepeatinn.co.uk**

DUNDEE Apex City Quay ££

1 West Victoria Dock Rd, Dundee DD1 3JP **Tel** *0131 441 0440* **Rooms** *152*

A contemporary hotel complex overlooking City Quay and Dundee's waterfront, near the riverside walk and historic maritime attractions, five minutes' walk from the city centre. Modern rooms and suites, plus a lively bar-restaurant area and a Yu Spa offering treatments, a pool and a gym. **www.apexhotels.co.uk**

EDINBURGH The Glenora Guest House ££

14 Rosebery Crescent, Edinburgh, EH12 5JY **Tel** *0845 1800 045* **Rooms** *11*

Set in a beautiful Georgian townhouse in the city centre, the Glenora offers luxurious accommodation and an excellent restaurant. The interior is modern and stylish and the award-winning restaurant serves superb organic Scottish breakfasts. Well located close to all amenities. **www.glenorahotel.co.uk**

EDINBURGH Walton Guest House £££

79 Dundas St, Edinburgh, EH3 6SD **Tel** *0131 556 1137* **Rooms** *10*

Located in Edinburgh's New Town, the Walton Guest House occupies a fine Georgian townhouse. The accommodation comprises compact doubles, larger triples and family rooms, all decorated to a high standard. Close to the city centre and ideal both for tourists and those on business. **www.waltonhotel.com**

EDINBURGH The Balmoral £££££

1 Princes St, Edinburgh, EH2 2EQ **Tel** *0131 556 2414* **Rooms** *188*

Boasting the best known address in Edinburgh, The Balmoral is favoured by those who are accustomed to the very best in life. This elegant hotel has luxurious, tastefully furnished suites and rooms, with Internet access, TVs, and more. Also offers conference facilities, a spa and excellent eateries. **www.thebalmoralhotel.com**

EDINBURGH The Bonham ££££££

35 Drumsheugh Gardens, Edinburgh, EH3 7RN **Tel** *0131 274 7400* **Rooms** *48*

Ultra-smart town house, boasting a rich interior with a perfect blend of many original features and some contemporary touches, including modern works of art and furniture. The oak-panelled restaurant is popular and the cooking is skilled. Offers elegant and well-equipped rooms. **www.thebonham.com**

EDINBURGH The Scotsman ££££££

20 N Bridge, Edinburgh, EH1 1YT **Tel** *0131 556 5565* **Rooms** *69*

This stylish hotel is housed in the converted former offices of *The Scotsman* newspaper, and offers great views of the city. The luxurious rooms and suites are decorated with authentic Scottish estate tweeds, and feature amenities such as DVD and CD players, TVS, Internet access, coffee makers and more. **www.thescotsmanhotel.co.uk**

EDNAM Edenwater House · ⊞ · ££

Ednam, Kelso, Roxburghshire, TD5 7QL **Tel** *01573 224070* **Rooms** *4*

A quiet, family-run traditional guesthouse located on the edge of the village. This stone building is comfortably furnished, and offers lovely views of the surrounding Cheviot Hills. The delicious home-cooked meals, made with local produce, are accompanied by a particularly interesting wine list. Closed winter. **www.edenwaterhouse.co.uk**

GLASGOW Citizen M · ⊞ · £

60 Renfrew St, Glasgow, G2 3BW **Tel** *0203 519 1111* **Rooms** *198*

This affordable boutique hotel with cool decor and features is close to Glasgow's cultural and nightlife hangouts. Design classics fill the welcoming lounge area, cocktail bar and 24-hour Canteen M. Futuristic guest rooms have large beds, high-tech gadgets, free Wi-Fi, mood lighting and power showers. **www.citizenm.com**

GLASGOW Blythswood Square · ⊞ · £££

11 Blythswood Square, Glasgow, G2 4AD **Tel** *0141 208 2458* **Rooms** *93*

So much more than a hotel, the Blythswood is the latest addition to the Townhouse Company's group of hotels. This stylish establishment offers luxurious accommodation, excellent levels of service, wonderful food and a state-of-the-art spa. **www.townhousecompany.com/blythswoodsquare**

GLASGOW Radisson SAS · ⊞ · £££

301 Argyle St, Glasgow, G2 8DL **Tel** *0141 204 3333* **Rooms** *250*

This contemporary, award-winning hotel is mainly recognized for its innovative design. Hosts lavishly furnished rooms, suites and an apartment, well-equipped with many innovative features. Also has conference rooms, a popular bar and a good restaurant. A definite choice for those who appreciate modern surroundings. **www.radisson.com**

GLASGOW Hotel du Vin at One Devonshire Gardens · ⊞ · ££££

One Devonshire Gardens, Glasgow, G12 0UX **Tel** *0141 339 2001* **Rooms** *49*

A beautiful town house, located in the city's trendy and leafy West End. The rooms have been glamorously furnished and opulently decorated, and the food in the three AA Rosettes restaurant is extremely refined. Well equipped with a high standard of service to match – a place for a serious treat. **www.hotelduvin.com**

GLENROTHES Balbirnie · ⊞ · £££££

Balbirnie Park, Markinch, Glenrothes, Fife, KY7 6NE **Tel** *01592 610066* **Rooms** *30*

This elegant Georgian mansion is set in 160 ha (400 acres) of gorgeous parkland. The hotel is family run and has been frequently recognised for its quality of service and dining. The ambience is luxurious and proves popular with corporate and leisure customers. Has opulent and comfortable rooms. **www.balbirnie.co.uk**

GULLANE Golf Inn · ⊞ · ££

Main St, Gullane, East Lothian, EH31 2AB **Tel** *01620 843259* **Rooms** *13*

An intimate inn, set in a lovely village in East Lothian – a short drive from Edinburgh – which makes it popular for day trips. Decorated with pine furnishings and crisp colour schemes. The accommodation here is comfortable, but not too expensive, and the appetizing meals are of excellent value. **www.golfinn.co.uk**

HEITON Roxburghe · ⊞ · ££££

Heiton, Kelso, Roxburghshire, TD5 7SF **Tel** *01573 238018* **Rooms** *22*

Grand, Jacobean-style house, set in acres of beautiful estate grounds. The house is luxuriously appointed in traditional style, with comfortable rooms. This hotel is a perfect base to enjoy the scenic Borders. Offers a range of outdoor activities such as golf, fishing, mountain biking, walks and more. **www.roxburghe.net**

JEDBURGH Hundalee House · ⊞ · £

Hundalee, Jedburgh, Roxburghshire, TD8 6PA **Tel** *01835 863011* **Rooms** *5*

Stylish B&B in a refined, Georgian-style property, which has been tastefully maintained. The classic interior, a welcoming ambience and good home cooking offers excellent value to its guests. This part of the Borders is perfectly placed for experiencing the scenic environs. **www.accommodation-scotland.org**

LINLITHGOW Champany Inn · ⊞ · £££

Champany, Linlithgow, West Lothian, EH49 7LU **Tel** *01506 834532* **Rooms** *16*

Stylish restaurant-with-rooms. Has spacious bedrooms, with en suite facilities, tasteful and elegant furnishings, bow windows with tartan curtains, and modern amenities. Serves an excellent Scottish breakfast. Located close to several sightseeing attractions and golf courses. **www.champany.com**

LUSS The Lodge on Loch Lomond · ⊞ · ££££

Luss, Argyll, G83 8PA **Tel** *01436 860201* **Rooms** *47*

This is a family-run hotel offering a high standard of service and facilities. Public areas and bedrooms are luxurious and comfortable, and the restaurant prides itself on the use of quality local produce. The hotel boasts a stunning location with views of Loch Lomond. **www.loch-lomond.co.uk**

MELROSE Burts Hotel · ⊞ · £££

Market Square, Melrose, Roxburghshire, TD6 9PL **Tel** *01896 822285* **Rooms** *20*

Family-run, traditional hotel, carefully maintained over the years. Has a well-earned reputation, both locally and abroad. The restaurant and bar serve superb local produce in convivial surroundings. Offers a warm welcome and good service. Situated close to several golf courses. **www.burtshotel.co.uk**

MELROSE The Townhouse Hotel
£££

Market Square, Melrose, Roxburghshire, TD6 9PQ **Tel** *01896 822645* **Rooms** *11*

A smart hotel, decorated in a sensitive, yet modern style. The owners have a long-standing reputation as welcoming hosts. The chic brasserie serves tasty contemporary cooking. A good place from which to explore this delightful corner of the Borders. **www.thetownhousemelrose.co.uk**

ST ANDREWS The Scores Hotel
£££

76 The Scores, St Andrews, Fife, KY16 9BB **Tel** *01334 472451* **Rooms** *30*

Popular with golfers, this hotel enjoys enviable views over the coastline of St Andrews and is centrally located to suit all pursuits in the area. Bedrooms are well appointed; some have sea views. There are formal and informal dining options, as well as a bar. **www.bw-scoreshotel.co.uk**

ST ANDREWS Old Course Hotel
£££££

Old Station Rd, St Andrews, Fife, KY16 9SP **Tel** *01334 474371* **Rooms** *144*

Situated just on the edge of the town, this hotel boasts splendid views of Old Course – the legendary sea-side links. Features glamorous interiors and exemplary amenities. The luxurious rooms and suites are decorated in a contemporary style. Also has specially designed rooms for disabled guests and wonderful spa facilities. **www.oldcoursehotel.co.uk**

ST BOSWELLS Dryburgh Abbey Hotel
£££

St Boswells, Melrose, Dumfriesshire, TD6 0RQ **Tel** *01835 822261* **Rooms** *38*

An imposing, red sandstone baronial mansion, located in a picturesque setting on the edge of River Tweed. The ruined abbey adjacent to the building adds to the character of the setting. Offers large rooms, and is a popular destination for weddings, conferences and other celebrations. **www.dryburgh.co.uk**

ST FILLANS Four Seasons
£££

St Fillans, Perthshire, PH6 2NF **Tel** *01764 685333* **Rooms** *12*

Set in particularly stunning countryside, with a waterfront location, this small hotel has comfortable rooms, with en suite facilities and striking views of Loch Earn. Also hosts six self-catering log cabin chalets for those who want to enjoy a more intimate stay. This cosy retreat is ideal for a romantic getaway. **www.thefourseasonshotel.co.uk**

TIGHNABRUAICH Royal An Lochan
££

Shore Rd, Tighnabruaich, Argyll, PA21 2BE **Tel** *01700 811239* **Rooms** *11*

Fine, family-run hotel, set on the picturesque shore. Offers comfortable and spacious accommodation. Dining here can be on a formal or informal basis, and the quality of food and ingredients is extremely high. The service is efficient and friendly. **www.anlochan.co.uk**

TROON Highgrove House Hotel
££

Old Loans Rd, Troon, Ayrshire, KA10 7HL **Tel** *01292 312511* **Rooms** *9*

An intimate and stylish hotel, designed by a sea captain in the 1920s, with fantastic views over the Firth of Clyde to the Isle of Arran and beyond. A popular place with golfers and for weddings, it's a haven to relax, enjoy good food and convenient for many Ayrshire attractions. **www.costleyhotels.co.uk**

TURNBERRY The Westin Turnberry Resort
£££££

Turnberry, Ayrshire, KA26 9LT **Tel** *01655 331000* **Rooms** *219*

One of the trendiest places to stay in Scotland. Boasts championship golf courses, a spa, and conference facilities. The well-appointed, en suite rooms are elegantly furnished, with modern amenities. Also has rooms with facilities for disabled guests. Allows pets. Six bars and restaurants to choose from. **www.turnberryresort.co.uk**

YARROW Tibbie Shiels Inn
£

St Mary's Loch, Selkirk, Selkirkshire, TD7 5LH **Tel** *01750 42231* **Rooms** *5*

Once a hostelry favoured by Sir Walter Scott, this 18th-century inn remains a popular place to eat and stay while in the area. Many original features of this B&B have been retained. Has simply furnished, clean rooms, as well as camping facilities. Offers good food, warm service and a genuine welcome. **www.tibbieshiels.com**

THE HIGHLANDS AND ISLANDS

ABEFELDY Fortingall Hotel
££££

Fortingall, Aberfeldy, Perthshire, PH15 2NQ **Tel** *01887 830367* **Rooms** *10*

This country hotel is a great example of the best that Scottish hospitality has to offer. It is located amidst stunning scenery at the foot of Glen Lyon, and comfortable sofas and roaring log fires greet guests in winter. The AA Rosette-awarded restaurant delights, with imaginative cuisine that uses local seasonal produce. **www.fortingall.com**

ABERDEEN Udny Arms
£

Main St, Newburgh, Aberdeenshire, AB41 6BL **Tel** *01358 789444* **Rooms** *30*

A comfortable, traditional hotel. The bright, cheerful bedrooms have attached bathrooms, and are decorated with antique furnishings and several modern conveniences. The public rooms are relaxing and welcoming. Located close to three championship golf courses. Also offers facilities for biking and archery. **www.udnyarmshotel.com**

Key to Price Guide *see p556* **Key to Symbols** *see back cover flap*

ABERDEEN Ardoe House Hotel 🅿 🖼 🍴 🛏 📺 £££

S Deeside Rd, Aberdeen, Aberdeenshire, AB12 5YP Tel 01224 860660 Rooms 109

Located 5 km (3 miles) from the city centre, this is one of Aberdeen's best hotels. The rooms at this luxurious retreat are tastefully decorated. The suites have four-poster beds. All rooms offer striking views of the countryside. Also has amenities such as a Jacuzzi, tennis courts and beauty salons. Pets allowed. **www.mercure-uk.com**

ABERDEEN Marcliffe at Pitfodels 🖼 🍴 📺 ♿ ££££

N Deeside Rd, Pitfodels, Aberdeenshire, AB15 9YA Tel 01224 861000 Rooms 42

Situated on the outskirts of the city, this up-market hotel has beautiful interiors and a warm and welcoming ambience. The stylish bedrooms offer en suite facilities and many other modern amenities. The conservatory restaurant is bright and airy, and the menus feature Aberdonian quality produce. **www.marcliffe.com**

ACHILTIBUIE Summer Isles 🅿 🍴 £££

Achiltibuie, Ross-shire, IV26 2YG Tel 01854 622282 Rooms 13

A remote and picturesque setting overlooking the Summer Isles makes this charmingly low-key place an idyllic retreat. The hotel interior is understated, with well-appointed bedrooms. The restaurant serves food made with locally grown ingredients. Check opening timings. **www.summerisleshotel.co.uk**

APPLECROSS Applecross Inn 🅿 🍴 ♿ £££

Applecross, Wester Ross, IV54 8LR Tel 01520 744262 Rooms 7

Boasting a stunning rural location with views across the bay to Skye, this inn retains all its character and charm while offering high-quality accommodation and dining. An award-winning hotel with a warm, family atmosphere and some of the best seafood in Scotland. **www.applecross.uk.com**

ARISAIG Old Library Lodge 🍴 ££

Road to the Isles, Arisaig, Perthshire, PH39 4NH Tel 01687 450651 Rooms 6

Modest and well-run restaurant-with-rooms, set on the Road to the Isles. Housed in a 200-year-old former stable, the hotel offers great views and comfortably furnished rooms. Dining here is a rich culinary experience. Sometimes closed Nov, Dec. **www.oldlibrary.co.uk**

AULDEARN Boath House 🅿 🍴 ♿ £££££

Auldearn, by Nairn, Inverness-shire, IV12 5TE Tel 01667 454896 Rooms 8

Known as a "jewel in the Highland crown", this gorgeous mansion is a must-see attraction. The rooms are elegantly furnished with antiques, works of art and modern amenities; all offer excellent views of the estate and the gardens. Also hosts a beauty salon and spa, and serves award-winning cuisine. **www.boath-house.com**

BALLATER Darroch Learg 🅿 🍴 ♿ ££££

Braemar Rd, Ballater, Royal Deeside, Aberdeenshire, AB35 5UX Tel 013397 55443 Rooms 17

Set on a hill in Ballater, amid attractive gardens, this charming Victorian hotel offers splendid views of Lochnagar. The accommodation is comfortable, and the cooking is highly skilled, using the best local produce. A superb wine list completes the experience. **www.darrochlearg.co.uk**

BEAULY Lovat Arms Hotel 🅿 🍴 ♿ ££

Beauly, Inverness-shire, IV4 7BS Tel 01463 782313 Rooms 28

This family-run, traditional hotel is more than 200 years old. The rooms are en suite, equipped with modern amenities such as TVs, modem outlets, coffee makers and more. Plenty of golfing and fishing opportunities nearby. Good Scottish fare served by friendly staff, featuring local game fish. **www.lovatarms.com**

CRINAN Crinan Hotel 🖼 🅿 🍴 ♿ £££££

Crinan, by Lochgilphead, Argyll, PA31 8SR Tel 01546 830261 Rooms 20

A popular base from where to enjoy the panoramic views over Loch Fyne and Jura Sound. The distinctive whitewashed building accommodates a bar and restaurant, where seafood is a speciality. The bedrooms are simply, but tastefully decorated. A friendly and bustling place. **www.crinanhotel.com**

DUNKELD The Pend 🅿 🍴 £

5 Brae St, Dunkeld, Perthshire, PH8 0BA Tel 01350 727586 Rooms 3

High-quality accommodation in a quiet, Georgian town house, located just off High Street. The interiors are furnished with many antiques and period pieces. Welcoming hosts offer the best of Scottish hospitality, and serve imaginative and superbly-prepared dishes. **www.thepend.com**

DURNESS Mackays Rooms 🅿 🍴 £££

Durness, Sutherland, IV27 4PN Tel 01971 11202 Rooms 7

This small hotel provides comfortable accommodation in the heart of Mackay country. Rooms vary in size and facilities; the deluxe rooms have oversized, feather-topped beds and flat-screen TVs. The superb restaurant focuses on traditional Highland dishes and local seafood including Loch Eriboll crab, lobster and scallops. **www.visitmackays.com**

ERISKA Isle of Eriska Hotel 🅿 🍴 🛏 📺 ♿ £££££

Ledaig, by Oban, Argyll, PA37 1SD Tel 01631 720371 Rooms 17

Family-run country estate, located on an island. Houses individually decorated rooms, as well as private cottages; all equipped with modern amenities. This luxurious, romantic hideaway offers several leisure facilities and elaborate dinners. Tranquil and peaceful surroundings. **www.eriska-hotel.co.uk**

FORRES Cluny Bank Hotel　　　　　　　　　　　P ¶¶　　£££

69 St Leonard's Rd, Forres, Moray, Inverness-shire, IV36 1DW **Tel** *01309 674304* **Rooms** *8*

This historic, family-run hotel is located in the quiet residential part of Forres, and retains many of its original features. The bedrooms are comfortable and tastefully decorated, while the public rooms are welcoming and airy. The friendly staff can help arrange outdoor pursuits such as golfing, fishing, cycling and more. **www.clunybankhotel.co.uk**

FORT WILLIAM Ashburn House　　　　　　　　　　P　　£££

4 Achintore Rd, Fort William, Perthshire, PH33 6RQ **Tel** *01397 706000* **Rooms** *7*

This traditional, Highland B&B overlooking Loch Linnhe, extends a typical Scottish welcome. The bedrooms of this Victorian house are attractively decorated and well equipped to ensure a comfortable stay. Located a short walking distance from the town centre. Offers hearty breakfasts. **www.ashburnhouse.co.uk**

FORT WILLIAM The Grange　　　　　　　　　　　　£££

Grange Rd, Fort William, Perthshire, PH33 6JF **Tel** *01397 705516* **Rooms** *4*

This historic B&B has been skilfully and lovingly restored. Enjoys lovely views across Loch Linnhe, and is run by welcoming hosts. The interior is beautifully decorated with great attention to detail, and the rooms are individually furnished with antique beds and lavish bathrooms. Serves a generous breakfast. **www.thegrange-scotland.co.uk**

INVERGARRY Tomdoun Hotel　　　　　　　　　P ¶¶ &　　£

Invergarry, Invernesshire, PH35 4HS **Tel** *01809 511218* **Rooms** *10*

Surrounded by wonderful scenery, this remote, period hotel is the perfect rural retreat. There are no TVs or telephones in the guestrooms, and the cosy public areas are warmed by log fires. The traditional bar is stocked with over 100 malt whiskies, and the restaurant menu highlights Scotch beef, game and seafood. Dogs welcome. **www.tomdoun.com**

INVERNESS Glenmoriston Town House　　　　　　¶¶　　£££

20 Ness Bank, Inverness, Inverness-shire, IV2 4SF **Tel** *01463 223777* **Rooms** *30*

A traditional town-house hotel that has been tastefully and luxuriously upgraded. The hotel overlooks the River Ness and is only minutes from the town centre. The rooms are furnished in a contemporary style, with modern amenities. Boasts an award-winning French restaurant. **www.glenmoristontownhouse.com**

ISLE OF HARRIS Scarista House　　　　　　　　P ¶¶　　££££

Sgarasta Bheag, Isle of Harris, HS3 3HX **Tel** *01859 550238* **Rooms** *6*

Set in a Georgian-style house, this hotel offers traditional comfort in well furnished, comfortable rooms, all with stunning views of the surrounding remote scenery. There is a library with an open fire and no television to disturb the peace and tranquility of the area. The hotel restaurant is excellent. **www.scaristahouse.com**

ISLE OF IONA Argyll Hotel　　　　　　　　　　¶¶　　££

Isle of Iona, Agryll and Bute, PA76 6SJ **Tel** *01681 700334* **Rooms** *16*

A relaxing retreat with views over the Sound of Iona, with a comfortable and welcoming ambience, enhanced by log fires. The bright, cheerful rooms are simply decorated and furnished with modern facilities. Also boasts a sunny conservatory, and serves good home-grown food and delicious bread. **www.argyllhoteliona.co.uk**

ISLE OF LEWIS Galson Farm　　　　　　　　　　　　££

S Galson, Isle of Lewis, Outer Hebrides, HS2 0SH **Tel** *01851 850492* **Rooms** *4*

Charming, 18th-century farmhouse on the west coast of Lewis. Offers simple, homely accommodation. This working farm is set in a beautiful location, with striking views of the surroundings. Serves good home cooking with interesting vegetarian options. Bunkhouse accommodation also available. **www.galsonfarm.co.uk**

ISLE OF SKYE Duisdale　　　　　　　　　　　　¶¶　　££

Sleat, Isle Ornsay, Isle of Skye, Inverness-shire, IV43 8QW **Tel** *01471 833202* **Rooms** *18*

Friendly Victorian house set on a hill, with magnificent views of the Sound of Sleat. This small hotel has been flamboyantly decorated and has lots of character. The rooms are spacious and comfortably furnished. Also offers delicious food and lovely gardens. **www.duisdale.com**

ISLE OF SKYE Flodigarry Hotel　　　　　　　　P ¶¶　　£££

Flodigarry, Isle of Skye, Inverness-shire, IV51 9HZ **Tel** *01470 552203* **Rooms** *18*

This award-winning country house hotel is located in ancient woodland overlooking the sea towards mainland Scotland. The hotel occupies the former home of Scottish heroine Flora MacDonald and offers comfortably furnished rooms, all with stunning views. This is an excellent base from which to embark on outdoor activities. **www.flodigarry.co.uk**

ISLE OF SKYE Three Chimneys　　　　　　　P ¶¶ &　£££££

Colbost, Dunvegan, Isle of Skye, Inverness-shire, IV55 8ZT **Tel** *01470 511258* **Rooms** *6*

Arguably the finest restaurant-with-rooms in Scotland, this intimate hotel is recognized for the excellence of its cooking and hospitality of the owners. Features modern and luxurious accommodation. The retreat's spectacular location makes for a memorable visit. **www.threechimneys.co.uk**

KILLIECRANKIE Killiecrankie Hotel　　　　　　¶¶ &　　£££

Killiecrankie, by Pitlochry, Perthshire, PH16 5LE **Tel** *01796 473220* **Rooms** *10*

A relaxing and informal hotel, set by the scenic wooded cliffs of the Killiecrankie Pass – a Royal Society for the Protection of Birds reserve. The decor is stylish and bright, and the accommodation is comfortable and spacious. Known for serving good food; light meals are also available. **www.killiecrankiehotel.co.uk**

Key to Price Guide *see p556* **Key to Symbols** *see back cover flap*

KINGUSSIE The Cross

P ‖ ££££££

Tweed Mill Brae, Ardbroilach Rd, Kingussie, Perthshire, PH21 1LB **Tel** *01540 661166* **Rooms** *8*

Highly acclaimed restaurant-with-rooms, located in a converted tweed mill near the Cairngorms. The smartly refurbished and attractively decorated interior is light and bright. An ideal base for those interested in exploring this area. Three AA Rosettes restaurant, excellent wine list and caring hosts. **www.thecross.co.uk**

LOCHINVER The Albannach

P ‖ ££££££

Lochinver, Sutherland, Inverness-shire, IV27 4LP **Tel** *01571 844407* **Rooms** *5*

Set on a hill on the outskirts of Lochinver, this small hotel is ideal for those who enjoy the finer things in life. Offers great views of the countryside. The cooking is quite superb, making innovative use of fresh local produce. Welcoming and hospitable owners. Three suites also available. Closed Jan, Feb. **www.thealbannach.co.uk**

LOCHRANZA Apple Lodge

🗐   £

Lochranza, Isle of Arran, Bute, KA27 8HJ **Tel** *01770 830229* **Rooms** *4*

This charming guesthouse is an excellent base for exploring the sights of Arran. Close to the Kintyre ferry with fine views over the nearby castle. Bedrooms are prettily floral; there is also a self-contained cottage annexe. Serves good home cooking. **www.a1tourism.com/uk/applelodge2**

MUIR OF ORD The Dower House

‖   £££

Highfield, Muir of Ord, Inverness-shire, IV6 7XN **Tel** *01463 870090* **Rooms** *4*

This attractive, 18th-century hotel is one of the best-kept secrets in the Highlands. Offers tastefully decorated, pleasant rooms, equipped with modern amenities. The restaurant is renowned for its appetizing home-cooked meals, which emphasize the versatility of good local produce. **www.thedowerhouse.co.uk**

MULL Tiroran House

P ‖ &   £££

Isle of Mull, PA69 6ES **Tel** *01681 705232* **Rooms** *8*

Set in a Victorian country house surrounded by beautiful gardens and stunning loch-side views, this boutique hotel provides luxury accommodation on the Isle of Mull. Rooms are all en suite, with quality furnishings; self-catering cottages are also available. Dinner comprises fresh organic produce from the kitchen garden. Dog-friendly. **www.tiroran.com**

OBAN Manor House

P ‖ &   £££

Gallanach Rd, Oban, PA34 4LS **Tel** *01631 562087* **Rooms** *11*

Housed in a late Georgian property, the Manor House is perched on a hill overlooking Oban Bay and boasts superb views. The well-appointed rooms are all en suite, with period features sitting alongside modern amenities. A changing seasonal menu is on offer in the restaurant, and less formal lunches are available at the bar. **www.manorhouseoban.com**

ORKNEY ISLANDS Foveran

P ‖   ££

St Ola, Kirkwall, Orkney, KW15 1SF **Tel** *01856 872389* **Rooms** *8*

A fine, family-run hotel, with splendid views over Scapa Flow. The hotel has been tastefully refurbished to a high standard, and the staff gives a true taste of Orcadian hospitality. A wonderful base for exploring these magical islands. Offers superb cooking and pleasant accommodation. **www.foveranhotel.co.uk**

PITLOCHRY Atholl Palace

🖳 P ‖ 🏊 🎾 &   ££££

Pitlochry, Perthshire, PH16 5LY **Tel** *01796 472400* **Rooms** *106*

This grandiose hotel is an excellent example of Scottish baronial architecture. The accommodation is on a large scale with spacious bedrooms and public areas. Features a wide range of leisure and spa facilities, as well as varying dining options to suit all tastes. **www.athollpalace.com**

PLOCKTON Plockton Hotel

‖ &   ££

Harbour St, Plockton, Ross-shire, IV52 8TN **Tel** *01599 544274* **Rooms** *15*

A comfortable and tastefully furnished hotel, set across the waterfront, with breathtaking views of the countryside. The bedrooms are stylishly simple, with en suite facilities; many overlooking the loch and the mountains. Serves good food, using fresh local produce. **www.plocktonhotel.co.uk**

STRONTIAN Kilcamb Lodge

‖   £££££

Strontian, Argyll, PH36 4HY **Tel** *01967 402257* **Rooms** *10*

This elegant country house is located on the quiet Ardnamurchan peninsula. A lovely place to relax and enjoy the striking views over a winding sea loch. Welcoming hosts, excellent food and intimate ambience complete the experience. Dinner included. **www.kilcamblodge.co.uk**

TORLUNDY Inverlochy Castle

P ‖   ££££££

Torlundy, Fort William, Perthshire, PH33 6SN **Tel** *01397 702177* **Rooms** *17*

A grand, luxurious castle, set amid beautiful grounds, on the outskirts of Fort William. The interior is decorated in a traditional, classic style. Offers high standards of food, accommodation and service. Dining here is a memorable experience. Fishing, tennis and croquet facilities are also available. **www.inverlochycastlehotel.com**

ULLAPOOL Tanglewood House

🗐   ££

Ullapool, Ross-shire, IV26 2TB **Tel** *01854 612059* **Rooms** *3*

This modern, highly individual house commands panoramic vistas of Loch Broom from its huge picture windows. The hotel is tastefully furnished and extremely comfortable. The hostess is a highly accomplished cook, who serves imaginative and innovative cuisine. Bring your own alcohol. **www.tanglewoodhouse.co.uk**

WHERE TO EAT

British food need strike no terrors to the visiting gourmet's heart; the UK's restaurant scene has moved far from its once dismal reputation. Foreign chefs and cooking

Hakkasan in central London
(see p609)

styles have ensured a wide range of cuisine throughout Britain, with the greatest choice in London and the other major cities. British chefs are today among the most innovative in the world, and the indigenous cooking (once thought to consist only of fish and chips, meat pies and lumpy custard) has improved out of all recognition. Whatever your budget, it is

possible to eat well and at most times of day in large towns. Less elaborate, but well-prepared, affordable food is available in all types of restaurants and cafés; modern approaches combine fresh produce and dietary common sense with influences from around the world. Pub fare has perhaps undergone the greatest transformation with a wide variety of food found in all kinds of pubs. Gastropubs in particular focus on quality cuisine. The restaurant listings *(see pp608–651)* feature some of the very best places, as well as those with a steady track record.

WHAT'S ON THE MENU?

The choice seems endless in large cities, particularly in London. Cuisines from all over the world are represented, as well as their infinite variations – Thai, Tex-Mex, Turkish, Tuscan, Tandoori, Bhel Poori and Balti. There are many more unusual styles of cooking such as Ethiopian, Polish, Caribbean and Pacific Rim. French and Italian restaurants are still highly regarded, offering everything from pastries and espresso coffee to the highest standards of *haute cuisine*. Outside the major cities the food scene is more limited, but creative cooking can be found in the most rural areas,

and more and more Rosette-awarded pubs and restaurants are popping up. The vague term "modern European cuisine" adopted by many restaurants disguises a diverse rag-bag of styles. The spectrum ranges from French to Asian recipes, loosely characterized by the imaginative use of fresh, high-quality ingredients, which are cooked simply with imaginative seasonings.

Nostalgic yearnings for British food have produced a revival of hearty traditional dishes such as steak and kidney pie and treacle pudding *(see p607),* though "Modern British" cooking adopts a lighter, more innovative approach. The distinctions between British and

modern European food are starting to blur, as young chefs apply Oriental and Mediterranean flavours to home-grown ingredients. This mixing-up of flavours is referred to as "fusion" cuisine.

BREAKFAST

It used to be said that the best way to enjoy British food was to eat breakfast three times a day. Traditional British breakfast starts with cereal and milk followed by bacon, eggs and tomato, perhaps with fried black pudding *(see p606)* in the North and Scotland. It is finished off with toast and marmalade washed down with tea. Or you can just have black coffee and fruit juice, with a croissant or two (known as Continental breakfast in hotels). The price of breakfast is often included in hotel tariffs in Britain.

LUNCH

The most popular lunchtime foods are sandwiches, salads, baked potatoes with fillings and ploughman's lunches *(see p606).* A traditional Sunday lunch of roast chicken, lamb or beef is served in some pubs and restaurants. Many establishments offer reasonably priced set lunches that make dining in upmarket restaurants much more affordable.

Bibendum, sophisticated French cuisine in London (see p615)

AFTERNOON TEA

No visitor should miss the experience of a proper English afternoon tea, which rivals breakfast as the most enjoyable meal of the day (see p606). Some of the most palatial teas are offered by country-house and top London hotels such as the Ritz or Browns. The area that is best known for its classic "cream teas" is the West Country; these always include scones, spread with clotted cream, butter and jam. Wales, Scotland, Yorkshire and the Lake District also offer tasty teas with regional variations; in the North Country a slice of apple pie or fruit cake is served hot with a piece of North Yorkshire Wensleydale cheese on top.

An afternoon tea including sandwiches, cakes and scones

DINNER

At dinner time, the grander restaurants and hotels offer elaborately staged meals, sometimes billed as five or six courses (though one may be simply a sorbet, or coffee with *petits fours*). Taster menus, which can sometimes be up to 20 courses, are a great way to sample the best a restaurant has to offer.

Generally, you can choose to take your dinner before 6pm or after 9pm only in larger towns, where restaurants and bars often have longer opening hours. Confusingly, in the North of England and Scotland "lunch" can be called "dinner" and "dinner" may be called "tea".

Leith Docks in Edinburgh, a centre of good pubs, bars and restaurants

PLACES TO EAT

Eating venues are extremely varied, with brasseries, bistros, wine bars, tearooms, *tapas* bars and theatre cafés competing with the more conventional cafés and restaurants. Many pubs also serve excellent food, often at reasonable prices (see pp652–5). Some of the finest restaurants are in grand hotels.

BRASSERIES, BISTROS AND CAFES

French-style café-brasseries are now popular in Britain. Sometimes they stay open all day, serving coffee, snacks and fairly simple dishes along with a selection of beers and wines. Alcoholic drinks, however, may only be available at certain times of day. The atmosphere is usually young and urbane, with decor to match. Drinks such as imported bottled beers, exotic spirits or cocktails may be fairly expensive.

The café at Tate St Ives, Cornwall (see p629)

Wine bars are similar to brasseries, but with a better selection of wines, which may include English varieties (see p160). Some bars have a good range of ciders and real ales as well (see p604). Bistros are another French import, serving full meals at lunch and dinner with less formality and more moderate prices than you would expect at a restaurant. You should expect to pay anything from £15 to £30 for a standard three-course meal in a bistro.

RESTAURANTS-WITH-ROOMS AND HOTELS

Restaurants-with-rooms are a new breed of small establishments with only a handful of bedrooms and usually excellent food. They tend to be expensive and are usually in a rural location.

Many hotel restaurants happily serve non-residents. They tend to be expensive, but the best can be unparalleled. Hotels serving a high standard of food are also included on pages 556–99.

RESTAURANT ETIQUETTE

As a rule of thumb, the more expensive the restaurant, the more formal the dress code – though very few restaurants expect men to wear a shirt and tie. Ring ahead to check.

A total smoking ban in public places was implemented throughout the UK in 2007. However, smoking outside is still permitted in some cases.

Raymond Blanc's Le Manoir Aux Quat'Saisons *(see p620)*, one of Britain's most acclaimed restaurants-with-rooms

ALCOHOL

Britain's laws concerning the sale of alcohol, the "licensing laws", were once among the most restrictive in Europe. Now they are much more relaxed, with some restaurants operating extended opening hours, especially at weekends. Some establishments, however, may only serve alcohol at set times with food. Some unlicensed restaurants operate a "Bring Your Own" policy; a corkage fee is often charged. It is illegal to sell alcohol to under 18s.

VEGETARIAN FOOD

Britain is ahead of many of its European counterparts in providing vegetarian alternatives to meat dishes. Few places in this section serve only vegetarian meals, but most restaurants offer at least one vegetarian option. Vegetarians who want a wider choice should seek out South Indian and other ethnic restaurants which have a tradition of vegetarian cuisine.

FAST FOOD AND CHAIN RESTAURANTS

Fast food usually costs well under £10. Apart from the ubiquitous fish and chip shop, there are many of the usual fast food chains, as well as some more upmarket

options such as PizzaExpress and Yo! Sushi. Other chains offering good-value, quality food, as well as facilities for children include Ask, Giraffe, Gourmet Burger Kitchen and Leon. Sandwich bars are very popular and are often good value; some also have seating. Budget cafés, nicknamed "greasy spoons", serve simple, inexpensive food, often in the form of endless variations of the breakfast fry-up *(see p606)*.

BOOKING AHEAD

It is always safer to book a table first before making a special journey to a restaurant; city restaurants can be very busy, and some of the more renowned establishments can be fully booked a month in

Fifteen restaurant overlooking Watergate Bay *(see p628)*

advance. Fridays, Saturdays and Sunday lunchtimes are particularly busy, and booking is essential. Famous gourmet restaurants can require a booking months in advance.

CHECKING THE BILL

All restaurants are required by law to display their current prices outside the door. These amounts include Value Added Tax (VAT), currently at 20 per cent. Service and cover charges (if any) are also specified.

Wine is always pricey in Britain, and extras like coffee or bottled water can be disproportionately expensive.

Service charges (usually between 10 per cent and 15 per cent) are often automatically added to your bill. If you feel that the service has been poor, you are entitled to subtract this service charge. If no service charge has been added, you are expected to add 10 to 15 per cent to the bill, but it is your decision.

Look out for additional charges: some restaurants may leave the "total" box of credit card slips blank, hoping customers will add something extra to the service charge. A few smart restaurants may also add a "cover charge" for flowers, bread and butter, etc. The majority of restaurants accept credit cards.

MEALTIMES

Breakfast is a moveable feast. It may be as early as 6:30am in a city business hotel (most hoteliers will make special arrangements if you have a plane to catch or some other reason for checking out early) or as late as 10:30am in relaxed country house establishments. Few hoteliers relish cooking bacon and eggs that late, however, and some insist you are up and about by 9am sharp if you want anything to eat. But you can find breakfast all day long in some urban restaurants. The American concept of Sunday "brunch" (a leisurely halfway house between breakfast and lunch) is becoming increasingly popular in some hotels, restaurants and cafés.

Lunch in pubs and restaurants is usually served between noon and 2:30pm. Try to arrive in time to order the main course before 1:30pm, or you may find choice restricted. Most tourist areas have plenty of cafés, fast-food diners and coffee bars where you can have a snack at any time of day. During peak hours there may be a minimum charge.

If you are lucky enough to be in one of the places where you can get a traditional afternoon tea, it is usually served between 3pm and 5pm.

Dinner is usually served from 6pm until 10pm; some places, especially ethnic restaurants, stay open later. In guest houses or small hotels, dinner may be served at a specific time. In cities, many restaurants are closed on Sunday evenings and on Mondays.

CHILDREN

The continental norm of dining out *en famille* is steadily becoming more acceptable in Britain, and visiting a restaurant may no longer entail endless searches for a babysitter. Many places welcome junior diners, and

Langan's Brassserie, a popular choice for Anglo-French cuisine *(see p610)*

Ice-cream parlour sign

some actively encourage families, at least during the day or early evening. Formal restaurants sometimes cultivate a more adult ambience at dinner time, and some impose age limits. If you want to take young children to a restaurant, check when you book.

Italian, Spanish, Indian, fast-food restaurants and ice-cream parlours nearly always welcome children, and sometimes provide special menus or high chairs for them. Even traditional English pubs, which were once a strictly adult preserve, accommodate families and may even provide special rooms or play areas.

The places that welcome and cater for children are indicated in both the pubs guide *(see pp652–55)* and the restaurant listings.

DISABLED ACCESS

As in most walks of life, restaurant facilities in Britain could be better for disabled visitors, but things are gradually improving. Modern premises usually take account of mobility problems, but it's always best to check first if you have special needs.

PICNICS

Eating outside is becoming more popular in Britain, though it is more likely that you will find tables outside pubs in the form of a beer garden, than outside restaurants. One inexpensive option is to make up your own picnic; most towns have good delicatessens and bakeries where you can collect provisions, and in Britain you do not usually have to worry about shops closing at mid-day as they often do on the Continent.

Look out for street markets to pick up fresh fruit and local cheeses at bargain prices. Department stores like Marks & Spencer and supermarkets such as Sainsbury's and Tesco often sell an excellent range of pre-packed sandwiches and snacks; large towns usually have several sandwich bars to choose from. Your hotel or guest house may also be able to provide a packed lunch. Ask for it the night before.

An option for a chillier day is a hot takeaway meal; fish and chips with salt and vinegar all wrapped in paper is not only a British cliché but a national institution.

Eating alfresco at Grasmere in the Lake District

The Traditional British Pub

Beer label
c.1900

Every country has its bars, but Britain is famous for its pubs or "public houses". Ale was brewed in England in Roman times – mostly at home – and by the Middle Ages there were inns and taverns which brewed their own. The 18th century was the heyday of the coaching inn as stage coaches brought more custom. In the 19th century came railway taverns for travellers and "gin palaces" for the new industrial workers. Today, pubs come in all styles and sizes and many cater to families, serving food as well as drink *(see pp652–55)*.

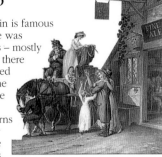

Early 19th-century coaching inn – also a social centre and post office

THE VICTORIAN PUB

A century ago, many pubs in towns and cities had smart interiors, to contrast with the poor housing of their clients.

Elaborately etched glass is a feature of many Victorian interiors.

Pub games, *such as cribbage, bar billiards, pool and dominoes are part of British pub culture. Here some regular customers are competing against a rival pub's darts team.*

Beer gardens *outside pubs are a favourite venue for family summer treats.*

Pint glasses (containing just over half a litre) are used for beer.

The Red Lion pub name is derived from Scottish heraldry *(see p26)*.

Old-fashioned cash register contributes to the period atmosphere of the bar.

Pewter tankards, seldom used by drinkers today, add a traditional touch.

WHAT TO DRINK

Draught bitter is the most traditional British beer. Brewed from malted barley, hops, yeast and water, and usually matured in a wooden cask, it varies from region to region. In the north of England the sweeter mild ale is popular, and lagers served in bottles or on tap are also widely drunk. Stout, made from black malt, is another variation.

Beer pump

Draught bitter is drunk at cellar temperature.

Draught lager is a light-coloured, carbonated beer.

Guinness is a thick, creamy Irish stout.

Pavement tables, crowded with city drinkers during the summer months

A village pub, offering a waterside view and serving drinks in the garden

Bottles of spirits, as well as the popular port and sherry, are ranged behind the bar.

Glass lamps imitate the Victorian style.

Wine, once rarely found in pubs, is now increasingly popular.

A deep-toned mahogany bar forms part of the traditional setting.

Draught beer, served from pumps or taps, comes from national and local brewers.

Optics dispense spirits in precise measures.

Mild may be served by the pint or in a half-pint tankard (as above).

Top cocktails are gin-and-tonic (right) and Pimm's.

PUB SIGNS

Early medieval inns used vines or evergreens as signs – the symbol of Bacchus, the Roman god of wine. Soon pubs acquired names that signalled support for monarchs or noblemen, or celebrated victories in battle. As many customers could not read, pub signs had vivid images.

The George *may derive from one of the six English kings of that name, or, as here, from England's patron saint.*

The Bat and Ball *celebrates cricket, and may be sited near a village green where the game can be played.*

The Green Man *is a woodland spirit from pagan mythology, possibly the basis for the legend of Robin Hood (see p336).*

The Magna Carta *sign commemorates and illustrates the "great charter" signed by King John in 1215 (see p48).*

The Bird in Hand *refers to the ancient country sport of falconry, traditionally practised by noblemen.*

The Flavours of Britain

A rich agriculture that provides meat and dairy products such as well as fruit, vegetables and cereals, gives the British table a broad scope. Traditional dishes – cooked breakfasts, roast beef, fish and chips – are famous, but there is much more on offer, varying from region to region. Many towns give their names to produce and dishes. Seasonal choices include game and seafood, while other produce can be seen at the increasingly popular farmers' markets. Britons still have a penchant for pies and puddings, and most regions have cakes and buns they can call their own. Scotland has its own distinctive cuisine *(see p488)*.

Asparagus

Local fresh beetroot on sale at a greengrocer's shop

CENTRAL AND SOUTHERN ENGLAND

All tastes are catered for in the metropolis, and the surrounding countryside has long been given over to its demands. The flat lands of East Anglia provide vegetables and root crops; the South Downs have been shorn by sheep; geese have made Nottingham famous; and the county of Kent is known as "the Garden of England" for its glorious orchards and its fields of soft fruits. From around the coast come Dover sole, Whitstable oysters (popular since Roman times) and the Cockney favourites, cockles and whelks. The game season runs from November to February, and pheasant is often on the menu.

WEST OF ENGLAND

The warmest part of England is renowned for its classic cream teas, the key ingredient provided by its dairy herds. In Cornwall, pasties have long been a staple. Once eaten by tin miners and filled with meat at one end and jam the other, to give two courses in one, they are now generally made with meat and veg-

Cornish Yarg   Cider-washed   Dorstone goats'-   Cropwell
                Celtic Promise   milk cheese   Bishop Stilton
Montgomery
Cheddar

Ewes'-milk
Wigmore

Selection of fine, farm-produced British cheeses

TRADITIONAL BRITISH FOOD

Though many traditional dishes, such as Lancashire hotpot, beef Wellington and even fish and chips, can be harder to hunt down than tapas, pizza or chicken tikka masala, other reliable regulars remain. Among them are shepherd's pie (minced lamb with mashed potatoes), steak and kidney pie (beef and kidney in gravy baked in a pastry crust), or game pie and "bangers and mash" (sausages with mash potatoes and onion gravy). For pudding there is a variety of trifles, pies, tarts and crumbles, often eaten with custard, as well as a lighter summer pudding of seasonal fruit. A "full English breakfast" is a fry-up of sausages, eggs, bacon, tomatoes, mushrooms and bread, perhaps with black pudding or laverbread. Lunchtime snacks include a "Ploughman's lunch" of cheese and pickles with a "doorstep" of bread.

Dover sole *This is the most tasty flatfish, best served simply grilled with lemon, spinach and new potatoes.*

Display of British breads at a local farmers' market

etables. The clear waters around the peninsula offer up such seafood as sardines, mackerel and crab in abundance, and many of the region's best restaurants specialize in fish. Bath gives its name to special biscuits and buns.

NORTH OF ENGLAND

Cumberland sausage, Lancashire hotpot, Goosnargh duck and Yorkshire pudding – the names tell you exactly where the food on your plate originated. These are the staples, but restaurants these days are creating new dishes from old, such as trout with black (blood) pudding, and even being adventurous with "mushy" peas. Bradford, with its large Asian community, is the best place to eat Indian food.

WALES

The green grass of Wales is appreciated by sheep, who turn into fabulous lamb that is simply roasted and eaten with mint sauce – a favourite all over Britain. The grass is

A Cornish fishmonger displays a locally caught red mullet

good for dairy products, too, including white, crumbly Caerphilly. Cheese is the principal ingredient of Welsh rarebit (pronounced rabbit), made with cheese grilled on toast and occasionally augmented with beer. Look out for prize-winning Welsh Black beef – prime fillets are often accompanied by horseradish sauce. The Irish Sea provides plenty of fish, but there is also freshwater trout and salmon. A curiosity of the South Wales seashore is laver, a kind of sea spinach, which is mixed with oatmeal and fried in small cakes called *bara lawr*, or laverbread, to be served with sausage and bacon for breakfast.

BRITISH CHEESES

Caerphilly Fresh, white, mild cheese from Wales.

Cheshire Crumbly, silky and full-bodied cheese.

Cheddar Often imitated, never bettered; the best comes from the West Country.

Double Gloucester Mellow flavoured, smooth and creamy.

Sage Derby Flavoured with green veins of sage.

Stilton The king of British cheeses, a strong, blue-veined cheese with a creamy texture. Popular at Christmas.

Wensleydale Young, moist and flaky-textured, with a mild, slightly sweet flavour.

Cornish mackerel *The ideal partner for this rich fish is a piquant sauce make of English gooseberries.*

Roast beef *Horseradish sauce is a traditional accompaniment, as are crisp Yorkshire puddings made of batter.*

Welsh lamb with leeks *The leek is the national vegetable of Wales, and perfectly complements roast lamb.*

Choosing a Restaurant

The restaurants in this guide have been selected across a wide range of price categories for their good value, exceptional food and interesting location. This chart lists the restaurants by region, starting with London. It also highlights some of the factors that may influence your choice. For pub listings, see pages 652–657.

PRICE CATEGORIES
For a three-course meal for one, half a bottle of house wine, and all unavoidable extra charges such as cover, service, VAT:
£ under £20
££ £20–£35
£££ £35–£55
££££ £55–£75
£££££ over £75

LONDON

WEST END AND WESTMINSTER Busaba Eathai £
106–110 Wardour St, W1F 0TR **Tel** *020 7255 8686*   **Map** *11 A2*

The immense popularity of Busaba Eathai rests on its reasonably priced Thai food and efficient service. Get there early, as the queue here can be of legendary proportions after 7pm. However, be prepared to share a table whatever time you arrive. Food is good – try Thai calamari and the rose apple wok dish. One of three branches.

WEST END AND WESTMINSTER Bam-Bou ££
1 Percy St, W1T 1DB **Tel** *020 7323 9130*   **Map** *11 A1*

A nice bar upstairs lures you in for a few drinks before you descend to the restaurant proper. Seated at a low table with just candlelight playing off dark wood, you feel a million miles from London. This is not your average Pan-Asian restaurant. The food is excellent and the atmosphere relaxed and warm. Private rooms are also available.

WEST END AND WESTMINSTER Belgo Centraal ££
50 Earlham St, WC2H 9LJ **Tel** *020 7813 2233*   **Map** *11 B2*

Nice and handy for Neal Street, Belgo Centraal remains popular every night. The cool young staff whip up a great variety of Belgian cuisine, from *moules marinières* to more exotic creations featuring Belgium's famous beers. Meat-eaters are also catered for. Eat at the long refectory tables and enjoy the fun.

WEST END AND WESTMINSTER Café Mode ££
57 Endell St, WC2H 9AJ **Tel** *020 7240 8085*   **Map** *11 C2*

Great salads, pizzas and vegetarian dishes, and warm, friendly staff all contribute to a winning formula at Café Mode. Always great value and very popular, this restaurant is also preferred by lone diners. The little Med-inspired gem is a cool retreat from the hustle and bustle of Covent Garden.

WEST END AND WESTMINSTER Café Pacifico ££
5–6 Langley St, WC2H 9JA **Tel** *020 7379 7728*   **Map** *11 B2*

Café Pacifico is frequented by the young and young-at-heart. Occasional Mexican live music and a buzzy atmosphere promise a lively night, though those looking for a romantic dinner might want to stay away. A few cocktails followed by some filling and reasonably priced food will send you singing out into the street.

WEST END AND WESTMINSTER Chor Bizarre ££
16 Albemarle St, W1S 4HW **Tel** *020 7629 9802*   **Map** *10 F3*

Serving dishes from regional India, this restaurant is always busy. Try the lamb with fenugreek, spinach and ginger, and the aubergine with peanut sauce. Waiters can lose interest – keep them on their toes if you do not want to be forgotten – but they are friendly and willing to help you choose from the large menu.

WEST END AND WESTMINSTER Loch Fyne ££
2–4 Catherine St, WC2B 5JS **Tel** *020 7240 4999*   **Map** *11 C2*

At Loch Fyne, a seafood restaurant, the fish and shellfish are brought in fresh from Scotland. The wine list is suitably chosen to match the crustaceans and other edible sea creatures on offer. Portions are generous whether you choose a platter of oysters or a large plate of poached smoked haddock.

WEST END AND WESTMINSTER Mekong ££
46 Churton St, SW1V 2LP **Tel** *020 7630 9568*   **Map** *19 B2*

This long-standing Vietnamese eatery still fills up on account of its wallet-friendly food. The ground-floor dining area can seem cramped, and the rustic walls painted in clashing pink and green leave something to be desired, but the kitchen delivers some tasty treats. Delightful staff and sought-after outdoor tables add to the experience.

WEST END AND WESTMINSTER Palm Court Brasserie ££
39 King St, WC2E 8JS **Tel** *020 7240 2939*   **Map** *11 C2*

A good location and a sophisticated interior make Palm Court Brasserie a firm favourite with the locals. Mediterranean flavours are well infused with the southern sunshine. Sharing platters are good fun and great value, while a roast rump of lamb is quite filling. There are special pre-theatre and mid-week deals, too. Reservations strongly recommended.

Key to Symbols *see back cover flap*

WEST END AND WESTMINSTER Porter's English Restaurant
17 Henrietta St, WC2E 8QH **Tel** *020 7836 6466*

££

Map 11 C2

A great place for proper fish and chips, Porter's is known for serving hearty British "grub" with tasty pie dishes such as steak and Guinness, cod, salmon and prawn. Desserts are equally large and not for those on a diet. Prices are good for the location – there is a lunch deal for £22.95 –, and the staff are cheerful.

WEST END AND WESTMINSTER Rasa W1
6 Dering Street, W1S 1AD **Tel** *020 7629 1346*

££

Map 10 E2

With seven restaurants around London, the Rasa chain are the foremost exponents – in India and abroad – of the distinctive, mainly vegetarian, cuisine of Kerala in South India. As well as some of London's most interesting vegetarian food, branches have seafood, meat and other specialities. Seasonings are more subtle and fragrant than hot.

WEST END AND WESTMINSTER Thai Metro
38 Charlotte St, W1F 2NN **Tel** *020 7436 4201*

££

Map 3 A5

Thai Metro offers top-notch Thai cuisine at affordable prices. The green curry is a must-try, but be warned about the chillies. The zingy flavours that characterize Thai food are all here in abundance. If the weather is warm, you can enjoy your food in the fresh air. Service is brisk, which may not be ideal for a relaxed meal. Good lunch deals.

WEST END AND WESTMINSTER The Ebury
11 Pimlico Rd, SW1W 8NA **Tel** *020 7730 6784*

££

Map 18 D2

Diners come to this sleek restaurant housed in a converted pub to enjoy a varied modern European menu with British and Mediterranean accents. First-rate ingredients are used in dishes such as ricotta and herb gnocchi, and slow-cooked pork belly with Parmesan polenta. The dining room is bright and airy, exuding understated elegance.

WEST END AND WESTMINSTER Vasco & Piero's Pavilion
15 Poland St, W1F 8QE **Tel** *020 7437 8774*

££

Map 11 A2

Of Umbrian heritage, the owner of this restaurant ensures that chickpeas and lentils feature frequently on the largely Italian menu which changes twice daily. The pasta is made in-house, with the finest quality ingredients. The truffles, particularly, make the place worth a visit. In season, black or white truffles are imported from Umbria.

WEST END AND WESTMINSTER Al Duca
4–5 Duke of York St, SW1Y 6LA **Tel** *020 7839 3090*

£££

Map 11 A3

Just off Piccadilly, this bright, modern Italian restaurant offers great value in an expensive area, with set-price menus. Classic north Italian dishes are nicely presented, including grilled fish, pastas and richly flavoured risottos. Excellent wine list and a great range of Italian liqueurs for after your meal.

WEST END AND WESTMINSTER Christopher's American Grill
18 Wellington St, WC2E 7DD **Tel** *020 7240 4222*

£££

Map 11 C2

Rather more formal than you might expect from an American restaurant, but then this is a superior establishment. There are plenty of American favourites to choose from, including delicious ham hocks, large steaks and excellent lobsters. There is a Martini bar on the ground floor, and views over Waterloo Bridge from the upstairs restaurant.

WEST END AND WESTMINSTER Elena's L'Etoile
30 Charlotte St, W1T 2NG **Tel** *020 7636 7189*

£££

Map 11 A1

This long-standing local eatery is extremely busy at lunchtime, with advertising media people from surrounding ad agencies and TV companies. The time-tested menu delivers classic French bistro food under the gaze of celebrity pictures that cover the walls. It's not cheap but guarantees quality and that indefinable extra – real atmosphere.

WEST END AND WESTMINSTER Hakkasan
8 Hanway Place, W1T 1HD **Tel** *020 7927 7000*

£££

Map 11 A1

A very expensive Chinese restaurant, Hakkasan has maintained a consistently high turnover. The decor is superbly stylish and the food even more so. No windows mean you can't peer in to check it out before entering. Though busy, it's a great choice for gourmets who can afford it. Don't miss the dim sums.

WEST END AND WESTMINSTER Il Convivio
143 Ebury St, SW1W 9QN **Tel** *020 7730 4099*

£££

Set within a beautiful Georgian town house, this Italian restaurant has a conservatory with a retractable roof that offers an outdoor dining experience throughout the summer. Fare includes seared diver scallops with Catalonian chicory pasta and a great choice of desserts. For a more modest meal, choose from the great value fixed-price menus. Closed Sun.

WEST END AND WESTMINSTER Indigo
1 Aldwych, WC2B 4RH **Tel** *020 7300 0400*

£££

Map 12 D2

This stylish restaurant offers an eclectic mix of modern European and International dishes, all beautifully presented. Enjoy a drink in the Grand Bar upstairs before descending in the lift to the plush dining room. Plenty of choice for all tastes and a useful "mix and match" salad and pasta course. On Sundays, they have a brunch-and-movie deal.

WEST END AND WESTMINSTER J Sheekey
32 St Martin's Court, WC2N 4AL **Tel** *020 7240 2565*

£££

Map 11 B2

Sheekey's fish restaurant first opened near Leicester Square in 1896. It was sadly neglected for years, but since its revamp by the Caprice group its wonderful Victorian interior is again thronged with Theatreland crowds. British fish classics – a celebrated fish pie – are finely done, and the catch-of-the-day fish are superb. There is also an oyster bar.

WEST END AND WESTMINSTER Langan's Brasserie
6 Stratton St, W1J 8LB **Tel** 020 7491 8822
♪   ⓔⓔⓔ
Map *10 F3*

The original and perhaps still the best in this chain of restaurants, Langan's faithfully adheres to the style of its late eponymous owner. Service is discreetly attentive and the staff are friendly. Try and get a table downstairs where they serve soufflé with anchovy sauce. Try the house speciality, Langan's bangers and mash with white onion sauce.

WEST END AND WESTMINSTER L'Escargot Marco Pierre White
48 Greek St, W1D 4EF **Tel** 020 7439 7474
🍴   ⓔⓔⓔ
Map *11 A1*

Another Soho institution, this restaurant is run by Marco Pierre White, a legendary chef. Expect high standards but be surprised by the very reasonable prices. In the Picasso Room you can look at some of the master's works while eating artistically crafted fine food. Try the parfait of foi gras *en gelée* with toasted Poilane. Closed on Sundays.

WEST END AND WESTMINSTER Momo
25 Heddon Street, W1B 4BH **Tel** 020 7434 4040
♪ &   ⓔⓔⓔ
Map *10 F2*

Popular ever since it opened in 1995, Momo gave a newly fashionable appeal to North African food. Classic tagines and couscous, as well as less familiar dishes, are infused with fresh flavours of cumin, mint and coriander, amid decor that stylishly evokes old Marrakech. There's great live music in the bar every Tuesday.

WEST END AND WESTMINSTER National Gallery Dining Rooms
Sainsbury Wing, National Gallery, Trafalgar Sq, WC2N 5DN **Tel** 020 7747 2525
🚶 🍴 &   ⓔⓔⓔ
Map *11 B3*

Museum and gallery cafés tend to be dull and functional, but the National Gallery has changed all that with this lively and modern brasserie. It's open for breakfast, lunch and dinner, so at various times you can enjoy tea and cakes, grills, pastas, or cocktails. There's also a generous children's menu.

WEST END AND WESTMINSTER Sofra
36 Tavistock St, WC2E 7PB **Tel** 020 7240 3773
🚶   ⓔⓔⓔ
Map *11 C2*

A reputed London institution, Sofra has been serving superior Turkish food for many years. The speciality is the healthy option involving a variety of little dishes to share. Bread and olives come free throughout the meal, while dips such as hummous and *tzatziki* always taste fresh and clean.

WEST END AND WESTMINSTER The Gaucho Grill
125–126 Chancery Lane, WC2A 1PU **Tel** 020 7242 7727
🚶 &   ⓔⓔⓔ
Map *12 E1*

There are a few of branches of the Gaucho around London and they remain of consistent value. The star attraction is still its delicious steak. A large wine list helps wash down an enormous meal and the cocktails are good too. Ideal for a pleasant, no-frills dining, it's a well-priced place in a reasonably expensive area. Closed Sundays.

WEST END AND WESTMINSTER The Wolseley
160 Piccadilly, W1J 9EB **Tel** 020 7499 6996
🚶 &   ⓔⓔⓔ
Map *10 F3*

London never had many 19th-century "grand cafés", but in 2003 this fine Piccadilly building was made into a great modern equivalent. Chandeliers hanging from lofty ceilings aid the glamorous, buzzing atmosphere. Menus offer plenty of variety, from salads to grills and seafood. Also open daily for breakfast and afternoon tea.

WEST END AND WESTMINSTER Rules
35 Maiden Lane, WC2E 7LB **Tel** 020 7836 5314
&   ⓔⓔⓔⓔ
Map *11 C2*

London's oldest restaurant, opened in 1798, has kept its fascinating decor and its standards as a temple of fine British cooking. The roast beef is definitive, served with fabulous horseradish sauce. Game, fresh from Rules' own hunting estate, is also a speciality. Upstairs are wonderfully Dickensian private rooms.

WEST END AND WESTMINSTER The Criterion
224 Piccadilly, W1J 9HP **Tel** 020 7930 0488
🚶 🍴   ⓔⓔⓔⓔ
Map *11 A3*

The giant Criterion is a monument of a restaurant, right on Piccadilly Circus. Dating from the 1870s, it has fabulous Arabian-fantasy decor with a glittering mosaic ceiling; there are few more impressive places to sit and escape the city outside. On the menu is adventurous Franco-British cuisine. There is also a fine wine list.

WEST END AND WESTMINSTER Umu
14–16 Bruton Place, W1J 6LX **Tel** 020 7499 8881
& 🍴   ⓔⓔⓔⓔ
Map *10 E3*

Seriously expensive but extremely stylish, the Michelin-starred Umu offers a beautiful interior, traditional Kyoto cuisine and friendly service by great staff. With a remarkable sake list, this is one of the few places in London where you can find genuine Japanese *kaiseki*. There's also a good, though expensive, tasting menu. Closed 24 Dec–7 Jan.

WEST END AND WESTMINSTER Wilton's
55 Jermyn St, SW1Y 6LX **Tel** 020 7629 9955
& 🍷 🍴   ⓔⓔⓔⓔ
Map *11 A3*

A landmark institution, there has been a Wilton's in London since 1742. A quintessential expensive club-dining experience. Morecambe Bay potted shrimps, grilled Dover sole, Scottish lobster thermidor and West Mersey Oysters are the main attractions here, but you will also want to bask in the atmosphere and in the attentive and well-mannered service.

WEST END AND WESTMINSTER Hélène Darroze at the Connaught
Connaught Hotel, Carlos Place, W1K 2AL **Tel** 020 7107 8880
& 🍷 🍴   ⓔⓔⓔⓔⓔ
Map *10 E3*

The Connaught Hotel's restaurants have enjoyed an august reputation since the hotel opened in the early 1900s. Renowned French chef Hélène Darroze has two Michelin stars. Her cooking is hugely inventive, blending French traditions with rare, intricate spicings. Dinner prices are high, but there is a more accessible lunch menu. Book ahead.

Key to Price Guide *see p608* **Key to Symbols** *see back cover flap*

SOUTH KENSINGTON AND HYDE PARK Island Restaurant & Bar

Royal Lancaster Hotel, Lancaster Terrace, W2 2TY **Tel** *020 7551 6070*

Map *8 F2*

The Island Restaurant's location in a hotel on a busy junction can seem unexciting, but inside it's a bright contemporary bar-brasserie with friendly, fast-moving staff. Menus feature an enjoyable mix of modern European dishes, from steaks to fresh seafood, plus salads, pasta and child-friendly options.

SOUTH KENSINGTON AND HYDE PARK Whits

21 Abingdon Road, W8 6AH **Tel** *020 7938 1122*

Map *15 C1*

A neighbourhood restaurant on a side lane off busy High Street Kensington. Because of its position it does not attract the masses. Try the house special, King & Queen Scallop Risotto, or the roast duck confit. Other mains include pork with crackling or Elwy lamb. Food is consistently good and very seasonal, but always very affordable.

SOUTH KENSINGTON AND HYDE PARK Amaya

15 Halkin Arcade, off Motcomb Street, SW1X 8JT **Tel** *020 7823 1166*

Map *10 D5*

A very distinguished Indian restaurant, Amaya is spacious, stylish and with the kitchen on honest display. Specializing in grills, it has three stations – tandoori, sigra and tawa – in action all evening. The range of meats and vegetables is brilliant and the presentation and service faultless. Though it is expensive, it's worth dining here.

SOUTH KENSINGTON AND HYDE PARK Cambio de Tercio

163 Old Brompton Rd, SW5 0LJ **Tel** *020 7244 8970*

Map *16 F2*

This unmistakably Spanish restaurant offers traditional Spanish cuisine such as plump king prawns cooked with chilli and garlic. Most of the ingredients are brought over from Spain and the wine list consists entirely of Spanish wines. It was once voted "best Spanish restaurant outside of Spain" by the Spanish Ministry of Agriculture, Fishing and Food.

SOUTH KENSINGTON AND HYDE PARK Fifth Floor at Harvey Nichols

Harvey Nichols, Knightsbrige, SW1X 7RJ **Tel** *020 7235 5250*

Map *9 C5*

Harvey Nichols is a favourite among London's big stores, and its top-floor restaurant has a special verve. Lunch and dinner menus are a set price, and all offer intricate, delicious modern cuisine and extravagantly subtle desserts. The adjacent café has a snack menu and an outside terrace.

SOUTH KENSINGTON AND HYDE PARK L'Étranger

36 Gloucester Rd, SW7 4QT **Tel** *020 7584 1118*

Map *16 E1*

L'Étranger is a gem of a place serving extremely good French-Asian fusion food in very stylish surroundings. People rave about the caramelized black cod with miso and with good reason. Every dish on the menu is delectable and there's a massive wine list that has been created with passion and love. You can dance in the club downstairs.

SOUTH KENSINGTON AND HYDE PARK Nahm

The Halkin Hotel, 5 Halkin St, SW1X 7DJ **Tel** *020 7333 1234*

Map *10 D5*

This remarkable Thai restaurant has a Michelin star so you can arrive with high expectations. The set menu doesn't disappoint. A recommended appetizer is *ma hor* (minced prawns and chicken simmered in palm sugar with deep fried shallots, garlic and peanuts, served on pineapple and mandarin orange). Not cheap but worth the price.

SOUTH KENSINGTON AND HYDE PARK Racine

239 Brompton Rd, SW3 2EP **Tel** *020 7584 4477*

Map *17 B1*

Racine sets out to showcase French cuisine and succeeds very well. Genuine French food, French waiters and great atmosphere all combine to keep locals coming back for more. The venison, when in season, is excellent and the menu changes regularly. The service is good.

SOUTH KENSINGTON AND HYDE PARK Zafferano

5 Lowndes St, SW1X 9EY **Tel** *020 7235 5800*

Map *18 D1*

Zafferano has long been recognized as one of the capital's premier Italian restaurants. It's a discreet place, where the emphasis is firmly on the food. Dishes such as risotto with white wine truffle and char-grilled lamb with aubergine (eggplant) allow the quality of the ingredients to shine through.

SOUTH KENSINGTON AND HYDE PARK Le Gavroche

43 Upper Brook Street, W1K 7QR **Tel** *020 7408 0881*

Map *10 D2*

First opened by brothers Michel and Albert Roux in 1967, Le Gavroche has long set the benchmark for fine dining in London. Michel Roux Jr is now in charge, aided by English chef Rachel Humphrey, but the restaurant remains true to its traditions of timeless luxury and superb French-based haute cuisine. A majestic wine list and superb service.

SOUTH KENSINGTON AND HYDE PARK Nobu

Metropolitan Hotel, 19 Old Park Lane, W1K 1LB **Tel** *020 7447 4747*

Map *10 E4*

London's sleekest, hippest Japanese restaurant was the first European showcase for acclaimed chef Nobu Matsushita. Famous for celebrity diners, it's also a landmark for quality: fresh fish and seafood are supreme, and modern Japanese dishes are prepared with immense skill and panache.

SOUTH KENSINGTON AND HYDE PARK Tom Aikens

43 Elystan St, SW3 3NT **Tel** *020 7584 2003*

Map *17 B2*

Chef Aikens is the twinkliest star in the cooking firmament with other chefs praising his cooking no end. That said, some people find the cuisine a touch rich but everyone loves the experience. Dishes are lovingly constructed and beautifully plated with flavours finely balanced with a watchmaker's care. Very popular so book ahead.

SOUTH KENSINGTON AND HYDE PARK Zuma

5 Raphael St, SW7 1DL **Tel** 020 7584 1010

Map 9 C5

Zuma is a very fashionable restaurant, right opposite Harrods. Celebrities can be spotted here but they come for the great food just like everyone else. Great sashimi, *nigiri*, sushi and tempura with fancy service and fancy prices. It's definitely an experience, but be prepared to dig deep into your pocket.

REGENT'S PARK AND BLOOMSBURY Fino

33 Charlotte Street (entrance on Rathbone Street), W1T 1RR **Tel** 020 7813 8010

Map 11 A1

A smart, comfortable variation on the Spanish tapas bar in a bright basement north of Oxford Street. The menu consists of refined, imaginative presentations of traditional Spanish tapas. The wine list features great modern Spanish wines, and an especially good choice of fine sherries.

REGENT'S PARK AND BLOOMSBURY Ishtar

10–12 Crawford St, W1U 6AZ **Tel** 020 7224 2446

Map 1 C5

Modern Turkish, so no exotic dancers and no photos of the Istanbul landmarks, either. You can dine on two levels, including under some romantic cellar arches and the dishes are familiar but updated. Go for pan-fried sea bass with potatoes and saffron sauce or some well-marinated kebabs. Leave room for some pastries too.

REGENT'S PARK AND BLOOMSBURY Salt Yard

54 Goodge St, W1T 4NA **Tel** 020 7637 0657

Map 3 A5

Given modern London's international flavour it is no surprise that the city has its own take on the traditional Spanish tapas bar. Instead of using only Spanish ingredients, the award-winning Salt Bar also uses first-rate Italian and British produce in irresistible small delights like salt cod fritters with orange alioli or duck and spinach gnocchetti.

REGENT'S PARK AND BLOOMSBURY Caffe Caldesi

118 Marylebone Lane, W1U 2QF **Tel** 020 7847 0753

Map 10 D1

This airy Italian restaurant offers classic dishes and a very reasonable wine list, with a slightly more formal dining space upstairs. Sit down to a traditional home-cooked dinner. Try the fresh ravioli stuffed with beetroot and ricotta with sage and butter sauce. There is also a patisserie, a delicatessen and a bar.

REGENT'S PARK AND BLOOMSBURY Galvin Bistrot de Luxe

66 Baker Street, W1U 7DJ **Tel** 020 7935 4007

Map 1 C5

Brothers Chris and Jeff Galvin run their four restaurants with a blend of originality and thorough French culinary training. The Baker Street branch has the look of a classic Paris bistro, along with a menu of flavour-rich, robust but sophisticated dishes, including wonderful versions of classics like confit of duck. Lunchtime menus are a bargain.

REGENT'S PARK AND BLOOMSBURY Queen's Head & Artichoke

30–32 Albany Street, NW1 4EA **Tel** 020 7916 6206

Map 2 E4

Handily located near Regent's Park and Euston station, this friendly gastropub is rightly popular. Sit outside on the terrace or inside in a bustling, wood-panelled Victorian bar or quieter dining room. The fare includes Mediterranean-inspired tapas, steaks, seafood and other dishes made from high-quality ingredients. Good wine selection too.

REGENT'S PARK AND BLOOMSBURY Locanda Locatelli

8 Seymour Street, W1H 7JZ **Tel** 020 7935 9088

Map 9 C2

Giorgio Locatelli is a star among London chefs, producing some of the city's most refined Italian cuisine. Seasonally based menus change frequently, and subtle use of Mediterranean herbs and truffles is a hallmark. The dining room is elegant, the service is smooth, and every detail is given its due attention. Reserve well ahead.

THE CITY AND SOUTHWARK Leon

86 Cannon Street EC4N 6HT **Tel** 020 7623 9699

Map 13 B2

The Leon chain hits the spot with its bright, modern cafés. Choose from a range of mostly Mediterranean-inspired dishes such as grilled halloumi, "superfood" salads, fresh soups and more. Drinks include beers, wines and fresh juices. This is one of nine branches around London. It's open for breakfast, and you can eat in or take away.

THE CITY AND SOUTHWARK Baltic

74 Blackfriars Rd, SE1 8HA **Tel** 020 7928 1111

Map 12 F4

Located inside a former coach house with exciting high ceilings, Baltic exudes charm. The eastern European influence is noticeable in Baltic's beetroot and vodka cured salmon. There's a massive range of vodkas and the food constantly surprises with dishes such as roast saddle of wild boar.

THE CITY AND SOUTHWARK Bengal Cuisine

12 Brick Lane, E1 6RF **Tel** 020 7377 8405

Map 6 E5

Just about every building in Brick Lane is an Indian restaurant, but the quality varies. Bengal Cuisine is certainly a lot more modern than most of them. The food is very good value and the cook goes easy on the chilli to suit the Western palate. Staff are happy to advise on dishes if asked. There's a good Sunday buffet as well.

THE CITY AND SOUTHWARK Haz

9 Cutler St, E1 7DJ **Tel** 020 7929 7923

Map 14 D1

Lively, fun and a little posh too, this is a true touch of Turkey in the city. Go for a mixed *meze* starter. They just keep coming and they're all delicious. Go for the well-marinated meat dishes and kebabs and mop up the juice with the lovely flat bread. The office workers throng into Haz at lunchtime so get here before noon.

Key to Price Guide see p608 **Key to Symbols** see back cover flap

RESTAURANTS AND PUBS

THE CITY AND SOUTHWARK Mar I Terra

14 Gambia St, Waterloo, SE1 0XH **Tel** *020 7928 7628*   **Map** *12 F4*

Described as a little gem by its fans, this local Spanish restaurant has also been steadily building custom. The quality of the ingredients is one of its secrets as is its location off the main drag. This means the diners are discerning gourmets who have come for the food and the cheerful atmosphere.

THE CITY AND SOUTHWARK Rajasthan

49 Monument St, Monument, EC3R 8BU **Tel** *020 7626 1920*   **Map** *13 C3*

Rajasthan is bright and airy, with fresh flowers on show and not a Bengal tiger or Taj Mahal in sight. The staff are happy to help you avoid the usual curry cliché dishes, but are equally happy to give you chicken tikka masala if that's what you require. Or try something extra special such as a whole poussin. Closed Sundays.

THE CITY AND SOUTHWARK Story Deli

5 Dray Walk, The Old Truman Brewery, 91 Brick Lane, E1 6QL **Tel** *020 7247 3137*

The menu at this refreshing, organic pizzeria and café uses innovative ingredients, ranging from prawns to pumpkin, to top its tasty, thin-crust pizzas. A great alternative lunch option, with fresh juices and soups as well as tea, coffee and wine. Very popular so bag a seat early. Open daily until 10:30pm.

THE CITY AND SOUTHWARK Tapas Brindisa

18–20 Southwark Street, SE1 1TJ **Tel** *020 7357 8880*   **Map** *13 B4*

The Brindisa company, based in the adjacent Borough Market, has led the way in importing fine Spanish foods into the UK – superb Serrano hams, peppers and more. Their tapas bar showcases these delights in fabulous small dishes prepared with as much skill as grand cuisine. Very popular, so you may have to wait for a table.

THE CITY AND SOUTHWARK Eyre Brothers

70 Leonard Street, EC2A 4QX **Tel** *020 7613 5346*   **Map** *5 C4*

This elegantly comfortable Shoreditch bistro oozes panache in its design, service and exceptional food. The brothers who own it are much travelled, and menus are predominantly Spanish- or Portuguese-based, with many original touches. The meats are superb, and the mostly Iberian wine list is equally good. Great tapas at the bar.

THE CITY AND SOUTHWARK St John

26 St John Street, EC1M 4AY **Tel** *020 3301 8069*   **Map** *4 F5*

Under its founder-chef Fergus Henderson, St John has been a leader in the revival of British food. It's known particularly for its quality meats – not just fabulous beef, but also half-forgotten, gutsy old favourites such as pig's feet and braised mutton. Dishes are richly flavoured, and excellent value. The freshly baked bread is worth the visit by itself.

THE CITY AND SOUTHWARK The Chancery

9 Cursitor St, EC4A 1LL **Tel** *020 7831 4000*   **Map** *12 E1*

This little gem is a stylish new-wave restaurant tucked away down a side street. The well-cooked food is adventurous, modern and very reasonably priced. Try the parfait of foie gras and chicken livers, quince chutney and toasted brioche, or peppered monkfish tail, sweetcorn and pancetta chowder.

THE CITY AND SOUTHWARK The Don

The Courtyard, 20 St Swithin's Lane, EC4N 8AD **Tel** *020 7626 2606*   **Map** *13 B2*

This used to be a wine warehouse so it's no surprise that it has an excellent winelist. It also has very attentive staff, who go out of their way to be helpful. A good sommelier and a range of interesting and unique dishes make this a very popular restaurant indeed and reservations are pretty much obligatory. Closed Sundays.

THE CITY AND SOUTHWARK The Lobster Pot

3 Kennington Lane, SE11 4RG **Tel** *020 7582 5556*   **Map** *20 F2*

The French owners set out to recreate Brittany (even down to seagull soundtracks) and succeed brilliantly. The eight-course "surprise" menu is fantastic, and the fish is always superbly fresh. Do book in advance, as it's not very big. Downstairs is a brasserie serving classic French fare at slightly lower prices, and there is a wine bar upstairs. Closed Sun, Mon.

THE CITY AND SOUTHWARK Moro

34–36 Exmouth Market, EC1R 4QE **Tel** *020 7833 8336*   **Map** *4 E4*

Moro is well known for its Spanish-Moroccan cuisine and serves up consistently good food to regulars. Courgette (zucchini) and mint tortilla is an example of light, flavoursome food and there are some very good breads. Buy ingredients next door and take their famous cookbook home with you.

THE CITY AND SOUTHWARK Oxo Tower Restaurant, Bar & Brasserie

Barge House Street, SE1 9PH **Tel** *020 7803 3888*   **Map** *12 E3*

The top floor of the Oxo building (once a factory producing Oxo stock cubes) enjoys one of London's finest riverside views. Run by Harvey Nichols, the brasserie and slightly smarter restaurant both offer deliciously subtle modern food. Prices can be high (especially for wines), but the view makes a meal here something special.

THE CITY AND SOUTHWARK Tentazioni

2 Mill St, SE1 2BD **Tel** *020 7237 1100*   **Map** *14 E5*

Although a bit more expensive than the average Italian eatery, Tentazioni matches the price with its very high standards. Excellent food is on offer and the five-course tasting menu is a delight, especially at the very reasonable price. A busy and friendly restaurant that's well worth making the walk from Tower Bridge.

FURTHER AFIELD Base

71 Hampstead High St, NW3 1QP **Tel** *020 7431 2224*

£ £

During the day, Base is a gourmet bar serving Mediterranean cuisine. In the evening it becomes a bistro serving sumptuous Mediterranean fusion food with an emphasis on fresh ingredients. The menu changes regularly and is complemented by an extensive wine list. Another branch is located at 195 Baker Street.

FURTHER AFIELD Brown's West India Quay

Hertsmere Road, E14 8JJ **Tel** *020 7987 9777*

£ £

The Brown's empire began in Brighton and is now established throughout the country. The main draw is its solid British cooking while the decor – dark wooden café chairs, palms and ceiling fans – create a colonial feel. Al fresco dining is possible in this former sugar warehouse near Canary Wharf.

FURTHER AFIELD Cibo

3 Russell Gardens, W14 8EZ **Tel** *020 7371 6271*

£ £

Map *7 A5*

Cibo has been around long enough to become a dependable local institution. Its clever mix of tried and trusted northern Italian favourites, combined with more adventurous dishes, never fails to satisfy its young crowd. There's plenty of bread and olives to savour while waiting at the table. The wine list matches the restaurant's high quality.

FURTHER AFIELD Haché Burger

329–331 Fulham Rd, SW10 9QL **Tel** *020 7823 3515*

£ £

Map *16 F4*

This chic, modern "bespoke" hamburger place is popular with cinema-goers and posh teenagers. Gourmet burgers are served on a fresh ciabatta bun with rocket, tomato, sweet red onion and the special Haché mayonnaise. Choose from a range of beef, lamb, venison, chicken, fish, duck or veggie burgers.

FURTHER AFIELD Manna

4 Erskine Road, Primrose Hill, NW3 3AJ **Tel** *020 7722 8028*

£ £

Open since the 1960s, Manna is heaven for many London vegetarians. In place of the tired "meat-free" choices of many veggie cafés, it has a ground-up approach to vegetarian cooking, producing dishes full of tantalizing flavours. Choices include root vegetable masala, tempura mushrooms, exciting salads and good desserts.

FURTHER AFIELD Mosob

339 Harrow Rd, W9 3RB **Tel** *020 7266 2012*

£ £

Located a short walk from Westbourne Park tube, this family-run restaurant serves Eritrean food in a colourful dining room decorated with African-flavoured furnishings. All dishes on the menu are served with *injera*, a typically Eritrean bread that also doubles as an eating utensil. The vegetarian menu is 100 per cent vegan.

FURTHER AFIELD North Pole

131 Greenwich High Rd, SE10 8JA **Tel** *020 8853 3020*

£ £

A little Greenwich gem, North Pole is comfortably warm with a nice bar downstairs and a fire in the grate upstairs. A small piano tinkles away in the background. Traditional Sunday roasts of beef or chicken are available with all the trimmings but whatever the choice, the food is of a very high standard.

FURTHER AFIELD The Lane Restaurant

12–20 Osborn St, E1 6TE **Tel** *020 7377 1797*

£ £

Map *14 E1*

Located at the south end of famous Brick Lane, but not an Indian restaurant. It's actually a rather cool and trendy place doing a variety of dishes at very reasonable prices. The cocktail bar is nice too. It's in an up-and-coming area, so you may find yourself surrounded by young people with cool clothes and a disposable income.

FURTHER AFIELD The Real Greek

14–15 Hoxton Market, N1 6HG **Tel** *020 7739 8212*

£ £

Map *5 C3*

Join the crowd at Mezedepolio and choose from a massive selection of Greek dishes. The home-style cooking is unique, and many of the dishes on the menu have never been seen in the country before. They're all very tempting but be warned to keep an eye on the prices. The Real Greek wine bar serves Greek wines as well.

FURTHER AFIELD Le Vacherin

76–77 South Parade, W4 5LF **Tel** *020 8742 2121*

£ £ £

Le Vacherin is a chef-patron restaurant in deepest Chiswick, a lovely area of London. Here they have re-created a charming Parisian bistro, serving top-notch food in a nice unpretentious way to a loyal local clientele. Sunday brunch is particularly popular. October to March they serve the speciality cheese, le Vacherin, baked with black truffles, almonds and white wine.

FURTHER AFIELD Lots Road Pub & Dining Room

114 Lots Road, SW10 0RJ **Tel** *020 7352 6645*

£ £ £

Map *16 F5*

A smart take on gastropub style, the Lots Road Pub is located on the far western side of Chelsea. There is a bright, modern dining area alongside a relaxed bar where punters can sample the excellent beers. Regulars on the menu include lively salads, rich meats such as daube of fine beef and superior-quality burgers with perfect chips.

FURTHER AFIELD Morgan M

50 Long Lane, EC1A 9EJ **Tel** *020 7609 3560*

£ £ £

Chef Morgan Meunier is renowned for his modern French menu featuring delicate flavours created from luxury ingredients. The speciality is the six-course tasting menu, but the restaurant also caters for vegetarians, and there are pre-theatre menus. Every detail is outstanding. Reservations are essential.

Key to Price Guide *see p608* **Key to Symbols** *see back cover flap*

FURTHER AFIELD Rivington Bar and Grill   £££

178 Greenwich High Rd, Greenwich, SE10 8NN **Tel** *020 8293 9270*

Located next to the cinema, Rivington is a great spot for lunch, dinner or drinks before or after a movie or tour around historic Greenwich. Hearty British cuisine is served in a modern dining room with exposed brickwork, crisp white linen tablecloths and low lighting. The Market Breakfast is good.

FURTHER AFIELD The Belvedere   £££

Holland House, Abbotsbury Road, W8 6LU **Tel** *020 7602 1238*   **Map** *7 B5*

Tucked away in leafy Holland Park, the Belvedere has a perfect location. The opulence of the main room doesn't get reflected in the bill. Instead, a brilliant variety of dishes is effortlessly combined with a very fair price. "Gastropub" type food means hearty and heartening meals that comfort the senses while tickling the palate.

FURTHER AFIELD The Engineer   £££

65 Gloucester Avenue, Camden, NW1 8JH **Tel** *020 7722 0950*

One of the longest-running gastropubs, and still a model of its kind, The Engineer features a varied, interesting menu that uses fresh ingredients. The bar and dining room are both enjoyably relaxing, and for summer there are tables in a pretty garden. Unusually, it also opens for breakfast, from 9am. Very popular so tables can be hard to get.

FURTHER AFIELD The Spread Eagle   £££

1–2 Stockwell St, SE10 9JN **Tel** *020 8853 2333*

Fiercely championed by locals, this place radiates confidence with its innovative French cuisine. Small, intimate booths to dine in and a real, roaring fire in winter all conspire to make you want to stay long after the coffee has been cleared away. The food is rich and satisfying and the whole experience is equal to the West End and at half the price.

FURTHER AFIELD Bibendum   ££££

Michelin House, 81 Fulham Road, SW3 6RD **Tel** *020 7581 5817*   **Map** *17 B2*

Bibendum's location, in the 1930s former Michelin tyre building, makes any meal here a special occasion. The dining area is surrounded by spectacular Art Deco tiles and stained glass showing Michelin men on bicycles. Seafood is the speciality here, and the creative haute cuisine is consistently impressive. Save space for the delicately scrumptious desserts.

FURTHER AFIELD Gordon Ramsay   £££££

68 Royal Hospital Rd, SW3 4HP **Tel** *020 7352 4441*   **Map** *17 C4*

Awarded with three Michelin stars, this restaurant strives for perfection and the effort reflects in everything from place settings to service. For an astonishing average of £110 per person, it is reputedly the best restaurant in London as well as all of England. As a souvenir of London, meal memories here will last a lifetime.

FURTHER AFIELD The River Café   £££££

Thames Wharf, Rainville Rd, Hammersmith, W6 9HA **Tel** *020 7386 4200*

The michelin-starred River Café is a well-established favourite among Londoners and tourists alike. With outstanding service, beautifully prepared rustic Italian dishes such as buffalo ricotta and turbot, and an excellent wine list, it's well worth the price. Floor-to-ceiling windows offer lovely views of the gardens and river beyond.

THE DOWNS AND CHANNEL COAST

ARUNDEL Amberley Castle   £££££

Amberley, nr Arundel, West Sussex, BN18 9LT **Tel** *01798 831992*

Nestled in some wonderfully imposing 18-m (60-ft) walls with a 12th-century portcullis, this fine restaurant offers a seasonally adjusted menu of local treats. Afternoon tea is served Mon–Thu. Its popularity as a wedding venue makes it necessary to book ahead.

BRIGHTON Seven Dials   ££

1 Buckingham Place, Seven Dials, Brighton, East Sussex, BN1 3TD **Tel** *01273 885555*

A bustling eatery much beloved by Brighton's Sunday supplement set, Seven Dials is housed in a converted bank. The menu makes good use of Sussex farmland and local organic produce. Private dining is provided in the downstairs Vault, while a summer terrace offers the perfect spot for al fresco people-watching.

BRIGHTON Terre à Terre   ££

71 East Street, Brighton, East Sussex, BN1 1HQ **Tel** *01273 729051*

This ground-breaking vegetarian restaurant is one of the first to have combined all-vegetarian cooking with sophisticated culinary skills and careful sourcing of the finest ingredients. Menu options are enormously varied and full of vibrant flavours, while the ambience is informal. Always busy, particularly at weekends, so book in advance.

BRIGHTON Seattle Restaurant   £££

Hotel Seattle, Brighton Marina, Brighton, East Sussex, BN2 5WA **Tel** *01273 679799*

A sleek Brighton favourite overlooking the Marina, this restaurant lays stress on mod-European flavours and seafood delicacies. It also serves up a decent selection of pastas. Try the salmon and dill fishcakes or the pan-seared skate served with capers and lemon. The well-stocked and busy cocktail bar adds to the chic buzz.

BRIGHTON Hotel du Vin
Ship St, Brighton, East Sussex, BN1 1AD **Tel** *01273 718588*

Part of the reliable, cheerful Hotel du Vin mini-chain, this natty bistro is tucked away in the Lanes. The menu opts for modern European with French influence. Vegetarians are also catered for. Some choice selections from the extensive wine list are on offer. The Pub du Vin next door serves traditional pub fare with ales and wine.

CANTERBURY The Goods Shed
Station Road West, Canterbury, Kent, CT2 8AN **Tel** *01227 459153*

At this farmers' market diner-cum-café, there's a simple blackboard menu offering well-constructed treats. The simple home cooking uses the best of the day's produce from the myriad stalls. As it is increasingly popular with local foodies, seating is at quite a premium during peak times. Closed Mondays; lunch only Sundays.

CHICHESTER Amelie and Friends
31 North St, Chichester, West Sussex, PO19 1LY **Tel** *01243 771444*

By day this deli-café, set in a Georgian townhouse has a modern vibe and serves inventive salads, main dishes, coffee and home-made cakes and pasties. By night it is transformed – the chefs have a Michelin-starred background and their three-course evening menus are creative and seasonal.

CHICHESTER The George and Dragon Inn
North St, Chichester, West Sussex, PO19 1NQ **Tel** *01243 785660*

This smartly refurbished pub now features a comfortable and relaxed restaurant in the conservatory, with tables spilling over on to the courtyard in the summer months. The menu offers quality home-made food as well as bar snacks. Located on the North Walls walk, near the famous Chichester Festival Theatre.

CHICHESTER Comme Ça
67 Broyle Rd, Chichester, West Sussex, PO19 6BD **Tel** *01243 788724*

Just around the corner from Chichester's historic centre, Comme Ça is a busy centrepiece for full-blooded Normandy cooking genially served in a comfortably rustic ambience. Outside dining is available on the terrace during the summer months, while the Garden Room is a popular spot for private functions. Closed Mon.

DEAL 81 Beach Street
81 Beach Street, Deal, Kent, CT14 6JB **Tel** *01304 368136*

Housed in an 18th-century former shop in Deal's charming old town, this friendly bistro provides excellent, mostly traditional, British food with an inventive modern twist. Sunday roast lunches are particularly popular, and great value; other specialities include delicious smoked haddock and vegetarian pancakes.

EAST CHILTINGTON The Jolly Sportsman
Chapel Lane, East Chiltington, East Sussex, BN7 3BA **Tel** *01273 890400*

This acclaimed gastropub is a relaxed rural retreat, famed for its free-range chicken and duck, with enjoyable Euro stylings elsewhere on a surprisingly refined menu. Contemporary art adorns the walls, while the shaded terrace has a distinctly Moroccan feel. Microbrewery on the premises. Closed Sunday evening, Mondays.

EAST LAVANT Royal Oak
Pook Lane, East Lavant, West Sussex, PO18 0AX **Tel** *01243 527434*

Once the local watering hole in an off-the-beaten-track Downland village close to Goodwood, the Royal Oak is now a highly reputed gastropub and still maintains its original 200-year-old charm. On the menu you'll find high-class renditions of pub classics plus specials with a more modern accent. Accommodation is also available.

EMSWORTH 36 on the Quay
47 South St, Emsworth, Hampshire, PO10 7EG **Tel** *01243 375592*

Located in a fishing village overlooking the bay, this bright and affable dining room focuses largely on fish. In addition, plenty of landlubber local produce feature on the menu. The "Little Big" tasting menu allows diners to enjoy a little bit of everything. Overnight accommodation available. Closed Sun, Mon.

EVERSLEY New Mill Restaurant
New Mill Rd, Eversley, Hampshire, RG27 0RA **Tel** *01189 732277*

Rural honey pot perched on the banks of River Blackwater and the Millpond. The main restaurant is home to à la carte lighter fare, while the grill room, basing itself on the rural gastropub template, is the place for belt-loosening, comfort classics. There's an award-winning wine list.

FAVERSHAM Read's Restaurant with Rooms
Macknade Manor, Canterbury Rd, Faversham, Kent, ME13 8XE **Tel** *01795 535344*

Traditional Georgian manor house with self-styled "restaurant-with-rooms", Read's is set in its own wooded grounds. The kitchen produces a delicious range of seasonal, modern British fare. Plenty of vegetables, fresh from its own walled garden, are accompanied by locally caught game and fish.

HAYWARDS HEATH Jeremy's at Borde Hill
Borde Hill Gardens, Balcombe Rd, Haywards Heath, West Sussex, RH16 1XP **Tel** *01444 441102*

Overlooking a walled Victorian garden, this family-run restaurant cooks up modern European dishes, with a strong Mediterranean influence. Local artwork on the walls and friendly service add to the pleasingly relaxed air. The outdoor dining on the terrace is a perfect spot for Sunday lunch.

Key to Price Guide *see p608* **Key to Symbols** *see back cover flap*

HYTHE BAY Hythe Bay Seafood Restaurant

Marine Parade, Hythe Bay, Kent, CT21 6AW **Tel** *01303 233844*

This beachfront charmer conjures up a whole range of innovative recipes with the local catch. The oysters are a house speciality. Vegetarian dishes are on offer too. There is a sunny terrace for dining al fresco in good weather, and morning coffee and drinks are served at the bar from 10am. Occasional complimentary wine offers.

JEVINGTON The Hungry Monk

Jevington, nr Polegate, East Sussex, BN26 5QF **Tel** *01323 482178*

Local game and fish jostle for position and are given a Gallic twist on the enjoyable menu on offer at this 14th-century flint cottage. A one-time monastic retreat, complete with log fireplaces, candlelight and assorted antiques, the Hungry Monk is at its finest when the nights are drawing in. Half of the extensive wine list is under £20 a bottle.

LEWES Bill's Produce Store

56 Cliffe High St, Lewes, East Sussex, BN7 2AN **Tel** *01273 476918*

People come from miles around and from as far as London to eat at this deli/café/restaurant. The amazing variety of dishes is served in generous portions and beautifully presented. There is always a queue, but it moves fast, and the service is friendly and efficient. There are other branches in Brighton, Reading, London and Cambridge.

NEWBURY Dew Pond

Old Burghclere, Newbury, Berkshire, RG20 9LH **Tel** *01635 278408*

A cosy country-house restaurant on the edge of Watership Down, Dew Pond specializes in Scottish beef. Closer to home, Hampshire cheeses and local game also feature on the menu. Oak beams and outside decking add to the allure. Watch out for a series of monthly gastro evenings featuring five-course dinners with specially selected wines.

PORTSMOUTH A Bar Bistro

58 White Hart Rd, Portsmouth, Hampshire, PO1 2JA **Tel** *02392 811585*

There's much to enjoy in this affable seafood restaurant overlooking the fish market. The A Bar Bistro has an airy feel, with French windows and a terrace. For mains, try the salmon wellington, mussels or local catch of the day. Certainly not ideal if you are just having drinks, though you can get yourself a passable martini here.

RIPLEY Drakes

The Clock House, High Street, Ripley, Surrey, GU23 6AQ **Tel** *01483 224777*

A fine Queen Anne town house with variegated brickwork and a very attractive garden, Drakes is becoming an increasingly popular destination for London foodies. Well-crafted modern French favourites are created by a confident young chef, whose impressive CV includes stints with über-chefs Marco Pierre White and Nico Landenis.

RYE Landgate Bistro

5–6 Landgate, Rye, Sussex, TN31 7LH **Tel** *01797 222829*

The Landgate Bistro is famed for its agreeably uncomplicated modern British fare that has a growing army of fans. Its fishcakes and other clever tricks with seafood are much celebrated. Also on offer are local meats and game. Among the menu highlights are the delicious leek and Roquefort tarts. Closed Mondays and Tuesdays.

SEAVIEW Priory Bay Hotel

Priory Drive, Seaview, Isle of Wight, PO34 5BU **Tel** *01983 613146*

Dating back to the medieval times, this hotel has a pair of hotel dining rooms set on the bay itself, with their own private beach. The Priory Oyster specializes in seafood and light mod-Med flavours that come with a good and healthy zing. It also welcomes children, unlike the Island Room, which is preferred by the less calorie-conscious.

STOCKBRIDGE The Greyhound

31 High St, Stockbridge, Hampshire, SO20 6EY **Tel** *01264 810833*

Superior gastropub serving modern English cuisine, the Greyhound makes plentiful use of produce from the nearby New Forest and the River Test, which runs through the grounds. On the menu, meat options outweigh the fish-based dishes. Though the place can get loud, there's much to recommend here. Closed Sun dinner, Mon.

TUNBRIDGE WELLS Thackeray's

85 London Rd, Tunbridge Wells, Kent, TN1 1EA **Tel** *01892 511921*

Thackeray's offers agreeable modern French flavours in a Grade II listed building, once home to the eponymous novelist. The warm, chatty atmosphere draws a contended clientele, both local and from further afield. Cocktails are served beforehand in the Gold Room, and a post-meal Scotch in the gold leaf-lined Throne Room. Closed Sun dinner, Mon.

WHITSTABLE Wheelers Oyster Bar

8 High St, Whitstable, Kent, CT5 1BQ **Tel** *01227 273311*

Justly celebrated shellfish emporium that closes at 9pm, Wheelers Oyster Bar is the oldest fish and shellfish establishment in Britain. It doesn't have a licence so bring your own wine to the Oyster Parlour, tucked behind the main seafood bar, or nip over to the pebble beach for an impromptu picnic. Closed Wednesdays.

WHITSTABLE Whitstable Oyster Fishery Company

Horsebridge, Whitstable, Kent, CT5 1BU **Tel** *01227 276856*

This is a popular seafood restaurant based in an old Naval warehouse overlooking the North Sea. There's a busy open kitchen with skilled staff getting to grips with fish freshly caught by the company's own band of fishermen. The nautically themed decor is enthusiastic but stops short of going overboard. Closed Mon evenings.

WILMINGTON Crossways Hotel   🏠   ££££

Wilmington, nr Polegate, East Sussex, BN26 5SG **Tel** *01323 482455*

A short stroll from the famed Long Man of Wilmington, the Crossways is a great spot for those visiting Glyndebourne. Its modern British cuisine uses fresh local ingredients. Though the classic dining room may not impress the style-conscious, it's well worth the experience.

WINCHESTER The Chesil Rectory   🏠👤🏠   ££££

1 Chesil Street, Winchester, Hampshire, SO23 0HU **Tel** *01962 851555*

The oldest, continually occupied house in Winchester, dating from 1450, is wonderfully atmospheric, with half-timbered walls and massive oak beams in its snug rooms. Under chef Damian Brown the restaurant has hit a new high, with creative, flavour-rich, modern British cooking highlighting local ingredients. Superb wine list, plus a wine shop.

EAST ANGLIA

ALDEBURGH 152 Aldeburgh   🏃👤   ££

152 High St, Aldeburgh, Suffolk, IP15 5LD **Tel** *01728 454594*

A leisurely pebble's throw from the beach, chic little 152 Aldeburgh serves up modern European cooking with a bias towards flavours from south of the Alps. Open for breakfast, lunch and dinner, the restaurant benefits from a well-travelled kitchen and the bountiful fresh produce on its doorstep. Closed first two weeks of January.

ALDEBURGH Regatta Restaurant and Wine Bar   🏃🏠   ££

171–173 High St, Aldeburgh, Suffolk, IP15 5AN **Tel** *01728 452011*

Favoured spot for seasonal asparagus, this cheery, family-run restaurant waves the flag for Suffolk's acclaimed regional produce. Specialities include good fish from the beach and game from the surrounding estates in winter. A worthy addition to Aldeburgh's burgeoning foodie scene. Closed Sun dinner.

BURY ST EDMUNDS Maison Bleue   🏃👤🏠   ££

31 Churchgate St, Bury St Edmunds, Suffolk, IP33 1RG **Tel** *01284 760623*

This award-winning restaurant specializes in Gallic fish, though the daily-changing menu does include a special "butcher's corner" for the meat-lovers. The smart dining room is well served by a kitchen that conjures up interesting, yet simple, fare using the best of the local catch. The nautical-themed bar is decorated with paintings of the sea.

CAMBRIDGE Cambridge Chop House   🏃   ££

1 Kings Parade, Cambridge, Cambridgeshire, CB2 1SJ **Tel** *01223 359506*

As the name suggests, meat is the headliner at this atmospheric venue where modern versions of British classics are cooked with imagination and first-rate local ingredients. Fish dishes also feature, and there are great fruity desserts. The wine list is varied, and the set-price lunch menu, with three courses for just £16, is excellent.

CAMBRIDGE Graffiti at Hotel Felix   🏃👤   ££

Whitehouse Lane, Huntingdon Rd, Cambridge, Cambridgeshire, CB3 0LX **Tel** *01223 277977*

Overlooking landscaped gardens, this handsome hotel dining room is set in a converted Victorian mansion. The menu features a selection of mod-Med dishes as well as a choice of game. Despite being just a short distance away from the bustle of Cambridge city centre, the place is quite peaceful. There is a good-value three-course lunch deal.

CAMBRIDGE Restaurant 22   🏠   ££££

22 Chesterton Rd, Cambridge, Cambridgeshire, CB4 3AX **Tel** *01223 351880*

Small but perfectly formed, Restaurant 22 is set in a smart Victorian town house that serves British and French favourites, with the odd Asian twist added for extra interest. The decent wine list is predominantly French, but does travel further afield to good effect.

CAMBRIDGE Midsummer House   🏃👤🏠   ££££

Midsummer Common, Cambridge, Cambridgeshire, CB4 1HA **Tel** *01223 369299*

On the banks of the River Cam, Midsummer House is a plush restaurant that boasts an array of awards. The elegant ambience is well served by a kitchen with a heavy French accent. A slate floor and warm shades add to the charm and give a distinctly Mediterranean feel to proceedings. Closed Sun, Mon; Tue lunch.

CLAVERING The Cricketers   🏃🏠   £££

Whyken Rd, Clavering, nr Saffron Walden, Cambridgeshire, CB11 4QT **Tel** *01799 550442*

This award-winning rural retreat has become a popular destination for London foodies. The extra allure is provided by the fact that this is actually TV chef Jamie Oliver's family home. Menus change seasonally, with the robust cooking treading that well-worn path between the UK and Italy. Good selection of wine and real ales.

COLCHESTER The Warehouse Brasserie   🏃👤🏠   ££

The Old Chapel, Chapel St North, Colchester, Essex, CO2 7AT **Tel** *01206 765656*

One of the better dining options in the area, the Warehouse Brasserie is set in the heart of Colchester. A decent collection of British comfort food classics is served to an appreciative mix of diners in a relaxed, friendly atmosphere. The attentive service here makes for a pleasant dining experience. Closed Sun, Mon.

Key to Price Guide *see p608* **Key to Symbols** *see back cover flap*

CROMER Bolton's Bistro

The Cliftonville Hotel, Seafront, Cromer, Norfolk, NR27 9AS Tel 01263 512543

There's a really traditional feel to this seafront bistro affair with its daily-changing blackboard menu displaying prepared-to-order fresh fish specialities, including some fine seasonal Cromer crab and lobster. Red meat-eaters and vegetarians get their share of goodies too, while the ice cream has a local fan club.

FRESSINGFIELD EYE The Fox and Goose Inn

Church Rd, Fressingfield Eye, Suffolk, IP21 5PB Tel 01379 586247

Once a poorhouse, the Fox and Goose Inn has been a local favourite since the mid-1800s. The restaurant serves modern British cuisine and has perfected its interpretation of regional specialities, with a pro-European touch added occasionally. Closed Mondays; first two weeks in Jan.

HOLKHAM The Victoria at Holkham

Holkham Estate, nr Wells-Next-The-Sea, Norfolk, NR23 1RG Tel 01328 716008

A stroll from the windswept sands of Holkham Beach, this neat hotel diner serves local shellfish, organic delicacies and wild game. Thornham oysters, crab and mussels are the house specialities; the venison, beef and game come from the Holkham Estate. Booking is essential.

HOLT Morston Hall

Holt, Norfolk, NR25 7AA Tel 01263 741041

Increasingly popular honeypot for happy-go-lucky locals and yachting types from nearby Morston Quay, Morston Hall is an inviting, relaxed place. The five-course daily-changing menu features superior cooking with French foundations. Afternoon tea is served daily by the open fire. Closed first three weeks in Jan.

HUNTINGDON The Pheasant

Keyston, Huntingdon, Cambridgeshire, PE28 0RE Tel 01832 710241

This thatched inn, with oaked-beam dining room, is home to some heartening Anglo-French fare. The secret of its outstanding cooking lies in the successful blending of classical French techniques with the pick of local game. The well-considered wine list includes a wide by-the-glass choice.

IPSWICH Il Punto

Neptune Quay, Ipswich, Suffolk, IP4 1AX Tel 01473 289748

A former Belgian gunboat dating from the 1800s, Il Punto now serves as a floating brasserie with a distinctly Gallic outlook. The interior makes good use of its original fittings, while there's plenty of outside deck dining to be enjoyed when waters are calmer. No lunch served on Saturdays.

MELBOURN Sheene Mill

Station Rd, Melbourn, Cambridgeshire, SG8 6DX Tel 01763 261393

The cosy interior and chatty, informal air belie the meticulous kitchen at this restored rural mill. Proudly waving the flag for British cuisine, albeit with plenty of influences from sunnier climes, the cooking here is of a very high quality. The vegetables and herbs are all from the garden on the premises.

NORWICH Tatlers

21 Tombland, Norwich, Norfolk, NR3 1RF Tel 01603 766670

A long-standing brasserie, Tatler's is situated in the heart of town, just around the corner from the cathedral. The staff dispense modern British fare to an appreciative mix of diners in an informal atmosphere. The seasonal menu uses local ingredients and includes decent vegetarian options. Closed Sunday evenings.

NORWICH St Giles House Restaurant

41–45 St Giles St, Norwich, Norfolk, NR2 1AB Tel 01603 275180

The philosophy of this restaurant specializing in modern European cuisine is simple: offering top-quality food made with the finest local and seasonal ingredients. There is an extensive wine list covering both the old and new worlds, and a wide range of wines by the glass. Located in a Grade II listed building in the centre of town.

OULTON BROAD The Crooked Barn Restaurant

Ivy House Country Hotel, Ivy Lane, Oulton Broad, Suffolk, NR33 8HY Tel 01502 501353

An 18th-century thatched barn, Crooked Barn Restaurant is ideal for candlelit dining in a light and spacious room. The excellent cooking, which uses local free-range and organic produce, is predominantly British. The odd garnish from further afield is also added to good effect, with touches from southern Europe, as well as Down Under.

SOUTHWOLD The Promenade

Southwold Pier, North Parade, Southwold, Suffolk, IP18 6BN Tel 01502 722105

Fans rate The Promenade as one of the best fish and chip cafés in England. It certainly has a great location, above the sea on the 19th-century pier in fashionable Southwold. You can eat in or take away. They also offer very generous full English breakfasts. Other options on the Pier are the Boardwalk restaurant and the Clockhouse pub-café.

STANTON The Leaping Hare Restaurant

Wyken Hall, Stanton, Bury St Edmunds, Suffolk, IP31 2DW Tel 01359 250287

This well-known restaurant stands in a converted 18th-century barn. The attractive dining room is set on the edge of a country estate, nestled among woods, vineyards and perfect gardens. An appealing rustic menu featuring Suffolk fare matches the ambience. The excellent wine list includes wines produced from the Wyken vineyard.

WELLS-NEXT-THE-SEA The Crown Hotel   🚶 ♿ 🍷   ££
The Buttlands, Wells-Next-The-Sea, NR23 1EX **Tel** *01328 710209*

Restored from a 16th-century coaching inn, the Crown serves decent British fare with a few interesting Pacific Rim touches. The kitchen enjoys the best of fresh produce caught in the picturesque harbour town on the Norfolk coast. Lighter bites are available in the bar, with an open fire and old oak beams. Two-course set menu Mon–Thu.

WOODBRIDGE Crown & Castle   🚶 ♿ 🍷   £££
Orford, Woodbridge, Suffolk, IP12 2LJ **Tel** *01394 450205*

Sitting in the shadows of a Norman castle, this relaxed, elegant hotel dining room plays to its strengths: a quintessentially English menu for such a perfect English setting. The private dining room is home to a large round table, and suitable for small dinner parties.

WYMONDHAM Number 24 Restaurant   🚶 ♿ 🍷   £££
24 Middleton St, Wymondham, Norfolk, NR18 0AD **Tel** *01953 607750*

Located in a charming Grade II listed building, this restaurant has a seasonal menu featuring contemporary English cuisine. The fixed-price Sunday lunch, however, tends to follow a more traditional route of roast beef plus a variety of other options. Closed Sunday dinner and all day Monday.

THAMES VALLEY

BRAY-ON-THAMES The Fat Duck   🚶 🍷   £££££
High St, Bray, Berkshire, SL6 2AQ **Tel** *01628 580333*

One of the most exquisite restaurants in the region, Fat Duck is located in a 15th-century listed building. The exterior gives way to clean, modernist decor, where diners undergo a once-in-a-lifetime experience. Multiple, double-figure courses include such culinary inventions as snail porridge and egg and bacon ice cream.

BUCKINGHAM Prego Restaurant and Wine Bar   🚶 ♿ 🍷   ££
4 High St, Buckingham, Buckinghamshire, MK18 1NT **Tel** *01280 821205*

This friendly family restaurant exudes sunny Mediterranean ambience. Well located on Buckingham high street, it specializes in authentic Italian home cooking including fine pizza and pasta dishes. Free parking is available directly opposite the restaurant.

DINTON La Chouette   🚶   £££
Westlington Green, Dinton, Buckinghamshire, HP17 8UW **Tel** *01296 747422*

Forget calories and fat content as you enter this Belgian restaurant situated on the village green. The fabulously rich menu caters to the indulgent food-lover. Dishes are modern European blended with a little Belgian stodge. Perfect place for jazz-loving beer connoisseurs, but watch out for low beams as you walk away from the bar.

EASINGTON The Mole and Chicken   🚶 ♿ 🍷   ££
Easington, nr Long Crendon, Buckinghamshire, HP18 9EY **Tel** *01844 208387*

Well-heeled diners come from afar to this former 19th-century village store for views of the Buckinghamshire and Oxfordshire countryside. The adventurous cooking features modern European cuisine using local produce. There's also a good wine list. While it's open-plan and snug inside, visitors flock to the garden in summer. Book in advance.

GODSTOW The Trout Inn   🚶 ♿ 🍷   ££
195 Godstow Rd, Lower Wolvercote, Oxford, Oxfordshire, OX2 8PN **Tel** *01865 510930*

Built in 1133 and steeped in history, the Trout Inn was where Lewis Carroll dreamt up *Alice in Wonderland*, and Colin Dexter, the creator of Inspector Morse, regularly sunk a pint. On the banks of Oxford Canal, punters enjoy passing boats and feed the fish, ducks, swans and peacocks as they tuck into European fare.

GREAT MILTON Le Manoir aux Quat' Saisons   ♿ 🍷   £££££
Church Rd, Great Milton, Oxford, Oxfordshire, OX44 7PD **Tel** *01844 278881*

Acclaimed as an art gallery for the taste buds, this restaurant has a two-acre kitchen garden producing the vegetables and herbs used in their imaginatively crafted dishes. The new season milk-fed lamb is one of the specialities. Lovingly prepared picnic hampers sustain explorations around the surrounding countryside.

GREAT MISSENDEN La Petite Auberge   🚶 🍷   ££££
107 High St, Great Missenden, Buckinghamshire, HP16 0BB **Tel** *01494 865370*

Set in the idyllically quiet Chiltern village, La Petite Auberge is a quaint French restaurant run by a self-effacing French couple. Though the decor is modest and traditional, the impeccable authentic French cuisine more than makes up for it. The restaurant has a loyal following of locals and travellers.

KINTBURY The Dundas Arms   🚶 🍷   ££
53 Station Rd, Kintbury, Berkshire, RG17 9UT **Tel** *01488 658263*

Nestled on the banks of the River Kennet and Kennet and Avon Canal, the Dundas Arms is a late 18th-century restaurant-pub. Local produce is imaginatively whipped up into creative dishes and served amid simple but effective decor. The beer and wine selections are handsome, beefed up by local Rambury and West Berkshire brews.

Key to Price Guide *see p608* **Key to Symbols** *see back cover flap*

MAIDENHEAD The Waterside Inn
The Waterside Inn, Ferry Rd, Bray, Berkshire, SL6 2AT **Tel** *01628 620691*

Boasting three Michelin stars, the jewel in chef entrepreneur Michel Roux's restaurant empire is a formal establishment offering French dining at its very finest. Enjoy roasted Challandais duck with lemon, while the Thames refracts throughout this riverside gem. Finish up with indulgent digestifs in one of the summerhouses or by the fire. Open Wed–Sun.

MOULSFORD The Boathouse at the Beetle and Wedge
Ferry Lane, Moulsford-on-Thames, Oxfordshire, OX10 9JF **Tel** *01491 651381*

Beetle and Wedge is encircled by beautiful gardens running alongside the river immortalized in Kenneth Grahame's *The Wind in the Willows.* The relaxed Boathouse Restaurant is not to be missed during long evenings when dishes are grilled to perfection. Inside, the dining room can be used for private parties. Booking ahead is a must.

OXFORD Browns
5–11 Woodstock Rd, Oxford, Oxfordshire, OX2 6HA **Tel** *01865 511995*

A branch of the booming brasserie chain, Browns is a firm favourite with business folk and weekend lunchers. The menu is filled with contemporary dishes, such as asparagus and wild mushroom risotto, to complement snacks and salads, sandwiches and steaks. There is also a set menu. Pretty seating spills out onto the pavement in summer.

OXFORD Jamie's Italian
24–26 George Street, Oxford, Oxfordshire, OX1 2AE **Tel** *01865 838383*

At Jamie's Italian, exuberant TV chef Jamie Oliver offers enjoyable, Italian-based food in a casual setting. Prices are reasonable, and bookings cannot be made, so be prepared to queue. The Oxford branch was the first to open but there are now several Jamie's Italians around Britain.

OXFORD Cherwell Boathouse
Bardwell Rd, Oxford, Oxfordshire, OX2 6SR **Tel** *01865 552746*

With a riverfront location at a punting station, Cherwell Boathouse is a favourite with wine buffs and romancers. Simple, but flawless, modern European cooking is enhanced by a well-priced and famously good wine selection. Try the honed-to-perfection goat's cheese or adventurous dishes such as pan-fried pollock.

OXON Sir Charles Napier
Sprigg's Alley, nr Chinnor, Oxon, Oxfordshire, OX39 4BX **Tel** *01494 483011*

A favourite with showbiz types seeking retreat, this isolated pub-restaurant in the Chiltern hills is not easily accessed, but the stunning views make it more than worth it. The British menu is slightly pricey, but features some rare dishes. Check the restaurant website as the menu is constantly changing. Remarkable garden sculptures and paintings.

PENN STREET VILLAGE Hit or Miss Inn
Penn St Village, Penn St, Amersham, Buckinghamshire, HP7 0PX **Tel** *01494 713109*

Hit or Miss is a gastropub in the most traditional sense. Its location, opposite a cricket club, makes it a favourite destination for locals or walkers strolling from Penn Wood. The menu is vast, covering everything from crayfish to a reasonable set Sunday roast. Watch out for special Morris dancing, jazz events and a beer fest in July.

READING London Street Brasserie
2–4 London St, Reading, Berkshire, RG1 4SE **Tel** *01189 505036*

This brasserie prides itself on being an antidote to generic, conveyor-belt eateries. Waiting staff wear black, but are allowed to express individuality in no set uniform. The menu mixes British, French and Mediterranean cuisine, yet manages to avoid becoming confusing, while the contemporary decor makes this brasserie a romantic dining destination.

READING L'Ortolan
Church Lane, Shinfield, Reading, Berkshire, RG2 9BY **Tel** *01189 888500*

One of the best restaurants in the country, this British and French eatery is an absolute pleasure. Its lovely setting in luxurious gardens is complemented by the terrace and conservatory. Wine-tasting evenings emphasize their focus on fine drinking as well as dining. Set lunches and menus are tasty and affordable.

REED The Cabinet at Reed
The Cabinet, High St, Reed, nr Royston, Hertfordshire, SG8 8AH **Tel** *01763 848366*

Boasting a unique blend of English, French and transatlantic fare, the Cabinet is a rising star in the quiet Hertfordshire countryside. It is housed in a 16th-century building, with a pleasant decor comprising beamed ceilings and leather chairs. Outside, it is stunning with a large al fresco dining area and a wood-burning rotisserie.

SPEEN The Old Plow Bistro & Restaurant
Flowers Bottom, Speen, Buckinghamshire, HP27 0PZ **Tel** *01494 488300*

A 17th-century building set in the heart of the Chiltern countryside, Old Plow is famed for a very high quality of modern eclectic cuisine. Specialities are French dishes with wonderful sauces, and seafood which arrives direct from the Devon coast. Good value fixed-price menu and friendly service. Closed Sun, Mon.

STREATLEY The Swan at Streatley
Streatley-on-Thames, Berkshire, RG8 9HR **Tel** *01491 878800*

The restaurant at this efficient business and leisure hotel serves carefully prepared dishes with the best local produce. The star attraction on the menu is the roast breast of Gressingham duck with citrus fruits. Adjourn from the Riverside Terrace to the Drawing Room Bar for a coffee or liqueur for the full dining experience.

THAME The Thatch
29–30 Lower High St, Thame, Oxfordshire, OX9 2AA **Tel** *01844 214340*

Set in a 16th-century half-timbered building, the Thatch offers a well-considered menu, which makes excellent use of seasonal and ethically produced ingredients. The restaurant also boasts an airy dining room, open fires and a secluded patio garden. The attentive staff ensure eating and drinking here is a relaxed affair.

THURLEIGH The Jackal
3 High St, Thurleigh, Bedfordshire, MK44 2DB **Tel** *01234 771293*

This pub-restaurant offers outstanding and award-winning bistro-style food. With a huge outdoor garden and an inviting interior filled with sofas and easy chairs, it's the perfect place to spend an evening or lunch time. The home-made sticky toffee pudding is fast becoming famous across the district.

WINDSOR Al Fassia
27 St Leonards Rd, Windsor, Berkshire, SL4 3BP **Tel** *01753 855370*

Shining out among the traditional Windsor restaurants, Al Fassia serves a host of North African delights. The caring concern of a family-run business is matched with a strictly professional attention to detail. The fluffy, melt-in-the-mouth couscous is well worth a try. Some specialities must be ordered a couple of days ahead.

WINDSOR Mango Lounge
9 Datchet Rd, Windsor, Berkshire, SL4 1QB **Tel** *01753 855576*

With views across to Windsor Castle, this is a stylish and contemporary Indian restaurant. The innovative menu reflects the entire Indian sub-continent, including Goan, Bengali, Gujarati and Rajasthani influences. Try the king prawn moilee, cooked in a coconut and curry leaf sauce, or the Karai chicken, flavoured with chilli flakes and cumin.

WOBURN Paris House
Woburn Park, Woburn, Bedfordshire, MK17 9QP **Tel** *01525 290692*

A mock-Tudor building set in the grounds of Woburn Abbey, Paris House is a fancy, but friendly, restaurant serving contemporary French cuisine. Varied menus range from gastronomic to special occasions (such as *Phantom of the Opera* evenings) to fine à la carte choices. Don't miss the wonderfully dripping hot raspberry soufflé.

WOODSTOCK The Feathers Hotel
Market St, Woodstock, Oxfordshire, OX20 1SX **Tel** *01993 812291*

Situated near to historic landmarks such as Blenheim Palace and the Oxford University's "dreaming spires", the Feathers successfully combines modern cuisine with traditional dishes. Originally seven separate 17th-century houses, the building has a cosy and charismatic interior, with roasting log fires and interesting antique furniture.

WESSEX

AVEBURY The Circle Restaurant
High St, Avebury, Marlborough, Wiltshire, SN8 1RF **Tel** *01672 539514*

Wholefood fans rave about this counter-service restaurant beside the ancient stone circle. Using local products, they serve up wonderful home-made soups and organic teas – all at an extremely reasonable price. It's a perfect place to allow the wonder of Avebury stone circle to properly sink in, along with their nutritious flapjacks.

AXMINSTER River Cottage Canteen
Trinity Sq, Axminster, Devon, EX13 5AN **Tel** *01297 631715*

Part of Hugh Fearnley-Whittingstall's River Cottage empire, this local-produce store and café-restaurant showcases the best of the region's local and seasonal food, with an eye on local producers. Expect the likes of fresh, line-caught fish from Lyme Bay, and plenty of goodies to take away. Closed Sun, Mon dinner all year & Sun–Wed dinner in winter.

BATH Café Retro
18 York St, Bath, Somerset, BA1 1NG **Tel** *01225 339347*

This independent café down a side street behind the Abbey is a long-standing favourite with Bathonians. Particularly favoured for lunch, its boho atmosphere draws people in for all-day breakfasts, ciabattas, toasted and club sandwiches, and tea and cakes. It's open seven days a week but closed in the evenings and during private functions.

BATH Browns
Orange Grove, Bath, Somerset, BA1 1LP **Tel** *01225 461199*

Inside a Georgian building once used as a police station and magistrates court, Browns serves up classic Brit cuisine in a classy atmosphere. The restaurant is open for breakfast, lunch and dinner and is a popular spot for afternoon tea, while the outdoor patio is ideal for sipping cocktails during the summer months.

BATH Demuths
2 North Parade Passage, off Abbey Green, Bath, Somerset, BA1 1NX **Tel** *01225 446059*

This Bath institution is great not just for vegetarians and vegans but for anyone who enjoys world food. Delights such as beetroot risotto with toasted pistachios, goats' cheese and rocket, and roast pineapple with red chilli jelly, cashew and coconut cheese are served up in the pretty dining room of a grand Georgian building.

Key to Price Guide *see p608* **Key to Symbols** *see back cover flap*

BATH Hole in the Wall 🧍♿🍷 ££

16 George St, Bath, Somerset, BA1 2EN **Tel** *01225 425242*

This vaulted restaurant has been refurbished to bring sleek minimalism to dazzling period features. The old-fashioned service and subdued atmosphere merely adds to its glamour. The contemporary British cuisine, with a French flair, is superb. Don't miss the buttered cabbage. Good-value lunch and pre-theatre menus.

BATH Jamie's Italian 🧍♿🍷 ££

10 Milsom Place, Bath, Somerset, BA1 1BZ **Tel** *01225 510051*

It's not difficult to find an Italian restaurant in Bath, but Jamie's – one of his national chain – is among the best. The service here is good, the ingredients fresh and the flavours lip-smacking. Expect rustic Italian specials and an Italian wine list, with bottles and 500ml carafes to choose from. Great atmosphere and much beloved in the city.

BATH Sally Lunn's 🧍 ££

24 North Parade Passage, Bath, Somerset, BA1 4NX **Tel** *01225 461634*

Located in Bath's oldest building, dating from 1482, this famous tea shop and eating house includes a kitchen museum where Sally Lunn, a young French refugee, created the original Bath bun. Spread over three floors it serves traditional English cooking such as poached salmon and roast lamb and beef.

BATH Hudson's Steakhouse ♿ £££

14 London St, Bath, Somerset, BA1 5BY **Tel** *01225 332323*

One of Hudson's special cocktails is a good way to begin a visit to this acclaimed steakhouse in a former Victorian pub, close to the city centre. Its steaks, notably Angus and Limousin, are sourced from Staffordshire farms and matured for 35 days. Chicken and seafood are on offer too, as well as imaginative starters and desserts.

BATH The Olive Tree 🧍🍷 ££££

4–7 Russell St, Bath, Somerset, BA1 2QF **Tel** *01225 447928*

Inside the Queensberry Hotel, The Olive Tree restaurant is a stylish haven serving up modern British fare. The menu includes dishes like seared Cornish scallops, liquorish roast loin of venison and sticky toffee pudding. The emphasis is on local West Country ingredients, and prices are reasonable for the quality.

BATH The Bath Priory 🧍♿🍷 £££££

Weston Road, Bath, Somerset, BA1 2XT **Tel** *01225 331922*

This top-notch establishment stands in a 19th-century Bath hotel, surrounded by four acres of award-winning gardens. Executive chef Michael Caines has two Michelin stars and is renowned for his innovative modern-European cuisine. Tasting and seasonal menus are available. Private dining is also possible.

BEAMINSTER Bridge House Hotel 🧍♿🍷 £££

Prout Bridge, Beaminster, Dorset, DT8 3AY **Tel** *01308 862200*

A few minutes from the Dorset coast, among beautiful countryside, this restaurant makes a great refreshment break. Local produce is transformed into dishes that change daily, but are likely to include fresh scallops or their speciality – organic pork, chicken and lamb. A brasserie section overlooks the walled garden.

BEAMINSTER Wild Garlic 🧍♿🍷 £££

4 The Square, Beaminster, Dorset, DT8 3AS **Tel** *01308 861446*

Mat Follas, the owner of this restaurant, won UK MasterChef 2009 for his hearty, tasty food. His restaurant centres on local produce, with occasional wild ingredients and edible flowers foraged from local hedgerows. Menu options include lamb with wild garlic pesto and a five-dessert tasting platter.

BOURNEMOUTH Chez Fred 🧍♿🍷 £

10 Seamoor Rd, Westbourne, Bournemouth, Dorset, BH4 9AN **Tel** *01202 761023*

The only place to eat fish and chips by the seaside, Chez Fred is famous for its interpretation of the national delicacy as well as mouthwatering puddings. Quintessentially British, the setting of this family-run eatery is welcoming and the atmosphere children-friendly and lively. No bookings accepted.

BOURNEMOUTH Urban Reef Café 🧍🎵♿🍷 ££

The Overstrand, Undercliff Dr, Boscombe, Bournemouth, Dorset, BH5 1BN **Tel** *01202 443960*

Urban Reef Café and Deli is all about bright colours, trendy fixtures and stunning views of the sea. By day it's a funky cosmopolitan café serving coffee, cakes and a wide range of lunches; by night it's a restaurant. Mains include free-range New Forest chicken breast stuffed with leek and wrapped in bacon, and plenty of seafood specials.

BOURNEMOUTH Gilbey's 🧍♿🍴 £££

Liston Hotel, 5 Wollstonecraft Rd, Bournemouth, Dorset, BH5 1JQ **Tel** *01202 394588*

Murals of Bournemouth's pier in Edwardian times decorate the walls of this award-winning restaurant in the family-owned Liston Hotel, five minutes' walk from the long, sandy beach. The fare is English/French with international touches and, in the summer, can be enjoyed on the garden terrace. Portions are generous.

BRADFORD-ON-AVON Woolley Grange 🧍♿🍷 ££££

Woolley Green, Bradford-on-Avon, Wiltshire, BA15 1TX **Tel** *01225 864705*

This intriguing 17th-century Jacobean manor house, built of Bath stone, is beautifully surrounded by 14 acres of leafy grounds. The extensive menu features everything from children's food to fine international cuisine using locally sourced produce. A casual, cosy atmosphere prevails in the dining room decorated with Oriental rugs and antiques.

BRISTOL Arnolfini Café & Bar   🚹♿🚇🅿️   ⓔ
16 Narrow Quay, Bristol, BS1 4QA **Tel** *0117 9172300*

Bristol's key contemporary art gallery houses a bijou café and bar, with tables spilling out onto the popular quayside in summer. The salads, soups, sandwiches and home-made cakes all come highly recommended, while the wine list is small but perfectly formed. Arrive early to bag a seat; Arnolfini stays open until 6pm.

BRISTOL Social Maitreya   🚹♿   ⓔⓔ
89 St Mark's Rd, Easton, Bristol, BS5 6HY **Tel** *0117 9510100*

Take a taxi ride to this much-garlanded vegetarian restaurant off the beaten track. Café Maitreya specializes in unpretentious, organic vegetarian cuisine and tapas. There are flourishes of inspiration, and the presentation is beautiful. It gets busy in the evening, so be sure to book ahead; it's open for lunch and dinner.

BRISTOL Spyglass   🚹🎵♿🚇   ⓔⓔ
Welsh Back, Bristol, BS1 4SB **Tel** *0117 9277050*

Just along the quayside from its sister restaurant, The Glassboat, Spyglass serves year-round barbecue food at fantastic prices. Mediterranean-style meat, fish and vegetable dishes are served al fresco, and there are heaters and marquees to keep you warm and dry when it's cold. Open Apr–Sep.

BRISTOL The Glassboat   🚹♿🚇🅿️   ⓔⓔ
Welsh Back, Bristol, BS1 4SB **Tel** *0117 9290704*

Moored at one of Bristol's most romantic settings, this upmarket floating restaurant serves French-influenced dishes. Snails, rabbit and lobster are favourites on a menu that includes great lunchtime and early evening offers. Dining at night is by candlelight.

BRISTOL Goldbrick House   🚹♿🚇🅿️   ⓔⓔⓔ
69 Park St, Bristol, BS1 5PB **Tel** *0117 9451950*

One of Bristol's top and most fashionable restaurants, Goldbrick House has a number of dining options, from the casual downstairs café – good for brunch and afternoon coffee – to the secluded club-like rooms for cocktails. There is also an upstairs restaurant serving good, classically British food. The white tablecloths are spotless and the service impeccable.

BRISTOL Hotel du Vin   🚹♿🅿️   ⓔⓔⓔ
The Sugar House, Narrow Lewins Mead, Bristol, BS1 2NU **Tel** *0117 9255577*

Bristol's best restaurant has a dash of Gallic flair as well as a clubby atmosphere. Open for lunch and dinner, the classic European cuisine includes ham hock, roast partridge, chargrilled rib-eye steak and pan-fried red mullet. Children eat free, but an adult-only dining room is more the norm at night. The in-house sommelier is fantastic.

BRISTOL Riverstation   🚹♿🅿️   ⓔⓔⓔ
The Grove, Bristol, BS1 4RB **Tel** *01179 144434*

Formerly a harbourside police station left in decline, Riverstation has fully exploited its potential to become one of the city's top restaurants offering modern European cuisine. Of its two floors, the dock floor has a bar and kitchen which is busy and buzzing all day long. The other floor is a light and airy restaurant.

COLERNE Lucknam Park   ♿🅿️   ⓔⓔⓔⓔⓔ
Colerne, Chippenham, Wiltshire, SN14 8AZ **Tel** *01225 742777*

Situated in a splendid country manor with hotel, spa and equestrian facilities, the restaurant is a suitably posh addition. Enjoy Michelin-starred cuisine in the Park restaurant or local specials in the relaxed brasserie. The hotel is steeped heavily in tradition and the dress code is casual but smart. No children under five in the restaurant.

CRUDWELL The Rectory   🚹♿🚇🅿️   ⓔⓔⓔ
Rectory Hotel, Crudwell, Malmesbury, Wiltshire, SN16 9EP **Tel** *01666 577194*

This upmarket, modern restaurant is located within the Rectory hotel, in the heart of the Cotswolds. The oak-panelled dining room overlooks the gardens and sunken Victorian pool. On the menu are British classics, an impressive dessert selection and plenty of locally sourced cheeses. Outdoor dining is available during the summer months.

LACOCK At the Sign of the Angel   🚹♿🅿️   ⓔⓔⓔ
Church St, Lacock, Wiltshire, SN15 2LB **Tel** *01249 730230*

The only sheep that this converted 15th-century wool merchant's house comes across now, is in the form of delicious roast lamb. The ambience is that of a quaint village restaurant, with log fires, oak panelling, low beams and squeaky floorboards, all teeming with history and character. Friendly, informal staff and good Sunday roasts.

LYME REGIS Hix Oyster and Fish House   🚹🅿️   ⓔⓔⓔ
Cobb Rd, Lyme Regis, Dorset, DT7 3JP **Tel** *01297 446910*

Mark Hix, formerly of The Ivy in London, is the brains behind this fresh fish restaurant, with the best location in town. There are meat dishes as well as a variety of oysters on offer daily, plus the catch of the day. The set lunch menu is great value, and the Lyme Bay fish soup is recommended.

MAIDEN NEWTON Le Petit Canard   🅿️   ⓔⓔⓔ
Dorchester Road, Maiden Newton, Dorchester, DT2 0BE **Tel** *01300 320536*

Enjoy fine dining at this rustic, France-meets-West Country restaurant. Their success is reflected in the deliciously unique dishes such as the loin fillet of local venison with redcurrant sauce. The service is impeccable and the cottage environment endearing.

Key to Price Guide *see p608* **Key to Symbols** *see back cover flap*

MIDSOMER NORTON The Moody Goose

*The Old Priory Hotel, Church Sq, Midsomer Norton, nr Bath, Somerset, BA3 2HX **Tel** 01761 416784*

Fifteen miles from Bath, in the rolling Somerset countryside, The Moody Goose occupies a former priory and has all the grandeur you would expect. The food is excellent, with choices such as rabbit terrine and hot and cold-steamed smoked salmon. There is a good selection of vegetarian dishes. Closed Sunday evenings.

POOLE Museum Inn

*Farnham, nr Blandford Forum, Dorset, DT11 8DE **Tel** 01725 516261*

With a cosy dining room, a log fire in a huge inglenook fireplace, flagstoned floors and wooden tables, this is a classic English pub-restaurant. The weekly menu is reasonable and perfectly executed. Ingredients are largely locally sourced and include free-range poultry and fresh fish from Brixham.

POOLE Storm Fish Restaurant

*16 High Street, Poole, Dorset, BH15 1BP **Tel** 01202 674970*

With a rustic interior and a cosy, intimate atmosphere, Storm is perfect for a romantic dinner. Owner Pete Miles is a fisherman by day and chef by night, serving up the freshest produce in what is reputedly Poole's finest seafood restaurant. Specialist fish cookery courses are also available.

SALISBURY The Jade

*109a Exeter St, Salisbury, Wiltshire, SP1 2SF **Tel** 01722 333355*

Located in the heart of the city, just a short walk from Salisbury Cathedral, this Cantonese restaurant is a firm favourite with locals. Seafood dominates the menu, and the chef's special is a whole live lobster braised, Cantonese style. Great service and friendly staff.

SHEPTON MALLETT Sharpham Park Shop and Harlequin Café

*Kilver Court, Kilver St, Shepton Mallet, Somerset, BS4 5NF **Tel** 01749 340410*

Sharpham Park is an organic farm based near Glastonbury. Owned by Roger Saul, the founder of the Mulberry designer label, it has a café and a farm shop at Kilver Court. The café is decorated in stylish fabrics, with bleached wood furniture. Fare includes sandwiches, soups and other simple meals.

SOMERSET Lord Poulett Arms

*Hinton St George, Somerset, TA17 8SE **Tel** 01460 73149*

This celebrated gastropub in south Somerset is the perfect stop on a Sunday for its legendary roasts. More exotic lunch choices include Thai red curry with Cornish mussels. There is also a selection of gourmet sandwiches, while dinner options include pan-roasted Venison loin. Local ciders and home-made seasonal cordials complement the menu.

SOMERSET The Pilgrims at Lovington

*Pilgrims Rest Inn, Pilgrims Way, Lovington, Somerset, BA7 7PT **Tel** 01963 240600*

Robust, restaurant-quality food served in a relaxed pub atmosphere in the depths of Somerset. The menu changes on a monthly basis, but the one thing you can be sure to find are excellent local cheeses. This is one of the very best dining pubs in Somerset. There is no children's menu, but smaller portions can be made up specially.

STON EASTON Sorell

*Ston Easton Park Hotel, Ston Easton, nr Bath, Somerset, BA3 4DF **Tel** 01761 241631*

Overlooking the River Nor and Ston Easton Park's beautiful gardens, this Georgian restaurant harks back to a bygone era. The food, however, is modern British, with European influences, made with fresh local produce. Open to both residential and non-residential hotel guests. Dine al fresco on the terrace in summer.

STURMINSTER NEWTON Plumber Manor

*Sturminster Newton, Dorset, DT10 2AF **Tel** 01258 472507*

In the middle of Thomas Hardy's "Vale of Little Dairies" and in the centre of a triangle of charming country towns, this family-run country house and restaurant is an idyllic stopping point. Portraits adorn the walls and friendly Labradors greet guests as they come to enjoy fine food, particularly fish as well as delightful desserts.

SWANAGE Cauldron Bistro

*5 High St, Swanage, Dorset, BH19 2LN **Tel** 01929 422671*

Quality ingredients fresh from the sea have long been the secret to the success of this town-centre restaurant close to the quay, with French posters adding to the classic bistro atmosphere. Firm, juicy scallops are heavenly. Invigorate the palate with the ginger ice cream. Booking essential.

TAUNTON The Devonshire Arms

*Long Sutton, Langport, Somerset, TA10 9LP **Tel** 01458 241271*

This Grade II listed former hunting lodge is home to the perfect English pub, overlooking the village green. Inside, the stylish modern restaurant serves lunch and dinner, with local produce and British gastropub-style classics at the heart of the menu, including Gloucester Old Spot pork belly and Cornish mussels steamed in cider.

TAUNTON Brazz

*Castle Hotel, Castle Green, Taunton, Somerset, TA1 1NF **Tel** 01823 272671*

Once a Norman fortress, this castle has been welcoming travellers since the 12th century, and has been run by the same family since the 1950s. While the antiquated interior is preserved, the food is the main focus in the Brazz brasserie, such as local rabbit and pigeon with bean cassoulet.

TAUNTON Willow Tree   £££

3 Tower Lane, Taunton, Somerset, TA1 4AR **Tel** *01823 352835*

This small, intimate restaurant occupies a 17th-century listed building near the town centre. It serves modern British fare based on home-grown and local produce, such as fricasse of mussels and breast of duck with garlic and creamed cabbage. It has won several awards; booking is essential.

WARMINSTER The Mulberry Restaurant   ££££

Bishopstrow House, Warminster, Wiltshire, BA12 9HH **Tel** *01985 212312*

Named after a tree in Bishopstrow House's beautiful grounds, golden-yellow Mulberry Restaurant is gracious with a Georgian feel. It may look old and rambling but its clientele is young. Enjoy light lunches and dinners overlooking acres of land and opt for the set meals. Private dining also available.

WEST BAY Riverside   £££

West Bay, Bridport, Dorset, DT6 4EZ **Tel** *01308 422011*

This restaurant boasts wonderful service, superb food and a festive atmosphere indoors. Its position as one of the best fish restaurants in the Southwest is quite an achievement, since most coastal places serve seafood. The langoustines with mayonnaise or pan-fried mackerel with chips are heavenly.

WEST BEXINGTON Manor Hotel   ££

Beach Rd, West Bexington, Dorchester, Dorset, DT2 9DF **Tel** *01308 897785*

Just when you think you've taken one coastal path too far, you'll hit upon this gorgeous old stone inn. The restaurant serves a range of delicious dishes, while the daily-changing menu features local produce and seafood. The Cellar Bar offers a selection of wines from around the world.

WILTSHIRE The Compasses Inn   ££

Lower Chicksgrove, Tisbury SP3 6NB **Tel** *01722 714318*

The Compasses Inn is situated in a designated area of outstanding natural beauty. This superbly run restaurant is housed in a traditional thatched cottage and has a pleasant, relaxed atmosphere. The award-winning imaginative English and modern European menu is complimented by a good choice of wines and friendly service.

YEOVIL Little Barwick House   ££££

Little Barwick House, Barwick, Yeovil, Somerset, BA22 9TD **Tel** *01935 423902*

Located right on the Dorset and Somerset border, this idyllic family-run hotel is a great place to stop for food while touring each county's gorgeous scenery. The decor is elegantly country-house, which matches the fine British food, such as the roast breast of Gressingham duck. Children over five years welcome.

DEVON AND CORNWALL

AVONWICK Avon Inn   ££

Avonwick, Totnes, Devon, TQ10 9NB **Tel** *01364 73475*

On the banks of the Avon, this traditional English pub is a perfect respite during a river walk. British food is prepared with a Continental twist. Specialities include the steak and ale pie and the beer-battered cod. Enjoy with fine wines or real ales.

BARNSTAPLE Terra Madre   ££

Broomhill Art Hotel, Muddiford Rd, Barnstaple, Devon, EX31 4EX **Tel** *01271 850262*

Part of a intriguing sculpture garden art gallery and hotel, this restaurant provides a three-course gourmet lunch that can last the entire afternoon, and even push on late into the evening. An advocate of the slow food movement, expect local meat, fish and dairy; organic wine and fresh bread.

BARNSTAPLE The Grove Inn   ££

Kings Nympton, nr Barnstaple, North Devon, EX37 9ST **Tel** *01769 580406*

The award-winning Grove Inn is a firm foodie favourite in the North Devon area. Ploughmans and Sunday lunches are much recommended, as are the home-made puddings. Regular special events such as food and wine tasting evenings, complement the seasonal menus.

BIGBURY Oyster Shack   £££

Milburn Orchard Farm, Stakes Hill, Bigbury, Devon, TQ7 4BE **Tel** *01548 810876*

The name suggests that Oyster Shack is little more than a shack with a tarpaulin, but it is in fact an excellent seafood restaurant serving unmissable food: local mussels and oysters, pan-fried sardines, potted shrimp, shell-on prawns or whatever the catch of the day might be. Booking is essential.

CHAGFORD 22 Mill Street   ££££

22 Mill St, Chagford, Devon, TQ13 8AW **Tel** *01647 432244*

Nestled behind a dark green shop front, this modern European restaurant is run by a couple who even make their own butter. The atmosphere is relaxing. Attention to detail, clear flavours and attractive presentation make the place good value. Tasting menu and private dining available.

Key to Price Guide *see p608* **Key to Symbols** *see back cover flap*

CHAGFORD Gidleigh Park

Gidleigh Park, Chagford Devon, TQ13 8HH **Tel** *01647 432367*

Officially one of the best restaurants this country has to offer, Gidleigh Park has two Michelin stars. The attention to detail is what sets it apart. Menus change according to the season, but expect fine quality whatever the month. The wine choice is also among the nation's best. Perfect for special occasions.

DARTINGTON Cott Inn

Dartington, Totnes, Devon, TQ9 6HE **Tel** *01803 863777*

Charming Cott Inn is a 14th-century restaurant-with-rooms with all the antiquated extras: exposed beams, open fireplace, horse brasses, soft lights. The restaurant has cosy cushioned pews, wall lanterns and a very reasonable menu. Check the blackboard for daily specials, and don't miss the three-course Sunday roast.

DARTMOUTH The New Angel

2 South Embankment, Dartmouth, Devon, TQ6 9BH **Tel** *01803 839425*

Run by notorious chef John Burton-Race, this fine-dining restaurant features local produce like line-caught mackerel in the first floor dining room and cocktails with a view on the second floor. Unlike formal dining rooms, families are welcome in an unpretentious environment. Get there at 8:30am for coffee, croissants and cooked breakfast.

DARTMOUTH The Seahorse

5 South Embankment, Dartmouth, South Devon, TQ6 9BH **Tel** *01803 835147*

Located in the heart of the historic Naval town of Dartmouth, this award-winning seafood and meat grill restaurant takes full advantage of its maritime setting. Menu options include prawns, lobster, crab, bass, scallops, turbot and more. Stylish and cosy.

DODDISCOMBSLEIGH The NoBody Inn

Doddiscombsleigh, nr Exeter, Devon, EX6 7PS **Tel** *01647 252394*

A 16th-century country inn set in the rolling Devon countryside, NoBody Inn was renamed after an unfortunate incident when an empty coffin was buried at the funeral of one of its landlords. Enjoy the traditional interior and fresh local produce as well as its imaginative wine and whisky list. Unspoilt old-world charm.

EXETER Abode

Cathedral Yard, Exeter, Devon, EX1 1D2 **Tel** *01392 319955*

Local superstar chef Michael Caines presides over this fine dining restaurant situated close to Exeter Cathedral. An overnight stay at Abode, plus dinner, offers fantastic value for money. The tasting menu is outstanding; skip dessert for the superb southwest cheese selection. Champagne bar and café too.

EXETER Thai Orchid

5 Cathedral Yard, Exeter, Devon, EX1 1HJ **Tel** *01392 214215*

Authentic Thai cuisine is on offer in the 16th-century building, where the stone-masons who built Exeter's glorious cathedral originally boarded. Fresh orchids on each table are a thoughtful finishing touch. Momospice, the restaurant's private dining experience, is not to be missed.

EXETER The Jack in the Green

Rockbeare, nr Exeter, Devon, EX5 2EE **Tel** *01404 822240*

Winner of a multitude of awards, The Jack specialises in British classics using locally-sourced ingredients. Whether you dine in the pub or opt for the tasting menu in the restaurant, the standard is top class. There's a large wine list, separate vegetarian menu and hearty Sunday lunch offering too.

EXMOOR The Mason's Arms

Knowstone, North Devon, EX36 4RY **Tel** *01398 341231*

Cosy 13th-century thatched inn on the Devon/Somerset border, with views of Exmoor. The Michelin-starred restaurant is headed by the former head chef of Michel Roux's Waterside Inn in Bray. Expect Modern British and French classics. The pub itself is popular with locals. Restaurant closed Sunday night and Monday.

FALMOUTH Gylly Beach Café

Cliff Rd, Falmouth, Cornwall, TR11 4PA **Tel** *01326 312884*

Friendly, award-winning beach café with spectacular coastal views of the Lizard Peninsula and Pendennis Castle. During the day it's perfect for ice-cream and coffee; by night it becomes a trendy dining spot. Dishes are made with the freshest Cornish ingredients, brunch is popular and there is occasional live music.

HONITON Combe House Hotel and Restaurant

Gittisham, Devon, EX14 3AD **Tel** *01404 540400*

This restaurant has a deserved reputation for fine food and friendly, dedicated service. Choose from select cuts of meat and game in season, including wood pigeon and pork tenderloin, or locally caught fish. All vegetables are sourced from the restaurant's kitchen garden.

KINGSBRIDGE Buckland-Tout-Saints Hotel

Goveton, Kingsbridge, Devon, TQ7 2DS **Tel** *01548 853055*

Set in a wonderful 1690 Grade II listed residence in the middle of lush woodland countryside, Buckland-Tout-Saints is a magnificent manor house from Queen Anne's time, with plenty of character. The restaurant serves British cuisine and focuses on local produce including West Country cheese. Menus change daily.

LAUNCESTON Blagdon Manor
Ashwater, Cornwall, EX21 5DF **Tel** *01409 211224*

This country-house hotel has some superb dining options for foodies, with local produce at the heart of its menus. Expect game from the nearby woods, local cheeses and fish fresh from the sea. Blagdon Manor is a Grade II listed building with flagstone floors and beams dating to the 1600s. Open for lunch Fri–Sun & dinner Wed–Sun. Book in advance.

LEWDOWN Lewtrenchard Manor
Lewdown, Okehampton, Devon, EX20 4PN **Tel** *01566 783222*

Mentioned in the *Domesday Book* of 1086, this impressive manor was once a popular hangout of knights. Today, diners are treated to generous helpings of wholesome modern English food; seared scallops, roast duck and the like are on the menu. The showpiece attraction is The Purple Carrot, a chef's table with private view of the world-class kitchen.

LIFTON The Arundell Arms Hotel
Fore St, Lifton, Devon, PL16 0AA **Tel** *01566 784666*

The Arundell Arms serves as an escape from the hustle and bustle. The lovely surrounding area provides activities such as fishing, riding, walking and golf. The restaurant serves fixed-price menus featuring local game and fish, created by Steve Pigeon, one of Britain's official master chefs. Bar snacks are also available for lunch or dinner.

LOSTWITHIEL Muffins Tea Rooms
32 Fore St, Lostwithiel, Cornwall, PL22 0BN **Tel** *01208 872278*

You can't go far in Cornwall without being offered a cream tea, so why not have one of the best? Muffins is the top pick in the county for Cornish clotted cream, scones and jam. They also do great Ploughman's lunches and have a deli selling local Cornish produce. Located 5 miles (8 km) east of the Eden Project. Closed Sun, Mon.

LYNMOUTH The Rising Sun
Harbourside, Lynmouth, Devon, EX35 6EG **Tel** *01598 753223*

Percy Bysshe Shelley stayed at this 14th-century thatched smugglers' inn that overlooks a picturesque harbour and Lynmouth Bay. Lobster, fresh from the bay, literally lands at their door, as well as local Exmoor game and salmon fished from the River Lyn. Dinner is served in the romantic candlelit, oak-panelled dining room.

MARLDON Church House Inn
Village Rd, Marldon, Devon, TQ3 1SL **Tel** *01803 558279*

Located in the centre of the village, delightful Church House Inn is as old as the 14th-century church beside it. The restaurant, renowned for its traditional menu with a Mediterranean twist, serves as the centre of the local community. A perfect slice of quintessential countryside life comes with a full-bodied pint.

MAWGAN PORTH The Scarlet
Tredragon Rd, Mawgan Porth, Cornwall, TR8 4DQ **Tel** *01637 861800*

The restaurant at this design-conscious hotel has a view to rival the best in Britain. The floor-to-ceiling windows offer spectacular panoramas of the rugged Cornish coastline. The menu is pricey but impressive, with dishes such as pan-fried skate wings and roast loin of venison. Good local cider and wine-matching menu available.

NEWQUAY Fifteen Cornwall
On the beach, Watergate Bay, Cornwall, TR8 4AA **Tel** *01637 861000*

Situated right on the beach, Jamie Oliver's Fifteen is justly famous for its British food with an Italian twist. The restaurant is a short drive from bustling Newquay and is open for breakfast, lunch and dinner. This is a popular spot for dinner, so book ahead to avoid disappointment.

PADSTOW St Petroc's
New St, Padstow, Cornwall, PL28 8EA **Tel** *01841 532700*

This bright and bustling bistro is tucked away behind the busy fishing harbour and is one of seafood chef Rick Stein's numerous eateries in Padstow. The international range of dishes includes pigeon breast salad and bavette Bordelaise steak (only served rare). Booking advisable.

PADSTOW The Seafood Restaurant
Riverside, Padstow, Cornwall, PL28 8BY **Tel** *01841 532700*

This imaginative fish and shellfish restaurant has been around since 1975. Just across the quay from the lobster boats and trawlers, it procures much of the fish literally straight off the boats. Overseen by celebrity chef Rick Stein, seafood is fresh and succulent. Platters of oysters, sushi and sashimi are on offer. Children welcome up to 7pm.

PENZANCE The Cove
Lamorna, nr Penzance, Cornwall, TR19 6XH **Tel** *01736 731411*

This cosy restaurant and café is nestled in the tiny picturesque fishing village of Lamorna and has nice views over the cove. Perfect for walkers on the Cornish coastal path, the menu includes plates of charcuterie, wild mushroom risotto and delicious, chocolatey desserts. Children's high tea is available between 6 and 7 pm.

PENZANCE Bay Restaurant
Britons Hill, Penzance, Cornwall, TR18 3AE **Tel** *01736 366890*

This stylish two AA Rosette restaurant has an outdoor deck that opens out in summer for magnificent views across Mount's Bay and over the rooftops to Penzance Harbour. Generous and creative European cuisine is served by knowledgeable staff. Local fish, vegetables and herbs are complemented by excellent Cornish wine.

Key to Price Guide *see p608* **Key to Symbols** *see back cover flap*

PENZANCE Harris's ⬥ ⬥ £££
46 New St, Penzance, Cornwall, TR18 2LZ Tel 01736 364408

Run by the Harris family since 1972, this small restaurant wins acclaim for freshly made dishes served with local produce and fish from nearby Newlyn market. The daily-changing menu highlights modern British cuisine with an excellent range of fresh seafood dishes. The crab Florentine comes highly recommended.

PLYMOUTH The Barbican Kitchen ⬥ ⬥ £££
Black Friars Distillery, 60 Southside St, The Barbican, Plymouth, PL1 2LQ Tel 01752 604448

TV chefs Chris and James Tanner opened their brasserie in Plymouth's historic gin distillery building. The fare is a mix of classic British and Continental alongside more innovative offerings, such as the Pork Plate, comprising loin, glazed belly and black pudding. The interior is bright and funky, and the cocktails are great.

PLYMOUTH The View ⬥ ⬥ ⬥ £££
Treninnow Cliff Rd, Millbrook, Cornwall, PL10 1JY Tel 01752 822345

A real find, The View overlooks Whitsand Bay on a wild stretch of coast in north Cornwall. This modern, unpretentious restaurant offers a seasonal menu with fresh fish and seafood during the warmer months and more meat dishes towards winter. All ingredients are locally sourced, and the sunset views are fantastic.

POLPERRO Kitchen ⬥ ⬥ £££
The Coombes, Polperro, Cornwall, PL13 2RQ Tel 01503 272780

This delightful little restaurant serves mainly home-made food. Bread is baked daily and ice cream is made nearby. Delicious fish is garnered from Cornish day boats, with the exception of the odd exotic dish. The atmosphere is cosy and diners can often go into the kitchen for a chat and tour afterwards.

PORT ISAAC Slipway Hotel and Seafood Restaurant ⬥ ⬥ £££
The Habour Front, Port Isaac, Cornwall, PL29 3RH Tel 01208 880264

This quaint fish restaurant offers a perfect sample of Cornish fishy fare in season. Though there's no live music inside, diners can hear the tuneful noise of fisherman singing by the harbour. Reasonably-priced and consistently good, with a 40-plus wine list to boot.

SALCOMBE Winking Prawn ⬥ ⬥ ££
Waterfront Brasserie and Garden, North Sands, Salcombe, Devon, TQ8 8LD Tel 01548 842326

In a thickly wooded valley, this little place appears beside an empty beach. There's an evening barbecue of steak and king prawns that can be taken outside on fine days. When it rains, the restaurant offers bowls of soup and *fruits de mer*. There are also cream teas and good ice creams.

ST IVES Tate Café and Restaurant ⬥ ⬥ £
Porthmeor Beach, St Ives, Cornwall, TR26 1TG Tel 01736 796226

Enjoy the views over the old town of St Ives and Porthmeor Beach from this art-gallery brasserie while tucking into whole-food dishes made from produce created by Cornish growers and suppliers where possible. They stock and sell premium Cornish goods, ranging from cheese to fish, potatoes to ice cream and cider to wine. Lunch and afternoon tea only.

ST IVES Alba ⬥ ⬥ ⬥ ££
Old Lifeboat House, Wharf Rd, St Ives, Cornwall, TR26 1LF Tel 01736 797222

With spectacular views of the bay, mesmerizing Alba is housed in the old lifeboat building. Equally breathtaking is the award-winning cuisine, predominantly line-caught seafood and seasonal vegetables, all sourced locally. The accompanying wine list is as impressive. There is a separate vegetarian menu.

ST IVES Porthminster Café ⬥ ⬥ ⬥ £££
Porthminster beach, St Ives, Cornwall, TR26 2EB Tel 01736 795352

Located on the superb Porthminster beach, this bright and friendly café serves Mediterranean and Asian fare alongside local Cornish dishes. Oysters served with lemon or grilled with chorizo, wasabi and yuza mayonnaise are a speciality. Come for lunch to make the most of the view.

ST MAWES Hotel Tresanton ⬥ ⬥ ⬥ ££££
27 Lower Castle Rd, St Mawes, Cornwall, TR2 5DR Tel 01326 270055

Situated at the edge of the unspoiled village of St Mawes, the Tresanton was created in the 1950s as a yachtsmen's club. The lovely restaurant has pretty views of the sea, looking towards St Anthony's Lighthouse. The food, with a hint of Italian flair, is exquisite and benefits from the local seafood easily available. Breakfast menu and picnics available.

SUMMERCOURT Viners ⬥ ⬥ ⬥ £££
Carvynick, Summercourt, Cornwall, TR8 5AF Tel 01872 510544

This bar and restaurant is run by executive chef Kevin Viner, the first-ever chef in Cornwall to win a Michelin star. The interior has been tranformed with flair. The owner-chef strives to keep the dishes simple. The emphasis is on the stand-alone strength of first-rate local fish and shellfish, Cornish lamb and beef. Good vegetarian options too.

TAVISTOCK The Horn of Plenty ⬥ ⬥ ££££
Gulworthy, Tavistock, Devon, PL19 8JD Tel 01822 832528

With stunning views over the tranquil Tamar Valley near Tavistock in Devon, this inviting country-house hotel is set in five acres of immaculate gardens and wild orchards. The award-winning restaurant excels itself under the baton of its executive head chef, Peter Gorton. Children welcome at lunchtimes. Cookery courses available.

TOPSHAM La Petite Maison 🚶 🍷 ⓔⓔⓔ
35 Fore St, Topsham, Devon, EX3 0HR **Tel** *01392 873660*

Situated in the attractive town of Topsham on the Exe Estuary, this small, fine-dining restaurant is popular with local diners. Lyme Bay crab and roast chump of local lamb are among the dishes served in a warm and friendly atmosphere. Make sure you save room for the West Country cheeses.

TORQUAY The Elephant 🚶 ♿ 🍷 ⓔⓔⓔ
3&4 Beacon Terrace, Torquay, Devon, TQ1 2BH **Tel** *01803 200044*

On Torquay's harbourfront, the Elephant is one of Devon's most stylish restaurants. Local fresh food is the order of the day, and diners may choose between The Room, with its fine dining and Michelin-starred taster menu, or The Elephant, which offers a brasserie-style menu in a more relaxed atmosphere. Closed during winter.

TOTNES Willow 🚶 🎵 🍷 ⓔⓔ
87 High St, Totnes, Devon, TQ9 5PB **Tel** *01803 862605*

Willow holds the crown in the area for vegetarian and vegan cuisine, offering reasonably-priced wholesome dishes and an organic wine list amid cheerful decor with a pretty courtyard at the back. The staff are helpful, and welcoming towards children. Even if you aren't vegetarian, it's still worth a visit.

TREBURLEY Springer Spaniel 🚶 ♿ 🍷 ⓔⓔ
Treburley, nr Launceston, Cornwall, PL15 9NS **Tel** *01579 370424*

Picturesque, award-winning Springer Spaniel is a country-food pub, set in an attractive 18th-century beamed building. The menu changes frequently, reflecting the owner's desire to use local produce, including home-grown vegetables and salads. There is also a Little Jack Russell menu for children. Staff are friendly and laid-back.

TRURO The Lugger Restaurant 🚶 ♿ 🛏 ⓔⓔⓔ
Portloe, Truro, Cornwall, TR2 5RD **Tel** *01872 501322*

The boutique Lugger Hotel has superb views of pretty Portloe and the coast. The restaurant here is open for lunch and dinner and serves British and European-inspired cuisine – with a French chef at the helm, its worth trying the seafood *bouillabaisse*. In summer, the sun-drenched terrace is perfect for sipping aperitifs.

VIRGINSTOW Percy's ♿ 🍷 ⓔⓔⓔⓔ
Coombeshead Estate, Virginstow, Devon, EX21 5EA **Tel** *01409 211236*

Award-winning dishes burst with colour and flavour at this restaurant and hotel. The kitchen, supervised by one of Devon's top female chefs, Tina Bricknell-Webb, creates consistently good contemporary country cuisine, with a wine selection to match. The home-reared lamb is particularly recommended.

WOOLACOMBE Trimstone Manor 🚶 ♿ 🛏 ⓔⓔⓔ
Trimstone, nr Woolacombe, North Devon, EX34 8NR **Tel** *01271 862841*

Just a short drive from the North Devon coast, this 17th-century hotel is set in lovely grounds. The restaurant here serves timeless classics such as grilled lemon sole, confit of duck leg and pork tenderloin. There is a bar for pre-dinner drinks and a good selection of malt whisky. A popular Sunday lunch destination, so book in advance.

THE HEART OF ENGLAND

ANSLOW The Burnt Gate 🚶 ♿ ⓔⓔ
59 Hopley Rd, Anslow, Burton upon Trent, Staffordshire, DE13 9PY **Tel** *01283 563664*

Friendly pub and restaurant with a homely decor featuring dark wood beams and an open coal fire. This award-winning eatery serves traditional dishes made with fresh, local produce, and is well known for steak, gammon, poultry, seasonal game and a variety of seafood. Also has dedicated menus for vegetarians and coeliacs.

BIRMINGHAM Chez Jules 🚶 ⓔⓔ
5a Ethel St, Birmingham, B2 4BG **Tel** *0121 633 4664*

Located in the heart of Birmingham, this busy French bistro offers simple, tasty food at surprisingly low prices. The menu includes old favourites such as *blanquette de veau* (veal stew), beef tenderloin, crème brûlée and chocolate mousse, all using produce from local markets. Relaxed and friendly atmosphere.

BIRMINGHAM Titash Balti Restaurant 🚶 ♿ ⓔⓔ
2278 Coventry Rd, Birmingham, B26 3JR **Tel** *0121 722 2080*

A must-try speciality here is Balti, a spicy, aromatic dish that was originally introduced by the city's large Kashmiri Pakistani community, and is cooked in a wok-like pot. The restaurant has been awarded the title "Curry Chef of the Year". An à la carte menu offers delicious food and a range of accompanying breads.

BIRMINGHAM Berlioz Restaurant 🚶 ♿ ⓔⓔⓔ
6 Burlington Arcade, 126 New St, Birmingham, B2 4JQ **Tel** *0121 633 1737*

Bright and airy, and with an undeniable historical grandeur, Berlioz is comfortably relaxed and offers impressive views over the New Street shopping area. The food has an unexpected Scottish influence, with steak, salmon and even haggis on offer.

Key to Price Guide *see p608* **Key to Symbols** *see back cover flap*

BIRMINGHAM Purnell's
55 Cornwall St, Birmingham, B3 2DH **Tel** *0121 212 9799*

Glynn Purnell's Michelin-starred restaurant has forged a reputation as one of the finest in the city. Featured on the superb à la carte menu are red mullet with green mustard, daube of beef and caramelized apple parfait. There's also a good-value, three-course lunch menu. Reservations recommended. Closed Sun, Mon.

BIRMINGHAM The Brasserie Malmaison
One Wharfside St, Birmingham, B1 1RD **Tel** *0121 246 5000*

The Malmaison is beautifully designed and offers a traditional French brasserie dining experience with a modern British twist and plenty of charisma. The food is beautifully presented and divinely tasty, prepared with fine-quality locally sourced ingredients. Try the assiette of rabbit or the baked cod fillet with garlic mash.

CHELTENHAM Brasserie Blanc
The Promenade, Cheltenham, Gloucestershire, GL50 1NN **Tel** *01242 266800*

Fine dining under the helm of award-winning chef Raymond Blanc. Set in an elegant Georgian building, this modern, vibrant brasserie is as well known for its cocktail bar as it is for its rich, French food. The kids menu offers a mix of haute cuisine and popular favourites such as gratinèed macaroni cheese and home-made French fries.

CHELTENHAM Le Champignon Sauvage
24–26 Suffolk Rd, Cheltenham, Gloucestershire, GL50 2AQ **Tel** *01242 573449*

Renowned French restaurant and winner of several awards. The interior is lovingly decorated in cream, with modern art on the walls and large, comfortable chairs for an informal dining experience. The seasonal menu has a strong emphasis on local ingredients. Wood pigeon, Cinderford lamb and sea bream are some of the favourites here.

CHIPPENHAM Bybrook Restaurant
Manor House Hotel and Golf Club, Castle Combe, nr Bath, Wiltshire, SN14 7HR **Tel** *01249 782206*

Outstanding food in a breathtaking setting in the Manor House hotel on the southern edge of the Cotswolds. Named after the Bybrook River that runs beside the hotel, this restaurant uses fresh produce from the house's kitchen garden and orchards. Stained-glass windows offer views over the Italian garden and the adjacent golf course.

GLOUCESTER The Fountain Inn
Westgate Street, Gloucester, Gloucestershire, GL1 2NW **Tel** *01452 522562*

With a pretty patio and delightful flower garden, this place is great for al fresco dining in the summer. Everyone is catered for, with a good mixture of mediterrannean dishes, seafood and traditional pub fare. The Sunday menu is particularly tempting.

HEREFORD Garway Moon
Garway Common, Hereford, Herefordshire, HR2 8RQ **Tel** *01600 750270*

Overlooking the village green this delightful pub retains its community atmosphere, whilst serving up robust, locally sourced food of a very high standard. Look for the pizza-and-a-pint deals on Wednesday, the curry-and-pint deals on Thursday, or choose from the extensive specials board.

HEREFORD Castle House
Castle St, Hereford, Herefordshire, HR1 2NW **Tel** *01432 356321*

Award-winning restaurant in the Castle House hotel. The seasonal menu here draws on fresh meat and produce delivered daily from the hotel's farm nearby. Try the Hereford prime beef and finish with a rhubarb mousse with ginger ice. Also hosts a cocktail bar for a pre-meal apéritif.

LEAMINGTON SPA Mallory Court
Harbury Lane, Leamington Spa, Warwickshire, CV33 9QB **Tel** *01926 330214*

Modern European dining, either in the brasserie or the more formal dining room, surrounded by lush Warwickshire countryside. The fixed-price menu offers a good choice from the likes of Everleigh Farm venison with beetroot or pan-fried fillet of wild sea bass with chorizo.

LEDBURY Scrumpy House
W H Weston's Cider, The Bounds, Ledbury, Herefordshire, HR8 2NQ **Tel** *01531 660626*

Once a cowshed, and now the café-restaurant of the visitor centre at Weston's cider-makers, the Scrumpy House is a brilliant way to discover the best of the local apple crop. Enjoy dishes such as roast breast of local chicken with pork and cider faggots, washed down with one of the many different ciders available.

LITTLE BEDWYN The Harrow at Little Bedwyn
Little Bedwyn, Marlborough, Wiltshire, SN8 3JP **Tel** *01672 870871*

Rated by the *Wine Spectator* as having one of the finest restaurant wine lists in the world. This Michelin-star eatery is primarily known for its extensive collection of Australian premium wines, and diners can opt for the "tasting menu with Aussie wines" meal. Also serves an à la carte menu.

LUDLOW The Clive Restaurant with Rooms
Bromfield, Ludlow, Shropshire, SY8 2JR **Tel** *01584 856565*

This converted farmhouse, with 15 bedrooms, has been decorated to emphasize many of the building's original features, including whitewashed walls and wood-beamed ceilings. The seasonal menu serves high-quality British fare, using produce from the surrounding countryside. The atmosphere is warm and informal.

PAXFORD The Churchill Arms
*Paxford, Chipping Campden, Gloucestershire, GL55 6XH **Tel** 01386 594000*

Pub with four rooms on a B&B basis, set in a small, working Cotswolds village. Offers an appetizing menu of local produce to accompany the popular real ales from local breweries. The menu is constantly updated, but dishes such as grilled fish, braised local lamb shank and poached chicken are regular favourites.

SALT Holly Bush Inn
*Salt, nr Stafford, Staffordshire, ST18 0BX **Tel** 01889 508234*

This picturesque country inn with a large beer garden is one of England's oldest pubs. Serves award-winning food. Dishes range from green shelled mussels to home-made steak and kidney pudding, as well as pan-fried Cornish brie. Ideal for a family stop-off point.

STRATFORD-UPON-AVON Marlowe's Restaurant
*18 High St, Stratford-upon-Avon, Warwickshire, CV37 6AU **Tel** 01789 204999*

Two restaurants housed in an Elizabethan town house, in the heart of Stratford. Opt for the silver-service formal restaurant – perfect for business clients and posh events – or book a private party in the more informal bistro. Autographed pictures of visiting glitterati such as Vanessa Redgrave and Sir Alec Guinness line the bar.

SWINDON Pear Tree Restaurant
*Church End, Purton, Swindon, Wiltshire, SN5 4ED **Tel** 01793 772100*

AA Rosette-winning restaurant in an elegant Cotswold stone hotel on the outskirts of Purton. Has 17 luxury bedrooms and a small conservatory dining room with great views over the Marlborough Downs. Menu offers modern English cooking, including pan-fried sea bass, roast loin of venison and delicious desserts.

TETBURY The Trouble House Inn
*Cirencester Rd, Tetbury, Gloucestershire, GL8 8SG **Tel** 01666 502206*

Excellent local food in a stunning historical setting. Offers everything from the local ale to a fabulous three-course meal. Specials such as Gloucester Old Spot sausages with creamy mashed potato and onion gravy are a clear favourite. Features an atmospheric dining room with polished wooden floors, black beams and ancient fireplaces.

TITLEY The Stagg Inn & Restaurant
*Titley, Kington, Herefordshire, HR5 3RL **Tel** 01544 230221*

Small hotel and restaurant overlooking the beautiful border country. A well-reputed wine list accompanies its classic menu of regional English fare. Diners have a choice of eating in the bar, the non-smoking dining room or the garden. The produce, which includes organic rare breed pork and home-cured bacon, is sourced from local shops.

WINCHCOMBE 5 North Street
*5 North St, Winchcombe, Gloucestershire, GL54 5LH **Tel** 01242 604566*

Small, Michelin-starred restaurant, set in a picturesque village. The cosy interior features heavy wood beams, and has a cottage-like feel. Presents a tasty menu of traditional English fare with a French twist. Serves the likes of breast and confit leg of poussin, and line-caught sea bass.

WINCHCOMBE Wesley House
*Wesley House, High St, Winchcombe, Gloucestershire, GL54 5LJ **Tel** 01242 602366*

Hotel and restaurant in the old Cotswolds town of Winchcombe. The food here is simple, with an emphasis on seasonal local ingredients. Specialities to look out for include grilled monkfish and roasted duck breast. Keep some space for the delicious home-made desserts, such as the outstanding bakewell tart.

WISTANSTOW The Plough Inn
*Wistanstow, Craven Arms, Shropshire, SY7 8DG **Tel** 01588 673251*

Timeless village pub with a warm and welcoming ambience. The inn may look unexceptional from outside, but the menu makes it well worth the visit. A great choice for family Sunday lunches. Home-made chutneys and sauces all add to the charm. Fabulous real ale is provided by the brewery located next door.

WORCESTER King Charles II Restaurant
*29 New St, Worcester, Worcestershire, WR1 2DP **Tel** 01905 22449*

Historic restaurant serving international cuisine. The decor is stylish, and features fine lace tablecloths, crystal glasses and an elegant ambience. It was from here that King Charles II escaped Cromwell's forces after his defeat in the Battle of Worcester in 1651. There is a dungeon situated in the restaurant.

EAST MIDLANDS

BAKEWELL Piedaniels
*Bath St, Bakewell, Derbyshire, DE45 1BX **Tel** 01629 812687*

An attractively converted barn houses this relaxed restaurant serving traditional French cuisine made from fresh local produce. Starters might include warm chicken and duck liver mousse, to be followed by Derbyshire beef with Roquefort butter. If there's room, try one of the original and beautifully presented desserts.

Key to Price Guide *see p608* **Key to Symbols** *see back cover flap*

BASLOW Fischer's

Baslow Hall, Calver Rd, Baslow, Derbyshire, DE45 1RR Tel 01246 583259

An award-winning restaurant, located in a popular country-house hotel on the edge of the Chatsworth estate. The Michelin-starred menu serves dishes made using the local produce; some from Chatsworth's farm shop. Venison, wild hare and spring lamb provide the seasonal highlights. Dress code is smart casual.

BECKINGHAM Black Swan

Hillside, Beckingham, Lincolnshire, LN5 0RQ Tel 01636 626474

Fabulous country inn serving French and modern English cuisine. This friendly and welcoming restaurant has been winning awards for the past 20 years. Dishes are made from locally sourced produce. Favourites such as Colston Bassett Stilton make its mark on the three-course table d'hote menu. Patio dining available in summer.

CAUNTON Caunton Beck

Main St, Caunton, Newark, Nottinghamshire, NG23 6AB Tel 01636 636793

Lovingly run gastropub in a delightfully restored 16th-century ale house. The family friendly restaurant has a welcoming ambience, and a modern European menu that is served at any time of the day. Also features a large and popular outdoor terrace in the summer.

CHESTERFIELD Buckinghams

85–87 Newbold Rd, Newbold, Chesterfield, Derbyshire, S41 7PU Tel 01246 201041

Hotel and unusual restaurant, with just one table that seats up to ten diners. The chef consults with the guests before the meal, and provides a unique, "surprise" seasonal menu depending on their requirements and wishes. The setting is cosy, and the decor elegant. The hotel also offers cooking courses.

CLIPSHAM Olive Branch

Main St, Clipsham, Oakham, Rutland, LE15 7SH Tel 01780 410355

A country pub, housed in three adjacent cottages that were joined in 1890 and later renovated. This delightful eatery has a reputation for fine dining and holds a Michelin star. In addition to a wide range of delicious regional dishes, the gastropub also offers sloe gin and damson vodka. The decor is traditional, with antique furnishings.

COLSTON BASSETT Martins Arms Inn

School Lane, Colston Bassett, Nottingham, Nottinghamshire, NG12 3FD Tel 01949 81361

Well-reputed for its game and fish, not to mention the Stilton produced in the village of Colston Bassett itself. Provides a great stopping-off point in the agricultural haven of the Vale of Belvoir. The food is modern European making the most of local ingredients. A welcoming fire and comfortable sofas add to the informal ambience.

DAVENTRY Fawsley Hall

Fawsley, Daventry, Northamptonshire, NN11 3BA Tel 01327 892000

Magnificent Tudor country-house hotel with a choice of restaurants offering varying degrees of formality. Offers some of the best desserts in the region. The main courses include dishes such as stuffed saddle of Cornish lamb or butter-poached guinea fowl. The menu changes regularly.

FOTHERINGHAY The Falcon Inn

Fotheringhay, Northamptonshire, PE8 5HZ Tel 01832 226254

Welcoming inn known as much for its selective wine list as it is for its real ales. International menu featuring pub fare as it should be served. Whole roast sea bass, rack of lamb and sirloin steak with roasted tomatoes are some of the notable options. Log fires and eclectic decoration add to the effect.

LEICESTER Sayonara Thali

49 Belgrave Rd, Leicester, Leicestershire, LE4 6AR Tel 0116 2665 888

Popular South Indian restaurant on Leicester's Golden Mile, so-called for its gold jewellery shops. Serves thali food – curry dishes served on a large metal plate along with chapatis and deep fried bread made with plain flour. Delicious milk drinks flavoured with pistachio and cardamom are also available.

LEICESTER Alloro

29 Millstone Lane, Leicester, Leicestershire, LE1 5JN Tel 0116 291 0004

Elegant restaurant in a converted factory; the menus here present a wide range of traditional Italian dishes including seafood risotto and fillet steak. The two-course lunch and dinner specials are good value and there is a bar area where you can enjoy a coffee after dinner.

LEICESTER The Case

4–6 Hotel St, St Martins, Leicester, Leicestershire, LE1 5AW Tel 0116 251 7675

A modern European menu with an English twist. This trendy restaurant has built a reputation for innovative and imaginative cuisine. Specials might include grilled lemon sole with prawn, lemon and caper brown butter, and Cajun-spiced monkfish on bubble and squeak. Features wine-tasting evenings.

LINCOLN Jews House

15 The Strait, Lincoln, Lincolnshire, LN2 1JD Tel 01522 524851

Reputedly Lincoln's oldest building, this 12th-century, Jewish merchant's house is also the town's most famous restaurant. Located beside the town's cathedral, the venue is small, cosy and exclusive; advance booking is recommended. A well-stocked wine cellar accompanies a menu featuring a mix of British and French cuisines.

MATLOCK The Red House

Old Rd, Darley Dale, Matlock, Derbyshire, DE4 2ER **Tel** *01629 734854*

Country-house hotel with just ten bedrooms. This small, AA Rosette-awarded restaurant is well reputed in Derbyshire for its panoramic dining room and home-made cuisine. Locally sourced ingredients create such dishes as lamb shank or mushroom cream cheese roulade. The dress code is smart casual.

MELTON MOWBRAY The Grinling Gibbons

Stapleford Park, nr Melton Mowbray, Leicestershire, LE14 2EF **Tel** *01572 787015*

A highly renowned restaurant, set in a tranquil country hotel and spa. The menu is traditionally English with an emphasis on fish, including wild halibut with caramelized cauliflower and roast John Dory with baby squid. Also offers a children's menu. Smart casual attire is requested in the restaurant.

NEWHAVEN Carriages Italian Restaurant

Newhaven, nr Hartingdon, Buxton, Derbyshire, SK17 0DU **Tel** *01298 84528*

Heartwarming Italian welcome followed by an appetizing variety of traditional Sicilian cuisine and fresh seafood. The decor features two railway carriages bedecked with velvet armchairs and period style table lamps. Favourites include *saltimbocca alla Romana* (veal medallions) and *filetto al Dolcelatte* (fillet steaks with blue cheeses and port).

NEWTON-LINFORD The Grey Lady

Sharpley Hill, Newtown Linford, Leicestershire, LE6 0AH **Tel** *01530 243558*

Scenic restaurant set in a quaint thatched cottage. This charming eatery prides itself on using the freshest ingredients for preparing its dishes. House specialities include steak, braised shank of lamb and grilled Dover sole. Also features a delightful selection of home-made puddings. An idyllic, relaxing spot.

NORTH KILWORTH Wordsworth Restaurant

Lutterworth Rd, N Kilworth, Leicestershire, LE17 6JE **Tel** *01858 880058*

This elegant restaurant is located in the Kilworth House Hotel, and provides an attractive setting for an evening meal. The classy interior features glittering chandeliers, a domed ceiling and stained-glass windows. Treats such as three-way duck and tri-colour ravioli may be on offer. .

NOTTINGHAM Hart's

1 Standard Court, Park Row, Nottingham, Nottinghamshire, NG1 6GN **Tel** *0115 911 0666*

Impressive hotel and restaurant, well known for its fantastic British cooking. Food is sourced locally, but given an international twist, which produces such dishes as pan-fried pollock with rosti potato. Fabulous desserts include a range of home-made ice creams and sorbets.

NOTTINGHAM Sinatra

8–16 Chapel Quarter Nottingham, NG1 6JQ **Tel** *0115 941 1050*

Offering excellent-value fare, Sinatra is located in Nottingham's Chapel Quarter, close to Market Square. There is a bistro for snacks and light lunches, and a more formal restaurant serving evening meals. Coffees and cocktails are available at the bar. This is a popular place for Sunday lunch, so book in advance.

NOTTINGHAM Ye Olde Trip to Jerusalem

Brewhouse Yard, Nottingham, Nottinghamshire, NG1 6AD **Tel** *0115 947 3171*

With ancient cellar rooms and engravings on the walls, the atmosphere of Britain's oldest pub doesn't disappoint. The food is typical pub fare with a strong local influence. Sirloin steak and chicken tikka masala make an appearance, as do nachos and mini-burgers to share.

NOTTINGHAM World Service

Newdigate House, Castlegate, Nottingham, Nottinghamshire, NG1 6AF **Tel** *01158 475587*

An award-winning restaurant, this eatery has fast gained a reputation for serving outstanding local produce with an Eastern twist. Organic salmon might come with beetroot and orange salsa, while lamb rump might be served with sheep's milk purée. The bar provides the perfect setting for a pre-meal drink.

PLUMTREE Perkins

Old Railway Station, Plumtree, Nottingham, Nottinghamshire, NG12 5NA **Tel** *0115 937 3695*

Friendly restaurant and bar, occupying a converted, late 19th-century village station. The main restaurant extends into a conservatory and garden patio. The seasonal menu changes every four weeks, and features everything from leek and rosemary soup to local Clipston fillet steak.

STAMFORD The George

71 St Martin's, Stamford, Lincolnshire, PE9 2LB **Tel** *01780 750750*

The oak-panelled restaurant at this renowned hotel has a reputation for fine dining. You might choose seared calves' liver with pan-fried sage polenta from the extensive à la carte menu, but be sure to leave space for a scrumptious dessert or the distinguished cheeseboard which features a selection of local cheeses.

WINTERINGHAM Winteringham Fields

Silver St, Winteringham, Lincolnshire, DN15 9ND **Tel** *01724 733096*

Gastronomic hotspot in a rambling old 16th-century manor house hotel, beautifully set in a peaceful country village. With two AA Rosettes, the award-winning menu doesn't disappoint. Try the six-course surprise menu for the region's and season's best cuisine. A wide variety of seafood, poultry, game and delicious desserts.

Key to Price Guide *see p608* **Key to Symbols** *see back cover flap*

LANCASHIRE AND THE LAKES

AMBLESIDE Drunken Duck Inn 🚶 ♿ 🅿 €€€
Barngates, Ambleside, Cumbria, LA22 0NG **Tel** *0153 9436347*

Oak beams and open log fires create a traditional setting in this 400-year-old inn. Serves imaginative dishes in a relaxed and informal atmosphere. The varied menu features specialities such as pork belly and faggots, and monkfish with saffron mash. Guests can also sample the delicious home-brewed beers.

AMBLESIDE Rothay Manor Hotel and Restaurant 🚶 ♿ 🅿 €€€
Rothay Bridge, Ambleside, Cumbria, LA22 0EH **Tel** *01539 433605*

Renowned for its afternoon teas, this comfortable, family-run hotel and restaurant offers outstanding service. Venison cobbler, fell-bred lamb and rolled fillet of plaice stuffed with mousseline of salmon might be among the tempting dishes offered.

AMBLESIDE The Samling 🚶 🅿 €€€€
Ambleside Rd, Ambleside, Cumbria, LA23 1LR **Tel** *015394 31922*

This delightful, award-winning restaurant offers dining in unashamed comfort. Line-caught sea bass, hand-dived scallops and succulent Herdwick lamb are some of the dishes on the gourmet menu. The well-stocked cellar holds choice wines from across the world, plus some fine old whiskies.

BLACKBURN Northcote 🚶 ♿ 🅿 €€€€
Northcote Rd, Langho, Blackburn, Lancashire, BB6 8BE **Tel** *01254 240555*

Set within the refined luxury of a 19th-century country house, the emphasis in this award-winning restaurant is on superlative cooking. Chef Nigel Haworth's inventiveness focuses on seasonal regional produce, creating some unique twists to local dishes. Black pudding and pink trout served with mustard and nettle sauce is a signature dish.

BLACKPOOL Seniors 🚶 ♿ €
106 Normoss Road, Blackpool, Lancashire, FY3 8QP **Tel** *01253 393529*

This excellent fish and chip restaurant has a host of loyal customers. As well as the usual cod and haddock, other fish varieties include John Dory fillets, silver hake, halibut, monk tail and lemon sole, plus a regular catch of the day. Bright and colourful dining environment and friendly atmosphere.

CARLISLE Keez Bistro 🚶 €€
50–52 Cecil St, Carlisle, Cumbria, CA1 1NT **Tel** *01228 590670*

This contemporary bistro offers simple classic dishes from around the world. The small menu changes each month, and the ingredients are largely locally sourced. There's also a good choice of hand-picked wines. Friendly, professional staff and flocks of returning customers. Closed Sun, Mon.

CARTMEL Uplands 🚶 ♿ 🅿 €€€€
Haggs Lane, Cartmel, Cumbria, LA11 6HD **Tel** *01539 536248*

A family-run hotel and restaurant, which enjoys several repeat customers. Serves modern British cooking in the relaxed and comfortable setting of an Edwardian gentleman's residence. The four-course set dinner provides options at each course, and includes a tureen of home-made soup served with delicious bread, hot from the oven.

CARTMEL L'Enclume Restaurant with Rooms ♿ 🅿 €€€€€
Cavendish St, Cartmel, Cumbria, LA11 6PZ **Tel** *01539 536362*

Dining at this former village smithy is nothing short of a culinary adventure; a definite stop for discerning foodies. Award-winning chef Simon Rogan's bold and creative style explores unusual ingredients such as myrrh and ancient herbs. Choose from the à la carte menu or try one of the taste-and-texture menus offering 20 mini-taster courses.

COCKERMOUTH Quince and Medlar 🚶 🅿 €€€
11–13 Castlegate, Cockermouth, Cumbria, CA13 9EU **Tel** *01900 823579*

A historic, Georgian building near Cockermouth Castle is home to this family-run, vegetarian restaurant. The stylish surroundings enhance the intimate candlelit dinners. For over 20 years, this eatery has been serving imaginative dishes, exploiting modern vegetarian cuisine to the full and drawing inspiration from around the world.

GRANGE-OVER-SANDS Lymestone Restaurant 🚶 🅿 €€€
Kents Bank Rd, Grange-over-sands, Cumbria, LA11 7EY **Tel** *01539 533076*

Set in the family-run Lymehurst hotel, the Lymestone Restaurant is headed by chef Kevin Wyper. The menu features British classics, often with a modern twist, that are made up of only the best locally sourced seasonal ingredients. Choose from the three-course dining menu or the daily specials board.

GRASMERE The Jumble Room €€
Langdale Rd, Grasmere, Ambleside, LA22 9SU **Tel** *01539 435188*

This small, colourful restaurant at the heart of Grasmere village serves an eclectic mix of food, based around the ethos of organic localism. Expect South African Dithose chicken, stuffed with sunflower and pumpkin seeds, or maybe lamb koftas, as well as fish and chips in organic beer batter.

KENDAL New Moon Restaurant   ♦ & £ £

129 Highgate, Kendal, LA9 4EN **Tel** *01539 729254*

With its popular British menu, New Moon is one of the best restaurants in the area. It has a contemporary interior, along with a relaxed atmosphere, and offers good-value, two-course set lunches and early-evening dinners. The chef is more than happy to adapt dishes to suit dietary sensitivities, so do ask. Occasional wine-tasting evenings too.

KENDAL The Grainstore   £ £

Brewery Arts Centre, Highgate, Kendal, Cumbria, LA9 4HE **Tel** *01539 725133*

The simple exterior of this arts centre bistro belies the quality of the food on offer. A commitment to the highest quality produce from the Cumbrian countryside means you can expect chicken from the Eden Valley, fell-bred lamb and beef, and even Lake District ice cream. The smoked Cumberland sausage is always a favourite.

LIVERPOOL Bistro Franc   ♟ £ £

1 Hanover St, Liverpool, L1 3DW **Tel** *0151 708 9993*

Popular with the pre-theatre crowd, this busy city-centre eatery labours its French theme a little in the decor, so it may come as no surprise that the food also features accessible versions of Gallic classics. Specials such as *roti du canard* appear on a changing menu that may also include roast lamb on pearl barley risotto.

LIVERPOOL 60 Hope Street   ♦ ♟ £ £ £

60 Hope St, Liverpool, L1 9BZ **Tel** *0151 707 6060*

Ideal for a casual meal, the Café Bar in the basement serves a range of light meals, from sandwiches and salads to more substantial dishes. For a formal setting, choose the restaurant, which offers modern European cuisine within relaxed and unpretentious surroundings. The wine selection complements the food.

LIVERPOOL The Side Door   ♦ & ♟ £ £ £

29A Hope St, Liverpool, L1 9BQ **Tel** *0151 707 7888*

Located midway between the city's two cathedrals, this friendly restaurant offers imaginative modern British and European cooking, but biased towards local cuisine. Expect to be guided through the carefully selected wine list, which features many unusual varieties from both the old and new world.

LONGRIDGE The Longridge Restaurant   ♦ & ♟ £ £ £

104–106 Higher Rd, Longridge, Preston, Lancashire, PR3 3SY **Tel** *01772 784969*

Opened in 1990, this is acclaimed chef Paul Heathcote's flagship restaurant. Traditional local dishes such as black pudding and bread-and-butter pudding appear beside more flamboyant creations based on Goosnargh chicken and duck. The reasonably priced, two-course lunch is of great value.

MANCHESTER Earth Café   ▤ ♦ £

16–20 Turner Street, Northern Quarter, Manchester, M4 1DZ **Tel** *0161 834 1996*

This popular, award-winning vegetarian restaurant is located in the basement of the Manchester Buddhist Centre. As you would expect, the food is fair-trade and vegan, befitting Buddhist spiritual principles. An excellent place for creative wholesome dishes; the vegan dark chocolate cheesecake is superb.

MANCHESTER El Rincon de Rafa   ♦ £ £

Off St Johns Street, 244 Deansgate, Manchester, M3 4BQ **Tel** *0161 839 8819*

Standout tapas from this popular, lively and atmospheric Spanish basement restaurant. Try the *patatas bravas*, *albondigas* and the *chorizo al vino*; the paella is also excellent. Wash it all down with a jug of sangria. It can get very busy here, so book ahead, especially at weekends.

MANCHESTER Harvey Nichols Second Floor   & ♟ £ £ £

21 New Cathedral St, Manchester, M1 1AD **Tel** *0161 828 8898*

The stylish second-floor restaurant in Manchester's iconic store is a great place to relax after a hard day's shop. In understated surroundings you can enjoy confit leg of Goosnargh duck, or olive-oil poached cod, and perhaps follow it with a popcorn panna cotta or a beetroot parfait.

MANCHESTER Restaurant Bar & Grill   ♦ & £ £ £

14 John Dalton St, Manchester, M2 6JR **Tel** *0161 839 1999*

This vibrant, modern restaurant, close to many of Manchester's major venues, is a popular city-centre meeting place, both at lunch time and in the evening. Asian influences colour the à la carte menu with dishes such as Malay spiced chicken or crispy duck on Chinese greens.

MANCHESTER The River Bar and Restaurant   ♦ & £ £ £

Lowry Hotel, 50 Dearman's Place, Salford, M3 5LH **Tel** *0161 827 4003*

This chic, modern restaurant offers a high level of personalized service and meticulous attention to detail. The executive head chef and his team have created a British menu that draws upon the finest seasonal and local ingredients, with an emphasis on classic foods and flavours.

MANCHESTER Yang Sing   ♦ & ♟ £ £ £

34 Princess St, Manchester, M1 4JY **Tel** *0161 236 2200*

A highly acclaimed Chinese restaurant, and a culinary experience not to be missed. Expert waiters guide you through the extensive, 400 dish menu to create an individual banquet that perfectly suits your taste. Features a good range of Chinese beers.

Key to Price Guide *see p608* **Key to Symbols** *see back cover flap*

MELMERBY Village Bakery

Melmerby, Penrith, Cumbria, CA10 1HE **Tel** *01768 881811*

The smell of fresh bread and home baking greet guests as they enter this popular restaurant. Noted for its warm and unfussy service, the eatery makes use of the best seasonal and organic produce available locally. Fare includes hearty breakfasts, wholesome lunches (with hot and cold selections) and teas, as well as tasty treats through the day.

NEAR SAWREY Ees Wyke Country House

Ees Wyke Country House, Near Sawrey, Cumbria, LA22 0JZ **Tel** *015394 36393*

Formerly the holiday home of Beatrix Potter and close to Hill Top, this charming restaurant is set in one of the most beautiful parts of the Lake District. The five-course set dinner is served in a small and intimate dining room. The menu changes daily and only local produce is used. Eight rooms are available for accommodation.

PENRITH The George and Dragon

Clifton, Penrith, CA10 2ER **Tel** *01768 865381*

Cosy, warm and welcoming, with bare wood tables, The George and Dragon occupies an 18th-century coaching inn. The gourmet menu is concocted with imagination, and the seasonal produce is supplied by the Lowther estate. A strong wine list matches the excellent menu. There are lovely rooms upstairs for those wishing to stay the night.

PRESTON Angelos Ristorante and Pizzeria

33–35 Aversham St, Preston, PR1 3BN **Tel** *01772 257133*

This traditional Italian restaurant is located in the city centre and offers a wide range of old Italian favourites. There's a large selection of pizzas as well as good risottos and meat grills. The wine list is made up exclusively of Italian wines, all sourced directly from small, family-run vineyards in Italy. Closed on Mondays.

SILVERDALE Wolf House Gallery

Lindeth Rd, Silverdale, Lancashire, LA5 0TX **Tel** *01524 701405*

Set within a discerning arts and crafts gallery, in lovely limestone countryside overlooking Morecambe Bay, this friendly café, which is open during the day, has home-made soups, tasty snacks and a tempting range of home baking. On Friday and Saturday evenings, it offers an unusual venue for fine dining, but bring your own wine.

TROUTBECK Queens Head

Queen's Head, Troutbeck, Windermere, Cumbria, LA23 1PW **Tel** *01539 432174*

Flag floors, oak beams and an Elizabethan four-poster bar are some of the timeless features of this 17th-century inn. The atmosphere is homely, and the food traditional. Try the Goosnargh chicken with a herb mash. While there is a good choice of wines, it is a great place to taste local ales such as Hartleys XB.

ULLSWATER Sharrow Bay Country House Hotel

Lake Ullswater, Penrith, Cumbria, CA10 2LZ **Tel** *01768 486301*

Traditional country house, superbly located in its vast grounds beside idyllic Ullswater. Sample Michelin-starred cuisine from a six-course menu that has evolved over time, but where time-honoured favourites such as Stilton, onion and spinach soufflé or fillet of salmon with lemon and martini sauce make regular appearances. Caters for children over ten.

ULVERSTON The Bay Horse Hotel

The Bay Horse Hotel, Canal Foot, Ulverston, Cumbria, LA12 9EL **Tel** *01229 583972*

An 18th-century inn, once serving coaches crossing the Morecambe Bay sands. This comfortable, family-run hotel and restaurant on the banks of Leven enjoys outstanding views of both the Cumbrian and Lancashire fells. The menu is equally superb and draws on fresh local ingredients such as shrimps, wild salmon and salt marsh lamb.

WATERMILLOCK The Rampsbeck Country House Hotel

Watermillock, Ullswater, Cumbria, CA11 0LP **Tel** *01768 486442*

Fantastic views and fine dining are some of the highlights of this 18th-century country house, located on the shores of Ullswater, in one of the most picturesque corners of the Lake District. The AA Rosette-winning restaurant serves imaginative dishes, using regional delicacies such as wild salmon, rabbit, Cumbrian ham and local lamb.

WHITEWELL Inn at Whitewell

Whitewell, Forest of Bowland, Clitheroe, Lancashire, BB7 3AT **Tel** *01200 448222*

Dating back to the 15th century, this remote inn originally provided a welcome rest to travellers passing through the wilds of the Trough of Bowland, on their way to Lancaster. The stunning location is matched by the cooking of chef Jamie Cadman, whose contemporary style of British cooking incorporates many seasonal local specialities.

WINDERMERE Miller Howe

Rayrigg Rd, Windermere, Cumbria, LA23 1EY **Tel** *01539 442536*

A delightful restaurant that serves fine gourmet food in striking surroundings. Try the tasting menu, which includes recommendations from the extensive wine list, or pick from the imaginative à la carte. Also offers a range of good value lunch options. Occasional live music.

WINDERMERE Holbeck Ghyll Country House Hotel

Holbeck Lane, Windermere, Cumbria, LA23 1LU **Tel** *01539 432375*

Set in a 19th-century hunting lodge, this intimate, Michelin-star restaurant has good views across the lake. Serves English cuisine which reflects just a hint of France. The set dinner offers a range of choices at each course, such as scallops or langoustine followed by beef, pigeon or venison in a pumpkin purée.

WRIGHTINGTON BAR The Mulberry Tree　🛗 ♿ 🍷　££

9 Wood Lane, Wrightington Bar, Standish, Wigan, Lancashire, WN6 9SE **Tel** *01257 451400*

The restaurant of this former local pub has an enviable reputation for imaginative cuisine. French influences add an unexpected twist to typically English dishes. Try the entrée of black pudding topped with a poached egg and hollandaise sauce, followed by roast loin of cod on a saffron and spring pea risotto. Look for reasonably priced specials.

YORKSHIRE AND THE HUMBER REGION

ASENBY Crab and Lobster　🛗 🎵 ♿　£££

Crab Manor, Dishforth Rd, Asenby, Thirsk, North Yorkshire, YO7 3QL **Tel** *01845 577286*

Step back into time at this charming seafood eatery, decorated with antiques and artifacts. The chef's signature dish is lobster Thermidor, but the fish and chips is equally good. Lamb and chicken dishes are also featured on the menu. Located in the quiet countryside of the Vale of York and not far from Ripon.

BOLTON ABBEY Devonshire Arms Brasserie　🛗 ♿ 🍷　££££

The Devonshire Arms Country House Hotel, Bolton Abbey, Skipton, North Yorkshire, BD23 6AJ **Tel** *01756 710710*

Fringing the Yorkshire Dales and close to Bolton Priory, this characterful coaching inn has been in the family of the Duke and Duchess of Devonshire since 1753. The setting here is informal and relaxed, and the cuisine is a blend of modern British and French. A good vegetarian menu is also available.

BOROUGHBRIDGE thediningroom　🛗 🍷　£££

20 St James Square, Boroughbridge, North Yorkshire, YO51 9AR **Tel** *01423 326426*

Overlooking the Georgian square of a small market town, this cosy and friendly eating place is highly popular with the locals. Fish features prominently on the menu, which offers dishes best described as modern English. Everything is home-made and locally sourced where possible, and there is a good selection of wines and champagne.

BRADFORD Mumtaz　♿　££

Great Horton Rd, Bradford, West Yorkshire, BD7 3HS **Tel** *01274 571861*

In a city famous for its curry houses, Mumtaz has been attracting plaudits for over 25 years. The inspiration comes from the Kashmiri heritage of the owner's family, and the results can be breathtaking. The restaurant is alcohol-free but mango lassi is a popular alternative. It can get very busy, particularly at weekends, so book.

BURNSALL The Devonshire Fell Hotel and Bistro　🛗 ♿ 🍷　£££

Burnsall, Skipton, North Yorkshire, BD23 6BT **Tel** *01756 729000*

Originally a club for 19th-century gentlemen mill owners, this hotel and restaurant is situated on a hillside, and offers spectacular views over Wharfedale. A bright and colourful bar leads to an inviting dining room. The menu is a medley of new cuisine with French overtones.

EAST WITTON The Blue Lion　🛗 ♿ 🍷　£££

E Witton, nr Leyburn, North Yorkshire, DL8 4SN **Tel** *01969 624273*

Former coaching inn full of character, on the edge of the Yorkshire Dales and not far from Jervaulx Abbey. The home-prepared food, available both in the bar and restaurant, ranges from traditional hearty dishes, such as steak and kidney pudding, to more exotic creations reflecting Asian influences. Extensive wine list and hand-drawn beers.

ELLAND La Cachette　🍷　£££

31 Huddersfield Rd, Elland, West Yorkshire, HX5 9AW **Tel** *01422 378833*

A busy and highly popular brasserie-style restaurant serving modern British food in a Mediterranean ambience. Fish features prominently on the menu, and there is a good choice of daily specials as well. The light, two-course lunch is of great value and the three-course dinner includes a half bottle of wine. The à la carte menu is extensive.

FERRENSBY The General Tarleton Inn　♿ 🍷　££

Boroughbridge Rd, Ferrensby, nr Knaresborough, North Yorkshire, HG5 0PZ **Tel** *01423 340284*

Named after a British general in the American War of Independence, this former, 18th-century coaching inn is renowned for its excellent fish dishes such as seafood thermidor. Although the wine list is extensive, real ale fans can opt for a pint of Black Sheep or Timothy Taylor's, two of the best beers in the area.

HALIFAX Design House　🛗 ♿ 🍷　££

Dean Clough (Gate 5), Halifax, West Yorkshire, HX3 5AX **Tel** *01422 383242*

A stylishly modern restaurant set within a former mill, which has found a new lease of life as the Dean Clough Arts and Business Complex. There is a distinct Mediterranean feel to the place. Tapas and lighter meals are popular during the day. The three-course set menu is of excellent value, and there are sharing platters too.

HAROME The Star Inn　🛗 ♿ 🍷　£££

Harome, nr Helmsley, North Yorkshire, YO62 5JE **Tel** *01439 770397*

This attractive, 14th-century thatched inn exudes rustic charm, with original cow byres and a dormitory formerly used by travelling monks. The intimate, award-winning restaurant serves traditional British fare, and is justifiably popular. Advance reservations are recommended. The same menu is served in the bar.

Key to Price Guide *see p608* **Key to Symbols** *see back cover flap*

HARROGATE Drum and Monkey

5 Montpellier Gardens, Harrogate, North Yorkshire, HG1 2TF **Tel** *01423 502650*

Elegant, but unpretentious, the old world ambience of this superb fish and seafood restaurant reflects the traditional character of the famous spa town of Harrogate. Dine in either the bar or the restaurant above. Dishes such as queen scallops with cheese and garlic butter, fisherman's pie and the shellfish platter are popular choices.

HAWORTH Weaver's

15–17 W Lane, Haworth, West Yorkshire, BD22 8DU **Tel** *01535 643822*

This long-established restaurant is set within three 17th-century weaver's cottages that once incorporated a café frequented by the Brontës. Flagged floors, bric-à-brac, low lighting and intimate alcoves in the dining room add to the atmosphere. Northern regional cooking is the hallmark, a popular choice being the Whitby fisherman's pie.

HETTON Angel Inn

Hetton, Skipton, North Yorkshire, BD23 6LT **Tel** *01756 730263*

Pioneering gastropub in the heart of the Yorkshire Dales. Wooden beams, nooks and crannies and log fires re-create the atmosphere of a bygone era. Dine in either the elegant restaurant or the more informal bar-brasserie. The separate menus offer a range of interesting dishes, including a substantial choice of vegetarian and gluten-free options.

ILKLEY Box Tree

35–37 Church St, Ilkley, West Yorkshire, LS29 9DR **Tel** *01943 608484*

Enjoy fine dining in the luxurious setting of one of Ilkley's oldest buildings. Awarded a Michelin star, the cuisine is modern French and draws upon the best of local and regional produce. The menu changes constantly, but dishes such as the hand-dived scallops served with white truffle oil are highly recommended.

LEEDS Sous le Nez en Ville

The Basement, Quebec House, Quebec Street, Leeds, LS1 2HA **Tel** *0113 244 0108*

Renowned for its good food and excellent service, the long-established Sous le Nez is one of the most acclaimed restaurants in Leeds. The menu is typically French – try the gateau of fillet steak stuffed with shallots – and there is an excellent-value early evening *menu de soire* that includes half a bottle of wine.

LEEDS Chino Latino

Boar Lane, Leeds, West Yorkshire, LS1 6EA **Tel** *0113 380 4080*

Located in the city centre, Chino Latino offers an innovative fusion of Far East cuisine combining the delicate flavours of Chinese, Thai, South East Asian and modern Japanese food. Before dining, try a cocktail in the Latino bar. Relaxed atmosphere and good wine list.

LEEDS Anthony's Restaurant

19 Boar Lane, Leeds, West Yorkshire, LS1 6EA **Tel** *0113 245 5922*

Close to the station, passers-by would be surprised to find a restaurant of such gastronomic ambition among the everyday shops and bars. Complex constructions and compelling flavour juxtapositions are what to expect: roast duck with apple or seared tuna with broccoli puree and roast rhubarb, for instance.

OSMOTHERLEY Golden Lion

6 West End, Osmotherley, North Yorkshire, DL6 3AA **Tel** *01609 883526*

Traditional country pub in a picturesque village of 17th-century stone cottages. Serves as a starting point for the Lyke Wake Walk, and is close to Mount Grace Priory. Very popular with hill walkers, the pub offers well cooked, wholesome food using fresh local produce. The steak and kidney pie and tasty casseroles are firm favourites. Vegetarian options too.

RAMSGILL The Yorke Arms

Ramsgill, Pateley Bridge, nr Harrogate, North Yorkshire, HG3 5RL **Tel** *01423 755243*

Acclaimed chef Frances Atkins is one of only six female chefs in the country to gain the coveted Michelin star. Her creative dishes in the modern British style are superb, using seasonal meats, fish and game in unusual combinations. Discreet service in the relaxing ambience of this 17th-century shooting lodge makes dining here a real pleasure.

RIDGEWAY The Old Vicarage

Ridgeway Moor, Ridgeway Village, Sheffield, South Yorkshire, S12 3XW **Tel** *01142 475814*

Michelin-starred restaurant set within a Victorian vicarage. Welcoming winter log fires and an attractive garden terrace for apéritifs on balmy evenings are some of the attractions here. Produce from the kitchen garden and seasonal delicacies, often combined with unexpected ingredients, are at the heart of the inventive dishes on offer.

RIPLEY The Boar's Head Hotel

Ripley, Harrogate, North Yorkshire, HG3 3AY **Tel** *01423 771888*

A former coaching inn beside the castle, in the heart of a charming estate village. The menus are nothing short of inspirational, whether you dine in the elegant restaurant or the more casual and informal setting of the bistro. Seasonal fish, meat and game feature prominently on the menu.

ROBINS HOOD'S BAY Wayfarer Bistro

Station Road, Robin Hood's Bay, Nr Whitby, North Yorkshire, YO22 4RL **Tel** *01947 880240*

Excellent fish and seafood dishes are a feature of this successful bistro-cum-B&B on the stunning North Yorkshire coast. Meat options include great chargrilled steaks and vegetarians are also catered for. Great value and warm, welcoming atmosphere. Rooms available.

SHEFFIELD Zeugma   🏃 ⚫   ⓔ
146 London Road, Sheffield, S2 4LT **Tel** *0114 2582223*

Marvellous Turkish grills are the speciality here. Diners can watch their *cop shish* (marinated chunks of lamb) or *kaburga* (lamb spare ribs) being cooked over hot charcoal. Other options include grilled vegetable kebabs and plenty of meat-free starters. Bring your own wine (£3.95 corkage fee).

SHEFFIELD Greenhead House   🏃 ⚫ 🍷   ⓔⓔⓔⓔ
84 Burncross Rd, Chapeltown, Sheffield, South Yorkshire, S35 1SF **Tel** *0114 246 9004*

Set within a 17th-century house to the north of Sheffield. Features a delightful walled garden, a comfortable lounge warmed by open fires and an intimate dining room that creates a distinctively homely feel. The husband and wife team offer carefully prepared dishes in an all-inclusive meal, supported by a comprehensive selection of wines.

STOKESLEY Chapter's   🏃 ⚫ 🍷   ⓔⓔⓔ
27 High St, Stokesley, North Yorkshire, TS9 5AD **Tel** *01642 711888*

Set in a refurbished and characterful Grade II listed building, this stylish eatery overlooks Stokesley's market square, below the northern escarpment of the Cleveland Hills. Dine in the gourmet restaurant or the more casual brasserie bar. Serves a variety of seafood, game and poultry dishes.

SUTTON-ON-THE-FOREST The Rose and Crown Inn   🏃 ⚫ 🍷   ⓔⓔⓔ
Main St, Sutton-on-the-Forest, York, YO61 1DP **Tel** *01347 811333*

Informal dining in this village inn restaurant, which specializes in fish dishes presented in a classic brasserie style. Surrounded by pleasant gardens and set in the rural heart of Yorkshire, it is well placed between the attractive centres of Helmsley and York, and surrounded by a wealth of stately homes and abbeys.

WATH-IN-NIDDERDALE The Sportsman's Arms   🏃 ⚫ 🍷   ⓔⓔⓔ
Wath-in-Nidderdale, Pateley Bridge, Harrogate, North Yorkshire, HG3 5PP **Tel** *01423 711306*

Set within an old farmhouse and converted barn, this characterful inn emanates the charm of a former age. The food, served in a comfortable room, is cooked with a French influence, and includes fresh, seasonal fish and seafood brought from Whitby. Steaks, lamb, duck and guinea fowl also appear on the menu.

WHITBY Magpie Café   🏃 ⚫ 🍷   ⓔⓔ
14 Pier Rd, Whitby, North Yorkshire, YO21 3PU **Tel** *01947 602058*

Looking out across the historic port towards St Mary's Church and the abbey, this distinctive black-and-white, former merchant's house became a café in the 1930s. Specialities revolve around seafood and fish and chips, of which there are some eight different varieties. However, there is also a wide selection of other dishes too.

WHITBY Estbek House   🍷   ⓔⓔⓔ
East Row, Sandsend, Whitby, North Yorkshire, YO61 3SY **Tel** *01947 893424*

A delightfully understated restaurant with rooms, tucked into a wooded inlet on the North Yorkshire Heritage Coast. The daily changing menu reflects the catches of the day, but might include local turbot or plaice, served in simple sauces. The seafood pie is very popular.

YORK Goji   🏃 ⚫ 🍴   ⓔⓔ
36 Goodramgate, York, YO1 7LF **Tel** *01904 622614*

This refreshing café serves wholesome and imaginatively prepared vegetarian food using fresh seasonal produce. Try the tasty Goji hotdog (tofu frankfurter), the mushroom burger or – for something mildly spicy – the vegetable korma. Vegan and gluten-free options are also available, as well as organic wines. Excellent coffee and restorative teas too.

YORK Melton's Too   🏃 ⚫   ⓔⓔ
25 Walmgate, York, North Yorkshire, YO1 9TX **Tel** *01904 629222*

Located in a former saddler's, this open-plan bistro retains many original features, but has a distinctively modern feel. While losing nothing of the original Melton's dedication to home-made food, this place has a more informal appeal; an ideal venue whether you want just a light bite or a full dinner. The bar has a good range of speciality beers.

YORK The Blue Bicycle Restaurant   🏃 🎵 🍷   ⓔⓔⓔ
34 Fossgate, York, North Yorkshire, YO1 9TA **Tel** *01904 673990*

Seafood and modern European dishes are the specialities at this atmospheric restaurant. Situated beside River Foss, in a building that housed a 19th-century brothel, it still retains some of the original booths in the cellar. A guitarist provides an added attraction on Saturday evenings.

NORTHUMBRIA

AYCLIFFE The County   🏃 🍷   ⓔⓔ
13 The Green, Aycliffe, Darlington, County Durham, DL5 6LX **Tel** *01325 312273*

Overlooking Aycliffe village green, the County is a historic building with a contemporary interior. The relaxed setting extends to the menu, you can combine dishes to get exactly what you want. The food is simply cooked and focuses on traditional and modern British cuisine. The wines are from the New World and there's a good range of real ales.

CARTERWAY HEADS The Manor House Inn

Carterway Heads, Shotley Bridge, Northumberland, DH8 9LX **Tel** *01207 255268*

Located in isolation, this 18th-century inn has stunning views across the open moors. Dine in a quiet, relaxed atmosphere, either in the restaurant or more informally at the bar, which is popular with walkers and cyclists. The home-made food is good and a small shop sells some of the chutneys, jams and ready meals on the menu.

DURHAM Bistro 21

Aykley Heads House, Aykley Heads, Durham, County Durham, DH1 5TS **Tel** *0191 384 4354*

Set within an early 18th-century building, originally a farmhouse, this popular bistro retains a distinct bucolic feel and, in summer, tables appear in the courtyard for al fresco dining. The cuisine is modern British with overtones of the Mediterranean and there's an ever-changing list of special dishes exploiting seasonal fresh produce.

GATESHEAD Eslington Villa Hotel

8 Station Rd, Low Fell, Gateshead, Tyne and Wear, NE9 6DR **Tel** *0191 487 6017*

This stunning 19th-century house combines the charm of an earlier age with modern creativity and offers dining in the comfortable restaurant or the less formal setting of the conservatory. The award-winning kitchen team are passionate about food and conceive eclectic menus featuring the best in contemporary and original cuisine.

GATESHEAD Six Restaurant

BALTIC Centre for Contemporary Art; Gateshead Quays, South Shore Road, Gateshead, NE8 3BA **Tel** *0191 4404948*

Enjoy the splendid views of the River Tyne and the famous Tyne Bridges from the rooftop of this beautifully converted flour mill. Excellent modern British food is served in a crisp, contemporary dining room by attentive and informative waiting staff. Kick-start the evening with a drink at the bar.

GATESHEAD The Sage

St Mary's Square, Gateshead Quayside, Gateshead, NE8 2JR **Tel** *0191 4444654*

You don't have to be waiting for a show to start to enjoy the dining experience at the Sage's excellent brasserie. Expect to find the best of market fish on a modern British/European menu that might also include tarragon-stuffed chicken wrapped in Parma ham, or caramelized shallot tarte tatin with Northumberland goats' cheese.

HEXHAM Barrasford Arms

Barrasford, Hexham, Northumberland, NE48 4AA **Tel** *01434 681237*

An unpretentious country pub-restaurant with rooms, the Barrasford Arms is a popular destination for diners as well as a properly functioning local pub. The food is English with a French twist, reflecting the chef's training under the legendary Albert Roux. The real ales are also well kept.

HEXHAM Valley Connection 301

Market Place, Hexham, Northumberland, NE46 3NX **Tel** *01434 601234*

This Bangladeshi restaurant enjoys a pretty location off the main street beside Hexham Abbey. Unique dishes include Mr Daraz's very own *bhuna gosht* (stir-fired lamb) and *bongo po curry*, created around king prawns from the Bay of Bengal. The winner is *shat kora*, flavoured with a variety of lemon found in the valley of Sylhet in Bangladesh.

HUTTON MAGNA The Oak Tree Inn

Hutton Magna, County Durham, DL11 7HH **Tel** *01833 627371*

Unassuming Oak Tree Inn is local favourite and a real gem. The chef at this restaurant hails from the Savoy, bringing imaginative fine cuisine to the informality of an 18th-century village pub. A warm salad of crispy pork belly with black pudding precedes royal sea bream with wild mushroom and asparagus noodles. Booking is essential.

MATFEN Matfen Hall Country House Hotel

Matfen, Northumberland, NE20 0RH **Tel** *01661 886500*

This beautifully restored 19th-century country mansion, set within its own extensive grounds, offers a dining experience to remember. Both the library and smaller print room provide a truly atmospheric candlelit setting for an intimate meal. The food is superb and the service is discreet, but attentive.

NEWCASTLE At Bangkok Café

39–41 Low Friar Street, Newcastle Upon Tyne, NE1 5UE **Tel** *0191 260 2323*

The aim of this popular Thai eatery is to serve authentic dishes in a relaxed and informal atmosphere. Only the freshest herbs are used to create traditional, spicy green curries and warming, pungent soups. Daily set menus offer great value, as do the occasional buffet lunches.

NEWCASTLE Paradiso

1 Market Lane, Newcastle upon Tyne, Tyne and Wear, NE1 6QQ **Tel** *0191 221 1240*

This stylish eatery is one of Newcastle's most popular restaurants. It combines old and new, its contemporary design blending well with the exposed brickwork of the traditional building. Diners can enjoy modern Italian cuisine with unusual influences from Africa, Asia and beyond. Sandwiches and snacks are served throughout the day. Closed Sun.

NEWCASTLE The Cherry Tree

9 Osborne Road, Jesmond, Newcastle upon Tyne **Tel** *0191 239 9924*

The Cherry Tree offers some of the best modern British food in the northeast. The imaginative menu includes grilled halibut, Kielder venison and Ingram Valley lamb. Set lunches and early evening menus offer great value, and live jazz in the evening is a welcome addition.

NEWCASTLE Fisherman's Lodge ££££

Jesmond Dene, Jesmond, Newcastle upon Tyne, Tyne and Wear, NE7 7BQ **Tel** *0191 281 3281*

Close to the city centre, but lying in the secluded wooded valley of Jesmond Dene, Fisherman's Lodge has earned an outstanding reputation for its fine dining. Seafood dishes are the speciality, but local meat and game also feature prominently on the menu. Exotic deserts and a carefully selected cheese board round off the meal.

PONTELAND Café Lowrey £££

33–35 The Broadway, Darras Hall Estate, Ponteland, Newcastle upon Tyne, NE20 9PW **Tel** *01661 820357*

Café Lowrey offers bistro-style dining with a distinct French influence to the food. Ingredients are locally sourced, the service is friendly and the atmosphere relaxed, though there's generally a lively buzz to the place at the weekend. However, go mid-week when there's usually a quiet corner to be had.

REDWORTH Barcelo Redworth Hall Hotel £££

Redworth, Bishop Auckland, Darlington, County Durham, DL5 6NL **Tel** *01388 770600*

Built in 1693 as a private house, Redworth Hall retains many of its original features and stands in 150 acres of beautifully kept grounds. The elegant 1744 dining room, named after the year in which it was added, offers fine dining in luxurious surroundings.

ROMALDKIRK The Rose and Crown Inn £££

Romaldkirk, Barnard Castle, County Durham, DL12 9EB **Tel** *01833 650213*

This traditional stone-built coaching inn dates from the 18th century and stands on the green beside the church in the heart of a County Durham village. Dine in style in the oak-panelled restaurant at tables bedecked in crisp white linen or choose the more rustic setting of the brasserie, perhaps selecting only one or two courses as you please.

STOCKSFIELD Feathers Inn ££

Hedley on the Hill, Stocksfield, Nortumberland, NE43 7SW **Tel** *01661 843 607*

A village pub with a growing reputation for good food and real ale. Local game, meat and vegetables feature on a daily changing menu that might include home-made black pudding and poached egg for starters, followed by red leg partridge or North Sea plaice. Look for blackboard specials. No food on Mondays.

YARM Judges House ££££

Kirklevington Hall, Kirklevington, Yarm, Cleveland, TS15 9LW **Tel** *01642 782878*

Fine dining at this popular country house hotel might begin with a mosaic of young rabbit, followed by locally reared beef fillet served with dumpling, foie gras and truffle. Round it off with a warm chocolate cake with caramelized bananas. Booking is advised. Less formal dining options are available.

NORTH WALES

ABERDOVEY Penhelig Arms ££

Aberdyfi, Gwynedd, LL35 0LT **Tel** *01654 767215*

This small, friendly hotel has a reputable restaurant that enjoys panoramic views of the Dovey estuary. On offer is a good range of locally sourced fish and meat. Indulge in a glass of champagne and fresh dressed crab, or try the reasonably priced fixed menu.

ABERSOCH Porth Tocyn Country Hotel ££££

Abersoch, Gwynedd, LL53 7BU **Tel** *01758 713303*

Panoramic hotel restaurant Porth Tocyn has appeared in good food guides for over 50 years. There's a choice between a three- and two-course evening menu. Ask for a table at the "picture window" for the best views over the peninsula. Tables in the garden for informal lunchtime dining.

BEAUMARIS Ye Olde Bull's Head Inn ££££

Castle St, Beaumaris, Isle of Anglesey, LL58 8AP **Tel** *01248 810329*

Locally known as "the Bull", this restaurant-with-rooms is based in the centre of town. An ancient coaching inn, built in 1472, the building provides an elegant setting for the main restaurant in its oldest part. There's also a less formal brasserie and a popular bar.

CAPEL COCH Tre-Ysgawen Hall £££

Capel Coch, Llangefni, Isle of Anglesey, LL77 7UR **Tel** *01248 750750*

Hotel and spa with seasonal menu and excellent accompanying wine list, Tre-Ysgawen Hall has a delicious evening menu. The chef provides vegetarian and low-calorie fare on request. Residents have use of a gym and a golf course, available to help burn off the calories. There's also an atmospheric bar.

DOLGARROG The Lord Newborough ££

Dolgarrog, Conwy, LL32 8JX **Tel** *01492 660549*

The Lord Newborough prides itself on its simple, but tasty cuisine and friendly dining atmosphere. Using the best of Snowdonia's ingredients, the menu features Welsh lamb shank, Conwy Valley steak, Welsh potato bake (with leeks) and a delicious cheese board.

Key to Price Guide *see p608* **Key to Symbols** *see back cover flap*

DOLGELLAU Bwyty Dylanwad Da 　　　　　　🏃🍴　　££

*2 Ffos-y-felin, Dolgellau, Gwynedd, LL40 1BS **Tel** 01341 422870*

Small friendly café-restaurant with a long and impressive reputation, Bwyty Dylanwad Da also offers one of the best cappuccinos in town. Menu features traditional dishes such as faggot with spiced apple sauce, Welsh beef steak and Welsh honey and almond ice cream. Closed Jan–Mar.

HARLECH Castle Cottage 　　　　　　　　🏃🍴　　£££

*Y Llech, Harlech, Gwynedd, LL46 2YL **Tel** 01766 780479*

The award-winning restaurant (with rooms) at the Castle Cottage is a popular destination for locals and visitors alike. The seasonal menu features locally caught lobster, sea bass and black bream, and there is also venison from the Brecon Beacons National Park. The restaurant has won a Visit Wales Gold Award.

LLANBEDROG Glyn-Y-Weddw Arms 　　　　🏃♿🍴　　££

*Lon Pin, Llanbedrog, Pwllheli, Gwynedd, LL53 7TH **Tel** 01758 740212*

This low-key village pub and restaurant serves good, hearty food using fresh local produce. Daily specials and fixed-price menus include vegetarian options. Draught ales are also available and there is a lovely beer garden. A carvery is held on Sundays and there is an international buffet every Saturday.

LLANBERIS The Gwynedd Hotel & Restaurant 　　🏃♿　　£££

*Llanberis, Gwynedd, LL55 4SU **Tel** 01286 870203*

Fabulously situated at the foot of Mount Snowdon, this restaurant prides itself on the varied menu of local and seasonal cuisine. The owners, Mark and Dita Bartlett, pay meticulous attention to every detail. Dinner and lunch come complete with sightseeing information.

LLANDUDNO The Seahorse 　　　　　　　　🏃　　££

*7 Church Walks, Llandudno, LL30 2HD **Tel** 01492 875315*

The dining room of this Grade II listed Victorian building boasts a lovely view of Corfu – courtesy of local mural artists. There's more artistry in the kitchen where the finest local ingredients are used to create a fresh seafood menu featuring baked hake with crab in a thermidor sauce. Theme nights are popular, including Thai and Spanish.

LLANDRILLO Tyddyn Llan 　　　　　　　🏃♿🍴　　££££

*Llandrillo, nr Corwen, Denbighshire, LL21 0ST **Tel** 01490 440264*

The rural location of this restaurant-with-rooms makes it the perfect stopping-off point after a hearty walk in the countryside. Set in a small elegant Georgian house, it is famed for the award-wining cuisine by owner Brian Webb. The imaginative menu, featuring local lamb and beef, justifies its reputation as one of Wales's finest restaurants.

LLANGOLLEN The Corn Mill 　　　　　　　🏃🍴　　££

*Dee Lane, Llangollen, Denbighshire, LL20 8NN **Tel** 01978 869555*

Informal restaurant in a heritage building, The Corn Mill is a preferred family destination. Children can enjoy fishcakes or sausages, while their parents dine on venison sausage with parsnip, carrot and potato mash or panfried steak on black pudding, paté and Brie.

NORTHOP Stables Bar Restaurant 　　　　🏃♿🍴　　£££

*Soughton Hall, Northop, Flintshire, CH7 6AB **Tel** 01352 840577*

Part of the luxurious Soughton Hall Hotel, Stables Bar Restaurant offers a truly atmospheric setting with open fires, cobbled floors and timber-roofs. The menu features modern British cuisine. Evening dinner is served in the Stables and the accompanying wine is chosen from the extensive restaurant cellars.

PENMAENPOOL Penmaenuchaf Hall 　　　🏃♿🍴　　££££

*Penmaenpool, Dolgellau, Gwynedd, LL40 1YB **Tel** 01341 422129*

The reputation of Penmaenuchaf Hall rests on its award-winning cuisine. Modern British cooking, thoughtfully kept simple and light, is served in the elegant dining room with fine linen, silver cutlery and crystal wine glasses. Welsh beef and lamb make a good showing. A Celtic cheese board is also available.

PORTMEIRION Hotel Portmeirion 　　　　🏃♿🍴　　££££

*Off A487, Portmeirion, Gwynedd, LL48 6ET **Tel** 01766 770228*

Designed by Clough Williams-Ellis in 1931, the formal hotel (*see p591*) dining room has fabulous views overlooking the estuary. The modern Welsh menu uses the best of local Welsh produce. Castell Deudraeth gastropub, another restaurant on the premises, specializes in fresh seafood, while the Town Hall Restaurant serves meals and snacks.

PWLLHELI Plas Bodegroes 　　　　　　　🏃♿🍴　　££££

*Nefyn Rd, Pwllheli, Gwynedd, LL53 5TH **Tel** 01758 612363*

One of Wales's most well-known restaurants, award-winning Plas Bodegroes may be pricey, but it's more than worth the expense. Locally reared meat, fish and freshly caught game make for a great menu, but the desserts are the main draw. Try the heart-shaped cinnamon biscuit of rhubarb and apple with elderflower custard.

RHOS-ON-SEA Forte's Restaurant 　　　　　🏃　　£

*Penrhyn Avenue, Rhos-on-Sea, Conwy, LL28 4NH **Tel** 01492 544662*

With contemporary decor, Forte's is a perfect lunch venue for families exploring Rhos-on-Sea. It doubles as an ice cream parlour with a delicious range of sundaes, all made with the house ice cream. The restaurant closes at 5:30pm, except during July and August when it remains open in the evening. Lovely views of the harbour.

RHYDLYDAN Y Giler Arms

Rhydlydan, nr Betws-y-Coed, Conwy, LL24 0LL **Tel** *01690 770612*

Friendly country pub and hotel with its own fishing lake, the Giler Arms serves a flavourful seasonal menu in its atmospheric bar-restaurant. There's a good range of local ales, including Batham's traditional draught beers. Enjoys stunning views of the lake.

RHYL Barratts of Tyn Rhyl

Tyn Rhyl, 167 Vale Rd, Rhyl, Denbighshire, LL18 2PH **Tel** *01745 344138*

A surprising find in the seaside town of Rhyl, Tyn Rhyl occupies a quiet plot in an otherwise unremarkable setting. This restaurant with rooms however, has been turning heads for some years now. Diners are drawn here by the promise of fine, home-cooked cuisine at relatively affordable prices.

RUTHIN Manorhaus

10 Well St, LL15 1AH **Tel** *01824 704830*

This super-stylish restaurant with rooms is housed in a listed Georgian stone building in the heart of historic Ruthin. The seasonal menu, featuring such Welsh delights as salt marsh lamb and Menai mussels, is served in the design-conscious dining room, where local art adorns the walls. Relax with an after-dinner Welsh whisky in the cosy bar.

TALSARNAU Maes-y-Neuadd

Talsarnau, Gwynedd, LL47 6YA **Tel** *01766 780200*

Housed in a scenic country house hotel, the restaurant at Maes-y-Neuadd serves an innovative four-course menu. Fresh meats and cheese come from local farms, fish from Cardigan Bay, and fresh vegetables and strawberries from the hotel garden. The courses in the set menus are carefully crafted to maintain harmony.

TAL-Y-BONT Ysgethin Inn

Tal-y-bont, nr Barmouth, Gwynedd, LL43 2AN **Tel** *01341 247578*

Informal family pub in a converted mill house on the banks of the River Ysgethin, serving a mix of simple bar snacks, classic roasts and house specials, such as Ysgethin steak pie. There's an extensive children's menu. Riverside patio and children's adventure playground. The Black Rock grill restaurant cooks on volcanic stone.

SOUTH AND MID-WALES

ABERAERON The Hive on the Quay

Cadwgan Place, SA46 0BU **Tel** *01545 570445*

The award-winning home-made honey ice cream is just one of the reasons to come to this café-restaurant in a converted wharf. On offer is a wide variety of food, from savoury pancakes to seafood platters and Ploughman's lunches to Cardigan Bay crab sandwiches. Almost everything is sourced locally and made on the premises.

ABERGAVENNY The Walnut Tree Inn

Llandewi Skirrid, NP7 8AW **Tel** *01873 852797*

This legendary restaurant is a firm fixture on the foodie trail thanks to an eclectic menu and a carefully chosen wine list. The menu changes daily and often includes cassoulet of duck, pork and sausage; Taleggio cheese and lentil tart; chestnut ice cream and prune and armagnac tart. The rural setting is great for a relaxed special occasion.

BRECON Felin Fach Griffin

Felin Fach, Brecon, Powys, LD3 0UB **Tel** *01874 620111*

Award-winning pub with rooms midway between Brecon and Hay-on-Wye, the Felin Fach Griffin has been acclaimed as exceptional by critics. A delicious lunch and supper menu of traditional Welsh cuisine is on offer. Starters include gnocchi with wild rabbit, while mains range from fresh salted cod to local Welsh rib-eye. Great local cheese board.

BRIDGEND Eliot Restaurant

Coed-y-Mwstwr Hotel, Coychurch, Bridgend, CF35 6AF **Tel** *01656 860621*

In a country-house hotel, Coed-y-Mwstwr ("whispering trees"), Eliot Restaurant provides fabulous views over the picturesque Vale of Glamorgan. Daily table d'hôte menu offers great value lunches, whilst the evenings are à la carte. There's also a family Sunday lunch menu.

BUILTH WELLS The Drawing Room

Cwmbach, Builth Wells, Powys, LD2 3RT **Tel** *01982 552493*

Five-star restaurant-with-rooms in the heart of Wales, the Drawing Room occupies an elegant Georgian country residence. Its location in the lush Wye Valley provides plenty of delicious seasonal ingredients, including prime Welsh black beef and lamb from local farms.

CARDIFF Mimosa Kitchen and Bar

Mermaid Quay, Cardiff Bay, CF10 5BZ **Tel** *02920 491900*

Welsh, stylish and tasty: three adjectives that describe the food in this fashionable gastropub. Seasonal, organic regional produce is the order of the day, with food served from breakfast through to dinner. Welsh slate, leather seats and stylish windows attract an arty media crowd.

Key to Price Guide *see p608* **Key to Symbols** *see back cover flap*

CARDIFF Sequoias Restaurant
New House Country Hotel, Thornhill, Cardiff, CF14 9UA **Tel** *02920 520280*

The panoramic restaurant at this country-house hotel on the outskirts of Cardiff, is known to blend international flavours with the best local produce from the Vale of Glamorgan. Traditional Sunday lunch menu offers discounts for children. Ask for a table on the patio if you don't want to feel that you are dining at a hotel.

CARDIFF Woods
Pilotage Building, Stewart St, Cardiff, CF10 5BW **Tel** *02920 492400*

Contemporary brasserie-style dining in a building once occupied by the harbour pilots. The table d'hôte is good value, but à la carte is also available for eclectic dishes such as carrot and cumin fritters with smoked baba ganoush. Everything is sourced as locally as possible, including the dish of the day.

CRICKHOWELL Nantyffin Cider Mill
Brecon Road, Crickhowell, Powys, NP8 1SG **Tel** *01873 810775*

Pretty country restaurant in a converted mill at the base of the Black Mountains, the Nantyffin remains popular with locals and tourists alike. Dining is split between the bar and the high-beamed, stone-walled restaurant. Dishes are a mix of the local (Glanusk pheasant) and the international (feta, artichoke and olive tart).

FISHGUARD Diners' Circle
Tregynon, Gwaun Valley, nr Fishguard, Pembrokeshire, SA659TU **Tel** *01239 820531*

A 14th-century farmhouse restaurant, Diner's Circle has been steadily building itself a reputation since it first opened over 25 years ago. All food is made on the premises by the owner, with an emphasis on beef and lamb reared on the nearby land. Only members can book to eat here, but one-night membership is available and well worth it.

HAVERFORDWEST The Shed Fish and Chip Bistro
Porthgain, Haverfordwest, Pembrokeshire, SA26 5BN **Tel** *01348 831518*

For a decade the Shed was an unlikely but successful bistro, the eponymous building sitting by the quay in the tiny harbour village of Porthgain. Now it has pared down its menu, but still serves the freshest locally caught fish in a variety of ways, alongside delicious home-made chips.

HAY-ON-WYE Three Cocks Hotel & Restaurant
Three Cocks, nr Hay-on-Wye, Brecon, Powys, LD3 0SL **Tel** *01497 847215*

Listed hotel-restaurant on the main Hereford to Brecon road, the Three Cocks serves tasty home-made dishes using the best of local cuisine. The dining room is quiet, but inviting, with stone fireplaces, comfortable chairs and great views over the hotel garden. Booking recommended.

LLANWRTYD WELLS The Lasswade Country House Hotel & Restaurant
Station Rd, Llanwrtyd Wells, Powys, LD5 4RW **Tel** *01591 610515*

The Lasswade, an Edwardian country-house hotel, is renowned for its fresh and locally sourced, mostly organic, produce. This AA Rosette restaurant won the "True Taste of Wales" and "Sustain Food Challenge" awards and has a sustained reputation for quality. The Welsh black beef is a speciality. Booking is recommended.

MONMOUTH The Stone Mill
Rockfield, Monmouth, Monmouthshire, NP25 5SW **Tel** *01600 716273*

On the edge of the Forest of Dean, the picturesque Stone Mill occupies a converted 16th-century barn with oak beams and vaulted ceiling offset by modern furnishings. The menu features the best of Welsh cuisine, including locally sourced Longhorn beef, pork from Raglan, chicken from Chepstow and game from the area.

MUMBLES Verdi's
Knab Rock, SA3 4EN **Tel** *01792 369135*

The perfect place to stop after a bracing walk along Mumbles seafront. This glass-fronted Italian café serves up the best pizza this side of Naples, as well as focaccia sandwiches and daily pasta specials. Tasty desserts include tiramisu and delicious Turkish delight ice cream, or you could just enjoy a coffee and admire the view of Swansea Bay.

PEMBROKE George Wheeler Restaurant
Old Kings Arms Hotel, Main St, Pembroke, Pembrokeshire, SA71 4JS **Tel** *01646 683611*

Award-winning restaurant in Pembrokeshire's oldest hotel, George Wheeler showcases the best of Wales's local produce, especially fish, sourced daily from Milford Haven. Traditional dishes, such as seared Welsh lamb fillet, sit neatly alongside more modern fare, such as the ever-popular king prawns in smoked bacon.

SKENFRITH The Bell at Skenfrith
Skenfrith, Monmouthshire, NP7 8UH **Tel** *01600 750235*

Renovated 17th-century coaching inn with guestrooms, the Bell is well worth the short drive out of Monmouth. The restaurant menu here ties in with the farmer's market at nearby Abergavenny. Welsh beef, lamb and wild mushrooms popularly feature on the menu. Caters for children over nine.

SOLVA The Old Pharmacy
5 Main St, Solva, Pembrokeshire, SA62 6UU **Tel** *01437 720005*

Formerly a chemist shop, this quaint little restaurant in the harbour village of Lower Solva specializes in local fish and seafood. The menu's star attraction is the bouillabaisse with freshly baked olive oil bread. The Solva lobster and crab, and Welsh organic beef and lamb are good too. There's a charming riverside patio. Children's menu available.

ST DAVIDS Warpool Court Hotel

St Davids, Pembrokeshire, SA62 6BN **Tel** *01437 720300*

Rosette-awarded hotel-restaurant with enviable views over St Davids peninsula, the Warpool Court boasts a delicious daily changing menu of modern British fare. Look for slow-cooked salt marsh lamb, wild sea bass, and locally grown rhubarb in the desserts.

SWANSEA Hanson at the Chelsea

Ty Castell House, 17 St Mary St, SA1 3LH **Tel** *01792 464068*

The yellow dining room might be small, but this award-winning fish restaurant is big on flavour. The locally caught sea bass is a popular choice; meat dishes include slow-cooked pork belly and chargrilled 28 day aged beef. Puddings are worth leaving space for, too.

SWANSEA Patrick's with Rooms

638 Mumbles Rd, Mumbles, Swansea, SA3 4EA **Tel** *01792 360199*

Fantastic restaurant-with-rooms overlooking the Mumbles, Patrick's caters for everyone. The food is delicious with an accompanying wine list. Many of the ingredients used are sourced from the nearby countryside and sea, such as the tasty Gower mussels with leek and laver bread and St Iystydd cheese gratin.

TALYBONT-ON-USK Usk Inn

Talybont-on-Usk, Brecon, Powys, LD3 7JE **Tel** *01874 676251*

Fabulous country pub with rooms in the heart of the Brecon Beacons National Park, Usk Inn sources its ingredients daily from all over Wales: fresh milk and cheese from Brecon, vegetables from Merthyr, meat from Bwlch. The menu caters for everything from bar snacks to three-course table d'hôte.

USK Three Salmons Hotel

Bridge St, Usk, Monmouthshire, NP15 1RY **Tel** *01291 672133*

Restaurant in a beautifully timbered 17th-century coaching inn, Three Salmons Hotel, in the market town of Usk, serves a carefully crafted menu of fresh, local fare with an Italian twist. The carpaccio of beef and baked salmon with pistachio and Parmesan crust, gives a flavour of what is on offer; however, the menu changes regularly.

WHITEBROOK The Crown at Whitebrook

Whitebrook, nr Monmouth, Monmouthshire, NP25 4TX **Tel** *01600 860254*

Elegant restaurant in a charming hotel just outside of Monmouth, The Crown at Whitebrook dates back to 1670. Head chef James Sommerin uses local ingredients but classic French training to create a mouthwatering menu, which mixes game with local beef, lamb and fish.

WOLFSCASTLE Wolfscastle Country Hotel

Wolfscastle, Haverfordwest, Pembrokeshire, SA62 5LZ **Tel** *01437 741225*

One of Wales's grandest country-house hotel-restaurants, the Wolfscastle occupies a panoramic old riverside vicarage near to Haverfordwest and Fishguard. The menu is, unsurprisingly, big on fish with salmon, monkfish and halibut making a good showing next to Welsh beef, lamb and duck. Gourmet breaks available.

THE LOWLANDS

ANSTRUTHER The Cellar

24 E Green, Anstruther, Fife, KY10 3AA **Tel** *01333 310378*

Housed in one of Fife's oldest buildings, this cosy restaurant has won numerous culinary awards. Chef Peter Jukes serves excellent seafood cuisine, with fish, crabs, lobsters and scallops playing a prominent role. Uses fresh local produce. Ideal for those looking for an intimate, romantic meal.

AYR Browne's Restaurant at Enterkine House

By Ayr, Ayrshire, KA6 5AL **Tel** *01292 520580*

This is one of the most elegant country houses in the area. The dining room is beautifully furnished and offers outstanding service. The menu uses only the best locally sourced produce, such as Buccleuch beef, and the skillfully prepared dishes are artfully presented.

CUPAR Ostlers Close

25 Bonnygate, Cupar, Fife, KY15 4BU **Tel** *01334 655574*

A cosy, comfortable restaurant serving modern Scottish cuisine. The menu features a variety of seafood, as well as poultry and seasonal game. Uses fresh local produce. The wild mushrooms are highly recommended. Open for dinner from Tuesday to Saturday; lunch is offered only on Saturday.

DIRLETON The Open Arms

Main St, Dirleton, East Lothian, EH39 5EG **Tel** *01620 850241*

Situated on the edge of the village green, overlooking the 13th-century Dirleton Castle, this popular, family-owned country hotel has a well deserved reputation for good food. Guests can choose between the elegant, formal restaurant or the bright, informal brasserie. The convivial surroundings add to the charm.

Key to Price Guide *see p608* **Key to Symbols** *see back cover flap*

DUNDEE Jute Café
152 Nethergate, Dundee, DD1 4DY Tel 01382 909246

This is a buzzing meeting place for Dundee's cultural set, along with families and weekend revellers, within the DCA Arts Centre. The menu changes monthly but might include sea bass with a spicy risotto and chargrilled chicken with a mozzarella melt. The interior is sleek and contemporary; service can be a tad slow when busy.

EDINBURGH The Dogs
110 Hanover Street, Edinburgh, EH2 1DR Tel 0131 220 1208

This is a curious but welcome member of the Edinburgh restaurant scene. The superb cooking champions Scottish ingredients with classics such as sweetbreads on toast, game pie and lemon thyme posset served with oat biscuits. A charming eatery with quirky crockery and excellent-value fare.

EDINBURGH Angels With Bagpipes
343 High St, Royal Mile, Edinburgh, EH1 1PW Tel 0131 220 1111

Superb-value dining on the Royal Mile, in a medieval tenement building with a courtyard at the rear. Straightforward menus feature local seafood and game in European-influenced Scottish dishes, such as hake with chorizo, tomato, aubergine and anchovy. The staff are very welcoming.

EDINBURGH Le Café St Honore
34 N W Thistle St Lane, Edinburgh, EH2 1EA Tel 0131 226 2211

Located close to the main shopping streets, but in a quiet lane, this traditional French restaurant with a typical Parisian-style interior, is a favourite of many. All produce is of the finest quality, the dishes are imaginative and skilfully cooked and the staff are friendly and helpful.

EDINBURGH Restaurant Martin Wishart
54 The Shore, Edinburgh, EH6 6RA Tel 0131 553 3557

Possibly the finest dining experience in all of Scotland. Chef Martin Wishart's creative and innovative cuisine is in great demand by lovers of fine food, and justifiably so. Serves modern French fare, using the best produce available. The service is excellent, the ambience welcoming and the experience truly memorable.

EDINBURGH The Balmoral Number One
The Balmoral Hotel, 1 Princes St, Edinburgh, EH2 2EQ Tel 0131 557 6727

This classy and upmarket restaurant is located in The Balmoral Hotel, and has its own entrance on Princes Street. Acclaimed chef Jeff Bland is renowned for his skill, imagination and passion for fine Scottish cuisine. The service at this Michelin-starred and multiple award-winning dining venue is also exceptional.

EDINBURGH The Kitchin in Leith
78 Commercial Quay, Edinburgh, EH6 6LX Tel 0131 555 1755

A contemporary eatery in Edinburgh's trendy Leith Waterfront area. Chef Tom Kitchin has deservedly earned a reputation for his innovative menus and presentation. Fish and seafood feature alongside traditional British meats such as venison and beef. More unusual choices include ox tongue and bone marrow. All produce is locally sourced.

ELIE Sangster's
51 High St, Elie, Fife, KY9 1BZ Tel 01333 331001

Located in a popular, coastal East Neuk village, this small, fine restaurant is run by one of Scotland's most recognized and skilled chefs, Bruce Sangster. Specialities include twice baked cheese soufflé, slow cooked noisette of lamb and delicious desserts. Closed on Monday, as well as for dinner on Sunday and for lunch on Tuesday and Saturday.

GLASGOW Firebird
1321 Argyle St, nr Museum of Transport, Glasgow, G3 8TL Tel 0141 334 0594

A popular bar-restaurant hang-out for drinks and an informal evening meal. All produce is of the freshest and highest quality, and the pizzas are among the best in Glasgow. It can get quite noisy at the weekends; if you like it quieter, go during the week instead.

GLASGOW Wee Curry Shop
41 Byres Road, G11 5RG Tel 0141 339 1339

The Wee Curry Shop has three branches in Glasgow offering excellent Indian cuisine, often with a Scottish twist. Haggis pakora and spiced haddock are among the more unusual dishes on the menu. All the food is freshly prepared on the premises and is excellent value. A popular choice in the West End of Glasgow.

GLASGOW City Merchant
97–99 Candleriggs, Glasgow, G1 1NP Tel 0141 553 1577

A warm and welcoming, family-run restaurant located in Glasgow's Merchant City. This bustling venue serves excellent seafood cuisine with a Scottish influence and uses the best local produce. The ambience is informal and rustic. Can accommodate up to 120 guests. Offers good value for money.

GLASGOW Gamba
225A W George St, Glasgow, G2 2ND Tel 0141 572 0899

Popular, seafood restaurant, recognized for its high quality, varied cuisine. The food is meticulously prepared, using fresh seasonal produce such as fish, lobsters and oysters, and beautifully presented. The interior of this city centre eatery is modern, stylish and comfortable, while the ambience is cosy.

GLASGOW Stravaigin　　　　　　　　　　　　　　　　🏃 🍷　　£££

*28 Gibson St, Hillhead, Glasgow, G12 8NX **Tel** 0141 334 2665*

Well placed in the popular Gibson Street, in the Glasgow University neighbourhood. Features a popular café-bar and a highly successful restaurant. Serves award-winning pub fare: the best of Scottish produce flavoured with the world's sauces, herbs and spices.

GLASGOW Two Fat Ladies at the Buttery　　　　　　🏃 ♿ 🍷　　£££

*652 Argyle St, Glasgow, G3 8UF **Tel** 0141 221 8188*

Although located in a less than salubrious part of the city centre, this is one place that is well worth seeking out. This attractive pub has been converted into an elegant dining room, but retains elements of its past. Largely a fish restaurant, it also serves hearty Scottish fare, made from fresh local produce. Also offers a wide selection of desserts and cheeses.

GLASGOW Ubiquitous Chip　　　　　　　　　　　　🏃 ♿ 🍷　　£££

*12 Ashton Lane, Glasgow, G12 8SJ **Tel** 0141 334 5007*

A Glasgow West-End institution, this prestigious restaurant serves traditional Scottish cuisine, made with fresh local ingredients, and has been a home of culinary excellence for over 30 years. Great atmosphere and a friendly staff make this a notable place.

GULLANE La Potinière　　　　　　　　　　　　　　　🍷　　£££

*Main St, Gullane, East Lothian, EH31 2AA **Tel** 01620 843214*

Superior restaurant situated in a pretty East Lothian village. The menu changes from season to season, and offers well-prepared food, using fresh local produce. Boasts a caring and hospitable staff, as well as a private parking facility. The restaurant is closed on Monday and Tuesday.

INVERKEILOR Gordon's Restaurant　　　　　　　　　　🍷　　££££

*Main Street, Inverkeilor, DD11 5RN **Tel** 01241 830364*

One of Scotland's finest dining establishments, this family-run restaurant is set in the tiny Angus village of Inverkeilor. The menu features Scottish seasonal ingredients such as Arbroath Smokie, North Sea halibut and Isle of Mull Tobermory cheddar; all dishes are beautifully presented. Rooms are available for overnight stays.

KIPPFORD The Anchor Hotel　　　　　　　　　　　　🏃 ♿　　££

*Main St, Kippford, Dalbeattie, Kirkudbrightshire, DG5 4LN **Tel** 01556 620205*

This seaside hotel and pub is situated on the waterfront in the pretty village of Kippford, with great views of the coastal activity. The friendly bar serves appetizing pub food, using seasonal, locally sourced produce. A popular spot to enjoy real ale and a filling meal. The hotel is comfortable and of good value. Open summer only.

LARGS Nardinis　　　　　　　　　　　　　　　　　　🏃 ♿　　£££

*The Esplanade, Largs, KA30 8NF, Ayrshire, **Tel** 01475 475000*

A splendid Art Deco interior sets the scene of this seafront lounge café. This well-known Scottish institution is definitely worth a visit if in the area. Breakfasts, cakes and Italian and British dishes are served all day. A perfect place to relax, sit back and read the paper. Extremely popular with both locals and tourists.

LINLITHGOW Champany Inn　　　　　　　　　　　　🏃 ♿ 🍷　　£££

*Champany, nr Linlithgow, West Lothian, EH49 7LU **Tel** 01506 834532*

Located on the outskirts of Linlithgow, not far from Edinburgh, this charming restaurant has a well-earned reputation for offering some of the best steaks in Scotland. Diners can choose from strip loin, rib eye, fillet and porterhouse; all cooked to perfection. Must-try specialities include delicious Loch Gruinart oysters and succulent hot smoked salmon.

PEEBLES The Adam Room, Tontine Hotel　　　　　　🏃 ♿ 🍷　　££

*High Street, Peebles, EH45 8AJ **Tel** 01721 720892*

This hotel is one of the best places to enjoy good Scottish fare. The menu includes local lamb, beef and fish dishes, and the service is friendly and accomplished. Dine in the smart Georgian Adam Room or opt for the less formal bistro. Both offer excellent value for money and beautifully presented dishes.

PERTH The Bothy　　　　　　　　　　　　　　　　　🏃 ♿　　££

*33 Kinnoull Street, Perth, PH1 5EN **Tel** 0845 659 5907*

This stylish restaurant, in the centre of Perth, has earned itself a well-deserved reputation for serving great seafood and quality Scottish favourites such as black pudding with scallops. The service is friendly and efficient, and the varied menu has something for everyone. The pre-theatre menu is a bargain.

PERTH 63 Tay Street　　　　　　　　　　　　　　　　🍷　　£££

*63 Tay St, Perth, Perthshire, PH2 8NN **Tel** 01738 441451*

63 Tay Street has won awards for its customer service and attention to detail. The modern Scottish cuisine is superb, with menus that feature the best regional produce available. Outstanding dishes include rack of lamb and plaice served with West Coast scallops.

PERTH Let's Eat　　　　　　　　　　　　　　　　　🏃 ♿ 🍷　　£££

*77–79 Kinnoull St, Perth, Perthshire, PH1 5EZ **Tel** 01738 643377*

Local ingredients and passionate owners play a prominent role in this restaurant's success. Offers relaxing and comfortable surroundings, seasonal menus and skilled cooking. Fish, beef, venison and lamb are the mainstays of the delicious meals and are usually accompanied by fresh vegetables and creative sauces.

Key to Price Guide *see p608* **Key to Symbols** *see back cover flap*

PORTPATRICK Knockinaam Lodge ⚑♿🍷 ££££

Off A77, nr Portpatrick, Dumfries and Galloway, DG9 9AD **Tel** *01776 810471*

This attractive country house has an idyllic location overlooking the sea, and even boasts its own small private beach. Comfort and pampering are top priority at this beautiful and stylish lodge. The dining room serves international cuisine, with modern Scottish influences. A welcoming ambience adds to the charm.

ST ANDREWS The Peat Inn ♿🍷 ££££

On B940, Cupar, by St Andrews, Fife, KY15 5LH **Tel** *01334 840206*

Highly accomplished modern cooking, using regional produce and seasonal vegetables, has established this smart hotel-restaurant as one of the best in Britain. The innovative cuisine is prepared by renowned chef Geoffrey Smeddle, whose passion for good Scottish fare is evident in his creations. Lunch is particularly good value.

ST ANDREWS The Seafood Restaurant ♿🍷 ££££

Bruce Embankment, St Andrews, Fife, KY16 9AS **Tel** *01334 479475*

Located in an enviable seafront location, this superb restaurant offers a memorable dining experience, along with striking views of the coastline. The menu features a variety of seafood, which is carefully prepared and beautifully presented. The ambience at this stylish eatery is warm and cosy.

ST MONANS Craig Millar @ 16 West End ♿🍷 £££

16 West End, St Monans, Fife, KY10 2BX **Tel** *01333 730327*

Set in a stunning water's edge location, this fine, modern restaurant is attractively and elegantly fitted out. Serves a wide range of fresh, seasonal fish and seafood, including prawns, crabs, scallops and more. Craig Millar, former partner-chef at the Seafood Restaurant here, serves fine, fresh marine delights.

SOUTH QUEENSFERRY Orocco Pier ⚑♿🍷 £££

17 High St, S Queensferry, Edinburgh, EH30 9PP **Tel** *0870 118 1664*

Situated on the main street in South Queensferry, a short distance from Edinburgh city centre. Open all day for light snacks, coffees and meals, this elegant restaurant is a great place to enjoy the splendid views of the Forth estuary and its bridges. Fish and seafood play a prominent role in the menu.

TROON Highgrove House Hotel ⚑♿🍷 £££

Old Loans Rd, Troon, Ayrshire, KA7 7HL **Tel** *01292 312511*

Perched high on Dundonald Hill, this hotel-restaurant occupies a retired sea captain's house, and enjoys magnificent views over the Firth of Clyde and the Mull of Kintyre. The atmosphere is comfortable and welcoming. Serves informal meals from a varied menu, featuring some old favourites and newer innovations.

THE HIGHLANDS AND ISLANDS

ABERDEEN Priory 🍷 £££

Mary Culter House Hotel, South Deeside Rd, Aberdeen, Aberdeenshire, AB12 5GB **Tel** *01224 732124*

Located on the banks of the River Dee, the Priory restaurant provides a lovely setting for a romantic candle-lit dinner, with its stone walls, open fire and intimate atmosphere. The menu is modern European with a Scottish twist, and every dish on it is prepared using excellent local produce. Closed Sun.

ABERDEEN The Udny Arms ⚑🍷 £££

Main St, Newburgh, Nr Aberdeen, Aberdeenshire, AB41 6BL **Tel** *01358 789444*

This family-run, village hotel has a bistro and pub that is cosy, full of character, and serves up honest, wholesome food. The locals rate this place very highly, not least because it is great value for money. The staff are friendly and efficient which makes for a pleasant dining experience.

ABERDEEN The Silver Darling ⚑♿🍷 ££££

Pocra Quay, Footdee, N Pier, Aberdeen, Aberdeenshire, AB11 5DQ **Tel** *01224 576229*

A superb seafood bistro restaurant located on the north side of Aberdeen harbour. This well-established venue is one of the best places to enjoy the daily catch, which has been carefully cooked and presented. Try and sit by the window if you can to make the most of the splendid coastline views. Closed Sun.

ALEXANDRIA Cameron House ♿🍷 £££££

Off A82, Loch Lomond, Alexandria, West Dunbartonshire, G83 8QZ **Tel** *01389 722504*

A formal dining room at this luxurious country house, situated on the tranquil shores of Loch Lomond and set amid beautiful grounds. The elegant and stylish Martin Wishart restaurant has won several awards, and offers exquisitely prepared meals in comfortable surroundings. The staff are well trained and friendly.

AUCHTERARDER Andrew Fairlie @ Gleneagles 🍴🍷 £££££

Gleneagles Hotel, Auchterarder, Perthshire, PH3 1NF **Tel** *0800 704705*

One of the finest dining experiences in Scotland. This elegant restaurant is set within the luxurious Gleneagles Hotel. The highly acclaimed chef presents imaginative French cuisine with a Scottish flavour. Standouts include home-smoked lobster, butter-poached turbot and the "textures of chocolate" dessert..

BALLATER Darroch Learg

Braemar Rd, Ballater, Aberdeenshire, AB35 5UX **Tel** *013397 55443*

A great restaurant, with a well-deserved reputation for excellence, set within a Victorian shooting lodge. The modern British cuisine is particularly outstanding, as the best local produce is used to create imaginative and flavoursome dishes. The setting of this award-winning venue is relaxed, and the adjacent conservatory adds to the charm.

CAIRNDOW Loch Fyne Oyster Bar

Clachan, Cairndow, Argyll, PA26 8BL **Tel** *01499 600236*

Highly renowned restaurant offering an impressive array of fish and seafood. The menu features an excellent selection of both hot and cold meals, including delicious oysters, mussels, two veggie options and a lobster platter. Also offers steaks, lamb, and chicken dishes, as well as vegetarian choices.

CARNOUSTIE Ganges

11 Park Ave, Carnoustie, Angus, DD7 7JA **Tel** *01241 853336*

Located in a former Masonic hall just off Carnoustie's high street, this Indian restaurant has already earned a reputation for its tasty food and affordable prices. All the classic Indian dishes can be found here, cooked to an excellent standard. Closed Mon.

COLBOST BY DUNVEGAN Three Chimneys

Colbost, Dunvegan, Isle of Skye, Inverness-shire, IV55 8ZT **Tel** *01470 511258*

Situated a short distance from Dunvegan, on the western shores of the loch. Once a stone-built crofter's cottage, this award-winning restaurant offers seafood and game, lovingly prepared with fresh local produce. The ambience is peaceful and relaxed, and the service friendly. One of the "not to miss" places in Scotland.

DRYMEN The Pottery

The Square, Drymen, Argyll, G63 OBJ **Tel** *01360 660458*

Delightful pub-restaurant and coffee shop, located in the square of the pretty little village of Drymen. Offers good, home-cooked food all day and delicious afternoon teas and lunches – all prepared fresh. Boasts a charming terrace. A popular stopping point for locals as well as tourists exploring the area.

DUFFTOWN A Taste of Speyside

10 Balvenie St, Dufftown, Moray, AB55 4AB **Tel** *01340 820860*

Set amid the mountains and glens of the Spey Valley, this restaurant has been offering an enjoyable culinary experience to customers for many years. The food here is wholesome and simply prepared, showing a strong commitment to quality local produce such as fish, poultry and game.

DUNKELD Howie's Bistro

23 Atholl St, Dunkeld, Perthshire, PH8 0AR **Tel** *01350 728847*

Located in the town centre, Howie's Bistro offers a modern European menu alongside Scottish favourites. All ingredients are locally sourced and include fresh salmon and organic steaks. The dining room is contemporary, with exposed brick walls, modern furniture and large windows. There is an open fire and free Wi-Fi.

FORT WILLIAM Crannog Seafood Restaurant

The Waterfront, Fort William, Perthshire, PH33 6DB **Tel** *01397 705589*

Nothing can detract from the simple pleasure of eating exquisitely fresh seafood while overlooking a panoramic loch view. The helpings at this restaurant are generous, the atmosphere is warm and relaxing and the service quite efficient.

INVERNESS Culloden House

Culloden, Inverness, Inverness-shire, IV2 7BZ **Tel** *01463 790461*

A historic building with loads of character, set in lovely grounds, close to the Culloden Visitor Centre. Offers Scottish country house-style food, with sauces, jellies, sorbets and mousses interspersing a wide variety of hearty and appetizing meat, game and fish dishes. Accommodation is also available.

KILBERRY Kilberry Inn

Kilberry, by Tarbert, Loch Fyne, Argyll, PA29 6YD **Tel** *01880 770223*

This former post office is now run as a pub in a quiet coastal village. Serves modern Scottish cuisine, with a constantly changing menu. However, a good selection of old favourites is also featured so not to disappoint the regular customers. Has a warm and cosy atmosphere.

KILLIECRANKIE Killiecrankie Hotel

Off A9, nr Pitlochry, Perthshire, PH16 5LG **Tel** *01796 473220*

Attractive, well-appointed hotel, which has the feel of a village inn. The food served here is healthy and wholesome, with some unusual, yet innovative twists. The excellent bar meals supplement the fine, dinnertime fare, both of which are served in cosy and inviting surroundings. The staff are friendly and hospitable.

KILLIN Bridge of Lochay Hotel and Restaurant

Aberfeldy Road, Killin, Perthshire, FK21 8TS **Tel** *01567 820272*

Situated just on the outskirts of the village of Killin, this hotel-restaurant has established a well-deserved reputation for the quality of its food and friendly service. The menu offers tasty and inventive dishes prepared using plenty of local ingredients. In fine weather, a good selection of single malt whiskies can be enjoyed on the terrace.

Key to Price Guide *see p608* **Key to Symbols** *see back cover flap*

KINCRAIG The Boathouse Restaurant

Loch Insh, Kincraig, Inverness-shire, PH21 1NU **Tel** *01540 651272*

Charming log-cabin restaurant overlooking Loch Insh. Features a traditional Scottish menu with local fish, haggis and steak, and serves tea, coffee, snacks and home-baked dishes throughout the day. Offers a special menu for children, and encourages outdoor meals on the balcony in summer. Also has a gift shop and a bar.

KIRKWALL, ORKNEY Foveran Restaurant

Kirkwall, Orkney, KW15 1SF **Tel** *01856 872389*

One of the best restaurants on Orkney, the Foveran is expertly run by the Doull family. The menu makes good use of the abundant local produce, including beef and fresh seafood, with the famous Highland Park whisky used in some dishes. The lovely dining room has a relaxed and friendly atmosphere.

KYLESKU The Kylesku Hotel

On A894 by Lairg, Sutherland, IV27 4HW **Tel** *01971 502231*

Lochs and mountains provide a magnificent backdrop to this hotel, which is located on the quayside. The bar and restaurant menus are extensive, and feature an array of local dishes. However, the speciality here is the freshly caught fish. The tranquil surroundings create an excellent setting in which to unwind and relax.

LOCH EPORT Langass Lodge

Loch Eport, Isle of North Uist, Outer Hebrides, HS6 5HA **Tel** *01876 580285*

One of the finest dining experiences to be found in the Hebrides, set in a beautiful location on this wild island. The wonderful menu takes in the freshest of local seafood, game and beef. All vegetables are homegrown. Reservations are essential if not lodging at the hotel.

OBAN Wide Mouthed Frog

Dunstaffnage Bay, by Oban, Argyll, PA37 1PX **Tel** *01631 567005*

Situated between the villages of Connel and Oban, this restaurant is a popular meeting place, particularly with the sailing fraternity. Good food and convivial surroundings make this a deservedly bustling venue. The menus feature local produce and the food is well cooked and presented. Accommodation also available in summer.

OBAN Ee'usk

N Pier, Oban, Argyll, PA34 5QD **Tel** *01631 565666*

This stylish restaurant occupies a great waterside setting, and has something for everyone. Serves mouthwatering seafood, using fresh catches of the day. A must-visit for those who enjoy fish. A favoured choice of many, this eatery also offers great views of the coastline. Excellent-value set menus are available.

OBAN The Knipoch Hotel

On A816, nr Oban, Argyll, PA34 4QT **Tel** *01852 316251*

Situated on the outskirts of Oban, this traditional country hotel has been a popular stopping place for many years. The bar meals here are excellent, while the dinners range from three to five courses. In addition, the huge array of vegetables and flamboyant puddings are as eyecatching as they are tasty.

PLOCKTON Plockton Shores Restaurant

Harbour St, Plockton, Ross-shire, IV52 8TN **Tel** *01599 544263*

Nestled on the shores of Loch Carron is this restaurant specializing in fish and shellfish. Diners can take in the spectacular views from across the bay while enjoying dishes such as Cullen skink (smoked haddock in a potato and parsley soup) or seared fillets of Mallaig sea bass served with aubergines and oven-roasted tomatoes.

PORT APPIN The Airds Hotel

Port Appin, Argyll, PA38 4DF **Tel** *01631 730236*

This hotel-restaurant is set on a fine waterfront location in Appin, and has a cheerful and comfortable interior. Offers a well balanced menu, with a variety of seafood, poultry and game, and uses fresh local produce to prepare appetizing dishes. The service is excellent, and the ambience warm and inviting.

SGARASTA BHEAG Scarista House

Sgarasta Bheag, Isle of Harris, HS3 3HX **Tel** *01859 550238*

This Georgian house boasts stunning views of the surrounding ocean and mountains. The restaurant keeps things simple with a compact menu, and the sensational food is all locally sourced. Tasting the locally caught seafood is a particular treat. Guest rooms are available, and two nearby cottages can be rented.

STANLEY, NR PERTH Ballathie Hotel Restaurant

Kinclaven, Stanley, Perthshire, PH1 4QN **Tel** *01250 8883268*

A short drive from Perth, this country-house hotel is beautifully located on the banks of the River Tay. Dine in the hotel's main restaurant, where specialities include local venison and fine Scottish beef, or visit the bar for a lighter snack. It is popular for Sunday lunch, and during the summer months afternoon tea is served on the lawns.

ULLAPOOL The Ceilidh Place

14 W Argyle St, Ullapool, Sutherland, IV26 2TY **Tel** *01854 612103*

An interesting arts venue and hotel, with a great atmosphere. Situated in an award-winning hotel with its own book-shop, rooms and bar, this restaurant serves superbly skilled and imaginative dishes, which are unashamedly local and of the highest quality. Meals incorporate fish, meat, poultry, vegetables and fruits – all prepared simply, yet excellently.

British Pubs

No tour of Britain could be complete without some exploration of its public houses. These are a great social institution, descendants of centuries of hostelries, ale houses and stagecoach halts. Some have colourful histories or fascinating contents, and occupy a central role in the community, staging quiz games and folk dancing. Many of those listed below are lovely buildings, or have attractive settings. Most serve a variety of beers, spirits and wine by the glass.

A "free house" is independent and will stock several leading regional beers, but most pubs are "tied" – this means that they are owned by a brewery and only stock that brewery's selection.

Many pubs offer additional attractions such as live music and beer gardens with picnic tables. Traditional pub food and more varied gastropub cuisine is often served at lunchtime, and increasingly, in the evenings as well. Traditional pub games take many forms, including cribbage, shove ha'penny, skittles, dominoes and darts.

LONDON

Bloomsbury: *Lamb*
94 Lamb's Conduit St, WC1.
Tel 020 7405 0713. **Map** 3 C5
Unspoilt Victorian pub with lovely cut-glass "snob screens" and theatrical photographs. Small courtyard at the rear. 🍴 🎵 📷 🚶

City: *Black Friar*
174 Queen Victoria St, EC4.
Tel 020 7236 5474. **Map** 12 F2
Eccentric inside and out, with intriguing Art Nouveau decor. Attentive service. 🍴 🚶

City: *Ye Olde Cheshire Cheese*
145 Fleet St EC4.
Tel 020 7353 6170. **Map** 12 E1
Authentic 17th-century inn that evokes shades of Dickens's London. Its stark glory is best enjoyed in front of the open fires. 🍴 🚶

Hammersmith: *Dove*
19 Upper Mall, W6.
Tel 020 8748 9474.
One of west London's most attractive riverside pubs – you can watch rowing crews from the terrace. 🍴 📷

Hampstead: *Spaniards Inn*
Spaniards Lane, NW3.
Tel 020 8731 8406.
Famous Hampstead landmark dating from the 16th century, once part of a tollgate. 🍴 📷 🚶

Kensington: *Windsor Castle*
114 Campden Hill Rd, W8.
Tel 020 7243 8797. **Map** 7 C4
A civilized Georgian inn with oak furnishings and open fires.

The walled garden attracts well-heeled crowds in summer. Hearty English food. 🍴 📷 🚶

Southwark: *George Inn*
77 Borough High St, SE1.
Tel 020 7407 2056. **Map** 13 B4
Quaint coaching inn with unique galleried courtyard. Rooms ramble upstairs and downstairs, and the overspill sits outside. Morris dancers may be seen performing here at times *(see p120).* 🍴 📷 🚶

THE DOWNS AND CHANNEL COAST

Alciston: *Rose Cottage Inn*
Alciston nr Polegate.
Tel 01323 870377.
In a creeper-covered cottage, this rural Sussex pub is decorated in classic rustic style, with beamed ceilings and open fireplaces. The local ales and busy kitchen add to its warmth. 🍴 📷

Brighton: *Market Inn*
Market St, BN1 1HH.
Tel 01273 329483.
Once home to the Prince of Wales's chimney sweep, this is now something of a Brighton institution, spilling out onto The Lanes in the summer months. 🍴 📷

Charlton: *The Fox Goes Free*
Charlton nr Chichester.
Tel 01243 811461.
This lovely 16th-century inn serves local ales and cider straight from barrels. Full à la carte menu and great selection of bar meals. Live music on Wednesdays. 🍴 🎵 📷 🚶 ♿

Ditchling: *The Bull Hotel*
2 High St, BN6 8TA.
Tel 01273 843147.
Housed in a 14th-century building, the main bar is large, rambling and pleasantly traditional with characterful old wooden floorboards, beams and furniture, and a blazing fire. 🍴 🎵 📷 🚶

Faversham: *White Horse Inn*
The Street, Boughton.
Tel 01227 751343.
Chaucer gave this place a passing mention in *The Canterbury Tales*. Among hop gardens and orchards, this genial country pub resounds with echoes from the past. Thirteen en suite bedrooms. 🍴 🎵 📷 🚶 ♿

Isle of Wight:
The Wight Mouse Inn
Newport Rd, Chale.
Tel 01983 730431.
This pub draws in the locals with its range of real ales. Jazz music on Thursdays. 🍴 🎵 📷 🚶

Lewes: *Six Bells Inn*
Chiddingly, nr Lewes.
Tel 01825 872227.
Once a stopover for stagecoaches, this cosy drop-in now does a fine job of reviving weary ramblers and thirsty locals. Supposedly haunted by a grey cat and one Sara French, hanged in 1852 after serving her husband a pie seasoned with arsenic. 🍴 🎵 📷 🚶 ♿

Romsey: *The Star Inn*
East Tytherley, nr Romsey.
Tel 01794 340225.
Popular watering hole on the edge of the New Forest, overlooking the village cricket pitch. The rivers Test and Dunn are nearby. Overnight accommodation available. 🍴 📷 🚶

Rye: *The Mermaid*
Mermaid St. *Tel 01797 223065.*
Dating from 1136, this is one of the country's oldest inns. Constructed from old ship timbers, The Mermaid is an evocative slice of England's nautical history. Sit by the open fire and spot the celebrities having a quiet drink. 🍴 📷 🚶

Walliswood: *The Scarlett Arms*
Walliswood Green Rd.
Tel 01306 627243.
Handsome inn with flagstone bar, wooden benches and a grand inglenook fireplace. The staff make the experience all the more congenial. Occasional live music. 🍴 🎵 📷 🚶 ⚡

EAST ANGLIA

Cambridge: *The Boathouse*
14 Chesterton Rd. **Tel** 01223 460905.
This riverside pub boasts a natty
nautical theme and exceedingly
comfortable armchairs. The beer
garden is always warm and toasty,
courtesy of heaters, allowing you
to watch the river flow all year
around. 🍴 🎵 🚲 ♿ ✈

Itteringham:
The Walpole Arms
The Common. **Tel** 01263 587258.
Oak-beamed inn that has been
serving locally brewed ales since
the 1700s. The restaurant is also
highly regarded. 🍴 🚲 🚹 ♿

Kings Lynn: *The Lord Nelson*
Walsingham Rd, Burnham Thorpe.
Tel 01328 738241.
This watering hole was once one
of Lord Nelson's favourite haunts.
Kick back on any of the old high-
backed benches, and wait for the
attentive staff to take your order.
Private functions are held in the
handsome, flagstoned Victory
Barn. Quiz Tuesday lunchtime. 🍴
🎵 🚲 🚹 ♿

Norfolk: *Red Lion*
Wells Rd, Stiffkey. **Tel** 01328 830552.
The oldest parts of the simple
bars have oak beams, aged
flooring tiles or bare boards, and
big open fires. A back gravel
terrace has seats and tables for
enjoying the bar food on a sunny
day, and some pleasant walks are
nearby. Real ale and 30 malt
whiskies are available.
🍴 🎵 🚲 🚹 ♿

Norwich: *The Fat Cat*
49 W End St. **Tel** 01603 624364.
Rightly famed for its extensive
real ale selection, The Fat Cat
is full of attractions, starting
with the well-stocked bar and
the lively local clientele. 🍴 ♿

Ringstead: *The Gin Trap Inn*
6 High St. **Tel** 01485 525264.
Close to the Norfolk coastline
and just on the edge of the
Ringstead Downs nature reserve,
this classic country pub features
hand-pumped real ales and cosy
log fires. The restaurant has a
devoted following. Overnight
accommodation available. Quiz
every other Sunday. 🍴 🚲 🚹 ♿

Southwold: *The Crown Hotel*
High St. **Tel** 01502 722275.
The pub remains the star of this
converted hotel, though the chic
restaurant is becoming a firm local
favourite. Excellent selection of
wines at the bar. 🍴 🚹 ♿

Stowmarket:
The Buxhall Crown
Mill Rd, Buxhall. **Tel** 01449 736521.
Local real ales take pride of
place in this old village pub
that also does a roaring trade in
home-cooked food with locally
sourced ingredients. Good list
of wine by the glass. 🍴 🚲 🚹

Suffolk:
The Six Bells at Bardwell
Bardwell, Bury St Edmunds.
Tel 01359 250820.
This village green charmer, dating
from the 1500s, offers superb food
and peaceful accommodation.
🍴 🚲 🚹

Walden: *Queen's Head Inn*
High St, Littlebury, Saffron Walden.
Tel 01799 522251.
Attractive coaching inn with a
relaxed, family ambience. Stocks a
decent selection of ales and has a
heady wine list. There are six en
suite rooms. 🍴 🎵 🚲 🚹 ✈

THAMES VALLEY

Aylesbury: *The King's Head*
Kings Head Passage, Market Sq,
Buckinghamshire. **Tel** 01296 718812.
A small oasis in the heart of a
pretty market town, this airy pub
has award-winning food and ales
and a courtyard for whiling away
long summer afternoons. 🍴 🚲

Bedford: *The Park*
98 Kimbolton Rd, Bedfordshire.
Tel 01234 273929.
This warm and friendly pub has
traditional features such as oak
beams and old fireplaces. Good,
wholesome food on offer. 🍴 🎵
🚲 🚹 ♿

Bicester: *The Hundred Acres*
Hart Place, Oxfordshire.
Tel 01869 329981.
A homely pub serving food
and open late on weekends.
Welcomes children until 8pm.
🍴 🚲 🚹 ✈

Chipping Norton:
The Falkland Arms
Great Tew, Chipping Norton,
Oxfordshire. **Tel** 01608 683653.
Award-winning cask ales and a
wonderful atmosphere. You can
try beer tasters before you buy at
this traditional gem of a place.
🍴 🎵 🚲 ✈

Faringdon: *The Trout Inn*
Tadpole Bridge, Buckland Marsh,
nr Faringdon. **Tel** 01367 870382.
Always busy and bustling, this
17th-century pub boasts a river-

front garden where customers
can savour local dishes.
🍴 🚲 🚹 ♿

Great Hormead:
The Three Tuns
High Street, Hertfordshire.
Tel 01763 289405.
A traditional thatched and beamed
village pub with a cosy open fire
in winter and a patio in summer.
Hearty and reasonably priced
food. 🍴 🚲 🚹 ♿ ✈

Luton: *The Bricklayers Arms*
High Town Rd, Bedfordshire.
Tel 01582 611017.
A friendly pub with ice-cold beers
and plenty of quiz machines. Order
whatever's on the left-hand pump,
since its contents are changed
constantly. ✈

Newbury: *The Monument*
Northbrook St, Berkshire.
Tel 01635 41964.
The busiest pub around, there
are different events every night
of the week and a wide range
of pub games. There is also a
beer garden. 🎵 🚲 ✈

Oxford: *The White Horse*
52 Broad St. **Tel** 01865 728318.
This cosy pub has loads of
character, with pictures of old
sports stars on the walls and a
great range of beers. 🍴

Watton-at-Stone: *The Bull*
113 High St, Herts. **Tel** 01920 831032.
Sit around the open-hearth fire
at this 14th-century inn, or in the
picturesque garden. 🍴 🚲 🚹 ✈

WESSEX

Abbotsbury: *Ilchester Arms*
Market St, Dorset. **Tel** 01305 871243.
A prominent landmark in this
quaint village, the 18th-century
stone Grade II listed inn features
a deluxe conservatory. 🍴 🚲 🚹
♿ ✈

Bath: *The Bell*
103 Walcot St, Bath, Avon.
Tel 01225 460426.
Splendid little pub, with billiards,
live music and organic beers.
Soak in the friendly atmosphere
while tucking into tasty sandwiches
and snacks. 🎵 🚲 🚹 ✈

Bridport: *Shave Cross Inn*
Shave Cross, Marshwood Vale,
Dorset. **Tel** 01308 868358.
Award-winning inn with fine ales
as well as English, Caribbean and
international food. Five rooms.
🍴 🎵 🚲 🚹 ✈

Pensford: *Carpenter's Arms*
Stanton Wick, nr Pensford, Somerset.
Tel *01761 490202.*
Overlooking the lovely Chew
Valley, this welcoming pub is set
among a row of small miners'
cottages. It has an excellent menu
and a comprehensive wine list.

Salisbury: *Haunch of Venison*
1 Minster St, Salisbury, Wiltshire.
Tel *01722 411313.*
The severed, mummified hand of
an 18th-century card player is on
display (along with more pleasant
antiques) at this 650-year-old pub.
The restaurant is a must-visit for a
good meal. Keep an eye out for
the resident ghost.

Salisbury: *The New Inn*
41/47 New St, Wiltshire.
Tel *01722 326662.*
The low-beamed ceilings and
intimate interior lighting here
are offset by fine views of the
cathedral spire opposite. The
menu is broad and vegetarian-
friendly.

DEVON AND CORNWALL

Dawlish: *The Mount Pleasant*
Mount Pleasant Rd, Dawlish Warren,
Devon. **Tel** *01626 863151.*
This pub is renowned for its views
over Exmouth from the dining
area. Drinkers visit once and
become loyal customers for years.
The warm ambience makes a
winning combination with super
value for money.

Exeter: *The Bridge Inn*
Bridge Hill, Topsham, Devon.
Tel *01392 873862.*
With its pink exterior, you can't
miss this riverside pub, which has
been run by the same family since
1899. Its several separate rooms
with fireplaces are truly snug
in winter, while the garden is
gorgeous on sunny days. A pub
with no bar, they serve drinks and
bar snacks through a hatch in the
corridor.

Falmouth: *Pandora Inn*
Restronguet Creek, Mylor Bridge,
nr Falmouth, Cornwall.
Tel *01326 372678.*
Medieval pub with a thatched
roof by the waterside. Full of cosy
corners, low wooden ceilings, panelled walls and a variety of maritime
memorabilia.

Knowstone: *Masons Arms*
Inn Devon. **Tel** *01398 341231.*
An atmospheric Grade II listed
cottage that is full of character.

The decor includes farm tools
and a bread-oven fireplace.
Delicious restaurant food and
friendly hosts.

Lynton: *Fox and Goose*
Parracombe, Barnstaple.
Tel *01598 763239.*
A friendly and welcoming pub/
B&B with very good food and
beer. The log fire, plank ceiling
and assorted mounted antlers and
horns give a proper Exmoor feel
to the place. Serves real ale and
local cider.

Newton Abbot: *Two Mile Oak*
Totnes Rd.
Tel *01803 812411.*
An old coaching inn with a beamed
lounge and an alcove just for two.
A mix of wooden tables and chairs,
and a fine winter log fire.

Penzance: *The Pirate Inn*
Alverton Rd, Alverton, Cornwall.
Tel *01736 366094.*
Recommended by the local youth
hostel, this is a friendly stop for a
beer and sandwich. Visitors often
invest in the souvenir T-shirts sold
here.

Porthleven: *Harbour Inn*
Commercial Rd, Cornwall.
Tel *01326 573876.*
Watch the sun go down and sip
a top-quality pint as you sit by
Porthleven's harbour. Two
hundred years old, this pub retains
its original character, the modern
sofas and coffee tables notwith-
standing.

Saltash: *Rod and Line*
Church Rd, Tideford, Cornwall.
Tel *01752 851323.*
This friendly old Cornish pub is set
just off the main A38 road. Popular
with locals, it has a single bar with
a log fire. The interesting menu
features local seafood.

Tiverton: *The White Ball Inn*
Bridge St, Devon. **Tel** *01884 251525.*
Although the decor is slightly
generic, there is an unusual visible
well with a glass top. Vertigo
sufferers should not look down.

THE HEART OF ENGLAND

Alderminster: *The Bell*
Warwickshire. **Tel** *01789 450414.*
Smart 18th-century coach inn
just 6.4 km (4 miles) out of
Stratford-upon-Avon, The Bell
also boasts a high-class restaurant.
Great views over Stour Valley
from the garden and conservatory.

Armscote: *Fox & Goose*
Warwickshire. **Tel** *01608 682293.*
This atmospheric bar-restaurant
(and B&B) is perfect for a light
supper or relaxing drink. Sit in the
vast lawns during summer. The
bar has an open fire in winter.

Ashleworth: *Queen's Arms*
The Village, Gloucestershire.
Tel *01452 700395.*
Sixteenth-century inn with a
noticeable Victorian makeover,
this pub features wood-beamed
ceilings and antique furnishings.
The fantastic kitchen serves
traditional pub food as well as
more international flavours.

Bickley Moss:
Cholmondeley Arms
Malpas, Cheshire. **Tel** *01829 720300.*
The menu in this family-friendly
pub includes the very best of
traditional local cuisine. Children
will adore the desserts – baked
syrup sponge, black cherry
Pavlova, bakewell tart, ice creams
and sorbets. Accommodation is
also available.

Bretforton: *Fleece Inn*
Near Evesham. **Tel** *01386 831173.*
This real ale pub with its half-
timbered façade is also a National
Trust property. Beautifully located
in the Vale of Evesham. Rooms
available. Parking in village square.

Farnborough:
Inn at Farnborough
Near Banbury. **Tel** *01295 690615.*
Classy inn in a Grade II listed
free house from the 1700s. This
inn serves delicious local cuisine,
including sumptuous organic
steak burgers. Large garden and
conservatory.

Shrewsbury: *Armoury*
Welsh Bridge, Victoria Quay.
Tel *01743 340525.*
This converted 18th-century
warehouse, with views over the
river, is a popular open-plan
venue. Go early if you want
to enjoy a leisurely sit-down
meal.

Welford-on-Avon:
The Bell Inn
Nr Stratford-upon-Avon,
Warwickshire. **Tel** *01789 750353.*
This lovely 17th-century country
pub serves wonderful real ale and
traditional bar food. The Bell Inn
lies just a short distance southwest
of Stratford-upon-Avon. There is
a delightful seating area in the
garden.

Key to Symbols *see back cover flap*

Wenlock Edge:
Wenlock Edge Inn
Hilltop, nr Much Wenlock, Shropshire.
Tel 01746 785678.
This award-winning pub is
popular with walkers – there
is a comprehensive selection
of maps and guidebooks on
stand-by. A fairly homely affair,
Wenlock Edge Inn serves good
bar food and ales. Three rooms
are available on a bed and breakfast basis. 🍴 🖼 🧍 ♿

EAST MIDLANDS

Alderwasley: *The Bear Inn*
Belper, Derbyshire. *Tel 01629 822585.*
Friendly country pub with real
olde-worlde charm, The Bear Inn
serves a good range of real ales
and delicious cuisine. Popular with
locals and visitors alike. Ten rooms
are also available. 🍴 🖼 🧍 ♿

Birchover: *Druid Inn*
Main St, nr Matlock Derbyshire.
Tel 01629 650302.
In the lovely village of Birchover,
the old but beautifully revamped
Druid Inn has an excellent local
menu. Legend has it that the nearby Row Tor rocks were once a
place of Druid rituals. 🍴 🎵 🖼
🧍 ↗

Grimsthorpe: *Black Horse*
Grimsthorpe Bourne, Lincolnshire.
Tel 01788 591093.
Nestled just below Grimsthorpe
Castle, this early 18th-century
inn has been renovated into a
high-class pub-eaterie. Lovers
of the outdoors will enjoy the
rambling grounds and lakeside
nature trail. Return to enjoy the
cosy atmosphere of the bar
and spend the night in one of
the three charmingly old-fashioned
rooms. 🍴 🖼 🧍

Hathersage:
Plough Inn
Leadmill Bridge, Hope Valley,
Derbyshire. *Tel 01433 650319.*
Enjoying an idyllic location
on the banks of River Derwent,
the 16th-century Plough Inn is set
on nine acres of private parklands
and offers the perfect summer stop
off. Fabulous food, great views
and six en suite rooms. 🍴 🖼 🧍

Lyddington:
Old White Hart
51 Main St, Rutland.
Tel 01572 821 703.
Charming country inn with an
award-winning à la carte menu.
The Old White Hart has lovingly
retained the oak-beamed ceilings,
exposed brick walls and open
fires of the renovated 17th-century
stone building. 🍴 🖼 🧍 ↗

Mumby: *Red Lion*
Hogsthorpe Rd, Lincolnshire.
Tel 01507 490391.
Run by the local Bateman's
Brewery, this pub is an excellent
choice to sample the flavours of
Lincolnshire. On the menu are
traditional dishes prepared with
locally sourced ingredients.
🍴 🖼 🧍 ♿

Nottingham: *Cock and Hoop*
25 High Pavement, Nottingham.
Tel 0115 852 3231.
This traditional Victorian Ale
House offers a friendly, civilised
retreat where punters can enjoy
superb real ale and excellent wines.
The restaurant serves excellent
British home cooking. Small dogs
welcome. 🍴 🧍

Stamford:
The George of Stamford
71 St Martins, Lincolnshire.
Tel 01780 750750.
One of England's most famous
coaching inns, the George's bar,
restaurant and rooms are all rich
in history. Other than the award-
winning restaurant menu, there
are also more informal pub food
choices served in the ivy-covered
courtyard and in the York Bar.
🍴 🎵 🖼 🧍 ♿

LANCASHIRE AND THE LAKES

Ambleside: *The Britannia Inn*
Elterwater, Cumbria.
Tel 015394 37210.
This traditional inn began life
as a farmhouse and cobbler's.
Standing on the village green and
surrounded by stunning scenery, it
is a delightful place to unwind in
after a day's walk. There are also
nine en suite rooms. 🍴 🖼 🧍

Clitheroe: *The Shireburn Arms*
Hurst Green, Lancashire.
Tel 01254 826678.
Located in a picturesque village,
this characterful 17th-century inn
was one of author JRR Tolkein's
favourite haunts. The Shireburn
Arms takes its name from the family who built Stonyhurst College and
nearby almshouses. 🍴 🖼 🧍 ♿

Downham: *Assheton Arms*
Downham, Lancashire.
Tel 01200 441227.
Previously known as The George
and Dragon, this pub was renamed
following the elevation of the local
squire, Ralph Assheton, to Lord
Clitheroe. Facing the old church in
a pretty village of stone cottages,
it has even been featured in films
and television series. Specialities
on the menu include seafood
and stone-cooked steaks. 🍴 🧍

Hawkshead:
Queen's Head Hotel
Main St, Cumbria. *Tel 01539 436271.*
Situated at the heart of one of the
prettiest Lake District villages.
The superb food ranges from
simple sandwiches at the bar to
full meals at the restaurant. William
Wordsworth was schooled in this
village. 🍴 🖼 🧍

Hawkshead: *Tower Bank Arms*
Near Sawrey, Hawkshead, Cumbria.
Tel 01539 436334.
Standing in a picturesque village,
this 17th-century inn is very close
to Hill Top, where the legendary
children's book author Beatrix
Potter once lived. It even features
in one of her well-known stories,
The Tale of Jemima Puddle-Duck.
Three letting rooms. 🍴 🖼 🧍

Liverpool: *Ship and Mitre*
133 Dale St, Merseyside.
Tel 0151 236 0859.
Close to the city centre, this traditional pub has a reputation for
serving a wide range of real ales.
Hot food served daily. Pub quiz
on Thursdays. 🍴 🧍

Lonsdale: *Snooty Fox Tavern*
Main St, Kirkby Lonsdale, Cumbria.
Tel 01524 271308.
A listed Jacobean coaching inn in
the centre of the town, the Snooty
Fox lies in the picturesque Lune
Valley. Its rambling bars and
cobbled courtyard exude a quaint
charm. 🍴 🎵 🖼 🧍 ♿ ↗

Manchester: *Lass o' Gowrie*
36 Charles St. *Tel 0161 273 6932.*
Famous for its cask ales, this lively
pub is popular with students. The
menu offers a range of freshly
cooked food. Entertainment
comes in the form of live music
and comedy nights. 🍴 🎵 🧍 ↗

YORKSHIRE AND HUMBERSIDE

Askrigg: *Kings Arms*
Market Place, N Yorks.
Tel 01969 650817.
Fans of James Herriot's *All
Creatures Great and Small* will
recognize this as "The Drover's
Arms". There is a broad menu of
appetizing food and five real ales
on tap in the bar. 🍴 🖼 🧍 ↗

Driffield: *Wellington Inn*
19 The Green, Lund, Driffield, E
Yorks. *Tel 01377 217294.*
Just north of the minster town
of Beverley, this attractive pub
overlooks a charming village
green. Its fine food and friendly
service have won it an enviable
reputation. 🍴 🖼 🧍 ♿ ↗

Flamborough: *The Seabirds*
Tower St, Flamborough, E Yorks.
Tel *01262 850242.*
Near the bird sanctuary *(see pp400–401)* on the chalk cliffs of Flamborough Head, this pub is popular with both locals and walkers. The specialities on the menu revolve around fish, but a range of other dishes is on offer too. 🍴 🛏 🚶

Lancaster:
The Game Cock Inn
The Green Austwick, via Lancaster, N Yorks. **Tel** *01524 251226.*
Close to the Yorkshire "Three Peaks", this 17th-century coaching inn is the focal point of the tiny village. The award-winning food is home-cooked by a French chef, and the menus offer a range of options – everything from a simple snack to an elaborate dinner. Dog friendly and rooms available. 🍴 🛏 🚶 ♿

Leyburn: *The Blue Lion*
E Witton, Leyburn, N Yorks.
Tel *01969 624273.*
An 18th-century coaching and drover's inn within a charming Wensleydale village, it retains many original features. Open fires warm the rooms in winter. The food is traditional, but often with an unusual twist.
🍴 🛏 🚶 ♿

Pickering: *New Inn*
Cropton, Pickering, N Yorks.
Tel *01751 417330.*
With an award-winning bewery in the backyard, it's no wonder that this popular pub on the edge of the Moors can get busy. The warren of rooms includes several characterful dining areas. Brewery tours are available. 🍴 🎵

Skipton: *The Red Lion Hotel*
By the bridge, Burnsall, N Yorks.
Tel *01756 720204.*
Before the bridge was built across the Wharfe at Burnsall, this 16th-century inn used to operate a ferry across the river. Today, it has a reputation for fine food and its generous range of real ales and wine. Dogs welcome. 🍴 🛏 🚶 ♿

NORTHUMBRIA

Barnard Castle: *The Morritt Arms*
Greta Bridge, Barnard Castle,
Co Durham. **Tel** *01833 627232.*
Located between Carlisle and London, this 17th-century stone farmhouse eventually became a coaching inn. Dickens stayed here while writing *Nicholas Nickleby*. A mural by local artist John Gilroy depicts Dingley Dell from *The Pickwick Papers*. 🍴 🛏 🚶 ♿

Key to Symbols *see back cover flap*

Consett: *Lord Crewe Arms*
Blanchland, nr Consett, Co Durham.
Tel *01434 675251.*
Built in 1160 as the abbot's house, this delightful hotel faces an unusual enclosed cobbled square at the heart of a very pretty village. Dine in the formal restaurant or opt for the more casual style and menu at the bar. Dog friendly. Accommodation available. 🍴 🛏 🚶

Cornhill on Tweed: *Black Bull*
Etal Village, Northumb.
Tel *01890 820200.*
Close to the Norman castle in this attractive estate village, the award-winning Black Bull is famous as the only thatched pub in Northumberland. Ingredients for the home-cooked food are sourced locally wherever possible and the menu always includes tasty vegetarian options. 🍴 🛏 🚶 ♿ 🌿

Craster: *Jolly Fisherman*
Haven Hill, nr Alnwick, Northumb.
Tel *01665 576461.*
Unassuming local pub with lovely sea views. Home-made crab soup and seafood are specialities.
🍴 🛏 🚶 ♿ 🌿

Hedley on the Hill:
The Feathers Inn
Stocksfield, Northumb.
Tel *01661 843607.*
This family-run pub is popular with foodies, and serves traditional British fare. There is always a good selection of vegetarian dishes too and at least four guest ales on tap at the bar. 🍴 🎵 🛏 🚶 🌿

Hexham: *Dipton Mill Inn*
Dipton Mill Rd, Northumb.
Tel *01434 606577.*
Originally an 18th-century mill, this family-run pub lies beside Dipton Burn in a wooded valley. The characterful bar stocks a range of beers brewed next door, and serves home-made food. 🍴 🛏 🚶 ♿ 🌿

Kielder Water:
The Pheasant Inn
Stannersburn, Falstone, Northumb.
Tel *01434 240382.*
This 17th-century farmhouse has functioned as a pub for the last 250 years. Popular with visitors to Kielder Water and the surrounding forest. Meals are served at the bar, with the dining room opening for Sunday lunch and evening dinner.
🍴 🛏 🚶 ♿ 🌿

Newton: *Cook and Barker Inn*
Morpeth, Northumberland.
Tel *01665 575234.*
Once a forge, the inn got its name from its first proprietors, a Captain Cook who married a Miss Barker.

Dine à la carte in the restaurant, where the original fireplace and well remain. Hearty pub meals are available at the bar. Accommodation available. 🍴 🛏 🚶 ♿

Seahouses: *The Olde Ship Hotel*
Northumb. **Tel** *01665 720200.*
Situated above the tiny fishing harbour with a view across Farne Islands. Interesting nautical memorabilia decorate the bars. Pleasant beer garden. Accommodation is also available. 🍴 🛏 🚶 ♿

NORTH WALES

Capel Curig: *Bryn Tyrch Hotel*
Conwy. **Tel** *01690 720223.*
Pretty country inn in the heart of Snowdonia National Park, this is a popular stop-off point for walkers and climbers. Traditional Welsh cuisine. Great views of Mt Snowdon from the bar. 🍴 🛏 🚶 🌿

Ganllwyd: *Tyn-y-groes*
Dolgellau, Gwynedd.
Tel *01341 440275.*
Picturesque 16th-century inn in the heart of the Snowdonia National Park, Tyn-y-groes hotel and pub offers a friendly base for walking, mountain biking and fishing in the park. 🍴 🛏 🚶 ♿ 🌿

Glanwydden: *Queen's Head*
Llandudno. **Tel** *01492 546570.*
This bustling village pub has a reputed bar menu. Tables at the Queen's Head fill quickly so it is wise to arrive early. Great range of real ales. 🍴 🛏 🚶

Maentwrog: *Grapes Hotel*
Blaenau Ffestiniog, Gwynedd.
Tel *01766 590365.*
Said to be haunted, this Grade II listed coaching inn serves fine ales and home-made cuisine in a stunning setting. Pitch pine pews, exposed stone walls and a roaring fire in winter all add to the effect. 🍴 🎵 🛏 🚶 ♿

Holywell: *The Black Lion*
Babell, Holywell, Flintshire.
Tel *01352 720239.*
The Black Lion can trace its roots back to the 13th century. Today this quiet country pub, near the A55, is popular with diners and Real Ale enthusiasts. 🍴 🛏

Mold: *Glasfryn*
Raikes Lane, Sychdyn, Mold.
Tel *01352 750500.*
Pretty village pub known for its theatre-going clientele (Theatre Clwyd is just next door), Glasfryn is a converted farmhouse pub with a warm welcome. Good menu and wine list. 🍴 🛏 🚶 ♿

Nant Gwynant: *Pen-y-Gwryd*
Gwynedd. *Tel* 01286 870211.
Hotel with a bustling pub in
the shadow of Mt Snowdon. It is
here that the 1953 Everest team
holed up here while training for
the ultimate ascent. Popular with
walkers for its prime location, it
also serves great food and drink.
🍴 🛏 🐕 ♿

Overton Bridge:
Cross Foxes Inn
Erbistock, Wrexham, Clwyd.
Tel 01978 780380.
Fabulous food in a fabulous
setting, Cross Foxes Inn, on the
banks of the River Dee, is a very
welcoming 18th-century coaching
inn with a distinctive dining room.
Good choice of real ales.
🍴 🛏 🐕 ♿

SOUTH AND MID-WALES

Aberaeron: *Harbourmaster*
Pen Cei, Ceredigion.
Tel 01545 570755.
Fabulous hotel-pub overlooking
the town's picturesque harbour.
This blue-washed building serves
tasty seafood such as Cardigan Bay
crab and lobster, Aberaeron mackerel and several other such freshly
caught delicacies in its restaurant.
Also has 13 rooms. 🍴 🛏 🐕 ♿

Aberystwyth: *Halfway Inn*
Devils Bridge Rd, Pisgah.
Tel 01970 880631.
Halfway between Aberystwyth and
Devil's Bridge (hence the name),
this large inn has steadily built a
strong reputation for its fine food
and fabulous real ale. Designated
restaurant area away from the bar.
🍴 🛏 🐕 🚶

Brecon: *Griffin at Felin Fach*
Felin Fach, Brecon.
Tel 01874 602111.
Comfy leather sofas piled with
soft cushions, roaring log fires in
winter and a gorgeous garden for
summer drinking and dining, the
Griffin has it all. Food and ales are
locally sourced (many ingredients
are home-grown) and there's a
great choice of fine wines, sherries
and spirits too. Seven beautifully
furnished and comfortable rooms
complete the picture. 🍴 🐕 ♿

East Aberthaw: *Blue Anchor*
Barry, S Glamorgan.
Tel 01446 750329.
This refurbished, thatched pub in
the seaside town of Barry is just
16 km (10 miles) from Cardiff,
Blue Anchor has a friendly little bar
as well as an elegant restaurant
serving superior cuisine. Estuary
walks nearby. 🍴 🛏 🐕 ♿

Hay-on-Wye: *The Pandy Inn*
Dorstone, Herefordshire.
Tel 01981 550273.
A picturesque pub with rooms
just over the border in Herefordshire, The Pandy Inn boasts a long
and illustrious history. Supposedly
the oldest pub in the county, it
played host to Oliver Cromwell
during the 17th-century Civil
War. The restaurant seats 50
and serves wholesome, filling
and tasty food. Dogs welcome.
🍴 🎵 🛏 🐕

Pembroke Ferry: *Ferry Inn*
Pembroke Dock.
Tel 01646 682947.
This early 17th-century inn
serves delicious seafood in a
prime location overlooking
the harbour. Ferry Inn has an
extensive waterfront terrace,
which is a perfect setting for
languid summer dining. Check
out the specials board for
locally caught fish.
🍴 🎵 🛏 🐕 ♿

Penallt: *Boat Inn*
Lone Lane. *Tel* 01600 712615.
With a stunning location on the
banks of River Wye, the beer
garden of Boat Inn is a great
place to relax with a chilled
drink on a warm summer's
day. Bar food is available.
Access is via a footbridge. 🍴 🎵
🛏 🐕

Tintern:
The Rose & Crown Inn
Monmouth Rd, Monmouthshire.
Tel 01291 689254.
On the banks of the River Wye, in
a designated Area of Outstanding
Natural Beauty, the Rose &
Crown dates back to at least
1835. Walkers and dogs welcome.
🍴 🐕 ♿

Usk: *Nag's Head*
Twyn Sq. *Tel* 01291 672820.
Atmospheric village pub with
an extensive menu that is very
reasonably priced for the size
of the portions. The warmly
welcoming establishment places
an emphasis on the home-made
food, but there is also a bustling
bar area. 🍴 🛏 🐕 ♿

THE LOWLANDS

Edinburgh:
Café Royal Circle Bar
West Register St. *Tel* 0131 556 1884.
This atmospheric pub features
tiled portraits of Scottish worthies
and ornate chandeliers. Sink back
into one of the comfortable leather
chairs for a drink before making
your way to the oyster bar and
restaurant. 🍴

Elie: *Ship Inn*
The Harbour, Fife. *Tel* 01333 330 246.
Quayside pub with nautical decor
and attractive views. Summer
barbecues. 🍴 🎵 🛏 🐕 🚶

Glasgow: *Horseshoe*
17–19 Drury St. *Tel* 0141 248 6368.
Busy Victorian pub with a long
bar and plenty of period features.
Good value bar snacks. Karaoke
in the evenings. 🍴 🎵 🐕

Isle of Whithorn: *Steam Packet*
Isle of Whithorn, Dumfries &
Galloway. *Tel* 01988 500 334.
Superb setting on a lovely harbour.
Pleasant eating areas and a good
selection of real ales. Boat trips
from the harbour. 🍴 🛏 🐕

THE HIGHLANDS AND ISLANDS

Applecross: *Applecross Inn*
Shore St, Wester Ross, Highland.
Tel 01520 744262.
Spectacularly located beyond
Britain's highest mountain pass,
this pub overlooks the Isle of Skye.
Local seafood is served, and there
is music once a week in season.
🍴 🎵 🛏 🐕 ♿

Dundee: *Fishermans Tavern*
10–16 Fort St, Broughty Ferry, Tayside.
Tel 01382 775941.
Choose between award-winning
real ales and the extensive
selection of malts, or savour a
little of both. Good seafront and
views of the Tay Rail Bridge.
Rooms available. 🍴 🐕 🎵

Isle of Skye: *Praban Bar at
Eilean Iarmain.* Isle Ornsay, Isle of
Skye. *Tel* 01471 833332.
Welcoming hotel bar. Lots of malts
and good bar food. Gorgeous
setting. 🍴 🎵 🛏 🐕 ♿

Loch Lomond: *Oak Tree Inn*
Balmaha, (E side). *Tel* 01360 870357.
Traditional stone inn with a well-
stocked bar, restaurant and B&B.
Sit by the roaring fires in winter
and snack on the tasty bar food
that is served all day. 🍴 🎵 🛏 🐕

Portsoy: *The Shore Inn*
The Old Harbour, Banffshire.
Tel 01261 842831.
A 300-year-old seafaring inn
nestled in a picturesque harbour.
Traditional cask ale and a real
open fire. 🍴 🎵 🐕 🚶

Ullapool: *Ferry Boat Inn*
Shore St, Highland. *Tel* 01854 612366.
Good whiskies, bar lunches and
fine views over the harbour. Coal
fires and big windows overlooking
the loch. 🍴 🎵 🐕

SHOPPING IN BRITAIN

While the West End of London (see pp148–51) is undeniably the most exciting place to shop in Britain, many of the regional towns and cities offer nearly as wide a range of goods. Moreover, regional shopping can be less stressful, less expensive, and remarkably varied, with craft studios, farm shops, street markets and factory

Vivienne Westwood's designer label

outlets adding to the enjoyment of bargain-hunting. Britain is famous for its country clothing: wool, waxed cotton and tweed are all popular, along with classic prints such as Liberty or Laura Ashley and tartan. Other particularly British goods include antiques, floral soaps and scents, porcelain, glass and local crafts.

Antiques stall at Bermondsey Market

SHOPPING HOURS

In general, shops in Britain open during the week from 9am or 10am, and close after 5pm or 6pm. Hours on Saturdays may be shorter. Many town centre shops open on Sundays. Some stores open late for one evening a week – Thursday in London's West End – while village shops may close at lunch-time, or for one afternoon each week. Market days vary from town to town.

HOW TO PAY

Most large shops all over the UK accept well-known credit cards such as Access and VISA. Charge cards such as American Express or Diners Club are acceptable in some places, but markets and some small shops do not take credit cards. Traveller's cheques can be used in larger stores, though exchange rates for non-sterling cheques may be poor. Take your passport with you for

identification. Few places accept cheques drawn on foreign banks. Cash is still the most popular way to pay for small purchases.

RIGHTS AND REFUNDS

If something you buy is defective, you are entitled to a refund, provided you have kept your receipt as proof of purchase and return the goods in the same condition as when you bought them, preferably in the same packaging. This may not always apply to sale goods clearly marked as seconds, imperfect, or shop-soiled. Inspect these carefully before you buy. You do not have to accept a credit note in place of a cash refund.

ANNUAL SALES

Sales take place during January, and in June and July, when nearly every shop cuts prices to get rid of old stock. But you may find special offers at any time of the year. Some

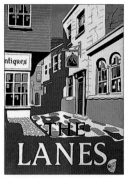

Sign for the Lanes, Brighton
(see p175)

shops begin winter sales just before Christmas. Department stores and fashion houses have some excellent bargains for keen shoppers; one of the most prestigious sales is at Harrods *(see p97)*, where queues form long before opening time.

VAT AND TAX-FREE SHOPPING

Value added tax (VAT) is charged on most goods and services sold in Britain – exceptions are food, books and children's clothes. It is usually included in the advertised price. Visitors from outside the European Union who stay less than three months may claim this tax back. Take your passport with you when you go shopping. You must complete a form in the shop when you buy goods and give a copy to the customs authorities when you leave the country. You may have to show your goods as proof of purchase. If you arrange to have goods shipped from the store, VAT should be deducted before you pay.

OUT-OF-TOWN SHOPPING CENTRES

These large complexes, built in the style of North American malls, are rapidly increasing around Britain. The advantages of car access and cheap parking are undeniable, and most centres are accessible by public transport too. The centres usually feature popular high street stores, with facilities such as cafés, crèches, restaurants and cinemas.

A traditional shop front in Stonegate, York *(see p404)*

DEPARTMENT STORES

A few big department stores, such as Harrods, are only found in London, but others have provincial branches. John Lewis, for example, has shops all over the country. It sells a huge range of fabrics, clothing and household items, combining quality service with good value. Marks & Spencer, with branches in most major towns and cities in Britain, is famed for its good-value clothing and pre-prepared food. Debenhams and British Home Stores (BHS) are other well-known general stores with inexpensive clothing and home furnishings. Habitat is a reputable supplier of modern furniture. The sizes of all these stores, and the range of stock they carry, differs from region to region.

Local Teesdale cheeses

CLOTHES SHOPS

Once again, London has the widest range, from *haute couture* to cheap and cheerful items ready-made. Shopping for clothing in the regions, however, can often be less tiring. Many towns popular with tourists – Oxford, Bath and York for instance – have independently owned clothes shops where you are likely to receive a more personal service. Or you could try one of the chain stores in any high street such as Laura Ashley or Next for smart, reasonably priced clothes, and Topshop, Oasis and Miss Selfridge for younger and cheaper fashions.

SUPERMARKETS AND FOODSHOPS

Supermarkets are a good way to shop for food. The range and quality of items is usually excellent. Several large chains compete for market share, and as a result prices are generally lower than in smaller shops. Sainsbury, Tesco, Asda, Morrisons and Waitrose are some of the national names. The smaller town-centre shops such as bakeries, green-grocers or farm shops, may give you a more interesting choice of regional produce, and a more personal service.

SOUVENIR, GIFT AND MUSEUM SHOPS

Buying presents is a must for most travellers. Most reputable, large stores can arrange freight of high-value

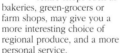

The Mustard Shop *(see p201)*, Norwich

items. If you want to buy things you can carry back in your suitcase, the choice is wide. You can buy attractive, well-made, portable craft items all over the country, especially in areas tourists are likely to visit. For slightly more unusual presents, have a look in museum shops and the gifts available in National Trust *(see p29)* and English Heritage *(see p671)* properties.

SECOND-HAND AND ANTIQUE SHOPS

Britain's long history means there are many interesting artifacts to be found. A visit to any of Britain's stately homes will reveal a passion for antiques. Most towns have an antique or bric-a-brac (miscellaneous second-hand items) shop or two. Look for auctions – tourist information centres *(see pp668–9)* can help you to locate them. You may like to visit a car boot sale or charity shop in the hope of picking up a bargain.

Book stall, Hay-on-Wye, Wales *(see p461)*

MARKETS

Large towns and cities usually have a central covered market which operates most week-days, selling everything from fresh produce to pots and pans. The information under each town entry in this guide lists market days. Many towns hold weekly markets in the main square, while Farmers' Markets have become increasingly popular and are a good place to source fresh, organic produce from British farms.

ENTERTAINMENT IN BRITAIN

L ondon is without a doubt the entertainment capital of Britain *(see pp152–5)*, with a whole wealth of shows, films and concerts to choose from, but many regional theatres, opera houses and concert halls also have varied programmes. Edinburgh, Manchester, Leeds,

Punch and Judy show

Birmingham, and Bristol in particular have a lot to offer and there are a number of summer arts festivals around the country such as those at Bath and Aldeburgh *(see pp62–3)*. Ticket prices vary but are usually cheaper outside the capital and when booked in advance.

SOURCES OF INFORMATION

In London, check the listings magazines, such as *Time Out*, or the *Evening Standard*, London's evening newspaper. All of the high-brow newspapers *(see p679)* provide comprehensive arts reviews and listings of the cultural events and shows throughout the country. Local newspapers, libraries, or tourist offices *(see p669)* can supply details of regional events. Specialist magazines such as *NME* give up-to-date news of the pop music scene and are available from any newsagent.

THEATRES

Britain has an enduring theatrical tradition dating back to Shakespeare *(see pp324–5)* and beyond. All over the country, amateurs and professionals tread the boards in auditoriums, pubs, clubs and village halls. Production and performance standards are generally high, and British actors have an

international reputation. London is the place to enjoy theatre at its most varied and glamorous *(see p152)*. The West End alone has more than 50 theatres *(see p153)* ranging from elaborate Edwardian, to Modernist-style buildings such as the National Theatre on the South Bank.

In Stratford-upon-Avon, the Royal Shakespeare Company presents a year-round programme of Shakespeare, as well as avant-garde and experimental plays. Bristol also has a long dramatic tradition, the Theatre Royal *(see p256)* is the oldest working theatre in Britain. Some of the best productions outside the capital can be found at the West Yorkshire Playhouse in Leeds, the Royal Exchange in Manchester *(see p372)* and the Traverse in Edinburgh. Open-air theatre ranges from the free street entertainment found in many

Street entertainer

city centres, to student performances on the grounds of university colleges, or a production at Cornwall's clifftop amphitheatre, the Minack Theatre *(see p276)*. Every fourth year, York also stages a series of open-air medieval mystery plays called the York Cycle. Perhaps the liveliest theatrical tradition in Britain is the Edinburgh Festival *(see p509)*. Ticket availability varies from show to show. For a midweek matinee, you may be able to buy a ticket at the door, but for the more popular West End shows tickets may have to be booked weeks or months in advance. You can book through agencies and some travel agents, and most hotels will organize tickets for you. Booking fees are often charged. Beware of tickets offered by touts *(see p67)* – these may be counterfeit. There are no age restrictions in Britain's theatres.

MUSIC

A diverse musical repertoire can be found in a variety of venues. Church choral music is a national tradition, and many churches and cathedrals host concerts. London, Manchester, Birmingham, Liverpool, Bristol and Bournemouth all have their own excellent orchestras. Major cities also have grand opera houses.

Rock, jazz, folk and country-and-western concerts are staged periodically in pubs and clubs. Wales has a strong musical tradition; northern England is known for its booming brass and silver bands; and Scotland has its famous bag-pipers *(see p480)*.

The Buxton Opera House, the Midlands

The multiplex Vue West End cinema, Leicester Square, London

CINEMAS

The latest films can be seen in any large town. Check the local papers or the tourist office to find out what is on.

Cinemas are having a revival, with luxurious multi-screen cinemas taking over from the local, single-screen cinemas. In larger cities a more diverse range of films is often on offer including foreign-language productions. These tend to be shown at arts or repertory cinemas. Mainstream English-speaking films are usually shown by the big chains. Age limits apply to certain films. Young children are allowed to see any feature film which is graded with a U (universal) or PG (parental guidance) certificate. Cinema prices vary widely; some are cheaper at off-peak times, such as Mondays or afternoons. For new releases it is advisable to book in advance.

CLUBS

Most cities have some sort of club scene, though London has the most famous venues (see p155). These may feature live music, discos, or DJ or dance performances. Some insist on dress codes or members only, and most have doormen, or "bouncers". Apart from the major cities, Brighton and Bristol have lively clubs.

DANCE

This covers a multitude of activities: everything from classical ballet and acid-house parties to traditional English Morris dancing or the Scottish Highland fling, which you may come upon in pubs and villages around the country.

Dance halls are rarer than they were, but ballroom dancing is alive and well. Other dance events you may find are ceilidhs (pronounced kay-lee), which is Celtic dancing and music; May Balls often held at universities (invitation only); dinner or tea dances and square dancing.

Birmingham is home to the Birmingham Royal Ballet and is the best place to see performances outside London. Avant-garde contemporary dance is also performed.

GAY

Most large communities will have some gay meeting places, mostly bars and clubs. You can find out about them from publications such as the free *Pink Paper* or *Gay Times* on sale in some newsagents, and in gay bars and clubs. London's gay life is centred around Soho (see p80) with its many European-style cafés and bars. Outside London, the most active gay scenes are in Manchester and Brighton. Gay Pride is the largest free outdoor festival in Europe.

Three revellers, Gay Pride Festival

CHILDREN

London offers children a positive goldmine of fun, excitement and adventure, though it can be expensive. From the traditional sights to something more unusual such as a discovery centre, London has a wide range of activities, many interactive, to interest children of all ages. The weekly magazine *Time Out* has details of children's events.

Outside London, activities for children range from nature trails to fun fairs. Your local tourist office or the local library will have information on things to do with children.

Pirate Ship, Chessington World of Adventures, Surrey

THEME PARKS

Theme parks in Britain are enjoyed by children of all ages. Alton Towers has conventional rides plus a motor museum. Chessington World of Adventures is a huge complex south of London. Based on a zoo, it includes nine themed areas, such as Forbidden Kingdom and Pirates Cove. Legoland is fantastic for younger children. Thorpe Park is a large, watery theme park full of model buildings and a peaceful pet farm.

Alton Towers
Alton, Staffordshire.
Tel 0871 222 3330.
www.altontowers.com

Chessington World of Adventures
Leatherhead Rd, Chessington, Surrey.
Tel 0871 663 4477.
www.chessington.co.uk

Legoland
Winkfield Rd, Windsor, Berkshire.
Tel 0871 222 2001.
www.legoland.co.uk

Thorpe Park
Staines Rd, Chertsey, Surrey.
Tel 0871 663 1673.
www.thorpepark.com

SPECIALIST HOLIDAYS AND OUTDOOR ACTIVITIES

Britain offers a wide variety of special interest holidays and courses, where you can learn a new sport or skill, practise an activity you enjoy, or simply have fun and meet people. If you prefer less structured activities, there are numerous options to choose from, such

Cycling on the Gower Peninsular, Wales

as walking in Britain's national parks, pony trekking in Wales, surfing in Cornwall or skiing in Scotland. There are also several spectator sports for those who like to watch rather than participate, including Premier League football, test match cricket and historic horse races.

Arvon Foundation writing week at Totleigh Barton in Devon

SPECIAL INTEREST HOLIDAYS

There are a number of special interest holidays and residential courses available in Great Britain. One advantage of this type of vacation is that you can attend a course alone, and yet have plenty of congenial company – most people are delighted to meet others who share their interests. Whatever your passion, you are likely to come across a holiday package that suits your needs.

Centres such as **Wye Valley Art Centre** in Gloucestershire and **West Dean College**, West Sussex, offer engaging, residential courses in arts and crafts. These can range from familiar activities such as drawing and painting to more esoteric subjects such as mosaic art and glass engraving. Those interested in writing can enroll at the **Arvon Foundation**, which organizes week-long courses in fiction, poetry, songwriting and TV drama at four rural retreats in Devon,

Shropshire, West Yorkshire and Invernesshire. The **Ashburton Cookery School** in Devon and **Cookery at the Grange** in Somerset offer fun cookery courses with lots of hands-on involvement. Non-carnivores might try the Vegetarian Society's **Cordon Vert School** in Cheshire, which has innovative cookery courses catering to chefs at all levels – from complete beginners to talented amateurs.

Companies such as **Hidden Britain Tours**, **Inscape Tours** and the **Back-Roads Touring Company** provide themed holidays. History lovers can opt for a tour of King Arthur's Country or Shakespeare's England. Other tours designed for motor enthusiasts, garden lovers or fans of rock and roll are also available.

The prices of such holidays include expert guidance, transport, entry fees to attractions and accommodation, which could be anything from a farmhouse to a medieval castle.

WALKING

Walking is a popular activity in Britain and a network of long-distance footpaths and shorter routes criss-crosses the country *(see pp36–7)*. It is also an excellent way to experience the spectacular variety of the British landscape, either by yourself or with a group. An advantage is that most routes are away from major tourist sites and often pass through picturesque villages that are off the beaten track.

The **Ramblers' Association** is Britain's main walking body, and its website provides useful information on most routes and walking areas. It also publishes a range of books, including *Walk Britain*, which lists many good walks as well as suitable hotels, bed and breakfasts and hostels along the way.

There is no shortage of companies providing guided and self-guided holidays for walkers. The cost of these holiday packages should cover

Walking on Holyhead Mountain near South Stack Anglesey, Wales

accommodation, transport and detailed route guides. **Ramblers' Countrywide Holidays** offers guided group walks through some of the country's most splendid landscapes. **Sherpa Expeditions** has a variety of self-led walks. Pick a challenging 15-day coast-to-coast walk, or a more leisurely ramble along South Downs Way. Individual companies will advise you on the level of fitness required and the type of clothing and footwear that will be needed.

If you are planning to walk on your own, especially in remote areas, remember that it is essential to not only be well equipped, but to also leave details of your route with someone.

Mountain biking in Yorkshire

CYCLING

The country's tranquil lanes, bridleways and designated tracks are perfect for cyclists who want to explore the back roads of Britain. Depending on your level of fitness, you may opt for demanding routes through mountainous areas such as the magnificent West Highland Way in Scotland *(see p494)*. Those who would like to take it easy can enjoy a relaxed tour along Devon's lanes and take the opportunity to stop off for a sinfully rich cream tea.

Country Lanes offers a good variety of guided holidays in small groups around the west of England. The price includes an experienced leader, high quality bicycle equipment, accommodation, meals and

entry to attractions along the way. **Compass Holidays** and **Wheely Wonderful Cycling** concentrate on self-led tours, with routes throughout the country. They also provide bicycles, accommodation, detailed route maps, (including details of pubs, cafés and places of interest along the way) and appropriate luggage transport. Such self-guided bicycling holidays are ideal for families or groups of friends.

If you wish to organize your own cycling holiday, you may contact the **Cyclists' Touring Club**, which is Britain's main recreational cycling body, and **Sustrans**, the organization that formed the National Cycle Network. Both can provide a wealth of information about cycling in the country, including advice on matters such as bringing a bike into Britain, taking your bike on the train and the rules of the road. *Cycling in the UK*, the official guide book for the National Cycle Network, has route details and maps for many of the best rides, and also offers tips on how to hire a bike and what to do along the way.

HORSE RIDING AND PONY TREKKING

There are good riding centres in most parts of Britain, but certain areas are especially suitable for this invigorating activity. The best of these locations include the New Forest *(see p168)*, the South Downs *(see p181)*, the Yorkshire Dales National Park *(see pp384–6)* and the Brecon Beacons on the border between Wales and England *(see pp468–9)*.

Pony trekking holidays are also becoming very popular, and generally include basic training, a guide, meals and accommodation. These vacations are perfect for novice riders and children since the ponies are very well-trained and rarely proceed above a canter. The **British Horse Society** has all the information on where to ride as well as a list of approved riding schools that offer training. You can also consult the **Equine Tourism** website for information on riding centres

Horse riding on a country bridleway *(see p37)*

and horse-riding holidays. National park information offices can also provide details of the many equestrian centres that organize riding holidays in or around national parks.

GOLF

Over a quarter of Britain's 2000-odd golf clubs are in Scotland, which is unsurprising given that the ancient game was invented here. The first formal club was established in Edinburgh in 1744.

Today, the best known clubs are Carnoustie and St Andrews in Scotland, Royal St George's in England and Celtic Manor in Wales. These high-profile clubs only admit players above a certain handicap. Most other clubs, however, are more relaxed and welcome visitors.

Green fees vary greatly, as do the facilities offered by various clubs. Some clubs may ask to see a valid handicap certificate before they allow a player on the course. Failing that, a letter of introduction from a home club may be sufficient.

Specialist operators such as **Golf Vacations UK** and **Great Golf Holidays** can smooth the way to the first hole considerably by booking golf packages. They will organize travel and accommodation, reserve tee times and pay the green fees. They will also help you get temporary membership of a club if required.

If you wish to go it alone, the **Golf Club of Great Britain** can provide information on where to play. They also have an affiliated website for nonresidents of the UK.

SURFING

The best areas for surfing are in the West Country and South Wales. Tuition is available at many resorts, and equipment can be hired.

The Cornwall-based **British Surfing Association** runs its own surf school with professional coaching catering to a range of abilities, from novices to advanced competition surfers. Other companies that offer good surfing courses include **Surf South West** in Devon and the **Welsh Surfing Federation Surf School** in South Wales.

Sailing in Cardigan Bay, Welsh coast

BOATING AND SAILING

The British are extremely enthusiastic about boating and sailing. The network of rivers, lakes and canals ensures an abundance of boating sites. Many excellent choices are available – the Isle of Wight and the south coast are full of pleasure crafts. Several inland areas such as the Lake District (*see pp354–69*) are among the most widely favoured. Canal cruising is also very popular (*see p689*) and the Norfolk Broads (*see p198*) provide one of the best inland boating experiences. Check with the **Broads Authority** for details.

Many sailing courses are available. The **Royal Yachting Association** can provide lists of approved courses and training centres around Britain. One of the most trusted is Dorset's **Weymouth & Portland National Sailing Academy**, which has a range of courses to suit all ages and levels of ability. The **Falmouth School**

of **Sailing** in Cornwall is a privately owned sailing and powerboat school, which conducts lessons in the enclosed, safe waters of the Fal Estuary. Courses include basic "taster sessions", one-to-one tuition for adults and children, as well as group lessons.

SKIING

Facilities for skiing are limited in the UK, especially since the weather is rather unreliable. However, skiing enthusiasts can head for Scotland, which has a range of challenging slopes. **Ski Scotland**, the official ski site of the Scottish Tourist Board, has information about ski packages, accommodation, up-to-date weather conditions and details of the main ski areas, including the Cairngorms and the Nevis Range. **Snowsport Scotland**, the governing body for all Scottish snowsports, provides information on other snow-based activities such as Nordic skiing and snowboarding.

FISHING

Fishing, both on the sea and in rivers, is one of Britain's most popular participation sports. Regulations, however, are strict and can be rather complicated. It is advisable to check for details about rod licences, close seasons and other restrictions at tourist offices or tackle shops, or with the **Angling Trust** in Leominster.

The best game fishing (trout and salmon) is in the West Country, the Northeast, Wales and Scotland. Also, there are several websites with links to specialist operators who arrange fishing holidays.

Solitary sea fisherman, England's southeast coast

SPECTATOR SPORTS

Football (soccer) is a passion for a large section of the population. The English Premier League is run by the **Football Association** and is home to some of the world's top clubs, including **Manchester United** (*see p375*), **Arsenal FC** and **Chelsea FC**. The domestic football season runs from August to May. Tickets for Premier League games can be expensive and difficult to obtain, but it is worth attempting to get hold of returned or unsold tickets directly from the clubs.

The main tennis event of the year is Wimbledon, which is held at the **All England Lawn Tennis Club (AELTC)** in London. This two-week event takes place in the last week of June and the first week of July. The tournament sparks off a period of tennis fever in England, especially when British players such as Andy Murray progress in the competition. Most tickets for Centre Court are allocated by a public ballot. Check the official website of the AELTC for details on how to procure tickets. Around 6,000 tickets are available on the day of play (payment by cash only), except for the final four days of the tournament.

Rugby Football is administered by the **Rugby Football Union** and also has a good following. Games are played in cities such as Edinburgh, London and Cardiff.

Cricket, the English national game, is played from April to September. Tickets for country matches are relatively cheap. International test matches are played on historic grounds such as **Surrey County Cricket Club's** ground at the Oval in London, and the **Yorkshire County Cricket Club** situated at Headingley in Leeds.

Both steeplechasing and flat-racing are very popular, and betting is big business. The Grand National is the best-known steeplechase and runs at **Aintree Racecourse** in early April. The main flat-race meeting is **Royal Ascot**, which takes place in Berkshire towards the end of June.

DIRECTORY

SPECIAL INTEREST HOLIDAYS

Arvon Foundation
42A Buckingham Palace Rd, London SW1. *Tel* 020 7324 2554. www.arvonfoundation.org

Ashburton Cookery School
Old Exeter Rd, Ashburton, Devon TQ13. *Tel* 08432 895555. www.ashburton cookery school.co.uk

Back-Roads Touring Company
107 Paver Rd, London W4. *Tel* 020 8987 0990. www.backroads touring.co.uk

Cookery at the Grange
The Grange, Whatley, Frome, Somerset BA11. *Tel* 01373 836579. www.cookeryatthegrange.co.uk

Cordon Vert School
The Vegetarian Society, Parkdale, Dunham Rd, Altrincham, Cheshire WA14. *Tel* 0161 9252014. www.cordonvert.co.uk

Hidden Britain Tours
28 Chequers Rd, Basingstoke, Hampshire RG2 7PU. *Tel* 01256 814222. www.hidden britaintours.co.uk

Inscape Tours
35 Whitehall, London SW1A 2BX. *Tel* 020 7839 3988. www.inscapetours.co.uk

West Dean College
West Dean, Chichester, W Sussex PO18. *Tel* 01243 811301. www.westdean.org.uk

Wye Valley Art Centre
Llandogo, Monmouthshire NP25. *Tel* 01594 530214. www.wyearts.co.uk

WALKING

Ramblers' Association
2nd Floor, Camelford Hse, 87–90 Albert Embankment, London SE1. *Tel* 020 7339 8500. www.ramblers.org.uk

Ramblers' Countrywide Holidays
Box 43, Welwyn Garden City AL8. *Tel* 01707 386 800. www.ramblers countrywide.co.uk

Sherpa Expeditions
131A Heston Rd, Hounslow TW5. *Tel* 020 8577 2717. www.sherpa-walking-holidays.co.uk

CYCLING

Compass Holidays
Cheltenham Spa Railway Station, Queens Rd, Cheltenham, Gloucester-shire GL51. *Tel* 01242 250642. www.compass-holidays.com

Country Lanes
Brokenhurst New Forest. *Tel* 01590 622627. www.countrylanes.co.uk

Cyclists' Touring Club
Parklands, Railton Rd, Guildford GU2. *Tel* 0844 736 8450.

Sustrans
National Cycle Network Centre, 2 Cathedral Sq, College Green, Bristol BS1. *Tel* 0845 1130065. www.sustrans.org.uk

Wheely Wonderful Cycling
Petchfield Farm, Elton, Ludlow, Shropshire SY8. *Tel* 01568 770755.

HORSE RIDING AND PONY TREKKING

British Horse Society
Abbey Park, Stareton, Kenilworth, Warwickshire CV8. *Tel* 0844 848 1666. www.bhs.org.uk

Equine Tourism
Holt Ball, Luccombe, Somerset TA24. *Tel* 01643 862785. www.equinetourism.co.uk

GOLF

Golf Club of Great Britain
338 Hook Rd, Chessington, Surrey KT6. *Tel* 020 8391 4666. www.golfclubgb.co.uk

Golf Vacations UK
Tel 01228 598098. www.golfvacationsuk.com

Great Golf Holidays
Tel 01637 879951. www.greatgolfholidays.com

SURFING

British Surfing Association
The International Surfing Centre, Fistral Beach, Newquay, Cornwall TR7. *Tel* 01637 876474. www.sup-surfing.org.uk

Surf South West
PO Box 39, Croyde, N Devon EX33. *Tel* 01271 890400. www.surf southwest.com

Welsh Surfing Federation Surf School
The Barn, The Croft, Llangennith, Swansea SA3. *Tel* 01792 386426. www.wsfsurfschool.co.uk

BOATING AND SAILING

Broads Authority
18 Colegate, Norwich, Norfolk NR3. *Tel* 01603 610734. www.broads-authority.gov.uk

Falmouth School of Sailing
Grove Place, Falmouth, Cornwall TR11. *Tel* 01326 211311. www.falmouth-school-of-sailing.co.uk

Royal Yachting Association
RYA House, Ensign Way, Southampton, Hampshire SO31. *Tel* 023 8060 4100. www.rya.org.uk

Weymouth & Portland National Sailing Academy
Osprey Quay, Portland, Dorset DT5. *Tel* 01305 866 000. www.wpnsa.org.uk

SKIING

Ski Scotland
www.ski.visitscotland.com

Snowsport Scotland
Caledonian House, South Gyle, Edinburgh EH12. *Tel* 0131 625 4405. www.snowsportscotland.org

FISHING

Angling Trust
6 Rainbow St, Leominster, Herefordshire HR6 8DQ. *Tel* 0844 770 0616. www.anglingtrust.net

Fishing Net
www.fishingnet.com

Fishing UK
www.fishing.co.uk

SPECTATOR SPORTS

Aintree Racecourse
Ormskirk Rd, Aintree, Liverpool L9. *Tel* 0151 909 3719. www.aintree.co.uk

All England Lawn Tennis Club (AELTC)
Church Rd, Wimbledon, SW19. *Tel* 020 8944 1066. www.wimbledon.org

Arsenal FC
Emirates Stadium, 2 Gilders Way, Highbury, London N5. *Tel* 020 619 5000. www.arsenal.com

Chelsea FC
Stamford Bridge, Fulham Rd, London SW6. *Tel* 0871 984 1955. www.chelseafc.com

Football Association
16 Lancaster Gate, London W2. *Tel* 0844 980 8200. www.thefa.com

Manchester United
Sir Matt Busby Way, Old Trafford, Manchester M16. *Tel* 0161 868 8000. www.manutd.com

Royal Ascot
Ascot Racecourse, Ascot, Berkshire SL5. *Tel* 0844 346 3000. www.ascot.co.uk

Rugby Football Union
Rugby Rd, Twickenham, Middlesex TW1. *Tel* 0871 222 2120. www.rfu.com

Surrey County Cricket Club
The Kia Oval, Kennington, London SE11. *Tel* 020 7820 5700. www.kiaoval.com

Yorkshire County Cricket Club
Headingley Carnegie Cricket Ground, Leeds LS6. *Tel* 0871 971 1222. www.yorkshireccc.com

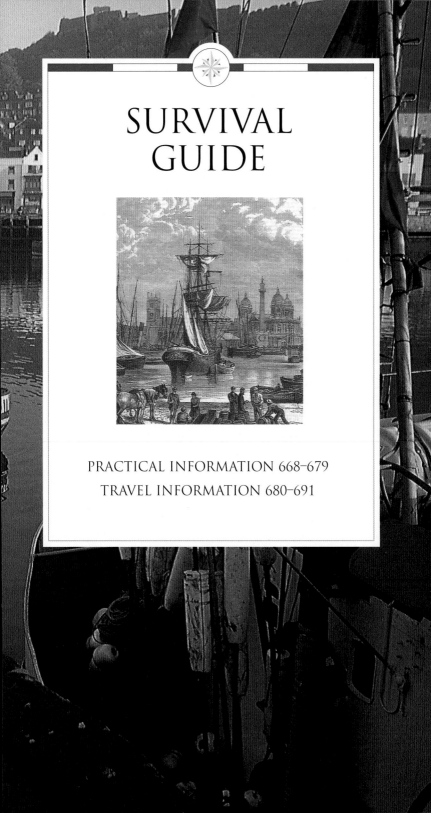

SURVIVAL
GUIDE

PRACTICAL INFORMATION 668–679

TRAVEL INFORMATION 680–691

PRACTICAL INFORMATION

Every year, millions of people from all over the world seek out what the British often take for granted: the country's ancient history, colourful pageantry, spectacularly varied countryside and wonderful coastline. The range of facilities on offer to visitors in Britain has improved considerably over the past few years. Be aware that prices vary within Britain, and regional differences can be very noticeable. London, not surprisingly, is the most expensive city, and the

A mounted sentry, London

knock-on effect extends to most of southern England, Britain's most affluent region. Food, accommodation, entertainment, transport and consumer items in shops are generally cheaper in other parts of the country. It is always advisable to plan your trip before you travel and to enjoy Britain fully, it is important to be aware of the basics of British life: when to visit, what to take, how to get around, where to find information and what to do if things go wrong.

Weymouth Beach, Dorset, on a busy public holiday weekend

WHEN TO GO

Britain's temperate climate does not produce many temperature extremes *(see p68)*. However, weather patterns shift constantly, and the climate can vary widely in places only a short distance apart. Since it is impossible to predict rain or shine reliably in any season, be sure to pack a mix of warm and cool clothes and an umbrella, irrespective of when you plan to visit. Always get an up-to-date weather forecast before you set off on foot to remote mountain areas or moorland. Walkers can be surprised by the weather, and the Mountain Rescue services are often called out due to unexpectedly severe conditions. Weather reports can be found on television and radio,

A sign for the Mountain Rescue

as well as in newspapers. They can also be provided by phone services *(see p678)*.

Britain's towns and cities are all-year destinations, but many attractions are open only between Easter and October. The main family holiday months, July and August, and public holidays *(see p65)* are always busy, and some hotels are full around Christmas. Spring and autumn offer a good compromise between reasonably good weather and a relative lack of crowds.

VISAS AND PASSPORTS

A valid passport is required to enter Britain. Visitors from the European Union (EU), the United States, Canada, New Zealand and Australia do not need visas to enter the country. Visit www.ukvisas.gov.uk to check your visa status. Visas can be arranged online at www.fco.gov.uk. When you arrive at any British air- or seaport, you will find separate queues at immigration control – one set for EU nationals, and another for everyone else. Residents of the EU are allowed to work in Britain with no permit, while Commonwealth citizens under the age of 27 may work part time for up to two years. North American students can get a Blue Card through their university. This enables them to work for up to six months, but it must

be obtained before arrival in Britain. BUNAC *(see p672)* is a student club that organizes exchange schemes for students to work abroad.

CUSTOMS INFORMATION

Britain is part of the European Union, so anyone who arrives here from a member country can pass through a blue channel. However, random checks are still being made to detect entry of prohibited goods, particularly drugs, indecent material and weapons. Never, under any circumstances, carry luggage or parcels through customs for someone else. For most EU members there is no limit to the amount of excise goods (such as tobacco or alcohol) that can be brought into Britain, provided these are for your own use. This legislation does not apply to some new member states; check if you are unsure.

Travellers entering from outside the EU have to pass through customs channels. Go through the green channel if you have nothing to declare over the customs allowances, and use the red channel if you have goods to declare. If you are unsure of importation restrictions, go through the red channel. On departure, non-EU residents can apply for a VAT refund on goods bought in Britain *(see p658)*.

Britain is free of rabies, and no live animals may be imported without a permit. Any animals found will be impounded and may be destroyed.

◁ **Fishing boats in Scarborough port, North Yorkshire**

TOURIST INFORMATION

Tourist information is available in many towns and public places, including airports and main rail and coach stations, and some places of historical interest. Look out for the tourist information symbol, which can indicate anything from a large and busy central tourist bureau to a simple kiosk or even simply an information board in a parking area.

Tourist offices will be able to help you on almost anything in their area, including places of interest and guided walks. Both the regional and national tourist boards produce comprehensive lists of local attractions and registered accommodation options. A range of leaflets is generally available for free at tourist offices, but a charge may be made for more detailed maps and booklets. For route planning, consider the excellent large-format motoring atlases produced by both the RAC and the AA (see p685). For rural exploration, Ordnance Survey maps are ideal (www.ordnancesurvey.co.uk).

It's wise to book accommodation well in advance of your visit. **VisitBritain** is a good resource for this. Out of season, you should have few problems booking transport, restaurants or even theatre performances at short notice, but in the high season, if you have set your heart on a luxury hotel, popular West End show or specific tour, you should try to book in advance. Contact VisitBritain in your country, or see a travel agent for advice and general information.

The most common English tourist information sign

OPENING HOURS

Outside of London and other main cities, many businesses and shops still close on Sundays, even though trading is legal. During the week, opening hours are generally from 9 or 10am until 5 or 5:30pm. Shop hours may include a late opening one evening a week, usually Thursday. In big city centres, particularly London, shops are generally open longer – often until 7pm and seven days a week.

Museums in London tend to operate late opening hours one day a week, while those outside the capital may be less flexible, sometimes closing in the morning or for one day a week, often on Mondays.

On public holidays, also known as bank holidays in Britain, banks, offices and some shops, restaurants and attractions often close, and transport networks run a limited service.

DIRECTORY

CUSTOMS AND IMMIGRATION

UK Border Agency
www.ukba.homeoffice.gov.uk/customs-travel

Home Office
Border & Immigration Agency, Lunar House, 40 Wellesley Rd, Croydon, Surrey.
Tel 0870 606 7766.
*www.*ind.homeoffice.gov.uk

For information on import or export restrictions, visit **www**.hmrc.gov.uk

EMBASSIES AND CONSULATES

Australian High Commission
Australia House, Strand, London WC2.
Tel 020 7379 4334.
www.uk.embassy.gov.au

Canadian High Commission
Canada House, Trafalgar Square, London SW1.
Tel 020 7258 6600.
www.canada.gc.ca

New Zealand High Commission
New Zealand House, 80 Haymarket, London SW1.
Tel 020 7930 8422.
www.nzembassy.com

United States Embassy
24 Grosvenor Sq, London W1.
Tel 020 7499 9000.
www.usembassy.org.uk

INTERNATIONAL TOURIST INFORMATION

VisitBritain Australia
Tel 02 9021 4400.
www.visitbritain.com

VisitBritain Canada
Tel 1416 646 6674.
www.visitbritain.com

VisitBritain Ireland
www.enjoyengland.ie

VisitBritain USA
Tel 212 850 0336.
www.visitbritain.com

REGIONAL TOURIST BOARDS

Britain
Thames Tower, Blacks Rd, London W6 9EL.
Tel 020 8846 9000.
www.visitbritain.com

Cumbria
Tel 01539 822222.
www.golakes.co.uk

East of England
Tel UK: 0333 320 4202; International: 01603 875 486.
www.visiteastofengland.com

East Midlands
www.discover eastmidlands.com

London
Tel 0870 156 6366.
www.visitlondon.com

Northumbria
Tel 03000 262626.
www.visitnortheast england.com

Northwest
Tel 01942 821222.
www.visitnorthwest.com

Scotland
Tel 0845 859 1006.
www.visitscotland.com

Southeast
Tel 023 8062 5400.
www.visitsoutheast england.com

Southwest
Tel 0117 230 1262.
www.swtourism.org.uk

Wales
Tel 0870 830 0306.
www.visitwales.co.uk

Yorkshire and the Humber Region
www.yorkshire.com

A Cotswolds church, one of hundreds of parish churches open to the public free of charge

PUBLIC CONVENIENCES

Although some old-style supervised public toilets still exist, these have been largely replaced by the modern, free-standing, coin-operated "superloos". Main railway stations usually have toilet facilities for which there is a small charge. Young children should never use these toilets on their own.

TIPPING, ETIQUETTE AND SMOKING

In Britain it is the norm to tip taxi drivers and waiting staff in restaurants. Between 10 and 15 per cent is standard. Many restaurants automatically add a service charge to the bill, so do check before leaving a tip. It is not customary to leave a tip when buying a drink in a pub or bar.

Smoking is now forbidden in all of Britain's public indoor spaces, including pubs, restaurants, nightclubs, transport systems, taxis, theatres and cinemas. For advice on smoking-related issues, contact **ASH** (Action on Smoking and Health). It is illegal to buy cigarettes if you are under the age of 18.

Age restrictions also apply in pubs and bars, where you must be over 18 to be served. Some bars are for over-21s only, and patrons may be asked for identification before being served.

ADMISSION PRICES

Admission fees for museums and sights vary widely, from a nominal 50p to in excess of £10 for the more popular attractions. Many of the major national museums are free, although donations are encouraged. The same is true of a few local authority museums and art galleries. Some sights are in private hands, run either as a commercial venture or on a charitable basis. Stately homes open to the public may still belong to the gentry who have lived there for centuries; a charge is usually made to offset the enormous costs of upkeep. Many of these houses, such as Woburn Abbey (see p230), have added safari parks or garden centres to attract larger numbers of visitors.

Great British Heritage Pass

Britain's thousands of small parish churches are among the country's greatest architectural treasures. None of these churches charges an entrance fee, although you may find that some are locked because of vandalism. Increasingly, many of the great cathedrals expect a donation from visitors.

Reductions are often available for groups, senior citizens, children and students. Proof of eligibility will be required when purchasing a ticket. Visitors from overseas may buy a Great British Heritage Pass, which gives access to more than 600 sights including Stonehenge (see pp262–3) and Warwick Castle (see pp322–3). The pass is also available as a Family Pass. Families of two adults and up to three children, aged 5–15, can benefit. The pass can be bought from VisitBritain offices abroad. In the UK, it is sold at the Britain Visitor Centre in Lower Regent Street in London, as well as at some ports of entry and tourist information centres across Britain (see p669).

TRAVELLERS WITH SPECIAL NEEDS

The facilities on offer for disabled visitors to Britain are steadily improving. Recently designed or newly renovated buildings and public spaces now offer lifts and ramps for wheelchair access (this information is given in the headings for each entry in this guide); specially designed toilets; grab rails; and, for the hearing-impaired, earphones. Buses are also becoming increasingly accessible, and, if given advance notice, train, ferry or bus staff will help any disabled passengers. Ask a travel agent about the Disabled Persons Railcard, which entitles you to discounted rail fares.

Many banks, theatres and museums now provide aids for the visually or hearing-impaired. Specialist tour operators, such as **Tourism for All**, cater for physically handicapped visitors.

If renting a car, Hertz (see p685) offers hand-controlled vehicles for hire at no extra cost. In order to use any of the disabled parking spaces, you need to display a special badge in your car.

For more general information on facilities for disabled travellers, contact **RADAR**.

This association also publishes two books that carry a wealth of information for disabled holiday-makers: *Holidays in Britain and Ireland* and *There and Back*. The latter is a comprehensive guide to non-local travel. It pays particular attention to the links between the different methods of transport, whether by air, rail, road or sea.

TRAVELLING WITH CHILDREN

Britain offers a wealth of activities and fun days out for those travelling with children. The VisitBritain website *(see p669)* is a great resource for offering ideas, tips and useful information for the family.

Peak holiday times – Easter, July and August – and half-term school holidays have most to offer in terms of entertainment for children. There is always something child-friendly going on at Christmas, too, like panto-mimes and winter skating rinks. It is worth checking the websites of individual muse-ums and art galleries, because these often host child-centred events at key times of year. A couple of useful websites for information on things to do with children are www. kidslovelondon.com and www.whatson4kids.com.

Discounts for children or family tickets are available for travel, theatre shows and other forms of entertainment.

The Natural History Museum, a great day out for the whole family

Choose a hotel that welcomes children, or opt for self-catering quarters with hard-wearing furnishings and lots of room in which to run around. Many hotels now provide baby-sitting or baby-listening services, and may offer reductions or even free accommodation for very young children *(see pp552–99)*.

Restaurants are also becom-ing more welcoming of tiny patrons, and many provide high chairs and special menus *(see pp600–51)*. Italian eateries are often the most friendly and informal, but even the traditional British pub, once resolutely child-free, has relented, with beer gardens and family rooms. Under-18s are not permitted near the bars, nor are they allowed to buy or consume alcohol. The over-16s however, are permitted to consume wine, beer or cider with a table meal provided the alcohol is bought by an adult.

Baby-changing facilities are often provided at larger shops, department stores and shopping centres, as well as at most large museums and art galleries. For those who don't want to travel with all the paraphernalia necessary for their offspring (baby food, nappies, sunscreen), **Tinytots-away** provides a great serv-ice. This web-based company will deliver everything you need for your trip directly to your accommodation.

DIRECTORY

HELPLINE

Action on Smoking and Health (ASH)
Tel 020 7739 5902.
www.ash.org.uk

TRAVELLERS WITH SPECIAL NEEDS

RADAR
Tel 020 7250 3222.
www.radar.org.uk

Tourism for All
Tel UK: 0303 3030146;
International: +1539 814683.
www.tourismforall.org.uk

TRAVELLING WITH CHILDREN

Tinytotsaway
www.tinytotsaway.com

The privately owned, admission-charging Hever Castle *(see p189)*

International Student Identity Card

STUDENT TRAVELLERS

Full-time students in posses-
sion of a valid International
Student Identity Card (ISIC)
are often entitled to discounts
on things such as travel,
entrance fees and sports
facilities. North American students can also get medical
cover, although it may be
very basic *(see p675)*. ISICs
can be purchased from **STA
Travel**, the **National Union of
Students** or online. Proof of
student status is required.

A **Hostelling International**
card enables you to stay in
Britain's youth hostels. Outside
of term time, inexpensive
accommodation is also available at many of the university
halls of residence, such as the
University of London. This is
a good way of staying in city
centres on a tight budget.
Those who are exploring
the wilder regions of Britain
can find affordable sleeping
quarters in camping barns
(dormitory-style bunkhouses).
Though spartan, they cost very
little. The YHA website (www.
yha.org.uk) has a full list of
camping barns across Britain.

US and Canadian students
interested in working in Britain should contact **BUNAC**.

ENGLISH HERITAGE AND THE NATIONAL TRUST

Many of Britain's historic
buildings, parks and gardens,
not to mention vast tracts of
countryside and coastline,
are cared for by associations
such as **English Heritage**
(EH), the **National Trust**
(NT) or the **National Trust
for Scotland** (NTS). Entrance
fees for these sights are often
quite steep, so if you wish to
visit several of them during
your stay, it may be worth
taking out an annual mem-
bership, which allows free
access to any of these
properties for a calendar
year. Be aware that many
may be closed in winter.

Many of the National Trust's
properties are "listed", meaning that they are recognized
as having special architectural
or historical interest and are
therefore protected from alterations and demolition. This
guide identifies EH, NT and
NTS properties at the beginning of each entry.

ENGLISH HERITAGE

**The sign and symbol
of English Heritage**

ELECTRICITY

The voltage in Britain is
220/240 AC, 50 Hz. Electrical
plugs have three rectangular
pins and take fuses of 3, 5
and 13 amps. Visitors from

abroad will need an adaptor
for appliances that have been
brought from home, such
as portable computers, hairdryers and phone chargers.
Most hotels will have two-
pronged European-style
sockets for shavers only.

**Clock at the Royal Observatory,
Greenwich (see p125)**

TIME

During the winter months,
Britain is on Greenwich
Mean Time (GMT), which is
five hours ahead of Eastern
Standard Time and 10 hours
behind Sydney. From about
the middle of March until
October, the clocks go for-
ward one hour to British
Summer Time (BST).

To check the correct time,
contact the Speaking Clock
service by dialling 123.

CONVERSION CHART

Britain is officially metric,
in line with the rest of
Europe. However, imperial
measures are still in use,
especially for road distances, which are measured in
miles. Imperial pints and
gallons are 20 per cent
larger than US measures.

Imperial to metric
1 inch = 2.5 centimetres
1 foot = 30 centimetres
1 mile = 1.6 kilometres
1 ounce = 28 grams
1 pound = 454 grams
1 pint = 0.6 litres
1 gallon = 4.6 litres

Metric to imperial
1 millimetre = 0.04 inch
1 centimetre = 0.4 inch
1 metre = 3 feet 3 inches
1 kilometre = 0.6 mile
1 gram = 0.04 ounce
1 kilogram = 2.2 pounds

Lorna Doone Cottage and National Trust Information Centre, Somerset

RESPONSIBLE TRAVEL

Like many European countries, Britain is aware of the need to be greener and is making a concerted effort to reduce emissions and waste. While most rubbish is still sent to landfill sites, there are recycling campaigns in every town and city, and the amounts of household waste are gradually diminishing.

Many holiday properties across the country publish their green policies, showing how they minimize energy use. Some lodgings even offer discounts to guests arriving by public transport or on foot, particularly in heavily congested areas such as national parks. These themselves vary in the environmental schemes they operate, but all are committed to encouraging green tourism. The **Green Tourism Business Scheme** is a national scheme that has vetted 1,500 places to stay in England, Scotland and Wales, from small B&Bs to

Colourful stalls at a farmers' market

luxury five-star hotels, as well as about 500 visitor attractions. The scheme requires owners to provide details on more than 145 criteria, ranging from energy and waste control to use of local produce and transport. A qualified environmental auditor visits each property and allocates an award based on the standards met. There are also more than 20 regional accommodation certification schemes across Britain, including **Green Leaf** (New Forest) and **Green Island** (Isle of Wight).

Another green accommodation solution is the great outdoors. Campsites are located across Britain, and pitches are available from as little as £4.50 per night. Note, however, that sites are often fairly far from the main towns and may not be served by public transport.

Organic and fair-trade products can be bought at most supermarkets. Many towns and cities hold a weekly food market, and farmers' markets are also on the increase. These stock locally sourced produce, and shopping here is a great way to give back to the local economy. Visit www. farmersmarkets.net. to find your nearest farmers' market. When in rural areas, look out for farm shops that stock fresh products from local farms. "Slow Food" fairs are held occasionally across the country. These tend to last several days and are a great opportunity for small vendors to set up stalls and for visitors to sample food from sustainable sources.

DIRECTORY

STUDENT TRAVELLERS

BUNAC
16 Bowling Green Lane, London EC1R 0QH.
Tel 020 7251 3472.
www.bunac.org

Hostelling International
Tel 01707 324170.
www.hihostels.com

National Union of Students
Tel 0845 521 0262.
www.nus.org.uk

STA Travel
Priory House,
6 Wrights Lane,
London W8 6TA.
Tel 020 7361 6262.
www.statravel.co.uk

University of London
Malet St,
London WC1.
Tel 020 7862 8880.
www.housing.lon.ac.uk

HERITAGE ORGANIZATIONS

English Heritage
Tel 0870 333 1181.
www.english-heritage.
org.uk

National Trust
Tel 0844 800 1895.
www.national
trust.org.uk

National Trust for Scotland
Hermiston Quay, 5
Cultins Rd, Edinburgh
EH11 4DF. *Tel 0844 493 2100.* www.nts.org.uk

RELIGIOUS ORGANIZATIONS

Baptist
London Baptist Assn,
235 Shaftesbury Ave,
London WC2. *Tel 020 7692 5592.* www.
londonbaptist.org.uk

Buddhist
Buddhist Society,
58 Eccleston Sq, London
SW1. *Tel 020 7834 5858.*
www.thebuddhist
society.org

Church of England
Great Smith St, London
SW1. *Tel 020 7898 1000.*
www.cofe.anglican.org

Evangelical Alliance
Whitefield House,
186 Kennington Park Rd,
London SE11.
Tel 020 7207 2100.
www.eauk.org

Jewish
Liberal Jewish Synagogue,
28 St John's Wood Rd,
London NW8. *Tel 020 7286 5181.* www.ljs.org

Muslim
Islamic Cultural Centre,
146 Park Rd, London
NW8. *Tel 020 7724 3363.* www.iccuk.org

Quakers
Friends House, 173–177
Euston Rd, London NW1.
Tel 020 7663 1000.
www.quaker.org.uk

Roman Catholic
Westminster Cathedral,
Victoria St, London SW1.

Tel 020 7798 9055.
www.westminster
cathedral.org.uk

United Synagogue (Orthodox)
Adler House,
735 High Rd, North
Finchley, London N12.
Tel 020 8343 8989.
www.theus.org.uk

RESPONSIBLE TRAVEL

Green Business
www.green-business.co.
uk

Green Island Tourism
www.greenisland
tourism.org

Green Leaf Tourist Scheme
www.thegreenforest.org

Green Tourism Business Scheme
www.green-business.co.
uk

Tourism Concern
www.tourismconcern.
org.uk

Personal Security and Health

Britain is a densely populated country that, like any other, has its share of social problems. However, it is very unlikely that you will come across any violence. If you do encounter difficulties, do not hesitate to contact the police for help. Britain's National Health Service can be relied upon for both emergency and routine treatment. Note that you may have to pay if your country has no reciprocal arrangement with Britain.

Police car

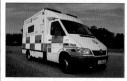
Ambulance

Fire engine

POLICE

The sight of a traditional bobby walking the streets is now less common than that of the police patrol car, but the old-fashioned police constable does still exist, particularly in rural areas and crowded city centres.

Unlike in many other countries, the police force in Britain does not carry guns, although 10 per cent of the London Metropolitan police are armed.

If you are lost, ask a police-man or woman – they are courteous, approachable and helpful. Traffic wardens may also be able to help you with directions. If you have been the victim of a robbery or an assault, contact the police by dialling 999. All Britain's major cities have community police support officers who patrol the city streets working alongside the police. They are able to deal with anti-social behaviour, can offer advice on crime prevention and can also help you with directions and information.

LOST AND STOLEN PROPERTY

If you lose anything or have anything stolen, report it at the nearest police station as soon as you are able. A writ-ten report from the local police is required to make a claim on your insurance for any theft. All of the main bus and rail stations have lost-property offices.

CRIME

Britain is not a dangerous place for visitors, and it is most unlikely that your stay will be blighted by crime. Due to terrorist threats, there are occasional security alerts, especially on the Under-ground, but these are mainly false alarms often due to peo-ple accidentally leaving a bag or parcel unattended. Always co-operate with the authori-ties if your bag has to be searched or if you are asked to evacuate a building.

WHAT TO BE AWARE OF

Make sure that your posses-sions are adequately insured before you arrive in Britain, and never leave them unat-tended in public places. Keep your valuables concealed (particularly mobile phones), especially in crowded places. Pickpockets love markets, busy shops and all modes of transport during rush hour. Keep handbags on your lap, never on the floor or on the back of your chair. It is advisable not to carry too much cash or jewellery with you. Take what you need for the day, and leave the rest in your hotel safe instead. It is also advisable not to leave any valuables on display in your hotel room.

At night, try to avoid desert-ed and poorly lit places such as back streets and car parks.

Begging is an increasingly common sight in many British cities, and foreign visitors are frequent targets for hard-luck stories. Requests for money are usually polite, but any abuse should be reported to the police immediately.

Female police constable

Traffic police officer

Male police constable

WOMEN TRAVELLERS

It is not unusual in Britain for women to travel unaccompanied or to visit a bar or restaurant with a group of female friends. However, caution is advisable in deserted places, especially after dark. Always summon a licensed taxi *(see pp690–91)* and do not walk through a quiet area at night, especially if you are not familiar with the district. Try to avoid using train carriages where there is just one other passenger or a group of young men.

It is illegal to carry any offensive weapons such as knives, guns and even tear gas around with you, even for self-defence. However, personal alarms are allowed.

IN AN EMERGENCY

The police, fire and ambulance services are on call 24 hours a day and can be reached by dialling 999. Along the coastal areas, this number will also put you in touch with Britain's voluntary coastguard rescue service, the Royal National Lifeboat Institute. Calls are free from any public or private phone, but they should be made only in real emergencies.

PHARMACIES

You can buy a wide range of over-the-counter drugs in Britain. **Boots** (www.boots.com) is the best-known chemist, with branches in most towns. Many medicines, however, are available only with a doctor's prescription. If you are likely to need medication, either bring your own or get your doctor to write out the generic (as opposed to the brand) name of the drug. If you are entitled to an NHS prescription, you will be charged a standard rate; if not, you will be charged the full cost of the drug. Do ask for a receipt for any insurance claim.

Some pharmacies are open until midnight; contact your local hospital for a list. You can call the NHS Direct 24-hour helpline (0845 4647) or go to a hospital casualty department any time. In an emergency, dial 999 for an ambulance.

Pharmacy sign

HEALTH INSURANCE

It is sensible to take out travel insurance to cover cancellation or curtailment of your holiday, theft or loss of money and possessions, and the cost of any medical treatment, which may include emergency hospital care, repatriation and specialists' fees. This is particularly important for visitors from outside the European Union. Emergency medical treatment in a British NHS casualty ward is free, but any kind of additional medical care could prove very expensive.

Those with a European Health Insurance Card (EHIC) are entitled to free treatment under the NHS. This applies to visitors from EU and European Economic Area (EEA) countries, as well as some Commonwealth countries, such as Australia and New Zealand. Be aware, though, that certain benefits covered by medical insurance will not be included. North American and Canadian health plans or student identity cards *(see p672)* may give you some protection against costs, but do always check the small print.

If you need to see a dentist while staying in Britain, be aware that you will have to pay. The cost varies, depending on your entitlement to NHS treatment and whether you can find an NHS dentist to treat you (many dental practices no longer take on NHS patients). Emergency dental treatment is available in some hospitals, but if you prefer to be seen by a private dentist, try looking in the *Yellow Pages (see p678).*

Royal National Lifeboat Institute logo

DIRECTORY

EMERGENCY NUMBERS

Police, Fire and Ambulance services
Tel 999.

Accident and Emergency Departments
For your nearest unit, check the phone directory or contact the police.

Emergency Dental Care
Tel 020 7188 7182 *(Guy's Hospital, London)* or 020 7188 8006 *(children only, 24 hours).*

HELPLINES

Alcoholics Anonymous
Tel 0845 769 7555. www. alcoholics-anonymous.org.uk

British Deaf Association
www.signcommunity.org.uk

British Pregnancy Advisory Service
Tel 08457 30 40 30. www.bpas.org

Childline
Tel 0800 1111 *(24-hour free phoneline for children in need of help).*
www.childline.org.uk

Dial UK
Tel 01302 310123 *(helpline for the disabled).*
www.dialuk.org.uk

Disabled Living Foundation
Tel 0845 130 9177.
www.dlf.org.uk

Frank
Tel 0800 77 66 00 *(24-hour substance-abuse helpline).*
www.talktofrank.com

NHS Direct
Tel 0845 4647.
www.nhsdirect.nhs.uk

Rape Crisis Centre
Tel 0808 802 9999.
www.rapecrisis.co.uk

Royal National Institute of Blind People
Tel 0303 123 9999.
www.rnib.org.uk

Samaritans
Tel 08457 90 90 90 *(24 hours).*
www.samaritans.org

Victim Support
Tel 0845 30 30 900.
www.victimsupport.org

Banking and Local Currency

The high-street banks usually offer the best rates of currency exchange, though commission fees may vary. However, if you do find yourself having to use one of the many privately owned bureaux de change that are found at nearly every major airport, train station and tourist area, take care to check the commission and minimum charges before completing any transaction.

Customers using ATMs outside a branch of Lloyds TSB

BUREAUX DE CHANGE

Private bureaux de change may be more conveniently located and have more flexible opening hours than banks. However, rates of exchange vary and commission charges can be high, so it is always worth shopping around. **Exchange International**, **Travelex**, **American Express** and **Chequepoint** all have branches throughout Britain and usually offer good exchange facilities. Marks & Spencer (www.marksand spencer.com) has bureaux de change in more than 110 of its stores across the UK. They charge no commission on foreign-currency travellers' cheques and only 1 per cent on sterling travellers' cheques.

BANKS

Every large town and city in Britain has a branch of at least one of these five high-street banks: Barclays, Lloyds TSB, HSBC, NatWest and Royal Bank of Scotland.

Banking hours vary but the majority are open 9am to 5:30pm Monday to Friday. Most main branches open on Saturday mornings, too. All banks close on public holidays (see p65).

If you run out of funds, it is possible to have money wired from your country to your nearest British bank. Branches of Travelex and American Express will also do this for you. North American visitors can get cash dispatched through **Western Union** to a bank or post office. Remember to take along your passport as proof of identity.

CASH DISPENSERS

Most banks have a cash dispenser, or ATM, from which you can obtain money with a credit card and your personal identification number (PIN). Cash machines can also be found in some supermarkets, post offices, petrol stations, train stations and London Underground stations. Some of the most modern ATMs have on-screen instructions in several languages. Some make a charge for cash withdrawals (typically £1.50 per transaction). American Express cards may be used at all cash-dispensing machines, but there is a 2 per cent handling charge for each transaction.

There have been some incidences of card crime at ATMs; be vigilant and cover the keypad with your hand when entering your PIN.

CREDIT CARDS

Credit cards are widely used throughout Britain. Indeed, a credit card is necessary in order to rent a car and for some hotel bookings. However, many small shops, guesthouses, markets and cafés may not accept them, so always check in advance of your purchase. Cards that are accepted are usually displayed on the windows of the establishment. Britain uses the "chip and PIN" system instead of a signature on a credit slip. You will need a four-digit PIN, so ask your bank for one before you leave.

A credit card allows you to obtain cash advances up to your credit limit at any bank and cash dispenser displaying the appropriate card sign. You will be charged the credit card company's interest rate for obtaining cash, and this will appear on your statement with the amount advanced. You will probably also incur a currency-exchange fee.

American Express
Tel 01273 696 933.
www.americanexpress.co.uk

Chequepoint
Tel 020 7225 4600.
www.chequepoint.com

Exchange International
Tel 020 7630 1107.

Travelex
www.travelex.co.uk

Western Union
Tel 0808 234 9168.
www.westernunion.co.uk

CURRENCY

Britain's currency is the pound sterling (£), which is divided into 100 pence (p). There are no exchange controls in Britain, so you may bring in and take out as much cash as you like. Scotland has

A Scottish one pound (£1) bank note

its own notes. Although these are legal tender throughout Britain, they are not always accepted in England and Wales. Travellers' cheques are the safest alternative to carrying large amounts of cash. Always keep the receipts from your

travellers' cheques separate from the cheques themselves. This simple precaution makes it easier to obtain a refund if your cheques are lost or stolen. Some high-street banks issue travellers' cheques free of commission to their account holders, but the normal rate is about 1 per cent. When changing money, ask for some smaller notes, since these are easier to use.

Bank Notes
English notes are produced in denominations of £5, £10, £20 and £50. Some shops may refuse the larger notes, so always get small denominations.

£50 note

£20 note

£10 note

£5 note

Coinage
Coins currently in use are £2, £1, 50p, 20p, 10p, 5p, 2p and 1p.

2 pounds (£2)

1 pound (£1)

50 pence (50p)

20 pence (20p)

10 pence (10p)

5 pence (5p)

2 pence (2p)

1 penny (1p)

Communications and Media

Modern BT phone box

With constantly improving telecommunication systems and email, staying in touch and making plans while travelling has never been easier. The telephone system in Britain is efficient and inexpensive. Charges depend on when, where and for how long you talk. The cheapest time to call is between 7pm and 8am Monday to Friday and throughout the weekend. Local calls made on public payphones, however, are charged at a fixed rate per minute.

PUBLIC TELEPHONES

You can use a payphone with coins or a card. All payphones accept 10p, 20p, 50p and £1 pieces; the newer ones also accept £2 coins. The minimum cost of a call is 40p. Phone cards are more convenient than coins and can be bought from newsagents and post offices. If you use a credit card, note that it carries a minimum charge and that your calls will be charged at a higher rate.

MOBILE PHONES

Mobile phones are widespread in Britain, and every high street has at least one mobile-phone shop, the most common being **Vodafone**, **O2**, **Carphone Warehouse**, **Orange** and **Phones4U**. The UK network uses the 900 or 1800 GSM system, so visitors from the United States (where the system is 800 or 1900 MHz band) will need to acquire a tri- or quad-band set. Contact your service provider for details. You may need to inform your network operator in advance of your trip, so that the "roaming" facility can be enabled. When abroad,

you will be charged for the calls you receive, as well as for the calls you make; in addition, you have to pay a substantial premium for the international leg of the call.

It is easier and cheaper to purchase a SIM card locally and top it up with credit. This will allow you to use the local mobile-phone networks, though you can only do this if your handset is not "locked" to a specific network. Alternatively, you could buy a brand-new phone and top up with a pay-as-you-go card. Make sure the phone you buy can accept international calls. Check that your insurance policy covers you in case your phone gets stolen, and keep your network operator's helpline number handy for emergencies.

ACCESSING THE INTERNET

Most cities and towns now have some form of public access to computers and the Internet, including specially adapted payphones in the street. Many hotels include Internet facilities as part of their service, and free Internet access is often available at libraries, though you may have to book a time slot. Many cafés now offer free Wi-Fi (wireless) Internet access, so you can use your laptop computer.

Internet cafés usually charge for computer use by the minute. Internet access is generally very cheap, but it is most reasonable during off-peak times. However, charges can build up quickly,

especially when including the cost of printing.

VoIP (Voice over Internet Protocol) is a way of communicating telephonically via your computer. Most Internet cafés will have at least one such system installed. In order to use it, you will need a Skype account (free to set up), a set of headphones and a microphone (usually provided by the café). It is free to call other Skype accounts. Calling land lines and mobiles is very cheap, but you need to buy Skype credits using credit/debit cards or PayPal.

DIRECTORY

The following services exist to help you find or reach a specific phone number. You will be charged more for enquiries if calling from a mobile phone.

BT Directory Enquiries
Tel 118 500 (charge applies).

International Directory Enquiries
Tel 118 505 (charge applies).

International Operator
Tel 155 (freephone).

Operator Assistance
Tel 100.

Overseas Calls
Tel 00 followed by country code: Australia (61), Canada (1), Ireland (353), New Zealand (64), South Africa (27), United States (1).

Yellow Pages
Tel 118 247 (charge applies).
www.yell.com
Provides numbers for shops or services in any area, as well as maps and driving directions.

DIRECTORY

Carphone Warehouse
www.carphonewarehouse.co.uk

Orange
www.orange.co.uk

O2
www.o2.co.uk

Phones4U
www.phones4u.co.uk

Vodafone
www.vodafone.co.uk

Round-the-clock Internet access at the Europe-wide chain easyInternetcafe

POSTAL SERVICES

Stamps can be bought at many outlets, including supermarkets and petrol stations. When writing to a British address, always include the post-code, which can be obtained from **Royal Mail**. Within the UK, letters and postcards can be sent either first or second class; second-class mail is cheaper and takes a day or two longer. The price of postage depends on the size and weight of your letter. For more details, visit the Royal Mail website or take your letter/parcel to any post office, where they will weigh it and give you the price of postage.

Pillar box

Large urban post office branches have a *poste restante* service where letters can be collected. Correspondence should be sent to the recipient at *Poste Restante*, followed by the address of the relevant post office branch. To collect your post, you will have to show your passport or other form of identification. Post is kept for one month. London's main post office is in William IV Street, WC2. The American Express office on Haymarket also has a *poste restante* service for customers.

Main post office branches offer all the mail services available. In more isolated areas, there are often small branches in newsagents, grocery stores and general information centres. In many villages, the post office is also the only shop.

Post offices are usually open from 9am to 5:30pm Monday to Friday, and until 12:30pm on Saturday.

Royal Mail
Tel 08457 740 740.
www.royalmail.com

POST BOXES

Post boxes can be found throughout cities, towns and villages in Britain. They may be either free-standing pillar boxes or wall safes, but they are always painted bright red. Collections are usually made several times a day during weekdays (less often on Saturdays and Sundays). The last collection time of the day is marked on the box.

MAILING ABROAD

Air letters go by Royal Mail's airmail service anywhere in the world; the cost depends on the destination. On average, it takes three days for them to reach cities in Europe, and four to six days for other destinations. Royal Mail also offers an express airmail service called **Airsure**, available from all post office branches. Mail goes on the first available flight to the country of destination.

Parcelforce Worldwide offers courier-style services to most destinations and is comparable in price to **DHL**, **Crossflight**, **Expressair** or **UPS**.

Airsure (Royal Mail)
Tel 08457 740 740.
www.royalmail.com

Crossflight
Tel 01753 776 000.
www.crossflight.co.uk

DHL
Tel 0844 248 0844.
www.dhl.co.uk

Expressair
Tel 020 7781 0036.
www.expressair.co.uk

Parcelforce Worldwide
Tel 08448 004466.
www.parcelforce.com

UPS
Tel 08457 877 877.
www.ups.com

NEWSPAPERS AND MAGAZINES

British national newspapers fall into two categories: quality papers, such as *The Times*, *The Daily Telegraph* and *The Guardian*; and those heavy on gossip, such as *The Sun* or the *Daily Mirror*. The weekend newspapers, more expensive than dailies, are packed with supplements of all kinds, including sections on the arts, entertainment, travel, listings and reviews. Free newspapers, with an emphasis on news and celebrity gossip, are given away, morning and evening, at main railway stations in major cities such as London and Manchester.

Specialist periodicals on just about every topic are available from newsagents. For a more in-depth analysis of current events, buy *The Economist*, *New Statesman* or *The Spectator*, while *Private Eye* cocks a satirical snook at public figures. A few foreign magazines and newspapers are available in large towns, often at main train stations, but mostly in London. One of the most popular is the *International Herald Tribune*, which is available on the day of issue.

Some of Britain's national newspapers

TELEVISION AND RADIO

The state-run BBC (British Broadcasting Corporation) operates eight channels and has a reputation for making some of the world's best television. These channels have no advertising breaks. Its commercial rivals include ITV, Channel 4 and Five. ITV is liked for its soap operas and game shows; Channel 4 caters for trendy and minority tastes (art films, documentaries, offbeat chat shows); and Five relies on US imports and TV movies.

The BBC also has a number of radio stations, ranging from pop music (Radio 1) to the middle-brow Radio 4. There are many local commercial radio stations.

Full TV and radio schedules appear in newspapers and listings magazines, as well as online and in the *Radio Times*, a weekly publication.

TRAVEL INFORMATION

Britain is an international gateway for both air and sea traffic, which translates into a variety of options in terms of travel. Visitors enjoy a large selection of air carriers linking Britain to the rest of Europe, North America and Australasia. Coach travel is a cheap, if rather slow, form of transport from Europe, while travelling by train has been transformed thanks to the Channel Tunnel. It takes less than two and a half hours from Paris to London on Eurostar. Travelling within Britain is also easy. There is an extensive network of roads to all parts of the country, and hiring a car can be a convenient way of travelling around. The railway network is efficient and far-reaching, especially around London. Travelling by coach is the cheapest option. The coach network reaches most areas but can be slow. If time is short, air travel is possible if expensive.

BRITISH AIRWAYS
British Airways logo

Eurostar trains at St Pancras International Station, London

TRAVELLING AROUND BRITAIN

Choosing the best form of transport depends on where and when you want to go, although the quickest and most convenient methods are generally also the most expensive. The **Transport Direct** website offers a number of alternative ways of getting to your chosen destination.

Distances between any two points within mainland Britain are relatively small, so air travel usually makes sense only between the extremes, such as London to Edinburgh.

Train travel is the best option if you want to visit Britain's major cities, though fares, especially at peak times, can be expensive. If you plan to do much travelling within Britain, invest in a rail pass (*see p686*). You can buy one before you arrive in the UK since several schemes cater for overseas visitors. **BritRail** has several options on offer, from a few days' to two weeks' worth of rail travel.

Coaches (*see p688*) cover a wide number of UK destinations and are cheaper than trains, but they take longer and may be less comfortable.

For a touring holiday, hiring a car (*see p685*) is easier than relying on public transport. Car rental can be arranged at major airports, large train stations and city centre outlets. Small local firms often undercut the large operators in price but may not be as reliable or convenient. To get the best deals, book from abroad.

For detailed exploration of smaller areas, such as Britain's national parks, you may prefer more leisurely forms of transport such as bike, narrowboat or horse. Sometimes there are picturesque local options, like the rowing-boat ferry between Southwold and Walberswick on the Blyth Estuary (*see p202*). Larger car ferries travel to Britain's islands.

Taxis (*see p690*) are available at all main coach and train stations; without a car you will avoid the stress of driving in congested city centres.

GREEN TRAVEL

With congestion charges in London and limited parking throughout the urban areas, driving in British cities is not recommended. Instead, make use of the country's extensive public transport network.

Covering a lot of ground without a car is possible, although this does take careful planning to ensure you catch all of your connections. Most areas are served by trains and/or buses, and services tend to be fairly regular. Travelling around the countryside without private transport, however, can be difficult, because bus services can be infrequent (particularly on Sundays). It may be sensible to hire a car.

Trains in Britain can be overcrowded at peak times, and they are often expensive, although booking tickets in advance can bring the cost down. The GroupSave ticket scheme allows discounted rail travel for groups of three or four, and various other discounts are available with a travel card.

The National Trust (*see p672*) offers some incentives, including discounted entry, to those who use public transport when visiting some of their sites.

The National Cycle Network provides more than 20,000 km (12,430 miles) of cycle paths across Britain. A bike can be taken on most off-peak trains, but you may have to book a spot for it. Check before you travel.

For more information on environmentally friendly travel options, contact **Sustrans**.

Arriving by Sea, Rail and Coach

Irrespective of how you are travelling from Europe, you will have to cross the English Channel or the North Sea. Ferry services operate from a huge number of ports on the European mainland and have good link-ups with international coaches, with services from most European cities to Britain. The Channel Tunnel means there is a non-stop rail link between Europe and Britain. Prices between the ferries and the tunnel services remain competitive, and both options are good green alternatives to flying.

FERRY SERVICES FROM EUROPE

A complex network of car and passenger ferry services links over a dozen British ports to many ports in northern and southern Europe.

Ferries can be convenient and economical for those travelling by car or on foot. Fares vary greatly according to the season, time of travel and duration of stay. Early booking means big savings – a Dover–Calais return crossing can cost as little as £22. The shortest crossings are not always the cheapest, since you often pay a premium for the speed of the journey.

CROSSING TIMES

Crossing times vary from just over an hour on the shortest routes to a full 24 hours on services from Spain and Scandinavia. If you take an overnight sailing, it is often worth paying extra for sleeping quarters to avoid feeling exhausted when you arrive.
Speed Ferries runs fast Seacat (catamaran) services between Dover and Boul-

ogne, in France, taking just under an hour. Catamarans can carry vehicles and lack the dip and sway of a conventional ship, so may be less painful for those who tend to get seasick.

SEAPORT BUREAUCRACY

Visitors from outside the EU should allow plenty of time for immigration control and customs clearance at British seaports (see p668).

CHANNEL TUNNEL

Thanks to the Channel Tunnel, there is access to Britain via **Eurostar** and **Eurotunnel** from the French and Belgian high-speed rail networks. In France and Belgium, trains reach speeds of up to 186 mph (300kmph). The cost is comparable to flying but the train is much more convenient and much less environmentally damaging. Typically, a ticket from London to Paris costs about £99 but can be as low as £59.

Passengers on buses and cars get on to a freight train run by Eurotunnel

EURO TUNNEL

Eurotunnel logo

that takes 35 minutes to travel between Calais and Folkestone. For those travelling by rail there are about 40 scheduled passenger-only Eurostar services, operated by the French, Belgians and British. They run direct services from Brussels, Paris, Lille and Calais to Ashford, Ebbsfleet and St Pancras in London. There are two passenger tunnels and one service tunnel, both lying 25–45 m (82–147 ft) below the sea bed.

INTERNATIONAL COACH TRAVEL

Although coach (bus) travel is considerably cheaper than other forms of travel, it is not the most comfortable. If you have a lot of spare time and want to stop off en route, however, it can be convenient. Once you have paid for your ticket, you will not have to pay extra for the ferry or the Channel Tunnel.

DIRECTORY

FERRIES, RAIL AND COACH TRAVEL

BritRail
www.acprailnet.com

Brittany Ferries
Tel 0871 244 0744.
www.brittany-ferries.co.uk

European Rail Travel
Tel 08448 484 064.
www.raileurope.co.uk

Eurostar
Tel 08432 186 186.
www.eurostar.com

Eurotunnel/Le Shuttle
Tel 08443 35 35 35.
www.eurotunnel.com

National Express
www.nationalexpress.com
(coaches)

Norfolk Line
www.norfolkline.com *(ferries)*

P&O Ferries
www.poferries.com

Speed Ferries
www.speedferries.co.uk

Transport Direct
www.transportdirect.info

GREEN TRAVEL

Sustrans
www.sustrans.org.uk

Ferry arriving at Dover

Arriving by Air

Britain has about 130 licensed airports, only a handful of which deal with long-haul traffic. The largest one, London's Heathrow, is the world's busiest international airport and one of Europe's main routing points for international air travel. Heathrow is served by most of the world's leading airlines, with direct flights from nearly all the major cities. Other international airports include Gatwick, Stansted, Manchester, Glasgow, Newcastle, Birmingham and Edinburgh. Smaller airports, such as London City, Bristol, Norwich and Cardiff, have daily flights to European destinations. Strict anti-terrorist measures are currently in force at all airports.

A British Airways 747 jet at Heathrow Airport

BRITISH AIRPORTS

Most of Britain's largest and best-known airports are run by the British Airports Authority (BAA); the rest are either owned by a local authority or in private hands. BAA airports offer up-to-date facilities, including 24-hour banking, shops, cafés, hotels and restaurants. Security is strict at all British airports, and it is important never to leave your luggage unattended.

For visitors to London, Heathrow, Gatwick or Stansted are equally convenient. If you plan to visit northern England, there are now many flights going to Birmingham, Newcastle and Manchester, while for Scotland you can fly to Glasgow or Edinburgh.

Heathrow has five terminals and other airports have two. Before you fly, check with the airport from which terminal your flight leaves.

During severe weather conditions in the winter months, your flight may be diverted to another airport. If this happens, the airline will organize transportation back to your original destination.

British Airways has flights to most of the world's important destinations. Other British international airlines include **Virgin Atlantic**, with routes to the USA and the Far East, and **Flybe**, which flies to Western Europe.

American airlines offering scheduled services to Britain include **Delta**, **US Air** and **American Airlines**. From Canada, the main carrier is **Air Canada**. From Australasia, the national carriers **Qantas** and **Air New Zealand** vie with several Far Eastern rivals.

Britain imposes an airport tax on all departing passengers. This is currently £10 for domestic and EU routes, and £20 for non-EU and long-haul flights. It is included in the price of the ticket.

TRANSPORT FROM THE AIRPORT

Britain's international airports lie some way from the city centres, but transport to and from them is efficient. The most convenient form of door-to-door travel is a taxi, but it is also the most expensive. In addition, taxis can be slow if there is road congestion. This is also a problem with buses or coaches, although they are a lot cheaper.

Heathrow and Newcastle airports are linked to the city centres by the Underground (see p691), which is efficient, quick and cheap. Visitors to London arriving at Heathrow can also take the Heathrow Express, the fast train to Paddington Station

AIRPORT	ℹ INFORMATION	DISTANCE TO CITY CENTRE	TAXI FARE TO CITY CENTRE	PUBLIC TRANSPORT TO CITY CENTRE
Heathrow	08700 000 123	23 km (14 miles)	£40–£45	Rail: 15 mins Tube: 45 mins
Gatwick	08700 002 468	45 km (28 miles)	£75	Rail: 30 mins Bus: 70 mins
Stansted	08700 000 303	60 km (37 miles)	£80	Rail: 45 mins Bus: 75 mins
Manchester	0161 489 3000	16 km (10 miles)	£15–£16	Rail: 15 mins Bus: 30 mins
Birmingham	08707 33 55 11	13 km (8 miles)	£12–£15	Bus: 30 mins
Newcastle	08718 821 121	8 km (5 miles)	£10–£12	Metro: 20 mins Bus: 20 mins
Glasgow	08700 400 008	13 km (8 miles)	£12–£15	Bus: 20 mins
Edinburgh	08700 400 007	13 km (8 miles)	£17–£18	Bus: 25 mins

Terminal 5 at Heathrow Airport

(www.heathrowexpress.com or 0845 600 1515). Trains run every 15 minutes from 5am until around midnight, taking 15 minutes from Terminals 1, 2 and 3, and 21 minutes from Terminal 5. Terminal 4 requires a change of train and takes a total of 23 minutes. Those arriving at Gatwick can take the Gatwick Express to London Victoria (www.gatwick express.com or 0845 850 15 30). Trains run every 15 minutes and take 30 minutes.

Stansted and Manchester also have regular express trains that are not too expensive and are a reliable method for travelling into the heart of the city.

National Express coaches (*see p688*) provide direct connections from major airports (London's Heathrow, Gatwick and Stansted, Luton, Birmingham, Liverpool, Manchester, Coventry, East Midlands and Bristol) to many British destinations. They also have a regular service between Gatwick and Heathrow.

CHOOSING A TICKET

Finding the right flight at the right price can be difficult. Promotional fares do come up, and it is always worth checking with the airlines. Cheap deals are often available from package operators

Signs for express railway services to London

and are advertised in newspapers and travel magazines. Even if you enjoy independent travel, it may be worth considering a package, since sometimes car rental or rail travel is included, and this can be cheaper than arranging it yourself once in Britain.

Fares are usually seasonal, the most expensive falling between June and September. The best deals can be had from November to April, excluding Christmas – if you want to travel then, be sure to book well in advance. APEX (Advance Purchase Excursion) fares are often the best value, though they must be booked up to a month ahead and are subject to restrictions. Charter flights offer even cheaper seats but are not usually flexible.

Budget airlines such as **easyJet** and **Ryanair** offer exceptionally cheap flights if booked long enough in advance. Always buy discount fares from a reputable operator, and do not part with any cash until you have seen your ticket and ensured your seat has been confirmed.

Students, the under-26s, senior citizens and frequent travellers may obtain a discount through student travel agencies. Children also travel at cheaper rates.

TRAVELLING WITHIN BRITAIN BY AIR

Internal air travel in Britain only makes sense over long distances, where it can save a great deal of time – for example, London to Scotland, or to one of the many offshore islands. Fares can be expensive, but if you book well ahead, they can be up to three times cheaper than if you just turn up at the airport. The British Airways shuttle flights that operate between London and cities such as Glasgow, Edinburgh and Manchester are very popular with business travellers. At peak times of the day, flights leave every hour, while at other times there is usually a flight every two hours. Even on domestic flights, security is strict. Never leave your bags unattended.

Travelling Around by Car

The most startling difference for most foreign motorists is that in Britain you drive on the left, with corresponding adjustments at roundabouts and junctions. Distances are measured in miles. Once you adapt, rural Britain is an enjoyable place to drive, though traffic density in towns and at busy holiday times can cause long delays – public holiday weekends near the south coast can be particularly horrendous. An extensive network of toll-free motorways and trunk roads has now cut travelling time to most parts of the country.

The A30 dual carriageway going through Cornwall

WHAT YOU NEED

To drive in Britain you need a current driving licence with an international driving permit, if required. You must also carry proof of ownership or a rental agreement in your vehicle, plus any insurance documents.

ROADS IN BRITAIN

Rush hour can last from 8 to 9:30am and from 5 to 7pm on weekdays in the cities; at these times, traffic can grind to a halt.

A good touring map is vital for driving in the country. The AA or RAC motoring atlases are fairly straightforward to use. For exploration of more rural areas, the Ordnance Survey series is the best. Motorways are marked with an "M" followed by their identifying number. "A" roads, sometimes dual carriageways (that is, with two lanes in each direction), are main routes, while "B" roads are secondary roads. The latter are often less congested and more enjoyable. Rural areas are criss-crossed by a web of tiny lanes.

ROAD SIGNS

Signs are mostly standardized in line with Europe. Directional signs are colour-coded: blue for motorways, green for major routes and white for minor routes. Brown signs indicate places of interest. Advisory or warning signs are usually triangles in red and white, with easy-to-understand pictograms. Watch for electronic notices on motorways that warn of roadworks, accidents or patches of fog.

Level crossings, found at railway lines, often have automatic barriers. If the lights are flashing red, it means a train is coming and you must stop.

The UK Highway Code Manual, available online at the Department of Transport website, is an up-to-date guide to all the current British driving regulations and traffic signs.

RULES OF THE ROAD

Speed limits are 30–40 mph (50–65 km/h) in built-up areas and 70 mph (110 km/h) on motorways or dual carriageways. Look out for speed signs on other roads. It is compulsory to wear seatbelts in Britain. Drink-driving penalties are severe; see the UK Highway Code Manual for legal limits. It is illegal to use a mobile phone while driving.

PARKING

Parking meters operate during working hours (usually 8am–6:30pm Mon–Sat). Be sure to keep a supply of coins for them. Some cities have "park and ride" schemes, where you can take a bus from an out-of-city car park into the centre. Other towns have parking schemes where you buy a card at the tourist office or newsagents, fill in your parking times and display it on your dashboard. Avoid double red or yellow lines at all times; single lines sometimes mean you can park in the evenings and at weekends, but check carefully. Traffic wardens will not hesitate to ticket, clamp or tow away your car. If in doubt, find a car park. Outside urban

DISTANCE CHART

LONDON												
492 / 792	ABERDEEN											
111 / 179	411 / 658	BIRMINGHAM										
114 / 182	490 / 784	88 / 101	BRISTOL									
150 / 240	493 / 789	102 / 163	44 / 70	CARDIFF								
74 / 118	563 / 901	185 / 296	189 / 302	228 / 365	DOVER							
372 / 600	121 / 194	290 / 464	369 / 590	373 / 597	442 / 707	EDINBURGH						
170 / 272	565 / 904	164 / 262	75 / 120	120 / 192	244 / 342	444 / 710	EXETER					
198 / 317	792 / 492	90 / 144	161 / 258	165 / 264	270 / 432	214 / 342	237 / 380	LIVERPOOL				
184 / 294	333 / 533	81 / 130	162 / 258	173 / 277	257 / 411	213 / 341	238 / 381	34 / 54	MANCHESTER			
274 / 438	228 / 365	204 / 326	288 / 461	301 / 482	343 / 549	107 / 171	364 / 582	155 / 248	131 / 210	NEWCASTLE		
56 / 90	473 / 757	63 / 101	70 / 112	104 / 166	129 / 206	353 / 565	141 / 226	153 / 245	144 / 230	254 / 406	OXFORD	
194 / 310	307 / 491	129 / 206	217 / 347	231 / 397	264 / 422	186 / 297	292 / 467	97 / 155	65 / 104	82 / 131	174 / 278	YORK

10 Distance in miles
10 Distance in kilometres

areas and popular tourist zones, parking is much easier. Look out for signs with a blue "P", indicating parking spaces. Never leave any valuables or luggage in your car: thefts are common, especially in cities.

PETROL

Large supermarkets often have the best deals; look out for branches of Asda, Tesco or Sainsbury's with petrol stations. Motorway service areas are generally more expensive. Petrol is sold in three grades: diesel, LRP (lead replacement petrol) and unleaded. Most modern cars in Britain use unleaded petrol, and any vehicle you hire will probably do too. Unleaded and diesel are cheaper than LRP. Most petrol stations in Britain are self-service, but the instructions at pumps are easy to follow.

Sign for a car park

BREAKDOWN SERVICES

Britain's major motoring organizations are the **AA** (Automobile Association) and the **RAC** (Royal Automobile Club). They provide a comprehensive 24-hour breakdown service for members, as well as many other motoring services. Both offer reciprocal assistance for members of overseas motoring organizations – before arrival, check with your own group to see if you are covered. You can contact the AA or RAC from the roadside SOS phones found on motorways. **Green Flag** is the other major rescue service in Britain.

Most car-hire agencies have their own cover, and their

charges include membership of the AA, the RAC or Green Flag. Be sure to ask the rental company for the service's emergency number.

If you are not a member of an affiliated organization, you can still call out a rescue service, although it will be expensive. Always follow the advice given on your insurance policy or rental agreement. If you have an accident that involves injury or another vehicle, call the police as soon as possible (*see p675*).

The Environmental Transport Association gives advice on reducing the impact of carbon emissions, as well as offering a number of ethical breakdown services.

CAR HIRE

Hiring a car in Britain can be expensive. Details of car-hire companies at Britain's airports are on the VisitBritain website (*see p669*). One of the most competitive national companies is **Autos Abroad**, but small local firms may undercut even these rates. Other reputable car-hire companies include **Avis**, **Hertz**, **Europcar** and **Budget**. It is illegal to drive without third-party insurance, and it is advisable to take out fully comprehensive insurance. Many companies prefer you to leave a credit card number; if not, you may have to part with a substantial cash deposit. You need your driving licence and a passport when you hire. Most companies will not hire cars to novice drivers, and may place age limits (normally 21–74). Automatic cars are also usually available for hire. If you are touring Britain for three weeks or more, you may find a leasing arrangement cheaper than hiring. Remember to add VAT and insurance costs when you check hire rates.

DIRECTORY

BREAKDOWN

AA
Tel 0800 085 272.
www.theaa.com

Environmental Transport Association
www.eta.co.uk

Green Flag
Tel 0845 246 2766.
www.greenflag.com

RAC
Tel 01922 437000.
www.rac.co.uk

CAR HIRE

Autos Abroad
Tel 0844 826 6536.
www.autosabroad.com

Avis
Tel 0844 581 0147.
www.avis.co.uk

Budget
Tel 0844 544 3439.
www.budget.co.uk

Europcar
Tel 0871 384 9950.
www.europcar.co.uk

Hertz
www.hertz.co.uk

National Car Rentals
www.nationalcar.co.uk

GENERAL INFORMATION

AA Disabled Line
Tel 0800 262 050.

AA Road Watch
Tel 0906 888 4322.

Department of Transport
www.dft.gov.uk

DVLA
www.dvla.gov.uk

Weather
www.metoffice.gov.uk/weather

HITCHHIKING

It is not advisable to hitchhike in Britain, and there is a risk in hitchhiking alone, especially for a woman. If you must, stand near a busy exit road junction. In rural or walking areas like the Lake District, tired hikers may well be offered a lift. It is illegal to hitch on motorways or their approach roads.

Lift-sharing is now a common practice. The small-ads magazine *Loot* (sold in London, Manchester and Bristol, and also available online) has a large section for lift-seekers.

A small petrol station in Goathland, North Yorkshire

Travelling Around by Rail

Britain has a privatized rail network that covers the whole of the country, serving more than 2,500 stations. Divided into regional sections, the system is generally efficient and reliable. Parts of the network are occasionally closed for repairs, mostly at weekends, so check with your local station or online before travelling. Journeys across the country may involve a number of changes, since most lines radiate from London, which has seven major terminals. There is also a rail link with continental Europe on Eurostar, from King's Cross St Pancras station in London and Ebbsfleet and Ashford in Kent (see p680).

The concourse at Liverpool Street Station, London

TICKETS

Large travel agents and all railway stations sell train tickets. First-class tickets cost about one-third more than standard fares, and buying a return fare is generally cheaper than buying two singles.

Allow plenty of time to buy your ticket, and always ask about any special offers or reduced fares. There are four types of discounted fares for adults. Apex tickets are available in limited numbers on some long-distance routes, but they have to be booked at least one week in advance. SuperApex fares, also available in limited numbers on a few mainline services, have to be purchased 14 days in advance. Savers can be used at weekends and on most weekday trains outside rush hours, while Supersavers cannot be used on Fridays or on any peak-hour services to, from or through London.

Inspectors can levy on-the-spot fines if you do not have a valid ticket, so it is wise to buy a ticket before boarding the train. Ticket offices in rural areas may close at weekends, but small branch lines have a conductor on board who sells tickets. Many stations have automatic ticket machines.

RAIL PASSES

If you plan to do much train travelling around Britain, buy a rail pass. This can be purchased from many agents abroad, such as **Rail Europe** or **Cie Tours International**. National Rail's All Line Rail Rover gives adults unlimited travel throughout England, Scotland and Wales for seven or 14 days. A Family & Friends Railcard saves one-third on adult and 60 per cent off kids' (aged 5–15) fares. A Young Person's Rail Card offers discounts to 16- to 25-year-olds or full-time students attending a UK educational establishment. The Senior Rail Card entitles those over the age of 60 to a discount of one-third on most fares. There are special passes for London transport, too, and a pass that covers London, Oxford, Canterbury and Brighton. Children aged five to 15 pay half fare; those under the age of five travel free. Disabled travellers qualify for many discounts.

Keep a passport-sized photograph handy for buying passes. If you have a pass, make sure you always show it when you buy a ticket.

GENERAL TIPS

Britain's fastest and most comfortable trains are those on the mainline routes. These are very popular services and get booked up quickly. It is always advisable to reserve your seat in advance, especially if you want to travel at peak times, such as Friday evenings. Mainline trains have dining cars and air-conditioning, and they are fast – travelling to Edinburgh from London, for example, takes just over four hours.

Porters are rare on British stations, although trolleys are often available for passengers to help themselves. If you are disabled and need help, call the Mobility Helpline to book assistance at least 24 hours

Mainline train at platform

Reconditioned steam trains on the tracks in North Yorkshire

ahead of your journey. A yellow line above a train window indicates a first-class compartment. Note that even if the train is full, you cannot sit in the first-class area without paying the full fare.

Trains sometimes split en route, each section proceeding to different destinations, so always check which section you should be on. Trains stop for only a minute at each station, so gather your belongings in advance and be ready to get on and off.

Some stations are a little way from town centres, but they are usually well signposted and mostly on a bus route. Trains on Sundays and public holidays can be slower and less frequent than normal.

SCENIC TRAIN RIDES

After motor transport made many rural railways redundant in the mid-20th century, some picturesque sections of track, as well as many old steam engines, were rescued and restored to working order by enthusiasts. These services are often privately run; the local tourist office, railway station ticket office or travel agents will provide you with more information. This is one of the best ways to enjoy Britain's spectacular scenery. Most of the lines are short – around 20 miles (32 km) – but cover some of the prettiest parts of the country. Lines include the Ffestiniog Railway *(see pp452–3)* in North Wales; the North York Moors Railway *(see p394)*; the Strathspey Steam Railway in the Cairngorm Mountains of the Scottish Highlands *(see p544)* and the La'l Ratty Railway in Cumbria *(see p364).*

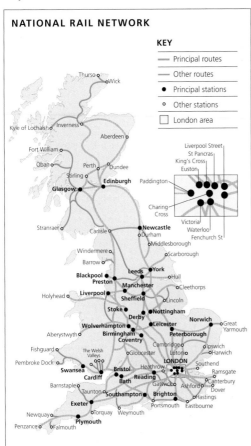

NATIONAL RAIL NETWORK

KEY

— Principal routes
— Other routes
● Principal stations
○ Other stations
▢ London area

Thurso
Wick
Kyle of Lochalsh
Inverness
Fort William
Oban
Perth
Dundee
Stirling
Edinburgh
Glasgow
Paddington
Liverpool Street
St Pancras
King's Cross
Euston
Charing Cross
Victoria
Waterloo
Fenchurch St
Stranraer
Carlisle
Newcastle
Durham
Middlesborough
Windermere
Scarborough
Barrow
Leeds
York
Blackpool
Hull
Preston
Manchester
Cleethorps
Holyhead
Liverpool
Sheffield
Lincoln
Stoke
Nottingham
Derby
Leicester
Norwich
Wolverhampton
Peterborough
Great Yarmouth
Aberystwyth
Birmingham
Coventry
Cambridge
Luton
Ipswich
Fishguard
Gloucester
Harwich
The Welsh Valleys
Heathrow
LONDON
Southend
Pembroke Dock
Swansea
Bristol
Reading
Ramsgate
Barnstaple
Cardiff
Bath
Gatwick
Ashford
Canterbury
Dover
Taunton
Southampton
Brighton
Hastings
Exeter
Portsmouth
Eastbourne
Newquay
Torquay
Weymouth
Penzance
Falmouth
Plymouth

DIRECTORY

UK RAIL NUMBERS

First Great Western Trains
Tel 08457 000 125 (bookings).

Mobility Advice Line
Tel 0121 454 3323.

Lost Property
Tel 0845 330 9882 (London Transport) or contact the relevant train company.

Midland Mainline
Tel 08457 22 11 25 (bookings).

National Express East Coast
Tel 08457 225 333 (bookings).

National Rail Enquiries Timetables
Tel 08457 48 49 50.
www.nationalrail.co.uk

Rail Europe
Tel 08448 484 064 (London).
www.raileurope.co.uk

Virgin Trains
Tel 08719 774 222 (bookings).

OVERSEAS RAIL NUMBERS

CIE Tours International
Tel +353 1703 1888 (Ireland).
www.cietours.com

Rail Europe
Tel 1-800-622-8600 (USA);
1-800-361-RAIL (Canada).

Travelling around by Coach

In Britain, the word "coach" refers to a long-distance express bus and one used for sightseeing excursions. What the British refer to as "buses" covers those vehicles that operate on regular routes with scheduled stops around or between villages, towns and cities. Many coach services duplicate rail routes but are generally cheaper. Journey times, however, are longer and much less predictable on crowded roads. Modern coaches are comfortable, sometimes with refreshments and toilets on board. Some city-to-city routes, especially at weekends, are so popular that it is a good idea to buy a reserved journey ticket, which guarantees you a seat. For ideas on visits to make, consult the VisitBritain website.

A coach tour on the Royal Mile, Edinburgh

NATIONAL COACH NETWORK

There are many regional coach companies, but the largest British coach operator is **National Express**, with a nationwide network of more than 1,200 destinations *(see pp16–19)*. Always book ahead for the more popular routes. The company offers a number of discounts, such as their £5 Funfares (50p booking fee), which are available online, to over 50 destinations. **Megabus** offers tickets for destinations all over Britain from as little as £1 (50p booking fee). As you would expect, you will need to book early, and the less popular destinations and travel times have the best deals.

The **Oxford Tube** and **Oxford Espress** run frequent, wheelchair-friendly services between Oxford and London, while **Scottish Citylink** is a major operator running regular services between London, the north and Scotland. Some

services run from Heathrow, Gatwick and Stansted airports. Allow plenty of time to buy your ticket before boarding.

Discounts are available for full-time students and anyone under 25. The over-50s can also qualify for a discount coach card, saving up to 30 per cent on many fares.

COACH TOURS

A range of coach tours, covering all interests, age groups and destinations, is available. Some include a tour guide. They may last anything from a couple of hours to two weeks or more, touring coast or countryside and visiting places of interest. Some are highly structured, organizing every break en route; others leave you to sightsee or shop at your own pace. You can opt for a prearranged route, or commission your own itinerary for a group. Visit the **Enjoy England** website for inspiration.

Any large town will have a selection of coach companies. Check the local Yellow Pages *(see p678)* or ask at your hotel or local tourist office. You can also book coach trips direct from overseas through a specialist travel agent.

Seaside resorts and tourist sites are destinations for many day trips, especially in high season. In some of the more popular rural areas, such as the Lake District, special small coaches operate for ease of movement. You can book these in advance, or just turn up before the coach leaves, although the tour is likely to be fully booked, especially in high season. The local tourist information point or travel agent will be able to tell you where these trips leave from, the cost and may even sell you tickets. It is customary to tip the guide after your tour.

REGIONAL BUSES

Regional bus services are run by a number of companies, some private and some operated by local authorities. Services to remote areas tend to be sporadic and expensive, with some buses running just once a week and many isolated villages having no service at all. Only a few rural buses are equipped for wheelchairs.

As a rule, the further you get from a city, the fewer the buses and the more expensive the fare. On the plus side, local buses can be a pleasant and often sociable

A National Express coach

way of travelling around Britain's lovely countryside.

Most buses run with just one operator – the driver. All drivers prefer you to have the correct fare, so always keep a selection of coins handy. Some routes do not operate on Sundays and public holidays; those that do are much reduced. Always check your routes, schedules and fares at the local tourist office or bus station before you depart on a bus to avoid being stranded somewhere with no return transport.

DIRECTORY

Enjoy England
www.enjoyengland.com

VisitBritain
www.visitbritain.com

COACH TRAVEL

Megabus
Tel 0871 266 3333.
www.megabus.com

National Express
Tel 08717 81 81 78.
www.nationalexpress.com

Oxford Bus Company
Tel 01865 785400.
www.oxfordbus.co.uk

Oxford Tube
Tel 01865 772250.
www.stagecoachbus.com/oxfordshire

Scottish Citylink
Tel 0871 266 3333.
www.citylink.co.uk

Victoria Coach Station
Tel 020 7027 2520.
www.tfl.gov.uk/vcs

FERRY & WATERWAY TRAVEL

British Waterways
Tel 01923 201120
(head office).
www.britishwaterways.co.uk

Caledonian MacBrayne
Tel 0800 066 5000.
www.calmac.co.uk

Waterscape
www.waterscape.com

Travelling Britain's Coasts and Waterways

Britain has thousands of miles of inland waterways and hundreds of islands scattered along its beautiful coastline. Cruising along a canal in the Midlands countryside or travelling on one of the small local ferries to a remote Scottish island are both wonderful experiences. Canal boats can be hired, and scores of ferries run between Britain's offshore islands. For information on Britain's canals, rivers and lakes and to book accommodation, a boat or a hotel boat, visit the Waterscape website.

A barge on the Welsh Backs, Bristol

CANALS

As industrial production grew in the 18th century, it became vital to find a cheap and effective way of transporting heavy loads. Canals fulfilled this need, and a huge network was built, linking most industrial areas in the north and sea ports.

The arrival of the railways and their immediate success for freight made most canals redundant, but there are still some 3,200 km (2,000 miles) left, most in the old industrial heartland of the Midlands.

Today these canals lure travellers who are content to cruise on old-fashioned, slow narrowboats, taking their time to enjoy the views and the canalside inns, originally built to satisfy the bargees' thirsts and to supply stabling for the barge horses. These canal holidays can be very relaxing if you have the time.

If you wish to hire a narrowboat, you can book with a specialist travel firm or contact **British Waterways**.

LOCAL FERRIES

Britain's local ferries can offer anything from a ten-minute river journey to a seven-hour sea cruise.

Many of Scotland's ferries are operated by **Caledonian MacBrayne**. They sail to lots of different destinations, such as the Isle of Skye to the Kyle of Lochalsh, or the five-hour journey from Oban to Lochboisdale in the Western Isles. They offer a variety of different ticket types, from unlimited rover tickets for a specific period of time, to island-hop passes or all-inclusive coach tour and ferry tickets. Not all the island ferries take cars.

River ferries make an interesting alternative to the more usual forms of transport. The ferry across the Mersey, between the cities of Liverpool and Birkenhead, is still

A car ferry travelling from Oban to Lochboisdale

used by many commuters. London's river trips, such as the one that runs from Westminster to Tower Bridge, offer a different perspective on the city and make a change from tubes, buses and cars. Local tourist information centres can give you information about ferries in their area.

Travelling within Cities

Urban public transport in Britain is efficient and can be fun – children love London's double-decker buses. Fares are good value, especially compared to the expense of parking a car. Most of the larger cities have good bus services. London, Newcastle and Glasgow also have an underground system, while Blackpool, Manchester and Nottingham have trams. Taxis are available at every train station and at ranks near hotels and city centres. The best way to see many cities is on foot, but whatever transport you opt for, try to avoid the rush hours, from 8am to 9:30am and 5pm to 6:30pm.

Double-decker buses on the Strand, in London

LOCAL BUSES

Buses come in all shapes and sizes, with automatic doors and comfortable interiors. They include driver-operated double-deckers, the single-decker "bendy" bus and even smaller single-deckers that are able to weave in and out of traffic more easily. The old "big red bus" with a conductor still exists in London, but only as Heritage route numbers 9 and 15 (through the West End and the City respectively).

On most buses you pay the driver as you enter. They will not always accept notes, so keep a few pound coins handy. Credit cards and cheques are not accepted. The fare depends on the distance you travel. If you are exploring a city by bus, a daily pass is a good idea. Many of the larger cities have daily or weekly passes that can be used on all public transport in that city; these can often be bought from newsagents. Check with the tourist office for schedules and fares.

Night services are available only in major cities, from about 11pm until early morning.

Day passes are valid on these until 4:30am. In London, night buses are prefixed with the letter "N", and most of them pass through Trafalgar Square. Be on your guard when travelling alone late at night, when there may be few other passengers on board.

At some stops, called request stops, the driver will not halt unless you signal that you want to get on or off. If you want to board, raise your arm as the bus approaches; if you want to get off, ring the bell once before your stop. Destinations are shown on the front of buses. If you are not sure which stop you need, ask the driver or conductor to alert you and stay on the lower deck. Always keep your ticket until the end of the journey in case an inspector gets on board. They can impose an on-the-spot fine if you are without a valid ticket.

Cities have bus lanes, intended to bypass car traffic jams during the rush hours. These can be effective, but your journey could still take a long time. Schedules are hard to keep to, so regard timetables as advisory.

DRIVING IN CITIES

Driving in city centres is increasingly discouraged. In 2003 London introduced a congestion charge – if you drive or park within the congestion zone from Monday to Friday (7am to 6pm), you will be charged a £9–12 fee to pay before 10pm that day at a newsagent, petrol station or post office. Not paying the charge will lead to a large fine. See **Transport for London**'s website for more information. Other cities are considering similar steps to keep drivers out of the centres. Parking in city centres is also strictly controlled to prevent congestion (see p684).

TAXIS

In large towns, taxis can be found at taxi ranks and train stations. Some operate by radio, so you have to phone. The local Yellow Pages (see p678), pubs, restaurants and hotels will all have a list of taxi numbers. Prices are usually regulated. Always ask the price before you start your journey if there is no taxi meter. If you are not sure of the correct fare, ask the local tourist information point.

The famous London black cabs are almost as much of an institution as the big red buses. These are the safest cabs to use in London since all the drivers are licensed and have undergone strict tests. All licensed cabs must display a "For hire" sign, which is lit up whenever they are free. The newer cab designs are equipped to carry wheelchairs. If a cab stops for you in London, it must by law take you anywhere within a radius of 6 miles (10 km) so long as it is within the Metropolitan Police District. This includes most of London and Heathrow Airport. All licensed cabs have meters that start ticking

One of London's black cabs

as soon as the driver accepts your custom. The fare will increase minute by minute or for each 311 m (1,020 ft) travelled. Most drivers expect a tip of between 10 and 15 per cent of the fare. If you have a complaint, note the serial number found in the back of the cab.

Do not use unlicensed minicabs – they may be mechanically unsound or even uninsured. Never accept an unbooked minicab ride in the street.

GUIDED BUS TOURS

Most major tourist cities offer sightseeing bus tours. Weather permitting, a good way to see the cities is from a traditional open-topped double-decker bus. Private tours can be arranged with many companies. Contact the local tourist information centre for more details.

TRAMS

Trams are making a comeback throughout Britain in clean, energy-efficient and more modern guises. One of the best tram schemes in Britain is Manchester's Metrolink. The oldest tramway is in Blackpool, which opened in 1885.

LONDON UNDERGROUND

The Underground network in London, known as the Tube, has more than 270 sta-

A tram along Blackpool's famous promenade

CYCLING

Cycling is one of the greenest ways of getting around town. Even modest towns have somewhere you can hire bikes. Cyclists may not use motorways or their approach roads, nor can they ride on pavements, footpaths or pedestrianized zones. Many city roads have cycle lanes and their own traffic lights. You can take a bike on most trains; see the **National Rail** website for more information. Never leave your bike unlocked, and always wear a helmet.

Cyclists stopped at a red light on a London street

tions, each of which is marked with the London Underground logo. The only other cities with an underground system are Newcastle and Glasgow. Newcastle's system is limited to the city centre, while Glasgow's skirts around the centre. Both are clean and efficient, running the same hours as London's.

A London Underground sign outside a station

London tube trains run every day, except Christmas Day, from about 5:30am until just after midnight. Fewer trains run on Sundays and bank holidays. Note that the tube can get very crowded during rush hour.

An Oyster card

The 11 tube lines are colour-coded and maps called Journey Planners are posted at every tube station, while maps of the central section are displayed in each train.

Most tube journeys between central destinations in London can be completed with only one or two changes of line. Smoking is not permitted on the Underground.

Tickets are purchased at the station, but many travellers use an Oyster card, an electronic card that can be topped up for use on buses, trains and the tube. Using an Oyster card is, by far, the cheapest way of travelling

on London Transport's tubes and buses. For information on how to get one, see the Transport for London website. Oyster cards can be purchased from abroad. There are similar electronic card schemes in other major British cities, such as Oxford.

WALKING IN CITIES

Once you get used to traffic on the left, Britain's cities can be safely and enjoyably explored on foot. Instructions written on the road will tell you from which direction you can expect the traffic to come.

There are two types of pedestrian crossing: striped zebra crossings and push-button crossings at traffic lights. At a zebra crossing, traffic should stop for you, but at push-button crossings, cars will not stop until the lights change in your favour. More and more cities and towns are creating traffic-free zones in the city centre for pedestrians.

DIRECTORY

National Rail
Tel 08457 48 49 50
(enquiries).
www.nationalrail.co.uk

Transport for London
Tel 0843 222 1234 *(voice-activated service).* **www**.tfl.com

General Index

Page numbers in **bold** type refer to main entries
100 Club (London) 154, 155
333 (London) 154, 155

A

A La Ronde 289
AA 685
Abbeys and priories
  Abbey Dore 316
  Bath Abbey 259, 260
  Bolton Priory 386
  Buckfast Abbey 291, 295
  Buckland Abbey **292**
  Byland Abbey **392**
  Cartmel Priory 369
  Castle Acre Priory 195
  Christchurch Priory 271
  Dryburgh Abbey 503
  Dunfermline Abbey 500
  Easby Abbey 351
  Fountains Abbey 12, 50, 347, **390–91**
  Furness Abbey 368, 369
  Glastonbury Abbey 253
  Hartland Abbey 286
  Hexham Abbey 422, 423
  Inchmahome Priory 495
  Jedburgh Abbey 503
  Kelso Abbey 503
  Kirkham Priory 351
  Kirkstall Priory 351
  Lanercost Priory 358
  Lindisfarne Priory 418, 419
  Llanthony Priory 461, 469
  Malvern Priory 317
  Melrose Abbey 503, **512**
  Mount Grace Priory 350, **394**
  North Country abbeys **350–51**
  Rievaulx Abbey 12, **393**
  Rosedale Abbey 395
  St Mary's Abbey (Llyn Peninsula) 453
  St Mary's Abbey (York) **350–51**, 408
  St Nicholas Priory (Exeter) 289
  Tintern Abbey **475**
  Torre Abbey 290
  Whalley Abbey 371
  Whitby Abbey 396
Abbotsbury 32, **268**
  hotels 570
  pubs 653
Abbotsford House **512**
Abefeldy, hotels 596
Aberaeron **463**
  pubs 657
  restaurants 644
Aberconwy see North Wales
Aberdeen 13, **538–40**
  hotels 596–7
  restaurants 649
Aberdeenshire see Highlands and Islands
Aberdovey, restaurants 642
Aberdyfi **455**
  hotels 590
Abergavenny,
  hotels 591
  restaurants 644
Abersoch
  hotels 590
  restaurants 642
Aberystwyth **462–3**
  hotels 592
  pubs 657
Achiltibuie, hotels 597
Achray, Loch 481
Act of Union (1535) 50, 437

Act of Union (1707) 53, 480, 482, 483
Adam, John 509
Adam, Robert 25, 55
  Audley End 208–9
  Bowood House 255
  Bury St Edmunds 206
  Culzean Castle 478, 522, 523
  Georgian House (Edinburgh) 504
  Harewood House 410
  Kedleston Hall 28–9
  Kenwood House (London) 124
  Pulteney Bridge (Bath) 259
  Saltram House 292
  Syon House (London) 126
Adam, William 502, 503, 514, 548
Adelphi Theatre (London) 153
Admission prices 670
The Adoration of the Kings (Bruegel) 82
The Adoration of the Magi (Rubens) 213
Afternoon tea 601
  Devonshire cream teas 287
Agincourt, Battle of (1415) 49
Agricola, Julius 44, 482
Aidan, St 46, 415, 418, 419
Aintree Racecourse 664, 665
Air Canada 682
Air New Zealand 682, 683
Air travel **682–3**
Airsure (Royal Mail) 679
Aislabie, John 390
Aitchison, Craigie 517
Alban, St 45
Albert, Prince Consort
  Albert Memorial (London) 97
  Balmoral 540
  Great Exhibition 57, 95, 96
  Manchester 373
  Osborne House 162, 164
  Victoria and Albert Museum (London) 98
  Windsor Castle 236
Albert Memorial (London) 97
  Street-by-Street map 97
Alciston, pubs 652
Alcohol 602, 671
  traditional British pub 604–5
Alcoholics Anonymous 675
Aldeburgh 11, **202–3**
  festivals 63, 203
  hotels 565
  restaurants 618
Alderminster, pubs 654
Alderwasley, pubs 655
Aldrich, Henry 227
Aldwych Theatre (London) 153
Alexandria, restaurants 649
Alfred the Great, King 47, 221, 247, 268
Alfriston 180
Alice in Wonderland (Carroll) **445**
All England Lawn Tennis Club 155, 664, 665
All Souls, Langham Place (London) 105
All Souls College (Oxford) 226
Allendale
  North Pennines tour 427
Alma-Tadema, Lawrence
  Etruscan Vase Painters 374
Alnwick Castle 344, **420**
Altarnun 285
Althorp House 343
Alton Towers 661
Alwinton 421
The Ambassadors (Holbein) 83

Ambleside **366–7**
  hotels 582
  pubs 655
  restaurants 635
Ambulances 675
American Airlines 682, 683
American Express 676
Amigoni, Jacopo 214
Ampleforth, hotels 586
Anglesey 442
  see also North Wales
Anglesey Abbey **208**
Angling Trust 664, 665
Anglo-Saxon Kingdoms **46–7**
Angus see Highlands and Islands
Anne, Queen 41, 54, 287
  Bath 260
  Blenheim Palace 217, 228
  death 101
  Hampton Court 173
  Kensington Gardens (London) 101
Anne of Cleves 180
Anne Hathaway's Cottage 327
  Midlands garden tour 321
Anslow, restaurants 630
Anstruther, restaurants 646
Antiques for Everyone 62
Antiques shops 659
  London 150, 151
Antonine Wall 44, 491
Apollo Theatre (London) 153
Applecross
  hotels 597
  pubs 657
Appledore **287**
Aquariums
  The Deep (Kingston upon Hull) 402, 403
  National Marine Aquarium (Plymouth) 292
  Sea Life Centre (Brighton) 175
Arbor Low
  Peak District tour 338
Architecture 24–5
  building with Cotswold stone **304–5**
  Durham Cathedral 429
  Georgian architecture 54–5
  rural architecture 32–3
  Scottish castles **486–7**
  stately homes 28–9
  Tudor manor houses 302–3
Argyll, Dukes of 496, 548
Argyll and Bute see Highlands and Islands
Arisaig, hotels 597
Aristocracy **30–31**
Arkwright, Sir Richard 55, 336, 339, 372
Arlington Court 287
Armscote, pubs 654
Armstrong, Lord 420
Arnolfini Portrait (Van Eyck) 82
Arnside, hotels 582
Arsenal FC 664, 665
Art
  canal boats 301
  shops 150, 151
  see also Museums and galleries
Arthur, King 47, 247, **285**
  Dozmary Pool 285
  Glastonbury 253
  Ruthin 445
  Snowdon 433
  Stirling Castle 496
  Tintagel 273, 285
  Winchester 170
Arthur, Prince 313, 318
Arts and Crafts movement 220–21, 328

Arundel
  Castle 172
  restaurants 615
Arvon Foundation 662, 665
Asenby, restaurants 638
Ashburton Cookery School 662, 665
Ashleworth, pubs 654
Ashmole, Elias 222, 224
Ashmolean Museum (Oxford) 222, 224
Ashness Bridge 363
Aske, Robert 351
Askrigg, pubs 655
Aspiring Forms (Wells) 277
Asquith, Henry 58
Astor, Nancy 162
Astor, William Waldorf 189
At the Theatre (Renoir) 83
Athelhampton 245, 269
Athelstan, King of Wessex 401
Atkinson, Thomas 402
Auchindrain Museum **548**
Auchterarder
  hotels 594
  restaurants 649
Audley End **208–9**
Augustine, St 46, 186
Auld Alliance 482
Auldearn, hotels 597
Austen, Jane
  Bath 258, 260
  grave 170
  Jane Austen's House (Chawton) 162, 172
Autos Abroad 685
Autumn in Great Britain 64
Avebury **263**
  restaurants 622
Aviemore 544
Avis 685
Avonwick, restaurants 626
Awe, Loch **547**
Axminster, restaurants 622
Ayckbourn, Alan 24, 397
Aycliffe, restaurants 640
Aylesbury
  hotels 568
  pubs 653
Ayr
  restaurants 646
Ayrshire *see* Lowlands (Scotland)
Aysgarth Falls 385

B

Babbacombe
  hotels 574
  Model Village 290
Babbage, Charles 291
Babworth, hotels 581
Back of the New Mills (Crome) 201
Back-Roads Touring Company 662, 665
Bacon, Sir Francis 232
Bacon, Francis 80, 91, 201
Baker, Ted 150, 151
Bakewell, restaurants 632
Bala **450**
Ballater
  hotels 597
  restaurants 649
  Royal Deeside tour 540
Ballet 661
  London 154
Balliol, Bernard 426
Balmoral 479, 525
  Royal Deeside tour 540
Balquhidder, hotels 594
Balston, Michael 233
BALTIC (Newcastle upon Tyne) 425

Bamburgh **420**
  Castle 417
Banbury 220
Banchory
  Royal Deeside tour 541
Bank holidays 65
Bank notes 677
Bankes, Sir John 270
Bankes family 271
Banking **676**
Banks, Iain 502
Bankside Power Station (London) **121**
Bannockburn, Battle of (1314) 49, 496
Banqueting House (London) **90**
  Street-by-Street map 89
Baptist Church 673
Barbican Concert Hall (London) 154
Bardon Mill
  North Pennines tour 427
Barlow, Bishop of St Davids 464
Barnard Castle **426**
  pubs 656
Barnby Moor, hotels 581
Barnsley, hotels 586
Barnstaple **287**
  hotels 574
  restaurants 626
Barra 529
Barrie, J M 101
Barrow-in-Furness 368
Barry, Sir Charles
  Houses of Parliament (London) 90
  Manchester Art Gallery 374
  Town Hall (Halifax) 412
Barry, E M 80
Baslow
  hotels 581
  restaurants 633
Bassenthwaite 360
  hotels 582
Bateman's (Burwash) 163
Bath 11, 21, 241, 248, **258–61**
  hotels 570
  International Music Festival 63
  pubs 653
  restaurants 622–3
  Street-by-Street map 258–9
Bath, Marquesses of 266
Bathurst, 1st Earl 329
Battersea Park (London) 75
Battle, hotels 563
Battle Abbey 181
The Battle of Culloden (Campbell) 537
Beachy Head 180
Beaker People 42, 43
Beale, Gilbert 234
Beale Park
  Thames Valley tour 234
Beaminster, restaurants 623
Beamish Open Air Museum 13, **424–5**
The Beatles 31, 60, 376, **377**
  Beatles Festival (Liverpool) 63
  The Beatles Story (Liverpool) 377
Beauchamp family 322, 323, 472
Beaulieu **164**
  hotels 563
Beauly, hotels 597
Beaumaris **444**
  Castle 432, 438–9, 444
  hotels 590
  restaurants 642
Beaumont, Guillaume 369
Becket, St Thomas à 48–9, 186, 187
Beckingham, restaurants 633
Becky Falls 295

Bed-and-breakfast 553
Beddgelert 448–9, **452**
  hotels 590
Bede, the Venerable 415, 419, 428
Bedford
  pubs 653
Bedford, Dukes of 11, 230
Bedford Square (London) 107
Bedfordshire *see* Thames Valley
Bedingfeld, Sir Edmund 195
"Beefeaters" 118
Beer **604–5**
Belfast, HMS (London) **117**
Belford, hotels 588
Bell, Alexander 481
Bell, Vanessa 163
Bellany, John 505
Bellini, Giovanni 224
Bempton Cliffs **400–401**
Ben MacDhui 545
Benbecula 529
Bennett, Arnold 311
Bere Regis 269
Berkshire *see* Thames Valley
Bermondsey Market (London) 149
Berrington Hall 313
Berwick Street market (London) 149
Berwick-upon-Tweed **418**
  hotels 588
Bess of Hardwick 334, 336
Betws-y-Coed **450**
  hotels 590
Bevan, Aneurin 437
Beverley **401**
  hotels 586
Bibury 304, 308
  hotels 578
Bicester
  hotels 568
  pubs 653
Bickley Moss, pubs 654
Bideford **286**
Big Ben (London) 10, 77, 90
  Street-by-Street map 89
Bigbury-on-Sea
  hotels 574
  restaurants 626
Biggar **513**
Biggin-by-Hartingdon, hotels 581
Birchover, pubs 655
Birds 34–5
  Bempton 400–401
  St Abb's Head 502
  Shetland seabirds 528
  see also Wildlife
Birkenhead 379
Birmingham **318–19**
  hotels 578
  restaurants 630–31
Bistros 601
Black Death 48, 49, 207, 318
The Black Isle **531**
Black Mountain 468
Black Mountains 469
Blackburn
  hotels 582
  restaurants 635
Blackmore, R D 251
Blackpool 12, **371**
  hotels 583
  Illuminations 64
  restaurants 635
Blackwell, hotels 578
Bladud, King 260
Blaenafon 457, **474**
Blaenau Ffestiniog **451**
Blahnik, Manolo 98, 150, 151
Blair, Tony 61
Blair Atholl, festivals 62
Blair Castle 487, **543**

Blairgowrie
  hotels 594
Blake, Peter 91
Blake, William 91, 412, 520
Blakeney Marshes
  North Norfolk coastal tour 197
Blanchland
  North Pennines tour 427
Blandford Forum, hotels 571
Blencathra 361
Blenheim Palace 11, 158, 217, **228–9**
Blickling Hall **198**
Blists Hill Victorian Town (Ironbridge Gorge) 315
Blockley, hotels 578
Bloomsbury (London) **103–7**
  area map 103
  hotels 558–9
  pubs 652
  restaurants 612
Bloomsbury Group 103, 107, **163**, 180
Bloomsbury Square (London) 107
Boadicea 44, 45, **195**
  Colchester 205
  St Albans 232
Boatbuilding (Constable) 204
Boateng, Ozwald 150, 151
Boats
  boating and sailing 664, 665
  canals 300, 301, 689
  ferries 681, 689
  punting on the Cam 214
  Thames boating tours 234
Bodiam Castle **182**
Bodleian Library (Oxford) **227**
Bodley, Thomas 227
Bodmin **284–5**
Bodmin Moor 11
Boer War 57
Boleyn, Anne
  Blickling Hall 198
  execution 117, 118
  Fountains Abbey 391
  Hever Castle 189
Bolton, hotels 583
Bolton Abbey, restaurants 638
Bolton Castle 385
Bolton Priory 386
Bonnie Prince Charlie (Dupré) 482
Book shops, London **150**, 151
Booth, Richard 461
Boots 675
Borders (Scotland)
  A Tour of the Borders 503
  see Lowlands (Scotland)
Borough Market (London) **120**, 149
Boroughbridge, restaurants 638
Borromini, Francesco 114
Borrowdale **363**
Boscastle 285
  hotels 574
Bosch, Hieronymus
  Christ Mocked 73
Bosham 171
Bossanyi, Erwin 187
Bosworth, Battle of (1485) 49
Botallack Mine
  Penwith tour 276
Bothwell, Earl of 511
Boucher, François 104
Bourgeois, Louise 121
Bournemouth **271**
  hotels 571
  restaurants 623
Bovey Tracey 295
Bow Fell 365
Bowder Stone 363
Bowness-on-Windermere 367
  hotels 583

Bowood House 255
Box Hill 172
Boyle, Danny 25
Boyne, Battle of the (1690) 53
Bracknell, hotels 568
Bradford **411**
  hotels 586
  restaurants 638
Bradford-on-Avon **255**
  hotels 571
  restaurants 623
Bradley, Thomas 412–13
Braemar Castle 486
Braemar Games 64
Braich-y-Pwll 453
Bramber 174
Branagh, Kenneth 327
Brangwyn, Sir Frank 466
Brasseries 601
Braunton Burrows 287
Braunton "Great Field" 287
Brawne, Fanny 123
Bray-on-Thames
  hotels 568
  restaurants 620
Breakdown services 685
Breakfast 600, 603
Brecon 469
  festivals 63
  hotels 592
  restaurants 644
Brecon Beacons 13, 433, **468–9**
Brentor 294
Bretforton, pubs 654
Brick Lane market (London) 149
Bridgend, restaurants 644
Bridgewater, 3rd Duke of 300
Bridport
  hotels 571
  pubs 653
Brighton 10, **174–9**
  festivals 62, 64, 65
  hotels 563
  pier 166–7, 174
  pubs 652
  restaurants 615–6
  Royal Pavilion 159, 175, 178–9
  Street-by-Street map 174–5
Bristol **256–7**
  hotels 571–2
  map 257
  restaurants 624
British Airports Authority 683
British Airways 682, 683
British Boot Company (London) 150, 151
British Broadcasting Corporation (BBC) 25
British Deaf Association 675
British Empire 22, 56
British Figure Skating and Ice Dance Championships 67
British Golf Open Championship 67
British Grand Prix 67
British Horse Society 663, 665
British Midland 682, 683
British Museum (London) 10, 73, **106–7**
British Pregnancy Advisory Service 675
British Surfing Association 664, 665
British Waterways 689
BritRail 680, 681
Brittany Ferries 681
Britten, Benjamin 203
Brixham 290
Brixton Academy (London) 154, 155
Brixton Market (London) 149
Broad Campden, hotels 578
Broad Haven, hotels 592

Broadlands 162
The Broads **198**
  windmills 199
Broads Authority 664, 665
Broadstairs 163
Broadway
  Midlands garden tour 320
Brockenhurst
  hotels 563
Brodick, Cuthbert 410
Brompton Oratory (London) **97**
  Street-by-Street map 97
Brontë, Anne 12, 397, **412**
Brontë, Charlotte 12, 339, **412**
Brontë, Emily 12, **412**
Brown, "Capability" 26
  Alnwick Castle 420
  Audley End 208
  Berrington Hall 313
  Blenheim Palace 229
  Bowood House 255
  Burghley House 342
  Chatsworth House 334
  Harewood House 410
  Longleat House 266
  Petworth House 172
  Stowe Gardens 230
Brown, Ford Madox 49, 373
  The Last of England 319
Brown, Gordon 61
Brownsea Island 270–71
Bruce, Sir George 501
Bruce, William Speirs 481
Bruce in Single Combat (Hassall) 482
Bruegel, Pieter the Elder
  The Adoration of the Kings 82
Brunel, Isambard Kingdom 256
Buckden, hotels 565
Buckfast Abbey 291, 295
Buckfastleigh **291**
Buckingham, restaurants 620
Buckingham, Dukes of 230
Buckingham Palace (London) 72, **86–7**
Buckinghamshire, 2nd Earl of 198
Buckinghamshire see Thames Valley
Buckland, hotels 578
Buckland Abbey **292**
Buckland-in-the-Moor 275, 295
Buckler's Hard 168
Buddhism 673
Bude **285**
  hotels 574
Budget (car hire) 685
Building materials 33
Builth Wells, restaurants 644
BUNAC 672, 673
Bunker Hill, Battle of (1775) 54
Bunyan, John 231
Burberry (London) 150, 151
Bureaux de change 676
Burford **220**
  hotels 568
Burford House Gardens 313
Burges, William
  Cardiff Castle 433, **472–3**
  Castell Coch 439
  Fountains Abbey 391
Burgh Island **291**
The Burghers of Calais (Rodin) 88
Burghley, William Cecil, 1st Lord 342
Burghley House 299, 332, **342–3**
Burlington, 3rd Earl of 126
Burlington Arcade (London)
  Street-by-Street map 84
Burne-Jones, Sir Edward 123, 319, 399
Burnham Market, hotels 565

Burns, Robert 65, 481, 505
  Burns Cottage 515
  Burns Night 65
Burnsall 386
  restaurants 638
Burrell, Sir William 520
Burrell Collection (Glasgow) 479,
  520–21
Burton Agnes Hall **400**
Burton Constable **402**
Bury St Edmunds **206–7**
  hotels 566
  restaurants 618
Buses 688–9
  guided tours 691
  local buses 690
Bute, 3rd Marquess of 439, 472, 500
Butler, Lady Eleanor 450
Buttermere **363**
  hotels 583
Buttertubs 385
Buxton 12, **334**
  hotels 581
  Peak District tour 338
Byland Abbey **392**
  pubs 655
Byron, Lord 31

C

Cabinet War Rooms (London) **89**
  Street-by-Street map 88
Cabot, John 50, 256
Cadbury, George 349
Caedmon's Cross (Whitby) 396
Caerleon **474**
Caernarfon **444**
Caernarfon Castle 13, 439, 441, 444
Caernarfonshire see North Wales
Caerphilly Castle 438
Caesar, Julius 44, 261
Café de Paris (London) 154, 155
Cafés 601
Cairndow, restaurants 649
Cairngorms 13, 479, 525, **544–5**
Caldey Island 466
Caledonian MacBrayne 689
Callander 495
Calne, hotels 572
Camber Sands 185
Cambrian Mountains 467
Cambridge 10–11, 20, 192, **210–15**
  Cambridge University 214–15
  festivals 63
  hotels 566
  King's College 211, 212–13
  pubs 653
  punting on the Cam 214
  restaurants 618
  Street-by-Street map 210–11
  University 159
Cambridge Theatre (London) 153
Cambridgeshire see East Anglia
Camden (London) **124**
Camden Lock Market (London) 149
Camden Passage (London) 149
Camilla, Duchess of Cornwall 61,
  235
Campbell, Colen 28, 266
Campbell, D
  The Battle of Culloden 537
Campbell, Donald 368
Campbell, Lady Grace 548
Campbell, Naomi 25, 60
Campbell clan 484, 548
Campden, Sir Baptist Hicks, 1st
  Viscount 327
Camping 555
Campsea Ashe, hotels 566
Canada Tower (London) 61

Canaletto, Antonio 420
  Entrance to the Arsenal 230
  Goodwood House 171
  View of Warwick Castle 323
  Wallace Collection (London) 104
Canals **689**
  Canals of the Midlands 300–301
  Industrial Revolution 348
  Leeds-Liverpool Canal 348
  Llangollen Canal 450
  Manchester Ship Canal 371, 372
  Monmouthshire and Brecon
    Canal 469
Canterbury 10, **186**
  Cathedral 159, 167, 186–7
  Festival 64
  hotels 563
  restaurants 617
Canute, King 47
  Bosham 171
  Buckfast Abbey 295
  Bury St Edmunds 206
Canynge, William 256
Capel Coch, restaurants 642
Capel Curig, pubs 656
Capel Garmon, hotels 590
Captain Thomas Lee (Gheeraerts) 91
Caravanning 555
Cardiff **470–73**
  hotels 592
  map 471
  restaurants 644–5
Cardiff Castle 433, 459, **472–3**
Carfax Tower (Oxford) 224
Cargo (London) 155
Carisbrooke Castle 164
Carlisle **358**
  hotels 583
  restaurants 635
Carlisle, Earls of 398, 399
Carlyle, Thomas 122
Carnegie, Andrew 481, 500–501
  Carnegie Birthplace Museum
    (Dunfermline) 501
Carnforth 370
Carnoustie, restaurants 649
Caro, Anthony 413
Carol concerts 65
Caroline, Queen 101
Caroline of Brunswick 179
Carpenter, Samuel 398
Carphone Warehouse 678
Carr, John 28, 408, 410
Carrawburgh Fort 423
Carrick Roads 280
Carroll, Lewis 225, 401, **445**
Cars **684–5**
  driving in cities 689
  hiring 680, 685
  racing 67
  see also Tours by car
Carterway Heads, restaurants 641
Cartier International Polo 67
Cartmel **369**
  restaurants 635
Carvoran Fort 422
Cash dispensers 676
Castell Coch 439
Castell-y-Bere 439
Castle Combe, hotels 572
Castle Drogo 295
Castle Howard 28, 347, **398–9**
Castlereagh, Lord 462
Castlerigg Stone Circle 43, 359, 361
Castles
  Scottish castles 486–7
  Welsh castles 438–9
  Aberystwyth 463
  Alnwick 344, 420
  Arundel 172

Castles (cont.)
  Balhousie Castle (Perth) 498
  Balmoral 479, 525, 540
  Bamburgh 417, 420
  Beaumaris 432, 438–9, 444
  Blair 487, 543
  Bodiam 182
  Bolton 385
  Braemar 486
  Bramber 174
  Caernarfon 13, 439, 441, 444
  Caerphilly 438
  Camber 185
  Cardiff 433, 459, 472–3
  Carisbrooke 164
  Carlisle 358
  Carreg Cennen 468
  Castell Coch 439
  Castell Dinas Brân 450
  Castell-y-Bere 439
  Cawdor 537
  Claypotts 486
  Cockermouth 362
  Colchester 205
  Conwy 13, 433, 438, 439, 443, 447
  Corfe 270
  Crathes 541
  Culzean 478, 522–3
  Dartmouth 290
  Dolbadarn 451
  Doune 498
  Dover 182, 183
  Drum 487, 541
  Drumlanrig 487, 514–15
  Duart 546, 547
  Duffus 486
  Dunrobin 487, 530–31
  Dunstaffnage 546–7
  Dunvegan 534
  Durham 429
  Edinburgh 13, 493, 506–7
  Eilean Donan 525, 530
  Exeter 288
  Floors 503
  Framlingham 203
  Glamis 491, 498–9
  Goodrich 317
  Guildford 172
  Harlech 13, 438, 454
  Helmsley 393
  Inverary 548
  Kilchurn 547
  Kisimul 529
  Lancaster 370, 371
  Leeds 10, 63, 165, 188
  Lewes 180
  Lincoln 340
  Lindisfarne 418
  Ludlow 312, 313
  Middleham 385
  Monmouth 474–5
  Neidpath 486
  Newcastle upon Tyne 424–5
  Nottingham 336
  Orford 203
  Oxford 225
  Pendennis 281
  Penrith 358
  Portchester 169
  Powis 460
  Restormel 284
  Richmond 384
  Ripley 389
  Rochester 188
  St Andrews 499
  Scarborough 397
  Sherborne 268
  Shrewsbury 312
  Skipton 386
  Stirling 13, 496–7

Castles (cont.)
Sudely 320
Taunton 252
Threave 515
Tintagel 285
Totnes 291
Tretower 469
Urquhart 536
Warkworth Castle 420
Warwick 12, 299, 321, 322–3
Winchester 170
Windsor 11, 158, 235, 236–7
Cathedrals
Aberdeen 538, 539
Beverley Minster 401
Bristol 257
Bury St Edmunds 206
Canterbury 159, 167, 186–7
Chester 310–11
Chichester 171
Coventry 319
Dunkeld 541
Durham 13, 347, 415, 428, 429
Edinburgh 509
Elgin 538
Ely 11, 159, 194–5
Exeter 288
Glasgow 516–17
Gloucester 329
Hereford 316
Kirkwall 528
Lincoln 299, 333, 341
Liverpool Anglican 379
Llandaff 471
Manchester 373
Metropolitan Cathedral of Christ
the King (Liverpool) 379
Newcastle upon Tyne 425
Norwich 200
Peterborough 194
Ripon 389
Rochester 188
St Albans 233
St Andrews 499
St Davids 13, 432, 464, 465
St Paul's (London) 73, 109, 110,
114–15
Salisbury 241
Southwark (London) 120
Truro 281
Wells 252–3
Winchester 23, 158, 170–71
Worcester 318
York Minster 12, 404, 406–7, 409
Catherine of Aragon 50
tomb of 194
Catherine the Great, Empress of
Russia 198
Caunton, restaurants 633
Cavell, Edith
grave of 200
Caves
Cheddar Gorge 254
Dan-yr-Ogof Caves 468
Fingal's Cave 547
Kents Cavern 290
Llechwydd Slate Caverns (Blaenau
Ffestiniog) 451
Mother Shipton's Cave
(Knaresborough) 388–9
St Fillan's Cave (East Neuk) 500
Stump Cross Caverns 386
Wookey Hole 252
Cawdor Castle **537**
Cawfields 422
Cecil, Robert 231
Cedd, St 209
Celts
chalk figures 221
Christianity 419

Celts (cont.)
in Wales 434, 436
Cemeteries, London 75
Central Hall (London) 88
Cenwulf 47
Ceramics
Coalport China Museum 315
Jackfield Tile Museum (Ironbridge
Gorge) 314
Staffordshire pottery 311
Cerne Abbas 269
Chagall, Marc 171
Chagford
hotels 574
restaurants 626–7
Chalk figures **221**
Cerne Abbas 269
Long Man of Wilmington 180
Sutton Bank 392
White Horse of Uffington 43, 221
Chamberlain, Neville 89
Chambers, William 80
Chanctonbury Ring 174
Changing of the Guard 87
Channel Coast 10, **165–89**
climate 69
hotels 563–5
pubs 652
restaurants 615–8
Channel Tunnel 60, 61, 681
Chapman, John 195
Charlbury, hotels 568
Charlecote Park 302
Charles, Prince of Wales
investiture 444
Warwick Castle 322
weddings 60, 61, 235
Charles I, King 41, 126
Banqueting House (London) 90
Bodiam Castle 182
Carisbrooke Castle 164
Civil War 52, 217
execution 52–3, 118
marriage 85
Powis Castle 460
and Scotland 483
Charles II, King 41, 174
Audley End 208
Crown Jewels 118
Great Fire of London 116
Holyroodhouse (Edinburgh) 510
The Mall (London) 85
Moseley Old Hall 303
Newmarket 207
Plymouth 292
Restoration 52, 53
Worcester 318
Charles, Thomas 450
Charles Dickens Museum (London)
107
Charleston (Lewes) 163, 180
Charlie, Bonnie Prince 54, 482, 483,
535
Abbotsford House 512
Battle of Culloden 537
Blair Castle 543
Drumlanrig Castle 515
Glenfinnan Monument 547
Holyroodhouse (Edinburgh) 510
Inverness 536
Jacobite Rebellion 525
Prince's Cairn 546
Scottish National Portrait Gallery
(Edinburgh) 505
Skye 529, 534
Traquair House 513
Charlotte, Queen 107
Charlton, pubs 652
Chartwell 10, 163, 189
Chatsworth House 12, 299, 331, **334–5**

Chatto, Beth 205
Chaucer, Geoffrey **186**
Canterbury Tales 24, 49, 186
memorial to 93
Chawton 162, 172
Cheddar Gorge **254**
Cheere, John 267
Cheese 607
Cheddar 254
Chelsea (London) **122**
Chelsea FC 664, 665
Chelsea Flower Show 62
Chelsea Physic Garden (London) 122
Cheltenham 24, **328**
hotels 572
restaurants 631
Cheltenham and Gloucester Trophy
67
Cheltenham Imperial Gardens
Midlands garden tour 320
Chequepoint 676
Cheshire see Heart of England
Chesil Bank 242, 268
Chessington World of Adventures 661
Chester 12, **310–11**
Chester-le-Street, hotels 588
Chesterfield, restaurants 633
Chesters Bridge 423
Chesters Fort 423
Cheviot Hills 416, **421**
Cheyne Walk (London) 122
Chichester 10, **171**
restaurants 616
Chiddingstone 166
Childline 675
Children **671**
entertainment 661
in restaurants 603
Chillida, Eduardo 413
Chinatown (London) **80**
Chinese New Year 65
Chippendale, Thomas 55
Burton Constable 402
Cawdor Castle 537
Harewood House 410
Stourhead House 267
Chippenham
restaurants 631
Chipperfield, hotels 568
Chipping, hotels 583
Chipping Campden **327**
hotels 579
Chipping Norton, pubs 653
Chisenhale Dance Space (London) 154
Chiswick (London) **126**
Chiswick House (London) 126
The Choice of Hercules (Poussin) 267
Choo, Jimmy 150, 151
Christ Church College (Oxford) 226
Christ Discovered in the Temple
(Martini) 379
Christ Mocked (Bosch) 73
Christ of St John of the Cross (Dalí)
517, 519
Christchurch College (Oxford) 217
Christchurch Priory 271
Christianity, Celtic **419**
Christmas 65
Church of England 50, 673
Churches (general)
architecture 32–3
wool churches 207
see also Cathedrals
Churches in London
All Souls, Langham Place 105
Brompton Oratory 97
Queen's Chapel 85
St Bartholomew-the-Great 112–13
St James Garlickhythe 110
St James's 84

Churches in London (cont.)
  St Margaret's 88
  St Mary Abchurch 111
  St Mary-le-Bow 110
  St Nicholas Cole Abbey 110
  St Paul's Cathedral 73, 109, 110, 114–15
  St Paul's Church 78, 79
  St Stephen Walbrook 111, 112
  Southwark Cathedral 120
  Westminster Abbey 73, 88, 92–3
Churchill, Sir Winston 60
  Blenheim Palace 228
  Chartwell 10, 163, 189
  Churchill Museum (London) 88, 89
  World War II 59
Churchill family 11
Churchill Museum (London)
  Street-by-Street map 88, 89
Church's Shoes (London) 150, 151
Chysauster 278–9
Cider, Somerset **252**
Cie Tours International 686, 687
Cinema see Film
Cinque Ports 181, **182**, 184
Cirencester **329**
Cissbury Ring 174
Cities, travelling in **690–91**
The City (London) **109–21**
  area map 109
  hotels 559–60
  pubs 652
  restaurants 612–3
  Street-by-Street map 110–11
Civil War 52, 217, 331
Clandon Park 172
Clans and tartans 531, **484–5**
Claude Lorrain 241
Claudius, Emperor 44, 183, 205
Clavering, restaurants 618
Claydon House (Winslow) 162
Claypotts Castle 486
Cley Windmill 191
  North Norfolk coastal tour 197
Clifford, Lady Anne 386
Clifford, Henry, Lord 386
Clifford, Robert de 386
Climate **68–9**, 668
Clipsham, restaurants 633
Clitheroe, pubs 655
"Clive of India"
  Clive Museum (Powis Castle) 460
Cliveden House 162
Cliveden Reach
  Thames Valley tour 234
Clothes
  in restaurants 601
  shops 150, 151, 659
Clovelly **286**
Clubs **661**
  London 154, 155
Clunie Foot Bridge
  Killiecrankie walk 542
Clyde Valley see Lowlands (Scotland)
Clydeside 483
Coach travel 680, 681, **688–9**
Coalbrookdale Museum of Iron 314
Coalport China Museum 315
Coast-to-Coast Walk 37, 363
Coats of arms 30
Cockington 290
Cockermouth **362**
  hotels 583
  restaurants 635
Cockington 290
Coggeshall **205**
  hotels 566
Coins 677
Colbost by Dunvegan, restaurants 650

Colchester **205**
  restaurants 618
Colchester, William 406
Coleridge, Samuel Taylor 289, 366
Colerne, restaurants 624
Colet, John 50
College of Arms (London) 30
  Street-by-Street map 110
Colman's Mustard 201
Colston Bassett, restaurants 633
Columba, St 525
  Iona 46, 547
  Loch Ness Monster 536
  Skye 534
Columbia Road market (London) 149
Colwall, hotels 579
Combe Martin 250, 288
Comedy Theatre (London) 153
Coming from the Mill (Lowry) 371
Communications **678–9**
Compass Holidays 663, 665
Coniston Water **368**
Conran, Sir Terence 31, 454
Conservative Party 60, 61
Consett, pubs 656
Constable, John
  Boatbuilding 204
  Christchurch Mansion (Ipswich) 203
  Constable walk 204
  Fitzwilliam Museum (Cambridge) 212
  The Hay Wain 83, 204
  Lake District 355
  Salisbury Cathedral 241
Constantine the Great, Emperor 45, 444
Consulates 669
Continental Airlines 683
Conversion chart 672
Conwy 435
  Castle 13, 433, 438, 439, 443, 447
  hotels 590
  Street-by-Street map 446–7
Conwy Castle (Sandby) 447
Cook, Captain James
  Captain Cook Memorial Museum (Whitby) 396
  Pitt Rivers Museum (Oxford) 225
  Plymouth 292
  Whitby 396
Cookham
  Thames Valley tour 235
Coookery at the Grange 662, 665
Cooper, Samuel
  James II 537
Corbridge **423**
Cordon Vert School 662, 665
Corelli, Marie 324
Corfe Castle **270**
Cornhill on Tweed, pubs 656
Cornwall 11, **273–85**
  climate 68
  Exploring Devon and Cornwall 274–5
  hotels 574–8
  Penwith tour 276
  pubs 654
  restaurants 626–30
  smugglers 280
Coronation Bridge
  Killiecrankie walk 542
Corpach
  Road to the Isles tour 547
Corpus Christi College (Cambridge) 214
Corpus Christi College (Oxford) 227

Corsham **255**
Cotehele 244, **293**
Cotman, John Sell 201
Cotswolds 298
  Midlands garden tour 320–21
  stone buildings 304–5
Country Lanes 663, 665
Countryside **34–5**
Courbet, Gustave 410
Courtauld Institute (London) 80
Covenanters 483
Covent Garden (London)
  Street-by-Street map 78–9
Coventry **319**
Coward, Noel 58, 291, 454
Coxwold **392–3**
Crabbe, George 203
Cragside 29
Cranmer, Thomas, Archbishop
  Martyrs' Memorial (Oxford) 222, 225
Crarae Gardens **548**
Craster, pubs 656
Crathes Castle and Gardens
  Royal Deeside tour 541
Credit cards 676
  in shops 658
Crediton, hotels 575
Cregennen lakes 455
Creccieth, hotels 590
Crich Tramway Village
  Peak District tour 339
Cricket 67, 664
Crickhowell
  hotels 592
  restaurants 645
Crime 674
Crimean War 56
Crinan, hotels 597
Crinkle Crags 365
Criterion Theatre (London) 153
Cromarty 531
Crome, John 201
  Back of the New Mills 201
Cromer, restaurants 619
Cromford 336
  Peak District tour 339
Cromwell, Oliver 41, 52
  Carlisle 358
  Ely Cathedral 194
  Huntingdon 208
  Oxford University 217
  Peterborough 194
  Ripley Castle 389
Cromwell, Thomas 351
Crookham, hotels 588
Crossflight 679
Crown Jewels **118**, 119
Crudwell, restaurants 624
Crufts Dog Show 62
Cruikshank, G 373
Crummock Water 357
Cuillins 534
Culbone 251
Culloden, Battle of (1746) 54, **537**
Culross **501**
Culzean Castle 478, **522–3**
Cumberland, Duke of 537, 539
Cumberland Terrace (London) 105
Cumbria see Lake District
Cumbrian Way 363
Cupar
  hotels 594
  restaurants 646
Currency **677**
Curthose, Robert 424
Curzon, Lord 182
Curzon family 28
Customs and immigration 668, 669

Cuthbert, St 360
  Lindisfarne 418, 419
  tomb of 415, 428
Cuthburga 271
Cuyp, Albert 212
Cycling 57, **663**, 665, 680, 691
Cyclists' Touring Club 663, 665

D

Dahl, Roald
  Roald Dahl Museum 230
Dale, David 514
Dalemain **358–9**
Dales Way 36
Dalí, Salvador
  Christ of St John of the Cross 517, 519
Dalston, hotels 583
Dan-yr-Ogof Caves 468
Danby, Earl of 224
Danby, Francis 257
Dance **661**
  London 154
Dance, George the Elder 111
Darby, Abraham I 314
Darby, Abraham III 315
Darling, Grace 418, 420
Darnley, Lord 510, 511
Dartington
  hotels 589
  restaurants 627
Dartington Hall 291
Dartmeet 295
Dartmoor
  hotels 575
  National Park 11, 240, 294–5
Dartmouth **290**
  restaurants 627
Darts 67
Darwin, Charles 163, 292
Daventry, restaurants 633
David, Gerard 504
David, St 434, 436, 464, 471
David I, King of Scotland
  Border abbeys 503
  Melrose Abbey 512
  Palace of Holyroodhouse 510
  St Margaret's Chapel (Edinburgh) 507
Davy, Sir Humphry 278, 348
Dawlish, pubs 654
de Morgan, William 221
de Quincey, Thomas 80, 366
Deal
  hotels 563
  restaurants 616
Dean's Yard (London)
  Street-by-Street map 88
Debenhams (London) 150, 151
Dedham, hotels 566
Dedham Church
  Constable walk 204
Dee, River 441
Deepdale 384
Deeside tour **540–41**
Defoe, Daniel
  Cheddar Gorge 254
  The Highland Rogue 494
  Robinson Crusoe 256, 500
Degas, Edgar 378
Delta Airlines 682, 683
Denbigh, pubs 656
Denbighshire see North Wales
Dennis Severs House (London) 125
Dentists 675
Department stores 659
  London 148
Department of Transport 685
Depression 58, 59, 483

Derain, André 400
Derbyshire see East Midlands
Derwent Gorge 336
Derwentwater 356, 360
Design Museum (London) **117**
Despenser family 472
Destailleur, Gabriel-Hippolyte 230
Devil's Bridge 463
  Wild Wales tour 467
Devil's Dyke 181
Devon 11, **273–5**, **286–95**
  climate 68
  Devonshire cream teas 287
  Exploring Devon and Cornwall 274–5
  hotels 574–8
  pubs 654
  restaurants 626–30
Devonshire, 4th Earl of 334
Devonshire, Dukes of 334, 369, 386
DHL 679
Dial UK 675
Diana, Princess of Wales
  Althorp House 343
  Kensington Gardens (London) 101
  Kensington Palace (London) 101
  Spencer House (London) 84
  wedding 60
Dibdin, Charles 455
Dickens, Charles **189**, 543
  Beaumaris 444
  Bleak House (Broadstairs) 163
  Bloomsbury (London) 103
  Charles Dickens Museum (London) 107
  Charles Dickens Museum (Portsmouth) 169
  George Inn (London) 120
  Great Yarmouth 199
Dinner 601, 603
Dinton, restaurants 620
Dirleton, restaurants 646
Disabled Living Foundation 675
Disabled travellers **670–71**
  in hotels 555
  in restaurants 603
Discovery, HMS (Dundee) 499
Disraeli, Benjamin 56, 57
  Hughenden Manor 233
Dissolution of the Monasteries 50, 101, 328, **351**, 503
Ditchling, pubs 652
Docklands (London) 61, **125**
Doddiscombleigh, restaurants 627
Dolgarrog, restaurants 642
Dolgellau **454–5**
  restaurants 643
Domesday Book 32, 48, 174, 329, 388
Dominion Theatre (London) 153
Dorchester **269**
  hotels 571
Dornoch **530–31**
Dorset see Wessex
Douglas, Sir James ("Black Douglas") 512, 515
Douglas family 485, 506
Doune Castle **498**
Dovedale
  Peak District tour 338
Dover 156, **183**
  hotels 563
Dover, Robert 327
Down House (Downe) 163
Downham, pubs 655
Downing Street (London) **89**
  Street-by-Street map 88

Downs and Channel Coast 10, **165–89**
  climate 69
  The Downs 181
  Exploring the Downs and Channel Coast 166–7
  hotels 563–5
  pubs 652
  restaurants 615–8
  wildlife 34
Doyle, Sir Arthur 294
  Sherlock Holmes Museum (London) 104
Dozmary Pool 284–5
Drake, Sir Francis 51, 292, **293**
Driffield, pubs 656
Druids 262
Drum Castle 487
  Royal Deeside tour 541
Drumlanrig Castle 487, **514–15**
Dryburgh Abbey
  Borders tour 503
Drymen, restaurants 650
du Maurier, Daphne **284**
Duchêne, Achille 228
Duchess Theatre (London) 153
Duddon Valley **365**
Dufftown, restaurants 650
Duffus Castle 486
Duich, Loch 525
Duke of York's Theatre (London) 153
Duke's Pass 495
Dulverton, hotels 572
Dumfries and Galloway see Lowlands (Scotland)
Dundee **499**
  hotels 594
  pubs 657
  restaurants 647
Dunfermline **500–501**
Dungeness 182–3
Dunkeld **541**
  hotels 597
  restaurants 650
Dunkery Beacon 251
Dunrobin Castle 487, 530–31
Dunster 251
Dunvegan Castle 534
Dunwich **202**
  hotels 566
Dupré, G
  Bonnie Prince Charlie 482
Durdle Door 243, 270
Durham **428–9**
  Cathedral 13, 347, 415
  hotels 589
  restaurants 641
Durham, County see Northumbria
Durness, hotels 597
Dysart, Elizabeth Countess of 126

E

Eardisland 313
Easby Abbey 351
Easington, restaurants 620
East Aberthaw, pubs 657
East Anglia 10–11, **191–215**
  climate 69
  hotels 565–7
  map 192–3
  North Norfolk coastal tour 196–7
  pubs 653
  restaurants 618–20
  wool trade 207
East Chiltington, restaurants 616
East End (London) **125**
East Grinstead hotels 564
East India Company 51
East Lambrook Manor 245
East Lavant, restaurants 616

East Midlands 12, **331–43**
  climate 69
  Exploring the East Midlands, 332–3
  hotels 581–2
  pubs 655
  restaurants 632–4
East Neuk **500**
East Street market (London) 149
East Witton
  hotels 586
  restaurants 638
Eastbourne **180**
  hotels 564
Easter 65
EasyJet 682, 683
Edale
  Peak District tour 338
Eden Camp **400**
Eden Project 11, **282–3**
Edinburgh 13, 479, **504–11**
  airport 682
  Castle 13, 493, 506–7
  Festival 24, 63, 491, 509
  Festival Fringe 63
  hotels 594
  map 505
  pubs 657
  restaurants 647
  Royal Mile 508–11
Edinburgh, Duke of 31
Edmund, St 206
Ednam, hotels 594
Edstone Aqueduct 301
Edward, Black Prince
  tomb of 187
Edward I, King 40, 49
  Beaumaris Castle 432, 438
  Caernarfon Castle 441, 444
  Conwy Castle 433, 443
  Eleanor crosses 225
  Harlech Castle 454
  Leeds Castle 188
  and Scotland 482
  Tower of London 118
  Welsh castles 436, 439
  Winchelsea 185
Edward II, King 40, 444
  Byland Abbey 392
  Caernarfon Castle 439
  tomb of 329
Edward III, King 40, 409
  Order of the Garter 30
  Windsor Castle 236
  wool trade 207
Edward IV, King 40
  "Princes in the Tower" 118, 119
Edward V, King 40
Edward VI, King 39, 41, 51
  Leeds Castle 188
  Sherborne School 268
Edward VII, King 41
  Anglican Cathedral (Liverpool) 379
  Sandringham 197
  Warwick Castle 323
Edward VIII, King (Duke of Windsor)
  41, 59, 291
Edward the Confessor, King 47
  Crown Jewels 118
  Westminster Abbey (London) 93
  Wimborne Minster 271
Edwin, King of Northumbria 406, 506
Eglwysfach, hotels 592
Eilean Donan Castle 525, 530
Eisenhower, Dwight D. 523
Elan Valley **462**
  Wild Wales tour 467
Eleanor, Queen 233
Electricity 672
Elgar, Sir Edward 313, 317
  birthplace 318

Elgin **538**
Elgin, Lord 106
Elie
  pubs 657
  restaurants 647
Eliot, George 122
  tomb of 124
Eliot, T S
  memorial to 93
  Cheyne Walk (London) 122
  Russell Square (London) 107
Elizabeth, the Queen Mother 499
Elizabeth I, Queen 41, 50, 256, 342
  childlessness 393
  Epping Forest 209
  and Francis Drake 293
  Hatfield House 217, 231
  Ipswich 203
  Knole 188
  and Mary, Queen of Scots 483
  Spanish Armada 51
Elizabeth II, Queen 41
  Buckingham Palace (London) 86–7
  coronation 60, 92
  in Edinburgh 509, 510
  Honours List 31
  Madame Tussaud's (London) 104
  Windsor Castle 236, 237
Elizabeth of York 170
Elland, restaurants 638
Elterwater 365
Ely **194–5**
  Cathedral 11, 159, 194–5
  hotels 566
Ely, Reginald 212
Embankment Galleries (London)
  80–81
Embassies 669
Emergencies 675
Emin, Tracey 91
Emmanuel College (Cambridge) 214
Emsworth, restaurants 616
English Heritage 672, 673
Enjoy England 555, 688, 689
Ennismore Mews (London) 95
Entertainment **660–61**
  London 152–5
Entrance to the Arsenal (Canaletto)
  230
Environmental issues
  holidays 673
  travel 680, 681
Environmental Travel Association 685
Epping Forest **209**
  Constable walk 204
Epstein, Sir Jacob
  Genesis 374
  Llandaff Cathedral 471
  St Michael Subduing the Devil 319
  Tate Britain 91
Equine Tourism 663, 665
Erasmus 50, 215
Eriska, hotels 597
Erpingham, Sir Thomas 200
Eskdale **364**
Essex see East Anglia
Ethelwulf, King 174
Etiquette 670
  in restaurants 601
Eton 24
Eton College 235
  Thames Valley tour 234
Etruscan Vase Painters (Alma-
  Tadema) 374
Etty, William
  Preparing for a Fancy Dress Ball 407
Europcar 685
European Rail Travel 681
European Union 21, 60
Eurostar 681
Eurotunnel 681

Evangelical Alliance 673
Evelyn, John 317
Evershot, hotels 572
Eversley, restaurants 616
Evesham, hotels 579
Ewloe, restaurants 643
Exchange International 676
Exeter **288–9**
  hotels 575
  pubs 654
  restaurants 627
Exmoor
  National Park 11, 240, 249, **250–51**
  restaurants 627
Expressair 679
Eyam
  Peak District tour 339
Eype, hotels 572

F

FA Cup Final 66
Faed, Thomas
  The Last of the Clan 531
Fairfax, Sir Thomas 393
Fairfax, Viscount 408
Fairhaven, Lord 208
Faith (London) 150, 151
Falkirk Wheel **501**
Falkland, Lord 220
Falkland Palace **500**
Falmouth **280–81**
  hotels 575
  pubs 654
  restaurants 627
Falmouth School of Sailing 664, 665
Farhi, Nicole 150, 151
Faringdon, pubs 653
Farmer's Bridge (Birmingham) 300
Farnborough, pubs 654
Farndale
  North York Moors tour 395
Farne Islands 12, **418**
Farrer, Reginald 548
Fashion
  London 150
Fast food 602
"Fat Betty" White Cross
  North York Moors tour 395
Faversham
  pubs 652
  restaurants 616
Fen Bridge
  Constable walk 204
The Fens **196**
  windmills 199
Ferrensby, restaurants 638
Ferries 681, **689**
Festival of Britain (1951) 60
Festivals 24, **62–5**
Ffestiniog Railway **452–3**
Fields 35
Fiennes, Ralph 24
Fife see Lowlands (Scotland)
Film 25, **661**
  London 153
Fingal's Cave 547
Fire service 675
First Great Western Trains 687
The First Marriage (Hockney) 91
Fishbourne Roman Palace 44–5, 171
Fishguard, restaurants 645
Fishing **664**, 665
Fishing Net 665
Fitzhamon, Robert 470, 472
Fitzherbert, Mrs 178, 179
Fitzwilliam Museum (Cambridge) **212**
The Five Sisters **530**
Flambard, Ranulph, Bishop of
  Durham 429

Flamborough
  hotels 586
  pubs 656
Flamborough Head **400–401**
Flaxman, John 80, 207
Fleming, Alexander 481
Flintshire *see* North Wales
Flitcroft, Henry 230, 266
Flodden, Battle of (1513) 50
Floors Castle
  Borders tour 503
Flowers
  The Countryside 34–5
  Flora of the Cairngorms 545
  Gardens through the Ages 26–7
Flowers (London) 150, 151
Foley, J H 399
Folkestone, hotels 564
Fontaine, Joan 284
Fontana, Lucio
  Spatial Concept "Waiting" 121
Food and drink 25
  Cheddar cheese 25
  Devonshire cream teas 287
  The Flavours of Britain 606–7
  The Flavours of Scotland 488
  The Garden of England 160–61
  pubs 652–7
  shops 659
  Somerset cider 252
  whisky 489
  see also Restaurants
Football 66, 664, 665
  Manchester United Museum
    (Salford Quays) 371, 375
Football Association 664, 665
Forbes, Stanhope 278
Forres, hotels 597
Forster, E M 163
Fort Amherst 188
Fort George **537**
Fort William
  hotels 598
  restaurants 650
  Road to the Isles tour 547
Forth Bridges **502**
Fortnum and Mason (London) 148, 149
Fortrose 531
Fortune Theatre (London) 153
Forum (London) 155
Foster, Norman 25, 201
Fotheringhay, restaurants 633
Fountains Abbey 12, 50, 347, **390–91**
Fowey **284**
  hotels 575
Foyles (London) 150, 151
Fragonard, Jean Honoré 104
Framlingham Castle **203**
Frampton, George 101
Frank 675
Fraser clan 485
French Connection (London) 150, 151
Fressingfield Eye, restaurants 619
Freud, Anna 123
Freud, Lucian 24
  Interior at Paddington 378
  Tate Britain (London) 91
Freud Museum (London) 123
Freud, Sigmund 123
Frink, Elisabeth 335, 379
Frith, William Powell 91
Frobisher, Martin 51
Fruit
  The Garden of England 160–61
Furness 349
Furness Peninsula **368–9**
Furry Dancing Festival (Helston) 62

G

Gaelic language 22, 480
Gainsborough, Thomas
  Anglesey Abbey 208
  Bath 258, 260
  Blickling Hall 198
  Christchurch Mansion (Ipswich) 203
  Gainsborough's House (Sudbury) 163, 206
  Harewood House 410
  Mr and Mrs Andrews 163
  Petworth House 172
  Sarah Siddons 54
  Tate Britain (London) 91
  Walker Art Gallery (Liverpool) 378
Galleries *see* Museums and galleries
Ganllwyd
  pubs 656
The Garden of England **160–61**
Gardens *see* Parks and gardens
Gardens of the Rose **233**
Gargoyles, stone **305**
Garrick, David 326
Garrick Theatre (London) 153
Gateshead, restaurants 641
Gatwick Airport 682
Gay and lesbian meeting places **661**
General Strike (1926) 59
Genesis (Epstein) 374
Geoffrey of Monmouth 285
Geology of the Lake District **352–3**
George I, King 41, 54
  Lamb House (Rye) 184
George II, King 41
  Jacobite Rebellion 483
  Marble Hill House (London) 126
George III, King 41
  Buckingham Palace (London) 101
  Cheltenham 328
  state coach 87
  Weymouth 268–9
  Windsor Great Park 235
George IV, King 41, 55
  Buckingham Palace (London) 86
  coronation 225
  Coronation Bridge 542
  Edinburgh 485, 509, 512
  and Mrs Fitzherbert 179
  Regent's Park (London) 103
  Royal Pavilion (Brighton) 159, 175, 178
  "royal route" 105
  Windsor Castle 236, 237
George V, King 41, 236
George VI, King 41
George Inn (London) **120**
Georgian Britain **54–5**
Gheeraerts, Marcus II
  Captain Thomas Lee 91
"The Gherkin" (London) 61
Giacometti, Alberto 201
Gibberd, Sir Frederick 379
Gibbons, Grinling
  Hampton Court 173
  Petworth House 172
  St Mary Abchurch (London) 111
  St Paul's Cathedral (London) 115
Gibbs, James
  King's College (Cambridge) 212
  Radcliffe Camera (Oxford) 227
  Senate House (Cambridge) 214
  Stowe Gardens 230
Gibson, John
  The Sleeping Shepherd Boy 378
  Tinted Venus 346
Gielgud Theatre (London) 153
Gieves & Hawkes (London) 150, 151

Gift shops 659
  London 150, 151
Gilbert and George 91
Gill, Eric 386
Gillingham, hotels 572
Gillow family 370
Giorgione 519
Girtin, Thomas 351
  Rievaulx Abbey 393
Gladstone, William Ewart 57
Glamis Castle 491, 498–9
Glanwydden, pubs 656
Glasgow 13, 516–21
  airport 682
  festivals 63
  hotels 595
  map 516
  pubs 657
  restaurants 647–8
Glastonbury 11, 253
Glastonbury Festival 63
Glencoe 543
Glencoe Massacre (1692) 53, 543
Glendurgan 244, 281
Glenfinnan Monument
  Road to the Isles tour 547
Glenridding 359
Glenrothes, hotels 595
Glewstone, hotels 579
Globe Theatre (London) 50, 120
Glorious Revolution (1688) 53, 537
Glossop, hotels 581
Gloucester 329
  restaurants 631
Gloucester, Humphrey, Duke of 227, 233
Gloucestershire *see* Heart of England
Glyndebourne Festival Opera 62
Glyndŵr, Owain 436
  Conwy Castle 433
  Harlech Castle 438, 454
  Machynlleth 462
Goathland
  North York Moors tour 395
Godiva, Lady 319
Godstow, restaurants 620
Golf 67, **499**, **663**, 665
Golf Club of Great Britain 663, 665
Golf Vacations UK 663, 665
Gonzalez-Foerster, Dominique 121
Goodrich Castle 317
Goodwood House 171
Goonhilly Earth Station 280
Gordale Scar
  Malham walk 387
Gordon clan 485
Gormley, Antony 413
Gower, Bishop of St Davids 464
Gower, George 51
Gower, John 120
Gower Peninsula 13, **466**
Goya, Francisco de 426, 520
Graham, J Gillespie 379
Grahame, Kenneth 234
Grand Christmas Parade (London) 65
Grand Union Canal 300
Grandisson, Bishop of Exeter 289
Grange-in-Borrowdale 363
  hotels 583
Grange-over-Sands, restaurants 635
Grant, Duncan 163
  Vanessa Bell at Charleston 163
Grasmere 355, **366**
  hotels 584
Grassington, hotels 586
Grassington Folk Museum 386
Grays Antiques market (London) 149
Great Autumn Flower Show
  (Harrogate) 64
Great Britain, ss 256

Great Chesters Fort 422
Great Dunmow, hotels 566
Great Exhibition (1851) 56, 57, 95, 96
Great Fire of London (1666) 53
  Monument 116
Great Gable 364
Great Golf Holidays 663, 665
Great Hormead, pubs 653
Great Malvern **317**
Great Milton, restaurants 620
Great Missenden, restaurants 620
Great Orme's Head 445
Great Plague (1665–6) 53
Great Tew **220**
  hotels 568
Great Whittington, restaurants 641
Great Yarmouth **199**
El Greco 227, 426, 520
Green, Benjamin 425
Green Flag 685
Green Island 673
Green Leaf Tourist Scheme 673
Green Park (London) 75
Green Tourism Business Scheme 673
Green travel 680, 681
Greenwich (London) **125**
Greenwich Market (London) 149
Greenwich Park (London) 75
Greg, Samuel 310
Gresham, Sir Thomas 111
Grevel, William 327
Greville, Sir Fulke 322, 323
Greville family 322
Grey, 2nd Earl 425
Greyfriars Bobby 511
Griffith, Sir Henry 400
Grimes Graves **194–5**
Grimsby **403**
Grimshaw, Atkinson 410
Grimspound 295
Grimsthorpe, pubs 655
Guards Polo Club (London) 155
Guest houses 553
Guildford **172**
  hotels 564
Guisborough, hotels 586
Gullane
  hotels 595
  restaurants 648
Gunpowder Plot (1605) 52
Guy Fawkes Night 64, 180

H

Hadrian, Emperor 44, 422
Hadrian's Wall 13, 44, 346, 415, **422–3**, 482
Halifax 348, **412–13**
  hotels 386
  restaurants 638
Hall, John 325
Hals, Frans 104, 212
Haltwhistle
  hotels 589
  North Pennines tour 427
Ham House (London) 126
Hamada, Shoji 407
Hambledon Mill
  Thames Valley tour 234
Hamilton, James
  The Massacre of Glencoe 543
Hamilton, Richard 91
Hamiltons Gallery (London) 150, 151
Hamley's (London) 150, 151
Hammersmith, pubs 652
Hampshire see Downs and Channel Coast

Hampstead (London) **123**
  pubs 652
Hampstead Heath (London) 75, **124**
Hampton Court 10, **173**
  Flower Show 63
  Privy Garden 26
Hampton Court (Leominster) 313
Handel, George Frederick 212
Hardie, Keir 483
Hardknott Pass 364
Hardraw Force 385
Hardwick Hall 302, 336
Hardy, Thomas **269**
Hare, David 24
Harewood House **410**
Harlech **454**
  Castle 13, 438
  hotels 590
  restaurants 643
Harlow Carr Gardens 388
Harold II, King 171
  Battle of Hastings 46, 47, 181
Harome, restaurants 638
Harpenden, hotels 568
Harris, Isle of 529
  hotels 598
Harrods (London) **97**, 148, 149
Harrogate **388**
  festivals 64
  hotels 586
  restaurants 638
Hartley, Jesse 377
Harvard, John 214, 327
Harvard House (Stratford-upon-Avon) 327
Harvest Festivals 64
Harvey Nichols (London) 148, 149
Harwich
  hotels 566
Hassall, John
  Bruce in Single Combat 482
Hastings **181**
Hastings, Battle of (1066) 46, 47, **181**
Hatchards (London) 150, 151
Hatfield House 217, **231**
Hathaway, Anne 327
Hathersage
  Peak District tour 339
  pubs 655
Haverfordwest, restaurants 645
Hawkins, John 51
Hawkshead 368
  hotels 584
  pubs 655
Hawksmoor, Nicholas 28
  Castle Howard 398
  Blenheim Palace 228
Haworth 12, **412**
  hotels 586
  restaurants 639
Hay Bluff 469
Hay-on-Wye 13, 24, **461**
  pubs 657
  restaurants 645
The Hay Wain (Constable) 83, 204
Haydon Bridge
  North Pennines tour 427
  restaurants 641
Haytor Rocks 295
Haywards Heath, restaurants 616
Health **674–5**
Heart of England 12, **307–29**
  climate 68
  Exploring the Heart of England 308–9
  hotels 578–80
  pubs 654–5
  restaurants 630–32
Heathrow Airport 682
Heaven (London) 155

Hebden Bridge 348, **412**
Hebrides 534
Heddon's Mouth 250
Hedley on the Hill, pubs 656
Heights of Abraham 336
Heiton, hotels 595
Helmsley **393**
  hotels 587
Helplines 675
Helston **280**
  festivals 62
Hengist 221
Hengistbury Head 271
Henley-on-Thames 11, 63
  hotels 568
  Royal Regatta 66
  Thames Valley tour 234
Henrietta Maria, Queen
  portrait of 407
  Queen's Chapel (London) 85
  Queen's House (London) 125
Henry I, King 40, 113
Henry II, King 40, 48
  coat of arms 30
  Dover Castle 183
  Orford Castle 203
  Rosa Mundi 233
  Windsor Castle 236
Henry III, King 40
  Clifford's Tower (York) 407
  Gloucester 329
  Lewes 180
  and Wales 436
  Westminster Abbey (London) 93
Henry IV, King 40, 436
Henry V, King 40
  Battle of Agincourt 49
  Monmouth Castle 475
  Portchester Castle 169
Henry VI, King 40
  All Souls College (Oxford) 226
  Eton College 234
  King's College (Cambridge) 212
  St Albans 232
Henry VII, King 40
  Act of Union 437
  King's College (Cambridge) 213
  Richmond Palace (London) 126
  Tudor rose 30
  Westminster Abbey (London) 92, 93
Henry VIII, King 39, 40
  Camber Castle 185
  Church of England 50
  Dissolution of the Monasteries 101, 328, 351, 503
  Epping Forest 209
  Falmouth 281
  Hampton Court 173
  King's College (Cambridge) 211
  Knole 188
  Leeds Castle 188
  Mary Rose 169
  Melrose Abbey 512
  navy 50
  portraits 212
  St James's Palace (London) 84
  St Michael's Mount 278
  and Scotland 482
  Trinity College (Cambridge) 215
Henry, George
  Japanese Lady with a Fan 519
Henry of Eastry 187
Henry Wood Promenade Concerts 63
Hepworth, Barbara 24, **277**
  Barbara Hepworth Museum and Sculpture Garden (St Ives) 277
  Madonna and Child 277
  Tate Britain (London) 91
  Yorkshire Sculpture Park 413
Her Majesty's Theatre (London) 153

Heraldry **30–31**
Herbert, St 360
Herbert family 460, 472
Hereford **316**
  hotels 579
  restaurants 631
Herefordshire *see* Heart of England
Hereward the Wake 48, 194
Heron, Patrick 240, 277
Hertford, 3rd Marquess of 104
Hertfordshire *see* Thames Valley
Hertz 685
Hervey, Bishop Lord Arthur 253
Herzog and de Meuron 121
Hetton, restaurants 639
Hever Castle **189**
Hexham **422–3**
  hotels 589
  North Pennines tour 427
  pubs 656
  restaurants 641
Hidcote Manor Gardens
  Midlands garden tour 321
Hidden Britain Tours 662, 665
Highgate (London) **124**
  Cemetery 75, 124
Highlands and Islands 13, **525–49**
  climate 69
  Exploring the Highlands and
    Islands 526–7
  The Flavours of Scotland 488
  Highland Clearances 483, 531
  hotels 596–9
  pubs 657
  restaurants 649–51
Hippodrome (London) 155
Hirst, Damian 91
History **39–61**
  Scotland 482–3
  Wales 436–7
Hitchcock, Alfred 284
Hitchhiking 685
Hoare, Henry 266, 267
Hobart, Sir Henry 198
Hobbema, Meindert 212
Hobbs (London) 150, 151
Hockney, David 24
  The First Marriage 91
  The Other Side 411
  Tate Britain (London) 91
  Walker Art Gallery (Liverpool)
    378
Hodgkin, Howard 91
Hogarth, William 55
  Pollok House (Glasgow) 520
  Portrait of Richard James 212
  St Bartholomew-the-Great
    (London) 113
  Sir John Soane's Museum (London)
    112
Hogmanay 65
Holbein, Hans 237
  The Ambassadors 83
Holburne of Menstrie, William 260
Holderness **403**
Holidays, public 65
Holkham, restaurants 619
Holkham Hall
  North Norfolk coastal tour 197
Holland, Henry
  Royal Pavilion (Brighton) 178,
    179
  Woburn Abbey 28, 230
Holland House (London) 122
Holland Park (London) 74, **122–3**
Holmes, Kelly 66
Holmes, Sherlock 104
Holt, restaurants 619
Holyroodhouse (Edinburgh) 13,
  510

Holywell Music Room (Oxford)
  224–5
Home Office 669
Honister Pass 352
Honiton 289
  restaurants 627
Honours List 31
Hoover, William 59
Hope, hotels 581
Hopetoun House **502**
Hopkins, Anthony 24
Hopkins, Sir Michael 374
Hops and hopping 160–61
Hornsea 403
Horse Guards (London)
  Street-by-Street map 89
Horse racing 66, 664
  Newmarket 207
Horse riding **663**, 665
Horse of the Year Show 64, 67
Hospitals 675
Hostelling International 672,
  673
Hotels **552–99**
  children in 671
  Devon and Cornwall 574–8
  Downs and Channel Coast 563–5
  East Anglia 565–7
  East Midlands 581–2
  Heart of England 578–80
  Highlands and Islands 596–9
  Lancashire and the Lakes 582–5
  London 556–62
  Lowlands (Scotland) 594–6
  North Wales 590–91
  Northumbria 588–90
  restaurants-with-rooms 601
  South and Mid-Wales 591–4
  Thames Valley 568–70
  Wessex 570–74
  Yorkshire and the Humber Region
    586–8
Hough on the Hill, hotels 5581
Hound Tor 295
Houses of Parliament (London) 77,
  90
  State Opening of Parliament 64
  Street-by-Street map 89
Housesteads Fort 423
Housesteads Settlement 422
Housman, A E 312, 313
Hovingham, hotels 587
Howard, Catherine 118
Howard, Sir Ebenezer 58
Howard, Admiral Edward 399
Howard, Lord 51
Howard family 398–9
Howell, Margaret 150, 151
Huddersfield, hotels 587
Hudson, George 349
Hughes, Thomas 221
Huguenots 125
Hull **402–3**
Humber Region 12, **381–413**
  Exploring Yorkshire and the
    Humber Region 382–3
  hotels 586–8
  pubs 655–6
  restaurants 638–40
Hume, David 481
Hundred Years' War 49
Hunstanton Cliffs
  North Norfolk coastal tour 196
Hunt, Charles
  Life Below Stairs 29
Hunt, Leigh 122
Hunt, William Holman 374
Huntingdon **208**
  hotels 567
  restaurants 619

Huntsman, H & Sons (London) 150,
  151
Hurlingham Club (London) 155
Husthwaite, restaurants 639
Hutchinson, Mary 366, 392
Hutton-in-the-Forest 358
Hutton-le-Hole **394**
  North York Moors tour 395
Hutton Magna, restaurants 641
Hyde Park (London) 72, 75,
  95–101
  area map 95
  hotels 557–8
  restaurants 611–12
Hythe Bay, restaurants 617

I

ICA (London) 154
Ice skating 67
Iceni **195**
Icknield Way 37
Ickworth House 206–7
Ideal Home Exhibition 62
Ightham Mote 188–9
Ilfracombe, hotels 575
Ilkley, restaurants 639
Ilmington, hotels 579
Immigration 23, 60
  Bradford's Indian community
    411
In the Car (Lichtenstein) 505
Inchmahome Priory 495
Indian community, Bradford
  411
Industrial Revolution 54
  Birmingham 318
  The Industrial Revolution in the
    North 348–9
  Ironbridge Gorge 314–15
  Quarry Bank Mill, Styal 310
  Scotland and 480, 491
Ingilby, William Amcotts 389
Ingleton, hotels 589
Inns, accommodation in 553
Inscape Tours 662, 665
Insurance, health 675
Interior at Paddington (Freud) 378
International Eisteddfod 63
International Festival of Folk Arts
  (Sidmouth) 63
International Highland Games 62
International Sheepdog Trials 64
Internet **678**
Inverary Castle **548**
Invergarry, hotels 598
Inverkeilor, restaurants 648
Inverness **536**
  hotels 598
  restaurants 650
Inverno (Twombly) 121
Iona 547
  hotels 598
Ipswich **203**
  hotels 567
  restaurants 619
Ireland, Robert 312
Ironbridge Gorge 298, **314–15**
  hotels 580
Islam 673
Islay **549**
Isle of Skye *see* Skye
Isle of Wight **168**
  Coastal Path 37
  pubs 652
Isles of Scilly 279
  hotels 575
Islington (London) **124**
Itteringham, pubs 653

J

Jackfield Tile Museum (Ironbridge Gorge) 314
Jacobite Movement 483, 525, **537**
　Battle of Culloden 537
　East Midlands 331
　Glencoe Massacre 53, 543
James I, King 41, 51, 52, 483
　Audley End 208
　Banqueting House (London) 90
　birth 507
　Campden Manor 327
　Epping Forest 209
　Hyde Park (London) 101
　Newmarket 207
　Stirling 496
　Trinity College (Cambridge) 215
　Warwick Castle 323
James I, King of Scotland 501
James II, King 41, 52, 53
　Jacobite Movement 537
　Knole 188
　Monmouth Rebellion 252
James II, King of Scotland 499, 506, 515
James II (Cooper) 537
James IV, King of Scotland 482, 500, 506
James V, King of Scotland 508
　Edinburgh Castle 506
　Falkland Palace 500
　Holyroodhouse (Edinburgh) 510
James VIII (the "Old Pretender") 537
James, Henry 122, 184
James, Richard 150, 151
James of St George **439**
Japanese Lady with a Fan (Henry) 519
Jazz, London 154, **155**
Jazz Café (London) 155
Jedburgh, hotels 595
Jedburgh Abbey
　Borders tour 503
Jeffreys, Judge 252
Jekyll, Gertrude 27
　Hestercombe Garden 252
　Lindisfarne Castle 418
Jenkins, J 402
Jenkins, Valentine 497
Jermyn Street (London)
　Street-by-Street map 85
Jesus College (Cambridge) 214
Jevington, restaurants 617
Jews 673
Jigsaw (London) 150, 151
John, King 40
　Beaulieu 168
　Liverpool 376
　Magna Carta 48, 217, 233, 235
　tomb of 318
John, Augustus 400
John, Tom 467
John of Beverley, St 401
John of Gaunt 388
John o'Groats **528**
John Lewis (London) 148, 149
Johnson, Dr Samuel 444
Jones, Sir Horace 116
Jones, Inigo 25
　Banqueting House (London) 89, 90
　Piazza (London) 79
　Queen's Chapel (London) 85
　Queen's House (London) 125
　St Paul's Church (London) 78, 79
　Wilton House 265
Jones, Mary 450
Joseph of Arimathea, St 253
Jubilee and Apple market (London) 149
Jura **548**

K

Kapoor, Anish 121
Katrine, Loch 492, 494
Keats, John 123, 212
Keats House (London) 123
Kedleston Hall 28–9, 336
Kelmscott **220–21**
Kelso Abbey
　Borders tour 503
Kelvingrove Art Gallery and Museum (Glasgow) 517, 519
Kendal **368**
　hotels 584
　restaurants 635–6
Kennedy, Joseph Jr 202
Kenneth McAlpin, King of Scotland 47, 482
Kensal Green Cemetery (London) 75
Kensington (London) *see* South Kensington
Kensington Gardens (London) 25, 74, 75, **101**
Kensington Palace (London) **101**
Kent *see* Downs and Channel Coast
Kent, William 28, 101
Kents Cavern 290
Kenwood House (London) 124, 154
Keswick **359**
　hotels 584
　restaurants 636
Kew (London) **126**
Kew Gardens (London) 74, 126
Keynes, J M 163
Kielder Water **420**
　pubs 656
Kiftsgate Court Garden
　Midlands garden tour 321
Kilberry, restaurants 650
Kilchrist Church 535
Killerton 289
Killiecrankie
　hotels 598
　Killiecrankie walk 542
　restaurants 650
Killin, restaurants 650
Kilpeck Church 316
Kimmeridge 270
Kincraig, restaurants 650
Kincraig Highland Wildlife Park 544
King, Bishop Oliver 260
King's College (Cambridge) 11, 211, **212–13**
King's College Choir (Cambridge) 212
King's Lynn **196–7**
　hotels 567
　pubs 653
Kings and queens **40–41**
King's Road (London) 122
Kingsbridge, restaurants 627
Kingsley, Charles 286
Kingston Lacy 271
Kingston upon Hull **402–3**
Kingussie, hotels 599
Kinski, Nastassja 269
Kintbury, restaurants 620
Kintyre **549**
Kipling, Rudyard 163, 286
Kippford, restaurants 648
Kirk, Dr John 408
Kirkham Priory 351
Kirkstall Abbey 351
Kirkwall (Orkney), restaurants 650
Kitaj, R B 91
Knaresborough **388–9**
Knebworth House **231**
Kneller, Sir Godfrey 228
Knighton 459, **461**
Knights Templar 112
Knightshayes Court 245, 289

Knole **188**
Knowstone, pubs 654
Knox, John
　Church of Saint John (Perth) 498
　John Knox House (Edinburgh) 511
　Presbyterian Church 483
　St Giles Cathedral (Edinburgh) 509
　statues of 482, 518
Koko (London) 155
Kylesku, restaurants 650
Kynance Cove 280
Kyrle, John 317

L

Labour Party 61
Lacock **255**
　hotels 572
　restaurants 624
Laguerre, Louis 229
Lainé, Elie 230
Lake District 12, 346, **355–69**
　climate 68
　Exploring Lancashire and the Lakes 356–7
　geology 352–3
　hotels 582–5
　major peaks 360–65
　Northern Fells and Lakes 360–61
　pubs 655
　restaurants 635–8
　traditional Cumbrian sports 358
　walking in 363
Lake Vyrnwy, hotels 592
Lamb and Flag (London)
　Street-by-Street map 78
Lambert, Daniel 343
Lampeter, hotels 592
Lancashire 12, 355, **370–79**
　climate 68
　Exploring Lancashire and the Lakes 356–7
　hotels 582–5
　pubs 655
　restaurants 635–8
Lancaster **370–71**
　hotels 584
　pubs 656
Landewednack, hotels 575
Land's End 242, 274
　Penwith tour 276
Landscape **34–5**
Landseer, Sir Edwin 543
Lanfranc, Archbishop of Canterbury 186
Langar, hotels 581
Langdale **365**
Langdale Pikes 353
Langland, hotels 592
Langley, Bishop of Durham 428
Languages
　Gaelic 22, 480
　Welsh 22, 434, 437
Lanhydrock 244, 284, 285
Lanyon Quoit
　Penwith tour 276
Large Two Forms (Moore) 413
Largs, restaurants 648
The Last of the Clan (Faed) 531
The Last of England (Brown) 319
Lastingham
　North York Moors tour 395
Laszlo, Henri de 499
Latimer, Bishop
　Martyrs' Memorial (Oxford) 222, 225
Lauderdale, Duke and Duchess of 126
Laugharne, hotels 592
Launceston, restaurants 628

Laurel and Hardy 368–9
Lavenham 10, **206**
  hotels 567
Lawrence, Sir Thomas 257
Leach, Bernard 277, 407
Leamington Spa, restaurants 631
Ledbury **317**
  restaurants 631
Leeds **410**
  hotels 587
  restaurants 639
Leeds Art Gallery 410
Leeds Castle 10, 63, 165, **188**
Legoland 661
Leicester, restaurants 633
Leicestershire *see* East Midlands
Leigh, Mike 25
Leighton, Lord 123
Leighton Hall **370**
Leighton House (London) 123
Leighton Moss Nature Reserve 370
Leith Hill 172
Lely, Sir Peter 543
Leominster **313**
Leonardo da Vinci 237
  'The Leonardo Cartoon' 82
  Queen's Gallery (London) 87
Levens Hall **369**
Lever, William Hesketh 349, 379
Lewdown, restaurants 628
Lewes **180**
  hotels 564
  restaurants 617
Lewis, Isle of 481, 529
  hotels 598
Lewis, Wyndham 91
Leyburn, pubs 656
Liberty (London) 148, 149
Libeskind, Daniel 375
Lichtenstein, Roy 121
  In the Car 505
Life Below Stairs (Hunt) 29
Lifton, restaurants 628
Lightholer, Thomas 402
Limestone Corner Milecastle 423
Lincoln 12
  Cathedral 299, 333
  restaurants 633
  Street-by-Street map 340–41
Lincoln College (Oxford) 226
Lincolnshire *see* East Midlands
Lindisfarne **418**, 419
Lindisfarne Gospels **419**
Linley Sambourne House (London)
  122–3
Linlithgow
  hotels 595
  restaurants 648
Linlithgow, Marquess of 502
Linlithgow Palace **501**
Linn of Tummel
  Killiecrankie walk 542
Lippi, Fra Filippo 82
  The Annunciation 82
Little Bedwyn, restaurants 631
Little Langdale 365
Little Malvern 317
Little Moreton Hall 302–3, 311
Live Aid 61
Liverpool 12, 355, 357, **376–9**
  festivals 63
  hotels 584
  map 376
  pubs 655
  restaurants 636
  Walker Art Gallery 378–9
Liverpool and Manchester railway 348
Livingstone, David 481, **514**, 517
Lizard Peninsula **280**
Llanaber, hotels 591

Llanbedrog, restaurants 643
Llanberis 433, **451**
  hotels 591
  restaurants 643
Llandaff Cathedral 471
Llandovery
  Wild Wales tour 467
Llandrillo
  hotels 591
  restaurants 643
Llandrindod Wells **461**
Llandudno **445**
  hotels 591
  restaurants 643
Llangollen 441, **450**
  hotels 591
  International Eisteddfod 450
  restaurants 643
Llanidloes
  Wild Wales tour 467
Llanigon, hotels 592
Llanthony Priory 461, 469
  hotels 593
Llanwrtyd Wells, restaurants 645
Lleyn Peninsula **453**
Llithfaen 453
Lloyd, Christopher 182
Lloyd George, David 437, 471
Lloyd's Building (London) **116**
Llyn y Fan Fach 468
Llywelyn the Great 436
  Beddgelert 452
  Castell-y-Bere 439
  statue of 446
Llywelyn the Last 436, 444
Lobb, John 150, 151
Loch Garten Nature Reserve 545
Loch Ness Monster **536**
Lochinver, hotels 599
Lochmaddy 529
Lochranza, hotels 599
Lombard Street (London)
  Street-by-Street map 111
Lomond, Loch 494
  pubs 657
London 10, **71–155**
  cemeteries 75
  The City and Southwark 109–21
  climate 69
  congestion charge 689
  entertainment 152–5
  festivals 62–5
  Further afield 122–6
  hotels 556–62
  map 17
  parks and gardens 74–5
  pubs 652
  Regent's Park and Bloomsbury
  103–7
  restaurants 608–15
  shops and markets 148–51
  South Kensington and Hyde Park
  95–101
  Street-by-Street maps
    The City 110–11
    Covent Garden 78–9
    Piccadilly and St James's 84–5
    South Kensington 96–7
    Whitehall and Westminster 88–9
  Street Finder 127–47
  travel in 690–91
  West End and Westminster 77–93
London Bed and Breakfast Agency 555
London Coliseum (London) 154
London Dungeon **117**
London Eye 10, **81**
London Film Festival 64
London Marathon 66
London Underground 24, 56, **691**
Londonderry, Marquess of 462

London's Transport Museum
  Street-by-Street map 79, 80
Long, Charles 237
Long, Richard 91
Long Crendon, hotels 568
Long Man of Wilmington 180
Long Meg and her Daughters 358
Long Mynd 312
Longleat
  hotels 572
  Longleat House 11, 266
Longridge, restaurants 636
Lonsdale, pubs 655
Looe 284
Lord Mayor's Procession and Show
  (London) 64
Lord Nelson pub (Burnham Market)
  North Norfolk coastal tour 196
Lord's Cricket Ground (London) 155
Lorton Vale 360
Losinga, Bishop of Norwich 200
Lost Gardens of Heligan 244, 281
Lost property 674, 687
Lostwithiel 284
  restaurants 628
Lothians *see* Lowlands (Scotland)
Louise, Princess 101
Louth, hotels 581
Lower Slaughter 304
  hotels 567
Lowestoft **199**
  hotels 567
Lowlands (Scotland) **491–523**
  climate 69
  Exploring the Lowlands 492–3
  The Flavours of Scotland 488
  hotels 594–6
  pubs 657
  restaurants 646–9
Lowry, L S 375
  Coming from the Mill 371
Lucas, Sarah 91
Lucy, Sir Thomas 302
Ludlow 309, **312–13**
  restaurants 631
Luib 535
Lulworth Cove 270
Lunch 600, 603
Lundy 286
  hotels 575
Lundy 286
  hotels 575
Luss 494
  hotels 595
Luton, pubs 653
Lutyens, Sir Edwin 379
  Castle Drogo 29, 295
  Great Dixter 182
  Hestercombe Garden 252
  Lindisfarne Castle 418
  Queen Mary's Dolls' House 237
Lyceum Theatre (London) 153
Lyddington, pubs 655
Lydford Gorge 294
Lyme Regis
  hotels 572–3
  restaurants 624
Lynmouth 250, **288**
  hotels 575
  restaurants 628
Lynton **288**
  pubs 654
Lyric Theatre (London) 153
Lytham St Annes, hotels 584
Lytton, 1st Earl of 231
Lytton, Lord 231

M

McCartney, Paul 549
  see also The Beatles
McCartney, Stella 150, 151

MacDonald, Flora 529, 534, 535
MacDonald clan 484, 543
Machynlleth **462**
Mackay clan 484
McKellen, Ian 24
Mackenzie, Osgood 530
Mackenzie clan 484
Mackintosh, Charles Rennie 13, **518**, 519
Maclean clan 546
MacLeod clan 484
McNally, Leonard 384
McQueen, Alexander 150, 151
McTaggart, William 519
Madame JoJo's (London) 155
Madame Tussaud's (London) **104**
Madame Tussaud's (Warwick Castle) 322
Madonna and Child (Hepworth) 277
Madonna and Child (Michelangelo) 84
Maentwrog, pubs 656
Magazines 679
    London 150, 151
Magdalen College (Oxford) 226
Magdalene College (Cambridge) 215
Magna **413**
Magna Carta 48
Magna Carta 217, 233, 235, 264
Magnus Barfud, King 549
Maiden Castle 43, 269
Maiden Newton, restaurants 624
Maidenhead
    hotels 569
    restaurants 621
Major, John 61
Malcolm III, King of Scotland 500
Maldon **209**
Malham 387
Malham Cove 387
Malham Lings 387
Malham Tarn 387
Malham Walk **387**
The Mall (London) 85, **85**, 86, 87
Mallaig
    Road to the Isles tour 546
Mallyan Spout
    North York Moors tour 395
Malmesbury, hotels 573
Malverns **317**
    hotels 580
Manchester 12, **372–5**
    airport 682
    hotels 584–5
    map 372
    pubs 655
    restaurants 636
Manchester Ship Canal 371, 372
Manchester United 664, 665
Manor houses, Tudor **302–3**
Mansfield, Isaac 228
Mansion House (London)
    Street-by-Street map 111
Mantegna, Andrea 173
Mappa Mundi **316**
Maps
    Ordnance Survey 36
    road maps 684
    Aberdeen 539
    Bath 255
    Borders tour 503
    Brecon Beacons 468–9
    Brighton 174–5
    Bristol 257
    Cairngorms 544–5
    Cambridge 210–11
    Cardiff 471
    Cheviot Hills 421
    clans and tartans 484–5
    climate 68–9

Maps (cont.)
    Constable walk 204
    Conwy 446–7
    Cotswold stone towns and villages 305
    Covent Garden (London) 78–9
    Dartmoor National Park 294–5
    Devon and Cornwall 274–5
    Downs and Channel Coast 166–7
    East Anglia 192–3
    East Midlands 332–3
    Edinburgh 505
    Europe 15
    Exmoor National Park 250–51
    Ffestiniog Railway 452–3
    Glasgow 516
    Great Britain 14–15
    Hadrian's Wall 423
    Heart of England 308–9
    Highlands and Islands 526–7
    houses of historical figures 162–3
    Ironbridge Gorge 315
    Isle of Skye 534–5
    Killiecrankie walk 542
    Lancashire and the Lakes 356–7
    Lincoln 340–41
    Liverpool 376
    London 72–3
        The City and Southwark 109, 110–11
        Greater London 17, 72
        parks and gardens 74–5
        Piccadilly and St James's 84–5
        Regent's Park and Bloomsbury 103
        South Kensington 96–7
        South Kensington and Hyde Park 95
        Street Finder 127–47
        West End and Westminster 77
        Whitehall and Westminster 88–9
    Lowlands (Scotland) 492–3
    Malham walk 387
    Manchester 372
    Midlands 298–9
    Midlands canal network 301
    Midlands garden tour 320–21
    national rail network 687
    North Country 346–7
    North Norfolk coastal tour 196–7
    North Pennines tour 427
    North Wales 442–3
    North York Moors 395
    Northern Fells and Lakes 360–61
    Northumbria 416–17
    Orkney 15, 527
    Oxford 222–3
    Peak District tour 338–9
    Penwith tour 276
    Regional Great Britain 16–19
    Road to the Isles tour 546–7
    Royal Deeside tour 540–41
    Scotland 478–9
    Shetland 15, 527
    South and Mid-Wales 458–9
    Southeast England 158–9
    Stratford-upon-Avon 324–5
    Thames Valley 218–19
    Thames Valley tour 234–5
    Tissington Trail 337
    The Trossachs 494–5
    Wales 432–3
    Walkers' Britain 36–7
    Wessex 248–9
    West Country 240–41
    West Country Gardens 244–5
    Wild Wales tour 467
    York 404–5
    Yorkshire and the Humber Region 382–3
    Yorkshire Dales 384

Mar, 1st Earl of 496
Marble Hill House (London) 126
Marcher Lords 436, 437
Marchesa Maria Grimaldi (Rubens) 271
Marconi, Guglielmo 58
Margaret, Queen of Scotland 502, 507
Margaret of Anjou 214
Margate **183**
Maris, Matthijs
    The Sisters 521
Markets 659
    London 149
Marlborough 263
Marlborough, 1st Duke of 217, 228–9
Marldon, restaurants 628
Marlow 219
    hotels 569
Marney, Sir Henry 205
Marshland 35
Martello towers 182
Martin, John 427
Martini, Simone
    Christ Discovered in the Temple 379
Martyrs' Memorial (Oxford) 222, 225
Marx, Karl 103
    tomb of 124
Mary, Queen, consort of George V 237
Mary, Queen of Scots 50, 51, 482–3, **511**
    Abbotsford House 512
    Bolton Castle 385
    Edinburgh Castle 507
    golf 499
    Holyroodhouse (Edinburgh) 510
    Inchmahome Priory 495
    Linlithgow Palace 501
    Oxburgh Hall 195
    Provand's Lordship (Glasgow) 518
    "Rough Wooing" 512
    Scone Palace 498
    Stirling 496
    Traquair House 513
Mary I, Queen 41, 50
    Framlingham Castle 203
    Protestant martyrs 51, 112, 180, 225
Mary II, Queen 41, 52, 173
Mary Arden's Farm 327
Mary of Guise 510
Mary Rose 50, 169
The Massacre of Glencoe (Hamilton) 543
Matfen, restaurants 641
Mather, Rick 224
Matlock **336**
    restaurants 634
Matlock Bath 336
    hotels 581
Maumbury Rings 269
Maundy Thursday 62
Mawddach Estuary 455
Mawgan
    hotels 576
    restaurants 628
May, Isle of 500
Mayflower 52, 168–9, 292
Media **679**
Megabus 688, 689
Melbourn, restaurants 619
Melmerby, restaurants 637
Melrose, hotels 595
Melrose Abbey **512**
    Borders tour 503
Melton Mowbray, restaurants 634
Membury, hotels 576
Memorial Arch
    Killiecrankie walk 542
Mercia 46

Merionethshire *see* North Wales
Merlemond, Oliver de 316
Merry Maidens
 Penwith tour 276
Merton College (Oxford) 227
Methodism **279**, 437
Methuen, Lady 255
Michelangelo
 Ashmolean Museum (Oxford) 224
 Madonna and Child 84
 Windsor Castle 237
Mid-Lavant, hotels 564
Mid-Wales 13, **457–75**
 climate 68
 Exploring South and Mid-Wales
 458–9
 hotels 591–4
 pubs 657
 restaurants 644–6
 Wild Wales tour 467
Middle Ages **48–9**
Middleham Castle 385
Middleton-in-Teesdale **426**
Midhurst, hotels 564
Midland Mainline 687
Midlands **297–343**
 building with Cotswold stone **304–5**
 Canals of the Midlands 300–301
 East Midlands 331–43
 Heart of England 307–29
 map 16–17, 298–9
 Midlands garden tour 320–21
 Tudor manor houses 302–3
Midnight Mass 65
Midsomer, restaurants 625
Mildert, William van, Bishop of
 Durham 428
Milebrook, hotels 593
Millais, Sir John Everett
 Ashmolean Museum (Oxford) 224
 Leighton House (London) 123
 Ophelia 56
 Tate Britain (London) 91
 Walker Art Gallery (Liverpool) 378
Miller, Hugh 531
Milton, hotels 569
Milton, John 231, 312
Minack Theatre
 Penwith tour 276
Minehead 251
Ministry of Defence 294
Ministry of Sound (London) 155
Minsmere Reserve 202
Mirren, Helen 24
Misericords **341**
Mr and Mrs Andrews (Gainsborough)
 163
Mobile phones 678
Mobility Helpline 687
Modigliani, Amedeo 201
Moffat, restaurants 648
Mold, pubs 656
Monarchy 23–4, **40–41**
 royal coat of arms 30
Monasteries 350
 Dissolution of 50, 101, 328, 351, 503
Monet, Claude 212
Money **676–7**
Monmouth **474–5**
 hotels 593
 restaurants 645
Monmouth, Duke of 252
Mons Meg **506**
Montacute House 245, 247, 268
Montfort, Simon de 180, 323
Montgomery, Viscount 31
Montrose, Duke of 495
Monument (London) **116**
Moore, Albert
 Seashells 378

Moore, Henry 24
 City Art Gallery (Leeds) 410
 Large Two Forms 413
 Recumbent Figure 91
 Sainsbury Centre for Visual Arts
 (Norwich) 201
 St Stephen Walbrook (London) 111,
 112
 Scottish National Gallery of Modern
 Art (Edinburgh) 505
 Tate Britain (London) 91
 Walker Art Gallery (Liverpool) 378
 Yorkshire Sculpture Park 12, 413
Moorland 34
Morar
 Road to the Isles tour 546
Moray *see* Highlands and Islands
More, Sir Thomas 50, 122
Morecambe Bay **370**
Moreton in Marsh, hotels 580
Moreton family 303
Morgan, Dr William 437
Morpeth, hotels 589
Morris, Roger 548
Morris, William
 Castle Howard 399
 Jesus College (Cambridge) 214
 Kelmscott 220–21
 Peterhouse (Cambridge) 215
Mortehoe, hotels 576
Morwellham Quay **293**
Mosaics, Roman 329
Moseley Old Hall 303
Motor homes 555
Motor racing 67
Mott, Hay and Anderson 425
Moulsford
 hotels 569
 restaurants 621
Mount Edgcumbe Park 292
Mount Grace Priory 350, **394**
Mountbatten, Earl 31, 162
Mousehole 278
 hotels 576
Moustafa, Ahmed 517
Muir of Dinnet Nature Reserve
 Royal Deeside tour 540
Muir of Ord, hotels 599
Mull **546**
 hotels 599
Mullion, hotels 576
The Mumbles 466
 hotels 593
 restaurants 645
Mumby, pubs 655
Muncaster Castle 364
Mungo, St 501, 516–17
Museums and galleries
 admission prices 670
 shops in 659
 1853 Gallery (Bradford) 411
 Abbot Hall Art Gallery and
 Museum of Lakeland Life (Kendal)
 368
 Aberdeen Art Gallery 539
 Aldeburgh Museum 203
 Alexander Keiller Museum
 (Avebury) 263
 American Museum (Bath) 261
 Anne of Cleves House (Lewes) 180
 Armley Mills Museum (Leeds) 410
 Arnolfini (Bristol) 256
 Ashmolean Museum (Oxford) 222,
 224
 Auchindrain Museum 548
 Barbara Hepworth Museum and
 Sculpture Garden (St Ives) 277
 Beamish Open Air Museum 13,
 424–5
 The Beatles Story (Liverpool) 377

Museums and galleries (cont.)
 Beatrix Potter Gallery (Hawkshead)
 367
 Big Pit Mining Museum (Blaenafon)
 457, 474
 Black House Museum (Arnol) 529
 Blackwell Arts and Crafts House
 (Bowness-on-Windermere) 367
 Blaenavon Ironworks 474
 Blists Hill Victorian Town
 (Ironbridge Gorge) 315
 Bodmin Town Museum 284, 285
 Border History Museum (Hexham)
 422, 423
 Bowes Museum (Barnard Castle)
 426
 Bradford Industrial Museum 411
 Brantwood (Coniston) 368
 Brewers' Quay (Weymouth) 268,
 269
 Bridewell Museum (Norwich) 201
 Bristol Blue Glass Factory and
 Shop 257
 British Golf Museum (St Andrews)
 499
 British Museum (London) 10, 73,
 106–7
 Brontë Parsonage Museum
 (Haworth) 412
 Burns Cottage 515
 The Burrell Collection (Glasgow)
 479, 520–21
 Butcher Row House (Ledbury) 317
 Buxton Museum and Art Gallery
 334
 Cabinet War Rooms (London) 88,
 89
 Cadbury World (Bournville) 319
 Captain Cook Memorial Museum
 (Whitby) 396
 Carnegie Birthplace Museum
 (Dunfermline) 501
 Cartwright Hall Art Gallery
 (Bradford) 411
 Castle Museum (Colchester) 205
 Castle Museum (Norwich) 200–201
 Center for Alternative Technology
 (Machynlleth) 462
 Central Museum and Art Gallery
 (Northampton) 343
 Ceredigion Museum (Aberystwyth)
 463
 Charles Dickens Museum (London)
 107
 Charles Dickens Museum
 (Portsmouth) 169
 Churchill Museum (London) 88, 89
 Cider Museum and King Offa
 Distillery (Hereford) 316
 City Museum (Lancaster) 370, 371
 City Museum and Art Gallery
 (Birmingham) 319
 City Museum and Art Gallery
 (Bristol) 257
 City Museum and Art Gallery
 (Hereford) 316
 Clive Museum (Powis Castle) 460
 Coalbrookdale Museum of Iron 314
 Coalport China Museum 315
 Corbridge Roman Town –
 Hadrian's Wall 423
 Corinium Museum (Cirencester)
 329
 Courtauld Institute (London) 80
 Coventry Transport Museum 319
 Craft in the Bay (Cardiff) 471
 Cromarty Courthouse 531
 Cromwell Museum (Huntingdon)
 208
 D-Day Museum (Portsmouth) 169

Museums and galleries (cont.)
Dales Countryside Museum (Hawes) 385
Dartmouth Museum 290
Dennis Severs House (London) 125
Design Museum (London) 117
DIG – An Archaeological Adventure (York) 407, 408
Dock Museum (Barrow-in-Furness) 368, 369
Doctor Who Experience (Cardiff) 470
Dorset County Museum (Dorchester) 269
Dove Cottage and the Wordsworth Museum (Grasmere) 366
Dylan Thomas Centre (Swansea) 466
Eden Camp 400
Elgar's Birthplace (Worcester) 318
Elgin Museum 538
Elizabethan House Museum (Great Yarmouth) 199
Embankment Galleries (London) 80–81
Etruria Industrial Museum 311
Eureka! (Halifax) 413
Falmouth Art Gallery 281
Fitzwilliam Museum (Cambridge) 212
Flambards Experience (Helston) 280
Folk Museum (Helston) 280
Fox Talbot Museum (Lacock) 255
Freud Museum (London) 123
Gainsborough's House (Sudbury) 163, 206
Gasworks Museum (Biggar) 513
Gladstone Court Museum (Biggar) 513
Gladstone Pottery Museum (Stoke-on-Trent) 311
Glasgow School of Art 518, 519
Gloucester Docks 329
Glynn Vivian Art Gallery (Swansea) 466
God's House Tower Museum of Archaeology (Southampton) 169
Grace Darling Museum (Bamburgh) 420
Grassington Folk Museum 386
Groam House Museum (Rosemarkie) 531
Grosvenor Museum (Chester) 310, 311
Hands on History (Kingston upon Hull) 402
Herbert Gallery and Museum (Coventry) 319
Heritage Centre (Ledbury) 317
HMS Belfast (London) 117
HMS Unicorn (Dundee) 499
Holburne Museum of Art (Bath) 260
Hollytrees Museum (Colchester) 205
House of the Tailor of Gloucester (Gloucester) 205
Hugh Miller Museum (Cromarty) 531
Hunterian Art Gallery (Glasgow) 519
Imperial War Museum North (Salford Quays) 371, 375
International Slavery Museum (Liverpool) 377
Inverness Museum and Art Gallery 536

Museums and galleries (cont.)
Ipswich Museum 203
Jackfield Tile Museum (Ironbridge Gorge) 314
Jorvik (York) 408
Judge's Lodgings (Lancaster) 370, 371
Keats House (London) 123
Kelvingrove Art Gallery and Museum (Glasgow) 517, 519
Keswick Museum and Art Gallery 359
King's Own Scottish Borderers Regimental Museum (Berwick-upon-Tweed) 418
Lady Lever Art Gallery (Port Sunlight) 379
Lake Village Museum (Glastonbury) 253
Laurel and Hardy Museum (Ulverston) 369
Leeds Art Gallery 410
Leeds City Museum 410
Linley Sambourne House (London) 122–3
Llandudno Museum 445
Llechwydd Slate Caverns (Blaenau Ffestiniog) 451
Loch Ness Centre and Exhibition 536
London Dungeon 117
London's Transport Museum 79, 80
Lowestoft Museum 199
Lowry Centre (Salford Quays) 371, 375
Ludlow Museum 312, 313
M-Shed (Bristol) 256
McManus Galleries (Dundee) 499
Madame Tussaud's (London) 104
Maeldune Centre (Maldon) 209
Magna 413
Manchester Art Gallery 374
Manchester Museum 374
Manchester Town Hall 373
Manchester United Museum (Salford Quays) 371, 375
Maritime Museum (Aberdeen) 539
Maritime Museum (Kingston upon Hull) 402
Maritime Museum (Lancaster) 370, 371
Market Hall (Warwick) 321
Merseyside Maritime Museum (Liverpool) 377
Moray Motor Museum (Elgin) 538
Morwellham Quay 293
Moyse's Hall (Bury St Edmunds) 206, 207
Museum and Art Gallery (Cheltenham) 328
Museum of Barnstaple and North Devon 287
Museum of Canterbury 186
Museum of Childhood (Edinburgh) 510, 511
Museum of the Gorge (Ironbridge Gorge) 314
Museum of Islay Life 549
Museum of the Isles 535
Museum of Liverpool 377
Museum of London 113
Museum of London, Docklands 125
Museum of Natural History and Archaeology (Kendal) 368
Museum of Nottingham Life 336
Museum of Oxford 225
Museum of Science and Industry (Manchester) 374
Museum of Somerset (Taunton) 252

Museums and galleries (cont.)
National Coal Mining Museum for England 413
National Fishing Heritage Centre (Grimsby) 403
National Football Museum (Manchester) 373
National Gallery (London) 10, 73, 82–3
National Gallery of Scotland (Edinburgh) 504
National Horseracing Museum (Newmarket) 207
National Maritime Museum (London) 125
National Maritime Museum Cornwall (Falmouth) 11, 281
National Media Museum (Bradford) 411
National Motor Museum (Beaulieu) 168
National Museum Cardiff 471
National Museum of Scotland (Edinburgh) 505, 511
National Portrait Gallery (London) 81
National Railway Museum (York) 408
National Roman Legion Museum (Caerleon) 474
National Trust Assembly Rooms and Museum of Costume (Bath) 260
National Waterways Museum (Gloucester) 329
Natural History Museum (London) 96, 100
Nelson Museum (Monmouth) 475
New Millennium Experience (New Lanark) 514
No. 1 Royal Crescent (Bath) 260
North Devon Maritime Museum (Appledore) 287
The Old Operating Theatre (London) 117
Owain Glyndŵr Centre (Machynlleth) 462
Peak District Mining Museum (Matlock) 336
Pencil Museum (Keswick) 359
Penlee House Gallery and Museum (Penzance) 278, 279
People's Palace (Glasgow) 519
Perth Museum and Art Gallery 498
Pier Arts Centre (Stromness) 528
Pitt Rivers Museum (Oxford) 225
Plymouth Mayflower Exhibition 292
Poldark Mine 280
Pollok House (Glasgow) 520
Poole Museum 270, 271
Potteries Museum and Art Gallery (Hanley) 311
Priest's House Museum (Wimborne Minster) 271
Prison and Police Museum (Ripon) 389
Provand's Lordship (Glasgow) 518
Quarry Bank Mill (Styal) 310
Queen's Gallery (London) 86, 87
Radnorshire Museum (Llandrindod Wells) 461
The Red House (Aldeburgh) 203
Regimental Museum (Fort George) 537
Regimental Museum (Monmouth) 474–5
Regimental Museum of Royal Northumberland Fusiliers (Alnwick Castle) 420
Riverside Museum (Glasgow) 518

Museums and galleries (cont.)
Roald Dahl Museum 230
Roman Baths (Bath) 260
Roman Museum (Ribchester) 371
Rotunda Museum (Scarborough) 397
Royal Academy (London) 81, 84
Royal Albert Memorial Museum and Art Gallery (Exeter) 289
Royal Armouries Museum (Leeds) 410
Royal Cornwall Museum (Truro) 281
Royal Naval Museum (Portsmouth) 169
Royal Observatory Greenwich (London) 125
Royal Pump Room Museum (Harrogate) 388
Russell-Côtes Art Gallery and Museum (Bournemouth) 271
Rydal Mount (Rydal) 366
Ryedale Folk Museum (Hutton-le-Hole) 394
Sainsbury Centre for Visual Arts (Norwich) 201
St Fagans' National History Museum (Cardiff) 471
St John's House Museum (Warwick) 321
St Mungo Museum of Religious Life and Art (Glasgow) 517
Salford Museum and Art Gallery 371
Salisbury and South Wiltshire Museum 265
Scarborough Art Gallery 397
Science Museum (London) 96, 100
Scottish Fisheries Museum (East Neuk) 500
Scottish Kiltmaker Visitor Centre (Inverness) 536
Scottish National Gallery of Modern Art One and Two (Edinburgh) 505
Scottish National Portrait Gallery (Edinburgh) 505
Sea City Museum (Southampton) 169
Sherlock Holmes Museum (London) 104
Shetland Museum (Lerwick) 528
Shibden Hall Museum (Halifax) 413
Shrewsbury Museum and Art Gallery 312
Sir John Soane's Museum (London) 112–13
Somerset Rural Life Museum (Glastonbury) 253
Southwold Museum 202
Stamford Museum 343
Stranger's Hall (Norwich) 201
Streetlife Museum of Transport (Kingston upon Hull) 402, 403
Swaledale Folk Museum (Reeth) 385
Swansea Museum 466
Tain Through Time 531
Tales of Robin Hood (Nottingham) 336
Tate Britain (London) 73, 91
Tate Liverpool 377
Tate Modern (London) 10, 121
Tate St Ives 11, 277
Techniquest (Cardiff) 470
Tenement House (Glasgow) 517
Thackray Medical Museum (Leeds) 410
Thinktank – The Birmingham Museum of Science and Discovery 319

Museums and galleries (cont.)
Tom Brown's School Museum (Uffington) 221
Torquay Museum 290
Torridon Countryside Centre 530
Totnes Elizabethan Museum 291
Tullie House Museum (Carlisle) 358
Turner Centre (Margate) 183
UK Border Agency National Museum (Liverpool) 377
University Museum (Oxford) 225
Usher Art Gallery (Lincoln) 341
V&A Museum of Childhood (London) 125
Verulamium Museum (St Albans) 232
Victoria and Albert Museum (London) 10, 72, 97, 98–9
Walker Art Gallery (Liverpool) 346, 377, 378–9
Wallace Collection (London) 104
Wells & Mendip Museum (Wells) 252
West Gate Museum (Canterbury) 186
Westgate Museum (Winchester) 170
Westminster Abbey (London) 93
Wheal Martyn China Clay Museum 281
Whitby Museum and Pannett Art Gallery 396
The Whithorn Story 515
Whitworth Art Gallery (Manchester) 374
William Wilberforce House (Kingston upon Hull) 402, 403
Windermere Steamboat Museum 367
Worcester Porcelain Museum 318
Wordsworth House (Cockermouth) 362
World of Beatrix Potter (Windermere) 367
World Museum Liverpool 379
York Art Gallery 407
York Castle Museum 405, 408
Yorkshire Museum (York) 404, 408
Yorkshire Sculpture Park 12, 413
Music **660**
London 154
The Music Lesson (Vermeer) 86
Muslims 673
Mylne, Robert 548

N

Nant Gwynant, pubs 657
Napoleon I, Emperor 55
Royal Military Canal (Romney Marsh) 183
Waterloo Bridge (Betws-y-Coed) 450
Napoleon III, Emperor 237
Nash, John 25, 55
Buckingham Palace (London) 86
John Nash's Regency London 105
Regent's Park (London) 103
Royal Mews (London) 87
Royal Opera Arcade (London) 85
Royal Pavilion (Brighton) 159, 178–9
Nash, Paul 80
Nash, Richard "Beau" **261**
Nasmyth, Alexander 505
View of Culzean Castle 522
National Car Rentals 685
National Coal Mining Museum **413**
National Express 681, 687, 688, 689
The National Forest 331
National Gallery (London) 10, 73, **82–3**
National Health Service 59
National Maritime Museum (London) 125

National Maritime Museum Cornwall 11
National Motor Museum (Beaulieu) 168
National parks
Brecon Beacons 433, 468–9
Dartmoor 11, 240, 294–5
Exmoor 11, 240, 249, 250–51
Lake District 360–61
North York Moors 395
Northumberland 421
Peak District 338–9
Pembrokeshire Coast 458
Snowdonia 13, 442, 448–9, 451
Yorkshire Dales 346
National Portrait Gallery (London) **81**
National Rail 691
National Rail Enquiries 687
National Theatre (London) 152, 153
National Trust 28, **29**, 672, 673
National Trust for Scotland 672, 673
National Union of Students 672, 673
Natural History Museum (London) **100**
Street-by-Street map 96
Neal Street (London)
Street-by-Street map 78
Neal's Yard (London)
Street-by-Street map 78
Neal's Yard Remedies (London) 150
The Needles 164
Neidpath Castle 486
Nelson, Admiral Lord Horatio 54
Battle of Trafalgar 55
coat of arms 31
HMS Victory 169
Lord Nelson pub (Burnham Market) 196
Monmouth 475
Neptune's Staircase
Road to the Isles tour 547
Ness, Loch **536**
Nettlefold, Archibald 291
Neville family 322, 472
New Change (London)
Street-by-Street map 110
New College (Oxford) 226
New Forest **168**
New Lanark **514**
New London Theatre (London) 153
New Milton, hotels 564
New Year 65
Newbury
hotels 569
pubs 653
restaurants 617
Newby Hall **389**
Newcastle upon Tyne 56, 417, **424–5**
airport 682
hotels 589
restaurants 641–2
Newhaven (Derbyshire), restaurants 634
Newlands Valley **362**
Newlyn
Penwith tour 276
Newlyn School 277, 278
Newman, John Henry 97
Newmarket 11, **207**
hotels 567
Newport, hotels 593
Newquay
hotels 576
restaurants 628
Newspapers 25, 679
Newton, pubs 656
Newton, Sir Isaac 52
portrait 342
statue of 215

Newton Abbot, pubs 654
Newton-Linford, restaurants 634
NHS Direct 675
Nicholson, Ben 212, **277**
  St Ives, Cornwall 277
Nicolson, Harold 189
Nightingale, Florence 56, 162
Ninian, St 515, 517
Noel Coward Theatre (London) 153
Norfolk *see* East Anglia
Norfolk, Dukes of 172
Norfolk, Earl of 203
Norfolk Coast Path 37
Norfolk Lavender
  North Norfolk coastal tour 196
Norfolk Line 681
Normans 46–7
  castles 48
  invasion of Britain 434, 438
  and Scotland 482
North Country **346–429**
  The Industrial Revolution in the
    North 348–9
  Lancashire and the Lakes 355–79
  map 18–19, 346–7
  North Country abbeys 350–51
  Northumbria 415–29
  Yorkshire and the Humber Region
    381–413
North Downs Way 37
North of England Open Air Museum
  (Beamish) **424–5**
North Kilworth, restaurants 634
North Pennines tour **427**
North Uist 529
North Wales 13, **441–55**
  climate 68
  Exploring North Wales 442–3
  hotels 590–91
  pubs 656–7
  restaurants 642–4
North Walsham, hotels 567
North York Moors **395**
North Yorkshire Moors Railway **394**
Northampton **343**
Northamptonshire *see* East Midlands
Northop, restaurants 643
Northumberland *see* Northumbria
Northumberland, Dukes of 126, 420
Northumbria 12–13, 46, 47, **415–29**
  climate 69
  Exploring Northumbria 416–17
  hotels 588–90
  pubs 656
  restaurants 640–42
Norton, hotels 580
Norwich **200–201**
  hotels 567
  pubs 653
  restaurants 619
Norwich School 201
Notting Hill (London) **123**
Notting Hill Carnival 63
Nottingham **336**
  hotels 582
  pubs 655
  restaurants 634
Nottingham Goose Fair 64
Nottinghamshire *see* East Midlands
Novello Theatre (London) 153
Nunnington Hall **393**

O

The O2 155
Oakehampton, hotels 576
Oakham, hotels 582
Oasis (London) 150, 151
Oast houses 160–61

Oban **546**
  hotels 599
  restaurants 651
Offa, King of Mercia 46, 233, 461
Offa's Dyke 436, 461
Offa's Dyke Footpath 36, 461
Office (London) 150, 151
Okehampton 294
The Old Operating Theatre (London)
  117
Old Royal Naval College (London)
  125
Old Sarum 263, 264
Old Spitalfields market (London) 149
Old Trafford, hotels 585
Old Vic (London) 152, 153
Oldenburg, Claes
  Soft Drainpipe – Blue (Cool) 121
Oliver, Isaac 231
Olivier, Laurence 174, 284
Olympic Games 61
Omega Workshops 163
Open-air theatre, London **153**
Opening hours 669
  shops 658
Opera **154**
  Royal Opera House (London) 79,
    80
Ophelia (Millais) 56
Orange 678
Ordnance Survey maps 36
Orford Castle 203
Orkney **528**
  hotels 599
  maps 15, 527
Orton, Joe 124
Orwell, George 124, 548
Osborne House 10, 162, 164
Osmotherley, restaurants 639
Osmund, St 264
The Other Side (Hockney) 411
Ottery St Mary 289
  hotels 576
Oulton Broad, restaurants 619
Outdoor activities **662–5**
Oval Cricket Ground (London) 155
Overbecks 244
Overton Bridge, pubs 657
Owen, Richard 312
Owen, Robert 514
Owen, Wilfrid 312
Oxburgh Hall and Garden 195
Oxford 11, **222–7**
  hotels 569
  pubs 653
  restaurants 621
  Street-by-Street map 222–3
  University 11, 158, 226–7
Oxford and Cambridge Boat Race 62,
  66
Oxford Bus Company 688, 689
Oxford Castle 225
Oxford Castle Unlocked 225
Oxford Tube 688, 689
Oxfordshire *see* Thames Valley
Oxon, restaurants 621

P

P&O Ferries 681
Pacha London 155
Packwood House 303
Padstow
  hotels 576–7
  restaurants 628
Paignton 273
Paignton Zoo 290
Paine, Tom 195
Painswick 305
Palace Theatre (London) 153

Palaces
  Blenheim Palace 11, 158, 217,
    228–9
  Buckingham Palace (London) 72,
    86–7
  Culross Palace 501
  Falkland Palace 500
  Hampton Court 10, 26, 173
  Holyroodhouse (Edinburgh) 13,
    510
  Kensington Palace (London) 101
  Linlithgow Palace 501
  St James's Palace (London) 84
  Scone Palace 498
  see also Stately homes
Pall Mall (London)
  Street-by-Street map 85
Palladio, Andrea 126
Palmerston, Lord 215
Pangbourne
  Thames Valley tour 234
Pannett, Robert 396
Pannini 399
Parbury, Kathleen 419
Parcelforce Worldwide 679
Paris, Matthew 40
Park Crescent (London) 105
Parking 684–5
Parks and gardens **26–7**
  Abbotsbury Sub-Tropical Gardens
    268
  Anglesey Abbey 208
  Armadale Castle Gardens 535
  Athelhampton House 245, 269
  Battersea Park (London) 75
  Beth Chatto Garden (Colchester)
    205
  Biblical Gardens (Elgin) 538
  Blenheim Palace 229
  Botanical Gardens (Edgbaston) 319
  Burford House Gardens 313
  Chatsworth House 334–5
  Chelsea Physic Garden (London)
    122
  Cheltenham Imperial Gardens 320
  Compton Acres (Bournemouth)
    271
  Cotehele 244, 293
  Crarae Gardens 548
  Crathes Castle and Gardens 541
  Dartington Hall 291
  East Lambrook Manor 245
  Eden Project 11, 282–3
  Gardens of the Rose 233
  Glendurgan 244, 281
  Great Dixter 182
  Green Park (London) 75
  Greenwich Park (London) 75
  Hampstead Heath (London) 75,
    124
  Hampton Court 173
  Hestercombe Garden 252
  Hidcote Manor Gardens 321
  Holland Park (London) 74, 122–3
  Hyde Park (London) 72, 75, 101
  Inverewe Garden 530
  Kensington Gardens (London) 25,
    74, 75, 101
  Kew Gardens (London) 74, 126
  Kiftsgate Court Garden 321
  Knightshayes Court 245, 289
  Lanhydrock 244, 284, 285
  Levens Hall 369
  London 74–5
  Lost Gardens of Heligan 244,
    281
  Midlands garden tour 320–21
  Montacute House 245, 247
  Morrab Gardens (Penzance) 278
  Mount Edgcumbe Park 292

Parks and gardens (cont.)
  National Botanic Garden of Wales
    466
  Newby Hall 389
  Overbecks 244
  Oxburgh Hall and Garden 195
  Parnham 245
  Powis Castle 460
  Regent's Park (London) 75
  RHS Harlow Carr Gardens 388
  Richmond Park (London) 74, 126
  Rosemoor Garden 286
  St James's Park (London) 75
  Sissinghurst Castle Garden 189
  Snowshill Manor 320
  Stanway House 320
  Stourhead 241, 245, 266–7
  Stowe Gardens 11, 230
  Sudely Castle 320
  Trebah 281
  Trelissick 244, 281
  Trengwainton 244, 276
  Trewithen 244, 281
  University Botanic Garden
    (Cambridge) 215
  University of Oxford Botanic
    Garden 224
  Waddesdon Manor 230
  Warwick Castle 321
  West Country gardens 244–5
  Windsor Great Park 235
  Wisley 172
  Woburn Abbey 230
Parliament (London) see Houses of
  Parliament
Parliament Hill (London) 124
Parnham 245
Parr, Catherine 320
Parracombe 250
Passports 668
Pavarotti, Luciano 104
Pavey Ark 365
Paxford, restaurants 631
Paxton, Sir Joseph 57, 334, 412
Peacock Theatre (London) 154
Peak District 12, 331, 332
  Peak District tour 338–9
  Tissington Trail 337
Peasants' revolt (1381) 49
Peddars Way 37
Peebles, restaurants 648
Peers of the realm 31
Pellegrini, Giovanni Antonio 398
Pembridge 313
Pembroke, restaurants 645
Pembroke, Earls of 265
Pembroke College (Cambridge) 214
Pembroke Ferry, pubs 657
Pembrokeshire Coast National Park
  458
Pembrokeshire Coastal Path 36
Pen-y-Cae, hotels 593
Pen y Fan 469
Penallt, pubs 657
Penmaenpool
  hotels 591
  restaurants 643
Penn Street Village, restaurants 621
Penn, William 231
Pennines
  North Pennines tour 427
  Pennine Way 36, 338, 421
Penrith **358**
  hotels 585
  restaurants 637
Pensford, pubs 654
Penshurst Place 189
Pentland Hills **513**
Pentre Ifan 42
Penwith tour **276**

Penzance **278–9**
  hotels 577
  pubs 654
  restaurants 628–9
Pepys, Samuel 215
Percy family 420
Personal security **674–5**
Perth **498**
  restaurants 648
Perth and Kinross see Highlands and
  Islands
Peter of Langtoft 285
Peter the Great, Tsar 198
Peter Jones (London) 148, 149
Peterborough **194**
Peterhouse (Cambridge) 215
Peterloo Massacre (1819) **373**
Petroc, St 284
Petrol 685
Petticoat Lane market (London) 23,
  149
Petworth House 10, 22, **172**
Pevsner, Sir Nikolaus 389
Pharmacies 675
Philip II, King of Spain 51, 293
Phoenix Theatre (London) 153
Phones4U 678
Photographers' Gallery (London) 150,
  151
Piazza and Central Market (London)
  79
Picabia, Francis 121
Picasso, Pablo
  Ashmolean Museum (Oxford)
    224
  Fitzwilliam Museum (Cambridge)
    212
  Manchester Art Gallery 374
  Sainsbury Centre for Visual Arts
    (Norwich) 201
  Scottish National Gallery of
    Modern Art One and Two
    (Edinburgh) 505
  Tate Modern (London) 121
Piccadilly (London)
  Street-by-Street map 84–5
Piccadilly Circus (London) **81**
  Street-by-Street map 85
Piccadilly Crafts (London) 149
Piccadilly Theatre (London) 153
Pickering, hotels 587
Picnics 603
Picts 482
Pied à Terre (London) 150, 151
Pike o'Stickle 365
Pilgrim Fathers 52, 53, 169, 292
Piper, John 379
Pitlochry **541**
  hotels 599
The Place (London) 154
Plaid Cymru 437
Plath, Sylvia 412
Plockton
  hotels 599
  restaurants 651
Plumtree, restaurants 634
Plymouth **292**
  hotels 577
  restaurants 629
Polanski, Roman 269
Police 674, 675
Polo 67
Polperro 284
  restaurants 629
Polruan 284
Ponsonby, Sarah 450
Pontcysyllte Aqueduct 450
Ponteland, restaurants 642
Pontyclun, pubs 657
Pony trekking **663**, 665

Poole 11, **270–71**
  restaurants 625
Poole, Henry & Co (London) 150, 151
Pop music, London 154, **155**
Pope, Alexander 317, 329
Porlock 251
  hotels 573
Porlock Weir, hotels 570
Port Appin, restaurants 651
Port Isaac 273
  restaurants 629
Port Sunlight 349, 379
Porth Neigwl 453
Porth Oer 453
Porthkerry, hotels 593
Porthleven, pubs 654
Portmeirion 13, 432, **454–5**
  hotels 591
  restaurants 643
Portobello Road (London) **123**, 149
Portpatrick, restaurants 648
Portree 535
Portsmouth **169**
  restaurants 618
Portsoy, pubs 657
Post boxes 679
Postal services **679**
Postbridge 294
Potter, Beatrix **367**
  Beatrix Potter Gallery (Hawkshead)
    367
  Dunkeld 541
  Hill Top (Near Sawrey) 367
  House of the Tailor of Gloucester
    (Gloucester) 329
  Newlands Valley 362
  World of Beatrix Potter
    (Windermere) 367
The Potteries 311
Poundbury Camp 269
Poussin, Nicolas 241, 378, 504
  The Choice of Hercules 267
Powis Castle **460**
Praxiteles 172
Pre-Raphaelites 91, 374
Prehistoric Britain **42–3**
  Arbor Low 338
  Avebury 263
  Carloway Broch 529
  Castlerigg Stone Circle 43, 359,
    361
  Cerne Abbas 269
  Chanctonbury Ring 174
  Cissbury Ring 174
  Flag Fen Bronze Age Centre 194
  Great Orme's Head 445
  Grimes Graves 194–5
  Grimspound 295
  Hillside Chalk Figures 221
  Kents Cavern 290
  Lake Village Museum (Glastonbury)
    253
  Long Man of Wilmington 180
  Long Meg and her Daughters 358
  Long Mynd 312
  Maes Howe 528
  Maiden Castle 43, 269
  Maumbury Rings 269
  Mousa Broch 528
  Old Sarum 263, 264
  Parc Le Breose 466
  Pentre Ifan 42
  Penwith tour 276
  Poundbury Camp 269
  Ring of Brodgar 528
  Rollright Stones 220
  Silbury Hill 262
  Skara Brae 528
  Standing Stones of Callanish 529
  Standing Stones of Stenness 528

Prehistoric Britain (cont.)
  Stonehenge 11, 43, 241, 248–9, 262–3
  Uffington Castle 221
  Uffington White Horse 43
  Vale of the White Horse 221
  Wayland's Smithy 221
  West Kennet Long Barrow 262–3
  Wiltshire's other prehistoric sites 262
Preparing for a Fancy Dress Ball (Etty) 407
Presbyterian Church of Scotland 480
Prestbury, hotels 580
Preston
  hotels 585
  restaurants 637
Priestley, Joseph 255
Prince Edward Theatre (London) 153
Prince of Wales Theatre (London) 153
Prince's Cairn
  Road to the Isles tour 546
"Princes in the Tower" 118, 119
Priories *see* Abbeys and priories
Pritchard, Dafydd 452
Proctor, Sir Stephen 390
Provost Skene's House (Aberdeen) **539**
Public conveniences 670
Public holidays 65
Pubs 22, **652–7**
  accommodation in 553
  signs 605
  traditional British pub 604–5
Pugin, A W N 379
Punting on the Cam **214**
Purbeck, Isle of **270**
Puritans **231**
Pwllheli, restaurants 643

Q

Qantas 682, 683
Quakers 673
Quarry Bank Mill (Styal) **310**
Queen Elizabeth Forest Park 495
Queen of Hoxton (London) 155
Queen Square (London) 107
Queen's Chapel (London) **85**
  Street-by-Street map 85
Queen's Club Real Tennis (London) 155
Queens' College (Cambridge) 214–15
Queen's College (Oxford) 226
Queen's Gallery (London) 86, **87**
Queen's House (London) 125
Queen's Theatre (London) 153
Quiller-Couch, Sir Arthur 284
Quiraing 535

R

RAC 685
RAC London to Brighton Veteran Car Rally 64
Rackham, Arthur 234, 445
RADAR 555, 670–71
Radcliffe Camera (Oxford) 219, 223, 227
Radio 679
Raeburn, Henry 504
  Rev. Robert Walker Skating on Duddingston Loch 504
Rahere 113
Rail Europe 686, 687
Railways 680, 681, **686–7**
  Bala Lake Railway 450
  Bodmin & Wenford Railway 284
  Ffestiniog Railway 451, 452–3
  from airports 681–2
  Industrial Revolution 348, 349

Railways (cont.)
  Keighley and Worth Valley Railway 412
  National Railway Museum (York) 408
  North Yorkshire Moors Railway 394
  Romney, Hythe and Dymchurch Light Railway 183
  Snowdon Mountain Railway 451
  South Devon Steam Railway 291
  Strathspey Steam Railway 544
Rainfall 68–9
Raleigh, Sir Walter 51, 292
Ramblers' Association 662, 665
Ramblers' Countrywide Holidays 663, 665
Ramsay, Allan 504
Ramsgill in Nidderdale, restaurants 639
Ransome, Arthur 368
Rape Crisis Centre 675
Raphael 224
Rattle, Sir Simon 319
Reading
  hotels 569
  restaurants 621
Rebecca, Biagio 209
Reculver Fort 183
Recumbent Figure (Moore) 91
Redfern Art Gallery (London) 150, 151
Redworth, restaurants 642
Reed, restaurants 621
Regency London **105**
Regent Street Christmas Lights 64
Regent's Park (London) 75, **103–7**
  area map 103
  hotels 558–9
  restaurants 612
Reilly, Michael 80
Reiss (London) 150, 151
Religious organizations 673
Rembrandt van Rijn
  Ashmolean Museum (Oxford) 224
  Kenwood House (London) 124
  Queen's Gallery (London) 87
  Self-portrait 521
  Walker Art Gallery (Liverpool) 378
  Wallace Collection (London) 104
Remembrance Day 64
Renoir, Pierre Auguste 212, 400
  At the Theatre 83
  The Two Sisters 256
Responsible travel **673**
Restaurants **600–51**
  children in 671
  Devon and Cornwall 626–30
  Downs and Channel Coast 615–8
  East Anglia 618–20
  East Midlands 632–5
  The Flavours of Britain 606–7
  The Heart of England 630–32
  Highlands and Islands 649–51
  Lancashire and the Lakes 635–8
  London 608–15
  Lowlands (Scotland) 646–9
  North Wales 642–4
  Northumbria 640–42
  restaurants-with-rooms 601
  South and Mid-Wales 644–6
  Thames Valley 620–22
  Wessex 622–6
  Yorkshire and the Humber Region 638–40
  see also Food and drink
Rev. Robert Walker Skating on Duddingston Loch (Raeburn) 504

Reynolds, Sir Joshua
  Art Gallery (Aberdeen) 540
  Castle Howard 399
  Cawdor Castle 537
  Harewood House 410
  Ickworth House 207
  National Gallery of Scotland (Edinburgh) 504
  Saltram House 292
  Woburn Abbey 230
Reynoldston, hotels 593
Reyntiens, Patrick 379
Rhinog moors 455
Rhodes, Zandra 150, 151
Rhos-on-Sea, restaurants 644
Rhydlydan, restaurants 644
Rhyl, restaurants 644
Ribble Valley **371**
Richard, Earl of Cornwall 285
Richard I, King 40
  coat of arms 30
  statue of 88
Richard II, King 40, 221
Richard III, King 40
  Middleham Castle 385
  "Princes in the Tower" 119
  Wars of the Roses 49
Richard of Haldingham 316
Richardson, John 361
Richmond (London) **126**
Richmond (Northumbria) 589
Richmond (Yorkshire) 384–5
  hotels 587
Richmond Park (London) 74, 126
The Ridgeway 37
Ridgeway Village, restaurants 639
Ridley, John 427
Ridley, Nicholas 427
  Martyrs' Memorial (Oxford) 222, 225
Rievaulx Abbey 12, **393**
Rievaulx Abbey (Girtin) 393
Ringstead, pubs 653
Ringwood, hotels 564
Ripley **389**
  restaurants 617, 639
Ripon **389**
  hotels 587
Ritz, Cesar 81, 84
Ritz Hotel (London) **81**
  Street-by-Street map 84
Rizzio, David 510
Road signs 684
Road to the Isles tour **546–7**
Roald Dahl Museum **230**
Rob Roy 494, **495**
  Abbotsford House 512
  Falkland Palace 500
Robert Adam (Willison) 522
Robert the Bruce 505
  Battle of Bannockburn 482, 496
  Drum Castle 541
  embalmed heart 503, 512, 515
  Pass of Brander 547
  Rathlin 549
  St Fillan's Cave (East Neuk) 500
  tomb of 500
Robin Hood **336**, 397
Robin Hood's Bay **397**
  restaurants 639
Robinson, Thomas 398
Rochester **188**
Rock, hotels 577
Rock music, London 154, **155**
Rodin, Auguste
  The Burghers of Calais 88
Rogers, Richard 25, 116
Roger's Antiques Galleries (London) 150, 151
"*The Rokeby Venus*" (Velázquez) 83
Rollright Stones 220

Rolls, Charles Stewart 475
Romaldkirk
 hotels 589
 restaurants 642
Roman Britain 21, **44–5**
 Antonine Wall 44, 491
 Bath 259, 260–61
 Birdoswald Roman Fort 358
 Boadicea and the Iceni 195
 Caerleon 474
 Carlisle 358
 Chedworth Roman Villa 329
 Chester 311
 Chew Green Camp 421
 Chysauster 278–9
 Cirencester 329
 Dorchester 269
 Fishbourne Palace 44–5, 171
 Hadrian's Wall 13, 44, 346, 415,
  422–3, 482
 Hardknott Fort 364
 Lincoln 340
 Richborough Roman Fort 183
 Roman Theatre (St Albans) 232
 Scotland 482
 Segontium (Caernarfon) 444
 Shrewsbury 312
 Verulamium (St Albans) 232
 Wade's Causeway 395
 York 408
Roman Catholic Church 673
Romney, George 229, 537
Romney, Hythe and Dymchurch Light
 Railway 183
Romney Marsh **182–3**
Romsey, pubs 652
Ronnie Scott's (London) 155
Rooksbridge, hotels 573
Rosedale 380, 382
Rosedale Abbey
 North York Moors tour 395
Rosemoor Garden 286
Ross-on-Wye **316–17**
 restaurants 631
Rossetti, Dante Gabriel
 Ashmolean Museum (Oxford) 224
 Kelmscott 220
 Manchester Art Gallery 374
 Nottingham Castle 336
 Tate Britain (London) 91
Rosslyn Chapel 513
Rosthwaite 363
Rothiemurchus Estate 544
Rothschild, Baron Ferdinand de 230
Roubiliac, Louis François 215
Rowing 66
Rowlandson, Thomas 224
Rowntree, Joseph 349
Roxburghe, Duke of 503
Royal Academy (London) **81**
 Street-by-Street map 84
 Summer Exhibitions 63
Royal Albert Hall (London) 154, 155
 Street-by-Street map 96
Royal Ascot 66, 664, 665
Royal coat of arms 30
Royal College of Music (London)
 Street-by-Street map 96
Royal Deeside 13, 479
Royal Deeside tour **540–41**
Royal Exchange (London)
 Street-by-Street map 111
Royal Highland Gathering (Braemar)
 64
Royal Highland Show 63
Royal Hospital (London) 122
Royal Mail 679
Royal Mews (London) **87**
Royal Mile (Edinburgh) **508–11**
Royal National Eisteddfod 63

Royal National Institute of Blind
 People 675
Royal Observatory Greenwich
 (London) 125
Royal Opera Arcade (London)
 Street-by-Street map 85
Royal Opera House (London) **80**, 154
 Street-by-Street map 79
Royal Pavilion (Brighton) 159, 175,
 178–9
Royal Shakespeare Company 152, **327**
Royal Show 63
Royal Tunbridge Wells **189**
 hotels 564
 restaurants 619
Royal Welsh Show 63
Royal Yachting Association 664, 665
Roydhouse, hotels 587
Rubens, Peter Paul 378
 The Adoration of the Magi 213
 Banqueting House (London) 90
 Marchesa Maria Grimaldi 271
Rugby (sport) 66, 664
Ruby Blue (London) 155
Rugby Football Union 664, 665
Runnymede 235
Rupert, Prince 312
Rural architecture **32–3**
Rush hours 684
Ruskin, John 368
Russell Square (London) 107
Ruthin **445**
 hotels 591
 restaurants 644
Ryanair 682, 683
Rydal **366**
Rye
 hotels 564
 pubs 652
 restaurants 617
 Street-by-Street map 184–5
Rylance, Mark 120
Rysbrack, Michael 228

S

Sackville, Thomas 188
Sackville-West, Vita 163, 188, 189
Sadler's Wells (London) 154
Safety **674–5**
Sailing **664**, 665
St Abb's Head **502**
St Albans **232–3**
 hotels 570
St Andrews **499**
 hotels 596
 restaurants 648
St Aubyn, Colonel John 278
St Austell **281**
St Bartholomew-the-Great (London)
 112–13
St Blazey, hotels 577
St Boswells, hotels 596
St Davids 432, 457, **464–5**
 Cathedral 13, 432, 464, 465
 hotels 593
 restaurants 645–6
St Fillans, hotels 596
St Fillan's Cave (East Neuk) 500
St George's Day 62
St Hilary, hotels 577
St Ives 240, **277**
 festivals 63
 hotels 577
 restaurants 629
St Ives, Cornwall (Nicholson) 277
St James Garlickhythe (London)
 Street-by-Street map 110
St James's (London)
 Street-by-Street map 84–5

St James's Church (London)
 Street-by-Street map 84
St James's Palace (London) 84
 Street-by-Street map 84
St James's Park (London) 75
St James's Square (London)
 Street-by-Street map 85
St John's College (Cambridge) 215
St John's College (Oxford) 227
St John's in the Vale 361
St John's, Smith Square (London) 154
St Leger, Sir Anthony 188
St Margaret's Church (London)
 Street-by-Street map 88
St Martin's Theatre (London) 153
 Street-by-Street map 78
St Mary Abchurch (London) 111
St Mary-le-Bow (London)
 Street-by-Street map 110
St Mary's Abbey (York) **350–51**
St Mawes
 hotels 577
 restaurants 629
St Michael Subduing the Devil
 (Epstein) 319
St Michael's Mount **278–9**
St Monans, restaurants 649
St Nicholas Cole Abbey (London)
 Street-by-Street map 110
St Patrick's Day 62
St Paul's Cathedral (London) 73, 109,
 114–15
 Street-by-Street map 110
St Paul's Church (London)
 Street-by-Street map 78
St Peter's-on-the-Wall (Maldon) 209
St Stephen Walbrook (London) **112**
 Street-by-Street map 111
Salcombe, restaurants 629
Sales 148, 658
Salford Quays **371**
Salisbury 11, **264–5**
 Cathedral 241
 hotels 573
 pubs 654
 restaurants 625
Salisbury, Marquess of 31
Salt, restaurants 632
Salt, Sir Titus 349, 411
Saltaire 349, 411
Saltash, pubs 654
Saltram House 292
Salvin, Anthony 444
Samaritans 675
Sambourne, Linley 123
Sandby, Paul
 Conwy Castle 447
Sandringham **197**
Sanquhar **514**
Savin, Thomas **463**
Sawrey
 hotels 585
 restaurants 637
Scafell Pike 352, 364
Scarborough **397**
 hotels 587
Science Museum (London) **100**
 Street-by-Street map 96
Scilly Isles 279
 hotels 572
Scone Palace 498
Scotland 21–2, **477–549**
 castles 486–7
 clans and tartans 484–5
 food and drink 488
 Highlands and Islands 13, 525–49
 history 482–3
 hotels 594–9
 Lowlands 13, 491–523
 map 18–19, 478–9

Scotland (cont.)
  portrait of 480–81
  pubs 657
  restaurants 646–51
  whisky 489
Scott, Captain 499
Scott, Sir George Gilbert
  Anglican Cathedral (Liverpool) 379
  Bath Abbey 260
  Martyrs' Memorial (Oxford) 225
  St Davids Cathedral 465
  Worcester Cathedral 318
Scott, Sir Giles Gilbert 121
Scott, Sir Walter 326, 481, **512**
  Abbotsford House 512
  grave 503
  Highlands and Islands 525
  Mons Meg 506
  Perth 498
  St John's in the Vale 361
  Scott's View 503
  The Trossachs 494
  Wayland's Smithy 221
Scottish Citylink 688, 689
Scottish National Party 483
Scott's View
  Borders tour 503
Scrope, 1st Lord 385
Scrope, Richard, Bishop of York 409
Seabury, Samuel 538
Seahouses 418
  pubs 656
Seashells (Moore) 378
Seathwaite 365
Seaview
  hotels 565
  restaurants 617
Secondhand shops 659
Security **674–5**
Self-catering accommodation 554
Selfridges (London) 148, 149
Selkirk, Alexander 256, 500
Selworthy 251
Senate House (Cambridge) 214
Serpentine (London) 101
Seven Dials (London)
  Street-by-Street map 78
Seven Sisters 180
Severs, Dennis 125
Severus, Septimius 45
Sewingshields Milecastle 423
Seymour, Jane 39
Shaftesbury 247, **268**
Shaftesbury Theatre (London) 153
Shakespeare, William 24, 50, 51
  Charlecote Park 302
  Glamis Castle 499
  grave 325, 326
  Great Bed of Ware 98
  Henry IV 420
  Macbeth 499, 537
  monument to 120
  Royal Shakespeare Company 327
  Shakespeare's Birthplace (Stratford-upon-Avon) 324, 326
  Shakespeare's Globe (London) 120
  Stratford-upon-Avon 12, 299, 307, 326
  Westminster Abbey (London) 93
Sharington, Sir William 255
Shaw, George Bernard 103, **233**, 317
Shaw, Norman 29, 455
Sheffield, restaurants 640
Sheldon, Gilbert, Archbishop of Canterbury 225
Sheldonian Theatre (Oxford) 222, 225
Shelley, Percy Bysshe **222**, 462
Shells 243
Shephard, Ernest 234

Shepton Mallet
  hotels 573
  restaurants 625
Sheraton, Thomas 537
Sherborne **268**
Sherlock, Cornelius 378
Sherlock Holmes Museum (London) **104**
Sherpa Expeditions 663, 665
Sherwood Forest 336
Shetland **528**
  maps 15, 527
  seabirds 528
  Up Helly Aa festival 480, 528
Shipping at the Mouth of the Thames (Turner) 91
Shoe shops, London **150**, 151
Shopping **658–9**
  London 148–51
Show jumping 67
Shrewsbury **312**
  hotels 580
  pubs 654
Shropshire *see* Heart of England
Sickert, Walter Richard 378
Siddons, Sarah 54
Sidmouth 289
  festivals 63
Signac, Paul 410
Signs
  long-distance paths 37
  pub 605
Silbury Hill 262
Silverdale, restaurants 637
Simonsbath 251
Simpson, James 480–81
Simpson, Wallis 59
Sinclair clan 485
Sir John Soane's Museum (London) **112–13**
Sisley, Alfred 410
Sissinghurst Castle Garden 189
The Sisters (Maris) 521
Six Nations Rugby Union 66
Skara Brae 43
Skeabost 534
Skene, Sir George 539
Skenfrith, restaurants 645
Sketch for Annabel Lee (Whistler) 519
Ski Scotland 664, 665
Skiddaw 353, 361
Skiing **664**, 665
Skinners' Hall (London)
  Street-by-Street map 111
Skipton
  Castle 386
  pubs 656
Skirlaw, Walter 409
Skye, Isle of 478, 526, **532–5**
  hotels 598
  pubs 657
Slate **451**
The Sleeping Shepherd Boy (Gibson) 378
Sloane, Sir Hans 106, 122
Sloane Square (London) 122
Sloley, hotels 567
Smirke, Robert 106
Smith, Adam 480
Smith, Paul 150, 151
Smoking 670, 671
  in restaurants 601
Smugglers, Cornwall **280**
Smythson, Robert 390
Snooker 66
Snowdon 433, **451**
Snowdonia National Park 13, 442, 448–9, 451
Snowshill Manor 298
  Midlands garden tour 320

Snowsport Scotland 664, 665
Soane, Sir John 112
Soft Drainpipe – Blue (Cool) (Oldenburg) 121
Soho (London) **80**
Soldier's Leap
  Killiecrankie walk 542
Solva, restaurants 645
Somerset *see* Wessex
Somerset House (London) **80–81**
Somerset, restaurants 625
Sonning Bridge
  Thames Valley tour 234
South Downs Way 37
South Kensington (London) **95–101**
  area map 95
  hotels 557–8
  pubs 652
  restaurants 611–12
  Street-by-Street map 96–7
South Queensferry, restaurants 649
"South Sea Bubble" (1720) 54
South Uist 529
South Wales 13, **457–75**
  climate 68
  Exploring South and Mid-Wales 458–9
  hotels 591–4
  pubs 657
  restaurants 644–6
South West Coast Path 250
Southampton **168–9**
  hotels 565
Southbank Centre (London) 154
Southeast England **157–237**
  Downs and Channel Coast 165–89
  East Anglia 191–215
  The Garden of England 160–61
  houses of historical figures 162–3
  map 158–9
  Thames Valley 217–37
Southwark, pubs 652
Southwark (London) **109–21**
  area map 109
  Cathedral 120
  hotels 559–60
  restaurants 612–3
Southwest Coastal Path 36, 242, 273
Southwold **202**
  hotels 567
  pubs 653
  restaurants 619
Souvenir shops 659
  London 150, 151
Sowerby Bridge 413
  restaurants 640
Spacey, Kevin 152
Spanish Armada (1588) 39, 50–1, 292, 293, 546
Spatial Concept "Waiting" (Fontana) 121
Speaker's Corner (London) 101
Specialist holidays **662–5**
Spectator sports **664**, 665
Speed Ferries 681
Speed limits 684
Speen, restaurants 621
Speke Hall (Liverpool) 379
Spence, Sir Basil 319
Spencer, 1st Earl 84
Spencer, Sir Stanley 336
  Swan Upping 235
Spencer House (London)
  Street-by-Street map 84
Sports 25
  London 155
  The Sporting Year 66–7
  traditional Cumbrian sports 358
Spring in Great Britain 62
Spurn Head **403**

STA Travel 672, 673
Staffa, Isle of 547
Stafford, hotels 580
Staffordshire see Heart of England
Staffordshire pottery **311**
Stained glass of York Minster **409**
Staite Murray, William 407
Stamford **343**
  hotels 582
  pubs 655
  restaurants 634
Standen 29
Stanhope
  North Pennines tour 427
Stanley, restaurants 651
Stannersburn, hotels 590
Stanpit Marsh 271
Stansted Airport 682
Stanton 305
  restaurants 619
Stanway House
  Midlands garden tour 320
Stapledon, Walter de 288
Stately homes **28–9**
  Althorp House 343
  Anglesey Abbey 208
  Arlington Court 287
  Athelhampton House 245, 269
  Audley End 208–9
  Berrington Hall 313
  Blickling Hall 198
  Bowood House 255
  Burghley House 299, 332, 342–3
  Burton Agnes Hall 400
  Burton Constable 402
  Castle Drogo 295
  Castle Howard 28, 347, 398–9
  Charlecote Park 302
  Chartwell 10, 163, 189
  Chatsworth House 12, 299, 331, 334–5
  Clandon Park 172
  Corsham Court 255
  Cotehele 293
  Cragside 29
  Dalemain 358–9
  Fountains Hall 390
  Glynde Place 180
  Goodwood House 171
  Ham House (London) 126
  Hardwick Hall 302, 336
  Harewood House 410
  Hatfield House 217, 231
  Hay Castle 461
  Hever Castle 189
  Holker Hall 369
  Holkham Hall 197
  Hopetoun House 502
  houses of historical figures 162–3
  Hughenden Manor 233
  Hutton-in-the-Forest 358
  Ickworth House 206–7
  Ightham Mote 188–9
  Kedleston Hall 28–9, 336
  Kelmscott Manor 220–21
  Kenwood House (London) 124
  Kingston Lacy 271
  Knebworth House 231Lacock
  Abbey 255Lanhydrock 244, 284, 285
  Layer Marney Tower 205
  Leighton Hall 370
  Levens Hall 369
  Little Moreton Hall 302–3, 311
  Longleat House 11, 266
  Marble Hill House (London) 126
  Minster Lovell Hall (Swinbrook) 220
  Montacute House 268
  Moseley Old Hall 303

Stately homes (cont.)
  Muncaster Castle 364
  Newby Hall 389
  Nunnington Hall 393
  Osborne House 162, 164
  Oxburgh Hall 195
  Packwood House 303
  Penshurst Place 189
  Petworth House 10, 22, 172
  Plas Newydd 450
  Plas-yn-Rhiw 453
  Quex House (Margate) 183
  Royal Pavilion (Brighton) 159, 175, 178–9
  Saltram House 292
  Sandringham 197
  Sizergh Castle 368
  Snowshill Manor 298
  Somerleyton Hall 199
  Speke Hall 379
  Spencer House (London) 84
  Standen 29
  Stokesay Castle 313
  Syon House (London) 126
  Temple Newsam House (Leeds) 410
  Traquair House 487, 513
  Uppark House 181
  Waddesdon Manor 230
  Wightwick Manor 303
  Wilton House 265
  Woburn Abbey 230
  see also Castles; Palaces
Stephen, King 40
Stephenson, George 394, 408
Sterne, Laurence 392, 393
Stevenson, Robert Louis 481
Steyning **174**
Stirling **496**
  Castle 13, 496–7
Stirling, James 377
Stirling Castle in the Time of the Stuarts (Vorstermann) 496
Stockbridge, restaurants 617
Stocksfield, restaurants 642
Stoke-on-Trent **311**
Stokesay Castle 313
Stokesley, restaurants 640
Ston Easton
  hotels 573
  restaurants 625
Stone, Nicholas 224
Stone buildings, Cotswolds **304–5**
Stone circles see Prehistoric Britain
Stone of Destiny 506
Stonehenge 11, 43, 241, 248–9, **262–3**
Stonethwaite 363
Stoney Middleton 331
Stoppard, Tom 24
Stornoway 529
The Storr 535
Story, Waldo 229
Stour, River 204
Stourhead 241, 245, **266–7**
  Festival 63
Stowe Gardens 11, **230**
Stowmarket, pubs 653
Strachan, Douglas 185, 538
Strata Florida
  Wild Wales tour 467
Stratfield Saye 162
Stratford-upon-Avon 12, 299, 307, **324–7**
  hotels 580
  restaurants 632
  Street-by-Street map 324–5
Strathpeffer **531**
Streatley, restaurants 621
Street, G E 257
Striding Edge 353
Strontian, hotels 599

Stuart Britain **52–3**
Stuart clan 485
Stubbs, George 171, 260
Student travellers **672**, 673
Studland Bay 270
Stump Cross Caverns 386
Sturminster Newton, restaurants 625
Sudely Castle
  Midlands garden tour 320
Suffolk see East Anglia
Suffolk, 1st Earl of 208, 209
Suffragettes 58
Summer in Great Britain 63
Summercourt, restaurants 629
Summerson, John 266
Sunshine 68–9
Supermarkets 659
Surf South West 664, 665
Surfing **664**, 665
Surrey see Downs and Channel Coast
Surrey, Thomas Holland, Duke of 394
Surrey County Cricket Club 664, 665
Surtees, Bessie 425
Sussex see Downs and Channel Coast
Sustrans 663, 665, 680, 681
Sutherland, Earls of 530
Sutherland, Graham 80
  Chichester Cathedral 171
  Coventry Cathedral 319
Sutton Bank **392**
Sutton on the Forest, restaurants 640
Swaffham **195**
Swaledale 384
Swan Upping (Spencer) 235
Swanage 270
  restaurants 625
Swansea **466**
  hotels 593
  restaurants 646
Sweeney, Oliver 150, 151
Swimming **397**
Swinbrook 220
Swindon
  restaurants 632
Sygun Copper Mines 452
Syon House (London) 126

T

Tain 531
Tal-y-Bont, restaurants 644
Talbot, William Henry Fox 255
Talisker Distillery 534
Talsarnau
  hotels 591
  restaurants 644
Talybont-on-Usk, restaurants 646
Tan-y-Bwlch 453
Tan-y-Grisiau 453
Tar Tunnel (Ironbridge Gorge) 315
Tarn Hows 368
Tarr Steps 251
Tartans **484–5**
Tate Britain (London) 73, **91**
Tate Modern (London) 10, **121**
Tate St Ives 11
Tatham, C H 347
Taunton **252**
  hotels 573
  restaurants 625
Tavistock
  hotels 577
  restaurants 629
Taxes
  Value Added Tax (VAT) 602, 658
Taxis 680, **689–90**
Teignmouth, hotels 578
Telephones **678**

Television 25, 679
Telford, Thomas **447**
　Caledonian Canal 536
　Neptune's Staircase 547
　Pontcysyllte Aqueduct 450
　Waterloo Bridge (Betws-y-Coed) 450
Temperatures 68–9
Temple (London) **112**
Tenbury Wells 313
Tenby **466**
　hotels 593
Tennis 66, 664
Tennyson, Alfred, Lord 285, 341
Tetbury, restaurants 632
Tettersells, Nicholas 174
Tewkesbury **328**
　hotels 580
Textiles, Scottish **515**
Thame, restaurants 622
Thames Path 37
Thames Valley 11, **217–37**
　climate 68
　Exploring the Thames Valley 218–19
　hotels 568–70
　pubs 653
　restaurants 620–22
　Touring the Thames 234–5
Thatcher, Margaret 24, 60, 61
Theakston Brewery 385
Theatre 24, **660**
　London 152–3
　Royal Opera House (London) 79, 80
　Royal Shakespeare Theatre and Swan Theatre (Stratford-upon-Avon) 325
　Shakespeare's Globe (London) **120**
Theatre Royal, Drury Lane (London) 153
Theatre Royal, Haymarket (London) 105, 153
Theft 674
Theme parks **661**
Theresa, Mother 31
Thermae Bath Spa 261
Thetford 195
Thirlmere 361
Thoky, Abbot 329
Thomas, Dylan 80, 435
　Dylan Thomas Centre (Swansea) 466
Thomson, James 520
Thornhill, Sir James 229
Thornton, John 409
Thornton Watlass, hotels 588
Thorpe Park 661
Threave Castle **515**
Thurleigh, restaurants 622
Thynne, John 266
Tickets, sporting events 67
Tighnabruaich, hotels 596
Tijou, Jean 115
Tillmouth Park, hotels 590
Time 672
Tintagel 273, **285**
Tinted Venus (Gibson) 346
Tintern
　hotels 593
　pubs 249
Tintern Abbey **475**
Tinytotsaway 671
Tipping 670
　in restaurants 602
Tisbury, restaurants 626
Tissington, festivals 62
Tissington Trail 298, 332, **337**

Titian
　Alnwick Castle 420
　Fitzwilliam Museum (Cambridge) 212
　Petworth House 172
　Wallace Collection (London) 104
Titley, restaurants 632
Tiverton, pubs 654
Tobermory 527
Togidubnus 45
Toilets, public 670
Tolpuddle Martyrs 56
Topsham, restaurants 630
Topshop (London) 150, 151
Torbay **290**
Torlundy, hotels 599
Torquay 275, 290
　hotels 578
　restaurants 630
Torridge Valley 286
Totnes **291**
　restaurants 630
Tourism Concern 673
Tourism for All 555, 670, 671
Tourist information 669
Tours by car
　Borders tour 503
　Midlands garden tour 320–21
　North Norfolk coastal tour 196–7
　North Pennines tour 427
　Peak District tour 338–9
　Penwith tour 276
　Road to the Isles tour 546–7
　Royal Deeside tour 540–41
　Thames Valley 234–5
　A Tour of the Borders 503
　Wild Wales tour 467
Tower Bridge (London) **116**
Tower of London 10, 73, **118–19**
Townend (Troutbeck) 366–7
Townsend, John 224, 231
Tradescant, John 224, 231
Trafalgar, Battle of (1805) 55
Trains *see* Railways
Trams 691
Transport Direct 680, 681
Transport for London 689, 691
Traquair House 487, **513**
Travel **680–91**
　air 682–3
　buses 690
　cars 684–5
　in cities 690–91
　coaches 680, 681, 688–9
　coasts and waterways 689
　cycling 691
　Devon and Cornwall 275
　Downs and Channel Coast 166
　East Anglia 193
　East Midlands 332
　ferries 681, 689
　Heart of England 308
　Highlands and Islands 526
　Lancashire and the Lakes 356
　London Underground 691
　Lowlands (Scotland) 493
　North Wales 443
　Northumbria 417
　rail 680, 681, 686–7
　South and Mid-Wales 458
　taxis 680, 689–90
　Thames Valley 218
　Wessex 249
　Yorkshire and the Humber Region 383
Travelex 676
Traveller's cheques, in shops 658
Trebah 281
Treburley, restaurants 630
Trelissick 244, 281
Tremayne family 281

Trengwainton 244
　Penwith tour 276
Trewithen 244, 281
Trinity College (Cambridge) 215
Trinity College (Oxford) 227
Trollope, Anthony 288
Troon
　hotels 596
　restaurants 649
Trooping the Colour 63
The Trossachs 478, 481, **494–5**
Troutbeck, restaurants 637
Trumpet, hotels 580
Truro **281**
　restaurants 630
Tudno, St 445
Tudor manor houses **302–3**
Tudor Renaissance **50–51**
Tunbridge Wells **189**
　hotels 564
　restaurants 617
Turnberry, hotels 596
Turner, J M W 319
　Ashmolean Museum (Oxford) 224
　Cheyne Walk (London) 122
　Petworth House 10, 172
　Shipping at the Mouth of the Thames 91
　Turner Bequest 91
　Usher Art Gallery (Lincoln) 341
　Walker Art Gallery (Liverpool) 378
Turpin, Dick 405
Tussaud, Madame 104
Twm Siôn Cati's Cave
　Wild Wales tour 467
The Two Sisters (Renoir) 256
Twombly, Cy
　Inverno 121
Twyning 328
Tyler, Wat 112
Tynemouth, restaurants 642

U

Uffington 221
Uffington White Horse 43, 221
The Uists 529
UK Border Agency 377, 669
Ullapool
　hotels 599
　pubs 657
　restaurants 651
Ullingswick, restaurants 632
Ullswater **359**
　hotels 585
　restaurants 637
Ulverston
　restaurants 637
United Synagogue (Orthodox) 673
University of London 672, 673
Up Helly Aa festival (Shetland) 480, 528
Upper Coquetdale 416
Upper Swarford 218
UPS 679
US Airways 682, 683
Usk
　hotels 594
　pubs 657
　restaurants 646
Uswayford Farm 421

V

V&A Museum of Childhood (London) 125
Vale, H H 378
Vale of the White Horse **221**
Valley of Rocks (Exmoor) 250
Value Added Tax (VAT) 602, 658
Van der Plas, Pieter 231

Van der Vaart, Jan 335
Van Dyck, Sir Anthony
  Alnwick Castle 420
  Merchant Adventurers' Hall (York)
    407
  Petworth House 172
  Wallace Collection (London) 104
  Wilton House 265
Van Eyck, Jan
  Arnolfini Portrait 82
Vanbrugh, Sir John 28, **398**
  Blenheim Palace 228
  Castle Howard 398
  Stowe Gardens 230
Vanessa Bell at Charleston (Grant) 163
Vaudeville Theatre (London) 153
Vegetarian food 602
Velázquez, Diego 504
  'The Rokeby Venus' 83
Ventnor, hotels 565
Vermeer, Johannes
  The Music Lesson 86
Verrio, Antonio 343
Victim Support 675
Victoria, Queen 41, 56–7, 231
  Balmoral 479, 525, 540
  Blair Castle 543
  Buckingham Palace (London) 86
  Crown Jewels 118
  Kensington Palace (London) 101
  Killiecrankie 542
  Osborne House 10, 162, 164
  Pitlochry 541
  Royal Pavilion (Brighton) 178, 179
  Victoria and Albert Museum
    (London) 98
Victoria and Albert Museum (London)
  10, 72, **98–9**
  Street-by-Street map 97
Victoria Coach Station 689
Victorian Britain **56–7**
Victory, HMS 169
View of Culzean Castle (Nasmyth) 522
Vikings 46, 47, 350, 525
  Up Helly Aa festival (Shetland) 480,
    528
  York 408
Vindolanda 422
Vintage Magazines (London) 150, 151
Virgin Atlantic 682, 683
Virgin Trains 687
Virginstow, restaurants 630
Visas 668
VisitBritain 689
Vivian, John Henry 466
Vodaphone 678
Vorstermann, Johannes
  Stirling Castle in the Time of the
    Stuarts 496
Vortex Jazz Club (London) 155
Vorticists 91

W

Waddesdon Manor **230**
Waddington Galleries (London) 150,
  151
Wade, General 542
Wade's Causeway
  North York Moors tour 395
Wainwright, A W 363
Walberswick 202
Walden, pubs 653
Wales 21–2, **431–75**
  castles 438–9
  history 436–7
  hotels 590–94
  map 16, 432–3
  North Wales 441–55
  portrait of 434–5

Wales (cont.)
  pubs 656–7
  restaurants 642–6
  South and Mid-Wales 457–75
Walker, Sir Andrew Barclay 378
Walker, William 171
Walker Art Gallery (Liverpool) 346,
  378–9
Walking **662–3**, 665
  in cities 691
  Constable walk 204
  Killiecrankie walk 542
  Lake District 363
  Malham walk 387
  Tissington Trail 337
Walkers' Britain 36–7
Wallace, Sir Richard 104
Wallace, William 482, 497
Wallace Collection (London) **104**
Walliswood, pubs 652
Walpole, Sir Robert 54, 88
Walsingham, Alan de 194
Walton, Izaak 170, 338
Wanamaker, Sam 120
Wareham, hotels 573
Warkworth Castle **420**
Warminster, restaurants 626
Warner Bros. Studio Tour – The
  Making of Harry Potter **233**
Warrior, HMS 169
Wars of the Roses 49, 232, 331, 437
Warwick 298, **321–3**
Warwick, Earls of 321, 322–3
Warwick, Richard Neville, Earl of 322,
  323, 385
Warwick Castle 12, 299, **322–3**
  Midlands garden tour 321
Warwickshire *see* Heart of England
Wasdale Head 364
Washingborough, hotels 582
Washington, George 261
Wastell, John 212
Wastwater 352, **364**
Waterfalls
  Aysgarth Waterfalls 385
  Becky Falls 385
  Devil's Bridge 463, 467
  Hardraw Force 385
  Mallyan Spout 395
  Scale Force 363
  Swallow Falls (Betws-y-Coed) 450
Waterhouse, Alfred 373, 374
Waterloo, Battle of (1815) 55
Watermillock, restaurants 637
Waterscape 689
Watersmeet 251, 288
Waterstone's (London) 150, 151
Wath-in-Nidderdale, restaurants 640
Watt, James 54, 480, 491
Watteau, Antoine 104
Watton-at-Stone, pubs 653
Waugh, Evelyn 124, 398
Weather 668
Weathercall 685
Webb, Aston 87, 99
Webb, Philip 29, 221
Wedgwood, Josiah 311
Welford-on-Avon, pubs 654
Well-dressing festivals (Tissington) 62,
  337
Wellington, Duke of 55, 162, 450
Wellington, hotels 573
Wells 11, 240, **252–3**
  hotels 574
Wells, John
  Aspiring Forms 277
Wells-next-the-Sea 193
  North Norfolk coastal tour 197
  restaurants 620
Welsh language 22, 434, 437

Welsh Surfing Federation Surf School
  664, 665
Welwyn Garden City 58–9
Wenlock Edge 312
  pubs 655
Wensleydale 385
Wesley, John 201, 226, **279**
Wessex 11, 46, 47, **247–71**
  Exploring Wessex 248–9
  hotels 570–74
  pubs 653–4
  restaurants 622–6
West Bay, restaurants 626
West Bexington, restaurants 626
West Country **239–95**
  climate 68
  coastal wildlife 242–3
  Devon and Cornwall 273–95
  map 240–41
  Wessex 247–71
  West Country gardens 244–5
West Dean College 662, 665
West End (London) **77–93**
  area map 77
  hotels 556–7
  restaurants 608–10
West Hatch, restaurants 626
West Highland Way 36, 494
West Kennet Long Barrow 262–3
Wester Ross **530**
Western Isles 525, **529**
Western Union 676
Westminster (London) **77–93**
  area map 77
  hotels 556–7
  restaurants 608–10
  Street-by-Street map 88–9
Westminster Abbey (London) 73, **92–3**
  Street-by-Street map 88
Westminster Pier (London) 89
Westward Ho 286
Westwood, Vivienne 60, 150, 151
Weymouth **268–9**
  hotels 574
Weymouth & Portland National
  Sailing Academy 664, 665
Wharfedale 386
Wharram Percy **400**
Wheelchair access *see* Disabled
  travellers
Wheeler, Sir Mortimer 474
Wheely Wonderful Cycling 663, 665
Whinlatter Pass 360
Whipsnade Zoo **231**
Whisky **489**
Whistler, James McNeill
  Sketch for Annabel Lee 519
Whistles (London) 150, 151
Whitby 25, 381, **396**
  Abbey 12, 396
  hotels 588
  restaurants 640
Whitchurch Mill
  Thames Valley tour 234
White Cube Gallery (London) 150, 151
White Horse of Uffington 221
Whitebrook, restaurants 646
Whitechapel Art Gallery (London)
  150, 151
Whitehall (London)
  Street-by-Street map 88–9
Whitewell
  hotels 585
  restaurants 637
Whithorn **515**
  pubs 657
Whitstable, restaurants 617
Whitworth, Sir Joseph 374
Wickham
  hotels 565

Widecombe-in-the-Moor 22
Widegate, hotels 578
Wightwick Manor 303
Wigmore Hall (London) 154
Wilberforce, William **402**
Wilde, Oscar 174
Wildlife
　Bempton 400–401
　Braunton Burrows 287
　Brownsea Island 270–71
　Buckfast Butterfly Farm and Otter
　　Sanctuary 291
　Cotswold Wildlife Park 220
　The Countryside 34–5
　Elan Valley 462
　Flora of the Cairngorms 545
　Harewood Bird Garden 410
　Kincraig Highland Wildlife Park
　　544
　Longleat House Safari Park 266
　Minsmere Reserve 202
　National Seal Sanctuary (Helston)
　　280
　St Abb's Head 502
　Scottish Sealife Sanctuary (Oban)
　　546
　Sea-Life and Marine Sanctuary
　　(Scarborough) 397
　Shetland seabirds 528
　Swannery (Abbotsbury) 268
　West Country Coastal Wildlife
　　242–3
Wilfrid, St 422
William II, King 40
　death 168
　Lake District 355
William III, King 41, 52
　Battle of the Boyne 53
　Glencoe Massacre (1692) 543
　Hampton Court 26, 173
　Hyde Park (London) 101
　Jacobite Movement 537
　and Scotland 483
William IV, King 41, 101
William the Conqueror, King 40, 171
　Battle Abbey 181
　Battle of Hastings 46, 47, 181
　coronation 92
　Domesday Book 329
　Exeter 288
　Gloucester 329
　Lewes 180
　Selby Abbey 350
　Tower of London 118
　and Wales 436
　Winchester 170
　Windsor Castle 236
　York 407
William the Lion, King of Scotland
　482
Williams, Dominic 425
Williams, Kit 328
Williams-Ellis, Sir Clough 432, 454
Williamson, Henry 286
Williamson, Matthew 150, 151
Willison, George
　Robert Adam 522
Willow Tea Room (Glasgow) 518
Willy Lott's Cottage
　Constable walk 204
Wilmington, restaurants 618
Wilton 265
Wilton House 265
Wiltshire *see* Wessex
Wimbledon Lawn Tennis Tournament
　66
Wimborne Minster **271**
Winchcombe 305
　hotels 580
　restaurants 632

Winchelsea 185
Winchester 10, **170–71**
　Cathedral 23, 158, 170–71
　hotels 565
　restaurants 618
Windermere **367**
　hotels 585
　restaurants 637
Windmills **199**
Windsor 11, **234–7**
　Castle 11, 158, 235, 236–7
　hotels 570
　restaurants 622
Windsor, Duke of (Edward VIII) 41,
　51, 291
Winslet, Kate 24
Wint, Peter de 341, 369
Winter in Great Britain 65
Winteringham, restaurants 634
Wisley 172
Wistanstow, restaurants 632
Withernsea 403
Witney 220
　hotels 570
Woburn Abbey 11, **230**
　restaurants 622
Wolf of Badenoch 538
Wolfscastle, restaurants 646
Wolsey, Cardinal
　Christ Church College (Oxford) 226
　Hampton Court 173
　Ipswich 203
Women travellers 675
Wood, John the Elder 241, 256, 258,
　261
Wood, John the Younger 241, 258,
　260, 261
Woodbridge
　hotels 567
　restaurants 620
Woodstock, restaurants 622
Woodville, Elizabeth 214
Wookey Hole 252
　hotels 574
Wool trade **207**
Woolf, Virginia 163
Woollacombe
　hotels 578
　restaurants 630
Wootton Bassett, hotels 574
Worcester **318**
　restaurants 632
Worcestershire *see* Heart of England
Wordsworth, Dorothy 366, 392
Wordsworth, William **366**
　Dove Cottage (Grasmere) 366
　Duddon Valley 365
　Plas Newydd 450
　Rydal Mount (Rydal) 366
　St John's College (Cambridge) 215
　Sutton Bank 392
　Tintern Abbey 475
　Ullswater 359
　Wordsworth House (Cockermouth)
　　362
World War I 58
World War II 58, 59
　Cabinet War Rooms (London) 88,
　　89
Worthing 174
　hotels 565
Wren, Sir Christopher 25, **114**
　Christ Church College (Oxford) 226
　Emmanuel College (Cambridge)
　　214
　Guildhall (Windsor) 235
　Hampton Court 173
　Monument (London) 116
　Old Royal Naval College (London)
　　125

Wren, Sir Christopher (cont)
　Pembroke College (Cambridge)
　　214
　Royal Hospital (London) 122
　St James Garlickhythe (London)
　　110
　St James's Church (London) 84
　St Mary Abchurch (London) 111
　St Nicholas Cole Abbey (London)
　　110
　St Paul's Cathedral (London) 109,
　　110, 114–15
　St Stephen Walbrook (London) 111,
　　112
　Sheldonian Theatre (Oxford) 222,
　　225
　Swanage Town Hall 270
Wrexham *see* North Wales
Wrightington Bar, restaurants 638
Wyatt, James 402
Wyatville, Sir Jeffry 237
Wycliffe, John 49
Wye Valley 309
Wye Valley Art Centre 662, 665
Wye Valley Walk 317
Wykeham, William of 227
Wymondham, restaurants 620
Wyndham's Theatre (London) 153

Y
Yarm
　hotels 586
　restaurants 642
Yarrow, hotels 596
Yattendon, hotels 570
Yeomen Warders, Tower of London
　118
Yeovil, restaurants 626
York 347, 383, **404–9**
　hotels 588
　restaurants 640
　Street-by-Street map 404–5
　York Minster 12, 404, 406–7, 409
York, Duke of 260
Yorkshire 12, **381–413**
　climate 69
　Exploring Yorkshire and the
　　Humber Region 382–3
　hotels 586–8
　pubs 655–6
　restaurants 638–40
Yorkshire County Cricket Club 664,
　665
Yorkshire Dales National Park 346,
　384–6
　map 384
Yorkshire Sculpture Park 12, **413**
Young, James 481
Young British Artists (YBAs) 91

Z
Zennor
　Penwith tour 276
Zoffany, Johann 543
Zoos
　Bristol Zoo Gardens 256
　Paignton Zoo 290
　Tropical World (Leeds) 410
　ZSL Whipsnade Zoo 231
　see also Aquariums; Wildlife
ZSL Whipsnade Zoo **231**

Acknowledgments

Dorling Kindersley would like to thank the following people whose contributions and assistance have made the preparation of this book possible.

MAIN CONTRIBUTOR
Michael Leapman was born in London in 1938 and has been a professional journalist since he was 20. He has worked for most British national newspapers and now writes about travel and other subjects for several publications, among them *The Independent, Independent on Sunday, The Economist* and *Country Life*. He has written 11 books, including the award-winning *Companion Guide to New York* (1983, revised 1995) and *Eyewitness Travel Guide to London*. In 1989 he edited the widely praised *Book of London*.

ADDITIONAL CONTRIBUTORS
Amanda Clark, Paul Cleves, Laura Dixon, Damian Harper, James Henderson, Lucy Juckes, John Lax, Marcus Ramshaw, Nick Rider, Victoria Trott.

ADDITIONAL ILLUSTRATIONS
Christian Hook, Gilly Newman, Paul Weston.

DESIGN AND EDITORIAL
MANAGING EDITOR Georgina Matthews
SENIOR ART EDITOR Sally Ann Hibbard
DEPUTY EDITORIAL DIRECTOR Douglas Amrine
DEPUTY ART DIRECTOR Gaye Allen
PRODUCTION David Proffit
PICTURE RESEARCH Ellen Root, Rhiannon Furbear
DTP DESIGNER Ingrid Vienings
MAP CO-ORDINATORS Michael Ellis, David Pugh
RESEARCHER Pippa Leahy
REVISIONS TEAM Eliza Armstrong, Sam Atkinson, Chris Bagshaw, Moerida Belton, Lydia Baillie, Josie Barnard, Sonal Bhatt, Hilary Bird, Louise Boulton, Julie Bowles, Nick Bruno, Roger Bullen, Robert Butt, Chloe Carleton, Deborah Clapson, Louise Cleghorn, Elspeth Collier, Gary Cross, Cooling Brown Partnership, Caroline Elliker, Guy Dimond, Nicola Erdpresser, Mariana Evmolpidou, Danny Farnham, Joy Fitzsimmons, Fay Franklin, Ed Freeman, Janice Fuscoe, Richard Hammond, John Harrison, Charlie Hawkings, Andy Hayes, Kaberi Hazarika, Martin Hendry, Andrew Heritage, Annette Jacobs, Gail Jones, Steve Knowlden, Nic Kynaston, Esther Labi, Kathryn Lane, Pippa Leahy, Carly Madden, Alison McGill, Caroline Mead, James Mills Hicks, Rebecca Milner, Kate Molan, Elaine Monaghan, Mary Ormandy, Catherine Palmi, Marianne Petrou, Chez Picthall, Clare Pierotti, Andrea Powell, Mani Ramaswamy, Mark Rawley, Jake Reimann, Carolyn Ryden, David Roberts, Sands Publishing Solutions, Mary Scott, Claire Smith, Meredith Smith, Alison Stace, Gillian Thomas, Hugh Thompson, Simon Tuite, Conrad Van Dyk, Karen Villabona, Mary Villabona, Alice Wright.

ADDITIONAL PHOTOGRAPHY
Max Alexander, Peter Anderson, Apex Photo Agency: Stephen Bere, Deni Bown, June Buck, Simon Burt, Lucy Claxton, Michael Dent, Philip Dowell, Tim Draper, Mike Dunning, Chris Dyer, Andrew Einsiedel, Gaizka Elordi, Philip Enticknap, Jane Ewart, DK Studio/Steve Gorton, Frank Greenaway, Alison Harris, Stephen Hayward, John Heseltine, Sean Hunter, Ed Ironside, Dave King, Neil Mersh, Robert O'Dea, Ian O'Leary, Stephen Oliver, Vincent Oliver, Roger Phillips, Kim Sayer, Karl Shone, Chris Stevens, Jim Stevenson, Clive Streeter, Harry Taylor, Conrad Van Dyk, David Ward, Mathew Ward, Alan Williams, Stephen Wooster, Nick Wright, Colin Yeates.

PHOTOGRAPHIC AND ARTWORK REFERENCE
Christopher Woodward of the Building of Bath Museum, Franz Karl Freiherr von Linden, Gendall Designs, NRSC Air Photo Group, The Oxford Mail and Times, and Mark and Jane Rees.

PHOTOGRAPHY PERMISSIONS
DORLING KINDERSLEY would like to thank the following for their assistance and kind permission to photograph at their establishments: Banqueting House (Crown copyright by kind permission of Historic Royal Palaces); Cabinet War Rooms; Paul Highnam at English Heritage; Dean and Chapter Exeter Cathedral; Gatwick Airport Ltd; Heathrow Airport Ltd; Thomas Woods at Historic Scotland; Provost and Scholars Kings College; Cambridge; London Transport Museum; Madame Tussaud's; National Museums and Galleries of Wales (Museum of Welsh Life); Diana Lanham and Gayle Mault at the National Trust; Peter Reekie and Isla Roberts at the National Trust for Scotland; Provost Skene House; Saint Bartholmew the Great; Saint James's Church; London St Paul's Cathedral; Masters and Wardens of the Worshipful Company of Skinners; Provost and Chapter of Southwark Cathderal; HM Tower of London; Dean and Chapter of Westminster; Dean and Chapter of Worcetser Cathedral and all the other churches, museums, hotels, restaurants, shops, galleries and sights too numerous to thank individually.

KEY
a = above; b = below/bottom; c = centre; f = far; l = left; r = right, t = top.

Works of art have been reproduced with the permission of the following copyright holders: © ADAGP, Paris and DACS, London 2011: 171t; © Alan Bowness, Hepworth Estate 277bl; © Fondazione Lucio Fontana 121tr; © The Estate of Patrick Heron/DACS, London 2011:240cb; © David Hockney: *The First Marriage (A Marriage of Styles I)* 1962, oil on canvas 1829–2140 mm, 91tr; *The Other Side* 1990-93, oil on 2 canvases, 72 x 132 in, 411t; © Estate of Stanley Spencer/DACS, London 2011 235t; © Cy Twombly 121clb; © Angela Verren-Taunt/DACS, London 2011:277br.

The work of Henry Moore, *Large Two Forms*, 1966, illustrated on page 413b *Recumbent Figure* 1938 illustrated on page 91c has been reproduced by permission of the Henry Moore Foundation.

The publisher would like to thank the following individuals, companies and picture libraries for permission to reproduce their photographs:

ABBOT HALL ART GALLERY AND MUSEUM, Kendal: 370b(d); ABERDEEN ART GALLERIES 540t; ABERDEEN AND GRAMPIAN TOURIST BOARD 479ca; ACTION PLUS: 67t; 480t; 434c; David Davies 67cr; Peter Tarry 66cla, 67bl; AIRPORT EXPRESS ALLIANCE: 683c; Printed by kind permission of MOHAMED AL FAYED: 97t; ALAMY IMAGES: Peter Adams Photography 11tr; Gina Calvi 373tl; Bertrand Collet 488cl; Nick Higham 375b; gkphotography 607 tl; Bjanka Kadic 671tr; B. O'Kane 683tl; Angus Palmer 217b; Edward Parker 11br; The Photolibrary Wales 607c, 662tc, 662b; Seb Rogers 663cl; Neil Setchfield 606cl; Andrew Wiard 61crb; AMERICAN MUSEUM, Bath: 261tl; ANCIENT ART AND ARCHITECTURE COLLECTION: 42cb, 44ca, 44clb, 45ca, 45clb, 46br, 48crb, 51ca, 232tl, 235br, 439t; THE ARCHIVE & BUSINESS RECORDS CENTRE, University of Glasgow: 483t; T & R ANNAN AND SONS: 516b(d); ASHMOLEAN MUSEUM, OXFORD: 47t. BARNABY'S PICTURE LIBRARY: 60ca; BEAMISH OPEN AIR MUSEUM: 424c, 415b, 425ca, 425cb, 425b; BLACKFRIARS CAFE BAR, NEWCASTLE: Andy Hook 602c; BIBENDUM RESTAURANT LTD.: 600bl; BRIDGEMAN ART LIBRARY, LONDON AND NEW YORK: Agnew and Sons, London 323t; Museum of Antiquities, Newcastle upon Tyne 44tl; Apsley House, The Wellington Museum, London 30tl; Bibliotheque Nationale, Paris *Neville Book of Hours* 322t(d); Birgmingham City Museums and Gallery 319t; Bonham's, London, *Portrait of Lord Nelson with Santa Cruz Beyond*, Lemeul Francis Abbot 54cb(d); Bradford Art Galleries and Museums 49clb; City of Bristol Museums and Art Galleries 256c; British Library, London, *Pictures and Arms of English Kings and Knights* 4t(d), 39t(d), *The Kings of England from Brutus to Henry* 26bl(d), Stowe manuscript 40tl(d), *Liber Legum Antiquorum Regum* 46t(d), *Calendar Anglo-Saxon Miscellany* 46–7t(d), 46–7c(d), 46–7b(d), *Decrees of Kings of Anglo-Saxon and Norman England* 47clb(d), 49bl(d), *Portrait of Chaucer*, Thomas Occleve 49br(d), *Portrait of Shakespeare*, Droeshurt 51bl(d), *Historia Anglorum* 40bl(d), 236tl(d), *Chronicle of Peter of Langtoft* 285b(d), *Lives and Miracles of St Cuthbert* 419bl(d), 419cl(d), 419cr(d), *Lindisfarne Gospels* 419br(d), *Commendatio Lamentabilis intransitu Edward IV*

436b(d), *Histoire du Roy d'Angleterre Richard II* 438t(d), 537b; Christies, London 445t; Claydon House, Bucks, *Florence Nightingale*, Sir William Blake Richmond 162t; Department of Environment, London 48tr; City of Edinburgh Museums and Galleries, *Chief of Scottish Clan*, Eugene Deveria 484bl(d); Fitzwilliam Museum, University of Cambridge, *George IV as Prince Regent*, Richard Cosway 179cb, 212bl, *Flemish Book of Hours* 350tl(d); Giraudon/ Musee de la Tapisserie, with special authorization of the city of Bayeux 47b,181b; Guildhall Library, Corporation of London, *The Great Fire*, Marcus Willemsznik 53bl(d), *Bubbler's Melody* 54br(d), *Triumph of Steam and Electricity*, The Illustrated London News 57t(d), *Great Exhibition, The transept from Dickenson's Comprehensive Pictures* 56–7, *A Balloon View of London as seen from Hampstead* 105c(d); Harrogate Museum and Art Gallery, North Yorkshire 388t; Holburne Museum and Crafts Study Centre, Bath 53t; Imperial War Museum, *London Field Marshall Montgomery*, J Worsley 31cbr(d); Kedleston Hall, Derbyshire 28br; King Street Galleries, London, *Bonnie Prince Charlie*, G Dupré 482tl; Lambeth Palace Library, London, *St Alban's Chronicle* 49t; Lever Brothers Ltd, Cheshire 349cra; Lincolnshire County Council, Usher Gallery, Lincoln, *Portrait of Mrs Fitzherbert after Richard Cosway* 179b; London Library, *The Barge Tower from Ackermann's World in miniature*, F Scoberl 55t; Manchester Art Gallery, UK, *Etruscan Vase Painters* 1871, Sir Lawrence Alma-Tadema 374b; Manchester City Art Galleries 373b; David Messum Gallery, London 447b; National Army Museum, London, *Bunker's Hill*, R Simkin 54ca; National Gallery, London, *Mrs Siddons the Actress*, Thomas Gainsborough 54t(d), 163ca; National Museet, Copenhagen 46ca; Phillips, the International Fine Art Auctioneers, *James I*, John the Elder Decritz 52b(d); Private Collections: 8–9, 30ca(d), 604tl, 48–9, 55cla, 55bl, 56clb, Vanity Fair 57br, 163t, *Ellesmere Manuscript* 188b(d), *Armada: map of the Spanish and British Fleets*, Robert Adam 298t, 396t, 422b; Royal Geographical Society, London 163cb(d); Royal Holloway & Bedford New College, the *Princes Edward and Richard in the Tower*, Sir John Everett Millais 121b; Smith Art Gallery and Museum, Stirling 496b; Tate Gallery, London: 56crb, 237t; Thyssen-Bornemisza Collection, Lugo Casta, *King Henry VIII*, Hans Holbein the Younger 50b(d); Victoria and Albert Museum, London 28t(d), 56b, 97c, 204t, 351cr, 393b, *Miniature of Mary Queen of Scots*, by a follower of Francois Clouet 511br, 537t(d); Walker Art Gallery, Liverpool 378c; Westminster Abbey, London, *Henry VII Tomb effigy*, Pietro Torrigiano 30br(d), 40bc(d); The Trustees of the Weston Park Foundation, *Portrait of Richard III*, Italian School 49cla(d); Christopher Wood Gallery, London, *High Life Below Stairs*, Charles Hunt 29c(d); Courtesy of British Airways: 680t; BFI London IMAX Cinema Waterloo: Richard Holttum 153c; British Library Board: *Cotton Faustina BVII folio 85* 49cb, 109cl; © The British Museum: 42cr, 43cb, 73tl, 85c, 103, 106–7 all except 107t and 107bl; © The Bronte Society: 412 all; BT Payphones: 678tl; Burton Constable Foundation: Dr David Connell 350t. Cadogen Management: 84b; CADW – Welsh Historic Monuments (Crown Copyright): 474t; Camera Press: Cecil Beaton 92bl; Cardiff City Council: 472tr, 473t, 473c; FkB Carlson: 605bcl; Castle Howard Estate Ltd: 399tl; Colin de Chaire: 197c; Trustees of the Chatsworth Settlement: 334b, 335b; Museum of Childhood, Edinburgh: 510b; Bruce Coleman Ltd: 35br; Stephen Bond 294b; Jane Burton 35cra; Mark N. Boulton 35cl; Patrick Clement 34cb; Peter Evans 544tl; Paul van Gaalen 250tl; Sir Jeremy Grayson 35bl; Harald Lange 34bc; Gordon Langsbury 545t; George McCarthy 34t, 35bl, 242b, 285br; Paul Meitz 528clb; Dr. Eckart Pott 34bl, 528t; Hans Reinhard 34cb, 35tc, 294t, 494tl; Dr Frieder Sauer 534t; N Schwiatz 35clb; Kim Taylor 35tl, 528cra; Konrad Wothe 528ca; Collections: Liz Stares 30tr, Yuri Lewinski 373tl; Colman Getty Consultancy: 150; Corbis: Bruce Burkhardt 295c; Ashley Cooper 12tr; Eurasia Press/Steven Vidler 437br; Tim Graham 3br, 95bl; John Heseltine 111br; Angelo Hornak 117tc; Sygma/Sandro Vannini 11bl; VIEW/HUFTON & CROW 518cr; Doug Corrance: 403b; Doug Corrance: 485b; John Crook: 171b; Design Musuem: Amelia Webb 117bl; EasyEverything: James Hamilton 678br; 1805 Club: 31t; 1853 Gallery, Bradford 411t; Empics Ltd: Nigel French 66bl; Tony Marshall 66tl, 66c; English Heritage: 126b, 208c, 208b, 209b,

248–9b, 263b, 350br, 351b, 394t, 419tr, 419c; Avebury Museum 42ca; Devizes Museum 42br, drawing by Frank Gardiner 423br; Salisbury Museum 42t, 42bl; Skyscan Balloon Photography 43t, 262b; 394t; 423bl; English Life Publications Ltd, Derby: 342tl, 342tr, 343t, 343b; Et Archive: 41tc, 41cr, 52cb, 53clb, 58crb, 162b; Bodleian Library, Oxford 48crb; British Library, London 48tl, 48ca; Devizes Museum 42cl, 43b, 262c; Garrick Club 436tl(d); Imperial War Museum, London 58clb(d), 59br; Labour Party Archives 60bc; London Museum 43cla; Magdalene College 50ca; National Maritime Museum, London 39b; Stoke Museum Staffordshire Polytechnic 41bc, 52tl; Victoria & Albert Museum, London 50t(d); Mary Evans Picture Library: 9 inset, 604tr, 40br, 41tl, 41cl, 41bl, 41br, 44bl, 44br, 46cb, 47cla, 51t, 51cb, 51br, 53crb, 54bl, 55br, 56tl, 58ca, 59ca, 59clb, 59crb, 79cb, 104t,105t, 157 inset, 162cb, 163b, 187c, 189c, 195b, 206c, 222bl, 228tl, 231c, 231bl, 231br, 234bl, 239 inset, 278t, 295 inset, 336b, 349t, 349cla, 420t, 447tl, 482b, 499b, 512bl, 514b, 515t, 535b, 667 inset. Chris Fairclough: 295b, 352b, 688b; Falkirk Wheel: 507b; Paul Felix: 234c; Fiotograff © Charles Aithie: 435t; Fifteen Cornwall: 602bc; Firmdale Hotels: 553br; Fishbourne Roman Villa: 45t; Louis Flood: 484br; Foreign and British Bible Society: Cambridge University Library 435c; Fotomas Index: 105cra. Garden Picture Library: J S Sira 27ct; John Glover 27rb; Steven Wooster 26–27t; Getty Images: 61cr, Travel Ink 673tc; Matthew Stockman 66crb; WireImage/Samir Hussein 61tc; Glasgow Museums: Burrell Collection 521ca, 520–1 all except 521bcl; Art Gallery & Museum, Kelvingrove 519t, 531b, 543b(d); Saint Mungo Museum of Religious Life and Art 517tl; John Glover: 62cr, 160cb, 205b; The Gore Hotel, London: 554c. Sonia Halliday and Laura Lushington Archive: 409t; Robert Harding Picture Library: 182t, 548t, 60cra; Jan Baldwin 287b; M H Black 288t; Teresa Black 674crb; L Bond 337b; Michael Botham 36br; C Bowman 661c; Nelly Boyd 374tl; Lesley Burridge 304tr; Martyn F Chillman 305bc; Philip Craven 103t, 200b, 324b; Nigel Francis 219b; Robert Francis 66–7; Paul Freestone 226b; Sylvain Gradadom 295tl; Brian Harrison 529b; Van der Hars 538t; Michael Jenner 45b, 529c; Norma Joseph 65b; Christopher Nicholson 253t; B O'Connor 37ca; Jenny Pate 161bc; Rainbird Collection 47crb; Roy Rainsford 37b, 168t, 298b, 338cr, 368t, 386t, 475b; Walter Rawling 25t; Hugh Routledge 2–3; Peter Scholey 299t; Michael Short 305br; James Strachen 384b; Julia K Thorne 486bl; Adina Tovy 61tl, 486br; Andy Williams 179t, 234br, 346c, 432t, 524; Adam Woolfitt 24t, 24c, 44tr, 45crb, 260b, 272, 287ca, 305bl, 439bl, 468tl, 544tr; Harewood House: 410c; Paul Harris: 36t, 62cl, 301bl(d), 338b, 367b, 666–7, 663tr; Harrogate International Centre: 389b; Hayward Gallery: Richard Haughton 273tl; Crown copyright is reproduced with the permission of the Controller of HMSO: 73br, 118bl, 118br, 119tl; Cathedral Church of the Blessed Virgin Mary and St Ethelbert in Hereford: 316b; Hertfordshire County Council: Bob Norris 58–9; John Heseltine: 76t, 102, 107t, 250tr, 250c, 469tl; Historic Royal Palaces (Crown Copyright): 4crb, 118cla, 173, 235 all; Historic Scotland (Crown Copyright): 497c, 506tr, 506c, 5-7bl; Peter Hollings: 348bl; Neil Holmes: 258b(d), 260c, 286t, 371b, 429tl, 429tr, 451b; Angelo Hornak Library: 406tl, 406bl, 406br, 409br; Reproduced by permission of the Clerk of Records, House of Lords: 483c; David Martin Hughes: 156–7, 164; Hulton-Deutsch Collection: 26c, 26tr, 31cl, 31cr, 53cla, 54c, 56c, 57cb, 58tl 58tr, 58b, 59t, 60bl, 162ca, 169c, 233b, 300t, 348c, 349crb, 350bl, 377b, 397b, 398br, 437t, 495b, 522tl, 536b; Hunterian Art Gallery: 519b; Hutchison Library: Catherine Blacky 604cb; Bernard Gerad 481t; Hutton in the Forest: Lady Inglewood 358t. The Image Bank, London: Derek Berwin 552t; Romilly Lockyer 604bl; Colin Molyneux 469bl; Trevor Wood 286b; Simon Wilkinson 180b; Terry Williams 112tc; Images Colour Library: 34cla, 43c, 221b, 234t, 249t, 250bl, 251b, 336t, 338cl, 339t, 352c, 686cl; Horizon/Robert Estall 438c; Landscape Only 37cb, 248, 365, 439br; Imperial War Museum North: 375t; Ironbridge Museum: 317b. Jarrold Publishers: 212br, 229t(d), 304bl; Jazz Cafe, Camden: 155tl; Michael Jenner: 304tl, 340b, 528b; Jorvik Viking Centre, York: 405t. Frank Lane Picture Agency: 400b(d); W Broadhurst 25b; Michael Callan 242crb; Andrew Lawson: 27c, 27cb, 244br, 245tl, 245tr, 245br; Langan's Brasserie: 603t; Leeds Castle Enterprises: 165b; Leighton House, Royal Borough of Kensington: 122br; The Leisure Pass Group: 670cr; published by kind permission Dean and Chapter of Lincoln: 340t, 341cb, 341bl; Lincolnshire County Council: Usher Gallery, Lincoln: c 1820 by William Ilbery

341bl; LLANGOLEN INTERNATIONAL MUSICAL EISTEDDFOD 450c; LONDON AMBULANCE SERVICE: 674cra; LONDON AQUARIUM: 3c; LONDON FILM FESTIVAL: 62t; LONDON TRANSPORT MUSEUM: 84t; LONGLEAT HOUSE: 266t; THE LOWRY COLLECTION, Salford: *Coming From the Mill*, 1930, L.S. Lowry 371tr. MADAME TUSSAUDS: 104b; MAGNA: 353b; MALDOM MILLENNIUM TRUST: 209t; MANSELL COLLECTION, London: 31clb, 40tr, 52ca, 55cb, 261tr, 323bl, 349clb, 402b; NICK MEERS: 22t, 238–9; METROPOLITAN POLICE SERVICE: 675t; ARCHIE MILES: 240ca; SIMON MILES: 352tr; MINACK THEATRE: Murray King 276b; MIRROR SYNDICATION INTERNATIONAL: 74b, 87b, 112; BTA/Juilian Nieman 604ca; MUSEUM OF LONDON: 44crb, 113t; NATIONAL EXPRESS LTD: 688bl; NATIONAL FISHING HERITAGE CENTRE, Grimsby: 403t; NATIONAL GALLERY, London: 73t, 82–3 all; NATIONAL GALLERY OF SCOTLAND: *The Reverend Walker Skating on Duddingston Loch*, Sir Henry Raeburn 504c(d); NATIONAL LIBRARY OF WALES: 436tr, 439c(d), 467b; NATIONAL MUSEUM OF FILM AND TELEVISION, Bradford: 411c; Board of Trustees of the NATIONAL MUSEUMS AND GALLERIES ON MERSEYSIDE: Liverpool Museum 379t; Maritime Museum 377t; Walker Art Gallery 346b, 378tl, 378tr, 378b, 379c; NATIONAL MUSEUMS LIVERPOOL: Mills Media 357br; NATIONAL MUSEUMS OF SCOTLAND: 505t, 511bl; NATIONAL MUSEUM OF WALES: 436c; By courtesy of the NATIONAL PORTRAIT GALLERY, London: *First Earl of Essex*, Hans Peter Holbein 351t(d); NATIONAL TRAMWAY MUSEUM, Crich: 339c; NATIONAL TRUST PHOTOGRAPHIC LIBRARY: *Bess of Hardwick (Elizabeth, Countess of Shrewsbury)*, Anon 334tl(d); Mathew Antrobus 302br, 390cl, 391bl; Oliver Benn 29br, 278c, 293bl, 390b; John Bethell 279c, 279bl, 279br, 303t; Nick Carter 255b; Joe Cornish 456; Prudence Cumming 267c; Martin Dohrn 50crb; Andreas Von Einsidedel 29bl, 302cb, 303ca; Roy Fox 271t; Geoffry Frosh 289t; Jerry Harpur 244t, 244bl; Derek Harris 244clb, 267t; Nadia MacKenzie 28cl; Nick Meers 266b, 267b, 320b, 672bl; Rob Motheson 292t; Cressida Pemberton Piggot 554t; Ian Shaw 460t; Richard Surman 303br, 362b; Rupert Truman 303br, 379; Andy Tryner 302bl; Charlie Waite 391t; Jeremy Whitaker 303bc, 393t, 460b; Mike Williams 302ca, 391c; George Wright 244crb, 292c; NATIONAL TRUST FOR SCOTLAND: 478b, 500b, 501c, 508b, 522tr, 523tl, 523tr, 523br; Glyn Satterley 523tr; Lindsey Robertson 523bl; NATIONAL WATERWAYS MUSEUM at Gloucester: 301bc, 301br; NHPA: Martin Garwood 395ca; Daniel Heuclin 282la; NATURE PHOTOGRAPHERS: Andrew Cleave 242cla; E A James 35cla, 360t; Hugh Miles 421t; Owen Newman 35ca; William Paton 528crb; Paul Sterry 34crb, 34br, 35cb, 35crb, 234c, 255t, 387t, 528cla; Roger Tidman 197b; NETWORK PHOTOGRAPHERS: Laurie Sparham 480b; NEW SHAKESPEARE THEATRE CO: 153t; NORFOLK MUSEUMS SERVICE: Norwich Castle Museum 201b; OXFORD SCIENTIFIC FILMS: Okapia 282lb; 'PA' NEWS PHOTO LIBRARY: John Stillwell 61cr. PALACE THEATRE ARCHIVE: 152c; PHOTOS HORTICULTURAL: 161tlc, 161cra, 161cb, 161crb, 244ca, 245c; PICTURES: 680t; PLANET EARTH PICTURES: David Phillips 27crca; POPPERFOTO: 31br, 59bl, 60cb, 60br, 61bc, 86tl, 160tr, 203t, 284cl, 444b; AFP/ Eric Feferber 61br; SG Forester 67br; PORT MERION LTD: 454cr, 454tl; PRESS ASSOCIATION: Martin Keene 62b; PUBLIC RECORD OFFICE (Crown Copyright): 48b. ROB REICHENFELD: 174t, 175c, 175b, 300b, 658b, 663t; RBS GROUP: 676bl, 676cb; REX FEATURES LTD: 31ca, 41tr, 60tl, 61lb, 236c, 237br; Barry Beattie 259cl; Peter Brooke 31bc, 678br; Nils Jorgensen 30c; Eileen Kleinman 661br; Hazel Murray 61tl; Tess, Renn-Burrill Productions 269b; Brian Rasic 63t; Nick Rogers 61tr; Tim Rooke 64cr, 66tr; Sipa/Chesnot 31bl; Today 25c; Richard Young 60tl; REX FEATURES: Jonathon Player 294cla; THE RITZ, London: 81t; ROYAL ACADEMY OF ARTS, London: 84ca; Royal Collection © 1995 Her Majesty Queen Elizabeth II: *The Family of Henry VIII*, Anon 38(d), 85c, 86tr, 86bl, 87t, 236tr,

237tl(d), 237tr, 237bl, *George IV, in full Highland dress*, Sir David Wilkie 485t; David Cripps 87c; John Freeman 88br; ROYAL COLLEGE OF MUSIC, London: 96c; ROYAL PAVILION, ART GALLERY AND MUSEUMS, Brighton: 178c, 178bl, 178br, 179cl, 179cr; ROYAL BOTANIC GARDENS, Kew:74ca; ROYAL SHAKESPEARE THEATRE COMPANY: 325tl; Donald Cooper 327c(d). ST. ALBAN'S MUSEUMS: Verulamium Museum 232b; ST. PAULS CATHEDRAL: Sampson Lloyd 114tr, 114cl, 114clb; SARTAJ BALTI HOUSE: Clare Carnegie 411b; SCOTTISH NATIONAL GALLERY OF MODERN ART: Roy Lichtenstein In the Car 507c; SCOTTISH NATIONAL PORTRAIT GALLERY: on loan from the collection of the Earl of Roseberry, *Execution of Charles I*, Unknown Artist 52–3; SIDMOUTH FOLK FESTIVAL: Derek Brooks 289b; SKYSCAN BALLOON PHOTOGRAPHY: 262t; JOHN SNOCKEN: 27cr, 27ra; SOUTHBANK PRESS OFFICE: 154t; SPORTING PICTURES: 66cra, 66bc, 66br, 67cl, 358b; STA TRAVEL GROUP: 672tt; STILL MOVING PICTURES: Doug Corrance 548b; Wade Cooper 483b; Derek Laird 482c; Robert Lees 65t; STB 544br, 545c, Paisley Museum 515b, Paul Tomkins 529tr; SJ Whitehorn 495t; DAVID TARN: 389tl; TONY STONE IMAGES: 604–5, 550–1; Rex A.Butcher 81c; Richard Elliott 64b; Rob Talbot 353ca; David Woodfall 440 © TATE BRITAIN: 73bl, 91all, ; © TATE MODERN: 121tr, 121clb, 121br; *Soft Drain Pipe – Blue (Cool) Version*, 1967 © Claes Oldenburg 121cr; © TATE ST. IVES: 277cr, 277clb, 277br; ROB TALBOT: 353cb; TRANSPORT FOR LONDON: 378cl, 691cb; TROIKA PRODUCTIONS LIMITED: Michael Walter 680cl; TUILLE HOUSE MUSEUM, Carlisle: 358c; URBIS: 372c; courtesy of the Board of Trustees of the VICTORIA AND ALBERT MUSEUM, London: 72b, 98–99; Vue 661tl; CHARLIE WAITE: 549t; © WALES TOURIST BOARD: 433c, 434b, 438–9, 468br, 469tr, 469br; Roger Vitos 468tl, 468bl; THE WALLACE COLLECTION, London: 104cb; DAVID WARD: 525b, 543t; FREDERICK WARNE & CO: 367t(d); © WARWICK CASTLE: 323cra; Roger Vitos 468tl, 468bl; Courtesy of the Trustees of THE WEDGWOOD MUSEUM, Barlaston, Staffordshire, England: 311b; WEST MIDLANDS POLICE: 674bl, 674br, 674tr; DEAN and CHAPTER of WESTMINSTER: 92cla, 93bl; Tony Middleton 92bc; JEREMY WHITAKER: 228tr, 228c, 229b; WHITBREAD PLC: 604bl; WHITWORTH ART GALLERY, University of Manchester: courtesy of Granada Television Arts Foundation 374c; CHRISTOPHER WILSON: 404bl; WILTON HOUSE TRUST: 265b; WINCHESTER CATHEDRAL: 171t; WOBURN ABBEY – by kind permission of the Marquess of Tavistock and Trustees of the Bedford Estate: 50–1, 230t; TIMOTHY WOODCOCK PHOTOLIBRARY: b; Photo © WOODMAN-STERNE, Watford, UK: Jeremy Marks 114t, 115t. YORK CASTLE MUSEUM: 405cb; YORK ART GALLERY: 407bl; DEAN & CHAPTER YORK MINSTER: 409cla, 409ca, 409cl; Peter Gibson 409cra, 409cr, 409cl; Jim Kershaw 406tr; Reproduced couresty of the YORKSHIRE MUSEUM: 408c; YORKSHIRE SCULPTURE PARK: Jerry Hardman Jones 413t. ZEFA: 64t, 154b, 263t, 269t, 486c, 659t, 682c, 684tr; Bob Croxford 63cr; Weir 197t.

Front Endpaper: All special photography except ROBERT HARDING PICTURE LIBRARY/Andy Williams tl, Adam Woolfitt bl; DAVID MARTIN HUGHES brl; NATIONAL TRUST PHOTOGRAPHIC LIBRARY/ Joe Cornish clc; TONY STONE IMAGES/David Woodfall cl. Back Endpaper: All special photography except JOHN HESELTINE tl, br.

JACKET: Front – PHOTOLIBRARY: Paul Thompson. Back – ALAMY IMAGES: Kelly Shannon Kelly cla; AWL IMAGES: David Bank clb; Fergus Kennedy tl; DORLING KINDERSLEY: Joe Cornish bl. Spine – PHOTOLIBRARY: Paul Thompson t.

All other images © Dorling Kindersley. For further information see www.DKimages.com

Central London

**REGENT'S PARK
AND BLOOMSBURY**
See pp102–107
Street Finder maps 1, 2, 3

REGENT'S
PARK

GLOUCESTER PLACE
MARYLEBONE ROAD
EUSTON ROAD
TOTTENHAM COURT ROAD
GOWER STREET
CLEVELAND STREET
GREAT PORTLAND STREET
PORTLAND PLACE
HARLEY STREET
BAKER STREET
MORTIMER STREET
PORTLAND PLACE
WIGMORE STREET
OXFORD STREET
SOHO SQUARE
WARDOUR STREET
OXFORD STREET
BROOK STREET
REGENT STREET
SHAFTES
CONDUIT STREET
MOUNT ST
PICCADILLY
ST JAMES'S ST
PALL MALL
BERKLEY ST

BAYSWATER ROAD
MARBLE ARCH
PARK LANE

KENSINGTON

HYDE PARK

Round
Pond

SERPENTINE ROAD

Serpentine

GREEN
PARK

THE MALL

ST
JAMES'
PARK

GARDENS

ROTTEN ROW

KENSINGTON PALACE GDNS
KENSINGTON ROAD

HYDE
PARK
CORNER
KNIGHTSBRIDGE
KNIGHTSBRIDGE

**Buckingham
Palace**

BUCKINGHAM
PALACE
GARDENS

BUCKINGHAM GATE

Wes
A

EXHIBITION ROAD
**Victoria and
Albert Museum**
BROMPTON ROAD

GROSVENOR PLACE
LOWER
GROSVENOR
PLACE

VICTORIA STREE

ROCHESTER ROW
REGENCY STREE

VAUXHALL BRIDGE

GREA

**SOUTH KENSINGTON
AND HYDE PARK**
See pp94–101
Street Finder maps 8, 9, 16, 17

**WEST END AND
WESTMINSTER**
See pp76–93
Street Finder maps 10, 11, 18, 19